CHRONOLOGY OF THE MEDIEVAL WORLD

800 to 1491

Companion volumes

CHRONOLOGY OF THE ANCIENT WORLD
10,000 B.C. – A.D. 799

By H.E.L. Mellersh

CHRONOLOGY OF THE EXPANDING WORLD
1492–1762

By Neville Williams

CHRONOLOGY OF THE MODERN WORLD
1763–1992 2nd Edition

By Neville Williams and Philip Waller

R.L. STOREY

Chronology of the Medieval World

800 to 1491

Helicon

Chronology of the Medieval World, 800-1491
by R.L. Storey

First published in 1973
Reissued in 1994 by
Helicon Publishing Ltd
42 Hythe Bridge Street
Oxford, OX1 2EP

Printed and bound in England

ISBN 0 09 178264 3

British Library Cataloguing in Publication Data
A catalogue record for this book
is available from the British Library

Contents

Introduction

Chronology of the Medieval World, 800 to 1491 is the third member of the series founded by Neville Williams' two volumes, *Chronology of the Modern World, 1763 to 1965* and *Chronology of the Expanding World, 1492 to 1762*. Here the starting point is the year when the coronation of Charlemagne as Emperor revived the imperial title in western Europe for the leader of the Germanic people which had won primacy in this part of the former Roman Empire. The last Carolingian emperor died within a century, but before then the empire itself had been broken up into kingdoms which themselves disintegrated with the growth of feudal principalities, and these also were weakened by centrifugal tendencies. With the onslaught of Vikings, Magyars and Saracens, western Europe was under siege. From the mid-tenth century, however, the tide turned in favour of stability with the foundation of monarchies destined to survive and, by slow and painful stages, eventually increase their authority until, at the close of this period, executions for treason indicate more exalted concepts of kingship and greater self-confidence. Except for its miraculous escape from Mongol conquest in 1242, western Europe was not again threatened by destruction from without. The development of its civilisation which can be traced in these pages suffered only one major check, from the Black Death of 1347–49; its toll is reflected in the decreased amount of information to be found about European culture in subsequent years, a setback soon remedied by the achievements of the Renaissance in Italy.

While western Europe dominates the pages of this *Chronology*, an attempt is made to show contemporary developments in other continents. The illiterate yet extensive empires of Negro Africa and the equally mysterious civilisations of the Americas have left little record of a kind digestible for quotation here. In contrast, the intellectual achievement of the Arab world stands out in the early centuries of this period; from the twelfth century, the west's debt to Muslim scholars appears in the notices of translations from Arabic of original work on the natural sciences, studies of Hindu mathematics and astronomy, and, above all else, philosophical and scientific texts from ancient Greece. Western relations with the Greek Empire were almost invariably hostile, the consequence of ecclesiastical schism. This eastern heir of the Roman Empire was the most persistent political entity in the medieval world, periodically renewing its command under vigorous emperors. The empires of Asia, of the ʿAbbasīd Arabs, the Seljuqs and Mongols in the west, and of the numerous Muslim dynasties in central Asia, have histories of rapid expansion and collapse; few survived three generations of rulers, and Asian capitals have records of destruction beside which not only Constantinople, but even the more recently created capitals of Europe, appear remarkably fortunate. In China also our annals disclose a recurring pattern of invasions and rebellions sweeping away and founding imperial dynasties, although here, as in Persia, the traditions of civilisation already had ancient roots which never lost their capacity to survive political vicissitudes.

In this volume, the pattern set in the preceding *Chronologies* for the arrangement of information with a full-scale index is followed with certain modifications. Political events are shown chronologically in the framework of the modern calendar-year on the left-hand pages, while the right-hand pages opposite show each year's contribution to religious, intellectual and artistic development. In order to facilitate reference from the index, information is arranged in lettered sections as follows:

LEFT-HAND PAGES: Events which can be set against precise days or months appear in sections lettered 'A' (January, February and March), 'B' (April, May and June), 'C' (July, August and September) and 'D' (October, November and December). Occasionally an incident cannot be more exactly dated than by season; it will be shown at the head of its appropriate quarter (*e.g.* 'D' for Autumn). Events datable by the year alone are placed in section 'E'. Here also are shown incidents which cannot be assigned to a particular year, or more general movements which demand a reference (like the westward movement of the Seljuq Turks); for such cases, where '*circa* this year' is intended, the entry is preceded by an asterisk. Also in section 'E' are events believed to have occurred between certain dates; they are shown under the first year of the accepted bracket, with the final date coming at the beginning of the entry (*e.g.* the capture of Kiev by Vikings is shown in 850 E preceded by the terminal date '(–860)'). In certain instances the consequences of particular dated incidents cannot themselves be dated but they are noted with the dated events.

RIGHT-HAND PAGES: Particulars are arranged under these headings:

F Law and Politics
G Economics, Science, Technology and Discovery
H Religion and Education
J Art, Architecture and Music
K Literature, Philosophy and Scholarship
L Births and Deaths

This pattern is different from that in the published *Chronology* volumes of more recent periods because here we are concerned with the medieval centuries when law-making and legal institutions were major instruments in the growth of a monarchy's political authority, when economics were a minor concern to governments and so can more realistically be grouped with advances in science, technology and exploration, and when education was almost entirely controlled by religious authorities. Under 'H' also appear notices concerning ecclesiastical institutions and canon law. Much more might properly have been shown in this section; nearly all the buildings noticed under 'Architecture' are churches or mosques, most of the works of art portray religious subjects, the majority of European authors in all sections were in holy orders and their work was usually inspired, in varying degrees, by religious motives. Nor is it only in Europe's cultural heritage that the rôle of the Church was paramount. Many of the political events shown on the left-hand pages directly concerned ecclesiastical authorities, most notably the Papacy, both in its character of Christ's Vicar and as a temporal principality. Before its rise to these heights about half-way through this era, the Papacy was periodically held by nominees of emperors or local factions. For these reasons the elections of Popes are recorded on the left-hand pages, as are events of a religious character in which laymen were active, like the Crusades and conflicts of 'Church and State'.

A major problem in the editing of this volume has been the assignment of writings to dates. Many of the entries on the right-hand pages are titles of works which cannot be dated with precision. Until the advent of printing, these texts were not published in the way we know; many, indeed, so far as can be discovered, were not reproduced until modern times. Other works have not survived at all, or only in part, and are known to have existed because they are mentioned in later medieval literature, such as Arabic biographical dictionaries or Chinese encyclopedias. Few authors dated their manuscripts; thus only one of Gerard of Cremona's numerous translations from Arabic is dated (1175 G). Modern scholarship has dated various medieval manuscripts, though rarely to particular single years. Except when such attribution is generally accepted, works by known authors are here shown in the years when they died. These entries are prefixed by daggers. An asterisk follows a dagger when only an approximate date of death is available. Anonymous works, and these are most commonly vernacular literature up to the thirteenth century, are assigned to approximate dates and also marked with asterisks. The pages recording dates with round number, the ends of centuries and their mid-points, are consequently inflated. The fullest page is that for 1200, where the unusually high content of literature points both to the achievements of the 'Twelfth Century Renaissance' and, because this total is not later surpassed, to our more certain knowledge of the authorship of later literature. In the case of historical writings, also shown in section 'K', the subject matter provides indications for dating; various annals and chronicles are shown under the last years they themselves report, although such attribution actually points to the earliest dates when they may have been completed; the dates of their authors' deaths are probably more acceptable as terminals.

The section for Births and Deaths is much smaller than in the published

Chronologies. The only class of personage whose birthdays were recorded with some frequency was the offspring of reigning monarchs, potentially their heirs; for most other men, even the year of birth is rarely an established fact. Notices of deaths are not given for authors and artists unless some supplementary information, like the actual day, can be given. The daggers in the entries under other right-hand page sections provide the majority, or total, of each year's obituary notices.

On both pages, the most obvious contrast with the two published *Chronology* volumes is that here most pairs of pages record more than one year. The explanation is equally obvious: less information is available. Until the close of the twelfth century, most pairs of pages show three years; two years appear on most subsequent pairs of pages. In order to reduce the size of the volume, headings for which there are no entries have been omitted. These omissions frequently occur until about 1070 in the right-hand pages. They are less common in the record of political events, while 1116 is unique as a year devoid of noteworthy detail on any account. Each page is headed with the date-span it records and notices of some of the items occurring below; these headlines do not necessarily single out all the events which might generally be thought 'the most important', because the objective governing their choice is to indicate continuity and contrast with developments in many lands.

Cross-references are provided in the text by means of dates given in brackets at the ends of entries. Thus the notice in 1255 G of the translation of Averroes' *al-Kullīyāt* ends with '(–1160)', referring to the first notice of the original text on the page for 1160. Here also appears a cross-reference to 1482, the year when the first printed edition of the work is recorded, again in section 'G'. In other cases, however, the terminal bracketed date does not indicate a reference but the extent of time attributed to a work. This usage is particularly frequent in respect of buildings. Under 1093 J, for instance, there appears a notice of Durham Cathedral including '(–1133)'; here it must be understood that the building operations extended from 1093 to 1133. On the left-hand pages these bracketed dates occasionally indicate cross-references but more commonly indicate the end of the matter here shown as beginning, such as the reign of a newly-acceded king or dynasty. As has already been pointed out in the description of section 'E', bracketed dates at the beginnings of lines serve another purpose. Sometimes the numbers of kings are given in brackets; this is because in the particular time of the notices these persons were not then kings but the number is given to assist identification (*e.g.* 'Henry (II)' in 1151 C).

THE INDEX

Entries for Persons, Places and Subjects and titles of books and works of art are listed in a single alphabetical sequence. Prefixes to surnames and place-names (like Le Mans) have been ignored, as have prepositions like *De* and other recurrent opening words of titles (*e.g. Liber de* and its Arabic equivalent *Kitāb al-*). There are numerous cross-references. A table of abbreviations used and a list of subject entries precede the index.

PERSONS: Each personal entry is followed by sufficient information to assist identification by nationality, occupation and date. In most cases when an entry ends with a single reference that is the year of death; if a person is known to have died in another year it is also cited. For rulers, the dates in brackets are those of reigns; for other persons, when these are available, the bracketed dates are for their lives. Dates of births of rulers are given when available, either in the brackets preceded by 'b.', or immediately afterwards, followed by 'L' (a reference). Bracketed dates for reigns are not given when these coincide with the two terminal references following. The 'occupations' cited in the index are not exhaustive; they refer only to the branches of knowledge to which these authors are here shown to have contributed.

As surnames were not common in Europe before the fourteenth century, most Europeans are shown in the index under their Christian names. These names are arranged in this order of precedence: (i) Popes; (ii) Emperors; (iii) Kings, who are placed in the alphabetical sequence of their kingdoms; (iv) other territorial princes, again in the alphabetical order of their real or titular domains; and (v) others in the alphabetical order of their places of origin or soubriquets. With the exception of sovereigns, persons with surnames are so indexed.

PLACES: All places are assigned to their country according to the current world map. Countries and cities for which entries are numerous have references arranged in sub-sections, with events in a first chronological series followed by religious, institutional, artistic and literary notices. Because of the personal involvement of monarchs in the public histories of their countries, the principal events of each reign will often be referred to only against the names of rulers. For this reason, lists of rulers, with their dates, are given in the entries for all the European kingdoms, for the Papacy, Empire, Greek Empire, Baghdād (for the Caliphate), Ottoman Empire, Jerusalem, Egypt and Delhi. Other Asian and African states receiving less detailed treatment give direct notices of their various dynasties and some include cross-references to their more outstanding rulers (*e.g.* China, Dai Viet (now North Vietnam) and Morocco).

SUBJECT ENTRIES: The most substantial of these take the form of lists of 'Occupations'—directing the reader to the names of those contributing to a particular branch of literature or learning. To facilitate both reference and comparison, these lists are divided into national sections. Thus the list of 'Astronomers' indicates the major role of Persia in the history of astronomy. It will be noted that there is a section in these lists for 'Arab' authors; these are men who wrote in Arabic but their precise nationalities have not been traced, and they could include Muslims from any land between Spain and India. The published *Chronology* volumes have subject entries for assassinations and civil wars. Such events were so common in the medieval world that a *passim* notice here must suffice. More appropriate for this period are the subjects Conversion (to Christianity), Feudalism and Charters of Liberties.

* * *

The compilation of this volume has been a 'Voyage of the Eyes through the Wonders of Kingdoms'. The greatest of my obligations are to the numerous scholars whose published works have provided the information assembled here. My colleagues in the History Department at Nottingham University have generously assisted in the elucidation of problems. The late Frank Seymour Smith enriched the volume by his contributions on literature and Rosemary Proctor has supplied particulars on art and music. I extend my warmest thanks also to Neville Williams, the General Editor, and to John Pattisson, of Barrie & Jenkins, not only for their advice in resolving editorial difficulties, but for their unfailing encouragement and kindness.

R. L. S.

CHRONOLOGY

800–801 Revival of Imperial Title in Western Europe

800

D **Nov**: 24th, Charlemagne, King of the Franks and Lombards, arrives in Rome to receive Pope Leo III's declaration of innocence from accusations made by his enemies in Rome.

Dec: 25th, revival of title of Emperor in Western Europe by Leo's coronation of Charlemagne (–814).

E Charlemagne arranges for defence of French Channel coast against the Vikings.

Ibrāhīm ibn-al-Aghlab, Emir of Mzab (Algeria), establishes Aghlabid dynasty of Kairāwan ruling north-west Africa in only nominal subjection to the Caliph of Baghdād (–909).

801

E Barcelona taken by Charlemagne from the Muslims.

800

G **Economics, Science, Technology and Discovery**

*Ibn-Wahshiyya, *Nabataean Agriculture.*

†*Al-Fazāri, the first astronomer in Islam.

†*Al-Batrīq, translations into Arabic of the major medical works of Galen and Hippocrates.

Water-mills for irrigation introduced to Japan from China.

H **Religion and Education**

The Athanasian Creed.

(or 801) Alcuin presents an improved version of the Bible to Charlemagne; many copies were made at Tours.

The Cha'an (or Meditation) Sect now becoming the strongest movement in Chinese Buddhism (better known by the Japanese name of Zen Buddhism; –1191, 1227).

J **Art, Architecture and Music**

*Monastery of Centula (or St. Riquier), near Abbeville, completed.

*Abbey gateway at Lorsch.

*Basilica of Sta. Anastasia, Rome.

K **Literature, Philosophy and Scholarship**

*Alcuin, *Works* (*i.e. Lives of the Saints*; some poems; other Latin writings on Ethics, Rhetoric and Grammar; together with some hundreds of letters, many to Charlemagne).

**Widsith* (anon. heroic legend in Old English; known by the name of the wandering minstrel, because the poem opens with this word; –975).

*Cynewulf, *Elene* (and three other religious poems, in Old English, including perhaps *The Dream of the Rood*; –975).

* ?*Hildebrandslied* (a Lay, in Old High German; incomplete).

†*Paul the Deacon, *Historia Langobardorum* (*History of the Lombards*).

801

G **Economics, Science, Technology and Discovery**

Chia Tan, *Map of China and some of the barbaric countries within the seas.*

K **Literature, Philosophy and Scholarship**

T'ung tien (*Comprehensive Compendium*; the first Chinese historical encyclopedia).

L **Births and Deaths**

Sept. 8th, Anskar b. (–865).

802

A Mar: assembly of magnates at Aachen take new oath of fidelity to Charlemagne as Emperor.

E Irene, the Greek Empress, deposed by her minister of finance who succeeds as Nicephorus I (–811); thus end her (alleged) negotiations with Charlemagne for their betrothal.

Egbert succeeds Beorhtric as King of Wessex (–839).

The Maurice dynasty of locally elected dukes (*i.e.* Doges) of Venice ends; Obelerius succeeds (–811).

The monastery of Iona sacked by Vikings.

803

E Hārūn-ar-Rashīd, Caliph of Baghdād, destroys the Barmakids, the Persian dynasty responsible for the administration of his (the 'Abbasid) Empire.

804

E Charlemagne depopulates much of northern Saxony and Nordalbingia in one of his last measures for the subjection and conversion of the Saxons; with the end of this war, Germany to the River Elbe is incorporated into the Frankish dominions.

Hārūn-ar-Rashīd sacks Ankara.

802

F **Law and Politics**

An assembly of nobles and other subjects at Aachen accepts Charlemagne's codification of laws (Capitularies); his system of annual *missi* (itinerant surveyors of justice, royal rights, etc.) is now fully developed.

H **Religion and Education**

A council of the Frankish Church at Aachen receives the collection of canons made by Dionysius Exiguus (*Dionysio-Hadriana* or *liber canonum*).

Alfonso establishes an archbishopric at his capital, Oviedo.

J **Art, Architecture and Music**

Foundation of Oviedo Cathedral, of which the Cámara Santa survives.

803

F **Law and Politics**

*Codes of laws of Saxons, Frisians and Thuringians.

H **Religion and Education**

Oct. 12th, Ethelheard, Archbishop of Canterbury, holds a provincial council at Clovesho which confirms abolition of the Archbishopric of Lichfield.

L **Births and Deaths**

Aug. 9th, the ex-Empress Irene d. (*c.* 53).

804

G **Economics, Science, Technology and Discovery**

Lu Yü, *Ch'a ching* (the earliest treatise on tea).

J **Art, Architecture and Music**

Fridugis becomes Abbot of St. Martin's, Tours; its *scriptorium* flourishes under his rule.

*(or 918?) 'St. Columba's House' (*i.e.* church), Kells.

†Ibrāhīm al-Mawsili, court-musician of Hārūn-ar-Rashīd.

L **Births and Deaths**

May 19th, Alcuin of York d. (69).

805

E Charlemagne conquers Venetia, Dalmatia and Corsica; while his son Charles campaigns in Bohemia against the Chekhs (–806).
Nicephorus defeats Slavs attacking Patras.

806

A **Feb**: 6th, Charlemagne, ignoring his position as Emperor, makes his first plan for the division of his territories among his sons Charles, Louis and Pepin.

E Charlemagne takes Pampeluna and Novara.
Charles, his son, defeats the Sorbs (Slavs of the Elbe–Saale area), enforcing their submission, but achieves no result in a further campaign against the Chekhs.
Hārūn-ar-Rashīd takes Heraclea and other places in Cappadocia in a campaign which forces Nicephorus to resume his payment of tribute.
Al-Hakam I, Emir of Spain, massacres rebels in Cordova and Toledo.
Grimoald II succeeds Grimoald I as Prince of Benevento (–818).
Death of Kammu, Emperor of Japan, who had founded his capital at Heian (*i.e.* Kyōto).

807

E Nicephorus I sends a fleet to reassert Byzantine authority in Venice and Dalmatia.
First Viking raid on Ireland.

808

E Charlemagne founds Hamburg and creates the county of Brandenburg.
Göttrik, King of Denmark, begins defensive earthworks (the 'Danework') to defend his southern frontier.

805

G **Economics, Science, Technology and Discovery**

A capitulary of Charlemagne lists places on the eastern frontier (*e.g.* Magdeburg) where merchants may cross to trade with Slavs and Avars.

H **Religion and Education**

Saichō, returning to Japan from an embassy to China, introduces the Tendai Sect of Buddhism; its monastic centre was founded on Mount Hiei.

Another of Charlemagne's capitularies makes regulations for schools.

J **Art, Architecture and Music**

†Chia Tan, *New T'ang History* (of China; includes itineraries in Asia).

†Kisā'i, Persian grammarian.

806

H **Religion and Education**

Kūkai, on returning from an embassy to China, founds the important Shingon Sect of Buddhism in Japan.

J **Art, Architecture and Music**

Oratory (extant but restored) of the palace built by Theodulf, Bishop of Orleans, at Germigny-des-Prés.

807

G **Economics, Science, Technology and Discovery**

Hārūn-ar-Rashīd presents a water-clock to Charlemagne.

808

K **Literature, Philosophy and Scholarship**

Imube Hironari, *Kogo shūi* (treatise on Japanese customs, language, etc.).

809

A **Mar**: 24th, the Caliph Hārūn-ar-Rashīd dies after suppressing a revolt in Samarqand; his empire now divided between his sons al-Ma'mūn (–833) and al-Amīn (–813).

E Nicephorus raids Pliska, the Bulgar capital, in retaliation for the sack of Sofia by Krum, Khan of the Bulgars.

810

C **Jul**: 8th, death of Pepin, King of Italy, after failing to take Venice. The Venetians resume nominal recognition of Byzantine authority and begin their city on the Rialto. Bernard succeeds as King of Italy (–818).

E Göttrik, King of Denmark and southern Sweden and Norway, murdered; his nephew, Hemming, succeeds, and makes peace with Charlemagne.

811

C **Jul**: 26th, Nicephorus I, after taking Pliska, killed in the destruction of his army by the Bulgars; succeeded by Michael I Rangabe (–813).

E Formation of the Spanish March completed with the surrender of Tortosa to Louis, son of Charlemagne.

A Frankish army sent into Pannonia in (probably) the last campaign against the Avars; they are now finally subjected to Charlemagne and converted to Christianity.

Obelerius, Doge of Venice, deposed, and succeeded by Angelo Particiaco (–827).

812

B **Apr**: ambassadors of the Byzantine Emperor, Michael I, recognise Charlemagne as Emperor, while he renounces his claim to dominion over Venice.

E The Wiltzi (a Slav tribe living on the southern shore of the Baltic) temporarily submit to Charlemagne.

809

G **Economics, Science, Technology and Discovery**

†Hārūn-ar-Rashīd founded the first hospital in Baghdād. He is credited with establishing the postal service in his empire and to have contemplated making a canal through the Suez Isthmus.

H **Religion and Education**

Charlemagne, in opposition to Pope Leo III, orders the retention of *Filioque* in the Creed.

810

F **Law and Politics**

Establishment in Japan of the Bureau of Archives to draft imperial decrees and transmit petitions to the Emperor.

G **Economics, Science, Technology and Discovery**

†Jābir ibn-Hayyān of Kufa, 'father of Arabic alchemy'; credited with *The Book of the Composition of Alchemy* (–1144, 1473).

K **Literature, Philosophy and Scholarship**

†Nennius, *Historia Britonum* (chronicle and geography, notable because it contains the earliest direct reference to 'Arthur' as a battle-leader of the Celts).

†*Abū Nuwās, court-poet of Hārūn-ar-Rashīd.

†*Georgios Syncellos, *Chronicle* (from the Creation to 284; –817).

811

F **Law and Politics**

Promulgation of (the third) Japanese law-code.

G **Economics, Science, Technology and Discovery**

The T'ang Emperors now issuing 'flying-cash' (money-drafts repayable at the capital) to meet shortage of specie—despite large-scale production of a copper coinage; these drafts were exchanged by merchants and thus formed a paper currency (–1024).

812

F **Law and Politics**

†Tu Yü, *T'ung tien* (encyclopedia on Chinese government and economics).

J **Art, Architecture and Music**

*Church of S. Donato, Zara, built during the Frankish occupation of Dalmatia (–876).

813

B **Jun**: 22nd, Michael defeated by the Bulgars at Versinicia (near Adrianople). He was consequently deposed in favour of Leo V the Armenian (–820), while the Bulgars took Adrianople and attacked Constantinople.

C **Sep**: 11th, in an assembly of magnates at Aachen, Charlemagne gives the imperial crown to Louis, his only surviving son.
25th: al-Ma'mūn reunites the 'Abbasid Empire by the capture of Baghdād and murder of his brother, al-Amīn.

814

A **Jan**: 28th, Charlemagne dies; succeeded by Louis the Pious (–840).

B **Apr**: 14th, Krum, Khan of the Bulgars, dies; succeeded by Omortag, who made peace with Leo V (–831).
May: al-Hakam I crushes a new revolt in Cordova; some of the Muslim exiles founded a kingdom at Alexandria (–827).

C **Aug**: Louis creates dependent kingdoms of Bavaria and Aquitaine for his sons Lothar (–817) and Pepin (–838).

815

E Egbert of Wessex conquers Cornwall.

816

B **May**: 25th, Pope Leo III dies.
Jun: 22nd, Stephen IV crowned as Pope (–817).

813

G **Economics, Science, Technology and Discovery**

The brothers Ben Shaku measure the degree of meridian at the order of al-Ma'mūn (–833).

H **Religion and Education**

The tomb of St. James the Greater identified at Santiago de Compostela; it attracts pilgrimages from western Europe.

J **Art, Architecture and Music**

†Archbishop Hildebold began rebuilding Cologne Cathedral on a great scale on the 'new', 'Roman' plan.

814

G **Economics, Science, Technology and Discovery**

Introduction (unsuccessful) of tea-growing in Japan.

†Li Chi-fu, *Map of the Commands and Kingdoms* (of the Chinese Empire).

J **Art, Architecture and Music**

Priory church of St. Philibert-de-Grandlieu, Déas (–819).

L **Births and Deaths**

Feb. 18th, St. Angilbert d.

815

G **Economics, Science, Technology and Discovery**

*Māshā'allāh wrote on astrology, the astrolobe and meteorology; his book on prices is the oldest extant scientific book in Arabic.

H **Religion and Education**

Mar., Leo V deposes the Patriarch Nicephorus and holds a synod of the Greek Church which reaffirms the inconoclastic decrees of the council of 754.

†Ma'rūf al-Karkhi of Baghdād, the first Sūfī (mystic) saint.

J **Art, Architecture and Music**

The basilica of S. Stefano degli Abessini, Rome, completed by now.

K **Literature, Philosophy and Scholarship**

Shinsen Shōjiroku (*New Compilation of the Registers of Families*, giving genealogies of 1,182 Japanese noble families).

816

F **Law and Politics**

An assembly called by Louis the Pious to discuss his laws is poorly attended by the nobles; such general assemblies are now in decline.

H **Religion and Education**

Kūkai founds the monastic headquarters of the Shingon sect on Mount Koya, Japan.

817

A **Jan**: 24th, Pope Stephen IV dies.
25th, Paschal I crowned as Pope (–824).

C **Jul**: *Divisio imperii*: in a council at Aachen, Lothar created Emperor as the colleague of his father, Louis (–831), whose other sons, Pepin and Louis the German respectively receive Aquitaine and Bavaria as sovereign yet dependent kingdoms (–838; –876).
Al Ma'mūn causes a revolt in Baghdād (–819) by appointing ʻAli al-Rida, leader of the Shias, his heir.

818

B **Apr**: 17th, Bernard, King of Italy, dies in consequence of his being blinded upon his submission, after a brief revolt, to the Emperor Louis.

C **Aug**: Louis enforces temporary submission by the Bretons, whose leader, Morvan, is killed in a skirmish.

E Murder of Grimoald II, Prince of Benevento.
Death of ʻAli al-Rida, al-Ma'mūn's heir.

819

E Al-Ma'mūn suppresses the revolt in Baghdād and thus at last gains possession of his capital.

817

H **Religion and Education**

In the *Pactum Hlodovicianum*, Louis the Pious confirms the Papal States in Italy.

He also orders all monasteries of his empire to observe the Rule of St. Benedict of Nursia.

J **Art, Architecture and Music**

Basilica of Sta. Prassede, Rome.

Mosaics in the apses of Sta. Maria in Domnica, Sta. Prassede and Sta. Cecilia, Rome (–824).

K **Literature, Philosophy and Scholarship**

†*Li Ho, *Poems* (regarded as one of the greatest poets of the T'ang Dynasty).

†*Theophanes Confessor, continuation of Syncellos' *Chronicle* (–810; Theophanes' *Chronicle* was continued to 961).

818

H **Religion and Education**

Louis establishes the bishopric of Hildesheim.

†Theodulf of Orleans was one of the first bishops to attempt to set up schools in his diocese; he also tried to produce a critical version of the Bible.

819

J **Art, Architecture and Music**

Consecration of (the second) abbey-church of Fulda, a building which greatly influenced the development of architecture in western Europe.

Dedication of the extension to Mittelzell Minster, on Reichenau.

K **Literature, Philosophy and Scholarship**

†Liu Tsung-yuan, Chinese poet.

820

D **Dec**: 25th, murder of the Greek Emperor, Leo V; succeeded by Michael II (–829), founder of the Amorian dynasty (–867).

E Repulse of attempt by Vikings to land at the mouth of the Seine.
Tāhir appointed as the Caliph's governor of Khurāsān (eastern Persia); he founded the Tāhirid dynasty (–872).

821

E Death of Coenwulf, King of Mercia and principal English king (his successors are obscure and not known after 883).
Vikings, after sailing round Brittany, sack the Isle of Rhé.
Conquest of Tibet by the Chinese.

822

E Louis does public penance for the death of Bernard of Italy.
Al-Hakam I, Emir of Spain, dies; succeeded by his son, ʿAbd-ar-Rahmān II (–852).
Michael II, with Bulgarian support, defeats a rebellion.

823

E Lothar, son of Louis, crowned as King of Italy (–850) by Pope Paschal.

820

F **Law and Politics**

†Al-Shāfi'ī founded an Islamic law-school at Medina.

Institution in Japan of the Examiners of Misdeeds, who soon developed into a police force (as the Police Commissioners).

H **Religion and Education**

†Al-Shāfi'ī, founder of the Shāfi'ite rite of Islam.

J **Art, Architecture and Music**

*Manuscript plan for a monastery, at St. Gall.

K **Literature, Philosophy and Scholarship**

**Heliand* (an Old Saxon version of the Gospels in the form of a secular epic).

† ?Sankara, Hindu philosopher.

821

J **Art, Architecture and Music**

Einhard's church at Steinbach; he built another on his estate at Seligenstadt.

†Arno was patron of the *scriptorium* at Salzburg, where he was Bishop (later Archbishop) from 785.

822

H **Religion and Education**

Corvey on Weser founded by monks from Corbie, Picardy.

The bishop and chapter of Sens make the earliest known division of cathedral property.

Louis orders the reform of schools.

J **Art, Architecture and Music**

Consecration of the chapel of St. Michael, Fulda.

*Church of St. Peter, Fulda (–836).

K **Literature, Philosophy and Scholarship**

†Farrā', Persian grammarian.

L **Births and Deaths**

Feb. 11th, St. Benedict of Aniane (*c.* 72).

823

J **Art, Architecture and Music**

Buildings on Skellig Michael (*cf.* 860).

K **Literature, Philosophy and Scholarship**

†Al-Wāqidi, *Kitāb al-Maghāzi* (*History of the Wars*, of Muhammad); *Kitāb al-Tabaqāt al-Kabīr* (*The Great Book of the Classes*; biographies of the Prophet and his associates).

†Al-'Attābī, Arab poet.

824

A **Feb**: (?) 11th, Pope Paschal I dies; succeeded (by June 6) by Eugenius II (–827).

825

E Egbert of Wessex, after defeating the Mercians at 'Ellendun' (now Neither Wroughton), conquers Kent, Sussex and Essex.

Michael II defeats Thomas the Slav, a pretender (as 'Constantine VI') to the Byzantine throne supported by Caliph al-Ma'mūn.

Hamsavati (now Pegu) founded as the capital of the Mon kingdom of south Burma.

826

E Louis recognises Nomenoë as chief of the Bretons and receives his homage.

Harold, the exiled King of Denmark, baptised at Mainz.

827

B **Jun**: Ziyādat Allāh I of Kairāwan, exploiting a Christian revolt against Greek rule, begins the conquest of Sicily.

C **Aug**: Pope Eugenius II dies; succeeded by Valentine, who died in September.

D **Dec**: Pope Gregory IV elected (–844).

E Angelo Particiaco, Doge of Venice, dies; succeeded by his son, Giustiniani (–829).

Muslim fugitives from Cordova, on their expulsion from Alexandria, take Crete from the Greeks and make it a centre for piracy in the Aegean (–961).

824

F **Law and Politics**
Lothar of Italy publishes the *Constitutio Romana* defining imperial authority in the Papal States.

K **Literature, Philosophy and Scholarship**
†Han Yü, Chinese poet and philosophical essayist.

825

G **Economics, Science, Technology and Discovery**
Lock-gates in canals first mentioned in China.
Dicuil, *De mensura orbis terrae* (geographical compilation; includes account of an Irish voyage to Iceland in 795).

J **Art, Architecture and Music**
*Mico of St. Riquier compiles a work on prosody.

826

J **Art, Architecture and Music**
A water-organ built at Aachen.

L **Births and Deaths**
Nov. 11th, Theodore the Studite d. (67).

827

G **Economics, Science, Technology and Discovery**
Al-Hajjāj, translation into Arabic of Ptolemy's *Almagest* (astronomy).
Al-Asma'ī, *Kitāb al-Khail* (on the horse); *Kitāb al-Ibil* (on the camel).

J **Art, Architecture and Music**
Mosaics of the apse of San Marco, Rome (–844).
Mosque at 'Amr (with the earliest pointed arch in Egypt).

L **Births and Deaths**
Jan. 2nd, St. Adelard d. (*c.* 72).

828–831 Rebellion against Louis the Pious

828

E Louis the German repels Bulgarian invasion of Pannonia.

829

E Louis the Pious grants Alsace and other territories to his youngest son, Charles (the Bald), thus antagonising his eldest son, Lothar, to whom they had previously been assigned.

Egbert of Wessex (temporarily) conquers Mercia.

Saxony raided by Vikings.

Death of Michael II, the Greek Emperor; succeeded by his son, Theophilus (–842).

Death of Giustiniani Particiaco, Doge of Venice; succeeded by his brother, Giovanni I (–837).

Nanchao (the Thai state in Yunnan, south China) invades Szechuan (–873).

830

B Apr: Pepin and Louis the German lead a considerable Frankish revolt against their father, Louis the Pious. In the autumn, a reaction in Louis the Pious' favour enables him to regain command.

831

A Feb: Louis the Pious deprives Lothar of the imperial title and assigns more territories to his other sons, Pepin (in France), Louis (in Germany) and Charles (in the Rhineland and Provence).

C Sep: Palermo taken by the forces of Ziyādat-Allāh I of Kairāwan.

E Following the death of their Khan, Omortag, the Bulgars resume their attacks on the Byzantine Empire.

828

K **Literature, Philosophy and Scholarship**

†*Abu-al- 'Atāhiyah, 'the father of Arabic sacred poetry'.

829

K **Literature, Philosophy and Scholarship**

*Einhard, *Annales regni Francorum* (chronicle of the period 741–829).

†St. Nicephorus, *Short History* (602–769); *Short Chronography* (from the Creation to 829).

830

G **Economics, Science, Technology and Discovery**

*Mahāvīri, *Ganitasārasamgraha* (*Brief explanation of the compendium of calculation*; Hindu mathematical treatise).

J **Art, Architecture and Music**

(–835) Eastern part of the abbey-church, St. Gall.

*Church of S. Julián de los Prados, near Oviedo.

*Great Mosque of al-Qayrawān (Kairāwan; –*c.* 890).

K **Literature, Philosophy and Scholarship**

Al-Ma'mūn founds the Bayt al-Hikmah ('House of Wisdom'; a library, academy and translation bureau), Baghdād (–856).

*Einhard begins his *Vita Karoli Magni* (*Life of Charlemagne*).

831

H **Religion and Education**

Foundation of the bishopric of Hamburg in newly converted lands.

*Paschasius Radbertus, *De sacramento Corporis et Sanguinis Domini nostri* (asserting the transubstantiation of bread and wine in the Eucharist).

K **Literature, Philosophy and Scholarship**

Yüan Chen, Chinese poet.

832–836 Loss of personal authority by Emperors in China, Japan and Europe, and by the Caliph

832

E Louis the German and Pepin again revolt against Louis the Pious.

Nanchao destroys the kingdom of the Pyu people, the earliest known inhabitants of Burma.

The Uighurs, a Turkish confederation in Manchuria, begin to break up (–840).

833

B **Jun**: 24th, at 'The Field of Lies' (near Colmar), following Pope Gregory's attempt to mediate between Louis the Pious and his again rebellious sons, Lothar, Louis and Pepin, Louis senior is deserted by his followers and surrenders.

C **Aug**: 7th, death of the Caliph al-Ma'mūn while preparing an expedition to Constantinople; succeeded by his brother, al-Mu'tasim (–842). The almost all Turkish army which al-Ma'mūn had created now in control of the Caliphate (–946).

D **Oct**: 1st, Louis the Pious declared to be deposed, and imprisoned.

E Alfonso II, King of Oviedo (Leon), abdicates; succeeded by Ramiro I (–850).

Death of Junna, Emperor of Japan; his (Heian) dynasty continued but effective power exercised by the Fujiwara family.

The Chinese Emperor Wen-tsung's attempt to regain power from the eunuchs fails with the massacre of his ministers in 'the Sweet Dew incident'.

834

A **Mar**: 1st, Louis the Pious restored as emperor in consequence of a breach between Lothar and his brothers Louis and Pepin.

E Vikings ravage Frisia and thereafter make almost annual descents on the Channel coast of France.

Al-Mu'tasim expels the Jalt (gypsies) from Iraq.

835

B **Jun**: Louis the Pious despatches *missi* (itinerant officers) to restore order.

E Vikings resume their raids on England and (about now) begin to establish camps for their operations in Ireland.

836

E Vikings sack London.

Al-Mu'tasim transfers his capital from Baghdād to Sāmarra (–892); here he and his successors as Caliph were virtually prisoners of their Turkish bodyguard.

'Amrān succeeds his father as governor of Sind, an indication of the decline of the Caliph's authority there.

832

J **Art, Architecture and Music**
*Utrecht Psalter.

833

F **Law and Politics**
†St. Ansegisus made collections of capitularies of Charlemagne and Louis the Pious.
Ryō no gige (commentary on the *Yorō Code*, the Japanese law-code of 718).

G **Economics, Science, Technology and Discovery**
†The Caliph al-Ma'mūn founded an observatory at Baghdād and encouraged geographical exploration.

J **Art, Architecture and Music**
*S. Vincenzo in Prato, Milan (a vaulted basilica which is the earliest Lombard church in the 'first Romanesque' style).

L **Births and Deaths**
July 20th, St. Ansegisus d.

834

835

G **Economics, Science, Technology and Discovery**
First reference to a printed book in China.

836

J **Art, Architecture and Music**
Church of St. George, Oberzell.
The apse of the priory-church of St. Philibert-de-Grandlieu, Déas, demolished, and the sanctuary bay and a new apse built (–847).

837–840 Raids by Vikings on France and Saracens on Italy

837

B **Jun**: 29th, Giovanni I Particiaco, Doge of Venice, deposed; succeeded by Pietro Tradonico (–864).

E 'Abd-ar-Rahmān II crushes a revolt in Toledo.
Saracens of Sicily relieve the siege of Naples by Sikard, duke of Benevento, at the request of Andreas, duke of Naples; they next sack Brindisi.
Magyars, established in the Don-Danube area, assist the Bulgars against rebels.

838

B **Jun**: 13th, al-Mu'tasim sacks Amorium after defeating the Emperor Theophilus on the River Iris, but abandons his attempt to take Constantinople.

D **Dec**: 13th, death of Pepin I, King of Aquitaine.

E Saracens sack Marseilles and establish a base in southern Italy.

839

B **May**: 30th, by a new division of the Frankish Empire made at Worms, Louis the Pious assigns lands west of the Meuse, Moselle and western Alps to Charles the Bald, and to the east to Lothar, excepting Bavaria (which remains to Louis the German). Although Charles is invested as King of Aquitaine, he is opposed by Pepin II, son of Pepin I, who was proclaimed King there.

E Death of Egbert, King of Wessex and principal English king; succeeded by his son, Ethelwulf (–855).
Death of Sikard, duke of Benevento, leads to the duchy's division into principalities centred on Benevento and Salerno; while Amalfi becomes independent under Byzantine suzerainty.

840

B **Jun**: 20th, death of Louis the Pious on his return from an expedition against Louis the German; succeeded as emperor by his son, Lothar (–855).

E Vikings sail up the Seine, for the first time, to Rouen.
Saracens from Sicily take Taranto and Bari, then plunder the Adriatic coast to Venice.
(and later) The Uighurs driven from their empire on the Orkhan River by the Khirgiz and settle in the Tarim basin (Turfan).

837

G **Economics, Science, Technology and Discovery**
First notice of a carrier-pigeon service in the Arab Empire.

838

839

840

G **Economics, Science, Technology and Discovery**
*The gold altar of Sant'Ambrogio, Milan, has the earliest pictorial representation of a stirrup.

K **Literature, Philosophy and Scholarship**
*Agnellus, *The Lives of the Archbishops of Ravenna* (remarkable because of the author's research into primary sources).
†Einhard, *Epistolae*.

841

B **Jun:** 25th, the Emperor Lothar, supported by Pepin II of Aquitaine, defeated at Fontenoy by his brothers, Louis the German and Charles the Bald, who oppose his claims to authority under the *Constitutio* of 817.

842

A **Jan:** 5th, death of the Caliph, al-Mu'tasim; succeeded by his son, al-Wāthiq (–847).
20th, death of the Greek Emperor, Theophilus; succeeded by his son, Michael III (–867), with the Empress Theodora as regent (–855).
Feb: 14th, Louis the German and Charles the Bald, at Strasbourg, reaffirm their alliance against Lothar.

B **Jun:** 15th, Lothar, deserted by his followers, makes peace with Louis and Charles.

E London and Quentovic sacked by the Vikings.
Radelchis, prince of Benevento, subjected by the Saracens whom he had engaged against Sikonolf of Salerno.
Piast (traditionally) elected duke of Poland (–861).
Langdarma, King of Tibet, attempting to suppress Buddhism, murdered by a lama; the collapse of his empire followed.

843

C **Aug:** Treaty of Verdun partitioning the Carolingian Empire; Lothar retains the title (only) of Emperor and receives 'the Middle Kingdom' (of Italy, lands between the Rhine and Rhône–Saône–Scheldt, and Frisia), while Louis receives Germany (–876) and Charles France and the Spanish March (–877).

E Scotland first united when Kenneth MacAlpin, King of the Scots, becomes King of the Picts (–858).
Vikings establish a camp at Noirmoutier, on River Loire.
Saracen conquest of Sicily almost completed with the capture of Messina.

844

A **Jan:** 25th, death of Pope Gregory IV; succeeded by (John ?, then later by) Sergius II (–847).

C **Sep:** Vikings, who had already raided the Garonne basin, repulsed at Lisbon by Moors, but then sacked Cadiz, Seville and Cordova.

D **Oct:** in a meeting at Yütz, near Thionville, the Emperor Lothar, Charles the Bald and Louis the German, establish principles of fraternal co-operation.

E An expedition sent to Aquitaine by Charles the Bald fails to defeat Pepin II.

841

H **Religion and Education**

†Agobard, Archbishop of Lyons, *Liber contra insulsam vulgi opinionem de grandine et tonitruis* (against magic).

J **Art, Architecture and Music**

Apse of abbey-church of St. Germain, Auxerre, begun.

842

H **Religion and Education**

With the collapse of the Uighurs (840–3), the Manichean monasteries in China lost their patronage, were closed and the religion banned.

K **Literature, Philosophy and Scholarship**

The oaths of Strasbourg (*see* A) provide the first distinction between the French and German languages.

*Georgios Monachos, *World Chronicle* (Greek; from the Creation to 842; –948).

843

H **Religion and Education**

Mar. A synod of the Greek Church repeals the iconoclastic decrees and re-establishes Orthodoxy; end of the Iconoclast Controversy.

K **Literature, Philosophy and Scholarship**

Nithard, Abbot of St. Riquier, *History of the Sons of Louis the Pious* (Charlemagne's grandson's history of his own time, down to 843).

844

845

A **Jan**: 1st, baptism of fourteen Bohemian nobles at the court of Louis the German.

B **Jun**: by the Treaty of St. Benoît sur Loire, Charles the Bald recognises, and receives the homage of, Pepin II as King of Aquitaine, from whose lands the duchy of Aquitaine is detached and conferred on Rainulf I, count of Poitiers.

D **Nov**: 22nd, the Bretons, led by Nomenoë, defeat an army sent by Charles the Bald to enforce their subjection, at Ballon.

E Paris sacked by Vikings, whom Charles subsequently pays to leave.
Death of Turgeis, the Viking conqueror of northern Ireland.
Hamburg sacked by Danes under King Horik.
Saracens from Sicily take Ponza and Ischia as naval bases for raids on the Italian coast.

846

C **Aug**: 26th, the basilica of St. Peter and other places outside the walls of Rome plundered by Saracens.

E Charles the Bald, in a treaty with Nomenoë, recognises the independence of Brittany; he also agrees to leave Lambert, a count of the Breton March, in possession of Maine, despite his rebellion.
Louis the German defeats Mojmír, ruler of Moravia, and appoints Rostislav as his successor (–870).
Vijayālaya captures Tanjore, in the Pāndya kingdom of South India; this event marks the birth of the Chola Empire (–1279).

847

A **Jan**: 27th, death of Pope Sergius II.

B **Apr**: 10th, Leo IV crowned as Pope (–855); he soon began the walling of St. Peter's, so forming the 'Leonine City'.

C **Aug**: 10th *or* 11th, death of the Caliph al-Wāthiq; succeeded by his brother, al-Mutawakkil (–861).

E The Emperor Lothar and King Charles and Louis meet at Meerssen, near Maastricht, and agree to guarantee the inheritances of their children.
Louis, Lothar's son, defeats Saracens and takes Benevento.

845

H **Religion and Education**

Alien religions prohibited in China; Buddhist property confiscated.

J **Art, Architecture and Music**

**Li-tai Ming-hua chi* (*A Record of the Famous Paintings of All Periods*; compilation inspired by the destruction of works of art during the suppression of Buddhist monasteries in China).

K **Literature, Philosophy and Scholarship**

†*Abū-Tammām, *Dīwān* (collection of Arabic poetry); *Dīwān al-Hamāsah* (poems celebrating valour in battle).

846

G **Economics, Science, Technology and Discovery**

*Ibn-Khurdādhbih, first edition of his *al-Masālik w-al Mamālik* (*Book of Routes and Kingdoms* in Asia; geography based on itinerary of Arabic postal services).

K **Literature, Philosophy and Scholarship**

*Po-Chü-i, *Po-shih Ch'ang-ch'ing chi* (the works of famous Chinese poet, including *Ch'ang-hen ko—The Song of Everlasting Remorse*).

847

F **Law and Politics**

Charles the Bald's Capitulary of Meerssen orders every free man to choose himself a lord in order to facilitate the levy of an army.

G **Economics, Science, Technology and Discovery**

Vikings colonise Iceland.

J **Art, Architecture and Music**

(–861) Mosque at Sāmarra (the oldest surviving ruin of the 'Abbasīd period).

†Al-Wāthiq, the first Caliph-musician (lutanist and composer).

K **Literature, Philosophy and Scholarship**

*Ennin, diary (Japanese) of his stay in China (838–47).

848

B **Jun**: 6th, Charles the Bald crowned as King of Aquitaine following Pepin II's desertion by his subjects.

E Saracen fleet from Sicily destroyed by storm when on its way to Rome.

849

E Traditional date for the fortification of Pagan (on R. Irrawaddy), the capital of an emerging Burmese kingdom (–1287).

850

B **Apr**: Louis II, son of Lothar, crowned in Rome as Emperor and King of Italy (–875).

E Ramiro I succeeded by Ordoño I as King of Oviedo (–866).
Death of Jayavarman II, who has reunited the Khmers of Cambodia in independence from Java, founding his capital at Hariharalaya (near Angkor).
*Vikings now operating from camps on the Rhine, Scheldt, Somme, Seine, Loire and Garonne.
(–860) Kiev taken from the Khazars by Askold and Dir, Vikings (–878); this was the beginning of the Varangian empire of the Ros (the Swedish name for seamen, whence 'Russia').

848

J **Art, Architecture and Music**

Consecration of the vaulted church of Sta. Mariá de Naranco, near Oviedo.

*Vaulted church of S. Miguel de Linio, near Naranco.

K **Literature, Philosophy and Scholarship**

†Sedulius Scottus, *De rectoribus Christianis* (verse compilations on the New Testament); commentaries on grammar.

849

H **Religion and Education**

Gottschalk condemned as a heretic because of the predestinarian views of his *Confessio Prolixior*; this was refuted by Hincmar, in *De prædestinacione Dei*, and by Erigena (–851).

†Walafrid Strabo, *Glossa Ordinaria* (compilation of patristic commentaries on the Bible which became a standard work in twelfth-century monasteries).

†Abu-Sulaymān al-Dārānī, the Sūfī saint.

J **Art, Architecture and Music**

The echelon added to the apse of the abbey-church of St. Germain, Auxerre (–859).

K **Literature, Philosophy and Scholarship**

†Walafrid Strabo, *De imagine Tetrici* (poem); *De cultura hortorum* (the first medieval 'Georgic', describing herbs).

L **Births and Deaths**

— Alfred b. (–901).

850

G **Economics, Science, Technology and Discovery**

†Al-Khwārizmī, *Hisāb al-Jabr w-al Muqābalah* (*The Calculation of Integration and Equation*; when 'algebra' possibly originates; –1145, 1187, 1307); *Sūrat al-Ard* (*Image of the World*, with a map of the world and heavens); astronomical tables (–1126).

Al-Tabarī, *Firdaws al-Hikmah* (*Paradise of Wisdom*; Arabic compendium of medicine).

*Earliest Chinese reference to gunpowder.

H **Religion and Education**

Appearance of the collection of canons known as *The False Decretals* of the self-styled Isidore, Bishop of Seville (*alias* Pseudo-Isidore).

†Fulgentius Fenandus of Carthage, *Breviatio canonum* (compilation of African canons).

851

A **Mar**: 7th, death of Nomenoë, ruler of Brittany; succeeded by his son, Erispoë.

E Ethelwulf defeats the Danes at Oakley; they then first winter in England, in Thanet.
Danes led by King Oscar ravage Aquitaine, then sail to Rouen and plunder in the Beauvaisis.

852

B **May**: 28th, execution of the Saracen leader, Masar, by Louis II in his second expedition to recover Benevento; the Sicilian Saracens respond with the devastation and occupation of Calabria.

C **Sep**: Pepin II of Aquitaine delivered to Charles the Bald and imprisoned.
22nd, death of ʿAbd-ar-Rahmān II, Emir of Spain; succeeded by Muhammad I (–886).

853

B **May**: 22nd, a Greek expedition captures Damietta.

E Olaf the White, son of the King of Norway, receives the submission of Vikings and Danes in Ireland and makes Dublin his capital.
Tours burnt by Danes.
The nobles of Aquitaine offer their crown to Louis the German.
(or later?) Mufarrij-ibn-Sālim establishes an independent Saracen dynasty at Bari; it becomes a base for plundering central Italy.

854

E The death, in battle, of Horik, King of Denmark, leads to the disintegration of his kingdom.
Blois and Orleans sacked by Danes.
Pepin II reassumes the crown of Aquitaine.

851

G **Economics, Science, Technology and Discovery**
Silsilat al-Tawārikh (anon. Arabic account of journeys by Sulaymān the merchant from the Persian Gulf to India and China; a source of the stories of Sindbād the Sailor).

H **Religion and Education**
Johannes Scotus Erigena, *De divina prædestinatione* (refuting Gottschalk; –849).

852

H **Religion and Education**
ʿAbd-ar-Rahmān II of Spain holds a synod of Christian subjects and forbids them from seeking martyrdom.

K **Literature, Philosophy and Scholarship**
†*Frechulph of Lisieux, *History of the World.*

853

J **Art, Architecture and Music**
†Kudara-no-Kawanari, Japanese painter.

854

H **Religion and Education**
†Al-Tabarī, *Kitāb al-Dīn w-al-Dawlah* (defence of Islam, citing the Bible).

855

B **Jun**(?): Charles, son of Charles the Bald, crowned as King of Aquitaine (–866).

C **Jul**: 17th, death of Pope Leo IV and election of Benedict III (–858).
Aug: election of Anastasius as pope.
Sep: 24th, expulsion of Anastasius.
28th–29th, death in retirement, of the Emperor Lothar; he had partitioned his lands among his three sons, *viz.* the Emperor Louis II (Italy), Lothar II (from Frisia to the Alps, called *Lotharii regnum*, *i.e.* Lorraine) and Charles (the kingdom of Provence).

D **Nov**: 20th, the Greek Emperor, Michael III, begins his personal rule on the murder of (St.) Theoctistus the Logothete, the principal minister of Michael's mother, Theodora, as regent.

E Ethelbald deposes and succeeds his father, Ethelwulf, as King of Wessex (–860).
The Caliph al-Mutawakkil's last expedition to Caucasia completes its conquest.

856

A **Feb**: 10th, by the treaty of Louviers, Charles the Bald recognises Erispoë as King of Brittany.

C **Aug**: Vikings, led by Sidroe, establish a camp on the Seine, at Pitres, and ravage as far as the Loire.

D **Dec**: 28th, Paris burnt by Vikings.

E Expedition sent by Michael III reaches the Euphrates.

857

E *Garcia Ximenez establishes the kingdom of Navarre (–880).

855

H **Religion and Education**

†Ahmad ibn-Hanbal, founder of the Hanbalite sect of Islam, *Musnad* (collection of 30,000 traditions).

856

H **Religion and Education**

†Rabanus Maurus, *De institutione clericorum* (treatise on education); Biblical encyclopedia.

K **Literature, Philosophy and Scholarship**

*Al-Mutawakkil refounds the 'House of Wisdom', Baghdād, under Hunayn (–830).

L **Births and Deaths**

Feb. 4th, Rabanus Maurus d. (80).

857

F **Law and Politics**

Foundation of the perpetual regency of the Fujiwara family, which continued even when the Japanese emperors were of age (–1867).

G **Economics, Science, Technology and Discovery**

†Yuhannā ibn-Māsawayh, *Daghal al-'Ain* (*Disorder of the Eye*; oldest extant, systematic treatise on ophthalmology in Arabic).

858

A **Jan**: 13th, death of Ethelwulf, former King of Wessex.

B **Apr**: 17th (?), death of Pope Benedict III.
24th, Nicholas I crowned as Pope (–867).

C **Sep**: Louis the German takes possession of France, Charles the Bald being abandoned by the French magnates.

E Death of Kenneth MacAlpin, first King of Scotland; succeeded by his brother, Donald I (–862).

859

E Charles the Bald regains possession of France on the desertion by its magnates of Louis the German.
Vikings raid Algericas.
Conquest of Sicily by the Saracens completed.
Ashot I founds the Bagratide dynasty of Armenia (–890).

860

B **Jun**: 1st, Charles the Bald and Louis the German make peace at Coblenz.
18th, Vikings from Russia repulsed in an attack on Constantinople.

E Death of Ethelbald, King of Wessex; succeeded by his brother, Ethelbert (–865).
Vikings ravage the Balearic Islands and Provence.

861

B **May**: 28th, Paris again burnt by Vikings.

D **Dec**: 11th, the Caliph al-Mutawakkil murdered by his Turkish guard and succeeded by his son, al-Muntassir (–862).

E Charles the Bald fails in an attempt to seize the kingdom of Provence.
Pisa taken by Vikings.
Lothar II divorces his wife and marries his mistress.
Ziemovit succeeds his father, Piast, as Duke of Poland (–892).

858

H **Religion and Education**

(–867) Nicholas I declares that bishops are his delegates, contrary to the custom of their subjection to secular monarchs.

Dec. 25th, the election of Photius as Patriarch in succession to Ignatius, who had 'retired', was to cause a dispute with the Pope.

859

H **Religion and Education**

Mar. 11th, Eulogius, Archbishop of Toledo, executed by the Moors; he was the author of martyrologies and of anti-Muslim polemic.

860

F **Law and Politics**

Hincmar, Archbishop of Reims, *De divortio Lotharii* (treatise opposing Lothar's desire to divorce his childless wife and marry his mistress; the first medieval tract of a political nature).

G **Economics, Science, Technology and Discovery**

*Muhammad, Ahmad and Hasan, sons of Mūsā ibn-Shakir, *Book of Artifices* (the earliest extant treatise on mechanics).

H **Religion and Education**

†Dhu-al-Nūn, Sūfī theosophist.

J **Art, Architecture and Music**

The church and cells on Skellig Michael built (now? –*cf.* 823) on the island's resettlement by monks.

861

862

B **May**: 29th, al-Musta'in succeeds his brother, al-Muntassir, as Caliph (–866).

E Constantine I, son of Kenneth, succeeds Donald I as King of Scotland (–877).
Charles the Bald, by the new method of fortifying bridges, begins to hamper Danish raiders.
Ordoño I takes Salamanca.
Riurick (of Jutland) founds the first dynasty of Princes of Russia at Novgorod (–873).

863

A **Jan**: 25th, death of Charles, King of Provence, without issue; Louis II and Lothar II share his lands.

C **Sep** (and **Oct**): victories of Michael III over the Arabs of Armenia which mark a turning point in the wars between Byzantium and the Muslims.

E Charles the Bald invests his son-in-law, Count Baldwin I, in a 'march' against the Vikings, thus creating the origin of the county of Flanders.
Pyinbya, King of Nanchao, takes Hanoi (–866).

864

A **Mar**: 15th, Pietro Tradonico, Doge of Venice, murdered; succeeded by Orso Particiaco (–881).

E Michael III compels Boris I, Khan of the Bulgars, to receive baptism as a Christian.

862

H **Religion and Education**

At the request of Rostislav of Moravia, the Emperor Michael sends the brothers Constantine (later called Cyril) and Methodius to convert Slovakia; Cyril devised a Slavonic script ('Glagolitic' *i.e.* Cyrillic script) and translated the Bible and liturgical texts into Slavonic.

J **Art, Architecture and Music**

Reims Cathedral dedicated.

K **Literature, Philosophy and Scholarship**

†Servatus Lupus, Abbot of Ferrières, philologist.

L **Births and Deaths**

July 2nd, St. Swithin, Bishop of Winchester, d.

863

H **Religion and Education**

Aug. Pope Nicholas orders the restoration of Ignatius as Patriarch of Constantinople and the removal of Photius, whom he excommunicates.

Oct. Nicholas declares the Archbishops of Cologne, Trier and Ravenna to be deposed; such depositions by a pope were a novelty.

Caesar Bardas founds a secular university in Constantinople under Leo the Mathematician.

864

865–866 Danish victories in England and France—Nanchao invades Annam

865

A **Jan:** Pope Nicholas I orders Archbishop Hincmar of Reims to reinstate Rothad as Bishop of Soissons.

Feb: Charles the Bald and Louis the German meet at Douzy and agree to partition Lothar II's lands when he dies.

B **Jun:** Lothar II, who had submitted to the judgment of Nicholas I, obeys the Pope's order to take back his wife, Theutberga.

E Constantinople besieged by Vikings from Russia.

(or 866) Death of Ethelbert, King of Wessex; succeeded by his brother, Ethelred (–871).

866

A **Jan:** 24th, the Caliph al-Musta'in deposed by his Turkish guard and succeeded by his brother, al-Mu'tazz (–869).

B **Apr:** 21st, the Logothete Bardas murdered by Michael III.

May: 17th, death of Ordoño I, King of Oviedo; succeeded by his son, Alfonso III (–910).

C **Aug:** Boris I, in revolt against Michael III who had refused to allow a Bulgarian ecclesiastical establishment, sends an offer of allegiance to Pope Nicholas I.

Sep: 29th, death of Charles, King of Aquitaine; succeeded by his brother, Louis the Stammerer (–879).

D **Nov:** 1st, the 'Great Army' of the Danes, who had established a base in East Anglia, takes York.

E Robert the Strong, marquess of Neustria, who had successfully fought the Danes in the Loire Valley, killed in battle at Brissarthe.

Charles the Bald pays ransom to Danes who had reached Melun.

Louis II makes his third expedition against the Saracens in south Italy.

Chinese repel Nanchao from the Red River Delta.

865

G **Economics, Science, Technology and Discovery**

†Leon the Iastrosophist, a medical encyclopedia; he was said to have invented an optical telegraph.

H **Religion and Education**

†St. Anskar, Bishop of Hamburg (from 826), the 'apostle of the north', had founded Christianity in Denmark and Sweden.

*The Khazars (living between the Sea of Azov and the Lower Volga) converted to Judaism.

K **Literature, Philosophy and Scholarship**

*Johannes Scotus Erigena, *De Divisione Naturæ* (a dialogue, condemned as pantheistic and later placed on the Index; it was 'the one purely philosophical argument of the middle ages'—*W. P. Ker*).

L **Births and Deaths**

Feb. 3rd, St. Anskar d. (64).

Apr. 26th, Paschasius Radbertus d.

866

G **Economics, Science, Technology and Discovery**

Oldest dated Arabic paper manuscript (in Leyden University Library).

867

A **Mar:** 21st, Aelle, King of Northumbria, killed by Danes; his successors were Danish puppets (–875).

C **Sep:** 24th, the Greek Emperor, Michael III, murdered and succeeded by Basil I (–886), founder of the Macedonian dynasty (–963).

D **Nov:** 3rd, Basil deposes Photius and restores Ignatius as Patriarch of Constantinople.
13th, death of Pope Nicholas I.
Dec: 14th, Adrian II crowned as Pope (–872).

E Ya'qūb ibn-al-Layth al-Sāffar, governor of Sijistān, establishes the Saffārid dynasty (–908).

868

E By raising the siege of Ragusa by Muslim forces, the Greek Empire completes its control over the Balkans.
Ahmad-ibn-Tūlūn, the Turkish governor of Egypt, makes himself independent of the Caliph; he founded the Tulunid dynasty (–905).

869

B **Jun:** 16th, the Caliph al-Mu'tazz deposed by his Turkish guard and succeeded by his brother, al-Muhtadī (–870).

C **Aug:** 8th, death of Lothar II, King of Lorraine, without legitimate issue.
Sep: rebellion of the negro slaves employed in the saltpetre mines in Iraq (–883).
9th, Charles the Bald, ignoring the rights of Louis II and his own agreement with Louis the German (–865), crowned as King of Lorraine.

E Saracens of Kairāwan conquer Malta.

867

H **Religion and Education**

Photius anathematizes Nicholas in a council at Constantinople, and condemns the inclusion of *Filioque* in the Procession of the Holy Ghost in the Roman Church.

The Paulicians (an extensive heretical movement reviving Manichaeism and flourishing in Armenia) take Ephesus.

868

G **Economics, Science, Technology and Discovery**

Printed roll, dated 11 May 868, of Chinese translation of the Buddhist Diamond Sutra (the earliest surviving work in print).

K **Literature, Philosophy and Scholarship**

*Otfrid of Weissenburg, *Evangelienbuch* (a version of Gospel history in rhyming verse, intended to be sung, by the first German poet of whom there is any record).

869

G **Economics, Science, Technology and Discovery**

†Sābūr ben Sahl, a pharmacopeia.

H **Religion and Education**

*Adrian II appoints Methodius as Bishop of Moravia.

K **Literature, Philosophy and Scholarship**

†Al-Jāhiz, *Kitāb al-Hayāwan* (*Book of Animals*; by the first writer of Arabic *belles-lettres*).

L **Births and Deaths**

Feb. 14th, St. Cyril d.

Oct. 30th, Gottschalk d.

870

A **Feb**: Boris, Khan of the Bulgars, accepts the ecclesiastical authority of the Patriarch of Constantinople.

B **Jun**: 21st, the Caliph al-Mutadi murdered by his Turkish guard; succeeded by his cousin, al-Muʿtamid (–892).

C **Aug**: 8th, after invading Lorraine, Louis the German meets Charles the Bald at Meerssen and agrees to partition the kingdom.

D **Nov**: 20th, St. Edmund, King of East Anglia, killed by Danes.

E Charles the Bald occupies Provence and commits it to the charge of Boso; he also grants Anjou to Ingelger (–888).

Rostislav, Prince of Moravia, captured and deposed by his nephew, Svátopluk (–894), and Carloman, son of Louis the German; Carloman conquers Moravia.

871

A **Jan**: the West Saxons, at Ashdown, drive the Danes back into their camp at Reading.

Feb: 2nd, Louis II, with Byzantine naval assistance, takes Bari from the Saracens; he later defeats Saracens from Salerno at Capua.

B **Apr**: death of Ethelred, King of Wessex; succeeded by his brother, Alfred (–899).

E London occupied by the Danes.

Charles the Bald suppresses a revolt by his son, Carloman, whom he blinded.

Svátopluk expels the Germans from Moravia.

872

D **Dec**: 14th, John VIII crowned as Pope in succession to Adrian II (–882).

E Charles the Bald expels Vikings from Angers.

Basil I defeats the Paulicians, destroys their fortress at Tephrice, and effects their conversion to the Orthodox Church.

Al-Saffār destroys the Tāhirid dynasty of Khurāsān.

873

E *Death of Riurik of Novgorod; succeeded by his son, Igor, with Oleg as regent (–913).

870

H **Religion and Education**

†Al-Bukhārī, *al-Sahīh* (*The Genuine Collection*; a system of Muslim theology and law).

Methodius imprisoned at the instance of German prelates when en route for his mission to Moravia (–874, E).

871

K **Literature, Philosophy and Scholarship**

†Al-Hakam, *Futūh Misr w-al-Maghrib* (history of the Muslim conquest of Egypt, North Africa and Spain).

872

G **Economics, Science, Technology and Discovery**

*Ibn Tūlūn founds the first hospital in Cairo; hospitals now common in the Muslim countries.

J **Art, Architecture and Music**

A cathedral dedicated at Hildesheim.

873

G **Economics, Science, Technology and Discovery**

†Hunayn, *al-ʿAshr Maqālāt fi al-ʿAyn* (*The Ten Treatises on the Eye*); translations into Arabic from Greek of scientific works by Aristotle, Euclid, Galen and Hippocrates.

K **Literature, Philosophy and Scholarship**

†Al-Kindī, Arab Neo-Platonic philosopher, alchemist, astrologer, optician and musical theorist.

874

E Burgred, the last King of Mercia, expelled by the Danes.

By the Treaty of Forchheim, peace made between Louis the German and Svátopluk of Moravia who, for a time, becomes a tributary to the German king; in consequence, the Germans release Methodius.

Alfonso III defeats the Moors of Toledo at the Orbedo.

Nasr ibn-Ahmad founds the Sāmānid dynasty of Transoxiana (-999); its capital at Bukhāra becomes the centre for a Persian cultural revival.

A peasant rising led by Wang Hsien-chih and Huang Ch'ao takes control of eastern China.

875

C **Aug**: 12th, death of Louis II, the Emperor and King of Italy; Basil I subsequently takes possession of Bari.

D **Dec**: Louis the German invades Lorraine but withdraws on his failure to win local support.

25th, Charles the Bald crowned as Emperor by Pope John VIII in Rome (-877).

E Catalonia, formerly the Spanish march of the Carolingian Empire, now being ruled by the counts of Barcelona in only nominal subjection to the French king.

(or 876) Halfdan founds the Danish kingdom of York (-954); Danes now settling here.

*Bořivoj I, Prince of Bohemia, baptised by Methodius.

876

A **Jan**: 31st, Charles the Bald accepted as King of Italy at Pavia.

C **Aug**: 28th, death of Louis the German; his lands divided by his sons Carloman (Bavaria and the East March; -880), Louis the Younger (Saxony and Franconia; -882), and Charles the Fat (Alemannia; -888).

D **Oct**: 8th, Charles the Bald defeated at Andernach, on the Rhine, by Louis of Saxony.

877

B **May**: 7th, Charles the Bald orders the payment of a tax (*tributum Normannicum*) to pay Danes to leave the Seine area.

D **Oct**: 6th, death of Charles the Bald after his return from Italy, where the French nobles deserted him.

Dec: 8th, coronation of his son, Louis II the Stammerer, as King of the French (-879).

E Danes, driven from Exeter to Gloucester, begin to settle in western Mercia; others (about now) settling in the eastern part, establishing 'the Five Boroughs' of Lincoln, Stamford, Nottingham, Derby and Leicester.

Halfdan, the Danish king of York, killed in the battle of Strangford Lough against Baraidh, a Norse leader in Ireland.

Constantine I succeeded as King of Scotland by his brother, Aed (-878).

Ibn-Tūlūn of Egypt seizes Syria.

874

H **Religion and Education**

*A Greek archbishop sent as a missionary to Russia following a treaty between the Emperor and the Swedes of Kiev.

†Ibn-al-Hajjāj, *al-Sahīh* (the second of this name in the Muslim canon; –870).

875

J **Art, Architecture and Music**

*Levy Hradec, near Prague, the earliest surviving church in Bohemia.

*Basilica of S. Pietro, Agliate, near Milan.

K **Literature, Philosophy and Scholarship**

†*Hanzala of Badghis, Persian poet.

L **Births and Deaths**

Oct. 28th, St. Remi, Archbishop of Lyons, d. (*c.* 75).

876

J **Art, Architecture and Music**

S. Satiro, Milan (a church in the Byzantine style)

Ibn Tūlūn Mosque, Cairo, begun.

L **Births and Deaths**

— Henry the Fowler b. (–936).

877

F **Law and Politics**

June 14th, a capitulary of Charles the Bald issued in an assembly at Quierz seemingly recognises the hereditability of fiefs though it was designed to order government in his absence; while it may not be regarded as a charter for 'the feudal system', feudalism had effectively come into being in Charles' time by his grants to vassals, *e.g.* the practical establishment of Richard the Justiciar as the first Duke of Burgundy (*and see* 870 E).

G **Economics, Science, Technology and Discovery**

Al-Battānī begins his astronomical observations in al-Raqqah (–918).

H **Religion and Education**

Photius restored as Patriarch of Constantinople on the death of Ignatius.

L **Births and Deaths**

Oct. 23rd, St. Ignatius d.

— Johannes Scotus Erigena d. (*c.* 64).

878

A Jan: Alfred of Wessex takes refuge from the Danes in Athelney.

B May: Alfred defeats the Danes at Edington; by the peace of Wedmore, their leader, Guthrum, baptised as a Christian.
21st, Ibrāhīm II of Kairāwan destroys Syracuse.

C Sep: 7th, second coronation of Louis II by Pope John VIII, at Troyes.

E Aed, King of Scotland, succeeded by his nephew, Eochaid (–889).
Death of Rhodri the Great, King of Gwynedd, Powys and Seisyllwg; his kingdom now disintegrates.
Bourges sacked by the Danes.
Pope John VIII pays tribute to obtain peace from the Saracens.
The Chinese peasant leader, Wang Hsien-chih, defeated and executed by the Sha-t'o, the Turkish allies of the emperor.
*Oleg, regent of Novgorod, seizes Kiev; Askold and Dir killed.

879

B Apr: 10th, death of Louis II of France; succeeded by his sons, Louis III (–882) and Carloman (–884), after abortive invasion by Louis of Saxony.

D Oct: 15th, Boso crowned as King of Provence (–887).
Nov: 30th, Louis III and Carloman defeat Vikings on the Loire.

E Chinese rebels led by Huang Ch'ao sack Canton.
Nepal makes itself independent of Tibet.

880

A Feb: 2nd, Bruno, who had emerged as the tribal duke of Saxony by leading its defence against the Danes and Wends, killed in battle with the Danes on Lüneburg Heath.
Mar: Treaty of Ribemont: partition of France between Louis III (Francia and Neustria) and Carloman (Burgundy and Aquitaine).

E Death of Carloman of Bavaria; succeeded by his brother, Louis of Saxony (–882).
Fortunus succeeds his father, Garcia Ximenez, as King of Navarre (–905).
Basil I takes Taranto and expels the Saracens from Calabria.
Varagunavarman II of Pāndya, attempting to crush the Cholas, defeated at Sri Parambiyan by Āditya I and his overlord, Nriputungavarman of Pallava.
Huang Ch'ao declares himself Emperor of China (–884).

878

H **Religion and Education**

Disappearance of Muhammad al-Muntazar, twelfth Imām of the Ismā'ite sect of the Shī'ites (al-Mahdī, the 'Hidden Imām', whose followers still await his return).

J **Art, Architecture and Music**

Foundation of the Abbey of St. Michel, Cuxa.

879

F **Law and Politics**

Basil publishes a revised compilation of Roman Law (–886).

G **Economics, Science, Technology and Discovery**

120,000 'foreigners' said to have been killed in Canton (despite its exaggeration, this figure indicates the size of foreign, *viz.* Arab, Persian, etc., trading communities who at this time dominate China's export trade, particularly with Korea and Japan).

J **Art, Architecture and Music**

A double cathedral at Santiago de Compostela (–896).

L **Births and Deaths**

Sep. 17th, Charles the Simple b. (–929).

880

H **Religion and Education**

The Greek Church makes peace with the Pope.

John VIII licenses the use of Slavonic in the liturgy.

881

A **Feb**: 12th, Charles the Fat of Alemannia crowned as Emperor by John VIII (–888).

C **Aug**: 3rd, Louis III defeats Vikings at Saucourt (on the Somme).

E Death of Orso I Particiaco, Doge of Venice; succeeded by his son, Giovanni II (–888).
(and 882) Vikings sack Liège, Tongres, Cologne, Bonn, Stavelot, Prüm, Aachen and Trier.

882

A **Jan**: 20th, death of Louis of Saxony and Bavaria; succeeded by Charles the Fat, who thus reunites Germany (–888).

C **Aug**: 5th, death of Louis III; succeeded by his brother and co-king, Carloman.
Sep: Richard the Justiciar, on behalf of Charles the Fat, takes Vienne and expels his brother Boso, the usurping King of Provence.

D The Viking army, having been paid by Charles the Fat to leave the Rhineland, invades eastern France, sacking Reims.
Dec: 15th, murder of Pope John VIII; succeeded by Marinus I (also known as Martin II; –884).

883

E The Caliph's forces finally suppresses the negro rebellion (–869) after it had caused immense slaughter.

884

B **May**: 15th, death of Pope Marinus I.
17th, Adrian III crowned as his successor (–885).

C Carloman pays the Viking army to leave France; the main part goes to England, the rest into Lorraine.

D **Dec**: 12th, death of Carloman; succeeded, on the invitation of the French nobles, by Charles the Fat, who thus reunites the empire of Charlemagne (–888).

E Diego de Porcelos founds Burgos, which becomes the capital of Castile.
The usurping emperor, Huang Ch'ao, defeated and killed by the Turkish Sha-t'o; their leader Li K'o-yung now disputes control of North China with Chu Wen, Huang's lieutenant.

881

K **Literature, Philosophy and Scholarship**
*The *Ludwigslied* (in praise of Louis of Bavaria and his victory in 881; the first historical ballad in German literature).

882

L **Births and Deaths**
Dec. 21st, Hincmar d. (*c.* 75).
— ʿUbaydullāh b. (–934).

883

G **Economics, Science, Technology and Discovery**
†Avantivarman, King of Kashmīr, promoted irrigation schemes.

K **Literature, Philosophy and Scholarship**
*Nokter Balbulus (?), *Gesta Karoli Magni* (Charlemagne epic).

884

885

C **Jul**: 25th, the Viking army enters Rouen.
Sep: death of Pope Adrian III; succeeded by Stephen V (–891).

D **Nov**: 24th, the Viking army under King Sigefrid lays siege to Paris, where the defence is led by Odo, son of Robert the Strong, Marquess of Neustria. Charles the Fat pays the Vikings to leave, for Burgundy.

E Death in battle of Godefrid, a Viking king ruling on the Lower Rhine by the grant of Charles the Fat, thus ending Viking rule in Frisia.
Ashot I the Great recognised as King of Armenia by both the Emperor Basil I and the Caliph Al-Muʿtamid; he was effectively independent.

886

C **Aug**: 29th, death of Greek Emperor, Basil I the Macedonian; succeeded by his son, Leo VI (–912).

E Alfred expels the Danes from London and, in a treaty with Guthrum, defines the frontier of the Danelaw.
Death of Muhammad I, Emir of Spain; succeeded by his son, al-Mundhir (–888).

887

A **Jan**: 11th, death of Boso, who was still holding the kingdom of Provence; succeeded by his son, Louis (–927).

B **Apr**: 17th, a popular rising in Venice compels the Doge Giovanni II Particiaco to abdicate; succeeded by Pietro Candiano.

C **Sep**: Pietro Candiano killed in battle against the Slavs and Giovanni Particiaco resumes office as Doge.

E An assembly of German magnates at Tribur, near Darmstadt, deposes the Emperor, Charles the Fat.
Leo finally deposes Photius.

885

H **Religion and Education**

Following the death of Methodius (below), Stephen V bans the Slavonic liturgy, and Svátopluk consequently expels Methodius's followers from Moravia.

J **Art, Architecture and Music**

Dedication of the Abbey-church of Corvey on Weser.

K **Literature, Philosophy and Scholarship**

**La Vie de Sainte Eulalie* (anon.; the first extant French poem—a fragment; –1040).

L **Births and Deaths**

Apr. 6th, Methodius d.

886

F **Law and Politics**

**Basilica* (a new Greek version of Roman Law of Justinian) in sixty volumes, prepared by order of Basil I, and published by his son, Leo VI.

G **Economics, Science, Technology and Discovery**

†Abū Ma'shār, Persian astrologer and astronomer, treatise on tides.

J **Art, Architecture and Music**

*Apse mosaics in Sancta Sophia, Salonika.

L **Births and Deaths**

— Abū Ma'shar of Balkh (Albumazar) d. (100).

Apr. 16th, Jocelin, Bishop of Paris, d.

887

K **Literature, Philosophy and Scholarship**

**Rikkokushi* (*Six National Histories*; official court histories written in Chinese on the model of Chinese court records covering Japanese affairs 791–887).

888–890 End of Carolingian and Mayan Empires

888

A **Jan:** 13th, death of Charles the Fat, followed by dismemberment of his empire; his German vassals declare his successor to be Arnulf of Carinthia, illegitimate son of Carloman of Bavaria (–899); in Italy, Berengar, Marquess of Friuli, and Guy, Duke of Spoleto, contend for the crown; Boso's son, Louis, held Provence; Rudolph of Auxerre, Duke of Jurane Burgundy, establishes a kingdom of Burgundy (–911); while in France, surviving royal authority disintegrates.

Feb: 29th, Odo, Marquess of Neustria, crowned as King of France (–898).

B **Apr:** death of Giovanni II Particiaco, Doge of Venice; by the new principle of popular election, Pietro Tribuno chosen to succeed him (–912).

Jun: 24th, Odo defeats the Vikings at Montfaucon (on the Argonne).

D **Oct:** King Arnulf recognises Rodolph I as King of Jurane Burgundy, on the latter's cession of claims to Alsace and Lorraine.

E Death of Ingelger of Anjou; succeeded by his son, Fulk the Red (–938).

Al-Mundhir, Emir of Spain, poisoned and succeeded by his brother ʿAbdallāh (–912).

The Saracens establish a camp at Garde-Freinet, Provence.

889

A **Feb:** Guy, Duke of Spoleto, who had defeated Berengar, Marquess of Friuli, on the Trebbia, crowned at Pavia as King of Italy (–894).

E Donald II, son of Constantine I, succeeds Eochaid as King of Scotland (–900).

Last periodic *stelae* in Mayan cities of South Yucatán; end of the Old Empire, with migration to the north, where the New Empire emerges (–987).

890

E Louis recognised as King of Provence by Arnulf and Pope Stephen V.

Death of Ashot I the Great, King of Armenia; succeeded by Smbat I (–914).

Death of Mihira Bhoja I, founder of an empire in northern India centred on Kanauj.

*Hamdān Qarmat establishes the headquarters of the (future) Qarmatian sect of Ismāʾites, the Dār al-Hirjah, near al-Kūfah, Iraq (–899).

888

G **Economics, Science, Technology and Discovery**
†Ibn-Firnās attempted flight, with feathers, and built a planetarium.

J **Art, Architecture and Music**
†Ibn-Firnās taught the science of music in Andalusia.

889

J **Art, Architecture and Music**
†Indravarman I of Cambodia built Bakong Temple (the first terraced stone pyramid), Angkor; his successor, Yasovarman I, builds the first city there.

K **Literature, Philosophy and Scholarship**
†Ibn-Qutaybah, *Kitāb al-Maʿārif* (*Book of Knowledge*; Arab manual of history).

890

K **Literature, Philosophy and Scholarship**
**Taketori Monogatari* (*The Story of the Bamboo Gatherer*; the earliest Japanese prose narrative).
*The Saxon Poet (Poeta Saxo) writes about Charlemagne.

891

A **Feb**: 11th, King Guy crowned as Emperor by Pope Stephen V (–894).

B **Apr**: 16th, by his victory at Polei (now Aguilar), the Emir ʿAbdallāh defeats the revolt of ibn-Hafsūn; he also this year suppresses a rebellion in Seville.

Jun: 26th, Danish army defeats Count Arnulf and Archbishop Sunderold of Mainz at La Guele, in Lorraine.

C **Sep**: 1st, Arnulf defeats the Danes at Louvain.

14th, death of Pope Stephen V.

D **Oct**: 6th(?), Formosus crowned as his successor.

King Arnulf defeats the Danes on the Dyle, in Brabant; but they subsequently defeat Odo of France in Vermandois.

E Benevento briefly occupied by the Greeks.

892

D **Oct**: 15th, death of the Caliph, al-Muʿtamid; succeeded by his son, al-Muʿtadid (–902), who restores the capital to Baghdād (–1258).

E Danish army leaves France for England; here Alfred was fortifying centres ('Burhs') to resist them.

Svátopluk defeats King Arnulf's expedition into Moravia.

Leszek succeeds his father, Ziemovit, as Duke of Poland (–913).

893

A **Jan**: 28th, following a revolt against Odo organised by Archbishop Fulk of Reims, Charles the Simple, the posthumous son of Louis II, crowned as King of France (–929).

E Alfonso III defeats and kills Ahmād ibn-Muʿāwiya, who claimed to be the Mahdī, at Zamora.

Vladimir, Khan of the Bulgars, deposed by his brother, Symeon (–927).

894

D **Dec**: death of the Emperor, Guy; succeeded by his son and co-emperor, Lambert of Spoleto (–898).

E In an expedition to Italy, King Arnulf takes Bergamo; Milan, Pavia and other northern cities surrender to him.

Death of Svátopluk, prince of Moravia, who had subjected Bohemia, Silesia and adjacent territories; his sons, Mojmir and Svátopluk II, succeed, recognise Arnulf's supremacy, and engage in civil war.

891

G **Economics, Science, Technology and Discovery**

†Al-Ya'qūbī, *Kitāb al-Buldān* (*Book of Countries*).

K **Literature, Philosophy and Scholarship**

†Photius compiled *Myriobiblon* (a *Library*; an enormous collection of note-books on works read, with learned commentaries and judgments on style, quotations and citations from Greek authors whose writings would otherwise have disappeared).

†Al-Ya'qūbī, compendium of universal history (to 872).

892

K **Literature, Philosophy and Scholarship**

(–899) Alfred the Great translates St. Gregory, *Cura Pastoralis*; Orosius, *Historia adversus Paganos* (a universal history of 410 with geographical information); Bede, *Historia Ecclesiastica*; Boethius, *De Consolatione Philosophiæ*; St. Augustine, *Soliloquies*.

†Al-Balādhurī, *Futūh al-Buldān* (*Conquest of the Lands*, by the Arabs).

893

H **Religion and Education**

A hospice for pilgrims to the shrine of St. James at Santiago de Compostela is recorded.

J **Art, Architecture and Music**

The vaulted church at Val de Dios dedicated.

894

K **Literature, Philosophy and Scholarship**

*Asser, *Annales rerum gestarum Ælfredi magni* (*Life of King Alfred*).

895

E By blocking the River Lea, Alfred drives the Danes led by King Haesten from their camp near London.

King Arnulf creates his son Zwentibold King of Burgundy, but without effect because Rodolph I remains in possession.

Spytihněv, son of Bořivoj I, regains Bohemia's independence from Moravia and accepts the supremacy of Arnulf of Germany.

Leo VI prompts the Magyars (settled between the Dneiper and the Danube) to attack Bulgaria. The Khan, Symeon, retaliates by inciting the Pechenegs, recent arrivals on the Dneiper, to invade Magyar territory. Consequently the Magyars, after their expulsion from Bulgaria, are forced to seek lands elsewhere and settle in central Europe, on the Theiss.

896

A **Feb**: after forcing his way into Rome, King Arnulf crowned as Emperor by Pope Formosus, who had invoked his aid against the Romans. When Arnulf is subsequently forced to leave Italy, Lambert of Spoleto retrieves ground as its king.

B **Apr**: 4th, death of Pope Formosus; succeeded by Boniface VI.

May: death of Pope Boniface VI; succeeded by Stephen VI (–897), who conducts a trial and condemnation of Formosus' corpse.

E The Danish army disperses and settles in northern England.

The Bulgarian Khan, Symeon, defeats a Byzantine army at Bulgarophygon and forces Leo VI to pay tribute.

897

C **Jul** (and **Aug**): in a revolt in Rome, Pope Stephen VI murdered and replaced by Romanus.

D **Nov**: Pope Romanus succeeded by Theodore II (until December ?).

E Odo recovers the French crown and pardons Charles the Simple.

Āditya I defeats and kills Aparājita, the last Pallava King, whose lands are now annexed by the Cholas.

898

A **Jan**: 1st, death of Odo, King of France; succeeded by Charles the Simple.

B **Jun**: John IX elected Pope (–900).

D **Oct**: 15th, death, without issue, of King Lambert of Italy; succeeded, unopposed, by Berengar, Marquess of Friuli (–900).

E Richard the Justiciar, Count of Autun (in Burgundy), defeats Vikings at Argenteuil, near Tonnerre.

Magyar raid into the Veneto.

895

H **Religion and Education**
Consequent to Spytihněv's settlement with Arnulf (*see* E), Bohemia accepts the Latin liturgy and the ecclesiastical jurisdiction of a German bishop (? Regensburg).

K **Literature, Philosophy and Scholarship**
†Al-Dīnawarī, *al-Akhbār al-Tiwāl* (*Long narratives*; Persian universal history).

896

897

K **Literature, Philosophy and Scholarship**
†Anastasius Bibliothecarus, chief scholar at Rome, translations from Greek.

L **Births and Deaths**
— Al-Isfahānī b. (–967).

898

899

C King Berengar routs Magyar raiders on the Brenta, but on
Sep: 24th, they defeat Italian forces and ravage Lombardy.

D **Oct**: 26th, death of King Alfred the Great of Wessex; succeeded by his son, Edward the Elder (–924).
Nov or Dec: death of King Arnulf of Germany; succeeded by his son, Louis the Child (–911).

E Atenolf I of Capua conquers Benevento.
*The Qarmatians establish an independent state at Bahrain, on the Persian Gulf, whence they mount terrorist raids (–*c.* 1200).

900

B **May**: death of Pope John IX; succeeded by Benedict IV (–903).

D **Oct**: King Louis of Provence crowned as King of Italy at Pavia; Berengar deserted by his vassals.

E Death of Donald II, King of Scotland; succeeded by his cousin, Constantine II (–943).
Murder of Archbishop Fulk of Reims by Count Baldwin II of Flanders; succeeded by Hervé (–922).
Magyars raid Italy and Bavaria.
The Samanid ruler, Ismāʿil, seizes Khurāsān from the Saffārids; Transoxiana now under Muslim rule.
*Harold Fairhair completes the unification of Norway by his victory in Hafrsfjord (–933).

901

A **Feb**: Louis (III), King of Italy and Provence, crowned as Emperor by Pope Benedict IV (–905).

E Carinthia ravaged by the Magyars.

902

A **Mar**: 6th, death of the Caliph, al-Muʿtadid; his successors were, generally, ephemeral puppets (*e.g.* 908).

C **Aug**: 1st, Ibrāhīm II of Kairāwan destroys Taormina, the last Greek fortress in Sicily; he is subsequently killed attacking Cosenza.

E Berengar of Friuli expels Louis III from Pavia.

899

900

G **Economics, Science, Technology and Discovery**
*Al-Battānī, *Zij* (astronomical).

J **Art, Architecture and Music**
*The *Nea* (New Church) built for Basil I.

901

G **Economics, Science, Technology and Discovery**
†Thābit ibn Qurra, translation into Arabic of Greek astronomical and mathematical works.

902

K **Literature, Philosophy and Scholarship**
†Sugawara Michizane, Japanese poet.

903

C **Jul**: death of Pope Benedict IV; succeeded by Leo V.
Sep: death of Pope Leo V; succeeded by Christopher (–904).

E Tours burnt by the Vikings.

904

A **Jan**: 29th, following Christopher's expulsion, Sergius III crowned as Pope (–911); this is the beginning of the period in Papal history known as 'the Pornocracy' (–963).

C **Jul**: 31st, Arab fleet under Leo of Tripoli sacks Salonika.

E Chu Wen sacks Chiang An and sets up a puppet emperor (–907).

905

C **Jul**: 21st, Berengar of Friuli captures the Emperor, Louis III, at Verona, blinds him, and expels him from Italy to his kingdom of Provence.

E Sancho Garcia I succeeds his brother, Fortunus, as King of Navarre (–926).
With the extinction of the Tulunid dynasty, the Caliph recovers control of Syria and Egypt.

906

E *After defeating a German and Slav army at Pressburg, the Magyars overrun Moravia and destroy its empire; they also raid Saxony.

907

E The Russian ruler, Oleg, sacks the suburbs of Constantinople.
The imperial Chinese dynasty of the T'ang extinguished with the murder of its last emperor by the peasant leader, Chu Wen, who declared himself to be Emperor (–923); thus begins the 'Period of the Five Dynasties and the Ten Kingdoms' (–960), with the empire disintegrating. Yeh-lü A-pao-chi declares himself Emperor of the Khitan (semi-nomadic Mongol tribes of north China, also known as 'Kitai', whence 'Cathay').

903

G **Economics, Science, Technology and Discovery**

*Ibn al-Faqīh, *Kitāb al-Buldān* (*Book of the Countries*; Persian geographical compilation).

†Ibn-Rustah, *al-Aʿlaq al-Nafīsah* (*Precious Bags of Travelling Provisions*; Arab geography).

J **Art, Architecture and Music**

The Church of St. Martin, Tours, rebuilt (–918; it had the first ambulatory with radiating chapels).

L **Births and Deaths**

Jul. 8th, Grimbald d.

Dec. 7th, al-Sūfī b. (–986).

904

J **Art, Architecture and Music**

The cathedral of the Saviour rebuilt as St. John in Lateran, Rome (–928).

905

J **Art, Architecture and Music**

*Vaulted church of Sta. Cristina de Lena.

K **Literature, Philosophy and Scholarship**

Ki no Tsurayuki, Ōshikōchi no Mitsune, Mibu no Tadamine and Ki no Tomonori, *Kokinshū* (an anthology of about 1,100 Japanese and Chinese poems; completed 922).

906

F **Law and Politics**

*Regino of Prüm, legal collection including *Canon episcopi* (laws against witchcraft).

907

908

D **Dec:** 17th, al-Mustada is Caliph for one day, before being deposed and murdered.

E The Magyars defeat the Bavarians, killing the Margrave Liutpold, and raid Saxony and Thuringia.

The Sāmānids finally extinguish the Saffārids of Sijistān.

*Origin of tribal dukes in Germany: the Bavarians elect Arnulf as their Duke (–937) to organise defence against the Magyars; almost simultaneously, Burchard is elected in Swabia (–926), Conrad in Franconia (–918), and Reginar (grandson of Lothar I) in Lorraine.

909

D **Dec:** 7th, following his destruction of the Aghlabid dynasty of Kairāwan, Saʿid ibn-Husayn proclaimed as ʿUbaydullāh al-Mahdī (–934) in Tunis and so founds the Fātimid dynasty (–1171).

910

C **Aug:** 5th, Edward the Elder defeats Danes raiding Mercia at Tettenhall, Staffordshire; Halfdan, King of York, killed.

D **Dec:** King Alfonso III of Oviedo abdicates in favour of his son, Garcia I (–914).

E Danes pillage in Berri and kill the Archbishop of Bourges.

The Magyars defeat King Louis the Child near Augsburg.

911

A **Jan:** 21st, death of King Louis the Child, the last Carolingian ruler of Germany.

B **Apr:** 14th, death of Pope Sergius III; succeeded by Anastasius III (–913).

D **Oct:** 25th (or 912), death of King Rodolph I of Burgundy; succeeded by his son, Rodolph II (–937).

Nov: Duke Conrad of Franconia elected King of the Germans (–918). Charles the Simple of France accepted as King of Lorraine.

E Death of Ethelred, earldorman of Mercia; his wife, Ethelfleda (daughter of Alfred) rules: she became known as 'the Lady of the Mercians'. Edward the Elder of Wessex consequently occupies London.

Charles the Simple receives the homage of Rollo, the Norse leader established on the Seine, at St. Clair-sur-Epte; Rollo baptised as a Christian and granted Rouen, Lisieux, Evreux, etc. (–931). Thus begins the duchy of Normandy, while Viking raids on north France come to an end.

*Treaty of peace concluded between the Greek Empire and the Russians at Kiev.

908

K **Literature, Philosophy and Scholarship**
†Ibn al-Muʿtazz, Arab poet.

909

H **Religion and Education**
Sep: 11th, Abbey of Cluny founded, with the monks installed in a Gallo-Roman villa.

910

911

912

B **Apr** or **May**: Arabs destroy a Byzantine fleet off Chios.
May: 12th, death of the Greek Emperor, Leo VI; succeeded by his brother, Alexander (–913).

D **Oct**: 15th, death of ʿAbdallāh, Emir of Spain; succeeded by his grandson, ʿAbd-ar-Rahmān III, whose state, as a result of rebellion, is almost confined to Cordova (–932, 961).

E Death of Pietro Tribuno, Doge of Venice; succeeded by Orso Particiaco II (–932).

913

B **Jun**: death of Pope Anastasius III; succeeded by Lando (–914).
6th, death of the Greek Emperor, Alexander; succeeded by Constantine VII, the son of Leo VI (–959).

C **Aug**: an invasion by Symeon, Khan of the Bulgars, reaches the walls of Constantinople.

D **Dec**: 20th, Muslim rebels holding Seville surrender to ʿAbd-ar-Rahmān III.

E Ziemonyslas succeeds his father, Leszek, as Duke of Poland.
Death of Oleg, who had established control over Southern Russia; Prince Igor (a second of this name?) begins his personal rule (–945).

914

A **Mar**: John X crowned as Pope in succession to Lando (–928).

D **Oct**: Edward the Elder begins the conquest of the Danelaw.

E Death of Garcia I; succeeded by Ordoño II (–923), who transfers the capital from Oviedo to Leon, whence the kingdom now takes its name.
King Smbat I of Armenia executed by the Sājid emir Yūsuf, governor of Azerbaijan; succeeded by Ashot II (–928).
ʿUbaydullāh takes Alexandria.

915

D **Dec**: Berengar of Friuli crowned by Pope John X as Emperor (–922).

E Hugh the Black, son of Richard the Justiciar, Duke of (French) Burgundy, now the first count of the Franche Compté of Burgundy (–952).
Duke Henry of Saxony defends his independence in a revolt against King Conrad.
On the initiative of John X, the Saracen base on the Garigliano destroyed by Byzantine and Italian forces, thus ending the Saracen presence in central Italy and reducing their devastations.
*Parāntaka I, the Chola King, conquers the Pāndya kingdom.

912

G **Economics, Science, Technology and Discovery**
†Leo VI, *Tacticon* (on warfare).

J **Art, Architecture and Music**
(–913) Monks fleeing from Cordova (there was much migration of Christians from Muslim Spain now because of the new official intolerance) introduce the 'Mozarabic style' into Northern Spain in the monastery built for them at S. Miguel de la Escalada.

K **Literature, Philosophy and Scholarship**
Nokter Balbulus, a musician, develops the sequence in Church poetry, writing *The Sequentia.*

L **Births and Deaths**
Nov. 22nd, Otto I b. (–973).

913

914

915

J **Art, Architecture and Music**
Armenian church on Achthamar, Lake Van (–921).
†Regino of Prüm, *De armonica institutione* (treatise on music).

K **Literature, Philosophy and Scholarship**
†Regino of Prüm, World Chronicle (from A.D. 1 to 908).

916

E King Indra III of Rāshtrakūta takes Kanauj; its King, Mahīpala, recovers possession, but his empire is now in decline.

917

A **Jan:** 21st, King Conrad executes the rebel count palatine, Erchanger.

C **Aug:** 20th, the Khan Symeon, demanding that he should be recognised as Greek Emperor, defeats the imperial forces near Anchialus, on the Achelous; he next invades Thrace and makes himself master of the Balkans.

E Edward the Elder conquers Bedfordshire and destroys the Danish kingdom of East Anglia.

Duke Arnulf of Bavaria forcibly recovers his duchy after being deprived for rebellion against Conrad.

Magyars raid south Germany, Alsace and Burgundy, sacking Basel; the French nobles refuse to join King Charles in resisting them.

Death of Omar ibn-Hafsūn, a Muslim rebel leader in south Spain.

'Ubaydullāh conquers Sicily.

918

A **Jan:** 2nd, murder of Baldwin II of Flanders; succeeded by his son, Arnold I (–965).

B **Jun:** 12th, death of Ethelfleda, 'Lady of the Mercians'; end of Mercian independence, as Edward the Elder takes control. He also conquers the Danish midlands.

D **Dec:** 23rd, death of King Conrad I of Germany.

919

B **May:** Henry the Fowler, Duke of Saxony, crowned as King (Henry I) of the Germans (–936).

C **Sep:** 15th, Niall Black-knee, High King of Ireland, killed in battle against the Norsemen near Dublin.

E King Rodolph II of Burgundy prevented, by his defeat at Winterthür, from extending his domains to the east of the Rhine.

Ragnald, a Viking from Ireland, seizes York, becomes King of Northumbria, and acknowledges the lordship of Edward the Elder.

916

917

918

919

J **Art, Architecture and Music**
Foundation of (Mozarabic) church of Santiago de Peñalba.

920

D **Dec:** 17th, by a *coup d'étât*, Romanus I Lecapenus becomes joint—and effective—Greek Emperor (–944).

E 'Abd-ar-Rahmān defeats Ordoño II of Leon and Sancho of Navarre at Val de Junqueras.

921

D **Nov:** 7th, Charles the Simple meets Henry I at Bonn and is recognised by him as King of Lorraine.

E Robert, Marquess of Neustria, expels Danes from his lands but allows them to settle near Nantes.
Death of Richard the Justiciar, first Duke of Burgundy; succeeded by his son, Raoul (–923).
St. Ludmilla, the widow of Bořivoj I of Bohemia, murdered by her daughter-in-law, Drahomira of Stodor, the widow of Vratislav I and guardian of their sons, Wenceslas and Boleslav.

922

A **Feb:** Rodolph II of Burgundy crowned as King of Italy (–926).

B **Jun:** Robert, Marquess of Neustria, crowned as King of France in a revolt against Charles the Simple.

C **Jul:** 2nd, death of Archbishop Hervé of Reims; the usurping king, Robert, secures the see for Seulf (–925).

E Ashot II of Armenia assumes the title of 'King of Kings' in his attempt to assert supremacy in Caucasia.

923

B **Jun:** 15th, Charles the Simple defeated at Soissons by his rival, Robert, who is killed.

C **Jul:** 13th, in succession to Robert, Duke Raoul of Burgundy crowned as King of France (–936); he cedes the duchy to Gisilbert, who is challenged by Robert's brother, Count Hugh the Black, and by Hugh the Great (–938).
17th, King Rodolph defeats Berengar of Friuli, the ex-king of Italy, at Fiorenzuola, near Piacenza.
Sep: death of Ordoño II of Leon; succeeded by his brother, Froila II; outbreak of civil war (–924).

E Danes raid Aquitaine and the Auvergne.
Adrianople taken by Symeon.
Murder of Chu Wen, Emperor of China; succeeded by Li K'o-yung, leader of the Sha-t'o, who founded the [Later] T'ang dynasty (–936).
(or 924) capture and imprisonment of Charles the Simple by Count Herbert of Vermandois.

920

G **Economics, Science, Technology and Discovery**

*Earliest European reference to a collar in the harness of horses (which would permit the drawing of heavy loads and ploughs).

*Abū Zaid, *Akhbār al-Sīn w-al-Hind* (*Information about China and India*; edition of accounts by Arab travellers).

921

C **Economics, Science, Technology and Discovery**

*Ibn-Fadlān, account of his journey to the Bulgars, in Russia, this year.

922

H **Religion and Education**

Execution of al-Hallāj, the first Sūfī martyr, by the ʿAbbāsid inquisition.

923

K **Literature, Philosophy and Scholarship**

†Al-Tabarī, *Ta'rīkh al-Rusul w-al-Mulūk* (*Annals of the Apostles and Kings*); and an annalistic world history (from the creation to 915; –1233).

924–926 Magyars and Danes raid western Europe—Moors sack Pampeluna

924

B **Apr**: 7th, murder of Berengar of Friuli.

C **Jul**: 17th, death of Edward the Elder, King of England; succeeded by his son, Athelstan (–939).

E King Raoul cedes Bayeux to the Duke Rollo of Normandy to buy peace.
Danes raiding Burgundy repulsed and settle on the Seine, near Melun.
The Magyars resume their raids: in Italy, they burn Pavia, but King Rodolph and Hugh of Arles, the effective ruler of Provence, drive them off into south France; they also invade Germany, where King Henry obtains a truce for Saxony which he uses to strengthen his duchy by building fortified towns.
Alfonso IV succeeds his uncle, Froila II, as King of Leon (–927).
'Abd-ar-Rahmān sacks Pampeluna, the capital of Navarre.
Symeon's final attempt to take Constantinople fails, but he is now styling himself 'emperor'.

925

E Northmen from Rouen and the Loire pillage northern France, despite King Raoul's success in a battle at Fauquembergue, in Artois.
Count Herbert of Vermandois has his son, Hugh (aged five), elected as Archbishop of Reims in succession to Seulf (–931).
Henry I takes possession of the kingdom of Lorraine and subjects it, as a duchy, to the German crown.
Zague, a Jewess, leads a rebellion which overthrows the ruling dynasty in Abyssinia (–1270).
*The viscounts of Anjou now being known as counts to mark their independence from the suzerainty of the dukes of Normandy; this is an illustration of the disintegration of authority in the French duchies.

926

B **May**: 2nd, Duke Burchard of Swabia killed on his way to assist King Rodolph against Hugh of Arles, Marquess of Provence, who had been elected King by Italians in revolt against Rodolph; the last now abandons Lombardy.

C **Jul**: Hugh of Arles crowned as King of Italy (–948).

E Eastern France raided by the Magyars.
Death of Sancho Garcia I of Navarre; succeeded by his son, Garcia I (–970).
Symeon defeated by Tomislav, the first King of Croatia.
The Khitan obtain the cession of North East Hopei province.

924

J **Art, Architecture and Music**
Church of Sta. María de Lebena, near Santander.

925

G **Economics, Science, Technology and Discovery**
†Al-Razi, *Kitāb al-Judari w-al-Hasbah* (*On Small-pox and Measles*); *al-Hāwī* (medical compendium in 20 volumes; –1279); *Kitāb al-Asrār* (*The Book of Secrets*, on alchemy; –1187).

L **Births and Deaths**
— John Tzimisces b. (–976).
— St. Dunstan b. (–988).

926

927

B **May**: 27th, death of Symeon, Khan of the Bulgars and self-styled emperor; succeeded by his son, Peter, who makes peace with the Greek Emperor; the Emperor thus recovers authority over Serbia, where Časlav, its Prince, had previously been subject to the Khan.

C **Jul**: 12th, in a meeting near Penrith, Cumberland, the Kings of Scotland and Strathclyde recognise Athelstan as their overlord.

E Death of Louis the Blind, King of Provence (–933).
Alfonso IV of Leon abdicates in favour of his brother, Ramiro II (–952).

928

B **May**: Pope John X deposed and murdered; succeeded by Leo VI.

D **Dec**: death of Pope Leo VI.

E Henry I takes the town of Brandenburg in his war against the Wends.
Abas I succeeds his brother, Ashot II, as King of Armenia (–952).
(or 929) Henry I compels Duke Wenceslas of Bohemia to acknowledge his supremacy.
Ziyarid dynasty established in Jurjan (Persia; –1043).

929

A **Jan**: Stephen VII (or VIII) crowned as Pope (–931).
16th, ʻAbd-ar-Rahmān III, Emir of Spain, begins to style himself Caliph, thus consummating his independence of Baghdād.

C **Sep**: 4th, Henry I's lieutenants defeat Wends in revolt at Lenzen, on the Elbe; they are compelled to submit and accept Christianity.
28th, (St.) Wenceslas of Bohemia murdered and succeeded by his brother, Boleslav I (–967), who asserts his independence of the German king.

D **Oct**: 7th, death of Charles the Simple, still the prisoner of Herbert of Vermandois.

E Henry I's son, Otto, marries Edith, daughter of Athelstan of England.

927

F **Law and Politics**

Engi Shiki (an elaboration of older Japanese law codes made in vain attempt to check the collapse of the fiscal system).

J **Art, Architecture and Music**

The first abbey-church of Cluny dedicated.

928

929

L **Births and Deaths**

—al-Battānī d.

930

E Qarmatians sack Mecca and remove the Black Stone (–951).

On the death of the Emperor Daigo of Japan, the Fujiwara family acquire full powers as regents.

931

A **Feb**: death of Pope Stephen VII; succeeded by John XI (believed to be the son of Sergius III; –935/6).

E Death of Duke Rollo of Normandy; succeeded by his son, William Longsword (–942).

King Raoul removes Hugh of Vermandois from the Archbishopric of Reims and appoints Artaud.

'Abd-ar-Rahmān takes Ceuta from the Berbers.

932

E Hugh of Arles, King of Lombardy, marries Marozia, Pope John XI's mother. In an ensuing Roman revolt, Hugh is expelled, the Pope imprisoned, and Marozia disappears. Alberic, another of her sons, who led the revolt, now rules Rome and becomes its Duke (–954).

Pietro Candiano succeeds Orso Particiaco II as Doge of Venice (–939).

Ramiro II of Leon takes Madrid from the Muslims.

With the capture of Toledo, 'Abd-ar-Rahmān completes his reunification of Muslim Spain (begun in 912).

Rebellion against Chinese rule in Annam (–939).

933

A **Mar**: 15th, Henry I defeats the Magyars at 'Riade', near Merseburg.

E King Raoul grants Avranches and Coutances to William Longsword of Normandy in order to gain his allegiance.

Hugh of Arles cedes his claims to Provence to Rodolph II of Burgundy, on the latter promising not to enter Italy; Provence thus united with the kingdom of Burgundy.

Death of King Harold Fairhair of Norway; succeeded by Eric (–938).

930

F **Law and Politics**

The Althing (general court) established in Iceland; it is the oldest national assembly in the world.

G **Economics, Science, Technology and Discovery**

* ?Bald, *Leech Book* (oldest extant leech-book in Old English).

J **Art, Architecture and Music**

*Church of St. Wipert, Quedlinburg.

K **Literature, Philosophy and Scholarship**

**Ecbasis Captivi* (an allegorical beast narrative about a calf captured by a wolf—perhaps the earliest of its kind in European literature).

931

G **Economics, Science, Technology and Discovery**

Central examinations introduced in the medical schools in Baghdād and Persia.

H **Religion and Education**

†Ibn Massara, Spanish Muslim theologian.

932

G **Economics, Science, Technology and Discovery**

Fêng Tao, Prime Minister of China, orders the printing of Confucian, Buddhist and Taoist canons. This was done with wooden blocks (–1019).

† ?Al-Isrā'īli, *Kitāb al-Hummayāt* (treatise on fever); *Kitāb al-Baul* (treatise on urine).

933

K **Literature, Philosophy and Scholarship**

†Ibn Duraid, *al-Jamhara fī-l-Lugha* (*The Collection of a Language*; Arabic dictionary in Persian).

934

E Athelstan makes a punitive expedition into Scotland, reaching Kincardineshire.
Henry I forces King Gorm the Old of Denmark to make peace and establishes the march of Schleswig; he also completes his subjection of the Wends of the Lower Oder.
'Ubaydullāh sacks Genoa, Corsica and Sardinia.
Death of 'Ubaydullāh al-Mahdī of Kairāwan; succeeded by his son, Muhammad al-Qā'im (–946).
A Magyar raid reaches Constantinople.
The Byzantine general, John Curcuas, takes Melitene (Malatiya), near the upper Euphrates.

935

A **Feb**: Muhammad al-Ikhshīd founds the Ikhshīdid dynasty of Egypt (–969).

E King Raoul repulses Magyars raiding Burgundy.
The Doge, Pietro Candiano, takes and burns Comacchio.
Wang Chien establishes himself as Emperor of China, founding the Later Chin Dynasty (–947).
Wang Kon reunites Korea on the extinction of the Silla dynasty; he founds the Koryō dynasty (whence 'Korea'; –1392), with the capital at Kaesōng.

936

A **Jan**: 3rd(?), Leo VII crowned as Pope in succession to John XI (recently dead; –939).
14th–15th, death of King Raoul of France.

B **Jun**: 19th, Louis IV d'Outremer, son of Charles the Simple, having been recalled from exile in England, crowned as King of France (–954).

C **Jul**: 2nd, death of King Henry I of Germany; succeeded by his son, Otto I (–973).

E Harold Bluetooth succeeds Gorm the Old as King of Denmark (–983).
The Khitan settle in northern China, making Peking their southern capital.

937

C **Jul**: death of Arnulf the Bad, Duke of Bavaria.
12th–13th, death of Rodolph II, King of Burgundy; succeeded by his son, Conrad, a minor (–993).

E Athelstan wins a defensive victory against a coalition of Scots, Strathclyde Welsh and Norsemen at 'Brunanburgh'.
Magyar force raids France as far west as Reims, and then moves through Berri and Burgundy to Italy.
Bretons led by Alain Barbe-Torte defeat Vikings at St. Brieuc.
'Abd-ar-Rahmān III takes Saragossa in a campaign against Leon and Navarre; the King of Navarre recognises his suzerainty.
Muhammad al-Ikhshīd of Egypt seizes Palestine and Syria.

934

935

K **Literature, Philosophy and Scholarship**

Ki no Tsurayuki, *Tosa nikki* (the earliest extant diary of travels in Japanese, with poems by the author).

†Al-Ash'arī of Baghdād, founder of Muslim scholastic philosophy.

936

J **Art, Architecture and Music**

'Abd-ar-Rahmān begins the palace of al-Zahrū', Cordova.

937

J **Art, Architecture and Music**

St. Gall burnt by the Magyars.

K **Literature, Philosophy and Scholarship**

*Ekkehard of St. Gall (the first of that name), *Waltharii Poesis* (*Waltharius and Hildegund*, in Latin hexameters; 'the fullest extant rendering of a famous German story'—*W. P. Ker*).

938

E Death of Count Fulk the Red of Anjou; succeeded by his son, Fulk II the Good (–958).
Louis IV invades Lorraine at the request of its Duke, Gilbert.
Duchy of Burgundy partitioned by a treaty between Giselbert, Hugh the Great and Hugh the Black.
Otto I seizes King Conrad of Burgundy and his kingdom, enforces recognition of his authority in Bavaria, and repulses a Magyar force in Saxony.
Haakon I succeeds Eric as King of Norway (–963).

939

B Otto I suppresses a rebellion in Saxony and Thuringia.

C **Jul:** death of Pope Leo VII; succeeded by Stephen VIII (or IX; –942).
22nd, Ramiro II of Leon defeats 'Abd-ar-Rahmān at Simancas.
Sep: Otto repels an invasion by Louis IV, who is supporting a German rebellion; this collapses after the deaths of Dukes Everard of Franconia and Gilbert of Lorraine in a skirmish at Andernach; Otto takes possession of Franconia.

D **Oct:** 27th, death of King Athelstan of England; succeeded by his brother, Edmund (–946).

Olaf Guthfrithson, King of Dublin, takes York.
Hugh the Great, Marquess of Neustria, and Count Herbert of Vermandois, rebelling against Louis IV, expel Archbishop Artaud from Reims and restore Hugh of Vermandois.
Death of Pietro Candiano II, Doge of Venice; succeeded by Pietro Badoero (–942).
Ngo Quyen defeats the Chinese and founds the kingdom of Dai-co-viet (North Vietnam), with his capital at Co-loa.

940

E Edmund cedes Northumbria and the Danelaw to Olaf Guthfrithson.
Otto I enters France at the request of Hugh the Great and Herbert of Vermandois, receiving their homage.
Saracens raid into Switzerland.

941

E Berenger of Ivrea takes refuge at Otto's court.
An attack on Constantinople by Igor, Prince of Kiev, is defeated.
John Curcuas resumes his conquests in Mesopotamia.

938

G **Economics, Science, Technology and Discovery**
*Hero of Byzantium, treatise on surveying.

939

K **Literature, Philosophy and Scholarship**
*Ise, *Monogatari* (the Japanese *Tales of Ise*).
†Eutychius (al-Bitriq), Patriarch of Alexandria, historian.

L **Births and Deaths**
— Almanzor b. (–1002).
— Romanus II b. (–963).

940

F **Law and Politics**
Louis IV grants the county of Reims to its Archbishop (an illustration of the continuing disintegration of the larger territorial units in France; in such cases of grants to ecclesiastical lords, however, the crown benefited when it could influence the election of bishops).

H **Religion and Education**
Dunstan appointed Abbot of Glastonbury; he initiates reforms which influence the English Church.

J **Art, Architecture and Music**
*Apse of S. Ambrogio, Milan.
Ibn ʿAbd Rabbih, *al-ʿIqd al-Farīd* (*The Unique Necklace*; lives of musicians).

941

H **Religion and Education**
†St. Odo, Abbot of Cluny, monastic reformer.

942–946 Edmund conquers Danish England—Buwayhid control of Caliphate

942

D **Oct:** death of Pope Stephen VIII; succeeded by Marinus II (called Martin III; –946).
Nov: Otto and Louis IV meet at Visé (on the Meuse) and are reconciled; this leads to the submission of Hugh the Great to Louis.
Dec: 17th, murder of William Longsword, Duke of Normandy, by Arnold I, Count of Flanders; succeeded by Richard I (–996).

E Edmund recovers the Danelaw south of the Humber.
Otto releases King Conrad of Burgundy as his vassal.
Death of Pietro Badoero, Doge of Venice; succeeded by Pietro Candiano III (–959).

943

E Death of Constantine II, King of Scotland; succeeded by his nephew, Malcolm I (–954).
Louis IV cedes suzerainty over French Burgundy to Hugh the Great.
Death of Count Herbert II of Vermandois; his sons divide his lands.

944

D **Oct:** Sayf ad-Dawla establishes himself in Aleppo and extends his authority over northern Syria (–967), founding the Hamdānid dynasty (–1003).
Dec: 16th, deposition of the Greek Emperor, Romanus I, by his sons; Constantine VII resumes rule and crushes a rebellion.

E Edmund expels the Norse kings from York.
Louis IV captured by the Vikings of Rouen, who deliver him to Hugh the Great.

945

E Edmund conquers Strathclyde (including Cumberland and Westmorland) and gives it to his ally, Malcolm of Scotland.
Louis IV surrenders his capital, Laon, to Hugh the Great, to obtain his release.
Berengar, Marquess of Ivrea, leads a revolt against King Hugh and seizes control of Lombardy.
Igor of Kiev makes peace with the Greek Empire, and is killed by rebels soon afterwards; succeeded by his son, Svjatoslav (–972), whose mother, Olga, acts as regent (–962).

946

A **Jan:** 17th, ‘Adud ad-Dawla, the Shi’ite ruler of western Persia, expels the Turks from Baghdād; his dynasty, the Buwayhids, now rules the Caliphate from their capital at Shīrāz and has the title of Sultan (–1055).

B **May:** 10th, Agapitus II crowned as Pope in succession to Marinus II (–955).
26th, murder of King Edmund of England; succeeded by his brother, Edred (–955).

E Louis IV, assisted by Otto of Germany, takes Reims, expels Hugh of Vermandois and restores Artaud as Archbishop.
Death of al-Qā’im, Caliph of Kairāwan; succeeded by his son al-Mansūr (–952).

942

H **Religion and Education**

Pilgrim, Bishop of Passau, begins the conversion of Hungary.

†Sa'id al-Fayyūmi, Arabic translation of the Old Testament.

K **Literature, Philosophy and Scholarship**

†Al-Jahshiyari, first version of *Alf Laylah wa-Laylah* (*A Thousand and One Nights—The Arabian Nights*; his heroines included Shahrazād—'Sheherazade').

943

944

K **Literature, Philosophy and Scholarship**

†Al-Maturīdī of Samarqand, a founder of Muslim scholastic philosophy.

945

H **Religion and Education**

Sept. 19th, Cabiz, a Muslim theologian, executed because he had argued that Christ was superior to Muhammad.

Further endowment of the college for Brahmins at Salatgi, south India.

946

J **Art, Architecture and Music**

The cathedral of Clermont Ferrand dedicated.

K **Literature, Philosophy and Scholarship**

†Liu Hsü, *Chiu T'ang shu* (official history of the T'ang Dynasty, 618–907).

947

E Otto grants the duchy of Bavaria to his brother, Henry, on the death of Duke Berthold (–976).

The Khitan destroy the Later Chin dynasty and claim the Chinese throne, founding the Liao dynasty of North China (–1125).

948

B **Apr**: 10th, death of Hugh of Arles, the expelled King of Italy; his son, Lothar II, already joint king, as the puppet of Berengar of Ivrea (–950). The kingdom of Provence, which Hugh administered, now ceases to exist.

Jun: a council meets at Ingelheim under a papal legate to resolve the dispute for the archbishopric of Reims; it pronounces in favour of Artaud, and the legate threaten Hugh the Great with excommunication for his rebellion against Louis IV.

E Edred expels Eric Bloodaxe, son of King Harold Fairhair of Norway, from Northumbria.

Arnold of Flanders seizes Montreuil-sur-Mer.

The Caliph of Kairāwan appoints Hasan ibn-Ali as governor of Sicily; the office continues in his family (the Kalbite dynasty) and it establishes an ordered state in Sicily.

949

D **Dec**: 10th, death of Duke Hermann of Swabia; Otto then grants the Duchy to his son, Liudolf (–954).

E Krishna III, the Rāshtrakūta king, defeats and kills Parāntaka's son, Rājāditya, at Takkōlam; he then took Tanjore, the Chola capital, and much other territory.

(or 950) Death of Hywel the Good, King of Deheubarth, Gwynned, Powys and Seisyllwg; this empire now disintegrates.

947

H **Religion and Education**

The Liao Dynasty (–1125), in their adoption of Chinese customs, formally observe Confucianism but actually patronise Buddhism.

948

F **Law and Politics**

†Qudāma ibn-Ja'far, *Kitāb al-Kharāj* (account of the land-tax of the Muslim Empire, with description of its postal service).

H **Religion and Education**

Otto establishes bishoprics at Brandenburg and Havelberg for the conversion of the Wends, and at Ribe, Aarhus and Schleswig for missions to the north.

K **Literature, Philosophy and Scholarship**

†Qudāma, *Criticism of Poetry*.

*Symeon the Logothete, continuation to 948 of the Chronicle of Monachos (–842).

949

F **Law and Politics**

†Hywel Dda, *Leges Walliae* (earliest code of Welsh laws).

950–952 Otto subjugates Bohemia and Italy

950

D **Nov:** 22nd, death of Lothar II, King of Italy, without issue.
Dec: 15th, Berengar (II), Marquess of Ivrea, and his son, Adalbert, elected Kings of Italy.

E By the mediation of Otto I, Hugh the Great submits to Louis IV and restores Laon to him.
Otto compels Boleslav I of Bohemia to recognise his suzerainty and resume the payment of tribute.

951

C **Sep:** Otto, in his first campaign against Berengar, enters Pavia and assumes the Italian crown; he marries Adelaide, Lothar's widow.

E Magyars devastate Aquitaine.
Qarmatians restore the Black Stone to Mecca.
Hou-Chou dynasty of China (–960).

952

C **Aug:** 7th, Otto agrees that Berengar and Adalbert might hold the kingdom of Italy as his vassals.

D **Dec:** 17th, death of Hugh the Black, Count of Burgundy.

E Eric Bloodaxe recovers the kingdom of York.
Death of Ramiro II of Leon; civil war until his son, Ordoño III, succeeds (–957).
Ashot III succeeds his father, Abas I, as King of Armenia (–977).
Death of al-Mansūr of Kairāwan; succeeded by his son, al-Mu'izz (–975).

950

F **Law and Politics**

†Al-Fārābī, *The Model City*.

G **Economics, Science, Technology and Discovery**

†*Al-Istakhri, *Masālik w-al-Mamālik* (geography, with maps).

* ?Heraclius, *De Coloribus et artibus Romanorum* (*On the paints and arts of the Romans*; a third section added in France, in the twelfth century; includes descriptions of refining, manufacture, etc., of metals and alloys).

H **Religion and Education**

*Gyula, the Magyar 'leader', baptised in Constantinople and returned with the first Hungarian bishop as a missionary.

J **Art, Architecture and Music**

*Vaulted church of Sta. María, Melque.

*Tower of Doña Urraca, Covarrubias.

*Dunstan adds towers and porches at Glastonbury.

†Al-Fārābī, the Turkish scientific encyclopedist, *The Grand Book on Music* (on musical theory).

K **Literature, Philosophy and Scholarship**

Anthologia Palatina (the *Greek Anthology* collected by Constantine Cephalas; ms. found in the library of the Elector Palatine, Heidelberg. It consists of poems and brief inscriptions by some 300 writers from the fifth century B.C. to the sixth century A.D.).

951

952

953

E Liudolf of Swabia leads a revolt, supported by Franconia and Bavaria, against his father, Otto.

Sayf ad-Dawla defeats a Byzantine army under Bardas Phocas near Germanicea (Mar'-ash).

954

B **Jun**: 16th, Liudolf's adherents submit to Otto.

C **Aug**: death of Alberic, Duke of Rome.

Sep: 10th, death of Louis IV of France; succeeded by his son, Lothair (–986).

D **Dec**: 7th, in the redistribution of territories forfeited in the recent rebellion, Otto grants Liudolf's former duchy of Swabia to Burchard, and Lorraine to Archbishop Bruno of Cologne, Otto's brother.

E Eric Bloodaxe, the last Scandinavian King of York, killed by rebels; Edred takes possession of the kingdom and so holds all England.

Death of Malcolm I, King of Scotland; succeeded by his cousin, Indulf (–962).

Magyars raid through Bavaria, Lorraine, Burgundy, Flanders and as far as Utrecht.

955

C **Aug**: 10th, Otto defeats the Magyars on the Lechfeld, near Augsburg; their raids on western Europe now cease and they begin a settled life in Hungary.

D **Oct**: 16th, Otto defeats the Wends in Mecklenburg.

Nov: 23rd, death of King Edred of England; succeeded by Edwy, the son of Edmund (–959).

Dec: death of Pope Agapitus II; succeeded by John XII, Alberic's young son (–963).

E ? Olga, regent of Kiev, baptised in Constantinople.

956

B **Apr**: 8th, death of Giselbert, ruler of French Burgundy; Hugh the Great inherits his lands (–960).

Jun: 17th, death of Hugh the Great, Duke of the Franks, and suzerain of Aquitaine, Burgundy and Normandy; his sons share his lands.

E Otto punishes a revolt by the Wends by ravaging their lands.

*Arrival of the Ghuzz (or Oghuz) Turks, led by Seljuq, from Turkestan, in Transoxiana (–1037).

953

954

K **Literature, Philosophy and Scholarship**

†Rūdakī, Persian poet.

955

H **Religion and Education**

Otto I founds a monastery at Magdeburg.

J **Art, Architecture and Music**

*The second abbey-church at Cluny (–981); it had a pair of belfries (belfries now being introduced into north-west Europe from Italy).

Abbey-church of St. Michel, Cuxa (–974).

L **Births and Deaths**

— Otto II b. (–983).

956

G **Economics, Science, Technology and Discovery**

†al-Mas'ūdi ('The Herodotus of the Arabs'), *Murūj al-Dhahab wa-M'ādin al Jawhar* (*Meadows of Gold and Mines of Gems*; a historico-geographical encyclopedia, it gives the earliest known description of windmills (in Sijistan, Persia) and mentions horse-racing and (?) tennis; –1234).

957

B **Jun**: the Byzantine general, Nicephorus Phocas, takes Hadāth.

C **Aug**: death of Ordoño III of Leon; succeeded by his brother, Sancho I, who was deposed, in civil war, by Ordoño the Bad (–960).

E Edwy exiles Dunstan, Abbot of Glastonbury, from England; the Mercians and Northumbrians renounce Edwy in favour of his brother, Edgar.

958

E Death of Fulk II, Count of Anjou; succeeded by his son, Geoffrey I (–987).
The Byzantine general, John Tzimisces, takes Somosata and defeats Sayf ad-Dawla at Raʿbān (Syria).

959

D **Oct**: 1st, death of King Edwy of England; succeeded by Edgar (–975), who recalled Dunstan.
Nov: 9th, death of the Greek Emperor, Constantine VII; succeeded by his son, Romanus II (–963).

E Otto sends a missionary to Russia at the request of Olga of Kiev.
Death of Pietro Candiano III; succeeded by his son, Pietro Candiano IV (–976).
A Magyar raid reaches Constantinople.

960

E In the partition of Hugh the Great's lands, King Lothair invests the oldest son, Hugh Capet, with Neustria (–987), and Otto with the Duchy of Burgundy (–965).
ʿAbd-ar-Rahmān, exploiting the civil war in Leon, takes Oviedo, and, with Garcia of Navarre, restores Sancho I as King of Leon (–967).
The Karakhanids of central Asia become the first Turkish tribe to be converted *en masse* to Islam.
Chao K'uang-yin (as T'ai-Tsu; –976) founds the Northern Sung dynasty of Chinese Emperors (–1279).

957

J **Art, Architecture and Music**
Dedication of the church of Sta. Cecilia, Montserrat.

958

F **Law and Politics**
In Korea, which followed the Chinese (Confucian) model of government, the examination system established for the civil service, even though Buddhism still flourished as the official religion.

J **Art, Architecture and Music**
*Abbey-church of S. Pere, Roda, near Gerona.
Chartres Cathedral (of 743) burnt; rebuilt (–1022).

K **Literature, Philosophy and Scholarship**
*Liutprand of Cremona, *Antapodosis* (record of events from 886 to 950; continued in *De Rebus Gestis Ottonis* (*I*) for 960–4).

959

F **Law and Politics**
†Constantine VII, *De administrando imperio*, *De cerimoniis aulæ Byzantinæ* and *De thematibus* (all about Byzantine government, the first being a handbook for his son); he also wrote a *Life of Basil I* and encouraged the production of encyclopedias.
(–975) Edgar recognises the special laws of the Danes settled in England.

960

J **Art, Architecture and Music**
†Ching Hao, *Notes on Brushwork*.
*Abbey-church of St. Philibert, Tournus, begun (–*c.* 1120).
(–992) Church of Montierender.

961–964 Otto I crowned Holy Roman Emperor—Ghaznavid empire founded

961

A Mar: Nicephorus Phocas recovers Crete from the Saracens.

B May: 26th, Otto, son of Otto I, crowned as King of Lorraine.

C Sep: Otto and his son, Otto, acknowledged as Kings of Italy on their capture of Pavia.

E Death of ʿAbd-ar-Rahmān III, Caliph of Spain; succeeded by al-Hakam II (–976).

962

A Feb: 2nd, coronation of Otto as Holy Roman Emperor (–973) by Pope John XII, who becomes his subject; the imperial title was thus restored in western Europe.

D Dec: Nicephorus Phocas (briefly) occupies Aleppo.

E Indulf, King of Scotland, killed by Danes; succeeded by Dub, son of Malcolm I (–966).
Svjatoslav I, Grand Prince of Kiev, begins his personal rule (–972).
Alptigīn founds the Turkish dynasty of the Ghaznavids (–1186) with the seizure of Ghaznī.

963

A Mar: 15th, death of the Greek Emperor, Romanus II.

C Aug: 16th, Nicephorus II Phocas crowned as Greek Emperor (–969).

D Dec: 4th, Otto deposes Pope John XII; Leo VIII elected as his successor (–965).
26th–31st, Otto captures King Berengar II of Italy.

E Harold II succeeds Haakon I as King of Norway.
Following his defeats by Count Wichman of Saxony, Mieszko I of Poland becomes the 'friend' and tributary of Otto.

964

B May: 14th, death of John XII, who had expelled Pope Leo VIII; Benedict V the Grammarian crowned as John's successor.
Jun: 23rd, Otto expels Benedict and restores Leo.

961

F **Law and Politics**

T'ang hui yao (*Assembled Essentials of the T'ang*; encyclopedic collection of materials on Chinese government and economics under the T'ang, 618–907).

H **Religion and Education**

St. Athanasius the Athonite establishes the first notable foundation on Mount Athos, the Great Laura.

Adalbert makes a mission as a bishop to Russia.

†'Abd-ar-Rahmān founded the University of Cordova (–976).

J **Art, Architecture and Music**

Foundation of monastery at Gernrode (the church is extant).

K **Literature, Philosophy and Scholarship**

†Al-Kindī, *Governors and Judges of Egypt*.

962

K **Literature, Philosophy and Scholarship**

*Hrotswith (or Roswitha), Six comedies in prose (in imitation of Terence; *e.g.* *Gallicanus* and *Sapientia*; adapted for moral teaching in the convent).

963

964

H **Religion and Education**

Nicephorus (ineffectively) prohibits new monastic foundations and further endowments to existing houses.

965

A **Mar:** death of Pope Leo VIII.
27th, death of Arnold I, Count of Flanders; King Lothair occupies Arras and other southern parts of the county, but the Flemings prevent full confiscation and proclaim Arnold's grandson, Arnold II, as their Count (–988).

C **Aug:** Nicephorus II regains Cyprus from the Saracens.
16th, he takes Tarsus in the conquest of Cilicia.

D **Oct:** 1st, John XIII crowned as Pope (–972).

E English invasion of Gwynned (North Wales).
Henry the Great succeeds his brother, Otto, as Duke of Burgundy (–1002).
Greek expedition to Sicily takes Syracuse briefly; its fleet destroyed by the Saracens off Messina.
*Svjatoslav of Kiev destroys the power of the Khazars.

966

E Dub, King of Scotland, killed; succeeded by Culen, son of Indulf.
Otto creates the Palatinate of the Rhine for Hermann.
Death of Berengar II, former King of Italy.
Mieszko I of Poland converted to Christianity, following his marriage to Dobrava, daughter of Boleslav I of Bohemia; the first (Roman) missionary bishop comes to Poland.
Nicephorus Phocas campaigns on the middle Euphrates.

967

A **Jan:** Paldolf I Ironhead of Capua-Benevento invested with the March of Spoleto by Otto, who thus extends his authority into southern Italy.
Feb: death of Sayf ad-Dawla, Emir of Aleppo.

D **Dec:** 22nd, Otto, son of Otto, crowned as Emperor by John XIII (–983).

E Brian Bórumha and his brother, Mahon, King of Munster, defeat the Danes near Tipperary and sack Limerick.
Murder of Sancho I the Fat of Leon; succeeded by his son, Ramiro III (–982).
Mieszko of Poland, aided by Boleslav of Bohemia, defeats an invasion by Wichman of Saxony, who is killed.
Death of Boleslav I, Duke of Bohemia; succeeded by Boleslav II the Pious (–999).
Svjatoslav of Kiev, urged by the Greek Emperor to attack the Bulgarians, occupies the Dobrudja.

965

G **Economics, Science, Technology and Discovery**
Ibrāhīm ibn-Ia'qub, a Spanish Jew, travels in the Slav lands of the Elbe.

H **Religion and Education**
*Baptism of Harold Bluetooth; he officially establishes Christianity in Denmark.

J **Art, Architecture and Music**
†Huang Ch'üan, Chinese painter.

K **Literature, Philosophy and Scholarship**
†Al-Mutannabī, Syrian poetry.

966

K **Literature, Philosophy and Scholarship**
*Flodoard of Reims, *Historia Remensis Ecclesiæ* and *Annales* (894–966).

967

G **Economics, Science, Technology and Discovery**
Earliest known charter of privileges for an urban community (now) in France, *viz.* Morville-sur-Seille.

H **Religion and Education**
*Foundation of St. George, Prague (the first Bohemian nunnery).

J **Art, Architecture and Music**
Foundation of Magdeburg Cathedral.
†Li Ch'eng, Chinese painter.

K **Literature, Philosophy and Scholarship**
†Al-Isfahānī, *Kitāb al-Aghāni* (*Great Book of Songs*; an anthology of quotations from Arabic poetry, with biographies of the poets and of the composers who set the words to melodies).

968

E Nicephorus II rebuffs Liutprand of Cremona's embassy sent to Constantinople by Otto.
Dinh Bo Linh, after succeeding as ruler of Dai-co-viet and suppressing all opposition, declares himself Emperor (with the name Dinh-Tien-hoang), with his capital at Hoa-lu (–979). The Sung Emperors of China recognise him as a vassal.

969

C **Jul**: 6th, the fourth Fātimid Caliph, al-Mu'izz, already ruling Tunis and Morocco, conquers Egypt and extinguishes the Ilkshidid dynasty; he builds his capital at Cairo, which becomes the centre of a Shi'ite empire (–1171).

D **Oct**: 28th, Antioch taken by Byzantine forces; Aleppo also taken in this campaign of reconquest which Nicephorus regarded as a crusade.
Dec: 10th, murder of the Greek Emperor, Nicephorus II Phocas; succeeded by John Tzimisces (–976).

E Svjatoslav defeats Pechenegs besieging Kiev; he also conquers eastern Bulgaria.

970

E Sancho II succeeds his father, Garcia I, as King of Navarre (–994).
Svjatoslav invades Thrace and is defeated at Arcadiopolis by the Greek general, Bardas Sclerus.

971

B **Apr**: 23rd, John Tzimisces defeats Svjatoslav at Silistra (Dorystolum).

C **Jul**: 21st, Tzimisces again defeats Svjatoslav and compels him to evacuate Bulgaria and the Crimea.

E Culen, King of Scotland, killed; succeeded by Kenneth II, brother of Dub (–995).
Egyptians attempt to take Antioch.
Canton submits to the Sung Emperor.

968

G **Economics, Science, Technology and Discovery**

Discovery of silver-bearing ore at Goslav; the production of copper, zinc and lead was also developed here later.

Jews first settle in Bohemia.

H **Religion and Education**

Jordan (according to tradition), the first Polish bishop, consecrated as Bishop of Poznań.

Creation of the Archbishopric of Magdeburg which John XIII limited to the land between the Elbe and the Oder so that the conversion of the Slavs should not be made under Otto's influence; Adalbert is the first Archbishop.

K **Literature, Philosophy and Scholarship**

*Liutprand of Cremona, *Relatio de legatione Constantinopolitana* (account of his embassy to the Greek court in 968).

969

970

H **Religion and Education**

*St. Ethelwold of Winchester, *Regularis Concordia* (rules for English monastic life).

K **Literature, Philosophy and Scholarship**

**Deor's Lament* (remarkable 'personal' poem in Old English).

**Beowulf* (probably first written down *c.* 700; ms. of this epic, the oldest complete poem of length in any modern language, written in a West Saxon dialect of Old English).

971

L **Births and Deaths**

Nov. 1st, Mahmud of Ghaznī b. (–1030).

972

B **(Spring):** Svjatoslav of Kiev killed in his defeat on the cataracts of the Dneiper by the Pechenegs led by Kurya; succeeded by his son, Jaropolk I (–977).

Apr: 14th, an alliance of the Greek and Western Empires made by the marriage of Otto's son, Otto, to Theophano, a niece of John Tzimisces.

C **Jul:** the Saracens of Garde-Freinet capture Mayeul, Abbot of Cluny.

Sep: 6th, death of Pope John XIII.

D **Oct:** 12th, John Tzimisces sacks Nisibis; he leaves Mesopotamia when Abū Taghlib, Emir of Mosul, promises to pay tribute.

E Mieszko of Poland defeats an invasion by Hodo, Margrave of the Eastern Mark, at Cidyny (*or* Zehden).

The Bulgarian Tsar, Boris II, abdicates, and Bulgaria is annexed by the Greek Empire.

Yūsuf Bulukkin, a Berber, who had been appointed governor of north-west Africa by the Fātimid Caliph, establishes the dynasty of Zīrids as independent rulers in eastern Algeria (–1148).

973

A **Jan:** 19th, Benedict VI crowned as Pope (–974).

Mar: Mieszko and the Margrave Hodo submit their quarrel to Otto's judgment.

B **May:** 7th, death of the Emperor Otto I the Great; succeeded as German King by his son, Otto II (–983).

11th, Edgar crowned at Bath as King of all England; he then went to Chester, where eight Scottish and Welsh kings rowed him on the Dee.

C **Jul:** 4th, Abū Taghlib of Mosul defeats a Byzantine army near Amida, on the Tigris.

E At the request of Boleslav II of Bohemia, Otto I detaches Bohemia from the diocese of Regensburg and establishes the bishopric of Prague under the Archbishop of Mainz.

974

B **Jun:** death of Pope Benedict VI (murdered by Crescentius?); succeeded by Boniface VII, who is expelled in a Roman revolt in July.

D **Oct:** Benedict VII crowned as Pope.

E Otto defeats Harold Bluetooth of Denmark.

In his second Mesopotamian campaign, John Tzimisces, supported by Ashot III of Armenia, enters Nisibis and (possibly) comes near to Baghdād before withdrawing.

An army of al-Hakam of Cordova extinguishes the Idrīsid dynasty of Fez.

972

H **Religion and Education**

Foundation of the Azhar Mosque, Cairo; it included a university (–1258).

*Edgar holds a council of the English church to organise monastic reform; it approves of Ethelwold's *Regularis Concordia* (–970).

973

J **Art, Architecture and Music**

Essen Minister (–1002); the west choir and a tower survive.

Bradford-on-Avon Church.

K **Literature, Philosophy and Scholarship**

*Widukind, monk of Corvey, *Gesta Saxonum* (*History of the Saxons*, 919–973).

L **Births and Deaths**

May 6th, Henry II b. (–1024).

— al-Bīrunī b. (–1048).

— Hishām III b. (–1036).

974

975

B **May**: 29th, John Tzimisces enters Baalbek (Heliopolis) in the course of his third campaign (or crusade), when he conquers northern Palestine, taking Caesarea.

C **Jul**: 8th, death of Edgar, King of England; succeeded by his son, Edward (–978).

D **Nov**: 24th, death of al-Mu'izz, Caliph of Egypt; succeeded by his son, al-'Azīz (–996).

F William, Count of Arles, expels the Saracens from Garde-Freinet.

976

A **Jan**: 10th, death of the Greek Emperor, John Tzimisces; succeeded by Basil II (–1025) and Constantine VIII (–1028), the sons of Romanus II. The Bulgarian war of independence follows, led by Samuel (–1014).

B **(Spring)**: Bardas Sclerus, claiming the Empire, leads a military revolt.
Jun: 11th, murder, in a revolt, of Peter Candiano IV, who had attempted to make himself the feudal lord of Venice.

C **Jul**: Henry the Wrangler deprived of the Duchy of Bavaria because of his rebellion against Otto II.
Aug: 12th, Pietro Orseolo elected as Doge of Venice (–978).

D **Oct**: 1st, death of al-Hakam II, Caliph of Spain; succeeded by Hishām II (–1009), whose vizier Muhammad ibn-abi-'Āmir (al-Mansur,-Almanzor) held effective power as regent (–1002).
Nov: 14th, death of Chao K'uang-yin (T'ai-Tsu), the first Sung emperor, who had almost reunited China; succeeded by his brother, T'ai Tsung (–997).

E Sicilian Saracens ravage Calabria.

977

E Otto II gives the duchy of Lower Lorraine to Charles, who had quarrelled with his brother, King Lothair of France.
Smbat II succeeds Ashot III as King of Armenia (–989).
Jaropolk I of Kiev murdered and succeeded by his brother Vladimir (–1015).

975

G **Economics, Science, Technology and Discovery**

*Abu Mansūr Muwaffaq of Herat, *The Foundations of the True Properties of Remedies* (in Persian; describes 585 drugs).

Ibn Hauqal, geographer and cartographer, *flor.*

H **Religion and Education**

Foundation of the bishoprics of Prague and Olomuc, for Bohemia and Moravia.

J **Art, Architecture and Music**

The Great Mosque, Cordova (begun 786), extended.

K **Literature, Philosophy and Scholarship**

**The Exeter Book* copied; contains Old English poets *Widsith* (*see* 800) and *Widsith spoke.*

976

F **Law and Politics**

The Chinese (Sung) regular army totals 378,000 men.

G **Economics, Science, Technology and Discovery**

*Al-Khwārizmī, *Māfātih al-'Ulūm*, (*The Keys of the Sciences*; a classification of sciences).

H **Religion and Education**

†Al-Hakam enlarged Cordova University, now preeminent in Europe and the Muslim world; he also founded free schools in the city.

K **Literature, Philosophy and Scholarship**

**Suda* (Greek dictionary).

977

J **Art, Architecture and Music**

Consecration of vaulted abbey-church, Ripoll.

†*Kuo Chung-shu, Chinese painter.

K **Literature, Philosophy and Scholarship**

Li Fang (principal editor), *T'ai-ping yü-lan* (Chinese encyclopedia with extracts from 1,690 works).

†Ibn-al-Qūtīyah, *Ta'rikh Iftitāh al-Andalus* (history of the Muslim conquest of Spain to *c.* 930).

978

A **Mar**: 18th, Edward the Martyr, King of England, murdered by servants of his step-brother, Ethelred II, who succeeds (–1016).
31st, the duchy of Bavaria deprived of its privileged status in the sentences following Otto's defeat of the rebellion known as 'The War of the Three Henries'.
Boleslav II of Bohemia does homage to Otto II.

B **Jun**: 19th, Bardas Sclerus defeats imperial forces on the Plain of Pancalia, and again, in the autumn, at Basilica Therma.
Sep: Pietro Orseolo retires to a monastery and is succeeded as Doge of Venice by Vitale Candiano (–979).

D **Oct**: Otto II invades France, harrying as far as Paris, in retaliation for Lothair's attempt to seize Lorraine.

E Harold II of Norway defeated and killed by the Danes.

979

A **Mar**: 24th, Bardas Sclerus finally defeated at Pancalia, near the Halys, by imperial forces assisted by Prince David of Tao, the most powerful ruler in Caucasia.

E Lothair has his son Louis (V) crowned as co-King of France and revives the Kingdom of Aquitaine for him but fails to recover direct royal authority there. ('France' proper did not extend south of the Loire.)
Death of Vitale Candiano, Doge of Venice; succeeded by Tribuno Memmo (–991).
*An expedition by Otto II fails to defeat Mieszko of Poland; they come to terms, when Mieszko does homage.

980

C **Jul**: Otto II and Lothair meet at Margut, on the Chiers, and swear to their friendship; Lothair abandons his claim on Lorraine.

D **Nov**: Otto begins his expedition to Italy.

E Vikings renew their raids on England.
Malachy II, King of Tara, defeats Olaf Sihtricson, the Danish King of Dublin, near Tara Hill; Olaf then withdraws to Iona.
Le Dai Hanh usurps the imperial throne of Dai-co-Viet (–1005).
*Mahīpāla I, King of Bengal, recovers his ancestral throne by expelling the Kāmbojas, a hill tribe.

981

A **Mar**: death of Pandolf I Ironhead; his dominions divided by his sons, Landolf IV (Capua-Benevento) and Paldolf (Salerno).

E Almanzor, Regent of Cordova, takes Zamora and subjugates Leon.
Vladimir takes Przemyśl, Czerwień, etc. ('Red Russia') from Poland.
Le Dai Hanh defeats a Chinese invasion of Vietnam.

978

G **Economics, Science, Technology and Discovery**
Completion of ʿAdud-ad-Dawla's teaching hospital, al-Bīmāristān al-ʿAdudi, Baghdād; its 24 physicians formed a medical faculty.
De Computo (treatise on the calendar; by Helperic of St. Gall?).

J **Art, Architecture and Music**
Mainz Cathedral begun.

L **Births and Deaths**
— Lady Murasaki b. (–*c*. 1031).

979

980

J **Art, Architecture and Music**
Church of St. Pantaleon, Cologne, dedicated.
*St. Ethelwold rebuilds Winchester Cathedral.

L **Births and Deaths**
— Otto III b. (–1002).
— Avicenna b. (–1037).

981

K **Literature, Philosophy and Scholarship**
†Hsieh Chü-chêng, *Chiu Wu-tai-shih* (official Chinese history of the Five Dynasties, 907–59).

North–South war in Vietnam—Civil war in France and Germany

982

C **Jul**: 13th, Otto II defeated at Basientello, in Apulia, by Saracens and Greeks.

D **Dec**: death of Ramiro III of Leon, following his defeat by rebels; succeeded by his uncle, Bermudo II (–999).

E Le Dai Hanh destroys Indrapura, capital of the Champa kingdom (South Vietnam).

983

C **Jul**: 10th, death of Pope Benedict VII; succeeded by John XIV (Peter, Bishop of Pavia; –984).

D **Dec**: 7th, death of the Emperor, Otto II; succeeded by his son, Otto III (–1002), under the guardianship of his mother, Theophano (–991).

E Wends revolt against German rule and restore their pagan religion.
Harold Bluetooth, King of Denmark, deposed by his son, Svein I Forkbeard (–1014).
Death of Ahmad ibn-Buwayh ʿAdud-ad-Dawla, ruler of the Caliphate, who had consolidated his control in Persia and assumed the title Shāhanshāh (King of Kings).
*The Caliph of Egypt now ruling over Palestine and southern Syria.

984

A **Jan**: Otto III seized by Henry the Wrangler, the former Duke of Bavaria.
Mar: Lothair takes Verdun, his only success in a campaign to seize Lorraine.
23rd, Henry proclaims himself King of Germany, but the Saxons and many others oppose him.

B **Apr**: John XIV deposed by the former Pope, Boniface VII.
Jun: 29th, a diet of German princes recognises Otto as King; Henry surrenders Otto to his mother, Theophano, and grandmother, Adelaide, and is restored Bavaria in compensation (–995).

C **Aug**: 20th, murder of the deposed Pope, John XIV.

985

B **May**: Lothair calls an assembly to condemn Archbishop Adalbero of Reims, who had organised a rebellion in the interests of Otto III, but it is dispersed by Hugh Capet, Duke of the Franks.

C **Jul**: death of Pope Boniface VII; succeeded by John XV (–996).
1st, Almanzor sacks Barcelona.

E Otto creates Dietrich II as hereditary Count of Holland (–988).
Basil II defeats a palace conspiracy and begins his personal rule as Greek Emperor.
(or 986) Mieszko of Poland does homage to John XV.

982

G **Economics, Science, Technology and Discovery**
Eric the Red begins the Viking colonisation of Greenland.
*Yasuyori Tamba, *Ishinō* (oldest extant Japanese treatise on medicine).

L **Births and Deaths**
*St. Adalbert, Archbishop of Magdeburg, d.

983

K **Literature, Philosophy and Scholarship**
†Minamoto no Shitagau, *Wamyōshō* (Sino-Japanese dictionary).

984

G **Economics, Science, Technology and Discovery**
Ahmad and Mahmud, sons of Ibrāhīm the astrolabist, of Isfahan, make the earliest dated astrolabe (now at Oxford).

L **Births and Deaths**
Aug. 1st, St. Ethelwold d.

985

G **Economics, Science, Technology and Discovery**
†*Al-Maqdisī, *Ahsan al-Taqāsīm fi Ma'rifat al-Aqālīm* (*The Best of Classification for the Knowledge of Regions*; description of his travels in Islamic countries of the Middle East).

J **Art, Architecture and Music**
Gumbaz-i Qābūs tower, Jurjan, Persia.

L **Births and Deaths**
— Giovanni Gualberti b. (–1073).

986

A **Mar**: 2nd, death of King Lothair of France; succeeded by his son, Louis V (–987).

C **Aug**: 17th, Basil II routed by the Bulgarians in 'Trajan's Gate'.

E Sabuktagīn of Ghaznī invades the Punjab.

987

B **May**: 21st or 22nd, death of Louis V *le Fainéant*, the last Carolingian King of France, without issue.

C **Jul**: 3rd, Hugh Capet, Duke of the Franks, the effective ruler of France, having been elected to succeed Louis, crowned as King of France (–996), so founding the Capetian dynasty (–1328). His March of Neustria consequently disappears, although in fact it had already disintegrated as his vassals, lay and ecclesiastical, had made themselves independent.

21st, death of Geoffrey I, Count of Anjou; succeeded by his son, Fulk III Nerra (–1040).

Sep: 14th, Bardas Phocas proclaims himself Greek Emperor.

D **Dec**: 30th, Hugh has his son, Robert, crowned as co-King of France and his heir. (This method of associating the heir with his father, the King, was the Capetian practice until Philip II abandoned it.)

E Samuel now established as ruler of the revived Bulgarian principality (–1014).

In Yucatán, Hunac Ceel expels the ruling Mayan dynasty from Chichén-Itzá and establishes the new Mayan Empire, under the Cocom dynasty, with its capital at Mayapán (–1441).

(or 988) The first treaty, for peace for seven years, made between the Greek Empire and Egypt.

988

A **Feb**: Vladimir of Kiev baptised as a condition of a marriage alliance with Basil (–989).

C **Summer**: Hugh fails in attempts to recover Laon from Charles, Duke of Lower Lorraine, who, as Lothair's brother, is claiming the French crown.

Bardas Phocas defeated at Chrysopolis by imperial forces assisted by Vladimir of Kiev. (This was the origin of the Greek Emperors' Varangian Guard, of Viking stock.)

E Death of Dietrich II, Count of Holland; succeeded by his son, Arnulf the Great (–1003/4).

Almanzor razes the city of Leon and makes its king tributary to Cordova.

Sabuktagīn takes Kabul from Jaipāl I, King of the Punjab.

986

G **Economics, Science, Technology and Discovery**

†Al-Sūfī, *Kitāb al-Kawākib al-Thābitah* (*Book of the Fixed Stars*, on his astronomical observations).

*Abbo of Fleury, *De numero mensura et pondere* (mathematical commentary).

L **Births and Deaths**

May 25th, al-Sūfī of Ray (Alsoufi) d. (83).

987

988

F **Law and Politics**

The Liao Emperors adopt the Chinese examination system for their civil service.

G **Economics, Science, Technology and Discovery**

Ibn-al-Nadīm, *Index of Sciences* (catalogue of Arabic works).

L **Births and Deaths**

May 19th, St. Dunstan d. (63).

989

A **Jan:** 23rd, death of Archbishop Adalbero of Reims; King Hugh appoints as his successor Arnulf, an illegitimate son of King Lothair (–991).

B **Apr:** 13th, Bardas Phocas defeated by imperial forces at Abydus.

C **Sep:** Archbishop Arnulf admits Charles of Lower Lorraine to Reims.

D **Oct:** 11th, Bardas Phocas surrenders to Basil II and renounces his imperial pretensions; he dies soon afterwards (by poison ?).

E Vladimir of Kiev temporarily seizes Cherson (Sebastopol) to force Basil to perform his agreement to give Vladimir his sister, Anna, in marriage.

Death of Smbat II the Conqueror, King of Armenia; succeeded by his brother, Gagik I (–1020).

990

991

A **Mar:** 29th, Bishop Asselin of Laon treacherously captures Charles of Lower Lorraine and Archbishop Arnulf of Reims on Hugh's behalf, so ending Charles' attempt to win France.

B **Jun:** 15th, death of the Empress Theophano, who had been ruling as 'Emperor' for Otto III; Adelaide, Otto I's widow, takes her place (–995).

18th, Hugh deprives Arnulf of the Archbishopric of Reims and (21st) appoints Gerbert of Aurillac (–998).

C **Aug:** Olaf Tryggvason defeats and kills Byrhtnoth, Earldorman of East Anglia, in the battle of Maldon; the Vikings are paid 'Danegeld' to leave.

E Death of Tribuno Memmo, Doge of Venice; succeeded by Pietro Orseolo II (–1009).

Basil subjugates Albania and begins his pacification of Bulgaria (–995).

989

F Law and Politics

A local Synod at Charroux announces a Truce of God. This example is followed by other French ecclesiastical assemblies in order to reduce anarchy (–1040, 1042).

J Art, Architecture and Music

*Novgorod Cathedral (wooden; –1045).

990

G Economics, Science, Technology and Discovery

†Al-Sāghānī, astronomer and instrument maker.

H Religion and Education

Foundation of the Orthodox Church in Russia.

J Art, Architecture and Music

*S. Stefano, Verona.
Mosque of al-Hākim, Cairo (–1012).

991

J Art, Architecture and Music

Church of the Tithe (Desiatinnaia), Kiev (–1039).

K Literature, Philosophy and Scholarship

(–992) Ælfric, *Catholic Homilies* (Old English).

992

B **Jun:** 27th, Fulk of Anjou defeats and kills Conan I of Brittany at Nantes.

E Death of Charles of Lower Lorraine, the last Carolingian.
The independence of Venice recognised in treaties with the Greek and Western Empires.
Death of Mieszko I, Duke of Poland; his lands (Poland as far west as the Oder, with Pomerania and Moravia), divided among his sons, one of whom, *viz.* Boleslav Khrobry (the Brave; –1025) subsequently reunites them.
The Īlek Khāns of Turkestan take Bukhāra.

993

E Otto recovers Brandenburg, which had been held by the Lusatians, in their revolt, for about three years.
*Death of Conrad, King of Burgundy; succeeded by his son, Rodolph III (–1032).
(or 994) Delhi founded by Ānangapāla, chief of the Tomara tribe.

994

B **May:** 10th, the Danes devastate Anglesey.

C **Sep:** 14th, a Byzantine army defeated near Antioch by the forces of al-'Azīz, Caliph of Egypt.

E London besieged by Svein of Denmark and Olaf Tryggvason, who retire on payment of Danegeld.
Death of Sancho II of Navarre; succeeded by his son, Garcia II (–1000).
Nūh II, the Sāmānid ruler, cedes Khurāsān (eastern Persia) to Sabuktagīn of Ghaznī.
*Fulk of Anjou builds one of the earliest known castles, at Langeais, as a means of strengthening his authority; yet, as in other cases, it becomes the stronghold of semi-independent vassals.

995

B **Apr:** Basil raises the siege of Aleppo by the Egyptians and campaigns as far south as Tripoli.

C **Aug:** death of Henry the Wrangler, Duke of Bavaria and Carinthia; succeeded (in Bavaria only) by his son, Henry (II as Emperor).

E Kenneth II of Scotland killed; succeeded by Constantine III, son of Culen (–997).
Olaf I Tryggvason succeeds as King of Norway (–1000).
Svein of Denmark becomes King of Sweden.
Basil completes his first subjugation of the Bulgarians.

992

H **Religion and Education**

The first Benedictine monastery in Bohemia founded at Břevnov, near Prague.

K **Literature, Philosophy and Scholarship**

†Leo the Deacon, *History* (of the Greek Empire; 959–75).

L **Births and Deaths**

Feb. 29th, St. Oswald, Archbishop of York, d.

993

H **Religion and Education**

John XV canonises Ulric, Bishop of Augsburg; this was the first canonisation by a Pope.

K **Literature, Philosophy and Scholarship**

**The Battle of Maldon* (Old English poem on the battle of 991, *q.v.*).

994

G **Economics, Science, Technology and Discovery**

†ʿAli ibn-al-ʿAbbas (Haly Abbas), *Kāmil al-Sinā ʿah al-Tibbīyah* (*The Whole Medical Art*; Persian encyclopedia of medicine, known in Latin as *Liber Regius*; –1127).

Al-Khujandī determines the obliquity of the ecliptic at Ray, Persia.

J **Art, Architecture and Music**

A new cathedral begun at Augsburg.

995

G **Economics, Science, Technology and Discovery**

†Al-Warrāq, *Fihrist al-ʿUlūm* (*Index of the Sciences*; bibliographical compilation on all branches of knowledge).

H **Religion and Scholarship**

John XV orders the deposition of Gerbert, Archbishop of Reims.

K **Literature, Philosophy and Scholarship**

The Caliph al-Hākim founds a 'House of Science' (library).

*Ælfric, *Lives of the Saints*; translation of Genesis.

†Ismāʿīl ibn-ʿAbbād, *Kitāb al-Muhīt* (Arabic dictionary).

996

A **Mar**: 12th, death of Odo (Eudes) I, Count of Chartres, who had gained possession of Dreux, Melun, Troyes, Meaux and Provins.

B **Apr**: death of Pope John XV.
May: 3rd, Gregory V crowned as Pope; he was Bruno of Carinthia, the first German Pope (–999).
21st, Otto III crowned as Holy Roman Emperor by Pope Gregory (–1002).

C **Sep**: Gregory expelled by the Romans.

D **Oct**: 14th, death of al-ʿAzīz, Caliph of Egypt; succeeded by his son, al-Hākim (–1021).
24th, death of Hugh, King of France; succeeded by his son, Robert II the Pious (–1031).

E Death of Richard I, Duke of Normandy; succeeded by his son, Richard II the Good (–1026).
Almanzor destroys Leon city.

997

B **Apr**: John Philagathus, Archbishop of Piacenza, crowned as Pope John XVI (–998).

E Constantine III of Scotland killed and succeeded by Kenneth III, the son of Dub (–1005).
Ardoin, Marquess of Ivrea, leading an Italian revolt, murders Peter, Bishop of Vercelli; Otto III restores some order.
Géza (St. Stephen) succeeds as Duke of Hungary (–1000); he is baptised by Adalbert.
Death of Stephen Držislav, King of Croatia, a Byzantine vassal.
Almanzor sacks the church of Santiago de Compostela in a raid into Galicia.
The Īlek Khāns extinguish the Sāmānid dynasty of Transoxiana.
Death of the Emperor T'ai Tsung; he had subdued the remaining Chinese provinces save for the northern area ruled by the Khitan.
(or 998) the Bulgarian leader, Samuel, proclaims himself Tsar; he aspires to create a Balkan empire.

998

A **Jan.** *or* **Feb**: Arnulf restored as Archbishop of Reims following Gerbert's flight to Otto III.
Feb: Otto removes John XVI and restores Gregory V as Pope.

B **Apr**: Otto executes Crescentius II, Patrician (the secular ruler) of Rome.

E In order to thwart Samuel, Basil grants the protectorate of Dalmatia to Venice.
Mahmūd, son of Sabuktagīn, deposes his brother, Ismāʾīl, and becomes Emir of Ghaznī (–1030).

996

H **Religion and Education**

Adalbert establishes a Benedictine community at Miedryrzecze, Poznania (Poland).

997

G **Economics, Science, Technology and Discovery**

†Abu'l-Wafā, translations and commentaries on Euclid, etc. (all lost); contributions to development of trigonometry and geometry.

H **Religion and Education**

†Adalbert martyred on a mission to convert the Prussians (Apr. 23rd).

J **Art, Architecture and Music**

St. Martin, Tours, burnt; rebuilt (–1014).
Destruction of Santiago de Compostela (*see* E).

K **Literature, Philosophy and Scholarship**

*Richer of Reims (*or* St. Rémi), *Historiae* (of France, to 996).

998

F **Law and Politics**

Otto III unites his chanceries for Germany and Italy, thus restoring the Carolingian system of a single secretariat.

K **Literature, Philosophy and Scholarship**

†Ethelweard, the earldorman, translation into Latin of *The Anglo-Saxon Chronicle.*

999

A **Feb**: 18th, death of Pope Gregory V.

B **Apr**: 3rd or 4th, election of Gerbert of Aurillac as Pope Silvester II; he was the first French Pope (–1003).

D **Autumn**: Basil's Syrian campaign restores imperial control after a military revolt.
Dec: 16th, death of the Empress, Adelaide.

E Malachy II, (now) High King of Ireland, and Brian Bórumha, defeat the Danes at 'Glenmana' and sack Dublin.
Death of Bermudo II of Leon; succeeded by his son, Alfonso V (–1027).
Death of Boleslav II, Duke of Bohemia, who had, like his father (Boleslav I), established control in the country through the agency of his own officials instead of nobles; succeeded by Boleslav III (–1003).
Quetzalcóatl, founder of the Mexican Toltec empire (–1168), expelled from its capital, Tollán; he stays (? rules) in Mayapán until his return to Mexico.

1000

A **Mar**: 31st, Boleslav crowned as King of Poland by Otto III. The Archbishopric of Gniezno is created for Poland, with Silesia and Pomerania subject to it; thus Poland is recognised as independent both politically and ecclesiastically.
31st, murder of David, Prince of Tao (Georgia); Basil consequently annexes his lands.

C **Aug**: 15th, Stephen crowned as King of Hungary (–1038); he had put the country under the protection of the Pope, from whom he received the crown and the establishment of a Hungarian ecclesiastical hierarchy, under the Archbishopric of Gran.

E Ethelred ravages Cumberland and the Isle of Man.
Svein of Denmark defeats and kills Olaf I at 'Svold', and thus conquers Norway (–1014).
Death of Garcia II of Navarre; succeeded by his son, Sancho III the Great (–1035).
Otto III makes his permanent residence in Rome.
Basil extends his empire to the Lower Danube with the occupation of the Dobrudja.
As a result of invasions by Dai-co-viet, Yang Po Ku Vijaya, King of Champa, transfers his capital from Indrapura to Vijaya.
*Sweden now united as a kingdom under Olaf the Tax-king, who established Christianity.

1001

A **Feb**: the Romans revolt and besiege Otto in his palace on the Aventine; he is relieved by Henry of Bavaria, but although peace is restored, he leaves Rome.

D **Nov**: 27th, Maḥmūd of Ghaznī defeats Jaipāl of the Punjab at Peshawar; Jaipāl commits suicide and Maḥmūd occupies his kingdom.

999

J **Art, Architecture and Music**
†Dhanga, King of Jejakabhukti, built several temples at Khajurāho.

1000

F **Law and Politics**
*School of (Lombard) law at Pavia.

G **Economics, Science, Technology and Discovery**
*Helperic, *Arithmetic*.

H **Religion and Education**
*(–*c.* 1170). Development of cathedral schools at Tours, Orleans, Utrecht, Reims, Chartres, Liège and Paris; they eclipsed the monastic schools and from some universities were to rise.
The Christian religion established in Iceland.

J **Art, Architecture and Music**
*Nave of St. Philibert-de-Grandlieu, Déas.
*Church of St. Mary Minor, Lund.
*Wooden palace at Lojsta, Gotland.

K **Literature, Philosophy and Scholarship**
*Sei Shōnagon, *Makura no Sōshi* (*The Pillow Book*; a Japanese court lady's commonplace book of reflections, odd facts and anecdotes, with short poems).
Utsubo Monogatari (Japanese tales).
Verses on the Captivity of Boethius (anon. fragment versified from *The Consolation of Philosophy*; these 250 lines are 'much the earliest specimen of French verse'—*Hallam*; –885).

1001

J **Art, Architecture and Music**
Abbey-church of St. Bénigne, Dijon (–1018).
Monastery and vaulted church of St. Martin-du-Canigou (–1026).
*Church of St. Michael, Hildesheim (–1033).

1002–1003 Defeat and death of Almanzor—German and Polish intervention in Bohemia

1002

A **Jan:** 23rd, death of Otto III, the Holy Roman Emperor; he was unmarried.
Feb: 15th, Ardoin, Marquess of Ivrea, the leader of an Italian revolt against German and ecclesiastical domination, crowned as King of Italy (–1004).

B **Apr:** 30th, murder of Eckhard, Margrave of Meissen, an aspirant to the German crown.
Jun: 7th, Henry of Bavaria crowned as King of the Germans (–1024).

C **Jul:** Boleslav of Poland recognises Henry II as Emperor and cedes his recent conquests, retaining Lusatia and Milsko; as Boleslav leaves the diet, an attempt is made to murder him, for which he blames Henry, so beginning a war (–1018).
Aug: 10th, death of Almanzor, regent of Cordova, after his defeat at Calatañazor by the Kings of Leon and Navarre; succeeded by his son, al-Muzaffar (–1008).

D **Oct:** 15th, death of Henry, Duke of Burgundy, without issue; the succession is disputed (–1015).
Nov: 13th (St. Brice's day), Danes resident in southern England massacred at the instigation of King Ethelred.

E Duke Boleslav III expelled from Bohemia and succeeded by Vladivoj, the brother of Boleslav of Poland; in order to win German support against his subjects, Vladivoj becomes the vassal of Henry II, who creates him Duke of Bohemia (–1002).
Venetian fleet defeats Muslims besieging Greeks in Bari.

1003

B **Spring:** Basil II defeats Samuel, the Bulgarian Tsar, near Skoplje.
May: 12th, death of Pope Silvester II. John Crescentius, the son of Crescentius, now ruling Rome as its Patrician.
Jun: John XVII crowned as Pope.

D **Oct:** 1st, the acceptance of Henry II as King of the Germans completed with the homage of Duke Hermann of Swabia, his former rival for the title.
Dec: death of Pope John XVII.

E Death of Vladivoj, Duke of Bohemia; succeeded by his son, Jaromir. Shortly afterwards, Boleslav of Polands expels him and restores Boleslav III, who proceeds to murder his former opponents. The Bohemians then call in Boleslav of Poland, who deposes and blinds Boleslav III, and rules Bohemia himself.
Brian Bórumha now High King of Ireland (–1014).
King Svein of Denmark invades England to punish the Massacre of St. Brice's Day.
Muslims devastate Leon.

1002

G **Economics, Science, Technology and Discovery**

†Wu Shu, *Shih lei fu* (Chinese scientific encyclopedia).

J **Art, Architecture and Music**

Imperial residence, Bamberg (–1012).

K **Literature, Philosophy and Scholarship**

†Ibn-Jinni, Arabic philologist.

1003

G **Economics, Science, Technology and Discovery**

Voyage of Leif Ericsson to North America, where he discovered 'Wineland' (Nova Scotia).

†Gerbert of Aurillac (Pope Silvester II); various mathematical works attributed, including treatises on the abacus, the astrolabe and Spanish-Arabic numerals.

K **Literature, Philosophy and Scholarship**

*Stephen Asolik, a universal history (in Armenian, to 1003).

1004

A **Jan**: John XVIII crowned as Pope (–1009).

B **May**: 14th, following the desertion and flight of Ardoin, Henry II crowned as King of Italy (–1024); an anti-German riot in Pavia that day is followed by the sack of the city.

C **Sep**: Henry restores Jaromir as Duke of Bohemia (–1012) in a war which follows Boleslav of Poland's refusal to do homage.

E Pisa sacked by the Saracens.
Stephen of Hungary conquers Transylvania.
In the treaty of Shan-yüan, the Sung Empire recognises the permanent establishment of the Khitan Liao and begins the regular payment of tribute.

1005

A **Mar**: 28th, Henry II makes an alliance with the Wends against Boleslav of Poland, who had seized territory between the Oder and the Elbe. He later invades Poland as far as Poznan and is defeated by Boleslav. A treaty is made, but its terms are not known.

E Kenneth III of Scotland killed and succeeded by Malcolm II, the son of Kenneth II (–1034).

1006

C **Sep**: a joint expedition by Henry II and Robert of France fails to recover Valenciennes from Baldwin IV of Flanders, who has also seized the castle of Ghent built by Otto I.

E Henry occupies Basel.
A Saracen fleet defeated near Reggio by the Pisans.

1004

K **Literature, Philosophy and Scholarship**

†Abbo of Fleury, *Epitome de Vitis Romanorum Pontificum* (history of the Papacy).

1005

F **Law and Politics**

Wang Ch'in-jo (principal editor), *T'sê-fu yüan-kuei* (encyclopedia of Chinese government; completed 1013 in 1,000 books).

G **Economics, Science, Technology and Discovery**

†Abe Seimei, Japanese astronomer.

H **Religion and Education**

Al-Hākim founds the Dār al-Hikmah ('Hall of Wisdom', a college of theology), Cairo.

J **Art, Architecture and Music**

Abbey-church of St. Remi, Reims, planned (–1049).

St. Germain-des-Prés, Paris (–1021).

Oldest extant illustrated Arabic manuscript (Al-Sūfī's geography, in Leningrad; –986).

K **Literature, Philosophy and Scholarship**

Ælfric appointed the first abbot of Eynsham.

†Ibn-Fāris, Persian philologist.

L **Births and Deaths**

— St. Nilus d.

— Lanfranc b. (–1089).

1006

1007

D **Nov**: 1st, Henry founds the Bishopric of Bamberg for the conversion of the Wends, but also in furthering the policy (followed by Otto I) of founding royal authority on the Church as a counter to feudal particularism.

E Henry compels Baldwin to surrender Valenciennes.
Boleslav of Poland raids into Germany as far as Magdeburg and recovers territories west of the Oder, including Lausitz.
Kakuyid dynasty of Hamadan and Isfahan founded (–1050).

1008

E Al-Muzaffar, regent of Cordova, poisoned and succeeded by his brother, ʻAbd-ar-Rahmān; the latter is soon afterwards killed by the populace, and the military now effectively rule in Cordova.
Georgia first united under King Bagrat III.

1009

A **Mar**: death of Pietro Orseolo II, Doge of Venice; succeeded by his son, Ottone (–1026).

C **Jul**: death of Pope John XVIII; succeeded by Sergius IV (–1012).
Aug: 1st, a large Danish army lands at Sandwich and attacks London.
Sep: 27th, the church of the Holy Sepulchre at Jerusalem destroyed by order of the Caliph al-Hākim.

E Henry grants Valenciennes to Baldwin of Flanders as an imperial fief.
Hishām II, the Caliph of Cordova, deposed; succeeded by Muhammad II, who in turn is deposed and succeeded by Sulaymān (–1010).
Mahmūd of Ghaznī conquers the principality of Ghūr. Muslims now settling in north-west India.

1007

G **Economics, Science, Technology and Discovery**

First known use of the word 'burgess' or 'bourgeois' (*burgensis*) in charter of Fulk Nerra of Anjou establishing the 'Free borough' of Beaulieu.

*Ibn-Yūnus, *The Hakemite Tables* (astronomical tables, compiled 990–1007, in the observatory, Cairo).

†*Al-Majrīti, planetary tables; treatise on the astrolabe.

J **Art, Architecture and Music**

Bamberg Cathedral (–1012).

K **Literature, Philosophy and Scholarship**

†Al-Hamadhānī, *Maqāmāt* (Arabic prose fiction).

†Heriger of Lobbes, history of the Bishopric of Liège.

L **Births and Deaths**

— Ou-yang Hsiu b. (–1072).

— Peter Damian b. (–1072).

1008

K **Literature, Philosophy and Scholarship**

†*Al-Jawhāri, Arabic lexicon.

1009

H **Religion and Education**

†Mar. 14th, Bruno martyred on a mission to convert the Jadźwingas (a Baltic tribe).

J **Art, Architecture and Music**

Cuxa Abbey rebuilt (–1040).

Paderborn Cathedral begun.

Mainz Cathedral burnt; rebuilt (–1036).

*Completion of the Siva Temple at Tanjore (the largest and most mature work of South Indian architecture in the Chola period).

1010

E Sulaymān of Cordova deposed and Muhammad II restored; the latter is then murdered and Hishām II restored (–1013).

Ly Thai-to usurps the imperial throne of Dai-co-viet (–1029), and founds a new capital at Thang-long; he founds the Ly dynasty (–1225).

1011

E Ethelred invades South Wales.

Death of Bernard I Billung, Duke of Saxony; succeeded by his son, Bernard II.

The Saracens again sack Pisa.

1012

A (early): death of John Crescentius, Patrician of Rome.

B **Apr**: 19th, St. Alphege, Archbishop of Canterbury, murdered by the Danes, who had been ravaging southern and central England since 1009. They now leave the country after the payment of Danegeld.

May: 12th, death of Pope Sergius IV. The election of his successor disputed: Gregory is elected on the nomination of the Crescentius family, but soon expelled by the Counts of Tusculum, who put Theophylact of Tusculum, as Benedict VIII, in possession (–1024).

E Jaromir of Bohemia deposed and succeeded by Oldřich (–1034).

Death without issue, of Duke Hermann III of Swabia, the last of a Carolingian line; Henry II grants the Duchy to Ernest of Babenburg (–1015).

1013

B **Apr**: 20th, Hīshām II, Caliph of Cordova, disappears on the capture of the city by Sulaymān, who resumes his rule (–1016).

May: 24th, by the Peace of Merseberg, Boleslav of Poland does homage to Henry II and is permitted to retain all his conquests with the exception of Bohemia; he is now able to make war in Russia.

E Svein of Denmark, having been accepted as king in Northumbria and the Danelaw, conquers Wessex; Ethelred II flees to Normandy (–1014).

1010

F **Law and Politics**

King Robert proclaims a Peace of God in France.

G **Economics, Science, Technology and Discovery**

*Bridferth of Ramsey, *Handboc* (astronomical and astrological compilation in Latin and Old English).

K **Literature, Philosophy and Scholarship**

*Murasaki Shikibu ('Lady Murasaki'), *Genji Monogatari* (*Tale of Genji*; the first psychological novel in literature).

†*Aimon of Fleury, *Historia Francorum* (*History of the Franks*, from their Trojan origins to 654).

1011

K **Literature, Philosophy and Scholarship**

Ch'ên P'êng-nien, revision of Lu Fa-yen's *Ch'ien-yun* (Chinese phonetic dictionary of seventh century).

1012

G **Economics, Science, Technology and Discovery**

Rice is introduced into China from Champa, and becomes the staple diet.

H **Religion and Education**

St. Romuald founds the Order of Camaldoli (of hermit-monks).

First prosecutions for heresy in Germany.

*Burchard, Bishop of Worms, *Decretum libri xx* (canon law).

1013

G **Economics, Science, Technology and Discovery**

†*Al-Zahrāwi (Abulcasis), *al-Tasrif li-Man 'an al-Ta'alif* (medical *vade-mecum*; includes the first Islamic treatise on surgery).

J **Art, Architecture and Music**

Greenstead Church, Essex (the only surviving example of a wooden Saxon church).

L **Births and Deaths**

July 18th, Hermann Contractus b. (–1054).

— Alphesi b. (–1103).

1014

A **Jan**: Henry II holds a synod at Ravenna which makes decrees for ecclesiastical reform.
Feb: 3rd, death of Svein Forkbeard, King of Denmark, Norway and England; succeeded by his sons, Harold, in Denmark (–1019), and Cnut, in England, but Ethelred restored by the English and Cnut leaves the country.
14th, Henry crowned as Holy Roman Emperor by Pope Benedict VIII (–1024). He suppresses an anti-German riot in Rome.

B **Apr**: 18th, in the battle of Clontarf, Brian Bórumha, High King of Ireland, killed while victorious over a great Viking confederation; Irish unity collapses but the Vikings in Ireland are thereafter peaceful and subject to Irish rulers.
May: 7th, death of Bagrat III, King of Georgia.
Jun: Henry returns to Germany; in Lombardy, there follows an anti-German outburst directed against the bishops.

C **Jul**: 29th, Basil II captures and blinds a Bulgarian army in the Pass of Kleidion.

D **Oct**: 6th, death of Samuel, the Bulgarian Tsar.

1015

B **May**: 31st, death of Ernest of Babenburg, Duke of Swabia; succeeded by his son, Ernest (–1030).

C **Jul**: Boleslav of Poland repulses an invasion by Henry II.
Aug (–Dec): Cnut invades England and conquers Wessex and Mercia.

D **Dec**: 14th, death of Ardoin, sometime King of Italy.

E The Duchy of Burgundy divided by a treaty whereby Henry, the son of King Robert of France, becomes Duke, and Otto-William, the adopted son of Duke Henry the Great, receives the County of Dijon.
Saracens from Spain conquer Sardinia (–1016).
Death of St. Vladimir I, Great Prince of Russia (Kiev); succeeded by his son(?), Sviatopolk I, after he has restored unity by murdering his brothers, Boris and Gleb; another brother, Jaroslav, holds Novgorod against him (–1019).

1014

K **Literature, Philosophy and Scholarship**
Wulfstan, Archbishop of York, *Sermo Lupi ad Anglos* ('an address to the English nation').

1015

F **Law and Politics**
Benevento establishes a commune for self-government.

G **Economics, Science, Technology and Discovery**
†Māsawayh al-Mārdini, a pharmacopeia, treatises on laxatives and emetics.

J **Art, Architecture and Music**
*A cathedral begun at Strasbourg.

K **Literature, Philosophy and Scholarship**
(–1030) Dudon of St. Quentin, *De moribus et actis primorum Normanniae ducum* (chronicle of Normandy from 911).

1016

B **Apr**: 23rd, death of Ethelred II the Redeless, King of England; succeeded by his son, Edmund Ironside.

May: Edmund reconquers Wessex while Cnut besieges London.

Jun: Pisa and Genoa expel Mujāhid of Denia from Sardinia.

(?): King Rodolph III of Burgundy recognises Henry II as his heir and receives his (ineffective) assistance against a rebellion by Otto-William, Count of Burgundy.

C **Jul**: 6th, Fulk Nerra of Anjou, in the process of extending his territories, defeats Count Odo II of Blois at Pontlevoi.

D Cnut and Edmund make a treaty partitioning England after Cnut's victory at Ashingdon, Essex.

Nov: 30th, death of Edmund Ironside; Cnut now accepted as sole King of England (–1035).

E Malcolm of Scotland defeats Uhtred, Earl of Northumbria, at Carham, on the Tweed, thus securing Scottish possession of Lothian.

Olaf Haroldson recovers Norway's independence from Denmark by his naval victory off Nesjar.

Sulaymān of Cordova deposed by 'Ali ibn-Hammūd (–1018) who founds the Hammūdid dynasty.

The first Normans arrive in southern Italy as military adventurers.

Mahmūd of Ghaznī captures Samarqand.

Death of Rājarāja the Great, King of the Cholas, who had made himself supreme in southern India and Ceylon.

1017

C **Aug–Sep**: Henry II, attacking Poland, fails to cross the Oder and retires through Bohemia without defeating Boleslav of Poland, who was campaigning there.

D **Nov**: Henry restores the Duchy of Bavaria to Henry of Luxemburg.

1016

1017

H **Religion and Education**
†Genshin, monk of Mount Hiei, *Ōjō yōshū* (*Essentials of Salvation*; a popular work, expounding the new form of Buddhism developing in Japan).

J **Art, Architecture and Music**
Chapel of St. Bartholomew, Paderborn.

L **Births and Deaths**
Oct. 28th, Henry III b. (–1056).

1018

A **Jan:** 30th, by the Treaty of Bautzen (Budziszyn), peace made between Henry and Boleslav on terms favourable to Poland.

Mar: in an assembly at Nijmegen, Henry establishes peace in Lorraine; he fails, however, to enforce his authority over the nobles of Burgundy.

C **Jul:** 21st, Boleslav defeats Jaroslav of Novgorod, who had seized Kiev, on the Bug.

Aug: 14th, entering Kiev, he restores his son-in-law Sviatopolk I to the throne, but is then forced to retire when Sviatopolk organises an anti-Polish rising; Boleslav, however, regains Czerwień and Przemyśl for Poland.

D **Oct:** Byzantine army defeats south Italian rebels at Cannae.

Dec: 20th, Mahmūd of Ghaznī takes Kanauj, the capital of the kingdom of Pañchāla.

E ʽAbd-ar-Rahmān IV, of the Umayyad dynasty, succeeds as Caliph of Cordova, soon being replaced by a Hammūdid (–1023).

1019

E Cnut of England takes possession of the Danish throne in succession to his brother, Harold (–1035).

Basil II completes his conquest of Bulgaria and its former empire in the Balkans; his western frontier now extends to the Adriatic and in the north along the Danube.

Jaroslav expels Sviatopolk and becomes Great Prince of Kiev (–1055).

1020

C **Aug:** Henry II captures Ghent from Baldwin of Flanders.

E Bernard II of Saxony revolts against Henry II.

On the death of Gagik I of Armenia, his kingdom divided among his sons and so declines.

1021

A **Feb:** 13th, murder of al-Hākim, Caliph of Egypt; succeeded by his son, al-Zāhir (–1035).

D **Dec:** Henry begins his third expedition to Italy in response to further Byzantine successes in Benevento which are endangering Rome.

E Saracen pirates sack Narbonne.

Basil II regains control in Georgia.

1018

H **Religion and Education**

In a council at Pavia, Benedict VIII promulgates decrees against clerical marriage and concubinage.

K **Literature, Philosophy and Scholarship**

†Thietmar, Bishop of Merseburg, *Chronicon* (908–1018; argues that Poland was under German imperial and ecclesiastical authority).

1019

F **Law and Politics**

Henry II pronounces, in a synod at Goslar, that the children of marriages of priests of servile birth are unfree.

J **Art, Architecture and Music**

Cathedrals begun at Basel and Trier.

1020

F **Law and Politics**

Alfonso of Leon issues the *fuero* (town charter) and other laws.

G **Economics, Science, Technology and Discovery**

Earliest Chinese reference to a floating magnet (for navigation).

*Śrīdhara the Learned, *Ganitasāra* (*Compendium of Calculation*).

J **Art, Architecture and Music**

Chartres Cathedral (of 958) and St. Emmeram, Regensburg, burnt; rebuilt.

Bamberg Cathedral consecrated by Benedict VIII.

K **Literature, Philosophy and Scholarship**

†Firdausī, *Shāh-Nāma* (*The Book of Kings*; Persia's national epic; –1335).

1021

1022

A Henry's Italian expedition checks the Byzantine advance; he takes Capua and Troia before sickness compels the German army to retire.

C **Aug**: 1st, a synod held at Pavia by Henry denounces the marriage of clergy in Lombardy. 11th, Henry meets Robert of France at Ivois where they discuss the reform of the Church.

1023

E ʻAbd-ar-Rahmān V becomes Caliph of Cordova and is murdered and succeeded by Muhammad III (–1025).

Aleppo lost to the Greeks with the establishment there of the independent Mirdāsid emirate (–1079).

1024

B **Apr**: death of Pope Benedict VIII; succeeded by his brother, Romanus, senator of Rome, as John XIX (–1032).

C **Jul**: 13th, death of the Holy Roman Emperor, (St.) Henry II, without issue; he was the last of the Saxon line of emperors.

Sep: 4th, Conrad (II) of Franconia, the first of the Salian line, elected King of the Germans (–1039).

D **Dec**: 25th, Boleslav crowned as King of Poland with the approval of Pope John XIX.

E Jaroslav divides Russia with his brother, Mstislav, after being defeated by him (–1035).

1022

H **Religion and Education**
An early instance of the burning of heretics (Cathari), at Orleans.
The Emperor promotes Church reform (*see* C).

K **Literature, Philosophy and Scholarship**
†Notker Labeo, the *Consolation* of Boethius translated into German.
†St. Simeon, *Loves of the Divine Hymns* (Greek).

L **Births and Deaths**
June 29th, Notker Labeo d. (*c.* 72).

1023

H **Religion and Education**
Earliest notice of a confraternity in a French town, *viz.* Arras.

K **Literature, Philosophy and Scholarship**
†Wulfstan, *Homilies* (Old English).

L **Births and Deaths**
Nov. 20th, St. Bernward, Bishop of Hildesheim, d.

1024

G **Economics, Science, Technology and Discovery**
The Sung government takes over the banks of Chengtu, in Szechwan, and their certificates of deposit then become official and thus the first paper currency in the world.

J **Art, Architecture and Music**
Abbey-church of Mont-St.-Michel (–1084).

L **Births and Deaths**
— Hugh of Semur b. (–1109).

1025

A **Jan**: Mahmūd of Ghaznī sacks Somnāth (*now* Dwārka), the great centre of Hinduism.

B **Jun**: 17th, death of Boleslav the Brave, King of Poland, whose kingdom bounded by the Elbe, Baltic, Dneiper, Danube and Theiss now collapses; succeeded by his son, Mieszko II (–1033, 1034).

D **Dec**: 15th, death of the Greek Emperor, Basil II the Bulgarslayer, without issue; his brother, Constantine VIII, already co-emperor, rules alone.
25th, the dukes of Lorraine submit to Conrad II on the collapse of their revolt.

E Conrad makes an alliance with Cnut of England and Denmark.
Ernest, Duke of Swabia, revolts against Conrad.
Muhammad III of Cordova murdered; succeeded by a Hammūdid (–1027).
The crown of Italy offered by its nobles to William V, Duke of Aquitaine; he accepts on behalf of his son, but soon gives it up.
Rājendra, King of the Cholas, destroys the Malay empire with his great naval expedition against Sumatra and Malaya.

1026

E Death of Richard II, Duke of Normandy; succeeded by his son, Richard III (–1027).
Anund Jacob succeeds as King of Sweden (–1056).
Cnut defeated in the sea battle of the Holy River by Kings Anund of Sweden and Olaf of Norway and Ulf, his own regent of Denmark.
Death of Henry of Luxemburg, Duke of Bavaria.
Conrad crowned as King of Italy (–1039).
Ottone Orseolo, Doge of Venice, deposed; succeeded by Pietro Barbolano (–1032).
Paldolf IV recovers Capua with Byzantine assistance.
Mahmūd of Ghaznī conquers Gujarāt.

1027

A **Mar**: 26th, Conrad II crowned as Holy Roman Emperor by Pope John XIX (–1039).

B **May**: 5th, Alfonso V of Leon killed at the siege of Viseu; succeeded by his son, Bermudo III (–1037).
14th, Henry, Duke of Burgundy, son of King Robert, crowned as King of France.

C **Jul**: Conrad grants Bavaria to his son, Henry, and deprives Ernest of the Duchy of Swabia, on his submission after rebellion.

E Malcolm of Scotland does homage to Cnut.
Death of Richard III, Duke of Normandy; succeeded by his brother, Robert I (–1035).
Hishām III, an Umayyad, proclaimed as Caliph of Cordova (–1031).

1025

J **Art, Architecture and Music**
Abbey-church of Limburg an der Haardt (–1045).
*Church of St. Hilaire, Poitiers (–1049), and Auxerre Cathedral (–1030).

1026

G **Economics, Science, Technology and Discovery**
†Adelbold, Bishop of Utrecht, mathematician.

K **Literature, Philosophy and Scholarship**
†Adelbold, *Life of the Emperor Henry II* (to 1004).

1027

K **Literature, Philosophy and Scholarship**
*William of Jumièges, *Chronicle of the Dukes of Normandy*.

L **Births and Deaths**
— St. Romuald d.
Dec. –, William I b. (–1087).

Cnut conquers Norway—Ceylon liberated—Muslim empire in India

1028

B **Apr**: 14th, coronation of Conrad's son, Henry, as King of the Germans.

E Cnut expels Olaf, King of Norway, from his kingdom, which he had united, with the chiefs of the Faroes, Orkneys and Shetlands recognising his rule.
Sancho II of Navarre unites Castile to his kingdom.
Conrad II makes an unsuccessful campaign against Poland.
By defeating the Hungarians, Břatislav, the son of Duke Oldřich, unites Moravia to Bohemia.
Paldolf IV of Capua takes Naples from its duke, Sergius IV.
Death of the Greek Emperor, Constantine VIII; succeeded by his son-in-law, Romanus III (–1034).

1029

E Vikramabāhu I expels the Cholas from Ceylon and becomes King (–1041).

1030

B **Apr**: 21st, death of Mahmūd, Emir of Ghaznī, founder of the Muslim empire in north-west India; succeeded by his son, Masʿūd I (–1040).

C **Jul**: 29th, (St.) Olaf killed in the battle of Stiklestad while attempting to recover his kingdom of Norway from the Danes.
Aug: Ernest, who had been restored to the Duchy of Swabia, killed in a fresh revolt against Conrad.

E Conrad leads an unsuccessful expedition against Stephen of Hungary, who in return takes Vienna but is defeated by Břatislav of Bohemia.
Paldolf of Capua expelled from Naples by Sergius, who enfeoffs the Norman adventurer, Rainulf, with Aversa in reward for his services.

1031

C **Jul**: 20th, death of Robert II the Pious, King of France; succeeded by his son, Henry I (–1060).

D **Nov**: 30th, the Spanish Caliphate abolished by the Cordovans with the deposition of Hishām III, the last Umayyad; a score of independent Moorish kingdoms arose in Andalusia.

E Stephen of Hungary makes peace with Conrad, restoring Vienna, and with Oldřich of Bohemia, to whom he cedes Moravia.
Mieszko II of Poland attacked by a coalition; the Russians take 'Red Russia' while he has to cede Lusatia to Conrad; then he is expelled in a rising which establishes his brother, Bezprym, as ruler of Poland.

1028

H **Religion and Education**
†Fulbert had promoted the great cathedral school, under Hildegaire, at Chartres (–1115).

J **Art, Architecture and Music**
The Kazandjilar Djami, Salonika (built as a Greek church).

L **Births and Deaths**
Apr. 10th, Fulbert, Bishop of Chartres, d.
— Marianus Scotus b. (–1086).

1029

K **Literature, Philosophy and Scholarship**
†Al-Musabbihi, *Akhbār misr wa-Faḍā'ilhā* (an enormous history of Egypt of which only a fragment survives).

1030

G **Economics, Science, Technology and Discovery**
*Movable wooden characters used in printing in China.

J **Art, Architecture and Music**
†Tower of Victory built by Mahmūd at Ghaznī.
*Cathedrals of Coutances (–1091) and Speyer (–1137).
†Fan K'uan, Chinese painter.

K **Literature, Philosophy and Scholarship**
†Ibn Maskauayh, a universal history (to 983).

1031

J **Art, Architecture and Music**
Einsiedeln Abbey (–1039).

L **Births and Deaths**
— William of Dijon d.
— Roger Guiscard b. (–1031).

1032–1034 Kingdoms of Burgundy and Poland extinguished—Castile created

1032

C **Sep**: 5th–6th, death of Rodolph III, King of Burgundy, without legitimate issue; although the reversion to the crown had been granted to Henry II (–1016), Rodolph's nephew, Odo II, Count of Blois and Champagne, attempts to seize it by invading the kingdom.

D **Nov**: death of Pope John XIX; succeeded by his nephew, Benedict IV (–1045).

E Henry of France grants the Duchy of Burgundy to his brother, Robert, in order to end a war of succession (–1075).

Domenico Orseolo succeeds Pietro Barbolano as Doge of Venice, and is himself replaced by Domenico Flabanico (–1043); with the end of the Orseolo dynasty, the power of the popular assembly to elect the Doge is restored.

Mieszko returns to Poland following the murder of Bezprym.

Edessa taken by the Byzantine commander, George Maniaces.

1033

A **Feb**: 2nd, Conrad crowned as King of Burgundy; this now becomes known as the kingdom of Arles and is attached to the German crown, although it has few resources and no real authority there.

B **May** *or* **Jun**: Henry of France meets Conrad at Deville, on the Meuse, and makes an alliance against Odo of Blois.

E Sancho III of Navarre creates the kingdom of Castile for his son, Ferdinand I (–1065).

Mieszko surrenders his title of King of Poland and does homage to Conrad at Merseburg.

The Pechenegs raid the Balkans.

1034

A **Mar**: 15th, death of Mieszko of Poland; succeeded by his son Casimir I, a minor (–1058). The immediately subsequent history of Poland is obscure: there is a resurgence of paganism in which the Church establishment is destroyed.

B **Apr**: 11th, death of the Greek Emperor, Romanus III; succeeded by Michael IV the Paphlagonian, who marries Romanus' widow, Zoe, daughter of Constantine VIII (–1041).

D **Nov**: 25th, death of Malcolm II of Scotland; succeeded by his grandson, Duncan I (–1040).

E Death of Oldřich, Duke of Bohemia; succeeded by his son, Břatislav I (–1055).

Genoa and Pisa take Bona (in north Africa).

(–1037) the sons of Tancred d'Hauteville arrive in south Italy.

1032

J **Art, Architecture and Music**

Jan. 1st, the new abbey-church of Ripoll dedicated.

1033

L **Births and Deaths**

— Anselm b. (–1109).

1034

K **Literature, Philosophy and Scholarship**

†Adhemar of Chabannes, *Chronicon Aquitanicum* (*Chronicle of Aquitaine*, to 1028).

1035

C **Jul**: 2nd, death of Robert I the Devil (*or* the Magnificent), Duke of Normandy; succeeded by his illegitimate son, William I (–1087).

Aug: 11th, murder of al-Zāhir, Caliph of Egypt; succeeded by his son, al-Mustansir (–1094).

D **Nov**: 12th, death of Cnut, King of England, Denmark and (nominally) Norway; succeeded by his son, Harthacnut, in Denmark (–1042), with Harold Harefoot, another son, his regent in England (–1037). In Norway, Magnus I, the son of St. Olaf, had been established as King in a revolt against Cnut (–1047).

E Death of Sancho III, King of Spain; succeeded in Navarre by his son, Garcia III (–1054); while another son, Ramiro I, had been established in the newly created kingdom of Aragon (–1065).

Jaroslav becomes the sole ruler of Russia on the death of his brother, Mstislav of Tmutarakan'.

Death of Rājendra-Choladeva I, King of the Cholas; he had conquered the Pegu kingdom in Burma and the Nicobar and Andaman Islands, and built a new capital at Gangaikonda-Cholapuram, in Trichinopoly.

1036

B **Jun**: on the marriage of Conrad's son, Henry, to Cnut's daughter, Gunnhild, Denmark cedes the Kiel district of Schleswig to the German King.

E Conrad crushes a revolt by the Lyutitzi, a pagan Wendish tribe living to the east of the Elbe.

The Pechenegs again raid the Balkans.

1035

G **Economics, Science, Technology and Discovery**

*Petrocellus of Salerno, *Practica* (medical treatise).

H **Religion and Education**

*A collection of approximately 10,000 religious paintings, books and manuscripts in Chinese, Tibetan, Uighur and other languages, walled-up for safety at Tun-huang, in the Hsi Hsia Kingdom (discovered in 1900).

1036

F **Law and Politics**

Jaroslav the Wise revises the *Pravda Russkaia* (*Russian Law*).

A law-code of the Liao (no longer extant), said to contain 547 items.

J **Art, Architecture and Music**

The priory-church of Abdinghof, Paderborn (the first German Cluniac house) dedicated.

*Chernigov Cathedral.

K **Literature, Philosophy and Scholarship**

*Ekkehard of St. Gall (the fourth of that name), *Casus Sancti Galli* (*Memoirs of the Monastery of St. Gall*).

L **Births and Deaths**

— Su Tung-p'o b. (–1101).

1037

A **Mar:** Conrad holds a diet at Pavia to determine Lombard disputes and arrests Archbishop Aribert of Milan; the latter's escape leads to Conrad's abortive siege of Milan.

D **Nov:** 15th, Odo II, Count of Blois and Champagne, killed in battle at Bar in an expedition to seize the German crown; he bequeathes Champagne to his son Stephen, the remainder of his lands to another son, Theobald III of Blois.
Dec: 25th, Conrad sacks Parma to punish its rebellion.

E Harold Harefoot recognised as King in England (–1040).
Ferdinand of Castile defeats Bermudo III of Leon at Tamaron and takes possession of his kingdom.
The Seljuq Turks, who had emigrated from central Asia late in the tenth century, are now, by conquest, established in Khurāsān (–1055).

1038

C **Aug:** 15th, death of St. Stephen I, King of Hungary; Peter the German elected as his successor (–1042).

E Henry of France defeats a plot to depose him in favour of his brother, Odo, by Stephen of Champagne and Theobald of Blois; he obtains the support of Geoffrey Martel of Anjou with the grant of Tours.
Conrad grants the Duchy of Swabia to his son, Henry, on the death of Duke Hermann.
Conrad takes Capua as Paldolf refuses to submit to him and grants it to Guaimar IV of Salerno; Conrad then returns to Germany.
Břatislav of Bohemia, meeting little resistance, sacks Cracow and Gniezno in the course of a plundering raid into Poland; he takes possession of Silesia.
Li Hüang-hao declares himself Emperor of the Tanguts of Hsi Hsia (Tibetan tribes in western China) and ceases paying tribute to the Sung.

1039

A **Mar:** 10th, Eudes of Poitiers, invading Anjou, defeated and killed near Mauzé by Geoffrey Martel.

B **Jun:** 4th, death of the Holy Roman Emperor, Conrad II; succeeded by his son, King Henry III (–1056).

E Gruffyd ap Llewelyn, King of Gwynned and Powys, defeats an English attack.
Guy-Geoffrey of Aquitaine seizes the Duchy of Gascony.
In a civil war in Sicily, the Emir Ahmad is assisted by the Byzantine general, George Maniaces, who engages Norman soldiers.
Casimir, the son of Mieszko II, returns to Poland and establishes himself as ruler with assistance from Conrad (–1058).

1037

F **Law and Politics**

Conrad's *Constitutio de feudis* assures Lombard sub-tenants against unjust eviction by their lords.

G **Economics, Science, Technology and Discovery**

†Ibn Sīna (Avicenna), *al-Qānūn fi al-Tibb* (*The Canon of Medicine*; encyclopedia codifying Greco-Arabic medical learning; –1187).

J **Art, Architecture and Music**

Abbey-churches of Hersfeld and Jumièges (–1066).

*Rouen Cathedral (–1063).

Kiev Cathedral, with mosaics (–1100).

K **Literature, Philosophy and Scholarship**

†Farrukhī, Persian poet.

1038

H **Religion and Education**

Buddhism now firmly re-established in Tibet.

(or 1039) St. John Gualberti founds the Order of Vallombrosa.

J **Art, Architecture and Music**

Abbey-church of St. Aurelius, Hirsau (–1071).

K **Literature, Philosophy and Scholarship**

†Al-Tha'ālibi, Arab anthologist.

1039

G **Economics, Science, Technology and Discovery**

†'Ali al-Hasan (Alhazen), *Kitab al-Manāzir* (on optics).

J **Art, Architecture and Music**

Henry III builds the Pfalz (Palace) at Goslar (–1056; rebuilt from 1132).

K **Literature, Philosophy and Scholarship**

Ting Tu, Sung Ch'i, and others, *Chi-yün* (Chinese phonetic dictionary).

1040

A **Feb**: Mas'ūd I of Ghaznī deposed following his defeat at Tāliqān by Turks led by the Seljuqs, Tughril Bey and Chagi Bey, who conquer the Ghaznavid territories in Persia.

Mar: 17th, death of Harold (I) Harefoot, King of England; succeeded by his brother, Harthacnut, King of Denmark (–1042).

B **Jun**: 21st, death of Fulk III Nerra, Count of Anjou; succeeded by his son, Geoffrey II Martel (–1060).

C **Aug**: Henry III invades Bohemia in response to an appeal from Queen Richsa, regent of Poland; the Bohemians defeat him at Sumava.

14th, Duncan I of Scotland murdered and succeeded by Macbeth (–1057).

E Melfi, in Apulia, seized from the Greeks by the six sons of Tancred d'Hauteville and becomes the centre of their (Norman) principality.

Stephen Vojuslav makes Zeta, in southern Yugoslavia, independent of the Greek Empire.

1041

B **May**: after a second, and successful, campaign in Bohemia, Henry III compels Břatislav to acknowledge his supremacy and surrender his Polish conquests except Silesia.

4th, in the battle of Monte Maggiore, Lombard rebels employing Normans defeat Greek forces.

D **Dec**: 10th, death of the Greek Emperor, Michael IV; succeeded by his nephew, Michael V (–1042).

E Siward, Earl of Northumbria, murders Eardwulf, Earl of Bernicia, and now rules all Northumbria (–1055).

Michael IV suppresses a Slav revolt led by Peter Deljan.

1040

F **Law and Politics**

A Truce of God proclaimed in Aquitaine; this was a measure to limit private warfare.

G **Economics, Science, Technology and Discovery**

Water-power employed in hemp-mills at Graisivaudan.

†*Ahmad al-Nasawi, *al-Muqni'fi al-Hisāb al-Hindi* (*The Convincer on Hindu Calculation*; on fractions, square and cubic roots, etc., using Hindu (so-called 'Arabic') numerals).

J **Art, Architecture and Music**

St. Mary in Capitol, Cologne, begun.

*Baptistery at Biella, near Novara.

K **Literature, Philosophy and Scholarship**

**La Vie de Saint Alexis* (anon. poem of 125 strophes each of 5 lines, considered to be the beginning of French literature).

L **Births and Deaths**

— Rashi b. (–1105).

1041

F **Law and Politics**

The Chinese army totals 1,259,000 during a war against Tibetan tribes.

K **Literature, Philosophy and Scholarship**

†Minūchihrī, Persian poet.

1042

B **Apr:** 11th, Obo crowned as King of Hungary following Peter's expulsion (–1044).
14th, the Greek Emperor, Michael V, deposed; succeeded by Theodora and Zoe, daughters of Constantine VIII.
Jun: 8th, death of Harthacnut, King of England and Denmark; succeeded in England by his adopted heir, Edward the Confessor, son of Ethelred II (–1066); and in Denmark by Magnus, King of Norway (–1047).
12th, Constantine IV Monomachus, Zoe's third husband, succeeds as Greek Emperor (–1055).

C **Aug:** Henry III makes an expedition into Hungary; its King, Obo, flees, but returns when Henry withdraws.

E Henry grants the Duchy of Bavaria to Henry, Count of Luxemburg.
The *popolani* of Milan (temporarily) expel the nobles.
Death of Abū'l-Qasim Muhammad, prime minister of the King of Seville, whom he had established as the paramount Muslim ruler in Spain.
The Ghaznavids extinguish the Ziyarids of Jurjan.

1043

A **Feb:** *or* **Mar:** George Maniaces, claiming the Greek Empire, defeats imperial forces at Ostrovo, in Macedonia, but is killed.

B **Apr:** 3rd, Edward the Confessor crowned as King of England.

D **Oct:** on a 'Day of Indulgence', Henry III announces his pardon of all his enemies and urges all his subjects to forget their private enmities (*cf.* 'Truce of God' in France, 1042 F).

E Henry forces Obo of Hungary to cede various territories, thereby establishing the Austro-Hungarian frontier (until 1919).
Domenico Contarino I succeeds Domenico Flabanico as Doge of Venice (–1071).

1044

C **Jul:** Henry III defeats Obo of Hungary on the Raab and restores Peter as king and as his vassal (–1046).
Aug: 21st, Geoffrey Martel defeats and captures Theobald of Blois at Nouy, and compels him to cede Tours and Touraine.

E Gruffyd defeats Danes from Ireland.
Henry deprives Godfrey of Lorraine and Verdun, because of his conspiracy; Godfrey now rebels openly.
Benedict IX driven from Rome by a revolt.
The Sung Emperor undertakes to pay tribute to the Hsi Hsia, after defeating their attempt to conquer China.
Aniruddha becomes (the first historical) King of Pagan (in Burma; –1077).
Ly Thai-tong of Dai-co-viet defeats and kills Jaya Simhavarman II, King of Champa, and sacks Vijaya, his capital.

1042

F **Law and Politics**

A Truce of God first proclaimed in Normandy.

1043

J **Art, Architecture and Music**

Dimensional description of Cluny Abbey recorded in the Consuetudinary of Farfa.

1044

G **Economics, Science, Technology and Discovery**

Wu Ching Tsung Yao (includes a recipe for gunpowder).

H **Religion and Education**

*Archbishop Aaron, monk of Brauweiler, begins the reconversion of Poland, establishing a see at Cracow (instead of Gniezno).

L **Births and Deaths**

Sept. 10th, St. Anastasius d. (90).
— 'Umar Khayyām b. (–1123).

1045

A **Jan**: 10th, Silvester III (Crescentius) elected as Pope.
Mar: 10th, Silvester is deposed.

B **Apr**: 7th, Henry grants the Duchy of Swabia to Otto, count palatine in Lower Lorraine.
May: 1st, Benedict IX resigns, selling the Papacy to John Gratian, who is elected as Gregory VI (–1046).

C **Jul**: the ex-Duke, Godfrey, surrenders to Henry.

E Edward makes Harold, son of Godwin, Earl of East Anglia.
Henry grants the March of Antwerp to Baldwin, son of Baldwin V of Flanders.
Constantine IX incorporates Ani (in Armenia) into the Greek Empire.
First Seljuq raid into Armenia.

1046

B **Apr**: Henry III recovers Flushing from Count Dietrich of Holland.
May: 8th, Guillaume d'Hauteville, Count of Apulia, defeats Greek forces at Trani.
18th, Henry restores Upper Lorraine to Godfrey, but grants his former County of Verdun to its Bishop. He also invests Adalbert with the Archbishopric of Bremen (which Adalbert moves to Hamburg).

C **Aug**: Peter the German, King of Hungary, deposed; succeeded by Andrew I (–1060).

D **Oct**: 25th, in a council held by Henry at Pavia, the corrupt ecclesiastical practice of simony is denounced.
Dec: 20th, in the Synod of Sutri held by Henry, Benedict IX and Gregory VI are deposed from the Papacy.
24th, Suidger, Bishop of Bamberg, elected as Pope Clement II (–1047).
25th, Clement crowns Henry as Holy Roman Emperor (–1056).

1047

D **Oct**: 9th, death of Pope Clement II.
25th, death of Magnus the Good, King of Denmark and Norway; succeeded in Denmark by Svein II Estrithson (–1074) and in Norway by Harold Hardrada (–1066).
Nov: 8th, Benedict IX returns to Rome and reassumes the Papacy.
Dec: 25th, Poppo, Bishop of Brixen, elected as Pope Damasus II (–1048).

E William assumes personal rule of his Duchy of Normandy and, assisted by King Henry, defeats Norman rebels at Val-ès-Dunes, near Caen.
Henry III again deprives Godfrey of Upper Lorraine for a fresh rebellion.
Casimir of Poland, with Russian assistance, recovers control of Masovia and Pomerania.
Greeks defeat a Seljuq raiding force near Erzurum.

1045

G **Economics, Science, Technology and Discovery**

Earliest dated use in China of (earthenware) movable type for printing, invented by Pi Shêng.

H **Religion and Education**

Constantine IX re-founds the University of Constantinople, establishing faculties of law and philosophy; the notable jurist, John Xiphilin, was first head of the new law school.

J **Art, Architecture and Music**

*Abbey of Ste. Foi, Conques.

Novgorod Cathedral burnt; rebuilt in stone.

1046

H **Religion and Education**

†Richard of St. Vannes, a Church reformer in Lorraine.

L **Births and Deaths**

— St. Stephen of Muret b. (–1124).

1047

G **Economics, Science, Technology and Discovery**

**Établissements de Saint-Quentin* (drawn up in 1151 but dating from 1047–80 and thus the earliest known code of laws and customs in a French town; –1076).

H **Religion and Education**

Jan., Clement II denounces simony in a council at Rome.

1048

C **Jul:** 17th, Damasus II enthroned as Pope following the expulsion of Benedict IX.
Aug: 9th, death of Damasus II.

D **Dec:** Bruno of Egisheim, Bishop of Toul, elected as Pope Leo IX (–1054).

E King Henry and William of Normandy ally to make war against Geoffrey Martel of Anjou. William takes Alençon and Maine.
The Pechenegs begin their continuous ravages in the Balkans.
The Seljuq Turks sack Erzurum.

1049

1050

E Henry III makes a treaty of peace with Andrew I after a campaign in Hungary.
Casimir of Poland recovers Silesia from Bohemia.
Tughril Bey, the Seljuq leader, takes Isfahan, which becomes the capital of his empire in Persia and Khurāsān (–1063); end of the Kakuyid dynasty.

1048

G **Economics, Science, Technology and Discovery**

Use of the term 'bourgeois' at St. Omer, signifying the beginning of municipal organisation (*cf.* 1007).

†Al-Bīrunī ('the master'), *Ta'rikh al-Hind* (*Description of India*); an astronomical encyclopedia; a summary of mathematics, astronomy and astrology.

K **Literature, Philosophy and Scholarship**

†Al-Bīrunī, *Chronology of Ancient Nations*.

L **Births and Deaths**

— Odilo, Abbot of Cluny, d.

1049

H **Religion and Education**

Oct., reforming decrees (against simony, etc.) enacted in church councils held by Leo IX at Reims and Mainz.

†Abu Sa'īd, Persian mystic.

J **Art, Architecture and Music**

Bayeux Cathedral (–1077).

Abbey-church of St. Remi, Reims, dedicated.

1050

G **Economics, Science, Technology and Discovery**

Water-power used in fulling-mills in Dauphiné.

†*Gariopontus of Salerno, *Passionarius* (medical encyclopedia).

H **Religion and Education**

Berengar of Tours, author of *De Caena Domini*, condemned for heresy by the council of Vercelli.

J **Art, Sculpture, Fine Arts, Architecture and Music**

*Mosaics in church of Nea Moni, Chios.

Schaffhausen Abbey (–1064).

*Westminster Abbey (–1065; by Edward the Confessor).

†Béranger, architect of Chartres Cathedral.

†Guido d'Arezzo, *Micrologus de Disciplina Artis Musicae* (his innovations include changing two-line stave into five-line stave, the system of hexacords, new notations and the ut-re-mi-fa-so-la names for notes).

K **Literature, Philosophy and Scholarship**

**Konjaku Monigatari* (collection of hundreds of stories in Japanese classic literature).

**Digenes Akritas* (Greek epic).

†Raoul Glaber, *Historiae sui temporis* (mainly French history, 900–1044).

L **Births and Deaths**

Nov. 11th, Henry IV b. (–1106).

1051

C **Sep**: Godwin, Earl of Wessex, is exiled in Flanders after the failure of his rebellion against Edward the Confessor.

E The people of Benevento accept Leo IX as their ruler in order to protect themselves from the Normans. A plot to murder all the Normans in southern Italy fails.

1052

A (early): William of Normandy visits Edward the Confessor (and is recognised as his heir?).

C **Sep**: 15th, Godwin returns to England with a strong force and compels Edward to restore the Earldom of Wessex.

E Henry III makes his last expedition into Hungary, where he suppresses a rebellion.

1053

B **Apr**: 15th, death of Godwin, Earl of Wessex; succeeded by his son, Harold (–1066).
Jun: 18th, in the battle of Civitate, the Normans led by Humphrey d'Hauteville, Count of Apulia, capture Pope Leo IX, who had proclaimed a 'holy war' against them; he renounces it to obtain his release.

E A rebellion against William of Normandy by William of Arques only ends when the latter is starved out; the duke had defeated an attempt by King Henry to relieve the rebel. (This incident illustrates the disorderly state of feudal principalities.)
Henry III grants lands in Benevento to the Papacy; he also (perhaps in this year) grants the Duchy of Bavaria to his son, Henry, after the rebellion of Duke Conrad (–1061).

1054

A **Feb**: King Henry, now as the ally of Geoffrey Martel, invades Normandy and is defeated by Duke William at Mortemer.
Mar: Henry III begins an expedition into Italy.

B **Apr**: 19th, death of Pope Leo IX.

C **Jul**: 17th, Henry, son of Henry III, elected King of the Romans.
27th, Siward of Northumbria and Malcolm defeat Macbeth at Dunsinane.
Sep: 3rd, Ferdinand I of Castile defeats and kills his brother, Garcia III of Navarre, at Atapuerca, near Burgos; Garcia's son, Sancho IV, succeeds as King of Navarre (–1076).

D (late): Gebhard of Eichstadt elected as Pope Victor II (–1057).

E In a diet at Quedlinburg, Henry III awards Silesia to Poland in its dispute with Bohemia.
Břatislav I of Bohemia (supposedly) decrees that the succession of his Duchy should be limited to the eldest member of the house of Přemysl.
Tughril Bey raids Greek Asia Minor but fails to take Manzikert.

1051

H **Religion and Education**

Cathars executed at Goslar (another early instance of execution for heresy).

1052

1053

1054

G **Economics, Science, Technology and Discovery**

†Hermann Contractus, monk of Reichenau, treatises on the abacus and astrolabe.

H **Religion and Education**

Cerularius, Patriarch of Constantinople, refuses to meet Cardinal Humbert and other legates (sent by Leo IX, now dead) who excommunicate him; this was the final breach between the Roman and Greek Churches.

†Lazarus founded the establishment of monks on Mt. Galisius, near Ephesus.

Art, Architecture and Music

†Hermann Contractus, treatise on music.

K **Literature, Philosophy and Scholarship**

†Hermann Contractus, *Chronicon* (to 1054).

L **Births and Deaths**

Sept. 24th, Hermann Contractus d. (41).

End of 'Golden Age of Kiev'—Seljuqs take Baghdād—Expansion of Pagan

1055

A **Jan**: 11th, death of the Greek Emperor, Constantine IX; the Empress Theodora again rules (–1056).

Feb: 7th, death of Jaroslav I, Great Prince of Russia; succeeded by his son, Isiaslav I, at Kiev (–1078). By his will, Jaroslav divides his lands among five sons; civil war follows (–1097), and the 'Golden Age of Kiev' thus ends.

D **Dec**: 18th, Baghdād surrenders to the Seljuq Turks, who thus end Bawayhid rule. Tughril Bey, proclaimed as Sultan, so asserts his supremacy over the Islamic lands, centring on Persia, which the Seljuqs had conquered. (The Caliph remains the spiritual ruler of Islam.)

E Death of Siward, Earl of Northumbria; succeeded by Tostig, son of Godwin (–1065).

Gruffyd ap Llywelyn, King of Gwynedd and Powys, completes the conquest of South Wales.

Death of Břatislav I, Duke of Bohemia; succeeded by Spytihněv II (–1061).

Henry III makes his second expedition to Italy.

1056

B **Jun**: 17th, Gruffyd of Wales defeats and kills Leofgar, Bishop of Hereford, at Cleobury; later this year, he is defeated by Harold of Wessex and Leofric of Mercia and so compelled to recognise the lordship of Edward the Confessor, who cedes to him lands west of the Dee.

C **Aug**: 21st, death of the Greek Empress, Theodora, the last of the Macedonian dynasty; succeeded by Michael VI the Aged (–1057).

D **Oct**: 5th, death of the Holy Roman Emperor, Henry III; succeeded by his son, Henry IV (–1105), with his widow, Agnes, as regent (–1062).

E The Lyutitzi defeat forces sent by Henry III to suppress their revolt.

Edmund Slemme succeeds as King of Sweden, and is killed and succeeded by Stenkil.

In Milan, the Paterines (a popular, puritanical but not heretical movement aspiring to reform the Milanese church) aim to secure control of their government by the establishment of a commune.

1057

C **Jul**: 28th, death of Pope Victor II.

Aug: Robert Guiscard succeeds as Count of Apulia.

2nd, Frederick of Lorraine elected as Pope Stephen IX (–1058).

15th, Macbeth, King of Scotland, defeated and killed at Lumphanan, in Mar, by Macduff and Malcolm Canmore; succeeded by his stepson, Lulach (–1058).

31st, the Greek Emperor, Michael VI, abdicates in favour of the general, Isaac Comnenus, whose troops had already proclaimed him as Emperor (–1059).

E The Seljuqs sack Malatiya, on the Asian frontier of the Greek Empire.

Aniruddha of Pagan defeats Makuta, King of the Mons of Thaton, and annexes the Irrawaddy Delta.

1055

1056

1057

1058

A **Mar**: 17th, Malcolm III Canmore, son of Duncan I, succeeds as King of Scotland (–1093) after killing Lulach.
29th, death of Pope Stephen IX.

B **Apr**: 5th, Cardinal John Mincius elected as Pope Benedict X (–1059) by Roman nobles who had seized control of Rome.

C **Aug**: William of Normandy defeats the invading forces of Henry I and Geoffrey Martel at Varaville.

D **Nov**: 28th, death of Casimir the Restorer, Duke of Poland, who had restored the unity of the Polish tribes, recovered lost territories and had the Church reconstructed; succeeded by his son, Boleslav the Bold (–1081).
Dec: Gerard, Bishop of Florence (a Burgundian), elected as Pope Nicholas II at Siena by the reforming party of cardinals under the protection of Godfrey the Bearded, Duke of Lorraine.

1059

A **Jan**: 24th, Nicholas II enthroned in Rome (–1061); Benedict X deposed.

B **Apr**: 14th, a decree governing the election of Popes is made in a council held at the Lateran by Nicholas II.
May: 23rd, coronation of Philip, son of Henry I, as King of France.

C **Aug**: by the treaty of Melfi, Nicholas invests Robert Guiscard as Duke of Apulia and Calabria and Count of Sicily, and his vassal (–1085).

D **Dec**: 25th, abdication of the Greek Emperor, Isaac Comnenus; succeeded by Constantine X Ducas (–1067).

E Peter Damian persuades the Milanese to resume their ecclesiastical subjection to Rome.
The Seljuqs raid into the Greek Empire as far as Sebastea.

1060

C **Aug**: 4th, death of Henry I, King of France; succeeded by Philip I (–1108) with Baldwin V, Count of Flanders, his guardian.

D **Nov**: 14th, death of Geoffrey II Martel, Count of Anjou; succeeded by his nephews, Geoffrey III the Bearded and Fulk IV Rechin (–1068, 1109).

E With the assistance of Boleslav of Poland, Béla I gains the Hungarian crown (–1063) by defeating and killing his brother, Andrew I.
Bhoja, King of Mālwā, defeated and killed by the Kings of Gujarāt and Chedi.

1058

F **Law and Politics**

†Al-Māwardi, *Kitabadāb al-Dunyā wa-l-Dīn* (*Book on the Principles of Government*).

K **Literature, Philosophy and Scholarship**

†*Solomon ben Gabīrōl (Avicebron), *Yanbū'al-Hayah* (*Fountain of Life*; Neo-Platonic Muslim philosophy; –1150).

†Al-Ma'arrī, Arabic poems; *Risālat al-Ghufrān* (*Treatise on Forgiveness*).

L **Births and Deaths**

— Algazel b. (–1111).

1059

G **Economics, Science, Technology and Discovery**

Fu Kung, *Hsieh-p'u* (treatise on crabs).

H **Religion and Education**

Hildebrand appointed archdeacon of the Roman church.

J **Art, Architecture and Music**

Matilda, Duchess of Normandy, founds L'Abbaye aux Dames, with church of Ste. Trinité, Caen (–1093).

Baptistery of S. Giovanni, Florence, consecrated.

*Abbey of La Charité-sur-Loire (–1107).

1060

G **Economics, Science, Technology and Discovery**

†Bhoja (*see* E) is said to have written on astronomy, architecture and poetry.

J **Art, Architecture and Music**

Rebuilding of Mainz Cathedral (–1137).

*The Nan Paya and the Manuha Temples, Pagan, Burma.

K **Literature, Philosophy and Scholarship**

*Ezzo of Bamberg, *Ezzolied* (*Anegenge*; long rhyming poem on religious themes from Genesis to the Resurrection).

Asadī of Tūs, *Lughat-i-Furs* (Persian lexicon).

Sung Ch'i, biographical section of *New History of the T'ang Dynasty*.

1061

A **Mar**: 20th, Geoffrey and Fulk of Anjou defeat William VIII of Aquitaine at Chef-Boutonne.

C **Summer**: Roger Guiscard begins the Norman conquest of Sicily with the capture of Messina; he had been invited into the island by Ibn ath-Thimna, one of the Saracen leaders in a civil war.
Jul: 22nd(?), death of Pope Nicholas II.
Sep: 30th, Anselm of Baggio, Bishop of Lucca, elected as Pope Alexander II (–1073).

D **Oct**: 28th, Cadalus, Bishop of Parma, crowned as Pope Honorius II in Basel, in the presence of Henry IV (–1062).

E Malcolm invades Northumberland.
Otto of Nordheim created Duke of Bavaria.
Death of Spytihněv II, Duke of Bohemia; succeeded by his brother, Vratislav II (–1092).
The Cumans migrate into southern Russia from Kazakhstan.

1062

A **Mar**: 25th, Honorius II forces his way into Rome, but Godfrey of Lorraine induces both papal contestants to withdraw from the city.

B **Apr**: Anno, Archbishop of Cologne, abducts Henry IV and so takes charge of his government, with Adalbert, Archbishop of Bremen, as co-regent (–1066).

D **Oct**: 27th, Alexander II declared to be the true Pope in a synod at Augsburg.

E William of Normandy seizes Le Mans and declares himself Count of Maine.

1063

B **May**: Harold of Wessex begins to conquer Wales.

C **Aug**: 5th, Gruffyd, in flight from Harold, murdered by his followers; Wales again divided among native princes.
Sep: 20th, death of Tughril Bey, Sultan (of Persia); succeeded by his nephew, Alp Arslan (–1072).

E Henry IV expels Béla from Hungary and enthrones Solomon, the son of Andrew I (–1074).

1061

H **Religion and Education**
†Cardinal Humbert, *Liber adversus Symoniacos.*

J **Art, Architecture and Music**
The new cathedral at Hildesheim dedicated.

L **Births and Deaths**
May 5th, Cardinal Humbert d.
— Godfrey of Bouillon b. (–1100).

1062

J **Art, Architecture and Music**
Abbey-church of S. Miniato, Florence, completed.

1063

H **Religion and Education**
*Bishopric of Olomuc, Moravia, re-established.
*The Rule for Augustinian Canons now known.

J **Art, Architecture and Music**
Pisa Cathedral and campanile ('Leaning Tower'; –1271).
S. Marco, Venice, with mosaics (–1095).

K **Literature, Philosophy and Scholarship**
Papias the Lombard, *Vocabularium* (Latin dictionary).

1064

E Ferdinand I of Castile captures Coimbra.
The Pechenegs ravage in Greece.
Alp Arslan conquers Ani (central Armenia) and the kingdom of Kars.
*Harold of Wessex (allegedly) does homage to William of Normandy.

1065

A **Mar**: 4th, Henry IV nominally comes of age; he gives Lorraine to Duke Godfrey (–1069).

B **May**: 8th(?), Ramiro I of Aragon killed attacking the Moors in Graus; succeeded by his son, Sancho Ramirez (–1094). His death attracts assistance from western Europe for the crusade against the Moors.

D **Dec**: 27th, death of Ferdinand I; succeeded by his sons, Sancho II in Castile (–1072) and Alfonso VI in Leon (–1109).

E In a rebellion in Northumbria, Tostig is expelled and Morcar elected in his place as Earl.
Alp Arslan makes conquests in Transoxiana; other Seljuq Turks invade Syria.

1066

A **Jan**: Henry IV begins his personal government in Germany after dismissing Archbishop Adalbert.
5th, death of Edward the Confessor, King of England.
6th, Harold of Wessex elected as his successor.

B **Jun**: murder of Godescalc, Duke of the Obotrites, a Wendish tribe whom he had converted to Christianity.
28th, Ariald, leader of the Patarenes in Milan, murdered by agents of Archbishop Guy.

C **Sep**: 25th, Harold Hardrada, King of Norway, and Tostig defeated and killed by Harold of England at Stamford Bridge; Harold of Norway succeeded by his sons Magnus II and Olaf III (–1068, 1093).
28th, William of Normandy lands at Pevensey in his invasion of England.

D **Oct**: 14th, Harold defeated and killed by William at Hastings.
Dec: 25th, William crowned as King of England (–1087).

1064

F **Law and Politics**

(–1069) Raymond-Berengar of Catalonia publishes the *Usatges* (the earliest feudal code).

H **Religion and Education**

†ʿAli ibn-Hazm, *al-Fasi fi al-Milal w-al-Ahwā' w-al-Nihal* (*The Decisive Word on Sects, Heterodoxies and Denominations*; the first work—by a Spanish Muslim—on comparative religion).

J **Art, Architecture and Music**

Minden Cathedral.

K **Literature, Philosophy and Scholarship**

†ʿAli ibn-Hazm, *Tawq al-Hamāmah* (*The Dove's Necklace*; anthology of love-poems, illustrating life in Muslim Spain).

1065

F **Law and Politics**

Examinations for the Chinese civil service, hitherto sporadic, were now held every three years.

G **Economics, Science, Technology and Discovery**

Chou-Ts'ung, *Ming-t'ien-li* (new Chinese calendar).

H **Religion and Education**

Foundation of the Nizāmīyah (theological college; the Nizāmī University), Baghdād (–1395); others soon followed at Neyshabur, Damascus, Jerusalem, Cairo and Alexandria.

J **Art, Architecture and Music**

Dec. 28th, consecration of Westminster Abbey.
St. Étienne (of Abbaye-aux-Hommes), Caen (nave; –1077).

1066

G **Economics, Science, Technology and Discovery**

A tidal-mill (already) in Dover harbour.

J **Art, Architecture and Music**

Abbey-church of Bec (–1077).

1067–1070 Almoravid empire founded—Saxon rebellion

1067

B **Apr:** 5th, Fulk Rechin imprisons his brother and co-count, Geoffrey of Anjou.
May: 21st, death of the Greek Emperor, Constantine X; his widow, Eudocia Macrembolitissa, now rules.

E Seljuqs sack Caesarea and defeat Greek armies at Malatiya and Sebastea.

1068

A **Jan:** 1st, Romanus IV Diogenes, who had married Eudocia Macrembolitissa, now crowned as Greek Emperor (–1071).

E William I suppresses a revolt in Yorkshire by Earls Edwin and Morcar.
Philip I recognises Fulk Rechin as sole Count of Anjou.
Yūsuf-ibn-Tāshfīn, a founder of the Murābit (*or* Almoravid, Berber) Empire, founds Marrakesh (Morocco) as his capital.
The Cumans defeat the Russian princes near Pereyslavl.
Ly Thanh-tong of Dai-co-viet (which he renames Dai Viet) defeats and captures Rudravarman III of Champa, and annexes his northern provinces.

1069

A **Jan:** 28th, Robert de Comines, the Norman Earl of Northumbria, killed in Durham by rebels, who subsequently overrun Yorkshire.
Feb: William restores order in this district.

B **Apr:** 28th, death of Magnus II, King of Norway.

C **Sep:** Svein of Denmark takes York; the Northumbrians rally to him; William then harries Yorkshire and County Durham to reassert his authority.

D **Dec:** 25th, death of Godfrey the Bearded, Duke of Lorraine.

E Death of ʻAbbād Muʻtadid, King of Seville; succeeded by his son Muʻtamid (who, by taking Cordova, makes his kingdom paramount in Muslim Spain).
Boleslav of Poland takes Kiev and restores his uncle, Isiaslav, as its Grand Duke; Boleslav abandons Kiev within a year but recovers Red Russia for Poland.

1070

C **Jul:** 14th, Alfonso VI of Leon defeats and captures his brother, Sancho II of Castile, at Valpellage.
Aug: Henry IV deprives Otto of Nordheim, because of his treason, of his estates in Saxony and of the Duchy of Bavaria; the latter is granted to Welf IV.
15th, William I deposes Stigand and appoints Lanfranc as Archbishop of Canterbury.

E Malcolm invades Northumberland.
*Vijayabāhu completes the destruction of Chola power in Ceylon.

1067

1068

F **Law and Politics**

In Japan there begins the 'Camera system' of rule by the retired emperors (the father and/or grandfather or the reigning emperor, usually a minor), in competition with the Fujiwara regents.

L **Births and Deaths**

— Henry I b. (–1135).

1069

J **Art, Architecture and Music**

Constance Cathedral (–1089).

1070

G **Economics, Science, Technology and Discovery**

Code of municipal customs in Cambrai (then in the Empire: –1047).
†Al-Andalusi, *Tabaqāt al-Umam* (*Classification of Nations*).
*Wang Kuan, *Yang-chou shao-yo-p'u* (treatise on the peony, describing 39 varieties).
†*Oliver, monk of Malmesbury, astrologer; had attempted flight with attached wings.

J **Art, Architecture and Music**

Canterbury Cathedral and abbey-church of Bury St. Edmunds begun.

1071–1072 Battle of Manzikert—Seljuqs take Jerusalem—Greeks expelled from Italy

1071

A **Feb**: 22nd, Arnold III the Unfortunate, Count of Flanders, killed when defeating Philip I of France at Cassel.

B **Apr**: with the capture of Bari, Robert Guiscard completes the expulsion of the Greeks from Italy.

C **Aug**: 19th, Alp Arslan destroys a Greek army at Manzikert, in Armenia, and captures Romanus IV, whom he frees for a ransom and the payment of tribute; the Seljuq Turks now complete their conquest of Armenia and overrun most of Asia Minor. In this year, they also conquer Syria and Atsiz ibn-Abaq takes Jerusalem (from the Egyptians).

D **Oct**: 24th, Michael VII, the son of Constantine X, proclaimed as Greek Emperor (–1078), and Romanus is deposed and imprisoned; Michael vainly appeals to western Europe for assistance against the Turks.

E William expels Hereward the Wake from the Isle of Ely.
Henry IV suppresses a Saxon revolt in favour of Otto of Nordheim.
Death of Domenico Contarino I, Doge of Venice; succeeded by Domenico Salvio (–1084).
Solomon of Hungary takes Belgrade after its Greek governor had instigated an invasion by the Pechenegs.

1072

A **Jan**: 10th, Robert Guiscard captures Palermo.

B **Spring**: by his campaign in Scotland, William compels Malcolm III to offer him homage.

D **Oct**: Sancho II of Castile murdered and succeeded by Alfonso VI of Leon (–1109).
Dec: 15th, the Seljuq Sultan, Alp Arslan, murdered while campaigning in Transoxiana; succeeded by his son, Malik Shah (–1092).

1071

J **Art, Architecture and Music**

The new abbey-church of Montecassino dedicated.

1072

F **Law and Politics**

†Ou-yang Hsiu developed the first censorship rules, in China.

**Pravda* (Compilation of Russian laws by Jaroslav's sons).

G **Economics, Science, Technology and Discovery**

†Ou-yang Hsiu, treatise on the peony.

H **Religion and Education**

Apr., a council of the English Church at Winchester affirms the primacy of Canterbury over York.

Alexander II gives his approval to the Order of Camaldoli.

†St. Peter Damian, *De Divina Omnipotentia*.

J **Art, Architecture and Music**

Lincoln Cathedral begun.

K **Literature, Philosophy and Scholarship**

†Ou-yang Hsiu, *Chi-ku-lu* (the first work on ancient inscriptions); histories of China.

L **Births and Deaths**

Feb. 22nd, St. Peter Damian d. (65).

Mar. 17th, Adalbert, Archbishop of Hamburg, d.

1073

B **Apr**: 21st, death of Pope Alexander II.
22nd, Hildebrand elected as Pope Gregory VII (–1085).

C **Aug**: Henry IV expelled from Saxony in a new rising under Otto of Nordheim.

E William recovers Le Mans from Fulk Rechin.
Sulaymān ibn-Qutlamish, a Seljuq, begins the systematic conquest of Asia Minor (–1077).

1074

A **Feb**: 2nd, Henry makes peace with the Saxons at Gerstungen.
Mar: Gregory excommunicates Robert Guiscard.

B **Apr**: 28th, death of Svein Estrithson, King of Denmark; a war of succession follows until his son, Harold, accedes (–1081).

E Normandy revolts against William.
Henry unsuccessfully campaigns in Hungary in an attempt to restore King Solomon, who had been expelled by Géza I (–1077).
Malik Shah captures Aleppo.

1075

A **Feb**: 24th–28th, Gregory suspends seven German bishops opposing clerical celibacy and, in an unpublished decree, condemns the practice of investiture of prelates by secular rulers.
Mar: in a riot in Milan, the Patarene leader, Erlembald, is murdered, and members of the sect are expelled from the city.

B **Jun**: 9th, Henry defeats the Saxons at Homburg-on-Unstrut.

D **Nov**: the Saxon nobles surrender to Henry, who punishes them with imprisonment and confiscation.
Dec: 25th, Henry's son, Conrad, accepted as his successor.

E William's lieutenants in England (during his absence in Normandy) defeat a revolt by Earls Waltheof of Northumbria, Ralf of East Anglia and Roger FitzOsbern of Hereford.
Both Henry and Gregory appoint candidates for the Archbishopric of Milan.
Géza I has himself crowned as King of Hungary with a crown sent by Michael VII.
Atsiz takes Damascus.

1073

F **Law and Politics**

Michael Attaleiata, *Ponema juris* (system of Graeco-Roman law).

H **Religion and Education**

†Chou Tun-i, founder of a Confucian revival in China, *T'ung Shu* and other philosophical treatises.

J **Art, Architecture and Music**

Abbey of St. Augustine, Canterbury, begun.

L **Births and Deaths**

— St. John Gualberti d. (88).

1074

G **Economics, Science, Technology and Discovery**

Henry IV grants a charter of privileges to Worms, the first such imperial charter conceded to citizens rather than their ruler. At Cologne, there is the first-known revolt of citizens against their episcopal overlord.

Malik Shah builds a new observatory (at Ray or Neyshabur), where 'Umar al-Khayyām is engaged to reform the old Persian calendar (–1079).

H **Religion and Education**

Gregory sends legates to France to reform the Church there; he announces the excommunication of married priests.

St. Stephen of Muret founds the monastic order of Grandmont.

1075

G **Economics, Science, Technology and Discovery**

Sureśvara, *Sabdapradīpa* (Sanskrit herbal).

H **Religion and Education**

Gregory VII, *Dictatus Papae* (detailing his vision of papal powers).

St. Robert founds the monastic order of Molesme.

J **Art, Architecture and Music**

*Cathedral of Santiago de Compostela (–1211); French masons recruited.

L **Births and Deaths**

Feb. 16th, Orderic Vitalis b. (–1143).

Dec. 4th, St. Anno, Archbishop of Cologne, d.

— Lothar II b. (–1137).

Kingdoms of Poland and Croatia—Sack of Ghana—Sultanate of Rūm

1076

A Jan: 24th, Henry responds to a letter from Gregory threatening excommunication by holding, at Worms, a council where the German bishops renounce their allegiance to Gregory; the Pope (in Lent) then excommunicates Henry.

B May: 31st, Earl Waltheof executed because of his rebellion against William.
Jun: 4th, Sancho IV of Navarre murdered; his kingdom seized by Sancho V Ramirez of Aragon and Alfonso of Castile and Leon.

D Oct: 16th, a diet of German princes at Tribur threatens to depose Henry IV.
Dec: 25th, Boleslav crowned as King of Poland with a crown sent by Gregory to reward his zeal in restoring the Church in Poland, under the direction of papal legates, and for supporting the Pope against Henry; in this year, Boleslav campaigns against Bohemia, with Russian assistance, and (supposedly) moves the Polish capital from Gniezno to Cracow.

E The Saxons again rebel against Henry.
Zvonimir crowned as King of Croatia by a papal legate and recognises the Pope's overlordship.
The Egyptians recover Jerusalem, but after a siege Atsiz again expels them.
The Berbers destroy Ghana, capital of the (Madingo) Negro Empire of Ghana (Western Sudan).
Ly Nhan-tong, Emperor of Dai Viet, wages war in southern China (–1078).

1077

A Jan: Henry submits to Gregory at Canossa and is absolved from excommunication.
Mar: 13th, in a diet at Forchheim, Henry's German enemies affirm that the German crown is elective and choose Rudolf, Duke of Swabia, as King.

B Apr: 25th, death of Géza I of Hungary; succeeded by his brother, Ladislas I (–1095).

E Robert Curthose leads a Norman rebellion against William, his father.
Robert Guiscard occupies the Lombard principality of Salerno.
Boleslav of Poland again restores Isiaslav as Grand Duke of Kiev at the request of Pope Gregory, to whom Isiaslav had presented Russia.
Sulaymān ibn-Qutlumish establishes the Seljuq sultanate of Rūm, with his capital at Nicaea (–1086, 1307).
Death of Aniruddha, first King of united Burma and founder of its Pagan dynasty.

1076

F **Law and Politics**

Dismissal of Wang An-Shih, Chief Councillor of the Sung Empire (from 1069), due to opposition to his extensive reforms of government.

H **Religion and Education**

A national university established in Dai Viet.

J **Art, Architecture and Music**

Old Sarum Cathedral begun.

K **Literature, Philosophy and Scholarship**

†Adam of Bremen, *Historia Hammaburgensis Ecclesiae* (*History of the Church* (*i.e.* Bishopric) *of Hamburg*; describes geography and ethnography of northern Europe and first mentions discovery of Vineland; –1003).

†Ibn Haiyān, *Kitāb al-Matīn* (or *Liber Solidus*; history of Muslim Spain in 60 volumes).

1077

J **Art, Architecture and Music**

Rochester Cathedral and St. Albans Abbey-church begun.

K **Literature, Philosophy and Scholarship**

*Lambert of Hersfeld, *Annales* (from the Creation to 1077).

†Shao Yung, *Kuan-wu* (*On the Study of Phenomena*; part of a larger work, now lost).

1078

A **Mar:** 31st, after a revolt in Constantinople, Michael VII abdicates and is succeeded by the general Nicephorus III Botaneiates, who had already been proclaimed Emperor (–1081).

C **Aug:** 7th, Rudolf of Swabia obliged to withdraw after an otherwise indecisive battle with Henry at Mellrichstadt.

D **Nov:** Gregory publishes a decree condemning lay investiture into spiritual offices.

E Isiaslav of Kiev killed while defeating his nephews; succeeded by his brother, Vsévolod I (–1093).

1079

A **Jan:** Kings William and Philip I routed at Gerberoy by William's son, Robert Curthose.

B **Apr:** 11th, death of St. Stanislaus, Bishop of Cracow, as the result of his mutilation for suspected treason against Boleslav of Poland.

E Malcolm devastates Northumberland.
Hugh I resigns the Duchy of Burgundy in order to enter a monastery.
Inge I succeeds Stenkil as King of Sweden (–1112).
Henry grants the Duchy of Swabia to Frederick, Count of Staufen, who marries his daughter.
Atsiz murdered on the order of Tutush, Malik Shah's brother, who takes over his semi-independent principality.

1080

A **Jan:** 27th, Henry defeated at Flarchheim and compelled to abandon Saxony.
Mar: 7th, Gregory pronounces in favour of Rudolf of Swabia and declares Henry to be deposed.

B **May:** 14th, Walcher, Bishop of Durham and Earl of Northumberland, murdered; William consequently ravages this area. He also invades Scotland and builds the castle at Newcastle-upon-Tyne.
Jun: 25th, Henry holds a council of bishops at Brixen which declares Gregory to be deposed and elects Guibert, Archbishop of Ravenna, as Pope Clement III (–1100).
29th, by the treaty of Ceprano, Gregory makes an alliance with Robert Guiscard and recognises his conquests.

D **Oct:** 15th, in a battle near Hohen-Mölsen, Henry is defeated but Rudolf is mortally wounded.

E William refuses to do fealty to Gregory.
Philip of France defeated by Hugh, lord of Le Puiset, one of the vassals in his domain lands.
*Roupen establishes himself as the ruler of the exiles from Armenia who were settling in Cilicia (Lesser Armenia).

1078

H **Religion and Education**

Legates sent by Gregory reorganise the English Church.

Gregory orders all bishops to found cathedral-schools.

K **Literature, Philosophy and Scholarship**

Michael Psellus, *The Chronography, 976–1078* (historical narrative of events in Constantinople and the Empire; personal commentary for the period of the writer's life).

1079

G **Economics, Science, Technology and Discovery**

Mar. 15th, the Jalālī Era computed by 'Umar al-Khayyām in his *Astronomical Calendar* adopted in Persia.

J **Art, Architecture and Music**

The present Winchester Cathedral begun.

†Wen T'ung, Chinese painter.

K **Literature, Philosophy and Scholarship**

†Scylitzes, continuation of Theophanes' chronicle (811–1079).

L **Births and Deaths**

— Peter Abelard b. (–1142).

1080

G **Economics, Science, Technology and Discovery**

†*Symeon Seth, dictionary on medical properties of foodstuffs; botanical dictionary; translations from Arabic to Greek.

J **Art, Architecture and Music**

*Bayeux Tapestry (a pictorial record of the Norman Conquest of England; *cf.* the Mongol Scroll –1293).

York Cathedral begun.

*Abbey of St. Sernin, Toulouse, founded.

*Rebuilding of S. Ambrogio, Milan, begun.

*Gniezno and Cracow Cathedrals.

1081

A **Mar**: the Greek Emperor, Nicephorus III, deposed in favour of Alexius I Comnenus (–1118).

B **Apr**: a rebellion in Poland forces Boleslav into exile; succeeded by his brother, Vladislav I Hermann, under whom the Polish territories disintegrate in civil war and its crown falls into abeyance (–1102).
17th, death of Harold III Whetstone, King of Denmark, a law reformer; succeeded by his brother, Cnut IV (–1086).
May: Henry unsuccessfully attempts to enter Rome.
Jun: the conquests east of the Dracon by Sulaymān, Sultan of Rūm, are recognised in a treaty with Alexius.
17th, Robert Guiscard, invading the Greek Empire, begins his siege of Durazzo; he occupies Corfù.

C **Aug**: 9th, Rudolf's former supporters elect Hermann of Salm as King of Germany.

D **Oct**: 18th, Guiscard defeats Alexius near Durazzo.

E William makes an expedition into South Wales, where Norman marcher lords are now established.
Alfonso VI of Castile exiles Rodrigo (*or* Ruy) Diaz de Vivar ('The Cid').

1082

A **Feb**: 21st, Guiscard takes Durazzo.

E William imprisons his brother Odo, Bishop of Bayeux and Earl of Kent.
Vratislav II of Bohemia defeats the Austrians at Mailberg.
Alexius grants Venice extensive rights to trade in the Greek Empire.

1083

A **Jan**: 11th, death of Otto of Nordheim.

B **Jun**: 3rd, Henry captures St. Peter's Rome; his negotiations with Gregory collapse.

E Maine revolts against William.
Greeks defeat Guiscard's son, Bohemond, at Larissa, and recover Durazzo.
Death of Boleslav the Bold, the former King of Poland.

1081

L **Births and Deaths**
Aug. 11th, Henry V b. (–1125).

1082

J **Art, Architecture and Music**
Abbey-church of SS. Peter and Paul, Hirsau (–1091).

1083

G **Economics, Science, Technology and Discovery**
† ?Franco of Liège, mathematical treatises.

K **Literature, Philosophy and Scholarship**
†Marianus Scotus, *Chronicon* (world history from the Creation to 1082; he corrected the accepted date for the Incarnation).

L **Births and Deaths**
Dec. 1st, Anna Comnena b. (–1148).

1084

A **Mar**: 21st, Henry enters Rome.
24th, Clement III crowned as Pope.
31st, he crowns Henry as Holy Roman Emperor.

B **May**: Guiscard expels the Germans from Rome and his Normans sack the city.

E Domenico Salvio, Doge of Venice, deposed; succeeded by Vitale Falieri (–1096).
Death of Michael, King of Serbia; his title had been conferred by Pope Gregory VII.

1085

B **May**: 25th, death of Pope Gregory VII the Great, at Salerno.
25th, Alfonso of Castile and Leon takes Toledo, then subjects the Muslim Kings of Valencia.
Jun: 15th, Vratislav II crowned as King of Bohemia; Henry had granted him the crown, for his life only, to reward his services in Italy, and also excused payment of tribute.

C **Jul**: 17th, death of Robert Guiscard; succeeded, as Duke of Apulia, by his son, Roger Borsa (–1111), who withdraws the Normans from Greece. Robert's brother, Roger, succeeds in Sicily and Calabria (–1101).

Disorders in Denmark prevent Cnut invading England, for which he had allied with Olaf of Norway and Robert of Flanders. This threat may explain why, on . . .

D **Dec**: 25th, William orders the survey of England subsequently recorded in *Domesday Book*.

E The Seljuqs take Ankara and Antioch from the Greeks, but Alexius compels them to restore Nicomedia.

1086

B **May**: 24th, Desiderius, Abbot of Montecassino, elected as Pope Victor III (–1087).

C **Jul**: 10th, St. Cnut IV, King of Denmark (who had conquered Livonia), murdered; succeeded by his brother Olaf IV (–1095).
Aug: 1st, William receives oaths of loyalty from all who hold land in England, at Salisbury.
11th, Henry defeated at Pleichfeld by Welf, Duke of Bavaria.

D **Oct**: 23rd, Yūsuf ibn-Tāshfīn, the Berber ruler, who had been called into Spain by al-Muʿtamid of Seville, defeats Alfonso of Castile and Leon at Azagal (*or* Zalaca, near Badajoz).

E Sulaymān, Sultan of Rūm, defeated and killed by Tutush while attempting to take Aleppo; succeeded by his son, Kilij Arslan I (–1107).

1084

H **Religion and Education**
St. Bruno founds his hermitage at Chartreuse (origin of the Carthusian Order).

J **Art, Architecture and Music**
Salerno Cathedral dedicated.
Worcester Cathedral begun.
†Benno of Osnabrück, master mason of Henry III and Henry IV.

1085

F **Law and Politics**
Henry extends the 'Peace of God' over the whole Empire.

J **Art, Architecture and Music**
Tomb-mosque of al-Juyūshī, Cairo.
Abbey-church of S. Salvador, Leyre, completed.

K **Literature, Philosophy and Scholarship**
*?Somadeva, *Ocean of the Streams of Story* (as translated from the collection of Sanskrit folk stories).

1086

G **Economics, Science, Technology and Discovery**
Earliest Chinese reference to a suspended magnetic needle (–1117).

K **Literature, Philosophy and Scholarship**
†Sšu-ma Kuang, *Tžu chih t'ung chien* (*Universal Mirror to Assist Government*; comprehensive history of China, 403 B.C.–A.D. 959, in 294 chapters; –1205).

1087

B **May**: 30th, Henry has his son, Conrad, crowned as King of Germany.

C **Sep**: 9th, death of William I the Conqueror, King of England, when suppressing the revolt in Maine; succeeded in Normandy by his son, Robert Curthose, who immediately faces a baronial rebellion he is never able to suppress completely (–1106).
16th, death of Pope Victor III.
26th, William II, son of William I, crowned as King of England (–1100).

E A combined fleet from Genoa and Pisa takes Madhīyah, in Barbary; this emphasises European control of the western Mediterranean.
The Pechenegs attempt to storm Constantinople; Solomon, the former King of Hungary, (possibly) killed in their ranks.

1088

A **Mar**: 12th, Cardinal Otto of Chatillon elected as Pope Urban II (–1099).

B **Jun**: William II suppresses a revolt in England led by Odo of Bayeux, Bishop of Rochester, who was supporting Robert Curthose.

C **Sep**: 28th, death of Hermann of Salm.

E Henry makes peace with the Saxons.

1089

C **Sep**: at the Council of Melfi, Urban begins negotiations with Alexius about a crusade against the Turks.

E Henry IV marries Praxedis (Adelaide) of Kiev.
Welf, son of the Duke of Bavaria, marries Matilda, Countess of Tuscany.
Sancho Ramirez of Aragon does homage as a papal vassal.
David III the Builder becomes King of Georgia (–1125) jointly with his father, George II.
The Fātamids recover Ascalon, Tyre and Acre from the Seljuqs.

1087

F **Law and Politics**

Nizām-al-Mulk regularises the system of military fiefs in the Seljuq Empire; these become hereditary and assist its disintegration.

G **Economics, Science, Technology and Discovery**

Domesday Book records 5,624 water-mills for corn south of the Trent and Severn, and some stamping-mills for crushing iron-ore, and hammer-mills.

†Al-Zarqāli (Arzachel), *Toledan Tables* (astronomical and geographical); treatise on an astrolabe of his invention.

†Constantine the African, first translation of Arab medical works into Latin.

J **Art, Architecture and Music**

Bāban-Nasr gateway, Cairo (with machicolation; for the earliest European example, *see* 1197).

London Cathedral ('Old St. Paul's') and abbey-churches of Gloucester and Tewkesbury begun.

1088

G **Economics, Science, Technology and Discovery**

†Nāsir-i-Khusraw, *Safar-nāma* (diary of travels in Syria, Egypt, Arabia and Asia).

J **Art, Architecture and Music**

Cluny 'III' (the largest of all abbey-churches; –1130).

*Tower of London ('The White Tower').

K **Literature, Philosophy and Scholarship**

Ansārī, *Munajat* (Persian poetry).

L **Births and Deaths**

Jan. 6th, Berengar of Tours d. (*c.* 88).

1089

J **Art, Architecture and Music**

S. Nicola, Bari (in a Romanesque style new to Italy).

L **Births and Deaths**

May 28th, Lanfranc, Archbishop of Canterbury, d. (84).

Almoravid Empire in Spain—Foundation of the Assassins—Norman conquest of Sicily completed

1090

B **Apr:** 29th, Alexius defeats the Pechenegs, who are settling in Bulgaria, at Mount Levunium.

C **Jul:** Henry begins the siege of Mantua.

D **Nov:** Yūsuf ibn-Tāshfīn, returning to Spain from Africa, takes Granada; he founds the Almoravid dynasty in Spain (–1147).

E Death of Halstan of Sweden; succeeded by Inge I (–1112).
Raymond-Berengar II, Count of Barcelona, becomes a papal vassal.
Roger Guiscard takes Malta.
Robert of Flanders fights for Alexius against the Turks.
Al-Hasan ibn-al-Sabbāh, founder of the Assassins, establishes himself in the castle of Alamūt, Iraq (–1124).

1091

B **Apr:** 11th, Henry takes Mantua and, subsequently, defeats the forces of Matilda of Tuscany at Tricontai.

E Malcolm III invades England but is forced by William to do homage.
William and Robert expel their youngest brother, Henry, from Normandy.
Raymond-Berengar of Barcelona takes Tarragona.
Yūsuf destroys, and unites, the Muslim kingdoms of Andalusia.
Roger Guiscard takes Butera, so completing the conquest of Sicily from the Saracens.
Ladislas of Hungary conquers Croatia.
Malik Shah makes Baghdād the Seljuq capital.

1092

D **Nov:** Death of Malik Shah, Sultan of Persia; succeeded by his son, Mahmūd I, who fights his brothers (–1094), while the Seljuq Empire disintegrates with the emergence of independent rulers.

E William seizes northern Cumberland and Westmorland from the Scots.
Philip I abducts and 'marries' Bertrada, Fulk Rechin's wife.
Death of Vratislav II, King of Bohemia; succeeded by his brother, Conrad, who dies this year and is succeeded by Vratislav's son, Břatislav II (–1100).
Kilij Arslan seizes Nicaea and Smyrna from independent Turkish rulers.
Assassination of Nizām-al-Mulk, Vizir of Malik Shah; he is the first political victim of the Assassins.

1090

G **Economics, Science, Technology and Discovery**
First dated Chinese reference to a flyer in silk-working machinery.

J **Art, Architecture and Machinery**
*Ely and Norwich Cathedrals begun.
†Kuo Hsi, Chinese painter.

1091

G **Economics, Science, Technology and Discovery**
(or 1092) Walcher of Malvern observes an eclipse of the moon (one of the earliest west European observations).
†Wilhelm, Abbot of Hirsau, *Astronomica*.

J **Art, Architecture and Music**
†Wilhelm of Hirsau, *Musica*.

1092

F **Law and Politics**
†Nizām-al-Mulk, *Siyāsat-nāmah* (treatise on the art of government).

G **Economics, Science, Technology and Discovery**
Su Sung, *Hsing-i-hsiang fa-yao* (astronomical treatise, with celestial maps).

H **Religion and Education**
The council of Soissons condemns Roscelin for his heretical speculation about the Trinity.

1093

B **Apr**: death of Rhys ap Tewdwr, the last independent native prince in South Wales.

C **Sep**: 22nd, death of Olaf III the Peace-King, King of Norway; succeeded by Magnus III (–1103).

D **Oct**: 4th, death of Robert I the Frisian, Count of Flanders, who had imposed the 'Peace of God' in his lands.

Nov: 13th, Malcolm III Canmore, King of Scotland, killed at Alnwick while invading England; succeeded by his brother, Donald Bane (–1097).

E Alfonso of Castile and Leon takes Santarem, Lisbon and Cintra.

Conrad, in revolt against his father, Henry IV, crowned as King of Lombardy.

Death of the Russian prince, Vsévolod I; succeeded by his nephew, Sviatopolk II (–1113).

1094

A **Feb**: 26th, 'Umar al-Mutawakkil, the last King of Badajoz, killed after the city surrenders to Yūsuf.

B **Jun**: death of Sancho V Ramirez of Aragon and Navarre; succeeded by his son, Pedro I (–1104).

D **Dec**: 29th, death of al-Munstansir, Caliph of Egypt; his north African empire now rapidly declines and the caliphate is held by a succession of powerless nonentities, several of whom are murdered.

E The Welsh expel the Normans from north-west Wales.

Duncan II, son of Malcolm III, briefly holds the Scottish throne with Anglo-Norman aid, until he is killed and Donald Bane resumes control.

Philip I thwarts William's attempt to conquer Normandy.

The Cid captures Valencia and holds it against the Moors (–1099).

Urban II regains possession of the Lateran Palace, so completing his recovery of Rome from adherents of the anti-pope, Clement III; Henry's cause in Italy is now ruined, although he is unable to leave; the Empress Adelaide deserts him.

Tutush seizes Aleppo from its independent ruler.

Barkiyāruq succeeds Mahmūd I as Seljuq Sultan (–1105).

1093

G **Economics, Science, Technology and Discovery**
†Shên Kua, *Mêng-ch'i* (*Essays from the Torrent of Dreams*; sections on mathematics, music, archaeology and other sciences, with earliest literary mention of a magnetic needle and description of printing with movable type).

J **Art, Architecture and Music**
Durham Cathedral (–1133); here ribs first appeared in the vaulting (as decoration).
Troia Cathedral begun.

L **Births and Deaths**
Nov. 16th, St. Margaret, Queen of Scotland, d. (47).

1094

G **Economics, Science, Technology and Discovery**
Al-Bakri, *Kitāb al-Masālik w-al-Mamālik* (*The Book of Roads and Kingdoms*; the earliest surviving geographical work by a Spanish Muslim).

H **Religion and Education**
Anselm, *Cur Deus Homo* (*Why did God become man?*).

J **Art, Architecture and Music**
Cluniac houses of Charlieu and S. Juan de la Peña dedicated.

K **Literature, Philosophy and Scholarship**
Leo of Ostia, *Chronica* (of Montecassino, 529–1075; –1139).

1095–1096 The First Crusade

1095

A **Feb**: 25th, in a council at Rockingham, Archbishop Anselm of Canterbury quarrels with William over the issue of episcopal obedience to the King and/or Pope.

Mar: in a council at Piacenza, Urban appeals to western Europe to rescue Constantinople.

C **Jul**: 29th, death of St. Ladislas I, King of Hungary; succeeded by his son, Coloman (–1114).

Aug: 18th, death of Olaf IV King of Denmark; succeeded by his brother, Eric I (–1103).

D **Nov**: 18th–28th, Urban holds a council at Clermont; here he excommunicates Philip I because of his adulterous 'marriage' with Bertrada, and (on the 27th) proclaims the First Crusade, granting an indulgence to participants. The Crusade's aim is to liberate Jerusalem.

Dec: 1st, Raymond IV, Count of Toulouse, is the first magnate to join the Crusade.

E William suppresses a rebellion led by Robert de Mowbray, Earl of Northumberland.

Alfonso of Castile and Leon enfeoffs Henry of Burgundy in the Country of Portugal (–1112).

Welf of Bavaria divorces Matilda of Tuscany.

Alexius repulses the Cumans (Turkish tribes) at Adrianople; he appeals to Urban for western aid against the Turks.

Death of the Seljuq prince, Tutush; his dominions disintegrate, as his sons, Ridwān and Duqāq, ruling Aleppo and Damascus respectively, cannot prevent other Turkish leaders from establishing themselves in Jerusalem, etc.

1096

B **May** and **June**: Crusaders in the Rhineland prompt attacks on the Jews there.

C **Aug**: 1st, Crusaders led by Peter the Hermit arrive in Constantinople.

D **Oct**: 21st, Kilij Arslan destroys the army of 'the People's Crusade' at Civetot.

E The Normans complete their conquest of south Wales and recover Anglesey.

William gains possession of Normandy as pledge for a loan to Robert, who is joining the Crusade.

Pedro of Aragon defeats the Moors at Alcaraz and takes Huesca.

Death of Vitale Falieri, Doge of Venice; succeeded by Vitale Micheli I (–1102).

Death of Werner, the first Count of Habsburg.

1095

G **Economics, Science, Technology and Discovery**
(–1123) At St. Bertin, water-power applied to water-lifting and irrigation wheels.

J **Art, Architecture and Music**
Abbey-church of St. Martial, Limoges, dedicated.

K **Literature, Philosophy and Scholarship**
*_Eiga Monogatari_ (_A Tale of Glory_; a romanticised chronicle of the Fujiwara family, 889–1092; thus the earliest known Japanese historical novel).
*_La Chanson de Roland_ (earliest extant example of a _chanson de geste_; 'eleventh century: certainly not later than 1095'—_Saintsbury_).
†*Rāmānuja, Hindu philosopher.

1096

H **Religion and Education**
Robert d'Arbrissel founds the monastic order of Fontevrault.

J **Art, Architecture and Music**
Abbey-church of Ste. Madeleine, Vézelay (–1104).

K **Literature, Philosophy and Scholarship**
*Simeon of Durham, _Historia Dunelmensis Ecclesiae_ (extending to 1096).

1097

A **Jan:** the Crusaders in Constantinople riot.

B **May:** 21st, they defeat Kilij Arslan outside Nicaea.
Jun: 19th, they take Nicaea.

C **Jul:** 1st, they defeat Kilij Arslan at Dorylaeum.
Aug: they take Iconium (*now* Konya), Kilij Arslan's capital.

D **Oct:** Archbishop Anselm begins his first exile from England.
Edgar the Atheling, the son of Malcolm III (by his second marriage, with St. Margaret), with Anglo-Norman assistance, deposes and succeeds Donald Bane, the last purely Celtic King of Scotland (–1107).
21st, the Crusaders begin their siege of Antioch.

E William unsuccessfully campaigns against the Welsh.
Henry IV returns to Germany from Italy.
The Russian princes descended from Jaroslav (–1055) meet at Liubech (near Kiev) and agree to unite against the Cumans who are now in occupation of the southern Russian steppes, to the Dneiper; they also agree to a doctrine of inheritance in order to prevent civil war.

1098

A **Feb:** 6th, Baldwin of Flanders takes Edessa and becomes its Count.

B **Jun:** 3rd, the Crusaders take Antioch.
28th, they defeat Kerboghā of Mosul, who had been blockading the city.

C **Aug:** 1st, death of Adhemar, Bishop of Le Puy, official leader of the Crusade.

E Magnus of Norway conquers the Orkneys, Shetlands and Isle of Man, and devastates Anglesey.
The Egyptians recover Jerusalem from the Turks.

1099

A **Jan:** 5th, Henry, son of Henry IV, elected as King of the Romans; Henry IV had now made peace with his enemies in Germany.

C **Jul:** 15th, the Crusaders take Jerusalem.
22nd, Godfrey of Bouillon elected as Defender of the Holy Sepulchre; thus, in effect, is the Latin Kingdom of Jerusalem founded.
29th, death of Pope Urban II.
Aug: 12th, the Crusaders defeat the Egyptians at Ascalon.
13th, Cardinal Rainer elected as Pope Paschal II (–1118).

E William II recovers control of Maine.
Death of the Cid; the Moors then recover Valencia.

1097

H **Religion and Education**

†St. Wulsi, a hermit who had lived for 70 years in a cave near Evesham.

J **Art, Architecture and Music**

Priory-church of St. Étienne, Nevers, dedicated.

Westminster Hall.

L **Births and Deaths**

— Roger II b. (–1154).

1098

H **Religion and Education**

Mar. 21st, Robert of Molesme founds Cîteaux Abbey (and the Cistercian Order).

Oct., representatives of the Roman and Greek Churches debate the Procession of the Holy Ghost in a council at Bari.

J **Art, Architecture and Music**

Trani Cathedral begun.

*Raymond Gayrard employed as architect for building of Conques abbey-church (–1118).

L **Births and Deaths**

— St. Hildegarde b. (–1179).

1099

H **Religion and Education**

Foundation of the Order of Knights of St. John of Jerusalem.

J **Art, Architecture and Music**

Modena Cathedral begun.

L **Births and Deaths**

Dec. 3–4th, St. Osmund, Bishop of Salisbury, d.

— Rodrigo Díaz de Vivar (El Cid) d. (*c.* 56).

1100

B Apr: the Emirs of Ascalon, Caesarea and Acre submit to Godfrey as tributaries.

C Jul: 18th, death of Godfrey of Bouillon, Defender of Jerusalem; succeeded by his brother, Baldwin I, as King of Jerusalem (–1118).
Aug: 2nd, William II Rufus, King of England, killed.
5th, coronation of his brother, Henry I, as King (–1135); he issues a 'charter of liberties' and recalls Anselm.
Sep: death of the anti-pope, 'Clement III'; a Roman faction has Theodoric crowned as his successor; he is expelled later this year.

E Břatislav II, Duke of Bohemia, murdered; succeeded by his brother, Bořivoj (–1107). Civil war breaks out.
Death of Constantine Bodin, King of Zeta, who had formed a Serbian state by the conquest of Rascia and Bosnia; this now breaks up.

1101

A Mar: Tancred, Prince of Galilee, assumes the regency of Antioch following the capture of its Norman prince, Bohemond, by the Danishmend Emir, Ghāzī.

B May: Baldwin takes Arsūf and Caesarea.
Jun: 22nd, death of Roger I, Great Count of Sicily; succeeded by his son, Simon (–1103).
23rd, a new crusading army, led from Constantinople by Raymond of Toulouse, takes Ankara.

C Jul: 17th, by the Treaty of Alton, Robert of Normandy cedes his claim to the English throne to Henry I.
27th, death of King Conrad.
Aug: Raymond's army is destroyed by the Danishmends at Mersivan, in Anatolia.
Sep: another crusading force is destroyed by the Turks at Heraclea.
4th, Baldwin defeats the Egyptians at Ramleh.

E Philip I of France purchases Bourges from its viscount, who is going to the Holy Land.
In a meeting at Konungahella, Kings Eric of Denmark, Inge of Sweden and Magnus Bareleg of Norway swear to maintain perpetual peace.

1100

F **Law and Politics**

*Irnerius establishes the glossatorial method in the rising law-school at Bologna. His successors were 'the Four Doctors', *viz.* Bulgarus, (–1166), Martinus, Jacobus and Hugo.

G **Economics, Science, Technology and Discovery**

*Discovery of alcohol by distillation (at Salerno?); used in medicine (–1110).

* ?Odo of Meung, *De viribus herbarum* (herbal, in hexameters).

*'Theophilus', *Diversarum artium schedula* (encyclopedia of arts and crafts; gives earliest European account of bell-founding and describes processes in metallurgy).

*Adelard of Bath translates Euclid into Latin from Arabic.

J **Art, Architecture and Music**

*Cathedrals of Braga (then the capital of Portugal) and Canosa, and S. Michele, Pavia, begun.

*S. Clemente, Rome, restored.

K **Literature, Philosophy and Scholarship**

*The *Dunstable Miracle Play* (the earliest extant).

*Dominicus Gundissalinus, Archdeacon of Segovia, a major translator from Arabic (and theologian), *flor.*

**Gesta Francorum et aliorum Hierosolimitanorum* (anon. chronicle of the First Crusade, 1096–99).

1101

H **Religion and Education**

Nathan ben Jeliel, the *Aruk* (Talmudic dictionary).

K **Literature, Philosophy and Scholarship**

†Su Tung-p'o, Poems and essays in Chinese.

L **Births and Deaths**

Oct. 6th, St. Bruno d.

1102

A **Feb**: Albert elected as 'pope' by a Roman faction; he is soon deposed.

B **May**: 17th, the Egyptians defeat Baldwin of Jerusalem at Ramleh.
28th, he defeats them at Jaffa.

C **Jul**: 26th, death of Vladislav I Hermann, Duke of Poland; succeeded by his sons, Zbigniev (–1109) and Boleslav III (–1138), jointly. The latter begins to reconquer Pomerania.

E Henry I suppresses a revolt led by Robert of Bellême, Earl of Shrewsbury.
Matilda, Countess of Tuscany, grants 'the Patrimony of St. Peter' to the Papacy.
Death of Vitali Micheli I, Doge of Venice; succeeded by Ordelafo Falieri (–1117).

1103

B **Spring**: Bohemond is ransomed and resumes his rule at Antioch.
Apr: 27th, Anselm begins his second exile after quarrelling with Henry I.

C **Jul**: 11th, death of Eric I the Good of Denmark; there is an interregnum until 1105.
Aug: 24th, Magnus III Bareleg of Norway killed while invading Ireland in his defeat at Moycoba; succeeded by his sons, Eysten I (–1122), Olaf IV (–1116) and Sigurd I (–1130).

E Death of Simon of Sicily; succeeded by his brother, Roger II (–1154).

1104

A **Jan**: a Turkish civil war ends with the Sultan, Barkiyarūq, ceding Iraq and Syria to his brother, Muhammad; a third brother, Sanjar, already holds Khurāsān.

B **May**: Baldwin of Jerusalem takes Acre.
Bohemond and Baldwin II of Edessa defeated by the Turks when attempting to take Harran.

C **Sep**: 28th, death of Pedro I of Aragon and Navarre; succeeded by his brother, Alfonso I (–1134).

D **Dec**: 12th, Henry revolts against his father, the Emperor Henry IV.

E Philip of Spain absolved from excommunication on promising to part from Bertrada. He also yields to the Papacy on the principle of the lay investiture of bishops.

1102

G **Economics, Science, Technology and Discovery**
A public medical service organised in China.

1103

G **Economics, Science, Technology and Discovery**
†Joannes Afflacius (the Saracen) of Salerno, medical treatises and translations.

H **Religion and Education**
Pascal II sends a legate to reform the Polish Church.
†Isaac al-Fez (Alphesi), *Siphra* (*The Little Talmud*); *Halakot* (compendium on the legal part of the Talmud).

K **Literature, Philosophy and Scholarship**
†Frutolf, monk of Bamberg, *Breviarium de musica*; *Tonarius* (treatises on Gregorian music).

1104

G **Economics, Science, Technology and Discovery**
*Saewulf, monk of Malmesbury, account (Latin) of his early pilgrimage to Jerusalem, 1102–3 (the earliest extant pilgrim-narratives).

H **Religion and Education**
Consecration of the first Scandinavian archbishop, of Lund, Denmark, on the detachment of the diocese from the archbishopric of Hamburg.

1105

A **Feb**: 28th, death of Raymond IV, Count of Toulouse, while besieging Tripoli.

C **Aug**: 27th, Baldwin defeats the Egyptians in the third battle of Ramleh, ending their attempts to reconquer Palestine.

D **Nov**: 18th, some Italian nobles have Silvester IV elected as 'pope' (–1111).
Dec: Henry IV captured by his son, Henry, and forced to abdicate; he escapes early in 1106. Henry V thus succeeds as King of the Germans (–1125).

E Niels succeeds his brother, Eric, as King of Denmark (–1134).

1106

C **Aug**: 7th, death of the deposed Emperor, Henry IV.
Sep: death of Yūsuf ibn-Tāshfīn, the Almoravid emperor of Morocco and Muslim Spain; succeeded by his son, 'Alī (–1143).
28th, in the battle of Tinchebrai, Henry I gains the Duchy of Normandy by the defeat and capture of Robert, who is imprisoned (–1134).

E Count Lothar of Supplinburg becomes Duke of Saxony (–1136).

1107

A **Jan**: death of Edgar, king of Scotland; succeeded by his brother, Alexander I (–1124).

C **Jul**: Kilij Arslan I, Sultan of Rūm, killed near Mosul, which he had recently taken, in battle with other Turks; succeeded by his brother, Malik Shah (–1117).
Aug: Henry I and Anselm settle their disagreement over the investiture of bishops.

D **Oct**: 9th, Bohemond invades the Greek Empire, at Avlona, and attempts to take Durazzo.

E Bořivoj, Duke of Bohemia, deposed and succeeded by Svátopluk, lord of Olomuc (–1109).
A civil war in Poland ends with Zbigniev recognising the supremacy of his brother, Boleslav III.

1105

H **Religion and Education**
†Solomon ben Isaac (Rashi), commentaries on the Bible and Talmud.

J **Art, Architecture and Music**
Angoulême Cathedral begun.

1106

J **Art, Architecture and Music**
Parma Cathedral dedicated.

K **Literature, Philosophy and Scholarship**
†Li Lung-mien, Chinese painter.

1107

G **Economics, Science, Technology and Discovery**
*Daniel of Kiev, account (Russian) of his pilgrimage to Jerusalem, 1106–7.

J **Art, Architecture and Music**
The central tower of Winchester Cathedral collapses; rib-vaults introduced in its rebuilding.
†Mi Fei, an outstanding Chinese painter and calligrapher.

1108

B **May**: 29th, Alfonso of Aragon defeated by ʿAlī at Uclés, near Tarancón.

C **Jul**: 29/30th, death of Philip I, King of France; succeeded by his son, Louis VI (–1137).
Sep: by the Treaty of Devol, Bohemond, who had surrendered to Alexius, becomes the Emperor's vassal as Prince of Antioch.

E Coloman of Hungary grants his newly acquired kingdom of Croatia constitutional independence of Hungary.

1109

A **Mar**: Henry I rejects Louis VI's offer of personal combat; war follows.

B **Apr**: 14th, death of Fulk IV Rechin, Count of Anjou; succeeded by his son, Fulk V le Jeune (–1129).
Jun: 30th, death of Alfonso I of Castile and VI of Leon; succeeded by his daughter, Urracca, married to Alfonso I of Aragon (–1126), who styles himself Emperor of the Spains.

C **Jul**: 12th, Tripoli surrenders to Baldwin of Jerusalem.

E Henry V invades Poland on behalf of the exiled Zbigniev and is defeated near Wroclaw by Boleslav III. Zbigniev is subsequently permitted to return and Boleslav has him killed.
Svátopluk, Duke of Bohemia, murdered; civil war ensues.

1110

C **Aug**: Henry V begins his first expedition to Italy.

D **Dec**: 4th, Sidon surrenders to Baldwin.

E Rebels in Leon declare Alfonso of Aragon to be their King; he imprisons Urracca but she is rescued.

1108

G **Economics, Science, Technology and Discovery**

First embankment on the Red River, North Vietnam, to protect rice-fields from floods.

Chêng lei pên ts'ao (illustrated Chinese encyclopedia of *materia medica*).

*Walcher of Malvern, Lunar Tables for 1036–1112.

H **Religion and Education**

*William of Champeaux founds a theological school in the Abbey of St. Victor, Paris.

J **Art, Architecture and Music**

Dedication of the abbey-church of St. Benoît-sur-Loire (*or* Fleury).

1109

K **Literature, Philosophy and Scholarship**

Aelnoth dedicates his *Historia sancti Canuti* to Niels of Denmark.

L **Births and Deaths**

Apr. 21st, St. Anselm d. (73).

— Hugh of Semur, Abbot of Cluny, d. (85).

1110

G **Economics, Science, Technology and Discovery**

Henry of Mainz, *De imagine mundi* (with a map).

**Mappae Clavicula* (has earliest known account of preparation of alcohol).

**Anatomia porci* (describes dissection of a pig in the medical school, Salerno).

H **Religion and Education**

Basil, leader of the Bulgarian heretics (Bogomils), burnt by order of Alexius.

*Bishopric of Greenland established.

*Theobald of Étampes known as the first teacher at Oxford.

J **Art, Architecture and Music**

*Nave of Tournai Cathedral.

*Temple of Anantapanna (*or* Ananda), Pagan (the greatest work of Burmese architecture).

K **Literature, Philosophy and Scholarship**

†Pedro Alfonso, *Disciplina clericalis* (a popular collection of tales; a source for Reynard the Fox and other stories appearing in Chaucer and Shakespeare; –1481).

†*Nestor of Kiev, *The Ancient Chronicle* (the first Russian chronicle, from the Deluge to 1110).

1111

A **Feb**: death of Bohemond I, Prince of Antioch, in Apulia; his nephew, Tancred, continues to rule in Antioch.
4th, by the Treaty of Sutri, Henry V compels Paschal II to agree to his terms for the settlement of the investiture controversy.
21st, death of Roger, Duke of Apulia; succeeded by his son, William I (–1127).

B **Apr**: 13th, Henry V crowned as Holy Roman Emperor (–1125).
13th, the anti-pope, Silvester IV, deposed.

D **Oct**: 26th, Alfonso defeats the adherents of Urracca, whom he had repudiated, at Campo de Espina.

E Amadeus III, Marquess of Maurienne, created Count of Savoy by Henry V.
Vladislav, the brother of Bořivoj, recognised as Duke of Bohemia in the settlement following his defeat by Boleslav of Poland, who invaded in support of Vladislav's brother, Soběslav (–1125).
Russian princes win a decisive victory over the Cumans on the Salnitsa.

1112

A **(Lent)**: Paschal withdraws his concession to Henry V on investitures.

B **May**: death of Henry of Burgundy, Count of Portugal; succeeded by his son, Afonso Henriques (–1185).

C **Sep**: Henry V excommunicated in the Synod of Vienne.

E Henry I suppresses a Norman rebellion and imprisons Robert of Bellême.
Death of Inge I the Pious, King of Sweden; an interregnum apparently follows.
Raymond-Berengar III, Count of Barcelona, gains possession of the County of Provence.
Urracca has her son, Alfonso, proclaimed as King of Galicia.

1113

A **Mar**: by the Treaty of Gisors, Louis VI recognises Henry I's overlordship of Brittany and Maine.

B **Apr**: 16th, death of Sviatopolk II of Kiev; riots ensue in the city and Vladimir Monomach succeeds by general invitation (–1125).

E A Saxon rebellion against Henry V defeated at the battle of Warmstadt.
Raymond-Berengar of Barcelona and the Pisans begin their conquest of the Balearic Islands from the Saracens (–1115).

1111

G **Economics, Science, Technology and Discovery**

†Al-Ghazzāli (Algazel), the Persian theologian and mystic (Sūfī), inspired Muslim intolerance to science and its study now declines in Islamic lands.

H **Religion and Education**

†Al-Ghazzāli, *Ihyā 'Ulum al-Dīn* (*The Revivification of the Sciences of Religion*).

K **Literature, Philosophy and Scholarship**

*Guibert of Nogent, *Gesta Dei per Francos* (history of the First Crusade, 1095–1101).

1112

H **Religion and Education**

*Foundation of the monastic order of Savigny (–1147).

K **Literature, Philosophy and Scholarship**

'Gallus anonymus' (Martin, the French chaplain of Boleslav III?), the first chronicle of Poland (ending 1112).

†Sigebert of Gembloux, *Chronographia* (world history, 381–1111; –1186).

1113

H **Religion and Education**

St. Bernard enters the convent of Cîteaux.

Peter Abelard opens a school for rhetoric, philosophy and theology in Paris.

Foundation of the second Cistercian house at La Ferté.

L **Births and Deaths**

Aug. 24th, Geoffrey Plantagenet b. (–1151).

— Odo of Tournai d.

1114

A **Jan**: 7th, Henry V marries Matilda, daughter of Henry I of England.

D **Oct**: 1st, Henry V defeated by rebels of the Rhineland at Andernach.
25th, Alfonso of Aragon and Urracca of Castile and Leon are separated at the Council of Palencia.

E The Duke of Bohemia recorded, for the first known time, as hereditary cupbearer to the Holy Roman Empire and thus as one of the Empire's foremost princes.
Death of Coloman, King of Hungary, who had conquered Dalmatia and Herzogovina; succeeded by his son, Stephen II (–1131).

1115

A **Feb**: 11th, Lothar of Saxony, in revolt against Henry V, defeats him at Welfesholz.

C **Jul**: 24th, death of Matilda, Countess of Tuscany; she bequeaths her lands to Henry V, setting aside a previous bequest to the Papacy.

D **Nov**: the revolt of Mainz against Henry V compels him to release its Archbishop, Adalbert.

E The Christian conquest of the Balearic Islands completed; Raymond-Berengar takes possession of Majorca and Iviza.
The Venetians partially suppress a revolt against their rule in Dalmatia.
A-ku-ta, leader of the Jürched (Ju-chen; Tungusic tribes in Manchuria) in rebellion against the Liao, declares himself Emperor, with the Chinese dynastic name of 'Chin' (–1122).

1116

1114

G **Economics, Science, Technology and Discovery**

Earliest record of the great international fairs of Champagne, at Bar-sur-Aube and Troyes.

H **Religion and Education**

Many Paulicians converted to Orthodoxy following Alexius' disputations with them at Philippopolis.

*Foundation of the Congregation of Thiron.

The third Cistercian house founded at Pontigny.

J **Art, Architecture and Music**

Benevento Cathedral rebuilt (–1279).

†Tower of Victory built by Mas'ūd III at Ghaznī.

L **Births and Deaths**

— Gerard of Cremona b. (–1187).

1115

H **Religion and Education**

The fourth and fifth Cistercian houses founded at Clairvaux (with Bernard as its first abbot) and Morimond.

Bernard, Chancellor of Chartres Cathedral, reorganises its famous school.

†Ivo of Chartres, *Panormia Decretum*; *Tripartite Collection* (canon law).

J **Art, Architecture and Music**

*The tympanum of the portal of Moissac priory-church, portraying Christ in majesty, signals the revival of sculpture in western Europe.

K **Literature, Philosophy and Scholarship**

*Guibert of Nogent, *De vita sua* (autobiography).

L **Births and Deaths**

July 7th, Peter the Hermit d.

Dec. 12th, Ivo, Bishop of Chartres, d.

1116

1117

A **Mar:** Paschal flees from Rome as Henry V approaches, and enters.

E Henry I fights in Normandy to suppress a rebellion led by William Clito, son of Robert Curthose, who is supported by Louis VI (–1120).
Ordelafo Falieri, Doge of Venice, killed in battle; succeeded by Domenico Micheli (–1130).
Death of Malik Shah, Sultan of Rūm; succeeded by Maʿsūd I, son of Kilij Arslan (–1156).

1118

A **Jan:** 18th, Paschal II returns to Rome, following Henry V's departure, and dies on the 21st.
24th, John of Gaeta elected as Pope Gelasius II (–1118).
Mar: 8th, Henry has Maurice Bourdin, Archbishop of Braga, elected as Pope Gregory VIII and installs him in Rome (–1121).

B **Apr:** 7th, Gelasius, in Capua, excommunicates Henry.
2nd, death of Baldwin I, King of Jerusalem; succeeded by Baldwin (II), Count of Edessa (–1131).

C **Aug:** Henry returns to Germany from Italy.
15th, death of the Greek Emperor, Alexius I Comnenus; succeeded by his son, John II (–1143).

D **Dec:** 19th, Alfonso of Aragon captures Saragossa from its Muslim ruler.

E Roger II, Count of Sicily, makes his first attempt to conquer Tunis.
Inge II succeeds as King of Sweden (–1129).
Sanjar of Khurāsān becomes supreme Seljuq Sultan on the death of Muhammad I (–1157).

1119

A **Jan:** 29th, Pope Gelasius II dies at Cluny.
Feb: 2nd, Guy, Archbishop of Vienne, elected as Pope Calixtus II (–1124).

B **Jun:** 28th, on 'the Field of Blood', the Frankish army of Antioch is destroyed by Ghāzī, the Danishmend ruler.

C **Aug:** 20th, Henry I defeats Louis VI at Brémule.

D **Nov:** 20th, Calixtus mediates between Henry and Louis at Gisors.

E At Reims, he renews the excommunication of Henry V.

1117

G Economics, Science, Technology and Discovery

Earliest Chinese reference to a compass (for navigation).

J Art, Architecture and Music

Rebuilding of Parma Cathedral after its destruction in an earthquake.

L Births and Deaths

July 15th, Anselm of Laon d.

1118

F Law and Politics

†Alexius had established a form of feudalism in the Greek Empire by a grant of estates conditional upon military service (*pronoia*; –1180).

**Leges Henrici Primi* (collection of English legal customs).

J Art, Architecture and Music

Peterborough abbey-church (*now* cathedral) begun.

K Literature, Philosophy and Scholarship

†Florence of Worcester, *Chronicon ex Chronicis* (compilation for 450 to 1082, then an independent source; continued to 1295).

Povest' Vremennykh Let (*Book of Annals*; final edition of this treatise on the origin and history of Kievan Russia to 1110).

1119

F Law and Politics

*Ballāl Sen, King of East Sengal, is said to have reorganised the Indian caste system.

G Economics, Science, Technology and Discovery

Guido the Geographer, *Geographica* (encyclopedia with two maps, of Italy and the world).

H Religion and Education

Dec. 23rd, Calixtus II confirms the Cistercian rule (*Carta Caritatis*).

The Order of Knights Templars founded in Jerusalem.

J Art, Architecture and Music

Fontevrault abbey-church dedicated.

Autun Cathedral; Gislebert's sculpture (–1130).

1120–1122 Almohad and Chin dynasties founded—End of Investiture Contest

1120

D **Nov**: 25th, William, the son and heir of Henry I, drowned with 'The White Ship'.

E Alfonso of Aragon defeats the Muslims at Cutanda and Daroca.
The Sung ally with the Jürched against the Liao.

1121

B **Apr**: Calixtus captures the anti-pope, Gregory VIII.
Jun: Calixtus returns to Rome.

C **Sep**: 29th, in a diet at Würzburg, Henry V makes peace with his German enemies.

D **Nov**: 27th, Muhammad ibn-Tūmart, leader of the Almohads of the Atlas mountains, hailed as Mahdī by his followers and begins his conquest of the Almoravid territories in north west Africa (–1129).
With the capture of Stettin, Boleslav of Poland completes his conquest of Pomerania.

1122

C **Sep**: 23rd, the Investiture Contest ends with the Concordat at Worms between Calixtus II and Henry V.

E The Greeks exterminate the Pechenegs.
David III, King of Georgia, takes Tiflis, the last surviving Muslim stronghold in Caucasia, and makes it his capital.
The Liao Empire collapses and A-ku-ta establishes the Chin dynasty in its place (–1234).

1120

G **Economics, Science, Technology and Discovery**

*Chui-chung, *Pei-shan Chiu ching* (treatise on the distillation of spirits).

*Lambert of St. Omer, *Liber Floridus* (geographical encyclopedia, with maps).

H **Religion and Education**

Norbert of Xanten founds the Premonstratensian Order of conventual canons.

J **Art, Architecture and Music**

Entrance-hall of monastery of Petersberg, near Erfurt (early German rib vaults).

Abbey-church of Ste. Madeleine, Vézelay, burnt; rebuilt (–1132).

Collapse of choir of Gloucester abbey-church; rebuilt.

Perigueux Cathedral and St. Étienne, Beauvais, begun.

*Southwell Minster begun.

K **Literature, Philosophy and Scholarship**

Ari the Wise, *Islendingabók* (Icelandic saga).

1121

G **Economics, Science, Technology and Discovery**

†Al-Khāzinī, *Kitāb mīzān al-Hikma* (*Book of the Balance of Wisdom*; on mechanics, hydrostatics and physics; argues a theory of gravity towards the centre of the earth).

H **Religion and Education**

Abelard condemned for erroneous theological opinions at the council of Soissons.

†William of Champeaux, a founder of Realist philosophy, the first famous master of the Cathedral School, Paris.

L **Births and Deaths**

— Frederick I b. (–1190).

1122

H **Religion and Education**

Peter Abelard, *Sic et Non?* (logical discussion of certain writings of the Christian Fathers).

Deposition of Pontius, Abbot of Cluny; succeeded by Peter the Venerable (–1156).

J **Art, Architecture and Music**

*Piacenza Cathedral and Murbach Abbey-church.

K **Literature, Philosophy and Scholarship**

†Al-Hariri, *Maqāmāt* (Arabic *belles-lettres*; 50 picaresque stories).

1123

B **Apr**: 18th, Baldwin II of Jerusalem captured and his army destroyed in a surprise attack on his camp near Gargar, on the Euphrates, by Balak of Khanzit.

May: 29th, an invading Egyptian army flees before the Franks at Ibelin; the Venetians destroy their fleet off Ascalon.

Jun: Balak takes Aleppo.

E William Clito leads another Norman rebellion against Henry I (–1125).

John II defeats the Serbians.

1124

B **Apr**: 22nd, death of Alexander I, King of Scotland; succeeded by his brother, David I (–1153).

May: 6th, death of Balak, Emir of Aleppo.

Jun: Baldwin released for ransom.

C **Jul**: 7th, the Egyptians surrender Tyre to Baldwin.

Aug: Henry V attempts to invade France as the ally of Henry I, but retires as the French vassals respond to Louis' summons to military service.

D **Dec**: 13th, death of Pope Calixtus II.

16th, election of Pope Honorius II (–1130).

E John II defeats the Hungarians.

Death of al-Hasan ibn-al-Sabbāh, founder of the Assassins.

(–1125) Lothar, Duke of Saxony, penetrates the lands of the pagan Slavs as far as the lower Oder and destroys their great temple at Retra.

1125

B **May**: Baldwin defeats il-Bursuqi of Mosul at Azaz.

23rd, death of Henry V, the last Salian Emperor, without issue.

C **Aug**: 30th, Lothar of Supplinburg, Duke of Saxony, elected as King of the Romans (*i.e.* Germany; –1137).

E Death of Vladislav I, Duke of Bohemia; succeeded by his brother, Soběslav (–1040).

Death of Vladimir II, Prince of Kiev; succeeded by his son, Mstislav I (–1132).

Death of David III, who had re-established the Kingdom of Georgia in Caucasia and Armenia, and ended its theoretical subjection to Constantinople; succeeded by his son, Demetrius I (–1155).

The Jürched take Peking and destroy the Liao, the ruling dynasty of the Khitan; they next advance against their former ally, the Emperor Hui Tsung, who abdicates.

1123

G **Economics, Science, Technology and Discovery**

†'Umar al-Khayyām, *Algebra*.

†Marbode, Bishop of Rennes, *Liber lapidum* (medical lapidary in hexameters).

H **Religion and Education**

Mar. 18th–Apr. 5th, Calixtus II holds the first general council of the Church in west Europe (the First Lateran Council); its condemns simony and the marriage of priests. He also sends a legate to complete the organisation of the Polish Church; three new bishoprics founded, including one for Pomerania.

The first Cistercian house in Germany founded at Kamp, near Krefeld.

J **Art, Architecture and Music**

Foundation of the priory and hospital of St. Bartholomew, Smithfield, London.

K **Literature, Philosophy and Scholarship**

†'Umar al-Khayyām, *Rubaiyat* (Persian quatrains).

1124

H **Religion and Education**

Otto, Bishop of Bamberg, begins his mission to convert western Pomerania.

J **Art, Architecture and Music**

Gardar Cathedral, Greenland, founded.

L **Births and Deaths**

— St. Stephen of Muret d. (76).

1125

G **Economics, Science, Technology and Discovery**

*Hsü Ching, Description of Korea (printed 1167).

(–1133) Tide-mills near mouth of the Adour.

J **Art, Architecture and Music**

The nave of Cluny abbey-church collapses; rebuilt with flying buttresses (–1130).

Mosque of al-Aqmar, Cairo.

K **Literature, Philosophy and Scholarship**

†Cosmas of Prague, *Chronica Bohemorum* (Chronicle of Bohemia).

*Benedeiz, *Navigatio sancti Brandani* (*Voyage of St. Brandon*).

†Vladimir Monomach, 'Testament' (brief autobiography in Russian).

*Philip of Thaon, *Li bestiaire* (bestiary, in French verse).

†*Ekkehard of Aura, *Chronicon universale*.

(–1149) Raymond, Archbishop of Toledo, organises the translation into Latin of Arabic texts of Aristotle's works.

1126

A **Feb**: Lothar invades Bohemia on behalf of Otto of Kolmutz, who claims the Duchy; he is defeated at Kulm by Soběslav, whom he then recognises as Duke.

Mar: 8th or 10th, death of Urracca, Queen of Castile and Leon; Alfonso of Aragon thus loses his title to rule there as she is succeeded by their son, Alfonso (II of Castile and VII of Leon; –1157).

E Alfonso of Aragon defeats the Muslims at Arinsol, near Lucena.

The Jürched take Kaifeng, the Sung capital; they expand to the east and west, Korea and Hsi Hsia becoming vassals, and south to the River Huai.

1127

A **Mar**: 2nd, Charles the Good, Count of Flanders, murdered.

23rd, William Clito elected as his successor at the instance of Louis VI (–1128).

C **Jul**: 20th, death of William I, Duke of Apulia, without issue; his cousin, Roger II of Sicily, takes possession of the Duchy.

D **Dec**: 18th, Lothar's enemies in Germany elect Conrad of Hohenstaufen as King.

E Louis destroys the monopoly which the Garlande family had held over the French offices of state.

Stephen II of Hungary invades Greek territory and takes Belgrade and Sofia.

'Imad ad-Dīn Zangī appointed atabeg (governor) of Mosul in succession to il-Bursuqi; he becomes the Muslim champion against the Franks (–1146) and founds the Zangid dynasty (–1262).

Kao Tsung, son of Hui Tsung, establishes the southern Sung dynasty, with his capital in Hangchow (–1279).

1128

B **Jun**: 17th, Henry I's daughter, Matilda, widow of Henry V, marries Geoffrey Plantagenet of Anjou; she is recognised in England as her father's heir.

29th, Conrad crowned as King of Italy (–1130).

C **Jul**: 27th, William Clito killed; Louis then recognises Thierry of Alsace whom the Flemings, in revolt, had elected as their Count (–1168).

Aug: 22nd, Honorius II invests Roger of Sicily as Duke of Apulia.

E Afonso Henriques, Count of Portugal, gains control of his government by defeating the forces of his mother, Teresa, at St. Mamede.

1126

G **Economics, Science, Technology and Discovery**

*Adelard of Bath translates al-Khwarizmī, *Astronomical Tables* (–850).

Earliest European notice of an artesian well (in *Artois*).

Gunpowder first recorded in use at the siege of Kaifeng by the Jürched.

H **Religion and Education**

Bernard of Clairvaux, *On the Love of God.*

L **Births and Deaths**

— Averroes b. (–1198).

1127

G **Economics, Science, Technology and Discovery**

Grant of the oldest extant charter to a Flemish city, *viz.* St. Omer. (It is probable that some other Flemish towns already had communes with powers of jurisdiction.)

Stephen of Pisa translates Haly Abbas, *Liber Regius* (–994).

H **Religion and Education**

The conversion of the Wends resumed.

K **Literature, Philosophy and Scholarship**

*Fulcher of Chartres, *Historia Hierosolymitana* (chronicle of First Crusade and Kingdom of Jerusalem extending to 1127).

† ?Ava, didactic and religious poems; she was the first woman poet in Old High German literature.

1128

G **Economics, Science, Technology and Discovery**

James of Venice translates Aristotle, *Organon.*

H **Religion and Education**

The first Cistercian house in England founded at Waverley.

Al-Shahrastānī, *Kitāb al-Milal w-al-Nihal* (*Book of Religions and Sects*; comprehensive history of religions).

1129

B **May**: Fulk V, Count of Anjou, joins Baldwin of Jerusalem and marries his daughter, Melisande; Fulk's son, Geoffrey, succeeds as Count of Anjou (–1151).

D **Nov**: Baldwin takes possession of the Assassins' fortress of Banyas, by arrangement, but his attempt against Damascus is repulsed.
Dec: 17th, death of Muhammad, the Almohad Mahdī; succeeded by 'Abd-al-Mu'min (–1163).

E Sverker I elected King of Sweden (–1150).

1130

A **Feb**: Bohemond II of Antioch and his army, *en route* to attack the Armenians, massacred by the Danishmends on the Jihan.
13th, death of Pope Honorius II; on the same day, both Gregory Papareschi (as Innocent II; –1143) and Peter Pierleoni (as Anacletus II; –1138) elected as Pope; Innocent is forced to leave Rome.
Mar: 26th, death of Sigurd I, King of Norway; succeeded by his son, Magnus IV the Blind and (also) Harold IV Gille (–1135).

C **Sep**: 27th, Roger undertakes to recognise Anacletus as Pope in return for his creation as King of Sicily and Apulia.

D **Dec**: 25th, coronation of Roger II as King of Sicily.

E Alfonso of Aragon takes Bordeaux.
Death of Domenico Micheli, Doge of Venice; succeeded by Pietro Polano (–1148).
*Yeh-lü Ta-shih, a surviving member of the Liao, founds the Kara-Khitai (or Western Liao) Empire in East Turkestan (–1211).

1131

A **Mar**: 22nd, Lothar meets Innocent at Liège and recognises him as Pope.

C **Aug**: 21st, death of Baldwin II, King of Jerusalem; succeeded by Fulk of Anjou (–1143).
Sep: 8th, the English barons confirm their allegiance to Matilda as Henry's heir.

D **Oct**: 25th, Louis, son of Louis VI, crowned as King of France by Innocent, at Reims.

E Niels of Denmark deposed and succeeded by Eric II (–1137); civil war ensues.
Stephen II, King of Hungary, abdicates (and dies); succeeded by his cousin, Béla II (–1141).
Dai Viet repulses an invasion by Suryavarman II of Cambodia.

1129

K **Literature, Philosophy and Scholarship**

*Simeon of Durham, *Historia Regum* (English history to 1129; –1154).

L **Births and Deaths**

— Henry the Lion b. (–1195).

1130

F **Law and Politics**

Pipe roll of the English Exchequer for 1129–30 (the earliest surviving example of an administrative record kept annually).

G **Economics, Science, Technology and Discovery**

*Earliest European reference to breast-strap harness for horses (allowing drawing of heavier loads, ploughs, etc.).

* ?Benevenutus Grassus, *Practica oculorum* (most popular European treatise on eye diseases).

†Adelard of Bath, *Quaestiones Naturales* (dialogue discussing scientific questions); *De opera astrolapsus* (treatise on the astrolabe).

†Baudry de Bourgueil, *Itinerarium* (account of travels in northern France and England).

H **Religion and Education**

Oct. 25th, Innocent II dedicates Cluny abbey-church.

J **Art, Architecture and Music**

*Conques abbey-church completed.

K **Literature, Philosophy and Scholarship**

Chanson des Chétifs (romance legend of the First Crusade).

†Eadmer, *Historia Novorum* (English history) and *Vita sancti Anselmi* (*Life of St. Anselm*, 1033–1109).

*The *Ancren Rewle* (written, in Middle English, for the guidance of anchoresses).

1131

H **Religion and Education**

St. Gilbert founds the Order of Sempringham.

J **Art, Architecture and Music**

Cefalù Cathedral begun.

Seo de Urgel Cathedral (–1175).

Tintern Abbey founded.

K **Literature, Philosophy and Scholarship**

ʿAin al-Qudāt al-Hamadhānī, *Apologia* (written when this great Sūfī mystic philosopher was in prison awaiting execution).

1132

C **Summer**: because of a revolt in his kingdom, Roger withdraws from Rome, so allowing Innocent's agents to gain control, expelling Anacletus.
Sep: Lothar begins an expedition into Italy to restore Innocent.

E Death of Mstislav of Kiev; succeeded by his brother, Jaropolk II (–1139).

1133

B **Jun**: 4th, Lothar III crowned as Holy Roman Emperor (–1137), by Innocent II, in Rome.
4th, Innocent (ineffectively) grants metropolitan authority in Poland and Pomerania to Archbishop Norbert of Magdeburg.

C **Aug**: Lothar returns to Germany.

E The rebels defeat Roger on the Sabbato but he subsequently restores order in Apulia.
Innocent partitions Corsica between Genoa and Pisa.

1134

B **Jun**: 4th, Niels defeated by Eric, his rival for the Danish crown.

C **Jul**: 17th, Alfonso of Aragon defeated by the Muslims at Fraga.
Sep: 7th, death of Alfonso I of Aragon and Navarre; succeeded in Aragon by his brother, Ramiro II (–1137), while Navarre recovers its independence under Garcia IV Ramirez (–1150), and Alfonso of Castile takes possession of Saragossa.

E Lothar grants the Margravate of Brandenburg to Albert the Bear.

1132

J **Art, Architecture and Music**
Palatine Chapel, Palermo (–1143).

1133

H **Religion and Education**
*Robert Pullus teaches at Oxford.

J **Art, Architecture and Music**
Foundation of St. Bartholomew's Fair, Smithfield, London; for over 700 years it was a place to hear music and see dancing and plays.

L **Births and Deaths**
Feb. 10th, Robert Curthose d. (82).
Mar. Henry II b. (–1189).
Mar. 28th, St. Stephen Harding, Abbot of Cîteaux, d.

1134

J **Art, Architecture and Music**
North tower of Chartres Cathedral begun (the first Gothic tower).
*Upsala Cathedral begun.

L **Births and Deaths**
Jun. 6th, St. Norbert of Xanten, Archbishop of Magdeburg, d.

1135

A **Jan:** Harold IV of Norway defeats and imprisons his co-king, Magnus IV.
Mar: in a diet at Bamberg, Conrad and Frederick Hohenstaufen of Swabia make their final submission to Lothar.

B **May:** 26th, Alfonso of Castile and Leon acclaimed as Emperor of Spain.
Jun: 25th, Niels of Denmark murdered.

C **Aug:** Lothar makes peace between Poland and Bohemia, receiving homage from Boleslav of Poland; he also settles the dispute over the succession to the Hungarian crown.

D **Dec:** 1st, death of Henry I, King of England.
14th, Harold IV of Norway murdered by his brother, Sigurd; succeeded by his sons, Sigurd II and Inge I (–1161).
26th, Stephen of Blois, nephew of William I, crowned as King of England (–1154).

1136

A **Jan:** Gruffyd ap Cynan leads a rising in South Wales (–1137).
Feb: Stephen cedes Cumberland to David of Scotland, who in return recognises Stephen as King of England.

B **May:** Louis VI invests Stephen as Duke of Normandy.

C **Aug:** 15th, when assembling his army for his Italian expedition, Lothar (probably now) invests Henry of Bavaria as Duke of Saxony, making him the most powerful prince in Germany (–1138).

E (–1137) Lothar overruns Apulia and Calabria, meeting little opposition because the inhabitants simultaneously revolt against Roger; before leaving, Lothar and Innocent invest Rainulf of Alife as Duke of Apulia (–1139).

1135

G **Economics, Science, Technology and Discovery**

†Al-Jurjānī, *Dhakhīra al-Khwārizmshāhī*, (*The Treasure of the King of Khwārizm*; immense medical encyclopedia, in Persian).

J **Art, Architecture and Music**

Ulu Cami (cathedral mosque), Kayseri (–1205).

Verdun Cathedral crypt.

Venosa Cathedral begun.

*Fountains Abbey (–1150).

†Hui Tsung, former Emperor of China, a painter and great patron of the arts; the catalogue of his collection shows he possessed 6,192 paintings.

1136

F **Law and Politics**

**Constitutio Domus Regis* (outlines the establishment of King Stephen's household).

G **Science, Technology and Discovery**

Discovery of silver-bearing ore at Freiberg, Saxony; a 'silver-rush' follows, and Freiberg becomes a centre for metallurgy.

*Al-Māzinī of Granada, *Tuhfat al-Albāb* (describes his visit to the Volga area of Russia in 1136; –1162).

1137

C **Jul**: 4th, by the treaty of Tuy, Afonso Henriques of Portugal recognises the suzerainty of Alfonso, Emperor of Spain.

22nd, Louis (VII) marries Eleanor of Aquitaine.

Aug: Fulk of Jerusalem surrenders the fortress of Montferrand to Zangī of Mosul, after its siege, but is allowed to go free.

1st, death of Louis VI the Fat, King of France; succeeded by his son, Louis VII (–1180).

8th, Louis crowned as Duke of Aquitaine.

29th, John II Comnenus, having conquered Lesser Armenia (Cilicia), begins to bombard Antioch, but withdraws when its Prince, Raymond of Poitiers, pays homage.

Sep: 18th, Eric II of Denmark murdered; succeeded by Eric III, grandson of Eric I (–1147).

D **Dec**: 4th, death of the Holy Roman Emperor, Lothar III.

E Death of Gruffyd ap Cynan, King of Gwynedd; succeeded by his son, Owain the Great (–1170).

Stephen successfully campaigns in Normandy against Geoffrey of Anjou.

Ramiro II the Monk, King of Aragon, abdicates; succeeded by his daughter, Petronilla (–1164), who marries Raymond-Berengar IV, Count of Barcelona.

1138

A **Jan**: 25th, death of the anti-pope, Anacletus II; on Roger's instigation, Victor IV elected to succeed him.

Mar: 3rd, Conrad of Hohenstaufen elected as King of the Romans. He is opposed by Henry the Proud.

B **Apr**: 20th, attempt by John Comnenus to take Aleppo repulsed.

May: Robert, Earl of Gloucester, begins a civil war in England by declaring himself against Stephen.

21st, John raises his siege at Shaizar when its emir promises to pay tribute; he then enters Antioch but leaves for Cilicia on the outbreak of anti-Greek riots.

29th, the anti-pope, Victor IV, resigns.

Jun: Zangī takes Homs from the ruler of Damascus.

C **Jul**: Conrad deprives Henry of Saxony but fails to expel him (–1139).

Aug: 22nd, in the Battle of the Standard, near Northallerton, English forces defeat David of Scotland; Stephen buys peace by ceding Northumberland to David.

E Boleslav III of Poland defeated while invading Russia, and dies; thus ends a period of Polish expansion. His lands partitioned by his sons; the eldest, Vladislav II, becomes the first Grand Prince of Poland, with Cracow as his capital; he possesses Silesia and Pomerania and is hereditary suzerain in all Polish lands. Civil war follows (–1146).

1137

G **Economics, Science, Technology and Discovery**
Oldest extant Chinese maps, engraved on a stone slab.

J **Art, Architecture and Music**
*West front of St. Denis', Paris (–1140).
Kirkwall Cathedral begun.

K **Literature, Philosophy and Scholarship**
*Geoffrey of Monmouth, *Historia Regum Britanniae* (*History of the Kings of Britain*—the apocryphal 'British history' with the story of Arthur as a heroic king-figure, introducing Merlin & Co.; it is the source of the stories about King Lear, Cymbeline, Gorboduc, etc.).

1138

G **Economics, Science, Technology and Discovery**
†Al-Kharaqī, *Muntāhā al-Idrāk fī taqsīm al-Aflāk* (*The Highest Understanding on the Division of Spheres*).

K **Literature, Philosophy and Scholarship**
†Abu-Bakr ibn-Bājjah (Avempace), *Tadbir al-Mutawahhid* (*The Regime of a Solitary*; philosophical treatise).
†Nicephorus Bryennius, Greek historian (–1148).

L **Births and Deaths**
— Saladin b. (–1193).

1139

B **Apr**: Innocent excommunicates Roger of Sicily.
30th, death of Rainulf of Alife, Duke of Apulia.
Jun: Stephen affronts English churchmen by his arrest of the Bishops of Salisbury and Lincoln.

C **Jul**: 22nd, Innocent defeated and captured by Roger on the Garigliano; by the treaty of Mignano (25 July), he gains his liberty by recognising Roger as King.
25th, Afonso Henriques defeats the Muslims at Ourique and hailed as King of Portugal by his troops (–1185).
Sep: 30th, Matilda comes to England to lead her partisans against Stephen.

D **Oct**: 20th, death of Henry the Proud, former Duke of Bavaria and Saxony; his son, Henry the Lion, claims to succeed but Conrad had granted Bavaria to Leopold of Austria and Saxony to Albert the Bear of Brandenburg.

E Death of Jaropolk II of Kiev; Vsévolod II seizes the city (–1146). The surviving political unity of the Russian federation now finally collapses with the rivalry of princes for leadership and the provincial separatism of their subjects.

1140

B **Apr**: the Saxons, who had rejected Albert the Bear, refuse to surrender to Conrad.

D **Dec**: Conrad defeats Welf (VI), Henry's uncle, who was leading opposition to the grant of Bavaria to Leopold; in the battle, at Weinsberg, there seemingly originate the appellations of 'Welf' (Guelf) and 'Weibling' (Ghibelline).

E Death of Soběslav, Duke of Bohemia; Vladislav II, son of Vladislav I, elected as his successor (–1173).

1139

H **Religion and Education**

Apr. 20th, Arnold of Brescia condemned by the Second Lateran Council, held by Innocent II; the Pope also makes the Augustinian rule compulsory for conventual canons.

(–1141) Gratian of Bologna, *Concordia discordantium canonum* (better known as the *Decretum*; it founded the codification of canon law).

J **Art, Architecture and Music**

Fontenay abbey-church (–1147).

K **Literature, Philosophy and Scholarship**

†Moses ben Ezra, *Kitāb al Muhādarah* (critical work in Arabic on Spanish-Hebrew poetry); *Tarshīsh* (Hebrew poems).

Ibn-Bashkuwāl, *Kitāb al-Sila fi Akhbar a'immat al-Andalūs* (biographies of the learned men of Muslim Spain).

*Peter the Deacon, continuation of Leo of Ostia's *Chronica* of Montecassino to 1139 (–1094).

1140

G **Economics, Science, Technology and Discovery**

The St. Gothard Pass now open as a commercial route; a bridge had been made over the Schollenen gorges.

*Raymond of Marseilles, *Liber cursuum planetarum* (astronomical treatise and tables).

H **Religion and Education**

Peter Abelard condemned at the council of Sens at the instance of St. Bernard.

The first Polish Cistercian and Premonstratensian houses founded.

J **Art, Architecture and Music**

The new west front of St. Denis', Paris, now completed with a façade, which in design and sculpture marks the beginning of Gothic architecture; Abbot Suger now begins a new east end, with 'Gothic' vaulting and stained glass windows (also an innovation).

Pontigny abbey-church (–1170).

*Sens Cathedral begun.

*S. Ambrogio, Milan, a Romanesque church, given a ribbed vault.

†Kakuyū ('Toba Sōjō'), Japanese painter.

K **Literature, Philosophy and Scholarship**

**Cantore di mio Cid* (*Poema del Cid Campeador: The Song of the Cid*; Spanish epic poem about the deeds of Rodrigo *or* Ruy Diaz de Vivar, d. 1099).

*Bernard de Morlaix, *De Contemptu Mundi* (verse satire).

*Judah ha-Levi, *Zion ha-lo tish'ali* (*Ode to Zion*; Hebrew poem); *Kitāb al-Khazarī* (dialogue in Arabic defending revealed religion from philosophy).

1141

A **Feb**: 2nd, Robert of Gloucester defeats and captures Stephen at Lincoln.
16th, death of Béla II, King of Hungary; succeeded by Géza II (–1161).
Mar: 3rd, Matilda proclaimed as Queen of England in Winchester.

C **Sep**: 9th, Sanjar, the Seljuq Sultan, defeated on the Qatwān Steppe, at Samarqand, by the Kara-Khitai, who are establishing an empire stretching from China to the Oxus (–1130).

D **Nov**: 1st, Stephen released in exchange for Robert of Gloucester, whom his partisans had captured.
Dec: death of the Danishmend Malik ('King'), Muhammad ibn Ghāzī; his territories in Anatolia disintegrate.

E Death of Vishnu-Vardhana, who had founded a state in Mysore with its capital at Halebīd; he had adopted his name on his conversion to Vishnuism from Jainism.
After murdering the general, Yo Fei, the landowners of southern China make peace with the Jürched by the payment of tribute.

1142

B **May**: the civil war in Germany terminated in a diet at Frankfurt; Conrad grants Saxony to Henry the Lion (–1180) and Bavaria to Henry Jasomirgott, brother of Leopold of Austria (now dead; –1156).

C **Sep**: 25th, John Comnenus reaches Baghras, after campaigning against the Turks in Anatolia, and sends Raymond orders to surrender Antioch to him; on Ramond's refusal, John withdraws into Cilicia.

E France under an interdict imposed by Innocent because Louis VII refuses to admit the Pope's candidate to the Archbishopric of Bourges (–1143).

1143

B **Apr**: 8th, death of the Greek Emperor, John II Comnenus, while on his way to attack Antioch; succeeded by his son, Manuel I (–1180). The Armenians (of Cilicia), led by Theodore II, begin a war to recover their independence.

C A republic proclaimed by Romans in rebellion against Innocent.
Sep: 24th, death of Pope Innocent II.
26th, election of Pope Celestine II (–1144).

D **Nov**: 10th, death of Fulk, King of Jerusalem; his widow, Melisande, assumes the government, with their young son, Baldwin III, as her colleague (–1163).

E Alfonso, Emperor of Spain, recognises Afonso I as King of Portugal; Afonso does homage to Innocent's legate, thus making Portugal a papal fief.
Vladislav of Bohemia, aided by Conrad, defeats a rebellion.

1141

H **Religion and Education**

†Hugh of St. Victor, *De sacramentis Christiane Fidei*; *Didascalicon de studio legendi* (encyclopedia of knowledge); *De arca Noë* (treatise on Noah's ark).

K **Literature, Philosophy and Scholarship**

*Orderic Vitalis, *Historia Ecclesiastica* (chronicle of England and Normandy extending to 1141, with details of social and monastic life).

*Peter of Toledo translates *Risalah* (*The Apology of Al-Kindi*; an account of Islam, in Arabic by an oriental Christian).

1142

J **Art, Architecture and Music**

The first Irish Cistercian house founded at Mellifont.

K **Literature, Philosophy and Scholarship**

†Peter Abelard, *Letters* (to Héloise; including the celebrated autobiographical *Historia Calamitatum Mearum*).

†*William of Malmesbury, *Historia Regum Anglorum* and *Historia Novella* (history of England to 1142); *Gesta Pontificum Anglorum* (the English Church to 1120).

L **Births and Deaths**

Apr. 21st, Peter Abelard d. (63).

1143

F **Law and Politics**

Venice begins the formation of its communal institutions with the establishment of the *Consilium sapientium*.

G **Science, Technology and Discovery**

Henry the Lion founds Lübeck as an outpost against the Slavs. Count Adolf of Holstein resumes colonisation by Germans.

Reorganisation of the state hospitals in China.

† ?Hermann the Dalmatian, Latin translations of Arabic works on astronomy, etc.

H **Religion and Education**

A papal legate begins to enforce clerical celibacy in Bohemia.

*Robert of Chester and Hermann the Dalmatian, first Latin translation of the Koran.

J **Art, Architecture and Music**

*Mosaics in the apse of the Palatine Chapel, Palermo.

1144

A **Mar**: 8th, death of Pope Celestine II.
12th, election of Pope Lucius II (–1145).

B **Apr**: 23rd, the conquest of Normandy by Geoffrey of Anjou completed with the surrender of Rouen.

D **Oct**: Lucius makes a truce with Roger of Sicily.
Dec: 25th, Zangī takes Edessa, massacring the Franks.

E Alfonso of Castile (temporarily) takes Cordova.

1145

A **Feb**: 15th, death of Pope Lucius II; Bernard of Pisa was elected as Pope Eugenius III (–1153).

C **Jul**: ‘Abd-al-Mu'min takes Oran.

E Suryavarman II of Cambodia conquers Champa (–1149).

1146

A **Mar**: 1st, Eugenius III proclaims the Second Crusade on God's behalf.

C **Sep**: 14th, Zangī of Mosul murdered; one son, Sayf-ad-Dīn Ghazī, succeeds in Mosul, while a second, Nūr-ad-Din Mahmūd, takes control of Aleppo (–1174).

E Roger of Sicily takes Tripoli, in north Africa.
Vladislav II, attempting to reunite Poland, defeated by his brothers Boleslav and Miecislas, and flees to Germany; Boleslav IV replaces him as Grand Prince (–1173).
Death of Vsévolod II of Kiev; succeeded by Isiaslav II (–1155).

1144

G **Economics, Science, Technology and Discovery**

Robert of Chester translates the Arabic *Book of the Composition of Alchemy*, attributed to 'Jabir' (–810; the first translation of a writing on chemistry).

H **Religion and Education**

Murder of the boy (St.) William of Norwich, supposedly by Jews.

K **Literature, Philosophy and Scholarship**

†Matthew of Urfah (Edessa), chronicle of Armenia (953–1136).

1145

G **Economics, Science, Technology and Discovery**

Robert of Chester, first Latin translation of al-Khwārizmī's *Algebra* (–850).

*First known autopsy in China.

†*Jābir ibn-Aflah, *Kitāb al-Hay'ah* (*Book of Astronomy*; with a chapter on trigonometry).

J **Art, Architecture and Music**

The Portail Royal, Chartres Cathedral, begun.

*The Great Mosque, Mosul (–1191).

*'The Friday Mosque', Isfahan.

*Mosaics in the apse of Sta. Maria in Trastavere, Rome.

K **Literature, Philosophy and Scholarship**

Suger, *Liber de rebus in administratione sua gestis* (account of his administration of the Abbey of St. Denis, Paris).

Kim Pu-sik, *Samguk sagi* (*History of the Three Kingdoms*, of Korea; compiled in Chinese).

*Joannes Zonaras, *Historical Epitome* (from the Creation to 1118).

1146

J **Art, Architecture and Music**

Lund Cathedral consecrated.

Maulbronn abbey-church (–1178).

Mausoleum of Halifet Gazi (a Danishmend), Amasya.

K **Literature, Philosophy and Scholarship**

*Otto, Bishop of Freising, *Chronica sive Historia de duabus civitatibus* (philosophical history of the spiritual and material worlds, to 1146; gives the first reference to 'Prester John').

1147

B **Apr**: 'Abd-al-Mu'min completes his conquest of the Almoravid kingdom of Morocco with the capture of Marrakesh; he then crosses into Spain, where the Almoravid kingdom had disintegrated into several kingdoms established in Cordova, Valencia, Murcia, etc.

May: Conrad and the German crusaders depart from Regensburg.

Jun: 8th, Louis VII and the French crusaders set off from Saint Denis.

26th, the Wends sack Lübeck.

29th, an assembly of Saxon nobles plans a crusade against the Wends.

C **Jul**: 31st, the Wends defeat the Danes.

Sep: the Saxons abandon their crusade.

D **Oct**: 25th, Conrad's crusading army destroyed by the Turks on the Bathys, near Dorylaeum.

25th, English and Flemish crusaders, interrupting their voyage, assist in the capture of Lisbon by Afonso of Portugal.

31st, death of Robert, Earl of Gloucester, Matilda's chief adherent.

Nov: Conrad, retiring, meets Louis in Nicaea; they advance to Ephesus, where Conrad falls ill and returns to Constantinople.

3rd, Nūr-ad-Dīn defeats Joscelin II, Count of Edessa, who was retiring after an attempt to recover Edessa; the city is then depopulated by Nūr-ad-Dīn.

E Eric III the Lamb, King of Denmark, abdicates, and dies; the succession is disputed by Svein III (–1157) and Cnut.

Alfonso of Castile besieges Almeria.

Roger of Sicily occupies Corfù.

The Knights of Calatrava (origin of the Knights of Alcántara) founded in Castile.

1148

A (early): Matilda leaves England, having abandoned hope of defeating Stephen.

Jan: 1st, Louis and his crusaders force their way through the Turks to cross the bridge to Antioch.

B **Apr**: 24th, the crusaders (including Conrad and Louis) confer at Acre and decide to attack Damascus.

C **Jul**: 24th, the crusaders camp outside Damascus.

28th, they retreat: so ends the Second Crusade.

Sep: 8th, Conrad leaves Palestine for Constantinople, where he and Manuel make an alliance against Roger of Sicily.

D **Nov**: Raymond of Antioch defeats Nūr-ad-Dīn at Famiya.

E Geoffrey of Anjou assumes the title of Duke of Normandy.

Raymond-Berengar takes Tortosa.

Death of Pietro Polano, Doge of Venice; succeeded by Domenico Morosini (–1156).

With Venetian assistance, the Greeks expel Roger from Corfù.

1147

G **Economics, Science, Technology and Discovery**

Woodcuts first used to illustrate manuscripts at Engelberg.

Roger II abducts silk-weavers from Thebes and Corinth to form a colony at Palermo.

H **Religion and Education**

The Savigniac Order united to the Cistercians.

St. Bernard preaches against heretics in Languedoc.

1148

H **Religion and Education**

Abortive trial of Gilbert de la Porrée before Eugenius III at Reims.

*St. Bernard, *De Consideratione.*

The Council of Reims condemns protectors of heresy in Gascony and Provence.

J **Art, Architecture and Music**

Mosaics in the apse of Cefalù Cathedral.

K **Literature, Philosophy and Scholarship**

†*Landnámabók* (Icelandic chronicle; family saga based on the work of Ari).

†Kalhana, *Rājatarangini* (*Stream of Kings*; verse history of all the Kings of Kashmir; one of the few extant Hindu chronicles).

†Anna Comnena, *Alexiad* (a rhetorical life of her father, Alexius I, and chronicle of his reign, 1081–1118, begun by her husband, Nicephorus Bryennius).

L **Births and Deaths**

Nov. 2nd, St. Malachy, Archbishop of Armagh, d.

— Ari the Wise d. (81).

1149

B Jun: 29th, Raymond of Antioch defeated and killed by Nūr-ad-Dīn.

C Jul: Louis lands in Calabria on his return from Palestine; he meets Roger, who persuades him to take part in an attack on Constantinople: this scheme is abortive.

D Nov: Henry the Lion resumes his claim to the Duchy of Bavaria.

E 'Abd-al-Mu'min completes his conquest of the Muslim kingdoms in Spain.
Jaya Harivarman of Champa recaptures Vijaya, his capital, from Suryavarman of Cambodia.

1150

A Feb: King Henry, son of Conrad, defeats a rebellion by Welf VI of Swabia which Roger of Sicily had incited.

B Apr: Nūr-ad-Dīn captures, blinds and imprisons Joscelin of Edessa.

D Nov: 21st, death of Garcia IV Ramirez of Navarre; succeeded by his son, Sancho VI (–1194).

E Henry (II) invested as Duke of Normandy (–1189).
Conrad creates Albert the Bear Elector of Brandenburg (–1170).
*Eric succeeds Sverker as King of Sweden (–1160).

1149

F **Law and Politics**

**Lo Codi* (summary of Roman law; the earliest in vernacular, *viz.* Provençal).

G **Economics, Science, Technology and Discovery**

Robert of Chester, astronomical tables (for London, 1149–50; based on al-Battānī; –877).

H **Religion and Education**

Vacarius possibly teaches civil law at Oxford and elsewhere in England.

J **Art, Architecture and Music**

July 15th, Church of the Holy Sepulchre, Jerusalem, dedicated.

K **Literature, Philosophy and Scholarship**

Hung Tsun, *Ch'üan-chih* (earliest extant work on history of Chinese coinage, with illustrations).

1150

G **Economics, Science, Technology and Discovery**

*Bhāskara, *Siddhāntaśiromani* (Hindu treatise on mathematics and astronomy).

H **Religion and Education**

Paucapalea, *Summa* (canon law).

*Peter the Lombard, *Sententiarum libri IV* (popular theological text-book).

J **Art, Architecture and Music**

*Cathedrals of Angers, Aversa, Le Mans, Lisbon, Noyon (choir, –1205), Pécs and Stavanger, and second abbey-church of Pontigny, begun.

*Hermitage of S. Baudelio, Berlanga, near Burgos (the last Mozarabic church) completed.

†Temple of Angkor Vat, the mausoleum of King Suryavarman II.

K **Literature, Philosophy and Scholarship**

**Le Pèlerinage de Charlemagne à Jérusalem* (*chanson de geste*; authorship doubtful; sometimes called *The Voyage of Charlemagne*, and notable for its comedy as well as the heroic element).

**The Black Book of Carmarthen* (twelfth-century collection of Welsh poetry in ms., containing a reference to King Arthur).

*Jaufre Rudel de Blaya, Provençal songs and love-poems.

**Le Jeu d'Adam* (the most ancient '*jeu*'—religious drama—in French literature; it is an Anglo-Norman dramatic piece on the Fall, Cain and Abel, in rhyming couplets).

**König Rother* (a poem of about 5,000 lines; 'Bavarian'—*Saintsbury*).

Pfaffe Konrad, *Ruolandesliet* (oldest German imitation of a French form—*chanson de geste*—on *The Song of Roland*; –1095).

**Fons vitae* (Latin translation of Avicebron's *Fountain of Life*; –1058).

*Michael Glycas, a world chronicle (from the Creation to 1118).

1151

C **Aug**: Henry (II), by a treaty made in Paris, cedes the Norman Vexin to Louis VII.
Sep: 7th, death of Geoffrey Plantagenet, Count of Anjou and Maine; succeeded by his son, Henry (II).

E Manuel makes his first attack on Hungary in a war which lasts, intermittently, until 1167.
Baldwin of Jerusalem frustrates an attempt by Nūr-ad-Dīn to take Damascus, with which, although it is Muslim, Baldwin is allied.
'Alā'-ad-Dīn Husayn, Sultan of Ghūr (Afghanistan), earns his title 'the World-Burner' by his destruction of Ghaznī.

1152

A **Feb**: 15th, death of Conrad III, King of the Romans.
Mar: 4th, Frederick I Barbarossa of Hohenstaufen, his nephew, elected King of the Romans (–1190).
21st, marriage of Louis VII and Eleanor of Aquitaine dissolved.

B **May**: 16th, Henry (II) marries Eleanor of Aquitaine.
18th, in a diet at Merseburg, Frederick adjudges Svein III to be King of Denmark.

E Death of Conrad, Duke of Zähringen (in Swabia).
Frederick creates Welf of Swabia Marquess of Tuscany and Duke of Spoleto.
Al-Mu'min conquers Algeria.

1153

A **Jan**: Henry (II) lands in England and begins his campaign of conquest.
Mar: 23rd, Eugenius and Frederick, at Constance, seal an alliance.

B **May**: 24th, death of David I, King of Scotland, who had established an administration on Anglo-Norman lines and created feudal tenures; succeeded by his grandson, Malcolm IV (–1165).

C **Jul**: 8th, death of Pope Eugenius III.
12th, Anastasius IV elected Pope (–1154).
Aug: 19th, the Egyptian garrison of Ascalon surrenders to Baldwin of Jerusalem.

D **Nov**: 7th, in the treaty of Wallingford, Henry recognises Stephen as King while Stephen accepts Henry as his heir.

E Frederick holds court at Besançon and receives the homage of the Burgundians.
Roger of Sicily takes Bona, in north Africa; his empire there now extends from Tripoli to Tunis.
The Jürched (Chin Emperors) move their capital from Manchuria to Peking.

1151

J **Art, Architecture and Music**

*Mosaics in the Martorana (S. Maria dell'Amiraglio), Palermo.

K **Literature, Philosophy and Scholarship**

*Li Ch'ing-chao, Chinese poems.

L **Births and Deaths**

Jan. 13th, Suger, Abbot of St. Denis, d. (70).

1152

H **Religion and Education**

A synod at Kells acknowledges the supremacy of the Pope in Ireland, where the church is organised under four archbishoprics (Armagh, Dublin, Cashel and Tuam) on a similar pattern to other parts of Roman Christendom.

J **Art, Architecture and Music**

Amiens (Romanesque) Cathedral consecrated.

*The 'Old Cathedral', Salamanca, begun (–*c.* 1180).

K **Literature, Philosophy and Scholarship**

John of Salisbury, *Historia Pontificalis* (history of western Europe, 1148–52).

1153

H **Religion and Education**

There are now 343 houses of the Cistercian Order.

†St. Bernard, Latin hymns and treatises, especially *De Diligendo Deo* and *De Gradibus Humilitatis* (on God, mankind and divine love).

J **Art, Architecture and Music**

The baptistery of Pisa Cathedral, designed by Diotisalvi, begun.

Senlis Cathedral (–1184).

L **Births and Deaths**

Aug. 20th, St. Bernard of Clairvaux d. (62).

— al-Shahrastānī d. (77).

1154–1155 Frederick Barbarossa crowned as Emperor—Roman republic destroyed

1154

A **Feb**: 26th, death of Roger II, King of Sicily; succeeded by his son, William I (–1165). The Greeks foment a rebellion against him.

B **Apr**: 25th, Nūr-ad-Dīn takes Damascus, thus completing his mastery of Muslim Syria.

D **Oct**: Frederick begins his first expedition to Italy.
25th: death of Stephen, King of England.
Dec: 3rd, death of Pope Anastasius IV.
4th: Nicholas Breakspear elected as Pope Adrian IV (the only English Pope; –1159).
19th: Henry II crowned as King of England (–1189).

E Svein III flees from Denmark.

1155

A **Jan**: Henry II appoints Thomas Becket his chancellor.
Mar: Adrian places an interdict on Rome and so causes the Romans to banish their leader, Arnold of Brescia, and make peace with the Pope (*and see* H).
After a siege of two months, Frederick takes Tortona (a Milanese dependency), and razes it to the ground.

B **Apr**: 17th, Frederick crowned as King of Lombardy in Pavia.
Jun: 18th, he is crowned as Holy Roman Emperor by the Pope; the Romans then attack his German troops, who repulse them but are unable to hold the city. Frederick then advances towards Naples, but fever in his army compels him to abandon the campaign and return to Germany.

D **Nov**: Adrian makes an alliance with the barons in revolt against William of Sicily. He also makes an alliance with Manuel, who captures Bari.

E Adrian grants Ireland to Henry II.
Demetrius I, King of Georgia, abdicates; succeeded, successively in this year, by his sons, David IV and George III (–1184).
Death of Isiaslav II of Kiev; succeeded by Juri, prince of Suzdal (–1157).
*'The Wars of Pretenders' begin in Norway and Sweden; they last until about 1230.

1154

G **Economics, Science, Technology and Discovery**

†Al-Tīfāshī, the Egyptian mineralogist, *Flowers of Knowledge of Precious Stones.*

*Al-Edrisi, a planisphere and *al-Kitāb al-Rujārī* (*Roger's Book*; description of the world, the most elaborate in medieval times, with maps. Both for Roger II of Sicily, d. 1154).

H **Religion and Education**

†St. Wulfric, a hermit at Haselbury, near Crewkerne, Somerset.

J **Art, Architecture and Music**

*Campanile of S. Marco, Venice, built by Buono.

K **Literature, Philosophy and Scholarship**

†Gilbert de la Porrée, *Liber de sex principiis* (treatise on Aristotelian philosophy).

†*William of Conches, *De philosophia mundi* (revised as *Dragmaticon*).

The Anglo-Saxon Chronicles (six extant; written from 880 onwards, recording events in England from A.D. 449–1154).

*John of Hexham continued Simeon of Durham's *Historia Regum* to 1154 (–1129).

*Henry of Huntingdon, *Historia Anglorum* (English history, 85 B.C.–A.D. 1154).

1155

H **Religion and Education**

Arnold of Brescia burnt as a heretic.

*The Carmelite Order (of friars) originates in the establishment of a community of hermits on Mount Carmel.

†Thierry of Chartres, *De septem diebus et sex operum distinctionibus.*

K **Literature, Philosophy and Scholarship**

*Wace (of Jersey), *Brut* (British Chronicle), or *Geste des Bretons* (based on Geoffrey of Monmouth's chronicle—1137; includes Arthurian traditions and a reference to the Round Table; –1200).

Collapse of Indian empire of Rāshtrakūta—Duchy of Austria created

1156

B **Spring**: Reynald of Châtillon, Prince of Antioch, and Thoros of Armenia ravage the (Greek) island of Cyprus.

May: 28th, William of Sicily defeats Greek forces outside Brindisi: he then recovers Bari.

Jun: by the Treaty of Benevento, Adrian recognises William as King of Sicily and receives his homage.

Frederick marries Beatrice, heiress of Upper Burgundy.

C **Sep**: Hungary recognises Byzantine overlordship.

17th, in a diet at Regensburg, Frederick creates the Duchy of Austria for Henry Jasomirgott and settles the Duchy of Bavaria on Henry the Lion of Saxony (–1180).

E Henry II defeats his brother Geoffrey's revolt in Anjou.

Svein restored as King of Denmark with Saxon aid.

Death of Domenico Morosini, Doge of Venice; succeeded by Vitale Micheli II (–1173).

Death of Masʿūd I, Sultan of Rūm; succeeded by his son, Kilij Arslan II (–1188).

Death of Vikrāmanka, King of Rāshtrakūta (in the Deccan); his kingdom, which had been the most powerful in India for three centuries, now collapses.

1157

B **May**: 4th, by the Treaty of Roeskild, Denmark divided by Svein and his rivals, Cnut and Waldemar.

7th, Svein holds a banquet where Cnut is murdered but Waldemar escapes.

C **Aug**: 21st, death of Alfonso, Emperor of Spain; by his will, his sons, Sancho III and Ferdinand II become Kings of Castile and Leon respectively (–1158, 1188).

D **Oct**: Frederick takes formal possession of the Kingdom of Burgundy. He rejects claims of papal supremacy implied in a letter from Adrian IV.

23rd, Waldemar I becomes King of Denmark (–1182) by defeating and killing Svein III at Viborg.

E Henry compels Malcolm of Scotland to surrender Northumberland, Cumberland and Westmorland.

Eric of Sweden conquers Finland.

William of Sicily sacks Greek ports in the Ægean.

After invading Poland, Frederick compels Boleslav IV to admit, in the Peace of Krzyszkowo, the imperial overlordship of Poland (for the last time).

Death of Juri, Grand Prince of Russia; succeeded by his son, Andrew (–1159).

Death of Sanjar, the Seljuq Sultan; the disintegration of his empire, centred on Persia, now accelerates.

1156

G **Economics, Science, Technology and Discovery**

Henchün Seiken, *Kō yō shō* (treatise on perfumery).

J **Art, Architecture and Music**

Dedication of Maria Laach abbey-church (Romanesque).

Bari Cathedral begun (Romanesque).

L **Births and Deaths**

— Peter the Venerable, Abbot of Cluny, d.

1157

G **Economics, Science, Technology and Discovery**

Henry the Lion founds Munich.

Foundation of the Bank of Venice.

Henry II grants protection to the Hanse of merchants of Cologne and associated towns settled in London.

H **Religion and Education**

The Council of Reims condemns Cathars.

L **Births and Deaths**

Sept. 8th, Richard I b. (–1199).

— Alexander Neckham b. (–1217).

1158–1159 Italian revolt against Frederick

1158

A **Jan**: 11th, in a diet at Regensburg, Frederick concedes the hereditary title of King of Bohemia to Vladislav II.

B **Apr**: Baldwin of Jerusalem defeats Nūr-ad-Dīn at Butaiha.

C **Jul**: Frederick begins his second Italian expedition with the capture of Brescia.
Aug: 31st, death of Sancho III of Castile; succeeded by his infant son, Alfonso VIII (–1214). Civil war begins.
Sep: 8th, after a siege, Milan surrenders to Frederick.

D **Oct**: Manuel makes an expedition into Cilicia; Thoros evades capture but Reynald of Antioch submits and receives pardon.
Nov: 11th, in a diet at Roncaglia, Frederick promulgates his peace constitution for the Empire.

E Henry II campaigns against the Welsh and gains the overlordship of Gwynned and Deheubarth. He also becomes overlord of Brittany on the death of his brother, Geoffrey of Anjou.
Adrian arranges a peace between William of Sicily and Manuel, who ends his military intervention in Italy.

1159

B **Apr**: 12th, Manuel makes a ceremonial entry into Antioch, then withdraws to the west.

C **Jul**: Frederick begins the siege of Crema. Several Lombard cities, Genoa the first, are revolting against his authority. William of Sicily engineers a league of the Papacy, Brescia, Milan and Piacenza against Frederick.
4th, death of Vladislav II, the former Grand Prince of Poland; Frederick has his sons restored to Silesia, so attaching it to German interests.
Sep: Henry II abandons his siege of Toulouse when Louis VII enters the city.
1st, death of Pope Adrian IV.
7th, Roland Bandinelli elected as Pope Alexander III (–1181) by a majority of the cardinals, but a party favouring Frederick elects Cardinal Octavian as Pope Victor IV (–1164); neither is able to control Rome.

E Kiev expels Andrew and elects Rostislav I of Smolensk as prince (–1167).

1158

G **Economics, Science, Technology and Discovery**

†Nikulas Saemundarson, account (Icelandic) of his journey to Rome, Constantinople and Jerusalem, 1151–54.

H **Religion and Education**

Frederick I grants his charter, 'The Authentic', to Bologna University.

J **Art, Architecture and Music**

Alcobaça Abbey (Romanesque; –1223).

Vladimir Cathedral (–1194).

K **Literature, Philosophy and Scholarship**

†Otto of Freising, *Gesta Frederici imperatoris* (life of Frederick I, to 1156).

L **Births and Deaths**

Sept. 22nd, Otto, Bishop of Freising, d.

1159

F **Law and Politics**

Henry II collects scutage from feudal tenants *in lieu* of military service.

*John of Salisbury, *Policraticus* (*Statesman's Book*).

1160

A **Jan:** the fall of Mahdīyah completes the loss, by insurrection, of all the conquests by the King of Sicily in north Africa.
27th, Frederick takes and destroys Crema.
Feb: 11th, a synod held at Pavia by Frederick declares Victor IV to be the Pope.
Mar: 24th, Alexander excommunicates Frederick.

B **May:** 18th, St. Eric, King of Sweden, killed in civil warfare.

C **Summer:** Henry the Lion begins the systematic conquest of Wendish territory east of the Elbe (–1162).

D **Nov:** Nūr-ad-Dīn captures Reynald of Antioch.
10th, William's unpopular Grand Emir (Admiral) of Naples, Maio of Bari, assassinated.
Dec: Henry II occupies the Norman Vexin.

E Malcolm subdues Galloway.
Taira Kiyomori, leader of a Japanese 'feudal' confederacy, wins control of the imperial government after defeating his rivals (–1185).

1161

A **Feb:** 3rd, Inge I of Norway murdered; succeeded by Haakon II (–1162).
Mar: 9th, William of Sicily captured by rebels but escapes.

B **Apr:** 16th, William crushes the rebellion in Sicily and then turns to subdue Apulia and Calabria.
May: 31st, death of Géza II of Hungary; succeeded by his son, Stephen III (–1173).

C **Jul:** 15th, Ladislas II crowned as King of Hungary (–1162).
Sep: Frederick begins the siege of Milan.

E Al-Mu'min conquers Tripoli.

1160

F **Law and Politics**

*Peter of Piacenza introduces the study of law from Bologna to the emerging University of Montpellier.

G **Economics, Science, Technology and Discovery**

Eugene of Palermo, translation of Ptolemy's *Almagest* from Greek to Latin.

*Ibn-Rushd (Averroes), *Kitāb al-Kullīyāt fī-al-Tibb* (*Generalities of medicine*; an encyclopedia; –1255, –1482).

*Andrew, Duke of Vladimir, builds Moscow.

J **Art, Architecture and Music**

Towers (Romanesque) of Tournai Cathedral completed.

*Laon (Gothic) Cathedral begun; it is the first to have a polygonal apse (–1205).

K **Literature, Philosophy and Scholarship**

Jean Bodel, *Le Jeu de St. Nicholas* (performed at Arras; the oldest extant miracle play in French literature).

†Theodorus Prodromus, *Dosicles and Rodanthe* (verse romance by a Byzantine poet).

*Benoît de Sainte Maure, *Roman de Troie* (long poem on the Trojan theme, based on early authors; notable for the episode of Troilus and Cressida, used by Chaucer, Shakespeare and other poets; –1287).

1161

G **Economics, Science, Technology and Discovery**

†Géza of Hungary admits Saxon colonists, granting them self-government.

Kilij Arslan II builds two baths at Kavza; the Seljuqs developed spas and also created a hospital service.

†Matthaeus Platearius, of Salerno, *De simplici medicina*, or *Circa instans* (popular treatise on simples and drugs).

K **Literature, Philosophy and Scholarship**

Chêng Ch'iao, *T'ung chih* (a history of China, objective and scientific in method).

L **Births and Deaths**

— Vincent Kadlubek b. (–1223).

1162

A **Jan**: 14th, death of Ladislas II of Hungary; succeeded by his brother, Stephen IV (–1163).
Feb: 10th, death of Baldwin III of Jerusalem; succeeded by his brother, Amalric (*or* Amaury) I (–1174).
Mar: Frederick makes an alliance against Sicily with Pisa and Genoa.
26th, Milan, having surrendered to Frederick, is sacked by his orders; he returns to Germany, later.

B **May**: Alexander, at Montpellier, renews his excommunication of Frederick.
Jun: 3rd, Thomas Becket consecrated as Archbishop of Canterbury.

C **Jul**: 6th, the Germans and Danes crusading against the Wends defeat them at Demmin; Henry the Lion's campaign ends soon afterwards with their surrender.
Aug: 8th, death of Raymond-Berengar IV, Count of Barcelona; succeeded by his son, Alfonso (II of Aragon; –1196).
Sep: 23rd, Alexander meets Louis VII and Henry II at Coucy-sur-Loire and is recognised by them as Pope.

E Haakon II of Norway defeated and murdered by the Jarl Erling, whose son, Magnus VI, succeeds as King (–1184).
Charles VII, nephew of Sverker, succeeds as King of Sweden (–1168).

1163

B **Apr**: 11th, death of Stephen IV of Hungary; Stephen III then regains control.
May: death of ʻAbd-al-Mu'min, the Almohad ruler of Muslim Spain and north west Africa; succeeded by his son, Yūsuf abū-Yaʻqūb (–1184).

D **Oct**: Frederick returns to Lombardy but meets such widespread opposition that he withdraws.
1st, Archbishop Becket refuses Henry's demand for the punishment of clergy in secular courts.

1162

F **Law and Politics**

Danegeld raised, for the last time, as a tax for Henry II.

G **Economics, Science, Technology and Discovery**

Al-Māzini, *Tuhfat al-Albāb wa Nukhbat al-a jāb* (*Gift to the Heart and Choice of Wonders*; world geography, describing peoples, spirits, creatures, fossils; –1136).

†Ibn-Zuhr (Avenzoar), *Kitāb al-Taysīr fi al-Mudāwāh w-al-Tadbīr* (*Book of Simplification concerning Therapeutics and Diet;* –1280).

H **Religion and Education**

The Council of Montpellier condemns temporal lords who refuse to exercise their power against heretics.

J **Art, Architecture and Music**

Iplikci Mosque, Konya (–1182; probably the first mosque to have a minaret).

Poitiers Cathedral (–*c.* 1350).

K **Literature, Philosophy and Scholarship**

†Henry Aristippus, translations of Plato's *Phaedo* and *Meno.*

1163

F **Law and Politics**

Representatives of towns attend the Cortes of Aragon.

G **Economics, Science, Technology and Discovery**

German settlers in the Swedish island of Gothland granted self-government.

J **Art, Architecture and Music**

Nôtre Dame Cathedral, Paris, planned and begun (–1220).

Choir (early Gothic) of St. Germain-des-Prés, Paris, consecrated.

The Bobrinskoy Bucket (in the Hermitage Museum, Leningrad; 'the most important piece of inlaid metal-work of the Seljuq period in Persia') made at Herat by Muhammad ibn-al-Wāhid, caster, and Ma'sūd ibn-Ahmad, inlayer.

1164

A Jan: in the Constitutions of Clarendon, Henry II defines the relations of Church and State in England.

B Apr: 20th, death of the anti-pope, Victor IV.
22nd, Guido of Crema (uncanonically) elected as his successor (Paschal III). Frederick gives him protection, but German prelates who had recognised Victor as Pope refuse to accept Paschal (–1168).

C Aug: 10th, Nūr-ad-Dīn defeats and captures Bohemond III of Antioch at Artah; he is ransomed.

D Oct: 8th, Becket condemned for his contempt of the King by the Council of Northampton.
Nov: 2nd, he begins his exile in France.

E Malcolm IV of Scotland defeats Norse and Celtic rebels led by Somerled of the Isles, who is killed, at Renfrew.
Petronilla of Aragon abdicates; succeeded by her son, Alfonso II, already Count of Barcelona (–1196).
The Muslims in Spain recapture Cordova and Almeria.
Alexander III confirms the Order of Knights of Calatrava.

1165

B May: Frederick, at Würzburg, exacts an oath from the German clergy that they will not recognise Alexander as Pope.
7th, death of William I the Bad of Sicily; succeeded by his young son, William II (–1189), with his widow as regent.

D Nov: 23rd, Alexander, returning from exile in France, enters Rome, and is established in the Lateran by Sicilian forces.
Dec: 9th, death of Malcolm IV the Maiden, King of Scotland; succeeded by his brother, William I the Lion (–1214).

E Henry II makes his last, unsuccessful attempt to subjugate the Welsh princes of Snowdonia.
An attempt by the Chin to conquer the Southern Sung defeated.

1164

K **Literature, Philosophy and Scholarship**

*Chrétien de Troyes, *Erec et Énide* (poetic romance in the Arthurian cycle).

L **Births and Deaths**

May 16th, Héloise d. (*c.* 63).
*Peter the Lombard, Bishop of Paris, d.

1165

G **Economics, Science, Technology and Discovery**

†Ibn-Daud (Avendeath), translations into Latin from Arabic of scientific and philosophical works, introducing 'arabic numbers' (*see* 1041); includes the most popular version of *Secretum secretorum*, falsely attributed to Aristotle.
†Al-Ghāfiqi, *Kitāb al-Adwiyah al-Mufradah* (on simples).

H **Religion and Education**

*Rufinus, *Summa*; gloss of *Decretum.*

J **Art, Architecture and Music**

Ciudad Rodrigo Cathedral (Romanesque; –1230).
*Brandenburg Cathedral (Romanesque).
Church of Nerez, near Skoplje, with Byzantine frescoes.

K **Literature, Philosophy and Scholarship**

*Marie de France, *Lais* (important verse narratives of Celtic and other folk legends, including a *lai* on the Tristan theme).

L **Births and Deaths**

Aug. 21st, Philip II b. (–1223).
— Henry VI b. (–1197).

1166

E Frederick begins his fourth expedition to Italy.
Alfonso VIII acclaimed as King of Castile and thereafter subdues a rebellion.
Boleslav IV of Poland defeated by the Prussians.

1167

A **Mar**: 18th, Amalric of Jerusalem, as the ally of the Fātamid Caliph of Egypt, defeated at Ashmūn by the Syrians.

B **Apr**: 27th, the Lombard League, formed to oppose Frederick, initiates the reconstruction of Milan.
May: 29th, imperial forces defeats the Romans, outside Rome.

C **Jul**: Frederick unsuccessfully besieges Ancona but makes peace with the city.
24th, he camps outside Rome, subsequently forcing an entry; the papal forces surrender, Alexander flees to Benevento and Paschal is installed.
Aug: Frederick's army destroyed by fever, so he hastily returns to Germany.
4th, Saladin, commanding the Syrian garrison of Alexandria, surrenders to Amalric and his Egyptian allies.

E Alfonso II of Aragon succeeds to the County of Provence on the death of his cousin, Raymond-Berengar II.
Death of Rostislav I of Kiev; his sons dispute the succession (–1169).
Bijjala, who had usurped the kingdom of Rāshtrakūta, murdered to avenge his mutilation of two holy men of the Lingāyat sect, which is reviving the Siva cult in the Deccan.
(–1168) the Lombard League builds the city of Alessandria to strengthen its defences against Frederick.

1166

F **Law and Politics**

Henry II, in the Assize of Clarendon, formulates measures for prosecution of criminals, originating (grand) juries to present the accused.

†Bulgarus, *De regulis juris* (treatise on Roman Law by one of the 'Four Doctors' of Bologna).

H **Religion and Education**

†St. Ailred, Abbot of Rievaulx, *Meditations*; *Rule of a Recluse.*

†'Abd-al-Qadir al-Jīlāni, founder of the Qādirite (the first Muslim fraternity).

J **Art, Architecture and Music**

Bonn Minster (Romanesque) dedicated.

K **Literature, Philosophy and Scholarship**

*A monk of Ely, *The Song of Canute.*

†St. Ailred, *Relatio de Standardo*; *Chronicon ab Adam ad Henricum I.*

1167

G **Economics, Science, Technology and Discovery**

†Abraham ben Ezra, translations of Arab astrology, etc., into Hebrew.

H **Religion and Education**

A council of Cathari (heretics) meets near Toulouse (–1205).

†Abraham ben Ezra, biblical criticism.

L **Births and Deaths**

Sept. 10th, the Empress Matilda d. (65).

Dec. 24th, John b. (–1216).

— Ghengiz Khan b. (–1227).

1168

C **Sep**: death of the anti-pope, Paschal III; Abbot John of Struma elected as his successor (Calixtus III; –1178) and recognised as Pope by Frederick.

D **Nov**: 4th, Amalric, invading Egypt, takes Bilbeis.
13th, he camps outside Cairo, but withdraws when the Caliph receives forces in response to his appeal to Nūr-ad-Dīn.

E Henry the Lion marries Matilda, the daughter of Henry II.
Charles VII of Sweden defeated, killed and succeeded by Cnut Ericson (–1192).
Death of Thoros, Prince of Armenia; succeeded by his son, Roupen II (–1186).
The Toltec Empire destroyed by barbarous tribes from northern Mexico (including Aztecs; –1325).

1169

A **Jan**: Shīrkūh, Nūr-ad-Dīn's lieutenant, seizes control of Egypt and becomes al-'Ādid's vizir.
6th, Louis VII and Henry II meet at Montmirail to make peace.
Mar: 8th, Andrew of Suzdal seizes and sacks Kiev; now the most powerful Russian prince, he assumes the title of Great Prince and establishes his capital at Vladimir (–1174).
23rd, death of Shīrkūh; his nephew, Salāh-ad-Dīn (Saladin), becomes Vizir of Egypt (–1171).

B **May**: 'The First Conquerors' land in Ireland; they are Normans from Wales enlisted by Dermot MacMurrough to recover his kingdom of Leinster.

C **Aug**: 15th, Henry (VI), Frederick's son, elected King of the Romans.

D **Dec**: 13th, Amalric and the Greeks abandon their siege of Damietta, in Egypt.

E Stephen Nemanja becomes Grand Župan of Rascia, Serbia (–1196).
Casimir of Poland invades Russia as far as the Lublin plateau.
Kilij Arslan takes Ankara in his conquest of the Danishmends.

H **Religion and Education**
*Etienne of Tournai, canonist, *Summa*.

J **Art, Architecture and Music**
The architect Mateo takes charge of work on Santiago de Compostela Cathedral.

1170

B Jun: 14th, Henry II's son, Henry, crowned as King of England.

C Jul: 22nd, Henry II and Becket reconciled, at Fréteval.
Aug: 25th, Richard FitzGilbert, Earl of Pembroke ('Strongbow') takes Waterford.
Sep: 21st, he captures Dublin.

D Nov: 18th, death of Albert I the Bear, Elector of Brandenburg.
23rd, death of Owain the Great, King of Gwynned.
27th, by their victory over Andrew Bogolyubsky, the citizens of Novgorod secure their liberties.
Dec: 29th, murder of St. Thomas Becket in Canterbury Cathedral.

E Death of Qutb-ad-Dīn of Mosul; his brother, Nūr-ad-Dīn, settles a succession dispute.
The Korean palace guards massacre civil officials and enthrone a new king; a period of civil war follows (–1196).

1171

A Mar: 12th, Manuel orders the arrest of all Venetians in his empire; Venice retaliates by attacking Dalmatia.

B May: Richard FitzGilbert succeeds Dermot Macmurrough as King of Leinster.

C Sep: 13th, death of the last Fātimid Caliph of Egypt, al-'Ādid; Egypt is now nominally subject to the Caliph of Baghdad, and actually ruled by Saladin (–1193).

D Oct: 16th, Henry II lands in Ireland, where he receives the submission of the native princes.

E Yūsuf abū Ya'qūb is now the supreme Muslim ruler in Spain.
Nūr-ad-Dīn seizes Mosul and Nisibis.
Order of Knights of Santiago founded.

1170

F **Law and Politics**

Henry II suspends all his sheriffs from office and orders an enquiry into English local government (the Inquest of Sheriffs).

G **Economics, Science, Technology and Discovery**

*Roger of Salerno, *Practica chirurgiae* (earliest European textbook on surgery).

H **Religion and Education**

Athanasius II, Greek Patriarch of Antioch (–1165), killed in an earthquake; Aimery, the Latin Patriarch, restored.

Peter Waldo, a merchant of Lyons, initiates the unorthodox movement of the Poor Men of Lyons (–1184).

*John of Faenza, canonist, *Summa*; gloss of *Decretum*.

J **Art, Architecture and Music**

Mantes Cathedral and choir of abbey-church of S. Remi, Reims, begun.

K **Literature, Philosophy and Scholarship**

Heinrich von Veldeke, *Servatius* (Dutch-German dialect courtly lyrics).

*Chrétien de Troyes, *Cligès* (Arthurian romance—1164).

*Etienne de Fougères, *Le Livre des Mancières* (poem on manners and morality, rewards and punishments—in afterlife; hence one of the earliest didactic poems in French literature).

Richeut (earliest extant example of the *fabliau* in French poetry).

*Thomas of Brittany, an Anglo-Norman poet, a narrative poem on the legend of Tristan and Iseult (the extant fragment—3,144 lines—being the earliest text on this theme—1200; 1294).

†*Hemacandra, *Abhidhānacintāmanināmamālā* (Sanskrit dictionary of synonyms); *Kumārapālacarita* (epic poem in Sanskrit and Prākrit, an Indian vernacular).

L **Births and Deaths**

— St. Dominic b. (–1221).

— St. Godric of Finchale d.

1171

J **Art, Architecture and Music**

Tarragona and Worms (Romanesque) Cathedrals begun.

K **Literature, Philosophy and Scholarship**

*Helmold, Chronicle (of Christian missions to Slavs, to 1171; –1212).

L **Births and Deaths**

— Baldwin I b. (–1206).

1172

B May: 21st, papal legates absolve Henry II for the murder of Becket, at Avranches.

E Manuel captures Stephen Nemanja in his subjugation of Dalmatia.

1173

A Jan: Henry II receives the homage of the Count of Toulouse.
Mar: his son, Henry, flees to join Louis VII, who supports the rebellion against Henry II by his sons.
Death of Stephen III of Hungary; Béla III succeeds as King (–1196).

B May: 27th, death of Vitale Micheli II, Doge of Venice; succeeded by Sebastiano Ziano (–1179).

D Oct: 30th, death of Boleslav IV, Grand Prince of Poland; succeeded by his brother, Mieszko III of Greater Poland (–1177).

E Vladislav II, King of Bohemia, abdicates in favour of his son, Frederick; there follows a period of civil war, with ten changes of ruler in twenty-four years, in which royal officials become established as feudal magnates; there is a simultaneous increase in German influence, and settlement, in Bohemia (–1197).
Saladin's brother, Tūrān-Shāh, conquers Sudan.

1174

B May: 15th, death of Nūr-ad-Dīn, ruler of Syria; his empire disintegrates as his heir, Ismā'il, is young (–1181); Saladin, ruling Egypt, declares his independence.

C Jul: 11th, death of Amalric I of Jerusalem; succeeded by his son, Baldwin IV (–1185).
12th, Henry does penance at Canterbury for Becket's murder.
13th, William of Scotland is captured while invading Northumberland; Henry has now suppressed the rebellion in England.
Aug: 14th, Henry makes peace with Louis, at Montlouis.
Sep: 30th, Henry makes peace with his sons.

D Oct: 29th, in his fifth Italian expedition, Frederick begins the siege of Alessandria; he buys Tuscany and Spoleto from Welf VI.
Nov: 26th, Saladin, aspiring to take over Nūr-ad-Dīn's empire, enters Damascus and takes possession.
Dec: by the Treaty of Falaise, Henry releases William on obtaining his recognition of Henry's feudal supremacy over Scotland.

E Murder of Andrew of Vladimir; succeeded by his brother, Michael (–1177).
Kilij Arslan of Rūm completes his conquest of the Danishmends (of eastern Anatolia).
Tūrān-Shāh conquers the Yemen.

1172

F Law and Politics

Henry II orders an enquiry into services due to him as Duke of Normandy.

J Art, Architecture and Music

Palermo Cathedral (Romanesque; –1185).

Mosque, with the Giralda Tower (minaret), Seville (–1195).

1173

F Law and Politics

Henry II of England introduces the formula *Dei gracia* in his royal style.

G Economics, Science, Technology and Discovery

†Bjarni Bergthorsson, Icelandic treatise on chronology.

†Benjamin ben Jonah of Tudela, *Masse'oth Rabbi Binyamin* (narrative, in Hebrew, of his journey from Castile to the Middle East, 1160–73; published in Constantinople, 1453).

J Art, Architecture and Music

*Lübeck Cathedral begun (Romanesque).

K Literature, Philosophy and Scholarship

*Chrétien de Troyes, *Le Chevalier au Lion* (poetic romance in the Arthurian cycle); *Percevale le Gallois* or *Le Conte du Graal* (this Arthurian romance contains the earliest reference to the Holy Grail).

1174

J Art, Architecture and Music

Monreale Cathedral (–1182).

The choir of Canterbury Cathedral destroyed by fire; the French mason, William of Sens, has charge of its rebuilding (–1179).

K Literature, Philosophy and Scholarship

Garnier de Point-Sainte-Maxence, *La Vie de Saint Thomas Becket* (a poem in alexandrines).

1175–1177 Saladin Sultan of Egypt and Syria—Ghūrid invasion of India—Battle of Legnano

1175

B Apr: 13th, Frederick abandons the siege of Alessandria.
16th, he makes the Treaty of Montebello with the Lombard League.
May: the Caliph of Baghdād recognises Saladin as Sultan of Egypt and Syria.

E Henry II commits the government of Aquitaine to Richard (I).
Muhammad of Ghūr begins his invasion of India (–1202).

1176

B Apr: 22nd, Saladin defeats Sayf-ad-Dīn of Mosul.
May: 29th, the Lombard League defeats Frederick at Legnano.

C Sep: 17th, Manuel, attempting to conquer the Danishmend lands, is trapped and his army destroyed by Kilij Arslan, at Myriocephalum.

D Oct: by the Treaty of Anagni, Frederick makes peace with Alexander, recognising him as Pope and so ending the schism.

E Tūrān-Shāh conquers southern Arabia.

1177

B May: Henry creates his youngest son, John, Lord of Ireland.

C Jul: 23rd, in the Treaty of Venice, Frederick makes a truce with the Lombard League and Sicily.

D Nov: 25th, Baldwin of Jerusalem defeats Saladin, invading from Egypt, at Montgisard.

E Henry II arbitrates between the Kings of Castile and Navarre.
Alfonso VIII of Castile takes Cuenca from the Muslims.
Sverre becomes joint King of Norway with Magnus (–1184).
Mieszko III the Old, Grand Prince of Poland, deposed; succeeded by his brother, Casimir II (–1194). Casimir enforces his suzerainty over Silesia.
Michael succeeded as Great Prince of Vladimir by his brother, Vśevolod III (–1212).
Jaya Indravarman IV of Champa sacks Angkor, Cambodia; Tribhuvanadityavarman, who had usurped the throne, is killed, and Jayavarman, son of Dharanindravarman II, assumes leadership of Cambodian resistance (–1181).

1175

G Economics, Science, Technology and Discovery

Stamping-mill (for metal) built at Leoben, Styria.

Gerard of Cremona, Latin translation from Arabic of Ptolemy's *Almagest* (his only dated translation).

H Religion and Education

Genkū (Hōnen Shōnin) founds the Pure Land Sect (Jodo) of Japanese Buddhism (–1207).

J Art, Architecture and Music

Raimundus the Lombard contracts to build Seo de Urgel Cathedral.

1176

F Law and Politics

In the Assize of Northampton, Henry II establishes common rules for criminal justice in England.

J Art, Architecture and Music

Saladin's Citadel, Cairo, begun.

K Literature, Philosophy and Scholarship

Eisteddfod held in Cardigan Castle, Wales.

1177

1178

C **Jul**: 30th, Frederick crowned as King of Burgundy, at Arles.
Aug: 29th, the anti-pope, Calixtus III, resigns.

D **Nov**: 11th, in a diet at Speyer, the Saxons make a formal complaint to Frederick about the oppressive rule of Henry the Lion, who is cited to answer.

1179

A **Mar**: 5th–19th, the Third Lateran Council, held by Alexander, condemns heretics, their protectors and defenders; it also refuses Christian burial to men killed in tournaments.

B **Apr**: 13th, death of Sebastiano Ziano, Doge of Venice; succeeded by Orio Malipiero (–1192).
Jun: 10th, Saladin defeats Baldwin of Jerusalem on the Litani.
24th, Henry the Lion is put under the ban of the Empire for failing to appear before Frederick to answer charges.

C **Sep**: an anti-pope, Innocent III, elected.

D **Nov**: 1st, Philip crowned and associated with his father, Louis, as King of France.

E Alfonso VIII of Castile and Alfonso II of Aragon conclude a treaty defining the boundary between their future conquests from the Muslims.
A naval expedition sent by Yūsuf, Emperor of Morocco, fails to take Lisbon.
Alexander recognises his vassal, Alfonso I, as King of Portugal. The Portuguese Order of Knights of Avis now known by this name.

1178

G **Economics, Science, Technology and Discovery**
Roger of Hereford, astronomical tables.
*Han Ch'an-chih, *Chü lu* (treatise on oranges; describes 27 varieties).

J **Art, Architecture and Music**
Fossanova abbey-church, near Rome (–1208).

L **Births and Deaths**
— Snorri Sturleson b. (–1241).

1179

F **Law and Politics**
*Richard fitz Nigel, *Dialogus de Scaccario* (description of the English Exchequer).

G **Economics, Science, Technology and Discovery**
The 'Naviglio Grande' for irrigation, in Lombardy (–1258).
†St. Hildegarde of Bingen, *Physica* (encyclopedia of natural history; gives earliest reference to hopped beer).

H **Religion and Education**
Mar: 5–19th, Alexander III holds the Third Lateran Council (*see* A).

J **Art, Architecture and Music**
William the Englishman succeeds William of Sens as mason in charge at Canterbury Cathedral; with him begins 'English Gothic' and the use of Purbeck marble.
Ulu Cami, Erzurum.

L **Births and Deaths**
Sept. 17th, St. Hildegarde of Bingen, the 'Sybil of the Rhine', d. (81).

A Jan: the anti-pope, Innocent III, deposed.
13th, in a diet at Würzburg, Henry the Lion sentenced, in his absence, to lose his Saxon fiefs.

B Apr: Philip II marries Isabel of Hainault, niece of Philip of Flanders and heiress to Artois.
13th, in a diet at Gelnhausen, Frederick divides the Duchy of Saxony between the Archbishop of Cologne (who receives Westphalia) and Bernard of Anhalt, who is created Duke.
Jun: 28th, Philip II and Henry II confer at Gisors.
29th, death of Sayf-ad-Dīn of Mosul; succeeded by his brother, 'Izz-ad-Dīn.

C Sep: 16th, in a diet at Altenburg, Frederick partitions the Duchy of Bavaria, also confiscated from Henry the Lion; Otto of Wittelsbach is created Duke; Styria detached as another Duchy.
18th, death of Louis VII of France; Philip II is now sole King (–1223).
24th, death of the Greek Emperor, Manuel I; succeeded by his son, Alexius II (–1182), with his widow, Mary of Antioch, acting as regent. Stephen Nemanja of Rascia now able to achieve Serbian independence.

E At the congress of Leczyca, Casimir II persuades the prelates and nobles present to abolish the Seniorate (of the Grand Prince) and establish the hereditary province of Cracow for himself.
Minamoto Yoritomo begins his revolt against the Taira rulers of Japan (–1185).

F **Law and Politics**

At the start of his rebellion, Minamoto Yoritomo sets up the Board of Retainers to direct his 'feudal' organisation.

†Manuel (Greek Emperor, 1143–80) had continued the policy of making grants of land conditional on military service (–1118) and with the admission of the hereditary principle their resemblance to western feudal tenures became closer; they also exemplify the decay of imperial authority.

*Ranulf Glanville (but more probably Hubert Walter?) *Legibus et Consuetudinibus Regni Angliæ* (the first reasoned account of legal procedure).

G **Economics, Science, Technology and Discovery**

Bruges now the principal international mart of north Europe.

Movable lock-gate at Damme, on the Bruges–North Sea Canal.

Earliest European reference to a stern-post rudder (instead of an oar for steering).

*First mention of a windmill in western Europe, at St. Sauvère de Vicomte, Normandy.

Sancho VI of Navarre, *Los paramientos de la caza* (regulations for the chase; gives notices of falconry).

H **Religion and Education**

*Hugoccio, canonist, *Summa*.

*Josce of London founds the first college in the emerging University of Paris, the Collège des Dix-huit.

J **Art,** Architecture and Music

*Lisieux Cathedral begun.

*Byzantine frescoes in church of St. George, Staraya Ladoga.

K **Literature, Philosophy and Scholarship**

André le Chapelain (Andreas Capellanus), *De arte honeste amandi* (treatise on courtly love as expressed by Provençal troubadours).

**Amis et Amile* (*Amis and Amiloun—chanson de geste*; later incorporated into the Charlemagne cycle).

*Eilhart von Oberg, *Tristan* (*t*) (the first text on this theme).

*Graindor de Douay, *Chanson d'Antioche* (romance of the First Crusade; –1225).

L **Births and Deaths**

Oct. 25th, John of Salisbury d. (*c.* 60).

1181

C **Aug**: 30th, death of Pope Alexander III.
Sep: 1st, Cardinal Ubald of Ostia elected as Pope Lucius III (–1185).

D **Dec**: 4th, death of Ismā'īl of Aleppo; succeeded by his cousin, 'Izz-ad-Dīn of Mosul, who thus reunites the Zangid lands.

E Henry II's sons again rebel (–1183).
Frederick, supported by Waldemar of Denmark, completes his dispossession of Henry the Lion when Lübeck surrenders; Henry submits and is banished (to England) for three years, retaining only Brunswick.
The Pomeranian princes of Stettin become vassals of the Empire; thus western Pomerania, where Germans had settled, leaves the Polish sphere of influence.
Béla III of Hungary seizes Dalmatia and parts of Croatia and Sirmium from the Greek Empire.
Jayavarman VII crowned as King of Cambodia (–*c.* 1218) following his expulsion of the Chams.

1182

B **May**: 12th, death of Waldemar I the Great of Denmark; succeeded by his son, Cnut VI (–1202) who refuses to do homage to Frederick.

C **Jul**: Saladin and Baldwin of Jerusalem fight indecisively at Belvoir, south of the Sea of Galilee.
Sep: Andronicus I Comnenus, nephew of John II, usurps the Greek Empire (–1185), murdering Alexius II, his mother and her advisers.

D **Oct**: Saladin takes Edessa and Nisibis.

E Reynald of Châtillon launches a piratical expedition on the Red Sea which plunders Muslim pilgrims and merchant shipping.
The claimants to the Duchy of Bohemia obey Frederick's command to submit to his decision; he awards the Duchy to Frederick and Moravia, as a margravate subject only to the Empire, to Conrad Otto.

1183

B **Jun**: 11th, death of King Henry, son of Henry II; a league against Henry II in Aquitaine then collapses.
18th, Saladin takes Aleppo.
25th, by the Treaty of Constance, Frederick makes peace with the Lombard League, freeing its members from his government.

C **Aug**: 24th, Saladin now makes Damascus his capital.

E The Taira rulers flee from Kyōto before the advance of Minamoto Yoshinaka.

1181

F **Law and Politics**

Henry II, in the Assize of Arms, redefines the military obligations of all Englishmen.

Plea-rolls, recording judicial proceedings, first known as being kept in England; the earliest extant date from 1194.

G **Economics, Science, Technology and Discovery**

Earliest known confirmation by the King of France of the detailed franchises of a town, *viz.* Bourges.

H **Religion and Education**

Cardinal-bishop Henry of Albano directs fighting against Albigensians in southern France.

J **Art, Architecture and Music**

Mainz Cathedral begun (Romanesque).

K **Literature, Philosophy and Scholarship**

†Romuald of Salerno, universal chronicle (to 1178).

L **Births and Deaths**

— St. Francis b. (–1226).

— Ibn al-Farid b. (–1234).

1182

J **Art, Architecture and Music**

Glastonbury Abbey burnt; rebuilt.

*Mosaics in Monreale Cathedral.

K **Literature, Philosophy and Scholarship**

Ibn-Munqidh, *Kitāb al-i'tibār* (*Learning by example*; autobiography of a soldier-poet, with much about hunting, hawking and fishing).

H **Births and Deaths**

— Accursius b. (–1260).

1183

H **Religion and Education**

The Brotherhood of the White-caped Friends of Peace (Capuciati), inspired by Durand Dujardin of Puy-en-Velay, a carpenter, spreads in France.

K **Literature, Philosophy and Scholarship**

*Joannes Cinnamos, chronicle of the Greek Emperors John and Manuel Comnenus (for 1118–1176).

1184

B **May**: Yūsuf invades Portugal.
Jun: 15th, Magnus VI of Norway defeated and killed by Sverre, who now rules alone (–1202).

C **Sep**: 10th, death of Yūsuf, the ruler of north west Africa and Muslim Spain, thus ending his attack on Portugal; succeeded by his son, Abū-Yūsuf Ya'qūb (–1199).

D **Oct**: Lucius and Frederick, meeting in Verona, fail to resolve their differences.
29th, Henry, Frederick's son, betrothed to Constance, the presumptive heiress to the kingdom of Sicily.

E Death of George III, King of Georgia; succeeded by his daughter, Thamar (–1212).
Cyprus revolts against Greek rule.
Minamoto Yoshitsune, brother of Yoritomo, defeats and kills his cousin Yoshinaka.

1185

A **Feb**: 11th, Frederick grants a charter of liberties to Milan and makes an alliance against the Pope.
Mar: death of Baldwin IV of Jerusalem; succeeded by his young nephew, Baldwin V (–1186).

B **Apr**: John begins his unsuccessful expedition to Ireland.
25th, the naval battle of Dan-no-ura finally destroys the Taira and establishes Minamoto Yoritomo as the effective ruler in Japan, with the title Sei-i-tai Shogun ('barbarian-suppressing generalissimo'). Feudal government is now effectively established in Japan, with its capital at Kamakura (near Tokyo; –1333).
Jun: William of Sicily takes Corfù and Durazzo in his invasion of the Greek Empire.

C **Jul**: by the Treaty of Boves with Philip of Flanders, Philip II acquires Amiens and other lands and titles in north-east France, thus doubling the extent of the royal domain.
Aug: the Normans of Sicily sack Salonika.
Sep: Henry the Lion returns to Germany.
12th, in a riot in Constantinople, Andronicus is killed; succeeded by his cousin, Isaac II Angelus (–1195), who defeats the Normans at Mosinopolis and expels them.

D **Nov**: 24th, death of Pope Lucius III.
25th, Humbert Crivelli, Archbishop of Milan, elected as Pope Urban III (–1187).
Dec: 6th, death of Afonso I, the first King of Portugal; succeeded by his son, Sancho I (–1211).

E Philip II suppresses the office of chancellor to avoid the danger of influential offices being held by magnates.
The Bulgarian brothers, Theodore and Asen, begin an anti-Greek revolt.

1184

G **Economics, Science, Technology and Discovery**

Mekhitur of Her, *Consolation in Cases of Fever* (Armenian medical treatise).

H **Religion and Education**

Danish missionaries begin the conversion of the Livs (of Latvia).

The Council of Verona held by Lucius and Frederick condemns Waldensians (Poor Men of Lyons), Cathars and Humiliati, and organises proceedings against heretics.

K **Literature, Philosophy and Scholarship**

*William of Tyre, *Historia rerum in partibus transmarinis gestarum* (history of the Crusades, 1095–1184).

†Hung Kua, *Li Shih* (collection of inscriptions of the Han period, 206 B.C.–A.D. 220, with facsimiles).

1185

G **Economics, Science, Technology and Discovery**

*Ibn-Jubayr, *Rahlat al-Kinānī* (account of his journey from Granada to the Middle East in 1183–85).

H **Religion and Education**

Oxford University apparently now established

J **Art, Architecture and Music**

*The third abbey-church of Pontigny, and rebuilding of the choir of Vézelay abbey-church, begun.

K **Literature, Philosophy and Scholarship**

Giraldus Cambrensis (Gerald of Wales, or Barry) *Expugnatio Hibernica* (chronicle of the conquest of Ireland, 1169–85).

**Slovo o polku Igorevé* (*The Campaign of Igor*; prose poem in epic form about the campaign of Igor of Novgorod-Sêveresk against the Cumans in 1185; the beginning of Russian literature).

*Marie de France, *Lanval* (poetic narrative, with King Arthur as a character); *Lai le Freine* (or *Frène*): *Fables* (sometimes called *Isopet*; modelled on Æsop).

†Ibn-Tufayl, *Hayy ibn-Yaqzan* (*The Living One*; philosophical romance — possibly a model for Robinson Crusoe).

1186

A **Jan**: 27th, Henry (VI) marries Constance of Sicily; he is crowned as King of Burgundy, Germany and Italy, and entitled *Cæsar*.

B **May**: 17th, Urban breaks with Frederick by consecrating the papal candidate for the Archbishopric of Trier.

C **Summer**: Urban encourages Archbishop Philip of Cologne to revolt against Frederick, who therefore returns from Italy; while Henry suppresses revolts in Romagna and the Campagna.

Aug: death of Baldwin V of Jerusalem; succeeded by his mother, Sibylla, the wife of Guy de Lusignan, whom she crowns as King of Jerusalem (–1192).

D **Autumn**: the brothers Theodore and Asen liberate Bulgaria while their allies, the Cumans, ravage Thrace.

Dec: an assembly of German prelates at Gelnhausen declare their support for Frederick against Urban.

E Muhammad of Ghūr destroys the Ghaznavid kingdom of the Punjab and takes Lahore.

1187

C **Jul**: 3rd, the army of the kingdom of Jerusalem, advancing to raise the siege of Tiberias, trapped and destroyed by Saladin at the Horns of Hattin; Guy captured and Reynald of Châtillon beheaded. Saladin now rapidly takes possession of Palestine.

D **Oct**: 3rd, Saladin takes Jerusalem.

20th, death of Pope Urban III.

21st, Albert of Morra elected as Pope Gregory VIII.

Nov: Conrad of Montferrat repulses Saladin's attack on Tyre.

Dec: 17th, death of Pope Gregory VIII who had just proclaimed the Third Crusade to liberate Jerusalem.

19th, Paul Scolari elected as Pope Clement III (–1197).

E Philip II makes an alliance with Frederick; his campaign against Henry II ends with a truce.

Isaac II makes a truce with Theodore and Asen, recognising Bulgarian independence *de facto*; Theodore (*now named* Peter) crowned as Tsar (–1197), although Asen actually rules.

1186

F **Law and Politics**

Milan first known to be governed by a *rector*.

K **Literature, Philosophy and Scholarship**

†Robert of Torigny, *Chronicle* of the Dukes of Normandy (851–1137); continuation to 1186 of Sigebert's universal history (–1112).

1187

G **Economics, Science, Technology and Discovery**

†Gerard of Cremona, translations into Latin from Arabic of nearly 100 Greek and Arab works on philosophy, mathematics, astronomy (–1175), physics, medicine, alchemy and astrology, including *The Book of the Seventy*, attributed to Jābir (–810), al-Rāzī's *Book of Secrets* (–925), Avicenna's *Canon of Medicine* (–1037), and al-Khwārizmī's *The Calculation of Integration and Equation* (–850; this became the principal textbook on mathematics in western Europe until the sixteenth century).

K **Literature, Philosophy and Scholarship**

†Gilbert Foliot, *Letters*.

*Svend Aagesön, Chronicles of the Kings of Denmark (300–1187; the first Danish historian).

L **Births and Deaths**

Feb. 18th, Gilbert Foliot, Bishop of London, d.

Sept. 5th, Louis VIII b. (–1226).

1188

A **Jan**: Henry II and Philip, meeting at Gisors to discuss a truce, are persuaded to make peace and go on Crusade; they impose Saladin tithes to finance their expeditions.
21st, death of Ferdinand II of Leon; succeeded by his son, Alfonso IX (–1230).
Mar: 27th, Frederick takes the Cross; by his order, Henry the Lion goes into exile.

C **Jul**: Saladin releases Guy of Jerusalem.

D **Nov**: 11th, Henry, Philip and Richard meet at Bonmoulins; Richard does homage to Philip, thus breaking with Henry.

E Kilij Arslan II, Sultan of Rūm, abdicates, dividing his kingdom among his 11 sons; the succession is disputed (–1204).

1189

B **Apr**: 3rd, in the Peace of Strasbourg, Clement and Frederick resolve their differences.
May: Frederick departs from Regensburg on Crusade.

C **Jul**: Sancho of Portugal takes Alvor and Silves, in the Algarve, with the aid of English crusaders bound for Palestine.
3rd, Philip takes Tours.
4th, Henry capitulates to Philip and Richard at Colombières.
6th, death of Henry II, King of England.
Aug: 28th, Guy of Jerusalem begins the siege of Acre.
Sep: 3rd, Richard I crowned as King of England (–1199); this date becomes the limit of legal memory (from 1290).

D **Oct**: Henry the Lion returns to Germany and recovers much of Saxony and Holstein.
4th, Saladin fails to dislodge the Franks besieging Acre; they are now being reinforced as crusaders arrive from Europe.
Nov: 18th, death of William II, King of Sicily, without issue; his bastard cousin, Tancred, Count of Lecce, seizes the throne, with Clement's encouragement, but has to face widespread revolt (–1194).
Dec: 12th, having raised money by the sale of offices and privileges, Richard leaves England for the Crusade, leaving William de Mandeville, Earl of Essex, and Hugh Puiset, Bishop of Durham, in charge of England as justiciars.

E Isaac defeats Stephen Nemanja of Serbia and forces him to cede his recent conquests.
Yoritomo destroys the Fujiwara of Kiraizumi and so completes his subjection of Japan.

1188

F **Law and Politics**

Alfonso IX holds the first Cortes of Leon known to have been attended by representatives of towns as well as prelates and nobles.

G **Economics, Science, Technology and Discovery**

Saladin sends Chinese porcelain to Damascus (known in China from the ninth century but the first notice in the Middle East).

J **Art, Architecture and Music**

Portico de la Gloria (Romanesque) of Santiago Cathedral.
*Wells Cathedral begun.
*Mausoleum of Kilij Arslan II, Konya.
*Mosque at Rabat, intended to be the largest in the Muslim world.

K **Literature, Philosophy and Scholarship**

Ilyās ibn-Yūsuf Nizāmī, *Laylā and Majnūn* (Persian romance).
Giraldus Cambrensis began his *Itinerarium Cambriæ* (*Description of Wales*).

L **Births and Deaths**

Feb. 4th, St. Gilbert of Sempringham d. (*c.* 106).
Apr. 20th, St. Hildegonda d.

1189

G **Economics, Science, Technology and Discovery**

Hamburg becomes an imperial free city.

K **Literature, Philosophy and Scholarship**

*Heinrich von Veldeke, *Lieder*; and an epic from the French, *Eneide* (*Eneit*).
*Hugo Falcandus, *Historia de rebus gestis in Siciliae regno* (1154–89).

1190

A **Feb**: by the treaty of Adrianople, Isaac II permits Frederick and his Crusaders to pass into Asia Minor.

Mar: a series of attacks on Jewish communities in England culminates in a massacre of 150 in York.

B **May**: Bernard of Anhalt defeats Henry the Lion at Segeberg.

18th, Frederick fights his way into Konya, the capital of Rūm.

Jun: 10th, he is drowned in the Saleph (*now* Göksu), in Cilicia; succeeded by his son, Henry VI (–1197).

21st, the survivors of the German contingent arrive in Antioch.

C **Jul**: 4th, Philip and Richard meet at Vézelay and set off on the Crusade.

D **Oct**: 4th, Richard's troops in Messina seize control of the town; while here, Richard appoints his chancellor, William Longchamp, Bishop of Ely, as justiciar in England.

E Isaac defeats Stephen Nemanja on the Morava; Stephen is able, however, to retain his conquests, including his former principality of Zeta.

The Bulgarians defeat Isaac's attempt to subjugate them.

Foundation of the Knights of the Cross (later known as the Teutonic Knights).

Ballāla II, the Hoysala King, completes the destruction of the Chalukya Empire in southern India.

1191

A **Mar**: Richard and Philip, still wintering at Messina, make a treaty allowing Richard to rescind his promise to marry Philip's sister, Alice.

1st, Henry VI grants a charter of liberties to Pisa, thus enlisting its fleet.

30th, Pope Clement III having died, Cardinal Hyacinth Bobo elected as Celestine III (–1198).

B **Apr**: Henry VI takes Tusculum for the Romans, who massacre its inhabitants and raze it to the ground.

15th, Celestine crowns Henry as Holy Roman Emperor; Henry then begins his conquest of his wife's kingdom of Naples.

20th, Philip arrives before Acre.

May: Richard conquers Cyprus from its independent Greek ruler, then joins the Crusaders before Acre.

C **Jul**: 12th, the Crusaders take Acre; it becomes the capital of the Kingdom of Jerusalem.

28th, the dispute between John, Count of Mortain, and William Longchamp, the justiciar, ends with their reconciliation.

Aug: the Empress Constance captured in a revolt in Salerno, while Henry is compelled by fever in his army to raise the siege of Naples and return to Germany.

3rd, Philip sails for home from Palestine.

Sep: 7th, Richard leads the Crusaders to victory over Saladin at Arsūf.

D **Oct**: 5th, order restored in England at a council held in Reading by Walter of Coutances, Archbishop of Rouen, who had been empowered by Richard to supersede Longchamp as justiciar.

E Ya'qūb recovers Silves, etc., from Portugal, restoring the Tagus as the Muslim frontier.

Henry the Lion defeated at Boizenburg by Adolf of Holstein and loses Lübeck.

Isaac II institutes the Order of Knights of Angelici.

1190

G **Economics, Science, Technology and Discovery**

Earliest European reference to a floating magnet (for navigation).

*Daniel de Merlac, *Liber de naturis inferiorum et superiorum* (treatise on astrological philosophy, based on Arabic work).

(–1230) notices of coal-mining for iron forges at Liège; coal was apparently first mined for this purpose, also in France.

H **Religion and Education**

Reformed Buddhism introduced into Burma from Ceylon.

J **Art, Architecture and Music**

The west front of Laon Cathedral, initiating the Gothic style of west façades.

*Avila Cathedral completed.

*Vladimir Church.

K **Literature, Philosophy and Scholarship**

**El Misterio de los Reyes Magos* (anon., the earliest extant Spanish religious drama).

*Friedrich von Hausen, poems and lyrics (in Middle High German, in praise of idealised love; earliest extant lyrics of the twelfth–thirteenth century *Minnesingers*).

**Girart de Roussillon* (a Provençal *chanson de geste*).

†Saigyō, Japanese poet.

1191

G **Economics, Science, Technology and Discovery**

Eisai also (*below*) introduced tea into Japan and wrote *Kissa-yōjō-ki* (on its merits).

H **Religion and Education**

Eisai introduces the Rinzai sect of Zen Buddhism (–800) into Japan from China.

K **Literature, Philosophy and Scholarship**

Alleged remains of King Arthur discovered at Glastonbury.

†Al-Suhrawardi, *Hikmat al-Ishraq* (*Wisdom of Illumination*; philosophical treatise by leading Sūfī pantheist).

1192 Saladin defeated—Richard captured in Austria

A **Jan**: Richard camps at Beit-Nuba, 12 miles from Jerusalem, then retires to refortify Ascalon.

Mar: Philip II takes possession of the county of Péronne.

B **Apr**: 5th, Guy of Lusignan deposed as King of Jerusalem, receiving Cyprus in compensation; Conrad, Marquess of Montferrat, elected as King.

28th, Conrad murdered by Assassins sent by Sinan (–1193); Henry of Champagne elected as King of Jerusalem (at Acre; –1197).

May: 23rd, Richard takes Daron, thus completing the recovery of the Palestinian coast.

Jun: he camps within sight of Jerusalem, but withdraws.

By the Concordat of Gravina, Celestine III recognises Tancred as King of Sicily.

21st, death of Orio Malipiero, Doge of Venice; succeeded by Enrico Dandolo (–1205).

C **Jul**: 30th, Saladin takes Jaffa.

31st, Richard expels him.

Aug: 5th, Richard defeats Saladin outside Jaffa.

Sep: Albert of Brabant consecrated as Bishop of Liège, Celestine having rejected Henry VI's candidate; thus a civil war begins in Germany.

2nd, Richard and Saladin conclude a treaty for a truce for three years; so ends the Third Crusade.

D **Oct**: 9th, Richard sails from Palestine.

Nov: 24th, Bishop Albert of Liège murdered by German knights; Henry VI is blamed.

Dec: 11th, Richard captured near Vienna by Leopold, Duke of Austria.

E John claims to be King of England.

Sverker II succeeds his father, Cnut Ericson, as King of Sweden (–1210).

The Empress Constance escapes from Salerno.

Prithvī Rāj (*or* Raī Pithōra), the ruler of Ajmēr and Delhi, defeated and killed at Tarāorī by Muhammad, Sultan of Ghūr, who thus conquered northern India.

K **Literature, Philosophy and Scholarship**

†Richard of Devizes, *Chronicon de rebus gestis Ricardi Primi* (chronicle of the reign of Richard I and the Third Crusade).

*Chand Bardāī, *Chand Raīsā* (epic poem in Hindi about Prithvī Rāj, the last Hindu ruler of Delhi, d. 1192).

1193

A **Jan**: by the Treaty of Vercelli, Henry VI secures the support of the towns of Lombardy.
Delhi taken by Aybak, Muhammad's viceroy, and becomes the Muslim capital in India.
Feb: 14th, Leopold surrenders Richard to Henry VI.
Mar: 3rd, death of Saladin; his dominions now disintegrate; one son, al-ʿAzīz, succeeds in Cairo (–1196).

B **Jun**: 29th, by the Treaty of Worms, Henry agrees to release Richard, who became his vassal.

C **Jul**: 9th, by the Treaty of Mantes, Richard's envoys recognise the conquest of Gisors and the Norman Vexin by Philip.
Aug: Philip, building an anti-English alliance, marries, as his second wife, Ingeborg, sister of Cnut VI of Denmark.

D **Oct**: Leo II of Armenia captures Bohemond III of Antioch and compels him to recognise his suzerainty; but Bohemond's subjects refuse to comply.

E Henry Břetislav, Bishop of Prague, succeeds as Duke of Bohemia (–1197).
Death of Rashīd ad-Dīn Sinān, the 'Old Man of the Mountain', ruler (from 1162) of the Syrian branch of Assassins, based on Masyad; the main branch, of Alamūt, now recovers control of the whole order.
The Muslims in India take the great Buddhist centre of Bihār.

1194

A **Jan**: Philip and John offer to buy Richard from Henry VI.
Feb: 3rd, Richard released at Mainz; as he returns, he builds up an anti-French coalition in the Rhineland and Low Countries.
20th, death of Tancred, King of Sicily; succeeded by his son, William III.
Mar: Henry VI makes peace with Henry the Lion.
12th, Richard returns to England.
28th, he captures Nottingham Castle, thus ending John's revolt.

B **Apr**: 17th, Richard again crowned.
May: death of Guy of Lusignan, ruler of Cyprus; succeeded by his brother, Amalric.
4th, death of Casimir II the Just, Grand Prince of Poland; civil war follows (–1201).
12th, Richard leaves England, having raised much money by the sale of fresh charters, etc.; he had imposed a tax called the Carucage which was a revival of the Danegeld.
Jun: 27th, death of Sancho VI the Wise, King of Navarre; succeeded by his son, Sancho VII (–1234).

C **Jul**: 4th, Richard routes Philip at Fréteval.
Summer: Henry rapidly subdues southern Italy; Naples surrenders, Salerno is sacked.

D **Nov**: 20th, Henry VI enters Palermo, completing his conquest of Sicily.
Dec: 25th, he is crowned as King of Sicily (–1197).

E Tekish of Khwārizm defeats Tughril, the Seljuq Sultan of Persian Iraq, and establishes himself as Sultan (–1200).
Muhammad of Ghūr conquers the kingdom of Kanauj.

1193

F **Law and Politics**

Florence first known to have a *rector*.

G **Economics, Science, Technology and Discovery**

†Burgundo of Pisa, translations of Galen's medical works from Greek into Latin.

†Fan Ch'êng-ta, *Kuei hai yü hêng chih* (on the geography and natural history of south China); *Fan ts'un chü p'u* (treatise on the chrysanthemum, describing 35 varieties).

J **Art, Architecture and Music**

Jami' or Quwwat al-Islām mosque, Delhi (–1199).

Byzantine frescoes in church of Agios Neophytos, Cyprus.

K **Literature, Philosophy and Scholarship**

†Benedict of Peterborough, *Gesta Henrici II.*

L **Births and Deaths**

— St. Clara b. (–1253).

— Albertus Magnus b. (–1280).

1194

F **Law and Politics**

Hubert Walter, the Justiciar (*i.e.* viceregent, in Richard I's absence), issues articles for the eyre (itinerant judicial enquiry), instituting the office of coroner to keep records of crown pleas; the earliest extant plea rolls date from this year, when the Exchequer of the Jews also is established and an enquiry made into land-tenures in England.

J **Art, Architecture and Music**

June 10th, Chartres Cathedral burnt, save for the west front; its rebuilding initiates 'High Gothic'.

*Meaux Cathedral begun.

L **Births and Deaths**

Dec. 26th, Frederick II b. (–1250).

— Ezzelin da Romano b. (–1259).

1195

B Apr: 2nd, Henry VI has a crusade proclaimed at Bari.
8th, the Greek Emperor, Isaac II, deposed by his brother, Alexius III (–1203).
May: Celestine annuls a sentence by French bishops dissolving the marriage of Philip and Ingeborg.

C Aug: 6th, death of Henry the Lion.

1196

A Jan: Richard and Philip make peace by the Treaty of Louviers.

B Apr: in a diet at Würzburg, Henry proposes to make the Holy Roman Empire hereditary.
25th, death of Alfonso II of Aragon; succeeded by his son, Pedro II (–1213).
Jun: Philip marries, irregularly, Agnes, daughter of the Duke of Meran (in Bavaria).

C Jul: Philip renews the war with Richard by seizing Aumâle.
Al-ʿĀdil, Saladin's brother, gains control of Egypt and much of Syria, styling himself Sultan (–1218).
18th, Berber forces sent by Yaʿqūb inflict a crushing defeat on Alfonso VIII of Castile at Alarcos (west of Ciudad Real); Yaʿqūb now assumes the title Al-Mansūr (Spanish, Almanzor, 'the Victorious').

D Nov: 17th, Celestine rejects Henry's proposal to make the Empire hereditary.
Dec: 25th, Henry's son, Frederick (II), elected King of the Romans.

E Death of Béla III of Hungary; succeeded by his son, Imre (–1204).
Asen I of Bulgaria murdered; the Tsar Peter now takes control.
Stephen Nemanja, Grand Župan of Rascia, abdicates, having founded a Serbian state independent of Constantinople; succeeded by Stephen (–1228).
Muhammad of Ghūr conquers Gwalior and Gujarat.
Ch'oe Ch'ung-hon, a Korean general, massacres his rivals, takes control of the kingdom and restores its unity; his family, the Ch'oe, retain power until 1258.

1195

F **Law and Politics**

July 15th, date of the earliest extant final concord, a triplicate record of the transfer of land (in England) with its 'foot' filed in the Treasury.

H **Religion and Education**

*Bernard of Pavia, canonist, *Summa* of decretals.

†*Theodore Balsamon, titular (Greek) Patriarch of Antioch, *Exegesis canonum*.

K **Literature, Philosophy and Scholarship**

†Bernart de Ventadour, *Chansons d'amour* (love lyrics of a Provençal troubadour).

Hartmann von Aue, *Der Arme Heinrich* (Middle High German original of Longfellow's *The Golden Legend*, a moral epic poem).

†Nakayama Tadachika, *Mizu-kagami* (*The Water-Mirror*; Japanese history, 660 B.C.–A.D. 850); also a diary.

L **Births and Deaths**

Aug. 15th, St. Anthony of Padua b. (–1231).

1196

K **Literature, Philosophy and Scholarship**

*Ambroise d'Évreux, *L'Estoire de la guerre sainte* (verse narrative history of the Third Crusade; the oldest French historical narrative dealing with contemporary events, Ambroise being a follower of Richard I).

*Ephraim of Bonn, *Emek habacha* (account of persecution of Jews in Germany, France and England, 1146–96).

1197

C **Sep**: 10th, death of Henry of Champagne, King of Jerusalem.
28th, death of the Holy Roman Emperor, Henry VI.

E Death of Henry Břetislav, Duke of Bohemia, who had conquered Moravia; succeeded by Vladislav Henry, who soon abdicates in favour of Přemysl Ottokar I (–1230); his recognition as Duke ends a period of civil war and the German Emperor's influence in ducal elections.

Peter, Tsar of Bulgaria, murdered; succeeded by his brother, Kalojan (–1207).

Henry VI recognises Amalric as King of Cyprus.

Muhammad of Ghūr conquers Anhilwara.

1198

A **Jan**: Leo II crowned as King of Armenia (–1219) with the assent of the Pope and of the Emperors Henry and Alexius.
Amalric of Cyprus crowned as King of Jerusalem (–1205).
8th, death of Pope Celestine; Lothar Conti elected as Innocent III (–1216).

Feb: 2nd, German crusaders besieging Toron flee on the approach of an Egyptian army.

Mar: 6th, Philip, Duke of Swabia, elected as King of the Romans (–1208).

B **May**: 17th, Frederick crowned as King of Sicily (–1250).

C **Jul**: the Welf, Otto IV, son of Henry the Lion, after capturing Cologne, crowned as King of the Romans (–1215); thus there is civil war in Germany between him and the Hohenstaufen party of Philip of Swabia.

Aug: 15th, Innocent III proclaims the Fourth Crusade to liberate Jerusalem and offers an indulgence to those who fight the Albigensians in southern France.

Sep: Richard routes Philip at Gisors and recovers the Norman Vexin.

D **Nov**: Frederick of Sicily becomes the ward of Pope Innocent, who takes possession of Spoleto and the Marches for the Papacy.

E Ottokar I crowned as King of Bohemia, at Mainz, in return for his support of Philip of Swabia; with the establishment of the Kingdom of Bohemia, its succession ceases to be a regular cause of dispute and civil war.

1197

G **Economics, Science, Technology and Discovery**

Notice of 'iron-mills' at Sorø, Denmark.

An assize (*i.e.* 'statute') establishes common weights and measures in England.

J **Art, Architecture and Music**

*Château Gaillard built by Richard I (with the earliest known European machicolation; *cf.* 1087).

1198

H **Religion and Education**

The series of Papal Registers, recording the Pope's correspondence, dates from 1198.

J **Art, Architecture and Music**

Juggernaut Pagoda, Orissa, completed.

Byzantine frescoes in church of St. Demetrius, Vladimir.

K **Literature, Philosophy and Scholarship**

†Ibn-Rushd (Averroes), commentaries on Aristotle (–1220, 1472).

†Petrus Comestor, *Historia Scolastica* (popular manual of sacred history).

*William of Newburgh, *Historia Rerum Anglicarum* (1066–1198).

L **Births and Deaths**

Dec. 12th, Abū'l-Walīd ibn-Rushd (Averroes) of Cordova d. (72).

1199 Civil war in Japan

A **Jan**: 13th, Richard and Philip make a treaty of truce.

B **Apr**: 6th, death of Richard I Coeur de Lion, King of England.
May: 27th, John, his brother, crowned as King (–1216).

E Death of the Almohad Emperor, Yaʿqūb; succeeded by his son, Muhammad al-Nasir (–1214).
Death of Minamoto Yoritomo, first Shogun of Japan; his followers retain control of government but fight for supremacy (–1219).

F **Law and Politics**

The series of Chancery Rolls originates in the Charter and Fine Rolls of 1 John.

G **Economics, Science, Technology and Discovery**

Novgorod grants privileges to the Germans (from Gothland) established in a trading factory there, so ending an embargo begun by the Germans in 1189 in retaliation to restrictions on their operations in Russia.

H **Religion and Education**

Innocent III taxes the universal church for the proposed Fourth Crusade, the first direct papal taxation of the church.

J **Art, Architecture and Music**

Qutb-Minār Mosque, Old Delhi (–1236).

K **Literature, Philosophy and Scholarship**

Alexander de Villedieu, *Doctrinale Puerorum* (a grammatical compilation which comes to be widely used).

†Richard I, *Rotrouenge* (*chansons français*).

†Michael of Antioch, Chronicle (Syriac) of world history (from Creation to 1196).

**Chronicle of Kiev* (Russian history, 1116–99).

*Ralph de Diceto, *Ymagines Historiarum* (English history, 1149–99).

A **Jan**: 13th, Innocent lays an interdict on France because Philip refuses to take back Ingeborg as his wife.

B **May**: 22nd, by the Treaty of Le Goulet, Philip recognises John as Richard's heir in all his French possessions, in which Brittany is to be held by Arthur as John's vassal; John cedes the Vexin and Évreux to Philip.

C **Aug**: 30th, John marries Isabel, the heiress of the count of Angoulême, thereby alienating her fiancé Hugh of Lusignan.

Sep: 7th, the papal interdict lifted from France following Philip's separation from Agnes of Meran.

E Llewelyn seizes Anglesey.

*Beginning of the domination of the Incas in the Cuzco Valley, Peru (–1438).

1200

L **Births and Deaths**

Nov. 16th, St. Hugh of Avalon, Bishop of Lincoln, d. (*c*. 65).

F **Law and Politics**

**Très Ancien Coutumier de Normandie* (compilation of legal customs of Normandy).

G **Economics, Science, Technology and Discovery**

*Ibn-al-ʿAwwam, *al-Filāhah* (treatise on agriculture; describes 585 plants).

H **Religion and Education**

*Foundation by Lambert le Bégue of the Béguins and Beghards, lay sects, at Liège.
*Foundation of the Trinitarian Order of friars.
*The Cistercian Order now has 530 houses.
Philip II's charter to Paris University provides the first documentary recognition of its corporate existence.

J **Art, Architecture and Music**

Rouen Cathedral burnt; rebuilt under the architects Jean d'Andeli and Enguerran.
*Bourges and Soissons Cathedrals, and towers of Nôtre Dame, Paris, begun.
ʿArhaī-Dīn-ka Jhomprā Mosque, Ajmēr (–1202).

K **Literature, Philosophy and Scholarship**

Béroul, *Tristan* (romance in Norman-French).
*Bertrand de Bar-sur-Aube, *Aimeri de Narbonne* (narrative *chanson de geste* about Charlemagne at the fall of Narbonne and of his knight Aimeri, who led the attack for the Emperor; prose versions were made in the fifteenth century).
*Layamon (Lawman), *Brut* (*i.e.* a history, or chronicle of England from Brutus to Cadwalader, A.D. 689; Middle English poem based on Wace's French version of Geoffrey of Monmouth's *Historia*—1137; includes the stories of Lear and Cymbeline).
*Walter Map (or Mapes), *De nugis curialium* (a miscellany, chiefly satirical).
*Nicholas de Guildford(?), *The Owl and the Nightingale* (a long poem written 'not far from the year 1200'—*Baugh*).
**Carmina Burana* (collection of satirical poems, lyrics and other Goliardic verses, intended to be sung; discovered in the convent at Benediktbeurin, Munich).
**Huon de Bordeaux* (*chanson de geste*; introduces the fairy named 'Oberon').
*The Five Icelandic Sagas: *The Saga of Burnt Njal* (*Njala*); the *Laxdaela* (*Laxdale*); the *Eyrbyggja*; *Egil's Saga* (*Egla*); and *The Saga of Grettir the Strong* (*Grettla*) (legends and stories either about the deeds of the hero, or about events connected with a region; –1120, –1148).
**La Nobla Leyczon* (famous poem of the Vaudois troubadours).
Das Nibelungenlied (folk epic in Old High German).
*Ormin, *The Ormulum* (long poetic paraphrase of Gospel narratives and of the life of Christ).
Shota Rustaveli, *The Man in the Panther's Skin* (as translated from the Georgian romantic epic).
Tsutsumi Chūnagon, *Monogatari* (collection of Japanese stories by various authors).
Fujiwara Kanezane, *Gyokuyō* (*Leaves of Jade*; diary of a Japanese courtier for 1164–1200).
*Kamban, *Rāmāyanam* (or *Rāmāvatāram*; outstanding epic poem in Tamil literature, which had its golden age under the Chola Empire of south India, *c.* 850–*c.* 1200).
†Chu Hsi, a leading influence in the establishment of Neo-Confucian orthodoxy, known as Chu Hsi-ism, which because of its rigidity led to scholasticism instead of speculative philosophy; he has consequently often been compared with St. Thomas Aquineas (–1274).

(*Continued opposite*)

1201–1203 Conversion of Latvia—Muslim conquest of Bengal—South Vietnam, conquered by Cambodia

1201

B **Apr:** Venice agrees, by treaty, to transport the Crusaders in return for half of their conquests.

Jun: 8th, by the Diploma of Neuss, Otto IV cedes imperial authority in Italy to the Pope.

C **July:** Innocent recognises Otto as King of the Romans.

D **Dec:** 11th, Innocent III appeals to Philip II to intervene in Languedoc.

E Mieszko III recovers the Grand Principality of Poland (–1202).

Albert, Bishop of Riga, founds Riga as a military and commercial centre and also as a base for the conversion of the Livs of Latvia.

1202

A **Mar:** 9th, death of Sverre of Norway, who had introduced a feudal administration under sheriffs; succeeded by Haakon III (–1204).

B **Apr:** 30th, Philip declares that John has forfeited his French lands because he failed to appear in Philip's court to answer the barons of Poitou, John's vassals in revolt against him.

C **Aug:** 1st, John defeats and captures Arthur of Brittany, Hugh of Lusignan and other rebels at Mirabeau, near Poitiers.

D **Nov:** 12th, death of Cnut VI the Pious, King of Denmark; succeeded by his brother, Waldemar II (–1241).

15th, the Crusaders take Zara from the King of Hungary, for Venice; here they agree to take Constantinople on behalf of Alexius Angelus, son of Isaac II.

E Innocent excommunicates Alfonso IX of Leon and puts his kingdom under an interdict.

Death of Mieszko III the Old, Grand Prince of Poland and ruler of Cracow; his title dies with him; succeeded by Leszek II, son of Casimir II, who revives the plan to make Cracow a suzerain, hereditary principality (–1227).

With the fall of Kālinjar, Muhammad of Ghūr completes his conquest of Upper India; other Muslims, under Ikhtiyār-ad-Dīn, seize Bengal.

1203

B **Apr:** 3rd(?), John (supposedly) murders Arthur of Brittany; in consequence, John's French vassals mostly desert him so that Philip easily overruns the Loire valley.

C **Jul:** 17th, the Crusaders force an entry into Constantinople; Alexius III flees and Isaac II is restored.

Aug: 1st, at the Crusaders' insistence, Alexius IV Angelus crowned as Greek Emperor (–1204).

E Otto IV confirms Ottokar as King of Bohemia, who is now supporting him against Philip.

Death of Muhammad, Sultan of Ghūr; succeeded by Shīhab-ad-Dīn Muhammad (–1206).

Jayavarman VII of Cambodia conquers and annexes Champa (–1220).

1201

G **Economics, Science, Technology and Discovery**
John grants a charter to the Jews in England.

K **Literature, Philosophy and Scholarship**
Roger of Hoveden (or Howden), *Chronica majora* (Latin chronicle history of England to 1201; –1259).
†Al-Katīb, *Kitāb al-Barq al-Sha'mi* (*The Syrian Lightning*; historical memoirs).

1202

G **Economics, Science, Technology and Discovery**
Leonardo Fibonacci of Pisa, *Liber Abaci* (earliest Latin account of Arabic (*i.e.* Hindu) numerals; –1041).

H **Religion and Education**
†Joachim of Flora, *The Everlasting Gospel* (heterodox eschatology; –1254).
†*Alan of Lille, 'the Universal Doctor', *Anticlaudianus* or *The Office of a Good and Perfect Man* (popular encyclopedic poem).

K **Literature, Philosophy and Scholarship**
Jean Bodel, *Congé* (a poem of farewell to friends, on being stricken with leprosy).
*Jocelyn of Brakelond, *Chronicle* (of abbey of Bury St. Edmunds and some English history, 1173–1202).

L **Births and Deaths**
Mar. 30th, Joachim of Flora d. (70).

1203

H **Religion and Education**
Siena University founded.

J **Art, Architecture and Music**
Lérida Cathedral (–1278).

1204 Fourth Crusade conquers Greek Empire—John expelled from Normandy

A **Jan:** an anti-Latin mob in Constantinople proclaims Nicholas Canabus as Emperor; Isaac II murdered.

1st, death of Haakon III of Norway; succeeded by Gottorm.

Feb: 8th, Alexius IV murdered and Canabus imprisoned; Alexius V Ducas Murtzuphlus assumes the Greek Empire.

Mar: 8th, Philip takes Château Gaillard.

B **Apr:** 12th, the Crusaders force their way into Constantinople; Alexius flees, as does Constantine XI Lascaris after being offered the throne by Greek nobles.

13th, the Crusaders sack Constantinople, for three days.

May: Alexius Comnenus, grandson of Andronicus I, seizes Trebizond and establishes a new Greek empire there (–1461).

16th, Baldwin, Count of Flanders, crowned as Latin Emperor of Constantinople (–1206).

Jun: 24th, with the fall of Rouen, Philip's conquest of Normandy is complete; only Gascony and the Channel Islands remain in English hands.

C **Aug:** death of Gottorm of Norway; succeeded by Inge II (–1217).

Sep: al-Adil and Amalric of Jerusalem make a treaty of peace for six years.

D **Oct:** Baldwin, the Venetians and Crusaders partition the Greek Empire by treaty; Venice had already secured the Adriatic coast, Rhodes, and the islands in the Ægean; other Crusaders are to hold their conquests (yet to be made) as fiefs; thus Otto de la Roche is invested with the lordship of Athens.

Nov: Pedro II of Aragon swears fealty to the pope in Rome.

8th, Kalojan crowned as King of Bulgaria (styling himself Emperor) by a papal legate, following his agreement with Innocent to accept the Roman Church.

Dec: Theodore Lascaris, brother of Constantine XI, who was establishing himself at Brusa, defeated by Baldwin near Poimanenon.

E Death of Imre of Hungary; succeeded by his son, Ladislas III (–1205).

The Crusaders defeat Michael Ducas at Koundoura in Messenia; this was a decisive victory in their conquest of the Morea.

Innocent grants a charter to the Sword Brothers, the military order founded by Bishop Albert of Riga to assist in the conversion of the Livs.

Kaykhusraw I succeeds as Sultan of Rūm (–1210).

G **Economics, Science, Technology and Discovery**
†Moses ben Maimōn (Maimonides), *Kitāb al-Fusūl fī al-Tibb* (*Aphorisms of Medicine*).
†*Al-Bitrūji (Alpetragius), *Kitāb al-Hay'ah* (*The Book of Astronomy*; –1217).

J **Art, Architecture and Music**
Choir (Romanesque) of Tarragona Cathedral consecrated.

K **Literature, Philosophy and Scholarship**
†Moses ben Maimōn, *Dalālat al-Hā'irīn* (*The Guide to the Perplexed*; philosophical treatise to reconcile Jewish theology and Muslim Aristotelianism).

L **Births and Deaths**
Apr. 1st, Eleanor of Aquitaine d.
Dec. 13th, Moses ben Maimōn d. (69).

1205–1206 Bulgarisan defeat Latins—Slave Kingdom of Delhi—Ghengiz Khan

1205

A **Jan:** John organises English defences against an expected French invasion.
6th, Philip of Swabia crowned as King of the Romans (–1208).
16th, Innocent III (vainly) urges Philip II to organise a crusade against the Albigensians.
Feb: Kalojan of Bulgaria attacks Adrianople in a war against the Latins.
Mar: the English barons refuse to fight for John in France.

B **Apr:** 1st, death of Amalric II of Jerusalem: his widow, Isabella, rules in her own right, and on dying (date unknown) is succeeded by her daughter, Maria. Hugh I succeeds as King of Cyprus (–1218).
14th, Kalojan defeats and captures Baldwin outside Constantinople.
Jun: 1st, death of Enrico Dandolo, Doge of Venice; succeeded by Pietro Ziano (–1229).

C **Jul:** 12th/13th, death of Hubert Walter, Archbishop of Canterbury, John's chancellor; the monks of Canterbury elect Reginald, their sub-prior, to succeed.

D **Dec:** 11th, on John's insistence, John Grey, Bishop of Norwich, elected as Archbishop of Canterbury.

E Azzo VI, Marquess of Este, recognised as lord of Ferrara.
Ladislas of Hungary deposed and succeeded by his uncle, Andrew II (–1235).
Roman, established by Leszek of Poland as Prince of Halich (Galicia), refuses to do homage; when invading Poland, Roman is killed in the battle of Zawichost.
The Seljuqs take Kayseri, the Danishmend capital in Anatolia.
Ikhtiyār, the Muslim ruler of Bengal, fails in an attempt to invade Assam (*or, possibly,* Tibet).

1206

A **Mar:** Innocent rejects John Grey's election to Canterbury.
15th, Muhammad of Ghūr murdered by Aybak, his viceroy in India, who assumes the title of Sultan, founding the dynasty of Slave Kings of Delhi (–1290).

B **Spring:** the Mongol prince, Temujin, who had united Mongolia and taken the title of Ghengiz Khan, recognised as Khan (–1227) in an assembly of Mongols; the Mongol Empire thus founded.
Jun: John begins a campaign in western France, exploiting a revolt against Philip by the barons of Poitou.

C **Jul:** 27th, Philip of Swabia defeats Otto IV at Wassenburg.
Aug: Kalojan destroys Adrianople.
20th, as Baldwin had died in captivity, his brother, Henry of Flanders, crowned as Latin Emperor of Constantinople (–1216); his daughter, Joanna, succeeds to the county of Flanders (–1214).

D **Oct:** 26th John and Philip make a truce, for two years, at Thouars.
Dec: the monks of Canterbury in Rome, under Innocent's influence, elect Cardinal Stephen Langton as Archbishop.

1205

H **Religion and Education**

Diego of Osma, assisted by Dominic, begins his mission to the Albigensians (Cathari) of southern France.

†The 'Spiritual Society', or Amaurists, a sect of mystics founded by Amaury of Chartres.

Innocent III issues *Vergentis in senium*: heretics and their heirs are to be deprived of all their property and goods.

J **Art, Architecture and Music**

The original Gothic cathedral of Laon being completed, its apse is demolished and the extension of the choir begun.

On the completion of Noyon (Gothic) Cathedral, its west façade begun.

The Çifte Medrese (College), Kayseri, founded.

†Takanobu, Japanese painter.

K **Literature, Philosophy and Scholarship**

†Yüan Shu, *T'ung-chien chi-shih pen-mo* (*Narratives from Beginning to End from the Comprehensive Mirror*; another version of Ssŭ-ma Kuang's history of China; –1086).

Shin kokinshū (*Ghe New Ancient and Modern Collection*; an imperial anthology of Japanese poetry).

*Fujiwara Teika, or Sadaie, *Hyakunin isshu* (*One Poem Each by a Hundred Persons*).

1206

F **Law and Politics**

Ghengiz Khan promulgates the Great Yasa (imperial law-code) for the Mongols.

G **Economics, Science, Technology and Discovery**

Al-Jazarī, treatise on mechanics and clocks.

†Fujiwara Nagatsune, a Japanese courtier, wrote the first known treatise on landscape gardening.

K **Literature, Philosophy and Scholarship**

*Guiot of Provins, *Bible* (French satirical poem).

*Nicetas Acominatos, History of Constantinople (1180–1206).

1207

A **Jan:** Philip of Swabia takes Cologne, so completing his dominance in Germany.

C **Sep:** Boniface, Marquis of Montferrat, King of Thessalonica, killed in an ambush by Bulgars.

D **Oct:** 8th, death of Kalojan, Emperor of Bulgaria; succeeded by his nephew, Boril (–1218).

Nov: 17th, Innocent III (vainly) urges Philip II to organise a Crusade against the Albigensians.

E Venice takes Corfù.

Marco Sanudo, a Venetian, begins to rule as Duke of the Archipelago (*i.e.* the Ægean islands he had seized, with his capital on Naxos).

Innocent confirms Ottokar as King of Bohemia.

Han T'o-chou, the Southern Sung Emperor, killed by the Chin when attempting to reconquer northern China.

1208

A **Mar:** 23rd, Innocent's interdict (because John refused to accept Langton as Archbishop and had taken measures against the Church) published in England.

B **Apr:** Theodore I Lascaris crowned as Greek Emperor in Nicaea (–1222).

Jun: 21st, Philip of Swabia, whom Innocent had just recognised as King of the Romans, murdered by Otto of Wittelsbach.

C **Jul:** 31st, the Franks of Constantinople defeat Boril of Bulgaria.

D **Nov:** 11th, Otto IV elected, unanimously, as King of the Romans.

17th, Innocent III appeals to the nobility in northern France to intervene against the Albigensians.

E Llewelyn seizes Powys.

Al-Nasir destroys the last Almoravid strongholds in North Africa.

1207

F **Law and Politics**

Innocent III summons an assembly of representatives of towns in the Papal States.

H **Religion and Education**

Japanese authorities persecute the Pure Land Sect (–1175).

J **Art, Architecture and Music**

Magdeburg Cathedral burnt; Archbishop Albrecht orders that the new cathedral should be built in the Gothic style.

L **Births and Deaths**

Oct. 1st, Henry III b. (–1272).

— St. Elizabeth b. (–1231).

1208

H **Religion and Education**

Feb. 24th, probable date when St. Francis' vocation is revealed to him.

Innocent III taxes the church in France for the Albigensian Crusade.

Innocent approves the rule of the Society of Poor Catholics, consisting of former heretics in southern France.

J **Art, Architecture and Music**

Choir of Lincoln Cathedral, designed by Geoffrey de Noyer, completed (replaced; –1256).

K **Literature, Philosophy and Scholarship**

*Saxo Grammaticus, *Gesta Danorum* (history of the legendary kings of Denmark, based on folklore and poems; with the story of Amleth, *i.e.* Hamlet).

1209

B **Jun:** 17th, Raymond VI, Count of Toulouse, submits to the papal legate and is absolved from excommunication incurred by his sympathy for the Albigensian heresy prevailing among his subjects.

C **Jul:** 22nd, Béziers is sacked by the Albigensian crusaders.
Aug: 2nd, John, after invading Scotland, makes a treaty of peace with William II.
15th, Carcassonne is taken by the Albigensian crusaders: Simon de Montfort is then elected leader and expropriates land, becoming lord of Béziers and Carcassonne.

D **Oct:** Welsh princes do homage to John.
4th, Innocent crowns Otto IV as Holy Roman Emperor.
Nov: John's excommunication by Innocent published in France.

E Philip completes the walls of Paris.
Geoffrey of Villehardouin assumes the title of Prince of Achaea, founding another feudal Latin dynasty in the Morea (known as 'Romania' in the west).
Thamar, Queen of Georgia, takes Kars in a victorious campaign against the Turks.

1210

B **Spring:** Theodore defeats and kills Kaykhusraw of Rūm who, aided by Latins, was attempting to restore Alexius III.
Jun: John makes an expedition to Ireland, enforcing his authority there (–August).

C **Jul:** 17th, Sverker II of Sweden defeated, killed and succeeded by Eric X Cnutson (–1220); Eric is the first Swedish King to be anointed at his coronation, by the Archbishop of Upsala.

D **Oct:** 3rd, John of Brienne, having married Maria, crowned as King of Jerusalem (at Acre: –1225).
Nov: Otto opens his campaign to conquer Apulia and is therefore excommunicated by Innocent, who frees Otto's subjects from obedience, thus starting a rebellion in Germany.
Death of Aybak, Sultan of Delhi; his dominions disintegrate.

E Herman de Salza, the Grand Master, obtains papal privileges for the Teutonic Order.
Waldemar of Denmark conquers Danzig (Gdansk) and east Pomerania.

1209

H **Religion and Education**

Three thousand scholars said to have left Oxford, some for Cambridge (the earliest notice of a *studium* there); many returned to Oxford in 1214.

L **Births and Deaths**

Jan. 5th, Richard of Cornwall b. (–1272).

1210

F **Law and Politics**

*Most ancient Burmese law code dates from reign of Jayasura II (d. 1210).

G **Economics, Science, Technology and Discovery**

*Alfred of Shareshel, *De motu cordis* (*The Movement of the Heart*).

H **Religion and Education**

Innocent III verbally sanctions St. Francis' Order (the Friars Minor).

The study of certain of Aristotle's works forbidden at the University of Paris.

*Johannes Zemecke Teutonicus, *Glossa ordinaria* (on *Decretum*; –1139).

J **Art, Architecture and Music**

Reims Cathedral begun; the architects were, successively, Jean d'Orbais, Gaucher of Reims, Jean le Loup, Bernard of Soissons.

K **Literature, Philosophy and Scholarship**

*Gottfried von Strassburg, *Tristan und Isolde* (Old High German narrative poem in couplets).

*Latin translation of Aristotle's *Metaphysics*.

†*Gervase of Canterbury, *Gesta regum* (chronicle of England from Brutus to 1210).

1211

A **Mar**: 27th, death of Sancho I of Portugal; succeeded by his son, Afonso II (–1223).
30th, Innocent again excommunicates Otto, who has returned to Germany to defeat the rebellion.

B **May**: John makes war on Llewelyn.

C **Sep**: in a diet at Nuremburg, German princes in revolt against Otto offer the crown to Frederick II.

D **Oct**: 15th, Henry of Flanders defeats Theodore I on the Rhyndacus, near Brusa, and takes Pergamum.

E Ghengiz Khan destroys theKara-Khitai Empire in east Turkestan and invades China (–1215).

1212

A **Jan**: Joanna of Flanders marries Ferrand of Portugal (–1233).

C **Jul**: Frederick enters Germany.
16th, on a crusade, Alfonso VIII of Castile, Sancho VII of Navarre and Pedro II of Aragon win a great victory over the Muslims at Las Navas de Tolosa.
Sep: John abandons his preparations for a campaign against Llewelyn because of a baronial plot to murder him.
26th, in a Golden Bull, Frederick confirms Ottokar as King of Bohemia and generally recognises Bohemia as a largely autonomous fief of the Empire.

D **Nov**: 19th, by the Treaty of Toul, Frederick and Philip make an alliance against John and Otto.
Dec: 9th, Frederick crowned as King of the Romans.

E The Venetians occupy Crete.
Juri II succeeds Vsévolod III as Great Prince of Vladimir (–1238).
Death of Thamar the Great, Queen of Georgia; succeeded by her son, George IV (–1223).

1211

J **Art, Architecture and Music**

Nevers Cathedral burnt; rebuilt.

*Toulouse Cathedral.

1212

F **Law and Politics**

A survey of military tenures in England ordered by John is completed.

G **Economics, Science, Technology and Discovery**

†*Gervase of Tilbury, *Otia Imperialia* (miscellany of natural and topographical lore).

H **Religion and Education**

(–1214) Alfonso VIII establishes the first Spanish university at Palencia; it survived until *c.* 1250.

The Children's Crusade: the French contingent wrecked off Sardinia and its survivors captured by Saracens.

K **Literature, Philosophy and Scholarship**

*Wolfram von Eschenbach, *Parzival* (Middle High German epic on the Grail theme, introducing Lohengrin; continued in *Titurel* and *Willehalm*; –1230, –1336).

†Arnold of Lübeck, continuation of Helmold's Chronicle (–1171; to 1209).

Kamo Chōmei, *Hōjō-ki* (*Annals of ten-feet square*; on his eremetical bliss, with historical events of his time; a Japanese classic).

1213

B **Apr:** 8th, Philip formally accepts Innocent's mandate to conquer England.
19th (–29th), Innocent II proclaims the Fifth Crusade and removes the indulgences for the Albigensian Crusade.
May: 13th, John accepts the Pope's terms for ending the interdict, receiving Langton as Archbishop; he also resigns his kingdom to Innocent and receives it again as a papal fief, promising to pay tribute.
30th, his fleet destroys that of the French, massed for the invasion of England, at Damme, near Bruges.
Jun: by the death of his sister-in-law, Philip gains possession of St. Quentin, Valois and the remainder of Vermandois.
3rd, John makes a truce with Llewelyn.

C **Jul:** 12th, by the Golden Bull of Eger, Frederick recognises the Papacy's territorial claims in Italy and renounces imperial control over the Church in Germany.
Sep: 12th, Simon de Montfort and his crusaders defeat Raymond of Toulouse and kill his ally, Pedro II of Aragon, at Muret; Pedro's heir in Aragon is his young son, James I (–1276), and civil war follows there (–1227).
28th, Magyar nobles murder Queen Gertrude of Hungary.

D **Oct:** 13th, John's allies in the Low Countries defeat Duke Henry of Brabant at Steppes, near St. Trond.

E Alfonso of Castile defeats an invasion by the Almohads at Febragaen.
Kalinga Vijaya-Bāhu conquers Ceylon and founds a dynasty.

1214

A **Feb:** 15th, John begins his campaign in western France.

B **May:** by the Treaty of Metz, Frederick recognises Waldemar of Denmark's conquests in northern Germany.

C **Jul:** 27th, Philip defeats John's allies, among them Otto IV, at Bouvines; by capturing the Counts of Flanders and Boulogne, he establishes French control there. As Otto's defeat also assists Frederick's cause in Germany, the battle is considered one of the most important in European history.
Sep: 18th, John makes a truce with Philip at Chinon.

D **Oct:** death of Alfonso VIII of Castile; succeeded by his son, Henry I (–1217), a minor, and so civil war follows.
Dec: the Emperors Theodore and Henry make a demarcation treaty.
4th, death of William II the Lion, King of Scotland; succeeded by his son, Alexander II (–1249).
25th, death of al-Nasir, the Almohad emperor; succeeded by Yūsuf II (–1224).

E Frederick invests the Wittelsbachs with the Rhine Palatinate.
'Alā-ad-Dīn Muhammad, the Khwārizm Shah, takes Ghaznī; he had now conquered most of Persia and Transoxiana.

1213

F **Law and Politics**

Nov. 15th, knights representing shires are called, for the first known time, to a council held at Oxford by John.

K **Literature, Philosophy and Scholarship**

†*Geoffroi de Villehardouin, *De la Conquête de Constantinople* (*c.* 1198–1207, the crusader-historian taking part: –1216; 'the first great French prose book'—*Saintsbury*).

†Nicetas Chroniates, history of Byzantium 1118–1206; *De Statuis* (listing works of art destroyed in Constantinople by the crusaders).

1214

G **Economics, Science, Technology and Discovery**

†Maurus (of Salerno), *Anatomia Mauri* (one of the earliest Latin texts on anatomy).

H **Religion and Education**

Earliest constitution of Oxford University.

K **Literature, Philosophy and Scholarship**

*Robert de Borron, *Joseph d'Arimathie* (the first Grail romance).

L **Births and Deaths**

— Roger Bacon b. (–1294).

1215

A **Jan:** 8th, Simon de Montfort elected Lord of Languedoc in a council at Montpellier.

B **Apr:** Louis VII musters his troops at Lyons on the way to the Albigensian Crusade.
May: 17th, the barons in revolt against John take possession of London.
Jun: 19th, John and his opponents agree on terms for peace, published (from the 24th) in Magna Carta, whereby the King agrees to various curtailments of his powers and concedes 'liberties' to different classes of his subjects.

C **Jul:** 25th, Frederick, having secured general recognition, is again crowned as King of the Romans.
Aug: 28th, commissioners appointed by Innocent III announce the excommunication of John's opponents and suspend Archbishop Langton from office.
Sept: John receives Innocent's bull annulling Magna Carta.

D **Oct:** 13th, John resumes the civil war by laying siege to Rochester castle.
Nov: 11th–30th, Innocent III legislates at the Fourth Lateran Council for the organisation of the Fifth Crusade, especially concerning taxation; Simon de Montfort is confirmed in his lands in southern France.

E Michael Ducas, the Greek ruler of Epirus, who had taken Larissa, Durazzo, Corfù, etc., murdered; succeeded by his half-brother, Theodore (–1230).
Ghengiz Khan takes Peking; the Chin then make Kaifeng their capital (–1234).

1216

A **Jan:** 14th–23rd, John harries southern Scotland.

B **May:** 21st, Louis (VIII), Philip's son, lands in England in response to the invitation of John's opponents to become King of England.
Jun: 11th, death of Henry of Flanders, the Latin Emperor of Constantinople; succeeded by Peter de Courtenay (–1221).

C **Jul:** 16th, death of Pope Innocent III.
18th, Cencio Savelli elected as Pope Honorius III (–1227).
Aug: 24th, Beaucaire falls to Raymond VII of Toulouse: the first substantial defeat for the Albigensian crusaders.

D **Oct:** 19th, King John dies at Newark, after losing his baggage when crossing the Wash.
28th, his son, Henry III, crowned at Gloucester (–1272). William the Marshal, Earl of Pembroke, appointed his guardian.
Nov: 12th, Henry's council re-issues Magna Carta.
Dec: Tran Thai-tong, married to the daughter of the last Ly Emperor of Dai Viet, proclaimed as Emperor (–1225).

E Ottokar of Bohemia has his eldest son, Wenceslas, crowned as King, so establishing the principle of primogeniture.
Leo of Armenia takes Antioch (from Bohemond IV).
Māravarman Sundara, the Pāndya ruler, drives Kulottunga III, the Chola Emperor, into (temporary) exile; the second Pāndya Empire is now founded.

1215

F **Law and Politics**

The court of Common Pleas permanently established at Westminster in accordance with Magna Carta.

A document of Alfonso IX of Leon indicates that the emancipation of Christian serfs has begun there.

G **Economics, Science, Technology and Discovery**

Foundation of St. Thomas' Hospital, London.

H **Religion and Education**

Nov. 11th–30th, the Fourth Lateran Council provides for the reform of diocesan organisation and of the Benedictine and Augustinian Orders; it imposes the first papal tithe on the clergy; and orders that Jews should wear distinctive dress.

A synod of the Polish Church swears to accept clerical celibacy.

*Tancred, canonist, *Ordo Judiciarius*.

J **Art, Architecture and Music**

Choir of Auxerre Cathedral begun.

K **Literature, Philosophy and Scholarship**

†Hartmann von Aue, minnesinger.

L **Births and Deaths**

Apr. 25th, St. Louis b. (–1270).

— Kublai Khan b. (–1294).

1216

G **Economics, Science, Technology and Discovery**

The coal trade of Newcastle-upon-Tyne now established.

H **Religion and Education**

Innocent III sanctions St. Clare's Order of Poor Ladies of St. Damian (*or* Poor Clares).

Dec. 22nd, Honorius III recognises St. Dominic's Order of Friars Preachers (*or* Dominicans).

K **Literature, Philosophy and Scholarship**

*Henri de Valenciennes, *Istoire del'Empereur Henri* (prose narrative of the Fourth Crusade, 1207–16, continuing Villehardouin's history; –1213).

B May: 20th, William the Marshal, leading the loyalists, defeats Louis and the rebels at Lincoln.

Jun: death of Henry I of Castile; succeeded by his sister, Berenguela, the divorced wife of Alfonso IX of Leon.

C Aug: 23rd, the French fleet destroyed by the English off Sandwich.

31st, Berenguela abdicates in favour of her son, Ferdinand III (–1252).

Sep: 12th, by the Treaty of Kingston, the English rebels make peace with Henry III and Louis is paid to leave.

c. 25th, Afonso of Portugal defeats the Muslims at Alcazar do Sal.

D Nov: the first contingents of the Fifth Crusade (among them, briefly, Andrew of Hungary) take and sack Baisan, in Palestine.

6th, Henry's council again re-issues Magna Carta.

E Haakon IV succeeds Inge II as King of Norway (–1263).

Bishop Albert of Riga defeats the Esthonians at Fellin.

James I of Aragon succeeds to the County of Roussillon.

Stephen of Rascia crowned as King of Serbia with the assent of Honorius III (–1228).

Theodore Ducas, Despot of Epirus, captures Peter de Courtenay, whose wife, Yolande, then acts as regent in Constantinople.

G **Economics, Science, Technology and Discovery**
Michael Scot, translation from Arabic of Alpetragius, *Liber Astronomiæ* (–1204).
†Alexander Neckham, *De naturis rerum* (scientific encyclopedia).

H **Religion and Education**
St. Francis holds a chapter of his order which makes its first constitution.
The first Friars Preachers arrive in Paris.
The Waldensians of Provence and Lombardy hold a conference.

J **Art, Architecture and Music**
Darussifa Hospital, with mausoleum of Kaykavus I, Sivas.
Le Mans Cathedral choir begun.
Gregory of Bridlington, *De arte musices* (treatise on music).

1218

A **Jan:** 10th, death of Hugh I, King of Cyprus; succeeded by his son, Henry I (–1253).
Feb: 18th, death of Berthold V, the last Duke of Zähringen; the Duchy is then partitioned and its rectorate of Burgundy reverts to the Empire.
Mar: Henry makes peace with Llewelyn, at Worcester.

B **May:** Frederick creates Berne an imperial free city.
19th, death of the former Holy Roman Emperor, Otto IV.
29th, the Fifth Crusade lands outside Damietta.
Jun: 25th, Simon de Montfort killed at the siege of Toulouse, where Raymond VI had been restored by a revolt.

C **Aug:** 1st, Honorius III proclaims a new Albigensian crusade.
25th, the Crusaders take a fort outside Damietta.
31st, death of the Sultan al-Adil; succeeded by his sons, al-Kāmil in Egypt (–1238) and al Mu'azzam in Damascus (–1227).
Sep: the Crusaders receive further reinforcements and Cardinal Pelagius arrives as their leader.

D **Nov:** Cardinal Pandulf arrives to replace Cardinal Guala as papal legate in England.

E John Asen II, the son of Asen I, deposes and succeeds Boril as Emperor of Bulgaria (–1241).
(–1219) Waldemar of Denmark invades Esthonia and builds a castle at Revel.

1219

B **Spring:** Raymond, the son of Raymond VI, defeats the crusaders led by Amauri de Monfort at Basiège.
May: 2nd, death of Leo II, the first King of (Lesser) Armenia.
14th, death of William the Marshal, the *rector* of Henry III and England.

C Aug: 1st, Louis VII abandons his second Albigensian Crusade.

D Nov: 5th, the Fifth Crusade takes Damietta.

E Ghengiz Khan invades the Khwarismian Empire (Transoxiana and Persia).
Murder of Minamoto Sanetomo, Shogun of Japan, the only surviving member of Yoritomo's family; Hōjō Yoshitoki, leader of the triumphant faction, assumes power as regent of the Shogunate and defeats a bid for power by the retired Emperor, Go-Toba, in the Shōkyū War. The Hōjō family retains this power until 1333.

1218

F **Law and Politics**

Meeting of the first Cortes of Catalonia known to have representatives of towns.

J **Art, Architecture and Music**

Amiens and Coutances Cathedrals burnt; rebuilt (–1220).

Abbey of San Galgano, near Siena, begun.

†Jayavarman VII of Cambodia rebuilt and walled the city of Angkor Thom; the temple of Bayon is his greatest building.

L **Births and Deaths**

May 1st, Rudolph I b. (–1291).

1219

H **Religion and Education**

Aug. St. Francis preaches in Egypt, to both the Sultan and the Crusaders; missions of his friars sent to France, Germany, Hungary and Spain.

Honorius III bans the teaching of Roman Law in the University of Paris.

J **Art, Architecture and Music**

Lausanne Cathedral begun.

The south porch of Chartres Cathedral, which has a tympanum portraying the Last Judgment (a great Gothic sculpture), begun.

Ferguniye and Alaeddin Mosques, Konya; the architect of the second was Muhammad ibn-Kaulan of Damascus.

A **Feb**: Ghengiz Khan takes Bukhāra; it is depopulated and destroyed.

B **Apr**: 26th, by his charter of privileges granted at Frankfurt, Frederick grants sovereign rights to German prelates in order to secure the election of his son, Henry, as King of the Romans (–1235).
May: 17th, Henry III again crowned, at Westminster.

C **Aug**: the army of the Fifth Crusade, advancing into Egypt from Damietta, trapped by the Nile floods and the Muslim army; Pelagius therefore accepts al-Kamil's terms.
Sep: 8th, the crusaders therefore evacuate Damietta; end of the Fifth Crusade.

D **Nov**: 22nd, Honorius crowns Frederick II as Holy Roman Emperor (–1250).
Dec: 'Alā'-ad-Dīn dies in flight from Ghengiz Khan who has conquered Transoxiana; succeeded by his son, Jalāl-ad-Dīn (–1231).

E Honorius excommunicates Afonso and lays an interdict on Portugal.
John I, the son of Sverker II, succeeds Eric X as King of Sweden (–1223).
Bohemond recovers Antioch from Raymond-Roupen of Armenia.
Jaya Parameshvaravarman II becomes King of Champa on the withdrawal of the Khmers (of Cambodia).

G **Economics, Science, Technology and Discovery**

Earliest statutes of the medical school of Montpellier University.

Leonardo Fibonacci, *Practica geometriae* (on geometry and arithmetic).

John of Garland (*see* K) refers to a brace and (possibly) a woodplane (not known in Europe since classical times; –1424).

H **Religion and Education**

May: St. Francis resigns the government of his Order.

May: the first general chapter of the Dominican Order rejects its ownership of property and makes a constitution; this embodies the principle of representation of the Order's provinces in general chapters.

Alfonso IX of Leon founds the University of Salamanca.

J **Art, Architecture and Music**

Nôtre Dame Cathedral, Paris, completed according to the plan of 1163 (–1250).

May 16th, Henry II lays the foundation stone of a new Lady Chapel at Westminster Abbey, thus beginning the new abbey-church (–1245).

Salisbury Cathedral begun; Nicholas of Ely is architect.

Amiens Cathedral begun; the architects are, successively, Robert de Luzarches and Thomas de Cormont.

*Naves of Bamberg, Séez and Wells Cathedrals begun.

Ray (*or* Rhages), the centre of the Persian ceramic industry, destroyed by the Mongols.

K **Literature, Philosophy and Scholarship**

?John of Garland, *Compendium grammaticae* (influential treatise on grammar).

**L'Histoire de Guillaume le Maréchal* (life, in French verse, of William the Marshal, 1146?–1219).

*Renaud de Beaujeu, *Guinglain, ou, Le Bel Inconnu* (metrical romance belonging to the Arthurian cycle; English version: *The Fair Unknown*, *c.* 1330).

**Aucassin and Nicolette* (anon. romance—early thirteenth century; in Provençal literature, part prose, part verse).

*Gaucelm Faidit, *Le Triomphe de l'amour* (and other poems of an Italian troubadour).

*Caesarius von Heisterbach, *Dialogus miraculorum* (miscellany of stories and legends).

*The *Poetic*, or *Elder*, *Edda* (poem on Norse mythological and heroic themes; –1222).

*Michael Scot, translation of Averroes' commentaries on Aristotle (–1198).

*Jien, *Gukanshō* (*Jottings of a Fool*; first critical, analytical work on Japanese history).

L **Births and Deaths**

Mar. —, Charles of Anjou b. (–1285).

1221–1223 Mongol victories in Georgia, Russia and Afghanistan

1221

A **Feb:** George IV of Georgia defeated by the Mongols at Khunani, near Tiflis.
Mar: 25th, Robert de Courtenay crowned as Latin Emperor of Constantinople (–1228) as Peter had died in captivity.

C **Jul:** the legate Pandulf withdraws from England.

D **Nov:** 24th, Ghengiz Khan defeats Jalāl-ad-Din and destroys his army in Afghanistan; the Mongols next invade India.

1222

B **May:** 31st, a Mongol army defeats the Russians and Cumans on the Kalka, near the Sea of Azov.
Jun: Ghengiz Khan takes Herat and massacres its population; he had now conquered Afghanistan.

C **Aug:** death of Raymond VI, the deposed Count of Toulouse; his son, Raymond VII, inherits his claims.

E Alexander II conquers the Viking settlements in Argyll.
Death of Theodore I Lascaris, the Greek Emperor of Nicaea; succeeded by John III Ducas Vatatzes (–1254).

1223

A **Mar:** 25th, death of Afonso II the Fat, King of Portugal; succeeded by his son, Sancho II (–1248).

B **Apr:** Honorius declares that Henry of England is competent to rule.
May: 20th, Honorius III taxes the church in France for the Albigensian Crusade.

C **Jul:** 14th, death of Philip II Augustus, King of France.
Aug: 6th, (*or* 8th), his son, Louis VIII, crowned (–1226); he was the first Capetian King not to have been crowned in his father's lifetime.

E Death of John I of Sweden; succeeded by Eric XI, son of Eric X (–1250).
Death of George IV of Georgia; succeded by his sister, Rusadan.

1221

G **Economics, Science, Technology and Discovery**
Chiu Ch'ang-ch'un, journey from Peking to Persia (–1224; described by Li Chih-ch'ang, *Hsi yu chi*).

H **Religion and Education**
Aug: Dominican Friars arrive in England.

J **Art, Architecture and Music**
Burgos (choir, in the French Gothic style) and Toul Cathedrals, St. Martin, Ypres, and the Dominican church, Bologna (as a shrine for St. Dominic), begun.

L **Births and Deaths**
Aug. 6th, St. Dominic d. (51).
— St. Bonaventura b. (–1274).
— Alfonso X b. (–1284).

1222

F **Law and Politics**
Andrew of Hungary grants his Golden Bull, a charter of liberties (*cf.* Magna Carta, –1215).
Ottokar of Bohemia grants ecclesiastical and, later, secular lords sole jurisdiction over their tenants.

G **Economics, Science, Technology and Discovery**
†*Giles of Corbeil, *De urinis*, *De pulsibus*, etc. (medical lore in verse).

H **Religion and Education**
Padua University established.

K **Literature, Philosophy and Scholarship**
*Snorri Sturlason, *The Edda* (the prose, *i.e.* 'The Younger' *Edda*: Icelandic myths, from an earlier poetic version, written by Snorri, 'about 1222, in prose, with verse quotations from old heathen poems'—*W. P. Ker*; –1200; 1225).

1223

H **Religion and Education**
Nov. 29th, Honorius III confirms the final form of rules for the Friars Minor.

J **Art, Architecture and Music**
Alaeddin Mosque, Nigde.
Mosque of the Sultan Iltutmish, Badaun.

K **Literature, Philosophy and Scholarship**
†Vincent Kadlubek, *Historia Polonica* (the first Polish chronicle by a Pole, to 1200).

1224

A Jan–Apr: Henry III recovers control of royal castles which had been held by various barons since the civil war.

Feb: Amauri de Montfort cedes the conquests by the Albigensian Crusade in Toulouse to Louis VIII.

B May: 5th, Louis declares war on Henry III; he then overruns Poitou and most of Gascony north of the Garonne.

C Aug: 14th, with the capture of Bedford castle, Henry III suppresses the revolt of Fawkes de Breauté.

E Andrew, Bishop of Prague, dies in Rome; he was in exile because of his quarrel with Ottokar, due to his claiming clerical immunity from secular jurisdiction and taxation.

Bishop Albert of Riga takes Yuriev from the Russians and Esthonians.

Theodore Ducas of Epirus takes Salonika, from William of Montferrat, and is crowned as Greek Emperor.

Death of the Almohad Emperor, Yūsuf II; the disintegration of his empire in Morocco and Spain accelerates.

Ghengiz Khan destroys the state of Hsi Hsia, in north China.

1225

A Feb: 11th, the definitive reissues of Magna Carta and the Charter of the Forests made by Henry III in return for the grant by the barons of a general tax; this pays for an expedition to Gascony under Richard (Earl of Cornwall, 1227).

15th, Honorius condemns Raymond VII of Toulouse as a heretic.

D Nov: 7th, Archbishop Engelbert of Cologne, Frederick's viceregent in Germany, murdered.

9th, Frederick marries Queen Yolande, the daughter of John of Brienne, who had abdicated; he thus assumes the Kingdom of Jerusalem (–1250).

E Ferdinand III of Castile takes Andujar in his first campaign against the Muslims.

John Ducas defeats the Latins supporting a rebellion by Theodore I's sons, at Poimanenon.

Jalāl-ad-Dīn liberates Persia from the Mongols; after defeating the Georgians at Garnhi, he sacks Tiflis.

Tran Thai-tong becomes sole Emperor of Dai Viet (–1258), founding the Tran dynasty (–1400).

1224

G **Economics, Science, Technology and Discovery**
Andrew II grants judicial autonomy to German settlers in Transylvania.

H **Religion and Education**
Aug: St. Francis receives the *stigmata*.
Sept. 10th, Franciscan Friars arrive in England.
June 5th, Frederick II founds Naples University.

J **Art, Architecture and Music**
Kizil Kule (The Red Tower—castle), Alaiye.

K **Literature, Philosophy and Scholarship**
†*William the Breton, *Philippis* (Latin poem on the battle of Bouvines, 1214).

1225

F **Law and Politics**
*Eike von Repkowe, *Sachsenspiegel* (Latin treatise on Saxon cuxtoms; the oldest German legal writing).
Definitive re-issue of Magna Carta.

G **Economics, Science, Technology and Discovery**
Leonardo Fibonacci, *Flos super solutionibus quarundam quaestionum*; *Liber quadratorum* (mathematical treatises of great originality).
Qaisar ibn-Abī-al-Qasīm makes a celestial globe (extant).

J **Art, Architecture and Music**
Visby Cathedral, Gothland, dedicated after rebuilding.
The Carolingian choir of Beauvais Cathedral burnt (–1235).
Geneva Cathedral and choir of Ste. Gudule, Brussels, begun.
*Beverley Minster begun.

K **Literature, Philosophy and Scholarship**
Francis of Assisi, *Il Cantico di Frate Sole* (*Canticle of Brother Sun*; earliest masterpiece of Italian poetry).
The 'Lille' Book of Stories (earliest native French prose fiction).
**Cycle de la Croisade*: (1) *Chanson d'Antioche*, by Graindor de Douay (on the First Crusade, 1096–9); (2) *Conquête de Jérusalem*, by Graindor de Douay; (3) *Le Chevalier au Cygne*, and the *Roman de Godefroi Bouillon*; (4) *La Naissance de Chevalier au Cygne* (the whole forming a group of poems on the theme of the Crusades).
**La Razón feita de amor* (anon. Castilian lyric).
*Pierre de Beauvais, *Mappemonde* (couplets on geography and description of the world).
*Snorri Sturlason, *Heimskringla* (Norse and Icelandic history of kings; in two parts: (1) *The Olaf Sagas*, 968–1030; and (2) *The Norse Sagas*, to 1177 (–1200, 1222, 1284).
**Petition of Daniil Zatochnik* (satirical work in Russian).

1226

A **Jan**: 30th, Louis VIII assumes direction of the crusade against Raymond of Toulouse.
Mar: 6th, a second Lombard League, against Frederick II, formed by Milan, Bologna, Brescia, Mantua, Bergamo, Turin, Vicenza, Padua, and others.

B **Apr**: 5th, by the Treaty of Melun, Louis releases Ferrand of Flanders on receiving his admission of French suzerainty.

D **Nov**: 8th, death of Louis VIII, on completing his conquest of Toulouse; succeeded by his son, Louis IX (–1270), with his widow, Blanche of Castile, acting as regent (–1236).
27th the first league of Rhenish towns, directed against the Archbishop of Mainz, suppressed by Frederick.

E Ezzelin da Romano wins control of Verona and named as its Podestà.
The Polish prince, Konrad of Masovia, grants Chelmno to the German Order of the Cross (the Teutonic Knights) as a base for their conquest and conversion of the Prussians.

1227

A **Jan**: 8th, Henry III declares himself to be of full age.
Mar: 16th, by the Treaty of Vêndome, Blanche of Castile ends a revolt by the Count of Brittany and others.
18th, death of Pope Honorius III.
19th, Ugolino dei Conti elected as Pope Gregory IX (–1241).

C **Jul**: 22nd, Waldemar of Denmark defeated at Bornhöved by the allies of the Count of Schwerin; he thus loses Lübeck and other conquests in north Germany. German colonisation towards the east now resumes.
Aug: 24th, death of Ghengiz Khan; succeeded as Great Khan by his son, Ogodai (–1241). Ghengiz's empire is divided: Ogodai rules eastern Asia from the capital at Karakorum; Chaghadai, his brother, Turkestan; Tuluy, another brother, in Mongolia; and Batu, grandson of Ghengiz, Kazakhstan and European Russia (origin of 'The Golden Horde'; –1255).
Sep: 15th, the Almohad Abū-l-'Alā' Idrīs (al-Ma'mūn) declares himself the Muslim ruler of Spain.
29th, Gregory excommunicates Frederick for his failure to go to Palestine (on the Sixth Crusade).

D **Nov**: 11th, Leszek II of Cracow and Little Poland murdered by Swietopelk, the independent ruler of Pomerania; succeeded by his son, Boleslav V.
11th, death of al-Mu'azzam of Damascus; al-Kāmil of Egypt then seizes Jerusalem.

E James of Aragon ends the civil war by a convention with his nobles.
Bishop Albert of Riga defeats the Osilians; their conversion follows.

1226

G **Economics, Science, Technology and Discovery**
Lübeck made an imperial free city.

H **Religion and Education**
**Quinque Compilationes Antiquae* added to canon law (superseded by *Extra* –1234).

L **Births and Deaths**
Oct. 3rd, St. Francis of Assisi d. (45 ?).

1227

F **Law and Politics**
The Mongol army numbered about 129,000 at the death of Ghengiz Khan.

H **Religion and Education**
Dōgen introduces the Sōtō sect of Zen Buddhism into Japan.

J **Art, Architecture and Music**
Foundation stone of Toledo Cathedral laid; it was built in 'the French style' with Martin and Petrus Petri successively its architects.

K **Literature, Philosophy and Scholarship**
*Henry of Latvia, *History of Livonia* (1186–1227).

L **Births and Deaths**
— St. Thomas Aquinas b. (–1274).

1228

B **Jun**: 28th, Frederick sails for Palestine; Gregory then excommunicates him again.

C **Sep**: Henry III relieves the siege of Montgomery by Llewelyn ap Jorwerth.

E James of Aragon conquers the Balearic Islands (–1235).
Death of Robert de Courtenay, Latin Emperor of Jerusalem; succeeded by his son, Baldwin II (–1261) with John of Brienne as regent and entitled Emperor (–1237).
Death of Stephen of Serbia; succeeded by his sons, Radoslav and Vladislav (–1243).

1229

A **Feb**: 8th, Iltutmish, who had subjected the Muslim conquests, recognised as Sultan of India by the Caliph of Baghdād.
18th, Frederick makes a treaty of peace with al-Kāmil, whereby Jerusalem is partitioned; the Holy Places thus come under Christian control and the Sixth Crusade so ends without any fighting.
Mar: 18th, Frederick crowns himself as King of Jerusalem, in Jerusalem.

B **Apr**: 11th, the Treaty of Paris ends the Albigensian Crusade; Raymond VII submits to Louis IX, ceding the Duchy of Narbonne and the reversion to Toulouse, which he was to hold for his life.
Jun: al-Ashraf takes Damascus; as he recognises the supremacy of his brother, al-Kāmil, the Ayyūbid (Saladin's) Empire is now reunited.
10th, Frederick returns to Italy and defeats papal troops, led by John of Brienne, attempting to conquer Sicily as a crusade.

C **Jul**: 29th, Muhammad ibn-Hūd, who had seized Murcia and Granada, defeats al-Ma'mūn near Turifa.

D **Dec**: 31st, James of Aragon takes Palma, in Majorca.

E Alfonso IX of Leon takes Badajoz.
Ferdinand of Castile sends an army to Africa which restores his ally al-Ma'mūn as Emperor of the Almohads; the latter permits Castilians to settle at Marrakesh.
Death of Piero Ziano, Doge of Venice; succeeded by Jacopo Tiepolo (–1249).
Waldemar of Denmark surrenders Holstein, Mecklenburg and Pomerania in his treaty of peace with the Count of Schwerin.
Death of Bishop Albert of Riga.
The invading Shān tribe of Āhōm founds the Kingdom of Assam.

1228

G **Economics, Science, Technology and Discovery**
Dockyard at Alaiye.
Mental hospital, Divrigi.

J **Art, Architecture and Music**
Church and convent of S. Francesco, Assisi (–1239).
The old cathedral at Troyes destroyed by storm; the new cathedral already begun.
Dual foundation of the Ulu Cami (cathedral mosque) and mental hospital, Divrigi, begun.

K **Literature, Philosophy and Scholarship**
*Gerbert de Montreuil, *Roman de la Violette.*

L **Births and Deaths**
Apr. —, Conrad IV b. (–1254).
July 9th, Stephen Langton, Archbishop of Canterbury, d.

1229

G **Economics, Science, Technology and Discovery**
First treaty between German merchants and the Duke of Smolensk.
†Yāqūt, *Mu'jam al-Buldān* (geographical dictionary).

H **Religion and Education**
Nov: the Inquisition established in Toulouse.
Foundation of Angers University.

J **Art, Architecture and Music**
The Sultan Han (caravanserai) on the Konya-Aksaray road.

K **Literature, Philosophy and Scholarship**
*Guido Fava of Bologna, *La Gemma Purpurea* (example of the first literary prose in Italian).
†Yāqūt, *Mu'jam al-Udaba'* (biographical dictionary of learned men).

1230

B **Apr**: John Asen of Bulgaria defeats and captures Theodore Ducas of Epirus at Klokotinitza; the Bulgarian Empire now extends from the Black Sea to the Danube, Adriatic and Thessaly.

May: 3rd, Henry III arrives in Brittany as the ally of Peter of Dreux (Mauclerc), who is regent for his son, the Count.

C **Jul**: 23rd, by the Treaty of San Germano, Frederick makes peace with Gregory.

Aug: 10th, Kayqubād, Sultan of Rūm, defeats Jalāl-ad-Dīn at Erzinjān, and then occupies Erzurum.

Sep: 23rd, death of Alfonso IX of Leon; succeeded by his son, Ferdinand III of Castile, who thus finally unites the two kingdoms (–1252).

D **Oct**: Henry returns to England after his expedition from Brittany to Bordeaux.

E Muhammad ibn-Yūsuf seizes Granada (–1273), founding the Nasrid dynasty (–1492).

Death of Přemesyl Ottokar I, King of Bohemia; succeeded by his son, Wenceslas I (–1253).

Herman von Salza, the Grand Master, takes possession of Chelmno; the Knights now begin their conquest of Prussia.

*Bang Klang T'ao (assuming the title Indrapatindraditya) becomes King of Sukhodaya, the first Thai (Siamese) state to free itself from Cambodia (–1376).

1231

A **Feb**: 2nd, Sancho of Navarre and James of Aragon make a treaty of mutual adoption, at Tudela.

B **May**: Henry, King of the Romans, concedes the 'Constitution in favour of the princes', granting them territorial sovereignty.

26th, he emancipates the people of the Swiss canton of Uri from the Habsburgs in order to secure control of the St. Gothard Pass.

C **Jul**: 5th, Henry and Louis make a truce, for three years.

Aug: 15th, Jalāl-ad-Dīn murdered while in flight from the Mongols, who had reconquered Persia; Kayqubād now occupies Ahlat and Queen Rusudan reoccupies Tiflis.

Sep: 16th, Lewis I, Duke of Bavaria, murdered.

D **Dec**: Henry ends his second Welsh campaign by making a truce with Llewelyn.

25th, in a diet at Ravenna, Frederick (ineffectively) legislates against the formation of municipal corporations in Germany.

E Death of Vladislav III, Grand Prince of Poland.

Michael, son of Michael Ducas, establishes himself as Despot of Epirus (–1271).

The Mongols begin their campaigns to conquer Korea (–1258).

1230

F **Law and Politics**

*The jurist university founded at Montpellier in addition to its ancient law-school.

†*Azzo of Bologna, *Summa codicis et institutionum* (summary of Roman Law).

G **Economics, Science, Technology and Discovery**

*Iron production important in Westphalia, Swabia and Hungary.

*Earliest Muslim literary reference to a compass.

*Chia Sšu-tao, *Ts'u chih ching* (earliest treatise on crickets, kept by Chinese for their chirping).

J **Art, Architecture and Music**

Yuriev-Polskij Cathedral (–1234).

*Siena Cathedral begun.

K **Literature, Philosophy and Scholarship**

*Minnesingers (approximate end of a long period of German court poets and singers who wrote love lyrics of a formal style and aristocratic beauty. Among the most eminent names was Wolfram von Eschenbach —1220; also Walter von der Vogelweide—died this year?).

†Ibn-Hammād, *Akhbār Mulūk Bani 'Ubaid* (history of Fātimid Egypt, 909–1171).

†'Attār, Persian poet.

1231

F **Law and Politics**

Frederick II promulgates his *Liber* (or *Lex Augustalis*) for the Kingdom of Sicily (the first medieval code of laws based on Roman jurisprudence).

G **Economics, Science, Technology and Scholarship**

Frederick initiates the *augustales* (the first gold coinage in western Europe).

Frederick orders that medical teachers and practitioners should be examined by the University of Salerno.

H **Religion and Education**

Gregory appoints inquisitors against heresy in Germany.

Gregory exempts the Friars Preachers and Minor from episcopal jurisdiction.

His bull, *Parens Scientiarum,* gives privileges to Paris University, exempting it from control by the cathedral.

J **Art, Architecture and Music**

The upper part of Suger's choir in St. Denis, Paris, removed; in its rebuilding, Pierre de Montereau, the architect, is the first to put windows in a triforium. The Carolingian nave was subsequently replaced.

Mausoleum of 'Sultan Ghari' (Nāsir ad-Dīn Mahmūd, son of Iltutmish), Delhi.

L **Births and Deaths**

June 13th, St. Antonio of Padua d. (36).

Nov. 19th, St Elizabeth of Hungary d. (24).

1232

B **May**: 2nd, Richard Filangieri, Frederick's legate in Palestine, defeats, at Casal Imbert (near Tyre), the forces of John of Ibelin, Lord of Beirut, leader of the barons of 'Outremer' who are opposing Frederick's claim to royal authority there.
Jun: 15th, John defeats Filangieri at Agridi, in Cyprus.

C **Jul**: 29th, Henry III dismisses the justiciar, Hubert de Burgh, Earl of Essex, and begins the centralisation of royal finances under Peter des Rivaux.

D **Oct**: 16th, death of the Almohad Emperor, al-Ma'mūn; succeeded by his son, 'Abd-al-Wāhid, but Muhammad ibn-Yūsuf of Granada proclaims himself King in Spain (–1273).

E Frederick confirms 'The Constitution in favour of the princes'.
The Muslims of Minorca surrender to James of Aragon.
John Asen of Bulgaria breaks relations with the Papacy.

1233

B **Apr**: with the surrender of Kyrenia to John of Ibelin, Filangieri's forces are expelled from Cyprus and Henry of Lusignan restored as its King.

C **Aug**: Richard the Marshal, Earl of Pembroke, in alliance with Llewelyn, begins his revolt against Henry III.

D **Nov**: 25th, he defeats royal forces near Monmouth.

1232

F **Law and Politics**

In Sicily, Frederick holds an assembly attended by representatives of towns.

Jōei shikimoku (codification of the Minamoto family law regulating the Japanese warrior class, drawn up by the Administrative Board, the central organ of the Shogun's feudal government).

G **Economics, Science, Technology and Discovery**

Outbreak of disorder in Abbeville; there were similar disturbances, due to conflict between artisans and richer citizens, in other west European towns in the thirteenth century.

H **Religion and Education**

Elias elected the first minister-general of the Friars Minor.

J **Art, Architecture and Music**

Mustansirhya Mosque, Baghdād.

Shuīa ibn-Hanfar of Mosul makes a brass ewer inlaid with silver (in British Museum; a good example of Muslim inlaid metal-work, which reached its highest level in the mid-twelfth century).

K **Literature, Philosophy and Scholarship**

†*Samuel ben Tibbon, translation from Arabic to Hebrew of works of Maimonides (–1204), etc.

1233

F **Law and Politics**

†*Hugolinus, *Summa digestorum* (Roman law).

H **Religion and Education**

Apr: Gregory IX organises the Holy Office (Inquisition).

July 30th, Conrad of Marburg, the priest leading a savage persecution of alleged heretics in Germany is murdered.

Penitentiary movement, 'The Great Hallelujah', in north Italy.

Gregory IX confirms the establishment of the University of Toulouse and grants the scholars privileges.

K **Literature, Philosophy and Scholarship**

†Ibn-al-Athīr, *Kitāb al-Kāmil fi-al-Ta'rikh* (*The Complete Book of Chronicles*; abridges al-Tabari's work (–923) and continues Arab history to 1231).

1234

B **Apr**: 7th, death of Sancho VII the Strong, the last Spanish King of Navarre; his subjects elect his adopted heir, Theobald IV, Count of Champagne.

15th, Richard the Marshal murdered in Ireland.

25th, Louis IX attains his majority.

May: he marries Margaret of Provence.

In the outcry following Richard's murder, Henry dismisses Peter des Rivaux and is reconciled with the magnates.

E Gregory proclaims a crusade against the city of Rome, after a revolt there has forced him into flight.

Henry I, Prince of Wroclaw (*i.e.* Lower Silesia) becomes Grand Prince of Poland (–1238).

The Mongols take Kaifeng and destroy the Chin dynasty.

1235

A **Mar**: 7th, death of Andrew II of Hungary; succeeded by his son, Béla IV (–1270).

C **Jul**: in a diet at Worms, Henry deposed as King of the Romans following his revolt against Frederick, his father.

15th, Frederick marries, as his third wife, Isabella, the sister of Henry III.

E With the capture of Iviza, James of Aragon completes his conquest of the Balearic Islands.

John Asen makes a marriage alliance with John Vatatzes against the Latins ruling (now only) Constantinople, but their combined attack fails.

1234

H **Religion and Education**

The decretals of Gregory IX (known as *Extra*) added to the body of canon law.
Feb: the Peace Constitution bans the Inquisition in Germany.
The Caliph al-Mustansir founds al-Mustansīryah University, Baghdād (–1395).

1235

F **Law and Politics**

Earliest notice of law school of Orleans University (already a century old?).

G **Economics, Science, Technology and Discovery**

Wenceslas I grants privileges to (the present) 'Old Town' of Prague to encourage its settlement by Germans.

H **Religion and Education**

Franciscan Friars arrive in Wroclaw.
Robert le Bougre appointed inquisitor in France.

J **Art, Architecture and Music**

Church of St. Elizabeth, Marburg, and Liebfrauenkirche, Trier, begun.
*Beauvais Cathedral designed.
*Supposed mausoleum of Sultan Iltutmish, Delhi.
*Villard de Honnecourt, the French mason, visits Hungary.

K **Literature, Philosophy and Scholarship**

*Gonzalo de Berceo, *Vida de Sancto Domingo de Silos*; *Los Milagros de Nuestra Senora*; and *Vida de Santa Oria* (the three principal religious and devotional poems of a prolific Castilian poet, whose great distinction is that he is the first Spanish poet known by his name).
*Raoul de Houdenc, *Méraugis de Portlesguez* (an Arthurian romance).
†Rabbi David Qimhī, a Hebrew grammar.
†Michael Scot, translations of Aristotle from Arabic and Hebrew.
†Ibn-al-Farīd, Egyptian mystic poet.

1236

A **Jan**: 14th, Henry III marries Eleanor of Provence; his reception and patronage of her relatives in England arouses discontent.

Feb: 7th, Muhammad ibn-Hūd, King of Murcia and Granada, murdered.

B **Apr**: 29th, death of Iltutmish of Delhi; succeeded, briefly, by Fīrūz I, then by his daughter Radiyya (–1240).

Jun: 29th, Ferdinand of Castile and Leon takes Cordova, the capital of a Muslim kingdom.

C **Jul**: in a diet at Piacenza, Frederick announces his intention of recovering Italy for the Empire; Gregory replies by claiming the supreme temporal dominion of the Papacy under the *Donation of Constantine* (–1440 H).

D **Nov**: Frederick burns Vicenza, then returns to Germany.

E Ezzelin da Romano becomes lord of Vicenza.

The Teutonic Knights complete their conquest of the Pomezanians, of west Prussia.

The death of John of Ibelin, Lord of Beirut, leads to a worsening of the anarchy among the lords of Outremer.

A Mongol army led by Batu, grandson of Ghengiz Khan, conquers the Volga Bulgars.

Georgia also conquered by the Mongols.

1237

A **Jan**: Henry confirms the Charters (*i.e.* Magna Carta and the Charter of the Forest) and appoints three baronial councillors in return for the grant of a tax.

Frederick confers the status of imperial city on Vienna.

Feb: his son, Conrad, elected as King of the Romans.

Ezzelin da Romano takes Padua, and, later, Treviso.

Mar: 23rd, death of John of Brienne, co-Emperor of Constantinople.

C **Sep**: 25th, by the Treaty of York with Henry III, Alexander II renounces Scottish claims to Northumberland, Cumberland and Westmorland; the Anglo-Scottish Border was now defined by mutual agreement.

D **Nov**: 27th, Frederick defeats the Lombard League at Cortenuova; by insisting on unconditional surrender, however, he stimulates further resistance.

Dec: 21st, Batu's Mongol army destroys the city and principality of Riazan, Russia.

E James of Aragon conquers Murcia.

Pope Gregory confirms the union of the Sword Brothers of Livonia to the Teutonic Knights.

Kayqubād of Rūm murdered and succeeded by his son, Kaykushraw II (–1246); the Sultanate, which had achieved its greatest prosperity in his reign, now declines.

1236

F **Law and Politics**

Jan: the Statute of Merton (the first declaration on points of law known by the name 'statute' made after deliberation by Henry III and the barons).

J **Art, Architecture and Music**

Nave and transepts of Amiens Cathedral now complete.

Byzantine frescoes in Mileševo church.

1237

F **Law and Politics**

Examination system abandoned in north China (–1315).

G **Economics, Technology and Discovery**

Ch'ên Tzŭ-ming, *Fu-jên ta-ch'üan liang-fang* (treatise on women's diseases).

† ?Jordanus Nemorarius, *Arithmetica* and other original mathematical treatises.

H **Religion and Education**

Statutes of Gregory IX for the reform of the Benedictine Order.

J **Art, Architecture and Music**

(–1238) Foundation by Huand Hatun of mosque, with her mausoleum, a medrese (college) and a bath, at Kayseri.

K **Literature, Philosophy and Scholarship**

*Guillaume de Lorris, *Le Roman de la Rose* (the most famous of all narrative and—in part—allegorical poems of the Middle Ages, with some satirical sections in the later continuation; –1305).

**Sächsische Weltchronik* (Old High German: history of the world, the oldest extant in German literature).

†Roger of Wendover, *Flores Historiarum* (a chronicle of world history from the Creation to 1237, most important for English history in the author's lifetime).

L **Births and Deaths**

Dec. 4th, Roger of Wendover d.

1238

A **Jan**: 7th, Simon de Montfort, Earl of Leicester, marries Eleanor, Henry's sister.
Feb: 8th, Batu takes Vladimir, and then destroys Moscow and other central Russian cities, massacring their inhabitants.
Mar: 4th, he defeats the princes of northern Russia on the Sita, near Yaroslavl; Juri II, Great Prince of Vladimir, who is killed, succeeded by his brother, Jaroslav II (–1246). After failing to take Novgorod, Batu withdraws to the Don basin.
8th: death of al-Kāmil of Egypt and Damascus; civil war among his family, the Ayyūbids, follows.

C **Aug**: 3rd, Frederick begins the siege of Brescia.
Sep: James of Aragon takes Valencia.

D **Oct**: 9th, Frederick abandons the siege of Brescia.

E He makes his son Enzio King of Sardinia.
Death of Henry I, Grand Prince of Poland; succeeded by his son, Henry II (–1241).

1239

A **Mar**: 20th, Gregory excommunicates Frederick; in Germany, only Bavaria and Bohemia rebel in consequence.
20th, death of Herman of Salza, Grand Master of the Teutonic Knights.

B **Jun**: Frederick invades the Romagna and Tuscany.

C **Sep**: 1st, a new Crusade, led by King Theobald of Navarre, arrives at Acre.

D **Oct**: after six weeks, Frederick abandons his siege of Milan.
Nov: 13th, part of the crusading army defeated by the Egyptians at Gaza.
Dec: 7th, an-Nāsir of Karak expels the Latin garrison from their citadel in Jerusalem and destroys the city's fortifications.

E Jaroslav of Vladimir begins the payment of tribute to the Mongols in Russia (the 'Golden Horde').
*Béla IV of Hungary permits the Cumans, a pagan, nomadic tribe in flight from the Mongols, to settle between the Danube and the Theiss.

1238

H **Religion and Education**

*Some Carmelite Friars migrate from Palestine to Sicily and south France; the Order then spreads over Europe.

Scholars migrating from Oxford set up universities at Salisbury (–1278) and Northampton (–1264?).

1239

F **Law and Politics**

First notice of the King of France holding a *parlement* (law court; –1254).

H **Religion and Education**

Gregory IX deposes Elias from the general-ministership of the Friars Minor in response to protests against his despotic rule.

J **Art, Architecture and Music**

The central tower of Lincoln Cathedral collapses.

L **Births and Deaths**

Jun. 17–18th, Edward I b. (–1307).

A **Feb**: 22nd, Frederick reaches the outskirts of Rome, but withdraws to Sicily when Gregory rouses the Romans to resist. Gregory, ineffectively, orders a crusade against Frederick in Germany.

B **Apr**: 11th, death of Llewelyn ap Jorwerth, the Great, King of Gwynned (North Wales); succeeded by his son David (–1246).
22nd, Radiyya, Queen of Delhi, deposed in favour of Muʿizz-ad-Dīn Bahrām (–1242).

C **Jul**: 15th, Alexander Nevski of Novgorod defeats the Swedes on the Neva.
Aug: Frederick takes Ravenna.
Sep: Theobald of Navarre leaves Palestine; end of this Crusade.
Raymond Trencavel leads a revolt by the city of Toulouse.

D **Oct**: Radiyya of Delhi murdered.
Dec: 6th, Batu takes and sacks Kiev, then ravages Galicia.
20th, Frederick recognises the inhabitants of the three Swiss Forest Cantons of Schwyz, Uri and Unterwalden as freemen immediately subject to the Empire.

E *Sundiata, leader of a Madingo-Negro confederation in Kangaba, defeats Sumanguru, the dominant ruler in the former Empire of Ghana; Sundiata thus founds the Empire of Mali (–1337).

F **Law and Politics**

Waldemar II of Denmark publishes a collection of Cimbric Laws.

G **Economics, Science, Technology and Discovery**

†Bartholomew Anglicus (the Englishman), *De Proprietatibus Rerum* (encyclopedia on physical science in 19 volumes; –1398; first printed *c.* 1470).

†*Alexander de Villedieu, *Carmen de algorismo* (poem on arithmetic).

*The Mongol empire, by permitting safe travel through Asia, allows the first European contact with China (–*c.* 1340). There is also contact with western Asia and China receives the influence of Persian culture and Muslim religion, while Chinese civilisation influences central and western Asia.

J **Art, Architecture and Music**

Tours Cathedral choir begun.

Tournai Cathedral begun.

K **Literature, Philosophy and Scholarship**

*Der Stricker, *Der Pfaffe Amis* (oldest examples of the Middle High German folklore and stories, especially about rogues and their tricks, like those of Till Eulenspiegel; see also *Schwänke* in *Chronology 1492–1762*).

**Gudrun* (North German saga in Middle High German).

†Jacques de Vitry, *Historia Orientalis et Occidentalis* (history of the Holy Land to 1218).

†Jacopo da Lentini, Sonnets and other Italian poems.

*Jehan de Tuim, *Li Hystore de Jules César* (trans. from Lucan).

†Ibn-ʿArabī, *al-Fūtūhāt al-Makkīyah*; *Fusūs al-Hikam* (treatises giving Sūfī pantheism its philosophical framework).

L **Births and Deaths**

Nov. 16th, St. Edmund Rich, Archbishop of Canterbury, d.

1241–1242 Mongol conquest of central Europe—Henry III defeated in France

1241

A **Mar**: 28th, death of Waldemar II the Victorious, King of Denmark; succeeded by his son, Eric IV (–1250).

B **Apr**: Frederick takes Faenza and Benevento.
9th, a Mongol army led by Khaidu, after sacking Cracow, defeats the Poles, Silesians and Teutonic Knights at Leignitz; Duke Henry II the Pious killed. The Mongols ravage Silesia; repulsed by the Bohemians, they go through Moravia into Hungary.
11th, the main army, under Batu, defeats the Hungarians on the Sajo, at Mohi; they ravage the Danube plain, but are repulsed at Grobnok by the Croatians. A crusade proclaimed against them in Germany.
May: 3rd, Frederick's fleet captures prelates on their way to a general council in Rome.
Jun: death of John Asen II, Emperor of Bulgaria; succeeded by his infant son, Koloman (–1246).

C **Aug**: 21st, death of Pope Gregory IX.
Sep: 10th, Archbishop Siegfried of Mainz, Frederick's viceregent in Germany, leads a revolt against him.

D **Oct**: 25th, Goffredo Castiglione elected as Pope Celestine IV.
Nov: 10th, he dies; the cardinals had dispersed, and there is a vacancy while Frederick attempts to influence the next election.
Dec: 11th, death of Ogodai, Great Khan of the Mongols.
22nd, Lahore taken and destroyed by the Mongols.
25th, Batu takes Buda[pest].

E Henry III leads an expedition into Wales to enforce David's submission.
The Muslim King of Murcia becomes the vassal of Ferdinand of Castile and Leon.
Kaykhusraw II of Rūm suppresses a revolt inspired by dervishes.

1242

A **Feb**: 2nd, a council of barons refuses to grant Henry III a tax.

B **Spring**: the Mongols evacuate central Europe, where they were harrying Austria and Dalmatia, in order to return to their capital, Karakorum, to elect Ogodai's successor (–1246). Batu now organises his empire in Russia (the Khanate of Kypchak, or 'The Golden Horde') as an autonomous Mongol state (–1255).
Apr: 5th, Alexander Nevski, Prince of Novgorod, defeats the Teutonic Knights on Lake Peipus.
May: Raymond VII of Toulouse and the Lusignans, in Poitou, revolt against Louis; Henry supports the Lusignans.
15th, Bahrām of Delhi murdered by his soldiers, who elect ʿAlā-ad-Dīn Maʿsūd to succeed him (–1246).

C **Jul**: 21st, Louis defeats Henry at Taillebourg.
22nd, after an engagement at Saintes, Henry withdraws from France and Louis suppresses the revolt.

E Death of King Henry, son of Frederick II.
Swietopelk of East Pomerania organises a revolt by the Prussians against the Teutonic Knights.
*Béla of Hungary defeats Duke Frederick of Austria on the Leitha in a war to recover lands which he had ceded as the price of Frederick's hospitality when Béla fled from the Mongols.

1241

G **Economics, Science, Technology and Discovery**

Following the Mongol invasion, the Polish principalities are transformed by the massive influx of Germans replacing the natives massacred by the Mongols; Wroclaw, for instance, becomes Breslau (it had been destroyed by Batu Khan); land is reclaimed.

Hamburg and Lübeck form a peace-keeping league (which has been regarded as the origin of the Hanseatic League).

Louis IX founds Aigues-Mortes (one of the last 'new' French towns in the Middle Ages and the first French royal port on the Mediterranean; the walls—still standing—built 1268–80).

J **Art, Architecture and Music**

Reims Cathedral completed but for the transepts; the west front begun (architect: Jean le Loup).

The Black Pagoda, Konarak, Orissa, completed.

L **Births and Deaths**

Sept. 22nd, Snorri Sturleson d. (62).

1242

G **Economics, Science, Technology and Discovery**

*Narahari, *Rājanighantu* (dictionary of *materia medica*).

J **Art, Architecture and Music**

Sirçali Medrese (college), Konya.

1243

A **Jan**: Raymond of Toulouse submits to Louis by the Treaty of Lorris.

B **Apr**: 7th, Louis and Henry make a truce in the Treaty of Bordeaux.
Jun: 25th, Sinibaldo dei Fieschi elected as Pope Innocent IV (–1254).
26th, the Mongols defeat Kaykhusraw II of Rūm and his Greek allies at Köse Dagh, near Erzinjan; he becomes their tributary, as does Queen Rusadan of Georgia.

E Boleslav V established as Grand Prince at Cracow by the other Polish princes (–1279).
Stephen Uroš I, son of Stephen Nemanja, succeeds as King of Serbia (–1276).

1244

A **Mar**: 31st, Frederick's plenipotentiaries agree to a treaty of peace with Innocent, which Frederick disavows.

B **Apr**: 16th, Jājnagar, Raja of Jaipur, defeats the Muslim governor of Bengal on the Mahānādi.

C **Aug**: 23rd, the Christians finally expelled from Jerusalem, and the city sacked, by the Khwarizmian exiles employed by Ayyūb of Egypt in his war against Damascus.

D **Oct**: 17th, the Egyptians defeat the Christian army of Outremer and its Muslim allies of Damascus at Harbiyāh (*or* La Forbie), near Gaza.
Nov: a council of prelates and barons refuses to grant Henry a tax and puts forward a plan for the reform of his government.
Dec: 2nd, Innocent establishes the papal court at Lyons.

E Ferdinand of Castile and Leon and James of Aragon ratify, at Almizra, the convention of 1179 defining their frontier in the Muslim lands.

1243

G **Economics, Science, Technology and Discovery**

'Sidrach', *Fontaine de toutes les sciences* (popular, simple encyclopedia in French).

H **Religion and Education**

Dec: the Order of Friars Hermit of the Order of St. Augustine (Austin Friars) originates in the appointment by Innocent IV of a protector for some Tuscan eremetical communities.

The Jews of Belitz, near Berlin, all burnt in the earliest known case of a massacre due to an alleged desecration of the Host.

J **Art, Architecture and Music**

*Sainte Chapelle, Paris (–1248).

1244

G **Economics, Science, Technology and Discovery**

*Thomas de Chantimpré, *De natura rerum* (popular scientific encyclopedia).

H **Religion and Education**

Montségur, last refuge of heretics in southern France, falls to the Catholics.

1245

C **Jul**: 17th, in the General Council at Lyons, Innocent formally declares Frederick deposed from the Empire.

E Innocent appoints Afonso (III), Count of Boulogne, as curator of Portugal because of the incompetence of his brother, King Sancho II.
Daniel of Halich, the dominant prince in eastern central Europe, does homage to Batu.
The Mongols take Mūltan, in the Punjab.

1246

A **Jan**: Provence becomes part of France with the marriage of Beatrice, heiress of Raymond-Berengar IV (d. 1245), to Charles of Anjou, Louis' brother.
Feb: 25th, death of David of Gwynned; succeeded by Llewelyn ap Gruffyd (–1282).

B **May**: 22nd, at the instigation of Innocent, Henry Raspe, Landgrave of Thuringia, elected as King of the Romans (–1247).
Jun: 10th, Mas'ūd of Delhi deposed by 'The Forty' (Turkish nobles with effective power in Muslim India) in favour of Nāsir-ad-Dīn Mahmūd (–1266).

C **Aug**: Guyuk elected as Great Khan of the Mongols (–1248); he receives Innocent IV's envoy.
Sep: 30th, death of Jaroslav II, Grand Prince of Vladimir, at the Mongol court in Karakorum.

D **Nov**: Michael Asen, who had succeeded Koloman as Emperor of Bulgaria, confirms John Vatatzes' conquests since Koloman's death; he had occupied the empire of Thessalonica.

E Muhammad of Granada cedes Jaen to Ferdinand and becomes his vassal.
Death of Frederick the Valiant, the last Babenberger Duke of Austria; Ottokar of Bohemia elected in his place.
Frederick suppresses a revolt in Sicily and deports its last Muslim inhabitants to Lucera.

1245

F **Law and Politics**

James of Aragon issues the *Compilación de Canellas* (or *de Huesca*; a legal compilation).

G **Economics, Science, Technology and Discovery**

Strikes by employees in the cloth-weaving industry at Douai countered by the municipal authorities.

Gautier de Metz, *L'Image du Monde* (poem in couplets based on a Latin original concerning scientific topics, metaphysics and geography).

Ch'ên Jên-yü, *Chün p'u* (treatise on mushrooms).

H **Religion and Education**

June 24th, opening of the General Council of Lyons.

Innocent IV's declaration permitting the Friars Minor to hold property, which leads to the division of the Order into its 'Conventual' and 'Spiritual' branches.

Innocent sends John de Plano Carpinis, a friar minor, to the court of the Great Khan at Karakorum; this embassy leads the establishment of Christian missions in China until *c.* 1368.

Innocent confirms the privileges of the University of Toulouse after the university had declined substantially.

†Alexander of Hales, *Summa Theologiae* (printed 1475).

J **Art, Architecture and Music**

Westminster Abbey-church begun (architect: Henry of Reynes).

K **Literature, Philosophy and Scholarship**

Roger Bacon, Questions on Aristotle's *Metaphysics.*

Albertano of Brescia, *De arte loquendi et tacendi* (treatise on language).

L **Births and Deaths**

May, Philip III b. (–1285).

Aug. 27th, Alexander of Hales d.

1246

J **Art, Architecture and Music**

*S. Maria Novella, Florence, begun.

1247

A **Feb:** 17th, death of Henry Raspe.

B **Jun:** 16th, Parma seized by Frederick's enemies; he therefore breaks off his journey to Lyons to besiege the city.

C **Aug:** 20th, Ferdinand of Castile and Leon begins his siege of Seville.

D **Oct:** 3rd, William, Count of Holland, elected as King of the Romans (–1256).
15th, the Egyptians take Ascalon.

E Guyuk, the Great Khan, appoints Alexander Nevski as Prince of Kiev and his brother Andrew as Grand Duke of Vladimir (–1252).

1248

A **Feb:** 18th, the Parmesans defeat the imperial forces, nearly capturing Frederick.
Mar: Innocent IV sends another embassy of friars to the Mongol court.

B **Apr:** death of Guyuk, Great Khan of the Mongols; vacancy (–1251).

C **Aug:** 26th, Louis IX sails from France on Crusade (–1254).

D **Dec:** 22nd, Seville surrenders to Ferdinand.

E Death of Sancho II of Portugal; succeeded by his brother, Afonso III (–1279).
The Bohemian nobles, headed by Přemysl Ottokar (II), revolt, nominally in protest against Wencelas' order to join Innocent's crusade against Frederick.
The Genoese conquer Rhodes from the Greeks.

1247

F **Law and Politics**

Louis initiates the *ênqueteurs* (itinerant commissioners to receive complaints of maladministration).

**Konungs skuggsjá* (*King's Mirror*; Norwegian encyclopedic treatise, scientific but also on kingship).

G **Economics, Science, Technology and Discovery**

Ch'in Chiu-Shao, *Shu-shu Chiu-chang* (*Nine Sections of Mathematics*).

H **Religion and Education**

Innocent confirms the new rule for the Carmelite Friars.

J **Art, Architecture and Music**

*The Sircali Kumbet (mausoleum), Kayseri.

1248

G **Economics, Science, Technology and Discovery**

†Al-Baytār, *Kitāb al-jāmi* (*Collection of Simple Drugs*; lists 1,400; of great botanical value).

†Al-Qiftī, *Ikhbār al'Ulamā' bi 'Ulamā' bi-Akhbar al-Hūkamā'* (*History of Philosophers*; biographies of 414 Greek, Syrian and Islamic physicians, astronomers and philosophers).

Li Yeh, *Ts'e-yüan hai-ching* (*Sea-mirror of Circle Measurement*; algebraic treatise).

*Sung Tz'ŭ, *Hsi-yüan lu* (*Instructions to Coroners*; treatise on forensic medicine).

H **Religion and Education**

Piacenza University founded (–1398).

J **Art, Architecture and Music**

Apr. 30th, the Carolingian Cathedral, Cologne, burnt; foundation stone of the present cathedral laid on Aug. 15th (architect: Gerhard; he planned the west towers built in the nineteenth century).

Clermont-Ferrand Cathedral begun (architect: Jean des Champs).

K **Literature, Philosophy and Scholarship**

†Ibn-al-Hajib, *al-Kafiya* (epitome of Arabic grammar).

†Roderigo Jiménez de Rada, *Chronica Hispaniae* (world history from Creation to 1243, giving first general history of Spain, *i.e.* Muslim as well as Christian).

1249

B **May**: 26th, the Bolognese defeat and capture Frederick's son, Enzio, King of Sardinia, at La Fossalta.
Jun: 5th, Louis lands in Egypt, from Cyprus.
6th, he enters Damietta, without opposition.

C **Jul**: 8th, death of Alexander II, King of Scotland; succeeded by his son, Alexander III (–1286).
9th, death of Jiacopo Tiepolo, Doge of Venice; succeeded by Marino Morosini (–1252).
Sep: 27th, death of Raymond VII, Count of Toulouse; succeeded by his son-in-law, Alfonse of Poitiers, the brother of Louis IX (–1271).

D **Nov**: 23rd, death of Ayyūb, Sultan of Egypt; succeeded by his son, Tūrān Shāh (–1250).

E The Swedish Earl Birger conquers western Finland.

1250

A **Feb**: 2nd, death of Eric XI of Sweden; succeeded by his nephew, Waldemar I (–1275), with Birger, his father, as regent (–1266).
8th, Louis defeats the Egyptians at Mansūrah.

B **Apr**: 6th, Louis defeated and captured by the Egyptians while withdrawing from Mansūrah.
May: 2nd, Tūrān Shāh, the last Ayyūbid Sultan of Egypt, murdered by his Mamlūk (*i.e.* slave) guards, who elect their commander 'Izz-ad-Dīn Aybāk as regent while Shajar-ad-Durr, Ayyūb's widow, is nominal ruler. After 80 days, Aybāk marries her and assumes the Sultanate (–1257), founding the Mamlūk dynasty (–1382).
6th, Louis surrenders Damietta as part of the price for his release; he leaves for Acre, where he is accepted as ruler of Outremer.

C **Jul**: 9th, the Ayyūbid, an-Nāsir of Aleppo, takes Damascus (formerly held by Tūrān Shāh).
Aug: 9th–10th, Eric IV of Denmark murdered; succeeded by his brother, Abel (–1252).

D **Dec**: 13th, death of the Holy Roman Emperor, Frederick II, '*Stupor mundi*'; his son, Conrad IV, King of the Romans, succeeds as King of Sicily and (nominal) King of Jerusalem (–1254).

E The Gascons revolt against Simon de Montfort, Henry's lieutenant in Gascony.
Afonso of Portugal cedes the Algarve to Alfonso (X), son of Ferdinand of Castile and Leon.
*Otto and John of Brandenburg found Frankfurt on Oder and establish the Neumark in Lubusz and other lands formerly parts of Poland and Pomerania.

1249

H **Religion and Education**

University College, Oxford, founded.

†William of Auvergne, *Magisterium divinale* (theological treatise, showing appreciation of psychology).

1250

F **Law and Politics**

*Representatives of towns first called to the Cortes of Castile.

**Grand Coutumier de Normandie* (major compilation of legal customs of Normandy).

G **Economics, Science, Technology and Discovery**

*Illustration of a wheel-barrow (a medieval invention in Europe, although known in China in A.D. 231).

*Walter of Henley, *Hosebondrie* (treatise on husbandry and estate-management).

H **Religion and Education**

The Dominicans found the first school of oriental studies at Toledo.

J **Art, Architecture and Music**

*Towers of Bamberg Cathedral, choirs of Coutances and Naumberg Cathedrals, and north tower and transepts (architect: Jean de Chelle) of Nôtre Dame, Paris.

*Nave of Lichfield Cathedral begun.

Mausoleum of Malik Gazi, Kirşehir.

*Byzantine frescoes in Sopačani church.

*Sculptures in Mainz, Naumberg and Meissen Cathedrals, by 'the Master of Naumberg'.

K **Literature, Philosophy and Scholarship**

**The Lay of Havelok the Dane* ('written *c.* 1250; minor revision after 1310'—*Baugh.* A minstrel's verse-romance in rhyming couplets, some 3,000 lines in a Lincolnshire dialect, and thus one of the oldest extant verse narratives in English literature).

**Genesis and Exodus* (about 4,000 lines of verse belonging to the Middle English period, 1200–50).

**King Horn* (earliest English verse romance; companion to it, *Horn Childe*, appears in fourteenth century).

**Physiologus* (*i.e. The Bestiary*; important work of Middle Ages, based on an earlier Latin original).

†Frederick II, *De arte venandi cum avibus* (*The Art of Falconry*).

1251

A **Jan**: 7th, Florence admits the exiled Guelfs (anti-imperialists).
Feb: 2nd, Aybāk defeats an-Nāsir, invading Egypt, at Abbasa.
Mar: risings against Conrad in the Kingdom of Sicily.

B **May**: Simon de Montfort suppresses the Gascon rebellion.

C **Jul**: the Ghibellines (imperialists) exiled from Florence.
1st, Mongka elected Great Khan of the Mongols (–1259).

D **Nov**: Conrad enters Italy from Germany.

E The 'Crusade of the Pastoureaux' (shepherds), in France, suppressed on becoming disorderly.
War breaks out between Ottokar of Bohemia, as Duke of Austria, and Béla of Hungary, for possession of Styria.
Innocent IV sends a crown to Mindovg of Lithuania, for his coronation, in consequence of Mindovg's (feigned) conversion to Christianity.

1252

A **Mar**: 8th, a league of Guelf (pro-papal) Lombard cities (ineffectually) concluded at Brescia.
25th, William of Holland again elected as King of the Romans; Innocent directs the Germans to accept him.
31st, Ezzelin da Romano and Oberto Pelavicini, the tyrants of Verona and Cremona respectively, form a league of Ghibelline (imperialist) Italian cities.

B **May**: Simon de Montfort defends himself and quarrels with Henry when answering charges arising from his government of Gascony.
30th, death of St. Ferdinand III, King of Castile and Leon; succeeded by his son, Alfonso X (–1284).
Jun: Conrad rejects Innocent's proposal for the separation of Sicily from the Empire.
29th, Abel of Denmark defeated and killed by the Frisians; succeeded by his brother, Christopher I (–1259).

C **Jul**: William of Holland holds a diet outside Frankfurt when Conrad is, again, deprived of the Duchy of Swabia.

E Death of Marino Morosini, Doge of Venice; succeeded by Ranieri Zeno (–1268).
The *popolo* of Rome, in revolt against Innocent, establish a constitution under a podestà.
The Teutonic Knights found Memel, in Lithuania, where Mindovg had admitted them.
Alexander I Nevski appointed Grand Duke of Vladimir following the expulsion of Andrew by the Mongols (–1263).

1251

K **Literature, Philosophy and Scholarship**

†John Vanagan, history of Armenia.

1252

F **Law and Politics**

†*Sentenario* (law-code) of Ferdinand III of Castile.

G **Economics, Science, Technology and Discovery**

An ordinance of Afonso III regulates prices and the wages of labourers in Portugal.

Florence begins to coin the gold florin.

The merchants of Hamburg and Lübeck receive privileges in Flanders for themselves and their German associates.

Bruno da Longoburgo, *Chirurgia Magna*.

†Richard of Wendover, *Micrologus* (short medical encyclopedia).

*Giordano Ruffo, *Liber mareschalchiae* (treatise on medical treatment of horses).

H **Religion and Education**

Innocent IV's bull *ad extirpanda* orders the use of torture in the examination of heretics.

J **Art, Architecture and Music**

Consecration of the choir of Ely Cathedral.

K **Literature, Philosophy and Education**

†John Basing, *Donatus Graecorum* (Latin translation of a Greek grammar).

1253 Innocent IV returns to Rome

B **Apr**: an-Nāsir cedes Palestine to Aybāk of Egypt in a treaty of peace.

C **Jul**: 8th, death of Theobald I of Navarre; succeeded by his son, Theobald II (–1270).

D **Oct**: Donato Brancaleone, the podestà of Rome, compels Innocent to return to the city. 10th, Conrad completes his suppression of the Sicilian rebellion with the recovery of Naples.

E Death of Wenceslas II of Bohemia; succeeded by his son, Přemysl Ottokar II (–1278).
Louis IX sends the friars, William of Rubruck and Bartholomew of Cremona, to the court of the Great Khan at Karakorum to seek his alliance against the Muslims of Syria and Egypt.
Swietopelk of East Pomerania and the Teutonic Knights make peace.
Hūlāgū, a grandson of Ghengiz Khan, begins his conquest of the Islamic Empire (–1258).
Kublai Khan conquers the Kingdom of Nanchao (in Yunnan); its Thai people migrate to Siam (–1351). He also attacks Dai Viet.

G **Economics, Science, Technology and Discovery**

†Robert Grosseteste, *Compendium spherae* (on astronomy).

*Giovanni Campano da Novara, Latin translation of Euclid's *Elements* (printed 1482).

William of Rubruck travels in Central Asia on his embassy to Karakorum for Louis IX (–1255).

H **Religion and Education**

Innocent IV forms the *Perigrinantes propter Christum*, of Friars Preachers and Minor (the first European missionary society).

J **Art, Architecture and Music**

Çifte Medrese (college), Erzurum.

K **Literature, Philosophy and Scholarship**

Libro de los engaños e los asayamientos de las mugeres (*The Book of Sindibad*; a collection of Arabic stories translated into Spanish).

†Theobald I, King of Navarre, Lyrical poems, religious verse and some *chansons.*

†Robert Grosseteste had founded philosophical studies at Oxford; commentaries on Aristotle.

Date of the last Sanskrit inscription in Champa, where Indian cultural influences, dating from the fourth century A.D., had been destroyed.

L **Births and Deaths**

Aug. 11th, St. Clara d. (60).

Oct. 9th, Robert Grosseteste, Bishop of Lincoln, d.

A **Mar**: 6th, Henry concludes an agreement with papal envoys whereby his second son, Edmund, is to become King of Sicily (after its conquest).

B **Apr**: 9th, Innocent once more excommunicates Conrad.

22nd, by the Treaty of Toledo, peace and an alliance are made between Henry of England and Alfonso of Castile.

24th, Louis departs from Palestine, where civil war soon breaks out among the barons of Outremer.

May: 21st, death of Conrad IV, King of the Romans, Sicily and Jerusalem, when on his way to recover control in Germany; succeeded in Sicily by his son, Conrad II (Conradin; –1258).

C **Jul**: 11th, Louis returns to France.

13th, a group of Rhineland towns makes a confederation for mutual protection.

Sep: 13th, King Hethoum of Armenia received at the Mongol court and accepted as a vassal by Mongka.

D **Oct**: 6th, in a meeting at Worms, the Rhenish League makes an edict for peace-keeping.

11th, Innocent enters the Kingdom of Sicily to receive recognition as its sovereign.

(late), Edward (I), son of Henry III, marries Eleanor, sister of Alfonso of Castile; Edward is now endowed with Gascony, where he resides.

Nov: 2nd, Manfred, illegitimate son of Frederick II, begins an anti-papal revolt in the Regno with the seizure of Lucera.

3rd, death of the Greek Emperor (of Nicaea), John III Vatatzes; succeeded by his son, Theodore II Lascaris (–1258).

Dec: 2nd, Manfred defeats the papal army near Foggia; he thus won the loyalty of Apulia.

7th, death of Pope Innocent IV.

12th, Rinaldo Conti elected as Pope Alexander IV (–1261).

E Llewelyn makes himself the sole Welsh ruler.

The Teutonic Knights found Königsberg, naming it in honour of Ottokar of Bohemia, who had assisted in their recovery of western Prussia.

Daniel crowned as King of Halich by an agreement with Innocent IV.

F **Law and Politics**

A council of prelates and magnates refuses to grant Henry III a tax without the assent of knights and lesser tenants. A subsequent assembly of knights elected by shires refuses to grant a tax (26th Apr.).

Afonso of Portugal holds the first Cortes attended by representatives of towns.

An ordinance of Louis IX regulates the conduct of baillis and seneschals (his regional governors).

Registers of the Parlements (of Paris) date from 1254, *viz.* the series *Olim* (–1319).

Alfonso X of Castile and Leon publishes the *Fuero Real* (legal code, influenced by Roman law).

William of Holland holds a diet at Worms where German towns are represented for the first time.

H **Religion and Education**

Gerard de Borgo San Donnino publishes *The Introduction to the Everlasting Gospel* of Joachim of Flora (–1202, 1256).

J **Art, Architecture and Music**

Le Mans Cathedral choir completed.

*Utrecht Cathedral choir begun (–*c.* 1300).

K **Literature, Philosophy and Scholarship**

†Rudolf of Ems, a world chronicle.

L **Births and Deaths**

— Marco Polo b. (–1324).

— Chao Mêng-fu b. (–1322).

1255

B **Apr**: 9th, Alexander confirms Edmund's investiture as King of Sicily.

C **Sep**: the papal troops in the Regno surrender to Manfred.

D **Nov**: the Romans expel their imperialist podestà, Brancaleone; Alexander is then able to reside there.

E *Death of Batu, Khan of 'the Golden Horde'; succeeded by his son, Sartak (–1256).

1256

A **Jan**: 28th, death of William of Holland, King of the Romans.

B **Jun**: 19th, the papal legate leading the crusade proclaimed against Ezzelin by Alexander takes Padua.

C **Sep**: 24th, Louis' award (*dit*) of Péronne ends a civil war in Flanders.

D **Dec**: a Mongol army under Hūlāgū (recently appointed Ilkhan of Persia; –1265) besieges the Assassins' stronghold at Alamūt; their Grand Master, Rukn-ad-Dīn Kūrshāh, surrenders and is put to death. The Mongols now annihilate the Assassins in Persia.

E *Death of Sartak, Khan of 'the Golden Horde'; succeeded by Ulagchi (–1258).

1257

A **Jan**: 13th, Richard, Earl of Cornwall, elected King of the Romans by a majority of the College of Seven Electors (now mentioned for the first time; –1272).

B **Apr**: 1st, the other members of the college elect Alfonso of Castile (–1275).
15th, Aybāk, Sultan of Egypt, murdered by order of his wife, Shajar, who is then killed by the women of Aybāk's harem; succeeded by his son, Nūr-ad-Dīn 'Ali (–1259).
May: a revolt in Rome (engineered by Manfred?) restores Brancaleone as podestà; Alexander has to leave.
17th, Richard crowned as King of the Romans, at Aachen.

D **Dec**: the Mongols raid the Punjab.

E The Rhenish League disintegrates.
Alfonso of Castile and Muhammad of Granada expel the last Almohads from Spain.
Alexander excommunicates Afonso, and puts Portugal under an interdict, because the King has repudiated his wife and married Beatrix de Guzman.
Martino della Torre assumes the government of Milan.
The Mongols sack Hanoi but Tran Thai-tong forces them to leave Dai Viet.

1255

G **Economics, Science, Technology and Discovery**

Bonacosa, a Jew of Padua, translation of Averroes' *Kullīyāt* (entitled *The Colliget*; –1160).

Riots of the coppersmiths of Dinant.

J **Art, Architecture and Music**

*Leon Cathedral.

K **Literature, Philosophy and Scholarship**

*Ulrich von Lichtenstein, *Frauendienst* (autobiographical poem, with lyrics; the oldest work of its kind in German literature).

†Thomas of Celano, biography of St. Francis; hymn *Dies Irae.*

1256

F **Law and Politics**

(–1263) Alfonso X supervises the compilation of the *Siete Partidas* (or *Leges de Partidas*).

G **Economics, Science, Technology and Discovery**

Ch'ên Ching-i, *Ch'üan-fang pei-tsu* (botanical encyclopedia).

H **Religion and Education**

Alexander IV recognises the Austin Friars as a mendicant order.

Condemnation of *The Introduction to the Everlasting Gospel* as heretical (–1254).

J **Art, Architecture and Music**

Choir of St. John, Osnabrück (–1292).

'Angel Choir' of Lincoln Cathedral (–1320).

K **Literature, Philosophy and Scholarship**

Albert von Stade, *Annales* (from the Creation to 1256).

Albertus Magnus, *De Unitate Intellectus contra Averroem.*

†Jacob Anatoli, translation into Hebrew of works of Averroes (–1198).

1257

G **Economics, Science, Technology and Discovery**

*Aldobrandon of Siena, *Le règime du corps* (treatise on hygiene and diet).

H **Religion and Education**

†*Adam Marsh, principal founder of the Franciscan school at Oxford.

K **Literature, Philosophy and Scholarship**

†Ibn-al-Jawzi, *Mir'āt al-Zamān fi Ta'rīkh al-Ayyām* (universal Arab history from Creation to 1256).

A **Jan:** 11th, the Mongols defeat the Caliph at Anbar.
Feb: 10th, they take and destroy Baghdād.
20th, the last 'Abbāsid Caliph, al-Musta'sim, and his family are put to death by Hūlāgū's orders.
Mar: Llewelyn ap Gruffydd assumes the title of Prince of Wales; he now has possession of Anglesey, Snowdonia and Powys.

B **May:** 2nd, Henry accepts the baronial demand that his government should be reformed by a committee of twenty-four appointed by himself and the barons.
11th, Louis and James of Aragon make peace in the Treaty of Corbeil.
28th, Louis and Henry agree to the terms of a treaty of peace.
Jun: 11th, by the Provisions of Oxford, baronial control over Henry's government is established.

C **Aug:** death of the Greek Emperor (at Nicaea), Theodore II Lascaris; succeeded by his son, John IV (–1261).
10th, Manfred assumes the crown of Sicily (–1266).

D **Dec:** John IV and Michael VIII Palaeologus (–1282) crowned as Greek Emperors.
Alexander cancels the grant of Sicily to Edmund.

E Alexander lays an interdict on Denmark because of Christopher's quarrel with the Archbishop of Lund.
Ezzelin takes Brescia.
Alexander Nevski suppresses a riot in Novgorod protesting against a census (of all lands under Mongol control) ordered by Mongka.
Death of Ulagchi, Khan of 'the Golden Horde'; succeeded by Berke (a Muslim; –1266).
Partition of Georgia; its rulers remain vassals of the Mongols.
Kublai Khan invades China.
Following the murder of the last Ch'oe dictator, Korean resistance to the Mongols ends; the Koryō kings remain as vassals.

F **Law and Politics**

Louis IX forbids private warfare.

H **Religion and Education**

†Bartholomew of Brescia, *Glossa ordinaria decreti.*

†'Ali al-Shādhili, founder of the Shādhilite (Muslim fraternity of north-west Africa).

Robert de Sorbon begins to establish a college for theologians of the University of Paris (the first foundation for mature, *i.e.* graduate, scholars).

Following the sack of Baghdād, the al-Azhar Mosque, Cairo, becomes the chief university for Islam (in theology and law).

J **Art, Architecture and Music**

Salisbury Cathedral dedicated.

*West front of Vienna Cathedral.

Foundation of the Ince Minareli Medrese (college), Konya.

K **Literature, Philosophy and Scholarship**

Sa'dī, *Gulistan* (*The Rose-Garden*; moral reflections and humorous pieces in Persian prose, with rhymes); *Bustan* (*The Tree-Garden*) and *Ghazals* (didactic poems and sonnets).

1259

B Apr: Alexander recognises Richard as King of the Romans.
May: Siena accepts Manfred as its overlord to have his protection against Florence.
29th, death of Christopher I of Denmark; succeeded by his son, Eric V (–1286).

C Aug: 1st, Henry makes peace with Llewelyn.
11th, death of Mongka, Great Khan of the Mongols.
Sep: the Mongols invade Syria.
16th, the Milanese defeat and capture Ezzelin at Cassano.

D Oct: 1st, death of Ezzelin da Romano.
Dec: Nūr-ad-Dīn ʿAli, Sultan of Egypt, deposed and succeeded by Sayf-ad-Dīn Qutuz (–1260).
4th, Louis and Henry make peace in the Treaty of Paris: Henry renounces Normandy, Maine, Anjou and other lost Angevin territories and does homage for Gascony to Louis, who cedes lands on its eastern borders which cannot be precisely defined.

E With the death of Donato Brancaleone, Rome returns to papal control.
Ottokar of Bohemia occupies Styria when it revolts against Béla of Hungary.
Poland, Lithuania and Galicia devastated in punitive raids by Mongols and Russians.
John Palaeologus routs the forces of Michael Ducas of Epirus at Pelagonia.

1260

A Mar: 1st, Damascus surrenders to the Mongols, who now occupy all Syria, extinguishing the Ayyūbid Sultanate; Hūlāgū is soon forced to withdraw most of his forces because of a succession dispute: about now, Kublai and Ariqboga, brothers of Mongka, are both separately elected Great Khan of the Mongols (–1261).

C Jul: the Lithuanians defeat the Teutonic Knights at Durben; there follow the revolt of Kurland against the Knights and the apostasy of Mindovg, who conquers Livonia.
12th, Ottokar defeats Béla and his Russian, Polish and Bulgarian allies on the March, at Kroissenbrunn; Béla cedes Styria to Ottokar.
Sep: 3rd, the Egyptians, led by Baybars, destroy the remaining Mongol army at ʿAyn Jālūt, in Palestine, and then occupy Syria.
4th, Manfred's forces defeat the Florentines at Montaperto.

D Oct: 24th, Baybars murders Qutuz, Sultan of Egypt.

1259

F **Law and Politics**

The Provisions of Westminster, a plan for legal reforms, enacted in a baronial council (13 Oct) at the instance of the 'bachelry' (knights?) of England.

Louis IX abolishes the judicial duel.

G **Economics, Science, Technology and Discovery**

Al-Tūsī, employed by Hūlāgū, founds an observatory at Marāghah.

League of Lübeck, Rostock and Wismar (*cf.* 1241).

J **Art, Architecture and Music**

Byzantine frescoes in Boiana church.

K **Literature, Philosophy and Scholarship**

†Matthew Paris, *Chronica Majora* (chronicle of the world from the Creation, but more particularly of England in the author's lifetime); *La Vie de Seint Auban* (attributed to Matthew, who is thought to have written and illustrated the unique ms. of this poem).

L **Births and Deaths**

— Al-Ghazi Othman b. (–1326).

1260

F **Law and Politics**

†Accursius (Francisco Accorso), the last great glossator-jurist of Bologna, *Glossa ordinaria* (or *Accursiana*; standard work on civil law).

*Pierre de Fontaines, *Conseil à un Ami* (on the legal customs of Vermandois).

**Livre de Jostice et de Plet* (on legal customs of Orleans).

G **Economics, Science, Technology and Discovery**

Journey of Maffeo and Nicolò Polo, Venetian merchants, to China (–1269).

H **Religion and Education**

Kublai Khan, as ruler of China (–1294), upholds the cult of Confucius, although the Mongols' toleration of all religions antagonises the Chinese; Islam and Christianity thus enter, and Buddhism and Taoism revive, while the Mongols themselves prefer Lamaism (the debased Tibetan form of Buddhism).

Flagellants tour Italian cities.

J **Art, Architecture and Music**

Consecration of Burgos Cathedral.

Nicolò Pisano, Pulpit in the Baptistery, Pisa (sculpture).

K **Literature, Philosophy and Scholarship**

Chronique de Reims, or *Récits d'un Ménestrel de Reims*.

Al-Juwainī, *Ta'rīkh-i-jahān gushā* (*History of the World Conqueror*, *viz.* Ghengiz Khan; history in Persian of the Mongols, Assassins, etc., to 1258).

†*Minhāj-ud-Dīn, history of Muslim India.

1261

A **Mar:** 13th, in the Treaty of Nymphaeum, the Genoese undertake to assist Michael VIII to recover Constantinople in return for trading concessions hitherto enjoyed by the Venetians.

B **May:** 25th, death of Pope Alexander IV.
Jun: 12th, Henry publishes Alexander's bull absolving him from his oath to observe the Provisions and dismisses the baronial officials.

C **Jul:** 4th, Baybars assumes the Sultanate of Egypt (–1277).
25th, Michael VIII recovers Constantinople and is crowned there, deposing John IV; end of the Latin Empire of 'Romania'.
Aug: 29th, James Pantaléon of Troyes elected as Pope Urban IV (–1264). He offers the crown of Sicily to Charles of Anjou.

E The Muslim vassal King of Murcia revolts against Alfonso of Castile.
Kublai establishes his supremacy as Great Khan (–1294); he continues the conquest of China, where Peking is rebuilt as his winter capital. (His summer capital in eastern Mongolia, Shang-tu, is Coleridge's 'Xanadu').

1262

B **Jun:** Pedro, son and heir of James of Aragon, marries Constance, daughter and heir of Manfred of Sicily.

C **Aug:** Richard recognises Ottokar as ruler of Austria and Styria.
Sep: 14th, Alfonso of Castile takes Cadiz.

E Llewellyn begins his attacks on England.
James of Aragon creates the kingdom of Majorca for his son, James (–1311).
Outbreak of war between the Ilkhan Hūlāgū and Berke, Khan of 'the Golden Horde'; it is inconclusive but saves Egypt from Mongol attack (–1269).
Death of Ganapati, the Kākatīya ruler (in southern India); succeeded by his daughter, Rudrāmbā (Rudradeva Mahārāja; –1295).

1261

J **Art, Architecture and Music**

Thomas Aquinas, *Lauda Sion* (hymn).

K **Literature, Philosophy and Scholarship**

†Albert von Stade, *Troilus* (an epic on the Trojan theme).

Thomas Aquinas and William of Moerbeke begin translation of Aristotle's works (–1269).

1262

F **Law and Politics**

Ordinances of Louis IX bring French municipal finances under royal control.

G **Economics, Science, Technology and Discovery**

Judah Cohen and Isaac ben Sid of Toledo compile the *Alfonsine Tables* (lists of planetary movements, for Alfonso X; –1272).

H **Religion and Education**

Baybars establishes the first of a series of puppet Caliphs of the ʿAbbāsid dynasty in Cairo (–1517).

Brethren of the Free Spirit (heretical mystics) first appear in Augsburg.

†Shinran, a follower of Hōnen (–1175), founds the Shinsū (True) Sect of Japanese Buddhism.

J **Art, Architecture and Music**

The choir of St. Urbain, Troyes, begun by Johannes Anglicus.

Valencia Cathedral (Romanesque) begun.

K **Literature, Philosophy and Scholarship**

*Adam de la Halle ('Le Bossu'), *Le Jeu de la feuillée* (a comedy and satire; the first French farce).

L **Births and Deaths**

— Albertino Mussato b. (–1329).

1263

A **Jan**: Henry re-issues the Provisions of Westminster.
Mar: 29th, Urban excommunicates Manfred again.

B **Apr**: Simon de Montfort returns to England to lead a new baronial movement against Henry.
4th, Baybars attacks Acre and sacks its suburbs.

C **Jul**: 16th, Henry makes peace with his baronial opponents by accepting their terms; de Montfort and his allies occupy London.

D **Oct**: 3rd, in the battle of Largs, Alexander of Scotland defeats Haakon of Norway, who is attempting to subjugate the Hebrides, having already received the submission of Iceland and the colonists in Greenland; Alexander then subdues the Hebrides.
Nov: 14th, death of Alexander I Nevski, Grand Duke of Vladimir; succeeded by his brother, Jaroslav III (–1272).
Dec: death of Martino della Torre, tyrant of Milan; succeeded by his brother, Filippo. Urban had put the city under an interdict for its refusal to accept Otto Visconti as Archbishop.
15th, death of Haakon IV of Norway, in the Shetlands, where he had enforced an act of union with Norway by its people and those of the Orkneys; succeeded by his son, Magnus VII (–1280).

E Alfonso of Castile takes Cartagena; he also cedes the Algarve to Dinis, son of Afonso of Portugal.
Murder of Mindovg, Prince of Lithuania (from 1246), which he had expanded; his death assists the Teutonic Knights, who now complete their near-extermination of the Sambians in the suppression of their rebellion.
The Venetians defeat the Genoese, Michael VIII's allies, in a naval battle off Settepozzi.

1264

A **Jan**: 23rd, in the Mise of Amiens, Louis, as arbitrator, pronounces in favour of Henry against the barons.

B **Apr**: 7th, with his capture of Northampton, Henry renews the civil war.
May: 14th, Simon de Montfort defeats and captures Henry at Lewes.
Jun: 28th, Henry accepts a 'form of government' giving control to de Montfort's party.

D **Oct**: 2nd, death of Pope Urban IV.
21st, Guy Foulquoi, the papal legate in England, excommunicates Henry's opponents.

E Death of Daniel, first King of Halich.
The Poles inflict a great defeat on the Jadźwingas at Zawichost.
Manfred's domination of Tuscany completed with the submission of Lucca.
The Venetians defeat the Genoese off Trapani.

1263

H **Religion and Education**

Urban IV renews the papal prohibition on the study of Aristotle at the University of Paris (–1210).

†Bernard of Botone, *Glossa ordinaria* (on the Decretals).

J **Art, Architecture and Music**

Thomas Aquinas, *Pange lingua* (hymn, 'Now my tongue, the mystery telling').

1264

G **Economics, Science, Technology and Discovery**

Boleslav V grants a charter to Jews who, with Germans, are settling in Poland.

H **Religion and Education**

Jan. 7th, Walter de Merton founds Merton College, Oxford.

K **Literature, Philosophy and Scholarship**

**The Song of Lewes* (Latin poem about the battle reflecting sentiments of Simon de Montfort's partisans).

†*Vincent of Beauvais, *Speculum maius* (encyclopedia of universal knowledge and history; –1481).

1265

A **Feb**: Filippo della Torre of Milan and Obizzo d'Este of Ferrara form a new Lombard League of anti-imperial cities.
5th, Guy Foulquoi elected as Pope Clement IV (–1268).
8th, death of Hūlāgū, the Mongol Ilkhan of Persia; succeeded by his son, Abāqa (–1282).

B **Apr**: Clement grants the Kingdom of Sicily to Charles of Anjou.
Jun: 28th, he invests Charles as King and appoints him to lead the crusade against Manfred.

C **Aug**: Napoleone della Torre proclaimed as lord of Milan.
4th, Henry and Edward defeat and kill Simon de Montfort at Evesham.

D **Dec**: the rebels holding Axholme surrender to Henry.

E Baybars takes Caesarea and Arsūf.

1266

A **Jan**: 6th, Charles of Anjou crowned as King of Sicily (–1285).
Feb: 18th, death of Mahmūd, Sultan of Delhi; succeeded by his lieutenant, Balban (–1287).
26th, Charles defeats and kills Manfred at Benevento.

B **Apr**: 4th, death of John I, co-Margrave of Brandenburg; succeeded by his three sons.
Jun: Henry begins his siege of 'The Disinherited' in Kenilworth Castle.

C **Jul**: 2nd, in the Treaty of Perth, Magnus of Norway renounces his claims to the Hebrides and Isle of Man to Alexander of Scotland.
23rd, Baybars wins control of Galilee by taking the Templars' fortress of Safed.
Aug: 24th, a second Mamlūk army defeats the Armenians near Sarventikar and ravages Cilicia.

D **Oct**: 31st, in the Dictum of Kenilworth, Henry grants terms to de Montfort's adherents.
Dec: 14th, the defenders of Kenilworth surrender.

E Alfonso of Castile, aided by James of Aragon, conquers Murcia.
Death of Świetopelk, Prince of Pomerania.
The Genoese take and rebuild Kaffa, in the Crimea.
Death of Berke, Khan of 'the Golden Horde', ending his war with the Ilkhan (–1262); succeeded by Mangu-Temir (–1280).

1265

F **Law and Politics**

Jan. 20th, the Parliament held under Simon de Montfort is the first attended by elected shire-knights and burgesses.

†Odofredus of Bologna, commentaries on civil law.

H **Religion and Education**

†Simon Stock, first general prior of the Carmelite Friars and founder of houses in England, Paris and Bologna.

J **Art, Architecture and Music**

Nicolò Pisano and assistants, pulpit in Siena Cathedral (–1268; sculpture).

K **Literature, Philosophy and Scholarship**

*Jacobus de Voragine, *Legenda Aurea* (Lives and legends of the Saints: *The Golden Legend* –1483).

L **Births and Deaths**

May 30th(?), Dante Alighieri b. (–1321).

1266

G **Economics, Science, Technology and Discovery**

Louis IX introduces the *gros tournois* in his reform of the French currency.

H **Religion and Education**

*Mangu-Temir exempts the Russian clergy from the payment of taxes to 'the Golden Horde'.

K **Literature, Philosophy and Scholarship**

Azuma Kagami (*Mirror of the Eastland*; Japanese historical chronicle of events from 1180 to 1266, written in Chinese).

*Frate Guidotto of Bologna (?), *Fiore* (collections of sayings and 'flowers' of wisdom).

Roger Bacon, *Opus Maius* (on metaphysics).

1267

B **Apr:** Clement appoints Charles as peace-maker in Tuscany; a pro-papal government established in Florence.

9th, Gilbert de Clare, Earl of Gloucester, occupies London against Henry.

Jun: the Romans revolt against Clement.

Through the mediation of the papal legate, Ottobuono Fieschi, Henry is finally reconciled with his former opponents.

C **Aug:** Sicily revolts against Charles.

Sep: 29th, by the Treaty of Montgomery, Henry recognises Llewelyn as Prince of Wales as his vassal.

E Alfonso of Castile and Afonso of Portugal define their frontier in the Convention of Badajóz; Algarve now annexed to Portugal.

Charles occupies Corfù.

1268

A **Mar:** 7th, Baybars takes Jaffa.

B **Apr:** 4th, Michael VIII makes peace with the Venetians and restores their trading privileges.

17th, Clement appoints Charles as imperial vicar in Tuscany; he also cedes him the office of Senator of Rome.

May: 21st, Baybars takes Antioch and destroys the city with unprecedented slaughter.

Jun: 9th, Rudolph of Habsburg gains possession of Fribourg and the lordship of Berne.

C **Jul:** 23rd, death of Ranieri Zeno, Doge of Venice; succeeded by Lorenzo Tiepolo (–1275).

Aug: 23rd, Conradin, invading to recover his father Conrad IV's Kingdom of Sicily, defeated by Charles at Tagliacozzo.

D **Oct:** 29th, Charles has Conradin executed, extinguishing the house of Hohenstaufen; Conradin had also been nominally King of Jerusalem.

Nov: 29th, death of Pope Clement IV; there is a vacancy as Charles tries to secure the papacy for his nominee (–1271).

E Khaidu, a grandson of Ogodai, revolts and seizes the Khanate of Chaghadai (Turkestan; –1301).

1267

F **Law and Politics**

Nov. 18th, in the Statute of Marlborough, Henry III re-enacts the clauses of the Provisions of Westminster safeguarding sub-tenants against their lords.

K **Literature, Philosophy and Scholarship**

*Brunetto Latini of Florence, *Li livres dou tresor* (encyclopedia of popular knowledge and morality, in French).

1268

F **Law and Politics**

†Henry de Bracton, *De Legibus et Consuetudinibus Angliæ* (treatise on English law, the first systematic summary, citing cases).

H **Religion and Education**

†Benedict d'Alignan, *Tractatus Fidei*.
Foundation of Balliol College, Oxford.

J **Art, Architecture and Music**

Kesik Köprü Han (caravanserai), Kirşehir.

K **Literature, Philosophy and Scholarship**

†Philippe Mousqués, *La Chronique rimée* (history in verse of the French kings to the thirteenth century).

L **Births and Deaths**

— Philip IV b. (–1314).

1269–1270 Establishment of Marinids of Morocco and Solomonids of Abyssinia

1269

B **Apr**: in his fourth and last visit to Germany, Richard of Cornwall holds a diet of Rhenish princes at Worms, where a land-peace is sworn.

C **Sep**: 24th, Hugh III of Cyprus crowned as King of Jerusalem (at Acre; –1284).

E Ottokar of Bohemia succeeds, by treaty, to the Duchy of Carinthia, with Carniola and Istria; Verona and some other Italian cities recognise his overlordship.

Ya'qūb III takes Marrakesh and finally destroys the Almohads; he founds the Marīnid dynasty (–1465).

Abāqa, the Ilkhan, and Mangu-Temir make peace (–1262).

Death of Jatāvarman Sundara, the Pāndya ruler, who had made himself supreme in south India and Ceylon; succeeded by Māravarman Kulaśekhara (–1308/9).

The Mongols invading Sung China lay siege to the twin cities of Hsiang-yang (–1273).

1270

B **Apr**: 27th, a parliament, including some knights, grants a tax to finance Prince Edward's crusade.

C **Jul**: Charles finally suppresses the revolt in Sicily.

1st, Louis sails from France on Crusade.

18th, he lands at Carthage, having been diverted from Palestine by Charles.

25th, he takes Tunis.

Aug: 25th, death of St. Louis IX, King of France; succeeded by his son, Philip III (–1285).

D **Nov**: 1st, Charles, now leader of the Crusade, makes a treaty of peace with the Emir of Tunis, who resumes payment of the tribute formerly paid to the Hohenstaufen Kings of Sicily.

23rd, the crusaders' fleet destroyed by storm at Trapani, thus preventing Charles from directing it against Constantinople.

Dec: 5th, death of Theobald II, King of Navarre; succeeded by his brother, Henry I, Count of Champagne (–1274).

E Pisa, Siena, Turin, Alessandria and Brescia submit to Charles' dominion.

Death of Béla IV of Hungary; succeeded by Stephen V (–1272).

Yekuno Amlak overthrows the Zague dynasty of Kings of Abyssinia and founds the Solomonid dynasty (which traces its origin from Solomon and the Queen of Sheba).

1269

G **Economics, Science, Technology and Discovery**

Petrus Peregrinus of Maricourt, *Epistola de Magnete* (on the lodestone for a compass).

J **Art, Architecture and Music**

Oct. 13th, dedication of Henry III's abbey-church, Westminster.

Mosque of Baybars I, Cairo.

†Ibn-Sab'in, *Kitāb al-Adwār al-Mansūb* (treatise on related musical notes).

K **Literature, Philosophy and Scholarship**

*Adam de la Halle ('Le Bossu'), *Lyrics*; and a *Congé* (satirical farewell on departing from Arras in 1269 to go into enforced exile).

Phagspa devises a new Mongol alphabet for Kublai Khan.

1270

F **Law and Politics**

†*Établissements de Saint-Louis* (actually for the most part customals of (i) Orléannais and (ii) Touraine and Anjou).

Balban of Delhi confiscates lands granted on quasi-feudal terms when the tenants are unable to perform service in person.

*Hemādri, minister of the Yādava kingdom (south India), *Caturvargacintāmani* (encyclopedic Sanskrit digest of Hindu law).

G **Economics, Science, Technology and Discovery**

Population of Hangchow (the Sung capital) estimated to be 391,000 households.

†Ibn-abi Usaybi'ah, *'Uyūn al-Anbā' fi Tabaqāt al-Atibbā'* (*Valuable Information on the classes of Physicians*; biographies of some 600 Greek and Arab physicians).

Earliest notice of a map being used in navigation (in St. Louis' Crusade).

H **Religion and Education**

†Hōjō Sanetoki founds a school and library at Kanazawa, Japan.

J **Art, Architecture and Music**

*Choir of Séez and nave of Minden Cathedrals begun.

*Tomb of Shah Bahā' al-Haqq Zakarīya, Multan.

K **Literature, Philosophy and Scholarship**

†*Sordel di Goito (Sordello of Mantua), *Poems*.

1271

A **Mar:** 13th, Henry of Almain, the son of Richard of Cornwall, murdered in Orvieto by Guy, son of Simon de Montfort.

B **Apr:** 8th, Baybars takes the Knights Hospitallers' fortress of Krak des Chevaliers.
May: 9th, Edward arrives at Acre on crusade.

C **Aug:** 21st, death of Alfonse of Poitiers; his nephew, Philip III of France, thus inherits the counties of Poitou and Toulouse, which are absorbed into the royal domain; while Philip presents the Comtât Venaissin, east of the Rhône, to the Papacy.
Sep: 1st, Tedald Visconti of Piacenza elected as Pope Gregory X (–1276).

E Stephen of Hungary makes Bulgaria tributary.
Death of Michael II, Despot of Epirus; his lands partitioned.
Kublai Khan adopts the Chinese dynastic name of Yüan (–1368).

1272

B **Apr:** 2nd, death, in England, of Richard, Earl of Cornwall, King of the Romans.
May: 22nd, Baybars makes a treaty of peace for ten years with the Kingdom of Acre.
Jun: 16th, at Baybars' instigation, an Assassin attempts to murder Edward at Acre.

C **Aug:** death of Stephen V of Hungary; succeeded by Ladislas IV the Cuman (–1290).
Sep: 22nd, Edward sails from Palestine.

D **Nov:** 16th, death of Henry III of England.
20th, his son, Edward, proclaimed as King by hereditary right (–1307).
Dec: the Archbishop of Lyons (technically in the Empire) takes an oath of fealty to Philip of France.

E Death of Jaroslav III, Grand Duke of Vladimir; succeeded by his brother, Vasili (–1276).

1271

F **Law and Politics**

Durandus, *Speculum judiciale* (synthesis of civil and canon law; first printed 1474).

G **Economics, Science, Technology and Discovery**

Robert the Englishman, *De astrolobio canones.*

*Foundation of the surgeons' guild, Paris.

†*Villard de Honnecourt, architectural sketch-book (includes plans of water-driven machinery, *viz.* saw-mills, and a screw-jack for lifting—a recent invention ?).

Marco Polo leaves Venice on his journey to China (–1295).

H **Religion and Education**

†Hostiensis, *Summa Aurea* or *Summa Hostiensis* (of canon law).

J **Art, Architecture and Music**

Foundation of the Gök and Çifte Medresi (colleges), Sivas.

K **Literature, Philosophy and Scholarship**

†Vardan the Great, universal chronicle (in Armenian, from the Creation to 1267).

1272

G **Economics, Science, Technology and Discovery**

Twisting mills, for manufacture of silk, erected at Bologna.

*Manufacture of paper introduced to Italy (from Muslim sources in Sicily or Spain ?).

H **Religion and Education**

*Raymond Lull translates into Catalan, from Arabic, his own *Libre de contemplació en Deu* (encyclopedia of practical theology).

J **Art, Architecture and Music**

The choirs of Narbonne and Toulouse Cathedrals begun (architect, of both: Jean des Champs).

Regensburg Cathedral begun.

K **Literature, Philosophy and Scholarship**

†Hermann the German, translations of Averroes' commentaries (–1198).

1273

A Jan: 21st, death of Muhammad I, King of Granada; succeeded by his son, Muhammad II (–1302).

D Oct: 1st, Rudolf, Count of Habsburg, elected as King of the Romans (–1291) at the instigation of the enemies of Ottokar of Bohemia, who is excluded from the election.

E The Genoese defeat Charles of Sicily.

The Teutonic Knights complete their suppression of the rebellion of the previously conquered (and converted) tribes of West Prussia.

Michael VIII makes peace with Nogay, the Mongol ruler of the Lower Danube.

The Mongols take Hsiang-yang.

1274

C Jul: 6th, Michael VIII's ambassadors at the General Council of Lyons take an oath accepting the Pope's supremacy; Gregory then causes Charles to make a truce with Michael.

Aug: 19th, Edward I crowned as King of England.

Sep: 26th, Gregory recognises Rudolf as King of the Romans.

D Oct: 26th, Genoa makes an alliance with the imperialists of Lombardy, who recognise Alfonso of Castile as King of the Romans.

E Death of Henry I the Fat, King of Navarre and Count of Champagne; succeeded by his daughter, Joanna I (–1305).

In a diet at Regensburg, Ottokar of Bohemia declared to have forfeited Austria, Styria and his other recent acquisitions.

A fleet sent by Kublai Khan to conquer Japan repulsed at Hakata Bay and subsequently destroyed by a storm.

1273

G **Economics, Science, Technology and Discovery**

Alfonso first organises the Mesta (corporation of sheep-owners) of Castile.

Complaints in London about pollution from burning 'sea-coal' (from Newcastle).

H **Religion and Education**

Raymond Lull begins his missions to Muslims.

†Al-Rūmī's followers establish the Dervish Order of the Mevlevīye.

J **Art, Architecture and Music**

Choir of Limoges Cathedral begun (architect: Jean des Champs).

†Muhammad al-Ghālib founds the Alhambra Palace, Granada.

K **Literature, Philosophy and Scholarship**

†Al-Rūmī, *Masnavī-i ma'navī* (Sūfī mystical poem in six books, explaining by means of fables and anecdotes the mystic Sūfī doctrine); *Divan-i Shams-i Tabriz* (lyrical odes by the greatest Persian mystic poet).

William of Tripoli, *Tractatus de Statu Saracenorum* (account of history, faith and law of Islam, designed to assist Christian apologetic, by a Latin resident in Syria).

1274

F **Law and Politics**

Edward orders an enquiry into English local government; its reports are recorded on 'The Hundred Rolls'.

The examination system abandoned in South Chine (–1315).

†Thomas Aquinas, *De regimine principum* (unfinished political treatise).

G **Economics, Science, Technology and Discovery**

The first 'national' debt established at Genoa.

Exodus of weavers and fullers from Ghent, after they had failed to obtain improved terms of employment.

John Bate, treatise on the astrolabe.

†Al-Tūsī, *al-Zīj al-Īl-Khāni* (astronomical tables).

*Witelo, treatise on optics.

H **Religion and Education**

May 7th, Gregory X opens the General Council of Lyons, held to end the schism with the Greek Church.

The Council recognises the Dominican, Franciscan, Carmelite and Austin Friars, and orders the suppression of all smaller mendicant orders.

†Thomas Aquinas, *Summa Theologiae*.

K **Literature, Philosophy and Scholarship**

†Geoffroi de Beaulieu, *Vita Ludovici IX*.

May: Dante meets Beatrice (–1300).

†Ibn-Mālik, *Alfīya* (Persian poems).

Arnold Fitz Thedmar, *De Antiquis legibus liber* (Chronicle of London).

L **Births and Deaths**

Mar. 7th, St. Thomas Aquinas d. (47).

July 11th, Robert Bruce b. (–1329).

July 14th, St. Bonaventura ('Doctor Seraphicus') d. (53).

1275

B **Spring**: Baybars raids Cilicia.

C **Aug**: Gregory persuades Alfonso to renounce the Kingship of the Romans.
16th, death of Lorenzo Tiepolo, Doge of Venice; succeeded by Jacopo Contarino (–1279).
Sep: 8th, Ya'qūb of Morocco defeats Alfonso near Ecija.

D **Oct**: Gregory obtains German support in north Italy by an agreement with Rudolf; Charles' influence now wanes.
Nov: 10th, Charles defeated at Roccavione by Thomas, Marquess of Saluzzo, and thus loses control of Piedmont.

E Death of Waldemar I of Sweden; succeeded by Magnus I (–1290).

1276

A **Jan**: 10th, death of Pope Gregory X.
21st, Peter of Tarantaise elected as Pope Innocent V.

B **Jun**: 22nd, death of Innocent V.

C **Jul**: 11th, Ottobuoni Fieschi elected as Pope Adrian V.
25th, death of James I the Conqueror, King of Aragon; succeeded by his son, Pedro III (–1285), who, at his coronation (16 Nov.), renounces Aragon's vassalage to the Papacy.
Aug: 18th, death of Pope Adrian V.
Sep: 8th(?), Peter Juliani (of Portugal) elected as Pope John XXI (–1277).

D **Nov**: 25th, following Rudolf's siege of Vienna and a revolt in Bohemia, Ottokar, by the Treaty of Vienna, surrenders Austria, Styria, Carinthia, and all his other lands except Bohemia and Moravia, for which he does homage to Rudolf. Rudolf then makes Vienna the capital of his (Habsburg) lands.

E Philip III attempts to intervene in a dispute in Castile over the future succession to Alfonso X; his army is so badly organised that its march ends before the Pyrenees.
John XXI sanctions Charles' acquisition of the titular Kingdom of Jerusalem.
Stephen Uroš I of Serbia deposed and succeeded by his son, Stephen Dragutin (–1282).
Death of Vasili, Grand Duke of Vladimir; succeeded by his nephew, Dmitri I (–1293).
Kublai Khan takes Hangchow, the Sung capital.

1275

F **Law and Politics**

Edward holds his first Parliament attended by lords and elected knights and burgesses; it makes the first grant of customs on wool and leather. The first Statute of Westminster, *inter alia*, corrects abuses in local government.

**Schwabenspiegel* (compilation of Swabian laws).

G **Economics, Science, Technology and Discovery**

William of Saliceto, *Chirurgia* (surgery; refers to human dissection).

Marco Polo arrives at the court of Kublai Khan.

Florence V of Holland grants a charter of privileges to Amsterdam.

H **Religion and Education**

The Nestorian patriarch of Baghdād creates an archbishopric of Peking; some Mongols were Nestorian Christians, Kublai Khan's mother being one.

J **Art, Architecture and Music**

München-Gladbach Cathedral completed (architect: Gerhard of Cologne?).

*Nave of Strasbourg Cathedral completed (architect: Rudolf of Strasbourg?).

*Nave of Essen Cathedral.

Tower of Minster, Freiburg im Breisgau (–1340?).

K **Literature, Philosophy and Scholarship**

Raymond Lull, *Libre del orde de cavayleria* (Catalan treatise on chivalry).

1276

F **Law and Politics**

Magnus the Law-Mender establishes a common law in Norway.

H **Religion and Education**

Raymond Lull founds a college of friars for the study of Arabic at Miramar.

J **Art, Architecture and Music**

Döner Kümbet (mausoleum), Kayseri.

K **Literature, Philosophy and Scholarship**

Philippe de Rémy de Beaumanoir, *La Manekine* (metrical romance of adventure).

†Guideo Guinicelli, *Ballata*; love lyrics; *canzone*: *Al cor gentil ripara sempre amore* (poems by Dante's poetic 'father' and inspiring influence).

†James I of Aragon, *Libre del feyts* (chronicle of his deeds, in Catalan).

1277

B **Apr**: Baybars invades Anatolia and defeats the Mongols at Elbistan: he withdraws on the approach of an army sent by the Ilkhan Abāqa, which restores Mongol control over the Sultanate of Rūm.

May: 20th, death of Pope John XXI.

Jun: 24th, Edward begins his first Welsh campaign following Llewelyn's refusal to do homage.

C **Jul**: 1st, death of Baybars, Sultan of Egypt and Syria; succeeded by his son, Baraka (–1279).

D **Nov**: 9th, Llewelyn submits to Edward in the Treaty of Conway.

25th, John Gaetan elected as Pope Nicholas III (–1280).

E The Teutonic Knights exterminate the Pogezanians.

An army sent by Kublai Khan defeats Khaidu at Karakorum, but he survives this and later attempts to suppress his rebellion.

1278

A **Jan**: Charles of Sicily crowned as King of Jerusalem.

21st, Otto Visconti defeats Napoleone della Torre at Desio and expels him from Milan; the city accepts Otto as its Archbishop and lord (–1295).

B **May**: Rudolf surrenders the imperial claims to lordship over the Romagna to Nicholas III.

1st, death of William de Villehardouin, Prince of Achaea; succeeded by Charles of Sicily.

24th, Charles surrenders his vicariate of Tuscany and senatorship of Rome to Nicholas.

C **Aug**: 28th, Přemysl Ottokar II of Bohemia defeated and killed by Rudolf and Ladislas of Hungary at Dürnkrut, on the Danube near Stillfried; succeeded by his son, Wenceslas II (–1305), in Bohemia only, where civil war breaks out.

E Pierre de la Broce, chamberlain of Louis IX and Philip III, hanged.

1277

F **Law and Politics**

†Mu'ayyad Alhilli, *Sharāi-al-Islam* (digest of Shiah jurisprudence).

G **Economics, Science, Technology and Discovery**

†Pope John XXI (Petrus Hispanus), *Commentaries of Isaac* (on diets and medicine); *Thesaurus pauperum* (medical textbook); *De anima* (on psychology).

H **Religion and Education**

The Inquisition in France condemns Siger of Brabant for his Averroist writings.

†Raymond Martin, *Pugio fidei adversus Mauros et Judaeos* (*Defence of the Faith against Moors and Jews*).

J **Art, Architecture and Music**

The west façade of Strasbourg Cathedral begun (architect: Erwin).

Arnolfo di Cambio, Statute of Charles of Anjou.

1278

F **Law and Politics**

Edward I initiates judicial enquiries into the titles whereby (*quo warranto*) franchises were held.

Earliest surviving regulations for procedure in Parlement (now permanently installed in the royal palace, Paris, as the supreme court of law in France).

J **Art, Architecture and Music**

Nicolò and Giovanni Pisano, Fountain in the Piazza, Perugia (sculpture).

K **Literature, Philosophy and Scholarship**

Philippe de Rémy de Beaumanoir, *Jehan et Blonde* (romance).

†Martin of Troppau, *Chronicon pontificum et imperatorum* (chronology of popes and emperors to 1277).

L **Births and Deaths**

— Nicolò Pisano d. (*c.* 56).

1279 Extinction of Sung Dynasty

A **Jan:** death of Afonso III of Portugal; succeeded by his son, Dinis (–1325).

Feb: 14th, Rudolf recognises the superior authority of the Papacy over the Empire and cedes all claims to sovereignty over the Papal States and southern Italy.

Mar: death of Jacopo Contarino, Doge of Venice; succeeded by Giovanni Dandolo (–1289).

B **May:** 23rd, by the Treaty of Amiens, Philip cedes Agenais, on the Garonne, to Edward, and recognises his recent occupation of Ponthieu.

C **Aug:** Baraka, Sultan of Egypt and Syria, forced to abdicate in favour of his brother Salāmish; Qalāwūn, the leader of the coup, soon afterwards assumes the Sultanate (–1290).

D **Nov:** 26th, Alfonso of Castile and Philip of Spain make a truce by Edward's mediation.

Dec: 10th, death of Boleslav V the Chaste, Grand Prince of Poland, whose reign had been a period of disintegration; succeeded by Leszek the Black (–1288).

E Florence, Lucca, Siena, and others form a Tuscan Guelf League, with a customs union, and jointly employing an army.

The Greeks put John Asen III on the Bulgarian throne (–1280).

Balban of Delhi crushes a rebellion in Bengal.

A Mongol raid into the Punjab repulsed.

Māravarman Kulaśekhara of Pāndya defeats Rājendra III, the last Chola ruler.

Kublai Khan completes the Mongol conquest of China with a naval victory, near Macao; the southern Sung dynasty extinguished.

G **Economics, Science, Technology and Discovery**

Faraj ben Sālim of Girgenti translates, as *Liber Continens*, Rhazes' *al-Hāwī* (–925; first printed 1486).

Lapidario of Alfonso the Wise (a compilation on stones; it also gives one of the earliest western illustrations of a ship with two lateen sails and thus—unlike the square-rigged, simple masted ships of northern Europe—able to sail into the wind.)

**Ch'in ching* (earliest surviving version, of a possibly much older, Chinese treatise on ornithology).

H **Religion and Education**

Nicholas III's decree *Exiit qui seminat* attempts to reconcile the division among the Franciscans over whether they should own property.

In the course of a dispute with John Pecham, Archbishop of Canterbury, Edward I, in the Statute of Mortmain, forbids grants of land to the Church—the first act of anti-clerical legislation in England.

J **Art, Architecture and Music**

Turumta mausoleum Amasya

1280

A **Feb**: 10th, death of Margaret II, Countess of Flanders; succeeded, through the support of Philip III, by Guy of Dampierre, her son (–1305); Flanders thus comes under French influence, as Guy had been challenged by John of Avesnes, who had imperial backing.

B **May**: 9th, death of Magnus VII of Norway; succeeded by his son, Eric II (–1299).

C **Aug**: 22nd, death of Pope Nicholas III.

D **Oct**: 20th, the Mongols sack Aleppo.

E Petro of Aragon establishes a protectorate over Tunis.
William de la Roche succeeds to the lordship of Athens and styles himself Duke.
John Asen III of Bulgaria deposed by George I Terter.
Death of Mangu-Temir, Khan of 'the Golden Horde'; his brother, Tuda-Mangu, succeeds (–1287), but Nogay assumes joint rule in Russia as Khan of the Nogay Horde, ruling between the Dneiper and Danube (–1299). Tuda-Mangu ravages Vladimir and replaces Dmitri with his brother, Andrew, as Grand Duke (–1305).

1281

A **Feb**: 22nd, Simon de Brie elected Pope Martin IV (–1285); he appoints Charles of Sicily as Senator of Rome.

B **Apr**: 10th, Martin excommunicates the Greeks and renounces the union of 1274.

C **Jul**: 3rd, in the Treaty of Orvieto, the Venetians undertake to assist Charles to restore the Latin Empire in Constantinople; Martin declares Michael VIII deposed.
Aug: 15th and 16th, a second fleet sent by Kublai Khan to conquer Japan destroyed by a typhoon while being held to a small beachhead at Hakata Bay.

D **Oct**: 30th, Qalāwūn of Egypt defeats the Mongols, Armenians and Knights Hospitallers at Homs.

E Pedro of Aragon makes an alliance with Michael VIII (against Charles).

1280

F **Law and Politics**

*Philippe de Beaumanoir, *Coutumes de Clermont en Beauvaisis* (examination of local legal customs but a major work of jurisprudence by a royal lawyer, being also a study in comparative law and of legal principles).

G **Economics, Science, Technology and Discovery**

Riots by employees in the cloth-weaving industry in Flanders.

Paravicius translates, as *Theisir*, Avenzoar's *Facilitation of Treatment* (–1162).

Kuo Shou-ching, *Shouh-shih li* (calendar).

Notice of the spinning-wheel in Drapers' Statutes, Speyer.

H **Religion and Education**

†Mechthild of Magdeburg, *Book of the Flowing light of the Godhead* (Low German, by a poetess-mystic).

†Albertus Magnus, *Summa theologica*; also numerous scientific works.

J **Art, Architecture and Music**

Nave of Exeter Cathedral begun.

S. Maria sopra Minerva (the only Gothic church in Rome; –1450).

*Walter Odington, *De speculatione musices* (explains mensural music).

*Cimabue, *Madonna enthroned with angels* (painting).

K **Literature, Philosophy and Scholarship**

†*Rustico di Filippo, sonnets and poems (the first Italian poet to choose humorous themes).

*Jakemon Saquet (Jakemes), *Le Châtelain de Couci* (*Le Roman du Castelain de Couci et de la Dame de Fayel*; metrical tale).

Adenet le Roi, *Chansons de geste.*

L **Births and Deaths**

Nov. 14th, Albertus Magnus of Cologne d. (87).

1281

G **Economics, Science, Technology and Discovery**

Henry Bate, *Liber servi Dei* (autobiography of an astrologer).

J **Art, Architecture and Music**

North transept (Portail des Libraires), Rouen Cathedral, begun.

1282

A **Mar**: 21st, David, Llewelyn's brother, begins a widespread Welsh revolt against Edward.
30th, the French garrison in Palermo massacred in the 'Sicilian Vespers'; the revolt spreads, leading to Charles' loss of the island of Sicily, whose people offer the crown to Pedro of Aragon, as Manfred's heir.

B **Apr**: 1st, death of Abāqa, Ilkhan of Persia (with his capital at Tabriz); succeeded by his brother Tekuder, who announces his conversion to Islam, taking the style 'Sultan Ahmad' (–1284).
Jun: 18th, Pedro, making for Sicily, lands in north Africa, ostensibly on crusade.

C **Aug**: Edward begins his second Welsh campaign.
30th, Pedro lands in Sicily, soon taking possession as King Peter I (–1285).

D **Nov**: 18th, Martin declares Pedro deprived of the crown of Aragon and proclaims a crusade against him.
Dec: 11th, death of the Greek Emperor, Michael VIII Palaeologus; succeeded by his son, Andronicus II (–1328), who immediately renounces the reunion with Rome.
11th, Llewelyn, Prince of Wales, killed while invading Builth; David assumes his title (–1283).
27th, in a diet at Augsburg, Rudolf invests his sons Albert and Rudolf Habsburg with the Duchies of Austria and Styria respectively.

E Leszek of Poland avenges a devastating raid by the Jadźwingas with their final destruction.
The Mongols ravage the Kingdom of Halich, destroying its political importance, and go on into Poland.
Stephen Dragutin appoints his brother, Stephen Uroš II, joint-king and effective ruler of Serbia (–1321); Stephen Uroš takes Skoplje from the Greeks.

1283

B **Apr**: 25th, the Welsh revolt against Edward collapses with the surrender of Harlech castle and capture of David.

D **Oct**: 3rd, David executed as a traitor against Edward, for the newly defined crime of 'raising war against the king' and by the new penalty of hanging, drawing and quartering.

E Skurdo, the last Prussian leader, flees to Lithuania; the Teutonic Knights have now exterminated or subjugated the Prussians, whose lands are colonised by Germans and Poles.
Andrew flees from Vladimir after a rising and Nogay supports the restoration of Dmitri as Grand Duke.
Indravarman V successfully resists a seaborne Mongol invasion of Champa (–1284).

1282

F **Law and Politics**

Eric II grants a charter of liberties to the Danish nobles.

The Priors of the Arts established as the governing body in Florence.

G **Economics, Science, Technology and Discovery**

Alliance of Lübeck, Riga and Visby for the protection of their trade in the Baltic.

Ristoro d'Arezzo, *Della Composizione del Mondo* (encyclopedia on structure of the world, astrology, etc., in Italian).

H **Religion and Education**

†Nicheren founded the Nicheren (*or* Lotus) Sect of Japanese Buddhism (a popular, nationalistic movement; *cf.* friars).

J **Art, Architecture and Music**

Albi Cathedral (–1390).

*Arnolfo di Cambio, tomb of Cardinal de Braye, Orvieto.

K **Literature, Philosophy and Scholarship**

*Adanet le Roi, *Cléomadès* (romance about *Le Cheval de Fust*—a wooden horse which flies through the air, bringing its riders fantastic adventures).

†Ibn-Khallikān, *Wafayāt al'yān wa-Anbā' al-Zamān* (dictionary of 865 Muslim biographies).

†George Acropolites, chronicle of Constantinople (1204–61).

1283

F **Law and Politics**

Pedro III concedes the *Privilegio General* to the Union of Aragon (association of nobles and municipalities).

Creation of the Court of the Consulate of the Sea for commercial affairs at Valencia; a compilation of commercial law, the *Llibre del Consolat de Mar*, had now appeared.

G **Economics, Science, Technology and Discovery**

Lübeck and other Baltic towns, with some princes, make an alliance for their mutual protection.

Compass now known by Islamic, French and Italian seamen.

*Burchard of Mount Sion, *Descriptio Terrae Sanctae* (account of his journey in Palestine).

†Al-Qazwini, *'Ajā'ib al-Makhluqāt wa-ghara' ib al-Mawjudāt* (*Marvels of created things and their singularities*; cosmographical encyclopedia); *'Ajā'ib al-Buldān* (*Marvels of the countries*; geographical encyclopedia).

K **Literature, Philosophy and Scholarship**

Adam de la Halle ('Le Bossu'), *Le Jeu de Robin et de Marion* (pastoral, an early example of a comic *singspiel*; music perhaps written by the poet).

Jacob van Maerlant, *Spieghel Historiael* (Flemish chronicle of world history).

*Raymond Lull, *Blanquerna* (religious romance in Catalan).

1284

A Jan: a revolt in Rome destroys Charles' authority there.

Feb: Philip of France accepts Martin's offer of the crown of Aragon; it was granted by Martin to Philip's second son, Charles of Valois.

Mar: 4th, death of Hugh III, King of Cyprus and Jerusalem; succeeded by his son, John I (–1285).

B Apr: 4th, death of Alfonso X the Wise, King of Castile and Leon; a civil war follows; his second son, Sancho (IV; –1295), elected King by the nobles despite his will bequeathing the crown to his grandson, Ferdinand de la Cerda.

Jun: 5th, the Genoese, Roger Loria, defeats the Angevin navy in the Bay of Naples and captures Charles' heir, Charles, who is delivered to Peter of Aragon.

C Aug: 6th, Pisa ruined by the destruction of its fleet by the Genoese off the island of Meloria.

10th, the Ilkhan Tekuder murdered in an anti-Muslim revolt; succeeded by his brother, Arghūn (–1291).

16th, Philip (IV), son of Philip III, marries Joanna I, Queen of Navarre and Countess of Champagne.

1285

A Jan: 7th, death of Charles I of Anjou, King of Sicily; succeeded by his son, Charles II (–1309).

Mar: 9th, Mongols invading the Punjab kill Balban's heir, Muhammad Khan.

28th, death of Pope Martin IV.

B Apr: 2nd, Jacopo Savelli elected as Pope Honorius IV (–1287).

May: 20th, death of John I, King of Jerusalem and Cyprus; succeeded by his brother, Henry II (–1324).

Jun: 27th, Philip invades Aragon on his 'crusade' and begins the siege of Gerona.

C Jul: 7th, Dietrich Holzschuh, who claimed to be the Emperor Frederick II, burnt to death; Rudolf thus suppresses a revolt.

Sep: 7th, Philip takes Gerona; he now withdraws, as his army is ravaged by disease.

D Oct: 5th, death of Philip III the Bold, King of France; succeeded by his son, Philip IV the Fair (–1314).

31st, Magnus of Sweden, whose arbitration Eric of Norway is compelled to accept by the Hanse's blockade, pronounces in favour of the German towns in their dispute over trading privileges.

Nov: 2nd, death of Pedro III the Great; succeeded by his sons, Alfonso III in Aragon and James in (the island of) Sicily (–1291).

E The Teutonic Knights found Strassburg, on the Drewenz; thus begins their occupation, colonisation and conversion of Lithuania.

1284

F **Law and Politics**

Edward's Statute of Rhuddlan provides English government for the Principality of Wales.

G **Economics, Science, Technology and Discovery**

A Venetian law refers to reading glasses and, apparently, spectacles ('roidi da ogli').

†Alfonso the Wise had translations made of Arab works on astronomy, astrology, clocks, etc.

Al-Māristan al-Mansūri (Qalāwūn's hospital, school and mosque), Cairo.

H **Religion and Education**

Foundation of Peterhouse, the first college at Cambridge.

J **Art, Architecture and Music**

Collapse of the vault of the choir of Beauvais Cathedral; rebuilt.

Façade of Siena Cathedral begun (architect: Giovanni Pisano).

K **Literature, Philosophy and Scholarship**

†Alfonso X, King of Castile (El Sabio—The Wise or Learned), *Cantigas de Santa María* (poems in Galician); *Grande y general historia* (the first general history of Spain in Spanish, to 1252); *Septennario* (encyclopedia). A treatise written for him gives the first description of the game of chess in a European language.

*Sturla Thordsson, *Sturlunga Saga* (Icelandic history of the house of Sturla; –1225).

L **Births and Deaths**

Apr. 25th, Edward II b. (–1327).

1285

F **Law and Politics**

Edward I's Statutes of Westminster II (*De donis conditionalibus*—concerning feudal tenures) and Winchester (for the maintenance of public order). The former follows a royal enquiry into tenures of the crown known as 'Kirkby's Quest'.

*Giles of Rome, *De regimine principum* (*The Government of Princes*; printed from 1473).

G **Economics, Science, Technology and Discovery**

William of St. Cloud observes the sun through a *camera obscura* (–1290).

J **Art, Architecture and Music**

*Duccio (?), *Rucellai Madonna* (painting).

K **Literature, Philosophy and Scholarship**

*Jacques Bretel, *Le Tournoi de Chauvency* (a poem on the tournament and on chivalry).

1286

A **Mar**: 19th, death of Alexander III of Scotland; his heir was his granddaughter, Margaret, the daughter of Eric of Norway (–1290).

D **Nov**: Eric V Clipping, King of Denmark, murdered; succeeded by his son, Eric VI Menved (–1319).

E Kublai Khan's army invading Dai Viet defeated; he therefore abandons his preparations for the conquest of Japan.
(and 1287) Nogay raids Poland and Galicia.

1287

B **Apr**: 3rd, death of Pope Honorius IV.
20th, the Egyptians take Lattakieh.
May: 31st, the Genoese defeat the Venetian fleet off Acre and blockade the coast of Outremer.
Jun: 23rd, James repulses an Angevin invasion of Sicily and Roger Loria defeats the Angevin fleet off Castellammare.

C **Jul**: 15th, Edward of England and Alfonso of Aragon make a treaty of alliance at Oléron.

E Abdication of Tuda-Mangu, Khan of 'the Golden Horde'; succeeded by Tele-Buga (–1291).
Death of Balban of Delhi; succeeded by his grandson, Kaiqubād (–1290).
Mongols invading the Punjab massacred near Lahore.
Kublai Khan's army invading Dai Viet repelled but then invades Burma and destroys the Kingdom of Pagan; its fall allows the emergence of several principalities of the Thais, who had recently been moving southward into Burma and Cambodia, while Burma itself is divided into three states.

1286

F **Law and Politics**

In the writ of *Circumspecte agatis*, Edward defines the issues triable only in ecclesiastical courts.

G **Economics, Science, Technology and Discovery**

Philip IV introduces the Gabelle (royal monopoly for the sale of salt) in France (–1341).

H **Religion and Education**

*Durandus, *Rationale divinorum officiorum* (on liturgy; first printed 1459).

K **Literature, Philosophy and Scholarship**

†William of Moerbeke translated from Greek Aristotle's *Politics*, *Nicomachean Ethics*, etc.

†Bar Hebraeus, *Syriac Grammar*.

Giovanni Balbi, *Catholicon* (treatise on study of Latin, with a dictionary; first printed 1460).

1287

F **Law and Politics**

Alfonso of Aragon confirms the Privilege of the Union (–1283).

G **Economics, Science, Technology and Discovery**

A storm causes many deaths by drowning in the extension of the Zuider Zee, which reaches its limits about this time.

Rabban Sauma, a Nestorian monk of Peking, visits European courts as a Mongol envoy; his travels are recorded.

K **Literature, Philosophy and Scholarship**

Fra Salimbene of Parma (*i.e.* Ognibene di Adamo), *Chronica* (from 1167 to 1287, with much personal and valuable historical material on the early history of the Franciscans).

*Guido Columnis (of Messina), *Historia Trojana* (prose version, in Latin, of Benoît's *Roman de Troi*—1160).

†*Conrad (Konrad) von Würzburg, *Der Schwanenritter* (narrative on the Lohengrin theme, in rhymed couplets); *Der Trojanische Krieg* (epic poem in rhymed couplets on the Trojan theme).

1288

A **Feb**: Jerome of Ascoli elected as Pope Nicholas IV (–1292); he soon receives an ambassador from the Ilkhan Arghūn who had been visiting the European kings to organise a joint crusade against Egypt.

C **Jul**: 7th, John I, Duke of Brabant, defeats and captures Archbishop Siegfried of Cologne at Worringen, so winning possession of the Duchy of Limburg.

D **Oct**: 27th, by the Treaty of Campofranco, made by Edward's mediation, Alfonso of Aragon releases Charles II of Naples.

Dec: Obizzo II, Marquess of Este, accepted as lord of Modena (–1293).

E Death of Leszek III the Black, Grand Prince of Poland; there are several candidates for the succession. The Mongol raids into Poland (since 1282) now cease.

1289

B **Apr**: 26th, Qalāwūn takes and destroys Tripoli.

May: 29th, Nicholas crowns Charles as King of Sicily.

Jun: 2nd, Florence defeats Arezzo at Campaldino and so establishes her supremacy in Tuscany.

D **Nov**: death of Giovanni Dandolo, Doge of Venice; succeeded by Pietro Gradenigo (–1311).

6th, in the Treaty of Salisbury, Eric of Norway and the guardians of Scotland make terms with Edward for his custody of Margaret.

E Dinis of Portugal makes a concordat with the Papacy which regulates the relations of the crown and clergy.

Ugolino, the tyrant of Pisa, starved to death in its Tower of Hunger.

Obizzo becomes lord of Reggio.

1288

G **Economics, Science, Technology and Discovery**

Jacob ben Makir, treatise (in Hebrew) on the quadrant, making improvements.

Bartholomew of Parma, *Breviloquium geomantiae* (on astrology).

†Ibn-al-Nafīs, *Kitāb Mūjiz al-Qānūn* (*Commentary on the Canon* (of medicine of Avicenna –1037; includes a theory of the circulation of the blood).

J **Art, Architecture and Music**

Palazzo Communale, Siena (–1309).

K **Literature, Philosophy and Scholarship**

'Irāqī, *Lama'āt* (Persian poetry).

Matfré de Bezier, *Breviari d'amor*.

L **Births and Deaths**

— Levi ben Gerson b. (–1344).

1289

G **Economics, Science, Technology and Discovery**

A printing block used at Ravenna.

Completion of extension of the Chinese Grand Canal (of *c.* A.D. 605) to link Peking with the Yellow River.

John of Monte Corvino sent by the Pope to the Ilkhan of Persia (–1290) and the Great Khan (–1295).

H **Religion and Education**

Nicholas grants half the papal revenues to the College of Cardinals.

Gloucester Hall (now Worcester College) founded for Benedictine monks at Oxford.

J **Art, Architecture and Music**

Ali Şerefeddin Arslanhane Mosque, Ankara.

L **Births and Deaths**

Oct. 4th, Louis X b. (–1316).

1290–1291 Hungarian succession dispute—Outremer conquered by Egypt

1290

B **Jun**: 13th, Kaiqubād, the last Slave King of Delhi, murdered; succeeded by Fīrūz II (–1295), founder of the Khaljī dynasty (–1320).

C **Jul**: 18th, by the Treaty of Brigham, the guardians of Scotland agree to the marriage of Margaret to Edward (II), son of Edward I.

19th, Ladislas IV of Hungary murdered by Cumans; succeeded by his adopted heir, Andrew III, grandson of Andrew II (–1301); Rudolf invests his own son, Albert, as King, while Nicholas IV favours Charles Martel of Anjou, who is crowned by a papal legate.

Sep: Margaret, Queen of Scotland, 'the Maid of Norway', dies on her way from Norway.

8th, William of Montferrat, hitherto dominant in Lombardy, captured and imprisoned at Alessandria (–1292).

D **Nov**: 10th, death of Qalāwūn, Sultan of Egypt; succeeded by his son, al-Ashraf Khalīl (–1293).

Dec: 18th, death of Magnus I Barn-lock, King of Sweden, who had established feudalism; succeeded by his son, Birger II (–1319).

E Przemyslav II cedes Little Poland to Wenceslas II of Bohemia, who also acquires Cracow.

1291

A **Feb**: Philip of France and Alfonso of Aragon make peace by the Treaty of Tarascon. Alfonso restores Majorca to his uncle, James.

B **Apr**: 6th, al-Ashraf begins the siege of Acre.

May: 10th, Edward holds an assembly of Scottish lords at Norham which accepts his claim for recognition as overlord before he determines the succession to the Scottish throne.

18th, al-Ashraf takes and destroys Acre.

Jun: 18th, death of Alfonso III of Aragon; he bequeaths the kingdom to his brother, James II (–1327), provided that the latter cedes Sicily to their brother, Frederick; James, in fact, retains Sicily (–1295).

C **Jul**: 15th, death of Rudolf I of Habsburg, King of the Romans.

31st, with the fall of Beirūt to the Egyptians, the Latin presence in Palestine and Syria (Outremer) liquidated.

Aug: 1st, the Three Forest Cantons of Schwyz, Uri and Unterwalden form a defensive league (against the Habsburgs).

D **Oct**: 16th, Uri and Schwyz make a (short-lived) alliance with Zurich.

E At the request of Polish nobles, Wenceslas of Bohemia assumes the title of Grand Duke of Cracow.

Following the fall of Acre, the Teutonic Knights move the headquarters of the Grand Master to Venice.

Nogay deposes and kills Tele-Buga and has Tokhta proclaimed as Khan of 'the Golden Horde' (–1312).

1290

F **Law and Politics**

Edward I's statutes of Westminster III (*Quia emptores*—on the sale of feudal tenures) and *Quo warranto* (establishing the accession of Richard I in 1189 as the limit of legal memory).

G **Economics, Science, Technology and Discovery**

Edward expels the Jews from England.

William of St. Cloud determines the obliquity of the ecliptic at Paris.

H **Religion and Education**

Earliest extant constitution of the Austin Friars.

Dinis founds a university at Lisbon (–1308).

J **Art, Architecture and Music**

†Chi'en Hsuan, Chinese painter.

K **Literature, Philosophy and Scholarship**

Lohengrin (anon. German narrative poem—1220; 1336).

L **Births and Deaths**

June 9th, Dante's Beatrice d.

Nov. 28th, Eleanor of Castile, queen of Edward I, d.

1291

G **Economics, Science, Technology and Discovery**

Venetian glass factories are confined to the Island of Murano.

H **Religion and Education**

Assessment of English benefices for papal taxation, recorded as the *Taxatio* of Pope Nicholas IV.

J **Art, Architecture and Music**

Charing Cross, London, and nine other stone crosses raised to mark the stops of Queen Eleanor's funeral cortege (–1294); their ogee arches mark the beginning of the 'curvilinear' style of English Gothic.

Nave of York Minster begun.

L **Births and Deaths**

— Stefano Masuccio b. (–1388).

— Richard of Wallingford b. (–1335).

— Philippe de Vitry b. (–1361).

1292

A **Feb**: William V the Great, Marquess of Montferrat, dies in the iron cage in which he was kept at Alessandria (–1290).

B **Apr**: 4th, death of Pope Nicholas IV.
May: 10th, Adolf, Count of Nassau, elected as King of the Romans (–1298).

D **Nov**: 17th, Edward awards the Scottish crown to John Balliol (–1296).

E Albert of Habsburg defeats the Swiss Confederation but fails to take Zurich.
Monguls invading Muslim India are repulsed at Sunām.
Kublai Khan sends a fleet to conquer Java.

1293

A **Feb**: 13th, death of Obizzo d'Este; his son, Azzo VIII, elected as perpetual lord of Modena and Reggio (–1306).

B **May**: 15th, Anglo-Gascon and Norman ships fight off Saint-Mahé, Brittany.

C **Jul**: 5th, Peter, the hermit of Monte Murrone, elected as Pope Celestine V.

D **Dec**: 13th, Celestine abdicates.
13th, al-Ashraf, Sultan of Egypt, murdered; succeeded by his son, an-Nāsir (–1294; 1298–1308; 1309–40).

E Torkil Knutson conquers Karelia and founds Vyborg.
Tokhta ravages Vladimir, Moscow, etc., in re-establishing Andrew as Grand Duke in place of Nogay's vassal, Dmitri I.
Repulse of Kublai Khan's expedition to Java.
*Nogay invades Serbia; King Stephen Uroš becomes his vassal.

1292

F **Law and Politics**

Edward I orders the judges to provide training for the English legal profession (origin of education for the bar by the Inns of Court).

G **Economics, Science, Technology and Discovery**

†*Giovanni Campano invents an improved version of the quadrant.
Marco Polo leaves China and visits Java and Sumatra.
William of St. Cloud, table of planets.

H **Religion and Education**

†John Pecham, *Perspectiva Communis*; *De summa Trinitate et Fide Catholica.*
*Durandus, *Pontificale.*

J **Art, Architecture and Music**

St. Stephen's Chapel, Westminster, begun (origin of 'Perpendicular' architecture?).

K **Literature, Philosophy and Scholarship**

†Roger Bacon, *Compendium philosophiae* (encyclopedia).

L **Births and Deaths**

Dec. 8th, John Pecham, Archbishop of Canterbury, d.

1293

F **Law and Politics**

Ordinances of Justice enacted in Florence to prevent disorder due to the strife of the 'Black' and 'White' Factions.

G **Economics, Science, Technology and Discovery**

*Simon of Genoa, *Synonyma medicinae* (or *Clavis sanationis*; dictionary of *materia medica*).

H **Religion and Education**

†Henri de Gand, *Summa theologiae.*

I **Art, Architecture and Music**

*The Mongol Scroll (a pictorial record of the repulse by the Japanese of the Mongol invasions, 1274, 1281; *cf.* Bayeux Tapestry, 1080).

L **Births and Deaths**

— Philip VI b. (–1350).
— Jan Ruysbroeck b. (–1381).

1294 Anglo-French War

A **Jan**: Edward, by proxy, answers his summons to the Parlement of Paris to answer for attacks by Gascon on French seamen, and agrees to surrender castles in Gascony during an enquiry; the consequent French seizure of Gascony leads to war.

B **Jun**: John Balliol subjected to a baronial committee as a result of Scottish opposition to Edward's domination.

C **Aug**: 24th, in the Treaty of Nuremburg, Edward and Adolf make an alliance against France.

Sep: 30th, the Welsh revolt and prevent Edward from invading France.

D **Dec**: 23rd, Benedict Gaetani elected as Pope Boniface VIII (–1303).

E The Treaty of Tönsberg concludes a dispute between Eric of Norway and the Hanse in the latter's favour.

Philip imprisons Guy of Dampierre, Count of Flanders, following the betrothal of Guy's daughter to Edward (II).

The Genoese defeat the Venetians in a naval battle off Laiazzo, in Cilicia.

Przemyslav II of Greater Poland inherits East Pomerania from its last prince, Mszczvj.

'Alā'-ad-Dīn sacks Deogīr, the capital of a Hindu kingdom in West Deccan.

Death of Kublai Khan, Great Khan and Mongol (Yüan) Emperor of China; succeeded by his grandson, Temür (–1307).

F **Law and Politics**

Wenceslas II summons the Italian jurisconsult, Gozzo of Orvieto, to codify Bohemian law.

G **Economics, Science, Technology and Discovery**

*Gozzo compiles the mining code, *Ius regale montanorum* (the silver-mines of Kutná Hora were now flourishing).

H **Religion and Education**

*John of Monte Corvino establishes a Christian mission in Peking (–1307).

J **Art, Architecture and Music**

Florence Cathedral begun (architect: Arnolfo).

†Safī ad-Dīn, *Kitāb al-Adwār* (*Book of Musical Modes*); *Risālat al-Sharafīya* (treatise on music).

K **Literature, Philosophy and Scholarship**

*Thomas of Erceldoune (Thomas the Rhymer), *Sir Tristrem* (narrative poem first introducing to English literature the Tristram and Iseult theme).

†Guittone d'Arezzo, *Letters*; also many love lyrics and some political verse.

*Bauduins Butors, *Le roman des fils du roi Constant* (a new Arthurian prose-romance).

L **Births and Deaths**

— Charles IV b. (–1328).

1295

A **Mar**: 5th, Edward's forces defeat the Welsh at Maes Moydog, near Montgomery.

B **Jun**: Boniface arranges a treaty of peace, at Agnani, between Philip of France, Charles of Sicily and James of Aragon, who cedes Sicily to Charles.
26th, Przemyslav II of Greater Poland and Pomerania, who was emerging as the accepted ruler over Poland, crowned its King, with papal consent.

C **Jul**: 5th, Scotland and France seal a treaty of alliance ('the Auld alliance').
19th, 'Alā'-ad-Dīn Muhammad proclaimed as Sultan of Delhi following his murder of Fīrūz, his uncle (–1316).
Aug: 9th, death of Otto Visconti, Archbishop of Milan; his great-nephew, Matteo, succeeds as ruler of Milan and is imperial vicar in Lombardy.

E Otto IV, Count of Burgundy, cedes his county (Franche Comté, in the Empire) to France.
Death of Sancho IV of Castile and Leon; succeeded by his son, Ferdinand IV (–1312), and a civil war.
Death of Charles Martel of Anjou, the papal nominee to the Hungarian throne.
Ghazan, Ilkhan of Persia, adopts Islam as the state religion and, styling himself Sultan, declares his independence of the Great Khan.
*Rama Khamheng, (second) King of Sukhodaya, conquers the Mekong and Menam valleys (in Cambodia) and the Malay Peninsula.

1296

A **Jan**: 15th, the Sicilians elect Frederick II of Aragon as their King (–1337).
Feb: 8th, Przemyslav II, King of Poland, murdered at the instigation of Otto of Brandenburg; succeeded by his son, Vladislav Lokietek, as Grand Prince (–1300).
29th, Boniface, in his bull *Clericis Laicos*, forbids kings to tax the clergy.
Mar: 30th, Edward takes Berwick as he begins his campaign to subdue Scotland.

B **Apr**: 27th, he defeats the Scots at Dunbar.
Jun: 28th, Florence V, Count of Holland, murdered.

C **Jul**: 10th, John Balliol surrenders to Edward and abdicates.
Aug: Edward returns from Scotland, bringing 'the Stone of Destiny' from Scone.
Sep: Boniface modifies *Clericis Laicos* with his *Ineffabilis Amor*.

E Mangrai, a Thai leader, founds Chiang Mai (now in Siam), the capital of the new kingdom of Lan Na (–1775).

1295

F Law and Politics

Edward I holds his second (*cf.* 1275) Parliament attended by knights and burgesses (the so-called 'Model Parliament').

G Economics, Science, Technology and Discovery

Philip IV begins to debase the French coinage.

(–1296) Marco Polo returns to Venice.

K Literature, Philosophy and Scholarship

†Brunetto Latini, *Tesoretto* (*Tesoro*: a didactic allegory in verse—the earliest extant example of this form in Italian poetry); *Rettorica in volgar Fiorentino*.

*Girard d'Amiens, *Charlemagne* (epic poem on the Emperor from childhood to maturity).

**The Harrowing of Hell* (Middle English; the earliest extant miracle play in English literature; based on the apocryphal *Gospel of Nicodemus*).

†Sancho IV of Castile, *Lucidario* (a sort of encyclopedia).

1296

G Economics, Science, Technology and Discovery

Lanfranchi of Milan, *Chirurgica Magna* (on surgery).

William of St. Cloud, calendar for Queen Marie.

H Religion and Education

†Durandus, *Repertorium aureum juris* (printed 1474).

J Art, Architecture and Music

Master Honoré decorates a breviary, possibly for Philip IV (in the Bibliothèque Nationale; he is one of the first identified French miniaturists).

K Literature, Philosophy and Scholarship

†Wang Ying-lin, *Yü hai* (*The Sea of Jade*; encyclopedia).

†*Al-Būsīri, *al-Burdah* (*The Prophet's Mantle*; Arabic ode).

L Births and Deaths

Nov. 1st, Guilelmus Durandus, Bishop of Mende, d. (*c.* 66).

— Philippe de Rémy, lord of Beaumanoir, d. (*c.* 50).

A **Jan**: 30th, Edward outlaws the English clergy for their refusal to pay taxes; they surrender and are pardoned.

Feb: 2nd, Edward makes an alliance with Count Guy of Flanders.

24th, in a Parliament held by Edward at Salisbury, the magnates refuse to serve him in Gascony.

Mar: Sciarra Colunna attacks a convoy of papal treasure.

B **May**: William Wallace leads a Scottish rising against Edward.

23rd, Boniface excommunicates the Colunnas and proclaims a crusade against them.

C **Jul**: 31st, under pressure from Philip IV, Boniface renounces his claims in *Clericis Laicos* in the bull *Etsi de statu*.

Aug: he canonises Louis IX of France.

20th, Guy of Flanders defeated by French forces at Furnes.

24th, Edward sails to Flanders to lead his allies of the Low Countries against France.

Sep: 11th, Wallace defeats the English forces at Stirling Bridge.

D **Oct**: 7th, Edward makes a truce with France at Vyve-Saint-Bavon.

10th, Edward's regent re-issues Magna Carta and the Charter of the Forest, with supplementary articles, in a parliament, to allay protests against Edward's administration by the magnates and London.

Nov: 5th, Edward confirms this re-issue.

E The Bishoprics of Metz and Toul, in the Empire, subjected to French rule.

Boniface organises a crusade by Charles of Naples, James of Aragon, and the Genoese, against Frederick of Sicily.

The Venetians sack the Genoese port of Kaffa, in the Crimea; the Genoese ravage the Venetian island of Crete and are assisted by the Emperor Andronicus in massacring Venetian merchants in the Greek Empire.

'Alā'-ad-Dīn conquers the Hindu kingdom of Gujarāt.

Sultan Malik al-Saleh is the first Muslim ruler of Samudra, in north Sumatra.

Law and Politics

The Shogunate cancels all debts of its retainers in order to relieve their growing impoverishment—the consequence of high living standards and partible inheritances; the Japanese 'feudal' structure is collapsing under these strains.

First Irish parliament with elected members.

G **Economics, Science, Technology and Discovery**

†*Guido Bonatti of Forli, *Liber astronomicus.*

J **Art, Architecture and Music**

Giovanni Pisano, Pulpit in S. Andrea, Pistoia (–1301; sculpture).

K **Literature, Philosophy and Scholarship**

*Chou Ta-kuan, *Chên la fêng t'u chi* (description of Cambodian customs observed on his embassy, 1296–7).

1298–1299 Venice closes the Great Council—The 'Golden Horde' reunited

1298

A **Jan**: 31st, Edward and Philip make a truce, at Tournai.

B **Jun**: 23rd, the German electors depose Adolf of Nassau.

C **Jul**: 2nd, in a battle near Göllheim (near Worms), Adolf is defeated and killed by Albert of Habsburg.
22nd, Edward defeats the Scots at Falkirk but is unable to subdue Scotland.
27th, Albert elected King of the Romans (–1308).
Sep: Boniface's 'crusade' against the Colunnas concludes with the surrender of Palestrina, which he razes to the ground; he employs the lands confiscated from the Colunnas to found a state for his nephew, Peter Gaetani.
8th, the Genoese destroy the Venetian navy off the Dalmatian island of Curzola; as a result, Venice 'closes' her Great Council (*i.e.* restricts its membership).

E Nogay ravages the Crimea after defeating Tokhta.

1299

B **Apr**: 3rd, the magnates constrain Edward to re-issue the Charters.
27th, Ghazan, Ilkhan of Persia, defeats and kills Sulamish, his rebellious governor of Rūm, at Eskishehir.
May: Matteo Visconti negotiates a peace between Genoa and Venice, ending their war (since 1261) to control trade with the Greek Empire.
Jun: 27th, Boniface upholds Scottish independence in his bull *Scimus fili*.

C **Jul**: 4th, the fleets of Genoa and Aragon defeat Frederick of Sicily of Cape Orlando.
Sep: 5th, Philip of France and Albert, King of the Romans, make an alliance by the Treaty of Strasbourg.

D **Nov**: the Scots capture Stirling Castle.
10th, death of John I, Count of Holland and Zeeland; his uncle, John of Avesnes, Count of Hainault, seizes the counties despite the opposition of Albert.
23rd, Ghazan of Persia defeats the Egyptians at Salamia, near Homs.

E Death of Eric II of Norway; succeeded by his brother, Haakon V (–1319).
Tokhta defeats and kills Nogay on the Kagamlyk; the Mongols in eastern Europe are thus reunited.
'Alā'-ad-Dīn repulses a Mongol army outside Delhi.

1298

G **Economics, Science, Technology and Discovery**

Early English notice of use of the spinning-wheel in the manufacture of woollen yarn.

The English victory at Falkirk demonstrates the value of the longbow.

*Marco Polo, *Travels to Tartary and China* (thought to have been dictated in French from travel notes, and taken down by a fellow-prisoner, one Rusticiano of Pisa, at Genoa, after the battle of Curzola; the first European account of the geography, economy, civilisation and government of China).

H **Religion and Education**

Boniface VIII publishes *Liber Sextus* (the *Sext*; an additional compilation of canons).

His constitution *Cum ex eo* permits absenteeism by beneficed clergy attending universities.

J **Art, Architecture and Music**

Choir of Barcelona Cathedral (–1329).

Mosque of Zayn ad-Dīn Yūsuf, Cairo.

K **Literature, Philosophy and Scholarship**

†Jacobus de Voragine, *Chronicon Januense* (chronicle of Genoa to 1297).

L **Births and Deaths**

Aug. 19th, St. Louis of Anjou, Bishop of Toulouse, d. (23).

1299

G **Economics, Science, Technology and Discovery**

Li K'an, *Ch'u p'u hsiang lu* (treatise on bamboo).

J **Art, Architecture and Music**

*Giovanni Pisano, *Madonna* (in ivory), Pisa Cathedral.

Palazzo Vecchio, Florence (–1301).

1300 Bohemia subjects Poland—Ottoman Turks in Turkey

A **Jan:** Damascus surrenders to Ghazan.

Feb: Boniface proclaims a Jubilee in Rome; he also initiates a war against Margaret Aldobrandeschi, Countess Palatine of the Patrimony in Tuscany, the estranged wife of his great-nephew, Loffred Gaetani.

Mar: in response to baronial demands, Edward again issues the Charters and 'the articles on the charters'.

B **May:** Guy of Flanders surrenders to Philip and is imprisoned.

Jun: 14th, Roger Loria of Genoa wins a second naval victory over Frederick of Sicily.

C **Jul:** Edward takes Caerlaverock castle, in south-west Scotland.

Aug: Albert abandons his siege of Nijmegen in the war against John of Hainault; this failure is followed by a revolt of the Rhenish princes.

D **Dec:** Frederick defeats Charles of Naples at Falconaria, near Trapani.

E Wenceslas II of Bohemia takes possession of Greater Poland and Pomerania, deposing Vladislav; having thus reunited most of Poland, he was crowned as its King (Václav).

The Milanese expel Matteo Visconti and permit the Torriani to return.

The Shāns in Burma defeat a punitive Mongol expedition from China.

*A new wave of Turks ('Ottoman'), driven westward by the Mongols, are in occupation of western Anatolia, where the Greek Empire holds only Nicaea, Heraclea, Symrna, etc.

*The Aztecs paramount in Mexico.

G **Economics, Science, Technology and Discovery**

Wenceslas II, in a currency reform, issues the *groschen* of Prague.

*Leprosy now declining in western Europe.

*'Marc the Greek', *Liber Ignium* (gives the first western recipe for gunpowder).

H **Religion and Education**

Boniface VIII announces the Jubilee Year.

The Russian Metropolitan transfers his see from Kiev to Vladimir.

Execution of Segarelli of Parma, the founder of a heretical movement in Italy and Germany.

Foundation of Lérida University, Aragon.

J **Art, Architecture and Music**

*Franciscan church of S. Croce, Florence, begun (architect: Arnolfo di Cambio).

*Tomb of Shāh Shams-i Tabrīz, Mūltan.

*Giotto(?), Frescoes in S. Francesco, Assisi.

*Arnolfo di Cambio, bust and tomb of Boniface VIII.

K **Literature, Philosophy and Scholarship**

*Dante Alighieri completes *Vita Nuova* (begun *c.* 1294; consists of 25 sonnets, 4 canzoni and a ballata, with linking prose: the story of the poet's love for Beatrice from their first meeting in 1274).

†Guido Cavalcanti, *Donna mi prega*: *canzone* (sonnets and other poems by Dante's friend).

**King Alisaunder* (epic romance in verse on the life and deeds of Alexander the Great).

†*Kuan Han-ch'ing, Chinese plays (comedies and tragedies; drama—and the novel—flourished in China in the Mongol period).

1301

A **Jan**: 14th, death of Andrew III of Hungary, the last of the Árpád dynasty; Wenceslas of Bohemia declines the crown, but his son Wenceslas is elected and crowned, taking the Hungarian name of Ladislas (–1304); Boniface supports the candidature of Charles Robert of Anjou.

Feb: 7th, Edward revives the title Prince of Wales and confers it on his son, Edward (II).

14th, Edward makes (his last) confirmation of the Charters in response to demands in the Parliament of Lincoln.

B **Apr**: 13th, Boniface summons Albert, King of the Romans (whom he refuses to recognise as such), to answer for the murder of Adolf of Nassau.

May: the Black faction expelled from Florence.

C **Jul**: Edward begins his sixth campaign in Scotland.

27th, Ghāzī 'Osmān, founder of the Ottoman dynasty, defeats Greek forces at Baphaeum (?Koyunhisār), near Nicaea.

D **Nov**: 1st, Charles, Count of Valois, whom Boniface had called into Italy as 'Peacemaker', enters Florence; he allows the Blacks to return.

Dec: Boniface, in his bulls *Salvator Mundi* and *Ausculta Fili*, rebukes Philip of France for misgovernment and announces his trial, thus responding to Philip's proceedings against Bernard Saiset, Bishop of Pamiers, for treason.

E Death of Khaidu, still holding the Khanate of Chaghadai (Turkestan).

1302

A **Jan**: 27th, the Black faction, which had seized power in Florence, sentences it opponents (including Dante) to death or exile.

B **Apr**: 8th, death of Muhammad II of Granada; succeeded by his son, Muhammad III (–1308).

10th, Philip holds the first known meeting of the Estates General in Paris to rally national opinion against Boniface.

May: Boniface appoints Charles of Valois captain-general of the papal and Neapolitan forces.

18th, the French garrison massacred in the 'Matins of Bruges'; the Flemings revolt against the French occupation.

C **Jul**: 11th, the Flemish craftsmen defeat Philip at Courtrai.

Sep: 24th, following the destruction of Charles of Valois' army by malaria, a truce is made, by the Treaty of Caltabellotta, between Charles of Naples and Frederick of Sicily, whose kingdom is named Trinacria; thus ends the War of the Sicilian Vespers. Frederick's Catalan troops form the Grand Company and go to Greece.

D **Nov**: 18th, in the bull *Unam Sanctam*, Boniface asserts the superiority of the Pope's spiritual authority over secular princes.

E Albert subdues the Elector of the Rhineland.

1301

F **Law and Politics**

'Alā'-ad-Dīn of Delhi initiates regular taxation and prohibits consumption of wine; his anti-Hindu legislation is a departure from the Muslim tradition of toleration.

H **Religion and Education**

Philip IV restricts the powers of the Dominican Inquisition in Languedoc.
St. Gertrude inspires the cult of the Sacred Heart.

J **Art, Architecture and Music**

Al-Kāshānī, treatise on Persian pottery; includes description of the Chinese technique of glazing earthenware (faïence).

1302

F **Law and Politics**

First Estates-General of France (*see* B).
John of Paris, *De potestate regia et papali* (anti-papal defence of French sovereignty).

G **Economics, Science, Technology and Discovery**

Bartolomeo de Varignana of Bologna conducts the first *post mortem* examination.

H **Religion and Education**

Foundation of the College of Cardinal Lemoine, Paris.

J **Art, Architecture and Music**

Nave of Bayonne Cathedral begun.
Brunswick town hall begun.
Giovanni Pisano, Pulpit in Pisa Cathedral (–1310; sculpture).
Cimabue, *St. John* (mosaic in Pisa Cathedral).

L **Births and Deaths**

? Arnolfo di Cambio d. (70).

1303

A **Mar**: Philip publishes 'La Grande Ordonnance' for 'the reform of the kingdom' in response to baronial pressure.

B **Apr**: Boniface demands Philip's submission under pain of excommunication.
30th, he recognises Albert as King of the Romans.
May: Edward begins his seventh campaign in Scotland, a military progress to Elgin.
20th, Philip and Edward make peace in the Treaty of Paris; Gascony restored to Edward.
Jun: 24th, Philip calls the European princes to a general council to hear charges against Boniface.

C **Sep**: Philip releases Count Guy after an unsuccessful campaign in Flanders.
Boniface, in *Super Petri solio*, releases the French from their allegiance to Philip.
7th, an Italian force, led by Philip's agent, Guillaume de Nogaret, arrests Boniface at Anagni.
12th, Boniface released in a rising by the people of Anagni.

D **Oct**: 12th, death of Pope Boniface VIII.
22nd, Niccolò Boccasini elected as Pope Benedict XI (–1304).

E Eric VI confirms the privileges of the Danish church, ending the dispute begun in 1254.
Andronicus engages the Grand Company.
The Egyptians defeat the Mongols of Persia at Marj as-Saffar and recover Damascus for an-Nāsir.
Mongols unsuccessfully besiege Delhi.

1304

A **Mar**: the Scots submit to Edward in a parliament at St. Andrews.
Death of Daniel, Prince of Moscow, who had extended his state by conquest; succeeded by his son, Juri (–1324).

B **Apr**: 26th, the Florentine factions reconciled on the initiative of Benedict XI.
Jun: 10th, the extreme Blacks raise a fire which destroys the centre of Florence.

C **Jul**: 7th, death of Pope Benedict XI.
Aug: 18th, the French defeat the Flemings, but not decisively, at Mons-en-Pévèle, between Lille and Douai.

E A revolt in Hungary causes Ladislas (Wenceslas) to return to Bohemia. Albert invades Bohemia but retires on failing to take Kutná Hora. Wenceslas II expelled from Poland and Vladislav restored (–1333).
The Genoese seize Chios from the Greeks.
'Osmān takes Nicaea. The Grand Company raises the siege of Philadelphia by the Turks and then plunders Greek territory.
Mongols raiding India defeated.

1303

G **Economics, Science, Technology and Discovery**

Edward I's *Carta Mercatoria* in favour of alien merchants.

Pietro d'Abano, *Conciliator differentiarum philosophorum et praecipue medicinorum* (treatise attempting to reconcile conflicting opinions on scientific—and specially medical subjects); *Lucidator astronomiae* (likewise for astronomy).

Bernard de Gordon, *Lilium medicinae* (medical textbook; first printed 1480).

Chu Shih-chieh, *Ssŭ-yüan yü-chien* (*Precious Mirror of the Four Elements*; mathematical treatise).

†Taddeo Alderotti, a founder of the medical school at Bologna, *De conservanda sanitate* (on hygiene).

H **Religion and Education**

Boniface founds a university in Rome.

K **Literature, Philosophy and Scholarship**

Robert Mannyng, *Handlyng synne* (didactic poem of pastoral theology, with anecdotes).

L **Births and Deaths**

— Bridget of Sweden b. (–1373).

1304

G **Economics, Science, Technology and Discovery**

Hopped beer reported to have been common in the Low Countries for 30–40 years.

H **Religion and Education**

John of Monte Corvino baptises 6,000 converts in China.

J **Art, Architecture and Music**

The Cloth Hall, Ypres (destroyed in World War I).

Choir of Vienna Cathedral begun.

L **Births and Deaths**

Feb. 24th, Ibn Battūtah b. (–1377).

July 20th, Petrarch b. (–1374).

1305

A **Mar:** death of Guy, Count of Flanders; succeeded by his son, Robert, held captive by Philip of France (–1322).

B **Apr:** 4th, Roger de Flor, captain of the Grand Company, murdered in Constantinople; his followers defeat the imperial troops and plunder Thrace.
2nd, death of Joanna, Queen of France and Navarre; succeeded in the second by her son, Louis (X of France).
Jun: in the Treaty of Athis-sur-Orge, Philip restores Flanders to Robert for the payment of an indemnity.
5th, Bertrand de Got elected as Pope Clement V (–1314).
21st, death of Wenceslas II of Bohemia; succeeded by his son, Wenceslas III, who made peace with Albert of Austria.

C **Aug:** 4th, Wenceslas III of Bohemia murdered; end of the Přemyslid dynasty.
23rd, William Wallace executed in London as a traitor against Edward.
Sep: Edward enacts an ordinance for the government of Scotland.

D **Oct:** Albert, King of the Romans, compels the Bohemians to elect his son, Rudolf of Habsburg, as their King (–1307).
Nov: 14th, Clement V crowned as Pope at Lyons.
Dec: 29th, he licenses Edward to renounce his oaths confirming the Charters.

E Death of Andrew III, Grand Duke of Vladimir; succeeded by Michael II, Prince of Tver (–1319).

1306

A **Jan:** Modena and Reggio revolt against Azzo d'Este.
10th, Robert Bruce, Earl of Carrick, kills John Comyn, his rival as a claimant to the Scottish crown.
Feb: 12th, at Edward's instance, Clement suspends Robert Winchelsey, Archbishop of Canterbury, who then goes into exile.
Mar: 25th, Robert Bruce crowned as King of Scotland (–1329).

B **Apr:** 10th, Pistoia surrenders, after 11 months' siege, to Florence and Lucca; they divide its territories.
May: 7th, the Bolognese revolt against the Papacy and expel Cardinal Napoleon Orsini, the rector.
Jun: 26th, English forces defeat Bruce at Methven; his power in Scotland now collapses.

C **Aug:** 11th, Bruce again defeated at Dalry.

D **Nov:** the Knights Hospitallers begin their conquest of Rhodes from the Greeks with the capture of Philermo.

E A Mongol invasion of India defeated on the Indus.

1305

F **Law and Politics**

Edward I's ordinance of trailbaston empowers the king to appoint judicial commissions to try the perpetrators of particular outrages; it indicates the decline of public order.

H **Religion and Education**

Clement V organises a crusade against the heretical movement initiated by Fra Dolcino.

J **Art, Architecture and Music**

*Giovanni Pisano, *Madonna* in Arena Chapel, Padua (sculpture).

K **Literature, Philosophy and Scholarship**

†?Jean de Meun (Jean Clopinel), *Le Roman de la Rose* (continued from the poem by Guillaume de Lorris—1237); *Le Testament maistre Jehan de Meung.*

†Moses de Leon, The *Zohar* (the classic compilation on cabalistic literature, first studied in Jewish circles).

*Melis Stoke, *Rijmkroniek* (history of Holland, in Dutch verse, 694–1305).

1306

F **Law and Politics**

Pierre Dubois, *De recuperatione Terrae Sanctae* (*The Recovery of the Holy Land*; treatise upholding the sovereignty of the King of France against the Pope and Emperor).

†Wagaru, *Manu-Dhammasattham* (Burmese law-code).

G **Economics, Science, Technology and Discovery**

Philip expels the Jews from France.

†Al-Dimyāti, *Fadl al-Khayl* (*The Excellence of the Horse.* The Mamlūk sultans kept studs of race-horses).

H **Religion and Education**

Clement V formally recognises the University of Orleans.

J **Art, Architecture and Music**

James II founds Palma Cathedral, Majorca.

*Giotto, Frescoes in the Arena Chapel, Padua (–1309).

K **Literature, Philosophy and Scholarship**

†Jacopone da Todi, *Laudi spirituali*; *Stabat Mater* (religious verse, hymns and early dramatic poetry).

L **Births and Deaths**

Dec. 25th, Jacopone da Todi d. (*c.* 86).

1307 French prosecution of Knights Templars—Decay of Mongol rule in China

A **Jan**: 20th, Edward holds his last Parliament in Carlisle; it criticises papal exactions.

B **May**: Bruce, returning from Ireland, defeats English forces in Ayrshire.
Frederick of Meissen defeats Albert at Lucka.

C **Jul**: death of Rudolf of Habsburg, King of Bohemia.
7th, death of Edward I, King of England, leading an army to Scotland; succeeded by his son, Edward II (–1327).
Aug: Edward II campaigns in Scotland, briefly; on his withdrawal, Bruce establishes himself.
6th, Edward creates his favourite, Piers Gaveston, Earl of Cornwall.
15th, Henry, Duke of Carinthia, elected as King of Bohemia (–1310). Albert invades Bohemia.

D **Oct**: 6th, Corso Donati killed while evading arrest; an aristocrat and leader of the Blacks, he had planned a coup to reverse the recent reform of the Florentine constitution produced as a result of financial depression and popular unrest. Donati's failure and death closes the period when ancient noble families had been dominant in Florence.
13th, Philip orders the wholesale arrest of the Knights Templars in France and seizure of their property; the judicial investigation of their alleged crimes follows.
Nov: 7th, William Tell is said to have shot Hermann Gessler, the Austrian governor of Tyrol, on this day.
Dec: 25th, Bruce defeats the Earl of Buchan at Staines.

E The Milanese elect Guido della Torre as captain of the people (*i.e.* their despot).
Andronicus recognises the seizure of Anchialus and Mesembria by Theodore Svetoslav, the Bulgarian Tsar.
The Mongols annex Rūm, extinguishing the Seljuq sultanate.
Rāmachandra, the Hindu King of Deogīr, compelled to pay tribute to ʿAlāʾ-ad-Dīn.
Death of Temür, the Great Khan; Mongul rule in China now declines in dissension and civil war (–1333).

G **Economics, Science, Technology and Discovery**

By putting an embargo on trade, German merchants gain privileges for their settlement at Bruges.

Master Jacob of Florence, treatise on mathematics (including al-Khwārizmī's quadratic equations; –850).

*Dietrich of Freiburg, *De iride et radialibus impressionibus* (treatise on optical meteorology, particularly the rainbow).

†Pietro dei Crescenzi of Bologna, *Opus Ruralium* (or *Ruralia Commoda*; an agricultura handbook).

H **Religion and Education**

Clement appoints John of Monte Corvino Archbishop of Peking.

K **Literature, Philosophy and Scholarship**

Li Tse, *An-nam chih-lüeh* (history and description of Annam, from 202 B.C.; with an autobiography to 1293).

*Peter Langtoft, *Chronicle* (of England, from Brutus to 1307, in French verse; –1338).

*Wu-ch'in Yen, *Hsüeh-ku-pien* (treatise on Chinese seals); *Chou ch'in k'o shih shih yin* (on stone inscriptions).

1308

A **Jan**: 25th, Edward II marries Isabella, daughter of Philip of France.
31st, death of Azzo VIII d'Este, lord of Ferrara; he bequeaths the succession to his illegitimate son, Folco.
Feb: 25th, Edward crowned, taking a new form of coronation oath.

B **Apr**: Clement claims Ferrara as a papal fief and disowns Folco d'Este.
May: Philip holds another meeting of the Estates-General to uphold his proceedings against the Templars.
1st, Albert of Habsburg, King of the Romans, murdered by Duke John of Swabia.
18th, the magnates force Edward to banish Piers Gaveston.

C **Jul**: Clement gives way to Philip's demands for the further prosecution of the Templars.
Aug: 15th, the city of Rhodes surrenders to the Hospitallers; it becomes their headquarters.

D **Nov**: 12th, the Teutonic Knights, having been admitted to Danzig (Gdansk) as allies of Vladislav Lokietek, Grand Prince of Poland, seize the city and massacre its inhabitants.
27th, Henry (VII), Count of Luxemburg, elected as King of the Romans (–1313).

E Bruce defeats the Comyns of Buchan, takes Aberdeen, conquers Galloway, and begins his raids on northern England.
Haakon V of Norway makes an (ineffective) ordinance resuming feudal grants and abolishing baronial powers.
The Hungarian nobles acclaim Charles Robert of Anjou as their King (–1342).
The Ilkhan Uljāytū invades Syria and reaches Jerusalem.
Pratāparudradeva II, the Hindu King of Telingāna, forced to pay tribute to 'Alā'-ad-Dīn.

1309

A **Mar**: 14th, Muhammad III of Granada deposed and succeeded by his brother, Nasr (–1314).
27th, Clement declares that Venice is no longer a Christian state because it supports Folco d'Este.

B **May**: 8th, death of Charles II of Naples; succeeded by his son, Robert (–1343).
Jun: 3rd, Henry VII recognises the Swiss Confederation.

C **Jul**: 27th, in a Parliament at Stamford, the magnates accept Edward's recall of Gaveston when he grants their petitions for reform.
Aug: at Tedaldo, papal forces defeat the Venetians in the War of the Ferrarese Succession.

E The Teutonic Knights complete their seizure of East Pomerania; their Grand Master moves his headquarters from Venice to Marienburg.
Guzmán el Bueno takes Gibraltar from the Muslims; Valencia permanently annexed to Aragon.

1308

H **Religion and Education**

Dinis transfers the University of Lisbon to Coimbra.
Perugia University founded.

J **Art, Architecture and Music**

Duccio, *Maestà* for Siena Cathedral (–1311; painting).

K **Literature, Philosophy and Scholarship**

†Duns Scotus, *Quaestiones super IV libros sententiarum* (of Peter the Lombard; –1150), etc.

1309

F **Law and Politics**

An ordinance of Philip IV names his audit office as the *Chambre des Comptes*, which is now becoming a permanent, specialised organ of government.

H **Religion and Education**

Clement V begins his (and the Papacy's) residence at Avignon (–1376).

J **Art, Architecture and Music**

Naves of Auxerre and Nevers Cathedrals begun; the Romanesque nave of Auxerre demolished as it was 'rudely planned'.

K **Literature, Philosophy and Scholarship**

Jean, Sire de Joinville, *Mémoires; ou Histoire de Chronique du très chrétien roi Saint Louis* (eye-witness record, including an account of the private life of Louis IX and his deeds on crusade).

1310–1311 Edward II and the Ordainers—Council of Ten—Muslim subjection of south India

1310

B **May**: 16th, the magnates compel Edward to appoint a commission of reform (the Lords Ordainers).

Jun: 15th, the Papacy and Venice make peace; Clement makes Robert of Naples his vicar in Ferrara.

15th, the Council of Ten instituted at Venice following the failure of the plot of Bajamonte Tiepolo and Mario Querini.

C **Aug**: 30th, Elizabeth, daughter of Wenceslas II of Bohemia, marries John, son of Henry VII, who invests him as King of Bohemia; this follows a rising against Henry of Carinthia. John soon afterwards peacefully recovers Moravia from Duke Frederick of Austria.

E Lyons incorporated into France on its occupation by Philip's forces, who arrests its Archbishop.

The Grand Company ravages Thessaly.

'Alā'-ad-Dīn sends an army to plunder southermost India and compels the Kings of Dvāravatīpura and Madura to pay tribute.

1311

A **Jan**: 6th, Henry crowned as King of Lombardy in Milan.

Feb: 5th, Thomas, Earl of Lancaster, Leicester and Derby, succeeds to the earldoms of Lincoln and Salisbury on the death of his father-in-law, Henry de Lacy.

Mar: 15th, the Grand Company defeats and kills Walter of Brienne, Duke of Athens, on the Cephissus, in Boeotia.

C **Aug**: 13th, death of Pietro Gradenigo, Doge of Venice; succeeded by Marino Giorgio (–1312).

16th, a Parliament meets in which Edward accepts the Ordinances for the reform of his government and banishes Gaveston.

Sep: Henry takes Brescia and punishes it for rebellion.

Edward leads an ineffective campaign in Scotland (–Nov.).

E On leaving north Italy for Rome, Henry appoints Matteo Visconti as imperial vicar of Milan, and Can Grande della Scala as vicar of Verona, thus legitimising their despotisms. Florence appoints Robert of Naples as its lord to defend it against Henry (–1322).

Death of Mangrai, first King of Lan Na, which is now divided (–1325).

1310

G **Economics, Science, Technology and Discovery**

John Maudwith, treatises on trigonometry and astronomy.

Earliest notices of water-powered machinery for silk and iron manufacture in China.

H **Religion and Education**

Marguerite Porrette, a mystic, burnt as a witch in Paris.

†Henry Bate, *Speculum divinorum et quorundam naturalium* (theological encyclopedia with scientific digressions).

J **Art, Architecture and Music**

Mosaics in the monastery of Chora (now the Kahrieh Djami), Constantinople (–1320).

The Doges' Palace, Venice.

**Sumer is icomen in* (English round-song).

K **Literature, Philosophy and Scholarship**

Dante Alighieri, Convivio (*Convito—The Banquet*; prose commentaries on some of the poet's shorter poems, begun 1308).

†*Al-Mawsili, *Tayf al-Khayāl fi Ma'rifat Khayāl al-Zill* (*Phantoms of the Imagination on the Knowledge of the Shadow-Play*; unique example of Arabic dramatic poetry).

1311

F **Law and Politics**

The Ordinances establish the Privy Seal Office by ordering the Keeper's detachment from Edward II's Household.

G **Economics, Science, Technology and Discovery**

Philip expels the Lombards from France, seizing their property.

Pietro Vesconte, the earliest dated *portolano* (navigational map, of the Mediterranean and Black Sea); he also made atlases (–1327).

†Arnold of Villanova, physician and writer on alchemy and witchcraft, *Libellus de improbatione maleficiorum*; *Remedia contra maleficia*; *Opera medica* (printed 1504); *Tractatus de vinis* (treatise on wines).

†Al-Shirāzi, *Nihāyat al-idrak fī dirāyat al-aflak* (*Highest Understanding of the Knowledge of Spheres*).

H **Religion and Education**

Oct. 16th, assembly of the General Council of Vienne: at the instance of Raymond Lull, it decrees the creation of chairs in Arabic and Tartar at Paris, Louvain and Salamanca; it also suppresses the Béguins and Beghards.

J **Art, Architecture and Music**

ʻA'lā'i-Darwāza gateway to the Quwwat al-Islām, Old Delhi.

Frauenlob (Henry of Miessen) founds the Mastersingers at Mainz (–1876).

K **Literature, Philosophy and Scholarship**

†Giordano de Rivalto, *Sermons* (noted for the purity and grace of the prose style, thought to be the best of the period in Italian literature).

†Ibn-Manzūr, *Lisān al-ʻArab* (Arabic dictionary).

1312
B **Apr**: Clement declares the suppression of the Order of Knights Templars.
Jun: death of Marino Giorgio, Doge of Venice; succeeded by Giovanni Soranzo (–1327).
19th, Gaveston, who had returned to England, captured and killed by the Earls of Lancaster and Warwick; his death causes a split among Edward's baronial opponents.
29th, Henry VII crowned as Holy Roman Emperor in Rome, in the Lateran because St. Peter's is held by hostile Romans supported by Robert of Naples.

C **Sep**: 17th, death of Ferdinand IV of Castile and Leon; succeeded by his infant son, Alfonso XI (–1349), and civil war.

D **Oct**: 31st, Henry abandons his attempt to take Florence by storm.
Dec: 22nd, Edward makes peace with the magnates.

E Robert of Flanders concedes the castellanies of Lille, Douai and Béthune to Philip in lieu of the indemnity promised in 1305.
Death of Malatesta, the first lord of Rimini.
The Grand Company established in the Duchy of Athens as governors for the Emperor Frederick II *qua* King of Sicily.
Death of Tokhta, Khan of 'the Golden Horde'; succeeded by Uzbeg (–1341), a Muslim who completed the conversion of the horde to Islam.
The Shān leader, Thihathura, establishes his capital at Pinya, in north Burma.

1313
A **Jan**: 13th, Scots expel the English garrison from Perth.

B **Apr**: 26th, Henry declares Robert guilty of treason against the Empire.
Jun: 13th, under pressure from Philip, Clement declares Naples to be under papal protection.

C **Aug**: 24th, death of Henry VII, while leading an army against Naples.

D **Nov**: Lewis of Wittelsbach, Duke of Upper Bavaria, defeats an invasion by Frederick the Handsome, Duke of Austria, at Gammelsdorf.

E Tran Anh-tong, Emperor of Dai Viet, occupies Champa and establishes Che Nang, of the Cham royal dynasty, as puppet ruler (–1318).
*The Scots recover the Isle of Man.

1312

F **Law and Politics**

John II of Brabant saves himself from bankruptcy by conceding to his towns (Brussels, etc.) for their aid, the establishment of an elected council to preserve communal privileges.

*Dante Alighieri, *De Monarchia* (treatise in Latin on the poet's theories about divine government of the world).

H **Religion and Education**

May 6th, close of the General Council of Vienne.

J **Art, Architecture and Music**

Choir of Gerona Cathedral planned.

Church of the Holy Apostles (with mosaics), Salonika.

Hudavend Hatun mausoleum, Nigde.

K **Literature, Philosophy and Scholarship**

*†Cecco Angiolieri, *Il Canzioniere* (songs and sonnets).

*Walter of Guisborough (*alias* Hemingburgh), *Cronica* (English history, 1066–1312; –1347).

L **Births and Deaths**

Nov. 13th, Edward III b. (–1377).

— K'o Chiu-ssu b. (–1365).

1313

G **Economics, Science, Technology and Discovery**

†Alessandro della Spina, associated, with Salvino degl'Armati, with the invention of spectacles.

*Berengar of Valencia, translations of Arabic medical works.

Berthold Schwarz invents gunpowder.

H **Religion and Education**

Clement V publishes his additions to the *corpus* of canon law, the *Clementinae*.

K **Literature, Philosophy and Scholarship**

Abū Haiyān, *Kitāb al-idrāk lilisān al-Atrāk* (earliest extant treatise on Turkish grammar).

L **Births and Deaths**

Apr. —, John Balliol, former King of Scotland, d. (*c.* 63).

— Giovanni Boccaccio b. (–1375).

— Cola di Rienzo b. (–1354).

— Ibn-al-Khatīb b. (–1374).

1314

A **Feb**: 19th, Nasr, King of Granada, abdicates after a rebellion; succeeded by his nephew, Ismā'īl I (–1325).

Mar: 18th, Jacques de Molay, former Grand Master of the Templars, burnt in Paris.

B **Apr**: 20th, death of Pope Clement V.

Jun: 14th, Uguccione della Faggiuola, despot of Pisa, wins control of Lucca through a rising organised by Castruccio Castracani.

23rd, Bruce repulses English forces attempting to relieve Stirling castle.

24th, he defeats Edward at Bannockburn and so completes his expulsion of the English from Scotland.

C **Sep**: Philip makes peace with Flanders after a brief campaign.

D **Oct**: 19th, Frederick of Austria elected as King of the Romans (–1325).

20th, Lewis of Bavaria also elected (–1347); civil war ensues.

Nov: 28th, Philip forbids further collection of the tax voted for the Flemish campaign; it is causing revolts by provincial leagues of lesser nobles and towns.

30th, death of Philip IV of France; succeeded by his son, Louis X (–1316).

E The Egyptians establish a Muslim as King of Dongola (north Sudan), ending a Monophysite Christian monarchy dating from 543; from this time Arabs fleeing Mamlūk rule begin to settle in the Sudan.

1315

A **Jan**: 20th, Edward holds a Parliament when the barons make him purge his council.

Mar: 17th, Lewis recognises the Swiss federation by summoning it to a diet.

B **Spring**: Louis grants charters to various provincial leagues in order to appease their grievances.

Apr: 30th, Enguerrand de Marigny, Philip IV's finance minister, hanged.

May: 25th, Edward, brother of Robert of Scotland, invades Ireland.

C **Aug**: Louis fails in a campaign to conquer Flanders.

29th, Uguccione of Pisa routes the forces of Florence and Naples at Montecatini.

Sep: 10th, Edward Bruce defeats English forces near Connor.

D **Oct**: Matteo Visconti of Milan takes Pavia.

Nov: 15th, the Swiss defeat Duke Leopold of Austria at Morgarten.

E Death of Otto IV, Count of Burgundy (Franche Comté); succeeded by his daughter, Joanna, the wife of Philip (V of France).

The Bohemian nobles force King John to expel his German advisers and employ Bohemian lords.

Frederick of Trinacria assumes the title of King of Sicily, thus provoking a new war with Naples.

Gedymin succeed as Grand Prince of Lithuania (–1341) and takes Brest Litewski.

1314

F **Law and Politics**

Philip IV holds the fourth Estates-General in Paris and, for the first time, seeks its consent to taxation.

Candeśvara, *Nitiratnākara* (*Jewel-mine of Politics*; Hindu treatise on the science of government).

G **Economics, Science, Technology and Discovery**

Hereford *Mappa Mundi.*

Wang Chên, *Nung shu* (treatise on agriculture); this book is the first printed with wooden movable (revolving) type (–1045).

H **Religion and Education**

Foundation of the Colleges of Navarre and Montaigu, Paris, and Exeter College, Oxford (by Walter Stapeldon).

J **Art, Architecture and Music**

Byzantine frescoes in Studenitza church, Serbia.

K **Literature, Philosophy and Scholarship**

*Dante Alighieri, *Divina Commedia* begun: the *Inferno* in 34 cantos, *Purgatorio* in 33 cantos and *Paradiso* in 33 cantos (the greatest poetic work of the Middle Ages, and regarded as the maker of the Italian language; –1472).

Rashīd al-Dīn, *Jāmiʿal-tawārīkh* (*Collection of Histories*; universal history based on Arabic, Persian, Mongol and Chinese source-material. The dated manuscript is the first of the great Persian illustrated books).

Dalimil completes *Chronicle of Bohemia* (in Bohemian, rhymed).

*Hayton, an Armenian, *Fleur des histores de la terre d'Orient* (history and geography of Asia).

1315

F **Law and Politics**

The nobility of Esthonia forms the Landtag of Pernau (a constitutional assembly).

Restoration of examinations for recruitment to the Chinese civil service.

G **Economics, Science, Technology and Discovery**

The harvest in England and elsewhere in western Europe ruined by rain (–1316).

*John of Gaddesden, *Rosa anglica* (or *Rosa Medicinae*; medical treatise, including description of a 'pelican' for extracting teeth; first printed 1492).

J **Art, Architecture and Music**

Church of St. Mary the Virgin Pammakaristos (now the Fetiyeh Cami), with mosaics, Constantinople.

Simone Martini, *Maestà* (fresco) in Siena Town Hall.

L **Births and Deaths**

Sept. 20th, Raymond Lull d. (80).

1316

A **Jan:** 2nd, death of ʿAlā'-ad-Dīn, Sultan of Delhi; succeeded by his son, Shihan ad-Dīn ʿUmar.
Feb: Edward confirms the Ordinances and appoints Lancaster his chief councillor.

B **Apr:** 1st, Qutb-ad-Dīn Mubārak succeeds as Sultan of Delhi (–1320).
May: 2nd, Edward Bruce crowned as King of Ireland.
Jun: 5th, death of Louis X of France; with his widow pregnant, his brother, Philip, Count of Poitiers, becomes regent.

C **Aug:** 7th, Jacques Duèse elected as Pope John XXII (–1334).
10th, Phelim O'Connor, King of Connaught, defeated and killed by English forces at Athenry, in Galway.

D **Nov:** 14th, birth of John I, King of France, the posthumous son of Louis X.
19th, death of John I.

E Ghiberto da Correggio expelled from Parma and a republic established.
The Valencian Order of Knights of Montesa formerly constituted.
Death of Uljāytū, Sultan of Persia; succeeded by his nephew, Abū Saʿīd (–1335).

1317

A **Jan:** 9th, Philip (V) of Poitiers crowned as King of France (–1322).
Feb: Robert Bruce joins Edward to campaign in Ireland (–May).
Mar: 31st, John XXII claims imperial rights in Italy for the Papacy.

C **Aug:** 15th, the citizens of Ferrara, having massacred the Neapolitan garrison, elect Rinaldo, Obizzo and Nicolò d'Este as their rulers.

D **Dec:** Eric, Duke of Södermanland, leader of the baronial opposition in Sweden, captured by King Birger, his brother, and presumably murdered; a general rebellion follows.

E Uguccione expelled from Pisa and Lucca.
Robert of Naples promotes a general peace in Tuscany.
Mubārak of Delhi annexes the Hindu Kingdom of Deogīr.

1316

F **Law and Politics**
By the Peace of Fexhe, the Prince-Bishop of Liège concedes control of legislation to his subjects.

G **Economics, Science, Technology and Discovery**
Famine in western Europe causes heavy mortality, presumably arresting population growth.
Mondino de'Luzzi, *Anatomia*. He introduced the practice of dissection at Bologna University.

K **Literature, Philosophy and Scholarship**
*Abū-l-Barakāt, *Al-sullam al-Kabīr* (*Scala Magna*; Coptic-Arabic vocabulary).

L **Births and Deaths**
May 16th, Charles IV b. (–1378).
Dec. 22nd, Aegidius Colonna (Giles of Rome), Archbishop of Bourges, d. (69).

1317

H **Religion and Education**
John XXII publishes the *Extravagantes* (addition to the *corpus* of canon law).

J **Art, Architecture and Music**
Byzantine frescoes in Nagoričino church, Serbia.
Simone Martini, *St. Louis of Toulouse* painted for Robert of Naples.

1318

A **Feb**: peace made between the victorious Can Grande of Verona and the republic of Padua.
Mar: 27th, Philip makes peace with the Burgundians; end of the Movement of the Leagues.

B **Apr**: 8th, Bruce takes Berwick upon Tweed.
May: he raids as far as Ripon, exacting tribute.

C **Jul**: Padua accepts Giacomo da Carrara as its lord.
Robert of Naples raises the siege of Genoa by Frederick of Sicily.
19th, Duke Leopold of Austria makes a truce with the Swiss Forest Cantons.
Aug: 9th, in the Treaty of Leake, Edward confirms the Ordinances; at the instance of Aymer de Valence, Earl of Pembroke, and other magnates, Thomas of Lancaster loses his position of influence.

D **Oct**: 14th, Edward Bruce, King of Ireland, defeated and killed by English forces at Faughard, near Dundalk.

E George V becomes sole King of Georgia (–1346).
Tran Minh-tong, Emperor of Dai Viet, deposes Che Nang of Champa and appoints Che A-nan as military governor (–1326).

1319

A **Jan**: 19th, Robert of Naples accepts the lordship of Brescia.

B **May**: 8th, death of Haakon V of Norway; succeeded by his grandson, Magnus VIII (–1343), son of Eric of Södermanland.
Jun: 26th, Ismā'īl of Granada defeats a Castilian invasion.

C **Jul**: 23rd, John appoints Cardinal Bertrand du Poujet as legate in Italy.
Aug: Edward lays siege to Berwick upon Tweed.
Sep: Magnus of Norway elected King of Sweden (–1363), in place of Birger, who had fled to Denmark.
20th, a Scottish force led by Sir James Douglas defeats the forces raised by Archbishop Melton of York at Myton, in Swaledale; Edward then abandons the siege of Berwick.

D **Nov**: 1st, death of Uguccione while serving Can Grande at the siege of Padua; Frederick of Austria, King of the Romans, raises the siege.
13th, death of Eric VI Menved, King of Denmark, without issue.

E Dinis founds the Portuguese Order of Knights of Christ.
Michael, Grand Duke of Vladimir, executed for opposing his deposition by Uzbeg and the appointment of Juri of Moscow, who now succeeds as Grand Duke (–1322).

1318

G **Economics, Science, Technology and Discovery**

Mar. 13th, Jean de Murs determines the epoch of the spring equinox.

†Rashīd, *Jami 'al-tasanīf al-Rashīdī* (encyclopedia of Chinese medicine).

H **Religion and Education**

John XXII creates ten suffragans for the Archbishop of Sultānīyah (Persia); he delimits the Asian mission fields, assigning Greater Armenia, Persia and India to the Dominicans and northern Asia, including China, to the Franciscans.

Four Spiritual Franciscans burnt in the persecution of this branch of the Order directed by John XXII.

A papal bull appears to indicate that Cambridge University is a new foundation.

J **Art, Architecture and Music**

Church of St. Ouen, Rouen, planned.

Mosque of al-Nasir, Cairo (–1335).

L **Births and Deaths**

July 18th, Rashīd al-Dīn d. (71).

— Giovanni Dondi dall' Orologio b. (–*c.* 1385).

(–1319) Duccio di Buoninsegna d. (*c.* 63).

1319

G **Economics, Science, Technology and Discovery**

The death of Eric of Denmark ends his attempts to suppress the trading operations of the Hanse. It forms a settlement at Bergen and expels the English and Scots, so gaining a monopoly of trade with Norway.

Cannon possibly used at the English siege of Berwick.

J **Art, Architecture and Music**

The chapter house of Wells Cathedral completed (it introduces the late Gothic characteristic of using ribs solely for the decoration of the vault).

Ambrogio Lorenzetti, *Madonna* (painting).

L **Births and Deaths**

Apr. 26th, John II b. (–1364).

— Jean, Sire de Joinville, d. (95).

1320

A **Jan**: 20th, Vladislav Lokietek crowned as King of Poland.
25th, Christopher II succeeds his brother, Eric VI, as King of Denmark (–1326, 1330), on promising to accept baronial control.

B **Apr**: 14th, Mubārak of Delhi murdered by his favourite, Khusraw Khan, who assumes the throne.
26th, sealing of the Declaration of Arbroath, wherein the earls and barons of Scotland announce to the Pope their rejection of English rule and their loyalty to Robert I.
May: 5th, by the Treaty of Paris, Philip makes peace with Robert of Flanders.

C **Sep**: 5th, Khusraw killed after his defeat by Ghāzi Malik, who assumes the throne of Delhi as Ghiyāth-ad-Dīn Tughluq (–1325).

D **Oct**: 26th, Can Grande makes peace with Padua.

E Castruccio Castracani elected as captain-general of Lucca, for life.
John of Bohemia abandons the government of the country to Henry of Lipa and other nobles so that he can pursue a career of knight-errantry.
Gedymin of Lithuania defeats the princes of Kiev on the Irpen.

1321

B **Spring**: a league of Marcher lords seizes the Welsh estates of Hugh Despenser, the elder, in retaliation for his attempts at aggrandisement through Edward's favour.
Apr: Milan takes Vercelli.
Jun: 28th, Thomas of Lancaster holds a northern 'parliament' at Sherburn-in-Elmet.

C **Aug**: 19th, Edward compelled in Parliament to banish Hugh Despenser and his son, Hugh.

D **Oct**: 31st, Edward takes Leeds Castle, Kent, to punish Lord Badlesmere.

E Stephen Uroš II of Serbia succeeded by his illegitimate son, Stephen Uroš III (Dečanski; –1336).
Andronicus opens his rebellion against his grandfather, Andronicus II (–1325).

1320

F **Law and Politics**

An ordinance of Philip V reorganises the *Chambre des Comptes*.

**Modus tenendi parliamentum* (propaganda treatise by a political partisan on how the English parliament *should* function).

G **Economics, Science, Technology and Discovery**

*Henry de Mondeville, *Cyrurgia* (textbook on surgery, the first by a Frenchman).

†*Al-Fārisī, *Tanqīh al-Manāzur* (*Correction of the Optics*; including theory on the rainbow).

J **Art, Architecture and Music**

Bergen Cathedral completed.

Tomb of Shāh Rukn-i Alam, Mūltan (–1324).

*Byzantine frescoes in church of St. Demetrius, Mistra.

*Church of the Holy Cross, Schwäbisch Gmünd, begun (architect: Heinrich Parler. It initiates German 'late Gothic').

Simone Martini, Polyptych, Pisa (painting).

Pietro Lorenzetti, Polyptych, Arezzo (painting).

K **Literature, Philosophy and Scholarship**

**Cursor Mundi* (long religious poem in the Northern dialect of the second period of Middle English literature; written in couplets; 'perhaps as early as 1320'—*Saintsbury*).

**Guy of Warwick* (popular narrative poem).

1321

G **Economics, Science, Technology and Discovery**

Marino Sanuto, *Opus Terrae Sanctae*, with world map.

Levi ben Gerson, *Sefer ma'aseh hosheb* (*Work of the Computer*; Hebrew treatise on algebra and arithmetic).

Abū-l-Fidā', *Taqwīm al-Buldān* (*Table of Countries*; geography of Asia, Africa and Spain).

†*Ibn-al-Bannā, *Talkhīs fī a'māl al-hisāb* (*Summary of the operations of calculation*); *Kitāb al-manākh* (a calendar; hence *almanac*).

J **Art, Architecture and Music**

The Lady Chapel, Ely Cathedral, begun.

Foundation of Corporation of Minstrels in France.

K **Literature, Philosophy and Scholarship**

†Dante Alighieri, *De Vulgari Eloquentia*.

L **Births and Deaths**

Sept. 14th, Dante Alighieri d. (56).

1322–1323 Battles of Boroughbridge and Mühldorf—Papal siege of Milan

1322

A **Jan**: 2nd or 3rd, death of Philip V of France; succeeded by his brother, Charles IV (–1328).
5th, Milan takes Cremona.
Feb: 11th, Edward recalls the Despensers from exile.
Mar: 16th, he defeats Thomas of Lancaster at Boroughbridge.
22nd, Lancaster executed for treason.

B **May**: 2nd, Edward holds a Parliament at York when the Ordinances are repealed.
Jun: 24th, death of Matteo Visconti; his son, Galeazzo, accepted as ruler of Milan (–1328).

C **Aug**: an ineffective campaign by Edward in Scotland is followed by further Scottish raids into Yorkshire.
Sep: death of Robert of Béthune, Count of Flanders; succeeded by Louis of Nevers (–1323).
28th, Lewis the Bavarian, aided by John of Bohemia, defeats and captures Frederick of Austria on the Inn, at Mühldorf.

D **Oct**: 14th, Bruce defeats the English at Byland.

E Florence does not renew Robert of Naples' office as protector when his term expires.
Uzbeg deposes Juri and appoints Dmitri of Tver as Grand Duke of Vladimir (–1325).

1323

A **Feb**: Bertrand du Poujet opens his campaign against the Lombard 'Ghibellines' with the capture of Tortona and Monza.
Mar: 3rd, Andrew Hartley, Earl of Carlisle, executed as a traitor for making a treaty with Robert Bruce.

B **Jun**: a revolt in Bruges against Louis of Flanders leads to his capture and deposition in favour of his uncle, Robert of Cassel (–1328).
11th, du Poujet begins the siege of Milan.

C **Jul**: 28th, Milan reinforced by troops sent by Lewis and the siege abandoned.

D **Oct**: 8th, in consequence of Lewis claiming imperial authority in north Italy, John XXII asserts his right to confirm imperial elections and requires Lewis to surrender the Kingship of the Romans.

E Edward II makes a truce with Bruce.
James of Aragon seizes Sardinia from Pisa.
Michael Šišman of Vidin founds the last Bulgarian dynasty (–1330).
Tughluq of Delhi annexes the Hindu kingdom of Telingāna; its capital, Warangal, is renamed Sultānpur. A Mongol invasion of India repulsed.

1322

F **Law and Politics**

**The Assizes of Romania* (feudal customs of the Latin principalities in Greece) are reduced to writing.

J **Art, Architecture and Music**

Choir of Cologne Cathedral completed.

The central tower of Ely Cathedral collapses; replaced with a wooden lantern.

†Chao Mêng-fu, Chinese painter.

1323

F **Law and Politics**

The Cowick Ordinances and the Westminster Ordinances of 1324 and 1326 order the reorganisation of the Exchequer records, in the reforms of Walter Stapeldon, Bishop of Exeter, the Treasurer.

G **Economics, Science, Technology and Discovery**

Wên-jên Kuei, *Wên-jên Shih tou-chên lun* (treatise on smallpox).

Notice of water-driven bellows for an iron-forge at Briey, France.

H **Religion and Education**

John XXII condemns the doctrine of apostolic poverty in his bull *Cum inter nonnullos*, causing a revolt by the Spiritual Franciscans.

Bernard Gui, *Practica officii inquisitionis heretice pravitatis* (manual for officers of the Inquisition; provides definitions of witchcraft).

J **Art, Architecture and Music**

Foundation of academy for troubadours at Toulouse, with prizes for music competitions (now called Académie des Jeux Floraux).

K **Literature, Philosophy and Scholarship**

*Levi ben Gerson, commentaries on Averroes (–1198).

L **Births and Deaths**

— William of Wykeham b. (–1404).

1324

A **Mar**: 23rd, John excommunicates Lewis for his refusal to surrender the Kingship of the Romans.

B **May**: 22nd, in his manifesto, the Appeal of Sachsenhausen, Lewis denounces John and denies his claim to temporal authority in Germany.
Jun: 24th, he invests his son, Lewis, with Brandenburg (–1351).

C **Aug**: Charles invades Gascony; the Parlement of Paris had declared the province confiscated because Edward's lieutenant had sacked the French bastide of Saint-Sardos.

D **Dec**: 10th, Galeazzo Visconti of Milan takes Monza, previously du Poujet's headquarters.

E Charles I of Hungary completes his defeat of the rebellious nobles; he no longer holds parliaments.
Dmitri II of Vladimir kills Juri of Moscow.
Andrew and Leo, princes of Ruthenia, killed in a battle with Mongols.

1325

A **Jan**: 7th, death of Dinis of Portugal; succeeded by his son, Afonso IV (–1357).
Feb (*or* **Mar**): Tughluq of Delhi murdered and succeeded by his son, Muhammad II (–1351).
2nd, Andronicus III crowned as co-Emperor with Andronicus II to end the civil war in the Greek Empire (–1341).
Mar: Edward sends his wife, Isabella, to negotiate for peace with Charles IV; when in France, she becomes the mistress of Roger Mortimer, the exiled lord of Wigmore.
13th, Lewis makes a treaty releasing Frederick who renounces his claim to be King of the Romans.

C **Jul**: 8th, Ismāʿil I of Granada murdered: succeeded by his son, Muhammad IV (–1333).
Sep: 23rd, Castruccio Castracani of Lucca defeats Robert of Naples, Florence and other 'Guelfs' at Altopascio.

D **Nov**: 25th, the Ghibellines defeat the Bolognese at Zapolino.
Dec: 2nd, Florence creates Charles, Duke of Calabria, the son of Robert of Naples, as its lord.

E The Cortes of Castile declare that Alfonso XI is of age; the anarchy prevailing since 1312 soon ends.
Vladislav founds the Polish Order of the White Eagle.
Dmitri executed by Uzbeg for the murder of Juri of Moscow; Alexander of Tver appointed Grand Duke of Vladimir (–1328).
Sen Phu reunites the Siamese Kingdom of Lan Na.
In China, there is the first popular rising against the Mongol dynasty.
The Aztecs finally settle on an island in Lake Texcoco; this is the origin of Tenochtitlán (Mexico City).

1324

F **Law and Politics**

Marsilio of Padua, *Defensor Pacis* (treatise on government famous for its subordination of the Church to princely authority).

G **Economics, Science, Technology and Discovery**

Earliest European notice of cannon being made, of forged iron, at Metz.

H **Religion and Education**

John XXII reorganises the missionary *Societas Peregrinantium propter Christum* (–1253).

Earliest extant constitution of the Carmelite Friars.

Foundation of Oriel College, Oxford.

K **Literature, Philosophy and Scholarship**

William of Ockham, a Franciscan teaching at Oxford, called to the papal court at Avignon to answer charges of heresy, and imprisoned.

†Dino Compagni, *Cronica delle cose occorenti ne' tempi suoi* (history of Florence, 1280–1312).

L **Births and Deaths**

— Marco Polo d. (70).

1325

F **Law and Politics**

Muhammad of Delhi initiates the compilation of registers of the revenues and expenditure of his provincial governors.

G **Economics, Science, Technology and Discovery**

Ibn-Battūtah begins his travels (–1354).

J **Art, Architecture and Music**

Tomb of Nizām al-Dīn Auliyā (the Muslim saint), Delhi.

*Giotto, decoration of four chapels in Sta. Croce, Florence.

K **Literature, Philosophy and Scholarship**

†Dinis, King of Portugal, Lyrics and other poems.

†Amīr Khusraw of Delhi, Indian poet.

1326

B **Apr**: 6th, Ghāzi Orkhān, succeeding his father 'Osmān I as ruler of the Ottoman Turks (–1359), takes Brusa (Bursa) and makes it his capital.

Jun: 5th, du Poujet takes Modena in his 'crusade' against Milan.

C **Sep**: 24th, Isabella and Mortimer land at Orwell, Essex, and soon attract a considerable following.

30th, du Poujet takes Parma.

D **Oct**: 15th, the mob rises in London and kills Bishop Stapeldon of Essex, the Treasurer; Edward flees to Gloucester.

26th, Isabella enters Bristol; here Hugh Despenser, senior, taken and executed. Edward's son, Edward (III) proclaimed keeper of the realm in his father's 'absence'.

Nov: 16th, Edward II captured at Neath Abbey; also Hugh Despenser, junior, who is executed.

E Christopher of Denmark expelled (–1330).

At Pope John's instigation, Vladislav of Poland ravages the Mark of Brandenburg.

John of Gravina, Prince of Achaea, fails in an attempt to expel Greeks who had established themselves in the Morea.

Che A-nan, with Mongol support, defeats the Vietnamese and rules Champa independently (–1361).

1327

A **Jan**: 7th, a Parliament demands that Edward II be deposed.

20th, Edward abdicates in favour of Edward III (–1377).

Feb: 8th, du Poujet takes Bologna.

Mar: 31st, Charles and Edward end 'the War of Saint-Sardos' with the Treaty of Paris; Gascony restored to Edward.

B **May**: Lewis crowned as King of Lombardy in Milan.

C **Sep**: 21st, Edward II murdered.

D **Oct**: 31st, death of James II the Just, King of Aragon; succeeded by his son, Alfonso IV (–1336).

Dec: death of Giovanni Soranzo, Doge of Venice.

E After suppressing a Hindu revolt in the Deccan, Muhammad transfers his capital from Delhi to Deogīr (renamed Daulatābād).

1326

F **Law and Politics**

Representatives of Scottish burghs are first known to have attended a parliament held by Bruce at Cambuskenneth.

G **Economics, Science, Technology and Discovery**

Cannon used by the Florentines.

Richard Wallingford, *Canones de instrumento* (description of the astronomical clock he had built at St. Albans).

H **Religion and Education**

†St. Peter, the Russian Metropolitan (1308–26), makes his residence in Moscow.

Foundation of Clare Hall, Cambridge.

K **Literature, Philosophy and Scholarship**

*Peter of Duisburg, *Chronica* (history of the Teutonic Knights and Prussia, *c.* 1291–1326).

1327

G **Economics, Science, Technology and Discovery**

An illustration of cannon first appears in a manuscript of Walter of Milemete. Cannon now in England.

H **Religion and Education**

John XXII condemns Marsilio's *Defensor Pacis.*

Francesco degli Stabili, poet and astrologer, burnt by the Inquisition in Florence.

†Master Eckehart, German mystic.

J **Art, Architecture and Music**

Jean Pucelle, illuminated decoration of a Bible (in the Bibliothèque Nationale).

K **Literature, Philosophy and Scholarship**

*Petrarch, *Canzoniere* (inspired by his seeing Laura, 5–12 April 1327).

†Francesco degli Stabili (Cecco d'Ascoli), *Acerba* (poems of moral philosophy).

*The *Chester Cycle* (of Miracle Plays).

1328 End of Capetian dynasty—Treaty of Edinburgh

A **Jan**: 7th, Lewis enters Rome; he is crowned as Emperor by the Four Syndics of the Roman People. John declares a crusade against him.

8th, Francesco Dandolo elected as Doge of Venice (–1339).

24th, Edward marries Philippa, daughter of William I, Count of Hainault and Holland; he is forming an anti-French coalition in the Low Countries.

Feb: 1st, death of Charles IV, the last Capetian King of France; Philip of Valois becomes regent while Charles' widow is pregnant.

Mar: 17th, in the Treaty of Edinburgh, Edward makes peace with Scotland, recognising Bruce as King.

B **Apr**: 1st, Philip (VI) of Valois elected as King of France following the birth of a daughter to Charles' widow (–1350).

May: 4th, the Treaty of Edinburgh ratified by Edward in the Treaty of Northampton.

22nd, Lewis responds to John's declaration of a 'crusade' against him by having John declared deposed and having Peter of Corvara elected as 'Pope Nicholas V' (–1330).

24th, Andronicus II forced to abdicate, leaving Andronicus III the sole Greek Emperor.

C **Aug**: death of Galeazzo Visconti; his son, Azzo, succeeds as ruler of Milan (–1339).

4th, Lewis and his pope leave Rome.

23rd, Philip defeats the Flemings at Cassel; Louis of Nevers restored as Count.

Sep: 3rd, death of Castruccio Castracani of Lucca.

D **Nov**: 11th, death of Charles of Calabria, lord of Florence.

E Alexander II, Grand Duke of Vladimir, deposed on Uzbeg's orders by Ivan, son of Daniel, Prince of Moscow; Alexander of Suzdal appointed Grand Duke (–1332).

*The Karaman Turks take Konya, the former capital of Rūm, and extend their control here as the Ilkhanate of Persia disintegrates.

F **Law and Politics**

Ruprecht von Freising, *Rechtsbuch* (Codification of Bavarian laws).

G **Economics, Science, Technology and Discovery**

The manufacture of mirrors and silk now begun at Venice.

*John of Milan, *Flos Medicinae* (herbal).

H **Religion and Education**

†Agostino Trionfo (Augustinus Triumphus), *Summa de potestate ecclesiastica* (defence of papal supremacy).

Heinrich Suso, *Büchlein der Wahrheit* (on mysticism).

J **Art, Architecture and Music**

Simone Martini, Fresco in Siena Town Hall (portrait of Guidoriccio da Fogliano).

K **Literature, Philosophy and Scholarship**

†Nicholas Trivet, *Annales sex regum Angliae* (1136–1307).

William of Ockham escapes from Avignon and joins Lewis.

L **Births and Deaths**

Apr. 2nd, Agostino Trionfo d. (85).

Sept. 10th, Marsilio of Padua d.

— John of Jandun d.

*John of Monte Corvino, Archbishop of Peking, d.

1329

B **Jun**: 6th, Edward performs homage to Philip for Gascony at Amiens.
7th, death of Robert I Bruce, King of Scotland; succeeded by his son, David II (–1371).

C **Jul**: 22nd, death of Can Grande della Scala of Verona; succeeded by Mastino della Scala.

D **Dec**: Lewis returns to Germany; so ends the last attempt to restore imperial authority in Italy.
24th, Brescia accepts John of Bohemia as its lord; he raises Mastino's siege.

E Joanna II crowned as Queen of Navarre (–1349); this kingdom is thus separated from France. (She was the daughter of Joanna I and Louis X of France, and the wife of Philip of Évreux.)
John of Bohemia gains possession of Görlitz.
Andronicus recovers Chios from the Genoese, with Turkish assistance. He is defeated by Orkhān at Pelekanon.
Muhammad punishes the inhabitants of Delhi by ordering their removal to Daulatābād.

1330

A **Jan**: 13th, death of Frederick the Handsome, Duke of Austria.
Mar: 19th, Edmund, Earl of Kent, son of Edward I, executed as a traitor for opposing Isabella and Roger Mortimer, Earl of March.

B **Jun**: 14th, Pope John declares a crusade against the Grand Company in favour of Walter II, son of Walter de Brienne, Duke of Athens.
28th, Stephen Uroš III, King of Serbia, defeats and kills Michael Šišman, the Bulgarian Tsar, near Velbužd, and so establishes Serbian dominance in Macedonia; Michael succeeded by John Alexander (1331–61).

C **Jul**: 25th, the anti-pope, Nicholas V, resigns.
Aug: 4th, by the Treaty of Hagenau, the Habsburgs recognise Lewis as King.

D **Oct**: 19th, Edward arrests Mortimer and declares his intention to rule.
Nov: 29th, Mortimer, condemned as a traitor in Parliament, is executed.

E Joanna, widow of Philip V and Countess of Burgundy, marries Eudes IV, Duke of Burgundy.
Christopher returns to Denmark (–1331).
The Teutonic Knights occupy Riga.

1329

G **Economics, Science, Technology and Discovery**

Muhammad of Delhi unsuccessfully tries to introduce a fiduciary currency, with brass tokens decreed to have the value of silver.

Levi ben Gerson, *Sefer tekunah* (part of the *Milhamot—see* K; critical treatise on astronomy).

*Lu Yu, *Mo shih* (history of manufacture of ink in China).

J **Art, Architecture and Music**

Pietro Lorenzetti, The *Carmine Altar* (painting).

*T'ung Hou, *Hua chien* (history of Chinese painting from third century).

K **Literature, Philosophy and Scholarship**

†Albertino Mussato, 'the initiator of humanism', collected mss. of classical authors; *Historia Augusta* and *De Gestis Italicorum* (Italian history, 1310–21); *Eccerinis* (tragedy in Latin verse about Ezzelin da Romano, 1194–1259).

Levi ben Gerson, *Milhamot Adonai* (*The Wars of the Lord*; discussion of Aristotelian philosophy in relation to the Jewish faith).

1330

G **Economics, Science, Technology and Discovery**

*Odoric of Pordenone, *Description of the East* (records his travels in Persia, India, Sumatra, Java, Borneo, China, etc., 1316–30).

*Jordanus, *The Wonders of the East* (describing his travels; he went to India in 1330).

Pietro Buono, *Pretiosa margarita novella* (*The Precious Pearl*; treatise in defence of alchemy).

J **Art, Architecture and Music**

Andrea Pisano, southern (bronze) doors of the Baptistery, Florence (–1336).

*Salisbury Cathedral spire.

*Pietro Lorenzetti, Frescoes in S. Francesco, Assisi.

*Simone Martini, *Christ bearing the Cross* (painting).

K **Literature, Philosophy and Scholarship**

*Ramón Muntaner, *Chronica, o descripció dels fets e hazanyes del inclyt rey Don Iaume primer Rey Daragó* (Catalan chronicle, 1204–1328).

**I Fioretti di San Francisco* (*The Little Flowers of St. Francis*; narrations and legends of St. Francis and his friends, written down about now).

**Bevis of Hampton* (translation of an Anglo-Norman *chanson de geste* of the twelfth century—*Beuves de Haumtone*).

*Hamdallāh Mustawfī, *Ta'rīkh-i guzīda* (Persian annals from the Creation to 1330).

Date of last Sanskrit inscription in Cambodia, where Indian cultural influence (dating from seventh century A.D.) had been destroyed.

L **Births and Deaths**

June 15th, Edward (the Black Prince) b. (–1376).

1331

A **Mar**: 2nd, Orkhān takes Nicaea.

C **Sep**: 27th, Vladislav defeats the Teutonic Knights, who had been ravaging Poland, at Plowce.

E Go-Daigo, Emperor of Japan, who had refused to abdicate (according to custom) but attempted to rule, defeated and deposed by the Hōjō Regency (for the Shogun).

1332

B **Apr**: 8th, Philip passes sentence of banishment and forfeiture on Robert of Artois.

C **Jul**: John of Bohemia expelled from Brescia.
15th, Christopher II of Denmark dies in exile; Gerhard, Count of Holstein, continues to rule in the interregnum (–1340).
25th, Philip takes the Cross for a Crusade in Palestine planned by John XXII.
Aug: 12th, Edward, son of John Balliol, and other 'Disinherited' Scottish nobles, with English support, defeat and kill the Earl of Mar, regent of Scotland, at Dupplin Moor.
Sep: the League of Ferrara formed by Italian rulers against John of Bohemia and the legate, du Poujet.
24th, Edward Balliol crowned as King of Scotland.

D **Nov**: Azzo Visconti takes Pavia.
7th, Lucerne accedes to the confederation of the Swiss Forest Cantons.
25th, Charles, son of John of Bohemia, defeats the Estensi of Ferrara at San Felice.
Dec: 12th, Edward Balliol defeated by the Earl of Moray at Annan and flees into England.

E Walter of Brienne's 'crusade' fails to recover Athens.
Death of Alexander III, Grand Duke of Vladimir; succeeded by Ivan I Kalitá ('the Pouch') of Moscow (–1341). With the Metropolitan, Peter (–1342), also preferring to reside, Moscow was now the civil and ecclesiastical capital of Christian Russia.
'Amda Seyon I, Negus of Ethiopia, defeats invasions of the Sultan of Ifat, the leading Muslim ruler in northern Abyssinia.

1331

F **Law and Politics**

Ching-shih ta-tien (*The Great Standard of Administration*; Chinese official encyclopedia, mainly of Mongol institutions, with maps).

H **Religion and Education**

John XXII's constitution *Ratio juris* defines the functions of the court of audience of the papal palace (known from 1336 as the *Rota*).

*Alvaro Pelayo, *De planctu ecclesiae* (defence of papal authority, with criticisms of the Church).

J **Art, Architecture and Music**

'Perpendicular' work begun in Gloucester Abbey (now Cathedral).

†Mausoleum of Abū-l-Fidā', Hamāh.

K **Literature, Philosophy and Scholarship**

†Emanuel ben Solomon (Manoello Giudeo), The *Mahbaroth* (prose and verse miscellany by an Italian Jewish poet).

†Abū-l-Fidā', *Mukhtasar Ta'rīkh al-Bashar* (*Epitome of the History of Mankind*, to 1329).

1332

F **Law and Politics**

†Ahmād al-Nuwayrī, *Nihāyat al-Arab* (general encyclopedia for administrators, with large section on Muslim history).

G **Economics, Science, Technology and Discovery**

*The Black Death apparently originates in India.

*Introduction to France from Italy of techniques for distilling liqueurs.

H **Religion and Education**

Foundation of the College of Burgundy, Paris.

*Nicholas de Lyra, *Postilla litteralis super Biblia* (biblical exegesis; first printed 1471).

J **Art, Architecture and Music**

Taddeo Gaddi, Fresco *Life of the Virgin* in Sta. Croce, Florence (–1338).

L **Births and Deaths**

— Ibn-Khaldūn b. (–1406).

1333–1334 English intervention in Scotland—Extinction of Hōjō Regency

1333

A **Feb**: 6th, Bertrand du Poujet defeats the Ferrarese and takes Consadolo.
Mar: 2nd, death of Vladislav I, King of Poland; succeeded by Casimir III (–1370).

B **Apr**: 14th, du Poujet and John of Bohemia defeated before Ferrara.
May: Edward joins Edward Balliol at the siege of Berwick.
Jun: 8th, he orders the seizure of the Isle of Man from the Scots; the island is henceforth attached to England.

C **Jul**: 19th, he defeats the Scots at Halidon Hill.
20th, Berwick surrenders.
Aug: 25th, Muhammad IV of Granada murdered; succeeded by his brother, Yūsuf I (–1354).
Sep: Edward Balliol holds a parliament at Perth.
26th, Andrew of Hungary marries Joanna of Naples.

D **Oct**: John leaves Italy for Bohemia, where he puts Charles in charge of its government.

E The King of Granada takes Gibraltar from Castile.
Andronicus recovers possession of northern Thessaly.
Go-Daigo, assisted by Ashikaga Takauji, a great feudatory, defeats the Hōjō Regency and establishes himself as Emperor of Japan; the Hōjōs extinguished and the effective capital restored to Kyōto from Kamakura.

1334

B **May**: David II of Scotland arrives in France and Philip lodges him in the Château Gaillard.
Jun: 12th, by the Treaty of Newcastle-upon-Tyne, Edward Balliol recognises Edward III as his overlord and cedes Berwick and eight shires of southern Scotland to England.

C **Aug**: 17th, the Bolognese revolt and expel du Poujet.
Sep: a fresh rising in Scotland forces Balliol to flee to England.

D **Dec**: 4th, death of Pope John XXII.
20th, Jacques Fournier elected as Pope Benedict XII (–1342).

1333

F **Law and Politics**

†Muhammad ibn Jamā'a, *Tahrir al-ahkām* (treatise on the rights and duties of kings).

G **Economics, Science, Technology and Discovery**

A series of famines (–1347) and flooding of the Yellow River ruin the Chinese economy and further weaken the Yüan (Mongol) dynasty.

J **Art, Architecture and Music**

(–1335) Charles IV begins to build a new palace in Prague.

Simone Martini and Lippo Memmi, *Annunciation* (painting).

K **Literature, Philosophy and Scholarship**

*Hamdallāh Mustawfī, *Zafar-nāma* (*Book of Victory*; historical poem in Arabic, from Muhammad to 1331/2).

1334

H **Religion and Education**

Giovanni Valle, a minorite friar, founds a hermitage near Foligno; thus originate the Friars of the Strict Observance (of the Franciscan Order).

North-country masters migrating from Oxford attempt to establish a university at Stamford.

J **Art, Architecture and Music**

Giotto given charge of the building of Florence Cathedral; he built the campanile.

The Palace of the Popes, Avignon (–1352).

Taddeo Gaddi, Triptych (painting).

K **Literature, Philosophy and Scholarship**

†Ibn Sayyid al-Nas, biography of Muhammad.

1335–1336 Congress of Vyšehrad—Disintegration of Ilkhanate of Persia and Kingdom of Delhi

1335

A **Feb:** Edward abandons a projected Scottish campaign, having reached Roxburgh.

B **Apr:** 2nd, death of Henry, Duke of Carinthia; Lewis confers the Duchy and southern Tyrol on the Habsburgs, and northern Tyrol on his own sons, despite his promise to John of Bohemia that Henry's daughter, Margaret 'Maultasch' (married to John's son, John Henry), should inherit.

C **Jul:** Edward begins a campaign in southern Scotland.

D **Nov:** he returns to England; on his departure, Edward Balliol's authority in Scotland soon crumbles.

Kings John of Bohemia, Charles of Hungary and Casimir of Poland meet in congress at Vyšehrad, near Buda; the first two award that the Teutonic Knights should restore Kuyavia and Dobrzyń to Poland but retain Pomerania as Casimir's vassals; Casimir recognises Bohemian overlordship over Silesia, while John renounces his title to the Polish crown.

E Death of Abū Sa'īd, Sultan of Persia; the Mongol Ilkhanate of south-west Asia now disintegrates.

Muhammad prevented by disease from carrying out an expedition to Madura, in south India, where his governor, Hasan, had declared himself an independent Shah. Muhammad had begun to farm provincial revenues to his governors.

1336

A **Jan:** 24th, death of Alfonso IV of Aragon; succeeded by Pedro IV (–1387).

B **Apr:** 18th, Harihara I, who had led a Hindu revolt against Muslim rule, crowned in his newly built capital, Vijayanagar; foundation of the Sangama dynasty (–1486) of the Vijayanagar Empire of south India (–1649).

C **Jul:** Edward campaigns in the Highlands of Scotland.

Sep: 23rd, he obtains a large grant of taxes in a Parliament at Nottingham on complaining that Philip of France was refusing to restore Agenais and was sheltering David and aiding Scottish resistance.

D **Nov:** Edward makes his last visit to Scotland to strengthen Edward Balliol's position.

E Edward shelters Philip's enemy, Robert of Artois.

Benedict cancels the projected Crusade. Philip brings the fleet for it into the Channel, threatening England.

John of Bohemia ravages Austria; peace is made, whereby the Habsburgs are left holding Carinthia while Margaret is established in Tyrol.

Stephen Uroš III, King of Serbia, murdered and succeeded by his son, Stephen Uroš IV Dušan (–1355).

Mubārāk Shah rebels against Muhammad of Delhi and makes East Bengal independent (–1352).

Go-Daigo's attempt to restore imperial authority in Japan collapses; Ashikaga Takauji takes Kyōto and enthrones a new Emperor, but Go-Daigo escapes and sets up court at Yoshino, in south Yamoto.

1335

F **Law and Politics**

Matthew Blastares, *Syntagma canonum et legum* (compilation of Greek canon and civil law).

G **Economics, Science, Technology and Discovery**

†Richard of Wallingford, *Quadripartitum de sinibus demonstratis* (first original Latin treatise on trigonometry).

Guido da Vigevano, *Tesaurus regis Francie* (prescribes health-regime on crusade; a second section on military science).

H **Religion and Education**

Benedict XII, constitutions for the Cistercian Order.

*St. Sergius of Rádonezh founds the Trinity Monastery (Troitsa), one of the first Russian convents not in a town.

J **Art, Architecture and Music**

*Illustrated copy of the Persian epic, the Demotte *Shāh-nāma*, made at Tabriz ('probably Persia's greatest book'; –1020).

L **Births and Deaths**

May, Richard of Wallingford, Abbot of St. Albans, d. (44).

— Timur b. (–1405).

1336

F **Law and Politics**

†Cino da Pistoia, *Lectura in codicem* (commentary on part of the Code of Justinian).

G **Economics, Science, Technology and Discovery**

Aug. 12th, Edward prohibits the export of wool to Flanders, causing unrest there.

The failure of the harvest causes famine in India.

H **Religion and Education**

Benedict XII, constitutions for the Benedictine and Cluniac Orders.

K **Literature, Philosophy and Scholarship**

*Claus Wisse and Philip Colin, *Willehalm* (continuation of *Parzival*, by Wolfram von Eschenbach; –1212).

†Ramón Muntaner, *Sermó del passatge de Sardenya* (versified history; a 'Catalan epic').

L **Births and Deaths**

July 4th, St. Elizabeth, Queen of Portugal, d. (65).

Dec. 24th, Cino da Pistoia d. (66).

1337

A **Jan**: 25th, death of Frederick II of Sicily; succeeded by his son, Peter II (–1342).

B **Apr**: Edward sends an embassy to recruit allies in the Low Countries.
May: 24th, Philip announces the confiscation of Gascony because of Edward's 'rebellion'; its seizure began 'The Hundred Years War' (–1453).

C **Jul**: 15th, by the Treaty of Valenciennes, Lewis becomes Edward's ally against France.

D **Oct**: 7th, Edward claims the French crown through his mother, Isabella, daughter of Philip IV.
Dec: 28th, James van Artevelde accepted as the leader of the Flemings revolting against their Count because of the hardship caused by the English embargo on the export of wool to them.

E Azzo Visconti takes Piacenza.
Mastino della Scala of Verona takes Lucca; his dominion now reaches from the Alps to the Mediterranean.
Andronicus recovers possession of Epirus.
Orkhān takes Nicomedia (Izmit) from the Greeks.
Death of Mansa Musa, under whom the Empire of Mali had reached its greatest extent (it included Gao and Timbuktu; Niani, its capital, has disappeared).
(–1338) An army sent by Muhammad to conquer Tibet destroyed in the Himalayas.

1338

B **Jun**: a French fleet sacks Portsmouth.

C **Jul**: 16th, a majority of the German electoral princes assert, in the Declaration of Rense, their unfettered right to elect their King, thus rejecting papal claims to approve or confirm such elections.
16th, Edward lands at Antwerp.
Sep: 5th, he meets Lewis at Coblenz, who appoints him imperial vicar west of the Rhine.

E Ashikaga Takauji restores the Shogunate; it remained in his family until 1573, but its control of Japan was never complete and 'feudal' anarchy prevailed.

1337

G **Economics, Science, Technology and Discovery**
William Merlee kept records of the weather (–1344).

J **Art, Architecture and Music**
Ambrogio Lorenzetti, Frescoes in Siena Town Hall.
*Andrea Pisano, Reliefs on the campanile, Florence Cathedral.

K **Literature, Philosophy and Scholarship**
†Ferreto de' Ferreti, *Historia rerum in Italia gestarum* (1250–1318).

L **Births and Deaths**
Jan. 8th, Giotto di Bondone of Florence d. (70?).
Jan. 21st, Charles V b. (–1380).

1338

F **Law and Politics**
*Ashikaga Takauji, Shogun of Japan (from 1338) issues the *Kemmu Code*, organising his government, with its capital at Kyōto.

H **Religion and Education**
Benedict XII regulates the papal office of Grand Penitentiary.

K **Literature, Philosophy and Scholarship**
Robert Mannyng, translation in English verse of Langtoft's *Chronicle* (–1307).
†Shaikh Hasan-i Dihlavī, Indian poet writing Persian.

1339 Process of Warsaw—First Doge of Genoa

B **Jun**: 21st, at Laupen, the forces of the city of Berne, aided by the Forest Cantons, defeat the forces of Fribourg and local nobility opposing Berne's dominance in western Switzerland.

C **Aug**: 16th, death of Azzo Visconti; his uncle, Luchino, succeeds as ruler of Milan (–1349).

Sep: 15th, papal agents conclude their hearing, in 'The Process of Warsaw' (since 4 Feb.), of evidence of the occupation of Polish lands by the Teutonic Knights, who disregard the award in favour of Poland.

23rd, Simone Boccanera elected as the first Doge of Genoa after a popular rising.

D **Oct**: Philip and Edward abortively campaign against each other in Picardy.

31st, death of Francesco Dandolo, Doge of Venice; succeeded by Bartolomeo Gradenigo (–1342).

E Edward Balliol leaves Scotland, where he was unable to rule.

Venice makes her first conquest on the Italian mainland with the seizure of Treviso.

By the (second) Treaty of Vyšehrad, Casimir of Poland recognises his nephew, Lewis, son of Charles of Hungary, as his heir.

Casimir attempts to seize Halich (Galicia) and Volhynia on the murder of King Juri II; he is opposed by the Galicians, who elect Lubart, son of Gedymin of Lithuania, and he becomes King with Uzbeg's protection (–1349).

'Alī Shāh rebels against Muhammad and makes West Bengal independent of Delhi.

H **Religion and Education**

Benedict XII, constitutions for the Augustinian Canons.

Andronicus III sends an embassy to Benedict to negotiate the reunion of the Churches.

Foundation of Grenoble University (–1452).

J **Art, Architecture and Music**

A new cathedral begun at Siena; abandoned in 1357.

K **Literature, Philosophy and Scholarship**

Francesco Petrarch, *Africa* (epic poem, in Latin, on Scipio Africanus and the Second Punic War; unfinished).

L **Births and Deaths**

— Francesco Zabarella b. (–1417).

1340 Edward III 'King of France'—Battle on the Salado

A **Jan**: 25th, in Ghent, Edward assumes the title of King of France and is so recognised by the Flemings.

B **Jun**: 24th, the English win a naval victory over the French at Sluys.

C **Sep**: 25th, after some ineffectual skirmishing, Edward and Philip make a truce, at Esplechin; it was extended to 1345.

D **Oct**: 30th, Alfonso of Castile and Afonso of Portugal defeat a Muslim invasion from Africa on the Salado.

Dec: 1st, on his return to England, Edward purges his government and starts the prosecution of John Stratford, Archbishop of Canterbury, the dismissed chancellor.

E Gerhard, Count of Holstein, the ruler of Denmark, murdered; Waldemar IV, son of Christopher, elected as King (–1375).

Death of al-Nāsir, Sultan of Egypt; he is followed by a succession of 12 puppets, ruled (and removed) by their emirs (–1382).

F **Law and Politics**

Appointment of Robert de Bourchier as the first lay chancellor of England.

*Lupold of Bebenburg, *Tractatus de jure regni et imperii.*

G **Economics, Science, Technology and Discovery**

Muhammad of Delhi creates a department of agriculture because of the famine in India.

Philip VI first coins gold angels.

*Francesco Balducci Pegolotti, *Practica della mercatura* (handbook for international commerce, giving routes, tables of tariffs, dates, measures, etc.; including China).

William Merlee, *De futura aeris intemperie* (treatise on making weather-forecasts).

Hamdallāh Mustawfī, *Nuzhat al-Qulūb* (*Delight of the Hearts*; Persian encyclopedia of cosmography and science).

†Al-Baytar, *Kamil al-Sinā'atayn* (treatise on vetinerary medicine).

*'Gough Map' of England.

Iron blast-furnaces known in the Liège district; at Namur, water-power used to operate a tilt-hammer.

First European papermill at Fabriano, Italy.

H **Religion and Education**

Benedict sends John of Marignolli to China (–1353).

*Johannes Andreae, *Glossa ordinaria* on the *Sext* (–1298).

*Guiu Terrena, *Summa de haeresibus* (history and refutation of heresies).

J **Art, Architecture and Music**

Mosque of al-Maridani, Cairo.

Pietro Lorenzetti, *Madonna Enthroned* (painting).

K **Literature, Philosophy and Scholarship**

**El Caballero Cifar* (romance of chivalry and Arthurian legend, the first of its kind in Spanish literature).

L **Births and Deaths**

Mar. —, John of Gaunt b. (–1399).

Oct. 23rd, Nicholas de Lyra d. (61).

Nov. 30th, John, Duke of Berri, b. (–1416).

— David ap Gwilym b. (–1400).

— Gerard Groot b. (–1384).

*Geoffrey Chaucer b. (–1400).

A **Mar**: 15th, Lewis abandons his alliance with Edward and makes peace with Philip at Vincennes.

B **Apr**: 23rd, a Parliament meets in which Archbishop Stratford is exonerated from Edward's charges; under pressure, the king makes several concessions, among them assent to a request from the commons to accept baronial councillors.

30th, death of John III, Duke of Brittany; the succession disputed by his half-brother, John de Montfort, and his niece, Jeanne de Penthièvre, the wife of Charles of Blois, in whose favour the Parlement of Paris pronounces.

Jun: David returns to Scotland from France following his supporters' expulsion of the English from Edinburgh.

15th, death of the Greek Emperor, Andronicus III; succeeded by his son, John V (–1347, 1354–1391).

D **Oct**: 26th, John Cantacuzenus, Grand Domestic of the Greek Empire, proclaims himself its Emperor; so begins civil war, with the nobility supporting John Cantacuzenus while the populace defended John V (–1354).

Nov: Charles of Blois captures John de Montfort, who is imprisoned in France; John's wife, Jeanne, recognizes Edward as King of France and seeks his assistance to continue the Breton War of Succession.

E Mastino della Scala's empire collapses and only Verona and Vicenza remain in his hands.

Death of Gedymin, Grand Prince of Lithuania, who had extended his hold over western Russia and established his capital at Vilna; succeeded by his son, Olgierd (–1377).

Death of Ivan Kalitá, Prince of Moscow and Grand Duke of Vladimir; succeeded by his son, Simeon (–1353).

Death of Uzbeg, Khan of 'the Golden Horde'; succeeded by his son, Tinibeg (–1342).

Outbreak of rebellions by the Chinese against the Yüan Dynasty (–1368).

F **Law and Politics**

The Gabelle made general in France (–1286).

G **Economics, Science, Technology and Discovery**

*Musō Kokushi, a Zen monk, has the Tenryūji monastery, Kyōto, built from profits of a trading expedition to China; other monasteries follow suit, so participating in the contemporary growth of Japanese overseas trade; this is accompanied by increasing piracy.

H **Religion and Education**

Dispute in the Greek Church between mystics following Gregory Palamas, and (Latin) rationalists led by Barlaam (–1351).

Foundation of Queen's College, Oxford.

J **Art, Architecture and Music**

Francesco Petrarch, *Le Rime* (sequence of love poems). He is crowned as poet laureate on the Capitol, Rome.

Pietro Lorenzetti, Altarpiece with scenes from life of St. Humilitas (painting).

L **Births and Deaths**

Nov. 10th, Henry Percy b. (–1408).

1342

A **Jan**: Edward campaigns ineffectively in southern Scotland.

Feb: following a rising by the Tyrolese, Lewis declares Margaret 'Maultasch''s marriage to John Henry of Bohemia to be void; she then marries Lewis' son, Lewis, Margrave of Brandenburg.

Mar: 31st, with the capture of Roxburgh, the Scots complete their expulsion of the English.

B **Apr**: 25th, death of Pope Benedict XII.

May: 7th, Pierre Roger elected as Pope Clement VI (–1352).

Jun: Walter de Manny, with an English expedition, relieves Joan de Montfort, who had been holding Hennebont against Charles of Blois.

C **Aug**: 8th, death of Peter II of Sicily; succeeded by his son, Louis (–1355).

Sep: 8th, Walter de Brienne, titular Duke of Athens, who had been employed by Florence in a war against Pisa for possession of Lucca, proclaimed signore of Florence in a successful plot by the city magnates.

30th, the English in Brittany defeat Charles of Blois at Morlaix.

D **Oct**: Edward arrives in Brittany and campaigns against the French supporting Charles of Blois.

Dec: 28th, death of Bartolomeo Gradenigo, Doge of Venice.

E Death of Charles I of Hungary; succeeded by his son, Lewis I (–1382).

Janibeg deposes and succeeds his brother Tinibeg as Khan of 'the Golden Horde' (–1357).

1343

A **Jan**: 4th, Andrea Dandolo elected as Doge of Venice (–1354).

19th, Edward and Philip make a truce by the Treaty of Malestroit.

20th, death of Rober the Wise of Naples; succeeded by his granddaughter, Joanna I, wife of Andrew of Hungary (–1381).

C **Jul**: 8th, the Treaty of Kalisz ends the war between the Teutonic Knights and Casimir of Poland, who cedes Pomerania.

Aug: 1st, following an insurrection, Walter of Brienne surrenders the lordship of Florence; its commune thus restored.

E Magnus cedes the crown of Norway to his son, Haakon VI (–1380).

John Cantacuzenus conquers Thrace with Turkish support.

1342

F **Law and Politics**

Establishment of Confraternity of St. Nicholas, a guild of barristers and solicitors practising in the Parlement of Paris.

G **Economics, Science, Technology and Discovery**

Levi ben Gerson, Latin translation of his *De sinibus, chordis et arcubus* (an original treatise on trigonometry).

Joannes Actuarios, *Methodus medendi* (medical treatise).

J **Art, Architecture and Music**

Abbey-church of La Chaise-Dieu, near Clermont-Ferrand, rebuilt by Clement VI.

Simone Martini, *Christ returning to his parents after disputing with the Doctors* (painting).

Pietro Lorenzetti, *Birth of the Virgin* (painting).

Ambrogio Lorenzetti, *Presentation* (painting).

K **Literature, Philosophy and Scholarship**

Francesco Petrarch, *De Contemptu Mundi* or *Secretum.*

†Domenico Cavalca, *Specchio della Croce*, and other treatises (by 'the father of Italian prose').

L **Births and Deaths**

Jan. 15th, Philip the Bold b. (–1404).

— Robert of Artois d.

1343

G **Economics, Science, Technology and Discovery**

The first European commission of public health established in Venice.

Levi ben Gerson, *De harmonicis numeris* (treatise on arithmetic for the musician Philippe de Vitry).

Jean de Meurs, *Quadripartitum numerorum* (metrical treatise on mathematics, mechanics and music).

H **Religion and Education**

Foundation of Pisa University.

J **Art, Architecture and Music**

Choir of Augsburg Cathedral begun.

K **Literature, Philosophy and Scholarship**

*Juan Ruiz, *El libro de buen amor* (a Spanish poetic miscellany of satires and lyrics).

1344

A **Mar**: Alfonso of Castile takes Algericas.
29th, Pedro of Aragon reannexes the Balearic Islands to his kingdom, deposing King James II of Majorca (–1349).

D **Oct**: 28th, a crusading fleet organised by Clement VI takes Smyrna, a base for Turkish pirates.

E Clement pronounces in favour of Philip's right as King of France in negotiations between English and French embassies at Avignon.
Casimir of Poland defeats the Mongols on the Vistula.
Lewis of Hungary expels Mongols from Transylvania.

1345

B **May**: 20th, John de Montfort, who had escaped from France, does homage for Brittany to Edward.

C **Jul**: 24th, riots between the weavers and fullers of Ghent lead to the murder of the city's ruler, James van Artevelde.
Sep: death of William II of Hainault and IV of Holland; succeeded by his sister, Margaret, wife of Lewis the Bavarian.
25th, Stephen Dušan of Serbia takes Serres, in Macedonia.
26th, death of John de Montfort, Duke of Brittany; succeeded by his son, John IV (–1399).

D **Oct**: 21st, Henry of Grosmont, Earl of Lancaster, defeats the French at Auberoche, in Gascony.
Nov: 18th, Andrew of Hungary, King of Naples, murdered, supposedly at the instigation of his wife, Joanna; his brother, Lewis of Hungary, consequently makes war on Naples.

E In Florence, the great banking houses of Bardi and Peruzzi go bankrupt, following Edward's failure to pay his debts. The proletariat (*populo minuto*) makes its first attempt to win political significance and is defeated; its leader, Ciuto Brandini, hanged.
Lewis of Hungary conquers Croatia.
Muhammad vainly besieges local officials of the Deccan revolting against him in the citadel of Daulatābād; there are also rebellions in Warangal and Gujarāt.

1344

G **Economics, Science, Technology and Discovery**

The gold noble (6*s*. 8*d*.) first coined in England.

H **Religion and Education**

Clement VI erects the bishopric of Prague into an archbishopric, thus detaching Bohemia from the province of Mainz.

Art, Architecture and Music

Prague Cathedral (–1385; architect: Matthias of Arras –1352).

K **Literature, Philosophy and Scholarship**

†'Amda Seyon, Negus of Ethiopia, had chronicles written (1270–1344; continued to 1434).

†Abū Haiyān, treatises (now lost) on the Abyssinian and Persian languages.

L **Births and Deaths**

Apr. 20th, Levi ben Gerson (Gersonides) d. (56).

— Muhammad al-Damīrī b. (–1405).

— Simone Martini d. (*c*. 60).

1345

F **Law and Politics**

Harmenopulos, *Hexabiblos* (Byzantine adaptation of Roman law).

G **Economics, Science, Technology and Discovery**

†*Guido da Vigevano, *Anatomia*.

K **Literature, Philosophy and Scholarship**

†Jedaiah ha-Penini Bedersi, *Behinath 'Olam* (an Hebrew poem).

†Richard de Bury, *Philobiblon* (a personal work on the love of books by a learned collector; first printed 1473).

†Walter Burley, *De vita et moribus philosophorum* (printed 1467).

Lu T'ai, *Traibhumikatha* (*The History of the Three Worlds*; a Buddhist cosmological treatise in Siamese).

†John of Victring, *Liber certarum historiarum* (history of Austria and Carinthia, 1217–1342).

L **Births and Deaths**

Apr. 14th, Richard de Bury, Bishop of Durham, d.

1346

B **Apr**: by abandoning imperial claims in Italy, Charles of Bohemia receives the consent of Clement to his election as King of the Romans; Clement then orders the German electors to choose a King in place of Lewis.
16th, Stephen Dušan crowned as Emperor of the Serbs and Greeks in Skoplje.

C **Jul**: 11th, Charles IV elected as King of the Romans (–1378).
12th, Edward, seeking to exploit Norman disaffection against Philip, lands in the Cotentin, at Saint-Vaast de la Hougue.
26th, he takes Caen.
Aug: 20th, Joanna of Naples marries Louis of Taranto.
26th, Edward defeats the French at Crécy; among the killed on the French side are John of Bohemia (succeeded by Charles; –1378), and Louis of Nevers, Count of Flanders (succeeded by his son, Louis de Maele; –1384).
Sep: 4th, Edward begins the siege of Calais.

D **Oct**: 4th, Henry of Lancaster takes Poitiers.
17th, David of Scotland, invading England, defeated and captured at Neville's Cross, outside Durham.

E The Teutonic Knights annex the Danish provinces of Viro and Harju, in Esthonia, by purchase from Waldemar IV.
The Genoese recover Chios.
Mīrzā, in revolt against Muhammad, founds the Muslim kingdom of Kashmīr (–1589).

1347

A **Feb**: 3rd, John VI Cantacuzenus enters Constantinople; end of the civil war (–1354).

B **May**: 20th, the 'Roman People' give the title of Tribune and dictatorial powers to Cola di Rienzo.
Jun: 20th, Sir Thomas Dagworth defeats and captures Charles of Blois at Bégard, in Brittany.
25th, the French defeated in a naval battle at Le Crotoy, on the Somme.

C **Aug**: 3rd, Hasan, the leader of the Muslim rebels in the Deccan, acclaimed as Bāhman Shāh (–1358); he founds the Bāhmanī dynasty of Kulbarga (–1527).
4th, Calais surrenders to Edward, who expels its citizens and establishes an English colony.
Sep: 28th, he makes a truce with Philip.

D **Oct**: 11th, death of Lewis IV the Bavarian, King of the Romans; Charles had already been crowned and now receives general recognition.
Nov: 20th, Cola di Rienzo defeats the Roman nobles.
Dec: 15th, he abdicates and flees when the people rise against him.

E Ramadhipati, ruler of the (Thai) principality of U Thong, founds a new capital at Ayudhya (on an island in the Menam; –1350).

1346

G **Economics, Science, Technology and Discovery**

The Black Death in Georgia, and 'the Golden Horde'.

H **Religion and Education**

Valladolid University receives its first papal charter (although it had existed for about 100 years).

Bridget of Sweden founds the Brigittine Order of monks and nuns.

†John Baconthorpe, commentaries on the Bible, Aristotle and Averroes (–1198).

Pembroke College, Cambridge.

J **Art, Architecture and Music**

*Bernardo Daddi, *Madonna* in Or San Michele, Florence.

1347

F **Law and Politics**

Casimir III, Statutes of Wíslica and Piotrków (the first legal codes for Little and Greater Poland, respectively).

Magnus II completes his codification of Swedish laws.

G **Economics, Science, Technology and Discovery**

The Black Death in Constantinople, Naples, Genoa and south France.

The English use cannon at the siege of Calais.

H **Religion and Education**

The Benedictine house in Prague founded (or restored) by Charles permitted to use the Slavonic language and Cyrillic alphabet.

J **Art, Architecture and Music**

Andrea Pisano, sculpture at Orvieto Cathedral.

K **Literature, Philosophy and Scholarship**

†Adam of Murimuth, *Continuatio Chronicarum* (continuation of Guisborough's *Chronicle* of England, to 1346; –1312).

L **Births and Deaths**

— St. Catherine of Siena b. (–1380).

1348 Hungarian invasion of Naples—Order of the Garter

A **Jan**: 15th, Joanna of Naples sells Avignon to the Papacy.
24th, Lewis of Hungary takes Aversa in his invasion of the Kingdom of Naples.

B **Apr**: plague compels him to withdraw.
7th, Charles, as King of the Romans, confirms the imperial privileges of Bohemia and unites to it Upper Lusatia, Silesia and Moravia.

C **Jul**: 21st, after defeating the 'Union' of Valencian nobles at Epila, Pedro of Aragon abolishes the *Privilegio de la Unión* (–1283F).

E Edward founds the Order of the Garter.
The Teutonic Knights defeat the Lithuanian princes, Olgierd of Vilna and Kiejstut of Kovno, on the Strawa.

G **Economics, Science, Technology and Discovery**

The Black Death in Italy, Spain, central and northern France, and southern England.

Gentile da Foligno, *Consilium contra pestilentiam* (account of the Black Death).

Charles founds the 'New Town' of Prague.

Mechanical clock in Dover Castle (dated 1348 but possibly later).

*Felix Fabri, *Journey to Sinai* (pilgrim-narrative).

†Al-'Umari, *Masālik al-absār* . . . (*Voyages of the Eyes* . . .; geographical and historical compilation on Muslim lands, also Abyssinia and Mali).

H **Religion and Education**

†Johannes Andreae, *Novella* (commentaries on canon law).

Charles founds Prague University.

K **Literature, Philosophy and Scholarship**

†Giovanni Villani, *Nuova Cronica* (*i.e. Croniche Fiorentine*; of universal history but especially of Florence, from 1300; continued by others to 1364).

†Jean de Hocsem, *Gesta pontificum Leodensium* (chronicle of the prince-bishops of Liege, 1247–1348).

†*John of Winterthur, *Chronicon* (mainly of south Germany, 1198–1348).

L **Births and Deaths**

June 18th, Gentile da Foligno d. (*c.* 58).

July 7th, Johannes Andreae d. (*c.* 77).

— Giovanni Villani d. (*c.* 77).

— Andrea Pisano d. (*c.* 58).

? Pietro Lorenzetti d. (*c.* 42 ?).

? Ambrogio Lorenzetti d. (*c.* 40 ?).

1349 Expansion of France and Poland—Rise of Ayudhya

A **Jan**: 13th, Louis of Flanders takes Ghent, completing his suppression of the revolt of the Flemish weavers.

24th, death of Luchino Visconti; his brother, Archbishop Giovanni, succeeds as lord of Milan (–1354).

Mar: 26th, Alfonso XI of Castile dies, of the Black Death, while besieging the Muslims in Gibraltar; succeeded by his son, Pedro I (–1369).

B **May**: Philip of France buys Montpellier from James II of Majorca.

C **Jul**: 16th, Humbert II, Dauphin of Vienne, cedes the Dauphiné to Charles (V), son of John (II) of France.

D **Oct**: 8th, death of Joanna II, Queen of Navarre; succeeded by her son, Charles II (–1387).

25th, James II killed in an attempt to recover Majorca.

E Casimir of Poland conquers Galicia.

Ramadhipati compels Lu T'ai (Dharmaja II) of Sukhodaya to recognise his supremacy.

F **Law and Politics**

Stephen Dušan publishes his *Zakonnik* (Serbian law code).

G **Economics, Science, Technology and Discovery**

The Black Death in northern England, Ireland and Scandinavia; and in Germany and Switzerland, where Jews are massacred for their supposed responsibility for the pestilence. Flagellants, inspired by the plague, condemned as heretics by Clement VI.

†Thomas Bradwardine, *De arithmetica speculativa*; *De geometrica speculativa*; *De proporcionibus velocitatum* (mathematical treatises).

*Fra Niccolò da Poggibonsi, *Libro d'Oltramare* (travel narrative: Jerusalem, Egypt and the East).

*Wang Ta-yüan, *Tao-i-chi-lio* (*Description of the Barbarians of the Isles*; account by a Chinese merchant of his travels, 1330–49).

H **Religion and Education**

†Richard Rolle, *The Prick of Conscience* (a poem); *Melium*; *Incendium Amoris* (an outstanding work in English mystical literature).

Foundation of Florence University (–1472) and Gonville College, Cambridge.

J **Art, Architecture and Music**

Byzantine frescoes in Lesnovo church, Serbia.

K **Literature, Philosophy and Scholarship**

†Juan Manuel, *Cronica abreviada*; *Conde Lucanor*, or *Libro de Patronio*; *Libro del Caballero y del Escudero*; *Libro de los Estados* (Spanish romances; tales; proverbial, didactic dialogues).

*Ulrich Boner, *Der Edelstein* (a Middle High German anthology of fables from Aesop onwards, retold; printed 1461).

†William of Ockham's numerous philosophical works, attacking universals, establish the Nominalist tradition (–1390); as a polemicist, he also wrote anti-papal tracts for Lewis the Bavarian.

L **Births and Deaths**

Apr. 10th, William of Ockham d. (*c*. 49).

Aug. 25th, Thomas Bradwardine, Archbishop of Canterbury, d. (*c*. 59).

Sept. 29th, Richard Rolle of Hampole d.

1350 Anarchy in Papal States

A **Feb**: 14th, Charles cedes Brandenburg and Tyrol to the Wittelsbachs, in the Treaty of Bautzen.

17th, Giovanni de' Manfredi seizes Faenza, in the Papal States, where the Pope's temporal authority is now almost non-existent.

C **Aug**: 22nd, death of Philip VI of France; succeeded by his son, John II (–1364).

29th, Edward defeats Spanish privateers off Winchelsea.

D **Oct**: 23rd, Giovanni Visconti takes possession of Bologna.

Nov: 18th, Robert de Brienne, Constable of France, executed on charges of treason.

E Louis of Taranto, King of Naples, flees to Provence when Lewis of Hungary invades; Lewis withdraws after conquering Naples, but his rule is ineffective.

Ramadhipati crowned as the first King of Ayudhya (*i.e.* Siam).

F **Law and Politics**

Ramadhipati I, Siamese legal codes (–1359).

*Charles IV withdraws his *Maiestas Carolina* (law code) on opposition by the Bohemian estates.

G **Economics, Science, Technology and Discovery**

The Black Death in Scotland.

Jean de Linières, Catalogue of stars.

*Moses ben Joshua, *Orah hayyim* (*Road of Life*; Hebrew treatise on medicine, with astrological explanation for Black Death).

Cannon of cast bronze being used.

H **Religion and Education**

William Bateman, Bishop of Norwich, founds Trinity Hall, Cambridge.

K **Literature, Philosophy and Scholarship**

*Giovanni Boccaccio, The *Filostrato* (poem on the Troilus and Cressida theme).

**Abele Spelen* (four plays from Brabant, etc. in Middle Dutch, the earliest of their type in European literature).

**Cancioneiros* (songs and lyrics from Galicia and Portugal; mss. anthologies of the poems of many authors).

**Poema de Alfonso Onceno* (Spanish verse chronicle on the life and deeds of Alfonso XI the Avenger, King of Castile, 1312–50).

†Yoshida Kenkō, *Tsurezure-gusa* (trans. by George Sansom as *Essays in Idleness*).

*Simon of Couvin, *De judicio solis in conviviis Saturni* (poem on Black Death).

*Beginning of first Cambodian chronicles.

*Simhabhūpala of Rājakonda, *Rasārnavasudhākara* (major treatise on Hindu drama).

1351

A **Mar**: 20th, death of Muhammad Tughluq of Delhi, whose kingdom had disintegrated; succeeded by his cousin, Fīrūz (–1388).

27th, the 'Battle of the Thirty' fought between as many English (who lost) and the same number of Bretons and other champions of the Montfort party.

B **May**: 1st, Zurich accedes to the Swiss Confederation.

D **Oct**: 17th, a Milanese invasion of Florentine territory defeated.

Dec: 24th, Lewis I, Margrave of Brandenburg, abdicates in favour of his brothers, Lewis II and Otto V.

E The Chinese government provokes great revolts by impressing labour to rebuild dykes along the Yellow River, and loses control of much of central China.

1352

A **Jan**: 6th, John of France holds the first feast of the Order of the Star.

14th, Lewis of Hungary makes peace with Joanna of Naples.

Feb: 13th, indecisive naval battle in the Bosphorus between the Genoese and the Venetians, Aragonese and Greeks.

Mar: 2nd, the Ottoman Turks take Gallipoli; although they came as allies of John VI in his new war with John V, they remain, making this their base for conquests in Europe.

B **Apr**: 28th, Clement makes peace with Giovanni Visconti, granting him the vicariate of Bologna.

C **Aug**: the English in Brittany defeat the Montfort faction at Mauron.

D **Dec**: 6th, death of Pope Clement VI.

18th, Étienne Aubert elected as Pope Innocent VI (–1362); he sets aside the 'compromise' made by the cardinals before his election, which was designed to restrict papal prerogatives.

E Berne, Glarus and Zug join the Swiss Confederation.

Fīrūz founds Fīrūzābād, near Delhi, as his new capital.

Ilyās Shāh of West Bengal annexes East Bengal.

Acamapitzin elected as King of the Aztecs.

1351

F **Law and Politics**

Lewis I confirms the Golden Bull (–1222) and enshrines the rights of the Hungarian nobility as the permanent law of the constitution.

G **Economics, Science, Technology and Discovery**

The Statute of Labourers regulates wages in England; they are rising as a consequence of the Black Death.

Conrad of Megenburg, *Das Buch der Natur* (treatise on natural history, blaming earthquakes for the Black Death; first printed 1475).

Iron wire manufactured with water-power at Augsburg.

H **Religion and Education**

A Byzantine Church Council endorses the mystical theology of Gregory Palamas, an ascete of Athos ('Palamism').

Perpignan University founded.

The first Statute of Provisors forbids papal appointments to ecclesiastical benefices in England.

J **Art, Architecture and Music**

†Musō Kokushi, Japanese landscape gardens.

K **Literature, Philosophy and Scholarship**

Francesco Petrarch, *An Epistle to Posterity* (prose work).

L **Births and Deaths**

Oct. 15th, Gian Galeazzo Visconti b. (–1402).

1352

F **Law and Politics**

The Statute of Treasons defines treasonable offences against the King of England.

G **Economics, Science, Technology and Discovery**

The Black Death in Russia.

First illustration of spectacles in fresco at Treviso.

†*Opicinus de Canistris, Italian cartographer.

H **Religion and Education**

Corpus Christi College, Cambridge.

J **Art, Architecture and Music**

Choir of Antwerp Cathedral begun.

Peter Parler of Gmünd succeeds as architect of Prague Cathedral.

K **Literature, Philosophy and Scholarship**

Ranulf Higden, *Polychronicon* (Latin prose history of the world from the Creation to 1327, continued by others to 1357; –1387).

*Francesco Petrarch, *All'Italia* (patriotic ode).

†*Baranī, *Ta'rīkh-i-Firūz Shahī* (history of Muslim India).

1353

A **Mar**: 31st, in the Treaty of Sarzana, Milan makes peace with Florence and its Tuscan allies.

B **Jun**: 30th, Innocent appoints Cardinal Gil Albornoz as legate in the Papal States.

C **Aug**: 29th, Venice defeats Genoa in a naval battle off La Loiera, near Alghero, Sardinia; Genoa then puts itself under the lordship of Giovanni Visconti.

Sep: 23rd, Edward holds a quasi-parliamentary assembly which consents to regulations for the wool trade.

E Death of Simeon of Moscow, Grand Duke of Vladimir; succeeded by his brother, Ivan II (–1359).

Leaders of the Chinese rebellion against the Yüan begin to compete for supreme command.

Fa Ngum, a Thai prince who had conquered the Upper Mekong Valley, proclaimed at Luang Prabang as Ch'ieng Dong Ch'ieng Tong, King of Lan Ch'ang ('the country of a million elephants', *i.e.* Laos).

1354

A **Jan**: 8th, Charles of Navarre murders Charles d'Espagne, Constable of France; he conspires with Edward against John of France.

Feb: 15th, Florence, Siena and Perugia form a defensive alliance against Milan, to which Venice accedes.

B **Apr**: 6th, English and French embassies, at Guînes, prolong the truce and agree on preliminary terms for peace which the French subsequently reject.

Jun: 5th, by the Treaty of Montefiascone, Albornoz receives the submission of Giovanni di Vico, Prefect of Rome, who had built a state in the Papal States, including Viterbo and Orvieto.

C **Aug**: 1st, Albornoz establishes Cola di Rienzo as Senator of Rome.

D **Oct**: Charles IV begins his expedition into Italy.

5th, death of Giovanni Visconti, Archbishop of Milan; his nephews, Bernabò (–1385), Galeazzo II (–1378) and Matteo II (–1355) Visconti, succeed as lords of Milan.

7th, death of Andrea Dandolo, Doge of Venice; succeeded by Marino Falieri (–1355).

8th, Cola di Rienzo killed in a popular revolt against his repressive government in Rome.

19th, Yūsuf I of Granada murdered; succeeded by his son, Muhammad V (–1359).

Nov: John VI Cantacuzenus forced to abdicate, leaving John V as the sole Greek Emperor (–1391).

4th, the Venetian fleet defeats the Genoese at Porto Longo, in the island of Sapientza.

1353

G **Economics, Science, Technology and Discovery**

Edward III transfers the wool staple from Bruges to England.

H **Religion and Education**

The first Statute of Praemunire prohibits appeals to the papal court concerning English benefices.

J **Art, Architecture and Music**

Taddeo Gaddi, Polyptych at Pistoia (painting).

K **Literature, Philosophy and Scholarship**

Giovanni Boccaccio, *Decameron.*

†Gilles le Muisit, Chronicle of Flanders (1294–1352).

L **Births and Deaths**

— Thomas Arundel b. (–1414).

1354

F **Law and Politics**

The Statute of the Staple, confirming the ordinance of 1353, affirms the supremacy of parliamentary legislation.

G **Economics, Science, Technology and Discovery**

*Ibn-Battūtah, *Tuhfat al-Nuzzār* . . . (*Gift to Observers dealing with the Curiosities of Cities and Wonders of Journeys*; account of his travels in the Middle and Far East and the interior of Africa, 1325–54).

J **Art, Architecture and Music**

Apse of choir of Freiburg Minster (architect: Johannes Parler).

Andrea Orcagna, Altarpiece in Strozzi Chapel, Florence (–1357; painting).

†Wu Chen and Huang Kung-wang, Chinese painters.

K **Literature, Philosophy and Scholarship**

†Kitabatake Chikafusa, *Jinnō shōtōki* (*Record of the Legitimate Descent of Divine Emperors*; Japanese history arguing legitimacy of the line of Go-Daigo; –1336).

1355

B **Apr:** 5th, Charles IV crowned in Rome as Holy Roman Emperor; he immediately returns to Germany.

17th, Marino Falieri, Doge of Venice, executed following the discovery, by the Council of Ten, of his conspiracy against the Venetian patricians.

May: 1st, Genoa makes peace with Venice.

Jun: 1st, Giovanni Gradenigo elected as Doge of Venice (–1356).

7th, in the Treaty of Gubbio, Galeotto Malatesta of Rimini, whom Albornoz had captured, cedes his conquests.

24th, Albornoz takes Ancona.

D **Oct:** 17th, death of Louis of Aragon, King of Sicily; succeeded by his brother, Frederick III (–1377).

Nov: Edward campaigns in Picardy for ten days; his son, Edward, Prince of Wales (the Black Prince), raids southern France, sacking Carcassone and Narbonne.

6th, the Scots take Berwick-upon-Tweed.

Dec: 2nd, in a meeting of the Estates-General of northern France, in Paris, Étienne Marcel leads a critical opposition.

E Charles (V), as Dauphin of Vienne, and Amadeus VI of Savoy define their frontier by treaty; the Franco-Savoyard border thus remained until 1601.

Casimir of Poland completes his subjection of Masovia with the submission of Ziemowit III, its last prince.

Death of Stephen Dušan when advancing to take Constantinople; his Serbian Empire now collapses.

1356

A **Jan:** 13th, Edward recaptures Berwick.

17th, Innocent declares a crusade against Francesco Ordelaffi, lord of Cesena and Forli.

20th, Edward Balliol abdicates as King of Scotland, selling his claims to Edward III, who now ravages as far as Edinburgh.

B **Jun:** 18th, Henry of Grosmont, Duke of Lancaster, lands in Normandy to support rebels against John of France.

C **Aug:** 8th, death of Giovanni Gradenigo, Doge of Venice; succeeded by Giovanni Delfino (–1361).

Sep: 19th, the Black Prince, raiding central France from Gascony, defeats and captures John at Maupertuis, near Poitiers.

D **Oct:** 17th, the Estates-General reassembles in Paris; Etienne Marcel leads the opposition to the government of the Dauphin Charles, now Regent of France.

Nov: 14th, Simone Boccanera elected as Doge of Genoa, having led the Genoese in expelling the Milanese.

E Outbreak of war between Hungary and Venice.

Janibeg conquers Azerbaijan from the Ilkhan.

Che Yüan-chang, leader of the Chinese peasants in revolt, takes Nanking.

1355

H **Religion and Education**

St. Scholastica's Day (10 Feb.), town and gown riot in Oxford.

Jean de Sy, partial translation of the Bible into French.

J **Art, Architecture and Music**

Choir of Aachen Cathedral begun.

Vestry (with fan vault) of Prague Cathedral.

Francesco Talenti commissioned to make a wooden model for Florence Cathedral (–1367).

K **Literature, Philosophy and Scholarship**

Gujarātī-Jaina, *Parikramanabūlavabodha* (on Jaina ethics, in Gujarātī—an Aryan vernacular of the Bombay area).

L **Births and Deaths**

Jan. 7th, Thomas of Woodstock b. (–1397).

1356

F **Law and Politics**

Dec: in a diet at Metz, Charles IV publishes his Golden Bull regulating procedure for the election of Kings of the Romans by a college of seven Electors, who are conceded regalian rights in their territories, which are to be indivisible.

In a campaign to enforce order in Bohemia, Charles authorises commoners to prosecute their lords in law-courts, where Bohemian is to be the official language.

Duke Wenceslas of Brabant concedes the *Joyeuse Entrée* (a charter of liberties) to his subjects, establishing an assembly, the Estates of Brabant.

G **Economics, Science, Technology and Discovery**

The Hanse puts an embargo on trade with Bruges in order to secure privileges there (–1360).

J **Art, Architecture and Music**

Madrasa of Sultan Hasan, Cairo (–1368).

*Kao Ming (?), *The Story of a Lute* (opera).

1357

A Mar: 23rd, in the Treaty of Bordeaux, England and France make a truce.

B May: 12th, death of Afonso IV of Portugal; succeeded by Pedro I (–1367).
Jun: 21st, Albornoz takes Cesena in his 'crusade' against Ordelaffi.

C Aug: 23rd, Androin de la Roche, Abbot of Cluny, replaces Albornoz as legate in the Papal States.
Sep: 17th, Lewis of Hungary takes Zara.

D Oct: 3rd, by the Treaty of Berwick, Edward releases David II, for a ransom, and makes a truce for ten years.

E Janibeg, Khan of 'the Golden Horde', murdered and succeeded by his son, Berdibeg (–1359).

1358

A Feb: death of Bāhman Shāh of Kulbarga; his kingdom now bestrides central India.
18th, Venice cedes Istria and Dalmatia to Lewis of Hungary; the republic of Ragusa also submits to him.
23rd, a Parisian mob led by Étienne Marcel compels Charles to confirm *La Grande Ordonnance*.
Mar: 27th, Charles escapes from Paris.

B Apr: Nicolò Acciajuoli, a Florentine, installed as lord of Corinth; he founds a dynasty (–1460).
May: 28th, the Jacquerie, a peasant revolt, breaks out in the Beauvaisis.
Jun: 24th, it is savagely suppressed.

C Jul: 31st, Marcel murdered in a riot in Paris.
Aug: 2nd, Charles returns to Paris and regains control.
Sep: 18th, Albornoz reappointed legate in the Papal States.

E Casimir of Poland finally suppresses the separatist confederation of the nobles of Great (western) Poland.
Death of Thinhkaba, who had founded a new kingdom in south Burma.

1359

A Mar: 24th, in the Treaty of London, John of France cedes Edward the lands of the Angevin Empire in sovereignty.

B May: 25th, the treaty rejected by the Estates-General.

C Jul: 4th, Ordelaffi of Forli surrenders to Albornoz.
Aug: 23rd, Muhammad V of Granada deposed; succeeded by his brother, Ismā'il II (–1360).

D Dec: 4th, Edward begins his siege of Reims in a new French campaign.

E Amadeus VI of Savoy takes possession of Piedmont.
Death of Orkhān, the Ottoman ruler, now styled Sultan, who had founded an organised state in control of western Anatolia and Thrace; succeeded by his son, Murād I (–1389).
Death of Ivan II, Grand Duke of Vladimir; succeeded by Dmitri III Donski, with Dmitri IV in opposition.
Berdibeg, Khan of 'the Golden Horde', murdered; succeeded by his brother, Kulpa (–1360).

1357

F **Law and Politics**

Mar. 10th, the Dauphin Charles, under pressure from the Estates-General, concedes *La Grande Ordannance* for the reform of French government.

Apr. 29th, Albornoz promulgates the *Egidian Constitutions*; these were the laws of the Papal States until the nineteenth century.

†Bartolus of Sassoferrato, *Commentaria in Codicem* (on Justinian's Code).

J **Art, Architecture and Music**

Cloisters (fan-vaulted) of Gloucester Abbey (*now* Cathedral) begun.

Choir of Basel Cathedral restored (architect: Johannes Parler).

Synagogue (*now* El Transito church), Toledo, completed.

K **Literature, Philosophy and Scholarship**

Francesco Petrarch, *I Trionfi* (*The Triumphs*; six allegorical poems).

†Ibn-Wafa, Egyptian poet.

1358

G **Economics, Science, Technology and Discovery**

Charles orders the establishment of vineyards in Bohemia.

1359

G **Economics, Science, Technology and Discovery**

†*Jean Buridan, *Quaestiones Octavi Libri Physicorum* (commentary on Aristotle's *Physics*, discussing gravity, etc.).

H **Religion and Education**

†St. Gregory Palamas, *Defence of those living in holy tranquillity*.

J **Art, Architecture and Music**

Andrea Orcagna, Tabernacle in Or San Michele, Florence (sculpture).

K **Literature, Philosophy and Scholarship**

†*Nicephorus Gregoras, *Roman* (*i.e.* Byzantine) *History* (1204–1359).

Isāmy, *Futuh-us-salatin* (the only extant contemporary history of the Bāhman kingdom of Kulbarga, south India; also of the Sultanate of Delhi, from 1302; in verse, modelled on Firdausī's *Shāh-Nāma*; –1020).

†John of Marignolli, *Cronaca di Boemia* (1335–58; includes account of his travels –1340).

1360

A **Jan**: 11th, Edward abandons the siege of Reims and raids Burgundy.
Mar: 17th, Albornoz takes possession of Bologna.

C **Apr**: 7th–12th, Edward besieges Paris, then withdraws to Chartres.
May: 8th, at Brétigny, he concludes the preliminary terms of a treaty of peace with France.

C **Jul**: 27th, Waldemar of Denmark destroys the Hanseatic centre of Visby; it never regains its importance as a market for fish.
12th, Ismāʿīl II of Granada murdered and succeeded by Muhammad VI (–1362).
Aug: 31st, the Hanse, Norway, Sweden and the Teutonic Knights make an alliance against Denmark.
Sep: the Milanese abandon their siege of Bologna on the arrival of Hungarian troops, allies of the Papacy; these are soon disbanded and the Milanese siege is renewed.

D **Oct**: 24th, the Treaty of Calais confirms the terms made at Brétigny; John is released, for a ransom, and cedes to Edward, in sovereignty, Aquitaine, Poitou, Ponthieu, etc.; while Edward gives up the title of King of France.

E Waldemar compels rebellious Danish nobles to make peace; he also conquers Scania, in Sweden.
Kulpa, Khan of 'the Golden Horde', murdered and succeeded by Nevruz (–1361).
Timur begins his conquest of Transoxiana with the seizure of Kesh.

1361

B **May**: John Hawkwood, with the White Company, begins his career as a condottiere in Italy.
Jun: 16th, papal forces defeat the Milanese at Rosillo, so ending the siege of Bologna.

D **Nov**: 21st, death of Philip de Rouvres, Duke of Burgundy, without issue; John of France takes possession of the Duchy.

E Death of Giovanni Delfino, Doge of Venice; succeeded by Lorenzo Celso (–1365).
Death of the Bulgarian Tsar, John Alexander, dividing his lands between his two sons; while a usurper, Duvrotik, takes the Dobrudja (named after him).
The Ottoman Turks take Serres and Demotika.
Nevruz, Khan of 'the Golden Horde', murdered and succeeded by Khidyr; the horde is now disintegrating, with its court involved in succession disputes.
Che Bong Nga succeeds as King of Champa and begins his attacks on Dai Viet (–1390).

1360

F **Law and Politics**

†Richard FitzRalph, *De Pauperie Salvatoris* (a tract against the mendicants, important for its theory on political authority).

Giovanni da Legnano, *Tractatus de bello* (*Treatise on war*, including its legal aspects; important as an early contribution to international law; –1388).

G **Economics, Science, Technology and Discovery**

Fīrūz Shah founds the city of Jaunpur.

Regulations against 'Schapsteufel' ('Schnaps fiend', *viz.* brandy, now common in Germany).

†*John of Rupescissa, *Liber de consideratione quintae essentiae* (alchemical treatise on the elixir of youth).

J **Art, Architecture and Music**

Alcazar Palace, Seville (–1402).

K **Literature, Philosophy and Scholarship**

Galeazzo Visconti establishes a library in Milan.

L **Births and Deaths**

Nov. 16th, Richard FitzRalph, Archbishop of Armagh, d.

1361

F **Law and Politics**

The Statute of Westminster institutes Justices of the Peace.

G **Economics, Science, Technology and Discovery**

Second outbreak of the Black Death in western Europe (–1362).

H **Religion and Education**

†John Tauler, a founder of the German mystical sect of the 'Friends of God'.

Foundation of Canterbury Hall, Oxford (–1539).

Pavia University founded (–1398).

J **Art, Architecture and Music**

†Philippe de Vitri, *Ars Nova* and *Ars contrapunctus* (theoretical treatises on the 'new style' of music, with shorter notes).

1362–1363 Decay of 'the Golden Horde'—Expansion of Hungary, Lithuania and Savoy

1362

B **Apr**: Pedro of Castile murders Muhammad VI and restores Muhammad V to Granada (–1392).
6th, united companies of *routiers* (disbanded soldiers living by organised brigandage) defeat French royal forces at Brignais, in Burgundy.
May: 26th, death of Louis of Taranto, King of Naples, as (the second) husband of Queen Joanna.

C **Jul**: Waldemar defeats the Hanse off Helsingborg; he detaches its allies, Norway and Sweden, with the marriage of Margaret, his daughter, to Haakon, their heir.
Sep: 12th, death of Pope Innocent VI.
28th, Guillaume de Grimoard elected as Pope Urban V (–1370).

E Margaret 'Maultasch' cedes Tyrol to Rudolf Habsburg, Duke of Austria.
Lewis of Hungary defeats and captures Strascimir of Bulgaria; he conquers northern Bulgaria, extending his control over the Balkans.

1363

A **Mar**: 3rd, Urban condemns Bernabò Visconti for heresy.

B **Apr**: John of France takes the cross in a crusade proclaimed by Urban.

C **Sep**: death of Giovanni de Vico; thus disappears an obstacle to the Papacy's control of its States.
6th, John grants the Duchy of Burgundy to his son, Philip the Bold (–1404).

D **Nov**: 26th, Urban dismisses Albornoz as legate in the Papal States.
30th, Albert II elected as King of Sweden (–1389); his father, Albert, Duke of Mecklenburg, had led a rebellion which deposed Magnus II.

E Death of Simone Boccanera, the first Doge of Genoa.
Amadeus of Savoy acquires the marquisate of Saluzzo.
Olgierd of Lithuania defeats the Mongols near the mouth of the Bug and reaches the Black Sea.
Fīrūz of Delhi regains control of Sind.

1362

G **Economics, Science, Technology and Discovery**
The English wool-staple established at Calais.

J **Art, Architecture and Music**
Nave of Westminster Abbey begun.

K **Literature, Philosophy and Scholarship**
Fritsche Closener, *Chronik* (one of the oldest extant chronicles in German; continued to 1415 by Jakob Twinger von Königshofen.

1363

G **Economics, Science, Technology and Discovery**
†Guy de Chauliac, *Chirurgia Magna* (includes description of Black Death).

H **Religion and Education**
Charles summons Conrad Waldhauser, the famous Austrian preacher, to Prague, where he urges the reform of the Church.

J **Art, Architecture and Music**
Nave and transepts of Canterbury Cathedral (–1400).

K **Literature, Philosophy and Scholarship**
†Al-Safadi, *Kitāb al-Wāfī bi-l-wafayāt* (the largest compilation of Muslim biographies)

L **Births and Deaths.**
Dec. 14th, Jean Gerson b. (–1429).

1364

A **Jan**: John returns to captivity in England when one of the hostages for payment of his ransom escapes.

Feb: 10th, by the Treaty of Brno, Charles IV grants Tyrol to Rudolf of Austria; both concede that, should the issue of either fail, the other and his heirs would inherit.

Mar: 3rd, Urban makes peace with Bernabò Visconti, to the latter's advantage.

B **Apr**: 8th, death of John II of France; succeeded by his son, Charles V (–1380).

May: 16th, Bertrand du Guesclin defeats the Captal de Buch, leading the army of Charles of Navarre in rebellion against Charles V, at Cocherel, on the Eure.

C **Sep**: in the Congress of Cracow, Casimir of Poland mediates between Charles IV and Lewis of Hungary; together with Kings Waldemar of Denmark and Peter of Cyprus they also consider a proposal to crusade against the Turks.

29th, the Montfort party in Brittany defeats and kills Charles of Blois, and captures Bertrand du Guesclin, at Auray.

E Crete revolts against Greek rule.

Thadominbya, a Thai prince, founds a new capital at Ava, in Upper Burma.

1365

A **Mar**: 6th, Charles V makes peace with Charles of Navarre.

12th, by the Treaty of Guérande, Charles V recognises John de Montfort as Duke of Brittany and receives his homage.

B **May**: Parliament repudiates King John's subjection of England to the Papacy (–1213) and annuls the payment of tribute.

Jun: 4th, after visiting Urban at Avignon, Charles IV crowned as King of Arles and Vienne at Arles; this is the last Burgundian coronation.

C **Aug**: 22nd, Charles V engages du Guesclin to enlist the Free Companies of *routiers*, in order to rid France of them, to serve Henry of Trastamare, illegitimate brother of Pedro of Castile.

D **Oct**: 10th, a Crusade led by Peter I of Cyprus takes Alexandria; it departs after sacking the town and massacring its population.

Nov: 22nd, the Hanse makes peace, unfavourably, with Waldemar of Denmark.

E Death of Lorenzo Celso, Doge of Venice; succeeded by Marco Cornaro (–1367).

1364

G **Economics, Science, Technology and Discovery**
Giovanni Dondi dall'Orologio, *Planetarium.*

H **Religion and Education**
Casimir III founds Cracow University (–1397).

J **Art, Architecture and Music**
Guillaume de Machaut, mass for the coronation of Charles V (polyphony, for four voices).

1365

H **Religion and Education**
Rudolf IV, Duke of Austria, founds Vienna University.

J **Art, Architecture and Music**
†K'o Chiu-ssu, Chinese painter.

K **Literature, Philosophy and Scholarship**
Prapañca, *Nagarakritāgama* (poem in old Javanese; gives information about Malayan peninsula and archipelago).

Ming Dynasty of China—Independence of Albania—Racial discrimination in Ireland

1366

A **Mar**: the Irish Parliament, in the Statute of Kilkenny, prohibits intermarriage between English and Irish and orders other measures dividing the two races.

5th, having expelled Pedro the Cruel, Henry of Trastamare crowned as King of Castile (–1379).

C **Aug**: 23rd, Amadeus of Savoy, crusading against the Turks, takes Gallipoli; he then rescues John V from Bulgaria by attacking Varna.

E Casimir wins possession of Volhynia.

Murād establishes the Ottoman capital in Adrianople.

1367

A **Jan**: 18th, death of Pedro I of Portugal; succeeded by his son, Ferdinand I (–1383).

20th, death of Marco Cornaro, Doge of Venice; succeeded by Andrea Contarini (–1382).

B **Apr**: 3rd, the Black Prince, invading Castile on behalf of Pedro, defeats Henry and captures du Gesclin, at Nájera; illness then forces him to withdraw and new rebellions against Pedro follow.

D **Oct**: 16th, Urban restores the Papacy to Rome.

Nov: 19th, in the League of Cologne, the Hanse, Sweden and Mecklenburg form an alliance against Denmark and Norway.

E Amadeus returns from Constantinople; the Turks recover Gallipoli.

Chu Yüan-chang, having defeated rival rebel leaders, takes Peking and expels Toghan Temur, the last Yüan (Mongol) Emperor; he becomes, as Hung-wu, founder of the Ming Dynasty (–1644), with his capital at Nanking.

*Timur consequently becomes effective ruler of the Asiatic Mongols, as Great Emir to puppet Great Khans.

1368

A **Mar**: 7th, Rudolf of Austria cedes Zug in a treaty of truce with the Swiss.

D **Nov**: 1st, Charles IV's queen crowned as Empress in Rome during his brief (and ineffective) expedition into Italy.

18th, Charles V accepts a judicial appeal from Gascon nobles against their governor, the Black Prince; thus, in effect, he renews the war against England.

E Charles Topia assumes the title of King of Albania on gaining control of the country.

1366

K **Literature, Philosophy and Scholarship**

Francesco Petrarch, *Rime in vita e morte di Madonna Laura.*

L **Births and Deaths**

Apr. —, Henry IV b. (–1413).
— Taddeo Gaddi d. (*c.* 66).

1367

F **Law and Politics**

The Kings of Kulbarga and Vijayanagar, in a treaty of peace, agree not to slaughter non-combatants in future wars (*cf.* 1360).

G **Economics, Science, Technology and Discovery**

Francesco Pizigano, *portolano* of the Mediterranean and north-west Europe.

Cannon used by both sides in the battle of Kauthal between Muslims of Kulbarga and Hindus of Vijayanagar.

H **Religion and Education**

With the accession of Timur, Islam spread through the Mongol lands and Christian missions to central Asia ceased.

Lewis I of Hungary founds Péc University.

J **Art, Architecture and Music**

Building of Florence Cathedral resumed, following Talenti's model (–1355).

The Jāmi' Masjid (mosque), Kulbarga.

*The Kremlin, Moscow.

K **Literature, Philosophy and Scholarship**

*Bianco da Siena, *Laudi spirituali* (religious lyrics and reflections).

1368

G **Economics, Science, Technology and Discovery**

Florentine dyers go on strike for higher pay.

Chia Ming, *Yin-shih-hsü-chih* (*Elements of Dietics*; explaining how the author reached the age of 100).

H **Religion and Education**

*John Milíč, reforming Bohemian preacher, *Tractate on Antichrist.*

K **Literature, Philosophy and Scholarship**

†*Fazio degli Uberti, Poems, lyrics, *canzoni* and *sonetti*; and *Dicta Mundi* (*Il Dittamondo*; didactic poem in imitation of Dante).

Hāfiz (*i.e.* Shams-ad-Dīn Muhammad), The *Dīwan* (collection of poems by the Persian lyrical poet—probably the greatest Persian poet next to Firdausī).

L **Births and Deaths**

June 28th, Sigismund of Luxemburg b. (–1437).
Dec. 3rd, Charles VI b. (–1422).
— Andrea Orcagna d. (*c.* 60).

1369

A **Jan**: a rebellion against Edward begins in Gascony.
Mar: 14th, Henry of Trastamare defeats Pedro at Montiel.
23rd, Henry kills Pedro I the Cruel, the former King of Castile; Henry (II) now in uncontested control.

B **Apr**: Charles V conquers Ponthieu.
22nd, Hugues d'Aubriot founds the Bastille, Paris.
May: 21st, Charles declares war on England.
Jun: 3rd, Edward reassumes the title 'King of France'.
19th, Philip of Burgundy marries Margaret, daughter and heir of Louis de Maële, Count of Flanders.

C **Sep**: John of Gaunt, Duke of Lancaster, raids France from Calais to Harfleur.

D **Oct**: John V, in Rome on a mission for aid against the Turks, accepted into the Roman Church.
Nov: 30th, by the Treaty of Stralsund, Waldemar of Denmark makes peace on terms favourable to the Hanse and its allies, who had conquered Scania.

E Venice repulses a Hungarian invasion.
Timur gains control of the Khanate of Chaghadai (*i.e.* Turkestan, with its capital Samarqand).
Hung-wu receives tribute-missions from Korea, Dai Viet and Champa.

1370

A **Feb**: 17th, the Teutonic Knights defeat the Lithuanians at Rudau.

C **Jul–Sep**: Sir Robert Knolles raids northern France.
Sep: 19th, the Black Prince sacks Limoges.
27th, Urban returns to Avignon.

D **Oct**: 2nd, Charles appoints Bertrand du Guesclin Constable of France.
17th, Pietro Gambacorta becomes ruler of Pisa (–1392); so ends its republic.
Nov: 5th, death of Casimir III the Great, King of Poland, the last of the Piast dynasty; Lewis of Hungary elected as his successor (–1382).
Dec: 4th, du Guesclin defeats Knolles, who was making for Brittany, at Pontvallain, in Maine.
19th, death of Pope Urban V.
30th, Pierre Roger de Beaufort elected as Pope Gregory XI (–1378).

E Kumāra Kampana, son of Bukka I of Vijayanagar, completes his conquest of the Muslim sultanate of Madura (*see* K).

1369

G **Economics, Science, Technology and Discovery**
Further outbreaks of the Black Death in England, France, etc.

J **Art, Architecture and Music**
†Simon Tunsted, *De quattuor principalibus musices* (practical treatise on music).

K **Literature, Philosophy and Scholarship**
Geoffrey Chaucer, *The Boke of the Duchesse.*
†*Thomas Grey, *Scalacronica* (English history to 1362).

1370

F **Law and Politics**
The *Pfaffenbrief* ('Priest's Charter') establishes a common public law among the members of the Swiss Confederation.

G **Economics, Science, Technology and Discovery**
First established example of insurance in northern Europe, at Bruges, involving a Genoese trader.
Henri de Vick instals a mechanical clock in the Palais Royal, Paris.
Earliest iron needles manufactured at Nuremburg.

H **Religion and Education**
†*Rulman Merswin, a member of the German sect of mystics, 'The Friends of God', *Book of the Nine Rocks.*

K **Literature, Philosophy and Scholarship**
Donato Velluti, *Cronica domestica* (description of the daily life of a rich merchant and his children).
The Pistill of Suete Susan (Scottish alliterative poet).
†Zākānī, *Akhlāq al-Ashrāf* (Persian poetry).
†Jean le Bel, *Chronique* (France, Germany, Belgium and England, 1326–61; one of Froissart's principal sources, –1400).
*Gangā Devi, *Madhurā Vijayam* (*The Conquest of Madura* by her husband, Kampana (1365–70); Sanskrit poem).

L **Births and Deaths**
Leonardo Bruni b. (–1444).
— Guarino b. (–1460).

1371

A **Feb**: 22nd, death of David II of Scotland, without issue; succeeded by his cousin, Robert II, the first Stewart (–1390).

Mar: Edward dismisses Bishops Wykeham, the Chancellor, and Brantingham, the Treasurer, and replaces them with laymen, following an anti-clerical outburst in Parliament.

C **Sep**: 26th, Murād defeats and kills King Vukašin of Serbia at Črnomen, on the Marica; he conquers Macedonia, while Constantinople and Bulgaria become Turkish tributaries.

E Albert of Sweden compelled to accept baronial control of his government.

Japan, Cambodia and Ayudhya (Siam) send tribute-missions to Hung-wu.

The Chams sack Hanoi.

1372

A **Mar**: John of Gaunt claims the throne of Castile, as Pedro's son-in-law. Henry of Castile, by besieging Lisbon, compels Ferdinand of Portugal to abandon his alliance with Gaunt.

B **Jun**: Sir Owain ap Thomas (self-styled Prince of Wales) takes Guernsey for Charles V. 23rd, in a naval battle off La Rochelle, Henry of Castile, as the ally of France, destroys an English fleet bringing John Hastings, Earl of Pembroke, Edward's lieutenant, to Gascony.

C **Aug**: 7th, the French recover Poitiers.

D **Dec**: Charles' conquest of Poitou completed.

1373

A **Mar**: 31st, Joanna of Naples recognises the independence of Sicily, where Frederick III takes the title of King of Trinacria.

B **Apr**: 28th, John IV of Brittany flees to England following a pro-French revolt by his subjects; only Brest remains in English hands.

May: 8th, Sir John Hawkwood, in papal service, defeats the Milanese at Chiesi. Amadeus of Savoy also ravages Milanese territory.

Jun: 16th, in the Treaty of London, England and Portugal make a perpetual alliance.

C **Aug**: Gaunt sets off from Calais on an expedition through Champagne and Burgundy. By the Treaty of Fürstenwalde, Otto Wittelsbach (son of Lewis the Bavarian) surrenders Brandenburg to Charles IV, who unites it to Bohemia.

D **Dec**: Gaunt arrives in Bordeaux at the end of his *chivauchée* through France, which had achieved little.

E The Genoese take Famagosta, in Cyprus.

1371

F **Law and Politics**

Charles IV promulgates the Westphalian Public Peace.

K **Literature, Philosophy and Scholarship**

**Le Livre du Chevalier de la Tour-Landry* (didactic collection of fables and stories for instruction of the author's three daughters after the death of their mother; English version printed by Caxton 1483–4).

L **Births and Deaths**

May 28th, John the Fearless b. (–1419).

1372

G **Economics, Science, Technology and Discovery**

Al-Damīrī, *Kitāb hayāt al-Hayāwan* (*The lives of Animals*; encyclopedia of animals, real and mythical; the greatest zoological work in Arabic).

K **Literature, Philosophy and Scholarship**

†'Sir John de Mandeville' (a *nom-de-plume*?; *alias* 'John of Burgundy'?), *Voiage and Travaile* (purports to describe the author's travels to Jerusalem, India, Java, China ('Cathay') and island utopias, and the wonders and monsters he saw; a largely derivative compilation; it enjoyed great popularity in western Europe, being translated into several languages (the earliest manuscript, in a Paris dialect, dated 1371); printed from 1480).

1373

F **Law and Politics**

John d'Arckel, Prince-Bishop of Liège, concedes 'the Peace of the Twenty-Two' to his subjects, admitting their representation in his government.

J **Art, Architecture and Music**

The two La Grange chapels, Amiens (first appearance of the 'Flamboyant' style of Gothic architecture).

K **Literature, Philosophy and Scholarship**

*John Barbour, *The Brus* (epic poem in 20 books on the life and deeds of Robert Bruce, d. 1329).

L **Births and Deaths**

Jul. 23rd, St. Bridget of Sweden d. (70).

1374

A **Feb**: 11th, the English and French make a truce for Picardy, at Bourbourg, and begin considering a settlement.

B **Jun**: Bernabò Visconti makes peace with Amadeus and a truce with Gregory.

1375

A **Feb**: 24th, death of Waldemar IV of Denmark; an interregnum follows (–1376).

B **Apr**: 13th, with the capture of Sis, the capital, the Egyptians and Turks finally liquidate the Kingdom of Armenia; Leo VI flees to western Europe.

Jun: 27th, English and French embassies, in conference at Bruges, conclude a general treaty of truce; Edward now holds only Calais, Brest, Bordeaux and Bayonne in France.

D **Oct**: Florence organises a league in the Papal States, causing rebellions against the Pope there.

E Dmitri of Moscow establishes his primacy in Russia on the surrender of Michael of Tver.

1374

F Law and Politics

Lewis the Great grants the first general charter of privileges to the Polish nobility, at Kessa.

G Economics, Science, Technology and Discovery

Hung-wu puts embargo on Japanese trade because of piracy (–1403).

†Ibn-al-Khatīb of Granada, *On Plague*.

H Religion and Education

*Gerhard Groot of Deventer forms the Brethren of the Common Life at Windesheim (–1386).

J Art, Architecture and Music

†Ni Tsan, Chinese painter.

K Literature, Philosophy and Scholarship

**Taiheiki* (Japanese novel about the period 1318–67).

†Ibn-al-Khatīb, *History of Granada*; numerous poetic, philosophical and geographical works.

L Births and Deaths

July 19th, Francesco Petrarch d. (70).

— Conrad von Megenburg d. (65).

1375

G Economics, Science, Technology and Discovery

Abraham Cresques (?), a Jewish mapmaker of Las Palmas, makes the first world map showing Marco Polo's travels, as a gift from Pedro of Aragon to Charles of France.

*Jules Protat of Mâcon uses a wooden block for printing.

K Literature, Philosophy and Scholarship

Coluccio Salutati appointed Latin secretary of Florence (–1406).

Hung-wu Chêng-yun (Chinese phonetic dictionary ordered by the Emperor Hung-wu).

†Beneš of Weitmil, *Vita Caroli* (biography of Charles IV, 1331–46); Chronicle of Bohemia (1283–1374).

*The *Mabinogion* (collection of eleven medieval Welsh folk tales, dating from perhaps the beginning of fourteenth century, or even earlier, and completed in their extant form by about 1425 in *The White Book of Ryydderch* (*c.* 1300–25) and *The Red Book of Hergest* (*c.* 1375–1425).

**Pearl* (remarkable elegiac poem, written in north western English dialect; anon., but perhaps by the poet who also wrote the following narrative poem).

**Gawain and the Green Knight*.

L Births and Deaths

Dec. 21st, Giovanni Boccaccio d. (62).

1376

A **Mar**: 19th, Bologna revolts against the Pope and declares its independence.
31st, Gregory excommunicates Florence, thus beginning the 'War of the Eight Saints'.

B **Apr**: 28th, the 'Good Parliament' meets (*see* F).
May: 13th, Olaf succeeds as King of Denmark (–1387) under the regency of his mother, Margaret, Queen of Norway, Waldemar IV's daughter.
Jun: 4th, formation of the League of Swabian Towns.
8th, death of Edward, Prince of Wales ('the Black Prince').
10th, Wenceslas, the eldest son of Charles IV, elected as King of the Romans.

C **Aug**: 14th, the Hanse obtains favourable terms from Haakon of Norway in the Treaty of Kallundborg.

E The Navarrese Company (mercenaries formerly employed in the war between France and Navarre) take Durazzo on behalf of Louis of Évreux.
John V grants Tenedos to Venice, while his son, Andronicus, who claims the imperial throne, grants the island to Genoa; thus a new war between Venice and Genoa begins.
Paramaraja I of Ayudhya reduces the King of Sukhodaya to the status of governor.

1377

A **Jan**: 17th, Gregory restores the Papacy to Rome.
27th, the 'Bad Parliament' meets and reverses the acts of the 'Good Parliament'; it grants a poll-tax.
Feb: 3rd, Robert of Geneva, the papal legate in the war against Florence, takes Cesena and massacres its inhabitants.
19th, Gaunt's intervention in an ecclesiastical court on behalf of John Wycliffe provokes a riot in London.

B **May**: 21st, at Reutlingen, Ulm and thirteen other Swabian cities defeat the forces sent by Charles IV to suppress their league.

Jun: 21st, death of Edward III of England; succeeded by his grandson, Richard II (–1399), with a council of regency.

C **Jul**: the French sack the Isle of Wight, and with the Castilians harass the English south coast.
27th, death of Frederick III of Trinacria; succeeded by his daughter, Maria (–1402). Pedro IV of Aragon now claims the Duchies of Athens and Neopatras.

E Death of Olgierd, Grand Prince of (eastern) Lithuania, who had conquered Podolia and the Ukraine, expelling the Mongols; succeeded by Jagiello (–1381).
Tran Due-tong, Emperor of Dai Viet, killed in his unsuccessful invasion of Champa; Che Bong Nga then sacks Hanoi again.
Hayam Wuruk, Emperor of Mājapāhit (Java), destroys the last remains of the Hindu Empire of Śrīvijaya (Sumatra).

1376

F **Law and Politics**

The 'Good Parliament' is the first to impeach the king's ministers, and the first when the Commons are known to have elected a Speaker; thereafter election of the Speaker became normal practice.

John Wycliffe, *De civili dominio* (denying the Church's temporal authority).

Philippe de Mézières, *Somnium viridarii* (*Le songe du vergier* is his French translation; dialogue defending royal prerogative against the Pope).

G **Economics, Science, Technology and Discovery**

John Arderne, *Practica de fistula in ano* (treatise on treatment of fistula).

†Al-'Abbās al-Rasūlī, Sultan of Yemen, *Bughyat al-fallāhīn* . . . (*The desired book of peasants on useful trees and aromatic plants*).

J **Art, Architecture and Music**

Jacopo di Paolo d'Avanzi, frescoes in church of S. Antonio, Padua.

Loggia dei Lanzi, Florence (–1382).

Town Hall, Bruges (–1421).

1377

G **Economics, Science, Technology and Discovery**

Returns of the poll-tax indicate that the English population (aged 14 and over) is 1,361,478.

The Teutonic Knights found Rhein (one of the last German colonies they established in 'the Wilderness' (south east Prussia), it being their policy to keep this area largely uninhabited).

In Ragusa (Dubrovnik) it is ordered that travellers from plague-infected areas should spend 30 days in quarantine.

H **Religion and Education**

Gregory XI condemns 19 conclusions in John Wycliffe's political writings.

J **Art, Architecture and Music**

Choir of Ulm Minster (–1449; architects: Heinrich and Michael Parler).

Court of Lions, Alhambra, Granada (–1391).

K **Literature, Philosophy and Scholarship**

William Langland, *The Vision, or Book, of Piers Plowman* (*William's Vision of Pierce Plowman*; a long allegorical poem in the west midlands dialect; started *c.* 1362, revised *c.* 1393).

†Guillaume de Machaut, *Le Jugement du roi de Navarre*; *La Prise d'Alexandrie*; and *Le Livre du voir-dit* (characteristic work of a court poet with some influence on Chaucer's early poems).

*Taillevent (Guillaume Tirel), *Le Viandier* (a recipe book).

L **Births and Deaths**

— Filippo Brunelleschi b. (–1446).

— John Arderne d. (70).

— Ibn-Battūtah d. (73).

1378 War of Chioggia—Revolution in Florence

A **Jan**: while visiting Paris, Charles IV grants the imperial vicariate of the Kingdom of Arles to the Dauphin Charles, son of Charles V.

Mar: 27th, death of Pope Gregory XI.

B **Apr**: 8th, Bartolomeo Prignano elected as Pope Urban VI (–1389).

Jun: the English take possession of Cherbourg by treaty with Charles II of Navarre (–1393).

C **Jul**: 21st, in the Revolt of the Ciompi, the *Popolo minuto* under Michele di Lando seize control of Florence.

28th, Florence and the Papacy make peace in the Treaty of Tivoli.

Aug: 4th, Gian Galeazzo Visconti succeeds his father, Galeazzo II, as joint ruler of Milan with his uncle, Bernabò (–1385, 1402).

9th, thirteen cardinals declare that the election of Urban VI is invalid.

31st, Michele di Lando suppresses a second rising by the *Popolo minuto*; a government representing a coalition of the different classes is established.

Sep: an English naval expedition fails to take St. Malo.

20th, the dissident cardinals, encouraged by Charles V, elect Robert of Geneva as Pope Clement VII (–1394).

D **Oct**: the Venetians take Tenedos from the Genoese in the 'War of Chioggia' (–1381).

Nov: Charles IV and England announce their recognition of Urban against Clement.

16th, Charles V declares his acceptance of Clement.

29th, death of the Holy Roman Emperor, Charles IV, King of Bohemia; succeeded by his son, Wenceslas (–1400, 1419) with his younger sons, Sigismund and John, being respectively endowed with the Mark of Brandenburg and the newly formed Duchy of Görlitz.

E Dmitri of Moscow defeats, on the Vozha, a Mongol army retaliating for his attack on them.

G Economics, Science, Technology and Discovery

*Joannes Jacobi, *Secretarium practicae medicinae* (or *Thesaurarum*; summary of medical treatises, written for Charles V of France).

*Guillem Sedacer, *Sedacina totius alchimiae.*

H Religion and Education

Beginning of the Great Schism, with papal courts at Rome and Avignon (–1417).

St. Catherine of Siena, *Dialogo* (treatise on the spiritual life, in Italian).

William of Wykeham founds Winchester College (a grammar school for poor scholars).

J Art, Architecture and Music

Nave of Canterbury Cathedral (architect: Henry Yevele; –1411).

†Meister Wilhelm of Cologne, painter.

K Literature, Philosophy and Scholarship

Giovanni da Firenze, *Il Pecorone* (collection of some 50 tales and short stories taken from old chronicles, *e.g.* from Villani—1348; perhaps the source of the plot of *The Merchant of Venice*).

L Births and Deaths

— St. Alexis, Metropolitan of Russia, d.
— John Hardyng b. (–*c.* 1465).
— Gerlac Petersen b. (–1411).
— Vittorino da Feltre b. (–1446).
— Lorenzo Ghiberti b. (–1455).

1379

A **Mar**: Gian Galeazzo takes possession of Asti.

B **Apr**: 28th, Alberico da Barbiano, leader of the condottieri Company of St. George, serving Urban, defeats the Breton force of Clement at Marino.
May: 29th, death of Henry II of Castile; succeeded by his son, John I (–1390).
Jun: Lewis of Hungary and Poland declares for Urban; Wenceslas persuades the German princes to do likewise.
20th, Clement establishes his papacy at Avignon, having been expelled from Naples.

C **Aug**: 3rd, John IV recovers Brittany following an anti-French rebellion due to Charles' confiscation of the Duchy.
16th, the Genoese take Chioggia from the Venetians.

E Ghent, led by Philip van Artevelde, revolts against Louis of Flanders, and defeats him.
The Navarrese Company, having left Durazzo on the death of Louis of Évreux, take Thebes, capital of the (Catalans') Duchy of Athens on behalf of Nerio Acciajuoli, lord of Corinth.

1380

A **Jan**: 14th, a Parliament meets which declares Richard II to be old enough to rule.

B **Jun**: 10th, the English defeat a Franco-Castilian fleet off Kinsale, Ireland.
22nd, the Venetians recover Chioggia, compelling the Genoese there to surrender.
29th, Joanna of Naples declares Louis, Duke of Anjou (brother of Charles V), to be her heir.

C **Jul**: 24th, an expedition led by Thomas of Woodstock, Earl of Buckingham, leaves Calais to raid Picardy, Champagne and the Loire Valley.
Aug: a French fleet raids the Thames and burns Gravesend.
Sep: 8th, Dmitri of Moscow leads the Russians to victory over 'the Golden Horde' at Kulikova Pole, on the upper Don; Moscow's supremacy in Russia was thus confirmed.
16th, death of Charles V the Wise, King of France; succeeded by his son, Charles VI (–1422).
23rd, Buckingham's expedition reaches Brittany.

D **Nov**: 5th, a Parliament meets and grants another poll-tax.
16th, the council ruling France for Charles VI abolishes all taxes in the face of public unrest.

E Death of Haakon VI of Norway; succeeded by his son, Olaf (V), King of Denmark (–1387). Albert of Sweden also claims Norway, and in the war following there develops the organisation of the 'Vitalian Brethren' which plunders Baltic shipping for the next 50 years.

1379

G **Economics, Science, Technology and Discovery**

The Hanse rejects demands of English merchants for free trade in its towns and in the Baltic (–1388).

Jehan de Brie, *Le Bon Berger* (manual for shepherds).

H **Religion and Education**

Henry of Langenstein, *Epistola Pacis* (advocates a general council to reunite the Church).

Clement VII recognises Erfurt University.

William of Wykeham founds New College, Oxford.

John Wycliffe, *De Ecclesia*; *De Potestate Papae.*

K **Literature, Philosophy and Scholarship**

*Benvenuto de'Rambaldi; *Commentum* (first important commentary on Dante).

L **Births and Deaths**

— Thomas à Kempis b. (–1471).

— Alfonso Borgia (Calixtus III) b. (–1458).

1380

F **Law and Politics**

Hung-wu, in suppressing a conspiracy, abolishes the office of Prime Minister and the Central Chancellery; henceforth Chinese emperors assume personal and autocratic rule.

H **Religion and Education**

Conrad of Gelnhausen, *Epistola Concordiae* (advocating a general council to reunite the Church).

*John Wycliffe, English translation of the Bible.

**Cloud of Unknowing* (by anonymous English mystic).

K **Literature, Philosophy and Scholarship**

**Zadonschchina* (Russian historical poem).

*Lal Ded, *Lallā-vakyāni* (*Lallā's Wise Sayings*; collection of verses attributed to the Kashmiri poetess-mystic, 'Granny Lal').

L **Births and Deaths**

Apr. 29th, St. Catherine of Siena d. (33).

Sep. 8th, St. Bernadino of Siena b. (–1444).

— Bernardo Daddi d.

A **Jan**: 15th, by the Treaty of Vincennes, John de Montfort ends his rebellion and is recognised by Charles as Duke of Brittany; Buckingham accordingly leaves Brittany, leaving a garrison in Brest, and a truce for six years is made with France.

B **May**: 19th, John of Castile announces his acceptance of Clement VII as Pope.
Jun: 1st, Urban, who had excommunicated Joanna, recognises her cousin, Charles, Duke of Durazzo, as King of Naples (–1386).
14th, in the Peasants' Revolt, the rebels occupying London kill Archbishop Sudbury, the Chancellor, and Robert Hales, the Treasurer.
15th, Richard meets Wat Tyler, the rebel leader, who is killed; the revolt now suppressed.
17th, the league of Rhenish towns (formed Jan. 20th) allies with the Swabian League.

C **Jul**: 26th, Charles of Durazzo enters Naples.
Aug: 8th, Venice and Genoa make peace in the Treaty of Turin.
29th, Ferdinand of Portugal, under pressure from England, revokes his acceptance of Clement and recognises Urban.

E Jagiello of Lithuania deposed by his uncle, Kiejstut (–1382).
Tokhtamysh, Timur's vassal ruling part of 'the Golden Horde', defeats Mamay (ruling the western part) on the Kalka and thus reunites the Horde (–1397).

G **Economics, Science, Technology and Discovery**

Printing by movable type at Limoges.

H **Religion and Education**

Henry of Langenstein, *Concilium Pacis* (arguing the superiority of general councils over the pope).

Pierre d'Ailly (?), *Epistola Leviathan* (advocating a general council to reunite the Church).

†Jan Ruysbroeck, Flemish mystic, *XII Béguines*; *The Book of Truth*; *Mirror of Simple Souls*; *The Kingdom of Lovers*; and other mystical writings.

John Wycliffe, *De Eucharistia* (denying transubstantiation).

K **Literature, Philosophy and Scholarship**

Geoffrey Chaucer, *The House of Fame*; *The Parliament of Fowles.*

†Lapo da Castiglionchio, *Epistola* (autobiographical, with descriptions of contemporary and family life).

L **Births and Deaths**

— Poggio Bracciolini b. (–1459).

— Jehan de la Fontaine b. (–*c.* 1431).

— St. Colette b. (–1447).

A **Jan**: 14th, Richard marries Anne of Bohemia in accordance with a treaty of alliance with her brother, Wenceslas.

Feb: new taxes cause a riot in Rouen ('La Harelle').

Mar: Joanna of Naples surrenders to Charles of Durazzo; she is imprisoned and presumably murdered.

1st, the *maillotins* of Paris riot against the new taxes; similar riots occur in southern France.

15th, the *Popolo grasso* recover power in Florence and establish an oligarchy.

B **May**: 3rd, the weavers of Ghent, led by Philip van Artevelde, take Bruges; other Flemish towns revolt.

30th, Clement crowns Louis of Anjou as King of Naples.

Jun: Louis leads an army into Italy.

10th, death of Andrea Contarini, Doge of Venice; succeeded by Michele Morosini.

C **Aug**: Ferdinand of Portugal makes peace with John of Castile, who was besieging Lisbon; an English expedition thus has to evacuate Portugal.

26th, Tokhtamysh sacks Moscow and then withdraws, having restored his suzerainty over Russia.

Sep: 11th, death of Lewis the Great, King of Hungary and Poland; one of his two daughters, Jadwiga, is elected as 'King' of Poland (–1399); the Hungarians elect the elder, Mary (–1395), betrothed to Sigismund of Bohemia, but Charles of Durazzo claims as the Angevin male heir and invades.

D **Oct**: 16th, death of Michele Morosini, Doge of Venice; succeeded by Antonio Vernieri (–1400).

Nov: 27th, a French army defeats the Flemish rebels at Roosebeke; Philip van Artevelde is killed.

E Jagiello recovers control of Lithuania by defeating and murdering Kiejstut.

Establishment of the Burji line (of Circassian origin) of Mamlūk Sultans of Egypt; its history is one of intrigue and murder, with a total of 23 sultans (–1517; *cf.* 1468).

Timur conquers Khurāsān.

Hung-wu completes the conquest of China and expulsion of the Mongols.

G **Economics, Science, Technology and Discovery**

†Nicholas Oresme, *De Moneta* (one of the earliest European treatises on currency); *Le Livre du Ciel et du Monde*; treatises on mathematics, mechanics, etc.

H **Religion and Education**

An English church council at Blackfriars condemns John Wycliffe's theological opinions; he is expelled from Oxford.

K **Literature, Philosophy and Scholarship**

*Geoffrey Chaucer, translation of *The Consolation of Philosophy* by Boethius.

†Nicholas Oresme, translations into French of Aristotle's *Politics* and *Ethics*.

L **Births and Deaths**

July 11th, Nicholas Oresme, Bishop of Lisieux, d.

1383

A **Jan**: the French army returning from Flanders restores royal control in Paris; taxes are reimposed.

Mar: 1st, death of Amadeus VI of Savoy, 'the Green Count', who had made Savoy an important state.

B **May**: an English expedition led by Henry Despenser, Bishop of Norwich, as a 'crusade' on behalf of Urban, fails to exploit unrest in Flanders, and withdraws.

D **Oct**: death of Ferdinand I of Portugal; he had recognised his son-in-law, John of Castile, as his heir.

E Poland and Lithuania united by the Treaty of Volkovysk, whereby Jadwiga marries Jagiello; Lithuania now accepts Christianity, so ending the Crusades of the Teutonic Knights, whose expansion had prompted this union.

Establishment of the Crispi dynasty in the Duchy of Archipelago (–1566).

1384

A **Jan**: John of Castile compels John, Master of the Order of Avis, the elected regent of Portugal for the former's wife, to surrender the government to him.

30th, death of Louis de Maële, Count of Flanders; succeeded by his son-in-law, Philip the Bold of Burgundy (–1404).

Feb: the Scots destroy Lochmaben Castle and raid Cumberland.

B **Apr**: an English expedition invades Scotland to Edinburgh.

C **Jul**: 26th, Wenceslas arranges a truce between the town leagues and princes of south west Germany, at Heidelberg.

Sep: John of Castile abandons the siege of Lisbon.

21st, Louis I of Anjou dies at Bari, while attempting to conquer Naples; succeeded by his son, Louis II.

D **Nov**: 20th, the Florentines occupy Arezzo.

1383

F **Law and Politics**

Wenceslas proclaims a public peace for Germany.

G **Economics, Science, Technology and Discovery**

Ships entering Marseilles are required to spend 40 days in quarantine.

†John of Ypres, collection of travellers' tales (*cf.* Hakeluyt).

H **Religion and Education**

John Wycliffe, *Trialogus* (summary of his doctrines).

K **Literature, Philosophy and Scholarship**

John Gower, *Vox Clamantis* (long poem in Latin about the Peasants' Revolt, 1381).

John Cantacuzenus, memoirs of his political career (1320–56).

*John Fordun, *Scotichronicon* (history of Scotland from Noah to 1383; –1449).

L **Births and Deaths**

Mar. 1st, Constantinus Harmenopulos d. (63).

June 15th, John Cantacuzenus (former Greek Emperor, as a monk, named Joasaph), d.

Dec. 31st (*or* 1 Jan. 1384?), John Wycliffe d. (*c.* 63).

1384

G **Economics, Science, Technology and Discovery**

John Dombleday, *Stella alchimie* (manual for alchemists).

K **Literature, Philosophy and Scholarship**

Geoffrey Chaucer, *Troylus and Cryseyde.*

†Kan'ami, founder of a hereditary line of performers of the Japanese *Nō* drama.

L **Births and Deaths**

Aug. 20th, Gerhard Groot d. (44).

1385–1386 Battles of Aljubarrota and Sempach—Turkish conquest of Balkans

1385

A **Feb**: 21st, the Rhenish and Swabian Leagues ally with the Swiss, at Constance.
Mar: 23rd, the nobles of Siena overthrow its democratic government.

B **Apr**: 6th, the Portuguese Cortes elects John, Master of Avis (and illegitimate son of Pedro I) as King of Portugal (–1433).
May: 6th, Gian Galeazzo seizes his uncle, Bernabò Visconti, and takes control of Milan.
21st, Clement invests Louis II of Anjou as King of Naples.

C **Jul**: the Scots, with French support, raid Northumberland.
Aug: Richard leads a retaliatory expedition which sacks Edinburgh.
14th, John of Portugal, with English support, decisively defeats John of Castile at Aljubarrota.

D **Dec**: 18th, the Peace of Tournai, between Philip the Bold and the weavers of Ghent, ends a period of social upheaval in Flanders.
18th, Bernabò Visconti murdered.

E The Turks take Sofia.
Timur partially conquers Azerbaijan.

1386

A **Feb**: 7th, Charles III of Durazzo, King of Naples, murdered in Hungary; succeeded by his son, Ladislas (–1414).
Mar: 4th, Jagiello of Lithuania crowned as King (Vladislav II) of Poland (–1434).

B **May**: 9th, the Treaty of Windsor, between Kings Richard and John, makes a perpetual alliance of England and Portugal.
Jun: 10th, Sigismund of Bohemia marries Mary of Hungary, whom he had rescued from Horwath, Ban of Croatia; on becoming King of Hungary (–1437), Sigismund cedes Brandenburg to Jošt, Margrave of Moravia.

C **Jul**: John of Gaunt lands at Corunna to open his campaign to win the crown of Castile.
9th, the Swiss defeat and kill Duke Leopold III of Austria at Sempach.

D **Oct**: the French council abandons its well-advanced preparations to invade England.
24th, Richard is compelled by the magnates to replace his senior ministers and appoint a commission of reform.

E Pedro of Aragon declares in favour of Clement VII.
Murād takes Nis and compels Lazar, Prince of Serbia, to become tributary.
Timur completes his conquest of Persia and sacks Tiflis, where he captures Bagrat V of Georgia. He is, however, compelled to withdraw from Azerbaijan after Tokhtamysh takes Tabriz.

1385

G **Economics, Science, Technology and Discovery**

*Leonardo Frescobaldi, account of his journey to the Near East and Egypt in 1384–85.

H **Religion and Education**

John de Burgh, chancellor of Cambridge University, *Pupilla Oculi* (manual for parish priests).

The Bohemians at Prague University gain more influence in consequence of a dispute with the Germans there.

Foundation of Heidelberg University.

J **Art, Architecture and Music**

*Chapel (in the 'flamboyant' style) in the former castle of Riom built by John, Duke of Berri.

†Wang Meng, Chinese painter.

K **Literature, Philosophy and Scholarship**

Baldasarre (Marchione Stefani), *Istoria fiorentina* (a chronicle of Florence from the Creation to 1385).

1386

F **Law and Politics**

Philip of Burgundy forms the 'chamber' in Flanders (origin of the judicial councils of Flanders, Brabant and Holland).

H **Religion and Education**

*Foundation of Windesheim (Augustinian) Abbey, near Zwolle; it became the centre of the mystical *devotio moderna* (–1374).

J **Art, Architecture and Music**

Gian Galeazzo Visconti lays the foundation stone of Milan Cathedral.

K **Literature, Philosophy and Scholarship**

López de Ayala, *Libro de las avas de caça* (Castilian treatise on falconry).

L **Births and Deaths**

— Donatello b. (–1466).

A **Jan**: 1st, death of Charles II the Bad, King of Navarre; succeeded by his son, Charles III (–1425).

5th, death of Pedro IV the Ceremonious, King of Aragon; succeeded by his son, John I (–1395).

B **Apr**: 8th, Louis, Duke of Touraine, brother of Charles VI, marries Valentina, daughter of Gian Galeazzo Visconti of Milan; she was to succeed to her father's dominions if he had no son.

May: in the Treaty of Troncoso, John of Castile makes a marriage alliance with John of Gaunt, who has abandoned his campaign in Galicia.

C **Aug**: 3rd, death of Olaf of Denmark and Norway; his mother, Margaret, elected to continue as regent in both countries for her lifetime (–1412).

25th, at Nottingham, Richard receives favourable answers to his questions to the judges about his prerogative powers.

D **Oct**: 19th, Gian Galeazzo takes Verona; Antonio della Scala, its ruler, flees.

22nd, Vicenza surrenders to Gian Galeazzo.

Nov: Timur destroys Isfahan.

17th, Richard accepts the demands of the Duke of Gloucester and Earls of Arundel and Warwick to call a Parliament to try his ministers whom they have impeached.

Dec: 20th, Henry, Earl of Derby, defeats Richard's supporter, Robert de Vere, Earl of Oxford, at Radcot Bridge, Oxfordshire. The magnates are reported to have considered deposing Richard at this time.

E Louis II of Anjou gains the Kingdom of Naples following the flight, because of a revolt, of Ladislas and his mother, Margaret, the regent (–1399).

Jagiello receives the homage of the rulers of Moldavia.

Tokhtamysh invades Transoxiana but fails to take Bukhāra; Timur retaliates by ravaging Khorezm.

H **Religion and Education**

†Sāyana, commentaries on the Veda (?same as Mādhava, author of *Sarvadarśana-samgraha*; summary of Hindu philosophies).

J **Art, Architecture and Music**

Jagiello founds Vilna Cathedral, the first in Lithuania (following its conversion).

K **Literature, Philosophy and Scholarship**

Jean d'Arras, *L'histoire de Lusignan* (prose romance on the Mélusine—fairy-wife—theme).

John de Trevisa, translation of the *Polychronicon* of Ranulf Higden (–1352) into English (one of the first sustained examples of native English prose; –1482).

*Geoffrey Chaucer begins *The Canterbury Tales* (–1475).

L **Births and Deaths**

Sept. 16th(?), Henry V b. (–1422).

1388–1389 The Merciless Parliament—Battle of Kosova—Collapse of Javanese Empire

1388

A **Feb**: 3rd, the 'Merciless Parliament' meets and convicts Richard's courtiers accused by the Lords Appellant (Gloucester, Warwick, Arundel, Derby and Norfolk), who take control of the government.

B **Apr**: 9th, the Swiss defeat Duke Albert III of Austria at Näfels.
May: 2nd, Nerio Acciajuoli of Corinth takes the Acropolis of Athens.

C **Aug**: 5th, James, Earl of Douglas, killed while defeating Henry Percy ('Hotspur') at Otterburn ('Chevy Chase'), Northumberland.
23rd, the count of Württemberg defeats the Swabian League at Döffingen.
Sep: 20th, death of Fīrūz of Delhi; succeeded by his grandson, Tughluq II (–1389).

D **Oct**: 28th, Charles VI announces his intention to rule; in practice he is dependent on old councillors of Charles V (*Les Marmousets*).
Nov: 6th, Rupert, the Elector Palatine, defeats the Rhenish League at Worms.
24th, Gian Galeazzo takes Padua.

1389

A **Feb**: 19th, Abū-Bakr revolts and deposes Tughluq of Delhi (–1390).
24th, defeat and capture of Albert of Sweden at Falköping; Margaret of Denmark now accepted as ruler of Sweden (–1412).

B **Apr**: 1st, Albert of Austria recognises the recent Swiss conquests in the Treaty of Zurich.
May: 3rd, Richard resumes personal government.
5th, Wenceslas promulgates a Public Peace for south Germany to end the wars between princes and towns.
19th, death of Dmitri of Moscow, Grand Duke of Vladimir; succeeded by his son, Vasili I (–1425).
Jun: 15th, Murād I killed in defeating the Serbians at Kossovopolje (*or* Kosova); succeeded by his son, Bāyezīd I (–1403). Lazar of Serbia also killed; in the disintegration of his dominions, Montenegro becomes independent.

D **Oct**: 15th, death of Pope Urban VI (of Rome).
Nov: 2nd, Pietro Tomacelli elected as Pope Boniface IX (–1404).

E Jagiello receives homage from the rulers of Wallachia and Bessarabia.
Tokhtamysh campaigns inconclusively against Timur in central Asia.
Death of Rajasanagara, King of Java (from 1350); his empire—almost the whole of modern Indonesia—now collapses.

1388

G **Economics, Science, Technology and Discovery**

The Hanse puts an embargo on trade with Flanders (–1392). It also makes a treaty with English merchants, permitting their return to Danzig (Gdansk) and other Prussian towns (–1400).

The Statute of Cambridge empowers Justices of the Peace to regulate wages.

H **Religion and Education**

Cologne University founded.

J **Art, Architecture and Music**

Nave of S. Petronio, Bologna (–1440).

K **Literature, Philosophy and Scholarship**

Honoré Bonet, *L'Arbre de batailles* (on war and its ethics; the layman's version of Legnano's *Tractatus*; –1360).

†Antonio Pucci, *Le Noie* (didactic poem); *Fiore di leggende cantari antichi* (lyrics and narrative poems); *Della Guerra di Pisa Confortando Lucca* (historical poem); and *Istorie* (tales in verse).

L **Births and Deaths**

— Stefano Masuccio d. (97).

— Torquemada b. (–1468).

1389

G **Economics, Science, Technology and Discovery**

First German paper-mill, at Nuremburg, founded by Nicholas Stromer.

H **Religion and Education**

†Taftāzani, commentary on the creed of Islam.

Foundation of Buda University.

J **Art, Architecture and Music**

Mausoleum of Fīrūz Shāh Tughluq, Old Delhi.

Claus Sluter, Portal and Well of Moses (sculpture), Champnol Charterhouse, Dijon (–1404).

K **Literature, Philosophy and Scholarship**

Philippe de Mézières, *Le Songe du vieil pelerin* (*The Song of the Old Pilgrim*; allegory of travel in Europe, Africa and Asia).

*Johannes de Hese, *Itinerarium ad Jerusalem per diversas mundi partes* (fantasy of travel in Asia, with tales from Arabian Nights).

L **Births and Deaths**

— Cosimo de' Medici b. (–1464).

— Hāfiz d. (69).

1390

A **Feb**: assassination of Che Bong Nga, King of Champa; his conquests in Dai Viet are abandoned by his successor, La Khai (–1400).

B **Apr**: Gian Galeazzo declares war against Florence and Bologna.
19th, death of Robert II of Scotland; succeeded by his son, Robert III (–1406).
Jun: 19th, Francesco da Carrara recovers Padua from the Milanese.

C **Aug**: Louis II of Anjou enters Naples.

D **Oct**: 9th, death of John I of Castile and Leon; succeeded by his son, Henry III (–1406), and civil warfare.
Dec: Muhammad, the son of Fīrūz, establishes himself as King of Delhi after expelling Abū Bakr (–1393).

E Robert III's brother, Alexander ('the Wolf of Badenoch'), burns Elgin Cathedral.

1391

A **Feb**: 16th, death of the Greek Emperor, John V Palaeologus; succeeded by his son, Manuel II (–1425).
24th, Charles VI cancels plans for a French expedition to Rome and Naples in expectation of a personal interview with Richard, who had threatened to attack France if Charles invaded Italy.

B **Jun**: 18th, Timur defeats Tokhtamysh on the Kondurcha but does not pursue him west of the Volga.

C **Jul**: 25th, John, Count of Armagnac, who was employed by Florence, defeated and killed by the Milanese outside Alessandria.

E Queen Maria of Sicily marries Martin of Aragon, who becomes King (–1409).
Vasili II of Moscow annexes Nizhni-Novgorod.

1390

F **Law and Politics**

An ordinance of Richard II permits only lords to grant liveries to their retainers.

*Jean Boutillier, *Somme Rurale* (synthesis of French regional legal customs).

*Jaques d'Ableiges, final form of *Le Grand Coutumier de France* (legal compilation).

G **Economics, Science, Technology and Discovery**

Illustration of a European tower-mill (a windmill which could be turned to catch the wind).

Simone Sigoli, *Viaggio al Monte Sinai* (account of his journey with Frescobaldi; –1385).

H **Religion and Education**

English anti-papal statutes of *Praemunire* and Provisors (–1353, 1351).

†Matthias of Cracow, *Speculum aureum de titulis beneficiorum*; *De squaloribus curiae Romanae* (anti-papal treatises by a Bohemian reformer).

K **Literature, Philosophy and Scholarship**

John Gower, *Confessio Amantis* (long English poem, the narrative embodying many stories from classical and later sources; printed by Caxton in 1481).

**Miracles de Notre-Dame par personnages* (collection of 42 French miracle plays by different anonymous authors).

Al-Ahmedī, *Iskandar-namā* (Turkish epic poem about Alexander the Great).

†Albert of Saxony, commentaries on Aristotle and Ockham (–1349).

L **Births and Deaths**

—Humphrey of Gloucester b. (–1447).

1391

H **Religion and Education**

Foundation of the Bethlehem Chapel, Prague, for preaching in Czech.

Jews in Spain massacred or forcibly converted to Christianity.

Ferrara University founded.

K **Literature, Philosophy and Scholarship**

†Gaston Phoebus, Count of Foix, *Le déduits de chasse* (or *Le Miroir de Phoebus*; on hunting; –1410).

**The Book of Ballymote* (mss. of Irish poetry and prose).

*Manuel Chrysoloras of Constantinople holds the first west European chair of Greek, at Florence (–1400).

L **Births and Deaths**

May 26th, Charles of Orleans b. (–1465).

1392

A **Jan**: Gian Galeazzo makes peace with Florence and her allies at Genoa.

B **Apr**: 11th, Florence, Bologna, Padua, Ferrara, etc., form the League of Bologna for mutual defence against Gian Galeazzo.

Jun: 13th, John of Brittany instigates an attempt to murder Oliver de Clisson, Constable of France.

C **Aug**: Charles becomes insane while leading an expedition towards Brittany; the Dukes of Burgundy and Berri take control of his government and dismiss the 'Marmousets' (–1388).

D **Oct**: 21st, Pietro Gambacorta, ruler of Pisa, killed in a riot instigated by Jacopo d'Appiano, who succeeds him.

E Death of Muhammad V of Granada; succeeded by his son, Yūsuf II (–1396).

Timur takes Baghdād.

A period of feudal warfare in Japan (since 1336) ends with the abdication of the southern emperor in favour of the northern emperor (at Kyōto), who is still controlled by the Ashikaga Shoguns (–1568).

Yi Sŏng-gye, a Korean general, usurps the throne, ending the Koryō dynasty and founding the Yi dynasty (–1910); he recognises Chinese supremacy.

1393

A **Jan**: 20th, death of Muhammad of Delhi; succeeded by his son Sikandar.

Mar: 8th, Sikandar dies and is succeeded by his brother, Mahmūd (–1413); the kingdom of Delhi is dissolving in feudal anarchy.

20th, John of Pomuk, vicar-general of Prague, murdered by Wenceslas.

C **Jul**: 10th, in the Covenant of Sempach, the Swiss Confederation regulates its military organisation.

Aug: 10th, Henry of Castile begins his personal rule.

D **Nov**: 29th, death, in Paris, of Leo VI, the last King of Armenia.

E The Turks complete their conquest of Bulgaria.

Timur campaigns against 'the Golden Horde' in Russia, reaching Moscow; he also completes his conquest of Persia and Iraq, extinguishing the last independent Mongol dynasties.

1392

G **Economics, Science, Technology and Discovery**

The Hanseatic League recovers its privileges in Flanders and Novgorod by placing embargoes on trade with them.

Earliest known use, in Korea, of metal movable type for printing.

*Playing cards printed with blocks for Charles VI.

H **Religion and Education**

*Tsong Kapa founds the reformed order of Tibetan Lamas, the S'a-ser ('Yellow Hats').

J **Art, Architecture and Music**

Façade of Lyons Cathedral.

K **Literature, Philosophy and Scholarship**

Geoffrey Chaucer, *Treatise on the Astrolabe* (in English; 'for little Lewis my son').

Giovanni Conversini appointed professor of rhetoric at Padua University.

1393

F **Law and Politics**

Yi Sŏng-gye reinstitutes the examination system for the Korean civil service (on the Chinese model); Confucianism has official acceptance while Buddhism declines and is partially suppressed.

The Ming army consists of 493 guard units (of 5,600 men each) under the Ministry of War.

G **Economics, Science, Technology and Discovery**

Population registers record 60,000,000 Chinese in 10,000,000 households, and land registers show 129,000,000 acres in use.

H **Religion and Education**

'The Great' Statute of *Praemunire*.

L **Births and Deaths**

Apr. 21st, John Capgrave b. (–1464).

1394

A **Jan**: 11th, Ladislas of Naples recognises Nerio Acciajuoli as Duke of Athens, which he had won from the Catalans.

B **Apr**: 12th, the Turks take Salonika.
May: Malik Sarvar founds the Muslim kingdom of Jaunpur, on the middle Ganges (–1479).
8th, the 'League of the Lords' in Bohemia temporarily arrests Wenceslas.
Jun: 7th, death of Anne of Bohemia, Richard II's queen.

C **Sep**: 16th, death of Clement VII, the Pope at Avignon.
28th, Peter de Luna elected to succeed him, as Benedict XIII (–1417).

D **Oct**: 2nd, Richard lands at Waterford at the start of his expedition to Ireland.

E Bāyezīd's conquest of the Karamans of Rūm is recognised in the grant to him of the title of Sultan by the Caliph of Egypt.
Yi Sŏng-gye establishes the Korean capital at Seoul.

1395

A **Feb**: Charles holds a council of the French clergy who endorse a proposal that both Popes should resign; Benedict XIII refuses to comply.

B **Apr**: 15th, Timur defeats Tokhtamysh on the Terek.
May: 11th, Wenceslas sells the title of Duke of Milan to Gian Galeazzo.
15th, Richard leaves Dublin for England, having received the submission of the Irish chieftains.
17th, death of Mary, Queen of Hungary; some Hungarians support the claims of Ladislas of Naples against her husband, Sigismund.
17th, the Hungarians and Wallachians defeat the Turks at Rovine; but Wallachia becomes tributary to the Turks, who also conquer the Dobrudja.
19th, death of John I of Aragon; succeeded by his brother, Martin I (–1410).
Jun: 17th, Margaret of Denmark and Norway releases and makes peace with Albert of Sweden by the Treaty of Lindholm; Stockholm is given to the Hanse, which had mediated, as a guarantee for the peace.

C **Aug**: 26th, Timur abandons his campaign against Moscow, having destroyed the economy of 'the Golden Horde'.

E Vitold of Lithuania seizes Smolensk.
Timur takes Erzinjan and Sivas, in Anatolia.

1394

G **Economics, Science, Technology and Discovery**

Antonio de Montulmo, *De iudiciis nativitatum* (textbook on astrology).

H **Religion and Education**

†Matthias of Janov, a famous Czech preacher, *De regulis veteris et novi testamenti* (critical of the Church).

J **Art, Architecture and Music**

Westminster Hall (architect: Henry Yevele; –1400).

*Nave of Winchester Cathedral (architect: William Wynford).

K **Literature, Philosophy and Scholarship**

**Le Ménagier de Paris* (a handbook of instruction for a wife by her anonymous husband, on domestic, moral and ethical matters, including cooking).

†Luigi Marsigli founds a humanist group at San Spirito, Florence.

L **Births and Deaths**

Mar. 4th, Henry the Navigator b. (–1460).

1395

H **Religion and Education**

*Union of the Nizāmīyah and Mustansīryah colleges, Baghdād (–1065, 1234).

K **Literature, Philosophy and Music**

*Franco Sacchetti, *Lyrics* (*ballate*; *madrigale*; including perhaps the first example of a burlesque heroic poem, *The Battle of the Young and Old*).

**Trecento Novelle* (collection of amusing short stories and witty dialogues, with moral reflections; about 258 extant).

L **Births and Deaths**

Mar. —, John Barbour d. (79?).

1396

A **Mar**: 12th, a treaty of truce for 28 years made between France and England; Charles' daughter, Isabella, betrothed to Richard.

B **Apr**: 2nd, John of Jenstein resigns as Archbishop of Prague, the outcome of a dispute between Wenceslas and the Bohemian clergy, whom he is attempting to subject. At about the same time, Wenceslas, through Sigismund's mediation, is obliged to allow the lords of Bohemia and Moravia control over his government.

C **Sep**: 25th, the Turks destroy the crusading army of Sigismund and his western allies at Nicopolis.
29th, France and Florence make an alliance to partition the Duchy of Milan.

D **Oct**: 27th, Charles and Richard meet near Calais.
Nov: 4th, Richard marries Isabella.
27th, the French take possession of Genoa, which had surrendered itself to Charles to end its internal strife (–1409).

E Yūsuf II of Granada succeeded by his son, Muhammad VII (–1408).
Pedro Bordo de San Superano, commander of the Navarrese Company, usurps the Principality of the Morea.

1397

A **Mar**: Gian Galeazzo's forces invade Mantuan territory.

B **Jun**: 12th, the English garrison evacuates Brest by treaty with John of Brittany.
17th, Margaret holds an assembly of Scandinavian nobles at Calmar for the coronation of her grand-nephew, Eric (VII) of Pomerania, as King of Denmark, Norway and Sweden (the 'Calmar Union'; –1436, 1439, 1448).

C **Jul**: 10th, Richard arrests the Duke of Gloucester and the Earls of Arundel and Warwick.
Aug: the League of Bologna defeats the Milanese at Governolo.
Sep: 29th, Richard holds a Parliament which condemns the actions of the Lords Appellant in 1387–8; Arundel is executed and Warwick imprisoned; Gloucester had already (presumably) been murdered.

E 'The Golden Horde' deposes Tokhtamysh as Khan and elects Timur-Kutlugh, with Edigey actually ruling (–1400). Vitold of Lithuania invades the Ukraine as Tokhtamysh's ally (–1399).

1396

H **Religion and Education**

†Walter Hilton, the *Scale of Perfection* (religious instructions written in the vernacular for laymen by an English mystic).

Gian Galeazzo Visconti founds the Charterhouse, Pavia.

J **Art, Architecture and Music**

Mīr 'Ali of Tabriz makes an illuminated copy of the *Khwājū Kirmānī*.

*John Siferwas, Sherborne Missal and Lectionary (illuminated mss.).

L **Births and Deaths**

Apr. 4th, George of Trebizond b. (–1484).

June 5th, Giannozzo Manetti b. (–1459).

June 30th, Philip the Good b. (–1467).

July 31st, William Courtenay, Archbishop of Canterbury, d.

— Antonio Bettini b. (–1487).

1397

F **Law and Politics**

First publication of *Ta-Ming lü* (*Laws of the Great Ming*; comprehensive code of Chinese criminal and administrative law).

H **Religion and Education**

Jagiello revives Cracow University with a new foundation (–1364).

J **Art, Architecture and Music**

The Wilton Diptych (painting of Richard II and other figures).

The Golden Pavilion, outside Kyōto (burnt 1952).

†Francesco Landino, composer and organist; invented new type of clavier, the *serena serenorum*.

K **Literature, Philosophy and Scholarship**

Gasparino da Barzizza, considered the greatest Latin scholar of his time, appointed professor of rhetoric at Padua (–1422).

L **Births and Deaths**

— Paolo del Pozzo Toscanelli b. (–1482).

— Henry of Langenstein d.

— Pisanello b. (–*c.* 1450).

— Paolo Uccello b. (–1475).

1398

A **Jan**: 31st, Richard holds a Parliament at Shrewsbury which extends his powers by appointing a commission to continue its work and granting him the wool customs for life.

B **Apr**: 5th, the Teutonic Knights take Visby, Gothland.
May: Pīr Muhammad, Timur's grandson, takes Multān, in the Punjab.
11th, Gian Galeazzo makes a truce for ten years with Francesco Gonzaga of Mantua.
14th, a council of the French clergy assembles; it proposes to withhold taxes due to Benedict to force him to resign.

C **Jul**: 28th, Charles announces France's withdrawal from obedience to Benedict; Henry of Castile follows to do likewise.
Sep: death of Jacopo d'Appiano, ruler of Pisa; his son, Gherardo, succeeds with support from Gian Galeazzo.
Timur invades the Punjab.
16th, Richard stops a judicial duel between the Dukes of Hereford and Norfolk and sends both into exile.

D **Dec**: 18th, Timur sacks Delhi.

E Vasili of Moscow defeated in an attempt to annex Novgorod.
Death of Hung-wu, founder of the Ming dynasty.

1399

A **Jan.–Mar**: Timur continues his massacres and ravages in India, causing a famine.
Feb: 3rd, death of John of Gaunt, Duke of Lancaster; Richard confiscates his estates and sentences his son, Henry, Duke of Hereford, to exile for life.
19th, Gian Galeazzo buys Pisa from Gherardo d'Appiano.

B **Jun**: 1st, Richard lands at Waterford on his second Irish expedition.

C **Jul**: 4th, Henry lands at Ravenspur, Yorkshire, and raises a rebellion against Richard, who therefore abandons his Irish expedition.
17th, death of Jadwiga, 'King' of Poland, without issue.
Aug: 5th, 'the Golden Horde' defeats Vitold's Lithuanian and Russian army on the Vorskla.
19th, Richard surrenders to Henry at Flint.
Sep: 6th, Siena accepts the lordship of Gian Galeazzo.
29th, Richard abdicates and is declared deposed in a quasi-parliamentary assembly; Henry of Lancaster claims and receives the crown, as Henry IV (–1413).

D **Oct**: 13th, coronation of Henry IV; in preparation, he founds the Order of the Bath.

E Louis II of Anjou expelled from Naples and Ladislas accepted as King.
Manuel begins his journey from Constantinople to Venice, Paris and London to seek western aid against the Turks.

1398

G Economics, Science, Technology and Discovery

John of Trevisa, translation into English of *On the properties of things* of Bartholomew the Englishman (–1240).

Shên Chi-sun, *Mo fa chi yao* (illustrated treatise on manufacture of ink).

*Pietro de Tossignano, *Receptae super nonum Almansoris* (textbook of therapeutics and *materia medica*); *Consilium pro peste evitanda* (*How to escape the Black Death*, by avoiding contagion, etc.).

H Religion and Education

Gian Galeazzo Visconti suppresses Pavia University and refounds Piacenza University (–1412).

*Pier Paolo Vergerio, *De Ingenuis Moribus et Liberalibus Studiis* (first humanist treatise on education).

K Literature, Philosophy and Scholarship

Honoré Bonet, *L'Apparicion maistre Jehan de Meun* (poem on the author's times).

Formation of the Confrérie de la Passion (to perform religious plays), Paris.

L Births and Deaths

— Inigo López de Mendoza b. (–1458).

— Juliano Cesarini b. (–1444).

1399

H Religion and Education

†Nicholas Eymeric, *Directorium inquisitorum* (manual for inquisitors).

K Literature, Philosophy and Scholarship

Christine de Pisan, *Épître au dieu d'amour* (in defence of women; translated into English by Thomas Hoccleve –1402).

L Births and Deaths

— Peter Parler d.

— Pier Candido Decembrio b. (–1477).

Gian Galeazzo threatens Florence—Timur in Syria

A **Jan**: 5th, a conspiracy by the Earls of Huntingdon, Kent and Salisbury fails in an attempt to murder Henry IV.

21st, Perugia accepts Gian Galeazzo's lordship, as, soon afterwards, do Assisi, Lucca and Spoleto.

Feb: 14th(?), death (by murder?) of Richard II.

Mar: 20th, Charles orders the patrons of French benefices to accept his nominees during the withdrawal of obedience from Benedict XIII.

21st, Gian Galeazzo makes peace with Venice, thus isolating Florence.

C **Aug**: 14th–29th, Henry campaigns in Scotland.

21st, the Rhenish Electors elect Rupert III of the Palatinate as King of the Romans (–1410) in place of Wenceslas, whom they declare deposed.

Sep: 16th, Owain Glyn Dwr begins his revolt.

24th, his first raids into England checked by his defeat by local English levies, at Welshpool.

D **Oct**: Henry campaigns in North Wales.

Dec: 1st, Michele Steno succeeds Antonio Vernieri as Doge of Venice (–1413).

E Henry of Castile sends a punitive expedition against North African pirates which takes Tetuan.

Timur defeats the Egyptians at Aleppo and Damascus, and sacks the cities of Syria.

Death of Timur-Kutlugh, Khan of 'the Golden Horde'; succeeded by Shadibeg, with Egidey continuing to rule (–1407).

Le Quy Ly deposes the last Tran Emperor of Dai Viet and becomes Emperor with the name Ho Quy; after eight months he abdicates in favour of his son, Ho Han Thuong (–1407).

F **Law and Politics**

Salutati, *De tyrrano* (humanist treatise on tyranny).

†Baldo degli Ubaldi, *Summula respiciens facta mercatorum* (treatise on mercantile law); commentaries on Roman and canon law.

G **Economics, Science, Technology and Discovery**

*The introduction of herring curing enables the Dutch of Brill to rival the Hanseatic merchants' fish trade; the Hanse is also hampered by the migration of herring from the Baltic during the fifteenth century.

*Hops introduced to England.

*Cannon first made of cast iron.

H **Religion and Education**

†*John Mirk, Prior of Lilleshall, *Instructions for Parish Priests* (1,934 lines of English verse); *Manuale Sacerdotis* (a more elaborate and learned work on the same theme); *Festiall* (sermons in English).

J **Art, Architecture and Music**

*Façade ('flamboyant') of Rouen Cathedral.

K **Literature, Philosophy and Scholarship**

*Jean Froissart, *Chronicles* (1307–1400; continued to 1467 by two others; translated by Lord Berners as *The Cronycles of England, Fraunce, Spayne*—1525).

*Climente Sánchez de Vercial, *Libro de los Gatos* (prose fables and satires, or *Enxemplos*, compiled from earlier books for the use of preachers).

*Jean le Maingre (known as 'Boucicaut') originates and contributes to *Les Cent Ballades*, written by princes and nobles at the court of Charles VI.

*Lo Kuan-chung, *San Kuo* (Chinese romance).

*Juliana Berners, *Treatyse perteynynge to Hawkynge*, *Huntyng* (printed 1486).

†Jean d'Outremeuse (*alias* Desprez), *Myreur des histors* (verse history from the Flood, partly fictional); *Geste de Liège* (*chanson de geste* on history of Bishopric of Liège).

†David ap Gwilym, Welsh poetry.

L **Births and Deaths**

Oct. 25th, Geoffrey Chaucer d. (*c.*60)

— Henry Yevele d. (*c.* 80).

— Theodore of Gaza b. (–1478).

— Luca della Robbia b. (–1482).

1401

A **Jan**: 18th, Jagiello agrees that his lieutenant-governor of Lithuania, Vitold, son of Kiejstut, should be its Grand Duke, as his vassal, for life (–1430).
Mar: Giovanni Bentivoglio proclaims himself lord of Bologna (–1402).
24th, Timur sacks Damascus.

B **Spring**: Wenceslas, after being besieged in Prague Castle by the 'League of the Lords', accepts a permanent committee of nobles to govern Bohemia with him.

C **Jul**: 9th, Timur destroys Baghdād to punish its revolt.
Aug: Sigismund released by the Hungarians who had imprisoned him for a few months.
5th, Amadeus VIII of Savoy acquires the Génevois.

D **Oct**: Henry's second Welsh campaign fails to crush the revolt.
Rupert, subsidised by Florence, repulsed by the Milanese garrison in an attempt to take Brescia.

1402

A **Feb**: Henry of Castile, on popular demand, resumes the country's obedience to Benedict.

B **Spring**: Sigismund imprisons his brother, Wenceslas.
May: 25th, death of Maria, Queen of Sicily; her husband, Martin, rules alone.
Jun: 22nd, Glyn Dwr defeats and captures Edmund Mortimer at Pilleth in Maelienydd.
26th, Gian Galeazzo defeats the forces of Florence and Bologna at Casalecchio.
27th, Bologna surrenders to him, recognising his lordship; Giovanni Bentivoglio murdered.

C **Jul**: 28th, Timur defeats the Ottoman Turks near Ankara; Bāyezid captured. Timur next takes Brusa.
Aug: the Earl of Northumberland and Henry 'Hotspur' defeat Scottish forces invading England at Humbledon Hill.
Sep: Henry IV again campaigns, without effect, in Wales.
3rd, death of Gian Galeazzo Visconti, first Duke of Milan; succeeded by his son, Giovanni Maria (–1412), with a Regency. Anarchy breaks out in Lombardy while the war against Florence ends.

D **Dec**: Timur expels the Hospitallers from Smyrna.

E Henry of Castile sends an expedition to conquer the Canary Islands; it fails (–1425).
The Teutonic Knights purchase the Neumark of Brandenburg from Sigismund; the Order's lands now extend from the Oder to the Narva.

1401

H **Religion and Education**

Statute *De Heretico Comburendo*; William Sawtry is the first Lollard to be burnt at Smithfield (2 Mar.).

†*Thomas of Štítný, *Books of Christian Instruction*; *Learned Entertainments* (Czech treatises for religious instruction).

J **Art, Architecture and Music**

The manufacture of decorated glassware in Syria ends as a result of Timur's ravages.

L **Births and Deaths**

— Nicholas of Cusa b. (–1464).

— Tommaso Masaccio b. (–1428).

1402

H **Religion and Education**

John Hus appointed to the Bethlehem Chapel, Prague.

J **Art, Architecture and Music**

Town Hall, Brussels (–1454).

Seville Cathedral (–1517).

K **Literature, Philosophy and Scholarship**

Thomas Hoccleve translates Christine de Pisan's *Épître au dieu d'amour* (–1399).

L **Births and Deaths**

— Denis the Carthusian b. (–1471).

1403

A **Jan or Feb**: Antonio I, son of Nerio Acciujuoli, takes the Acropolis from the Venetians who are now ruling the Duchy of Athens.

Mar: 8th, death in captivity of the Ottoman Sultan, Bāyezīd I; succeeded by his sons, Sulaymān (–1411) and Muhammad I (–1421).

11th, Benedict escapes from Avignon, where the French had been besieging him.

B **May**: 30th, France resumes its obedience to Benedict.

Jun: 3rd, Valais accedes to the Swiss Confederation.

C **Jul**: 6th, Glyn Dwr captures Carmarthen Castle.

21st, Henry defeats and kills Henry 'Hotspur' at Shrewsbury, so ending his revolt.

Aug: 5th, Ladislas of Naples crowned as King of Hungary, but soon withdraws from Hungary.

Sep: 29th, Henry recovers Carmarthen Castle.

D **Autumn**: Wenceslas escapes from Vienna to Bohemia and regains authority there.

Dec: Glyn Dwr takes Cardiff.

E Yung-lo, son of Hung-wu, usurps the Chinese throne (–1424).

1404

A **Jan**: 14th, Henry holds a Parliament which constrains him to name his councillors; it grants a novel tax on land revenues (–20 Mar.).

B **Apr**: 27th, death of Philip the Bold, Duke of Burgundy; succeeded by his son, John the Fearless (–1419).

May: Vitold of Lithuania recovers possession of Smolensk.

Jun: 14th, Glyn Dwr, having won control of Wales, assumes the title of Prince of Wales and holds a parliament.

C **Jul**: 14th, he makes an alliance with France.

Aug: death of Harihara II, who had consolidated the Vijayanagar Empire (south India).

D **Oct**: 1st, death of Boniface IX, the Pope at Rome.

6th, Henry holds a Parliament at Coventry which releases him from the restrictions imposed by that of January.

17th, Cosmo Migliorato elected as Pope Innocent VII (at Rome; –1406).

Nov: 25th, in the Treaty of Flensburg, Margaret of Denmark makes peace with the Teutonic Knights and Albert of Mecklenburg, who renounces the Swedish crown.

E Francesco of Padua seizes Verona and Brescia; he is attacked by Venice, which takes Verona and Vicenza.

Timur leaves Anatolia, having reinstated the Turkish princes and thus dismembered the Ottoman Empire.

1403

H **Religion and Education**

Prague University condemns John Wycliffe's works.

J **Art, Architecture and Music**

Lorenzo Ghiberti, bronze doors of the Baptistery, Florence (–1424; 1425–52).

K **Literature, Philosophy and Scholarship**

Pedro del Corral, *Crónica del rey don Rodrigo* (a fictional narrative about the invasion of Spain by the Moors).

Yung-lo Ta-tien (traditional date for completion of this Chinese encyclopedia in 22,937 volumes, none of which is extant; 2,000 scholars employed on this compilation of all Chinese knowledge).

*Frederigo Frezzi, *Quadiregio* (didactic narrative and theological poem in imitation of Dante: the progress of man through the four kingdoms—of love, Satan, the vices and the virtues).

†*Al-Shamī, *Zafar-nāma* (official biography of Timur, in Persian).

L **Births and Deaths**

Feb. 22nd, Charles VII b. (–1461).

— Bessarion of Trebizond b. (–1472).

1404

G **Economics, Science, Technology and Discovery**

First notice of an Archimedean screw driven by a windmill for drainage, in Holland.

J **Art, Architecture and Music**

Conrad of Soest, altarpiece (painting), Niederwildungen.

K **Literature, Philosophy and Scholarship**

Christine de Pisan, *Le Livre des faicts et bonnes meurs du sage roi Charles (V)*.

L **Births and Deaths**

Sept. 27th, William of Wykeham, Bishop of Winchester d. (82).

— George Châtelain b. (–1474).

— Domenico Capranica b. (–1458).

— Leone Battista Alberti b. (–1472).

1405

A **Feb:** 19th, Timur dies while leading an expedition to China; his heirs retain only Transoxiana and Khurāsān, with his son, Shāh Rūkh, ruling (eventually) from Herat (–1447). The Mamlūks recover Syria, the dynasty of Black Sheep Turkomans from Azerbaijan establish a dominion from eastern Anatolia to Baghdād, and the Safawi dynasty appears in Persia.

Mar: 11th, John Talbot defeats Glyn Dwr at Grosmont, Monmouthshire.

B **May:** 5th, Prince Henry defeats Glyn Dwr at Usk.

29th, a rebellion against Henry IV led by Richard Scrope, Archbishop of York, collapses on his arrest.

Jun: 8th, execution of Archbishop Scrope.

C **Aug:** the Dukes of Orleans and Burgundy raise armies against each other; Burgundy enters Paris and assumes control of the French government.

Glyn Dwr, with French military assistance, takes Carmarthen.

Sep: Henry IV recovers Carmarthen in an otherwise ineffective campaign.

14th, John, Archbishop of Mainz, and other princes form the alliance of Marbach against Rupert.

D **Oct:** 16th, Burgundy and Orleans make a truce.

Nov: Francesco Carrara II of Padua surrenders to Venice.

12th, Mallū Khan, the effective ruler of the diminished kingdom of Delhi, killed in his defeat by Khizr Khan, the Mongol ruler of the Punjab, near Pāk Pattan.

E Yung-lo, Emperor of China, recognises Paramesvara, founder of Malacca, as its King. (On his conversion to Islam, Paramesvara took the name of Megat Iskander Shah).

1406

A **Feb:** 17th, Francesco Carrara murdered in prison.

Mar: 1st, a parliament called by Henry IV meets at Westminster.

30th, James of Scotland captured by the English at sea while on his way to France.

B **Apr:** 4th, death of Robert III of Scotland; succeeded by his son, James I (–1437), during whose captivity in England his uncle, Robert, Duke of Albany, is regent (–1420).

C **Jun:** 18th, Innocent VII excommunicates Ladislas of Naples and declares him deprived of his kingdom.

D **Oct:** the Duke of Orleans invades Gascony in an unsuccessful campaign against the English.

9th, Florence annexes Pisa.

Nov: 6th, death of Innocent VII, the Pope at Rome.

30th, Angelo Correr elected as Pope Gregory XII (at Rome; –1415).

Dec: 22nd, Henry dismisses parliament, the longest ever held in medieval England; it had withheld grants of taxation until Henry announced the names of his councillors and accepted regulations for their conduct.

25th or 26th, death of Henry III of Castile; succeeded by his infant son, John II (–1454).

E Outbreak of war between Vitold of Lithuania and Vasili of Moscow.

Hūshang murders his father, Dilāvar Khan, governor of Mālwa, and declares himself its King (–1435).

1405

G **Economics, Science, Technology and Discovery**

The city of Lübeck constructs the Elbe–Trave canal.

Cheng Ho leads Chinese naval expeditions to south east Asia, Burma, India, Ceylon, east Africa and, possibly, Australia (–1433; –1436, 1451).

†Konrad Kyeser, *Bellifortis* (illustrated manual on military technology, in Latin verse; includes section on hydraulics and water-supply).

J **Art, Architecture and Music**

Peter von Prachatitz becomes the architect for Vienna Cathedral.

†The Rigistān (Timur's mausoleum), Samarqand.

'Abd-al-Qādir, *Jāmi' al-Alhān* (*Compiler of melodies*; Arabic treatise on Persian music).

K **Literature, Philosophy and Scholarship**

Johann von Tepl, *Ackerman aus Böhmen* (*Death and the Ploughman*; dialogue influenced by Italian humanist models).

†Timur played 'the greater game' of chess (with 110 squares); al-Tabrizī, a notable player at his court, described the game.

L **Births and Deaths**

Oct. 18th, Aeneas Silvius Piccolomini (Pius II) b. (–1464).

— Muhammad al-Damīrī d. (61).

— Lorenzo Valla b. (–1457).

1406

G **Economics, Science, Technology and Discovery**

Chu Hsiao, *Chiu huang pên ts'ao* (*Herbal to relieve famine*; illustrated herbal describing 414 species).

†*Eustace Deschamps, *Demonstrations contre sortileges* (French treatise against necromancy).

J **Art, Architecture and Music**

*Jacopo della Quercia, Caretto Tomb, Lucca Cathedral.

K **Literature, Philosophy and Scholarship**

†Ibn-Khaldūn, *Muqaddamah* (unique work on philosophy of history); history of the Arabs, Persians and Berbers.

L **Births and Deaths**

Jan. —, Claus Sluter d.

May 4th, Coluccio Salutati d. (75).

— Giovanni Conversini d. (59).

— Maffeo Vegio b. (–1458).

1407

A **Mar**: death of Francesco di Gonzaga of Mantua; succeeded by his son, Giovanni Francesco (–1444).

D **Nov**: 1st, Benedict XIII arrives at Savona for a meeting with Gregory XII, who excuses himself.
23rd, Louis, Duke of Orleans, murdered at the instigation of John, Duke of Burgundy.

E Edigey deposes Shadibeg and appoints Bulat-Saltan Khan of 'the Golden Horde' (–1410).
Muzaffar, the Shah of Delhi's governor, establishes the Sultanate of Gujarāt (–1583).
Yung-lo, Emperor of China, occupies Hanoi and annexes Dai Viet, extinguishing the Ho dynasty; Vietnamese resistance continues despite savage reprisals (–1418).

1408

A **Jan**: 28th, Gregory XII reaches Lucca but evades a meeting with Benedict XIII, who is at Porto Venere.
Feb: 19th, Henry Percy, Earl of Northumberland, invading from his exile in Scotland, defeated and killed at Bramham Moor.
28th, John of Burgundy returns to Paris and defends his murder of Louis of Orleans.

B **Apr**: 25th, Ladislas of Naples occupies Rome; Gregory therefore breaks off his negotiations with Benedict.
May: 11th, death of Muhammad VII, King of Granada; succeeded by his brother, Yūsuf III (–1417).
21st, a council of the French Church declares its neutrality between the rival popes.
Jun: 29th, the cardinals who had abandoned Gregory and Benedict meet at Leghorn and call for a general council of the Church to be held at Pisa.

C **Sep**: Vitold of Lithuania and Vasili of Moscow make peace, establishing their frontier along the Ugra.
23rd, John of Burgundy defeats the Bishop of Liège's rebelling subjects at Othée.

D **Dec**: Edigey unsuccessfully besieges Moscow but restores the 'Tartar Yoke'.

1407

G **Economics, Science, Technology and Discovery**

Foundation of St. George's Bank, Genoa.

†John Mirfield, *Breviarium* (medical encyclopedia).

K **Literature, Philosophy and Scholarship**

†López de Ayala, *Cronica de los reyes de Castillo* (history of Castile, by a participant, 1350–94); also *Court Rhymes*.

†Ulman Stromer, *Püchel von mein Geslechet* (chronicle of his Nuremburg family, 1349–1407).

1408

H **Religion and Education**

John Resby burnt as a Wycliffite in Scotland.

Doctrines of John Hus criticised in a Prague diocesan synod.

J **Art, Architecture and Music**

Donatello, *David* (marble statue), Florence Cathedral.

Nanni, *Isaiah* (statue), Florence Cathedral.

K **Literature, Philosophy and Scholarship**

Bogurodzico (a Battle Song—the beginning of Polish literature).

†Giovanni da Ravenna, *Rationarium vite* (autobiography of a humanist-educationalist).

L **Births and Deaths**

Jan. 6th, Bernardo Giustiniani b. (–1489).

— John Gower d. (*c.* 78).

1409

A **Jan**: the Welsh holding Harlech Castle surrender; Glyn Dwr's rebellion has now collapsed.

Mar: 25th, the general council called by the cardinals has its first session at Pisa.

B **Jun**: 5th, the Council of Pisa declares the deposition of Popes Benedict XIII and Gregory XII; the latter holds a council at Cividale.

26th, the cardinals at Pisa elect Cardinal Peter Philarges as Pope Alexander V (–1410).

C **Jul**: Venice reconquers Dalmatia from Sigismund.

24th, death of Martin of Sicily; Martin of Aragon annexes Sicily.

Sep: 3rd, the Genoese expel the French garrison.

D **Oct**: Ladislas expelled from the Papal States. Alexander supports Louis II of Anjou in an attempt to recover Naples.

Nov: 21st, Benedict XIII holds a 'general' council at Perpignan.

E The Chinese (temporarily) conquer Ceylon.

1410

A **Jan**: Henry, Prince of Wales, and his associates take control of Henry IV's government.

B **May**: 3rd, death of Pope Alexander V.

17th, Baldassare Cossa elected as Pope John XXIII (at Rome; –1415).

18th, death of Rupert of Wittelsbach, King of the Romans.

31st, death of Martin I of Aragon, without heirs; civil war ensues (–1412).

C **Jul**: 15th, in the Great Northern War, Jagiello of Poland and Vitold of Lithuania defeat the Teutonic Knights at Tannenburg (Grunwald).

Sep: 20th, Sigismund of Luxemburg, King of Hungary, elected as King of the Romans (–1437).

D **Oct**: 1st, Jošt, Margrave of Moravia, also elected as King of the Romans (–1411).

10th, the Poles again defeat the Teutonic Knights at Koronowo.

Nov: 2nd, John of Burgundy and the partisans of the late Louis of Orleans (the 'Armagnacs') make a (temporary) treaty of peace at Bicêtre.

E Death of Balat-Saltan, Khan of 'the Golden Horde'; succeeded by Timur-Khan (–1411).

Yung-lo campaigns in Mongolia, gaining the neutrality of the (western) Oirats and defeating the (eastern) Tatars.

1409

H **Religion and Education**

Council of Pisa (*see* A, B).
Wenceslas gives control of Prague University to the Czech masters.
Foundation of Leipzig University.

L **Births and Deaths**

— Réné of Anjou b. (–1480).

1410

G **Economics, Science, Technology and Discovery**

Benedetto Rinio of Venice, *Liber de Simplicibus* (herbal).

H **Religion and Education**

Archbishop Zbyněk of Prague burns works by John Wycliffe and excommunicates John Hus.
Dietrich of Neim, *De scismate libri III* (history of the Great Schism).

J **Art, Architecture and Music**

*Paul, Hans and Hermann Limburg, *Les très riches heures du Duc de Berry.*

K **Literature, Philosophy and Scholarship**

*Edward, Duke of York, *The master of game* (English version of *Le Miroir de Phoebus*; –1391).

L **Births and Deaths**

— John Morton b. (–1500).

1411

A **Jan**: 8th, death of Jošt of Moravia, rival King of the Romans; Brandenburg thus reverts to Sigismund who (later this year) mortgages it to Frederick of Hohenzollern, Burgrave of Nuremburg, in whose family it thereafter remains (–1415).

Feb: 1st, by the Treaty of Thorn (Toruń), the Teutonic Knights make peace with Poland and Lithuania, ceding Samogitia to the latter.

17th, Sulaymān, the Ottoman ruling in Europe, defeated and killed by his brother, Mūsa.

B **May**: 9th, Louis of Anjou defeats Ladislas of Naples at Roccasecca, then withdraws to France.

C **Jul**: 21st, Sigismund again, but unanimously, elected King of the Romans.

D **Nov**: 8th, John of Burgundy, supported by an English contingent, defeats the Armagnacs attempting to take Paris at St. Cloud.

Dec: Henry IV resumes control of his government.

E Timur-Khan assumes personal power and defeats Edigey, but is soon expelled by Jalāl-ad-Dīn, son of Tokhtamysh, who is supported by Vitold of Lithuania; the disintegration of 'the Golden Horde' thus continues (–1502).

1412

B **May**: 16th, Giovanni Visconti, Duke of Milan, murdered; succeeded by his brother, Filippo Maria (–1447).

18th, by the Treaty of Eltham, Henry IV makes an alliance with the Armagnacs against Burgundy.

Jun: 15th, John XXIII makes peace with Ladislas.

28th, a commission ends the succession dispute in Aragon by electing Ferdinand (I), uncle and regent of John II of Castile, as King (–1416).

C **Aug**: 22nd, the Burgundian and Armagnac factions make another treaty of peace at Auxerre.

D **Nov**: 27th, death of Margaret, Regent of Denmark, Norway and Sweden; Eric VII begins his personal rule.

E An expedition by Sigismund fails to recover Dalmatia from Venice.

Vitold fortifies the Dneiper to control its passage to the Black Sea; he employs in his garrisons some Mongol groups calling themselves Cossacks, a name also adopted by Russian Ukrainians of this area.

1411

G **Economics, Science, Technology and Discovery**

†Nicolò Falcucci, *Sermones medicales septem* (printed 1475); *Liber de medica materia*; *Commentaria super aphorismos Hippocratis.*

H **Religion and Education**

†Gerlac Petersen, a Flemish mystic, *Fiery Soliloquy with God.*

J **Art, Architecture and Music**

The Guildhall, London (–1426).

Donatello, *St. Mark* (statue), Or San Michele, Florence (–1412).

†*Jacquemart de Hesdin, miniaturist, *Grandes Heures du Duc de Berri*; also begins *Très Belles Heures de Turin.*

K **Literature, Philosophy and Scholarship**

Thomas Hoccleve, *De Regimine Principum* (didactic poem).

L **Births and Deaths**

Feb. 23rd, Lorenzo Buonincontro b. (–*c.* 1500).

1412

H **Religion and Education**

A papal interdict on Bohemia causes John Hus to leave Prague; he writes *Adversus indulgentias* and *Contra bullam pape.*

Pavia University re-established (–1398).

K **Literature, Philosophy and Scholarship**

Christine de Pisan, *Le Livre de Paix* (on government and peace).

John Lydgate, *The Hystorye, sege and dystruccyon of Troye* (*The Troy Book*).

L **Births and Deaths**

Jan. 6th(?), Joan of Arc b. (–1431).

— Juan de la Mena b. (–1456).

1413

A **Jan**: 30th, an assembly of the estates for northern France, meeting in Paris, refuses to grant taxation and demands reform of the government.

Feb: death of Mahmūd, (nominal) King of Delhi, so ending the Tughluq dynasty; Dawlat Khān Lōdī elected as his successor (–1414).

Mar: 20th, death of Henry IV, King of England; succeeded by his son, Henry V (–1422).

B **Apr**: 28th, the Bastille taken in the Cabochien riots in Paris.

May: 29th, despite the issue of the 'Ordonnance Cabochienne' reforming the government, fresh riots break out in Paris and the butchers establish a rule of terror.

Jun: 7th, Ladislas takes Rome; John XXIII flees to Bologna.

C **Jul**: Muhammad I, the youngest son to Bāyezīd, with support from the Greeks, defeats and kills his brother, Mūsa, at Jamurlu, in Serbia; he thus reunites the Ottoman dominions.

Aug: 4th, the Armagnacs restore royal authority in Paris.

Sep: 8th, the Parisian rebels savagely prosecuted and the 'Ordonnance Cabochienne' withdrawn.

D **Oct**: John XXIII's envoys accept Sigismund's demand that a general council of the Church should be called.

2nd, the Union of Horodlo, a charter of Jagiello of Poland and Vitold of Lithuania, reaffirms the unity of the two states but makes the autonomy of Lithuania permanent and cedes new privileges to its nobility.

Dec: 26th, death of Michele Steno, Doge of Venice.

1414

A **Jan**: 7th, Tomaso Mocenigo elected Doge of Venice (–1423).

9th, Henry V disperses a treasonable Lollard assembly organised by Sir John Oldcastle in St. Giles' Fields, outside London.

B **May**: 23rd, Henry makes a treaty of alliance with John of Burgundy.

28th, Khizr Khān, the Mongol ruler of the Punjab, takes Delhi as viceroy for Rūkh, Timur's successor; he thus establishes the Sayyid dynasty of Delhi (–1451).

31st, Henry appoints his first embassy to demand the French throne.

C **Aug**: the Armagnacs take Charles VI on an expedition against Burgundy.

6th, death of King Ladislas of Naples, thus ending his attempt to conquer the Papal States; succeeded by his sister, Joanna II (–1435).

D **Nov**: 5th, John XXIII opens the General Council of Constance.

E Fresh outbreak of war between the Teutonic Knights and Poland and Lithuania.

Yung-lo invades and defeats the Oirats of western Mongolia.

1413

H Religion and Education

A General Council of the Church held in Rome by John XXIII condemns the works of John Wycliffe.

*John Hus, *De Ecclesia*; *Exposition of Belief* (in Czech).

†*Juliana of Norwich, an English mystic, *Revelations of Divine Love*.

Henry Wardlaw, Bishop of St. Andrews, founds St. Andrews University.

J Art, Architecture and Music

Brunelleschi begins the dome of Florence Cathedral.

**Très Belles Heures du Duc de Berri* (illuminated ms).

Donatello, *St. John the Evangelist* (statue), Or San Michele, Florence (–1415).

1414

G Economics, Science, Technology and Discovery

†Jacopo da Forli, *In aphorismos Hippocratis expositiones* (printed 1473); *Super libros tegni Galeni* (1475).

J Art, Architecture and Music

Ghiberti, *St. John the Baptist* (statue), Or San Michele, Florence.

Quercia, *Fonte Gaia* (public fountain), Siena (–1419).

K Literature, Philosophy and Scholarship

†Al-Fīrūzābādī, *Al-Qāmūs* (*The Ocean*; Arabic dictionary).

L Births and Deaths

Feb. 12th, Jacopo da Forli d.

Feb. 19th, Thomas Arundel, Archbishop of Canterbury, d. (61).

July 22nd, Francesco della Rovere (Sixtus IV) b. (–1484).

— Piero de'Medici b. (–1469).

1415

A **Feb**: 23rd, by the Treaty of Arras, John of Burgundy makes another truce with his French enemies.

Mar: 14th, Henry V's second embassy to demand the French throne ends its negotiations in Paris with its minimum terms refused.

20th, John XXIII flees from Constance.

B **Apr**: 30th, Sigismund confers the Electorate of Brandenburg on Frederick of Hohenzollern.

May: 29th, the Council of Constance deposes John XXIII from the papacy.

C **Jul**: 4th, Gregory XII's representatives announce his abdication to the Council of Constance.

Aug: 5th, Richard, Earl of Cambridge, and Henry, Lord Scrope, executed as traitors against Henry V.

13th, Henry invades France.

21st, a naval expedition sent by John I of Portugal takes Ceuta.

Sep: 2nd, the nobility of Bohemia and Moravia protest against the execution of Hus.

5th, they form an association to oppose the Church authorities.

22nd, Henry takes Harfleur.

D **Oct**: 25th, Henry defeats the French at Agincourt.

Nov: 16th, he returns to England.

Dec: 13th, by the Capitulations of Narbonne, Sigismund obtains the accession of the Kings of Aragon, Castile and Navarre to the Council of Constance.

E The Swiss take Aargau from the Habsburgs.

Muhammad I recovers Ankara.

1416

A **Feb**: 9th, Sigismund creates Count Amadeus VIII as Duke of Savoy.

Mar: 1st, Sigismund arrives in Paris, proposing to mediate between France and England.

B **Apr**: 2nd, death of Ferdinand I of Aragon; succeeded by his son, Alfonso V (–1458).

C **Aug**: 15th, a Franco-Genoese fleet, attempting to recover Harfleur from the English, defeated in the Seine estuary.

15th, by the Treaty of Canterbury, Sigismund makes an alliance with Henry V.

D **Oct**: 6th, John of Burgundy meets Henry at Calais.

E The Venetians defeat the Turks off Gallipoli.

1415

G **Economics, Science, Technology and Discovery**

*Giovanni de'Fontana, *Bellicorum instrumentorum liber* (illustrated treatise on military technology; refers to rockets and torpedoes).

H **Religion and Education**

In the decree of *Haec Sancta*, the Council of Constance declares the supremacy of general councils in the Church. The Council also condemns John Hus as a heretic and he is burnt (Jul. 6th; *see* B–D).

†John Hus, *Letters*.

*Thomas Netter of Walden, *Doctrinale Fidei Ecclesiae Catholicae*; *Fasciculi Zizaniorum* (anti-Lollard tracts).

Foundation by Henry V of a Brigittine house (of nuns and monks) at Twickenham, transferred to Syon in 1431 (the last monastic foundation in England).

J **Art, Architecture and Music**

Pisanello, Frescoes (now destroyed) in the Doge's Palace, Venice (–1422).

**Agincourt Song* (tune now in English hymnal—*Deo Gracias*).

K **Literature, Philosophy and Scholarship**

*Christine de Pisan, *Le Livre de trois vertus* (didactic assertion of the right of women to receive a full education, and, as writers of their right to be regarded on equal terms with male authors).

†Manuel Chrysoloras, *Greek Grammar* (printed *c.* 1480).

L **Births and Deaths**

Apr. 15th, Manuel Chrysoloras d. (*c.* 60).

Sept. 20th, Owen Glyn Dwr d.

Dec. 23rd, Frederick III b. (–1493).

— Jan Dlugosz b. (–1480).

1416

G **Economics, Science, Technology and Discovery**

†Blasius of Parma, *Tractatus de ponderibus* (on statics and hydrostatics); also treatises on astrology.

H **Religion and Education**

May 30th, the Council of Constance burns Jerome of Prague as a heretic.

Sikander Butshikan (the Iconoclast), King of Kashmīr, destroys Hindu temples and forces conversions to Islam.

J **Art, Architecture and Music**

Gerona Cathedral completed with the building of its nave.

Donatello, *St. George* (statue), Or San Michele, Florence (–*c.* 1420).

K **Literature, Philosophy and Scholarship**

Alain Chartier, *Livre des quatres dames* (poem on the horrors of war and grief of the bereaved).

Poggio rediscovers Quintilian's *Institutio oratoria* at St. Gall.

L **Births and Deaths**

June 15th, John, Duke of Berri, d. (76).

— St. Francesco de Paolo b. (–1507).

— Joannes Argyropoulos b. (–1486).

1417

B **Apr**: 29th, death of Louis II, Duke of Anjou and ex-King of Naples; succeeded by his son, Louis III (–1434).

C **Jul**: 26th, the Council of Constance deposes Benedict XIII.
Aug: 1st, Henry V lands at Trouville to begin his campaign to conquer Normandy.
27th, Attendolo Sforza, the condottiere employed by Joanna of Naples, expels Braccio da Montone, another condottiere, from Rome.
Sep: 20th, Henry takes Caen.

D **Nov**: 11th, the Council of Constance elects Cardinal Odo Colonna as Pope Martin V (–1431).
Dec: 14th, Sir John Oldcastle executed as a traitor against Henry V and burnt as a heretic.

E Death of Maso degli Albizzi, the effective ruler of Florence.
Muhammad VIII succeeds Yūsuf III as King of Granada (–1445).

1418

B **Apr**: 22nd, dissolution of the Council of Constance.
May: 29th, the army of John of Burgundy admitted into Paris.
Jun: 12th, members of the Armagnac faction in Paris massacred, among them Bernard VII, Count of Armagnac.

C **Jul**: 29th, Henry V begins the siege of Rouen.
Sep: 29th, Cherbourg surrenders to Henry.

D **Dec**: 11th, Amadeus of Savoy acquires Piedmont.
26th, the Dauphin Charles proclaims himself Regent of France.

E Venice captures Friuli from Sigismund.
Le Loi, a Vietnamese peasant, organises national resistance to the Chinese occupation (–1428).

1417

F Law and Politics

By suspending the assizes, Henry V causes increased resort of litigants to Chancery; its jurisdiction in 'equity' (established under Richard II) becomes increasingly popular from this time.

Yung-lo has definitive editions of the Confucian classics published in order to exclude heterodox ideas; the restoration of traditional Confucianism is accompanied by the revival of the associated examination system for the Chinese civil service.

H Religion and Education

In its decree *Frequens*, the Council of Constance provides for the holding of further general councils after stipulated intervals.

The Great Schism ends with the election of Martin V (*see* D).

†Francesco Zabarella, *Glossa ordinaria* on *Clementinae* (–1313).

J Art, Architecture and Music

Petrus Christus, *Madonna and Child* (painting), Frankfurt.

K Literature, Philosophy and Scholarship

John Capgrave, *Chronicle* (of England, from the Creation to 1417).

**Gesta Henrici Quinti* (*The Deeds of Henry V*, King of England).

L Births and Deaths

Sept. 26th, Cardinal Francesco Zabarella d. (78).

1418

F Law and Politics

†Ahmad al-Qalqashandi, *Subh al-Aʿsha* (encyclopedic manual for Egyptian civil servants).

G Economics, Science, Technology and Discovery

The Hanseatic League makes its first legislative act, regulating the alliance and its trading operations; Lübeck recognised as its leading member.

†Domenico di Bandino, *Fons memorabilium universi* (encyclopedic treatise on cosmography, astronomy, geography, history, etc.).

(–1419) Madeira discovered by seamen sent by Henry the Navigator.

H Religion and Education

Establishment of the reformed religious community at Melk, Austria.

J Art, Architecture and Music

The Masjid-i Gauhar Shāh, Meshed.

Ghiberti, model of the dome for Florence Cathedral.

ʿAbd-al-Qādir, *Maqāsid al-Alhān* (*Purport of Melodies*).

K Literature, Philosophy and Scholarship

The Letters of the Paston Family (collected by Sir John Fenn in 1787; begin now and continue to 1506).

1419–1420 Hussite rebellion—Treaty of Troyes—Neapolitan war of succession

1419

A **Jan:** 19th, Rouen surrenders to Henry V, whose conquest of Normandy is thus complete.

C **Jul:** 22nd, the (Taborite) sect of extreme Hussites formed.
30th, a crowd of Hussites murders anti-Hussite town councillors of Prague by defenstration.
Aug: 16th, death of Wenceslas IV of Bohemia; succeeded by his brother, Sigismund, King of the Romans and of Hungary.
Sep: 10th, John the Fearless, Duke of Burgundy, murdered at Montereau during a conference with the Dauphin Charles; succeeded by his son, Philip the Good (–1467).

D **Oct:** 5th, Amadeus of Savoy acquires Nice.
Dec: 25th, Philip of Burgundy allies himself with Henry V against the Dauphin.

E Devarāya I decisively defeats Fīrūz, Shah of Kulbarga, at Pangal; Fīrūz has to abandon his conquests fromVijayanagar.

1420

A **Feb:** 21st, the Hussite extremists seize Austi and found Tabor, whence their sect is named.
Mar: 1st, Martin V declares a crusade against the Hussites.
25th, in the first battle of the Hussite wars, the Taborites, led by John Žiška, defeat the Bohemian Catholics at Sudomer.

B **May:** 21st, by the Treaty of Troyes, Charles VI recognises Henry V as Duke of Normandy and his own heir to the French throne.
Jun: 2nd, Henry marries Charles' daughter, Catherine.

C **Jul:** 14th, the Taborites defeat a crusading army led by Sigismund on the Vitkow (*now* Žiška's) Hill outside Prague. The 'Four Articles of Prague' defining the principles common to the Hussites now published.
Aug: Louis III of Anjou arrives in Naples following Martin V's proposal that he should be Queen Joanna's heir.
Sep: Naples occupied by the troops of Alfonson of Aragon and Sicily, whom Joanna adopts as her heir.
3rd, death of Robert Stewart, Duke of Albany and Regent of Scotland; succeeded by his son, Murdoch (–1425).
30th, Martin V enters Rome; the papal residence restored here following the partial pacification of the Papal States.

D **Nov:** 1st, the Hussites again defeat Sigismund under the Heights of Vyšehrad, near Prague: the first anti-Hussite crusade fails.
Dec: 1st, Henry V and Charles VI enter Paris.

E Yung-lo transfers the capital of China from Nanking to Peking, which is rebuilt.

1419

G **Economics, Science, Technology and Discovery**
Henry the Navigator founds the nautical school at Sagrez.

H **Religion and Education**
Rostock University founded.

J **Art, Architecture and Music**
Church of St. Jan, s'Hertogenbosch, burnt; rebuilt.
Ghiberti, *St. Matthew* (statue), Or San Michele, Florence (–1422).
Brunelleschi, Façade of the Foundling Hospital, Florence (–1463).

L **Births and Deaths**
Apr. 5th, St. Vincent Ferrer d. (69).
Nov. 22nd, John XXIII (the deposed Pope) d.

1420

F **Law and Politics**
Establishment of the Tung-ch'ang, Peking (the 'Eastern Yard', where the eunuchs in the Emperor's service kept secret files on official personnel).

G **Economics, Science, Technology and Discovery**
**Feuerwerkbuch* (manual on manufacture and use of cannon and gunpowder; describes a nitro-explosive, shrapnel, etc.).

H **Religion and Education**
*Jean Charlier de Gerson, *De Consolatione Theologiae*.

K **Literature, Philosophy and Scholarship**
*John Lydgate, *The Siege of Thebes* (historical poem).

L **Births and Deaths**
Aug. 9th, Pierre d'Ailly d. (70).

1421

A **Mar**: 22nd, the Dauphin's troops defeat the English at Baugé during Henry's absence in England; his brother, Thomas, Duke of Clarence, killed.

B **Apr**: 23rd, Philip of Burgundy buys Namur from its marquis, John III.
May: 4th, death of Muhammad I, the Ottoman Sultan; succeeded by his son, Murād II (–1451).
20th, death of Khizr Khan, the first Mongol ruler of Delhi; succeeded by his son, Mubārak, who styles himself Shah (–1435).
Jun: 1st, the estates of Bohemia and Moravia, meeting at Čâslav, renounce Sigismund as their king and form a government.
30th, Florence buys Leghorn from Genoa.

D **Oct**: 6th, Henry begins the siege of Meaux.
28th, Milan annexes Genoa (–1435).
Nov: 2nd, the Bohemians defeat a second invading crusade by German princes at Saaz: the second anti-Hussite crusade fails.

1422

A **Jan**: 6th, John Žiška defeats Sigismund at Kutná Hora.
10th, he again defeats Sigismund at Německý Brod.

B **May**: 10th, Meaux surrenders to Henry V.
16th, the Bohemians accept Korybut, nephew of Jagiello of Poland, as their King.
Jun: 8th, Murād II begins the siege of Constantinople.
30th, Carmagnola, the condottiere, defeats the Swiss at Arbedo, thus gaining the Val d'Ossola for Filippo Maria of Milan.

C **Aug**: Murād abandons the siege of Constantinople when his brother, Mustafā, rebels.
31st, death of Henry V, King of England; succeeded by his infant son, Henry VI, with the lords establishing a council to rule in his minority (–1436, 1461, 1470–1).
Sep: 27th, by the Treaty of Melno, the Teutonic Knights end their war with Poland and Lithuania.

D **Oct**: 21st, death of Charles VI, King of France; succeeded, according to the Treaty of Troyes, by Henry VI of England.
30th, the Dauphin Charles, son of Charles VI, assumes the title of King (Charles VII) of France (–1461).

E Ahmad deposes his brother Fīrūz and becomes Shah of Kulbarga (–1435); he defeats Viyayarāya of Vijayanagar on the Tungabhara and devastates his kingdom.
Yung-lo campaigns (inconclusively) against the Tatars (–1424).

1421

G **Economics, Science, Technology and Discovery**
The Jews expelled from Austria.

H **Religion and Education**
Establishment of the reformed monastic congregation of Santa Giustina, Padua (begins modern monasticism).

J **Art, Architecture and Music**
Church of S. Lorenzo, Florence (architect: Brunelleschi).
†Nanni, *The Four Saints* and *Assumption* (sculpture).

K **Literature, Philosophy and Scholarship**
Cicero's *De Oratore* rediscovered at Lodi.

L **Births and Deaths**
Dec. 6th, Henry VI b. (–1471).
— Jean le Maingre ('Boucicaut') d. (57).
— Bartolomeo Platina b. (–1481).
— Vespasiano da Bisticci b. (–1498).

1422

H **Religion and Education**
†Banda Nawāz, *Mi'raj al-'ashiqin* and *Hidāya nāma* (treatises on Muslim mysticism; earliest examples of Urdū prose).

J **Art, Architecture and Music**
Tomb of Fīrūz Shāh, Kulbarga, near Bīdar.

K **Literature, Philosophy and Scholarship**
Alain Chartier, *Quadrilogue invectif* (discussion between four characters: his country, France; its nobility; the clergy and the people: on the state of the nation and the disasters of the writer's own times).
†Filippo della Gazzaio, *Assempri* (collection of exemplary tales and legends of the saints).
*Thomas Walsingham, *Historia Anglicana* (1272–1422; the last in the series of chronicles of England produced at St. Albans Abbey).

L **Births and Deaths**
Nov. 29th, Benedict XIII (the deposed Pope) d.
*William Caxton b. (–1491).

1423

B **Apr**: 15th, death of Tomaso Mocenigo, Doge of Venice; succeeded by Francesco Foscari (–1457).
23rd, the General Council called by Martin V opened at Pavia.
27th, Žižka defeats the moderates at Hořic in the first battle of the Bohemian civil war.
May: Joanna of Naples begins operations to expel Alfonso from Naples and adopts Louis III of Anjou as her heir in his place.

C **Jul**: 21st, the General Council, transferred from Pavia, opened at Siena.
31st, Anglo-Burgundian forces defeat the French at Cravant.

E Florence declares war on Milan; hostilities continue until 1454.
Salonika ceded to Venice by the Greeks, who were unable to defend it from the Turks.
Murād II destroys Hexamilion and ravages the Morea.

1424

A **Jan**: 3rd, death of the condottiere, Sforza Attendolo; succeeded by his son, Francesco.
Mar: 7th, the General Council of Siena dissolved.
28th, by the Treaty of Durham, James I of Scotland is released and makes a truce for seven years with England.

C **Aug**: 17th, John, Duke of Bedford, the English regent in France, defeats the forces of Charles VII at Verneuil.

D **Oct**: 11th, death of John Žižka; his followers take the name of 'the Orphans'.
16th, Humphrey, Duke of Gloucester, begins his campaign to conquer the lands of his wife, Jacqueline of Bavaria, countess of Holland, Zeeland and Hainault, from Philip of Burgundy.

E The Turks take Smyrna.
Death of Yung-lo, the Chinese Emperor.

1423

G **Economics, Science, Technology and Discovery**

*Earliest illustration, in a Munich manuscript, of a crank and connecting-rod (operating a hand-mill); wood-boring apparatus also shown.

H **Religion and Education**

Jun: 10th, the college of cardinals at Peniscola created by Benedict XIII elects Gil Sanchez Muñoz as Pope Clement VIII (–1429), while a dissident cardinal elects another anti-pope, Benedict XIV.

J **Art, Architecture and Music**

Pisanello, *Annunciation* (painting; –1424).

Gentile, *The Adoration of the Magi* (painted altarpiece).

K **Literature, Philosophy and Scholarship**

*James I, King of Scotland, *The King's Quair* (an allegory in 'rhyme-royal', written during his captivity in England).

L **Births and Deaths**

Jul. 3rd, Louis XI b. (–1483).

— Richard Whittington d.

— Georg Puerbach b. (–1461).

1424

F **Law and Politics**

Origin of the committee of the Lords of the Articles, a select body to consider the principal business in Scottish parliaments.

G **Economics, Science, Technology and Discovery**

Earliest illustration of a carpenter's brace.

K **Literature, Philosophy and Scholarship**

†Giovanni Sercambi, *Novelle*.

1425

B **Apr**: Humphrey of Gloucester returns to England, abandoning Jacqueline to Philip of Burgundy—in favour of Eleanor Cobham, whom he subsequently marries.

May: 25th, James of Scotland, in his restoration of royal authority, has Murdoch, Duke of Albany, executed.

C **Jul**: 21st, death of the Greek Emperor, Manuel II, who ruled only Constantinople, while his brothers ruled other remaining fragments of the empire in Greece; succeeded by his son, John VIII (–1448).

Aug: 2nd, Le Mans surrenders to the English.

Sep: 8th, death of Charles III, King of Navarre; succeeded by his daughter, Blanche, wife of John of Aragon.

D **Oct**: 30th, fracas in London between citizens favouring Humphrey of Gloucester and the men of Henry Beaufort, Bishop of Winchester.

Dec: 3rd, Venice and Florence make an alliance against Milan.

E Portugal begins the conquest of the Canary Islands.

Vasili II succeeds his father, Vasili I, as Grand Duke of Moscow (–1462); his uncle Juri, Prince of Galich, unsuccessfully attempts to oppose his succession (–1433).

1426

A **Jan**: 27th, Alfonso of Aragon joins the league against Milan.

Feb: Venice declares war on Milan.

Mar: 12th, Humphrey of Gloucester and Henry Beaufort formally reconciled in the 'parliament of bats' at Northampton.

12th, the Bohemians defeat Duke Albert of Austria, whom they had expelled from Moravia, at Zwettl, in Austria.

B **Jun**: 16th, the Bohemians, led by Prokop the Great, destroy a German crusading army at Ústi: the third anti-Hussite crusade fails.

E Giovanni Francesco Gonzaga of Mantua takes Brescia from Milan.

Barsbāy of Egypt devastates Cyprus, and makes its King tributary.

1425

G **Economics, Science, Technology and Discovery**

†Ugolini da Montecatini, *De balneorum Italiae* (*Etruriae*) *proprietatibus et virtutibus* (one of the earliest treatises on bathing).

H **Religion and Education**

*Thomas à Kempis (*i.e.* Thomas Hemerken), *De imitatione Christi* (*The Imitation of Christ*; revised 1441; –1471).

Foundation of Louvain University.

J **Art, Architecture and Music**

Quercia, Reliefs, S. Petronio, Bologna (–1438).

Uccello, Mosaics in S. Marco, Venice (–*c.* 1430).

Gentile, *Quaratesi Altarpiece* (painting).

Jan van Eyck appointed court painter of Philip of Burgundy.

*Masaccio, Frescoes in Brancacci Chapel and, of the *Trinity*, in Sta. Maria Novella, Florence (–1428).

K **Literature, Philosophy and Scholarship**

*Alain Chartier, *La Belle Dame Sans Merci* (poem).

L **Births and Deaths**

Apr. —, Leonardo Dati d.

— Julius Pomponius Laetus b. (–1498).

1426

J **Art, Architecture and Music**

Church of Nôtre-Dame, Caudebec ('flamboyant'), begun.

Masaccio, *Madonna and Child* (painting; part of his dismembered Pisa Polyptych).

†Hubert and Jan van Eyck, *The Adoration of the Lamb* (painted polyptych, Ghent; –1432).

L **Births and Deaths**

Sept. 18th, Hubert van Eyck d. (*c.* 60).

— Giovanni Bellini b. (–1516).

— Thomas Hoccleve d. (*c.* 55).

1427–1429 Bohemians raid Germany—Liberation of Dai Viet—Joan of Arc relieves Orleans

1427

B **Apr:** 17th, the Bohemians expel their King, Korybut; then follows their first raid into Germany (Silesia and Lusatia).

C **Jul:** 11th, Eric of Denmark defeats the Hanse off Copenhagen; the war followed Eric's imposition of dues on ships passing the Sound between Sealand and Scania.
Aug: 27th, a crusading army led by Cardinal Beaufort flees from Stříbo on the approach of the Bohemians: the fourth anti-Hussite crusade fails.
Sep: 5th, the French defeat English forces at Montargis.

D **Oct:** 11th, Venetian forces led by Francesco Carmagnola defeat the Milanese at Maclodio, thus winning Bergamo.

E Outbreak in Poitou of a private war between Charles VII's favourite, Georges de la Trémoille, and Arthur of Brittany, Count of Richemont, the constable of France.
A revolt causes the flight of Muhammad VIII of Granada; Muhammad IX succeeds (–1429).

1428

B **Apr:** 19th, by the Peace of Ferrara, Milan cedes Brescia and Bergamo to Venice.

C **Jul:** 3rd, by the Treaty of Delft, Jacqueline of Bavaria recognises Philip of Burgundy as governor and her heir in Holland, Zeeland and Hainault.

D **Oct:** 7th, the English begin the siege of Orleans.

E Sigismund defeated in a campaign against the Turks on the Lower Danube.
Le Loi, having defeated the Chinese, declares himself Emperor of Dai Viet (as Le Thaito; –1433), establishing the Le dynasty (–1786); the Ming recognise him on his admission of Chinese suzerainty.

1429

A **Jan:** 10th, Philip of Burgundy establishes the Order of the Golden Fleece.
Feb: 12th, in 'the Battle of the Herrings' at Rouvray, the English defeat a French attack on supplies for their forces besieging Orleans.
23rd, Joan of Arc arrives at Chinon to meet Charles VII.

B **Apr:** 29th, Joan relieves Orleans.
May: 8th, the English abandon the siege.
Jun: 18th, the French defeat the English at Patay.

C **Jul:** 17th, Charles VII crowned as King of France at Reims.

D **Winter, 1429–30:** the Bohemians raid Saxony and Franconia.

E Muhammad IX of Granada murdered and Muhammad VIII restored.
Ahmad of Gujarāt recovers Bombay from Ahmad I of Kulbarga.

1427

J Art, Architecture and Music

Donatello, *Salome* (bronze relief), the Baptistery, Siena; *The Ascension*; tomb of John XXIII, in the Baptistery, Florence.

L Births and Deaths

— Gentile da Fabriano d. (*c.* 57).

1428

F Law and Politics

An act of James I requires the election of representatives of the sheriffdoms to Scottish parliaments.

H Religion and Education

Parliament rejects Martin V's demand for the repeal of the Statutes of Provisors (–1351, 1390).

J Art, Architecture and Music

Ghiberti, Bronze shrine of the Three Martyrs, Bargello, Florence; *St. Stephen* (statue), Or San Michele, Florence.

L Births and Deaths

May 3rd, Pedro Gonzalez de Mendoza b. (–1495).
Nov. 22nd, Richard Neville (Warwick 'the Kingmaker') b. (–1471).
— Pier Paulo Vergerio d. (79).
— Alessio Baldovinetti b. (–1499).
— Tommaso di Ser Giovanni di Mone (Masaccio) d. (27).

1429

H Religion and Education

Foundation of Lincoln College, Oxford.

L Births and Deaths

Mar. —, Margaret of Anjou b. (–1482).
July 12th, Jean Gerson d. (66).
— Giovanni de'Medici d.

1430

A **Mar:** 29th, Murād captures Salonika from the Venetians.

B **May:** 23rd, Burgundian troops capture Joan of Arc and deliver her to the English.

C **Aug:** 4th, Philip of Burgundy inherits the Duchies of Brabant and Limburg.

D **Oct:** 27th, death of Vitold, Grand Duke of Lithuania; Svidrigello, brother of Jagiello of Poland, elected as his successor (–1432).
Dec: 2nd, Niccolò Piccinino, the condottiere serving Milan, defeats Florentine forces under the Count of Urbino on the Serchio.

1431

A **Feb: 20th,** death of Pope Martin V.
Mar: 3rd, Gabriel Condulmer elected as Pope Eugenius IV (–1447).

B **May:** Eugenius excommunicates and wages war on the Colunna family.
Humphrey of Gloucester, lieutenant of England in Henry's absence, crushes a Lollard rising in Abingdon led by 'Jack Sharp'.
17th, Niccolò Piccinino and Francesco Sforza, the Milanese condottieri, defeat the Venetian forces under Carmagnola at Soncino.
23rd, the Genoese (subject to Milan) defeat a Venetian fleet on the Po.
30th, Joan of Arc burnt as a heretic at Rouen.

C **Jul:** 23rd, opening of the General Council of Basel.
Aug: 14th, a crusading army led by Cardinal Cesarini flees from Domažlice (Taus) on the approach of the Bohemians: the fifth anti-Hussite crusade fails.
27th, the Genoese fleet again defeats the Venetians near Portofino.

D **Dec:** 16th, Henry VI crowned as King of France in Paris.
18th, Eugenius orders the dissolution of the Council of Basel; it refuses to comply.

E John of Castile defeats the Moors of Granada at La Higuera; their King, Muhammad VIII, is deposed and succeeded by Yūsuf (–1432)
Paramaraja II of Ayudhya sacks Angkor, capital of Cambodia.

1430

F **Law and Politics**

A statute restricts the right to elect shire-knights to English parliaments to those who have freehold lands worth not less than 40*s*. *p.a.*

G **Economics, Science, Technology and Discovery**

'Mad Meg', the large cast-iron cannon (now in Ghent).

H **Religion and Education**

William Lyndwood, *Liber provincialis*, or *Provinciale* (collection of English provincial constitutions, with commentary).

Moses Arragel, *Bible of the House of Alba* (translation of the Bible from Latin and Hebrew into Castilian).

J **Art, Architecture and Music**

Capella Pazzi, Florence (–1443; architect: Brunelleschi).

K **Literature, Philosophy and Scholarship**

*Olivier Basselin (of Vire), *Vaux-de-vire* (drinking-songs from the valley of the River Vire—hence, it is said, the term *Vaudeville*).

†*Andrea da Barberino, *I Reali di Francia* (anthology of Carolingian epics in a prose rendering).

*Rodriguez de la Cámara, *El siervo libre de amor* (autobiographical novel).

†Adam of Usk, *Chronicon* (personal chronicle of England, 1377–1421).

L **Births and Deaths**

— Thomas Netter of Walden d.

— Bartholomew Diaz b. (–1500).

1431

G **Economics, Science, Technology and Discovery**

Jean Ganivet of Vienne, *Amicus Medicorum* (*Directory of Astrology made medical*).

(–1432) Portuguese discovery of the Azores.

H **Religion and Education**

Council of Basel (–1449; *see* A–D).

J **Art, Architecture and Music**

Pisanello, Frescoes in the Lateran Basilica (destroyed), Rome (–1432).

Lucca della Robbia, Cantoria ('Singing Gallery'), Florence Cathedral (sculpture).

†Minchō, Japanese painter.

L **Births and Deaths**

— Christine de Pisan d. (*c.* 68).

— Andrea Mantegna b. (–1506).

*Jehan de la Fontaine d. (*c.* 50).

*François Villon b. (–1466).

1432

B **May**: 5th, the Venetians execute Francesco Carmagnola, their condottiere captain.
7th, delegates of the Council of Basel meet Bohemian representatives at Cheb.
Jun: 24th, Yūsuf IV of Granada murdered; Muhammad VIII restored (–1445).

C **Aug**: 17th, Giovanni Caraccioli, the favourite of Joanna of Naples, murdered.
Sep: 1st, Svidrigello deposed as Grand Duke of Lithuania following his anti-Polish alliance with the Teutonic Knights; succeeded, and defeated, by Sigismund, brother of Vitold (–1440).

E Eric of Denmark, Norway and Sweden, finally defeated by the Count of Holstein, claiming the Duchy of Schleswig.
Murād II conquers Albania after the death of John Castriota I.
The Latin principality of Achaea surrenders to Thomas Palaeologus, ruler of the Morea.
Ahmad of Kulbarga completes his new capital at Bīdar.

1433

A **Jan**: 4th, Bohemian delegates arrive in Basel to discuss Hussite doctrines with the Council.

B **Apr**: Juri of Galich takes Moscow and proclaims himself Grand Duke; he soon withdraws.
26th, Milan and Venice make peace.
May: 31st, Eugenius crowns Sigismund as Holy Roman Emperor.
Jun: Georges de la Trémoille, Charles VII's favourite, seized by his enemies and compelled to retire from the King's court.

C **Aug**: 14th, death of John I the Great, King of Portugal; succeeded by his son, Edward (–1438).
Sep: 22nd, Sigismund creates Giovanni Francesco di Gonzaga as Marquess of Mantua.

D **Nov**: 30th, the delegates of the Council of Basel in Prague make terms for a settlement with the Bohemian moderates—the 'Compacts of Prague'.
Dec: 15th, Eugenius eventually recognises the Council of Basel.

1432

G **Economics, Science, Technology and Discovery**
Revolts of peasants in Saxony, Silesia, Brandenburg and the Rhineland.

H **Religion and Education**
Foundation of Caen and Poitiers Universities.

J **Art, Architecture and Music**
Ghiberti, bronze reliquary of St. Zenobius, Florence Cathedral (–1442).
Jan van Eyck, *Portrait of a Man* ('Leal Souvenir'); altarpiece in St. John's, Ghent.
*Fra Filippo Lippi, *The Relaxation of the Carmelite Rule* (frescoes).

K **Literature, Philosophy and Scholarship**
Mystère du Concile de Bâle (a morality play).
Lorenzo Valla, *De Voluptate*.

1433

H **Religion and Education**
Nicholas of Cusa, *Concordantia Catholica* (a moderate conciliarist's plea for unity and tolerance in the Church).
Juan de Torquemada, *Summa de Ecclesia* (defending papal supremacy).
Paul of Burgos, *Dialogus Pauli et Petri contra Judaeos* (Christian apologetics by an apostate Jew).

J **Art, Architecture and Music**
Sta. Maria degli Angeli, Florence (architect: Brunelleschi).
Perpignan Cathedral (–1509).
Donatello, Cantoria, Florence Cathedral (–1439).
Jan van Eyck, *Man in a red turban* (painting).
Fra Angelico, *Linaiuoli Madonna* (painting).

L **Births and Deaths**
Oct. 19th, Marsilio Ficino b. (–1499).
Nov. 10th, Charles the Bold b. (–1477).

1434–1435 Roman republic—Teutonic Knights defeated—Congress of Arras

1434

A **Feb**: 19th, Mubārak Shāh of Delhi murdered; his nephew, Muhammad, elected as his successor (–1446).

B **May**: 30th, in the Battle of Lipany, the Bohemian Catholics and Utraquists (moderate Hussites) defeat the extremist Taborites led by Andrew Prokop, who is killed.

31st, death of Jagiello (*or* Vladislav II) of Poland; succeeded by his son, Vladislav III (–1444).

Jun: 4th, Eugenius flees from Rome to Florence following the establishment of a republican government by the Colunnas and condottieri employed by Milan.

6th, death of Juri of Galich when again in possession of Moscow; his son Vasili Kosoy proclaims himself Grand Duke, but Vasili II is restored and has Vasili Kosoy blinded.

C **Aug**: 28th, Piccinino defeats Venetian and Florentine forces near Imola.

D **Oct**: 5th, Cosimo de'Medici returns from exile to Florence, becoming its effective ruler (–1464). Palla Strozzi is banished.

Nov: 15th, death of Louis III, Duke of Anjou and claimant to Naples; succeeded by his brother, Réné of Provence, Duke of Bar and Lorraine (–1480).

E The English suppress risings by the peasants of Lower Normandy.

The capital of Cambodia transferred to Phnom Penh.

1435

A **Feb**: 2nd, death of Joanna II of Naples; she bequeaths her kingdom to Réné of Anjou.

C **Jul**: 17th, by the Treaty of Vordingborg, the Hanse makes peace with Eric of Denmark, Norway and Sweden.

Aug: 5th, Alfonso of Aragon defeated and captured by the Genoese in a naval battle off the Isle of Ponza; he is soon afterwards released after making a treaty of alliance with Milan.

5th, English, French and Burgundian embassies begin the Congress of Arras.

Sep: 1st, Sigismund of Lithuania defeats the Teutonic Knights and Lithuanian rebels under Svidrigello at Wilkomierz.

6th, the English embassy abandons its negotiations for peace with France at Arras.

15th, death of John, Duke of Bedford, the English regent of France.

21st, by the Treaty of Arras, Philip of Burgundy makes peace with Charles VII of France.

D **Oct**: 28th, the French capture Dieppe; the English suppress a subsequent rising by the local peasants.

Dec: 27th, Francesco Spinola leads a rebellion in Genoa which recovers the city its independence from Milan.

31st, by the Peace of Brest, the Teutonic Knights cede Samogitia and Sudauen to Poland.

E Engelbrecht, the leader of a popular Swedish revolt against King Eric, holds a parliament at Arboga which elects him Regent of Sweden.

1434

J **Art, Architecture and Music**

Rebuilding of Nantes Cathedral begun.
Church of St. Maclou, Rouen ('flamboyant'), begun.
*Donatello, *David* (bronze).
Jan van Eyck, *Arnolfini marriage group*; *Madonna and Child* (paintings).

K **Literature, Philosophy and Scholarship**

Edward, King of Portugal, commissions Fernão Lopes to write his *Cronache*.

L **Births and Deaths**

— Nicholas de Clamanges d.

1435

G **Economics, Science, Technology and Discovery**

First known dredger, called the 'Scraper', built at Middelburg.

H **Religion and Education**

†Paul of Burgos, *Scrutinium Scripturae* (–1470).

J **Art, Architecture and Music**

Leone Battista Alberti, *Della Pittura* (treatise on painting).
Jan van Eyck, *Madonna of the Chancellor Rolin* (painting; –1436).
*Roger van der Weyden, *The Descent from the Cross* (painted altarpiece).
*Konrad Witz, *Heilspiegelaltar* (painted altarpiece).

K **Literature, Philosophy and Scholarship**

Lorenzo Valla, translation of Homer's *Iliad* (–1438).
Ibn 'Arabshāh, *'Ajā'ib al-maqdur fī nawā'ib Timūr* (Arabic biography of Timur).

L **Births and Deaths**

— Andrea della Robbia b. (–1525).

1436

B **Apr:** 13th, Paris taken from the English for Charles VII.

C **Aug:** 2nd, Philip of Burgundy compelled to abandon his attempt to take Calais.
15th, James of Scotland abandons his attempt to take Roxburgh castle from the English.
23rd, Sigismund enters Prague, having been accepted as King of Bohemia following his recognition of the Compacts of Prague.

D **Oct(?):** the minority of Henry VI ends and his personal rule begins.

E Engelbrecht, the Swedish leader, murdered. Amund Sigurdsson leads a revolt in Norway. King Eric pacifies both countries by his concessions to national (*i.e.* anti-Danish) sentiments.

1437

A **Feb:** 12th, Richard, Duke of York, the English lieutenant in France, takes Pontoise.
21st, murder of James I of Scotland; succeeded by his son, James II (–1460).

B **Apr:** a conspiracy against Charles VII by Dukes Charles I of Bourbon, John II of Alençon, Réné of Anjou and John V of Brittany, and Count John IV of Armagnac, collapses.

C **Jul:** 31st, the Council of Basel cites Eugenius to answer its charges of disobedience to its decrees.

D **Nov:** John VIII leaves Constantinople for Rome on a mission to seek assistance against the Turks.
Dec: 9th, death of Sigismund, the Holy Roman Emperor; succeeded as King of Hungary by Duke Albert V of Austria (–1439). The Bohemians, however, refuse to accept him as their King.

E A Portuguese expedition led by Prince Henry the Navigator fails to take Tangier.
Philip of Burgundy acquires the Duchy of Luxemburg by purchase.

1436

G **Economics, Science, Technology and Discovery**

The Hanse suspends trade with Flanders following an anti-German riot in Sluys (–1438).

Andreas Bianco, *Cartes hydrographiques*; map of Europe.

Fei Hsin, *Hsing-cha-sheng-lan* (*Description of the Star Raft*; eye-witness account of Cheng Ho's voyages, 1405–33).

H **Religion and Education**

Francesco de Paolo founds the Order of Minims.

J **Art, Architecture and Music**

Tomb of Ahmad Shāh of Kulbarga, Ashtur.

Uccello, Fresco in Florence Cathedral.

Jan van Eyck, *Madonna of Canon van der Paele*; *Jan de Leeuve* (paintings).

L **Births and Deaths**

Jan. 6th, Regiomontanus b. (–1476).

— Francisco Ximenes de Cisnéros b. (–1517).

1437

G **Economics, Science, Technology and Discovery**

Astronomers of Samarqand make the *Tables of Ulūgh Beg*.

**The Libel of English Policy* (poem describing English trade and urging its expansion and the exploitation of sea-power).

J **Art, Architecture and Music**

Pisanello, *St. George and the Princess* (painting; –1438).

Jan van Eyck, *St. Barbara* (drawing).

Fra Filippo Lippi, *The Tarquinia Madonna*; *Barbaderi Altarpiece* (paintings).

L **Births and Deaths**

— Isaac Abrabenel b. (–1508).

— Niccolò Niccoli d. (73).

1438

A Jan: 5th, Eugenius opens a General Council at Ferrara; he had transferred the General Council here from Basel, but most of its members refuse to comply.

24th, the Council of Basel decrees the suspension of Eugenius from the exercise of papal authority.

Mar: John VIII and a Greek delegation arrive to attend the Council of Ferrara.

18th, Albert (II) of Austria elected as King of the Romans (–1439).

B May: 21st, Piccino enters Bologna on behalf of Filippo Maria of Milan; with the renewal of war with Venice, he then invades Venetian territory.

C Jul: 7th, publication of the Pragmatic Sanction of Bourges, a declaration by a council of the French church held by Charles VII restricting papal authority in France.

Sep: 9th, death of Edward of Portugal; succeeded by his infant son, Afonso V (–1481).

E A baronial rebellion forces Eric VII to flee from Denmark to Gothland, where he resorts to piracy. The Swedes also revolt and a diet appoints Charles Knutson as Regent.

1439

A Jan: 10th, the Council of Ferrara reassembles in Florence.

B Jun: 25th, the Council of Basel declares Eugenius deposed from the Papacy.

C Jul: English and French embassies meeting in the Congress of Calais fail to make peace as the English will not renounce Henry VI's title to be King of France; but the English make a truce with Philip of Burgundy (on 28 Sep.).

6th, in the Council of Florence, the union of the Latin and Greek Churches is proclaimed; despite the subscription of John VIII and his delegation to the union, the citizens of Constantinople refuse to accept it.

Sep: 13th, the English garrison of Meaux surrenders to the French.

Oct: 27th, death of Albert II, King of the Romans; succeeded as King of Hungary by Vladislav of Poland (–1444).

Nov: 2nd, Charles publishes a 'grande ordonnance' designed to organise and discipline French troops.

5th, the Council of Basel elects Amadeus VIII, Duke of Savoy, as Pope Felix V (–1449); he abdicates the duchy in favour of his son.

9th, Francesco Sforza, serving Venice, defeats the Milanese under Piccinino near Riva.

E Eric VII declared deposed from the Danish throne.

1438

G **Economics, Science, Technology and Discovery**

The Hanse raises its embargo on trade with Flanders when Bruges cedes its demands.

H **Religion and Education**

Henry Chichele, Archbishop of Canterbury, founds All Souls College, Oxford.

K **Literature, Philosophy and Scholarship**

*Margery Kemp, *Her Book* (*The Book of Margery Kempe*; the earliest 'autobiography' in English literature, by a mystic).

L **Births and Deaths**

— Giacopo della Quercia d. (*c.* 53).
— Bernardo Pulci b. (–1488).

1439

G **Economics, Science, Technology and Discovery**

Paddles used to control flow of water at lockgates of Milanese canals.

H **Religion and Education**

Union of the Latin and Greek Churches (*see* C).
Foundation of Godshouse, Cambridge (a 'teachers' training college').

J **Art, Architecture and Music**

The spire of Strasbourg Cathedral completed (by Johannes Hültz).
Jan van Eyck, *Madonna of the Fountain*; *Portrait of his wife* (paintings).
Domenico Veneziano and Piero della Francesca, Frescoes (lost) in Sant'Egidio, Florence.

K **Literature, Philosophy and Scholarship**

Georgios Gemistos Plethon, a Greek delegate to the Council of Florence, prompts Cosimo de'Medici to found the Florentine Academy.
†Ambrogio Traversari, superior of the convent of Santa Maria degli Angeli, outside Florence (a meeting-place for humanists), translations of Greek Fathers.

L **Births and Deaths**

— Geoffroi Boussard b. (–1505).

A **Feb**: 2nd, Frederick (III) Habsburg, Duke of Styria, elected as King of the Romans (–1493).
15th, Charles calls his last meeting of the Estates-General of northern France to Bourges, but it is not held because of 'the Praguerie'. This baronial revolt headed by the Dauphin Louis and the Dukes of Bourbon, Brittany and Alençon, is defeated in a two months' campaign. Charles hereafter regularly raises taxes without calling for assent from the estates-general.
22nd, birth of Ladislas Posthumus, son of Albert II; the Bohemians accept him as their King (–1457).

B **Apr**: 9th, Christopher III of Bavaria, nephew of Eric VII, elected as King of Denmark (–1448); royal authority had now been lost to the nobles.
Jun: 29th, Florentine and Papal forces defeat Milanese forces under Piccinino at Anghiari; Florence thus gains Borgo San Sepulcro.

C **Jul**: the English recover Harfleur.
Sep: 20th/21st, death of Frederick I, Elector of Brandenburg; succeeded by his son, Frederick II (–1470).

D **Oct**: 26th, execution of Gilles de Rais, a Breton noble convicted of necromancy, infanticide, etc.
Nov: 2nd, the canton of Schwyz begins a war against the city of Zurich, which it prevents from seizing from Schwyz the lands of the last Count of Toggenburg.
24th, the judicial murder of William, Earl of Douglas, by James II's councillors begins a feud between the Scottish crown and the Douglas family.

E The Swiss canton of Uri recovers Leventina from Milan.
Queen Leonor deposed from being regent for her son, Afonso of Portugal, in favour of his brother, Peter.
Sigismund, Grand Prince of Lithuania, murdered; succeeded by Casimir, brother of Vladislav of Poland (–1492).
Eugenius declares a crusade against the Turks.
Death of Itzcoatl, fourth Aztec king; he had established his primacy in the valley of Mexico; succeeded by Montezuma I (–1469).

G **Economics, Science, Technology and Discovery**

Johann Gensfleisch (Gutenburg) invents printing by movable metal type, at Mainz.

H **Religion and Education**

Henry VI founds King's College, Cambridge.

Lorenzo Valla demonstrates the falsity of 'The Donation of Constantine' (–1236 C).

J **Art, Architecture and Music**

*Fra Angelico, Frescoes and altarpiece, S. Marco, Florence.

K **Literature, Philosophy and Scholarship**

Alain Chartier, *Tractus de vita curiali* (trans. by Caxton, 1484).

*The *Cancionero General* ('a collection of *canciones*—love songs—in Spanish, written between the age of Juan de la Mena (1416–1456)—and its publication by Castillo in 1517; contains the productions of 136 poets—much that is anonymous.'—*Hallam*).

†*Jordi de Sant Jordi, *Enuigs* (personal narrative in Catalan, written by a poet of Valencia).

Aeneas Silvius Piccolomini, *De Gestis Concilii Basiliensis* (*History of the Council of Basel*).

L **Births and Deaths**

July 9th, Jan van Eyck d.

1441

A **Feb**: 21st, Venice annexes Ravenna following a revolt there against the Pope, as secular ruler, assisted by Venetian forces.

B **Apr**: 2nd, Cardinal Giovanni Vitelleschi, commander of the papal forces, murdered.

C **Sep**: 8th, Christopher of Denmark and Norway elected as King of Sweden (–1448).
19th, the French take Pontoise, completing their recovery of the Île-de-France from the English.

D **Oct**: 23rd, an ecclesiastical court condemns Eleanor Cobham, wife of Humphrey of Gloucester, for sorcery in an alleged attempt on the life of Henry VI.
Nov: 20th, by the Treaty of Cavriana (published 10 Dec.), Milan and Venice make peace through the mediation of Francesco Sforza, the Venetian captain, who had married Bianca, daughter and heir of Filippo Maria of Milan.

E Vladislav of Poland and Hungary raises the siege of Belgrade by the Turks.
*Mayapán destroyed in a revolt; the New Mayan Empire disintegrates and its cities are abandoned.

1442

B **Jun**: 2nd, Réné of Anjou escapes from Naples on its capture by Alfonso of Aragon.
14th, Zurich allies with Frederick against the Swiss Confederation.

C **Aug**: 3rd, Charles takes Dax in a campaign against the English in Gascony.

E The Norwegians accept Christopher of Denmark and Sweden as their King, in place of Eric (–1448).
Frederick II of Brandenburg suppresses the civic liberties of his capital, Berlin-Kölln.
John Hunyadi defeats the Turks invading Transylvania.
Death of Alexander I the Great, King of Georgia, who had reunited the kingdom.

1441

F **Law and Politics**
Frederick III declares a public peace for Germany.

G **Economics, Science, Technology and Discovery**
The Peace of Copenhagen ends a commercial war between the Hanse and Flanders.
Revolt of serfs in Denmark.

H **Religion and Education**
Henry VI founds Eton College.
Foundation of Bordeaux University.

J **Art, Architecture and Music**
Fra Filippo Lippi, *Coronation of the Virgin* (painting; –1447).

K **Literature, Philosophy and Scholarship**
Leone Battista Alberti, *Della Famiglia* (dialogues on domestic, social and allied themes, including friendship).

1442

G **Economics, Science, Technology and Discovery**
First report of gipsies in Europe, as having landed at Barcelona.

J **Art, Architecture and Music**
Andrea del Castagno and Francesco da Faenza, Frescoes in S. Zaccaria, Venice.
Western towers of Burgos Cathedral (–1458; architect: John of Cologne).

K **Literature, Philosophy and Scholarship**
†Al-Maqrīzī, *Al-Mawā'iz w-al-I'tibār fi Dhikr al-Khitat w-al-Āthār* (*Sermons and learning by example on an account of the new settlements and remains*; on Egyptian topography, history and antiquities).

L **Births and Deaths**
Apr. 28th, Edward IV b. (–1483).
— William Grocyn b. (–1519).
— Tamas Bakócz b. (–1521).

1443 Papacy restored to Rome—Turkish reverses

A **Feb**: 26th, Alfonso of Aragon enters Naples, where he is recognised as King (–1458).

B **May**: 16th, the Council of Basel holds its last general session.
Jun: 5th, Bologna revolts and expels Piccinino.

C **Aug**: John Beaufort, Duke of Somerset, lands at Cherbourg in a campaign (planned) to relieve Gascony.
Sep: 28th, Eugenius returns to Rome. The General Council is transferred there from Florence (but its later history is not known).

D **Nov**: 10th, a crusading army led by John Hunyadi, Voivode of Transylvania, defeats the Turks at Niš; it also takes Sofia.
21st, Philip of Burgundy seizes Luxemburg city.
Dec: Somerset retires to Normandy after raiding Anjou.
12th, in the battle of Zlatica, the Turks repulse Hunyadi from Thrace.

E Skanderbeg (George Castriota) begins the revolt of Albania against the Turks (–1468).

F **Law and Politics**

The Parlement of Toulouse (temporarily established in 1420) reorganised as a court of appeal for south west France; it is thus the first provincial parlement.

G **Economics, Science, Technology and Discovery**

Commercial treaty between John of Castile and the Hanse.

J **Art, Architecture and Music**

Uccello, *The Four Prophets*; stained glass windows (–1445), all in Florence Cathedral.
Fra Filippo Lippi, *The Annunciation* (painting).
Jacques Coeur's house, Bourges (–1453).

K **Literature, Philosophy and Scholarship**

Ashikaga Yoshimasa, Shogun of Japan, has rules made for the Tea Ceremony.
†Bāisunqur Mīrzā, son of Shah Rūkh, great patron of Persian artists and founder of library at Herat.
†Zeami Motokiyo, writer and performer of Nō dramas, *Kadensho* (*Book of the Flowery Tradition*; chief theoretical work on this classic Japanese drama).

L **Births and Deaths**

Mar. 16th, Fernandez Gonsalvo da Córdoba b. (–1515).
Apr. 12th, Henry Chichele, Archbishop of Canterbury, d. (*c.* 80).
May 9th, Cardinal Niccolò Albergati d.
May 31st, Margaret Beaufort b. (–1509).
— Matthias Corvinus b. (–1490).
— Pierre Cauchon, Bishop of Beauvais, d.
— Rudolphus Agricola b. (–1485).

1444

A (early): Hunyadi defeats the Turks on Mount Kunovica.

B **May**: 28th, by the Treaty of Tours, Charles makes a truce for two years with Henry VI, who engages to marry Margaret, daughter of Réné of Anjou.

Jun: 12th, at Szeged, Murād makes a truce for ten years with the crusaders, with Skanderbeg, and with George Barnković, who is restored as Despot of Serbia.

C **Aug**: 26th, at St. Jakob on the Birs, the Swiss are defeated by French freebooters ('écorcheurs') sent by Charles VII to assist Frederick of Austria.

Sep: Cardinal Cesarini absolves Vladislav, Hunyadi and other crusaders from their oaths to keep the truce with Murād.

23rd, death of Giovanni Francesco di Gonzaga, Marquess of Mantua; succeeded by his son, Federico I.

D **Oct**: 15th, death of Niccolò Piccinino, the condottiere.

21st, by the Treaty of Zofingen, Charles makes peace with the Swiss Confederation.

Nov: 10th, Murād destroys the crusading army at Varna; Hunyadi escapes, Cesarini disappears, and Vladislav III of Poland and Hungary is killed.

E George of Poděbrady becomes leader of the Hussites in Bohemia.

1445

B **Apr**: 23rd, Henry VI marries Margaret of Anjou.

C **Jul**: 7th, Vasili of Moscow defeated and captured by forces of Ulug-Mahmed, Khan of 'the Golden Horde'; he is released and confirmed as Grand Duke; Ulug-Mahmed is subsequently murdered and succeeded by his son, Mahmudek.

D **Dec**: 26th, Zara Yakub of Abyssinia defeats an invasion by the Sultan of Ifat, near Egubba; the sultanate now declines.

E By a secret ordinance, Charles VII establishes a regular army of cavalry ('compagnies de Grande Ordonnance') which is first employed to clear unoccupied France of the 'écorcheurs'.

Muhammad VII of Granada deposed for the third (and last) time; succeeded by his nephew, Muhammad X, who is in turn expelled and succeeded by Saʿd al-Mustaʿīn (–1446).

John Hunyadi elected regent of Hungary.

1444

G **Economics, Science, Technology and Discovery**

Niccolò de Conti returns to Venice after travelling in Asia, including Java, for 25 years.

J **Art, Architecture and Music**

Konrad Witz, *Christ walking on the Water* (painting).

Castagno, stained glass windows, Florence Cathedral.

*Jean Fouquet, *Charles VII of France* (painted portrait).

K **Literature, Philosophy and Scholarship**

†Leonardo Bruni of Arezzo ('Aretino'), *Vita di Dante* (important source work); *De bello Italico adversus Gothos* (after Procopius; printed 1470); *De bello Punico* (1490); *Epistolae* (1472); *History of Florence* (incomplete).

*Enguerrand de Monstrelet, *Chronicle* (1400–44; may be considered as a continuation of Froissart –1400).

Aeneas Silvius Piccolomini, *Euryalus and Lucretia.*

L **Births and Deaths**

Mar. 9th, Leonardo Bruni d. (75).

May 20th, St. Bernardino of Siena d. (64).

— Donato d'Augnolo Bramante de Urbino b. (–1514).

— Sandro Botticelli b. (–1510).

1445

J **Art, Architecture and Music**

Choir of St. Lawrence, Nuremburg (–1471).

*Dieric Bouts, *Nativity* (painting).

*Castagno, *The Last Supper* and *Passion Scenes* (frescoes in S. Apollonia, Florence).

*Domenico Veneziano, *St. Lucy Altarpiece* (painting, now dispersed).

*Ucello, *The Deluge* (painting), Sta. Maria Novella, Florence.

*Piero della Francesca, *Madonna della Misericordia* (painted polyptych; –1462?); *Baptism of Christ* (–1450).

K **Literature, Philosophy and Scholarship**

Juan Alfonso de Baena, *Cancionero* (de Baena; famous anthology of about 600 Spanish poems; a standard work of classic status).

L **Births and Deaths**

Mar. 16th, Johann Geiler von Kaiserberg b. (–1510).

— Josquin des Prés b. (–1521).

1446

A **Feb**: Muscovite malcontents led by Dmitri Shemiaka, son of Juri of Galich, seize the city and blind Vasili II; he is imprisoned but soon released.

B **Jun**: 12th, by the Treaty of Constance, Frederick of Austria makes peace with the Swiss Confederation.

E Muhammad X recovers Granada (–1454).
'Alam succeeds Muhammad IV as Shah of Delhi (–1451).

1447

A **Feb**: 17th, Vasili returns to Moscow, following the flight of Dmitri Shemiaka.
23rd, death of Pope Eugenius IV.
23rd, death of Humphrey, Duke of Gloucester, while under arrest; it is soon rumoured that he has been murdered.
Mar: 6th, Tommaso Parentucelli elected as Pope Nicholas V (–1455).

B **May**: 2nd, Casimir, the Grand Prince, grants a great charter of liberties to the Lithuanian nobility at Vilna.
Jun: 25th, he is crowned as Casimir IV, King of Poland (–1492); it is now presumed that Vladislav III had been killed at Varna (–1444).

C **Aug**: 13th, death of Filippo Maria Visconti, Duke of Milan. The Milanese establish the Ambrosian Republic, but a war of succession follows. Francesco Sforza, claiming to be Visconti's heir, is opposed by Venice and Alfonso of Aragon, who also claims the Duchy. Charles, Duke of Orleans, also claims Milan.

E Death of Shah Rūkh, followed by dissolution of the Tīmūrid house of Herat; the Turkoman dynasty of the White Sheep now rules Persia (except for Khurāsān) from Tabriz.

1446

G Economics, Science, Technology and Discovery

Nuño Tristam, a Portuguese explorer, killed by natives at the Rio Grande.

Denis Fernandez discovers Cape Verde and the Senegal.

J Art, Architecture and Music

Choir vault of Vienna Cathedral.

*Fra Angelico, Frescoes in chapel of the Vatican (–1449).

*Roger van der Weyden, *The Last Judgement* (painting).

Façade of Palazzo Rucellai, Florence (architect: Alberti).

K Literature, Philosophy and Scholarship

Flavio Biondi, *Italia illustrata* (printed 1474).

Onmum ('vernacular writing'; phonetic system for writing) officially adopted in Korea.

L Births and Deaths

Apr. 15th, Filippo Brunelleschi d. (69).

— Vittorino da Feltre d. (68).

1447

H Religion and Education

Margaret of Anjou founds Queens' College, Cambridge.

J Art, Architecture and Music

Fra Angelico, *Last Judgement* (frescoes), Orvieto Cathedral.

L Births and Deaths

Mar. 6th, St. Colette of Corbie d. (66).

Apr. 11th, Cardinal Henry Beaufort, Bishop of Winchester, d. (*c.* 72).

1448

A **Jan**: 6th, death of Christopher of Bavaria, King of Denmark, Norway and Sweden; end of the Calmar Union.

Feb: envoys of Nicholas V conclude the Concordat of Vienna with Frederick III and other German princes; in return for the right to exercise some papal powers in their territories, they abandon the Council of Basel.

Mar: 16th, the English surrender Le Mans to the French.

B **Apr**: 28th, an ordinance of Charles VII establishes regular companies of 'Free Archers'.

May: outbreak of war between England and Scotland.

Jun: 20th, Karl Knutsson elected as (Charles VIII) King of Sweden (–1470).

C **Jul**: 7th, the surviving members of the Council of Basel move to Lausanne.

Sep: George of Poděbrady occupies Prague.

1st, Count Christian of Oldenburg elected as King of Denmark and Norway (–1481).

15th, Francesco Sforza defeats the Venetians at Caravaggio.

D **Oct**: 17th–19th, Murād II defeats Hunyadi at the (second) battle of Kossovopolje and thus regains control of the Balkans (excluding Albania).

19th, Sforza makes an alliance with the Venetians against Milan.

31st, death of the Greek Emperor, John VIII, without issue; succeeded by Constantine XI, Despot of the Morea (–1453).

Dec: Murād ravages the Morea.

1449

A **Mar**: 24th, English forces sack Fougères, in Brittany, and so give Charles VII cause to renew the war.

B **Apr**: 7th, the anti-pope, Felix V, abdicates in the Council (of Basel) at Lausanne.

25th, the council dissolves itself.

May: 20th, Afonso V of Portugal defeats a rebellion by his brother, Peter, who is killed, at Alfarrobeira.

D **Oct**: 21st, Christian of Denmark deposed as King of Norway and Charles of Sweden elected (–1450).

29th, the English surrender Rouen to Charles VII.

E Cheng-t'ung, the Chinese Emperor, defeated and captured while attacking the Oirats (western Mongols); they briefly besiege Peking, but withdraw when the defenders elect a new emperor.

1448

H **Religion and Education**

William Waynflete founds Magdalen College, Oxford.

J **Art, Architecture and Music**

*Donatello, *Gattamelata* (equestrian statue) and High Altar, the Santo, both in Padua.

Pisanello, Medals of Alfonso of Naples (–1449).

Mantegna, Frescoes in the Ovetari Chapel (destroyed, 1944), Padua (–*c.* 1455).

K **Literature, Philosophy and Scholarship**

John Capgrave, *Liber de Illustribus Henricis* (completed; a chronicle of the German emperors, 918–1198; of English kings named Henry; and others).

*Evfimi, Archbishop of Novgorod, organises the *Novgorodsko-Sofisky Svod* (*Novgorod-Sophian Digest*; compilation of Russian historical annals).

1449

J **Art, Architecture and Music**

Castagno, *The Assumption* (painting; –1450).

K **Literature, Philosophy and Scholarship**

Journal d'un Bourgeois de Paris (records of events and everyday life, and personal feelings, kept by an unknown Parisian, 1405–49).

†Walter Bower, continuation of Fordun's *Scotichronicon* to 1437 (–1383).

L **Births and Deaths**

Jan. 1st, Lorenzo de'Medici b. (–1492).

Oct. 21st, George, Duke of Clarence, b. (–1478).

Domenico Ghirlandaio b. (–1494).

1450

A **Jan**: 26th, the Commons in parliament begin the impeachment of Henry VI's favourite, William de la Pole, Duke of Suffolk.

Feb: 25th, after being besieged by Sforza, the Milanese agree to accept him as their Duke (–1466).

B **Apr**: 15th, the French defeat the last English force sent to Normandy at Formigny.

May: 2nd, the Duke of Suffolk murdered on his way into exile.

Jun: rebellion in Kent and Sussex led by 'Jack Cade'.

C **Jul**: 3rd–5th, the rebels control London.

12th, 'Cade' killed.

13th, Zurich rejoins the Swiss Confederation.

29th, Christian I of Denmark crowned as King of Norway, having compelled Charles of Sweden to renounce the Norwegian crown.

Aug: 12th, the English holding Cherbourg surrender; Charles VII's conquest of Normandy thus completed.

29th, the formal union of Denmark and Norway, under Christian, enacted at Bergen.

Sep: Richard, Duke of York fails in an attempt to make Henry VI reconstitute his council.

1451

A **Feb**: 3rd, death of Murād II, the Ottoman Sultan; succeeded by his son, Muhammad II (–1481).

B **Apr**: 19th, 'Alam Shah of Delhi 'cheerfully' resigns on the election of Bahlūl Lodī, an Afghan ruling the Punjab (–1489).

Jun: 12th, Bordeaux surrenders to Charles VII.

C **Aug**: 20th, the capture of Bayonne completes the French conquest of Gascony; England's only French possession now is Calais.

Sep: 28th–30th, Thomas Courtenay, Earl of Devon, besieges William, Lord Bonville, in Taunton castle, Somerset.

D **Oct**: Frederick III, as guardian of Ladislas Posthumus, appoints George of Poděbrady governor of Bohemia and John Hunyadi governor of Hungary.

1450

F **Law and Politics**

†Agnes Sorel, the first prominent mistress of a French King.

G **Economics, Science, Technology and Discovery**

*Paper currency abandoned in China.

H **Religion and Education**

Formation of the Bohemian and Moravian Communion of Brethren (–1467).
James Kennedy founds St. Salvator's College, St. Andrews.

J **Art, Architecture and Music**

The Jubilee in Rome finances the buildings (including the new St. Peter's) and library of Nicholas V.
Nave of Barcelona Cathedral completed.
*Nave of Berne Cathedral begun (architect: Matthaus Ensinger).
*S. Francesco, Rimini, alterations and additions by Alberti.
*Roger van der Weyden, *The Entombment*; *Madonna with Four Saints* (paintings).
Piero della Francesca, *St. Jerome with donor* (painting).
*Giovanni Bellini, *The Crucifixion*; *St. Ursula among her companions*; *Virgin and Child* (paintings; –1460).

K **Literature, Philosophy and Scholarship**

Volksbücher (prose sagas in German, started).
Nicholas of Cusa, *Idiota de Sapientia*.
*Gutierre Diaz de Gamez, *El Vitorial* (chronicle of the chivalrous deeds of Pero Niño, Count of Buelna, *c.* 1380–1449).

L **Births and Deaths**

— Francisco de Almeida b. (–1510).
*John Cabot b. (–1498).
*Aldus Manutius b. (–1515).

1451

G **Economics, Science, Technology and Discovery**

Commercial war of the Hanse against France and Burgundy (–1457).
Ma Huan, *Ying-yai-sheng-lan* (*Description of the Coasts of the Ocean*; eye-witness account of Cheng Ho's voyages, 1405–33).

H **Religion and Education**

Foundation of Glasgow University.

J **Art, Architecture and Music**

Piero della Francesca, *Sigismondo Malatesta and his patron saint* (fresco).
*Jean Fouquet, *The Melun Diptych* (painting).

K **Literature, Philosophy and Scholarship**

Koryŏ sa (*History of Korea* under the Koryō dynasty, 936–1392; an official compilation on the Chinese model).

L **Births and Deaths**

Mar. 9th, Amerigo Vespucci b. (–1512).
Apr. 23rd, Isabella of Castile b. (–1504).
Aug. 3rd, Ludovico Sforza b. (–1505).
*Christopher Columbus b. (–1506).

1452

A Feb: 22nd, James of Scotland personally murders William, Earl of Douglas.
Mar: Richard of York surrenders after the failure of his attempt to raise a rebellion against Henry VI.
19th, Nicholas V crowns Frederick III as Holy Roman Emperor.

B Apr: 18th, Frederick creates Borso d'Este as Duke of Modena and Reggio.
19th, Venice declares war on Milan.
27th, George of Poděbrady elected as regent of Bohemia.

C Jul: Alvaro de Luna, constable of Castile, executed as the result of a court plot, being accused of employing sorcery to win influence over King John.

D Oct: 23rd, a rising in Bordeaux enables the English to regain possession.

E Ladislas assumes personal rule in Hungary but Hunyadi remains as viceroy and captain-general.
A Mongol khanate established at Gorodets (renamed Kasimov) under the authority of Vasili of Moscow.

1453

A Jan: 6th, Frederick III erects Austria into an Archduchy.
7th, Stefano Porcaro executed for plotting to arrest Nicholas V and establish a republic in Rome.

B Apr: 7th, Muhammad begins the siege of Constantinople.
May: 29th, he takes the city by storm. Constantine XI is killed and the Greek Empire finally extinguished. Constantinople becomes the Ottoman capital.
29th, Jacques Coeur, the financier and councillor of Charles VII, sentenced to exile for peculation.

C Jul: 17th, the French victory at Châtillon ends the Hundred Years War; the English commander, John Talbot, Earl of Shrewsbury, killed.
23rd, Philip of Burgundy defeats rebels from Ghent at Gavre.
Aug: Henry VI becomes insane.

D Oct: 13th, his first (and only) child, Edward, is born.
19th, Bordeaux surrenders to Charles VII.
28th, Ladislas Posthumus crowned as King of Bohemia; he appoints George of Poděbrady as governor.

E Vasili II of Moscow establishes his authority over Novgorod.

1452

H **Religion and Education**
Foundation of Valence University, with Grenoble University incorporated.

J **Art, Architecture and Music**
Michelozzo Michelozzi, *Baptist* (statue), Florence Cathedral.
*Fra Filippo Lippi, *Virgin and Child*; Frescoes at Prato (–1464).
*Roger van der Weyden, *Nativity* (painted triptych); *Brague Triptych.*
*Piero della Francesca, *The True Cross* (frescoes in S. Francesco, Arezzo; –1459 ?).

K **Literature, Philosophy and Scholarship**
Poggio Bracciolini, *Liber Facetiarum* (a collection of stories, often satirical and humorous, about the clergy).

L **Births and Deaths**
Mar. 10th, Ferdinand of Aragon b. (–1516).
Sept. 21st, Girolamo Savonarola b. (–1498).
— Leonardo da Vinci b. (–1519).

1453

J **Art, Architecture and Music**
Tomb of Daryā Khān, Ahmadabad.
*Roger van der Weyden, *The Seven Sacraments* (painting).
*Castagno, *Famous Men and Women* (paintings).
Mantegna, *St. Luke* (painted polyptych; –1454).
†John Dunstable, the first English composer to influence music abroad.

L **Births and Deaths**
July 3rd, Jacques de Lalain, *le bon chevalier* (–1474), d.
— Alfonso d'Albuquerque b. (–1515).

1454

A **Feb**: Casimir incorporates Prussia into Poland at the request of the union of Prussian nobles and towns revolting against the Teutonic Order.

Mar: 22nd, death of Cardinal John Kemp, Archbishop of Canterbury, Chancellor of England.

27th, the lords in Parliament appoint Richard of York as protector of England during Henry's insanity.

B **Apr**: 9th, the Peace of Lodi ends the war between Milan and Venice and Florence.

May: Henry Holand, Duke of Exeter, raises a short-lived rebellion in Yorkshire.

C **Jul**: 21st, death of John II of Castile; succeeded by his son, Henry IV (–1474).

Aug: Milan, Venice and Florence make a league for 25 years, to which the Papacy and Alfonso of Aragon and Sicily acceded; the need of these states for permanent representatives with each other initiates the modern type of diplomacy.

Sep: 9th, the Teutonic Knights defeat Casimir at Chojnice.

D **Oct**: 31st, members of the Percy and Neville families fight a battle in their private war, at Stamford Bridge, Yorkshire.

Dec: 25th, Henry VI recovers his sanity; York is consequently dismissed from the protectorate.

E Muhammad X of Granada again defeated and succeeded by Sa'd (–1462).

Frederick II of Brandenburg buys the Neumark from the Teutonic Knights.

1455

A **Mar**: 24th, death of Pope Nicholas V.

B **Apr**: 8th, Alonso da Borgia elected as Pope Calixtus III (–1458).

May: 22nd, Richard of York and the Nevilles attack the court at St. Albans, capturing Henry VI and killing Edmund Beaufort, Duke of Somerset.

D **Nov**: 19th, York again appointed protector of England.

Dec: 15th, the Earl of Devon defeats Lord Bonville in 'the fight at Clyst', Devonshire.

E Muhammad II expels Chiara Giorgio, widow of Duke Nerio II, from Athens, and establishes Franco Acciajuoli as Duke.

1454

F **Law and Politics**

Casimir grants the Charters of Nieszawa conceding new liberties to the Polish gentry and recognising the crown's need for their consent to legislation in *sejmiki* (local assemblies).

Charles VII's ordinance establishing a *chambre des comptes* completes his reforms of the French financial system. Other ordinances reorganise the Parlement of Paris.

J **Art, Architecture and Music**

Uccello, the three *Battles* (paintings; –1457).

Piero della Francesca, painted altarpiece (Saints with Nicholas of Tolentino; –1469).

K **Literature, Philosophy and Scholarship**

Arnoul Gréban, *Mystère de la Passion* (a drama).

†Sharaf ad-Dīn 'Ali Yazdī, *Zafar-nāma* (official biography of Timur, in Persian).

L **Births and Deaths**

July 14th, Angelo Ambrogini Poliziana (Politian) b. (–1494).

1455

G **Economics, Science, Technology and Discovery**

Antoniotto Usodimare and Alvise da Cá da mosto explore the rivers Senegal and Gambia and discover five of the Cape Verde Islands (–1456).

H **Religion and Education**

*Reginald Peacock, *The Repressor of Over Much Blaming of the Clergy*.

J **Art, Architecture and Music**

†Ghiberti, *Commentarii* (important for information on fourteenth century Florentine art; also includes his autobiography, the first by an artist).

*Donatello, *Magdalen* (wooden statue), Florence Baptistery.

L **Births and Deaths**

Dec. 28th, Johann Reuchlin b. (–1522).

— Fra Angelico (Giovanni da Fiesole) d. (*c.* 60).

1456

A **Feb**: 25th, York is dismissed from the protectorate.

C **Jul**: 7th, a French ecclesiastical court rehabilitates Joan of Arc, declaring her trial in 1430–1 to be irregular.
22nd, Hunyadi defeats the Turks besieging Belgrade, forcing them to withdraw.
Sep: Charles confiscates the Dauphiné; the Dauphin, his son Louis, takes refuge with Philip of Burgundy.
10th, death of John Corvinus Hunyadi.

E The Turks take Athens, ending its Latin Duchy.

1457

B **Jun**: Charles VIII expelled from Sweden; succeeded by Christian of Denmark and Norway (–1464).
6th, the Poles take Marienburg; the Teutonic Knights then make Königsberg their headquarters.

C **Aug**: a French fleet under Pierre de Brézé sacks Sandwich.

D **Oct**: 23rd, Francesco Foscari, Doge of Venice, deposed by the Council of Ten; succeeded by Pasquale Malipiero (–1462).
Nov: 23rd, death of Ladislas V Posthumus, King of Hungary and Bohemia, without issue.

1456

F **Law and Politics**

The castle built at Yedo (now Tokyo), one of the first in Japan, symbolises the development of 'feudal' anarchy.

H **Religion and Education**

Reginald Pecock, *The Book of Faith* (anti-Lollard).

J **Art, Architecture and Music**

Sta. Maria Novella, Florence, alterations and additions by Alberti (–1470).

Castagno, *Niccolò da Tolentino* (fresco in Florence Cathedral).

K **Literature, Philosophy and Scholarship**

François Villon, *Le Petit Testament* (–1461).

L **Births and Deaths**

Oct. 23rd, St. John Capistrano d. (*c.* 70).

Nov. 25th, Jacques Coeur d.

— Juan de Mena d. (44).

1457

G **Economics, Science, Technology and Discovery**

The Treaty of Lübeck ends a commercial dispute between the Hanse and Philip of Burgundy.

*Judah Verga of Lisbon, description of his invention for determining the sun's meridian.

H **Religion and Education**

Following his trial, Reginald Pecock renounces his heretical opinions and is deprived of the bishopric of Chichester.

†Pietro da Monte, canonist, *Repertorium utriusque juris* (printed 1465).

Foundation of Freiburg University.

J **Art, Architecture and Music**

*Mantegna, *Madonna and Saints* (frescoes in S. Zeno, Verona).

K **Literature, Philosophy and Scholarship**

†Lorenzo Valla, 'founder of critical scholarship', *Elegantiae Latinae linguae* (printed 1471).

L **Births and Deaths**

Jan. 19th, Pietro da Monte d.

Jan. 28th, Henry VII b. (–1509).

Aug. 1st, Lorenzo Valla d. (52).

Aug. 19th, Andrea del Castagno d. (*c.* 34).

— Filippino Lippi b. (–1504).

1458

A **Jan:** 24th, Matthias Corvinus Hunyadi elected as King of Hungary (–1490).
Mar: 2nd, George of Poděbrady elected as King of Bohemia; he is also accepted in Moravia and Silesia (–1471).
25th, Henry VI effects a formal 'reconciliation' between York and the Nevilles and the families of their victims at the (first) Battle of St. Albans.

B **May:** 11th, the French occupy Genoa, which has ceded its lordship to gain protection against Alfonso of Aragon.
29th, Richard Neville, Earl of Warwick, defeats a Castilian fleet in the Channel.
Jun: 7th, defeat of Alfonso V the Magnificent, King of Aragon, Naples and Sicily; succeeded in Naples by his illegitimate son, Ferrante (–1494), and elsewhere by his brother, John II, King of Navarre (–1479).

C **Aug:** 6th, death of Pope Calixtus III.
19th, Aeneas Silvius Piccolomini elected as Pope Pius II (–1464).

1459

B **Jun:** 1st, Pius opens an ill-attended congress at Mantua, called to organise a crusade against the Turks.

C **Aug:** outbreak of rebellion against Ferrante of Naples.
Sep: 23rd, Richard Neville, Earl of Salisbury, defeats royal forces at Blore Heath, Staffordshire.

D **Oct:** 12th, the forces of York and the Nevilles flee before the royal forces in the 'Rout of Ludford'.
Nov: 20th, the 'Parliament of Devils' at Coventry attaints York and his allies as traitors against Henry VI.

E Turkish conquest of Serbia.
Abū-Sa'īd reunites the Tīmūrid kingdoms of Transoxiana and Khurāsān (–1469).

1458

H **Religion and Education**

Battista da Verona, *De ordine docendi et studendi* (manual on humanist education based on practice in the school of his father, Guarino, at Ferrara).

J **Art, Architecture and Music**

Pitti Palace, Florence (partly designed by Brunelleschi; –1470).
Jean Fouquet, illuminated ms. of *Les Grandes Chroniques de France*, completed.
Dieric Bouts, *St. Erasmus* (painted diptych).
Mantegna, *Cardinal Ludovico Mezzarota* (painting).

K **Literature, Philosophy and Scholarship**

Mystère du Vieil Testament produced at Abbeville.
†Inigo López de Mendoza, Marquis of Santillana, *Los Proverbios* (didactic poems).

L **Births and Deaths**

July 28th, Jacopo Sannazaro b. (–1530).
Sept. 1st, Cardinal Domenico Capranica d. (54).
— Maffeo Vegio d. (52).

1459

K **Literature, Philosophy and Scholarship**

†Gian Francesco Poggio (Bracciolini), *Historia Fiorentina* (unfinished); *De Varietate Fortunae*.
†Auziàs March, poems in Catalan of a metaphysical nature (in opposition to prevailing lyricism of the troubadours).

L **Births and Deaths**

Feb. 1st, Konrad Celtes b. (–1508).
Mar. 6th, Jacob Fugger b. (–1525).
Mar. 22nd, Maximilian I b. (–1519).
May 2nd, St. Antonini, Archbishop of Florence, d. (70).
Oct. 26th, Giannozzo Manetti d. (63).
Oct. 30th, Poggio Bracciolini d. (78).
Nov. 6th, Sir John Fastolf d.
— Adrian of Utrecht (Adrian VI) b. (–1523).
— John Fisher b. (–1535).
— Peter Martyr Anglerius b. (–1526 or 1527).

1460

A **Mar**: 5th, Christian of Denmark becomes Duke of Schleswig and Holstein on terms favourable to their nobility and guaranteeing the perpetual union of the two provinces.

C **Jul**: 7th, Ferrante defeated at Nola by John of Anjou, who is claiming the Neapolitan crown.
10th, Henry VI captured in the defeat of his supporters by the Nevilles at Northampton.
Aug: 3rd, James II of Scotland accidentally killed in his capture of Roxburgh Castle; succeeded by his son, James III (–1488).

D **Oct**: 31st, Henry accepts Richard of York as his heir to the English throne.
Dec: 30th, York killed in his defeat by 'Lancastrian' forces at Wakefield.

E The Turks take the Greek principality of the Morea and murder Franco Acciajuoli, the last Duke of Athens.

1461

A **Feb**: the German Electors agree to elect George of Poděbrady as King of the Romans, but through their subsequent dissension this scheme to depose Frederick III founders.
2nd(?), Edward, Duke of York, defeats 'Lancastrian' forces at Mortimer's Cross, Herefordshire.
17th, Henry VI rescued by Queen Margaret at her victory over Warwick at St. Albans.
Mar: 4th, Edward of York assumes the English crown (–1470, 1471–83).
29th, he defeats the 'Lancastrians' at Towton, Yorkshire; Henry then flees to Scotland.

B **Apr**: 25th, Henry cedes Berwick-upon-Tweed to Scotland.

C **Jul**: 22nd, death of Charles VII of France; succeeded by his son, Louis XI (–1483).
Aug: death of Don Carlos, son and heir of John of Aragon, who had deprived him of the Kingdom of Navarre; outbreak of civil war against John in Aragon and Navarre, while the Catalans attempt to establish a republic.
Sep: the Turks conquers the Greek Empire of Trebizond.

D **Nov**: 27th, Louis (temporarily) revokes the Pragmatic Sanction of Bourges.
Dec: George of Poděbrady rescues Frederick from his siege in Vienna by his brother, Albert VI of Austria.

1460

H **Religion and Education**

Jan. 18th, Pius II, in his bull *Execrabilis*, condemns all appeals to general councils.

Deniselle burnt as a witch at Arras; a witch-hunt follows locally.

Foundation of Universities of Basel and Nantes.

J **Art, Architecture and Music**

Façade ('flamboyant') of Toul Cathedral.

*Nave of Erfurt Cathedral.

*S. Sebastian, Mantua (architect: Alberti).

*Mantegna, *St. Sebastian* (painting); Frescoes of the Gonzaga family, *Camera degli Sposi*, Mantua Castello (–1474).

K **Literature, Philosophy and Scholarship**

†Jacopo Bracelli, *De bello Hispanico* (of Genoa, with Aragon, 1422–4).

(–1465) Réné of Anjou, *Livre des tournois* (on tournaments, etc).

L **Births and Deaths**

Nov. 13th, Prince Henry the Navigator d. (66).

Dec. 4th, Guarino da Verona d. (90).

*William Dunbar b. (–1520).

*John Skelton b. (–1529).

*Vasco da Gama b. (–1524).

1461

H **Religion and Education**

†St. Jonas, the first Metropolitan of Russia (from 1448) independent of the Greek Church.

K **Literature, Philosophy and Scholarship**

François Villon, *Le Grand Testament*; *Ballades* (–1456).

†Jean Chartier, *Grandes Chroniques de France* (printed 1476); *Histoire de Règne de Charles VII* (printed 1476–93).

L **Births and Deaths**

— Georg Puerbach d. (38).

— Domenico Veneziano d.

1462–1463 End of 'Tartar Yoke' in Russia—France annexes Roussillon and Cerdagne

1462

A **Mar**: 28th, death of Vasili II of Moscow; succeeded by his son, Ivan III (–1505). For the first time, the Khan of 'the Golden Horde' is not asked to confirm the succession, nor is tribute now paid to him; the 'Tartar Yoke' has ended.

B **May**: 5th, death of Pasquale Malipiero, Doge of Venice; succeeded by Cristofero Moro (–1471).
9th, by the Treaty of Bayonne, John of Aragon pledges the counties of Roussillon and Cerdagne to Louis in return for French military assistance against the Catalans; this army is destroyed by the climate.
Jun: 11th, the *Generalitat* (government) of Catalonia declares war on John.

C **Aug**: 18th, Ferrante of Naples, aided by Skanderbeg, defeats John of Anjou near Troia and so effectively ends the rebellion.

D **Oct**: 28th, Adolf of Nassau, claiming the Archbishopric, seizes Mainz.

E Henry of Castile takes Gibraltar.
'Abū-al-Hasan succeeds Sa'd as King of Granada (–1482).

1463

A **Jan**: 9th, the French take Perpignan in Louis' forcible annexation of Rouissillon and Cerdagne, which its people oppose.
13th, Louis persuades Henry of Castile and John of Aragon to make a truce.

D **Oct**: 22nd, Pius II publishes the last bull calling a crusade against the Turks.
Dec: Louis cedes his claims to Genoa to Francesco Sforza of Milan.
3rd, death of Albert VI, Archduke of Austria; his brother, Frederick, thus recovers possession of all Austria.
6th, Matthias Corvinus defeats the Turks and takes Jaysca, in Bosnia.

E Philip of Burgundy holds an Estates-General for his dominions at Bruges.
By overrunning Austria, Matthias compels Frederick to cede his claims to Hungary and end his intervention there; although their treaty of peace recognises that the Habsburgs might inherit Hungary if Matthias' issue should fail.

1462

G **Economics, Science, Technology and Discovery**

Alum discovered at Tolfa, in the Papal States; Pius II claims a monopoly of supply in Europe.

Citizens exiled from Mainz (*see* D) disperse printing in Germany.

J **Art, Architecture and Music**

Dieric Bouts, *Portrait of a Young Man* (painting).

K **Literature, Philosophy and Scholarship**

†*Antoine de la Salle, *L'Hystoire et plaisante chronique du petit Jehan de Saintre*; *La Salade* ('novels'); ? *Les Cent Nouvelles Nouvelles* (a collection of gay stories, free in style, and similar to Italian compilations, *e.g.* –1353, 1400).

L **Births and Deaths**

May 8th, Palla Strozzi d. (90).
June 27th, Louis XII b. (–1515).
Sept. 16th, Pietro Pomponazzi b. (–1525).
— Edmund Dudley b. (–1510).

1463

F **Law and Politics**

Sir John Fortescue, *De Natura Legis Naturae* (treatise on the idea of the monarchy).

J **Art, Architecture and Music**

Cambridge University confers a degree in music.

Andrea della Robbia, *The Foundling Children* on the façade, Foundling Hospital, Florence (–1466).

Mosque of Sultan Muhammad II, Constantinople (–1470).

K **Literature, Philosophy and Scholarship**

†Flavio Biondi of Forli, founder of classical archaeology, *Roma triumphans*; *Roma instaurata* (–1446).

L **Births and Deaths**

June 4th, Flavio Biondi d. (71).
Oct. 29th, Alessandro Achillini b. (–1512).
— St. Catherine of Bologna d. (50).
— Giovanni Pico della Mirandola b. (–1494).

1464

B **Apr**: 25th, Edward's forces defeat 'Lancastrians' invading from Scotland at Hedgeley Moor, Northumberland.

May: 1st, Edward privately marries Elizabeth Woodville, widow of John, Lord Grey of Ferrers.

15th, the 'Lancastrians' again defeated at Hexham.

C **Aug**: Charles VIII reinstated as King of Sweden.

1st, death of Cosimo de'Medici; succeeded, as virtual ruler of Florence, by his son, Piero (–1469).

14th, death of Pope Pius II at Ancona, while leading a small crusading army.

30th, Marco Barbo elected as Pope Paul II (–1471).

1465

B **Jun**: 5th, Henry IV of Castile declared deposed in favour of his brother, Alfonso; civil war follows.

C **Jul**: 16th, indecisive battle at Montlhéry in 'The War of the Public Weal', a baronial revolt against Louis led by Charles of Burgundy and the Dukes of Alençon, Bourbon and Brittany.

D **Oct**: 5th, Louis buys peace with the League of the Public Weal at Conflans.

Dec: 8th, Paul II declares George of Poděbrady to be deprived of the Kingdom of Bohemia as a heretic.

E Murder of 'Abd-al-Haqq II, last of the Marīnid rulers of Morocco; succeeded by the Wattāsids (–1549), who had been regents since his accession (in 1428).

1464

G **Economics, Science, Technology and Discovery**

June 19th, an ordinance of Louis XI creates the *poste*, organising relays of horses on the main roads for the king's business.

†Alvise de Cá da mosto, Portuguese navigator, *El libro de la prima navigatione per l'oceano a le terre de Negri della bassa Etiopa* (printed 1507).

H **Religion and Education**

Establishment at Bursfeld, Brunswick, of the first regular monastic congregation in Germany.

J **Art, Architecture and Music**

Dieric Bouts, *Five Mystic Meals* (painting: –1468).

Luca della Robbia, Bronze doors, The Sacristy, Florence Cathedral (–1469).

K **Literature, Philosophy and Scholarship**

Guillaume Alexis? *Maistre Pierre Pathelin* (a farce).

Andrea di Bossi, Bishop of Leira, first uses the term 'Middle Ages' with reference to the period between classical times and his own.

L **Births and Deaths**

June 16th, Roger van der Weyden d. (*c*. 64).

Aug. 11th, Cardinal Nicholas of Cusa d. (63).

Aug. 12th, John Capgrave d. (*c*. 64).

Aug. 14th, Aeneas Silvius Piccolomini (Pius II) d. (59).

1465

F **Law and Politics**

Matthias of Hungary establishes a standing army, universal conscription and permanent taxation.

G **Economics, Science, Technology and Discovery**

Sweynheym and Pannartz set up the first Italian press at Subiaco.

J **Art, Architecture and Music**

Uccello, Altarpiece, Urbino (–1469); *The Hunt* (paintings).

*Fra Filippo Lippi, *Virgin and Child and two Angels* (painting).

K **Literature, Philosophy and Scholarship**

†*John Hardyng, *Chronicle* (of England, from its Trojan origin, in English verse).

†John Bostock of Whethamstede, Abbot of St. Albans, *Registrum* (history of the house with some notice of English politics in his time).

†Charles, Duke of Orleans, *Poems and Ballads* (*Le Livre de la Prison*).

**The Ballad of William Tell* appears in Switzerland.

L **Births and Deaths**

Jan. 5th, Charles, Duke of Orleans, d. (74).

*Hans Holbein the Elder b. (–1524).

1466

A **Mar**: 8th, death of Francesco Sforza, Duke of Milan; succeeded by his son, Galeazzo Maria (–1476).

C **Jul**: Henry VI captured and imprisoned in the Tower of London.
James III kidnapped by Robert, Lord Boyd, who thus becomes governor of Scotland.

D **Oct**: 19th, the Peace of Toruń (Thorn) ends the Teutonic Knights' disastrous war (since 1454) with Poland; the Order accepts Polish sovereignty and cedes Pomerania, etc., retaining Königsberg.
Dec: 23rd, Paul II excommunicates George of Poděbrady and again declares his deposition.

E Skanderbeg defeats the Turks besieging his stronghold of Croya.

1467

B **Jun**: 15th, death of Philip the Good, Duke of Burgundy; succeeded by his son, Charles the Bold (–1477).

C **Aug**: 21st, Henry of Castile and the Infante Alfonso fight indecisively at Olmedo.

D **Oct**: 28th, Charles of Burgundy defeats a revolt by the citizens of Liège and repeals their privileges.

E Matthias defeats a revolt by Zoynich, Voivode of Wallachia and Moldavia.
Muhammad II conquers the Duchy of Herzegovina.

1466

G Economics, Science, Technology and Discovery

Earliest dated illustration of a ship (carrack) with three masts, the third having a lateen sail.

H Religion and Education

†Niccolò de'Tedeschi, *Summa* (of canon law).

J Art, Architecture and Music

Fra Filippo Lippi, Frescoes in Spoleto Cathedral (–1469).

K Literature, Philosophy and Scholarship

Michael Beheim, *Das Buch von den Wienern* (a poetic narrative).

L Births and Deaths

Dec. 13th, Donatello d. (80).
? François Villon d. (35 ?).
— John Colet b. (–1519).

1467

F Law and Politics

Frederick III holds a Reichstag at Nuremburg and promulgates a general peace in Germany for five years.

G Economics, Science, Technology and Discovery

Louis XI founds the silk industry at Lyons with a settlement of Italian workmen.

H Religion and Education

The Unity of the Brotherhood institutes its own church organisation in Bohemia.

L Births and Deaths

— Guillaume Budé (Budaeus) b. (–1540).
— Johannes Thurmair (Aventinus) b. (–1534).
— John Bourchier, Lord Berners, b. (–1533).

A **Jan**: 17th, death of Skanderbeg of Albania; succeeded by his son, John Castriota II (–1478).

Mar: 8th, in the treaty for the marriage of his daughter, Margaret, to James of Scotland, Christian of Denmark and Norway pledges the Orkneys (and, in 1469, the Shetlands) for her dowry; as this is unpaid, the islands are annexed to Scotland.

B **Apr**: 6th–14th, Louis holds his only meeting of an Estates-General at Tours.

C **Jul**: 3rd, death of Alfonso, the Infante of Castile and rival of his brother, Henry IV, for its throne; their sister, Isabella, refuses an offer of the crown, but is declared heiress to Henry, who has to repudiate his wife and daughter.

3rd, Charles of Burgundy marries Margaret, sister of Edward IV, who thus joins the confederation of French magnates against Louis.

Sep: 10th, Louis concludes a brief campaign in Brittany by making a treaty of peace with Duke Francis II, at Ancenis.

D **Oct**: 9th, Louis arrives in Péronne for an interview with Charles of Burgundy; when Liège revolts—at his instigation—Louis is virtually placed under arrest.

30th, Louis is compelled to attend Charles at the sack of Liège, and is soon afterwards released.

Nov: James III holds a parliament which condemns the Boyds for treason; Alexander is executed but Lord Robert escapes to England.

E Qā'it-bay succeeds as Sultan of Egypt; he survives longer than any other of the Burji Mamluk dynasty (–1495).

Sunni Ali, ruler of Gao (on the middle-Niger) takes Timbuktu; he founds the great African Empire of Gao (–1492).

Outbreak in Japan of the Ōnin War, 'feudal' warfare on an extensive scale (–1477); the Shogunate now has little real power.

F **Law and Politics**

Statute of Edward IV against livery and maintenance ('bastard feudalism'); another statute, designed to encourage archery, renewed the prohibition of dice, quoits and football and extended it to 'divers new imagined plays'.

*Sir John Fortescue, *De Laudibus Legum Angliae* (*In Praise of the Laws of England*, favourably comparing them with French laws).

H **Religion and Education**

†Zara Yakub, the Negus, reformed the Church in Abyssinia and suppressed heresy.

K **Literature, Philosophy and Scholarship**

Troan chronicle (the first printed Czech book).

*Jean Régnier, *Le Livre des Fortunes et Adversitez* (poetic expression of the author's philosophy).

L **Births and Deaths**

Sept. 26th, Cardinal Juan de Torquemada d. (80).

1469

B **May**: 3rd, Matthias of Hungary, invading Bohemia at the instigation of Paul II, declared King of Bohemia by rebels against King George.

9th, by the Treaty of St. Omer, Sigismund, Count of Tyrol, mortgages to Charles of Burgundy Upper Alsace and other lands already pledged to the Swiss.

Jun: Edward IV is drawn to Yorkshire by a rebellion led by 'Robin of Redesdale' (?Sir John Conyers) and planned by the Earl of Warwick.

The Bohemian estates accept Vladislav, son of Casimir of Poland, as George's heir.

C **Jul**: 11th, Warwick seals his alliance with George, Duke of Clarence, by the latter's marriage to his daughter, Isabel Neville.

26th, Warwick defeats and then executes William Herbert, Earl of Pembroke, at Edgecote.

28th, Warwick completes his coup d'etat with the arrest of Edward.

Aug: 1st, Louis XI founds the Order of St. Michael.

23rd, Alfonso, Duke of Calabria, son of Ferrante of Naples, defeats papal forces attacking Roberto Malatesta of Rimini.

Sep: a 'Lancastrian' rising in Yorkshire gives Edward the chance to free himself.

D **Oct**: 17th, Ferdinand, son of John of Aragon, marries Isabella, sister of Henry of Castile.

Dec: 2nd, death of Piero de'Medici; succeeded, as virtual rulers of Florence, by his sons Lorenzo (–1492) and Giuliano (–1478).

E Yādigār Muhammad succeeds Abū Sa'īd as the Tīmūrid ruler of Khurāsān (Herat; –1470); while Ahmad succeeds in Transoxiana (Samarqand: –1494).

Death of Montezuma I, the fifth Aztec King; he had extended his dominions to the Gulf of Mexico.

1470

A **Mar**: 12th, Edward disperses a Lincolnshire rising at Empingham ('Loosecoat Field'); learning of Warwick's implication, he turns against the Earl, who flees to France.

B **May**: the Turks capture Negropont from Venice.

15th, death of Charles of Sweden; an interregnum follows (–1483).

C **Jul**: 24th, Louis reconciles Margaret of Anjou and Warwick.

Aug: Husain Baiqara seizes Herat and is proclaimed Sultan of Persia (–1506).

D **Oct**: 6th, Warwick restores Henry VI as King; Edward flees to Holland.

E Frederick II abdicates as Elector of Brandenburg; succeeded by his brother, Albert III Achilles (–1486).

1469

G Economics, Science, Technology and Discovery
(–1471) Fernão Gomes crosses the Equator, reaching Cape Catherine.

H Religion and Education
Birth of Gurū Nānak, founder of the Sikhs (–1533).

J Art, Architecture and Music
Edward grants a charter of fraternity to the 'Minstrels of England' (–1756).

K Literature, Philosophy and Scholarship
Michael Beheim, *De Leben Friedrichs I von der Pfalz* (verse chronicle).
†Ibn-Taghri-Birdi, *Al-Nujūm al-Zāhirah fi Muluk Misr w-al-Qāhirah* (*The Brilliant Stars regarding the Kings of Egypt and Cairo*; history of Egypt, 640–1453).

L Births and Deaths
Mar. 14th, Jacob Fugger d.
May 3rd, Niccolò Machiavelli b. (–1527).
Oct. 9th, Fra Filippo Lippi d. (63).
Oct. 28th, Desiderius Erasmus b. (–1536).

1470

G Economics, Science, Technology and Discovery
*Athanasius Nikitin, a Russian merchant, Account of his travels in India.

H Religion and Education
Paul of Burgos, *Scrutinium Scripturae*, first printed in Rome (–1435).

J Art, Architecture and Music
S. Andrea, Mantua (architect: Alberti).
Tomb of Frederick III, St. Stephen's, Vienna (–1480; sculptor: Nicholas of Leyden).
†Tomb and mosque of Zain al-ʿAbidīn, Sultan of Kashmīr, Madani.
Jean Fouquet, illuminated ms. of Josephus, *History of the Jews*.
*Piero della Francesca, *Duke and Duchess of Urbino* (painted diptych); *The Resurrection* (fresco), Borgo San Sepulcro.
*Dieric Bouts, *Justice of the Emperor Otho* (two large painted scenes).
*Giovanni Bellini, *Pietà* (Milan); Altarpiece, S. Francesco, Pesara.
*Botticelli, *Fortitude*; *Return of Judith*; *Murder of Holofernes* (paintings).
*Hugo van der Goes, *The Vienna Diptych* (painting).

K Literature, Philosophy and Scholarship
*Sir Thomas Malory?; *Le Morte d'Arthur* ('reduced in to Englysshe' from the French Arthurian epical romances; –1485).
*Cristobulus of Imbros, a Greek panegyric of Muhammad II.

L Births and Deaths
May 26th, Pietro Bembo b. (–1547).
June 30th, Charles VIII b. (–1498).
Nov. 2nd, Edward V b. (–1483).
— Jean Mabuse (Jan Gossaert) b. (–1532).

1471 Edward IV recovers England—Growth of Inca Empire

A Jan: Louis invades Picardy in a campaign against Charles of Burgundy.
Mar: 21st, death of George of Poděbrady, King of Bohemia; succeeded by Vladislav II (–1516).

B Apr: 14th, Edward defeats and kills Warwick at Barnet, thus regaining the English throne.
Paul II creates Borso d'Este Duke of Ferrara.
May: 4th, Edward defeats Margaret's forces at Tewkesbury, capturing her and killing Edward, Prince of Wales, her and Henry VI's son.
21st, murder of Henry VI.
Jun: Frederick holds a Reichstag at Regensburg which grants a tax to defend Germany against the Turks (*and see* F).

C Jul: 3rd, Lorenzo de'Medici secures control of Florence when its Signoria appoints his nominees as the ten Accoppiatori to hold full powers of government.
26th, death of Pope Paul II.
Aug: the Portuguese conquer Tangier.
10th, Francesco della Rovere elected as Pope Sixtus IV (–1484).
11th, the Republic of Novgorod, after its defeat by Ivan III, becomes subject to the Dukes of Moscow.

D Oct: 10th, Sten Sture, nephew of Charles VIII, leading a popular rising, defeats the forces of Christian of Denmark at Brunkeberg, outside Stockholm; Sten is elected regent of Sweden (–1503).
Nov: 9th, death of Cristofero Moro, Doge of Venice; succeeded by Niccolò Trono (–1473).

E Le Thanh-tong, Emperor of Dai Viet, annexes the northern provinces of Champa.
Death of Inca Pachacuti; he had established the Inca Empire in Peru, Bolivia, Ecuador and northern Chile and Argentina (–1533).

F **Law and Politics**

Charles of Burgundy establishes a standing army.

Frederick, in the Reichstag (*see* B), promulgates a peace in Germany for four years and establishes a central court of justice (–1475).

G **Economics, Science, Technology and Discovery**

Catalonian serfs revolt and win freedom.

An ordinance of Louis XI appoints a master-general to control the mines in France.

Portuguese navigators discover Fernando Po.

Giovanni Matteo Ferrari, professor of medicine at Pavia, *Practicae pars prima et secunda* (printed).

H **Religion and Education**

Niccolò di Malermi, Italian translation of the Bible (from the Vulgate) first printed at Venice (–1477).

Thomas à Kempis, *De imitatione Christi*, first printed at Augsburg (–1425).

†Denis the Carthusian, mystic, *Speculum conversionis peccatorum* (printed 1473).

J **Art, Architecture and Music**

Mosque of Khwāja Mahmūd Gāwān, Bīdar.

K **Literature, Philosophy and Scholarship**

Lorenzo Valla, *Elegantiae Latinae Linguae*, first printed (–1457).

†Antonio Beccadelli, *De dictis et factis regis Alfonsi* (V), (printed 1485).

L **Births and Deaths**

Jan. 6th, Antonio Beccadelli (Panormita) d. (77).

Feb. 22nd, John of Rokycana, (Hussite) Archbishop of Prague, d.

Mar. 12th, Denis the Carthusian d. (69).

— St. Thomas à Kempis d. (92).

— Albrecht Durer b. (–1528).

*Francisco Pizarro b. (–1541).

1472

B **May**: 24th, death of Charles of France, brother of Louis XI, who is thus able to recover the Duchy of Guienne.

Jun: 27th, Charles of Burgundy attacks Beauvais in a campaign against Louis.

D **Oct**: 17th, Barcelona surrenders to John of Aragon; Catalonia makes peace and is reunited to Aragon.

Nov: 3rd, Louis makes a truce with Charles.

E By the Treaty of Prenzlau, Duke Eric of Pomerania recognises Albert of Brandenburg as his overlord.

A crusading fleet organised by Sixtus IV (temporarily) occupies Smyrna.

1473

A **Feb**: 1st, John of Aragon enters Perpignan in his recovery of Roussillon and Cerdagne following their revolt against French occupation.

Mar: 4th, the revolt of John V, Count of Armagnac, against Louis ends with the surrender of Lectoure and his fortuitous death.

C **Jul**: 28th death of Niccolò Trono, Doge of Venice; succeeded by Niccolò Marcello (–1474).

30th, Frederick III and Charles of Burgundy meet at Trier.

D **Oct**: 15th, Charles compels Réné II, the new Duke of Upper Lorraine, by the Treaty of Nancy, to allow passage to Burgundian troops.

Nov: 25th, Charles ends his conference with Frederick without persuading him to create Charles a king.

E Charles occupies Guelders and Zutphen.

1472

G **Economics, Science, Technology and Discovery**

†Giovanni Matteo Ferrari, *Consiliorum secundum vias Avicennae ordinatorum utile repertorium* (*Useful repertory of the precepts of Avicenna*, –1037; printed 1501).

H **Religion and Education**

The Florentine *studium* (university) transferred to Pisa.

J **Art, Architecture and Music**

*Piero della Francesca, *Madonna with the Duke of Urbino as Donor* (the 'Brera Madonna'); *The Nativity* (paintings; –1475).

K **Literature, Philosophy and Scholarship**

Dante's *Divine Comedy* first printed at Foligno (–1314).

**Gesta Romanorum* (famous Latin collection of legends, stories of chivalry, tales, historical narratives, written in fourteenth century) first printed at Utrecht.

L **Births and Deaths**

Nov. 19th, Cardinal Bessarion of Trebizond d. (69).

— Leone Battista Alberti d. (68).

— Lucas Cranach b. (–1553).

1473

F **Law and Politics**

By the *Dispositio Achillea*, Albert Achilles provides for the indivisible descent of his electorate by primogeniture (thus ensuring the unity of Brandenburg and allowing its growth into the Kingdom of Prussia).

Charles of Burgundy forms the Parlement of Malines as the central court for his dominions.

Edward IV empowers the council of his son Edward, Prince of Wales, to act as a court (anticipating the Tudor Council of the Marches).

G **Economics, Science, Technology and Discovery**

Andrew Hesz of Nuremberg sets up the first printing press in Hungary, at Buda.

Flos naturarum (work on alchemy attributed to 'Geber', *viz.* Jabir ibn Hayyān; –810) printed.

H **Religion and Education**

†Gedun-dub, the first Dalai Lāma of Tibet.

J **Art, Architecture and Music**

Sistine Chapel, Rome (–1481).

Master Francis (Fouquet?), illuminated ms. of St. Augustine's *City of God*.

*Giovanni Bellini, *Coronation of the Virgin* (painting).

K **Literature, Philosophy and Scholarship**

†Guillaume Fillastre, *Chronique de l'histoire de France* (printed 1517).

Niccolò Perotti, *Rudimenta grammatices*.

L **Births and Deaths**

Feb. 19th, Nicolaus Copernicus b. (–1543).

— Pierre Bayard ('the Chevalier Bayard') b. (–1524).

A **Mar**: 30th, by Louis' mediation, Sigismund of Austria recognises the independence and territories of the Swiss Confederation in return for its promise of assistance.

B **Apr**: 4th, in the Union of Constance, Sigismund, the Swiss and the 'Basse-Union' (Strasbourg, Schlestadt, Colmar and Basel) make a defensive alliance (against Charles of Burgundy).

C **Jul**: 25th, Edward and Charles make an alliance for the partition of France. Edward raises money for war by imposing a 'benevolence'.

Aug: Pietro Mocenigo raises the siege of Scutari by the Turks.

D **Dec**: 4th, death of Niccolò Marcello, Doge of Venice; succeeded by Pietro Mocenigo (–1476).

12th, death of Henry IV the Impotent, King of Castile.

13th, his sister, Isabella (–1504), and her husband, Ferdinand of Aragon, are proclaimed as Queen and King of Castile.

G **Economics, Science, Technology and Discovery**

Edward IV, in the Peace of Utrecht, ends war with the Hanse and restores its privileges in England.

†William Cannings of Bristol was the first English shipowner not himself directly engaged in trade.

Johannes Regiomontanus, *Ephemerides 1475–1500* (astronomical tables), printed at Nuremberg.

Lorenzo Buonincontro, *Commentaria in C. Manilii astronomicon.*

H **Religion and Education**

Hendrik Harphius, mystic, *Speculum aureum.*

J **Art, Architecture and Music**

Carlo Crivelli, *The Domidoff Altarpiece* (painting).

*Leonardo, *The Annunciation*; *Ginevra de' Benci* (paintings).

†Guillaume Dufay, Flemish composer of sacred and secular music.

K **Literature, Philosophy and Scholarship**

William Caxton prints and publishes, at Bruges, his first book in English, his own translation of *Recuyell of the Histories of Troye* (a French romance by Raoul le F'evre).

†George Châtelain, *Grand Chronique* (of Burgundy and France); *Histoire du bon Chevalier Jacques de Lalain* (d. 1453).

L **Births and Deaths**

Mar. 20th, George Châtelain d. (70).
Sept. 8th, Lodovico Ariosto d. (–1533).
Nov. 27th, Guillaume Dufay d.
— Lorenzo Campeggio b. (–1539).

1475

A **Feb**: the Castilians fight, indecisively, at Toro, against Afonso of Portugal, who is claiming their crown.

Mar: 10th, Perpignan recovered for France; so ends a savage war (since 1473) by which Louis reconquered Roussillon and Cerdagne.

B **Jun**: 19th, Frederick and Charles end inconclusive hostilities for control of Cologne with a treaty of peace.

C **Jul**: 4th, Edward lands at Calais to begin his invasion of France.

Aug: 29th, by the Treaty of Picquigny, he makes a truce for seven years with Louis, who promises to pay a pension.

Sep: 13th, by the Treaty of Souleuvres, Louis makes a truce for nine years with Charles of Burgundy.

29th, by the Treaty of Senlis, Francis of Brittany promises not to assist the enemies of Louis, who is now destroying a baronial coalition formed by Charles of Burgundy.

D **Nov**: Charles conquers the Duchy of Lorraine.

Dec: 19th, the Count of Saint-Pol executed as a traitor against Louis.

E Matthias of Hungary takes Savacz from the Turks.

Kaffa, the Genoese colony in the Crimea, taken by the Turks; the Mongol Khan of the Crimea becomes an Ottoman vassal.

1476

A **Feb**: 23rd, death of Pietro Mocenigo, Doge of Venice; succeeded by Andrea Vendramino (–1478).

Mar: 2nd, the Swiss defeat the Burgundian army at Grandson.

B **Jun**: 22nd, the Swiss again defeat Charles at Morat. Réné recovers his Duchy of Lorraine.

C **Jul**: 15th, John, Lord of the Isles, compelled to surrender to James III and renounce his pretensions to independence.

D **Dec**: 26th, Galeazzo Maria Sforza of Milan murdered; succeeded by his son, Gian Galeazzo, with his mother, Bona of Savoy, as regent.

E Ivan of Moscow refuses to pay tribute to Ahmad, Khan of 'the Golden Horde', and defeats him.

1475

F **Law and Politics**

With the death of Archbishop Adolph of Mainz, imperial chancellor, the central court in Germany (–1471) collapses.

†Matteo Palmieri, *Della vita civile* (dialogue on civics).

G **Economics, Science, Technology and Discovery**

†Regiomontanus, *De triangulis planis et sphaericis* (astronomy).

H **Religion and Education**

Sixtus IV permits Dominican convents to own property.

Foundation of St. Catherine's College, Cambridge.

J **Art, Architecture and Music**

Uspensky Cathedral, the Kremlin, Moscow (–1479; architect: Aristotle Fioravanti of Florence).

Appointment of Jean Fouquet as painter to King Louis (–1481 d. ?).

Hans Memling, *The Mystical Marriage of St. Catherine* (painting; –1479).

*Hugo van der Goes, *The Portinari Altarpiece* (painting).

*Leonardo, *Antique Warrior* (painting).

*Botticelli, *Adoration of the Kings* (painting).

K **Literature, Philosophy and Scholarship**

*Garcia de Montalvo, *Amadis de Gaula* (*Amadis of Gaul*; prose Spanish romance of chivalry written down about now from lost originals of the fourteenth century; 'A new age of Romance began'—*Hallam*).

L **Births and Deaths**

Mar. 6th, Michelangelo b. (–1564).

July 6th, Johann Müller (Regiomontanus), Bishop of Regensburg, d. (39).

Dec. 11th, Giovanni de' Medici (Leo X) b. (–1521).

— Paolo Uccello d. (78).

— Dieric Bouts d. (*c.* 60).

— Vasco Nuñez de Balbao b. (–1517).

*Thomas Wolsey b. (–1530).

*Gavin Douglas b. (–1523 ?).

*Alexander Barclay b. (–1552).

? Cesare Borgia b. (–1507).

1476

F **Law and Politics**

†Sir John Fortescue, *The Governance of England.*

H **Religion and Education**

Foundation of Upsala University.

K **Literature, Philosophy and Scholarship**

Masuccio, *Novellino* (50 stories), printed in Naples.

1477

A **Jan**: 5th, the Swiss defeat and kill Charles the Bold, Duke of Burgundy at Nancy. His heir is his daughter, Mary, but Louis rapidly seizes the Duchy and County of Burgundy and the Somme towns.

B **Apr**: 3rd, Guillaume Hugon, chancellor of Burgundy, murdered in Ghent.

C **Aug**: 4th, Jacques d'Armagnac, Duke of Nemours, executed as a traitor against Louis.
19th, Mary of Burgundy marries Maximilian of Austria; he now leads the defence of the Low Countries against Louis.

E Death of Mansur Shah, whose kingdom of Malacca comprised most of Malaya.
End of the Ōnin War (–1467) because of general exhaustion; civil warfare, however, remains endemic in Japan.

1478

A **Jan**: 18th, Novgorod surrenders to Ivan, after a rebellion.
24th, Maximilian and Mary of Burgundy make peace with the Swiss, at Zurich.
Feb: 18th, George, Duke of Clarence, murdered after being convicted in Parliament for treason against his brother, Edward IV.

B **Apr**: 26th, in the Pazzi Conspiracy, supported by Sixtus IV, Giuliano de' Medici is murdered but his brother Lorenzo escapes.
May: 6th, death of Andrea Vendramino, Doge of Venice; succeeded by Giovanni Mocenigo (–1485).
Jun: 1st, Sixtus excommunicates Lorenzo de' Medici; he allies with Naples in a general war against Florence, Venice and Milan.

C **Sep**: 15th, Louis calls a council of the Gallican Church to Orleans to protest against payments to the Papacy and to summon a general council of the Church.

D **Dec**: 7th, by the Treaty of Olomuc, Matthias of Hungary recognises Vladislav II as King of Bohemia, so ending their war over the Bohemian succession.

E Christian of Denmark founds the Order of the Elephant.
Albert of Brandenburg defeats attacks by Matthias, the Teutonic Knights, Pomeranians and Hanse.
The Turks conquer Albania.

1477

G **Economics, Science, Technology and Discovery**

Antonio Bettini, *Il Monte Sante di Dio*, printed; it has three copperplate engravings.

*Thomas Norton, *The Ordinall of Alchimy* (claims invention of a general-purposes alchemical furnace and gives earliest known illustration of a balance in a glass case).

H **Religion and Education**

Italian translation of the Bible, revised by Marine de Veneto, printed at Venice.

Foundation of Mainz and Tubingen Universities.

Ferdinand and Isabella establish the Inquisition in Spain.

J **Art, Architecture and Music**

*Botticelli, *Primavera* (painting).

K **Literature, Philosophy and Scholarship**

Anthony Woodville, Earl Rivers, translation, *The Dictes or Sayengis of the Philosophres* (the first book printed by William Caxton's press at Westminster).

*Caxton prints Chaucer's *Canterbury Tales* (–1387).

†Pier Candido Decembrio, *Vita Philippi Mariae ducis Mediolanensis* (1391–1447).

L **Births and Deaths**

Nov. 12th, Pier Candido Decembrio d. (78).

— Gregory of Sanok, Archbishop of Lwów, d.

1478

G **Economics, Science, Technology and Discovery**

Arnold Buckinck, map-engraver, edition of Ptolemy.

H **Religion and Education**

Christian I founds Copenhagen University.

J **Art, Architecture and Music**

*Hugo van der Goes, *The Trinity Altarpiece* (painting).

*Hans Memling, *Portrait of the Medallist Giovanni Candida* (painting).

Perugino, Frescoes at Castel Cerqueto (near Perugia).

K **Literature, Philosophy and Scholarship**

†Theodore of Gaza, *Greek grammar* (printed 1495).

William Worcestre, the first English antiquary, *Itineraries* (record of his travels in England, 1478–80).

L **Births and Deaths**

Feb. 22nd, Hendrik Harphius d.

Dec. 6th, Baldassare Castiglione b. (–1529).

— Giorgione b. (–1510).

— Giangiorgio Trissino b. (–1550).

— Thomas More b. (–1535).

1479

A **Jan**: 19th, death of John II of Aragon; succeeded by his son, Ferdinand II (–1516), and in Navarre by his daughter Eleanor.
26th, Muhammad II makes peace with Venice in the Treaty of Constantinople.
Feb: 12th, death of Queen Eleanor of Navarre; her husband, Francis Phoebus, Count of Foix, becomes King (–1483).

C **Aug**: 7th, an indecisive battle fought at Guinegate between Maximilian and French forces attempting to conquer Flanders.
Sep: Milan makes peace with the Canton of Uri, confirming its possession of Leventina.
4th, by the Treaty of Trujillo, Afonso of Portugal recognises Isabella as Queen of Castile.
7th, Ludovico il Moro becomes ruler of Milan in the minority of his nephew, Gian Galeazzo Sforza.
7th, Alfonso of Calabria defeats the Florentines at Poggibonzi.

E James III arrests his brothers, Alexander, Duke of Albany, and John, Earl of Mar; the latter dies but Albany escapes to England.
Buhlūl Shah of Delhi conquers the Muslim kingdom of Jaunpur.
Le Thanh-tong of Dai Viet takes Luang Prabang, capital of Laos.

1480

A **Jan**: Novgorod again surrenders to Ivan after another rebellion.
Mar: 6th, by the Treaty of Toledo, Ferdinand and Isabella recognise Afonso's African conquests, while he cedes the Canaries to Spain.
6th, by a personal mission to Ferrante, Lorenzo de' Medici makes a peace between Naples and Florence, to which the Papacy, Milan and Venice accede.

B **May**: 23rd, the Turks begin to besiege Rhodes.

C **Jul**: 10th, death of Réné II the Good, Duke of Anjou, titular King of Sicily, Jerusalem, etc.; Louis XI thus gains possession of Provence, Anjou, Maine and Bar.
28th, the Knights Hospitallers finally repulse the siege of Rhodes.
Aug: 10th, the Turks take Otranto.

E Persuaded by Louis XI, James III begins attacks on the English border.
Death of Eric Axelson, the independent ruler of Finland.

1479

J **Art, Architecture and Music**

Eltham Palace hall.

K **Literature, Philosophy and Scholarship**

Francesco Colonna, *Hypnerotomachia Polophili* (a prose allegory, a romance, a miscellany of classical archaeology written in a hybrid language—Lombardic Italian, Latin, Greek, Hebrew and Arabic. When printed and illuminated by Aldus (1499) one of the most beautiful books in the world).

Politian (Angelo Poliziano—Ambrogini), *Le Stanze per la Giostra* (an unfinished epic poem).

†Jorge Manrique, *Coplas por la muerte de su padre don Rodrigo* (elegy on the death of his father).

Bartolomeo Platina, *In vitas summorum pontificum ad Sixtum IV* (history of the Papacy).

1480

G **Economics, Science, Technology and Discovery**

First attempt by a ship from Bristol to discover the 'Isle of Brasil' (in mid-Atlantic).

Leonardo da Vinci designs a parachute.

Mittelalterliche Hausbuch (illustrated south German account of metallurgical processes).

J **Art, Architecture and Music**

King's College Chapel, Cambridge (–1515).

Vault of the Divinity School, Oxford (–1483).

Giovanni Bellini, *Dead Christ supported by Angels* (painting; –1485).

Ghirlandaio, *St. Jerome* (fresco).

*Hugo van der Goes, *The Death of the Virgin* (painting).

*Hans Memling, *Maria Portinari*; *The Virgin Enthroned* (paintings).

*Hieronymus Bosch, *The Crucifixion*; *Christ Mocked*; *The Epiphany* (paintings).

*Filippino Lippi, *Virgin and Child with St. Anthony* (painting).

*Ercole Roberti, *Altarpiece*, Milan (painting).

K **Literature, Philosophy and Scholarship**

Politian (Angelo Poliziano), *Favola di Orfeo* (first pastoral drama to be produced in Italy).

Rudolphus Agricola (Roelof Huysmann), *De Inventione Dialectica* (philosophical work by the greatest Dutch humanist and scholar of his age).

†Jan Dlugosz, *Historia Poloniae* (its history by one of Poland's greatest writers).

†Réné of Anjou, *Mortifiement de vaine plaisance* (moral treatise).

L **Births and Deaths**

— Lucretia Borgia b. (–1519).

*Ferdinand Magellan b. (–1521).

1481

B **May**: 22nd, death of Christian I of Denmark and Norway; succeeded by his son, John I (–1513).

C **Aug**: 28th, death of Afonso V the African, King of Portugal; succeeded by his son, John II (–1495).
30th, two Lithuanian princes executed for conspiring against Casimir IV at the instigation of Ivan of Moscow.
Sep: the Turks in Otranto surrender to Alfonso of Calabria.

D **Dec**: 22nd, Nicholas von Flüe, a hermit, intervenes in a diet at Stanz and averts a breach of the Swiss Confederation; Fribourg and Solothurn join it.

E Abū-al-Hasan of Granada seizes the Castilian castle of Zahara.
Death of Muhammad II, the Ottoman Sultan; succeeded by his son, Bāyezīd II (–1512), who is opposed by his brother, Djem.
Ahmad, Khan of 'the Golden Horde', murdered after abandoning a campaign against Moscow to restore the 'Tartar Yoke'.

1482

A **Feb**: 26th, the Castilians win Alhama from Granada.
Mar: 27th, death of Mary of Burgundy.

B **May**: 2nd, Venice, in alliance with the Papacy, declares war on Ferrara, which is supported by Florence, Milan and Naples (–1484).
Jun: 10th and 11th, by treaties made at Fotheringhay, Edward recognises Alexander of Albany as King of Scotland, as Edward's vassal; an English army then sent to invade Scotland.

C **Jul**: Scottish nobles led by Archibald ('Bell the Cat'), Douglas, Earl of Angus, imprison James and hang his 'base' favourites.
Aug: 21st, Roberto Malatesta, the condottiere employed by Venice and the Papacy, defeats Alfonso of Calabria at Campo Morto.
24th, Richard, Duke of Gloucester, ends his campaign in Scotland with the (final) recovery of Berwick for England.
Sep: 1st, Kiev (then in Lithuania) sacked by the Crimean Tartars, as Ivan's allies.

D **Dec**: 12th, Ercole of Ferrara makes peace with Sixtus IV.
23rd, by the Treaty of Arras, Louis makes peace with Maximilian, who recognises the French occupation of Burgundy, Picardy and Artois, and himself remains in possession of the Low Countries.

E Boabdil rebels against his father, Abū-al-Hasan, and seizes Granada (as Muhammad XI; –1483).

1481

F **Law and Politics**

†Thomas Littleton, *Of Tenures* (Latin treatise on the law of real property; 'the first great English law book since Bracton'—*Plucknett*).

G **Economics, Science, Technology and Discovery**

Louis XI, on gaining possession of Marseilles, proposes to make it an emporium for oriental merchandise.

J **Art, Architecture and Music**

Leonardo, *Adoration of the Kings* (painting).

Botticelli, Ghirlandaio and Perugino, Frescoes in the Sistine Chapel, Rome (–1482).

Verrocchio, Statue of Bartolomeo Colleone, Venice.

K **Literature, Philosophy and Scholarship**

William Caxton translates and prints a Flemish version of *Reynard the Fox* (*Roman de Renart*; it appears in French, German and English literature from *c.* 1200, perhaps 1172, to 1300). He also publishes *The Myrrour of the World* (an English version of Vincent of Beauvais' encyclopedia—1264; the first illustrated book printed in England).

L **Births and Deaths**

Mar. 7th, Baldassare Peruzzi b. (–1536).

Aug. 23rd, Thomas Littleton d.

— Bartolomeo Platina d. (60).

1482

G **Economics, Science, Technology and Discovery**

Diego Cão, a Portuguese mariner, reaches the Congo. The Portuguese make a settlement on the Gold Coast.

First printed Latin editions of Averroes' *Colliget* (Ferrara and Venice; –1160).

J **Art, Architecture and Music**

S. Mariapresso and S. Satiro, Milan (architect: Bramante).

K **Literature, Philosophy and Scholarship**

Luigi Pulci, *Morgante Maggiore* (28 cantos of a celebrated poem, in part burlesque, in part chivalrous and satirical, published in Florence and Venice).

Matteo Maria Boiardo, *Orlando Innamorato* (an unfinished epic on Charlemagne and his court); Songs and sonnets.

Caxton prints Trevisa's translation of Higden's *Polychronicon* (–1387), with his own continuation to 1460.

L **Births and Deaths**

Feb. 2nd, Luca della Robbia d. (82).

May 15th, Paolo del Pozzo Toscanelli d. (85).

Aug. 25th, Margaret of Anjou, former Queen of England, d. (53).

— Hugo van der Goes d. (*c.* 42).

— Antonio Telesio b. (–1534).

1483

A **Jan**: John of Denmark becomes King of Norway (–1513).
(*or* **Feb.**): death of Francis Phoebus, King of Navarre; succeeded by his sister, Catherine (who marries John d'Albret).
Feb: Sixtus IV joins the league against Venice in the War of Ferrara.

B **Apr**: 9th, death of Edward IV of England; succeeded by his son, Edward V.
23rd, the Castilians defeat the army of Granada besieging Lucena and capture Boabdil; Abū-al-Hasan then resumes the throne of Granada (–1485).
Jun: 21st, Ferdinand II, Duke of Braganza, executed for his part in a conspiracy crushed by John of Portugal, who is establishing a despotic government.
26th, Richard, Duke of Gloucester, begins to rule as Richard III (–1485), having deposed his nephew, Edward V; the latter and his brother, Richard, Duke of York, are soon afterwards murdered in the Tower of London.

C **Aug**: John of Denmark and Norway becomes King of Sweden.
30th, death of Louis XI of France; succeeded by his son, Charles VIII (–1498), whose sister, Anne of Beaujeu, acts as regent.

D **Nov**: 2nd, Henry Stafford, Duke of Buckingham, executed after the collapse of his rebellion against Richard III.

1484

A **Jan**: 5th–Mar. 11th, the Regent Anne holds an Estates General (for all France except Brittany) at Tours.

C **Aug**: 7th, the Treaty of Bagnolo ends the War of Ferrara.
12th, death of Pope Sixtus IV.
28th, John of Portugal personally slays the Duke of Viseu when repelling a conspiracy to assassinate him; he consequently forms a royal bodyguard.
29th, Battista Cybò elected as Pope Innocent VIII (–1492).
Sep: 21st, by the Treaty of Nottingham, Richard makes a truce for three years with James of Scotland.

E Ivan of Moscow annexes the principality of Tver.
The Turks take Kilia (in Moldavia) and Bialgorod.

1483

F **Law and Politics**

Code of Hong-duc (Vietnamese law-code).

H **Religion and Education**

Tommaso de Torquemada appointed inquisitor-general of Castile and Aragon.
Ferdinand of Aragon founds Palma University, Majorca.

J **Art, Architecture and Music**

Ashikaga Yoshimasa, the retired Shogun, builds the Silver Pavilion, Kyōto.
*Leonardo, *Lady with an Ermine* (painting); *The Virgin of the Rocks* (Louvre).
*Filippino Lippi, *The Annunciation*; *A Youth* (paintings).
Botticelli, *The Wedding-Feast* (painting).

K **Literature, Philosophy and Scholarship**

Caxton prints the English translation of Jacobus de Voragine's *Golden Legend* (–1265).

L **Births and Deaths**

Feb. 14th, Barbar b. (–1530).
Apr. 6th, Raphael Sanzio b. (–1520).
Nov. 10th, Martin Luther b. (–1546).
— Francesco Guicciardini b. (–1540).
— Thomas Parr (allegedly) b. (–1635!).

1484

F **Law and Politics**

Richard III empowers his council in Yorkshire to act as a judicial body (foreshadowing the Council of the North; –1537).
He also grants a charter to the College of Arms.

G **Economics, Science, Technology and Discovery**

Pietro Borgo, *Arithmetica*.

H **Religion and Education**

Summis desiderantes (bull of Innocent VIII against witchcraft).
Extravagantes Communes (completing the body of canon law).
Hélie de Bourdeille, *Defensio concordatorum* (printed 1520).

J **Art, Architecture and Music**

Albrecht Dürer, *Self-portrait* (aged 13).
*Filippino Lippi, Frescoes in Brancacci Chapel, Florence.

L **Births and Deaths**

Jan. 1st, Ulrich Zwingli b. (–1531).
Apr. 23rd, Julius Caesar Scaliger b. (–1558).
July 15th, Cardinal Hélie de Bourdeille, Archbishop of Tours, d.
— George of Trebizond d. (88).

1485

A **Jan**: 14th, Louis, Duke of Orleans, leading a coalition of French magnates, sends his defiance to the Regent Anne; 'La Guerre Folle' begins.

B **Jun**: 1st, Matthias of Hungary takes Vienna in his conquest of Austria (from Frederick III) and makes the city his capital.

C **Aug**: 1st, Henry Tudor, Earl of Richmond, sails from Harfleur to invade England.
22nd, Richard III killed at the Battle of Bosworth; Richmond succeeds as Henry VII (–1509), founding the Tudor dynasty (–1603).
Sep: Louis of Orleans submits to Anne; end of 'La Guerre Folle'.
15th, in an expedition to defend Moldavia against the Turks, Casimir of Poland receives the homage of its Voivode.

D **Oct**: 30th, Innocent begins a war against Ferrante of Naples.
Nov: 4th, death of Giovanni Mocenigo, Doge of Venice; succeeded by Marco Barbarigo (–1486).

E Abū-al-Hasan abdicates the throne of Granada in favour of his brother, Muhammad XII ('al-Zaghall'; –1489); Ferdinand and Isabella then release Boabdil to fight against Muhammad.

1486

A **Jan**: 18th, Henry VII marries Elizabeth, daughter of Edward IV.
Feb: 10th, the Breton Estates plan the marriage of Anne, the heir of Duke Francis, to Maximilian; he consequently attempts to invade France.
16th, Maximilian elected as King of the Romans (–1519); he proclaims a peace in Germany for ten years.
Mar: a plot by Francis, Viscount Lovel, to ambush Henry in Yorkshire fails.
11th, death of Albert III Achilles, Elector of Brandenburg; succeeded by his son, John Cicero (–1499).

B **May**: 7th, Alfonso of Calabria defeats Papal forces at Montorio.

D **Dec**: Louis of Orleans, Réné of Lorraine and other French nobles ally with the lords of Brittany in a new league against the Regent Anne.

E Agostino Barbarigo succeeds Marco Barbarigo as Doge of Venice (–1501).
Sāluva Narasimha, a virtually independent ruler of Chandragirirājya, in the disintegrating Vijayanagar Empire, deposes Praudharāya and founds the Sāluva dynasty (–1505).

1485

H **Religion and Education**

In the Treaty of Kutná Hora, Vladislav II confirms the Compacts of Prague (–1433 D) and other concessions to Hussite opinion.

J **Art, Architecture and Music**

Ivan III rebuilds the Kremlin.

Mantegna, *The Triumph of Caesar* (cartoons; –1494); **Virgin and Child and Angels* (painting).

*Filippino Lippi, *Madonna degli Otto* (painting).

Hans Memling, *The St. Christopher Triptych* (painting).

K **Literature, Philosophy and Scholarship**

Caxton prints his first edition of Sir Thomas Malory's *Morte d'Arthur* (–1470).

L **Births and Deaths**

Oct. 28th, Rudolphus Agricola d. (42).

— Sebastiano del Piombo b. (–1547).

— Hernando Cortez b. (–1547).

1486

G **Economics, Science, Technology and Discovery**

Rhazes, *Liber Continens* (–925, 1279), first printed at Brescia.

J **Art, Architecture and Music**

Ghirlandaio, Frescoes in Sassetti Chapel, Sta. Trinità, Florence, completed.

Filippino Lippi, *The Vision of St. Bernard* (painting).

*Giovanni Bellini, *The Transfiguration* (painting).

*Botticelli, *Giovanna degli Albizzi and the Cardinal Graces*; *Lorenzo Tornabuoni and the Liberal Arts* (paintings).

K **Literature, Philosophy and Scholarship**

Giovanni Pico della Mirandola, *De omni re scribili* (*Concerning All Things Knowable*); and *Oratio de hominis dignitate* (a treatise on Free Will).

†Guillaume Alexis, *Les Faintises du monde* (a philosophical poem); and *Le Blason de faulses amours* (a didactic poem).

†Erik Olai, *Chronica Regni Gothorum* (a chronicle, by the Father of Swedish historical writing).

*Henri Baude, *Les Lamentations Bourrien* (a verse satire in the style of Villon's satirical poems, directed against priests).

*Jacopo Sannazaro, *L'Arcadia* (a pastoral romance).

**Historiae Croylandensis Continuatio* (*Continuation of the History of Crowland*, the last English monastic chronicle).

L **Births and Deaths**

Aug. 11th, William Waynflete, Bishop of Winchester, d.

Sept. 19th, Arthur, Prince of Wales (–1502).

Nov. 13th, Johann Maier von Eck b. (–1543).

1487

A **Mar**: Anne's forces suppress the rebellion in Guienne.

B **May**: 24th, Lambert Simnel, pretending to be Edward IV's nephew, crowned in Dublin as 'King Edward V'.

Jun: 16th, Henry defeats and captures Simnel at East Stoke, near Newark; this is the last battle in 'The Wars of the Roses'.

C **Jul**: Frederick and Maximilian form the Swabian League of prelates, lords and towns to oppose the aggressions of the Wittelsbach Dukes of Bavaria.

Ivan subdues the Mongol khanate of Kazan and installs a vassal khan.

Aug: 11th, Innocent VIII makes peace with Ferrante of Naples.

13th, despite their inclusion in the peace, Ferrante massacres the Neapolitan nobles who had rebelled.

1488

A **Feb**: 5th, Maximilian held prisoner (until 16 May) by rebels in Ghent.

B **Jun**: 11th, James of Scotland murdered in flight from his defeat by rebelling nobles at Sauchieburn; succeeded by his son, James IV (–1513), who is in the rebels' custody.

C **Jul**: 27th, French royal forces defeat and capture Louis of Orleans at Saint-Aubin du Cormier.

Aug: 20th, by the Treaty of Sablé, Charles VIII makes peace with Francis of Brittany.

Sep: 9th, death of Francis II; succeeded by his daughter, Anne (–1491). Charles claims custody of the Duchy but the Bretons oppose him.

1487

F Law and Politics

Henry VII's (subsequently misnamed) 'Star Chamber Act' establishes a judicial sub-committee of his council.

Adoption of a set form for writing examination papers for the Chinese civil service.

G Economics, Science, Technology and Discovery

Ambrogio Contarini, *Viaggio al Ussum-Cassan, re di Persia* (describing his embassy from Venice to Persia, 1473–77, to the Court of Uzun Hasan).

H Religion and Education

Innocent VIII, Constitutions for monastic reform.

Malleus Maleficarum (*The Hammer of Witches*; infamous work encouraging the zeal of witch-hunters).

J Art, Architecture and Music

Filippino Lippi, Frescoes in Strozzi Chapel, Sta. Maria Novella, Florence (–1502).

Hans Memling, *St. Benedict* (painting).

L Births and Deaths

Oct. 22nd, Antonio Bettini, Bishop of Foligno, d. (91).

— Andrea del Sarto b. (–1531).

— Bernardino Ochino b. (–1564).

— Miles Coverdale b. (–1568).

1488

F Law and Politics

†Boromo Trailokanet, King of Ayudhya (Siam, from 1448), had formed a centralised administration, codified laws and organised society.

G Economics, Science, Technology and Discovery

Bartholomew Diaz, a Portuguese mariner, rounds the Cape of Storms (renamed the Cape of Good Hope by John II of Portugal).

H Religion and Education

Massacre of the Vaudois (Waldenses) heretics of Dauphiné.

Torquemada's rules for the Inquisition in Spain adopted.

A chair of Hebrew founded at Bologna University.

J Art, Architecture and Music

The *Būstān* of Bihzād, the Persian miniaturist.

Filippino Lippi, Frescoes in Caraffa Chapel, S. Maria Sopra Minerva, Rome (–1493).

*Giovanni Bellini, *St. Job* (painted altarpiece, Venice).

K Literature, Philosophy and Scholarship

†Bernardo Pulci, *Barlaam e Josafat* (religious drama).

L Births and Deaths

Apr. 22nd, Ulrich von Hutten b. (–1523).

1489

A **Feb**: 14th, by the Treaty of Dordrecht, Henry and Maximilian ally to assist the Bretons; an English contingent is subsequently sent to Brittany.

Mar: 14th, Venice buys Cyprus from Catherine Cornaro, last of the Lusignan dynasty of Kings of Cyprus.

27th, by the preliminary treaty of Medina del Campo, Ferdinand and Isabella project a marriage alliance with Henry VII.

B **Apr**: 28th, Henry Percy, Earl of Northumberland, killed by a mob when collecting a tax; Henry consequently goes to Yorkshire to suppress the rising.

C **Jul**: death of Buhlūl Lodi, Shah of Delhi; succeeded by his son, Sikandar (–1517).

Aug: 18th, Ferdinand takes Malaga.

D **Nov**: 25th, Muhammad XII of Granada surrenders to Ferdinand and Isabella at their capture of Baza; Boabdil resumes the Kingdom of Granada (–1492).

1490

A **Mar**: 16th, Maximilian obtains Tyrol by the grant of its Count, Sigismund Habsburg.

B **Apr**: 6th, death of Matthias Corvinus, King of Hungary, without lawful issue; the Habsburgs recover Austria in the disintegration of his empire.

C **Jul**: 11th, Vladislav of Bohemia elected as King of Hungary (as Ladislas VII; –1516).

D **Dec**: Maximilian marries Anne of Brittany by proxy.

E The Muslim kingdom of Kulbarga (the Deccan) disintegrates with the establishment of kingdoms by the governors of Bījāpur, Berar, Bīdar and Ahmadnagar.

1489

G **Economics, Science, Technology and Discovery**

A statute of Henry VII attempts to halt the depopulation of arable land by enclosure.

I-yü t'u-chih (*Pictures and descriptions of strange nations*, anon., of 1392–1430) printed.

H **Religion and Education**

A statute limits the abuse of clerical privilege in England.

J **Art, Architecture and Music**

Hans Memling, *The Shrine of St. Ursula* (painting).

Palazzo Strozzi, Florence, begun (by Benedetto da Maiano).

K **Literature, Philosophy and Scholarship**

Lorenzo de' Medici, *San Giovanni e San Paolo* (religious drama).

Politian, *Miscellanea* ('consisting of 100 observations illustrating passages of Latin authors'—*Hallam*).

Philippe de Commynes, *Mémoires* (completed in 1498; more than a chronicle of events in the times of Charles the Bold and Louis XI, as the author was the first critical and philosophical historian in European literature).

†Bernardo Giustiniani, *De origine urbis Venetiarum* (printed 1492).

L **Births and Deaths**

Mar. 10th, Bernardo Giustiniani d. (81).

July 2nd, Thomas Cranmer b. (–1556).

1490

J **Art, Architecture and Music**

*Botticelli, *The Annunciation* (painting).

*Signorelli, *Virgin and Child* (painting; –1495).

Ghirlandaio, Frescoes in choir, Sta. Maria Novella, Florence, completed.

K **Literature, Philosophy and Scholarship**

Joanot Martorell (d. 1488?), *Tirant lo blanc* (Catalan romance of chivalry).

*Robert Henryson, *The Testament of Cresseid* (continues Chaucer's poem –1384).

†*Laonicus Chalcocondylas, *Historiarum demonstrationes* (prose history, in Greek, of the Byzantine Empire, 1298–1453).

L **Births and Deaths**

*Francois Rabelais b. (–1553).

Hugh Latimer b. (–1555).

1491 Surrender of Granada—Brittany annexed to France

A Jan: 25th, Polish-Lithuanian forces decisively defeat the Transvolgan Tartars at Zaslaw and so end their ravages.

Feb: 20th, by the Treaty of Košice, the victorious Vladislav of Bohemia cedes lands in Silesia to his brother, Olbracht, who had been claiming the Hungarian crown.

D Nov: 7th, by the Treaty of Bratislava, Maximilian abandons his attempt to conquer Hungary and recognises Vladislav as its King.

25th, Boabdil concludes a treaty to surrender the city of Granada to Ferdinand and Isabella, which they have besieged since the spring.

Dec: 6th, Anne of Brittany marries Charles VIII and so ends the Duchy's independence of France.

E Henry raises money for a war with France by collecting 'benevolences'.

Perkin Warbeck is persuaded, in Cork, to impersonate a son of Edward IV.

The triple partition of Georgia completed.

G **Economics, Science, Technology and Discovery**

Apr. 17th, Ferdinand and Isabella sign their contract with Christopher Columbus concerning his proposed voyage of discovery.

? Seamen from Bristol possibly discover Newfoundland.

J **Art, Architecture and Music**

Hans Memling, *Altarpiece of the Passion*, Lübeck.

Carlo Crivelli, *The Virgin and Child* (painting).

K **Literature, Philosophy and Scholarship**

†John Rous, the two *Warwick Rolls* (providing illustrated history of armour); *Historia Regum Angliae* (legend and topography).

L **Births and Deaths**

Nov. 8th, Theofilo Folengo b. (–1544).

— William Caxton d. (69).

— Ignatius de Loyola b. (–1556).

— Martin Bucer b. (–1551).

— Jacques Cartier b. (–1557).

INDEX

The scheme of this Index is described in the Introduction, pp. x, xi. The main subject entries are as follows:

Agriculture
Alchemists
Anthologists
Arab literature
Archaeologists and antiquaries
Archbishoprics and bishoprics
Architects and masons
Architecture
Arthurian Legends
Astrologers
Astronomers
Astronomical instruments
Autobiographers
Bible
Biographers
Boroughs
Botanists
Canals
Cannon
Canon Law
Canonists
Cathedrals
Chansons de gestes
Charters of liberties
Chivalry
Church
Clergy
Coins
Colonisation
Conversion to Christianity
Councils, General
Crusades
Diarists
Dictionaries
Drama
Economics
Encyclopedias
Feudalism
Frescoes
Geographers
Government and politics
Grammarians
Herbals
Heresy
Historians and chroniclers
Humanists
Islam
Jews
Jurists
Kingdoms, Christian
Law
Madonna
Maps
Mathematicians
Medicine
Mendicant Orders
Meteorologists
Mills
Miracle Plays
Monasteries
Music
Mystics
Naturalists
Painters
Papacy
Parliaments
Philologists
Philosophers
Physicians
Poets
Printing
Religious Orders
Schools
Sculptors
Surgeons
Technology
Theologians
Trade
Translations
Travel-writers
Troy Theme
Universities
War
Witchcraft

Nationalities of Persons are abbreviated:

C. Chinese
E. English
Eg. Egyptian
F. French
G. German
Gk. Greek
It. Italian
Ja. Japanese
Je. Jewish
Per. Persian
Port. Portuguese
Sp. Spanish
Sp. M. Spanish Muslim

INDEX

A

Aachen, W. Germany, 802 A, F, H, 813 C, 817 C, 881 E; Palace, 805 J; organ, 826 J; Cathedral, 1355 J
Aagesön, Svend, Danish historian, 1187 K
Aargau, Switzerland, 1415 E
Aarhus, Denmark, Bishopric, 948 H
Aaron, Archbishop, monk of Brauweiler, 1044 H
Abacus, treatises on (Gerbert), 1003 G; (Hermann Contractus), 1054 G; (Fibonacci), 1202 G
Abano, Pietro d', It. philosopher of science (*c.* 1250–1318), 1303 G
Abāqa, Ilkhan of Persia, 1265 A, 1266 E, 1269 E, 1277 B, 1282 B
Abas I, King of Armenia, 928 E, 952 E
'Abbād, Ismā'īl ibn, Per. philologist (*c.* 937–95), 995 K
'Abbād Mu'tadid, King of Seville (1042–69), 1069 E
'Abbās (Haly Abbas), 'Alī ibn-al-, Arab physician (d. 994), 994 G, 1127 G
'Abbās al-Rasūlī, al-, Sultan of Yemen (1363–77), Arab botanist, 1377 G
Abbasa, Egypt, battle, 1251 B
'Abbasīd Caliph, Empire, *see* Baghdād, Caliphate of; period, ruin of, 847 J
Abbeville, France, 1232 F, 1458 K; abbey, *see* Centula
Abbeys. *See* Monasteries
Abbo of Fleury, F. mathematician and historian (954–1004), 1004 K
'Abd-al-Haqq II, Sultan of Morocco (1428–65), 1465 E
'Abd-al-Mu'min, Sultan of Morocco (b. 1101/2), 1129 D, 1145 C, 1147 B, 1149 E, 1152 E, 1158 E, 1161 E, 1163 B
'Abd-al-Wāhid II, Sultan of Morocco (1232–42), 1232 D
'Abd-ar-Rahmān II, Emir of Spain, 822 E, 837 E, 852 C, H
'Abd-ar-Rahmān III, Emir and Caliph of Spain (b. 889; 912–61), 912 D, 913 D, 917 E, 929 A, 931 E, 932 E, 936 J, 961 E, H; wars with Christians, 920 E, 924 E, 937 E, 939 C, 960 E
'Abd-ar-Rahmān IV, Caliph of Cordova, 1018 E
'Abd-ar-Rahmān V, Caliph of Cordova, 1023 E
'Abd-ar-Rahmān, Regent of Cordova, 1008 E
'Abdallāh, Emir of Spain, 888 E, 891 A, 912 D
Abe Seimei, Ja. astronomer, 1005 G
Abel, King of Denmark, 1250 C, 1252 B
Abelard, Peter, F. philosopher and theologian (1079–1142), 1079 L, 1113 H, 1121 H, 1122 H, 1140 H, 1142 K, L
Abele Spelen, 1350 K
Aberdeen, Scotland, 1308 E
Abingdon, England, 1431 B
Abhidhānacintāmaninămamālā (Hemacandra), 1170 K
Ableiges, Jacques d', F. jurist, 1390 F
Abraham ben Ezra, Sp. Je. translator and theologian (1092–1167), 1167 G, H
Abranel, Isaac, Je. philosopher (1437–1508), 1437 L
Abū-l-Barakāt, Eg. philologist and Coptic theologian (d. 1324), 1316 K
Abū-l-Fidā', Syrian soldier, geographer and historian (1273–1331), 1321 G, 1331 J, K
'Abū-al-Hasan 'Alī, King of Granada, 1462 E, 1481 E, 1482 A, E, 1483 B, 1485 E
Abū'l-Qāsim Muhammad, Prime Minister of Seville, 1042 E
Abū-Bakr, Shah of Delhi, 1389 A, 1390 D
Abū Haiyan al-Gharnāti, Sp. M. philologist (1256–1344), 1313 K, 1344 K
Abu Ma'shār (Albumazar), Per. astronomer and astrologer (786–886), 886 G, L
Abū Nuwas, Hasan ibn Hāni', Arab-Per. classic poet (762–810), 810 K
Abū Sa'īd, Sultan (Ilkhan) of Persia, 1316 E, 1335 E
Abū-Sa'īd, ruler of Transoxiana and Khurasan (1451–69), 1459 E, 1469 E
Abū Sa'id, Per. mystic (967–1049), 1049 H
Abulcasis. *See* Zahrāwi
Abydus, Turkey, battle, 989 B
Abyssinia, chronicles of, 1344 K; church, 1468 H; described, 1348 G; language, 1344 K
Zague dynasty estab., 925 E
Solomonid dynasty estab., 1270 E; *and see* 'Amda Seyon, Zara Yakub
Acamapitzin, Aztec king, 1352 E
Acciajuoli, Antonio I, Duke of Athens, 1403 E
Acciajuoli, Franco, Duke of Athens, 1455 E, 1460 E
Acciajuoli, Nerio I, Duke of Athens, 1379 E, 1388 B, 1394 A
Acciajuoli, Nerio II, Duke of Athens, 1455 E
Acciajuoli, Niccolò, lord of Corinth, 1358 B
Accursius (Francisco Accorso), It. jurist (1182–1260), 1182 L, 1260 F
Acerba (Cecco d'Ascoli), 1327 K
Achaea, Latin state in Greece, 1209 E, 1278 B, 1326 E, 1432 E
Achillini, Alessandro, It. philosopher and anatomist (1463–1512), 1463 L
Achthamar, on Lake Van, Turkey, church, 915 J
Ackermann aus Böhmen (Johann von Tepl), 1405 K
Acominatos, Nicetas, Gk. historian, 1206 K
Acre, Israel, 1089 E, 1100 B, 1104 B, 1148 B, 1189 C, D, 1191 B, C; capital of Kingdom of Jerusalem

Acre—*contd.*
(*q.v.* for Kings), 1191 C, 1239 C, 1263 B, 1271 B, 1272 B; naval battle off, 1287 B; taken by Egypt, 1291 B, E
Acropolites, George, Gk. historian, 1282 K
Actuarios, Joannes, Gk. physician, 1342 G
Adalbero, Archbishop of Reims, 985 B, 989 A
Adalbert, King of Italy (950–61), 950 D, 952 C
Adalbert, Archbishop of Bremen/Hamburg, 1046 B, 1062 B, 1066 A, 1072 L
Adalbert, St., Archbishop of Magdeburg (d. 982), 961 H, 968 H
Adalbert, Archbishop of Mainz, 1115 D
Adalbert, St. Bishop of Prague, 996 H, 997 E, H
Adam of Bremen, G. historian and geographer, 1076 K
Adam de la Halle, F. poet and satirist (*c.* 1240–88), 1262 K, 1269 K, 1283 K
Adenet le Roi, F. poet and romance writer (1240?–1300?), 1280 K, 1282 K
Adelaide, St. (931–999), German Empress, 951 C, 984 B, 991 B, 999 D
Adelaide (Praxedis) of Kiev, German Empress, 1089 E, 1094 E
Adelard, St., Abbot of Corbie, 827 L
Adelard of Bath, E. translator, astronomer and scientist, 1100 G, 1126 G, 1130 G
Adelbold, Bishop of Utrecht, G. mathematician and historian, 1026 G, K
Adhemar of Chabannes, F. historian (988–1034), 1034 K
Adhemar, Bishop of Le Puy, 1098 C
'Ādid, al-, Caliph of Egypt (1160–71), 1167 A, C, 1168 D, 1169 A, 1171 C
'Ādil, al-, Sayf-ad-Dīn, Sultan of Egypt and Syria, 1196 C, 1204 C, 1218 C
Āditya I, King of Cholas (871–907), 880 E, 897 E
Administrando imperio, De (Constantine VII), 959 F
Administratione, Liber de rebus in (Suger), 1145 K
Adolf of Nassau, King of the Romans (1292–8), 1292 B, 1294 C, 1298 B, C, 1301 B
Adolf, Count of Holstein, 1143 G, 1191 E
Adolf of Nassau, Archbishop of Mainz, 1462 D, 1475 F
Adoration of the Kings (Botticelli), 1475 J; (Leonardo), 1481 J
Adoration of the Lamb (Hubert and Jan van Eyck), 1426 J
Adoration of the Magi (Gentile), 1423 J
Adour, river, France, 1125 G
Adrian II, Pope (867–72), 867 D, 869 H, 872 D
Adrian III, Pope (884–5), 884 B, 885 C
Adrian IV (Nicholas Breakspear), Pope, 1154 D, 1155 A, B, D, 1156 B, 1157 D, 1158 E, 1159 C
Adrian V (Ottobuono Fieschi), Pope (1276), 1267 B, 1276 C
Adrian VI (Adrian of Utrecht), Pope (1522–3), 1459 L
Adrianople, Turkey, 813 B, 923 E, 1205 A, 1206 C; battle, 1095 E; Treaty of, 1190 A; Ottoman capital, 1366 E
'Adud-ad-Dawla, Buwayhid Sultan, 946 A, 978 G, 983 E
Adwār, Kitāb al- (Safī), 1294 J
Adwār al-Mansūb, Kitāb al- (ibn-Sab'in), 1269 J
Adwiyah al-Mufradah, Kitāb al- (al-Ghāfiqi), 1165 H
Aed, King of Scotland (877–8), 877 E, 878 E
Ælfric, E. ecclesiastic and writer (*c.* 955–*c.* 1010), 991 K, 995 K, 1005 K
Aelle, King of Northumbria, 867 A
Aelnoth, Danish historian, 1109 K
Aesop's *Fables*, 1185 K
Afghanistan, 988 E, 1221 D, 1222 B; *and see* Ghaznī, Ghūr
Aflah, Jābir ibn-, Arab astronomer and mathematician, 1145 G
Afonso I Henriques, Count and King of Portugal (b. 1110), 1112 B, 1128 E, 1137 C; King, 1139 C, 1143 E, 1147 D, 1179 E, 1184 B, C, 1185 D
Afonso II the Fat, King of Portugal (b. 1185), 1211 A, 1217 C, 1220 E, 1223 A
Afonso III, King of Portugal (b. 1210; 1248–79), 1245 E, 1248 E, 1250 E, 1252 G, 1254 F, 1257 E, 1267 E, 1279 A
Afonso IV, King of Portugal (b. 1290/1), 1325 A, 1340 D, 1357 B
Afonso V the African, King of Portugal (b. 1432), 1438 C, 1440 E, 1449 B, 1471 C, 1475 A, 1479 C, 1480 A, 1481 C
Africa, explored, 1354 G; *and see* Portugal. *See also* Negro Empires
Africa (Petrarch), 1339 K
Africa, North, Muslim conquest, 871 K; *and see* Egypt, Kairāwan, Morocco, Tunis
Agapitus II, Pope, 946 B, 955 D
Agenais, France, 1279 B, 1336 C
Aghānī, Kitāb al- (al-Isfahānī), 967 K
Aghlabid dynasty. *See* Kairāwan
Agincourt, France, battle, 1415 D
Agincourt Song, 1415 J
Agliate, Italy, basilica, 875 J
Agios Neophytos, Cyprus, church, 1193 J
Agnani, Italy, Treaty of, 1295 B
Agnellus, It. historian, 840 L
Agnes, German Empress (d. 1077), 1056 D
Agnes of Meran (irregular) wife of Philip II, 1196 B, 1200 C
Agobard, St., Archbishop of Lyons, writer on magic, 841 H
Agricola, Rudolphus (Roelof Huysman), Dutch scholar, philosopher and humanist (1443–85), 1443 L, 1480 K, 1485 L
Agriculture:
Department (Indian) of, 1340 G
enclosures, 1489 G
wheel-barrow, 1250 G
writings on:
Arab, 800 G, 1200 G
Chinese, 1314 G
European, 1250 G, 1307 G, 1379 G
See also Food, Horses
Agridi, Cyprus, battle, 1232 B
Ahlat, Turkey, 1231 C
Ahmad, Khan of the Golden Horde (1465–81), 1476 E, 1481 E
Ahmad, Shah of Gujarāt (1411–43), 1429 E
Ahmad I the Saint (Walī), Shah of Kulbarga (1422–35), 1422 E, 1429 E, 1432 E, 1436 J
Ahmad, Emir of Sicily, 1039 E
Ahmad, ruler of Transoxiana (1469–94), 1469 E
Ahmadābād, India, 1453 J
Ahmadnagar, Indian Muslim kingdom, 1490 E
Ahmedī, Ahmad ibn-Abrāhīm al-, Turkish poet (*c.* 1330–1413), 1390 K
Ahsan al-Taqāsim fi Ma'rifat (al-Maqdisī), 985 G
Aigues-Mortes, France, 1241 G
Ailly, Pierre d', Cardinal, F. theologian (1350–1420), 1381 G, 1420 L
Ailred, Abbot of Rievaulx, E. religious author and historian (*c.* 1110–66), 1166 H, K
Aimeri de Narbonne (Bertrand), 1200 K
Aimery, Patriarch of Antioch, 1170 H
Aimon, monk of Fleury, F. historian, 1010 K
'Aja'ib Timūr (ibn 'Arabshāh), 1435 K

Ajmēr, Pakistan, 1192 E; mosque, 1200 J
Akhbār al-Sīn w-al-Hind (Abū Zaid), 920 G
Akhbār al-Tiwāl (al-Dīnawarī), 895 K
Akhbār misr wa-Fadā'ilha (al-Musabbihi), 1029 K
Akhbār Mulūk Bani 'Ubaid (ibn-Hammād), 1230 K
Akhlāq al-Ashrāf (Zākānī), 1370 H
A-ku-ta, leader of Jürched and Chinese Emperor, 1115 E, 1122 E
'Alā'-ad- Dīn Muhammad, Sultan of Delhi (1295–1316), 1294 E, 1295 C, 1297 E, 1299 E, 1301 F, 1307 E, 1308 E, 1310 E, 1316 A
'Alā'-ad-Dīn Husayn 'the World-Burner', Sultan of Ghūr (1149–61), 1151 E
'Alā'-ad-Dīn Muhammad, Khwārizm Shah (1200–20), 1214 E, 1219 E, 1220 D
Alain Barbe-Torte, Breton leader, 937 E
Alaiye, Turkey, 1224 J, 1228 G
'Alam, Shah of Delhi, 1446 E, 1451 B
Alamūt, Iraq, 1090 E, 1256 D
Alan of Lille (de Insulis), F. philosopher, 1202 H
A'laq al-Nafīsah (ibn-Rustah), 903 G
Alarcos, Spain, battle, 1196 C
Alban, St. *See Vie de Seint Auban*
Albania, 991 E; kingdom, 1368 E; Turkish conquest, 1432 E, 1443 E, 1448 D, 1478 E; *and see* Skanderbeg
Albany, Dukes of. *See* Stewart
Albergati, Niccolò, It. cardinal, 1443 L
Alberic, Duke of Rome (932–54), 932 E, 954 C, 955 D
Albert, anti-pope, 1102 A
Albert I Habsburg, King of the Romans (b. 1248; 1298–1308)
  as Duke of Austria, 1282 D, 1292 E
  King of Hungary, 1290 C
  King of the Romans, 1298 C, 1305 D
  alliance with France, 1299 C
  revolts against, 1299 D, 1300 C, 1302 E, 1307 B
  relations with Pope, 1301 B, 1302 B
  war with Bohemia, 1304 E, 1305 B
  murdered, 1308 B
Albert II Habsburg, King of the Romans (b. 1397; 1438–9)
  as (Albert V) Duke of Austria, 1426 A
  King of Hungary, 1437 D
  King of the Romans, 1438 A, 1439 D
  posthumous son, 1440 A
Albert II, King of Sweden (1363–89) and Duke of Mecklenburg (d. 1412), 1363 D, 1367 D, 1369 D, 1371 E, 1380 E; deposed, 1389 A, 1395 B, 1404 D
Albert I the Bear, Margrave and Elector of Brandenburg, 1134 E, 1150 E, 1170 D; Duke of Saxony, 1139 E, 1140 B
Albert of Brabant, Bishop of Liège, 1192 C, D
Albert, Bishop of Riga, 1201 E, 1204 E, 1217 E, 1224 E, 1227 E, 1229 E
Albert of Saxony, G. philosopher, 1390 K
Albert von Stade, G. abbot, poet and chronicler (1200?–1261), 1256 K, 1261 K
Albertano of Brescia, It. philologist, 1245 K
Alberti, Leone Battista, It. architect, humanist and writer (1404–72), 1404 L, 1435 J, 1441 K, 1446 J, 1450 J, 1456 J, 1460 J, 1470 J, 1472 L
Albertus Magnus, G. philosopher, theologian and scientist (1193–1280), 1193 L, 1256 K, 1280 H, L
Albi, France, Cathedral, 1282 J
Albigensians. *See* Toulouse
Albizzi, Giovanna degli (Botticelli), 1486 J
Albizzi, Maso degli, ruler of Florence (1347–1417), 1417 E
Albornoz (Gil Alvarez Carillo), Sp. cardinal, legate in Papal States (d. 1367), 1353 B, 1354 B, C, 1355 B, 1357 B, C, F, 1358 C, 1359 C, 1360 A, C, 1361 B, 1363 D
Albrecht, Archbishop of Magdeburg, 1207 J
Albumazar. *See* Abu Ma'shār
Albuquerque, Alfonso d', Port. statesman (1453–1515), 1453 L
Albutenius. *See* Battānī
Alcántara, Spain, Knights of, 1147 E
Alcaraz, Spain, battle, 1096 E
Alcazar do Sal, Portugal, battle, 1217 C
Alchemists:
  Arab. *See* Jābir; Kindi
  Catalan. *See* Rupescissa, John; Sedacer, Guillem; Villanova, Arnold
  English. *See* Dombleday, John; Norton, Thomas
  Italian. *See* Buono, Pietro
  Persian. *See* Rāzī
Alchemy, Book of the Composition of, 810 G, 1144 G; cf. *Flos naturarum*, 1473 G
Alcobaça, Portugal, abbey, 1158 J
Alcohol, 1100 G, 1110 G, 1120 G; liqueurs, 1332 G; brandy, 1360 G
Alcuin of York, E. educator and writer (735–804), 800 H, K, 804 L
Alderotti, Taddeo, It. physician, 1303 G
Aldobrandeschi, Margaret, Countess of Tuscany, 1300 A
Aldobrandon of Siena, It. physician (d. 1287), 1257 G
Aldus Manutius (Aldo Manuzio), It. printer (1450–1515), 1450 L
Alemannia (*i.e.* Swabia, W. Germany and Switzerland), 876 C, 909 E
Alençon, France, 1048 E; Dukes of, 1437 B, 1440 A, 1465 C
Aleppo, Syria:
  capital of Hamdānids, 944 D; *and see* Sayf-ad-Dawla
  taken by Greeks, 962 D, 969 D, 995 B
  capital of Mirdāsids, 1023 E
  taken by Seljuqs, 1074 E, 1086 E, 1095 E, 1123 B
  attacked by Greeks, 1138 B
  capital of Zangids, 1146 C, 1181 D; *and see* Nūr-ad-Din, Ismā'īl
  taken by Ayyūbids, 1183 B; *and see* Nasir II
  sacked by Mongols, 1280 D
  battle, 1400 E
Alessandria, Italy, 1167 E, 1174 D, 1175 B, 1270 E, 1290 C, 1292 A; battle outside, 1391 C
Alexander II (Anselm of Baggio), Pope (1061–73), 1061 C, 1062 D, 1072 H, 1073 B
Alexander III (Roland Bandinelli), Pope, 1159 C, 1162 C, 1164 E, 1165 D, 1179 E, 1180 E; dispute with Frederick I, 1160 A, 1162 B, 1167 C, 1176 D; holds Lateran Council, 1179 A, H
Alexander IV (Rinaldo Conti), Pope, 1254 D, 1255 B, 1256 B, H, 1257 B, E, 1258 D, E, 1259 B, E, 1261 B
Alexander V (Peter Philarges), Pope, 1409 B, D, 1410 B
Alexander the Great:
  King Alisaunder, 1300 K
  Iskandar-namā, 1390 K
Alexander, Greek Emperor, 912 B, 913 B
Alexander I the Great, King of Georgia (1412–42), 1442 E
Alexander I, King of Scotland, 1107 A, 1124 B
Alexander II, King of Scotland (b. 1198), 1214 D, 1222 E, 1237 C, 1249 C
Alexander III, King of Scotland (b. 1241), 1249 C, 1263 D, 1266 C, 1286 A
Alexander I Nevski, Prince of Novgorod, 1240 C, 1242 B; Prince of Kiev, 1247 E; Grand Duke of Vladimir, 1252 E, 1258 E, 1263 D
Alexander II of Tver, Grand Duke of Vladimir, 1325 E, 1328 E

Alexander III of Suzdal, Grand Duke of Vladimir, 1328 E, 1332 E
Alexander, Bishop of Lincoln (d. 1148), 1139 B
Alexander of Hales, E. Franciscan and theologian, 1245 H, L
Alexander of Villedieu, F. grammarian and mathematician, 1199 K, 1240 G
Alexandria, Egypt, 814 B, 827 E, 914 E, 1167 C, 1365 D; University, 1065 H
Alexiad (Anna Comnena), 1148 K
Alexis, Life of St. (anon. French), 1040 K
Alexis, St., Metropolitan of Russia (1354–78), 1378 L
Alexis, Guillaume, F. poet and dramatist (1425–86), 1464 K, 1486 K
Alexius I Comnenus, Greek Emperor (1081–1118), 1081 A, 1082 E, 1090 B, 1095 E, 1110 H, 1114 H, 1118 C, F; wars with Turks, 1081 B, 1085 E, 1089 C, 1090 E; and Normans, 1081 D, 1083 E, 1108 C; life of, 1148 K
Alexius II, Greek Emperor (b. 1178), 1180 C, 1182 C
Alexius III, Greek Emperor (1195–1203; d. 1210), 1195 B, 1198 A, 1203 C, 1210 B
Alexius IV Angelus, Greek Emperor (1203–4), 1202 D, 1203 C, 1204 A
Alexius V Ducas Murtzuphlus, Greek Emperor, 1204 A, B
Alexius Comnenus, Emperor of Trebizond, 1204 B
Alf Laylah wa-Laylah (al-Jahshiyari), 942 K
Alfarrobeira, Portugal, battle, 1449 B
Alfiya (ibn Mālik), 1274 K
Alfonse of Poitiers, Count of Toulouse (1220–71), 1249 C, 1271 C
Alfonso I the Warrior, King of Aragon and Navarre (1104–34), 1104 C, 1114 D, 1130 E, 1134 C; Emperor of the Spains, 1109 B; takes Leon and Castile, 1110 E, 1111 D, 1126 A; wars with Muslims, 1108 B, 1118 D, 1120 E, 1126 E, 1134 C
Alfonso II, King of Aragon (b. 1152; 1164–96), as Count of Barcelona, 1162 C; as King, 1164 E, 1179 E, 1196 B; Count of Provence, 1167 E
Alfonso III, King of Aragon (b. 1265), 1285 D, 1287 C, F, 1288 C, 1291 A, B
Alfonso IV the Courteous, King of Aragon (b. 1299), 1327 D, 1336 A
Alfonso V the Magnificent, King of Aragon (b. 1385; 1416–58) and Naples, 1416 B; conquers Naples, 1420 C, 1423 B, 1426 A, 1435 C, 1442 B, 1443 A; claims Milan, etc., 1447 C, 1454 C, 1458 B; medals of, 1448 J; life of, 1471 K
Alfonso II the Chaste, King of Oviedo (Leon; 791–833; d. 842), 802 H, 833 E
Alfonso III the Great, King of Oviedo (b. 848; d. 912), 866 B, 874 E, 893 E, 910 D
Alfonso IV, King of Leon (d. 932), 924 E, 927 E
Alfonso V, King of Leon (b. 994), 999 E, 1002 C, 1020 F, 1027 B
Alfonso VI the Brave, King of Leon (b. 1030; 1065–1109) and Castile, 1065 E, 1081 E, 1109 B; conquers Castile, 1070 C, 1072 D; and Navarre, 1076 B; wars with Muslims, 1085 B, 1086 D, 1093 E, 1095 E
Alfonso VII, King of Castile and Leon (b. 1105/6; 1126–57), as King of Galicia, 1112 E; succeeds, 1126 A; conquests, 1134 C, 1144 E, 1147 E; Emperor of Spain, 1135 B, 1137 C, 1143 E, 1157 C
Alfonso VIII the Noble, King of Castile (b. 1155), 1158 C, 1166 E, 1177 E, 1179 E, 1196 C, 1212 C, H, 1213 E, 1214 D
Alfonso IX, King of Leon, 1188 A, F, 1202 E, 1215 F, 1217 B, 1220 H, 1229 E, 1230 C
Alfonso X the Wise, King of Castile and Leon (1252–84), 1221 L, 1250 E, 1252 B, 1254 B, D, 1267 E, 1284 B
King of the Romans, 1257 B, 1274 D, 1275 C
conquests from Muslims, 1257 E, 1261 E, 1262 C, 1263 E, 1266 E, 1275 C
war with France, 1276 E, 1279 D
as poet and historian, 1284 G, K
laws of, 1254 F, 1256 F, 1273 G
scientific works for, 1262 G, 1279 G
Alfonso XI the Avenger, King of Castile and Leon (b. 1310; 1312–49), 1312 C, 1325 E, 1333 E, 1340 D, 1344 A, 1349 A; poem about, 1350 K
Alfonso II, King of Naples (b. 1448; 1494–1500), as Duke of Calabria, 1469 C, 1479 C, 1481 C, 1482 C, 1486 B
Alfonso, brother of Henry IV of Castile (1453–68), 1465 B, 1467 C, 1468 C
Alfred the Great, King of Wessex, (871–99), 849 L, 871 B, 878 A, B, 886 E, 892 E, 895 E, 899 D, 911 E; translations by, 892 K; life of, 894 K
Alfred of Shareshel, E. physician, 1210 G
Algarve, Portugal, 1189 C, 1191 E, 1250 E, 1263 E, 1267 E
Algazel. *See* Ghazzālī
Algebra (al-Khwārizmī), 850 G, 1145 G, 1187 G; (al-Khayyām), 1123 G; (Li Yeh), 1248 G; (Levi ben Gerson), 1321 G
Algeria, 1152 E
Algericas, Spain, 859 E, 1344 A
Alhama, Spain, 1482 A
Alhambra Palace. *See* Granada
Alhazen. *See* Hasan
'Alī ibn-Yūsuf, Sultan of Morocco and Spain (1106–43), 1106 C, 1108 B, 1120 E, 1126 E, 1134 C
'Alī, Nūr-ad-Dīn, Sultan of Egypt, 1257 B, 1259 D
'Alī Shāh, ruler of West Bengal (1339–45), 1339 E
Alignan, Benedict d', F. theologian, 1268 H
Aljubarrota, Portugal, battle, 1385 C
Almagest (Ptolemy), 827 G, 1160 G, 1175 G
'Almanac', origin of, 1321 G
Almanzor (Muhammad ibn-abi-'Āmir al-Hājib al-Mansur), Regent of Muslim Spain (976–1002), 939 L, 976 D, 981 E, 985 C, 988 E, 996 E, 997 E, 1002 C
Almeida, Francisco de, Port. viceroy of India (1450–1510), 1450 L
Almeria, Spain, 1147 E, 1164 E
Almizra, Spain, Treaty of, 1244 E
Almohad dynasty. *See* Morocco
Almoravid dynasty. *See* Morocco
Alnwick, England, 1093 D
Alp Arslan, Sultan of Persia, 1063 C, 1064 E, 1065 E, 1071 C, 1072 D
Alpetragius. *See* Bitrūji
Alphabets: Cyrillic, 862 H; Mongol, 1269 K
Alphege, St., Archbishop of Canterbury, 1012 B
Alphesi. *See* Isaac
Alptigīn, founder of Ghaznavids (d. 976), 962 E
Alsace, France, 829 E, 888 D, 917 E; Upper, 1469 B
Alsoufī. *See* Sūfī
Altenburg, Austria, 1180 C
Althing, of Iceland, 930 F
Altopascio, Italy, battle, 1325 C
Alton, England, Treaty of, 1101 C
Alum, at Tolfa, 1462 G
Amadeus III, Marquess of Maurienne and Count of Savoy (1108–48), 1111 E
Amadeus VI, 'the Great Count', Count of Savoy b. 1334; 1343–83), 1355 E, 1359 E, 1363 E, 1367 E, 1373 B, 1374 B, 1383 A
Amadeus VIII, Count and Duke of Savoy (b. 1383; 1391–1439; d. 1451), 1401 C, 1418 D, 1419 D; created Duke, 1416 A; anti-pope as Felix V, 1439 D, 1449 B

Amadis de Gaula (Garcia de Montalvo), 1475 K
Amalfi, Italy, 839 E
Amalric (*or* Amaury) I, King of Jerusalem, 1162 A, 1167 A, C, 1168 D, 1169 D, 1174 D
Amalric II de Lusignan, King of Cyprus and Jerusalem (1198–1205), 1194 B, 1197 E, 1198 A, 1204 C, 1205 B
Amasya, Turkey, 1146 J, 1279 J
Amaurists (*or* 'Spiritual Society'), 1205 H
Amaury of Chartres, F. mystic, 1205 H
'Amda Seyon I, Negus of Abyssinia (1314–44), 1332 E, 1344 K
America, Central. *See* Maya, Mexico
America, North, discovered, 1003 G
America, South. *See* Peru
Amicus Medicorum (Jean Ganivet), 1431 G
Amida (*now* Diyarbakir), Turkey, battle, 973 C
Amiens, France, 1185 C, 1329 B; Cathedral, 1152 J, 1218 J, 1220 J, 1236 J; La Grange Chapels, 1373 J; Mise of, 1264 A; Treaty of, 1279 B
Amīn, al-, Caliph, 809 A, 813 C
Amis et Amile, 1180 K
Amorium, Turkey, 838 B
'Amr, Egypt, mosque, 827 J
'Amrān, governor of Sind, 836 E
Amsterdam, Holland, 1275 G
Anacletus II (Peter Pierleoni), Pope, 1130 A, C, 1132 C, 1138 A
Anagni, Italy, 1303 C; Treaty of, 1176 D
Ānangapāla, founder of Delhi, 993 E
Anastasius, anti-pope, 855 C
Anastasius III, Pope, 911 B, 913 B
Anastasius IV, Pope, 1153 C, 1154 D
Anastasius, apostle of Hungary (954–1044), 1044 L
Anastasius Bibliothecarius, It. scholar, 897 K
Anatoli, Jacob, It. Je. translator (1194–1256), 1256 K
Anatomia (Maurus), 1214 G; (Mondino), 1316 G; (Guido da Vigevano), 1345 G
Anatomia porci, 1110 G
Anatomist. *See* Māsawayh
Anatomy:
  circulation of the blood, 1288 G
  human dissection, 1275 G
  post mortem examination, 1302 G
Anbā' fī Tabaqāt al-Atibbā' (ibn-abi Usaybi'ah), 1270 G
Anbar, Iraq, battle, 1258 A
Ancenis, France, Treaty of, 1468 C
Anchialus, Bulgaria, 1307 E; battle, 917 C
Ancona, Italy, 1167 C, 1355 C, 1464 C
Ancren Rewle, 1130 K
Andalusi, Abu-al-Qāsim al-, Sp. M. geographer (1029–70), 1070 G
Andalusia (Muslim Spain)
  Umayyad dynasty (at Cordova). *See*
    Hakam I (796–822)
    'Abd-ar-Rahmān II (822–52)
    Muhammad I (852–86)
    Mundhir (886–8)
    'Abdallāh (888–912)
    'Abd-ar-Rahmān III (912–61)
    Hakam II (961–76)
    Hishām II (976–1013)
    Muhammad II (1009)
    Sulaymān (1009–16)
    'Abd-ar-Rahmān IV (1018)
    'Abd-ar-Rahmān V (1023)
    Muhammad III (1023–5)
    Hishām III (1027–31)
    Caliphate, 929 A, 1031 D
    Regents of. *See* Almanzor; Muzaffar; 'Abd-ar-Rahmān
  attacked by Vikings, 844 C
  dominated by Seville, 1042 E, 1069 E
  crusade against, 1065 B
  conquered by Almoravids (*see* Morocco), 1090 D, 1091 E
  conquered by Almohads (*see* Morocco), 1147 B, 1149 E, 1164 E, 1171 E
  treaties for Christian partition of, 1179 E, 1244 E
  expulsion of Almohads, 1212 C, 1213 E, 1227 C, 1257 E
  dominated by Granada, 1232 D; *and see* Granada
  histories of:
    Al-Hakam, 871 K
    Ibn-al-Qūtīyah, 977 K
    Ibn-Haiyan, 1076 K
  learned men of, biographies of, 1139 K
  persecution of Christians in, 852 H, 912 J
  poetry: ibn-Hazm, 1064 K
Andaman Islands, India, 1035 E
Andernach, West Germany, battles, 876 D, 939 C, 1154 D
André le Chapelain, F. court chaplain, 1180 K
Andreas, Duke of Naples, 837 E
Andrew I, King of Hungary (1046–60), 1046 C, 1050 E, 1060 E, 1063 E
Andrew II, King of Hungary (1205–35), 1205 E, 1217 D, 1222 F, 1224 G, 1235 A, 1290 C
Andrew III, King of Hungary, 1290 C, 1301 A
Andrew of Hungary, King of Naples (b. 1326; 1343–5), 1333 C, 1343 A, 1345 D
Andrew I Bogoljubsky, Prince of Suzdal, Kiev and Vladimir (b. 1110), 1157 E, 1159 E, 1160 G, 1169 A, 1170 D, 1174 E
Andrew II, Grand Duke of Vladimir, 1247 E, 1252 E
Andrew III, Grand Duke of Vladimir, 1280 E, 1283 E, 1293 E, 1305 E
Andrew, Bishop of Prague, 1224 E
Andronicus I Comnenus, Greek Emperor (1182–5), 1182 C, 1185 C, 1204 B
Andronicus II Palaeologus, Greek Emperor (d. 1332), 1282 D, 1297 E, 1303 E, 1307 E, 1321 E, 1325 A, 1328 B
Andronicus III Palaeologus, Greek Emperor (b. 1295/6; 1325–41), 1321 E, 1325 A, 1328 B, 1329 E, 1333 E, 1337 E, 1339 H, 1341 B
Andronicus Palaeologus, Gk. prince, 1376 E
Andujar, Spain, 1225 E
Angelici, Knights of, 1191 E
Angelico, Fra (Giovanni da Fiesole), It. painter (*c.* 1395?–1455), 1433 J, 1440 J, 1446 J, 1447 J, 1455 L
Angers, France, Cathedral, 1150 J; University, 1229 H
Anghiari, Italy, battle, 1440 B
Angilbert, St., F. poet, 814 L
Angiolieri, Cecco, It. poet (1260?–1312?), 1312 K
Angkor, Cambodia, 1177 E, 1431 E; temples, 889 J, 1150 J, 1218 J
Anhilwara, India, Hindu kingdom, 1197 E
Anglesey, Is., Wales, 994 B, 1096 E, 1098 E, 1200 E, 1258 A
Anglo-Saxon Chronicles, The, 998 K, 1154 K
Angoulême, France, Cathedral, 1105 J
Ani, Russia, Armenian kingdom, 1045 E, 1064 E
Anima, De (Petrus Hispanus), 1277 G
Animals, Book of (al-Jāhiz), 869 K
Animals, Lives of (al-Damīrī), 1372 G
Animals, tales of, 1110 K; *see also* Bestiaries
Aniruddha, King of Pagan (1044–77), 1044 E, 1057 E, 1077 E
Anjou, France, 870 E, 925 E, 1156 E, 1443 D
  Viscount of. *See* Ingelger (870–88)

Anjou—*contd.*
Counts. *See*
Fulk I (888–938)
Fulk II (938–58)
Geoffrey I (958–87)
Fulk III (987–1040)
Geoffrey II (1040–60)
Geoffrey III (1060–7)
Fulk IV (1060–1109)
Fulk V (1109–29)
Geoffrey IV (1129–51)
Henry II, Richard and John, Kings of England
renounced by Henry III, 1259 D
Dukes. *See*
Louis I (1356–84)
Louis II (1384–1417)
Louis III (1417–34)
Réné II (1434–80)
occupied by Louis XI, 1480 C
customal of, 1270 F
Ankara, Turkey, 804 E, 1085 E, 1101 B, 1169 E, 1415 E; battle, 1402 C; mosque, 1289 J
Anna, wife of Vladimir of Kiev, 989 E
Anna Comnena, Gk. chronicler, 1083 L, 1148 K
Annales (Albert von Stade), 1256 K
Annales regni Francorum (Einhard), 829 K
Annales rerum gestarum Aelfridi magni (Asser), 894 K
Annales sex regum Angliae (Nicholas Trivet), 1328 K
Annals of ten-feet square (Kamo Chōmei), 1212 K
An-nam Chih-lüeh (Li Tse), 1307 K
Annam, as Chinese province, 863 E, 866 E, 932 E
independent. *See* Dai-co-viet; Dai Viet:
literature: Li Tse, 1307 K
Annan, Scotland, battle, 1332 D
Anne of Bohemia, Queen of England, 1382 A, 1394 B
Anne of Beaujeu (*c.* 1462–1522), Regent of France, 1483 C, 1484 A, 1485 A, C, 1486 D, 1487 A, 1488 C
Anne, Duchess of Brittany, Queen of France (b. 1476; d. 1514), 1486 A, 1488 C, 1490 D, 1491 D
Anno, St., Archbishop of Cologne, 1062 B, 1075 L
Annunciation, The (Botticelli), 1490 J; (Leonardo), 1474 J; (Filippino Lippi), 1483 J; (Filippo Lippi), 1443 J; (Martini and Memmi), 1333 J; (Pisanello), 1423 J
Ansārī, Per. poet, 1088 K
Ansegisus, St., Abbot of St. Vaudrille, 833 F, L
Anselm, St., It. theologian and Archbishop of Canterbury (1033–1109), 1033 L, 1094 H, 1095 A, 1097 D, 1100 C, 1103 B, 1107 C, 1109 L; life (Eadmer), 1130 K
Anselm of Laon, F. theologian, 1117 L
Anskar, St., Bishop of Hamburg, 801 L, 865 H, L
Antapodosis (Liutprand), 958 K
Anthologia Palatina, 950 K
Anthologists:
Greek. *See* Cephalas
Indian. *See* Somadeva
Italian. *See* Guidotto of Bologna
Japanese, 1205 K; *and see* Tsutsumi Chūnagon
Persian. *See* Isfahānī; Tha'ālibi
Spanish. *See* Sánchez de Vercial
Antichrist, Tractate on (John Milíč), 1368 H
Antioch, Turkey:
held by Greeks, 969 D, 971 E, 994 C
taken by Turks, 1085 E
taken by Crusade, 1097 D, 1098 B
its Frankish armies destroyed, 1119 B, 1130 A
Greek campaigns against, 1137 C, 1138 B, 1142 C, 1143 B, 1159 B
relieved by Crusaders, 1148 A, 1190 B
taken by Armenians, 1216 E, 1220 E
destroyed by Egyptians, 1268 B
Patriarchs of, 1170 H, 1199 K
Princes of. *See* Bohemond I; Bohemond II; Raymond of Poitiers; Reynald of Châtillon; Bohemond III; Bohemond IV
Antioch, Chanson d', 1180 K
Antiquaries. *See* Archaeologists
Antique Warrior (Leonardo), 1475 J
Antonini, St., Archbishop of Florence, 1459 L
Antonio, St., of Padua, 1195 L, 1231 L
Antwerp, Belgium, 1045 E, 1338 C; Cathedral, 1352 J
Anund Jacob, King of Sweden (1026–56), 1026 E
Aphorismos Hippocratis expositiones, In (Jacopo da Forli), 1414 G
Aphorisms of Medicine (Maimonides), 1204 G
Apologia (al-Hamadhānī), 1131 K
Apparicion maistre Jehan de Meun, L' (Honoré Bonet), 1398 K
Appiano, Gherardo d', ruler of Pisa, 1398 C, 1399 A
Appiano, Jacopo d', ruler of Pisa, 1392 D, 1398 C
Apulia, Italy, 1210 D
Counts. *See* Hauteville, Guillaume; Hauteville, Humphrey
Dukes. *See*
Guiscard, Robert (1057–85)
Roger Borsa (1085–1111)
William I (1111–27)
Roger II (1127–54)
Rainulf of Alife (1136–8)
And see Sicily, Kings of
Aquinas, St., It. theologian, philosopher, translator and poet (1227–74), 1200 K, 1227 L, 1261 K, 1274 F, H, L; hymns of, 1261 J, 1263 J
Aquitaine, France
Kings. *See*
Louis (781–806/13)
Pepin I (814–38)
Charles the Bald (839–55)
Pepin II (839–*c.*864)
Charles son of Charles the Bald (855–66)
Louis II (866–79)
Carloman (880–4)
Kingdom offered to Louis the German, 853 E
raided by Danes, 923 E; by Magyars, 951 E
Hugh the Great suzerain of, 956 B
Duchy of, created, 845 B; *and see* William V; William VIII; Louis VII; Henry II; Richard I
Truce of God in, 1040 F
revolt in, 1183 B
English in, 1360 D; *see also* Gascony
Aquitaine, Chronicle of (Adhemar), 1034 K
Arab literature:
belles-lettres:
al-Jāhiz, 869 K
al-Jahshiyari, 942 K
al-Hamadhānī, 1007 K
al-Harīrī, 1122 K
ibn-Tufayl, 1185 K
dictionaries, 933 K, 995 K, 1008 K, 1311 K, 1414 K; biographical, 1229 K, 1270 G, 1282 K
history. *See* Historians
poetry:
anthologies, 967 K, 1038 K
sacred, 828 K
See also Poets
shadow-play, 1310 K
studied in Europe, 1276 H, 1311 H
Arab science, begins, 815 G; bibliographies of, 988 G, 995 G; declines, 1111 G; *see also* Alchemists, Astronomers (*etc.*); Translations
Arabian Nights, 942 K, 1389 K
'Arabī, Muhyi-al-Dīn ibn-, Sp. M. Sūfī philosopher (1165–1240), 1240 K

'Arabshāh, Ibn-, Syrian biographer (*c.* 1390–1450), 1435 K
Aragon, Spanish kingdom, created, 1035 D
  Kings. *See*
    Ramiro I (1035–65)
    Sancho V (1065–94)
    Pedro I (1094–1104)
    Alfonso I (1104–34)
    Ramiro II (1134–7)
    Petronilla (1137–64)
    Alfonso II (1164–96)
    Pedro II (1196–1213)
    James I (1213–76)
    Pedro III (1276–85)
    Alfonso III (1285–91)
    James II (1291–1327)
    Alfonso IV (1327–36)
    Pedro IV (1336–87)
    John I (1387–95)
    Martin I (1395–1410)
    Ferdinand I (1412–16)
    Alfonso V (1416–58)
    John II (1458–79)
    Ferdinand II (1479–1516)
    election of, 1412 B
    papal vassal, 1204 D, 1276 C
  civil wars in, 1213 C, 1227 E, 1410 B, 1461 C
  General Privilege of, 1283 F, 1287 F, 1348 C
  legal compilation, 1245 F
Arbedo, Italy, battle, 1422 B
Arbre de batailles, L' (Honoré Bonet), 1388 K
Arbrissel, Robert d', F. monastic founder, 1096 H
Arbroath, Scotland, Declaration of, 1320 B
Arca Noë, De (Hugh of St. Victor), 1141 H
Arcadia, L' (Jacopo Sannazaro), 1486 K
Arcadiopolis (*now* Lulebargaz) Turkey, battle, 970 E
Archaeologists and antiquaries:
  Chinese. *See* Chêng Ch'iao; Hung Kua; Hung Tsun; Ou-yang Hsiu; Shên Kua; Wu-ch'iu Yen
  Egyptian. *See* Maqrīzī
  English. *See* Rous, John; Worcestre, William
  Italian. *See* Biondi, Flavio
Archbishoprics and bishoprics
  created (for conversion). *See* Aarhus, Bamberg, Brandenburg, Cracow, Gniezno, Gran, Greenland, Hamburg, Havelberg, Hildesheim, Ireland, Lund, Magdeburg, Olomuc, Oviedo, Peking, Pomerania, Poznań, Prague, Ribe, Sultānīyah
  suppressed. *See* Lichfield
Archbishops and bishops, declared subject to Pope, 858 H; deposed by the Pope, 863 H, 995 H; suspended, 1075 A; *and see* Investiture Contest
Archimedean screw, 1404 G
Archipelago, Aegean islands, Duchy of the, 1207 E, 1383 E
Architects and masons:
  English. *See* Johannes Anglicus; Nicholas of Ely; William the Englishman; Wynford, William; Yevele, Henry
  French. *See* Béranger; Bernard of Soissons; Enguerran; Gayrard, Raymond; Gaucher of Reims; Henry of Reynes; Honnecourt, Villard d'; Jean d'Andeli; Jean des Champs; Jean de Chelle; Jean le Loup; Jean d'Orbais; Martin; Matthias of Arras; Noyer, Geoffrey de; Pierre de Montereau; Robert de Luzarches; Thomas de Cormont; William of Sens
  German. *See* Benno of Osnabrück; Erwin; Gerhard of Cologne; Hültz, Johannes; John of Cologne; Parler, Heinrich; Parler, Johannes; Parler, Michael; Parler, Peter; Prachatitz, Peter von; Rudolf of Strasbourg
  Italian. *See* Alberti, Leone Battista; Arnolfo di Cambio; Bramante di Urbino; Brunelleschi; Buono; Diotisalvi; Fioravanti, Aristotle; Ghiberti, Lorenzo; Giotto; Maiano, Benedetto da; Masuccio, Stefano; Mateo; Pisano, Giovanni; Raimundus the Lombard; Talenti, Francesco
  Spanish (?). *See* Petrus Petri
  Syrian. *See* Muhammad ibn-Kaulan
  Swiss. *See* Ensinger, Matthaüs
Architecture
  arch, pointed, 827 J
  belfries, 955 J
  Burmese, 1110 J
  Byzantine, in Italy, 876 J
  Cambodian, 881 J
  Carolingian, 819 J
  Gothic:
    begins, 1140 J
    'curvilinear', 1291 J
    English, 1179 J; late, 1319 J
    façade, 1190 J
    fan vaults, 1355 J, 1357 J
    Flamboyant, 1373 J, 1385 J, 1400 J, 1426 J, 1434 J, 1460 J
    French style, in Spain, 1221 J, 1227 J
    German, 1207 J, 1235 J; late, 1320 J
    'High', 1194 J
    Perpendicular, 1292 J, 1331 J
    polygonal apse, 1160 J
    tower, 1134 J
    triforium windows, 1231 J
  Indian, 1009 J
  machicolation, 1087 J, 1197 J
  models, 1355 J, 1418 J
  Mozarabic, 912 J, 919 J, 1150 J
  plans, 820 J, 1043 J, 1163 J
  Renaissance. *See* works *by* Alberti, Bramante, Brunelleschi, Maiano
  Romanesque:
    ambulatory, 903 J
    apses replaced, 836 J, 841 J
    demolished as 'rude', 1309 J
    'First', 833 J; called 'Roman' plan, 813 J
    flying buttresses, 1125 J
    in Italy, 1089 J
    late examples, 1204 J, 1262 J
    rib vaults, 1093 J, 1107 J, 1120 J, 1140 J
    towers, 1160 J
    vaulted church, 1001 J
  sketch-book, 1271 G
  wooden churches, 989 J, 1013 J
  See also Basilicas, Castles, Cathedrals, Monasteries, Mosques, Temples, Town-halls
Archives (Ja.), Bureau of, 810 F
Arckel, John d', Prince-Bishop of Liège, 1373 F
Arderne, John, E. physician, 1376 G, 1377 L
Ardoin, Marquess of Ivrea, King of Italy (1002–4), 997 E, 1002 A, 1004 B, 1015 D
'Aretino'. *See* Bruni, Leonardo
Arezzo, Italy, 1289 B, 1384 D; frescoes in, 1452 J
Arezzo, Guido d', It. musical theorist (995–1050), 1050 J
Argenteuil, France, battle, 898 E
Arghūn, Ilkhan of Persia (1284–91), 1284 C, 1288 A, 1289 G
Argentina, northern, 1471 E
Argyll, Scotland, 1222 E
Ari the Wise, Icelandic historian (1067–1148), 1120 K, 1148 K, L
Ariald, of Milan, Patarene leader, 1066 B

Aribert, Archbishop of Milan, 1037 A
Arinsol, Spain, battle, 1126 E
Ariosto, Lodovico, It. poet (1474–1533), 1474 L
Ariqboga, Great Khan of the Mongols (1260–1), 1260 A, 1261 E
Aristippus, Henry, It. translator, 1162 K
Aristotle, Gk. philosopher (d. 322 B.C.):
  Commentaries on (Gilbert de la Porrée), 1154 K; (Averroes), 1198 K, 1220 K, 1272 K; (Roger Bacon), 1245 K; (Grosseteste), 1253 K; (Levi ben Gerson), 1323 K, 1329 K; (Baconthorpe), 1346 H; (Buridan), 1359 G; (Albert of Saxony), 1390 K
  influence in Islam, 1204 K
  secretum secretorum (attrib.), 1165 G
  translations of, Arab, 873 G; Latin, 1125 K, 1128 G, 1210 K, 1235 K, 1261 K, 1286 K, 1382 K
  works forbidden at Paris, 1210 H, 1263 H
Arithmetica (Helperic), 1000 G; (Jordanus Nemorarius), 1237 G; (Thomas Bradwardine), 1349 G; (Pietro Borgo), 1484 G; *cf.* Levi ben Gerson, 1321 G, 1343 G
Arles, France, Count William of, 975 E; Kingdom of, 1032 E, 1178 C, 1365 B; vicariate of, 1378 A
Armagh, Ireland, Archbishopric of, 1152 H
Armagnac, France, Count John III of, 1391 C; Bernard VII, 1418 B; John IV, 1437 B; John V, 1473 A
'Armagnacs', 1410 D
Armati, Salvino degl', It. inventor of spectacles (d. 1317), 1312 G
Arme Heinrich, Der (Hartmann von Aue), 1195 L
Armenia, Turkey:
  Kings of Bagratide dynasty. *See*
    Ashot I (859–90)
    Smbat I (890–914)
    Ashot II (914–28)
    Abas I (928–52)
    Ashot III (952–77)
    Smbat II (977–89)
    Gagik I (989–1020)
  Greek campaigns against Arabs in, 863 C, 914 E
  Paulicians in, 867 H
  churches in, 915 J
  kingdom divided, 1020 E
  conquered by Seljuqs, 1045 E, 1080 E
  history (Asolik), 1003 K
Armenia, Lesser (in Cilicia, Turkey):
  kingdom founded, 1080 E
  war with Antioch, 1130 A
  conquered by Greeks, 1137 C, 1142 C
  war of independence, 1143 B, 1158 D; *and see* Theodore II, Thoros, Roupen II
  kingdom created, 1198 A; *and see* Leo II, Raymond-Roupen, Hethoum
  war with Egyptians, 1266 C, 1275 B, 1281 D
  conquered by Egyptians and Turks, 1375 B
  chronicles of, 1144 K, 1251 K, 1271 K
Armonica institutione, De (Regino of Prüm), 915 J
Armour, history of, 1491 K
Arno, Bishop and Archbishop of Salzburg, 821 J
Arnold I, Count of Flanders (918–65), 942 D, 948 E, 965 A
Arnold II, Count of Flanders (965–88), 965 A
Arnold III, Count of Flanders (1070–1), 1071 A
Arnold of Brescia, It. heretic and Roman leader, 1139 H, 1155 A, H
Arnold of Lübeck, G. chronicler, 1212 K
Arnold fitz Thedmar, E. chronicler, 1274 K
Arnolfini marriage group (Jan van Eyck), 1434 J
Arnolfo di Cambio, It. sculptor and architect, 1277 J, 1282 J, 1294 J, 1300 J, 1302 L
Arnulf of Carinthia, King of the Germans, 888 A, D, 890 E, 891 D, 892 E, 894 E, 895 E, H; Emperor, 896 A, 899 D
Arnuld the Bad, Duke of Bavaria, 908 E, 917 E, 937 C
Arnulf the Great, Count of Holland (988–1003/4), 988 E
Arnulf of Lorraine, Count, 891 B, C
Arnulf, Archbishop of Reims, 989 A, C, 991 A, B, 998 A
Árpád dynasty. *See* Hungary
Arques, William of, Norman rebel, 1053 E
Arragel, Moses, Sp. Je. translator, 1430 H
Arras, France, 964 A, 1460 H; confraternity, 1023 H; Congress of, 1435 C; Treaties of, 1415 A, 1482 D
Ars contrapunctus (Philippe de Vitry), 1361 J
Ars nova (Philippe de Vitry), 1361 J
Arsūf, Israel, 1101 B, 1265 E; battle, 1191 C
Artah, Syria, battle, 1164 C
Artaud, Archbishop of Reims, 931 E, 939 E, 946 E, 948 B
Arte honeste amandi, De (André le Chapelain), 1180 K
Arte loquendi et tacendi, De (Albertano of Brescia), 1245 K
Arte musices, De (Gregory of Bridlington), 1217 J
Arte venandi cum avibus, De (Frederick II), 1250 K
Artesian well, 1126 G
Artevelde, James van, Flem. leader, 1337 D, 1345 C
Artevelde, Philip van, Flem. leader, 1379 E, 1382 B, D
Arthur, King, alleged remains of, 1191 K
Arthurian Legends:
  Nennius, 810 K
  Geoffrey of Monmouth, 1137 K
  Black Book of Carmarthen, 1150 K
  Wace: *Brut*, 1155 K
  Chrétien de Troyes, 1164 K, 1170 K, 1173 K
  Marie de France, 1185 K
  Renaud de Beaujeu, 1220 K
  Rauol de Houdenc, 1235 K
  Bauduins Butors, 1294 K
  El Caballero Cifar, 1340 K
  Thomas Malory, 1470 K
Arthur of Brittany, 1200 B, 1202 C, 1203 B
Arthur, Prince of Wales (1486–1502), 1486 L
Artifices, Book of (sons of Mūsā ibn Shākir), 860 G
Artois, France, 1180 B, 1482 D; artesian wells, 1126 G
Arts, Essay upon various (Theophilus), 1100 G
Aruk (Nathan ben Jeliel), 1101 H
Arundel, England, Earl of. *See* FitzAlan
Arundel, Thomas, Archbishop of Canterbury, 1353 L, 1414 L
Arzachel. *See* Zarqāli
Asadī of Tūs, Per. philologist, 1060 K
Ascalon, Israel, 1089 E, 1100 B, 1153 C, 1192 A, 1247 D; battle, 1099 C; naval battle, 1123 B
Ascension, The (Donatello), 1427 J
Ascoli, Cecco d'. *See* Stabili, Francesco degli
Asen I, Bulgarian leader, 1185 E, 1186 D, 1187 E, 1196 E, 1218 E
Asen II, John, Emperor of Bulgaria, 1218 E, 1230 B, 1232 E, 1235 E, 1241 B
Asen III, John, Tsar of Bulgaria, 1279 E, 1280 E
Ash'arī, Abu'l-Hasan al-, Arab philosopher (873–935), 935 K
Ashdown, England, battle, 871 A
Ashikaga Takauji, Shogun of Japan (1338–58), 1333 E, 1336 E, 1338 E, F
Ashikaga Yoshimasa, Shogun of Japan (1443–73; d. 1490), 1443 K, 1483 J
Ashingdon, England, battle, 1016 D
Ashmūn, Egypt, battle, 1167 A
Ashot I, King of Armenia, 859 E, 885 E, 890 E
Ashot II, King of Armenia, 914 E; 'King of Kings', 922 E, 928 E

Ashot III, King of Armenia, 952 E, 974 E, 977 E
'Ashr Maqālāt fi al- 'Ayn (Hunayn), 873 G
Ashraf, al-, Sultan of Egypt, 1290 D, 1291 B, C, 1293 D
Ashraf I, al-, ruler of Damascus (1229–37), 1229 E
Ashtur, India, 1436 J
Askold, Viking leader in Russia, 850 E, 878 E
Asma'ī, 'Abd al-Malik ibn Quaraib al-, Arab philologist and naturalist (739–827), 827 G
Asolik, Stephen, Armenian chronicler, 1003 K
Asrār, Kitāb al- (al-Rāzī), 925 G, 1187 G
Assam, India, 1205 E; Shān kingdom, 1229 K
Assassins, order of, 1090 E, 1124 E, 1129 D, 1193 D; victims of, 1092 E, 1192 B, 1272 B; destroyed, 1256 D; history of, 1260 K
Asselin, Bishop of Laon, 991 A
Assempri (Filippo della Gazzaio), 1422 K
Asser, Welsh monk and chronicler (d. 910), 894 K
Assisi, Italy, 1400 A; S. Francesco, 1228 J; frescoes in, 1300 J, 1330 J
Assizes of Romania, 1322 F
Assumption, The (Castagno), 1449 J; (Nanni), 1421 J
Asti, Italy, 1379 A
Astrolabe, 984 G; treatises on: Arab, 815 G, 1007 G, 1087 G; Latin, 1003 G, 1054 G, 1130 G, 1271 G, 1274 G
Astrolabe, Treatise on the (Geoffrey Chaucer), 1392 K
Astrolobio canones, De (Robert the Englishman), 1271 G
Astrologers:
- Arab. *See* Kindī
- Belgian. *See* Bate, Henry
- English. *See* Bridferth; Daniel de Merlac; Oliver
- French. *See* Ganivet, Jean; Meurs, Jean de; (Jewish), Moses ben Joshua
- Italian. *See* Bartholomew of Parma; Blasius of Parma; Montulmo, Antonio do; Stabili; Francesco degli
- Persian. *See* Abu Ma'shār; Bīrunī

Astronomers:
- Arab, 1248 G. *See also* Aflah; Ben Shaku; Fazāri; Hajjāj; Māshā'allāh; Shāgānī; Thābit; Wafā
- Chinese. *See* Chou-Ts'ung; Kou Shou-ching; Su Sung
- Egyptian. *See* Qaisar; Yūnus
- English. *See* Adelard of Bath; Bate, John; Bridferth; Grosseteste, Robert; Maudwith, John; Robert of Chester; Robert the Englishman; Roger of Hereford; Walcher of Malvern; Wallingford, Richard
- French. *See* Linières, Jean de; Murs, Jean de; Oresme, Nicholas; Raymond of Marseilles; William of St. Cloud
- French Jews. *See* Jacob ben Makir; Levi ben Gerson
- German. *See* Hermann Contractus; Regiomontanus; Wilhelm of Hirsau
- Greek, 1248 G. *See also* Ptolemy
- Indian. *See* Bhāskara
- Irish. *See* Dicuil
- Italian. *See* Abano, Pietro d'; Bonatti, Guido; Buonincontro, Lorenzo; Campano, Giovanni; Dondi, Giovanni; Toscanelli, Paolo
- Japanese. *See* Abe Seimei
- Persian. *See* Abu Ma'shār; Battānī; Bīrunī; Kharaqī; Khayyām; Khujandī; Khwārizmī; Shīrāzi; Sūfī; Tūsī; *and see* Samarqand
- Portuguese Jew. *See* Verga, Judah
- Spanish Jews. *See* Cohen, Judah; Isaac ben Sid
- Spanish Muslims. *See* Bitrūji; Edrisi; Firnās; Majrīti; Zarqāli
- Scottish. *See* Scot, Michael

Astronomiae, Liber (Alpetragius), 1217 G
Astronomica (Wilhelm of Hirsau), 1091 G
Astronomical Calendar (al-Khayyām), 1079 G
Astronomical instruments:
- astrolabe, *q.v.*
- *camera obscura*, 1285 G
- celestial globe, 1225 G
- clock, 1326 G
- for measuring meridian, 1457 G
- planetarium, 888 G
- planisphhere, 1154 G
- quadrants, 1288 G, 1292 G
- *See also* Observatories

Astronomical tables:
- *Alfonsine Tables*, 1262 G
- al-Khwārizmī, 850 G, 1126 G
- Regiomontanus, 1474 G
- Robert of Chester, 1149 G
- Roger of Hereford, 1178 G
- *Toledan Tables*, 1087 G
- al-Tūsī, 1274 G
- *Ulūgh Beg, Tables of*, 1437 G
- ibn-Yunūs, 1007 G

Astronomicus, Liber (Guido Bonatti), 1297 G
Astronomy:
- Arab, translated, 1143 G, 1167 G, 1187 G
- degree of meridian, 813 G
- ecliptic, 994 G, 1290 G

Asturias, Kings of. *See* Leon
'Atāhiyah, Abu-al-, Arab poet (748–*c.* 828), 828 K
Atapuerca, Spain, battle, 1054 C
Atenolf I, Prince of Capua, 899 E
Athanasian Creed, 800 H
Athanasius, St., the Athonite, Gk. monastic founder, 961 H
Athanasius II, Patriarch of Antioch, 1170 H
Athelney, England, 878 A
Athelstan, King of Wessex, 924 C, 927 C, 929 E, 934 E, 937 E, 939 D
Athenry, Ireland, battle, 1316 C
Athens, Greece, Latin principality, 1204 D
- Duchy established, 1280 E
- conquered by Grand Company, 1311 A, 1312 E, 1330 B, 1332 E
- claimed by Aragon, 1377 C
- conquered by Acciajuolis (*q.v.*), 1379 E, 1388 B, 1394 A
- ruled by Venice, 1403 A
- conquered by Turks, 1455 E, 1456 E

Athīr, 'Izz-al-Dīn ibn-al-, Arab historian (1160–1233), 1233 K
Athis-sur-Orge, France, Treaty of, 1305 B
Atsiz ibn-Abaq, Seljuq leader, 1071 C, 1075 E, 1079 E
'Attābī, al-, Arab poet, 823 K
Attaleiata, Michael, Gk. jurist, 1073 F
'Attār, Per. poet, 1230 K
Auberoche, France, battle, 1345 D
Aubriot, Hugues d', founder of Bastille, 1369 B
Aucassin and Nicolette (anon.), 1220 K
Aue, Hartmann von, G. poet and crusader (1170?–1215), 1195 K
Augsburg, W. Germany, 1062 D, 1262 G, 1282 D; battle, 910 E; Bishop, Ulric, of, 993 H; Cathedral, 994 J, 1343 J
Augustine, St., *Soliloquies*, 892 K; *City of God*, 1473 J
Augustinian Order of Canons, 1063 H, 1139 H, 1215 H, 1339 H
Augustinian Order of Friars, 1243 H, 1256 H, 1274 H, 1290 H
Augustinus Triumphus. *See* Trionfo, Agostino
Aumâle, France, 1196 C

Auray, France, battle, 1364 C
Austi, Czechoslovakia, 1420 A
Australia (?), 1405 G
Austria:
frontier with Hungary, 1043 E
defeated by Bohemia, 1082 E
Count of. *See* Leopold IV
created Duchy, 1156 C; *and see* Henry Jasomirgott; Leopold V; Frederick II
ravaged by Mongols, 1242 B
conquered by Bohemia, 1246 E, 1262 C, 1274 E
under Habsburgs, 1276 D, 1282 D; *and see* Albert I, Albert II, Frederick III, Habsburgs
ravaged by Bohemia, 1336 E
Jews expelled from, 1421 G
created Archduchy, 1453 A
conquered by Hungary, 1485 B, 1490 B
history, 1345 K
Autobiographers:
Annamite. *See* Li Tse
Arab. *See* Munqidh
Belgian. *See* Bate, Henry
English. *See* Kemp, Margery
French. *See* Abelard; Guibert of Nogent
German. *See* Ulrich of Lichtenstein
Italian. *See* Ghiberti, Lorenzo; Ravenna, Giovanni da
Russian. *See* Monomach, Vladimir
Spanish. *See* James I of Aragon
Autopsy, 1145 G
Autun, France, Cathedral, 1119 J; Count of, *see* Richard the Justiciar
Auvergne, France, 923 E
Auxerre, France, abbey, 841 J; Cathedral, 1025 J, 1215 J, 1309 J; Treaty of, 1412 C
Ava, Burma, 1364 E
Ava, G. religious poet, 1127 K
Avantivarman, King of Kashmīr (855–83), 883 G
Avars, tribe in Hungary, 811 E
Avempace. *See* Bājjah
Aventinus (Johannes Thurmair), G. humanist (1467–1534), 1467 L
Avenzoar. *See* Zuhr
Averroes. *See* Rushd
Aversa, Italy, 1030 E, 1348 A; Cathedral, 1150 J
Avicebron. *See* Solomon ben Gabīrōl
Avicenna. *See* Sīna
Avignon, France, papacy at, 1309 H, 1324 H, 1328 H, 1344 E, 1348 A, 1365 B, 1367 D, 1370 C, 1377 A; rival papacy in, 1379 B, 1403 A; palace, 1334 J
Ávila, Spain, Cathedral, 1190 J
Avis, Portuguese Order of, 1179 E; master, 1384 A, 1385 B
Avranches, France, 933 E, 1172 B
'Awwam, Abu-Zakarīyā' ibn-al-, Sp. M. botanist and agriculturalist, 1200 G
Axelson, Eric, ruler of Finland, 1480 E
Axholme, Is., England, 1265 D
Ayala. *See* López de Ayala
Aybāk, 'Izz-ad-Dīn, Sultan of Egypt, 1250 B, 1251 B, 1253 B, 1257 B
Aybak, Qutb-ad-Dīn, Sultan of Delhi (1206–10), 1193 A, 1206 A, 1210 D
'Ayn Jālūt, Israel, battle, 1260 C
Ayudhya, Siamese kingdom, 1347 E, 1350 E, 1371 E, 1376 E, 1431 E, 1488 F
Ayyūb, Najm-ad-Dīn, Sultan of Egypt (1240–9), 1244 C, D, 1249 D
Ayyūbid dynasty. *See* Damascus, Egypt
Azagal, Spain, battle, 1086 D
Azaz, Syria, battle, 1125 B
Azerbaijan, Russia and Persia, 914 E; Mongols in, 1356 E, 1385 E, 1386 E; Black Sheep Turkomans, 1405 A
'Azīz, abu-Mansūr Nizār al-, Caliph of Egypt, 975 D, 983 E, 994 C, 995 B, 996 D
'Azīz, al-, Sultan of Egypt (b. 1138; d. 1198), 1193 A, 1196 C
Azores, Islands, 1431 G
Aztecs. *See* Mexico
Azuma Kagami, 1266 K
Azzo of Bologna, It. jurist, 1230 F

B

Baalbek (Heliopolis), Lebanon, 975 A
Bacon, Roger, E. philosopher and scientist (1214–92), 1214 L, 1245 K, 1266 K, 1292 K
Baconthorpe, John, E. theologian and philosopher, 1346 H
Badajóz, Spain, 1094 A, 1229 E; Convention of, 1267 E
Badaun, India, mosque, 1223 J
Badenoch, Scotland, 'Wolf of', 1390 E
Badlesmere, Batholomew, E. lord, 1321 E
Badoero, Pietro, Doge of Venice, 939 E, 942 E
Baena, Juan Alfonso de, Sp. editor and anthologist, 1445 K
Baghdād, Iraq, 813 C, 815 H, 817 C, 819 E
capital removed from, 836 E, 892 D
taken by Buwayhids, 946 A
threatened by Greeks, 974 E
taken by Seljuqs, 1055 D, 1091 E
destroyed by Mongols, 1258 A, H
taken by Timur, 1392 E, 1401 C
hospitals, 809 G, 978 G
'House of Wisdom' (library), 830 K, 856 K
medical schools, 931 G, 978 G
Mustansīryah mosque and university, 1232 J, 1234 H, 1395 H
Nizāmī University, 1065 H, 1395 H
observatory, 833 G
patriarch, 1275 H
Baghdād, Caliphate of (Islamic Empire):
'Abbāsid dynasty. *See*
Hārūn ar-Rashīd (786–809)
Amīn (809–813)
Ma'mūn (809–833)
Mū'tasim (833–42)
Wāthiq (842–7)
Mutawakkil (847–61)
Muntassir (861–2)
Musta'īn (862–6)
Mu'tazz (866–9)
Muhtadī (869–70)
Mu'tamid (870–92)
Mu'tadid (892–902)
Mustada (908)
Mustansir (1226–42)
Musta'sim (1242–58)
loss of authority in Africa, 800 E, 868 E; Asia, 836 E, 867 E; and Spain, 929 A
divided, 809 A, 813 C
controlled by Turkish army, 833 C, 836 E, 861 D, 866 A, 869 B, 870 B, 946 A
wars with Greeks, 856 E, 863 C, D
revolt of Negro slaves, 869 C, 883 E
regains Egypt and Syria, 905 E
controlled by Buwayhids, 946 A
controlled by Seljuqs, 1055 D
nominal subjection of Egypt, 1171 C, 1175 B

recognises Sultanate of Delhi, 1229 A
conquered and destroyed by Mongols, 1253 E, 1256 D, 1258 A
puppet, in Cairo, 1262 H
administration, 803 E; postal service, 809 G, 837 G, 846 G, 948 F; land tax, 948 F
Baghras, Turkey, 1142 C
Bagnolo, Italy, Treaty of, 1484 C
Bagrat III, King of Georgia, 1008 E, 1014 B
Bagrat V, King of Georgia, 1386 E
Bahlūl Lodī, Shah of Delhi, 1451 B, 1479 E, 1489 C
Bāhman, Shah of Kulbarga, 1347 C, 1358 A
Bāhmanī dynasty. *See* Kulbarga
Bahrain. *See* Qarmatians
Bahrām, Mu'izz-ad-Dīn, Shah of Delhi, 1240 B, 1242 B
Baisan, Israel, 1217 D
Bāisunqur Mīrzā, Per. patron, 1443 K
Bajjāh (Avempace), Abū-Bakr Muhammad ibn-, Sp. M. philosopher, 1138 K
Bakócz, Thomas, Hungarian statesman and cardinal (1442–1521), 1442 L
Bakrī, 'Abu- 'Ubayd 'Abdullāh al-, Sp. M. geographer, 1094 G
Balādhurī, Ahmad ibn-Yahya al-, Per. chronicler, 892 K
Balak of Khanzit, Seljuq leader, 1123 B, 1124 B
Balance of Wisdom (al-Khāzinī), 1121 G
Balban, Ghiyāth-ad-Dīn, Sultan of Delhi, 1266 A, 1270 F, 1279 E, 1285 A, 1287 E
Balbao, Vasco Nuñez de, Sp. explorer (1475–1517), 1475 L
Balbi, Giovanni, It. grammarian (d. 1298), 1286 K
Bald, E. leech, 930 G
Baldassare (Marchione Stefani), It. statesman and chronicler (1336–1385?), 1385 K
Baldovinetti, Alessio, It. artist (1428–99), 1428 L
Baldus. *See* Ubaldi
Baldwin I, (IX) Count of Flanders and Emperor of Constantinople (b. 1171), 1204 B, D, 1205 B, 1206 C
Baldwin II de Courtenay, Emperor of Constantinople (b. 1217; 1228–61; d. 1273), 1228 E
Baldwin I, King of Jerusalem, 1100 C, 1101 B, C, 1102 B, 1104 B, 1105 C, 1109 E, 1110 E, 1118 B
Baldwin II, Count of Edessa and King of Jerusalem (1118–31), 1104 B, 1118 B, 1123 B, 1124 B, C, 1125 B, 1129 B, D, 1131 C
Baldwin III, King of Jerusalem, 1143 D, 1151 E, 1153 C, 1158 B, 1162 A
Baldwin IV, King of Jerusalem, 1174 C, 1177 D, 1179 B, 1182 C, 1185 A
Baldwin V, King of Jerusalem (b. 1178), 1185 A, 1186 C
Baldwin I of Flanders, Count of Edessa, 1098 A
Baldwin I Iron-Arm, Count of Flanders (d. 879), 863 E
Baldwin II, Count of Flanders (879–918), 900 E, 918 A
Baldwin IV the Bearded, Count of Flanders (988–1036), 1006 C, 1007 E, 1009 E, 1020 C
Baldwin V the Debonnaire, Count of Flanders (1036–67), 1045 E, 1060 C
Baldwin VI, Count of Flanders (1067–70), 1045 E
Balearic Islands, Spain, 860 E; conquered by Barcelona and Pisa, 1113 E, 1115 E; by Aragon, 1228 E, 1229 D, 1232 E, 1235 E; *and see* Iviza, Majorca
Balkans, conquered by Bulgars, 917 C; by Greeks, 1019 E; raided by Pechenegs, 1033 E, 1036 E, 1048 E; *and see* Serbia
Ballades (François Villon), 1461 K
Ballāl Sen, King of (East) Bengal, 1119 F
Ballāla II, Hoysala King, 1190 E
Ballata and *canzone* (Guido Guinizelli), 1276 K
Balliol, Edward, King of Scotland (d. 1364), 1332 C, D, 1333 B, C, 1334 B, 1335 D, 1336 D, 1339 E; renounced title, 1356 A
Balliol, John. *See* John Balliol
Ballon, France, battle, 845 D
Ballymote, The Book of, 1391 K
Balneorum Italiae proprietatibus, De (Ugolini da Montecatini), 1425 G
Balsamon, Theodore, Gk. canonist, Patriarch of Antioch, 1195 H
Baltic Sea, piracy in, 1380 E; herring leave, 1400 G
Bamberg, W. Germany, 1135 A; Bishopric founded, 1007 D; Bishop Otto, 1124 H; Cathedral, 1007 J, 1020 J, 1220 J, 1250 J; imperial residence, 1002 J; monk of, *see* Frutolf
Bamboo, treatise on, 1299 G
Bamboo Gatherer, The (anon. Ja.), 890 K
Banda Nawāz, Al-Sayyid Muhammad, Indian Muslim mystic (1321–1422), 1422 H
Bandino, Domenico di, It. encyclopedeist, 1418 G
Bang Klang T'ao. *See* Indrapatindraditya
Banks, Chinese, 1024 G; of Venice, 1157 F; Florence, 1345 E; Genoa, 1407 G
Bannā, Abū-l-Abbās ibn-al-, Moroccan mathematician, 1321 G
Bannockburn, Scotland, battle, 1314 B
Banquet, The (Dante), 1310 K
Banyas, Syria, 1129 D
'Baphaeum' (?Koyunhisār), Turkey, battle, 1301 C
Baptism of Christ (Uccello), 1445 J
Baptist (Michelozzo), 1452 J
Bar, France, Duchy of, 1434 D, 1480 C
Bar-sur-Aube, France, battle, 1037 D; fair, 1114 G
Bar Hebraeus, Syrian Je. grammarian, 1286 K
Baraidh, Viking leader, 877 E
Baraka, Nāsir-ad-Dīn, Sultan of Egypt (b. 1260), 1277 C, 1279 C
Baranī, Ziyā-ad-Dīn, Indian Muslim historian, 1352 K
Barbadori Altarpiece (Filippo Lippi), 1437 J
Barbar, Mogul Emperor of India (1526–30), 1483 L
Barbarians of the Isles (Wang Ta-yüan), 1349 G
Barbarigo, Agostino, Doge of Venice (1486–1501), 1486 E
Barbarigo, Marco, Doge of Venice, 1485 D, 1486 E
Barbarossa. *See* Frederick I
Barberino, Andrea da, It. writer and editor (1370?–1430?), 1430 K
Barbiano, Alberico da, condottiere (d. 1409), 1379 B
Barbolano, Pietro, Doge of Venice, 1026 E, 1032 E
Barbour, John, Scottish poet (1316?–1395), 1373 K, 1395 L
Barcelona, Spain, 801 E, 985 C, 1442 G; Cathedral, 1298 J, 1450 J; Counts of, 875 E, *and see* Raymond-Berengar (I, II, III, IV); united to Aragon, 1164 E; *and see* Catalonia
Barclay, Alexander, Scottish poet (1475?–1552), 1475 L
Bardas Caesar, Gk. statesman, 863 H, 866 B
Bardas Phocas, Gk. general, 953 E
Bardas Phocas, claimant to Greek Empire, 987 C, 988 C, 989 B, D
Bardas Sclerus, Gk. general, 970 E, 976 B, 978 B, 979 A
Bardi, bankers of Florence, 1345 E
Bari, Italy, 1195 B, 1384 C; held by Saracens, 840 E, 853 E, 871 A; by Greeks, 875 C, 1002 E, 1155 D; by Normans, 1071 B, 1156 B; Cathedral, 1156 J; church, 1089 J; council, 1098 H

Barkiyarūq, Sultan of Persia (d. 1105), 1092 D, 1104 A
Barlaam, Gk. theologian, 1341 H
Barlaam e Josafat (Bernardo Pulci), 1488 K
Barmakids, Per. dynasty, 803 E
Barnet, England, battle, 1471 B
Barq al-Sha'mī, Kitāb al- (al-Katīb), 1201 K
Barsbāy, Sayfal-al-Dīn, Sultan of Egypt (1422–38), 1426 E
Bartolomeo de Varignana, It. surgeon (d. 1318), 1302 G
Bartholomew of Brescia, It. canonist, 1258 H
Bartholomew of Cremona, It. friar, 1253 H
Bartholomew (?Glanville) the Englishman, E. scientist, 1240 G, 1398 G
Bartholomew of Parma, It. astrologer, 1288 G
Bartolus of Sassoferrato, It. jurist (1314–57), 1357 F
Barzizza, Gasparino da, It. humanist (d. 1422?), 1397 K
Basel, Switzerland, 917 E, 1006 E, 1061 D, 1474 B; Cathedral, 1019 J, 1357 J; university, 1460 H
Basel, General Council of, 1431 C
  dispute with Pope, 1431 D, 1433 D, 1437 C, 1438 A, 1439 B
  negotiations with Bohemians, 1432 B, 1433 A, D
  elects anti-pope, 1439 D
  closing stages, 1443 B, 1448 A, C, 1449 B
  History of (Aeneas Silvius), 1440 K
  Mystère of, 1432 K
Bashkūwāl al Qurtabī, Abū-al-Qāsim ibn-, Sp. M. biographer (1101–83), 1139 K
Basiège, France, battle, 1219 B
Basientello, Italy, battle, 982 C
Basil I the Macedonian, Greek Emperor (867–86), 867 C, D, 872 E, 875 C, 879 F, 880 E, 885 E, 886 C, F, 900 J; *Life* of, 959 F
Basil II the Bulgarslayer, Greek Emperor (976–1025), 976 A, 985 E, 1025 D
  revolts against, 976 B, 978 B, 979 A, 987 C, 988 C, 989 B, D
  wars with Bulgars, 986 C, 991 E, 995 E, 1003 B, 1014 C
  relations with Kiev, 988 A, C, 989 E
  other Balkan conquests, 991 E, 1000 E, 1019 E
  treaties with Venice, 992 E, 998 E
  campaigns in Syria, 995 B, 999 D
  conquers Georgia, 1000 A, 1021 D
Basilica (Basil I), 886 F
Basilica Therma, Turkey, battle, 978 B
Basilicas. *See* Agliate, Milan, Rome
Basing, John, E. grammarian and translator, 1252 K
'Basse-Union' of German towns, 1474 B
Basselin, Olivier, F. song-writer, 1430 K
Bate, Henry, Belgian astrologer, autobiographer and theologian (1246–1310), 1281 G, 1310 H
Bate, John, E. astronomer, 1274 G
Bateman, William, Bishop of Norwich (d. 1355), 1350 H
Bath, England, 973 B
Bath, Order of the, 1399 D
Baths, Turkish, 1161 G, 1237 J; Italian, 1425 G
Batrīq, abu-Yahya ibn-al-, Arab translator, 800 G
Battānī (Albutenius), abu- 'Abdullāh ibn-Jabir al-, Per. astronomer (d. 929), 877 G, 900 G, 1149 G
Battle of the Young and Old, The (Franco Sachetti), 1395 K
Battles (Uccello), 1454 J
Battūtah, Ahmud-ibn- 'Abdullāh ibn-, Moroccan traveller, 1304 L, 1325 G, 1354 G, 1377 L
Batu, Mongol conqueror of Russia, 1227 C, 1236 E, 1237 D, 1240 E, 1241 B, D, G, 1242 B, 1245 E, 1255 E
Baude, Henri, F. poet and satirist (*c.* 1430–*c.* 1496), 1486 K
Baudry de Bourgueil, F. poet and travel writer (1046–1130), 1130 K
Baugé, France, battle, 1421 A
Baul, Kitāb al- (al-Isrā'ili), 932 G
Bautzen. *See* Budziszyn
Bavaria, West Germany and Austria:
  Carolingian Kings. *See*
    Lothar I (814–17)
    Louis the German (817–76)
    Carloman (876–80)
    Louis the Younger (880–2)
    Charles the Fat (882–8)
  raided by Magyars, 900 E, 908 E, 954 E
  Duchy, 908 E, 938 E, 978 A; *and see*
    Arnulf (908–37)
    Henry the Wrangler (947–95)
    Henry II, Emperor (995–1017)
    Henry of Luxemburg (1017–26)
    Henry III, Emperor (1024–42)
    Henry of Luxemburg (1042–7)
    Conrad of Zutphen (1049–53)
    Henry IV, Emperor (1053–61)
    Otto of Nordheim (1061–70)
    Wey IV (1070–1101)
    Wey V (1101–20)
    Henry the Proud (1126–39)
    Leopold IV (1139–42)
    Henry Jasomirgott (1142–56)
    Henry the Lion (1156–80)
  divided, 1180 C; *and see* Wittelsbachs
  rebellion in, 1239 A
  laws of, 1328 F
Bayard, Pierre, 'the Chevalier Bayard' (1473–1524), 1473 L
Baybars I, Rukn-ad-Dīn, Sultan of Egypt (1261–77), 1260 D, 1261 C, 1262 H, 1277 C; wars with Mongols, 1260 C, 1277 B; and Christians, 1263 B, 1265 E, 1266 C, 1268 A, B, 1271 B, 1272 B; against Armenia, 1275 B; mosque, 1269 J
Bayeux, France, 924 E; Bishop, *see* Odo; Cathedral, 1049 J; Tapestry, 1080 J
Bāyezīd I, Ottoman Sultan (b. 1347), 1389 B, 1393 E, 1394 B, E, 1395 B, 1396 C, 1402 C, 1403 A
Bāyezīd II, Ottoman Sultan (b. 1447; 1481–1512), 1481 E, 1484 E, 1485 C
Bayonne, France, 1375 B, 1451 C; Cathedral, 1302 J; Treaty of, 1462 B
Baytār, 'Abdullāh ibn-Ahmad ibn-al-, Sp. M. physician and botanist, 1248 G
Baytār, Abu-Bakr ibn-al-Mundhir al-, Eg. vetinerary surgeon, 1340 G
Baza, Spain, 1489 D
Beatrice, German Empress, 1156 B
Beatrice, heiress of Provence, 1246 A
Beatrice, met by Dante, 1274 K, 1290 L, 1300 K
Beauchamp, Guy, Earl of Warwick (d. 1315), 1312 B
Beauchamp, Thomas, Earl of Warwick (d. 1401), 1387 D, 1388 A, 1397 D
Beaufort, Edmund, Duke of Somerset, 1455 B
Beaufort, Henry, Cardinal and Bishop of Winchester, 1425 D, 1426 A, 1427 C, 1447 L
Beaufort, John, Duke of Somerset (d. 1444), 1443 C, D
Beaufort, Margaret, mother of Henry VII (1443–1509), 1443 L
Beaulieu, France, borough, 1007 G
Beaumanoir, Philippe de Rémy de, F. jurist, poet and romance writer (1248?–1296), 1276 K, 1278 K, 1280 F, 1296 L
Beauvais, France, 1472 B; Cathedral, 1225 J, 1235 J, 1284 J; St. Étienne, 1120 J
Bebenburg, Lupold, of, G. political writer, 1340 F

Bec, France, abbey, 1066 J
Beccadelli, Antonio (Panormita), It. poet and biographer (1394–1471), 1471 K, L
Becket, Thomas, Archbishop of Canterbury (1162–70), 1155 A, 1162 B; quarrel with Henry II, 1163 D, 1164 D, 1170 C; murdered, 1170 D, 1172 B
Becket, La Vie de Saint Thomas (Garnier), 1174 K
Bede, E. historian (d. 735), 892 K
Bedersi, Jedaiah ha-Penini, F. Je. poet, 1345 K
Bedford, England, 1224 C; Duke of, *see* John
Bedi Alzeman. *See* Hamadhānī
Beer, hopped, 1179 G, 1304 G; in England, 1400 G
Bégard, France, battle, 1347 B
Beghards, lay sect, 1200 H, 1311 H
Bégue, Lambert le, Belgian founder of sects, 1200 H
Béguins, lay sect, 1200 H, 1311 H
Beheim, Michael, G. poet (1416–1474?), 1466 K, 1469 K
Behinath 'Olam (Bedersi), 1345 K
Beirut, Lebanon, 1232 B, 1291 C
Bel Inconnu, Le (Renaud de Beaujeu), 1220 K
Béla I, King of Hungary, 1060 E, 1063 E
Béla II, King of Hungary, 1131 E, 1141 A
Béla III, King of Hungary, 1173 A, 1181 E, 1196 E
Béla IV, King of Hungary, 1235 A, 1239 E, 1242 E, 1251 E, 1259 E, 1260 C, 1270 E
Belgium, 850 E
  chronicles, 1186 K, 1370 K
  literature:
    Simon Couvin, 1350 K
    Jean d'Outremeuse, 1400 K
  See also Flanders; Liège
Belgrade, Yugoslavia, 1071 E, 1127 E, 1441 E, 1456 E
Belitz, E. Germany, 1243 H
Bellelettrists. *See* Arab literature
Bell-founding, 1100 G
Belle Dame sans merci, La (Alain Chartier), 1425 K
Bellicorum instrumentorum liber (Giovanni de' Fontana), 1415 G
Bellifortis (Konrad Kyeser), 1405 G
Bellini, Giovanni, It. painter (1426–1516), 1426 L, 1450 J, 1470 J, 1473 J, 1480 J, 1488 J
Bello Hispanico, De (Jacob Bracelli), 1460 K
Bello Punico, De (Leonardo Bruni), 1444 K
Belvoir, Israel, battle, 1182 C
Bembo, Pietro, It. humanist (1470–1547), 1470 L
Ben Shaku brothers, Arab astronomers, 813 G
Benedeiz, Anglo-Norman writer, 1125 K
Benedict III, Pope, 855 C, 858 B
Benedict IV, Pope, 900 B, 901 A, 903 C
Benedict V the Grammarian, Pope, 964 B
Benedict VI, Pope, 973 A, 974 B
Benedict VII, Pope, 974 D, 983 C
Benedict VIII (Theophylact of Tusculum), Pope, 1012 B, 1014 A, 1018 H, 1020 J, 1024 B
Benedict IX, Pope (b. *c.* 1024), 1032 D, 1044 E, 1045 B, 1046 D, 1047 D, 1048 C
Benedict X (John Mincius), Pope, 1058 B, 1059 A
Benedict XI (Niccolò Boccasini), Pope, 1303 D, 1304 B, 1305 C
Benedict XII (Jacques Fournier), 1334 D, 1336 E, 1338 H, 1339 H, 1340 H, 1342 B; monastic reforms, 1335 H, 1336 H, 1339 H
Benedict XIII (Peter de Luna), Pope at Avignon (1394–1417), 1394 C, 1395 A, 1422 L; loses French support, 1398 B, C, 1400 A, 1402 A, 1403 A, B; negotiates with Gregory, 1407 D, 1408 A, B; deposed, 1409 B, D, 1417 C, 1423 H
Benedict XIV, anti-pope, 1423 H
Benedict, St., of Aniane, F. monastic reformer, 822 L
Benedict, St., of Nursia (480–*c.* 545), Rule of, 817 H
Benedict of Peterborough, E. chronicler, 1193 K
Benedictine (monastic) Order, 1215 H, 1237 H, 1289 H, 1336 H
Beneš of Weitmil, Bohemian biographer, 1375 K
Benevento, Italy:
  Lombard princes of, 806 E, 818 E, 837 E, 839 E
  taken by Saracens, 842 E
  by Louis II, 847 E, 852 B
  by Greeks, 891 E, 1021 E
  by Capua, 899 E, 967 A, 981 A
  ruled by Pope, 1051 E, 1053 E, 1167 C
  Treaty of, 1156 B
  taken by Frederick II, 1241 B
  battle of, 1266 A
  Cathedral, 1114 J
  commune, 1015 F
Benevenutus Grassus, It. ophthalmologist, 1130 G
'Benevolence', 1474 C, 1491 E
Bengal, India and Bangladesh, Hindu Kings, 980 E, 1119 F; Muslim conquest, 1202 E, 1244 B, 1279 E; under independent rulers, 1336 E, 1339 E, 1352 E
Benjamin ben Jonah, Sp. Je. traveller, 1173 G
Benno of Osnabrück, G. mason, 1084 J
Benoît de Sainte-Maure, F. poet (*fl.* 1150), 1160 K, 1287 K
Bentivoglio, Giovanni, ruler of Bologna, 1401 A, 1402 B
Beorhtric, King of Wessex (786–802), 802 E
Beowulf, 970 K
Béranger, F. mason, 1050 J
Berar, India, Muslim kingdom, 1490 E
Berbers. *See* Morocco
Berdibeg, Khan of the Golden Horde, 1357 E, 1359 E
Berengar I, Marquess of Friuli and King of Italy (898–922), 888 A, 889 A, 898 D, 899 C, 900 D, 902 E, 905 C; Emperor, 915 D; deposed, 922 A, 923 C, 924 B
Berengar II, Marquess of Ivrea and King of Italy (950–61), 941 E, 945 E, 948 B, 950 D, 951 C, 952 C, 963 D, 966 E
Berengar of Tours, F. theologian and heretic, 1050 H, 1088 L
Berengar of Valencia, Sp. translator, 1313 G
Berenguela, Queen of Castile, 1217 B, C
Bergamo, Italy, 894 E, 1226 A, 1427 D, 1428 B
Bergen, Norway, 1318 G; Cathedral, 1320 J; Union of, 1450 C
Bergthorsson, Bjarni, Icelandic chronicler, 1173 G
Berke, Khan of the Golden Horde, 1258 E, 1262 E, 1266 E
Berlanga, Spain, hermitage, 1150 J
Berlin, Germany, 1442 E
Bermudo II, King of Leon, 982 D, 988 E, 999 E
Bermudo III, King of Leon, 1027 B, 1037 E
Bernard, King of Italy (b. 800), 810 C, 818 B, 822 E
Bernard I Billung, Duke of Saxony, 1011 E
Bernard II, Duke of Saxony, 1011 E, 1020 E
Bernard of Anhalt, Duke of Saxony, 1180 B, 1190 B
Bernard of Botone, It. canonist, 1263 H
Bernard, Chancellor of Chartres Cathedral, 1115 H
Bernard, St., of Clairvaux, F. poet and writer (1090–1153), 1113 H, 1115 H, 1140 H, 1146 A, 1153 L; works, 1126 H, 1148 H, 1153 H
Bernard, St., The Vision of (Filippino Lippi), 1486 J
Bernard de Morlaix, Anglo-French poet, 1140 K
Bernard of Pavia, It. canonist, 1195 H
Bernard of Soissons, F. mason, 1210 J
Bernardino, St., of Siena, It. mystic, 1380 L, 1444 L
Bernart de Ventadour, Provençal troubadour, 1195 K
Berne, Switzerland, 1218 B, 1268 B, 1339 B, 1352 E; Cathedral, 1450 J
Berners, John Bourchier, Baron, E. translator (1467–1533), 1467 L

Berners, Juliana, E. prioress and writer, 1400 K
Bernicia (*i.e.* Northumberland), England, 1041 E
Bernward, St., Bishop of Hildesheim, 1023 L
Béroul, Norman-French poet, 1200 K
Berri, France, Duke of. *See* John
Berthold, Duke of Bavaria, 947 E
Berthold IV, Duke of Zähringen, 1218 A
Bertrada, wife of Fulk of Anjou, 1092 E, 1095 D, 1104 E
Bertrand de Bar-sur-Aube, F. poet, 1200 K
Berwick upon Tweed, England, 1296 A, 1318 B, 1319 C, G, 1333 B, C, 1334 B, 1335 D, 1356 A, 1461 B, 1482 C; Treaty of, 1357 D
Besançon, France, 1153 E
Bessarabia, Russia, 1389 E
Bessarion of Trebizond, Gk. humanist and cardinal, 1403 L, 1472 L
Bestiaries:
  Ecbasis Captivi, 930 K
  Bestiaire (Philip of Thaon), 1125 K
  Physiologus, 1250 K
  Lives of Animals (al-Damīrī), 1372 G
Béthune, France, 1312 E
Bettini, Antonio, It. religious writer and Bishop of Foligno, 1396 L, 1477 G, 1487 L
Beverley, England, minster, 1225 J
Beuis of Hampton (anon.), 1330 K
Béziers, France, 1209 C
Bezprym, ruler of Poland, 1031 E, 1032 E
Bhāskara, Hindu mathematician and astronomer (1114–*c.* 1170), 1150 G
Bhoja I, Mihira, ruler of Kanauj, 890 E
Bhoja, King of Mālwā, 1060 E, G
Bialgorod, Russia, 1484 E
Bianco, Andreas, It. cartographer, 1436 G
Bianco da Siena, It. poet, 1367 K
Bible:
  Alcuin's version, 800 H
  cited by Muslim, 854 H
  encyclopedia of (Rabanus Maurus), 856 H
  exegesis:
    Abraham ben Ezra, 1167 H
    John Baconthorpe, 1346 H
    Paul of Burgos, 1435 H
    Nicholas de Lyra, 1332 H
    Solomon ben Isaac, 1105 H
  Glossa Ordinaria (Walafrid Strabo), 849 K
  poetic paraphrase (*Ormulum*), 1200 K
  themes in vernacular literature from:
    Ezzolied, 1060 K
    Genesis and Exodus, 1250 H
    Heliand, 820 K
  Theodulf's version, 818 H
  translations:
    Arabic, 942 H
    English, 995 K, 1380 H
    French, 1355 H
    Italian, 1471 H, 1477 H
    Slavonic, 862 H
    Spanish, 1430 H
Bible (Guiot of Provins), 1206 K
Bible of the House of Alba, 1430 H
Bibliographers:
  Arab. *See* Nadīm; Warrāq
  Greek. *See* Photius
Bicêtre, France, Treaty of, 1410 D
Bīdar, India, capital of Kulbarga, 1432 E; mosque, 1471 J; Muslim kingdom, 1490 E
Biella, Italy, 1040 J
Bihār, India, 1193 E
Bihzād, Per. miniaturist, 1488 J
Bījāpur, India, Muslim kingdom, 1490 E
Bijjala, usurper of Rāshtrakūta, 1167 E
Bilbeis, Egypt, 1168 D
Biographers
  Arab. *See* Safidi; Yāqūt
  Bohemian. *See* Beneš of Weitmil
  Egyptian. *See* Nas; Qiftī
  English. *See* Burley, Walter; Eadmer
  French. *See* Geoffroi de Beaulieu; Joinville, Jean de; Pisan, Christine de
  German. *See* Einhard; Otto of Freising
  Greek. *See* Anna Comnena; Cristobulus of Imbros
  Italian. *See* Agnellus; Beccadelli, Antonio; Decembrio, Pier Candido; Thomas of Celano
  Persian (official). *See* Shamī; Yazdī
  Spanish. *See* Diaz de Gamez, Gutierre
  Spanish Muslim. *See* Bashkūwāl
  Syrian. *See* ʿArabshāh; Khallikān; Usaybiʿah
  Welsh. *See* Asser
Biographical dictionaries. *See* Dictionaries
Biondi, Flavio, It. humanist and archaeologist, 1446 K, 1463 K, L
Birds, Chinese treatise on, 1279 G; *cf.* Falconry, Pigeons
Birger, Earl, Regent of Sweden, 1249 E, 1250 A
Birger II, King of Sweden (b. 1280, d. 1321), 1290 D, 1317 D, 1319 C
Birth of the Virgin (Lorenzetti), 1342 J
Bīrūnī, Abu Rayhān Muhammad al-, 'the Master', Per. astrologer, astronomer, geographer, historian, mathematician, physician and physicist, 973 L, 1048 G, K
Bishops. *See* Archbishops and Bishops
Bisticci, Vespasiano da, It. bookseller and patron (1421–98), 1421 L
Bitriq. *See* Eutychius
Bitrūji (Alpetragius), Nūr-ad-Dīn abū-Ishāq al-, Sp. M. astronomer, 1204 G, 1217 G
Black Death, 1332 G, 1346 G, 1347 G, 1348 G, 1349 A, G, 1350 G, 1351 G, 1352 G, 1361 G, 1369 G; quarantine against, 1377 G, 1383 G; writings on, 1348 G, 1350 G, K, 1351 G, 1363 G, 1374 G, 1398 G
Blanche of Castile, Queen and Regent of France (d. 1252), 1226 D, 1227 A
Blanche, Queen of Navarre (d. 1441), 1425 C
Blanquerna (Raymond Lull), 1283 K
Blasius (Biagio Pelacini) of Parma, It. astrologer and physicist, 1416 G
Blason de faulses amours, Le (Guillaume Alexis), 1486 K
Blastares, Matthew, Gk. jurist, 1335 F
Blois, France, 854 E; Counts of, *see* Odo II; Theobald III
Blore Heath, England, battle, 1459 C
Boabdil. *See* Muhammad XI
Bobrinskoy Bucket, 1163 J
Boccaccio, Giovanni, It. poet and writer, 1313 L, 1350 K, 1353 K, 1375 L
Boccanera, Simone, Doge of Venice, 1339 C, 1356 C, 1363 E
Bodel, Jean, F. poet, 1160 K, 1202 K
Boethius, *Consolation of Philosophy*, translations of:
  English, 892 K, 1382 K
  German, 1022 K
Boethius, Verses on the Captivity of (anon.), 1000 K
Bogomilism, Bulgarian heresy, 1110 H
Bogurodzica (Battle Song), 1408 K
Bohemia, Czechoslovakia:
  Princes of Přemyslid dynasty. *See*
    Bořivoj I, 875 E
    Spythiněv I, 895 E, H
    Vratislav I, 921 E
  Dukes. *See*
    Wenceslas, St. (921–9)

Boleslav I (929–67)
Boleslav II (967–99)
Boleslav III (999–1003)
Vladivoj (1002–3)
Jaromir (1003–12)
Oldřich (1012–34)
Břatislav I (1034–55)
Spytihněv II (1055–61)
Vratislav II (1061; King, 1085–92)
Conrad (1092)
Břatislav II (1092–1100)
Bořivoj II (1100–7)
Svátopluk (1107–9)
Vladislav I (1111–25)
Soběslav (1125–40)
Vladislav II (1040; King, 1158–73)
Frederick (1173–93)
Henry Břetislav (1193–7)
Vladislav Henry (1197)
Kings. *See*
Ottokar I (1197–1230)
Wenceslas I (1230–53)
Ottokar II (1253–78)
Wenceslas II (1278–1305)
Wenceslas III (1305)
Rudolf (1305–7)
Henry (1307–10)
John (1310–46)
Charles IV, Emperor (1346–78)
Wenceslas IV (1378–1419)
Sigismund (1419–21, 1436–7)
Korybut (1422–7)
Ladislas (VI) (1440–57)
George (1458–71)
Vladislav II (1471–1516)
Chekhs of, 805 E, 806 E
conversion to Christianity, 845 A, 875 E, H, 895 H, 967 H, 992 H
conquered by Moravia, 894 E, 895 E
dispute with Poland (from 999) for Silesia, *q.v.*
invaded by Poland, 1003 E, 1004 C, 1013 B, 1017 C, 1076 C
submits to Henry III, 1040 C, 1041 B
succession to duchy regulated, 1054 E
created a kingdom, 1085 B, 1158 A, 1198 E
civil wars in, 1100 E, 1109 E, 1111 E, 1126 A, 1143 E, 1173 E, 1182 E, 1197 E, 1276 D, 1278 C
status in Empire, 1114 E, 1212 D
reform of church, 1143 H
feudalism, 1173 E
ecclesiastical privileges, 1222 F, 1224 E
attacked by Mongols, 1241 B
end of Přemyslid dynasty, 1305 C
invaded by Albert I, 1307 C
under baronial rule, 1320 E, 1333 D
religious reforms, 1334 H, 1363 H, 1390 H. *See also* Hus, John; Jerome of Prague; Matthias of Cracow; Matthias of Janov; Milíč, John; Štítny, Thomas of
dispute of king and clergy, 1393 A, 1396 B
'League of the Lords', 1396 B, 1401 B
under interdict, 1412 H
Hussite movement, 1415 C
Taborites, 1419 C, 1420 A
crusades against, 1420 C, D, 1421 D, 1422 A, 1426 A, B, 1427 C, 1431 C
kings deposed, 1421 B, 1422 B, 1427 B
civil war, 1423 B
'the Orphans', 1424 D
raids into Germany, 1427 B, 1429 D
negotiations and settlement, 1432 B, 1433 A, D, 1434 B, 1436 C
succession dispute, 1437 D, 1440 A
rule of George of Poděbrady, *q.v.*
invaded by Hungary, 1465 D, 1466 D, 1469 B
concessions to Hussites, 1485 H
chronicles, 1125 K, 1278 K, 1359 K
Communion of Brethren, 1450 H, 1467 H
currency reform, 1300 G
German settlers, 1173 E, 1235 G
Jews in, 968 G
laws, 1294 F, 1356 F; *Maiestas Carolina*, 1350 F
literature:
Dalimil, 1314 K
Beneš of Weitmil, 1375 K
Johann von Tepl, 1405 K
Troan Chronicle, 1468 K
mining code, 1294 G
official language, 1356 F
vineyards ordered, 1358 G
Bohemond I, Prince of Antioch, 1083 E, 1101 A, 1103 B, 1104 B, 1107 D, 1108 C, 1111 A
Bohemond II, Prince of Antioch, 1130 A
Bohemond III, Prince of Antioch, 1164 C, 1193 D
Bohemond IV, Prince of Antioch, 1216 E, 1220 E
Boiana, Bulgaria, frescoes, 1259 J
Boiardo, Matteo Maria, It. poet (1441–94), 1482 K
Boizenburg, E. Germany, battle, 1191 E
Boke of the Duchesse, The (Geoffrey Chaucer), 1369 K
Boleslav I the Cruel, Duke of Bohemia (929–67), 921 E, 929 C, 950 E, 966 E, 967 E, 999 E
Boleslav II the Pious, Duke of Bohemia, 967 E, 973 E, 978 A, 999 E
Boleslav III, Duke of Bohemia, 999 E, 1002 E, 1003 E
Boleslav I Khobry (the Brave), Duke and King of Poland (b. 972), 992 E, 999 E; King, 1000 A, 1024 D; wars with Henry II, 1002 C, E, 1005 A, 1007 E, 1013 B, 1015 C, 1017 C, 1018 A; conquests, 1003 E, 1004 C, 1018 C, 1025 B
Boleslav II the Bold, Duke and King of Poland, 1058 D, 1060 E, 1069 E; King, 1076 D, 1077 E, 1079 B; expelled, 1081 A, 1083 E
Boleslav III Wrymouth, Duke of Poland (b. 1086), 1102 C, 1107 E, 1109 E, 1111 E, 1112 K, 1121 E, 1135 C, 1138 E
Boleslav IV, Grand Prince of Poland, 1146 E, 1157 E, 1166 E, 1173 D
Boleslav V the Chaste, Grand Prince of Poland (b. 1219), 1227 D, 1243 E, 1264 G, 1279 D
Bolivia, 1471 E
Bologna, Italy, 1226 A
revolts against Pope, 1306 B, 1325 D, 1327 A, 1334 C, 1360 A, 1376 A
wars with Milan, 1350 D, 1352 B, 1360 C, 1361 B, 1390 B, 1392 A, B, 1397 C, 1402 B, 1438 B, 1443 B
under Bentivoglio, 1401 A
churches, 1221 J, 1265 H, 1388 J, 1425 J
silk industry, 1272 G
University, 1158 H
chair of Hebrew, 1488 H
law school, 1100 F, 1139 H, 1160 F, 1166 F, 1260 F
medical school, 1275 G, 1302 G, 1303 G, 1316 G
Bombay, India, 1429 E; language, 1355 K
Bon Berger, Le (Jehan de Brie), 1379 G
Bona, Algeria, 1034 E, 1153 E
Bona of Savoy, Regent of Milan, 1476 D
Bonacosa of Padua, It. Je. translator, 1255 G
Bonatti, Guido, It. astronomer, 1297 G
Bonaventura, St., It. theologian and cardinal, 1221 L, 1274 L
Boner, Ulrich, Swiss fabulist, 1349 K

Bonet, Honoré, F. poet and writer (1345?–1406?), 1388 K, 1398 K
Boniface VI, Pope, 896 B
Boniface VII (Franco), Pope, 974 B, 984 B, 985 C
Boniface VIII (Benedict Gaetani), Pope, 1294 D, 1303 D
  makes peace, 1295 B
  Clericis laicos, 1296 A, C, 1297 C
  Italian affairs, 1297 A, B, E, 1300 A, 1301 D, 1302 B
  legislation, 1298 H
  Scottish affairs, 1299 B
  Jubilee, 1300 A, H
  relations with Hungary, 1301 A
  and Germany, 1301 B, 1303 B
  and France, 1301 D, 1302 B, 1303 B, C
  Unam Sanctam, 1302 D
  founds university, 1303 H
  bust of (Arnolfo), 1300 J
Boniface IX (Pietro Tomacelli), Pope, 1389 D, 1404 D
Boniface, Marquess of Montferrat and King of Thessalonica, 1207 C
Bonmoulins, France, 1188 D
Bonn, West Germany, 881 E, 921 D; Minster, 1166 J
Bonville, William, E. lord (d. 1461), 1451 C, 1455 D
Book of Faith (Reginald Pecock), 1456 H
Book of Margery Kemp, The, 1438 K
Book of Secrets (al-Rāzī), 925 G, 1187 G
Book of the Nine Rocks (Ralman Merswin), 1370 H
Book of the Seventy ('Jābir'), 1187 G
Book of Truth (Jan Ruysbroeck), 1381 H
Book of Victory (Mustawfī), 1333 K
Bordeaux, France, 1130 E, 1230 D, 1373 D, 1375 B, 1451 B, 1452 D, 1453 D; Treaties of, 1243 B, 1357 A; University, 1441 H
Bordo, Petro, commander of Navarrese Company, 1396 E
Borgia, Alonso da. *See* Calixtus III
Borgia, Cesare, Duke of Romagna (1501–7), 1475 L
Borgia, Lucrezia, Duchess of Ferrara (d. 1519), 1480 L
Borgo, Pietro, It. mathematician, 1484 G
Borgo San Sepulcro, Italy, 1440 B
Boril, Tsar of Bulgaria, 1207 D, 1208 C, 1218 E
Boris I, Khan of the Bulgars, 864 E, 866 C, 870 A
Boris II, Tsar of Bulgaria, 972 E
Boris, Russian prince, 1015 E
Bořivoj I, Prince of Bohemia, 875 E, 895 E, 921 E
Bořivoj II, Duke of Bohemia (1100–7), 1100 E, 1107 E, 1111 E
Bornhöved, W. Germany, battle, 1227 C
Boromo Trailokanet, King of Ayudhya (1448–88), 1488 F
Boroughbridge, England, battle, 1322 A
Boroughs, communes, etc.
  Brabant, 1312 F
  England, *burhs*, 892 E
  France, 1232 G; 1262 F. *See also* Beaulieu; Bourges; Cambrai; Morville-sur-Seille; St. Omer; St. Quentin
  Germany, 1231 D. *See also* Germany, cities
  Holland. *See* Amsterdam
  Italy. *See* Benevento; Florence; Lombard League; Milan; Venice
Bórumha, Brian. *See* Brian Bórumha
Bosch, Hieronymus, Dutch painter (*c.* 1450–1516), 1480 J
Bosnia, Yugoslavia, 1100 E
Boso, King of Provence (879–87), 870 E, 879 D, 882 C, 887 A
Bosphorus, Turkey, naval battle in, 1352 A
Bossi, Andrea di, It. scholar, Bishop of Leira, 1464 K
Bosworth, England, battle, 1485 C
Botanists:
  Arab. *See* ʿAbbas al-Rasūlī
  Chinese. *See* Ch'ên Ching-i; Chu Hsiao; Fan Ch'êng-ta; Han Ch'an-chih; Li K'an; Ou-yang Hsiu; Wang Kuan
  Greek. *See* Seth, Symeon
  Italian. *See* John of Milan; Rinio Benedetto
  Spanish Muslim. *See* ʿAwwam; Baytār; Ghāfiqi
  See also Naturalists
Botticelli, Sandro (Alessandro de' Mariano dei Filippi), It. painter (1444–1510), 1444 L, 1470 J, 1475 J, 1477 J, 1481 J, 1483 J, 1486 J, 1490 J
Boucicaut (Jean le Maingre), F. court poet, 1400 K, 1421 L
Bourbon, France, Dukes of, 1437 B, 1465 C
Bourbourg, France, Treaty of, 1374 A
Bourchier, Robert, Chancellor of England, 1340 F
Bourdeille, Hélie de, F. canonist and cardinal, 1484 H, L
Bourges, France, 878 E, 910 E, 1101 E; Archbishopric, 1142 E; Cathedral, 1200 J; communal franchises, 1181 G; house, 1443 J; Pragmatic Sanction, 1438 C, 1461 D
Boussard, Geoffroi, F. theologian (1439–1505), 1439 L
Boutillier, Jean, F. jurist, 1390 F
Bouts, Dieric, Dutch painter, 1445 J, 1458 J, 1462 J, 1464 J, 1470 J, 1475 L
Bouvines, France, battle, 1214 C; poem about, 1224 K
Boves, France, Treaty of, 1185 C
Bower, Walter, Scottish chronicler, 1449 K
Boyd, Robert, Lord, governor of Scotland, 1466 C, 1468 D
Brabant, Dukes of, 1213 D, 1288 C, 1430 C; communal liberties, 1312 F; estates, 1356 F
Braccio da Montone, Andrea, condottiere (1368–1424), 1417 C
Bracciolini, Poggio. *See* Poggio Bracciolini
Bracelli, Jacopo (d. 1466), It. historian, 1460 K
Bracton, Henry de, E. jurist, 1268 F
Bradford-on-Avon, England, church, 973 J
Bradwardine, Thomas, E. mathematician and Archbishop of Canterbury, 1349 G, L
Braga, capital of Portugal (1093–1147), Cathedral, 1100 J
Braganza, Duke Ferdinand II of, 1483 B
Brague Triptych (Roger van der Weyden), 1452 J
Brahmins, college for, 945 H
Bramante di Urbino, Donato d'Augnolo, It. architect (1444–1514), 1444 L, 1482 J
Bramham Moor, England, battle, 1408 A
Brancaleone, Donato, podestà of Rome, 1253 D, 1255 D, 1257 B, 1259 E
Brandenburg, East Germany, 928 E, 993 E; bishopric, 948 H; Cathedral, 1165 J
  Margraves of, Albert I (*q.v.*), 1250 E, 1266 B, 1296 A
    under Wittelsbachs, 1324 B, 1350 A, 1351 D
    united to Bohemia, 1373 D, 1378 D, 1386 B
  sold to Hohenzollerns (*q.v.*), 1411 A
  regulation (*Dispositio Achillea*), 1473 F
  Neumark, 1402 E, 1454 E
Brandini, Ciuto, Florentine rebel, 1345 E
Brandon, The Voyage of St. (Benedeiz), 1125 K
Branković, George, Despot of Serbia, 1444 B
Brantingham, Thomas, E. statesman and Bishop of Exeter (d. 1394), 1371 A
'Brasil, Isle of', 1480 G
Břatislav I, Duke of Bohemia (1034–55), 1028 E, 1030 E, 1034 E, 1038 E, 1041 B, 1054 E, 1055 E
Břatislav II, Duke of Bohemia, 1092 E, 1100 E

Bratislava (Pressburg), Czechoslovakia, battle, 906 E; Treaty of, 1491 D
Brauweiler, W. Germany, monk of, 1044 H
Breauté, Fawkes de, Norman mercenary, 1224 C
Bremen, West Germany, archbishopric, 1046 B
Brémule, France, battle, 1119 C
Brenta, River, Italy, battle, 899 C
Brescia, Italy, opposes Emperors, 1158 C, 1159 C, 1226 A, 1238 C, D, 1252 A, 1311 C; lords of, 1258 E, 1270 E, 1319 A, 1329 D, 1332 C; under Milan, 1401 D; taken by Padua, 1404 E, 1426 E; ceded to Venice, 1428 B
Breslau. *See* Wroclaw
Bressanone (Brixen), Italy, 1080 B
Brest, France, 1373 B, 1375 B, 1381 A, 1397 B
Brest Litewski, Russia, 1315 E; Peace of, 1435 D
Bretel, Jacques, F. poet, 1285 K
Brethren of the Free Spirit, 1262 H
Brétigny, France, Treaty of, 1360 B, D
Bretons. *See* Brittany
Breviari d'amor (Matfré de Bezier), 1288 K
Breviarium (John Mirfield), 1407 G
Breviarium de musica (Frutolf), 1103 K
Breviatio canonum (Fenandus), 850 H
Breviloquium geomantiae (Bartholomew of Parma), 1288 G
Břevnov, Czechoslovakia, monastery, 992 H
Brézé, Pierre de, F. admiral, 1457 C
Brian Bórumha, High King of Ireland (1003–14), 967 E, 999 E, 1003 E, 1014 B
Bridferth, monk of Ramsey, E. astronomer and astrologer, 1010 G
Bridget of Sweden, religious reformer, 1303 L, 1346 H, 1373 L
Brie, Jehan de, F. writer on shepherdry, 1379 G
Brienne, Robert de, constable of France, 1350 D
Brienne, Walter I de, Duke of Athens, 1311 A
Brienne, Walter II de, Duke of Athens (d. 1356), 1330 B, 1332 E; lord of Florence, 1342 C, 1343 C
Briey, France, iron-forge, 1323 G
Brigittine (monastic) Order, 1346 H, 1415 H
Brigham, Scotland, Treaty of, 1290 C
Brignais, France, battle, 1362 B
Brill, Holland, 1400 G
Brilliant Stars, The (ibn-Taghri-Birdi), 1469 K
Brindisi, Italy, 837 E; battle, 1156 B
Brissarthe, France, battle, 866 E
Bristol, England, 1326 D; seamen, 1474 G; exploration by, 1480 G, 1491 G
Britain, History of (Geoffrey of Monmouth), 1137 K, 1155 K
Brittany, France, subjected, 818 C
  independent chieftains. *See* Nomenoë; Erispoë
  kingdom, 846 E
  defeats Vikings, 937 E
  relations with Angevins, 992 B, 1113 A, 1158 E, 1200 B
  revolt against Louis IX, 1227 A, 1230 B, D
  War of Succession, 1341 D, 1342 B, C, D, 1351 A, 1352 C, 1364 C, 1365 A
  rebellion, 1373 B, 1379 C
  Dukes. *See* John IV; John V; Francis II
  War of Independence, 1486 A, 1488 C, 1489 A, 1490 D
  united to France, 1491 D
Brixen. *See* Bressanone
Brno (Brünn), Czechoslovakia, Treaty of, 1364 A
Broce, Pierre de la, F. courtier, 1278 E
Bruce, Edward, King of Ireland (1316–18), 1315 B, C, 1316 B, 1317 A, 1318 D
Bruce, Robert. *See* Robert I. *Cf. Brus*
Bruges, Belgium, 1474 K
  as commercial centre, 1180 G, 1353 G, 1370 G
  revolts in, ('Matins of Bruges') 1302 B, 1323 B, 1382 B
  relations with Hanse, 1307 G, 1356 G, 1438 G
  Treaty of, 1375 B
  Estates-General at, 1463 E
  canal to North Sea, 1180 G
  Town Hall, 1376 J
'Brunanburgh', Scotland (?), battle, 937 E
Brunelleschi, Filippo, It. architect (1377–1446), 1377 L, 1413 J, 1419 J, 1421 J, 1430 J, 1433 J, 1446 L, 1458 J
Bruni, Leonardo ('Aretino'), It. humanist and historian, 1370 L, 1444 K, L
Brunkeberg, Sweden, battle, 1471 D
Bruno, Archbishop of Cologne, 954 D
Bruno, Duke of Saxony, 880 A
Bruno, St., F. monastic reformer, 1084 H, 1101 L
Bruno da Longoburgo, It. surgeon, 1252 G
Bruno of Querfurt, St., G. missionary, 1009 H
Brunswick, W. Germany, 1181 E; Town Hall, 1302 J
Brus, The (John Barbour), 1373 K
Brusa, Turkey, 1204 D, 1326 B, 1402 C; battle, 1211 D
Brussels, Belgium, 1312 F; church, 1225 J; Town Hall, 1402 J
Brut (Wace), 1155 K; (Layamon), 1200 K
Brutus, mythical British King (of Trojan origin), 1200 K, 1210 K, 1307 K
Bryennius, Nicephorus, Gk. general and historian, 1138 K, 1148 K
Bucer, Martin, G. religious reformer (1491–1551), 1491 L
Buch, the Captal de (Jean de Grailly; d. 1377), 1364 B
Buch der Natur, Das (Conrad of Megenburg), 1351 G
Buch von den Wienern, Das (Michael Beheim), 1466 K
Buchan, Scotland, Earl of. *See* Comyn, John
Buchlein der Wahrheit, Das (Heinrich Suso), 1328 H
Buckinck, Arnold, Flemish map-engraver, 1478 G
Buckingham, England, Duke of, *see* Stafford, Henry; Earl of, *see* Thomas of Woodstock
Budapest, Hungary, 1241 D; University, 1389 H
Buddhism. *See* Burma, Ceylon, China, India, Japan, Korea, Tibet
Buddhist writings: *Diamond Sútra*, 868 G; Lu T'ai, 1345 K
Budé (Budaeus), Guillaume, F. humanist and philologist (1467–1540), 1467 L
Budziszyn (Bautzen), Poland, Treaties of, 1018 A, 1350 A
Bug, River, Poland and Russia, battles, 1018 C, 1363 E
Bughyat al-fellāhin (al- 'Abbās), 1376 G
Builth, Wales, 1282 D
Bukhāra, Russia, capital of Transoxiana, 874 E, 992 E, 1220 A, 1387 E
Bukhārī, Muhammad ibn-Ismā'il al-, Per. theologian (810–70), 870 H
Bukka I, King of Vijayanagar (1357–77), 1370 E
Bulat-Saltan, Khan of the Golden Horde, 1407 E, 1410 E
Buldān, 'Ajā'ib al- (al-Qazwini), 1283 G
Buldān, Kitāb al- (Ibn-al-Faqīh), 903 G; (al-Ya'qūbi), 891 G
Buldān, Mu'jam al- (Yāqūt), 1229 G
Bulgarophygon, Turkey, battle, 896 E
Bulgars:
  attack Greek Empire, 809 E, 811 C, 813 B, 831 E
  make peace, 814 B, 822 E
  invade Pannonia, 828 E
  relations with Magyars, 837 E, 895 E
  converted to Christianity, 864 E, 866 C, 870 A

Bulgars—*contd.*
invade Greek Empire, 896 E, 913 B, 917 C, 923 E, 924 E, 926 E, 927 B
attacked by Russians, 967 E, 969 E, 971 C
conquered by Greeks, 972 E
win independence, 976 A, 986 C, 987 E; *and see* Samuel
reconquered, 991 E, 995 E, 1003 B, 1014 C, 1019 E
Pechenegs settle among, 1090 B
Bogomil heresy of, 1110 H
independent. *See* Tsars:
Peter (1187–97)
Kalojan (1197–1207)
Boril (1207–18)
Asen II (1218–41)
Koloman (1241–6)
Michael Asen (1246–58)
Asen III (1279–80)
Michael Šišman (1323–30)
John Alexander (1330–61)
recognised as kingdom, 1204 D
extent of empire, 1230 B
tributary to Hungary, 1271 E
attacks on Greeks, 1307 E, 1366 C
disintegration of empire, 1361 E
conquered by Hungary, 1362 E
conquered by Turks, 1371 C, 1393 E
in Russia, 921 G, 1236 E
Bulgarus of Bologna, It. jurist, 1100 F, 1166 F
Bulukkin, Yūsuf, founder of Zīrid dynasty, 972 E
Buonincontro, Lorenzo, It. astronomer (1411–1501 ?), 1411 L, 1474 G
Buono, It. mason, 1154 J
Buono, Pietro, It. alchemist, 1330 G
Burchard I, Duke of Swabia, 908 E, 926 A
Burchard II, Duke of Swabia, 954 D
Burchard, G. canonist and Bishop of Worms (d. 1025), 1012 H
Burchard of Mount Sion, G. pilgrim-author, 1283 G
Burdah, al- (al- Būsīrī), 1296 K
'Burgess', first appearances of, 1007 G, 1048 G
Burgh, Hubert de, Earl of Essex (d. 1243), 1232 C
Burgh, John de, E. theologian, 1385 H
Burgos, Spain, capital of Castile, 884 E; Cathedral, 1221 J, 1260 J, 1442 J
Burgos, Paul of, Sp. theologian (apostate Jew) and Bishop of Cartagena (*c.* 1351–1435), 1433 H, 1470 H
Burgred, last King of Mercia (852–74), 874 E
Burgundo of Pisa, It. translator, 1193 G
Burgundy, France:
granted to Carloman, 880 A
raided by Magyars, 917 E, 935 E, 937 E, 954 E; by Danes, 924 E
Kings of. *See*
Rodolph I (888–911)
(Zwentibold, 895)
Rodolph II (911–37)
Conrad (937–93)
Rodolph III (993–1032)
kingdom taken by Emperors, 939 E, 1016 B, 1018 B, 1032 C
becomes kingdom of Arles, 1033 A
held by Emperors, 1153 E, 1156 B, 1157 D, 1178 C, 1186 A, 1218 A
last coronation, 1365 B
Duchy (French) of. *See*
Richard the Justiciar (?–921)
Raoul (921–3)
Gisilbert (923–56)
Otto (960–5)
Henry the Great (965–1002)
Henry Capet (1015–32)
Robert Capet (1032–75)
Hugh I (1075–9)
Eudes IV (1315–50)
Philip de Rouvre (1350–61)
Philip the Bold (1363–1404)
John the Fearless (1404–19)
Philip the Good (1419–67)
Charles the Bold (1467–77)
succession disputes, 923 C, 938 E, 956 B, 1002 D, 1015 E, 1032 E
raided by English, 1360 A, 1373 C
occupied by French king, 1361 D, 1363 C, 1477 A
Parlement for, 1473 F
standing army, 1471 F
history of (Châtelain), 1474 K
Franche Compté, 915 E, 952 D
ceded to France, 1295 E, 1315 E
united to Duchy, 1330 E
Buridan, Jean, F. philosopher and physicist, 1359 G
Burley, Walter, E. philosopher (1275–1345), 1345 K
Burma:
Pyu kingdom, 832 E
kingdom of Pagan, *q.v.*
Mon kingdoms. *See* Pegu; Thaton
invaded by Mongols, 1287 E
Shans of, 1300 E, 1312 E
Thai kingdoms, 1358 E, 1364 E
architecture of, 1110 J
law codes, 1210 F, 1306 F
reformed Buddhism in, 1190 H
Burnt Njal, Saga of, 1200 K
Bursfeld, W. Germany, monastery, 1464 H
Bursuqi, il-, atabeg of Mosul, 1125 B, 1127 E
Bury, Richard de, E. bibliophile and Bishop of Durham (1287–1345), 1345 K, L
Bury St. Edmunds, England, abbey, 1070 J; chronicle of, 1202 K
Būsīri, Sharaf al-Dīn al-, Egyptian poet (1213–*c.* 1296), 1296 K
Būstān, The (Sādi), 1258 K; ms. of (Bihzād), 1488 J
Butaiha, Syria, battle, 1158 B
Butera, Sicily, 1091 E
Butors, Bauduins, F. poet, 1294 K
Buwayhids. *See* Shīrāz
Byland, England, battle, 1322 D
Byrhtnoth, Earldorman of East Anglia, 991 C
Byzantine Empire. *See* Greek Empire

C

Cá da Mosto, Alvise de, Portuguese navigator (1432–64), 1455 G, 1464 G
Cabalistic literature: *Zohar*, 1305 K
Caballero Cifar, El, 1340 K
Cabiz, Muslim theologian, 945 H
Cabot, John, It. navigator (1450–98), 1450 L
'Cade, Jack', E. rebel-leader, 1450 B, C
Cadiz, Spain, 844 C, 1262 C
Cadwalader, supposed British King, 1200 K
Caen, France, 1346 C, 1417 C; abbeys, 1059 J, 1065 J; University, 1432 H
Caena Domini, De (Berengar), 1050 H
Caerlaverock, Scotland, castle, 1300 C
Caesarea, Israel, 975 B, 1067 E, 1100 B, 1101 B, 1265 E
Cairo, Egypt, 969 C, 1168 D; College, 1005 H; fortifications, 1087 J, 1176 J; hospitals, 872 G; 1284 G; library, 995 K; mosques, 876 J, 972 H, 990 J, 1085 J, 1125 J, 1258 H, 1269 J, 1284 G, 1298 J,

1318 J, 1340 J, 1356 J; observatory, 1007 G; puppet Caliphs, 1262 H, 1394 E; school, 1284 G; universities, 972 H, 1065 H, 1258 H
Calabria, Italy, 852 B, 880 E, 976 E; Dukes of, *see* Alfonso, Sicily
Calais, France, 1346 C, 1347 C, G, 1362 G, 1369 C, 1373 C, 1375 B, 1380 C, 1416 D, 1436 C, 1451 C; Congress of, 1439 C; Treaty of, 1360 D
Calatañazor, Spain, battle, 1002 C
Calatrava, Spain, Knights of, 1147 E, 1164 E
Calculation of Integration (al-Khwārizmī), 850 G, 1145 G, 1187 G
Calendars:
  almanac, 1321 G
  Chinese, 1065 G, 1280 G
  Persian, 1074 G, 1079 G
  William of St. Cloud, 1296 G
  treatise on (Helperic?), 978 G
Caliphs, *see* Baghdād; puppet, *see* Cairo
Calixtus II, Pope, 1119 A, D, E, H, 1121 B, 1122 C, 1123 H, 1124 D
Calixtus III, anti-pope, 1168 C, 1178 C
Calixtus III (Alonso da Borgia), Pope, 1379 L, 1455 B, 1458 C
Calligrapher, Chinese. *See* Mi Fei
Calmar, Sweden, Union of, 1397 B, 1448 A
Caltabellotta, Italy, Treaty of, 1302 C
Camaldoli, Italy, (monastic) Order of, 1012 H, 1072 H
Cambio, Arnolfo di. *See* Arnolfo di Cambio
Cambodia:
  Khmers of, reunited, 850 E
  Kings of. *See*
    Suryavarman II (1113–50)
    Jayavarman VII (1181–*c.* 1218)
  Thais in, 1230 E, 1287 E, 1295 E; *and see* Siam
  tributary to China, 1371 E
  capitals of. *See* Hariharalaya; Angkor; Phnom Penh
  customs of, 1297 K
  end of Indian culture, 1330 K
  first chronicle, 1350 K
Cambrai, France, customs of, 1070 G
Cambridge, England:
  Statute of, 1388 G
  University, 1209 H, 1318 H
    colleges:
      Corpus Christi, 1352 H
      Clare Hall, 1326 H
      Godshouse, 1439 H
      Gonville, 1349 H
      King's, 1440 H, 1480 J
      Pembroke, 1346 H
      Peterhouse, 1284 H
      Queens', 1447 H
      St. Catherine's, 1475 H
      Trinity Hall, 1350 H
  degree in music, 1463 J
Cambridge, Earl of, Richard, 1415 C
Cambuskenneth, Scotland, 1326 F
Camel, treatise on, 827 G
Campaldino, Italy, battle, 1289 B
Campano da Novara, Giovanni, It. translator, astronomer and mathematician, 1253 G, 1292 G
Campeggio, Lorenzo, It. cardinal (1474–1539), 1474 L
Campo de Espina, Spain, battle, 1111 D
Campo Morto, Italy, battle, 1482 C
Campofranco, Italy, Treaty of, 1288 D
Canals:
  Bruges-North Sea, 1180 G
  Chinese, 800 G, 825 G, 1289 G
  Elbe-Trave, 1405 G
  Japanese, 800 G
  Kashmīr, 883 G
  Lombard, 1179 G, 1439 G
  Suez, proposed, 809 G
  for irrigation, 800 G, 883 G, 1179 G
  lock-gates, 825 G, 1180 G, 1439 G
Canary Islands, 1402 E, 1425 E, 1480 A
Cancioneiros, 1350 K
Cancionera de Baena, 1445 K
Cancionero General, 1440 K
Candeśvara, Indian jurist, 1314 F
Candiano, Pietro I, Doge of Venice, 887 B, C
Candiano, Pietro II, Doge of Venice, 932 E, 935 E, 939 E
Candiano, Pietro, III, Doge of Venice, 942 E, 959 E
Candiano, Pietro IV, 959 E, 976 C
Candiano, Vitale, Doge of Venice, 978 B, 979 E
Candida, Giovanni (Hans Memling), 1478 J
Canistris, Opicinus de, It. mapmaker, 1352 G
Cannae, Italy, battle, 1018 D
Cannings, William, E. shipowner, 1474 G
Cannon:
  employed, 1319 G, 1326 G, 1347 G; in India, 1367 G
  illustrated, 1327 G
  'Mad Meg', 1430 G
  manufacture of, 1324 G, 1350 G, 1400 G
  treatise on, 1420 G
Cannosa, Italy, 1077 A
Canon episcopi (Regino of Prüm), 906 F
Canon Law:
  African canons, 850 H
  Decretals:
    Extra, 1234 H
    Sext, 1298 H; gloss on, 1340 H
    Clementinae, 1313 H
    Extravagantes, 1317 H
    Extravagantes Communes, 1484 H
    Glossa ordinaria on (Bernard of Botone), 1263 H
  Decretum, 1139 H
  Dionysius Exiguus, 802 H
  False Decretals, 850 H
  Quinque Compilationes, 1226 H
  See also Canonists
Canon of Medicine (Avicenna), 1037 G, 1187 G, 1288 G
Canones de instrumento (Richard Wallingford), 1326 G
Canonisation by Pope, earliest, 993 H
Canonists (ecclesiastical lawyers):
  African. *See* Fenandus, Fulgentius
  English. *See* Lyndwood, William
  French. *See* Bourdeille, Hélie de; Durandus; Étienne of Tournai; Ivo of Chartres
  German. *See* Burchard of Worms; Johannes Teutonicus; Regino of Prüm
  Greek. *See* Balsamon, Theodore
  Italian. *See* Bartholomew of Brescia; Bernard of Botone; Bernard of Pavia; Dionysius; Gratian; Hostiensis; Hugoccio; Johannes Andreae; John of Faenza; Monte, Pietro da; Paucapalea; Pullus, Robert; Rufinus; Tancred; Tedeschi, Niccolò de'; Zabarella, Francesco
  Spanish. *See* Isidore; Torquemada, Juan de
Canonum, Liber, 802 H
Canosa, Italy, Cathedral, 1100 J
Canterbury, England:
  Archbishops, disputed election of, 1205 C, D, 1206 A, D; primacy of, 1072 H. *See also* Alphege; Arundel, Thomas; Becket, Thomas; Bradwardine, Thomas; Chichele, Henry; Courtenay, William; Dunstan; Ethelheard; Kemp, John; Lanfranc; Langton, Stephen; Pecham, John; Rich, Edmund; Stigand; Stratford, John;

Canterbury, England—*contd.*
Archbishops—*contd.*
Sudbury, Simon; Walter, Hubert; Winchelsey, Robert
Cathedral, 1170 D, J, 1174 C, J, 1179 J, 1378 J
St. Augustine's abbey, 1073 J
Treaty of, 1416 C
Canterbury Tales, The (Geoffrey Chaucer), 1387 K, 1477 K
Cantico di Frate Sole (St. Francis), 1225 K
Cantigas de Santa Mariá (Alfonso the Wise), 1284 K
Canton, China, 879 E, G, 971 E
Cantore de mío Cid (anon.), 1140 K
Canute. *See* Cnut
Canzioniere, Il (Cecco Angiolieri), 1312 K
Canzioniere (Petrarch), 1327 K
Cão, Diego, Portuguese navigator, 1482 G
Cape of Good Hope, S. Africa, 1488 G
Cape Verde, Senegal, 1446 G
Cape Verde Islands, Portugal, 1455 G
Capetian dynasty. *See* France
Capgrave, John, E. chronicler, 1393 L, 1417 K, 1448 K, 1464 L
Capistrano, John, St., It. friar, preacher and legate, 1456 L
Capitularies. *See* Law
Cappadocia, Turkey, 806 E
Capranica, Domenico, It. cardinal, 1404 L, 1458 L
Capua, Italy:
battle of, 871 A
Capua-Benevento, Lombard princes of, 899 E, 981 A; *and see* Paldolf IV
taken by Emperors, 1022 A, B, 1038 E
Capuciati, Brotherhood of, 1183 H
Caraccioli, Giovanni, It. courtier, 1432 C
Caravaggio, Italy, battle, 1448 C
Caravanserais. *See* Kirsehir; Sultan Han
Carcassone, France, 1209 C, 1355 D
Cardiff, Wales, 1403 D
Cardigan, Wales, 1176 K
Cardinals, College of, 1289 H; *and see* Papacy
Carham, England, battle, 1016 E
Carinthia, Austria, 901 E
Duke of. *See* Henry the Wrangler
taken by Bohemia, 1269 E
under the Habsburgs (*q.v.*), 1276 D, 1335 B
Carlisle, England, 1307 A
Carloman, King of Bavaria (876–80), 870 E, 876 C, 880 E; illegitimate son of, 888 A
Carloman, King of France, 879 B, D, 880 A, 882 C, 884 C, D
Carloman, son of Charles the Bald, 871 E
Carlos, King of Navarre, 1461 C
Carmagnola, Francesco, condotierre, 1422 B, 1427 D, 1431 B, 1432 B
Carmarthen, Wales, 1403 C, 1405 C
Carmarthen, The Black Book of, 1150 K
Carmelite Order of Friars, 1155 H, 1238 H, 1247 H, 1265 H, 1274 H, 1324 H
Carmina Burana, 1200 K
Carmine Altar (Pietro Lorenzetti), 1329 J
Carniola, Yugoslavia, 1269 E
Carolingian dynasty. *See* Bavaria, Emperors, France, Germany, Italy
last members of, 992 E, 1012 E
Carpentry, tools for, 1220 G, 1424 G
Carrara, Francesco II da, lord of Padua, 1388 D, 1390 B, 1404 E, 1405 D, 1406 A
Carrara, Giacomo da, lord of Padua, 1318 C
Carta Caritatis, 1119 H
Cartagena, Spain, 1263 E
Carthage, Tunisia, 850 H
Carthusian (monastic) Order, 1084 H
Cartier, Jacques, F. navigator (1491–1557), 1491 L
Cartographers. *See* Maps
Casal Imbert, Israel, battle, 1232 B
Casalecchio, Italy, battle, 1402 B
Cashel, Ireland, archbishopric of, 1152 H
Casimir I the Restorer, Duke of Poland, 1034 A, 1039 E, 1047 E, 1050 E, 1058 D
Casimir II the Just, Grand Prince of Poland (b. 1138; 1177–94), 1169 E, 1177 E, 1180 E, 1194 B, 1202 E
Casimir III the Great, King of Poland (b. 1309), 1333 A, 1370 D
conquests, 1339 E, 1349 E, 1355 E, 1366 E
defeats Mongols, 1344 E
founds university, 1364 H
holds Congress of kings, 1364 C
legislation, 1347 F
subdues rebellion, 1358 E
treaties made by, 1335 D, 1339 C, E, 1343 C
Casimir IV, King of Poland (b. 1427; 1446–92), 1447 B, 1469 B
as Grand Prince of Lithuania, 1440 E, 1447 B
defeats Teutonic Knights, 1454 A, C, 1457 B, 1466 D
grants charters of liberties, 1454 F
war with Moscow, 1481 C, 1482 C
other campaigns, 1485 C, 1491 A
Čáslav, Czechoslovakia, 1421 B
Časlav, Prince of Serbia, 927 B
Cassano, Italy, battle, 1259 C
Cassel, Belgium, battles, 1071 A, 1328 C
Castagno, Andrea del, It. painter, 1442 J, 1444 J, 1449 J, 1453 J, 1456 J, 1457 L
Castellammare, Italy, naval battle, 1287 D
Castiglionchio, Lapo da, It. letter writer, 1381 K
Castiglione, Baldassare, It. courtier (1478–1529), 1478 L
Castile, Spain, county of, 1028 E
kingdom created, 1033 E. *And see*
Ferdinand I (1033–65)
Sancho II (1065–72)
Alfonso VI (of Leon; 1072–1109)
Urracca (Queen; 1109–26)
Alfonso VII (of Leon; 1126–57)
Sancho III (1157–8)
Alfonso VIII (1158–1214)
Henry I (1214–17)
Berenguela (Queen, 1217)
Ferdinand III (1217–)
(*Castile and Leon*)
Ferdinand III (1230–52)
Alfonso X (1252–84)
Sancho IV (1284–95)
Ferdinand IV (1295–1312)
Alfonso XI (1312–49)
Pedro I (1349–69)
Henry II (1366–79)
John I (1379–90)
Henry III (1390–1406)
John II (1406–54)
Henry IV (1454–74)
Isabella (Queen; 1474–1504)
capital of. *See* Burgos
chronicle of (López de Ayala), 1407 K
civil wars, 1158 C, 1214 D, 1276 E, 1284 B, 1295 E, 1312 C, 1325 E, 1365 C, 1366 A, 1367 B, 1369 A, 1390 D, 1465 B, 1467 C, 1468 C
claimed by John of Gaunt, 1372 A, 1386 C, 1387 B
Cortes of, 1250 F
laws of, 1252 F, 1254 F, 1256 F
Mesta, 1273 G

Order of Calatrava, 1147 E, 1164 E
poetry, 1225 K, 1235 K
Castles. *See* Château Gaillard; Ghent; Langeais; Yedo (Japan)
Castracani, Castruccio, lord of Lucca, 1314 B, 1320 E, 1325 C, 1328 C
Casus Sancti Galli (Ekkehard), 1036 K
Catalans, Grand Company of. *See* Greece
Catalonia, Spain:
as the Spanish March, 801 E, 811 E, 843 C, 875 E; rulers of, *see* Barcelona
united to Aragon, 1164 E
republic of, 1461 C, 1462 B, 1472 D
revolt of serfs, 1471 G
chronicles, 1330 K, 1336 K
Cortes, 1218 F
literature:
Raymond Lull, 1272 H, 1275 K, 1283 K
James I, 1276 K
Ramón Muntaner, 1330 K, 1336 K
Jordi de Saint Jordi, *Enuigs*, 1440 K
Auziàs March, poems, 1459 K
Joanot Martorell, novel, 1490 K
Usatges (feudal code), 1064 F
Cathari, heretics, 1022 H, 1051 H, 1167 H; *and see* Albigensians *under* Toulouse
'Cathay' (*i.e.* China), origin of, 907 E
Cathedrals:
Austria. *See* Vienna
Belgium. *See* Antwerp; Liège; Tournai
Czechoslovakia. *See* Prague
England. *See* Canterbury; Durham; Ely; Exeter; Gloucester; Lichfield; Lincoln; London; Norwich; Old Sarum; Rochester; Salisbury; Southwell; Wells; Winchester; Worcester; York
France. *See* Albi; Amiens; Angers; Angoulême; Autun; Auxerre; Bayeux; Bayonne; Beauvais; Bourges; Chartres; Clermont Ferrand; Coutances; Laon; Limoges; Lisieux; Lyons; (Le) Mans; Mantes; Meaux; Nantes; Narbonne; Nevers; Noyon; Orleans; Paris; Perigueux; Perpignan; Poitiers; Rouen; Séez; Sens; Soissons; Strasbourg; Toul; Toulouse; Tours; Troyes; Verdun
Germany. *See* Aachen; Augsburg; Bamberg; Bonn; Brandenburg; Cologne; Constance; Erfurt; Essen; Hildesheim; Lübeck; Magdeburg; Mainz; Meissen; Minden; München-Gladbach; Paderborn; Regensburg; Speyer; Trier; Ulm; Worms
Greenland. *See* Gardar
Holland. *See* Utrecht
Hungary. *See* Pécs
Italy. *See* Aversa; Bari; Benevento; Canosa; Cefalù; Florence; Milan; Modena; Monreale; Palermo; Parma; Piacenza; Pisa; Salerno; Siena; Trani; Troia; Venice; Venosa
Norway. *See* Bergen; Stavanger
Poland. *See* Cracow; Gniezno
Portugal. *See* Braga; Lisbon
Russia. *See* Chernigov; Kiev; Moscow; Novgorod; Vilna; Vladimir; Yuriev-Polskij
Scotland. *See* Kirkwall
Spain. *See* Ávila; Barcelona; Burgos; Ciudad Rodrigo; Gerona; Leon; Lérida; Oviedo; Palma; Salamanca; Santiago de Compostela; Seo de Urgel; Seville; Tarragona; Toledo; Valencia
Sweden. *See* Lund; Upsala; Visby
Switzerland. *See* Basel; Berne; Geneva; Lausanne
property of, first divided, 822 H
schools, 1000 H, 1078 H; *and see* Chartres, Paris
Catherine, Cape, Gabon, 1469 G
Catherine of France, Queen of England (1401–38), 1420 B
Catherine, Queen of Navarre, 1483 A
Catherine of Bologna, St., It. mystic, 1463 L
Catherine of Siena, St., It. mystic, 1347 L, 1378 H, 1380 L
Catholic Homilies (Aelfric), 991 K
Catholicon (Giovanni Balbi), 1286 K
Caturvargacintāmani (Hemādri), 1270 F
Caucasia, Russia/Turkey, 855 E, 922 E, 979 A, 1122 E
Cauchon, Pierre, Bishop of Beauvais, 1443 L
Caudebec, France, church, 1426 J
Cavalca, Domenico, It. friar and father of Italian prose, 1342 K
Cavalcanti, Guido, It. poet, 1300 K
Cavriana, Italy, Treaty of, 1441 D
Caxton, William, E. printer and translator (*c.* 1422–91), 1371 K, 1390 K, 1422 L, 1440 K, 1474 K, 1477 K, 1481 K, 1482 K, 1483 K, 1485 K, 1491 L
Cefalù, Sicily, Cathedral, 1131 J; mosaics, 1148 J
Celestine II, Pope, 1143 C, 1144 A
Celestine III (Hyacinth Bobo), Pope, 1191 A, B, 1192 B, C, 1195 B, 1196 D, 1198 A
Celestine IV (Goffredo Castiglione), Pope, 1241 D
Celestine V (Peter of Murrone), Pope, 1294 C, D
Celso, Lorenzo, Doge of Venice, 1361 E, 1365 E
Celtes, Konrad, G. humanist (1459–1508), 1459 L
Censorship, in China, 1072 F
Cent Ballades, Les, 1400 K
Cent Nouvelles Nouvelles, Les (Antoine de la Salle?), 1462 K
Centenarian. *See* Chia Ming
Centula, or St. Riquier, near Abbeville, France, monastery, 800 J; abbot of, *see* Nithard
Cephalas, Constantine, Gk. anthologist, 950 K
Cephissus, River, Greece, battle, 1311 B
Ceprano, Italy, Treaty of, 1080 B
Ceramics: Persian pottery, 1220 J, 1301 J; Chinese faïence, 1301 J
Cerdagne, France, 1462 B, 1463 A, 1473 A, 1475 A
Cerimoniis aulæ Byzantinæ, De (Constantine VII), 959 F
Cerularius, Patriarch of Constantinople, 1054 H
Cesarini, Juliano, It. cardinal and legate, 1398 L, 1431 C, 1444 C, D
Cesena, Italy, 1356 A, 1357 B, 1377 A
Ceuta (Sp. Morocco), 931 E, 1415 C
Ceylon, conquered by Cholas, 1016 E, 1029 E, 1070 E; by Kālinga, 1213 E; by Pāndya, 1269 E; by Chinese, 1409 E; reformed Buddhism in, 1190 H
Ch'a Ching (Lu Yu), 804 G
Chagi Bey, Seljuq leader, 1040 A
Chaghadai, ruler of Turkestan, 1227 C; Khanate of, 1268 E, 1369 E
Chaise-Dieu, La, France, abbey, 1342 J
Chalcocondylas, Laonicus, Gk. historian, 1490 K
Chalukya, India, Hindu empire, 1190 E
Chambre des comptes, 1309 F, 1320 F
Champa (South Vietnam), 1012 G
invaded by Dai Viet, 1000 E, 1044 E, 1068 E
wars with Cambodia, 1145 E, 1149 E, 1177 E, 1181 E, 1203 E, 1220 E
attacked by Mongols, 1283 E
conquered by Dai Viet, 1313 E, 1318 E, 1326 E
invade Dai Viet, 1361 E, 1371 E, 1377 E, 1390 A
tributary to China, 1369 E
invaded by Dai Viet, 1471 E
capital of. *See* Indrapura; Vijaya
end of Indian culture, 1253 K
Cha'an sect of Buddhism, 800 H

Champagne, France, Counts of. *See* Odo II, Stephen, Theobald I, Henry I, Joanna I
Fairs of, 1114 G
Chancery. *See* England, government
Chand Bardāī, Hindu poet, 1192 K
Chand Raisā (Chand Bardāī), 1192 K
Chandos, John, E. soldier, 1370 A
Chandragirirājya, India, 1486 E
Channel Islands, U.K., 1204 B
Chanson d'Antioche (Graindor de Douay), 1180 K
Chanson de Chétifs, 1130 K
Chanson de Roland, 1095 K, 1150 K
Chansons de gestes:
Amis et Amile, 1180 K
Girart de Roussillon, 1190 K
The Cid (Spanish), 1140 K
Le Pèlerinage de Charlemagne, 1150 K
Roulandesliet, 1150 K
Wace, *Brut*, 1155 K
Aimeri de Narbonne, 1200 K
Huon de Bordeaux, 1200 K
Adenet le Roi, 1280 K
Bevis of Hampton, 1330 K
Geste de Liège, 1400 K
Chansons d'amour (Bernart de Ventadour), 1195 K
Chansons françaises (Richard I), 1199 K
Chao K'uang-yin (T'ai-Tsu), Emperor of China, 927 L, 960 E, 971 E, 976 D
Chao Mêng-fu, Chinese painter, 1254 L, 1322 J
Charité-sur-Loire, La, France, abbey, 1059 J
Charlemagne, King of the Franks and Lombards, Emperor, 800 H, K, 805 J, 807 G, 809 H, 814 A
crowned as Emperor, 800 D
measures against Vikings, 800 E
conquests in Spain, 801 E, 806 E
constitutional measures, 802 A, 806 A, 813 C
relations with Greek Empire, 802 E, 812 B
capitularies, 802 F, 805 G, H, 833 F
conquests in Germany, 804 E, 808 E, 810 E, 812 E
conquers Venetia etc., 805 E
subjects Avars, 811 E
in literature:
Einhard, *Vita Karoli Magni*, 830 K
Nithard, *Gesta*, 843 K
Gesta Karoli, 883 K
Poeta Saxo, 890 K
Le Pèlerinage de Charlemagne, 1150 K
Amis et Amile, 1180 K
Bertrand de Bar-sur-Aube, 1200 K
Girard d'Amiens, 1295 K
I Reali di Francia, 1430 K
Boiardo, *Orlando Innamorato*, 1482 K
Charles the Bald, Emperor (b. 823; 875–7), 829 E, 831 A, 877 D
as King of Aquitaine, 839 B, 844 E, 845 B, 848 E, 852 C, 855 B
war against Lothar, 841 B, 842 A, B
King of France, 843 C
treaties with brothers, 843 C, 844 D, 847 E
defeated by Bretons, 845 D, 846 E, 856 A
measures against Vikings, 845 E, 862 E, 866 E, 872 E, 877 B
deprived of France, 858 C, 859 E
treaties with Louis the German, 860 B, 865 B
occupies Provence, 861 E, 870 E
grants counties, 863 E, 870 E
King of Lorraine, 869 C, 870 C
blinds his son, 871 E
crowned as Emperor, 875 D
King of Italy, 876 A, 877 D
defeated by Saxons, 876 D
capitularies of, 847 F, 877 F
Charles the Fat, Emperor (881–8), 876 C, 881 A, 882 C, D, 885 D, E, 887 E, 888 A; reunited Empire, 882 A, 884 D
Charles IV, King of Bohemia and Holy Roman Emperor (1355–78), 1316 L, 1376 B, 1378 D
Italian expeditions, 1332 D, 1354 D, 1368 D
ruling Bohemia, 1333 D, J
King of the Romans, 1346 B, C, 1347 D
as King of Bohemia, 1346 C, 1347 H, 1348 B, G, H, 1350 F, 1358 G, 1363 H
peace with Wittelsbachs, 1350 A
crowned Emperor, 1355 B
Golden Bull, 1356 F
treaty with Habsburgs, 1364 A
crowned at Arles, 1365 B
at Congress of Cracow, 1364 C
promulgates a peace, 1371 F
acquires Brandenburg, 1373 C
opposes Swabian League, 1377 B
visits Paris, 1378 A
recognises Urban VI, 1378 D
life of (Beneš of Weitmil), 1375 K
Charles, King of Aquitaine, 855 B, 886 C
Charles I, King of France. *See* Charles the Bald, Emperor
Charles II, King of France. *See* Charles the Fat
Charles III the Simple, King of France (893–929), 879 L, 893 A, 897 E, 898 A, 911 E, 917 E, 929 D, 936 A; King of Lorraine, 911 D, 921 D; defeated by revolt, 922 B, 923 B, E
Charles IV, King of France (1322–8), 1294 L, 1322 A, 1324 C, 1325 A, 1327 A, 1328 A, B
Charles V the Wise, King of France (1364–80), 1337 L, 1364 B, J, 1375 G, 1378 G, 1380 B, C, 1388 D
as Dauphin, 1349 C, 1355 E, 1357 F
Regent of France, 1356 D, 1357 A, 1358 A, C
revolt against, 1364 B, 1365 A
intervenes in Castile, 1365 C
war against England, 1368 D, 1369 B, 1370 D, 1372 B–D, 1374 A, 1375 B, 1377 C, 1380 B, C
visited by Emperor, 1378 A
promotes papal election, 1378 C, D
confiscates Brittany, 1379 C
life of (Christine de Pisan), 1404 K
Charles VI, King of France (1380–1422), 1368 L, 1380 C, 1392 H, 1422 D
as Dauphin, 1378 A
government in his minority, 1380 C, D, 1381 A, 1382 A, D, 1383 A, 1386 D
personal rule, 1388 D
Italian policy, 1391 A, 1396 C, D, 1409 C
relations with Richard II, 1391 A, 1396 A, D
insane, 1392 C
relations with Papacy, 1395 A, D, 1398 C, 1400 A, 1403 A, B
alliance with Welsh, 1404 C, 1405 C
riots against, 1413 A, B, C
expedition against Burgundy, 1414 C
attacked by Henry V, *q.v.*
regency of his son, 1418 D
treaty with Henry V, 1420 B, D
Charles VII, King of France (1422–61), 1403 L, 1422 D, 1453 B, 1461 C
as Dauphin and Regent, 1418 D
murders John of Burgundy, 1419 C, D
war with England, 1421 A, 1423 C, 1424 C, 1427 C
civil war under, 1427 E, 1433 B
receives Joan of Arc, 1429 A
crowned, 1429 C
peace with Burgundy, 1435 C
takes Paris, 1436 B

plots against, 1437 B, 1440 A
Pragmatic Sanction, 1438 C
reforms army, 1439 D, 1445 E, 1448 B
campaigns against English, 1442 C, 1444 B
relations with Swiss, 1444 C, D
expels English, 1449 A, D, 1450 B, C, 1451 C, 1452 D, 1453 D
reforms administration, 1454 F
quarrel with Dauphin Louis, 1456 C
attacks England, 1457 C
occupies Genoa, 1458 B
history of (Jean Chartier), 1461 K
mistress of, 1450 F
portrait of (Jean Fouquet), 1444 J

Charles VIII, King of France (1484–98), 1470 L, 1484 A, 1488 C, 1491 D; Regent for, *see* Anne of Beaujeu
Charles Martel, King of Hungary, 1290 C, 1295 E
Charles I Robert, King of Hungary (1308–42), 1301 A, 1308 E, 1324 E, 1335 D, 1339 E, 1342 E
Charles II the Bad, King of Navarre (b. 1332), 1349 D, 1354 A, 1364 B, 1365 A, 1376 E, 1378 B, 1387 A
Charles III, King of Navarre (b. 1361), 1387 A, 1415 D, 1425 C
Charles, King of Provence, 855 C, 863 A
Charles I of Anjou, King of Sicily (b. 1220; 1266–85), 1285 A
Count of Anjou and Provence, 1246 A
conquers Sicily, 1261 C, 1265 B, 1266 A
influence in Tuscany, 1267 B, 1268 B, 1270 E, 1278 B
suppresses revolt, 1267 C, 1270 C
attacks Greek Empire, 1267 E, 1270 D, 1274 C, 1281 C, E
Senator of Rome, 1268 B, 1278 B, 1281 A, 1284 A
defeats Conradin, 1268 C, D
intervenes in papal election, 1268 D
on Crusade, 1270 C, D
defeated in North Italy, 1273 E, 1275 D
King of Jerusalem, 1276 E, 1278 A
Prince of Achaea, 1278 B
defeated in Sicilian revolt, 1282 A, 1284 B
statue of (Arnolfo), 1277 J

Charles II, King of Sicily (Naples; b. 1248; 1285–1309), 1284 B, 1285 A, 1288 D, 1289 B, 1295 B, 1309 B; war against Sicily, 1297 E, 1300 D, 1302 C
Charles III of Durazzo, King of Naples, 1381 B, C, 1382 A, C, 1386 A
Charles VII, King of Sweden, 1162 E, 1168 E
Charles VIII (Karl Knutson), King of Sweden (1448–70), 1438 E, 1448 B, 1457 B, 1464 C, 1470 B; King of Norway, 1449 D, 1450 C
Charles of Blois, Duke of Brittany, 1341 B, D, 1342 B, C, D, 1347 B, 1364 C
Charles the Bold, Duke of Burgundy (1467–77), 1433 L, 1467 B, D, 1468 C, 1471 F, 1473 F, 1489 K
conflict with Louis XI, 1465 C, D, 1468 D, 1471 A, 1472 B, D, 1474 C, 1475 C
acquisitions, 1469 B, 1473 E, 1475 D
relations with Emperor, 1473 C, D, 1475 B
war with Swiss, 1474 B, 1476 A, B, 1477 A

Charles, Duke of Calabria, 1325 D, 1328 D
Charles I the Good, Count of Flanders, 1127 A
Charles, Duke of Guienne, 1472 B
Charles, Duke of Lower Lorraine, 977 E, 988 C, 989 C, 991 A, 992 E
Charles, Duke of Orleans, F. poet, 1391 L, 1447 C, 1465 K, L
Charles, Count of Valois (d. 1325), 1284 A, 1301 D, 1302 B, C
Charles, son of Charlemagne (d. 811), 805 E, 806 A, E
Charlieu, France, abbey, 1094 J
Charroux, France, 989 F
Charters of Liberties:
Aragon, 1283 F, 1287 F, 1348 C
Denmark, 1282 F
England, 1100 C; *and see* Magna Carta
Hungary, 1222 F
Lithuania, 1447 B
Poland, 1374 F, 1454 F
Portugal, 1287 F

Chartier, Alain, F. poet, 1416 K, 1422 K, 1425 K, 1440 K
Chartier, Jean, F. chronicler, 1461 K
Chartres, France, 1360 B; Cathedral, 958 J, 1020 J, 1050 J, 1134 J, 1145 J, 1194 J, 1219 J; cathedral school, 1000 H, 1028 H, 1115 H; Count of, 996 B
Chartreuse, France, monastery, 1084 H
Chase, Pleasures of the (Gaston Phoebus), 1391 K, 1410 K
Chase, regulations for (Sancho VI), 1180 G
Château Gaillard, France, 1197 J, 1204 A, 1334 B
Châtelain, George, F. chronicler, 1404 L, 1474 K, L
Châtelain de Couci, Le (Jakemon Saquet), 1280 K
Châtillon, France, battle, 1453 C
Chaucer, Geoffrey, E. poet (1340?–1400), 1340 L, 1369 K, 1381 K, 1382 K, 1384 K, 1387 K, 1392 K, 1400 L, 1477 K, 1490 K; sources of, 1110 K, 1160 K
Chauliac, Guy de, F. surgeon, 1363 G
Che A-nan, King of Champa (1326–61), 1318 E, 1326 E
Che Bong Nga, King of Champa, 1361 E, 1371 E, 1377 E, 1390 A
Che Nang, King of Champa, 1313 E, 1318 E
Cheb (Eger), Czechoslovakia, 1432 B; Golden Bull of Eger, 1213 C
Chedi, India, Hindu kingdom, 1060 E
Chef-Boutonne, France, battle, 1061 A
Chekhs. *See* Bohemia
Chelmno, Poland, 1226 E, 1230 E
Chemistry, instruments for, 1477 G. *See also* Alchemy
Chemists. *See* Chui-chung; 'Marc the Greek'
Chên la fêng t'u chi (Chou Ta-kuan), 1297 K
Ch'ên Ching-i, C. botanist, 1256 G
Ch'en Jên-yü, C. naturalist, 1245 G
Ch'ên P'êng-nien, C. philologist (961–1017), 1011 K
Ch'ên Tzŭ-ming C. physician, 1237 G
Chêng Ch'iao, C. historian and archaeologist (1104–62), 1161 K
Chêng-lei pên ts'ao, 1108 G
Cheng Ho, C. admiral and explorer, 1405 G, 1436 G, 1451 G
Cheng-t'ung, Emperor of China (b. 1427; d. 1464), 1449 E
Chengtu, China, banks of, 1024 G
Cheques. *See* Money drafts
Cherbourg, France, 1378 B, 1418 C, 1443 C, 1450 C
Chernigov, Russia, Cathedral, 1036 J
Chess, treatises on, 1284 K, 1405 K
Chester, England, 973 B
Chester Cycle (of miracle plays), 1327 K
Chevalier au Cygne, Le, 1225 K
Chevalier au Lion (Chrétien de Troyes), 1173 K
Chia Ming, C. physician and centenarian (*c.* 1268–*c.* 1374), 1368 G
Chia Ssŭ-tao, C. naturalist, 1230 G
Chia Tan, C. cartographer and historian (730–805), 801 G, 805 K
Chiang An, China, 904 E
Chiang Mai, Siam, capital of Lan Na, 1296 E
Chichele, Henry, Archbishop of Canterbury, 1438 H, 1443 L
Chichén-Itzá, Mexico, Mayan city, 987 E

Ch'ieh-yun (Lu Fa-yen, ed. Ch'ên P'êng-nien), 1011 K
Ch'ien Hsuan, C. painter (1235–90), 1290 J
Chiesi, Italy, battle, 1373 B
Chi-ku-lu (Ou-yang Hsiu), 1072 K
Children's Crusade, 1212 H
Chile, 1471 E
Chin dynasties. *See* China
Ch'in ching, 1279 G
Ch'in Chiu-Shao, C. mathematician, 1247 G
China:
  T'ang dynasty, 811 G, 817 K, 907 E
    conquers Tibet, 821 E
    attacked by Nanchao, 829 E, 863 E, 866 E
    'Sweet Dew incident', 833 E
    collapse of Uighurs, 842 H
    peasant rebellions, 874 E, 878 E, 879 E, 884 E, 904 E, 907 E; *and see* Huang Ch'ao, Chu Wen
  'Period of the Five Dynasties and the Ten Kingdoms', 907 E
    invasion by Khitan, 907 E, 926 E, 936 E
    Later T'ang dynasty, 923 E
    revolt of Annam, 932 E, 939 E
    Later Chin dynasty, 935 E, 946 E
    Hou-Chou dynasty, 951 E
  Liao (Khitan) dynasty of north China, 947 E, H, 988 F, 1004 E, 1036 F
    destroyed by Jürched, 1115 E, 1120 E, 1122 E, 1125 E
    Western. *See* Kara-Khitai
  Sung dynasty, 960 E, 976 E, 1024 G, 1041 F, 1065 F, 1076 F, 1126 E; *and see* Chao K'uang-yin, T'ai Tsung, Hui Tsung
    relations with Dai-co-viet, 968 E, 981 E, 1076 E
    pay tribute to Liao, 1004 E; and Hsi Hsia, 1038 E, 1044 E
    ally with Jürched, 1120 E, 1125 E, 1126 E
  Chin (Jürched) dynasty, 1122 E, 1141 E, 1153 E, 1165 E, 1207 E, 1215 E, 1234 E
  Southern Sung dynasty, 1127 E, 1141 E, 1165 E, 1207 E, 1279 E
  Mongol conquest, 1211 E, 1215 E, 1224 E, 1234 E, 1253 E, 1258 E, 1269 E, 1273 E, 1279 E
  Yüan (Mongol) dynasty, 1271 E, 1307 E, 1331 F; *and see* Kublai Khan, Temür
    famines ruin, 1333 G
    revolts against, 1341 E, 1351 E, 1353 E, 1356 E, 1367 E
  Ming dynasty (1367–1644), 1367 E, 1380 F, 1393 F, 1397 F, 1421 E, 1449 E; *and see* Hung-wu, Yung-lo
    army, 976 F, 1041 F, 1393 F
    calendar (Chou-Ts'ung), 1065 G
    called 'Cathay', 907 E
  canals, 800 G, 825 G; Grand Canal, 1289 G
  censorship, 1072 F
  currency paper, 811 F, 1024 G, 1450 G; history of coinage, 1149 K
  forensic medicine in, 1248 G
  government:
    coroners, 1248 G
    encyclopedias on, 812 F, 961 F, 1005 F, 1331 F
    examinations for civil service, 988 F, 1065 F, 1237 F, 1274 F, 1315 F, 1417 F, 1487 F
    model for Korea, 958 F
    Prime ministers, 932 G, 1380 F
    reforms by Sung, 1076 F
    secret files, 1420 F
  histories:
    encyclopedia, 801 K
    of the Five Dynasties, 981 K
    of inscriptions, 1072 K, 1184 K
    of T'ang dynasty, 805 K, 946 K, 1060 K
    official, 887 K, 946 K, 981 K
    T'ung chih (Chêng Ch'iao), 1161 K
    Universal mirror (Ssŭ-ma Kuang), 1086 K, 1205 K
  industry and technology:
    'compass', 1020 G, 1086 G, 1117 G
    faïence ware, 1301 J
    gunpowder, 850 G, 1044 G, 1126 G
    ink, 1329 G, 1398 G
    iron, 1310 G
    porcelain, 1188 G
    printing. *See* Printing
    silk, 1090 G, 1310 G
    wheel barrow, 1250 G
  law code, 1397 F; of Liao, 1036 F
  literature:
    poems of Li Ho, 817 K
    essays of Han Yü, 824 K
    poems of Po-Chü-i, 846 K
    poems in Japanese anthology, 905 K
    Sino-Japanese dictionary, 983 K
    phonetic dictionaries, 1011 K, 1039 K, 1375 K
    essays of Shên Kua, 1093 G
    poems and essays of Su Tung-p'o, 1101 K
    poems of Li Ch'ing-chao, 1151 K
    Sea of Jade (encyclopedia), 1296 K
    drama and novels; plays of Kuan Han-Ch'ing, 1300 K
    Story of a Lute (opera), 1356 J
    San Kuo (romance) of Lo Kuan-Chung, 1400 K
    The Great Chinese Encyclopedia, 1403 K
  maps, 801 G, 814 G, 1137 G, 1331 F
  paintings, 845 J, 1035 H; *and see* Painters
  population, 1270 G, 1393 G
  public health service, 1102 G, 1143 G
  religions:
    Buddhism, 800 H, 845 H, J, 947 H, 1191 H, 1260 H; texts printed, 868 G, 932 G
    Christian:
      Manichean, 842 H
      missions, 1245 H, 1260 H, 1275 H, 1304 H, 1340 H
    Confucianism, 947 H, 958 F, 1073 H; Neo- (Chu Hsi-ism), 1200 H; texts printed, 932 G; edited, 1417 F
    other, 1260 H
  rice introduced, 1012 G
  south, natural history of, 1193 G
  trade and communications, 879 G, 1240 G; with Arabs, 851 G; Europe, 1260 F, 1340 G; Japan, 805 H, 806 H, 1341 G, 1374 G
  travellers' accounts of, 847 K, 920 G, 1298 G
Ching Hao, C. painter, 960 J
Ching-shih ta-tien, 1331 F
Chinion, France, 1429 A; Treaty of, 1214 C
Chioggia, Italy, War of, 1378 D, 1379 C, 1380 B, 1381 C
Chios, is., Greece, 1304 E, 1329 E, 1346 E; church of Nea Moni, mosaics in, 1050 J; naval battle, 912 B
Chirurgia (William of Saliceto), 1275 G
Chirugia Magna (Bruno of Longoburgo), 1252 G; (Guy of Chauliac), 1363 G
Chirurgica Magna (Lanfranchi), 1296 G
Chiu Ch'ang-ch'un, C. traveller, 1221 G
Chiu huang pên ts'ao (Chu Hsiao), 1406 G
Chiu T'ang Shu (Liu Hsü), 946 K
Chiu Wu-tai-shih (Hsieh Chü-chêng), 981 K
Chi-yün (Ting Tu *e.a.*), 1039 K
Chivalry:
  The Ring of the Dove (Arabic), 1064 K
  L'Histoire de Guillaume le Maréchal, 1220 K

Raymond Lull, *Libre del orde de cavayleria*, 1275 K
Jacque Bretel, *Le Tournoi de Chauvency*, 1285 K
El Caballero Cifar, 1340 K
Réné of Anjou, *Livre des tournois*, 1460 K
Amadis of Gaul, 1475 K
Luigi Pulci, *Morgante Maggiore* (burlesque), 1482 K
Joanot Martorell, *Tirant lo blanc*, 1490 K
See also Chansons des gestes
Orders of. *See* Bath; Elephant; Garter; Golden Fleece; St. Michael; Star; White Eagle
Ch'oe Ch'ung-hŏn, Korean general (d. 1219), 1196 E
Ch'oe dictators of Korea, 1196 E, 1258 E
Chojnice, Poland, battle, 1454 C
Chola Empire of South India, 846 E, 1016 E, 1279 E; *and see* Āditya I; Parāntaka I; Rājarāja; Rajendra-Choladeva I; Kullotunga III
architecture of, 1009 J
capitals of. *See* Gaingaikonda-Cholapurum; Tanjore
literature under, 1200 K
See also Ceylon
Choniates, Nicetas, Gk. historian, 1213 K
Chou ch'in k'o shih shih yin (Wu-ch'iu Yen), 1307 K
Chou Ta-kuan, C. ambassador, 1297 K
Chou-Ts'ung, C. astronomer, 1065 G
Chou Tun-i, C. Confucian reformer and philosopher (1017–73), 1073 H
Chrétien de Troyes, F. poet (d. *c.* 1183), 1164 K, 1170 K, 1173 K
Christ, Knights of (Portuguese order), 1319 E
Christ bearing the Cross (Simone Martini), 1330 J
Christ mocked (Hieronymus Bosch), 1480 J
Christ returning (Simone Martini), 1342 J
Christ walking on the water (Konrad Witz), 1444 J
Christian I of Oldenburg, King of Denmark and Norway (b. 1426), 1448 C, 1449 D, 1450 C, 1468 A, 1478 A, H, 1481 B; King of Sweden, 1457 B, 1471 D; Duke of Schleswig-Holstein, 1460 A
Christian Instruction (Thomas of Štítný), 1401 H
Christopher, Pope, 903 C, 904 A
Christopher I, King of Denmark, 1252 B, 1258 E, 1259 B
Christopher II, King of Denmark (1320–32), 1320 A, 1326 E, 1331 E, 1332 C, 1340 E
Christopher III of Bavaria, King of Denmark, 1440 B, 1448 A; King of Sweden, 1441 C; King of Norway, 1442 E
Christus, Petrus, G. painter (d. 1472/3), 1417 J
Chronica Hispaniae (Roderigo of Toledo), 1248 K
Chronica Majora (Matthew Paris), 1259 K; (Roger of Howden), 1201 K
Chronica Regni Gothorum (Erik Olai), 1486 K
Chronica sive Historia de duabus civitatibus (Otto of Freising), 1146 K
Chronicle (Georgios Syncellos), 810 K
Chronicles. *See also* Histories
Chroniclers. *See* Historians
Chronicon (Adam of Usk), 1430 K; (Hermann Contractus), 1054 K; (Thietmar), 1018 K
Chronicon ab Adam ad Henricum I (Ailred of Rievaulx), 1166 K
Chronicon Aquitanicum (Adhemar), 1034 K
Chronicon de rebus gestis Ricardi Primi (Richard of Devizes), 1192 K
Chronicon ex Chronicis (Florence of Worcester), 1118 F
Chronicon Januense (Jacobus de Voragine), 1298 K
Chronicon pontificum et imperatorum (Martin of Troppau), 1278 K
Chronik (Fritsche Closener), 1362 K
Chronique de l'histoire de France (Guillaume Fillastre), 1473 K
Chronique de Reims (anon.), 1260 K
Chronique rimée, La (Philippe Mousqués), 1268 K
Chronographia (Sigebert of Gembloux), 1112 K
Chronography, Short (Nicephorus), 829 K
Chronography, The (Michael Psellus), 1078 K
Chronology, treatise on (Bergthorsson), 1173 G
Chronology of Ancient Nations (al-Bīrunī), 1048 K
Chrysanthemums, treatise on (Fan Ch'êng-ta), 1193 G
Chrysoloras, Manuel, Gk. grammarian, 1391 K, 1415 K, L
Chrysopolis, Turkey, battle, 988 C
Ch'u p'u hsiang lu (Li K'an), 1299 G
Chu Hsi, C. philosopher (1130–1200), 1200 K
Chu Shih-chieh, C. mathematician, 1303 G
Chü lu (Han Ch'an-chih), 1178 G
Chu Hsiao, C. botanist (d. 1425), 1406 G
Chu Wen (Chu Chüan-chung), C. peasant leader and Emperor (as T'ai-tsu), 884 E, 904 E, 907 E, 923 E
Chu Yüan-chang. *See* Hung-wu
Ch'üan-fang pei-tsu (Ch'ên Ching-i), 1256 G
Ch'üan-chih (Hung Tsun), 1149 K
Chui-chung, C. chemist, 1120 G
Chün p'u (Ch'ên Jên-yü), 1245 G
Church, reform of, 1014 A, 1018 H, 1019 H, 1022 C, H, 1046 D, 1058 D; *and see* Gregory VII, Humbert, Simony
See also Archbishoprics, Canon Law, Cathedrals, Clergy, Conversion, Councils, Greek Church, Heresy, Inquisition, Investiture Contest, Mendicant Orders, Monasteries, Popes, Religious Orders
Cicero, *De Oratore*, 1421 K
Cid, The (Rodrigo *or* Ruy Diaz de Vivar), Sp. hero (1043–99), 1081 E, 1094 E, 1099 E, L; *Song of*, 1140 K
Cidyny, Poland, battle, 972 E
Cilicia, Turkey, 965 C; Kingdom of Lesser Armenia in, *see* Armenia
Cimabue, It. painter, 1280 J, 1302 J
Cinnamos, Joannes, Gk. historian (*c.* 1143–1203), 1183 K
Cino da Pistoia, It. jurist and poet, 1336 F, L
Cintra, Portugal, 1093 E
Circa instans (Platearius), 1161 G
Circulation of the blood, 1288 G
Cistercian (monastic) Order, 1098 H, 1119 H, 1147 H, 1335 H; houses, 1113 H, 1115 H, 1123 H, 1128 H, 1140 H, 1142 J, 1153 H, 1200 H; *and see* Cîteaux, Pontigny
Cîteaux, France, abbey, 1098 H, 1113 H; abbot of, *see* Harding, Stephen
Civetot, Turkey, battle, 1096 D
Cividale, Italy, 1409 B
Civile, Della vita (Matteo Palmieri), 1475 F
Civili dominio, De (John Wycliffe), 1376 F
Civitate, Italy, battle, 1053 B
Clairvaux, France, abbey, 1115 H; abbot of, *see* Bernard
Clamanges, Nicholas de, F. theologian, 1434 L
Clara, St., It. monastic founder, 1193 L, 1216 H, 1253 L
Clare, Gilbert de, Earl of Gloucester (1243–95), 1267 B
Clarence, Dukes of. *See* George; Thomas
Clarendon, England, 1164 A, 1166 F
Classification of nations (al-Andalusi), 1070 G
Clavis sanationis (Simon of Genoa), 1293 G
Clement II (Suidger of Bamberg), Pope, 1046 D, 1047 D, H
Clement III (Guibert of Ravenna), anti-pope, 1080 B, 1084 A, 1094 E, 1100 C

Clement III (Paul Scolari), Pope, 1187 D, 1189 B, D, 1191 A
Clement IV (Guy Foulquoi), Pope (1265–8), 1264 D, 1265 A, B, 1267 B, 1268 B, D
Clement V (Bertrand de Got), Pope, 1305 B, D, H, 1306 A, H, 1307 H, 1308 B, C, 1309 A, C, H, 1310 B, 1312 B, 1313 H, 1314 B
Clement VI (Pierre Roger), Pope, 1342 B, J, 1344 D, E, H, 1346 B, 1349 G, 1352 B, D
Clement VII (Robert of Geneva), Pope at Avignon (1378–94), 1377 A, 1378 C, 1379 B, H, 1381 B, C, 1382 B, 1385 B, 1386 E, 1394 C
Clement VIII (Gil Sanchez Mũnoz), anti-pope (1423–8), 1423 H
Clementinae (Clement V), 1313 H; gloss on, 1417 H
Cleobury, England, battle, 1056 B
Cléomadès (Adenet le Roi), 1282 K
Clergy:
  absenteeism, 1298 H
  concubinage, 1018 H
  marriage, 1018 H, 1019 H, 1022 C, 1074 H, 1075 A, 1123 H, 1143 H, 1215 H
  privilege, 1489 H
  taxation, 1199 H, 1215 H, 1291 H, 1296 H
Clericis laicos (Boniface VIII), 1296 A, C, 1297 C
Clericorum, De institutione (Rabanus Maurus), 856 H
Clermont, France, 1095 D
Clermont Ferrand, France, Cathedral, 946 J, 1248 J
Cligès (Chrétien de Troyes), 1170 K
Clisson, Oliver de, constable of France (d. 1407), 1392 B
Clocks, 1348 G, 1370 G; astronomical, 1326 G; treatises on, 1206 G, 1284 G; water, 807 G
Clontarf, Ireland, battle, 1014 B
Closener, Fritsche, G. chronicler, 1362 K
Cloth industry, Flemish, 1245 G, 1280 G; spinning-wheel, 1280 G
Cloud of Unknowing (anon.), 1380 H
Clovesho, England, 803 H
Cluniac (monastic) Order, 1036 J, 1094 J, 1336 H
Cluny, France, abbey, 909 H, 927 J, 955 J, 1043 J, 1088 J, 1119 A, 1125 J, 1130 H; abbots of, *see* Hugh of Semur, Mayeul, Odilo, Odo, Peter the Venerable, Pontius; Roche, Adroin de la
Clyst, England, battle, 1455 D
Cnut, King of England (1016–35), 1014 A, 1015 C, 1016 B, D, 1027 E; King of Denmark, 1019 E, 1025 E, 1026 E, 1028 B, 1035 D, 1036 B; *History* of (Aelnoth), 1109 K; *Song of*, 1166 K
Cnut IV, St., King of Denmark, 1081 B, 1085 C, 1086 C
Cnut (V), contender for Danish crown, 1147 E, 1157 B
Cnut VI the Pious, King of Denmark, 1182 B, 1193 C, 1202 D
Cnut Ericson, King of Sweden, 1168 E, 1192 E
Coal, 1190 G, 1216 G, 1273 G
Cobham, Eleanor, Duchess of Gloucester, 1425 B, 1441 D
Coblenz, West Germany, 860 B, 1338 C
Cocherel, France, battle, 1364 B
Cocom dynasty. *See* Yucátan
Coenwulf, King of Mercia (796–821), 821 E
Coeur, Jacques, F. merchant and financier, 1443 J, 1453 B, 1456 L
Cohen, Judah, Sp. Je. astronomer, 1262 G
Coimbra, Portugal, 1064 E; University, 1308 H
Coins:
  Bohemian, 1300 G
  Chinese, 811 F; history of, 1149 K
  English, 1344 G
  Florentine, 1252 G
  French, 1266 G, 1340 G
  Indian (fiduciary currency), 1329 G
  Sicilian, 1231 G
Colet, John, E. humanist (1466–1519), 1466 L
Colette, St., of Corbie, F. mystic, 1381 L, 1447 L
Collection of Histories (Rashīd), 1314 K
Colleges. *See* Cambridge, Erzerum, Kayseri, Konya, Miramar, Oxford, Paris, St. Andrews, Salatgi, Sivas
Colleone, Bartolomeo, condottiere (1400–76), statue of, 1481 J
Colliget (Averroes), 1255 G, 1482 G
Co-loa, North Vietnam, capital of Dai-co-viet, 939 E
Colmar, France, 833 B, 1474 B
Cologne, West Germany, 881 E, 1198 C, 1207 A
  Archbishopric of, 1475 B
  Archbishops of, 863 H, 954 D, 1180 B, 1186 C, 1225 D, 1288 C; *and see* Anno
  Cathedral, 813 J, 1248 J, 1322 J
  churches, 980 J, 1040 J
  citizens revolt, 1074 G
  league made at, 1367 D
  merchants of, 1157 F
  University, 1388 H
Coloman, King of Hungary, 1095 C, 1108 E, 1114 E
Colombières, France, 1189 C
Colonisation, by Germans, 1227 C; in Bohemia, 1173 E, 1235 G; Holstein, 1143 G; Hungary, 1161 G, 1224 G; Lithuania, 1285 E; Poland, 1241 G, 1250 E, 1264 G; Prussia, 1283 E, 1377 G
Colunna, Roman family of, 1297 A, B, 1298 C, 1431 B, 1434 B
Colunna, Aegidius. *See* Giles of Rome
Colunna, Francesco, It. friar and prose writer (1432?–1527?), 1479 K
Coloribus et artibus Romanorum, De (Heraclius), 950 G
Columbus, Christopher, It. navigator (1451?–1506), 1451 L, 1491 G
Columnis, Guido de (of Messina), It. prose writer, 1287 K
Comacchio, Italy, 935 E
Comines, Robert de, Earl of Northumbria, 1069 A
Commentaria in C. Manilii astronomicon (Lorenzo Buonincontro), 1474 G
Commentaria in Codicem (Bartolus), 1357 F
Commentarii (Ghiberti), 1455 J
Commentum (Benvenuto de' Rambaldi), 1379 K
Common Pleas, English court, 1215 F
Communes. *See* Boroughs
Communications. *See* Post; Telegraph
Commynes, Philippe de, F. courtier and historian (*c.* 1447–1511), 1489 K
Comnena, Anna. *See* Anna Comnena
Comnenus dynasty. *See* Greek Empire; Trebizond
Compagni, Dino, It. chronicler and poet, 1324 K
Compass, Chinese, 1117 G; Muslim, 1230 G; European, 1283 G; lodestone for, 1269 G; *and see* Magnet
Compendium grammaticae (John of Garland), 1220 K
Compendium philosophiae (Roger Bacon), 1292 K
Compendium spherae (Robert Grosseteste), 1253 G
Compilación de Canellas (or *de Huesca*), 1245 F
Composizione del mondo (Ristoro d'Arezzo), 1282 G
Compostela. *See* Santiago de Compostela
Computer, Work of the (Levi ben Gerson), 1321 G
Computo, De (Helperic?), 978 G
Contemplació en Deu, Libre de (Raymond Lull), 1272 H
Comyn, John, contender for Scottish crown, 1306 A
Comyn, John, Earl of Buchan, 1307 D, 1308 E
Conan I, Count of Brittany, 992 B
Conciliar Movement. *See* Popes: Great Schism

Conciliator (Pietro d'Abano), 1303 G
Concilium Pacis (Henry of Langenstein), 1381 H
Concordantia Catholica (Nicholas of Cusa), 1433 H
Concordia discordantium canonum (Gratian), 1139 H
Conde Lucanor (Juan Manuel), 1349 K
Condottieri. *See* Barbiano, Alberico da; Carmagnola, Francesco; Colleone, Bartolomeo; Fogliano, Guidoriccio da; Hawkwood, John; Malatesta, Roberto; Braccio da Montone; Piccinino, Niccolò; Sforza Attendolo; Sforza, Francesco
Confessio Amantis (John Gower), 1390 K
Confessio Prolixior (Gottschalk), 849 H
Conflans, France, Treaty of, 1465 D
Confraternities. *See* Fraternities
Confucianism. *See* China, Korea
Congé (Jean Bodel), 1202 K; (Adam de la Halle), 1269 K
Congo, River, 1482 G
Connaught, Ireland, king of, 1316 C
Connor, Ireland, battle, 1315 C
Conques, France, abbey, 1045 J, 1098 J, 1130 J
Conquête de Jérusalem (Graindor de Douay), 1225 K
Conrad I, Duke of Franconia and King of the Germans (911–18), 908 E, 911 D, 915 E, 916 A, 917 E, 918 D
Conrad II of Franconia, Holy Roman Emperor, 1027 A, 1039 B
  as King of the Germans, 1024 C, D, E, 1027 C, 1030 C
  King of Italy, 1026 E, 1037 F
  grants etc. to son, Henry, 1027 C, 1028 B, 1036 B, 1038 E
  expeditions etc. to Poland, 1028 E, 1033 E, 1039 E
  war with Hungary, 1030 E, 1031 E
  conquers Lusatia, etc., 1031 E, 1036 E
  King of Burgundy, 1033 A
  alliance with France, 1033 B
  Italian campaign, 1037 A, D, 1038 E
Conrad, King of the Romans (b. 1074; 1087–1101), 1075 D, 1087 B, 1101 C; King of Lombardy, 1093 E
Conrad III Hohenstaufen, King of the Romans (b. 1093/4), 1138 A, 1143 E, 1150 E, 1152 A
  anti-king of Germany and Italy, 1127 D, 1128 B, 1135 A
  revolts against, 1138 C, 1139 D, 1140 B, D, 1142 B, 1150 A
  Crusades, 1147 B, D, 1148 B, C
Conrad IV, (I) King of Sicily and Jerusalem (1250–4), 1228 L, 1250 D, 1251 A, 1253 D, 1254 B; King of the Romans, 1237 A, 1251 D; quarrel with Pope, 1252 B, 1254 B; Duke of Swabia, 1252 C
Conrad II (Conradin), King of Sicily and Jerusalem, 1254 B, 1268 C, D
Conrad, King of Burgundy, 937 C, 938 E, 942 E, 993 E
Conrad, King of Jerusalem, 1192 B; as Marquess of Montferrat, 1187 D
Conrad of Zutphen, Duke of Bavaria (1049–53), 1053 E
Conrad, Duke of Bohemia, 1092 E
Conrad of Marburg, G. inquisitor, 1233 H
Conrad of Soest, G. painter, 1404 J
Conrad von Würzburg, G. poet, 1287 K
Conrad. *See also* Konrad
Conrad, Otto, Margrave of Moravia, 1182 E
Consadolo, Italy, 1333 A
Conseil à un Ami (Pierre de Fontaines), 1260 F
Conservanda Sanitate, De (Taddeo Alderotti), 1303 G
Consideratione, De (St. Bernard), 1148 H
Consideratione quintae essentiae, Liber de (John of Rupescissa), 1360 G
Consiliorum secundum vias Avicennae (Giovanni Matteo Ferrari), 1472 G
Consilium contra pestilentiam (Gentile da Foligno), 1348 G
Consilium pro peste evitanda (Pietro de Tossignano), 1398 G
Consolat de Mar, Llibre del, 1283 F
Consolation of Philosophy. See Boethius
Consolatione Theologiae, De (Jean Gerson), 1420 H
Constance, W. Germany, Cathedral, 1069 J; General Council of, 1414 D, 1415 A–D, H, 1416 H, 1417 C, D, H, 1418 B; Treaties of, 1153 B, 1183 B, 1385 A, 1446 B; Union of, 1474 B
Constance, Queen of Aragon, 1262 B
Constance, Queen of Sicily, 1184 D, 1186 A, 1191 B, C, 1192 E
Constantine, Emperor (306–37), (alleged) *Donation of*, 1236 C, 1440 H
Constantine VII Porphyrogenitus, Greek Emperor (b. 905), 913 B, 920 D, 944 D, 959 D; as historian, 959 F
Constantine VIII, Greek Emperor, 976 A, 1025 D, 1028 E; daughters of, 1034 B, 1042 B
Constantine IX Monomachus, Greek Emperor, 1042 B, 1045 E, H, 1055 A
Constantine X Ducas, Greek Emperor, 1059 D, 1067 B
Constantine Lascaris, Greek Emperor, 1204 B, D
Constantine XI Palaeologus, Greek Emperor, 1448 D, 1453 B
Constantine I, King of Scotland (862–77), 862 E, 877 E, 889 E
Constantine II, King of Scotland, 900 E, 927 C, 943 E
Constantine III, King of Scotland, 995 E, 997 E
Constantine the African, translator, 1087 G
Constantine. *Cf.* Cyril
Constantine Bodin, King of Zeta, 1100 E
Constantinople, Turkey:
  capital of Greek Empire, 867 H, 950 H, 955 E
  threatened by Arabs, 833 C, 838 B
  attacked by Bulgars, 813 B, 913 C, 924 E
  attacked by Vikings of Kiev, 860 A, 865 E, 906 E, 911 E, 941 E, 945 E
  attacked by Magyars, 934 E, 959 E
  attacked by Pechenegs, 1087 E
  Crusaders in, 1095 A, 1096 C, 1097 A
  riot in, 1185 C
  taken by Fourth Crusade, 1202 D, 1203 C, 1204 B, 1213 K
  Latin Emperors. *See* Baldwin I; Henry; Peter de Courtenay; Robert de Courtenay; Baldwin II; John of Brienne
  battle outside, 1205 B
  attacked by Greeks and Bulgars, 1235 E
  recovered by Greeks, 1261 A, C
  threatened by Charles of Anjou, 1270 D, 1281 C
  Black Death in, 1347 G
  besieged by Turks, 1422 B, C
  refuses church union, 1439 C
  falls; becomes Ottoman capital, 1453 B
  Treaty of, 1479 A
  Chora monastery, mosaics, 1310 J
  churches, 900 J; with mosaics, 1315 J
  histories of:
    Michael Psellus, 1078 K
    Nicetas Acominatos, 1206 K
    Nicetas Choniates, 1213 K
    George Acropolites, 1282 K
  mosque, 1463 J
  Patriarch, 870 A, 1054 H; *and see* Ignatius, Nicephorus, Photius
  University, 863 H, 1045 H

Constantinople, De la Conquête de (Villehardouin), 1213 K
Constitutio de feudis (Conrad), 1037 F
Constitutio Domus Regis (Stephen), 1136 F
Constitutio Romana (Lothar), 824 F
Contarini, Ambrogio, It. ambassador and author, 1487 G
Contarini, Andrea, Doge of Venice, 1367 A, 1382 B
Contarino, Domenico, Doge of Venice, 1043 E, 1071 E
Contarino, Jacopo, Doge of Venice, 1275 C, 1279 A
Conte du Graal (Chrétien de Troyes), 1173 K
Contemptu Mundi, De (Bernard de Morlaix), 1140 K; (Petrarch), 1342 K
Conti, Niccolò de, It. traveller, 1444 G
Contra insulam vulgi opinionem de grandine, Liber (Agobard), 841 H
Conversini, Giovanni, It. humanist, 1392 K, 1406 L
Conversion to Christianity. *See* Avars, Bohemia, Bulgars, England (Danes in), Denmark, Hungary, Iceland, Latvia, Lithuania, Normandy, Osilians, Poland, Pomerania, Prussians, Russia, Saxony, Slavs, Sweden, Wends
  See also Archbishoprics, Missions
Convivio (Dante), 1310 K
Conway, Wales, Treaty of, 1277 D
Copenhagen, Denmark, naval battle off, 1427 C; Treaty of, 1441 G; University, 1478 H
Copernicus, Nicolaus, Polish astronomer (1473–1543), 1473 L
Coplas por la muerte (Jorge Manrique), 1479 K
Corbeil, France, Treaty of, 1258 B
Corbie, France, abbey, 822 H; abbot, 831 H
Córdoba, Gonzalo Fernandez de, Sp. general (1443–1515), 1443 L
Cordova, Spain:
  capital of Muslim Spain, Ummayad rulers of. *See* Andalusia
  revolts in, 806 E, 814 B, 827 E, 1008 E, 1031 D
  sacked by Vikings, 844 C
  changes hands, 1013 B, 1069 E
  under Hammūdids, 1016 E, 1018 E, 1025 E
  taken by Castile, 1144 E, 1164 E, 1236 B
  Great Mosque, 975 J
  monks from, 912 J
  palace, 936 J
  schools, 976 H
  University, 961 H, 976 H
Corfù, is., Greece, 1081 B, 1147 E, 1148 E, 1185 B, 1207 E, 1215 E, 1267 E
Corinth, Greece, Latin lordship of, 1358 B, 1379 E
Cornaro, Catherine, titular queen of Cyprus, 1489 A
Cornaro, Marco, Doge of Venice, 1365 E, 1367 A
Cornwall, England, 815 E; Earls of, *see* Gaveston, Piers; Richard (King of the Romans)
Coroners, in England, 1194 F
Coroners, Instructions to (Sung Tz'ŭ), 1248 G
Corral, Pedro del, Sp. novelist, 1403 K
Correggio, Ghiberto da, despot of Parma, 1316 E
Corsica, Island of, France, 805 E, 934 E, 1133 E
Cortenuova, Italy, battle, 1237 D
Cortes. *See* Parliaments
Cortez, Hernando, Sp. explorer and soldier (1485–1547), 1485 L
Corunna, Spain, 1386 C
Corvey, West Germany, abbey, 822 H, 885 J; monk of, *see* Widukind
Cosenza, Italy, 902 C
Cosmas, Dean of Prague, Bohemian chronicler, 1125 K
Cosmologists:
  Persian. *See* Hamdallāh
  Siamese. *See* Lu T'ai
Cossacks, origin of, 1412 E
Coucy-sur-Loire, France, 1162 C
Councils, of Greek and Roman churches, 1098 H, 1274 C, 1439 C
Councils, General, of the (Latin) Church:
  First Lateran, 1123 H
  Second Lateran, 1139 H
  Third Lateran, 1179 A, H
  Fourth Lateran, 1215 H
  called to Rome, 1241 B
  Lyons (I), 1245 C, H
  Lyons (II), 1274 C, H
  Vienne, 1311 H, 1312 H
  Pisa, 1408 B, 1409 A, B
  Rome, 1413 H
  Constance, *q.v.*
  Pavia-Siena, 1423 B, C, 1424 A
  Basel, *q.v.*
  Ferrara-Florence, 1438 A, 1439 A, C, 1443 C
  called by Philip IV, 1303 B; by Louis XI, 1478 C
  condemned by Pius II, 1460 H
Count Lucanor (Juan Manuel), 1349 K
Courtenay, Thomas, Earl of Devon (1414–58), 1451 C, 1455 D
Courtenay, William, Archbishop of Canterbury, 1396 L
Courtrai, Belgium, battle, 1302 C
Coutances, France, 933 E; Cathedral, 1030 J, 1218 J, 1250 J
Coutances, Walter of, Archbishop of Rouen (d. 1207), 1191 D
Couvin, Simon of, Belgian poet (d. 1367), 1350 K
Covarrubias, Spain, 950 J
Coventry, England, 1404 D, 1459 D
Coverdale, Miles, E. bishop and translator of Bible (1487–1568), 1487 L
Crabs, treatise on (Fu Kung), 1059 G
Cracow, Poland, 1038 E, 1241 B
  Bishopric of, 1044 H, 1079 B
  capital of Poland, 1076 D, 1138 E
  Cathedral, 1080 J
  Congress of, 1364 C
  University, 1364 H, 1397 H
  province of, 1180 E, 1202 E; *and see* Leszek II, Boleslav V
  taken by Bohemia, 1290 E, 1291 E
Cranach, Lucas, G. artist (1472–1553), 1472 L
Cranmer, Thomas, Archbishop of Canterbury and Protestant martyr (1489–1556), 1489 L
Cravant, France, battle, 1423 C
Crécy, France, battle, 1346 C
Creeds, 800 H, 809 H
Crema, Italy, 1159 C, 1160 A
Cremona, Italy, 1252 A, 1322 A
Crescentius, Roman family of, 1012 B
Crescentius I, Patrician of Rome, 974 B
Crescentius II, Patrician of Rome, 998 B, 1003 B
Crescentius, Silvester. *See* Silvester III
Crescenzi, Pietro dei, It. writer on agriculture (d. 1320), 1307 G
Cresques, Abraham, Sp. Je. cartographer, 1375 G
Crete, is., Greece, 827 E, 961 A, 1212 E, 1297 E, 1364 E
Crickets, treatise on (Chia Ssŭ-tao), 1230 G
Crimea, Russia, 971 C, 1298 E; Khanate of, 1475 E, 1482 C; *and see* Kaffa
Crispi dynasty, Dukes of the Archipelago, 1383 E
Cristobulus of Imbros, Gk. historian, 1470 K
Crivelli, Carlo, It. painter (d. 1495), 1474 J, 1491 J
Črnomen, Yugoslavia, battle, 1371 C
Croatia, Yugoslavia, kingdom of, 926 E, 997 E, 1076 E; under Hungary, 1091 E, 1108 E, 1181 E, 1345 E, 1386 B; raided by Mongols, 1241 B

Cronache (Fernão Lopes), 1434 K
Cronica (Walter of Guisborough), 1312 K
Cronica abreviada (Juan Manuel), 1349 K
Cronica de los reyes de Castillo (Lopez de Ayala), 1407 K
Crónica del rey don Rodrigo (Pedro del Corral), 1403 K
Cronica delle cose occorenti (Dino Compagni), 1324 K
Cronica domestica (Donato Velluti), 1370 K
Cross, Knights of the. *See* Teutonic Knights
Crotoy, Le, France, naval battle off, 1347 B
Crowland, History of, 1486 K
Crucifixion (Giovanni Bellini), 1450 J; (Heironymus Bosch), 1480 J
Crusades:
  campaigns of John Tzimisces, 972 D, 974 E, 975 B
  'Holy War' against Normans in Italy, 1053 B
  against the Turks, 1089 C, 1095 A
    First, 1095 D, 1096 B, C, 1097 A–D, 1098 A–C, 1099 C; chronicles of, 1100 K, 1111 K, 1127 K; *Chansons*, 1130 K, 1180 K
    'The People's', 1096 C, D
    of Raymond of Toulouse, 1101 B, C
    Second, 1146 B, 1147 B, D, 1148 A–C
    History (William of Tyre), 1184 K
    Third, 1187 D, 1188 A, 1189 B–D, 1190 A–C, 1191 B, C, 1192 A–C; chronicles of, 1192 K, 1196 K
    German, 1195 B, 1198 A
    Fourth (diverted to Constantinople), 1198 C, 1201 B, 1202 D, 1203 C, 1204 B, D, E; chronicles of, 1213 K, 1216 K
    'The Children's', 1212 H
    Fifth, 1215 D, 1217 D, 1218 B, C, 1219 D, H, 1220 C
    poems on, 1225 K
    Sixth, 1227 C, 1228 B, 1229 A
    of Theobald of Navarre, 1239 A, D, 1240 C
    of St. Louis (Egypt), 1248 C, 1249 B, 1250 A, B
    'The Shepherds'', 1251 E
    of St. Louis (Tunis), 1270 C, D
    of Edward I, 1270 B, 1272 B, C
    proposed by the Ilkhan, 1288 A
    planned by John XXII, 1332 C, 1336 E
    takes Smyrna, 1344 D
    proclaimed by Urban V, 1363 B
    of Peter of Cyprus, 1364 C, 1365 D
    of Amadeus of Savoy, 1366 C, 1367 E
    destroyed at Nicopolis, 1396 C
    in the Balkans, 1440 E, 1441 E, 1443 D, 1444 A–D
    planned by Pius II, 1459 B, 1463 D, 1464 C
    occupies Smyrna, 1472 E
  against the Moors in Spain, 1065 B, 1212 C
  against the Wends, 1147 B, C, 1162 C
  against the Albigenses. *See* Toulouse
  against Frederick II, 1229 B, 1240 A, 1248 E
  against people of Rome, 1234 E
  against the Mongols, 1241 B
  against Ezzelin da Romano, 1256 B
  against Manfred, 1265 B
  against Pedro of Aragon, 1282 D, 1284 A, 1285 A, C
  against the Colunnas, 1297 B, 1298 C
  against Frederick of Sicily, 1297 E, 1302 C
  against Italian heretics, 1305 H
  against Milan, 1326 B
  against Lewis IV, 1328 A, B
  against the Grand Company, 1330 B, 1332 E
  against Francesco Ordelaffi, 1356 A, 1357 B, 1359 C
  against enemies of Urban VI, 1383 B
  against the Hussites. *See* Bohemia
Crusoe, Robinson, 1185 K
Cuenca, Spain, 1177 E
Cuidad Rodrigo, Spain, Cathedral, 1165 J
Culen, King of Scotland (966–71), 966 E, 971 E, 995 E
Cultura hortorum, De (Walafrid Strabo), 849 K
Cumans, Turkish tribe, in Russia, 1061 E, 1068 E, 1097 E, 1111 E, 1185 K; attack Greek Empire, 1095 E, 1186 D; defeated by Mongols, 1222 B; settle in Hungary, 1239 E, 1290 C
Cumberland, England, 945 E, 1000 E, 1092 E, 1136 A, 1157 E
Cur Deus Homo? (Anselm), 1094 H
Cura Pastoralis (Gregory the Great), translated, 892 K
Curcuas, John, Gk. general, 934 E, 941 E
Currency. *See* Money
Cursor Mundi, 1320 K
Cursuum planetarum, Liber (Raymond of Marseilles), 1140 G
Curzola, Island, Yugoslavia, battle, 1298 C, G
Cusa, Nicholas of, G. cardinal, legate, canonist, theologian and humanist, 1401 L, 1433 H, 1450 K, 1464 L
Customs (on wool, etc.), 1275 F
Cutanda, Spain, battle, 1120 E
Cuxa, Spain, abbey, 878 J, 955 J, 1009 J
Cycle de la Croisade, 1225 K
Cymbeline, mythical British king, 1137 K, 1200 K
Cynewulf, Anglo-Saxon poet, 800 K
Cyprus, Island, 965 C, 1156 B, 1184 E; conquered from Greeks, 1191 B, 1192 B, 1194 B; kingdom, 1197 E, 1205 B, 1218 A, *and see* Peter; civil war, 1232 B, 1233 B; raided by Egypt, 1426 E; sold to Venice, 1489 A
Cyril, St. (formerly Constantine), apostle of the Slavs, 862 H, 869 L
Cyrillic script, 862 H, 1347 H
Cyrurgia (Henry de Mondeville), 1320 G
Czechoslovakia. *See* Bohemia, Moravia, Slovakia
Czerwién, Poland, 1018 C

D

Daddi, Bernardo, It. painter, 1346 J, 1380 L
Daghal al-'Ain (Muhāsibī), 857 G
Dagworth, Thomas, E. soldier, 1347 B
Dai-co-viet (North Vietnam; *cf.* Annam):
  Kingdom founded, 932 E, 939 E; *and see* Dinh Bo Linh; Le Dai Hanh
  Ly dynasty, 1010 E, 1216 D; *and see* Ly Thai-to; Ly Thai-tong; Ly Thanh-tong; Ly Nhan-tong
  capitals. *See* Co-loa; Hanoi; Hoa-lu
  renamed Dai Viet, 1068 E
Dai Viet, 1068 E, 1131 E
  Tran dynasty, 1216 D, 1225 E, 1400 E; *and see* Tran Anh-tong; Tran Minh-tong; Tran Due-tong
  attacked by Mongols, 1253 E, 1257 E, 1286 E, 1287 E, 1326 E
  attacked by Champa, 1361 E, 1377 E, 1390 A
  tributary to China, 1369 E
  Ho dynasty, 1400 E
  conquered by China, 1407 E, 1418 E, 1428 E
  Le dynasty, 1428 E; *and see* Le Thanh-tong
  law code, 1483 F
  rice-growing, 1108 G
  university in, 1076 H
Daigo, Emperor of Japan, 930 E
Dalālat al-Ha'irin (Moses ben Maimon), 1204
Dalimil, Bohemian chronicler and poet, 1314 K
Dalmatia, Yugoslavia:
  Frankish conquest, 805 E, 807 E, 812 J
  held by Greeks, 807 E, 998 E, 1170 A, 1172 E
  under Venice, 998 E, 1115 E
  Hungarian conquests, 1114 E, 1181 E, 1358 A

Dalmatia, Yugoslavia—*contd.*
attacked by Mongols, 1242 B
conquered by Venice, 1409 C, 1412 E
Dalry, Scotland, battle, 1306 C
Damascus, Syria, 1075 E, 1095 E, 1138 B
attacked by crusaders, 1129 D, 1148 B, C
under Ayyūbids, 1151 E, 1154 B, 1175 D, 1183 C, 1218 C, 1229 E, 1244 C, D, 1250 C
taken by Mongols, 1260 A, 1300 A
recovered by Egypt, 1303 E
battle of, 1400 E
sacked by Timur, 1401 A
University, 1065 H
Damasus II (Poppo of Brixen), Pope, 1047 D, 1048 C
Damian, Peter, St., It. cardinal and Church reformer, 1007 L, 1059 E, 1072 H, L
Damietta, Egypt, 853 B, 1169 D, 1218 B, C, 1219 D, 1220 C, 1249 B, 1250 B
Damīrī, Muhammad ibn-Mūsā al-, Eg. zoologist (1344–1405), 1372 G, 1405 L
Damme, Belgium, 1180 G; naval battle, 1213 B
Dandolo, Andrea, Doge of Venice, 1343 A, 1354 D
Dandolo, Enrico, Doge of Venice (b. 1108), 1192 B, 1205 B
Dandolo, Francesco, Doge of Venice, 1328 A, 1339 D
Dandolo, Giovanni, Doge of Venice, 1279 A, 1289 D
Danegeld, 991 C, 994 E, 1012 E, 1162 F, 1194 B
Danelaw. *See* England
Danes. *See* Vikings
'Danework', 808 E
Daniel, Prince of Halich, 1245 E; King, 1254 E, 1264 E
Daniel, Prince of Moscow, 1304 A
Daniel, Prince of Moscow (1324–32?), 1328 E
Daniel of Kiev, Russian pilgrim-author, 1107 G
Daniel de Merlac, E. astrologer, 1190 G
Daniil Zatochnik, Petition of, 1225 K
Danishmends, Turkish tribe. *See* Sivas
Dan-no-ura, Japan, naval battle, 1185 B
Dante Alighieri, It. poet (1265–1321), 1265 L, 1274 K, 1302 A, 1321 L; works, 1276 K, 1290 K, 1300 K, 1310 K, 1314 K, 1321 K; on politics, 1312 F; commentary on, 1379 K; imitation of, 1403 K; printed, 1472 K
Dante, Vita de (Leonardo Bruni), 1444 K
Danzig. *See* Gdansk
Dār al-Hirjah, Iraq, 890 E
Dārāni, Abu-Sulaymān al-, Sūfī saint, 849 H
Daroca, Spain, battle, 1120 E
Daron, Israel, 1192 B
Dati, Leonardo, It. theologian and humanist, 1425 L
Daud, ibn- (Avendeath), Sp. Je. translator, 1165 G
Daulatābād (formerly Deogīr, *q.v.*), India, capital of Muslim India, 1327 E, 1329 E, 1345 E
Dauphiné of Vienne, France, 1050 G, 1349 C, 1456 C; Vaudois of, 1488 H
David III the Builder, King of Georgia, 1089 E, 1122 E, 1125 E
David IV, King of Georgia, 1155 E
David, King of Gwynned, 1240 B, 1241 E, 1246 A
David, I, King of Scotland, 1124 B, 1136 A, 1138 C, 1153 B
David II, King of Scotland (b. 1324), 1329 B, 1334 B, 1341 B, 1346 D, 1357 D, 1371 A
David, Prince of Tao (Georgia), 979 A, 1000 A
David ap Gruffyd, Welsh prince, 1282 A, 1283 B, D
David ap Gwilym, Welsh poet, 1340 L, 1400 K
David (Statues; Donatello), 1408 J, 1434 J
Dawlat Khan Lōdī, Shah of Delhi (d. 1414?), 1413 A
Dax, France, 1442 C
Dead Christ (Giovanni Bellini), 1480 J
Déas, France, church, 814 J, 836 J, 1000 J
Death and the Ploughman (Johann von Tepl), 1405 K
Decameron, The (Giovanni Boccaccio), 1353 K
Deccan, India, Hindu Kingdom, 1327 E; Muslim kingdom, *see* Kulbarga
Decembrio, Pier Candido, It. humanist and biographer, 1399 L, 1477 K, L
Decretals. *See* Canon Law
Decretum (Burchard of Worms), 1012 H; (Gratian), 1139 H; glosses on, 1165 H, 1170 H, 1210 H
Déduits de Chasse, Les (Gaston Phoebus de Foix), 1391 K, 1410 K
Defence of those living in holy tranquillity (St. Gregory Palamas), 1359 H
Defensor concordatorum (Hélie de Bourdeille), 1484 H
Defensor Pacis (Marsilio of Padua), 1324 F, 1327 H
Degree of Meridian, 813 G
Deheubarth, Wales, 1158 E; Kings of, *see* Hywel, Rhys
Dei gracia, English formula, 1173 F
Delfino, Giovanni, Doge of Venice, 1356 C, 1361 E
Delft, Holland, Treaty of, 1428 C
Delhi, India, 993 E
last Hindu king. *See* Prithvī Rāj
capital of Muslim India, 1193 A, 1327 E, 1329 E
attacked by Mongols, 1299 E, 1303 E
sacked by Timur, 1398 D
mausoleums, 1231 J, 1235 J, 1325 J, 1389 J
mosques, 1193 J, 1199 J, 1311 J
Delhi, Muslim Kingdom:
Slave Kings. *See*
Aybak (1206–10)
Iltutmish (1211–36)
Fīrūz I (1236)
Radiyya (queen; 1236–40)
Bahrām (1240–2)
Ma'sūd (1242–6)
Mahmūd I (1246–66)
Balban (1266–87)
Kaiqubād (1287–90)
Khaljī dynasty. *See*
Fīrūz II (1290–5)
'Alā'-ad-Dīn (1295–1316)
'Umar (1316)
Mubārak (1316–20)
usurped by Khusraw, 1320 B, C
Tuqhluqid dynasty. *See*
Tuqhluq I (1320–5)
Muhammad II (1325–51)
Fīrūz III (1351–88)
Tuqhlūq II (1388–9)
Abū-Bakr (1389–90)
Muhammad III (1390–3)
Sikandar I (1393)
Mahmūd II (1393–1413)
election of Dawlat Khān Lōdī, 1413 A
Sayyid (Mongol) dynasty. *See*
Khidr Khan (1414–21)
Mubārak II (1421–35)
Muhammad IV (1435–46)
'Alam (1446–51)
Lōdī dynasty. *See*
Bahlūl (1451–89)
Sikandar II (1489–1517)
disintegration of, 1335 E, 1336 B, E, 1339 E, 1345 E, 1346 E, 1347 C, 1393 A, 1405 D, 1406 E, 1407 E
feudalism in, 1270 F
fiduciary currency, 1329 G
government of, 1325 F, 1340 G
histories of, 1352 K, 1359 K
Delight of the Hearts (Mustawfī), 1340 G
Deluge, The (Uccello), 1445 J
Demetrius I, King of Georgia, 1125 E, 1155 E

Demmin, E. Germany, battle, 1162 C
Demonstrations contre sortileges (Eustace Deschamps), 1406 G
Demotika, Greece, 1361 E
Denis the Carthusian, Flemish mystic, 1402 L, 1471 H, L
Deniselle, F. witch, 1460 H
Denmark:
  Kings (early). *See* Göttrik, Hemming, Harold, Horik
  disintegration of, 854 E
  Kings. *See*
    Gorm the Old (–936)
    Harold I (936–83)
    Svein I (983–1014)
    Harold II (1014–19)
    Cnut (1019–35)
    Harthacnut (1035–42)
    Magnus I (1042–7)
    Svein II (1047–74)
    Harold III (1074–81)
    Cnut IV (1081–6)
    Olaf IV (1086–95)
    Eric I (1095–1103)
    Niels (1105–34)
    Eric II (1131–7)
    Eric III (1137–47)
    Svein III (1147–57)
    Waldemar I (1157–82)
    Cnut VI (1182–1202)
    Waldemar II (1202–41)
    Eric IV (1241–50)
    Abel (1250–2)
    Christopher I (1252–9)
    Eric V (1259–86)
    Eric VI (1286–1319)
    Christopher II (1320–6, 1330–1)
    interregnum, 1332 C
    Waldemar IV (1340–75)
    interregnum, 1375 A
    Olaf V (1376–87)
    Margaret (Regent, 1387–1412)
    Eric VII (1397–1439)
    Christopher III (1440–8)
    Christian I (1448–81)
    John I (1481–1513)
  Danish raiders. *See* Vikings
  defences of, 808 E
  conversion to Christianity, 865 H, 965 H
  defeats Norwegians, 978 E
  civil wars, 1074 B, 1131 E, 1134 B, 1147 E, 1157 B
  detached from see of Hamburg, 1104 H
  war with Wends, 1147 C, 1162 C
  sends missions to Latvia, 1184 H
  laws of, 1240 F
  under interdict, 1259 E
  charter of liberties, 1282 F
  privileges of church in, 1303 E
  barons control king, 1320 A, 1340 E
  revolts of serfs, 1441 G
  Order of the Elephant, 1478 E
  chronicles, 1109 K, 1187 K, 1208 K
Dentistry, 1315 G
Deogīr, India, Hindu Kingdom of, 1294 E, 1307 E, 1317 E; renamed, *see* Daulatābād
Deor's Lament, 970 K
Derby, England, 877 E; Earl of, *see* Henry IV
Dermot MacMurrough, King of Leinster, 1169 B, 1171 B
Dervishes, 1241 E, 1273 H
Descent from the Cross (Roger van der Weyden), 1435 J
Deschamps, Eustace, F. poet, 1406 G
Descriptio Terrae Sanctae (Burchard), 1283 G
Description of the Coasts of the Ocean (Ma Huan), 1451 G
Desio, Italy, battle, 1278 A
Despenser, Henry, Bishop of Norwich (d. 1406), 1383 B
Despenser, Hugh, Earl of Winchester, 1321 B, C, 1322 A, 1326 D
Despenser, Hugh, the younger, 1321 C, 1322 A, 1326 D
Desprez, Jean. *See* Outremeuse
Devarāya, I, Emperor of Vijayanagar (1406–22), 1419 E
Deville, France, 1033 B
Devol, Albania, Treaty of, 1108 C
Devon, Earl of. *See* Courtenay
Devotio Moderna, 1386 H
Dhakhira al-Khwārizmshāhī (al-Jurjānī), 1135 G
Dhanga, King of Jejākabhukti (950–99), 999 J
Dharanindravarman II, king of Cambodia, 1177 E
Dharmaja II, King of Sukhodya. *See* Lu T'ai
Dhu-al-Nūn, Eg. Sūfī theosophist, 860 H
Dialogo (St. Catherine of Siena), 1378 H
Dialogus de Scaccario (Richard fitz Nigel), 1179 F
Dialogus miraculorum (Caesarius von Heisterbach), 1220 K
Dialogus Pauli et Petri contra Judaeos (Paul of Burgos), 1433 H
Diamond Sūtra, 868 G
Diarists:
  Japanese. *See* Ennin; Fujiwara Kanezane; Ki no Tsurayuki; Nakayama Tadachika; Sei Shōnagon
  Persian. *See* Khusraw
Diaz de Gamez, Gutierre, Sp. biographer, 1450 K
Diaz de Novaes, Bartholomew, Port. explorer (1430–1500), 1430 L, 1488 G
Diaz de Vivar, Rodrigo. *See* Cid, The
Dicta Mundi (Fazio degli Uberti), 1368 K
Dictatus Papae (Gregory VII), 1075 H
Dictes or Sayengis of the Philosophres (Anthony Woodville), 1477 K
Dictionaries:
  Arabic, 933 K, 995 K, 1008 K, 1311 K, 1414 K
  biographical (Arabic), 1229 K, 1270 G, 1282 K
  botanical (Symeon Seth), 1080 G
  Coptic-Egyptian, 1316 K
  geographical (Yāqūt), 1229 G
  Greek, 976 K
  Indian, 1170 K
  Latin, 1063 K, 1286 K
  materia medica (Narahari), 1242 G
  Persian, 1060 K
  phonetic (Chinese), 1011 K, 1039 K
  Sino-Japanese, 983 K
  Talmudic, 1101 H
Dicuil, Irish astronomer and geographer, 825 G
Didascalion (Hugh of St. Victor), 1141 H
Diego de Porcelos, founder of Burgos, 884 E
Dieppe, France, 1435 D
Dies Irae (Thomas of Celano), 1255 K
Diet, treatises on, 1162 G, 1257 G, 1277 G
Dietics, Elements of (Chia Ming), 1368 G
Dietrich II, Count of Holland (d. 988), 985 E
Dietrich IV, Count of Holland (1039–49), 1046 B
Dietrich of Freiburg, G. meteorologist (d. *c.* 1311), 1307 G
Dietrich of Niem, G. notary and historian (*c.* 1345–1418), 1410 H
Digenes Akritas, 1050 K
Dihlavī, Husan-i, Shaikh, Indian poet, 1338 K

Dijon, France, Charterhouse, 1389 J; St. Bénigne abbey, 1001 J
Dilāvar Khan, governor of Mālwa, 1406 E
Diligendo Deo, De (Bernard of Clairvaux), 1153 K
Dimyāti, 'Abd-al-Mu'min al-, Eg. vetinerary surgeon, 1306 G
Din w-al-Dawlah, Kitāb al- (al-Tabarī), 854 H
Dinant, Belgium, 1255 G
Dīnawarī, Abū-Hanīfah Ahmad ibn-Dāwūd al-, Per. chronicler, 895 K
Dinh Bo Linh (Dinh-Tien-hoang), Emperor of Dai-co-viet (d. 979), 968 E
Dinis, King of Portugal (1279–1325), 1263 E, 1279 A, 1289 E, 1290 H, 1308 H, 1319 E, 1325 A; as poet, 1325 K
Dionysio-Hadriana (canons), 802 H
Dionysius Exigus, It. canonist (*c.* 500–*c.* 560), 802 H
Diotisalvi, It. architect, 1153 J
Diplomacy, 'Renaissance', 1454 C
Dir, Viking leader in Russia, 850 E, 878 E
Directorium inquistorum (Nicholas Eymeric), 1399 H
Disciplina clericalis (Pedro Alfonso), 1110 K
Diseases. *See* Black Death; fevers; leprosy; measles; small-pox; of the eye, *see* ophthamologists
'Disinherited, The ' (English), 1266 B, D; (Scottish), 1332 C
Dissection, human, 1275 G, 1316 G; of pig, 1110 G
Divan-i Shams-i Tabriz (al-Rūmī), 1273 K
Diversarum artium schedula, 1100 G
Divina Commedia (Dante), 1314 K, 1472 K
Divina Omnipotentia, De (Peter Damian), 1072 H
Divina praedestinacione, De (Erigena), 851 H
Divisio imperii, 817 C
Divisione Naturae, De (Erigena), 865 K
Divortio Lotharii, De (Hincmar), 860 F
Divrigi, Turkey, mosque and hospital, 1228 J; as Tephrice, 872 E
Diwān (Abū-Tammām), 845 K; (Hafiz), 1368 K
Diwān al-Hamāsah (Abū-Tammām), 845 K
Djem, Ottoman prince (1459–95), 1481 E
Dlugosz, Jan, Archbishop of Lwów, Polish historian, 1480 K, L
Dmitri I, Grand Duke of Vladimir (d. 1294), 1276 E, 1280 E, 1283 E, 1293 E
Dmitri II of Tver, Grand Duke of Vladimir, 1322 E, 1324 E, 1325 E
Dmitri III Donski, Grand Duke of Vladimir, 1359 E, 1375 E, 1378 E, 1380 C, 1382 C, 1389 B
Dmitri IV, claimant to Vladimir, 1359 E
Dmitri Shemiaka, Russian prince (d. 1453), 1446 A, 1447 A
Dneiper, river, Russia, 1412 E; battle on Cataracts of, 972 B
Dobrava, Polish princess, 966 E
Dobrudja, The, Rumania, 967 E, 1000 E, 1361 E, 1395 B
Dobrzýn, Poland, 1335 D
Doctrinale (Alexander of Villedieu), 1199 K
Doctrinale Fidei (Thomas Netter), 1415 H
Döffingen, W. Germany, battle, 1388 C
Dōgen, Ja. Buddhist reformer (1200–53), 1227 H
Dolcino, Fra, It. heretical leader, 1305 H
Domažlice (Taus), Czechoslovakia, battle, 1431 C
Dombleday, John, E. alchemist, 1384 G
Domenico Veneziano, It. painter, 1439 J, 1445 J, 1461 L
Domesday Book, 1085 D, 1087 G
Domidoff altarpiece (Carlo Crivelli), 1474 J
Dominic Guzman, St., founder of Friars Preachers, 1170 L, 1205 H, 1216 H, 1221 J, L
Dominicans. *See* Friars Preachers
Donald I, King of Scotland, 858 E, 862 E
Donald II, King of Scotland, 889 E, 900 E
Donald III Bane, King of Scotland, 1093 D, 1094 E, 1097 D
Donatello, It. sculptor, 1386 L, 1408 J, 1411 J, 1413 J, 1416 J, 1427 J, 1433 J, 1434 J, 1448 J, 1455 J, 1466 L
Donato, Corso, Florentine magnate, 1307 D
Donatus Graecorum (John Basing), 1252 K
Dondi dall'Orologio, Giovanni, It. astronomer (1318–*c.*1385), 1364 G
Dongola, Sudan, kingdom, 1314 E
Donna mi prega (Guido Cavalcanti), 1300 K
Dordrecht, Holland, Treaty of, 1489 A
Dorylaeum, Turkey, battles, 1097 C, 1147 D
Dosicles and Rodanthe (Theodorus Prodromus), 1160 K
Douai, France, 1245 G, 1312 E
Douglas, Archibald, Earl of Angus (d. 1513/14), 1482 C
Douglas, Gawain, Scottish poet (*c.* 1475–1523?) 1475 L
Douglas, James, Scottish knight, 1319 C
Douglas, James, Earl of Douglas, 1388 C
Douglas, William, Earl of Douglas, 1440 D
Douglas, William, Earl of Douglas, 1452 A
Douzy, France, 865 A
Dove's Necklace, The (ibn-Hazm), 1064 K
Dover, England, 1066 G, 1348 G
Dragmaticon (William of Conches), 1154 K
Drahomira of Stodor, widow of Vratislav I of Bohemia, 921 E
Drama:
  Arab:
    Shadow-Play, 1310 K
  Belgian:
    Abele Spelen (Middle Dutch), 1350 K
  Chinese (Kuan Han-ch'ing), 1300 K; *and see* Opera
  French:
    Le Jeu d'Adam, 1150 K
    farce:
      Adam de la Halle, 1262 K
      Guillaume Alexis (?), 1464 K
    pastoral (Adam de la Halle), 1283 K
    religious, company for, 1398 K
  Indian, 1350 K
  Italian:
    pastoral (Politian), 1480 K
    religious:
      Bernardo Pulci, 1488 K
      Lorenzo de'Medici, 1489 K
  Japanese:
    Nō Drama, 1384 K, 1443 K
  See also Miracle Plays
Dreux, France, 996 A
Dreux, Peter (Mauclerc) of, regent of Brittany, 1230 B
Drugs, Collection of Simple (al-Baytār), 1248 G; *see also* Pharmacologists
Dub, King of Scotland (962–6) 962 E, 966 E, 971 E, 997 E
Dublin, Ireland, 1170 C, 1395 B; 1487 B; Archbishopric of, 1152 H; battle, 919 C; Danish capital, 853 E, 980 E, 999 E, *and see* Olaf Guthfrithson
Ducas, Michael I, Despot of Epirus (1204–15), 1204 E, 1215 E, 1231 E
Ducas, Michael II, Despot of Epirus, 1231 E, 1259 E, 1271 E
Ducas, Theodore, Despot of Epirus, 1215 E, 1217 E, 1230 B; crowned as Emperor, 1224 E
Dubois, Pierre, F. polemical writer (*c.* 1250–*c.* 1321), 1306 F
Dubrovnik (republic of Ragusa), Yugoslavia, 868 E, 1358 A, 1377 G

Duccio di Buoninsegna, It. painter, 1285 J, 1308 J, 1318 L
Dudley, Edmund, E. councillor (1462–1510), 1462 L
Dudon of St. Quentin, F. historian (d. *c.* 1030), 1015 K
Dufay, Guillaume, Flemish composer, 1474 J, L
Dujardin, Durand, F. carpenter, 1183 H
Dunbar, Scotland, battle, 1296 B
Dunbar, William, Scottish poet (*c.* 1460–1520?), 1460 L
Duncan I, King of Scotland (1034–40), 1034 D, 1040 C, 1058 A
Duncan II, King of Scotland, 1094 E
Dundalk, Ireland, battle, 1318 D
Duns Scotus, John, Scottish philosopher and theologian, 1308 K
Dunsinane, Scotland, battle, 1054 C
Dunstable, John, E. composer and musician, 1453 J
Dunstable Miracle Play, 1100 K
Dunstan, St., E. Church reformer (925–88), 925 L; Abbot of Glastonbury, 940 H, 950 H, 957 E, 959 D; Archbishop of Canterbury, 988 L
Dunyā wa-l-Dīn, Kitabādāb al- (al-Māwardi), 1058 F
Dupplin Moor, Scotland, battle, 1332 C
Duqāq, Seljuq ruler of Damascus, 1095 E
Duraid, Abū Bakr Muhammad ibn-al-Hasan ibn-, Per. philologist (838–933), 933 K
Durandus, Guilelmus, F. jurist and canonist, Bishop of Mende (*c.* 1230–96), 1271 F, 1286 H, 1292 H, 1296 L
Durazzo, Albania, 1081 B, D, 1082 A, 1083 E, 1107 D, 1185 B, 1215 E, 1376 E, 1379 E
Durben, Latvia, Russia, battle, 1260 C
Dürer, Albrecht, G. artist (1471–1528), 1471 L, 1484 J
Durham, England, bishops of, *see* Bury, Richard de, and Puiset, Hugh du; Cathedral, 1093 J; history of (Simeon), 1096 K; Treaty of, 1424 A
Durham, County, 1069 A, C, 1080 B
Dürnkrut, Austria, battle, 1278 C
Duvrotik, ruler of the Dobrudja, 1361 E
Dvāravatīpura, India, Hindu kingdom, 1310 E
Dyle, river, Belgium, battle, 891 D

E

Eadmer, monk of Canterbury, E. chronicler and biographer, 1130 K
Eardwulf, Earl of Bernicia, 1041 E
East, Description of the (Odoric), 1330 G
East, Wonders of the (Jordanus,) 1330 G
East Anglia, England, kingdom, 870 D, 917 E; earldorman of, 991 C; earls, *see* Harold, Ralf
Eastern Mark, Germany, 972 E, 973 A
Ecbasis Captivi (anon.), 930 K
Eccerinis (Albertino Mussato), 1329 K
Ecclesia, De (John Hus), 1413 H; (John Wycliffe), 1379 H
Ecclesiastical History (Bede), 892 K; (Orderic Vitalis), 1141 K
Ecija, Spain, battle, 1275 C
Eck, Johann Maier von, G. theologian (1486–1543), 1486 L
Eckehart, Master, G. mystic, 1327 H
Eckhard, Margrave of Meissen, 1002 B; *cf.* Ekkehard
Economics:
  Chinese encyclopedia, 812 F
  De Moneta (Nicholas of Orsme), 1382 G
  first 'national debt', 1274 G
  See also Insurance; Money; Prices; Trade
Ecuador, 1471 E
Edda, The Elder, 1220 K
Edda, The Younger (Snorri Sturlason), 1222 K
Edelstein, Der (Ulrich Boner), 1349 K
Edessa (*now* Urfa), Turkey, 1032 E, 1098 A, 1144 D, 1147 D, 1182 D; Counts of, *see* Baldwin I, Baldwin II, Joscelin II
Edgar, King of England (b. 943; 959–75), 957 E, 959 D, F, 972 H, 973 B, 975 C
Edgar the Atheling, King of Scotland, 1097 D, 1107 A
Edgcote, England, battle, 1469 C
Edigey, ruler of the Golden Horde (d. 1420), 1397 E, 1400 E, 1407 E, 1408 D, 1411 E
Edinburgh, Scotland, 1341 B, 1356 A, 1384 B, 1385 C; Treaty of, 1328 A, B
Edington, England, battle, 878 B
Edith, wife of Otto I, 929 E
Edmund, St., King of East Anglia, 870 D
Edmund, King of Wessex (939–46), 939 D, 940 E, 942 E, 944 E, 945 E, 946 B, 955 D
Edmund Ironside, King of England, 1016 B, D
Edmund Slemme, King of Sweden, 1056 E
Edmund 'Crouchback', Earl of Lancaster (1245–96), 1254 A, 1255 B, 1258 D
Edmund of Woodstock, Earl of Kent (1301–30), 1330 B
Edred, King of Wessex and England, 946 B, 948 E, 954 E, 955 D
Edrisi (*or* Idrisi), Abū 'Abdullāh Muhammad al-, Sp. Mus astronomer and geographer (1099–1166), 1154 G
Education, treatise on (Rabanus Maurus), 856 H; *and see* Humanists
Edward the Elder, King of Wessex, 899 E, 910 C, 911 E, 914 D, 917 E, 918 B, 919 E, 924 C
Edward the Martyr, King of England, 975 C, 978 A
Edward the Confessor, King of England, 1042 B, 1043 B, 1045 E, 1050 J, 1051 C, 1052 A, C, 1056 B, 1066 A
Edward I, King of England (1272–1307), 1239 L, 1254 D, 1265 C, 1291 J, 1303 G, 1307 C
  on Crusade, 1270 B, 1271 B, 1272 B, C
  succeeds as King, 1272 D, 1274 C
  enquiries into government, etc., 1274 G, 1275 G, 1278 F, 1285 F
  parliaments of, 1275 F, 1295 F
  conquers Wales, 1277 B, D, 1282 A, C, 1283 B, D, 1284 F, 1294 C, 1295 A, 1301 A
  treaty with France, 1279 B
  mediates abroad, 1279 D, 1288 D
  relations with clergy, 1279 H, 1286 F, 1297 A, 1306 A, 1307 A
  alliance with Aragon, 1287 C
  intervenes in Scotland, 1289 D, 1290 C, 1291 B, 1292 D, 1294 B
  legal measures, 1290 F, 1292 F, 1305 F
  expels Jews, 1290 G
  war with France, 1294 A, C, 1297 A, C, D, 1298 A, 1303 B
  Scottish campaigns, 1296 A–C, 1297 B, 1298 C, 1300 C, 1301 C, 1303 B, 1304 A, 1305 C, 1307 C
  dispute with magnates, 1297 A, D
  confirms Charters, 1297 D, 1299 B, 1300 A, 1301 A, 1305 D
Edward II, King of England (1307–27), 1284 L, 1290 C, 1294 E, 1327 C
  created Prince of Wales, 1301 A
  succeeds as King, 1307 C, 1308 A
  wars with Scotland, 1307 C, 1311 C, 1314 B, 1319 C, 1322 C, D, 1323 E
  and Piers Gaveston, 1307 C, 1308 B, 1309 C

Edward II—*contd.*
baronial opposition to, 1310 B, 1311 C, F, 1312 B, D, 1315 A, 1316 A, 1318 C, 1321 B–D, 1322 A, B
war with France, 1324 C, 1325 A
deposed, 1326 C, D, 1327 A
Edward III, King of England (1327–77), 1312 L, 1326 D, 1327 A, 1345 E, 1348 E, 1377 B
relations with France, 1327 A, 1328 A, 1329 B
peace with Scotland, 1328 A, B
begins personal rule, 1330 D
wars with Scotland, 1333 B, C, 1334 B, 1335 A, C, 1336, C, D, 1342 A, 1356 A, 1357 D
war with France, 1336 C, E, 1337 B, 1339 D, 1340 B, C, 1343 A, 1346 C, 1347 C, 1354 A, B, 1355 D, 1357 A, 1359 A, B, D, 1360 A, B, D, 1369 B, 1374 A, 1375 B
regulates wool trade, 1336 G, 1353 C, G
claims French crown, 1337 D, 1340 A, 1344 E
German alliance, 1337 C, 1338 C, 1341 A
prosecutes Archbishop Stratford, 1340 D, 1341 B
intervenes in Brittany, 1342 B–D, 1345 B
defeats Spanish fleet, 1350 C
parliamentary criticism, 1371 A, 1376 B, F, 1377 A
alliance with Portugal, 1373 B
Edward IV, King of England (1461–83), 1442 L, 1461 A, 1464 B, 1469 J, 1483 B, 1486 A
measures against disorder, 1468 F, 1473 F
war with France, 1468 C, 1474 C, 1475 C
struggle with Warwick, 1469 B, C, 1470 A, D, 1471 B
peace with Hanse, 1474 G
condemns Clarence, 1478 A
war with Scotland, 1480 E, 1482 B, C
pretended son of, 1491 E
Edward V, King of England (1483), 1470 L; as Prince of Wales, 1473 F; murdered, 1483 B
Edward, King of Portugal, 1433 C, 1434 K, 1438 C
Edward, Prince of Wales ('The Black Prince'), 1330 L, 1355 D, 1356 C, 1367 B, 1368 D, 1369 A, 1370 C, 1376 B
Edward, Prince of Wales, 1453 D, 1471 B
Edward, Duke of York (*c.* 1373–1415), 1410 K
Edwin, Earl of Mercia (d. 1069), 1068 E
Edwy, King of England, 955 D, 957 E, 959 D
Egbert, King of Wessex, 802 E, 815 E, 825 E, 829 E, 839 E
Eger. *See* Cheb
Egidian Constitutions, 1357 F
Egil's Saga, 1200 K
Egypt:
Tulunid dynasty, 868 E, 905 E; *and see* Tūlūn
Ikhshīdid dynasty, 935 E, 969 C
Fātimid dynasty, 914 E, 969 C, 1171 C. *And see*
Mu'izz (969–75)
'Azīz (975–96)
Hākim (996–1021)
Zāhir (1021–35)
Mustansir (1035–94)
lose north west Africa, 972 E
first treaty with Greeks, 987 E
lose Jerusalem, 1071 C, 1076 E
recovery in Palestine, 1089 E, 1098 E
decline of Caliphate, 1094 D
wars with Franks, 1099 C, 1101 C, 1102 B, 1105 C, 1123 B, 1124 C, 1153 C
conquered by Ayyūbids, 1167 A, C, 1168 D, 1169 A, 1171 C
Ayyūbid dynasty. *See*
Saladin (1169–93)
'Azīz (1193–6)
'Ādil (1196–1218)
Kāmil I (1218–38)
Ayyūb (1240–9)
Tūrān Shāh (1249–50)
Crusades against, 1218 B, C, 1219 D, H, 1220 C, 1239 D, 1249 B, 1250 A, B
take Ascalon, 1247 D
Mamlūk dynasty:
Bahrī line. *See*
Aybāk (1250–7)
'Ali (1257–9)
Qutuz (1259–60)
Baybars I (1261–77)
Baraka (1277–9)
Salamish (1279)
Qalāwūn (1279–90)
Ashraf (1290–3)
Nāsir (1293 . . . 1340)
his successors, 1340 E
Burji line, 1382 E, 1468 E; *and see* Barsbāy
war with Mongols, 1260 C, 1288 A, 1299 E
invade Sudan, 1314 E
Crusade against, 1365 D
conquer Armenia, 1375 B
defeated by Timur, 1400 E
recover Syria, 1405 A
antiquities and topography (al-Maqrīzī), 1442 K
capital. *See* Cairo
Coptic-Egyptian vocabulary, 1316 K
encyclopedias of government, 1332 F, 1418 F
history, 871 K, 939 K, 961 K, 1029 K, 1230 K, 1332 F, 1442 K, 1469 K
poetry, 1235 K, 1296 K, 1357 K
racing-stud, 1306 G
Egypt, Governors and Judges, of, (al-Kindī), 961 K
Eiga Monogatari, 1095 K
Eilhart von Oberg, G. poet, 1180 K
Einhard, Frankish courtier and historian (*c.* 771–840), 821 J, 829 K, 830 K, 840 K
Einsiedeln, Switzerland, abbey, 1031 J
Eisai, Ja. Buddhist reformer (1141–1215), 1191 G, H
Eisteddfod, at Cardigan, 1176 K
Ekkehard of Aura, G. chronicler, 1125 K
Ekkehard of St. Gall (1), G. poet, 937 K
Ekkehard of St. Gall (4; d. *c.* 1060), G. chronicler, 1036 K
Elbe, river, W. Germany, 804 E, 806 E, 929 E, 965 H, 968 H
Elbistan, Turkey, battle, 1277 B
Eleanor of Aquitaine, wife of Louis VII, 1137 C, 1152 A; wife of Henry II, 1152 B, 1204 L
Eleanor of Castile, wife of Edward I, 1254 D, 1290 L; Crosses, 1291 J
Eleanor of Provence, wife of Henry III, 1236 A
Eleanor, Queen of Navarre, 1479 A
Eleanor, wife of Simon de Montfort (1215–75), 1238 A
Elegentiae Latinae linguae (Lorenzo Valla), 1457 K 1471 K
Elene (Cynewulf), 800 K
Elephant, (Danish) Order of the, 1478 E
Elgin, Scotland, 1303 B; Cathedral, 1390 E
Elias, minister-general of Friars Minor, 1232 H, 1239 H
Elixir of youth, 1360 G
Elizabeth, wife of John of Bohemia, 1310 C
Elizabeth of York, wife of Henry VII (d. 1503), 1486 A
Elizabeth, St., Queen of Hungary, 1207 L, 1231 L
Elizabeth, St., wife of Dinis of Portugal, 1336 L
'Ellendun' (Nether Wroughton), England, battle, 825 E
Eltham, England, palace, 1479 J; Treaty of, 1412 B
Ely, England, bishop of, *see* Longchamp; Cathedral, 1090 J, 1252 J, 1321 J, 1322 J; Isle of, 1071 E
Ely, Monk of, E. poet, 1166 K

Emanuel ben Solomon, It. Je. writer and poet, 1331 K
Emek habacha (Ephraim of Bonn), 1196 K
Emperors, restored in west, 800 D, 824 F
  Carolingian dynasty. *See*
    Charlemagne (800–14)
    Louis the Pious (814–40)
    Lothar I (817–31, 840–55)
    Louis II (850–75)
    Charles the Bald (875–7)
    Charles the Fat (881–8)
    Arnulf (896–9)
    empire of:
      Church in, 802 H
      extent of, 804 E
      occupies Dalmatia, 812 F
      decline of government, 816 F
      divided, 817 C, 839 B, 841 B, 843 C
      laws (capitularies) for, 802 F, 816 F, 847 F, 877 F
      missi of, 802 F, 835 B
      reunited, 884 D
      disintegrates, 888 A
      restoration of government of, 998 F
  others. *See*
    Guy of Spoleto (891–4)
    Lambert of Spoleto (892–8)
    Louis III (of Provence; 901–?5)
    Berengar of Friuli (915–22)
Emperors, Greek. *See* Greek Empire
Emperors, Holy Roman:
  Saxon. *See*
    Otto I (962–73)
    Otto II (967–83)
    Otto III (996–1002)
  Henry II (of Bavaria; 1014–24)
  Salian. *See*
    Conrad II (1027–39)
    Henry III (1046–56)
    Henry IV (1084–1105)
    Henry V (1111–25)
  Lothar II (of Saxony; 1133–7)
  Hohenstaufen. *See*
    Frederick I (1155–90)
    Henry VI (1191–7)
  Otto IV (of Saxony; 1209–?14)
  Frederick II (Hohenstaufen; 1220–50)
  Henry VII (of Luxemburg; 1312–13)
  Lewis IV (of Bavaria; 1328–47)
  Charles IV (of Bohemia; 1355–78)
  Sigismund (of Bohemia, 1433–7)
  Frederick III (Habsburg; 1452–93)
Empingham, England, battle, 1470 A
Empire, Greek (*alias* Byzantine). *See* Greek Empire
Empire, Holy Roman:
  College of Electors, 1257 A, B, 1356 F
  hereditary, proposal to make, 1196 B, D
  history of (Thietmar), 1018 K
  officers of, 1114 E
  peace constitution for, 1158 D
  regulated by Golden Bull, 1356 F
  rights in Italy of, 1201 B, 1278 B, 1279 A, 1317 A
  treatise on (Lupold), 1340 F
Encyclopedias:
  Arabic:
    historico-geographical, 956 G
    medical, 994 G
  Belgian:
    scientific, 1310 H
  Chinese:
    botanical, 1256 G
    governmental, 812 F, 961 F, 1005 F, 1331 F
    historical, 801 K
    literary, 977 K, 1296 K
    medical, *illustrated*, 1108 G
    scientific, 1002 G
    Yung-lo Ta-tien, 1403 K
  Egyptian:
    biographical, 1248 G
    governmental, 1332 F, 1418 F
    zoological, 1372 G
  English:
    medical, 1252 G, 1407 G
    scientific, 1217 G, 1240 G, 1245 K, 1266 K, 1292 K
  French, 1141 H, 1264 G, 1481 K
    geographical, 1120 G
    scientific, 1243 G, 1244 G
  German:
    natural history, 1179 G
    technical (?Theophilus), 1100 G
  Greek, 959 F
    medical, 865 G
  Indian (Hindu):
    legal, 1270 F
  Italian, 1267 K
    geographical, 1119 G, 1418 G
    geological, 1282 G
    medical, 1050 G
  Norwegian:
    scientific, 1247 F
  Persian:
    astronomical, 1048 G
    geographical, 1283 G
    medical, 1037 G, 1135 G, 1187 G
    of Chinese medicine, 1318 G
    scientific, 976 G, 1187 G, 1340 G
  Spanish, 1284 K, 1295 K
  Spanish Muslim:
    medical, 1160 G
  See also Dictionaries
Eneide (Heinrich von Veldeke), 1189 K
Engelberg, Switzerland, 1147 G
Engelbert, Archbishop of Cologne, 1225 D
Engelbrecht, Regent of Sweden, 1435 E, 1436 E
Engi shiki, 927 F
England:
  Principal King, *viz.* Coenwulf of Mercia, 821 E
  Kings of Wessex. *See*
    Beorhtric (786–802)
    Egbert (802–39)
    Ethelwulf (839–55)
    Ethelbald (855–60)
    Ethelbert (860–5)
    Ethelred (865–71)
    Alfred (871–99)
    Edward the Elder (899–924)
    Athelstan (924–39)
    Edmund (939–46)
    Edred (946–55)
  Kings of England, 954 E; *and see*
    Edwy (955–9)
    Edgar (959–75)
    Edward the Martyr (975–8)
    Ethelred II (978–1016)
    Svein (1013–14)
    Cnut (1014–35)
    Edmund Ironside (1016)
    Harthacnut (1035–7)
    Harold Harefoot (1037–40)
    Harthacnut (1040–2)
    Edward the Confessor (1042–66)
    Harold Godwinson (1066)
    Norman
    William I (1066–87)
    William II (1087–1100)

England—*contd.*
Kings of England—*contd.*
Henry I (1100–35)
Stephen (1135–54)
Angevin (*Plantagenet*)
Henry II (1154–89)
Richard I (1189–99)
John (1199–1216)
Henry III (1216–72)
Edward I (1272–1307)
Edward II (1307–27)
Edward III (1327–77)
Richard II (1377–99)
Lancaster
Henry IV (1399–1413)
Henry V (1413–22)
Henry VI (1422–61, 1470–1)
York
Edward IV (1461–70, 1471–83)
Edward V (1483)
Richard III (1483–5)
Tudor
Henry VII (1485–1509)
Viking raids, 835 E, 836 E, 842 E, 851 E
Danish armies in, 866 D, 867 A, 870 D, 871 A, E, 874 E, 875 E, 877 E, 878 A, B, 886 E, 892 E, 895 E, 896 E; conversion of, 878 A
Danelaw, 886 E, 892 E; conquered, 910 E, 914 D, 917 E, 918 E; lost, 940 E; reconquered, 942 E, 944 E, 948 E, 954 E; laws of, 959 F
Danish raids resumed, 980 E, 991 C, 994 E, 1002 D, 1003 E, 1009 E, 1012 E
Danish conquest, 1013 E, 1015 C, 1016 B, D
Norman conquest, 1066 D, 1068 E, 1069 A, C
land of Carlisle annexed, 1092 E
Scottish invasion defeated, 1138 C
civil war, 1138 B, 1139 C, 1141 A, D, 1148 A, 1153 A, D
rebellion, 1174 C
French invasion feared, 1205 A
under interdict, 1208 A
becomes papal fief, 1213 B, 1365 B
civil war, 1215 B–D, 1216 D, 1217 B–D
revolts, 1233 C, D, 1234 B
Barons' War, 1263 B, C, 1264 A, B, 1265 C, D, 1266 B, D
decline of order, 1305 F
Scottish raids, 1308 E, 1318 B, 1319 C, 1322 C, D, 1346 D
famine, 1315 G, 1316 G
Hundred Years War. *See* France
Black Death, 1348 G, 1349 G, 1361 G, 1369 G
French attacks, 1377 C, 1380 C, 1386 D
Peasants' Revolt, 1381 B, 1383 K
Scottish raids, 1384 A, 1385 C, 1388 C
Lollard risings, 1414 A, 1431 B
Cade's Rebellion, 1450 B, C
Wars of the Roses, 1450 C, 1451 C, 1452 A, 1454 B, D; first battles, 1455 B, D, 1458 A, 1459 C, D, 1460 C, D; York, 1461 A, 1464 B, 1469 B, C, 1470 A; Lancaster, 1470 C, D; York, 1471 B, 1483 B, D; Tudor, 1485 C, 1487 B
Church:
reforms, 940 H, 972 H
primacy in, 1072 H
reorganised, 1078 H
Constitutions of Clarendon, 1164 A
friars, 1221 H, 1224 H
mortmain, 1279 H
courts, 1279 H
taxatio, 1291 H
provisors, 1351 H, 1390 H, 1428 H
praemunire, 1353 H, 1390 H, 1393 H
heresy, 1382 H, 1401 H
privilege, 1489 H
government:
Domesday Book, 1085 D, 1087 G
Pipe Rolls, 1130 F
Stephen's household, 1136 F
Inquest of Sheriffs, 1170 F
Dialogus de Scaccario, 1179 F
Exchequer of Jews, 1194 F
Chancery rolls, 1199 F
survey of tenures, 1212 F
Hundred Rolls, 1274 G, 1275 G
Kirkby's Quest, 1285 F
Privy Seal Office, 1311 F
Ordinances, 1311 F, 1322 B
Exchequer reform, 1323 F
first lay Chancellor, 1340 F
Fortescue on, 1476 F
history. *See* Historians
Jews, attacked, 1190 A, 1196 K; charter to, 1201 F; expelled, 1290 G
law:
Leges Henrici Primi, 1118 F
trial by jury, 1166 F, 1176 F
'Glanville' on, 1180 F
plea rolls, 1181 F, 1194 F
coroner, 1194 F
final concord, 1195 F
Common Pleas, 1215 F
definitive charters, 1225 F
Statute of Merton, 1236 F
Statute of Marlborough, 1267 F
Bracton on, 1268 F
Statutes of Westminster, 1275 F, 1285 F, 1290 F
Quo warranto, 1278 F, 1290 F
legal profession, 1292 F
trailbaston, 1305 F
Statute of Treasons, 1352 F
supremacy of statute, 1354 F
justices of the peace, 1361 F
ordinance against liveries, 1390 F
Chancery jurisdiction, 1417 F
Fortescue on, 1468 F
statute against retaining, 1468 F
statute against sport, 1468 F
Council in the Marches, 1473 F
Littleton, *Tenures*, 1481 F
council in the north, 1484 F
'Star Chamber Act', 1487 F
literature, early:
Widsith, 800 K
Cynewulf, 800 K
Alfred's translations, 892 K
Bald, *Leech Book*, 930 G
Beowulf, 970 K
Deor's lament, 970 K
Widsith spoke, 975 K
Ælfric, 991 K, 995 K
Battle of Maldon, 993 K
Wulfstan, 1014 K, 1023 K
Dunstable Miracle Play, 1100 K
Song of Cnut, 1166 K
Layamon, *Brut*, 1200 K
The Owl and the Nightingale, 1200 K
Havelok the Dane, 1250 K
Genesis and Exodus, 1250 K
King Horn, 1250 K
Thomas the Rhymer, 1294 K
Harrowing of Hell, 1295 K
King Alisaunder, 1300 K
See also Poets; Translations

Orders: Garter, 1348 E; Bath, 1399 D
Parliament:
councils with knights, 1213 F, 1254 F
first 'full', 1265 F, 1275 F
'Model', 1295 F
Modus tenendi, 1320 F
concessions to, 1341 B
anti-clerical, 1365 B, 1371 B
'Good', 1376 B, 1377 A
speaker, 1376 F
impeachment, 1376 F, 1450 A
'Bad', 1377 A
'Merciless', 1387 D, 1388 A, 1397 C
of Henry IV, 1399 C, 1404 A, D, 1406 A, D
'of Bats', 1426 A
franchise, 1430 F
taxation:
Danegeld, 991 C, 1162 F
Saladin tithes, 1188 A
carucage, 1194 B
parliamentary, 1254 F, 1270 B
customs, 1275 F
poll-taxes, 1377 A, G, 1380 D
land, 1404 A
'benevolence', 1474 C, 1491 E
trade, with Hanse, 1379 G, 1388 G, 1474 G; wool, 1336 G, 1353 C, G, 1354 F, 1362 G; *Libel* on, 1437 G
travels in: Baudry, 1130 G; Worcestre, 1478 K
Enguerran, F. mason, 1200 J
Ennin, Ja. diarist, 847 K
Ensinger, Matthaüs, Swiss architect, 1450 J
Entombment (Roger van der Weyden), 1450 J
Enuigs (Jordi de Sant Jordi), 1440 K
Enzio, King of Sardinia, 1238 E, 1249 B
Eochaid, King of Scotland, 878 E, 889 E
Ephemerides (Regiomontanus), 1474 G
Ephesus, Turkey, 867 H, 1147 D
Ephraim of Bonn, G. Je. historian, 1196 K
Epila, Spain, battle, 1348 C
Epiphany (Hieronymus Bosch), 1480 J
Epirus, Greece, 1337 E; despots of, *see* Ducas
Epistola (Lapo da Castiglionchio), 1381 K
Epistola Concordiae (Conrad of Gelnhausen), 1380 H
Epistola Leviathan (?Pierre d'Ailly), 1381 H
Epistola Pacis (Henry of Langenstein), 1379 H
Epistolae (Einhard), 840 K
Epistle to Posterity, An (Petrarch), 1351 K
Epitome de Vitis Romanorum Pontificum (Abbo), 1004 K
Épître au dieu d'amour (Christine de Pisan), 1399 K, 1402 K
Equator, the, 1469 G
Erasmus, Desiderius, Dutch humanist (1469–1536), 1469 L
Erchanger, Count Palatine, 917 A
Erec et Énide (Chrétien de Troyes), 1164 K
Erfurt, E. Germany, Cathedral, 1460 J; University, 1379 H
Eric I the Good, King of Denmark (1095–1103), 1095 C, 1101 E, 1103 C, 1105 E, 1137 C
Eric II, King of Denmark, 1131 E, 1134 B, 1137 E
Eric III the Lamb, King of Denmark, 1137 C, 1147 E
Eric IV, King of Denmark, 1241 A, 1250 C
Eric V Clipping, King of Denmark, 1259 B, 1282 F, 1286 D
Eric VI Menved, King of Denmark, 1286 D, 1303 E, 1319 D, G
Eric VII of Pomerania, King of Denmark, Norway and Sweden (b. 1382, d. 1459), 1397 B, 1412 D, 1427 C, 1432 E, 1435 C; loses Sweden, 1435 E, 1436 E, 1438 E; and Norway, 1436 E; deposed, 1438 E, 1439 E
Eric I, King of Norway, 933 E, 938 E
Eric II, King of Norway, 1280 B, 1285 D, 1286 A, 1289 D, 1294 E, 1299 E
Eric, St., King of Sweden, 1150 E, 1157 E, 1160 B
Eric X Cnutson, King of Sweden (1210–20), 1210 C, 1220 E, 1223 E.
Eric XI, King of Sweden, 1223 E, 1250 A
Eric Bloodaxe, King of York, 948 E, 952 E, 954 E
Eric the Red, Viking leader, 982 G
Ericsson, Leif, Viking explorer, 1003 G
Erigena, Johannes Scotus, Irish philosopher and theologian (*c.* 813–77), 851 H, 865 K, 877 L
Erispoë, King of Brittany, 851 A, 856 A
Erlembald of Milan, Patarene, 1075 A
Erling, the Jarl, Norwegian king-maker, 1162 E
Ernest of Babenburg, Duke of Swabia, 1012 E, 1015 B
Ernest (II), Duke of Swabia, 1015 B, 1025 E, 1027 E, 1030 C
Erwin (? von Steinbach), G. mason (d. 1318), 1277 J
Erzinjān, Turkey, 1395 E; battle, 1230 C
Erzurum, Turkey, 1048 E, 1230 C; battle, 1047 E; college, 1253 J; mosque, 1179 J
Eschenbach, Wolfram von. *See* Wolfram
Eskishehir, Turkey, battle, 1299 B
Espagne, Charles d', constable of France, 1354 A
Esplechin, Belgium, treaty of, 1340 C
Essayists:
Chinese. *See* Su Tung-p'o
Persian. *See* Hamadhānī
Essays in Idleness (Yoshida Kenkō), 1350 K
Essays from the Torrent of Dreams (Shên Kua), 1093 G
Essen, W. Germany, Cathedral, 973 J, 1275 J
Essentials of Salvation (Genshin), 1017 H
Essex, England, 825 E; earl of, 1189 D
Este, Azzo VI d', lord of Ferrara (d. 1212), 1205 E
Este, Azzo VIII d', lord of Ferrara, 1293 A, 1306 A, 1308 A
Este, Borso d' (d. 1471), Duke of Modena and Reggio, 1452 B; Duke of Ferrara, 1471 B
Este, Ercole I d', Duke of Ferrara (1433–1505), 1482 D
Este, Folco d', lord of Ferrara, 1308 A, B, 1309 A
Este, Niccolò d', lord of Ferrara, 1317 C
Este, Obizzo II, Marquess of, 1265 A, 1288 D, 1289 E, 1293 A
Este, Obizzo d', lord of Ferrara, 1317 C
Este, Rinaldo d', lord of Ferrara, 1317 C
Esthonia, Russia, 1217 E, 1218 E, 1224 E, 1315 F, 1346 E
Estoire de la guerre sainte (Ambroise d'Évreux), 1196 K
Établissements de Saint-Louis, 1270 F
Établissements de Saint-Quentin, 1047 G
Ethelbald, King of Wessex, 855 E, 860 E
Ethelbert, King of Wessex, 860 E, 865 E
Ethelfleda, 'Lady of the Mercians', 911 E, 918 B
Ethelheard, Archbishop of Canterbury, 803 H
Ethelred, King of Wessex, 865 E, 871 A, B
Ethelred II the Redeless, King of England (b. 968/9, 978–1016), 978 A, 1000 E, 1002 D, 1011 E, 1013 E, 1014 A, 1016 B, 1042 B
Ethelred, earldorman of Mercia, 911 E
Ethelweard, earldorman, E. translator, 998 K
Ethelwold, St., Bishop of Winchester, 970 H, 972 H, 980 J, 984 L
Ethelwulf, King of Wessex, 839 E, 851 E; deposed, 855 E, 858 A
Ethiopia. *See* Abyssinia
Étienne of Tournai, F. canonist, 1168 H
See also Stephen

Eton, England, college, 1441 H
Eucharistia, De (John Wycliffe), 1381 H
Euclid, Gk. mathematician (*fl. c.* 300 B.C.), translated into Arabic, 873 G, 997 G; into Latin, 1100 G, 1253 G
Eudes IV, Duke of Burgundy (d. 1350), 1330 E
Eudes, Count of Poitiers, 1039 A
See also Odo
Eudocia Macrembolitissa, Greek Empress, 1067 B, 1068 A
Eugene of Palermo, Gk. translator (d. 1192), 1160 G
Eugenius II, Pope, 824 A, 826 H, 827 C
Eugenius III (Bernard of Pisa), Pope, 1145 A, 1148 H, 1152 H, 1153 B, C
Eugenius IV (Gabriel Condulmer), Pope, 1431 A, 1433 B, 1440 E, 1447 A; and General Council, 1431 D, 1433 D, 1437 C, 1438 A, 1439 B, D; expelled from Rome, 1434 B, 1443 C; wars of, 1431 B, 1440 B, 1441 A
Eulenspiegel, Till, 1240 K
Eulogius, Archbishop of Toledo, 859 H
Euphrates, river (Turkey, Syria, Iraq), 856 E, 966 E
Euryalus and Lucretia (Aeneas Silvius), 1444 K
Eutychius (*alias* Sa'id ibn-al-Bitriq), Patriarch of Alexandria, Eg. historian, 939 K
Evangelienbuch (Otfrid), 868 K
Everard, Duke of Franconia, 939 C
Everlasting Gospel, The (Joachim of Flora), 1202 H; *Introduction to* (Gerard de Burgo San Donnino), 1254 H, 1256 H
Evesham, England, 1097 H; battle, 1265 C
Evfimi, Archbishop of Novgorod, Russian historian (d. 1458), 1448 K
Évreux, France, 1200 B
Évreux, Ambroise d', Anglo-Norman poet, 1196 K
Examiners of Misdeeds (Japan), 820 F
Examinations. *See* China, government; Korea; Medicine
Exchequer. *See* England, government
Execrabilis (Pius II), 1460 H
Exegesis canonum (Theodore Balsamon), 1195 H
Exeter, England, 877 E; Bishop of, *see* Stapledon, Walter; Cathedral, 1280 J; Duke of, *see* Holand, Henry
Exeter Book, The, 975 K
Exploration, Arab, 833 G; *and see* Bristol, Navigation, Portugal, Travellers
Expugnatio Hibernica (Giraldus Cambrensis), 1185 K
Extra (decretals), 1234 H
Extravagantes (John XXII), 1317 H
Extravagantes Communes, 1484 H
Eyck, Hubert van, Flemish painter, 1426 J, L
Eyck, Jan van, Flemish painter, 1425 J, 1426 J, 1432 J, 1433 J, 1434 J, 1435 J, 1436 J, 1427 J, 1439 J, 1440 L
Eye. *See* Ophthamologists
Eymeric, Nicholas, Catalan inquisitor, 1399 H
Eynsham, England, Abbot of. *See* Aelfric
Eyrbyggja (saga), 1200 K
Eysten I, King of Norway (1103–22), 1103 C
Ezzelin da Romano, It. despot, 1194 L, 1226 E, 1236 E, 1237 A, 1252 A, 1256 B, 1258 E, 1259 C, D; poem on, 1329 K
Ezzo of Bamberg, G. poet, 1060 K
Ezzolied (Ezzo of Bamberg), 1060 K

F

Fa Ngum (Ch'ieng Dong Ch'ieng Tong), King of Laos (d. 1373), 1353 E
Fabliaux:
Richeut, 1170 K
Marie de France, 1185 K
Chevalier de la Tour-Landry, 1371 K
Libro de los Gatos, 1400 K
Fabri, Felix, It. pilgrim-author, 1348 G
Fabriano, Italy, 1340 G
Fabulists:
Arab. *See* Jahshiyari
Spanish Jew. *See* Pedro Alfonso
Facetiarum, Liber (Gian Francesco Poggio), 1452 K
Facilitation of Treatment (ibn-Zuhr), 1162 G, 1280 G
Fadl al-Khayl (al-Dimyāti), 1306 G
Fadlān, Ahmad ibn-, ibn-Hammād, Arab traveller, 921 G
Faenza, Italy, 1241 B, 1350 A
Faenza, Francesco da, It. painter, 1442 J
Faidit, Gaucelm, Provençal troubadour, 1220 K
Faintises du monde, Les (Guillaume Alexis), 1486 K
Fair Unknown, The, 1220 K
Falaise, France, Treaty of, 1174 D
Falconaria, Italy, battle, 1300 D
Falconry, 1180 G, 1386 K
Falconry, The Art of (Frederick II), 1250 K
Falcucci, Niccolò, It. physician, 1411 G
Falieri, Marino, Doge of Venice (b. 1274), 1354 D, 1355 B
Falieri, Ordelafo, Doge of Venice, 1102 E, 1117 E
Falieri, Vitale, Doge of Venice, 1084 E, 1096 E
Falkirk, Scotland, battle, 1298 C, G
Falköping, Sweden, battle, 1389 A
False Decretals, The, 850 H
Famagosta, Cyprus, 1373 E
Famiglia, Della (Leone Battista Alberti), 1441 K
Famiya, Turkey, battle, 1148 D
Famous Men and Women (Castagno), 1453 J
Fan Ch'êng-ta, C. geographer and botanist (1126–1193), 1193 G
Fan K'uan, C. painter (*c.* 990–1030), 1030 J
Fan ts'un chii p'u (Fan Ch'eng-ta), 1193 G
Fantastic romances:
Cléomadès, 1282 K
L'histoire de Lusignan, 1387 K
Faqīh, Abū Bakr ibn-al-, al-Hamadhānī, Per. geographer, 903 G
Fārābī, Muhammad ibn-Tarkhān abu-Nasr al-, Turkish philosopher and political and musical theorist, 950 F, J
Faraj ben Sālim, It. Je. translator (d. 1286), 1279 G
Farces. *See* Drama
Farfa, Italy, Abbey, consuetudinary of, 1043 J
Fārid, ibn-al-, Eg. mystic poet, 1181 L, 1235 K
Fāris, ibn-, Per. philologist, 1005 K
Fārisī, Kamāl al-Dīn al-, Per. meteorologist and writer on optics, 1320 G
Faroes, islands, 1028 E
Farrā', Per. grammarian, 822 K
Farrukhī, Per. poet, 1037 K
Fasciculi Zizaniorum (Thomas Netter), 1415 H
Fasl fi al-Milal w-al-Ahwā' w-al-Nihal, al- (ibn-Hazm), 1064 H
Fastolf, John, E. soldier, 1459 L
Fātamid dynasty, 909–69, *see* Kairāwan; 969–1171, *see* Egypt
Fauquembergue, France, battle, 925 E
Fava of Bologna, Guido, It. writer, 1229 K
Favola di Orfeo (Angelo Poliziano), 1480 K
Fayyūmi, Sa'id al- (*alias* Saadia ben Joseph), Je. translator (882–942), 942 H
Fazāri, Muhammad ibn-Ibrāhīm al-, Arab astronomer, 800 G
Fazio degli Uberti. *See* Uberti

Febragaen, Spain, battle, 1213 E
Fei Hsin, C. travel-author, 1436 G
Felim O'Conor, King of Connaught, 1316 C
Felix V, anti-pope. *See* Amadeus VIII
Fellin, Esthonia, battle, 1217 E
Feltre, Vittorino da, It. humanist schoolmaster (1378–1446), 1378 L, 1446 L
Fenandus, Fulgentius, of Carthage, canonist, 850 H
Fêng Tao, Prime Minister of China (d. 954), 932 G
Ferdinand I the Just, King of Aragon, 1412 B, 1415 D, 1416 B
Ferdinand II, King of Aragon (1479–1516), 1452 L, 1469 D, 1474 D, 1475 A, 1477 H, 1479 A, 1480 A, 1483 H, 1489 A, C, D, 1491 D, G
Ferdinand I, King of Castile, 1033 E, 1037 E, 1054 C, 1064 E, 1065 D
Ferdinand II, King of Leon, 1157 C, 1188 A
Ferdinand III, St., King of Castile and Leon (b. 1200), 1217 C, 1225 E, 1229 E, 1236 B, 1241 E, 1244 E, 1246 E, 1247 C, 1248 D, 1252 B, F
Ferdinand IV, King of Castile and Leon (b. 1286), 1295 E, 1312 C
Ferdinand I, King of Portugal (b. 1340), 1367 A, 1372 A, 1373 B, 1381 C, 1382 C, 1383 D
Ferdinand de la Cerda, claimant to Castile, 1284 B
Fernandez, Denis, Port. explorer, 1446 G
Fernando Po, African is. (of Spain), 1471 G
Ferrand of Portugal, Count of Flanders (d. 1233), 1212 A, 1214 C, 1226 B
Ferrante I, King of Naples (1458–94), 1458 B, 1459 C, 1460 C, 1462 C; wars with Pope, 1469 C, 1482 B, C, 1485 D, 1486 B, 1487 C; and Florence, 1478 B, 1480 A
Ferrara, Italy:
- ruled by Estensi, 1205 E; *and see* Este, *passim*
- war of succession to, 1308 B, 1309 A, C, 1310 B, 1317 C
- League of, and war, 1332 C, D, 1333 A, B
- war against Milan, 1392 B
- Peace of, 1428 B
- General Council at, 1438 A, 1439 A
- Duchy of, created, 1471 B
- War of, 1482 B–D, 1483 A, 1484 C
- school at, 1458 H
- University of, 1391 H

Ferrari, Giovanni Matteo, professor of medicine, 1471 G, 1472 G
Ferrer, Vincent, St., Catalan preacher (1350–1419), 1419 L
Ferreto de'Ferreti, It. humanist, poet and historian, 1337 K
Ferrières, France, abbot of. *See* Lupus, Servatus
Ferté, La, France, abbey, 1113 H
Festiall (John Mirk), 1400 H
Feudalism:
- Belgium, 863 E
- Bohemia, 1173 E
- Carolingian Empire, 847 F, 877 F
- Delhi, 1270 F, 1393 A
- England, 1159 F, 1194 F, 1212 F, 1267 F, 1285 F, 1290 F; 'bastard feudalism', 1390 F, 1468 F
- France, 870 E, 911 E, 921 E, 925 E, 943 E, 940 F, 987 C, 989 F, 994 E, 996 A, 1040 F, 1053 E, 1258 F
- Germany, 880 A, 908 E, 1007 D
- Greece (Romania), 1322 F
- Greek Empire, 1118 F, 1180 F
- Italy, 1037 B
- Japan, 1180 F, 1185 B, 1232 F, 1297 F
- Norway, 1202 A, 1308 E
- Scotland, 1153 B
- Seljuq Empire, 1087 F
- Spain, 875 E, 1064 F
- Sweden, 1290 D

Feuerwerkbuch, 1420 G
Fever, Consolation in Cases of (Mekhitur), 1184 G
Fevers, treatise on (al-Isrā'īlī), 932 G
Fexhe, Belgium, Peace of, 1316 F
Fez, Morocco, Idrisid dynasty of, 974 E
Fibonacci, Leonardo, It. mathematician (*c.* 1170–*c.* 1240), 1202 G, 1220 G, 1225 G
Ficino, Marsilio, It. philosopher (1433–99), 1433 L
'Field of Blood', Syria, 1119 B
'Field of Lies', Colmar, France, 833 B
Fiery Soliloquy with God (Gerlac Petersen), 1411 H
Fieschi, Ottobuono. *See* Adrian V
Fihrist al-'Ulum (al-Warrāq), 995 G
Filāhah, al- (ibn-al-'Awwam), 1200 F
Filangieri, Richard, imperial legate, 1232 B, 1233 B
Fillastre, Guillaume, F. historian, 1473 K
Filostrato (Boccaccio), 1350 K
Finland, 1157 E, 1249 E, 1293 E, 1480 E
Fioravanti, Aristotle, It. architect, 1475 J
Fiore (Guidotto of Bologna), 1266 K
Fiore di leggende (Antonio Pucci), 1388 K
Fiorenzuola, Italy, battle, 923 C
Fioretti di San Francisco, 1330 K
Firdausī, Abū'l Qāsim Mansūr, Per. poet (*c.* 940–1020), 1020 K, 1335 J, 1359 K
Firdaws al-Hikmah (al-Tabarī), 850 G
Firnās, Abū-al-Qāsim ibn-, Sp. M. astronomer and musical theorist, 888 G, J
Fīrūz I, Rukn-ad-Dīn, Sultan of Delhi, 1236 B
Fīrūz II, Jalal-ad-Dīn, Sultan of Delhi, 1290 B, 1295 C
Fīrūz III, Shah of Delhi (b. 1305), 1351 A, 1352 E, 1360 G, 1363 E, 1388 C; mausoleum, 1389 J
Fīrūz Shahī, Ta'rīkh-i- (Baranī), 1352 K
Fīrūz, Shah of Kulbarga (1397–1422), 1419 E, 1422 E, J
Fīrūzābād, India, 1352 E
Fīrūzābādī, Abū-l-Tāhir Muhammad al-, Per. philologist (1329–1414), 1414 K
Fisher, John, Bishop of Rochester (1459–1535), 1459 L
Fistula, treatise on, 1376 G
FitzAlan, Richard, Earl of Arundel, 1387 D, 1388 A, 1397 C
FitzGilbert, Richard de ('Strongbow'), Earl of Pembroke (d. 1176), 1170 C; King of Leinster, 1171 B
FitzRalph, Richard, Archbishop of Armagh, E. theologian, 1360 F, L
Five Mystic Meals (Dieric Bouts), 1464 J
Flabanico, Domenico, Doge of Venice, 1032 E, 1043 E
Flagellants, 1260 H, 1349 G
Flanders, Belgium:
- created a county, 863 E
- Counts. *See*
  - Baldwin I (863–79)
  - Baldwin II (879–918)
  - Arnold I (918–65)
  - Arnold II (965–88)
  - Baldwin IV (988–1036)
  - Baldwin V (1036–67)
  - Baldwin VI (1067–70)
  - Arnold III (1070–1)
  - Robert I (1071–93)
  - (Robert II)
  - (Baldwin VII)
  - Charles I (1119–27)
  - William Clito (1127–8)
  - Thierry (1128–68)
  - Philip (1168–91)

Flanders, Belgium—*contd.*
  Counts—*contd.*
    (Baldwin VIII)
    Baldwin IX (1195–1206)
    Joanna (1206–44)
    Ferrand (1212–33)
    Margaret (1244–80)
    Guy (1280–1305)
    Robert III (1305–22)
    Louis I (1322–3, 1328–46)
    Robert IV (1323–8)
    Louis II (1346–84)
    Philip the Bold (1384–1404)
    John the Fearless (1404–19)
    Philip the Good (1419–67)
    Charles the Bold (1467–77)
    Mary (1477–82)
    Maximilian (1477–82)
  raided by Magyars, 954 E
  French intervention, 965 A, 1127 A, 1128 C, 1280 A
  'Peace of God' in, 1093 D
  relations with Hanse, 1252 G, 1388 G, 1392 G, 1436 G, 1438 G, 1441 G
  civil war, 1256 C
  woollen industry, 1280 G, 1336 G
  revolts against France, 1302 B, C, 1303 C, 1304 C, 1305 A, B, 1312 E, 1314 C, D, 1315 C, 1320 B, 1323 B, 1328 C
  revolts against Count, 1337 D, 1379 E, 1382 B, D, 1385 D
  'crusade' in, 1383 B
  'chamber' (law court) of, 1386 F
  literature:
    Gilles le Muisit, 1353 K
    Jacob van Maerlant, 1283 K
Flarchheim, E. Germany, battle, 1080 A
Flensburg, W. Germany, Treaty of, 1404 D
Fleur des histores (Hayton), 1314 K
Fleury (St. Benoît-sur-Loire), France, abbey, 1108 J; monk of, *see* Aimon
Flight, attempts at, 888 G, 1070 G
Flint, Wales, 1399 C
Flodoard of Reims, F. chronicler (d. 972?), 966 K
Flor, Roger de, Catalan mercenary (b. 1262), 1305 B
Florence, Italy:
  as Guelf centre, 1251 A, C, 1259 B, 1260 C, 1267 B, 1279 E, 1288 B
  feud of Blacks and Whites, 1301 B, D, 1302 A, 1304 B, 1307 D
  takes Pistoia, 1306 B
  under Naples, 1311 E, 1322 E, 1325 D, 1328 D
  attacked by Henry VII, 1312 D
  war with Pisa, 1315 C, 1325 C
  under Walter of Brienne, 1342 C, 1343 C
  popular disturbances, 1345 E, 1368 G, 1378 C, 1382 A
  wars with Milan, 1351 D, 1353 A, 1354 A
  war with Pope, 1375 D, 1376 A, 1377 A, 1378 C
  takes Arezzo, 1384 D
  war with Milan, 1390 B, 1391 C, 1392 A, B, 1396 C, 1397 C, 1400 A, 1401 D, 1402 B, C
  annexes Pisa, 1406 D
  ruled by Maso degli Albizzi, 1417 E
  buys Leghorn, 1421 B
  war with Milan, 1423 E, 1425 D, 1430 D, 1434 C, 1440 B, 1454 B, C
  Eugenius IV in, 1434 B; holds General Council, 1439 A, C, K, 1443 C
  ruled by Medici, 1434 D, 1464 C, 1469 D, 1471 C
  wars with Pope, 1478 B, 1479 C, 1480 A, 1482 B, 1484 C
  Academy, 1439 K
  bankers of, 1346 G
  Bargello, bronze in, 1428 J
  burning in, 1327 H
  cannon used by, 1326 G
  Cathedral, 1294 J, 1355 J, 1367 J; baptistery, 1330 J, 1403 J, 1427 J; campanile, 1334 J, 1337 J; cantoria, 1431 J, 1433 J; dome, 1413 J, 1418 J; frescoes, 1436 J, 1456 J; reliquary, 1432 J; sacristy, 1464 J; statues, 1408 J, 1452 J, 1455 J; windows, 1443 J, 1444 J
  churches and chapels:
    Brancacci Chapel (Sta. Maria del Carmine), frescoes, 1425 J, 1432 J, 1484 J
    Capella Pazzi, 1430 J
    Or San Michele, 1346 J; sculpture in, 1359 J, 1411 J, 1413 J, 1414 J, 1416 J, 1419 J, 1428 J
    S. Apollonia, frescoes, 1445 J
    S. Croce, 1300 J; frescoes, 1325 J, 1332 J
    Sant'Egidio, frescoes, 1439 J
    S. Giovanni, baptistery, 1059 J
    S. Lorenzo, 1421 J
    S. Marco, frescoes, 1440 J
    Sta. Maria degli Angeli, 1439 K; frescoes, 1433 J
    Sta. Maria Novella, Abbey, 1246 J, 1456 J; frescoes, 1425 J, 1445 J, 1490 J; Strozzi chapels, 1354 J
    S. Miniato, Abbey, 1062 J
    S. Spirito, 1394 K
  coins florins, 1252 G
  Foundling Hospital, 1419 J, 1463 J
  government of, 1193 F, 1282 F, 1293 F, 1471 C
  histories of: Dino Compagni, 1324 K; Giovanni Villani, 1348 K; Baldassare, 1385 K; Leonardo Bruni, 1444 K; Poggio Bracciolini, 1459 K
  Latin secretary, 1375 K
  Loggia dei Lanzi, 1376 J
  Palazzi: Pitti, 1458 J; Rucellai, 1446 J; Strozzi, 1489 J; Vecchio, 1299 J
  University, 1349 H, 1472 H; chair of Greek, 1391 K
Florence V, Count of Holland (b. 1254), 1275 G, 1296 B
Florence of Worcester, E. chronicler, 1118 K
Flores Historiarum (Roger of Wendover), 1237 K
Florin, of Florence, 1252 G
Flos Medicinae (John of Milan), 1328 G
Flos naturarum (attrib. 'Geber'), 1473 G
Flos super solutionibus (Fibonacci), 1225 G
Flowers, plants, etc. *See* Bamboo, Chrysanthemum, Peony
Flowers of the Knowledge of Stones (al-Tīfāshī), 1154 G
Flowing Light of the Godhead (Mechthild), 1280 D
Flüe, Nicholas von, Swiss hermit, 1481 D
Flushing, Holland, 1046 B
Foggia, Italy, battle, 1254 D
Fogliano, Guidoriccio da, It. condottiere, 1328 J
Foix, France, Counts of. *See* Francis Phoebus; Gaston Phoebus
Folengo, Theofilo, It. poet (1491–1544), 1491 L
Foligno, Italy, 1334 H, 1403 K
Foligno, Gentile da, It. physician, 1348 G, L
Foliot, Gilbert, Bishop of London, 1187 K
Fons memorabilium universi (Domenico di Bandino), 1418 G
Fons Vitae (Avicebron), 1150 K
Fontaine, Jehan de la, F. poet, 1381 L, 1431 L
Fontaines, Pierre de, F. jurist, 1260 F
Fontana, Giovanni de', It. writer on warfare, 1415 G
Fontenay, France, abbey, 1139 J

Fontenoy, France, battle, 841 B
Fontevrault, France, abbey, 1119 J; Order of, 1096 H
Food, dictionary of, 1080 G; recipe-book, 1377 K; *and see* Beer, Herring, Mushrooms, Oranges, Rice, Salt, Tea, Wines
Football, 1468 F
Forchheim, W. Germany, 1077 A; Treaty of, 874 E
Fordun, John, Scottish chronicler (*fl.* 1363–84), 1383 K, 1449 K
Forests, Charter of the, 1225 A, 1237 A, 1297 D, 1298 B, 1300 A, 1301 A, 1305 D
Forgiveness, Treatise on (al-Ma'arri), 1058 K
Forli, Italy, 1356 A
Forli, Jacopo da, professor of medicine, 1414 G, L
Formigny, France, battle, 1450 B
Formosus, Pope, 891 D, 896 B
Fortescue, John, E. jurist (*c.* 1394–1476), 1463 F, 1468 F, 1476 F
Fortitude (Botticelli), 1470 J
Fortunae, De Varietate (Poggio Bracciolini), 1459 K
Fortunus, King of Navarre, 880 E, 905 E
Foscari, Francesco, Doge of Venice, 1423 B, 1457 D
Fossalta, La, Italy, battle, 1249 B
Fossanova, Italy, abbey, 1178 J
Fotheringhay, England, Treaties of, 1482 B
Fougères, France, 1449 A
Fougères, Étienne de, Bishop of Rennes, F. poet (d. 1178), 1170 K
Foundations of the True Properties of Remedies (Muwaffaq), 975 G
Fountain of Life (Avicebron), 1058 K, 1150 K
Fountains, England, abbey, 1135 J
Fouquet, Jean, F. painter and miniaturist (*c.* 1420–81?), 1444 J, 1451 J, 1458 J, 1470 J, 1475 J
See also Francis
Four Prophets (Uccello), 1443 J
Fraga, Spain, battle, 1134 C
France:
Kings of. *See*
Carolingians
Charlemagne (768–814)
Louis (814–40)
Charles (I) the Bald (843–77)
Louis II (877–9)
Carloman (879–84)
Louis III (879–82)
Charles (II) the Fat (884–8)
Odo (888–98)*
Charles (III) the Simple (893–929)
Robert I (922–3)*
Raoul (923–36)*
Louis IV (936–54)
Lothair (954–86)
Louis V (986–7)
See also Aquitaine
Capetians
Hugh (987–96)
Robert II (996–1031)
Henry I (1031–60)
Philip I (1060–1108)
Louis VI (1108–37)
Louis VII (1137–80)
Philip II (1180–1223)
Louis IX (1223–70)
Philip III (1270–85)
Philip IV (1285–1314)
Louis X (1314–16)
John I (1316)
Philip V (1317–22)
Charles IV (1322–8)
Valois
Philip VI (1328–50)
John II (1350–64)
Charles V (1364–80)
Charles VI (1380–1422)
Charles VII (1422–61)
Louis XI (1461–83)
Charles VIII (1483–98)
Viking raids, 800 E, 820 E, 821 E, 834 E, 840 E, 843 E, 844 C, 845 E, 850 E, 851 E, 853 E, 854 E, 856 C, 862 E, 863 E, 866 E, 872 E, 877 C, 878 E, 879 D, 881 C, 882 D, 884 C, 885 C, D, 888 B, 891 D, 892 E, 898 E, 902 E, 910 E, 911 E, 921 E, 923 E, 924 E, 925 E, 937 E
Saracen raids, 838 E, 888 E, 972 C, 975 E, 1021 E
Magyar raids, 917 E, 924 E, 926 E, 935 E, 937 E, 951 E
German invasions, 940 E, 1124 C
extent of, 979 E
reform of church, 1074 H
under interdict, 1142 E, 1200 A, C
annexes Toulouse, 1224 A, 1271 C; Provence, 1246 A; Franche Compté, 1295 E; Metz and Toul, 1297 E; Lyons, 1310 E; Dauphiné, 1349 C
first estates-general, 1302 B, 1308 B, 1314 F
prosecution of Templars, 1307 D, 1308 B, C, 1314 A
expulsion of Lombards, 1311 G
Movement of the Leagues, 1314 D, 1315 B, 1318 A
Hundred Years War
crown claimed by Edward III, 1337 B, D, 1340 A, 1344 E
English campaigns in, 1345 D, 1346 C, D, 1347 B, C, 1355 D, 1356 B, C, 1359 D, 1360 A, B; *and see* Brittany
Black Death in, 1347 G, 1348 G
estates-general, 1355 D, 1356 D, 1357 F, 1358 A
Jacquerie, 1358 B
treaties of peace, 1359 B, 1360 A, B
routiers, 1362 B, 1365 C
renewal of war, 1368 D, 1369 B, C, 1370 C, D 1372 B–D, 1373 C, D, 1374 A, 1375 B
attacks on England, 1377 C, 1380 B, C
English raids, 1378 B, 1380 C, 1381 A
truces, 1381 A, 1396 A
protests against taxation, 1380 D, 1382 A, 1383 A
clergy and Great Schism, 1395 A, 1398 B, 1400 A, 1403 A, B, 1408 B
war of Burgundy and Armagnacs, 1405 C, D, 1407 D, 1410 D, 1411 D, 1412 B, C, 1414 C, 1415 A, 1418 B
estates-general, 1413 A
renewal of war by Henry V, 1414 B, 1415 A–C, 1416 A, C; *and see* Normandy
Treaty of Troyes, 1420 B, 1422 D
English conquests, 1422 B, 1423 C, 1424 C, 1425 C, 1427 C, 1428 D, 1437 A, 1440 C
Joan of Arc's campaign, 1429 A, B
negotiations, 1435 C, 1439 C, 1444 B
expulsion of English, 1435 D, 1436 B, 1439 C, 1441 C, 1442 C, 1443 C, D, 1448 A, 1449 D, 1450 B, C, 1451 B, C, 1452 D, 1453 B–D
Pragmatic Sanction, 1438 C
Praguerie, 1440 A
dispute with Hanse, 1451 G
War of the Public Weal, 1465 C, D
estates-generals, 1468 B, 1484 A
English invasion, 1475 C
church council, 1478 C
La Guerre Folle, 1485 A, C
Brittany annexed, 1491 D

* Not Carolingians.

France—*contd.*
coinage reformed, 1266 G, 1340 G; debased, 1295 G
drama. *See* Drama
government:
offices suppressed, 1127 E, 1185 E
ênqueteurs, 1247 F
ordinance for baillis, 1254 F
Chambre des comptes, 1309 F, 1320 F, 1454 F
reforms conceded, 1303 A, 1357 F, 1413 B
poste, 1464 G
master of mines, 1471 G
history. *See* Historians
Jews persecuted, 1196 K; expelled, 1306 F
language, 842 K
law:
Peace of God, 1010 F
customals, 1200 F, 1250 F, 1260 F, 1270 F, 1280 F, 1390 F
parlement, 1239 F; *and see* Paris
private war banned, 1258 F
duel abolished, 1259 F
regional parlement, 1443 F
Orders: Star, 1352 A; St. Michael, 1469 C
poetry, early:
La vie de Sainte Eulalie, 885 K
On the Captivity of Boethius, 1000 K
La Vie de Saint Alexis, 1040 K
Congé (Jean Bodel), 1202 K
Thibaud of Navarre, 1253 K
Jakemon Saquet, 1280 K
See also Chansons de gestes; Poets
sovereignty of: John of Paris, 1302 F; Pierre Dubois, 1306 F
taxation:
tributum Normannicum, 877 B
Saladin tithes, 1188 A
gabelle, 1286 G, 1341 F
by estates-general, 1314 F
without consent, 1440 A
towns, laws of, 1047 G, 1070 G; confirmed by king, 1181 G; controlled by king, 1262 F
Francesca, Piero della, It. painter (*c.* 1415–92), 1439 J, 1445 J, 1450 J, 1451 J, 1452 J, 1454 J, 1470 J, 1472 J
Francesco de Paolo, St., It. religious reformer (1416–1507), 1416 L, 1436 H
Franche Compté. *See* Burgundy
Francia, French province, 880 A
Francis II, Duke of Brittany, 1465 C, 1468 C, 1475 C, 1486 A, 1488 C
Francis of Assisi, St., It. religious reformer (1181?–1226), 1181 L, 1208 H, 1210 H, 1217 H, 1219 H, 1220 H, 1224 H, 1226 L; as poet, 1225 K; biography of, 1255 K; *Fiore*, 1266 K; *Fioretti*, 1330 K
Francis (Fouquet?), Master, F. miniaturist, 1473 J
Francis Phoebus, Count of Foix, King of Navarre, 1479 A, 1483 A
Franciscans. *See* Friars Minor
Franco of Liège, Belgian mathematician, 1083 G
Franconia, W. Germany, 876 C; Duchy of, 908 E, 939 C, *and see* Conrad I
Frankfurt, W. Germany, 1142 B, 1220 A, 1252 C
Frankfurt on Oder, E. Germany, 1250 E
Franks:
annals of (Einhard), 829 K
Dukes of. *See* Hugh the Great; Hugh (Capet)
empire of. *See* Empire (Carolingian dynasty)
history of (Aimon), 1010 K
Fraternities:
French, first, 1023 H; of lawyers, 1342 F; for religious plays, 1398 K
Muslim: Qādirite, 1166 H; Shādhilite, 1258 H
Frauendienst (Ulrich von Lichtenstein), 1255 K
Frauenlob (Henry of Mainz), G. mastersinger, 1311 J
Fraxinetum. *See* Garde-Freinet
Frechulph, Bishop of Lisieux, F. chronicler, 852 K
Frederick I (Barbarossa) Hohenstaufen, Holy Roman Emperor (1155–90), 1121 L
King of the Romans, 1152 A, B, E
subjects Burgundy, 1153 E, 1156 B, 1157 D, 1178 C
first Italian expedition, 1154 D, 1155 A, B
subjects Poland, 1157 E, 1159 C
relations with Bohemia, 1158 A, 1182 E
peace constitution of, 1158 D
second Italian expedition, 1158 C, H, 1159 C, 1160 A, 1161 C, 1162 A
relations with Popes, 1153 B, 1157 D, 1160 A, 1162 B, 1176 D, 1184 D, H, 1185 A, 1186 B–D, 1189 B
supports anti-popes, 1164 B, 1165 B, 1166 C, 1168 C
third Italian expedition, 1163 D
fourth, 1166 E, 1167 B, C
promotion of son, Henry, 1169 C, 1184 D
fifth expedition, 1174 D, 1175 B, 1176 B, 1177 C
peace with Lombard League, 1183 B
proceeds against Henry the Lion, 1178 D, 1179 B, 1180 A–C, 1181 E
relations with Denmark, 1182 B
alliance with France, 1187 E
on crusade, 1188 A, 1189 B, 1190 A, B
life of (Otto of Freising), 1158 K; *and see* Friedrichs
Frederick II ('Stupor Mundi') Hohenstaufen, Holy Roman Emperor (1220–50), 1194 L, 1220 D, 1235 C, 1250 D
King of the Romans, 1196 D, 1211 C, 1212 C, D, 1214 C, 1215 C
King of Sicily, 1198 B, D, 1224 H, 1231 F, G, 1232 F, 1246 E
cession to Papacy, 1213 C
treaty with Denmark, 1214 B
concessions in Germany, 1214 E, 1218 B, 1220 B, 1232 E, 1240 D
King of Jerusalem, 1225 D, 1232 B, 1233 B
suppresses German towns, 1226 D, 1231 D
Lombard League against, 1226 A
dispute with Pope, 1227 C, 1228 B, 1229 B, 1230 C
on Crusade, 1228 B, 1229 A
revolt of son, Henry, 1235 C
plans for Empire, 1236 C
promotion of sons, 1237 A, 1238 E
campaigns in Italy, 1237 D, 1238 C, D, 1239 D, 1240 A, C, 1241 B, 1247 B, 1248 A, 1249 B
breach with Papacy, 1239 A, 1241 B, D, 1244 A, 1245 C, 1248 E
revolt in Germany, 1240 A, 1241 C, 1246 B
as author on Falconry, 1250 K
Athens ruled for, 1312 E
pretender as, 1285 C
Frederick III Habsburg, Holy Roman Emperor (1452–93), 1415 L, 1452 A, 1470 J
Duke of Styria, elected King of the Romans, 1440 A
war with Swiss, 1442 B, 1444 C, 1446 B
German peace-plans, 1441 F, 1467 F, 1471 B, F, 1475 F, 1487 C
concordat with Pope, 1448 A
titles granted by, 1451 D, 1452 B, 1453 A
plan to depose, 1461 A
war with brother, 1461 D, 1463 D
treaty with Hungary, 1463 E
relations with Burgundy, 1473 C, D, 1475 B
expelled from Austria, 1485 B, 1490 B

Frederick, King of Bohemia, 1173 E; Duke, 1182 E
Frederick II of Aragon, King of Sicily, 1291 B, 1295 A, 1297 E, 1299 C, 1300 B, D; King of Trinacria, 1302 C; resumes Sicilian title, 1315 E, 1318 C, 1337 A
Frederick III, King of Sicily (b. 1341), 1355 D; King of Trinacria, 1373 A, 1377 C
Frederick II the Valiant, Duke of Austria, 1242 E, 1246 E
Frederick, Count of Staufen and Duke of Swabia (d. 1105), 1079 E
Frederick Hohenstaufen (II), Duke of Swabia, 1134 A
Freiberg, E. Germany, silver mines, 1136 G
Freiburg im Breisgau, W. Germany, Minster, 1275 J, 1354 J; University, 1457 H
Freising, W. Germany, Bishop of. *See* Otto
Freising, Ruprecht von, G. jurist (*c.* 1272–*c.* 1330), 1328 F
Frescobaldi, Leonardo, It. travel-author (d. 1405), 1385 G, 1390 G
Frescoes:
  Byzantine. *See* Agios Neophytos, Boiana, Lesnovo, Milešovo, Mistra, Nagoričino, Nerez, Sopočani, Staraya Ladoga, Studenitza, Vladimir
  Italian. *See* Assisi, Florence, Mantua, Orvieto, Padua, Prato, Rome (Vatican), Siena, Spoleto, Treviso, Venice
Fréteval, France, 1170 C; battle, 1194 C
Frezzi, Frederigo, Bishop of Foligno, It. poet (*c.* 1350–1416), 1403 K
Friars. *See* Mendicant Orders
Friars Minor:
  founded by St. Francis, 1210 H
  government of, 1217 H, 1220 H, 1223 H, 1232 H, 1239 H
  history of (Salimbene), 1287 K
  missions by, 1253 H, 1318 H
  papal privileges, etc., 1231 H 1245 H, 1274 H
  Spiritual branch, 1245 H, 1279 H, 1318 H, 1323 H
  spread of, 1219 H, 1224 H, 1235 H
  Strict Observance, 1334 H
Friars Preachers:
  founded by St. Dominic, 1216 H
  government of, 1220 H
  missions by, 1253 H, 1318 H
  oriental studies of, 1250 H
  papal privileges, etc., 1231 H, 1274 H, 1475 H
  spread of, 1217 H, 1221 H
Fribourg, Switzerland, 1268 B, 1339 B, 1481 D
Fridugis, Abbot of St. Martin's, Tours, 804 J
Friedrichs I von der Pfalz (Michael Beheim), 1469 K
'Friends of God', German mystics, 1361 H, 1370 H
Frisia (Holland, W. Germany), 834 E, 885 E, 1252 B; laws of, 803 F
Friuli, Italy, 1418 E; marquess of, *see* Berengar
Froila II, King of Leon, 923 C, 924 E
Froissart, Jean, F. chronicler (1338–*c.* 1410), 1371 K, 1400 K, 1444 K
Frutolf, monk of Bamberg, G. musical theorist, 1103 K
Fu Kung, C. zoologist, 1059 G
Fu-jên ta-Ch'üan liang-fang (Ch'ên Tzŭ-ming), 1237 G
Fuero real (Alfonso X), 1254 F
Fugger, Jacob, G. financier, 1469 L
Fugger, Jacob, G. financier (1459–1525), 1459 L
Fujiwara family, Regents of Japan, 833 E, 857 F, 930 E, 1068 F, 1189 E; chronicle of, 1095 K
Fujiwara Kanezane, Ja. courtier and diarist (1130–1200), 1200 K
Fujiwara Nagatsune, Ja. courtier and writer on gardens (1169–1206), 1206 G
Fujiwara Teika (*alias* Sadaie), Ja. poet and anthologist, 1205 K
Fulbert, Bishop of Chartres, 1028 H, L
Fulcher of Chartres, F. chronicler, 1127 K
Fulda, W. Germany, 822 J; abbey, 819 J; abbot of, *see* Maurus, Rabanus; monk of, *see* Gottschalk
Fulk I the Red, Count of Anjou, 888 E, 925 E, 938 E
Fulk II, the Good, Count of Anjou, 938 E, 958 E
Fulk III Nerra, Count of Anjou, 987 C, 992 B, 994 E, 1007 G, 1016 C, 1040 B
Fulk IV Rechin, Count of Anjou, 1060 D, 1061 A, 1067 B, 1068 E, 1073 E, 1092 E, 1109 B
Fulk V le Jeune, Count of Anjou (b. 1092), 1109 B, 1129 B; King of Jerusalem, 1131 C, 1137 C, 1143 D
Fulk, Archbishop of Reims, 893 A, 900 E
Fulling-mills, in Dauphiné, 1050 G
Furnes, Belgium, battle, 1297 C
Fürstenwalde, E. Germany, Treaty of, 1373 C
Fusūl fī al-Tibb, Kitāb al- (Moses ben Maimon), 1204 G
Fūsus al-Hikam (ibn-'Arabī), 1240 K
Futūh al-Buldān (al-Balādhurī), 892 K
Futūh Misr w-al-Maghrib (al-Hakam), 871 K
Futuh-us-Salatin (Isāmy), 1359 K
Fūtūhāt al-Makkiyah, al- (ibn-'Arabī), 1240 K
Futura aeris intempericie, De (William Merlee), 1340 G

G

Gaddesden, John of, E. physician (*c.* 1280–1361), 1315 G
Gaddi, Taddeo, It. painter, 1332 J, 1334 J, 1353 J, 1366 L
Gaetani, Loffred, great-nephew of Boniface VIII, 1300 A
Gaetani, Peter, nephew of Boniface VIII, 1298 C
Gagik I, King of Armenia, 989 E, 1020 E
Galen, Gk. physician (d. 200 B.C.), translated into Arabic, 800 G, 873 G; into Latin, 1193 G; commentary on, 1414 G
Galich, Russia, prince of. *See* Juri
Galicia, Spain, 1387 B; King of, 1112 E; poetry, 1284 K, 1350 K
Galicia (Halich), Poland and Russia:
  prince established by Poles, 1205 E
  ravaged by Mongols, 1240 E, 1259 E, 1282 E, 1286 E
  becomes kingdom, 1254 E; *and see* Daniel, Juri II, Lubart
  conquered by Poland, 1339 E, 1349 E
Galilee, Israel, Latin principality, 1101 A, 1266 C
Gallicanus (Hrotswith), 962 K
Gallipoli, Turkey, 1352 A, 1366 C, 1367 E; battle off, 1416 E
Galloway, Scotland, 1160 E, 1308 E
Gama, Vasco da, Port. navigator (1460–1524), 1460 L
Gambacorta, Pietro, ruler of Pisa, 1370 D, 1392 D
Gambia, river, Gambia, 1455 G
Gammelsdorf, W. Germany, battle, 1313 D
Ganapati, King of Kākatīya, 1262 E
Gand, Henri de, Belgian theologian, 1293 A
Gangā Devi, Indian poetess, 1370 K
Gangaikonda-Cholapurum, India, Chola capital, 1035 E
Ganitasāra (Śrīdhara), 1020 G
Ganitasārasamgraha (Mahāvīri), 830 G
Ganivet, Jean, F. physician and astrologer, 1431 G

Gao, Mali, 1337 E; Negro Empire of, 1468 E
Garcia I, King of Oviedo (Leon), 910 D, 914 E
Garcia Ximinez, (first) King of Navarre, 857 E, 880 E
Garcia I, King of Navarre, 926 E, 937 E, 960 E, 970 E
Garcia II, King of Navarre, 994 E, 1000 E
Garcia III, King of Navarre, 1035 E, 1054 C
Garcia IV Ramirez, King of Navarre, 1134 C, 1150 D
Gardar, Greenland, Cathedral, 1124 J
Garde-Freinet (Fraxinetum), France, Saracen base, 888 E, 972 C, 975 E
Gardens, Japanese, 1351 J; treatise on, 1206 G
Garigliano, river, Italy, 915 E; battle, 1139 C
Gargar, Turkey, battle, 1123 B
Gariopontus of Salerno, It. physician, 1050 G
Garlande family, F. officials, 1127 E
Garnhi, Armenia, Russia, battle, 1225 E
Garnier de Point-Sainte-Maxence, F. poet, 1174 K
Garter, (English) Order of the, 1348 E
Gascony, France, Duchy of, 1039 E
  held by English Kings, 1204 B, 1259 D, 1329 B
  invaded by Louis VIII, 1224 B, 1225 A
  revolts against Simon de Montfort, 1250 E, 1251 B
  ruled by Edward (I), 1254 D
  first confiscation, 1294 A, 1303 B
  second confiscation, 1324 C, 1327 A
  third confiscation, 1337 B
  revolts against Black Prince, 1368 D, 1369 A
  English lieutenant defeated, 1372 B
  French invasion fails, 1406 D
  conquered by France, 1442 C, 1443 C, 1451 B, C, 1452 D, 1453 D
Gaston Phoebus, Count of Foix, F. writer on the chase (1331–91), 1391 K, 1410 K
Gattamelata (Donatello), 1448 J
Gaucher of Reims, F. mason, 1210 J
Gautier de Metz, F. poet, 1245 G
Gaveston, Piers, Earl of Cornwall, 1307 C, 1308 C, 1309 C, 1311 C, 1312 B
Gavre, Belgium, battle, 1453 C
Gawain and the Green Knight, 1375 K
Gayrard, Raymond, F. mason (d. 1118), 1098 J
Gaza, Egypt/Israel, battle, 1239 D
Gazzaio, Filippo della, It. didactic writer (1339–1422), 1422 K
Gdansk (Danzig), Poland, 1210 E, 1308 D, 1388 G
Gedun-dub, Dalai Lāma of Tibet, 1473 H
Gedymin, Grand Prince of Lithuania, 1315 E, 1320 E, 1339 E, 1341 E
Geiler von Kaiserberg, Johann, G. preacher (1445–1510), 1445 L
Gelasius II (John of Gaeta), Pope, 1118 A, B, 1119 A
Gelnhausen, W. Germany, 1180 B, 1186 D
Gelnhausen, Conrad of, G. theologian (d. 1390), 1380 H
Gemma Purpurea, La (Guido Fava), 1229 K
Genealogies, Japanese, 815 K
Generalities of Medicine (ibn-Rushd), 1160 G
Genesis and Exodus, 1250 K
Geneva, Switzerland, Cathedral, 1225 J; Génevois, 1401 C
Genji Monagatari or *The Tale of Genji* (Murasaki Shikibu), 1010 K
Genkū (Hōnen Shōnin), Ja. Buddhist saint (1133–1212), 1175 H, 1262 H
Genoa, Italy, 934 E
  western conquests by, 1016 B, 1034 E, 1087 E, 1133 E
  relations with Frederick I, 1159 C, 1162 A
  conquers Rhodes, 1248 E
  treaty with Greeks, 1261 A
  war with Venice, 1263 E, 1264 E
  occupies Kaffa, 1266 E, 1475 E
  war with Angevins, etc., 1273 E, 1274 D, 1284 B, C, 1287 B
  war with Sicily, 1297 E, 1299 C, 1300 B, 1318 C
  war with Venice, 1294 E, 1297 E, 1298 C, 1299 B
  occupies Chios, 1304 E, 1329 E, 1346 E
  first Doge, 1339 C, 1356 D, 1363 E
  Black Death in, 1347 G
  war with Venice, 1352 A, 1353 C, 1354 D, 1355 B
  under Milan, 1353 C, 1356 D
  takes Famagosta, 1373 E
  war (of Chioggia) with Venice, 1376 E, 1378 D, 1379 C, 1380 B, 1381 C
  Peace of, 1392 A
  under France, 1396 D, 1409 C
  alliance with France, 1416 C
  sells Leghorn, 1421 B
  war with Aragon, history of, 1460 K
  under Milan, 1421 D, 1431 B, C, 1435 C, D
  under France, 1458 B
  under Milan, 1463 D
  Bank, St. George's, 1407 G
  chronicle of (Jacobus de Voragine), 1298 K
  debt, 'national', of, 1274 G
Genshin, Ja. Buddhist monk and author (942–1017), 1017 H
Gentile da Fabriano, It. painter, 1423 J, 1425 J, 1427 L
Geoffrey I, Count of Anjou, 958 E, 987 C
Geoffrey II Martel, Count of Anjou (b. 1006; 1040–60), 1038 E, 1039 A, 1040 B, 1044 C, 1060 D; war with Normandy, 1048 E, 1054 A, 1058 C
Geoffrey III the Bearded, Count of Anjou (d. 1096), 1060 D, 1061 A, 1067 B
Geoffrey IV Plantagenet, Count of Anjou (1129–51), 1113 L, 1128 B, 1129 B, 1151 C; conquers Normandy, 1137 E, 1144 B, 1148 E
Geoffrey of Anjou, Count of Brittany, 1156 E, 1158 E
Geoffrey of Monmouth, Welsh chronicler (*c.* 1100–54), 1137 K, 1155 K, 1200 K
Geoffroi de Beaulieu, F. biographer, 1274 K
Geographers:
  Arab. *See* Hauqal; Istakhrī; Maqdisī; Mas'udi; Ya'qūbi; Yāqūt; Zaid
  Armenian. *See* Hayton
  Chinese, anon., 1489 G. *See also* Fan Ch'êng-ta; Hsü Ching
  Egyptian. *See* Maqrīzī
  French. *See* Lambert of St. Omer
  German. *See* Adam of Bremen; Henry of Mainz
  Irish. *See* Dicuil
  Italian. *See* Guido
  Persian. *See* Bīrunī; Faqīh; Khurdādhbih; Qazwini; Rustah; Sūfī
  Spanish. *See* Orosius
  Spanish Muslim. *See* Andalusi; Edrisi; Māzinī; Zarqāli
  Syrian. *See* Abū-l-Fidā; 'Umari
  See also Encyclopedias, Pilgrim-authors, Travellers
Geographica (Guido), 1119 G
Geology and mineralogy:
  Flowers of Knowledge of Precious Stones (al-Tīfashī), 1154 G
  Lapidario of Alfonso the Wise, 1279 G
  La Composizione del Mondo, 1282 G
Geometry, treatises on, 997 G, 1349 G
George of Poděbrady, King of Bohemia (b. 1420; 1458–71), 1458 A, 1471 A
  Hussite leader, 1444 E, 1448 E
  governor of Bohemia, 1451 D, 1452 B, 1453 D
  elected King of the Romans, 1461 A

relieves Frederick III, 1461 D
'Crusade' against, 1465 D, 1466 D, 1469 B
George I Terter, Tsar of Bulgaria, 1280 E
George II, King of Georgia (d. 1112), 1089 E
George III, King of Georgia, 1155 E, 1184 E
George IV, King of Georgia, 1212 E, 1221 A, 1223 E
George V, King of Georgia (1318–46), 1318 E
George, Duke of Clarence, 1449 L, 1469 C, 1478 A
George of Trebizond, Gk. scholar, 1396 L, 1484 L
George Castriota. *See* Skanderberg
Georgia, Russia:
united as kingdom, 1008 E
subjected by Greeks, 1021 E
independence restored. *See*
David III (1089–1125)
Dmetrius I (1125–55)
David IV (1155)
George III (1155–84)
Thamar (Queen; 1184–1212)
George IV (1212–23)
Rusadan (Queen; 1223–47)
conquered by Mongols, 1236 E, 1243 B, 1258 E
reunited by George V, 1318 E
Black Death in, 1346 G
invaded by Timur, 1386 E
reunited by Alexander I, 1442 E
partitioned, 1491 E
capital of. *See* Tiflis
epic: *Man in the Panther's Skin* (Rustaveli), 1200 K
Gerald of Wales (Giraldus Cambrensis; G. de Barri), Welsh chronicler (1146?–1223), 1185 K, 1188 K
Gerard de Borgo San Donnino, It. religious writer, 1254 H
Gerard of Cremona, It. translator, 1114 L, 1175 G, 1187 G
Gerberoy, France, battle, 1079 A
Gerbert of Aurillac. *See* Silvester II
Gerbert de Montreuil, F. poet, 1228 K
Gerhard, Count of Holstein, 1332 C, 1340 E
Gerhard of Cologne, G. mason, 1248 J, 1275 J
Germanicea (Mar'ash), Turkey, battle, 953 E
Germany:
Kingdom of, 843 C; divided 876 C, 882 A
Kings of (*alias*, eventually, Kings of the Romans):
Carolingian dynasty. *See*
Louis the German (843–76)
Charles the Fat (882–8)
Arnulf (888–99)
Louis the Child (899–911)
Conrad I (of Franconia; 911–18)
Saxon dynasty. *See*
Henry I (919–36)
Otto I (936–73)
Otto II (973–83)
Otto III (983–1002)
[Henry the Wrangler, 984]*,
Henry II (of Bavaria; 1002–24)
Salian dynasty. *See*
Conrad II (1024–39)
Henry III (1039–56)
Henry IV (1056–1105)
[Rudolf of Swabia, 1077–80]*
[Hermann of Salm, 1081]*
[Conrad, 1087–1101]†
Henry V (1105–25)
Lothar II (of Saxony; 1125–37)
Hohenstaufen dynasty. *See*
Conrad III (1127; 1138–52)
Frederick I (1152–90)
Henry VI (1190–7)
Philip (1198–1208)
[Otto IV, 1198–1215]*
Frederick II (1196; 1212–50)
[Henry, 1220–35]†
[Henry Raspe, 1246–7]*
Conrad IV (1250–4)
William of Holland (1247–56)
Richard, Earl of Cornwall (1257–72)
Alfonso, X of Castile (1257–75)
Rudolf I (1273–91)
Adolf of Nassau (1292–8)
Albert I (1298–1308)
Henry VII (1308–13)
Lewis IV (1314–47)
[Habsburg, Frederick, 1314–25]*
Charles IV (1346–78)
Wenceslas IV (1378–1400)
Rupert (1400–10)
Sigismund (1410–37)
[Jošt, 1410–11]*
Albert II (1438–9)
Frederick III (1440–93)
Maximilian (1486–1519)
Magyar raids, 900 E, 906 E, 908 E, 909 E, 910 E, 917 E, 924 E, 937 J, 954 E; defeated, 933 A, 938 E, 955 C
invasion of Odo of Blois, 1037 D
'Day of Indulgence', 1043 D
imperial charter to town, 1074 G
bishops oppose Pope, 1075 A, 1076 A
revolt against Henry IV, 1076 D, 1077 A
peace constitution, 1158 D
persecution of Jews, 1196 K
civil war, 1198 C, 1206 C, 1207 A, 1208 B, D
revolt against Otto IV, 1210 D, 1211 A, C, 1215 C
privilege to prelates, 1220 B
constitution for princes, 1231 B, 1232 E
ban on town corporations, 1231 D
revolt against Frederick II, 1240 A, 1241 C, 1246 B
diet with towns, 1255 F
Rhineland land-peace, 1269 B
civil war, 1314 D, 1322 C, 1325 A
Declaration of Rense, 1338 C
revolt against Lewis IV, 1346 C, 1347 D
Golden Bull of Charles IV, 1356 F
public peace, 1371 F, 1383 F, 1389 B
wars of towns and nobles, 1384 C, 1388 C, D, 1389 B
revolts against kings, 1400 C, 1405 C
Hussite raids, 1427 B, 1429 D
peasant revolts, 1432 G
public peace, 1441 F, 1467 F, 1486 A; court for, 1471 F, 1475 F
tax to oppose Turks, 1471 F
history. *See* Historians
Hospitallers. *See* Teutonic Knights
inquisition in, 1231 H, 1233 H, 1234 H
iron-industry, 1230 G
language, 842 K
law codes, 803 F, 1225 F, 1275 F, 1328 F
merchants. *See* Hanse
poetry:
Hildebrandslied, 800 K
Heliand, 820 K
Otfrid, 868 K
Lugwigslied, 881 K

* Claimant to the kingdom in opposition to the established king.

† Son of the reigning king who predeceased his father or was deposed by him.

Germany—*contd.*
poetry—*contd.*
Ekkehard, 937 K
Ava, 1127 K
Ruolandesliet, 1150 K
Das Nibelungenlied, 1200 K
Gottfried von Strassburg, 1210 K
Wolfram von Eschenbach, 1212 K
Gudrun, 1240 K
Frauendienst, 1255 K
Lohengrin, 1290 K
Volksbücher, 1450 K
Michael Beheim, 1466 K, 1469 K
Germigny-des-Prés, France, palace, 806 J
Gernrode, E. Germany, abbey, 961 J
Gerona, Spain, 1285 C; Cathedral, 1312 J, 1416 J
Gerson, Jean Charlier de, F. theologian, 1363 L, 1420 H, 1429 L
Gersonides. *See* Levi ben Gerson
Gerstungen, E. Germany, 1074 A
Gertrude, Queen of Hungary, 1213 C
Gertrude, St., the Great, G. mystic, 1301 H
Gervase of Canterbury, E. chronicler, 1210 K
Gervase of Tilbury, E. naturalist, 1212 G
Gessler, Hermann, governor of Tyrol, 1307 D
Gesta Danorum (Saxo Grammaticus), 1208 K
Gesta Dei per Francos (Guibert), 1111 K
Gesta Francorum, 1100 K
Gesta Frederici imperatoris (Otto of Freising), 1158 K
Gesta Henrici II (Benedict of Peterborough), 1193 K
Gesta Henrici Quinti, 1417 K
Gesta Karoli Magni (Notker Balbulus?), 883 K
Gesta Pontificum Anglorum (William of Malmesbury), 1142 K
Gesta Pontificum Leodiensium (Jean de Hocsem), 1348 K
Gesta regum (Gervase of Canterbury), 1210 K
Gesta Regum Anglorum (William of Malmesbury), 1142 K
Gesta Romanorum, 1472 K
Geste de Liège (Jean d'Outremeuse), 1400 K
Gestis concilii Basiliensis, De (Aeneas Silvius), 1440 K
Gestis Italicorum, De (Albertino Mussato), 1329 K
Géza, Duke and King of Hungary. *See* Stephen I
Géza I, King of Hungary, 1074 E, 1075 E, 1077 B
Géza II, King of Hungary (b. 1130), 1141 A, 1161 B, G
Ghāfiqi, Abu-Ja'far Ahmad ibn-, Sp. M. physician and botanist, 1165 G
Ghana, Negro Empire of, 1077 E, 1240 E
Ghazals (Sādi), 1258 K
Ghazan, Mahmūd, Ilkhan (or Sultan) of Persia (1295–1304), 1295 E, 1299 B, D, 1300 A
Ghāzī Gümüshtigin, Danishmend emir in Anatolia and Syria (1084–1134), 1101 A, C, 1119 B, 1130 A
Ghaznī, Afghanistan, 1030 J, 1114 J
Ghaznavid (Turkish) dynasty of. *See*
Alptigīn (962–76)
Sabuktagīn (976–97)
Ismā'il (997–8)
Mahmūd (998–1030)
Mas'ūd I (1030–40)
lose Persian empire, 1040 A
conquer Jurjan, 1042 E
destroyed by Ghūrids, 1151 E, 1186 E
conquered by Khwārizm-Shahs, 1214 E
Ghazzāli (Algazel), Abū-Hamid al-, Per. Sūfī theologian, 1058 L, 1111 G, H
Ghengiz Khan (Temujin), Khan of the Mongols (1206–27), 1167 L, 1206 B, F, 1227 C, F; conquests of, 1211 E, 1215 E, 1219 E, 1220 A, D, 1221 D, 1222 B, 1224 E; history of, 1260 K
Ghent, Belgium, 1006 C, 1020 C, 1274 G, 1432 J; revolts, etc., in, 1340 A, 1345 B, 1349 A, 1379 E, 1385 D, 1453 C, 1477 B, 1488 A
Ghibelline (Weibling), origin of, 1040 D; Italian party, 1251 C, 1252 A, 1274 D, 1322 A, 1325 D
Ghiberti, Lorenzo, It. sculptor and architect, 1378 L, 1403 J, 1414 J, 1418 J, 1419 J, 1428 J, 1432 J; as writer on art and autobiographer, 1455 J
Ghirlandaio, Domenico, It. painter (1449–94), 1449 L, 1480 J, 1481 J, 1490 J
Ghūr, Afghanistan, 1009 E
Sultans of. *See*
'Alā'-ad-Dīn (1149–61)
Muhammad (1163–1203)
Ghuzz (or Oghuz) Turks, 956 E
Gibraltar, 1309 E, 1333 E, 1349 A, 1462 E
Gift to Observers (ibn-Battūtah), 1354 G
Gilbert, Duke of Lorraine, 938 E, 939 C
Gilbert, St., of Sempringham, E. monastic reformer (b. *c.* 1083), 1131 H, 1188 L
Gilbert de la Porrée, Bishop of Poitiers, F. philosopher, 1148 H, 1154 K
Giles of Corbeil, F. physician, 1222 G
Giles of Rome (Aegidius Colonna), Archbishop of Bourges, It. polemical writer, 1285 F, 1316 L
Gilles le Muisit, Flemish chronicler, 1353 K
Ginevra de' Benci (Leonardo), 1474 J
Giordano Ruffo, It. vetinerary surgeon, 1252 G
Giorgio, Marino, Doge of Venice, 1311 C, 1312 B
Giorgione, It. painter (1478–1510), 1478 L
Giotto di Bondone, It. painter and architect, 1300 J, 1306 J, 1325 J, 1334 J, 1337 L
Giovanni da Firenze, It. short story writer, 1378 K
Gipsies, at Barcelona, 1442 G; *and see* Jalt
Girard d'Amiens, F. poet, 1295 K
Girart de Roussillon (anon.), 1190 K
Giselbert of Autun, F. sculptor, 1119 J
Gisilbert, Duke of Burgundy, 923 C, 938 E, 956 B
Gisors, France, 1119 D, 1180 B, 1188 A, 1193 C; battle, 1198 C; Treaty of, 1113 A
Giustiniani, Bernardo, It. historian, 1408 L, 1481 K, L
Glaber, Raoul, F. chronicler, 1050 K
Glanville, Bartholomew. *See* Bartholomew the Englishman
Glanville, Ranulf, justiciar of England (d. 1190), 1180 F
Glarus, Switzerland, 1352 E
Glasgow, Scotland, University, 1451 H
Glass manufacture, in Syria, 1401 J; at Venice, 1291 G, 1328 G
Glastonbury, England, 1191 K; abbey, 950 J, 1182 J; abbot of, *see* Dunstan
Gleb, Russian prince, 1015 E
Glendower. *See* Glyn Dwr
'Glenmana', Ireland, battle, 999 E
Glossa ordinaria (Walafrid Strabo), 849 H; (Johannes Teutonicus), 1210 H; (Bartholomew of Brescia), 1258 H; (Accursius), 1260 F; (Bernard of Botone), 1263 H; (Johannes Andreae), 1340 H; (Zabarella), 1417 H
Gloucester, England, 877 E, 1216 D; abbey (*now* Cathedral), 1087 J, 1120 J, 1331 J, 1357 J; Earls of, *see* Robert, Clare (Gilbert); Dukes of, *see* Thomas of Woodstock, Humphrey, Richard III
Glycas, Michael, Gk. chronicler, 1150 K
Glyn Dwr, Owain, Welsh leader, 1400 C, 1402 B, 1403 C, D; self-styled Prince of Wales, 1404 B, C, 1405 A–C, 1409 A, 1415 L
Gniezno, Poland, Archbishopric of, 1000 A, 1044 H; capital of Poland, 1038 E, 1076 D; Cathedral, 1080 J

Go-Daigo, Emperor of Japan (b. *c.* 1288, d. 1339), 1331 E, 1333 E, 1336 E, 1354 K
Godefrid, Viking King in Frisia, 885 E
Godescalc, Duke of Obotrites, 1066 B
Godfrey of Bouillon, Defender of the Holy Sepulchre, 1061 L, 1099 C, 1100 B, C; *Roman* about, 1225 K
Godfrey, Duke of Lorraine, 1044 E, 1045 C, 1046 B, 1047 E
Godfrey the Bearded, Duke of Lorraine, 1058 D, 1062 A, 1065 A, 1069 D
Godfric, St., of Finchale, E. hermit, 1170 L
Godwin, Earl of Wessex (d. 1053), 1045 E, 1051 C, 1052 C, 1053 B, 1055 E
Goes, Hugo van der, Flemish painter, 1470 J, 1475 J, 1478 J, 1480 J, 1482 L
Gold Coast, Ghana, 1482 G
Golden Bull of Charles IV, 1356 F
Golden Fleece, (Burgundian) Order of the, 1429 A
Golden Horde. *See* Russia
Golden Legend, The, 1265 K, 1483 K
Göllheim, W. Germany, battle, 1298 C
Gomes, Fernão, Portuguese navigator, 1469 G
Gonzaga, Federico I di, Marquess of Mantua (d. 1484), 1444 C
Gonzaga, Francesco di, ruler of Mantua, 1397 A, 1398 B, 1407 A
Gonzaga, Giovanni Francesco di, ruler of Mantua, 1407 A, 1426 E; Marquess, 1433 C, 1444 C
Gonzalo de Berceo, Sp. poet, 1235 K
Gorboduc, mythical British king, 1137 K
Gordon, Bernard de, physician (d. 1308), 1303 G
Görlitz, W. Germany, 1329 E; Duchy of, 1378 D; *cf.* Lusatia
Gorm the Old, King of Denmark, 934 E, 936 E
Gorodets, Russia, 1452 E
Goslar, W. Germany, 968 G, 1018 H, 1051 H; Pfalz, 1039 J
Gothic architecture. *See* Architecture
Gothland, island, Sweden, 1163 G, 1198 G, 1438 E
Goths, History of the (Leonardo Bruni), 1444 K
Go-Toba, retired Japanese Emperor, 1219 E
Gottorm, King of Norway, 1204 A, C
Gottfreid von Strassburg, G. poet, 1210 K
Göttrik, King of Denmark, Norway and Sweden, 808 E, 810 E
Gottschalk, monk of Fulda, G. heretical theologian, 849 H, 851 H, 869 L
Goulet, Le, France, Treaty of, 1200 B
Government and politics, writings on:
  Hincmar, *De divortio Lotharii*, 860 F
  al-Fārābī, *The Model City*, 950 F
  al-Māwardi, *Book of the Principles of Government*, 1058 F
  Nizām-al-Mulk, *Siyāsat-nāmah*, 1092 F
  John of Salisbury, *Policraticus*, 1159 F
  Richard fitz Nigel, *Dialogus de Scaccario*, 1179 F
  King's Mirror (Norwegian), 1247 F
  St. Thomas Aquinas, *De regimine principum*, 1274 F
  Giles of Rome, *De regimine principum*, 1285 F
  John of Paris, *De potestate regia et papali*, 1302 F
  Pierre Dubois, *De recuperatione terrae sanctae*, 1306 F
  Dante, *De monarchia*, 1312 F
  Candeśvara, *Jewel-mine of Politics*, 1314 F
  Marsilio of Padua, *Defensor Pacis*, 1324 F, 1327 H
  al-Jamā'a, *Tahrir al-ahkām*, 1333 F
  Lupold of Bebenburg, *Tractatus de jure regni et imperii*, 1340 F
  Richard FitzRalph, *De Pauperie Salvatoris*, 1360 F
  Philippe de Mézières, *Le songe du vergier*, 1376 F
  John Wycliffe, *De civili dominio*, 1376 F
  Salutati, *De tyranno*, 1400 F
  Thomas Hoccleve, *De Regimine Principum*, 1411 K
  Christine de Pisan, *Le Livre de Paix*, 1412 K
  John Fortescue, *De Natura Legis Naturae*, 1463 F; *The Governance of England*, 1476 F
  Matteo Palmieri, *Della vita civile*, 1475 F
  See also Encyclopedias
Governolo, Italy, battle, 1397 C
Gower, John, E. poet, 1383 K, 1390 K, 1408 L
Gozzo of Orvieto, It. jurisconsult, 1294 F, G
Gradenigo, Bartolomeo, Doge of Venice, 1339 D, 1342 D
Gradenigo, Giovanni, Doge of Venice, 1355 B, 1356 C
Gradenigo, Pietro, Doge of Venice (b. 1251), 1289 D, 1311 C
Gradibus Humilitatis, De (St. Bernard), 1153 K
Grail, The. *See* Holy Grail
Graindor de Douay, F. poet (*fl. c.* 1180), 1180 K, 1225 K
Graisivaudan, France, 1040 G
Grammarians:
  Arab. *See* Hajib
  English. *See* Basing, John; John of Garland
  French. *See* Alexander de Villedieu
  Greek. *See* Chrysoloras, Manuel; Theodore of Gaza
  Irish. *See* Sedulius Scottus
  Italian. *See* Balbi, Giovanni; Latini, Brunetto; Perotti, Niccolò
  Jewish. *See* Qimhī, David
  Persian. *See* Farrā'; Kisā'i
  Syrian Jew. *See* Bar Hebraeus
  See also Philologists
Gran, Hungary, Archbishopric of, 1000 C
Granada, Spain, 1090 D, 1229 C
  Nasrid dynasty. *See*
    Muhammad I (1230–73)
    Muhammad II (1273–1302)
    Muhammad III (1302–8)
    Nasr (1308–14)
    Ismā'il I (1314–25)
    Muhammad IV (1325–33)
    Yūsuf I (1333–54)
    Muhammad V (1354–9)
    Ismā'il II (1359–60)
    Muhammad VI (1360–2)
    Muhammad V (1362–92)
    Yūsuf II (1392–6)
    Muhammad VII (1396–1408)
    Yūsuf III (1408–17)
    Muhammad VIII (1417–45)
    Muhammad IX (1427–9)
    Yūsuf IV (1431–2)
    Muhammad X (1445, 1446–54)
    Sa'd (1445–6, 1454–62)
    'Abū-al-Hasan (1462–82, 1483–5)
    Muhammad XI (1482–3, 1489–92)
    Muhammad XII (1485–9)
  civil war and Spanish conquest, 1482 E, 1483 B, 1485 E, 1489 C, D, 1491 D
  Alhambra Palace, 1273 J, 1377 J
  History (ibn-al-Khatīb), 1374 K
Grand Chronique (George Châtelain), 1474 K
Grand Company. *See* Greece
Grand Coutumier de France (Jacques d'Ableiges), 1390 F; *de Normandie*, 1250 F
Grand Testament, Le (François Villon), 1461 K
Grande, Rio, Port. Guinea, 1446 G
Grande y general historia (Alfonso the Wise), 1284 K
Grandes Chroniques de France (illum. ms.), 1458 J; (Jean Chartier), 1461 K

Grandmont, France, order of, 1074 H
Grandson, Switzerland, battle, 1476 A
Gratian of Bologna, It. canonist, 1139 H
Graus, Spain, 1065 B
Gravesend, England, 1380 C
Gravina, Italy, Concordat of, 1192 B
Gravina, John of, Prince of Achaea, 1326 E
Gravity, theories of, 1121 G, 1359 G
Great Book of the Classes, The (al-Wāqidi), 823 K
Great Laura, Greek monastery, 961 H
Great Schism. *See* Papacy
Gréban, Arnoul, F. dramatist (1420–71?), 1454 K
Greece, 1064 E, 1157 E
  conquered by Latins, 1204 E
  as 'Romania', *Assizes of*, 1322 F; *and see* Achaea, Archipelago, Athens, Corinth, Morea, Salonika
  Grand Company in, 1302 C, 1303 E, 1304 E, 1305 B, 1310 E; *and see* Athens
Greek Anthology, The, 950 K
Greek Church:
  Iconoclastic dispute, 815 H, 843 H
  breach with Rome, 858 H, 863 H, 867 H, 880 H
  mission to Russia, 874 H
  new monasteries forbidden, 964 H
  final breach with Rome, 1054 H
  debate with Roman church, 1098 H
  union with Pope, 1274 C, H, 1281 B, 1282 D
  embassies to Pope, 1339 H, 1369 D
  'Palamist' dispute, 1341 H, 1351 H
  union with Pope, 1438 A, 1439 C, K
  authority in Russia ends, 1461 H
Greek Empire:
  Empress. *See* Irene
  Emperors. *See*
    Nicephorus I (802–11)
    Michael I (811–13)
    Leo V (813–20)
    Amorian dynasty
      Michael II (820–9)
      Theophilus (829–42)
      Michael III (842–67)
    Macedonian dynasty
      Basil I (867–86)
      Leo VI (886–912)
      Alexander (912–13)
      Constantine VII (913–59)
      Romanus I (920–44)*
      Romanus II (959–63)
      Nicephorus II (963–9)*
      John I (969–76)*
      Basil II (976–1025)
      Constantine VIII (976–1028)
      Romanus III (1028–34)*
      Michael IV (1034–41)*
      Michael V (1041–2)*
      Zoe (1042)
      Theodora (1042, 1055–6)
      Constantine IX (1042–55)*
      Michael VI (1056–7)*
    Comnenus dynasty
      Isaac I (1057–9)
      Constantine X (1059–67)*
      Eudocia (1067–8)*
      Romanus IV (1068–71)*
      Michael VII (1071–8)*
      Nicephorus III (1078–81)*
      Alexius I (1081–1118)
      John II (1118–43)
      Manuel I (1143–80)
      Alexius II (1180–2)
      Andronicus I (1182–5)
    Angelus dynasty
      Isaac II (1185–95, 1203)
      Alexius III (1195–1203)
      Alexius IV (1203–4)
      * * *
      Nicholas (1204)
      Alexius V (1204)
      Constantine XI (1204–8?)
      Theodore I (1208–22)
      John III (1222–54)
      Theodore II (1254–8)
      John IV (1258–61)
    Palaeologus dynasty
      Michael VIII (1258–82)
      Andronicus II (1282–1328)
      Andronicus III (1325–41)
      John V (1341–91)
      John VI (1341–54)*
      Manuel II (1391–1425)
      John VII (1425–48)
      Constantine XI (1448–53)
  war with Caliph, 804 E, 806 E, 833 C, 838 B
  attacked by Slavs, 805 E
  rule over Venice, 807 E, 810 C, 812 B
  war with Bulgars, 809 E, 811 C, 813 B, 814 B
  claimed by Thomas the Slav, 825 E
  loses Sicily, 827 B, 843 E, 859 E, 902 C
  loses Crete, 827 E
  attacked by Bulgars, 831 E
  rule in south Italy, 839 E
  takes Damietta, 853 B
  victories over Arabs, 856 E, 863 C
  attacked by Russians, 865 E, 907 E
  regains Balkans, 868 E
  rule in south Italy, 871 A, 875 C, 880 E, 891 E, 915 E
  war with Bulgars, 895 E, 896 E, 913 C, 917 C, 923 E, 924 E, 927 B
  attacked by Saracens, 904 C, 912 B
  treaties with Russians, 911 E, 945 E, 967 E
  Mesopotamian campaigns, 934 E, 941 E, 953 E, 957 B, 958 E, 962 D, 965 E, 966 E, 969 D, 972 D, 973 C, 974 E, 975 B
  attacked by Magyars, 959 E
  recovers Crete, 961 A; and Cyprus, 965 C
  Sicilian expedition, 965 E
  German embassies to, 968 E, K, 972 B
  attacked by Russians, 970 E, 971 B, C
  annexes Bulgaria, 972 E
  Bulgarian revolt, 976 A, 986 C
  revolt of Bardas Sclerus, 976 B, 978 B, 979 A
  revolt of Bardas Phocas, 987 C, 988 C, 989 B, D
  treaty with Egypt, 987 E
  alliance with Kiev, 988 C, 989 E
  Varangian guard formed, 988 C
  conquest of Bulgaria, 991 E, 995 E, 997 E, 1014 C, 1019 E
  treaties with Venice, 992 E, 998 E
  Syrian campaigns, 994 C, 995 B, 999 D
  controls Georgia, 1000 A, 1021 E
  occupies Dobrudja, 1000 E
  defends presence in Italy, 982 C, 1018 D, 1021 D, 1022 A, 1026 E
  loses Aleppo, 1023 E
  attacked by Pechenegs, 1033 E, 1036 E, 1048 E, 1064 E, 1071 E, 1087 E, 1090 B
  intervenes in Sicily, 1039 E
  expelled from Italy, 1040 E, 1041 B, 1046 B, 1071 B
  Serbian revolt, 1041 E
  revolt of George Maniaces, 1043 A

* *Not* member of the dynasty.

annexes Ani, 1045 E
attacked by Seljuqs, 1045 E, 1047 E, 1048 E, 1054 E, 1057 E, 1059 E
loses Armenia to Seljuqs, 1064 E, 1067 E, 1071 C, D, 1073 E, 1077 E, 1081 B, 1085 E
loses Belgrade, 1071 E
invaded by Guiscard, 1081 D, 1082 A, 1083 E, 1085 C
treaty with Venice, 1082 E
repels Cumans, 1095 E
First Crusade in, 1095 E, 1096 C, 1097 A–C
invaded by Bohemond, 1107 D, 1108 C
feudalism in, 1118 F, 1180 F
exterminates Pechenegs, 1122 E
Georgia independent of, 1125 E
Hungarian invasion, 1127 E
conquers Lesser Armenia, 1137 C
subjects Antioch, 1137 C, 1138 B, 1143 B, 1158 D, 1159 B
Syrian campaigns, 1138 B, 1142 C
Armenian revolt, 1143 B, 1156 B, 1158 D
Crusades in, 1147 C, 1148 C
invaded by Roger II, 1147 E, 1148 E, 1149 C
war with Hungary, 1151 E
takes Bari, 1155 D, 1156 B
attacked by William I, 1157 E, 1158 E
attacks Egypt, 1169 D
breach with Venice, 1171 A
subjugates Dalmatia, 1172 E
defeated by Seljuqs, 1176 C
loss of Balkans, 1180 C, 1181 E
invaded by William II, 1185 B, C
Bulgarian revolt, 1185 E, 1186 D, 1187 E, 1190 E
war with Serbia, 1189 E, 1190 E, 1196 E
Order of Angelici founded, 1191 E
recognises Armenian kingdom, 1198 A
taken by Fourth Crusade, 1202 D, 1203 C, 1204 A, B, D; *and see* Constantinople; Greece
Empire at Trebizond, 1204 B
capital at Brusa, 1204 D
dynasty in Epirus. *See* Ducas
capital at Nicaea, 1208 B
defeats Seljuqs, 1210 B
war with Latins, 1211 D, 1214 D, 1225 E, 1235 E
alliance with Seljuqs, 1243 B
loses Rhodes, 1248 E
recovers Constantinople, 1261 A, C
peace with Venice, 1268 B
war with Charles, 1270 D, 1274 C, 1281 C, E
intervenes in Bulgaria, 1279 E
loses Skoplje, 1282 E
war for trade in, 1299 B
Ottoman invasion, 1300 E, 1301 C, 1304 E, 1326 B, 1331 A, 1337 E, 1352 A, 1359 E, 1394 B
civil wars, 1341 D, 1343 E, 1347 A, 1352 A, 1354 D
claimed by Stephen Dušan, 1346 B
siege of Constantinople, 1422 B, C
Ottoman conquest of Greece, 1423 E, 1430 A
fall of Constantinople, 1453 B
government of, Constantine VII on, 959 F
history of. *See* Historians
law, 886 F, 1073 F, 1335 F

Greek language and literature:
Anthologia Palatina, 950 K
chair in, 1391 K
dictionary, 976 K
grammars, 1252 K, 1415 K, 1478 K
Myriobiblon (Photius), 891 K
poetry:
Digenes Akritas, 1050 K
Theodore Prodromus, 1160 K
See also Translations

Greenland, 982 G, 1263 D; bishopric, 1110 H, 1124 J
Greenstead, England, church, 1013 J
Gregoras, Nicephorus, Gk. historian, 1359 K
Gregorian music, 1103 K
Gregory I, St., Pope (590–604), *Cura Pastoralis* of, 892 K
Gregory IV, Pope, 827 D, 833 B, 844 A
Gregory V (Bruno of Carinthia), Pope, 996 B, C, 998 A, 999 A
Gregory, anti-pope, 1012 B
Gregory VI (John Gratian), Pope, 1045 B, 1046 D
Gregory VII (Hildebrand), Pope (b. *c.* 1023), 1073 B, 1085 B
Archdeacon of the Roman Church, 1059 H
relations with Sicily, 1074 A, 1080 B, 1084 B
reforms of, 1074 H, 1078 H
Dictatus Papae, 1075 H
Investiture Dispute with Henry IV, 1075 A, E, 1076 A, 1077 A, 1078 D, 1080 A, 1081 B, 1083 B, 1084 A, B
creates kings, 1076 D, E, 1084 E
relations with Russia, 1077 E
relations with England, 1080 E
Gregory VIII (Maurice Bourdin), anti-pope, 1118 A, 1121 B
Gregory VIII (Albert of Morra), Pope, 1187 D
Gregory IX (Ugolino dei Conti), Pope, 1227 A, 1230 H, 1231 H, 1232 E, 1233 H, 1234 E, H, 1237 E, H, 1239 H, 1241 C; dispute with Frederick II, 1227 C, 1229 B, 1230 C, 1236 C, D, 1239 A, 1240 A, 1241 B
Gregory X (Tedald Visconti), 1271 C, 1274 C, H, 1275 C, D, 1276 A
Gregory XI (Pierre Roger de Beaufort), 1370 D, 1373 B, 1374 B, 1375 D, 1376 A, 1377 A, H, 1378 A
Gregory XII (Angelo Correr), Pope (in Rome), 1406 D, 1407 D, 1408 A, B, 1409 B, 1415 C
Gregory of Bridlington, E. musical theorist, 1217 J
Grenoble, France, University, 1339 H, 1452 H
Grettir the Strong, Saga of, 1200 K
Grey, John, Bishop of Norwich (d. 1214), 1205 D, 1206 A
Grey, Thomas, E. chronicler, 1369 K
Grimbald, F. scholar, 903 K
Grimoald, I, Prince of Benevento, 806 E
Grimoald II, Prince of Benevento, 806 E, 818 E
Grobnok, Yugoslavia, battle, 1241 B
Grocyn, William, E. scholar (1442–1519), 1442 L
Groot, Gerhard, Dutch mystic, 1340 L, 1374 H, 1384 L
Grosmont, Wales, battle, 1405 A
Grosseteste, Robert, Bishop of Lincoln, E. philosopher and astronomer, 1253 G, K, L
Gruffyd ap Cynan, King of Gwynned (1081–1137), 1136 A, 1137 E
Gruffyd ap Llewelyn, King of Gwynned and Powys, 1039 E, 1044 E, 1055 E, 1056 B, 1063 C
Grunwald (Tannenburg), Poland, battle, 1410 C
Guaimar IV, Prince of Salerno, 1038 E
Guala, Jacopo, It. cardinal and legate (d. 1227), 1218 D
Gualberti, John, St., It. monastic reformer, 985 L, 1038 H, 1073 L
Guarino da Verona. *See* Verona
Gubbio, Italy, Treaty of, 1355 B
Gudrun, 1240 K; *see also Laxdaela Saga*
Guelders, Holland, 1473 E
Guele, La, France, battle, 891 B
Guelf (Welf), origin of, 1140 D; Italian party, 1251 A, 1252 A, 1265 A, 1279 E, 1325 C
Guérande, France, Treaty of, 1365 A
Guesclin, Bertrand du, Constable of France (1320–80), 1364 B, C, 1365 C, 1367 B, 1370 D

Gui, Bernard, F. theologian (*c.* 1261–1331), 1323 H
Guibert of Nogent, F. historian and autobiographer (1053–*c.* 1124), 1111 K, 1115 K
Guicciardini, Francesco, It. historian (1483–1540), 1483 L
Guide to the Perplexed (Maimonides), 1204 K
Guido, It. geographer, 1119 G
Guidotto of Bologna, It. anthologist, 1266 K
Guinegate, France, battle, 1479 C
Guînes, France, 1354 B
Guienne, France, Duchy of, 1472 B; *cf.* Gascony
Guinglain (Renaud de Beaujeu), 1220 K
Guinicelli, Guideo, It. poet, 1276 K
Guiot of Provins, F. poet, 1206 K
Guisborough (*alias* Hemingburgh), Walter, E. chronicler (*fl.* 1270–1315), 1312 K, 1347 K
Guiscard, Robert, Count of Apulia, 1057 C; Duke of Apulia, Calabria and Sicily, 1059 C, 1074 A, 1080 A, 1085 C; conquests, 1071 B, 1072 A, 1077 E, 1081 B, D, 1082 A, 1083 E, 1084 B
Guiscard, Roger. *See* Roger I
Guittone d'Arezzo, It. poet (1220–94), 1294 K
Gujarāt, India, Hindu kingdom, 1060 E; conquered, 1026 E, 1196 E, 1297 E, 1345 E; Muslim kingdom, 1407 E, 1429 E
Gujarātī-Jaina, Indian philosopher, 1355 K
Gukanshō (Jien), 1220 K
Gulistan (Sādi), 1258 K
Gundissalinus, Dominicus, archdeacon of Segovia, Sp. translator and theologian, 1100 K
Gunnhild, wife of Emperor Henry III, 1036 B
Gunpowder, in China, 850 G, 1044 G, 1126 G; European, 1300 G, 1313 G
Gurū Nānak. *See* Nānak
Gutenburg (Johann Gensfleich), G. printer, 1440 G
Guthrum, Danish king, 878 B, 886 E
Guy, Duke of Spoleto, 888 A; King of Italy, 889 A; Emperor, 891 A, 894 D
Guy de Lusignan, King of Jerusalem, 1186 C, 1187 C, 1188 C, 1189 C, D; deposed, rules Cyprus, 1192 B, 1194 B
Guy of Dampierre, Count of Flanders, 1280 A, 1294 E, 1297 A, C, 1300 B, 1303 C, 1305 A
Guy, Archbishop of Milan, 1066 B
Guy of Warwick, 1320 K
Guy-Geoffrey. *See* William VIII
Guyuk, Great Khan of the Mongols, 1246 C, 1247 E, 1248 B
Guzman, Beatrix de, wife of Afonso III, 1257 E
Gwalior, India, Hindu kingdom, 1196 E
Gwynned, Wales, 965 E
  Kings of. *See*
    Rhodri (844–78)
    Hywel (942–9)
    Gruffyd ap Llewelyn (1039–63)
    Gruffyd ap Cynan (1081–1137)
    Owain (1137–70)
    Llewelyn ap Jorwerth (1194–1240)
    David (1240–6)
    Llewelyn ap Gruffyd (1246–82)
  English conquest. *See* Edward I
Gyokuyō (Fujiwara Kanezane), 1200 K
Gyula, Hungarian leader, 950 H

H

Haakon I, King of Norway, 938 E, 963 E
Haakon II, King of Norway, 1161 A, 1162 E
Haakon III, King of Norway, 1202 A, 1204 A
Haakon IV, King of Norway (b. 1204), 1217 E, 1263 D
Haakon V, King of Norway, 1299 E, 1308 E, 1319 B
Haakon VI, King of Norway, 1343 E, 1360 C, 1362 C, 1367 D, 1376 C, 1380 E
Habsburg family, 1231 B, 1291 C, 1330 C, 1335 B, 1336 E
Habsburg, Albert I, Duke of Austria. *See* Albert I
Habsburg, Albert III, Duke of Austria (d. 1395), 1388 B, 1389 B
Habsburg, Albert V, Duke of Austria. *See* Albert II
Habsburg, Albert VI, Archduke of Austria, 1453 A, 1461 D, 1463 D
Habsburg, Frederick I, the Handsome, Duke of Austria, 1310 C, 1313 D, 1330 A; rival King of the Romans, 1314 D, 1319 D, 1322 C, 1325 A
Habsburg, Frederick, Duke of Styria. *See* Frederick III
Habsburg, Leopold II, Duke of Austria, 1315 D, 1318 C
Habsburg, Leopold III, Duke of Austria, 1386 C
Habsburg, Maximilian, Count of Flanders. *See* Maximilian
Habsburg, Rudolf I, Duke of Austria. *See* Rudolf I
Habsburg, Rudolf IV, the Ingenious, Duke of Austria (b. 1339), 1362 E, 1364 A, 1365 H, 1368 A
Habsburg, Rudolf, Duke of Styria, 1282 D
Habsburg, Sigismund, Count of Tyrol, 1469 B, 1474 A, B, 1490 A
Habsburg, Werner II, first Count of, 1096 E
Hadath, Lebanon, 957 B
Hadrian. *See* Adrian
Haestan, Danish king, 895 E
Hāfiz, Per. poet (1320–89), 1368 K, 1389 L
Hafrsfjord, Norway, battle, 900 E
Hafsūn, Omar ibn-, Sp. M. rebel, 891 B, 917 E
Hagenau, Austria, Treaty of, 1330 C
Hainault, Belgium, Counts of, *see* William III, William IV, Margaret, Jacqueline
Haiyān, Abū Marwān Haiyān ibn-, Sp. M. historian (987–1076), 1076 K
Haiyān. *See* Abū Haiyān
Hajjāj, ibn-Yūsuf ibn-Matar al-, Arab translator, 827 G
Hajjāj, Muslim ibn-al-, Arab theologian, 874 H
Hajib, ibn-al-, Arab grammarian, 1248 K
Hakam, al-, I, Emir of Spain (796–822), 806 E, 814 B, 822 E
Hakam, al-, II, Caliph of Spain, 961 E, 974 E, 976 D, H
Hakam, Ibn ʿAbd-al-, Eg. historian, 871 K
Hakata Bay, Japan, battles, 1274 E, 1281 C
Hakemite Tables (ibn-Yūnus), 1007 G
Hākim, Abu ʿAlī al-Mansur al-, Caliph of Egypt (b. 985; 996–1021), 990 J, 995 K, 996 D, 1005 H, 1009 C, 1021 A
Halakot (Isaac al-Fez), 1103 H
Halebīd, India, Hindu kingdom, 1141 E
Hales, Robert, Treasurer of England, 1381 B
Halfdan, King of York, 875 E, 877 E
Halfdan, King of York (*c.* 902–10), 910 C
Halich, *See* Galicia
Halidon Hill, Scotland, battle, 1333 C
Halifet Gazi, Danishmend noble, 1146 J
Hallāj, al- Sūfī martyr, 922 H
Halle, Adam de la. *See* Adam
'Hallelujah', 'The Great', 1233 H
Halstan, King of Sweden (1066–90), 1090 E
Haly Abbas. *See* ʿAbbās
Hamadan, Persia, Kakuyids of, 1007 E, 1050 E
Hamadhānī (Bedi Alzeman), Ahmad ibn-al-Husain al-, Per. essayist (967–1007), 1007 K

Hamadhānī, 'Ain al-Qudāt al-, Per. Sūfī philosopher (1098–1131), 1131 K
Hamāh, Syria, 1331 J
Hamburg, W. Germany, 808 E, 845 E, 1189 G, 1241 G, 1252 G; bishopric of, 831 H, *and see* Anskar; archbishopric of, 1046 B, 1104 H, *and see* Adalbert; *History of the Church of* (Adam of Bremen), 1076 K
Hamdānid dynasty. *See* Syria
Hamlet, Danish prince, 1208 K
Hammād, Abū 'Abdallāh Muhammad ibn-, Eg. historian, 1230 K
Hammūd, 'Ali ibn-, Caliph of Cordova (1016–18), 1016 E
Hammūdid dynasty. *See* Cordova
Hamsavati. *See* Pegu
Han Ch'an-chih, C. botanist, 1178 G
Han T'o-chou, Emperor of south China, 1207 E
Han Yü, C. poet and philosophical essayist (768–824), 824 K
Hanbal, Ahmad ibn-, Arab theologian (780–855), 855 H
Hanbalite sect of Islam, 855 H
Handboc (Bridferth), 1010 G
Handlyng synne (Robert Mannyng), 1303 K
Hangchow, China, 1127 E, 1270 G, 1276 E
Hanoi (*rectius* Thang-long, outside), N. Vietnam, capital of Annam, 863 E; capital of Dai-co-viet and Dai Viet, 1010 E, 1257 E, 1371 E, 1377 E, 1407 E
Hanse, league of German towns:
German merchants in England, 1157 G; Gothland, 1163 G; Russia, 1198 G, 1229 G
first leagues, 1241 G, 1259 G, 1282 G, 1283 G
in Flanders, 1252 G; embargoes on trade to, 1307 G, 1356 G, 1388 G, 1392 G, 1436 G, 1438 G, 1441 G, 1451 G, 1457 G
operations in Norway, 1285 D, 1294 E, 1318 G, 1376 C
wars with Denmark, 1360 C, 1362 C, 1365 D, 1367 D, 1369 D, 1427 C, 1435 C
relations with England, 1379 G, 1388 G, 1474 G
embargo on Novgorod, 1392 G
occupies Stockholm, 1395 B
fish trade, 1400 G
earliest legislation, 1418 G
treaty with Castile, 1443 G
dispute with France, 1451 G
war with Brandenburg, 1478 E
Hanzala of Badghis, Per. poet, 875 K
Harbiyāh, Israel, battle, 1244 D
Harding, Stephen, St., abbot of Cîteaux, 1133 L
Hardyng, John, E. chronicler, 1378 L, 1465 K
Harfleur, France, 1369 C, 1415 C, 1416 C, 1440 C, 1485 C
Harihara I, Rajāh of Vijayanagar (1336–57), 1336 B
Harihara II, Rajāh of Vijayanagar (1377–1404), 1404 C
Hariharalaya, Cambodia, 850 E
Harīrī, Abū Muhammad al-Qāsim al-, Arab belle-trist (1054–1122), 1122 K
Harju, Esthonia, Russia, 1346 E
Harlech, Wales, castle, 1283 B, 1409 A
Harmenopulos, Constantinus, Gk. jurist (1320–83), 1345 F, 1383 L
Harmonicis numeris, De (Levi ben Gerson), 1343 G
Harold, ex-king of Denmark, 826 E
Harold I Bluetooth, King of Denmark (d. 986), 936 E, 965 H, 974 E, 983 E
Harold II, King of Denmark (d. 1019), 1014 A
Harold III Whetstone, King of Denmark, 1074 B, 1081 B
Harold I Harefoot, regent in England, 1035 D; King, 1037 E, 1040 A
Harold II, Earl of East Anglia, 1045 E; Earl of Wessex, 1053 B, 1056 B, 1063 B, C, 1064 E; King of England, 1066 A, C, D
Harold I Fairhair, King of Norway (d. 933), 900 E, 933 E, 948 E
Harold II, King of Norway, 963 E, 978 E
Harold III Hardrada, King of Norway, 1047 D, 1066 C
Harold IV Gille, King of Norway, 1130 A, 1135 A, D
Harphius, Hendrik, Flemish mystic, 1474 H, 1478 L
Harran, Syria, battle, 1104 B
Harrowing of Hell, The, 1295 K
Harthacnut, King of Denmark and England, 1035 D, 1036 B, 1040 A, 1042 B
Hartley, Andrew, Earl of Carlisle, 1323 A
Hartmann von Aue, G. minnesinger, 1215 K
Hārūn ar-Rashīd, Caliph (786–809), 803 E, 804 E, J, 806 E, 807 G, 809 A, G, 810 K
Hasan, 'Jalal-ud-din, Shah of Madura (1335–40), 1335 E
Hasan (Alhazen), Abū 'Ali al-, Eg. mathematician (*c.* 965–1039), 1039 G
Hasan ibn-Ali, Governor of Sicily, 948 E
Hasan ibn-al-Sabbāh, founder of the Assassins, 1090 E, 1124 E
Hastings, England, battle, 1066 D
Hastings, John, Earl of Pembroke (1347–75), 1372 B
Hattin, Horns of, Israel, battle, 1187 C
Hauteville, Guillaume d', Count of Apulia, 1046 B
Hauteville, Humphrey d', Count of Apulia, 1053 B
Hauteville, Tancred d', of Normandy, sons of, 1034 E, 1040 E
Havelberg, E. Germany, bishopric, 948 H
Havelok the Dane (anon.), 1250 K
Hauqal, ibn-, Arab geographer and cartographer, 975 G
Hausen, Friedrich, von, G. minnesinger, 1190 K
Hawkwood, John, E. condottiere (d. 1394), 1361 B, 1373 B
Hawkynge, Treatyse perteynynge to (Juliana Berners), 1400 K
Hāwi, al- (al-Rāzī), 925 G, 1279 G
Hay'ah, Kitāb al- (ibn-Aflah), 1145 G; (al-Bitrūji), 1204 G, 1217 G
Hayam Wuruk, Emperor of Mājapāhit, 1377 E
Hayāwan, Kitāb al- (al-Jāhiz), 869 K
Hayāwan, Kitāb hayāt al- (al-Damīrī), 1372 G
Hayton, Armenian historian and geographer, 1314 K
Hayy ibn-Yaqzan (ibn-Tufayl), 1185 K
Hazm, 'Ali ibn-Ahmad ibn-, Sp. M. poet and theologian (994–1064), 1064 H, K
Heart, Movement of the (Alfred of Shareshul), 1210 G
Hebrew, chair of, 1488 H
Hebrew grammar (David Qimhī), 1235 K
Hebrew literature:
Immanuel ben Solomon, 1331 K
Jedaiah ha-Penini Bedersi, 1345 K
Johann Reuchlin, 1455 L
Hebrides, islands, Scotland, 1263 D, 1266 C; *and see* Isles
Hedgeley Moor, England, battle, 1464 B
Heian. *See* Kyōto
Heidelberg, W. Germany, 1384 C; University, 1385 H
Heilspiegelaltar (Konrad Witz), 1435 J
Heimskringla (Snorri Sturlason), 1225 K
Heisterbach, Caesarius von, G. chronicler (*c.* 1180–1240), 1220 K
Heliand (anon.), 820 K

Helmold, G. chronicler (d. 1177?), 1171 K, 1212 K
Héloise, F. nun, 1142 K, 1164 L
Helperic of St. Gall, G. mathematician, 978 G, 1000 G
Helsingborg, Sweden, battle, 1362 C
Hemacandra, Indian poet and philologist (1088–c. 1170), 1170 K
Hemādri, Indian statesman and legal writer, 1270 F
Hemingburgh, Walter of. *See* Guisborough
Hemming, King of Denmark, Norway and south Sweden, 810 E
Hemp mills, 1040 G
Henchün Seiken, Ja. writer, 1156 G
Henley, Walter of, E. writer on husbandry, 1250 G
Hennebont, France, 1342 B
Henricis, Liber de illustribus (John Capgrave), 1448 K
Henry I the Fowler, King of the Germans (919–36), 876 L; Duke of Saxony, 915 E; as King, 919 B, 921 D, 924 E, 925 E, 928 E, 929 C, 933 A, 934 E, 936 C
Henry II, St., Holy Roman Emperor (1014–24), 973 L, 1014 A, 1024 C
 Duke of Bavaria, 995 C, 1001 A
 King of the Germans, 1002 B, 1003 D, 1012 E, 1017 D, 1020 E
 wars with Poland, 1002 C, 1005 A, 1007 E, 1013 B, 1015 C, 1017 C, 1018 A
 King of Italy, 1004 B
 relations with Bohemia, 1004 C
 takes Basel, 1006 E
 Church reforms, 1007 D, 1014 A, 1019 H, 1022 C
 and Low Countries, 1006 C, 1007 E, 1009 E, 1018 A, 1020 C
 Italian expeditions, 1014 A, B, 1021 D, 1022 A, B
 and Burgundy, 1016 B
 Life of (Adelbold), 1026 K
Henry III, Holy Roman Emperor (1046–56), 1017 L, 1036 B, 1046 D, 1053 E, 1056 D
 Duke of Bavaria, 1027 C
 Duke of Swabia, 1038 E
 King of the Germans, 1028 B, 1039 B, J, 1042 E, 1046 B, 1084 J
 Bohemian campaigns, 1040 C, 1041 B
 Hungarian campaigns, 1042 C, 1043 E, 1044 C, 1050 E, 1052 E
 declares 'Day of Indulgence', 1043 D
 revolts in Germany, 1044 E, 1045 E, 1046 B, 1047 E, 1053 E, 1054 C, 1056 E
 in Flanders, 1045 E, 1046 B
 Church reforms, 1046 D
 Italian expeditions, 1054 A, 1055 E
 awards Silesia to Poland, 1054 E
Henry IV, Holy Roman Emperor (1084–1105), 1050 L, 1084 A, 1085 B, 1089 E, 1106 C
 Duke of Bavaria, 1053 E
 King of the Romans, 1054 C, 1056 D, 1061 D, 1065 A, 1066 A, 1074 G, 1075 D, 1079 E, 1084 J, 1087 B
 abducted, 1062 B
 Hungarian campaigns, 1063 E, 1074 E
 revolts in Saxony, 1070 C, 1071 E, 1073 C, 1074 A, 1075 B, D, 1076 E, 1080 A, 1088 E
 quarrel with Gregory VII, 1075 E, 1076 A, 1077 A, 1080 A, B
 revolts in Germany, 1076 D, E, 1077 A, 1078 C, 1080 D, 1081 C, 1086 C, 1093 E, 1099 A, 1104 D
 Italian campaigns, 1081 B, 1083 B, 1084 A, B, 1090 C, 1091 B, 1094 E, 1097 E
 declares 'Peace of God', 1085 F
 abdicates, 1105 D
Henry V, Holy Roman Emperor (1111–25), 1081 L, 1111 B, E, 1114 A, 1115 C, 1125 B
 King of the Romans, 1099 A, 1104 D, 1105 D, 1109 E
 Italian expeditions, 1110 C, 1117 A, 1118 A, C
 investiture dispute, 1111 A, 1112 A, C, 1118 A, B, 1119 D, 1122 C
 revolts in Germany, 1113 E, 1114 D, 1115 A, D, 1121 C
 invades France, 1124 B
Henry VI Hohenstaufen, Holy Roman Emperor (1191–7), 1165 L, 1191 B, 1196 B, D, 1197 C, E, 1198 A
 King of the Romans, 1169 C, 1190 B, 1194 A
 gains Sicily, 1184 D, 1186 A, 1191 B, C, 1194 C, D
 Italian campaigns, 1186 C, 1191 A, B, 1193 A
 dispute with Pope, 1192 C, D
 and Richard I, 1193 A, B, 1194 A
 proclaims crusade, 1195 B
Henry VII of Luxemburg, Holy Roman Emperor (1312–13), 1312 B
 King of the Romans, 1308 D, 1309 B, 1310 C
 King of Lombardy, 1311 A
 Italian campaign, 1311 C, E, 1312 D, 1313 B, C
Henry of Flanders, Emperor of Constantinople, 1206 C, 1208 C, 1211 D, 1214 D, 1216 B
Henry, Duke of Carinthia, 1335 B; King of Bohemia, 1307 C, 1310 C; daughter of, *see* Margaret 'Maultasch'
Henry I, King of Castile (b. 1204), 1214 C, 1217 B
Henry II of Trastamare, King of Castile and Leon (b. 1333), 1365 C, 1366 A, 1367 B; wins kingdom, 1369 A, 1372 A, B, 1377 C, 1379 B
Henry III, King of Castile and Leon (b. 1379), 1390 D, 1393 C, 1398 C, 1400 E, 1402 A, E, 1406 D
Henry IV the Impotent, King of Castile and Leon (b. 1425), 1454 C, 1458 B, 1462 E, 1463 A, 1465 B, 1467 C, 1468 C, 1474 D
Henry I de Lusignan, King of Cyprus (d. 1253), 1218 A, 1233 B
Henry I, King of England (1100–35), 1068 L, 1091 E, 1101 C, 1102 E, 1135 D
 Coronation charter, 1100 C
 quarrel with Anselm, 1103 B, 1107 C
 gains Normandy, 1106 C
 wars with Louis VI, 1109 A, 1119 C, D
 revolts in Normandy, 1112 E, 1117 E, 1123 E
 overlord of Brittany, etc., 1113 A
 alliance with Henry V, 1114 A, 1124 B
 succession to, 1120 D, 1128 B, 1131 C
 Leges of, 1118 F
Henry II, King of England (1154–89), 1133 L, 1152 B, 1154 D, 1157 F, 1173 F, 1189 C
 Duke of Normandy, 1150 E, 1151 C, 1172 F
 invades England, 1153 A, D
 and Thomas Becket, 1155 A, 1163 D, 1164 D, 1170 C, 1172 B, 1174 C
 campaigns in France, 1156 E, 1159 C, 1160 D, 1169 A, 1174 C
 wars with Scotland, 1157 E, 1174 C, D
 Welsh campaigns, 1158 E, 1165 E
 taxation by, 1159 F, 1162 F
 meets Pope, 1162 C
 Constitutions of Clarendon, 1164 A
 legal reforms, 1166 F, 1176 F
 alliance with Saxony, 1168 E
 son crowned, 1170 B
 Inquest of sheriffs, 1170 F
 Irish expedition, 1171 D
 revolts of sons, 1173 A, 1174 C, 1181 E, 1183 B
 grants to sons, 1175 E, 1177 B
 arbitrates in Spain, 1177 E
 relations with Philip II, 1180 B, 1187 E, 1188 A, D, 1189 C

Assize of Arms, 1181 F
Gesta (Benedict of Peterborough), 1193 K
Henry, son of Henry II, King of England (b. 1155), 1170 B, 1173 A, 1181 E, 1183 B
Henry III, King of England (1216–72), 1207 L, 1216 D, 1220 B, J, 1236 F, 1267 F, 1269 J, 1272 D
minority of, 1216 D, 1217 C, D, 1219 B, 1221 C, 1223 B, 1224 A, C, 1227 A
wars with Welsh, 1218 A, 1228 C, 1231 D, 1241 E, 1259 C, 1262 E, 1267 C
wars with France, 1224 B, 1225 A, 1230 B, D, 1231 C, 1242 B, C, 1243 B
reissues charters, 1225 A, 1237 A
reorganises government, 1232 C
revolts against, 1233 C, D, 1234 B
marriage alliances, 1235 C, 1236 A
treaty with Scotland, 1237 C
and Simon de Montfort, 1238 A, 1252 B
refused taxes, 1242 A, 1244 D, 1254 F
Sicilian scheme, 1254 A, 1255 B, 1258 D
treaty with Castile, 1254 B, D
Provisions of Oxford, etc., 1258 B, 1259 D
treaty with France, 1258 B, 1259 D
resumes control, 1261 B, 1263 A
wars with barons, 1263 B, C, 1264 A, B, D, 1265 C, D, 1266 B, D, 1267 B, F
Henry IV, King of England (1399–1413), 1366 L, 1413 A
Earl of Derby, Appellant, 1387 D, 1388 A
Duke of Hereford, exiled, 1398 C
Duke of Lancaster, deposes Richard, 1399 A, C, D
revolts against, 1400 A, 1403 C, 1405 B, 1408 A
Scottish campaign, 1400 C
Welsh campaigns, 1400 D, 1401 D, 1402 C, 1403 C, 1405 C
parliamentary criticism, 1404 A, D, 1406 A, D
government of Prince Henry, 1410 A, 1411 D
French alliance, 1412 B
Henry V, King of England (1413–22), 1387 L, 1413 A, 1415 H, 1417 F, 1421 A, 1422 C
Prince of Wales, 1405 B, 1410 A
revolts against, 1414 A, 1415 C, 1417 D
claims French crown, 1414 B, 1415 A
campaigns in France, 1415 C, D, 1417 C, 1418 C, 1419 A, 1420 D, 1421 D, 1422 B
alliance with Emperor, 1416 C
relations with Burgundy, 1416 D, 1419 D
Treaty of Troyes, 1420 B
Gesta, 1417 K
Henry VI, King of England (1422–61, 1470–1), 1421 L, 1440 H, 1441 D, H, 1445 B, 1453 D
minority, 1422 C, 1424 A, 1426 A, 1436 D
claiming French crown, 1422 D, 1431 B, D, 1435 C, 1439 C, 1444 B, 1448 A
criticism of government, 1450 A
and Richard of York, 1450 C, 1452 A
insane, 1453 C, 1454 A, D
civil war, 1455 B, D, 1456 A, 1458 A, 1459 C, D, 1460 C
accepts York as heir, 1460 D
flees to Scotland, 1461 A, B
captured, 1466 C
restored, 1470 D
murdered, 1471 B
Henry VII Tudor, King of England (1485–1509), 1457 L, 1485 C, 1486 A, 1487 F, 1489 A, G, 1491 E; revolts against, 1486 A, 1487 B, 1489 B, 1491 E
Henry I, King of France (1031–60), as Duke of Burgundy, 1015 E; King, 1027 B, 1031 C, 1033 B, 1038 E, 1058 B, 1060 C; relations with Normandy, 1047 E, 1048 E, 1053 E, 1054 A, 1058 C
Henry I of Champagne, King of Jerusalem, 1192 B, 1197 C
Henry II de Lusignan, King of Jerusalem and Cyprus (d. 1324), 1285 B
Henry I the Fat, Count of Champagne, King of Navarre, 1270 D, 1274 E
Henry, son of Conrad III, King of the Romans (d. 1150), 1150 A
Henry, son of Frederick II, King of the Romans (b. 1212), 1220 A, 1231 B; deposed, 1235 B, 1242 E
Henry Raspe, Landgrave of Thuringia, King of the Romans, 1246 B, 1247 A
Henry the Wrangler, Duke of Bavaria, 947 E, 976 C, 978 A, 984 A, B, 995 C
Henry of Luxemburg, Duke of Bavaria, 1017 D, 1026 E
Henry, Count of Luxemburg, Duke of Bavaria (1042–7), 1042 E
Henry the Proud, Duke of Bavaria (b. 1102; 1126–38) and Saxony, 1136 C, 1138 A, B, 1139 D
Henry the Great, Duke of Burgundy (965–1002), 965 E, 1002 D, 1015 E
Henry of Grosmont, Earl and Duke of Lancaster (d. 1361), 1345 D, 1346 D, 1356 B
Henry I the Bearded, Grand Prince of Poland, 1234 E, 1238 E
Henry II the Pious, Grand Prince of Poland, 1238 E, 1241 B
Henry of Burgundy, Count of Portugal, 1095 E, 1112 B
Henry the Lion, Duke of Saxony (1142–80; d. 1195), 1129 L, 1139 D, 1140 D, 1142 B, 1143 G, 1168 E, 1195 C, 1198 C
gains Bavaria, 1149 D, 1156 C, 1157 G
conquers Wends, 1160 C, 1162 C
proceedings against, 1178 D, 1179 B
deprived and exiled, 1180 A–C, 1181 E, 1185 C, 1188 A
recovers lands, 1189 D, 1190 B, 1191 E, 1194 A
Henry of Almain, E. prince, 1271 A
Henry of Huntingdon, E. chronicler, 1154 K
Henry of Latvia, Latvian chronicler, 1227 K
Henry of Mainz, G. geographer, 1110 G
Henry the Navigator, Port. prince, 1394 L, 1418 G, 1419 G, 1437 E, 1460 L
Henry of Reynes, F. mason, 1245 J
Henry of Susa. *See* Hostiensis
Henry Břetislav, Bishop of Prague, Duke of Bohemia, 1193 E, 1197 E
Henry Jasomirgott, Duke of Bavaria (d. 1177), 1142 B; and Austria, 1156 C
Henryson, Robert, Scottish poet (1430?–1506), 1490 K
Heraclea (*now* Ereghli), Turkey, 806 E, 1300 E; battle, 1101 C
Heraclius, Gk. craftsman, 950 G
Herat, Afghanistan, 1163 J, 1222 B; Timurid capital, 1447 E, 1469 E, 1470 C; library, 1443 K
Herbals:
Walafrid Strabo, 849 K
Sureśvara, 1075 G
Odo of Meung, 1100 G
John of Milan, 1328 G
Chu Hsiao, 1406 G
Benedetto Rinio, 1410 G
Herbert II, Count of Vermandois, 923 E, 925 E, 929 E, 939 E, 940 E, 943 E
Herbert, William, Earl of Pembroke, 1469 C
Hereford, England, Bishop of, 1056 B; Earl, 1075 E; Duke, *see* Henry IV; *Mappa Mundi*, 1314 G
Heresy:
Abyssinian, 1468 H

Heresy—*contd.*
European, 1012 H; burning of heretics, 1022 H, 1051 H, 1401 H; history of, 1340 H
See also Abelard; Albigenses (*under* Toulouse); Arnold of Brescia; Berengar of Tours; Brethren of the Free Spirit; Cathari; Dolcino; Flagellants; Gilbert de la Porrée; Gottschalk; Hus, John; Jerome of Prague; Joachim of Flora; Lollards; Ockham, William of; Pecock, Reginald; Raymond VII; Roscelinus; Segarelli; Siger of Brabant; Waldenses; Wycliffe, John
Greek. *See* Bogomolism; Paulicians
Muslim, 922 H, 945 H
Hereward the Wake, 1071 E
Hergest, Red Book of, 1375 K
Hériger, Abbot of Lobbes, Belgian historian, 1007 K
Hermann of Salm, King of the Romans, 1081 C, 1088 C
Hermann, first Count Palatine, 966 E
Hermann, Duke of Swabia, 948 D
Hermann III, Duke of Swabia, 1003 D, 1012 E
Hermann IV, Duke of Swabia, 1038 E
Hermann Contractus, monk of Reichenau, G. mathematician, astronomer, musical theorist and chronicler, 1013 L, 1054 G, J, K, L
Hermann the Dalmatian, translator, 1143 G, H
Hermann the German, translator, 1272 K
Hermits. *See* Godric of Finchale; Flüe, Nicholas von; Kamo Chōmei; Wulfric; Wulsi
Hero of Byzantium, Gk. surveyor, 938 G
Herring, 1400 G
Hersfeld, W. Germany, abbey, 1037 J
Hertogenbosch, Holland, 1419 J
Hervé, Archbishop of Reims, 900 E, 922 C
Herzegovina, Jugoslavia, 1114 E; Duchy, 1467 E
Hesz, Andrew, G. printer, 1473 G
Hethoum, King of Armenia, 1254 C
Hexabiblos (Harmenopulos), 1344 J
Hexamilion, Greece, 1423 E
Hexham, England, battle, 1464 B
Hidāya nāma (Banda Nawāz), 1422 H
Higden, Ranulf, E. chronicler (d. 1364), 1352 K, 1387 K, 1482 K
Higuera, La, Spain, battle, 1431 E
Hikma, Kitāb mizan al- (al-Khāzinī), 1121 G
Hikmat al-Ishraq (al-Suhrawardi), 1191 K
Hildebold, Archbishop of Cologne, 813 J
Hildebrand. *See* Gregory VII
Hildebrandslied (anon. lay), 800 K
Hildegaire, teacher at Chartres, 1028 H
Hildegarde of Bingen, St., G. mystic and naturalist, 1098 L, 1179 G, L
Hildegonda, St., G. monk, 1188 L
Hildesheim, W. Germany, bishopric of, 818 H; Cathedral, 872 J, 1061 J; church, 1001 J
Hilton, Walter, E. mystic, 1396 H
Hincmar, Archbishop of Reims (845–82), F. theologian, 849 H, 960 F, 865 A, 882 L
Hindu Calculation, The Convincer on (al-Nasawi), 1041 G
Hindu culture, etc. *See* India
Hippocrates, Gk. physician (d. 357 B.C.), translated, 800 G, 873 G; commentaries on, 1411 G, 1414 G
Hirsau, W. Germany, abbey, 1038 J
Hirsau, Switzerland, abbey, 1082 J
Hisāb al-Jabr w-al Muqābalah (al-Khwārizmī), 850 G, 1187 G
Hishām II, Caliph of Spain (b. 964), 976 D, 1009 E, 1010 E, 1013 B
Hishām III, Caliph of Spain (d. 1036), 973 L, 1027 E, 1031 D
Histoire de Guillaume le Maréchal, 1220 K
Histoire du Règne de Charles VII (Jean Chartier), 1461 K
Historia adversus Paganos (Orosius), 892 K
Historia Anglicana (Thomas Walsingham), 1422 K
Historia Anglorum (Henry of Huntingdon), 1154 K
Historia Augusta (Albertino Mussato), 1329 K
Historia Britonum (Nennius), 810 K
Historia calamitatum mearum (Abelard), 1142 K
Historia de rebus gestis in Siciliae regno (Hugo Falcandus), 1189 K
Historia Dunelmensis Ecclesiae (Simeon), 1096 K
Historia Ecclesiastica (Bede), 892 K; (Orderic Vitalis), 1141 K
Historia Fiorentina (Poggio Bracciolini), 1459 K
Historia Francorum (Aimon of Fleury), 1010 K
Historia Hammaburgensis Ecclesiae (Adam of Bremen), 1076 K
Historia Hierosolymitana (Fulcher), 1127 K
Historia Langobardorum (Paul the Deacon), 800 K
Historia Novella (William of Malmesbury), 1142 K
Historia Novorum (Eadmer), 1130 K
Historia Orientalis (Jacques de Vitry), 1240 K
Historia Poloniae (Jan Dlugosz), 1480 K
Historia Polonica (Vincent Kadlubek), 1223 K
Historia Pontificalis (John of Salisbury), 1152 K
Historia Regum (Simeon of Durham), 1129 K, 1154 K
Historia Regum Angliae (John Rous), 1491 K
Historia Regum Britanniae (Geoffrey of Monmouth), 1137 K
Historia Remensis Ecclesiae (Flodoard), 966 K
Historia Rerum Anglicarum (William of Newburgh), 1198 K
Historia rerum in Italia gestarum (Ferreto de' Ferreti), 1337 K
Historia rerum in partibus transmarinis gestarum (William of Tyre), 1184 K
Historia Scolastica (Petrus Comestor), 1198 K
Historia Trojana (Guido de Columnis), 1287 K
Historiae (Richer), 997 K
Historiae sui temporis (Glaber), 1050 K
Historians and chroniclers:
Abyssinian, 1344 K
Anglo-Norman. *See* Orderic Vitalis; Robert of Torigny; Wace
Annamite. *See* Li Tse
Arab. *See* Athīr; Jawzi*; Mas'ūdi; Wāqidi; Ya'qūbi*
Armenian. *See* Asolik, Stephen*; Hayton; Matthew of Urfah; Vanagan, John; Vardan*
Austrian. *See* Victring, John of
Belgian. *See* Gilles le Muisit; Hériger; Hocsem, Jean; Jean le Bel; Maerlant, Jacob; Sigebert of Gembloux*
Bohemian. *See* Cosmas; Dalimil; Martin of Troppau
Cambodian, 1350 K
Chinese. *See* Ch'êng Ch'iao; Chia Tan; Hsieh Chü-chêng; Liu Hsü; Ou-yang Hsiu; Sung Ch'i; Yüan Shu
Danish. *See* Aagesön, Svend; Aelnoth; Saxo Grammaticus
Dutch. *See* Stoke, Melis
Egyptian. *See* Eutychius; Hakam; Hammād; Kindī; Mazrīzī; Musabbihi; Nuwayrī; Taghri-Birdi
English, anon., 1154 K, 1417 K, 1486 K. *And see*, Ailred; Arnold fitz Thedmar; Bede; Benedict of Peterborough; Capgrave, John; Eadmer; Florence of Worcester; Gervase of Canterbury; Grey, Thomas; Guisborough, Walter of; Hardyng, John; Henry of Huntingdon; Higden,

Ranulph*; Joceyln of Brakelond; John of Hexham; John of Salisbury; Langtoft, Peter; Layamon; Murimuth, Adam of; Paris, Matthew*; Ralph de Diceto; Richard of Devizes; Roger of Hoveden*; Roger of Wendover; Rous, John; Simeon of Durham; Trivet, Nicholas; Walsingham, Thomas; Whethamstede, John; William of Malmesbury; William of Newburgh
French, anon., 1100 K. *And see* Abbo of Fleury; Adhemar of Chabannes; Aimon of Fleury; Chartier, Jean; Châtelain, George; Commynes, Philippe de; Dudon of St. Quentin; Fillastre, Guillaume; Flodoard of Reims; Frechulph of Lisieux*; Froissart, John; Fulcher of Chartres; Glaber, Raoul; Guibert of Nogent; (?) Martin Gallus (of Poland); Monstrelet, Enguerrand de; Nithard; Richer; Valenciennes, Henri de; Villehardouin, Geoffroi de; Vitry, Jacques de; William of Jumièges
German, anon., 881 K, 1237 K*. *And see* Adam of Bremen; Adelbold; Albert von Stade; Arnold of Lübeck; Beheim, Michael; Closener, Fritsche; Dietrich of Niem; Einhard; Ekkehard of Aura*; Ekkehard (IV); Heisterbach, Caesarius von; Helmold; Hermann Contractus; Lambert of Hersfeld; Notker; Otto of Freising*; Peter of Duisburg; Regino of Prüm*; Rudolf of Ems*; Stromer, Ulman; Thietmar; Twinger, Jakob; Widukind
German Jew. *See* Ephraim of Bonn
Greek. *See* Acominatos, Nicetas; Acropilites, George; Anna Comnena; Bryennius, Nicephorus; Chalcocondylas, Laonicus; Choniates, Nicetas; Cinnamos, Joannes; Glycas, Michael*; Gregorus, Nicephorus; John VI Cantacuzenus; Leo the Deacon; Monachos, Georgios*; Nicephorus, St.; Orosius; Psellus, Michael; Scylitzes; Simeon; Syncellos, George; Theophanes Confessor; Zonaras, Joannes
Icelandic. *See* Ari; Bergthorsson, Bjarni; Sturla Thordsson
Indian. *See* Kalhana
Indian Muslim. *See* Baranī; Isāmy; Minhāj
Irish. *See* Marianus Scotus*
Italian. *See* Agnellus; Baldassare; Bracelli, Jacopo; Bruni, Leonardo; Compagni, Dino; Ferreto de' Ferreti; Giustiniani, Bernardo; Hugo Falcandus; Leo of Ostia; Liutprand; Marignolli, John; Mussato, Albertino; Peter the Deacon; Pius II; Platina, Bartolomeo; Poggio Bracciolini; Romuald of Salerno; Salimbene; Villani, Giovanni; Voragine, Jacobus
Japanese, anon., 1266 K. *And see* Jien; Kitabatake Chikafusa; Nakayama Tadachika
Korean. *See* Kim Pu-sik
Latvian. *See* Henry of Latvia
of 'Outremer'. *See* William of Tripoli; William of Tyre
Persian. *See* Balādhurī; Bīrūnī; Dīnawarī*; Juwainī; Katīb; Miskawayh*; Mustawfī; Qutaybah; Rashīd*; Shahrastānī; Tabarī*
Polish. *See* Dlugosz, Jan; Kadlubek, Vincent
Portuguese. *See* Lopes, Fernão
Russian, anon., 1118 K, 1199 K, 1380 K. *And see* Evfimi; Nestor
Scottish. *See* Bower, Walter; Fordum, John
Spanish. *See* Alfonso X; López de Ayala; Roderigo Jiménez*
Spanish (Catalan). *See* Muntaner, Ramón; Terrena, Guiu
Spanish Muslim. *See* Haiyān; Khaldūn; Khatīb; Qūtīyah
Swedish. *See* Olai, Erik
Swiss, *See* Winterthur, John of
Syrian. *See* Abū-l-Fidā'; Michael of Antioch*; 'Umari
Welsh. *See* Asser; Geoffrey of Monmouth; Gerald of Wales; Nennius; Usk, Adam of
Historical Epitome (Zonaras), 1145 K
Historiarum demonstrationes (Laonicus Chalcocondylas), 1490 K
Historiarum, Liber certarum (John of Victring), 1345 K
History of the Three Worlds (Lu T'ai), 1345 K
History of the World (Frechulph), 852 K
History, philosophy of (ibn-Khaldūn), 1406 K
History, Short (Nicephorus), 829 K
History, siege and destruction of Troye, The (John Lydgate), 1412 K
Ho Han Thuong, Emperor of Dai Viet, 1400 E, 1407 E
Hoa-lu, N. Vietnam, capital of Dai-co-viet, 968 E, (1010 E)
Hoccleve, Thomas, E. poet and civil servant, 1402 K, 1411 K, 1426 L
Hocsem, Jean de, Belgian chronicler (1279–1348), 1348 K
Hodo, Margrave of the Eastern Mark, 972 E, 973 A
Hohen-Mölsen, E. Germany, battle, 1080 D
Hohenstaufen family, 1079 E, 1268 D; *and see* Germany (Kings), Swabia (Dukes)
Hohenzollern, Albert III Achilles, Elector of Brandenburg (b. 1414), 1470 E, 1472 E, 1473 E, 1478 E, 1486 A.
Hohenzollern, Frederick I, Elector of Brandenburg, 1411 A, 1415 B, 1440 C
Hohenzollern, Frederick II, Elector of Brandenburg (b. 1413, d. 1471), 1440 C, 1442 E, 1454 E, 1470 E
Hohenzollern, John Cicero, Elector of Brandenburg (1486–99), 1486 A
Hōjō Regency of the Shogunate, 1219 E, 1331 E, 1333 E
Hōjō Sanetoki, Ja. educational founder, 1270 H
Hōjō Yoshitoki, Ja. noble (1163–1224), 1219 E
Hōjō-ki (Kamo Chōmei), 1212 K
Holand, Henry, Duke of Exeter (1430–75), 1454 B
Holand, John, Earl of Huntingdon, 1400 A
Holand, Thomas, Earl of Kent, 1400 A
Holbein, Hans, the Elder, Flemish artist (1465–1524), 1465 L
Holland, Counts of, 985 E, 988 E, 1046 B, *and see* William (King of the Romans), Florence V, John I, John II, William III, William IV, Margaret, Jacqueline
  occupied by Philip of Burgundy, 1424 D, 1425 B, 1428 C
  literature:
    Melis Stoke, 1305 K
    Abele Spelen, 1350 K
    Johannes de Hese, 1389 K
  windmills in, 1404 G
Holstein, W. Germany, 1229 E; Counts of, 1143 G, 1189 D, 1191 E, 1332 C, 1340 E, 1432 E; united to Schleswig, 1460 A
Holy Grail, The (earliest references), 1173 K, 1212 K, 1214 K, 1336 K
Holy River, Sweden, battle, 1026 E
Holzschuh, Dietrich, pseudo-Frederick II, 1285 C
Homburg-on-Unstrut, W. Germany, battle, 1075 B
Homer's *Iliad*, translated, 1435 K
Homilies (Wulfstan), 1023 K
Homilies, Catholic (Ælfric), 991 K
Homs, Syria, battle, 1281 D

* These authors essayed world histories.

Hōnen Shōnin. *See* Genkū
Hong-duc, Code of, 1483 F
Honnecourt, Villard de, F. mason, 1235 J, 1271 G
Honoré, Master, F. miniaturist, 1296 J
Honorius II (Cadalus, Bishop of Parma; d. 1072), anti-pope, 1061 D, 1062 A, D
Honorius II, Pope, 1124 D, 1128 C, 1130 A
Honorius III (Cencio Savelli), Pope, 1216 C, H, 1217 E, 1218 C, D, E, 1219 H, 1220 D, E, 1223 B, H, 1225 A, 1227 A
Honorius IV (Jacopo Savelli), 1285 B, 1287 B
Hops. *See* Beer
Hořic, Czechoslovakia, battle, 1423 B
Horik, King of Denmark, 845 E, 854 E
Horne Childe, 1250 K
Horodlo, Russia, Union of, 1413 D
Horses, stirrups for, 840 G; collar, 920 G; breast-strap, 1130 G,
  racing, 956 G, 1306 G
  treatises on: al-Asmʿī, 827 G; Giordano Ruffo, 1252 G
Hosebondire (Walter of Henley), 1250 G
Hospitallers, German. *See* Teutonic Knights
Hospitallers, Knights, Order of, of St. John of Jerusalem, 1099 H, 1193 E, 1271 B, 1281 D; conquer Rhodes, 1306 D, 1308 C, 1480 B, C; expelled from Smyrna, 1402 D
Hospitals:
  Arab, 827 G, *and see* Baghdād, Cairo
  Chinese, 1143 G
  Seljuq, 1161 G, 1217 J; mental, 1228 J
Hostiensis (Henry of Susa), It. cardinal and canonist, 1271 H
Hou-Chou dynasty. *See* China
Hous of Fame, The (Geoffrey Chaucer), 1381 K
Hoysala, India, Hindu Kingdom, 1190 E
Hrotswith (*or* Roswitha), G. poetess (*c.* 932–1002), 962 K
Hsi Hsia, China, Tangut Empire, 1035 H, 1038 E, 1044 E, 1126 E, 1224 E
Hsiang-yang, China, 1269 E, 1273 E
Hsieh Chü-chêng, C. historian (912–81), 981 K
Hsieh-p'u (Fu Kung), 1059 G
Hsing-cha-sheng-lan (Fei Hsin), 1436 G
Hsing-i-hsiang fa-yao (Su Sung), 1092 G
Hsi-yüan lu (Sung Tz'ŭ), 1248 G
Hsü Ching, C. geographer, 1125 G
Hsüeh-ku-pien (Wu-ch'iu Yen), 1307 K
Hua chien (T'ung Hou), 1329 J
Huand Hatun, Seljuq lady, 1237 J
Huang Ch'ao, C. peasant leader, 874 E, 879 E; emperor, 880 E, 884 E
Huang Ch'üan, C. painter, 965 J
Huang Kung-weng, C. painter (1269–1354), 1354 J
Huesca, Spain, 1096 E
Hugh I de Lusignan, King of Cyprus, 1205 B, 1218 A
Hugh III, King of Cyprus (1267–84) and Jerusalem, 1269 C, 1284 A
Hugh Capet, Marquess of Neustria, 960 E; Duke of the Franks, 985 B; King of France, 987 C, D, 988 C, 989 A, C, 991 A, B, 996 D
Hugh of Arles, Marquess of Provence, 924 E; King of Italy, 926 B, C, 932 E, 933 E, 945 E, 948 B
Hugh the Black, Count of Burgundy, 915 E, 923 C, 938 E, 952 D
Hugh I, Duke of Burgundy, 1079 E
Hugh the Great, Marquess of Neustria (d. 956), 923 C, 938 E, 939 E, 940 E, 942 D, 943 E, 944 E, 948 B, 960 E; Duke of the Franks, 956 B, 960 E
Hugh of Avalon, St., Bishop of Lincoln, 1200 L
Hugh of Semur, Abbot of Cluny (1049–1109), 1024 L, 1109 L
Hugh of St. Victor, F. theologian, 1141 H
Hugh of Vermandois, Archbishop of Reims (b. 920), 925 E, 931 E, 939 E; expelled, 946 E, (948 B)
Hugo of Bologna, It. jurist, 1100 F
Hugo Falcandus, It. chronicler, 1189 K
Hugoccio, It. canonist, 1180 H
Hugolinus, It. jurist, 1233 F
Hugon, Guillaume, Chancellor of Burgundy, 1477 B
Hui Tsung, Emperor of China (1100–25), 1125 E, 1127 E; artist and patron, 1135 J
Hūlāgū, Ilkhan of Persia, 1253 E, 1256 D, 1258 A, 1259 C, 1260 A, C, 1262 E, 1265 A; astronomical tables of, 1259 G, 1274 G
Hültz, Johannes, G. mason, 1439 J
Humanist education, 1398 H; *and see* Feltre, Vittorino da; Ravenna, Giovanni da; Verona, Guarino da
Humanists:
  Dutch. *See* Agricola, Rudolphus
  German. *See* Cusa, Nicholas of
  Greek. *See* Bessarion of Trebizond
  Italina. *See* Alberti, Leone Battista; Barzizza, Gasparino da; Biondi, Flavio; Bruni, Leonardo; Conversini, Giovanni; Ferreto de'Ferreti; Manetti, Gianozzo; Marsigli, Luigi; Mussato, Albertino; Niccoli, Niccolò; Nicholas V; Petrarch; Pius II; Poggio Bracciolini; Salutati, Coluccio; Strozzi, Palla; Valla, Lorenzo; Vergerio, Pier Paulo
  Polish. *See* Sanok, Gregory of
Humbert II, Dauphin of Vienne, 1349 C
Humbert, It. cardinal and reformer, 1054 H, 1061 H, L
Humbledon Hill, England, battle, 1402 C
Hummayāt, Kitāb al- (al-Isrāʾīli), 932 G
Humphrey, Duke of Gloucester, 1390 L, 1424 D, 1425 B, D, 1426 A, 1431 B, 1441 D, 1447 A
Hunac Ceel, Mayan ruler, 987 E
Hunayn ibn-Ishāq al-Ibādi, Arab translator and ophthamologist (b. 809), 856 K, 873 G
Hundred Rolls, 1274 G
Hundred Years War, begins, 1337 B; ends, 1453 C; *and see* France
Hung Kua, C. archaeologist (1117–84), 1184 K
Hung Tsun, C. archaeologist (1120–74), 1149 K
Hung-wu, Emperor of China (b. 1328; 1367–98), as Chu Yüan-chang, peasant leader, 1356 E; first Ming Emperor, 1367 E, 1369 E, 1371 E, 1374 G, 1375 K, 1380 F, 1382 E, 1398 E, 1403 E
Hungary:
  as Pannonia, Avars in, 811 E; invaded by Bulgars, 828 E
  Magyars, 837 E; settle in Hungary, 895 E; conquer Moravia, 906 E; raids:
    Italy, 898 E, 899 C, 900 E, 924 E, 937 E
    Germany, 900 E, 906 E, 908 E, 909 E, 910 E, 917 E, 924 E, 937 J; and Flanders, 954 E; defeated, 933 A, 938 E, 955 C
    France, 917 E, 924 E, 926 E, 935 E, 937 E, 951 E
    threaten Constantinople, 934 E, 959 E
  conversion of, 942 H, 950 H, 997 E, 1044 L
  Kingdom created, 1000 C; *and see*
    Stephen I (1000–38)
    Peter (1038–46)
    Obo (1042–4)
    Andrew I (1046–60)
    Béla I (1060–3)
    Solomon (1063–74)
    Géza I (1074–7)
    Ladislas I (1077–95)
    Coloman (1095–1114)
    Stephen II (1114–31)

Béla II (1131–41)
Géza II (1141–61)
Stephen III (1161–73)
Ladislas II (1161–2)
Stephen IV (1162–3)
Béla III (1173–96)
Imre (1196–1204)
Ladislas III (1204–5)
Andrew II (1205–35)
Béla IV (1235–70)
Stephen V (1270–2)
Ladislas IV (1272–90)
Andrew III (1290–1301)
Wenceslas (III of Bohemia; 1301–4)
Charles I (1308–42)
Lewis I (1342–82)
Mary (1382–95)
Sigismund (1386–1437)
Albert (II; 1437–9)
Ladislas V (Vladislav III of Poland; 1439–44)
Ladislas VI (1444–57)
Matthias Corvinus (1458–90)
Ladislas VII (Vladislav II of Bohemia; 1490–1516)
loses Moravia, 1028 E
German campaigns in, 1042 C, 1043 E, 1044 C, 1050 E, 1053 E
frontier with Austria, 1043 E
wars with Greeks, 1124 E, 1151 E, 1156 C
loses Zara, 1202 D
murder of queen, 1213 C
Golden Bull of Andrew II, 1222 F, 1351 F
Cumans in, 1239 E, 1290 C
Mongol invasion, 1241 B, D, 1242 B, E
extinction of Árpád dynasty, succession dispute, 1290 C, 1301 A
succession disputes, 1382 C, 1386 A, 1395 B, 1403 C
defeats Turks, 1395 B
regency of John Hunyadi (*q.v.*), 1445 E
standing army, 1465 F
German colonies in, 1161 G, 1224 G
iron industry, 1230 G
visited by French mason, 1235 J
printing in, 1473 G
Hunt, The (Uccello), 1465 J
Huntingdon, England, Earl of. *See* Holand, John
Hunyadi, John Corvinus, Voivode of Transylvania, 1442 E, 1443 D, 1444 A–D, Regent of Hungary, 1445 E, 1448 D, 1451 D, 1452 E, 1456 C
Huon de Bordeaux, 1200 K
Hus, John, Bohemian reformer and martyr, 1402 H, 1408 H, 1410 H, 1412 H, 1413 H, 1415 H, L
Husain Baiqara, Sultan of Persia (1470–1506), 1470 C
Hūshang, King of Mālwa (1406–35), 1406 E
Hussite wars. *See* Bohemia
Hutten, Ulrich von, G. poet (1488–1523), 1488 L
Huysmann, Roelof. *See* Agricola, Rudolphus
Hydrographiques, Cartes (Andreas Bianco), 1436 G
Hydrostatics, 1121 G
Hygiene, treatises on, 1257 G, 1303 G
Hymns, 1153 H, 1261 J, 1263 J, 1306 K
Hypnerotomachia Polophili (Francesco Colonna), 1479 K
Hystoire et plaisante chronique, L' (Antoine de la Salle), 1462 K
Hywel the Good (Hywel Dda), King of Deheubarth, Gwynned, Powys and Seisyllwg, 949 E, F

I

Ibelin, Israel, battle, 1123 B
Ibelin, John of, Lord of Beirut, 1232 B, 1233 B, 1236 E
Ibil, Kitāb al- (al-Asma'ī), 827 G
Ibn ath-Thimna, Saracen, of Sicily, 1061 C
Ibrāhīm (I) ibn-al-Aghlab, Emir of Mzab, founder of Aghlabids (d. 811), 800 E
Ibrāhīm II of Kairāwan (874–902), 878 B, 902 C
Ibrāhīm ibn Ia'qub, Sp. J. traveller, 965 G
Iceland, 825 G, 847 G; Althing, 930 F; converted, 1000 H; submits to Norway, 1263 D
history and literature. *See* Sagas
other writers:
Nikulas Saemundarson, 1158 G
Bjarni Bergthorsson, 1173 G
Iconium. *See* Konya
Iconoclasm. *See* Greek Church
Idiota de Sapientia (Nicholas of Cusa), 1450 K
Idrāk lilisan al-Atrāk, Kitāb al- (Abū-Haiyan), 1313 K
Idrisi. *See* Edrisi
Idrīsid dynasty. *See* Fez
Ifat, Abyssinia, Sultans of, 1332 E, 1445 D
Ignatius, St., Patriarch of Constantinople, 858 H, 863 H, 867 D, 877 H, L
Ignium, Liber ('Marc the Greek'), 1300 G
Igor, Prince of Novgorod, 873 E; (?another), Prince of Kiev, 913 E, 941 E, 945 E
Igor of Novgorod-Sêveresk, poem about, 1185 K
Ihyā 'Ulum al-Din (al-Ghazzāli), 1111 H
Ikhbar al-'Ulamā' (al-Qiftī), 1248 G
Ikhshīd, Muhammad ibn-Tughj al-, Sultan of Egypt, 935 A, 937 E
Ikhshīdid dynasty. *See* Egypt
Ikhtiyār-ad-Dīn, Muslim conqueror of Bengal, 1202 E, 1205 E
Īlek Khāns. *See* Transoxiana
Ilkhans. *See* Persia
Iltutmish, Sultan of Delhi (1211–36), 1223 J, 1229 A, 1231 J, 1235 J, 1236 B
Ilyās, Shah of Bengal (d. 1358), 1352 E
Image du Monde, L' (Gautier de Metz), 1245 G
Image of the World (al-Khwarizmī), 851 G
Imagine mundi, De (Henry of Mainz), 1110 G
Imagine Tetrici, De (Walafrid Strabo), 849 K
Imitatione Christi, De (Thomas à Kempis), 1425 H, 1471 H
Imre, King of Hungary, 1196 E, 1204 E
Imube Hironari, Ja. philologist, 808 K
Inca Pachacuti, ruler of Incas (1438–71), 1471 E
Incarnation, date for, 1083 K
Incas. *See* Peru
Incendium Amoris (Richard Rolle), 1349 K
India:
Hindu Kingdoms. *See* Anhilwara; Bengal; Chalukya; Chedi; Chola; Deccan; Deogīr; Dvāravatīpura; Gujarāt; Gwalior; Halebīd; Hoysala; Jaīpur; Jejākabhutki; Kākatīya; Kanauj; Kashmīr; Madura; Mālwā; Pallava; Pañchāla; Pāndya; Punjab; Rāshtrakūta; Telingāna; Vijayanagar; Yādava
caste system, 1119 E
cultural influence in Cambodia, 1330 K; in Champa, 1253 K
dictionary of *materia medica*, 1242 G
languages:
Gujarātī, 1355 K
Prākrit, 1170 K
Sanskrit, 1330 K
Tamil, 1200 K
Urdū, 1422 H
laws, 1270 F

India—*contd.*
Hindu Kingdoms—*contd.*
literature:
anthology (Somadeva), 1085 K
Kalhana, 1148 K
dictionary of synonyms, 1170 K
Chand Bardāī, 1192 K
Kamban, 1200 K
drama, 1350 K
Gangā Devi, 1370 K
Lal Ded, 1380 K
philosophy (Sankara), 820 K
religions:
Buddhism, 1193 E
Hinduism, 1025 A
Jainism, 1141 E, 1355 K
Sikhs, 1469 H
Siva cult, 1167 E
Veda, 1387 H
Vishnuism, 1141 E
theologian. *See* Sāyana
trade with Arabs, 851 G, 920 G
Muslim settlements, 1008 E
Muslim invasions:
Ghaznavid, 1001 D, 1009 E, 1018 D, 1025 A, 1026 E
Ghūrid, 1175 E, 1186 E, 1192 E, 1193 A, 1194 E, 1196 E, 1197 E, 1202 E
Muslim kingdoms. *See* Delhi (*esp.*); Ahmadnagar; Bengal; Berar; Bīdar; Bījāpur; Gujarāt; Jaunpur; Kashmīr; Kulbarga; Madura; Mālwā
Black Death in, 1332 G
famines in, 1336 G, 1340 G
Mongol invasions, 1221 D, 1241 D, 1245 E, 1299 E, 1303 E, 1304 E, 1306 E, 1323 E, 1398 B–D, 1399 A; *and see* Delhi, Punjab
history, 1260 K, 1352 K, 1359 K
poetry, 1325 K, 1338 K, 1359 K
India, Description of (al-Bīrunī), 1048 G
Indra III, King of Rāshtrakūta, 916 E
Indrapatindraditya, King of Sukhodaya, 1230 E
Indrapura, S. Vietnam, Champa capital, 982 E, 1000 E
Indravarman I, King of Cambodia (877–89), 889 J
Indulf, King of Scotland (954–62), 954 E, 962 E, 966 E
Inge I, King of Norway, 1135 D, 1161 A
Inge II, King of Norway, 1204 C, 1217 E
Inge I the Pious, King of Sweden, 1090 E, 1101 E, 1112 E
Inge II, King of Sweden (1118–29), 1118 E
Ingelborg, wife of Philip II, 1193 C, 1195 B, 1200 A
Ingelger, Viscount of Anjou, 870 E, 888 E
Ingelheim, W. Germany, 948 B
Ink, Chinese treatises on, 1329 G, 1398 G
Innocent II (Gregory Papareschi), Pope (1130–43), 1133 E, 1139 H, 1142 E, 1143 C, E
abroad seeking recognition, 1130 A, H, 1131 A, D
returns to Rome, 1132 C, 1133 B
opposes Roger of Sicily, 1136 E, 1139 B, C
Innocent III, anti-pope, 1179 C, 1180 A
Innocent III (Lothar Conti), Pope, 1198 A, 1199 H, 1216 C
and Crusades, 1198 C, 1207 D, 1215 D
as temporal ruler, 1198 D, 1207 F
interdict on France, 1200 A, C
German policy, 1201 B, C, 1208 B, 1209 D, 1210 D, 1211 A
recognises Orders, 1204 E, 1210 E, H, 1216 H
relations with England, 1206 A, D, 1208 A, 1209 D, 1213 B, 1215 C
and other kingdoms, 1202 E, 1204 D, 1207 E
Lateran Council, 1215 D, H
Innocent IV (Sinibaldo dei Fieschi), Pope, 1243 B, 1245 E, 1251 E, 1254 D
regulates friars, 1243 H, 1245 H, 1247 H, 1253 H; and inquisition, 1252 H
crusade against Frederick II, 1244 A, 1245 C, 1248 E
at Lyons, 1244 D; General Council, 1245 C, H
missions to Mongols, 1245 H, 1246 C, 1248 B, 1253 H
intervenes in Germany, 1246 B, 1252 A
Roman revolt against, 1252 E, 1253 D
plans for Sicily, 1252 B, 1254 A, B, D
Innocent VI (Peter of Tarentaise), Pope, 1276 A, B
Innocent VI (Étienne Aubert), Pope, 1352 D, 1353 B, 1356 A, 1362 C
Innocent VII (Cosmo Migliorato), Pope (in Rome), 1404 D, 1406 C, D
Innocent VIII (Battista Cybò), Pope (1484–92), 1484 C, H, 1485 D, 1486 B, 1487 C; monastic reformer, 1487 H
Inquisition:
in France, 1229 H, 1235 H, 1277 H, 1301 H
in Germany, 1231 H, 1233 H, 1234 H
regulated, 1233 H, 1252 H
manuals for inquisitors, 1323 H, 1398 H
in Spain, 1477 H, 1483 H, 1488 H
Inscriptions, Chinese, treatises on, 1072 K, 1307 K
Insurance, early example of, 1370 G
Inventione Dialectica, De (Rudolphus Agricola), 1480 K
Investiture Contest, 1075 A, 1078 D; in Empire, 1076 A, 1077 A, 1080 A, B, 1111 A, 1112 A, B, 1122 C; England, 1106 C; France, 1104 E
Iona, island, Scotland, 980 E; monastery, 802 E
'Iqd al-Farid, al- (Rabbih), 940 J
Iraq, gipsies in, 834 E; revolt of slaves, 869 C, 883 E; under Seljuqs, 1104 A, 1194 E; conquered by Timur, 1393 E; *and see* Baghdād
'Irāqī, Per. poet, 1288 K
Ireland:
Vikings in, 807 E, 835 E, 845 E, 853 E, 877 E, 919 C
Danes in, 967 E, 994 B, 999 E, 1014 B, 1044 E
Norwegian invasion, 1103 C
Norman Conquest, 1169 B, 1170 C, 1171 D; chronicle of (Gerald of Wales), 1185 K
under John, 1177 B, 1185 B, 1210 B
first parliament, 1297 F
invaded by Scots, 1315 B, C, 1316 B, 1317 A, 1318 D
Black Death in, 1349 G
Statute of Kilkenny, 1366 A
French invasion attempted, 1380 A
Richard II in, 1394 D, 1395 B, 1399 B, C
Church in, 1152 H
Cistercians in, 1142 J
literature: *Book of Ballymote*, 1391 K
voyage to Iceland from, 825 G
Irene, Greek Empress, 802 E, 803 L
Iride et radialibus impressionibus, De (Dietrich of Freiburg), 1307 G
Iris, river, Turkey, battle, 838 B
Irnerius of Bologna, It. jurist, 1100 F
Iron manufacture, in China, 1310 G; in Europe, 1087 G, 1190 G, 1197 G, 1230 G, 1323 G, 1340 G; *and see* Cannon
Irpen, river, Russia, battle, 1320 E
Irrawaddy delta, Burma, 1057 E
Irrigation. *See* Canals
Isaac I Comnenus, Greek Emperor, 1057 C, 1059 D
Isaac II Angelus, Greek Emperor, 1185 C, 1187 E, 1189 E, 1190 A, E, 1191 E; deposed, 1195 B; restored, 1203 C; murdered, 1204 A; son, 1202 D
Isaac ben Sid, Sp. J. astronomer, 1262 G

Isaac Berrabi Jacob al-Fez (Alphesi), Moroccan J. Talmudic scholar, 1013 L, 1103 H
Isaac Judaeus. *See* Isrā'īli
Isabel, wife of King John, 1200 C
Isabel of Hainault, wife of Philip II, 1180 B
Isabella, wife of Frederick II (1214–41), 1235 C
Isabella, Queen of Castile (1474–1504), 1451 L, 1468 C, 1469 D, 1474 D, 1475 A, 1477 H, 1479 C, 1480 A, 1489 A, 1491 G; conquers Granada, 1481 E, 1482 A, 1483 B, 1489 C, D, 1491 D
Isabella, wife of Edward II (d. 1358), 1308 A, 1325 A, 1326 C, D, 1330 B, 1337 D
Isabella, wife of Richard II, 1396 A, D
Isabella, Queen of Jerusalem, 1205 B
Isaiah (Nanni), 1408 J
Isāmy, Indian Muslim poet and historian, 1359 K
Ischia, island, Italy, 845 E
Ise, Ja. poet, 939 K
Iseult. *See* Tristan
Isfahan, Persia:
  Kakuyid dynasty, 1007 E, 1050 E
  capital of Seljuq Empire, 1050 E, (1091 E)
  destroyed by Timur, 1387 D
  astrolabists of, 984 G
  'Friday Mosque', 1145 J
Isfahānī, Abū'l-Faraj al-, Per. anthologist and musicologist, 897 L, 967 K
Ishinhō (Yasuyori Tamba), 982 G
Isiaslav I, Prince of Kiev, 1055 A, 1069 E, 1077 E, 1078 E
Isiaslav II, Prince of Kiev, 1146 E, 1155 E
Isidore, *soi-disant* Bishop of Seville, 850 H
Iskandar-namā (al-Ahmedī), 1390 K
Islam:
  Caliph. *See* Baghdād; Cairo
  conversion to:
    China, 1240 G
    Karakhanids, 960 E
    Kashmīr, forced, 1416 H
    Malacca, 1405 E
    Mongols, 1282 B, 1295 E, 1312 E, 1367 H
    Transoxiana, 900 E
  countries described (al-Maqdisī), 985 G
  inquisition, 922 H
  law, 820 F, 1277 F
  scholastic philosophy, 935 K, 944 K
  sects, etc.: Dervishes, 1241 E, 1273 H; Hanbalite, 855 H; Ismā'ites, 878 H; Qādirite, 1166 H; Shādhilite, 1258 H; Shāfi'ite, 820 H; *and see* Assassins, Qarmatians, Shī'ites, Sūfī
  theologians. *See* Bukhārī; Cabiz; Dhu-al-Nūn; Ghazzālī; Hazm; Hajjāj; Taftazānī
  treatises on:
    in defence (al-Tabarī), 854 H
    Christian:
      Eulogius, 859 H
      Risalah, 1141 K
      William of Tripoli, 1273 K
  university, chief, in, 1258 H
Islendingabók (Ari the Wise), 1120 K
Isles, Scotland, Lords of the, 1164 E, 1476 C; *cf.* Hebrides
Ismā'īl, ruler of Aleppo (b. 1163), 1174 B, 1181 D
Ismā'īl, Sultan of Ghaznī (997–8), 998 E
Ismā'īl I, King of Granada, 1314 A, 1319 B, 1325 C
Ismā'īl II, King of Granada, 1359 C, 1360 C
Ismā'īl ibn-Ahmad, Sāmānid ruler (892–907), 900 E
Ismā'ites, sect of Shī'ites, 878 H; sect of, *see* Qarmatians
Isopet (Marie de France), 1185 K
Isrā'īli (Isaac Judaeus), Ishāq al-, Eg. J. physician (830?–932?), 932 G
Istakhri, al-, Arab geographer, 950 G
Istoire de l'Empereur (Henri de Valenciennes), 1216 K
Istoria fiorentina (Baldassare), 1385 K
Istorie (Antonio Pucci), 1388 K
Istria, Yugoslavia, 1269 E, 1358 A
Italia, All' (Petrarch), 1352 K
Italia illustrata (Flavio Biondi), 1446 K
Italy:
  Carolingian Kings. *See* Pepin; Bernard; Lothar I; Louis II; Charles the Bald; Charles the Fat
  Kingdom disputed, 888 A; *and see*
    Guy (889–94)
    Lambert (892–8)
    Berengar I (898–922)
    Louis III (900–5)
    Rudolph II (922–6)
    Hugh of Arles (926–48)
    Lothar II (948–50)
    Berengar II (950–61)
    Otto I, 951 C, 952 C; and Otto II, 961 C
    Ardoin (1002–4)
    Henry II (1004–24)
    offer of, 1025 E
    Conrad II (1026–39)
    Conrad III (1028–30?)
    Henry VI (1186–97)
    See also Lombards
  Saracen attacks, 837 E, 838 E, 840 E, 842 E, 845 E, 846 C, 847 E, 848 E, 852 B, 853 E, 878 E, 902 E, 976 E, 982 C, 1002 E, 1011 E; defeated, 866 D, 871 A, 880 E, 915 E, 1006 E
  Magyar raids, 898 E, 899 C, 900 E, 924 E, 937 E
  Greek rule in. *See* Greek Empire
  Black Death in, 1347 G, 1348 G
  history. *See* Historians
  map of, 1119 G
  poetry:
    St. Francis, 1225 K
    Jacopo da Lentini, 1240 K
    Sordello of Mantua, 1270 K
    Guideo Guinizelli, 1276 K
    Rustico di Filippo, 1280 K
    Guittone d'Arezzo, 1294 K
    Brunetto Latini, 1295 K
    Dante, 1276 K, 1290 K, 1300 K, 1310 K, 1314 K
    Cecco Angiolieri, 1312 K
    Petrarch, 1339 K, 1341 K, 1351 K, 1352 K, 1357 K, 1366 K
    Antonio Pucci, 1388 K
    Franco Sacchetti, 1395 K
    Frederigo Frezzi, 1403 K
    Angelo Poliziano, 1480 K
    Luigi Pulci, 1482 K
    Matteo Maria Boiardo, 1482 K
    Lorenzo de'Medici, 1489 K
  prose:
    Guido Fava, 1229 K
    Giordano da Rivalto, 1311 K
    Domenico Cavalca, 1342 K
    Boccaccio, 1350 K
    Giovanni da Firenze, 1378 K
    Lapo da Castiglionchio, 1381 K
    Sacchetti, *Trecento Novelle*, 1395 K
    Sercambi, *Novelle*, 1424 K
    Alberti, *Della Famiglia*, 1441 K
    Poggio, *Liber Facetiarum*, 1452 K
    Masuccio, *Novellino*, 1476 K
    Francesco Colonna, 1479 K
    Sannazaro, *L'Arcadia*, 1486 K
I'tibār, Kitāb al- (Ibn-Munqidh), 1182 K
Itineraries (William Worcestre), 1478 K
Itineraries in Asia, Chinese, 805 K

Itinerarium (Baudry de Bourgueil), 1130 K
Itinerarium ad Jerusalem (Johannes de Hese), 1389 K
Itinerarium Cambriae (Gerald of Wales), 1188 K
Itzcoatl, Aztec King, 1440 E
Iudiciis nativitatum, De (Antonio de Montulmo), 1394 G
Ivan I Kalitá of Moscow, 1328 E; Grand Duke of Vladimir, 1332 E, 1341 E
Ivan II of Moscow, Grand Duke of Vladimir, 1353 E, 1359 E
Ivan III, Grand Duke of Moscow (b. 1439; 1462–1505), 1462 A, 1481 C, 1482 C, 1484 E, 1485 J; defeats Mongols, 1476 E, 1481 E, 1487 C; subjects Novgorod, 1471 C, 1478 A, 1480 A
Iviza, island, Spain, 1115 E, 1235 E
Ivo, Bishop of Chartres, F. canonist, 1115 H, L
Ivois, France, 1022 C
Ivrea, Italy, Marquesses of. *See* Berengar; Ardoin
'Izz-ad-Dīn I, atabeg of Mosul (1176–93), 1180 B, 1181 D
I-yü t'u-chih (anon.), 1489 G

J

Jābir ibn-Hayyān, Arab alchemist, 810 G, 1144 G, 1187 G, 1473 G
Jacob of Florence, It. mathematician, 1307 G
Jacob ben Makir, F. J. astronomer (d. 1308), 1288 G
Jacobus of Bologna, It. jurist, 1100 F
Jacopo da Lentini, Sicilian courtier and poet, 1240 K
Jacopone da Todi, It. friar and poet, 1306 K, L
Jacqueline of Bavaria, Countess of Hainault, Holland and Zeeland (b. 1400, d. 1436), 1424 D, 1425 B, 1428 C
Jacquemart de Hesdin, Flemish miniaturist, 1411 J
Jacquerie, 1358 B
Jadwiga, 'King' of Poland (b. 1373), 1382 C, 1383 E, 1399 C
Jadzwingas, Baltic tribe, 1009 H, 1264 E, 1282 E
Jaen, Spain, 1246 E
Jaffa, Israel, battles, 1102 B, 1192 C, 1268 A
Jagiello (Vladislav II, King of Poland, 1386–1434; b. 1350), Grand Prince of Lithuania, 1377 E, 1381 E, 1382 E, 1383 E, 1387 J; as King, 1386 A, 1387 E, 1389 E, 1397 H, 1401 A, 1413 D, 1422 B, 1427 B, 1430 D, 1434 B; defeats Teutonic Knights, 1410 C, D, 1411 A, 1414 E, 1422 C
Jāhiz, abu-'Uthmān 'Amr al-, Arab belletrist, 869 K
Jahshiyari, al-, Arab fabulist, 942 K
Jaipāl I, King of the Punjab, 988 E, 1001 D
Jaīpur, India, Hindu kingdom, 1244 B
Jājnagar, Rajah of Jaīpur, 1244 B
Jalāl-ad-Dīn, Khan of the Golden Horde, 1411 E
Jalāl-ad-Dīn, Khwārizm Shah, 1220 D, 1221 D, 1225 E, 1230 C, 1231 C
Jalālī Era, 1079 G
Jalt (gipsies), 834 E
Jamā'a, Muhammad ibn-, Syrian writer on politics (1241–1333), 1333 F
James I the Conqueror, King of Aragon (b. 1208; 1213–76), 1213 C, 1217 E, 1227 E, 1231 A, 1244 E, 1245 F, 1258 B, 1262 B, E, 1266 E, 1276 C; conquests, 1228 E, 1229 D, 1232 E, 1235 E, 1237 E, 1238 C; autobiography, 1276 K; chronicle of, 1330 K
James II the Just, King of Aragon (1291–1327), King of Sicily, 1285 D, 1287 C, 1291 B, 1296 B; of Aragon only, 1297 E, 1299 C, 1323 E, 1327 D
James I (II), King of Majorca (d. 1311), 1262 E, 1291 A, 1306 J
James II (III), King of Majorca (1324–44), 1344 A, 1349 B, D
James I, King of Scotland (b. 1394), 1406 A, B, 1424 A, 1425 B, 1428 F, 1436 C, 1437 A; as poet, 1423 K
James II, King of Scotland (b. 1430), 1437 A, 1440 D, 1452 A, 1460 C
James III, King of Scotland (b. 1452), 1460 C, 1466 C, 1468 A, D, 1476 C, 1479 E, 1480 E, 1482 B, C, 1484 C, 1488 B
James IV, King of Scotland (b. 1473; 1488–1513), 1488 B
James, St., the Greater, tomb of, 813 H
James of Venice, It. translator, 1128 G
Jamhara fi-l-Lugha, al- (ibn-Duraid), 933 K
Jāmi, Kitāb al- (al-Baytār), 1248 G
Jāmi' al-Alhān ('Abd al-Qādir), 1405 J
Jāmi' al-tasanif (Rashīd), 1318 G
Jāmi' al-tawārikh (Rashīd), 1314 K
Jamurlu, Yugoslavia, battle, 1413 C
Jan de Leeuve (Jan van Eyck), 1436 J
Jandun, John of, F. polemicist, 1328 L
Janibeg, Khan of the Golden Horde, 1342 E, 1356 E, 1357 E
Japan:
- Fujiwara Regency founded, 833 E, 857 F, 930 E
- collapse of fiscal system, 927 F
- 'Camera system' begins, 1068 F
- feudal rule of Taira, 1160 E
- revolt against, 1180 E, F, 1183 E, 1184 E
- Shogunate founded, 1185 B, 1189 E, 1199 E
- Shōkyū War, 1219 E
- Hōjō regency of Shogunate, 1219 E, 1331 E, 1333 E
- Mongol attacks, 1274 E, 1281 C, 1286 E, 1293 J
- economic collapse of feudalism, 1297 F
- deposition of Go-Daigo, 1331 E, 1333 E, 1336 E
- Shogunate restored, 1338 E
- tribute to China, 1371 E
- civil war (1336–92), 1392 E
- Ōnin War, 1468 E, 1477 E
- Buddhism:
  - monasteries, 816 H, 1341 G
  - Nicheren sect, 1282 H
  - popular development, 1017 H, 1282 H
  - Pure Land sect, 1175 H, 1207 H
  - Shingon sect, 806 H, 816 H
  - Shinsū sect, 1262 H
  - Tendai sect, 805 H
  - Zen, 800 H
    - Rinzai sect, 1191 H
    - Sōtō sect, 1227 H
- Bureau of Archives, 810 F
- capitals. *See* Kyōto; Kamakura
- castle-building, 1456 F
- customs and language described, 808 K
- *Emperors, Descent of* (Kitabatake), 1354 K
- Examiners of Misdeeds, 820 F
- gardens, 1206 G, 1351 J
- genealogies, 815 K
- history, 1095 K, 1195 K, 1220 K, 1266 K; official, 887 K
- irrigation in, 800 G
- law-codes, 811 F, 833 F, 927 F; feudal, 1232 F, 1338 F
- literature:
  - *Monogatari* (romance, legend):
    - *Taketori*, 890 K
    - Ise, 939 K
    - *Utsubo*, 1000 K
    - *Genji*, 1010 K
    - *Konjaku*, 1050 K
    - *Eiga*, 1095 K
    - Tsutsumi, 1200 K

anthologies of poetry:
Kokinshū, 905 K
Shin Kokinshū, 1205 K
diaries:
Ki no Tsurayuki, 935 K
Sei Shōnagon, 1000 K
Nakayama, 1195 K
Fujiwara Kanezane, 1200 K
Sino-Japanese dictionary, 983 K
Azuma Kagami (chronicle), 1266 K
essays of Yoshida, 1350 K
Taiheiki (novel), 1374 K
Nō drama, 1384 K, 1443 K
medical treatise, first, 982 G
perfume, treatise on, 1156 K
Police Commissioners, 820 F
school and library in, 1270 H
tea, growing, 814 G, 1191 G; ceremony, 1443 K
trade, 879 G, 1341 G; and piracy, 1374 G
Jaromir, Duke of Bohemia, 1003 E, 1004 C, 1012 E
Jaropolk I, Prince of Kiev, 972 B, 977 E
Jaropolk II, Prince of Kiev, 1132 E, 1139 E
Jaroslav I the Wise, Prince of Kiev (1018–55), 1015 E, 1018 C, 1024 E, 1035 E, 1036 F, 1055 A, 1097 E
Jaroslav II, Great Prince of Russia, 1238 A, 1239 E, 1246 C
Jaroslav III, Grand Duke of Vladimir, 1263 D, 1272 E
Jatāvarman Sundara, Rajah of Pāndya (1251–69), 1269 E
Jaunpur, India, 1360 G; Muslim kingdom, 1394 B, 1479 E
Java, Indonesia, 1292 E, G, 1293 E; kingdom, 1389 E; *and see* Mājapāhit
Jawhāri, Abū-l-Fath 'Uthman ibn-Jinni al-, Turkish philologist, 1008 K
Jawzi, Sibt ibn-al-, Arab historian (1186–1257), 1257 K
Jaya Harivarman, King of Champa (d. 1166/7), 1149 E
Jaya Indravarman IV, King of Champa, 1177 E, 1181 E
Jaya Indravarman V, King of Champa, 1283 E
Jaya Parameshvaravarman II, King of Champa, 1220 E
Jaya Simhavarman II, King of Champa, 1044 E
Jayasura II, Burmese king, 1210 F
Jayavarman II, King of Cambodia, 850 E
Jayavarman VII, King of Cambodia (1181–*c.* 1218), 1177 E, 1181 E, 1203 E, 1218 J
Jaysca, Yugoslavia, 1463 D
Jazarī, al-, Arab writer on mechanics, 1206 G
Jean d'Andeli, F. mason, 1200 J
Jean d'Arras, F. romance writer, 1387 K
Jean le Bel, Belgian chronicler, 1370 K
Jean des Champs, F. mason, 1248 J, 1272 J, 1273 J
Jean de Chelle, F. mason, 1250 J
Jean le Loup, F. mason, 1210 J, 1241 J
Jean le Maingre. *See* Boucicaut
Jean d'Orbais, F. mason, 1210 J
Jeanne de Penthièvre, Breton claimant, 1341 B, D
Jehan et Blonde (Philippe de Remy), 1278 K
Jejākubhukti, India, Hindu kingdom, 999 J
Jerome of Prague, Bohemian reformer and martyr, 1416 H
Jerusalem:
sack of Holy Sepulchre, 1009 C
under Seljuqs, 1071 C, 1076 E, 1095 E
taken by Egyptians, 1098 E; Crusaders, 1099 C; Saladin, 1187 D, 1192 A, B; Egypt, 1227 D
partitioned with Frederick II, 1229 A, 1239 D
sacked, 1244 C
Mongols reach, 1308 E
Church of Holy Sepulchre, 1149 J
Orders in, 1119 H; *and see* Hospitallers
pilgrims to, accounts by, 1104 G, 1107 G, 1158 G, 1389 K
university, 1065 H
Jerusalem, kingdom of ('Outremer'), 1099 C; *and see*
Baldwin I (1100–18)
Baldwin II (1118–31)
Fulk (1131–43)
Melisande (1143)
Baldwin III (1143–63)
Amalric I (1163–74)
Baldwin IV (1174–85)
Baldwin V (1185–6)
Sibylla (1186)
Guy (1186–92)
(with capital at Acre, 1191 C)
Conrad (1192)
Henry (1192–7)
Amelric II (1198–1205)
Isabella (1205–)
Maria
John of Brienne (1210–25)
Frederick II (1225–50)
anarchy in, 1232 B, 1236 E, 1254 B
defeated by Egypt, 1244 D
Louis IX in, 1250 B, 1254 B
Edward I in, 1271 B, 1272 B, C
treaty with Egypt, 1272 B
conquered by Egypt, 1291 B, C
history of, 1127 K, 1225 K, 1240 K
Jeu d'Adam, Le (anon.), 1150 K
Jeu de la feuillée, Le (Adam de la Halle), 1262 K
Jeu de Robin et de Marion (Adam de la Halle), 1283 K
Jeu de St. Nicholas (Jean Bodel), 1160 K
Jewel-mine of Politics (Candeśvara), 1314 F
Jews:
in Bohemia, 968 G
in Germany, 1096 B, 1243 A
in England, 1144 H, 1190 A, 1194 F, 1201 G; expelled, 1290 G
ordered wear distinct dress, 1215 H
in Poland, 1264 G
expelled from France, 1306 F
massacres of, 1349 G
in Spain, 1357 J, 1391 H
expelled from Austria, 1421 G
History (Josephus), 1470 J
history of persecutions, 1196 K
theology (Maimonides), 1204 K; *and see* Talmudic scholars
conversion to, 865 H
Cabalistic literature, 1305 K
See also Hebrew literature
Jien, Ja. abbot and historian, 1220 K
Jihan, river, Turkey, battle, 1130 A
Jinnō shōtōki (Kitabatake), 1354 K
Joachim, Abbot of Flora, It. heterodox mystic (1132–1202), 1202 H, 1254 H, 1256 H
Joan of Arc, St., F. patriot-mystic, 1412 L, 1429 A, B, 1430 B; burnt, 1431 B; rehabilitated, 1456 C
Joanna I, Queen of Naples (b. 1326), 1343 A, 1348 A, 1352 A, 1373 A, 1380 B, 1381 B, 1382 A; husbands of, 1333 C, 1345 D, 1346 C, (1362 B)
Joanna II, Queen of Naples, 1414 C, 1417 C, 1420 C, 1423 B, 1432 C, 1435 A
Joanna I, Queen of Navarre (b. 1271; 1274–1305), 1274 E, 1329 E; Queen of France, 1284 C, 1305 B
Joanna II, Queen of Navarre (b. 1311), 1329 E, 1349 D
Joanna II, Countess of Burgundy, and Queen of France, 1315 E, 1330 E

Joanna, Countess of Flanders (d. 1244), 1206 C, 1212 A
Joannes Afflaccus (the Saracen) of Salerno, medical author and translator, 1103 G
Joannes Jacobi, Catalan physician, 1378 G
Jocelin, Bishop of Paris, 886 L
Jocelyn of Brakelond, E. monk and chronicler (*c.* 1155–1215?), 1202 K
Jōei shikimoku, 1232 F
Johannes Andreae (Giovanni d'Andrea), It. canonist (*c.* 1271–1348), 1340 H, 1348 H, L
Johannes Anglicus, E. mason, 1262 J
Johannes de Hese, Dutch writer, 1389 K
Johannes Zemecke Teutonicus, G. canonist (d. 1240), 1210 H
John (?Pope), 844 A
John VIII, Pope, 872 D, 875 D, 878 C, E, 880 A, H, 882 D
John IX, Pope, 898 B, 900 B
John X, Pope, 914 A, 915 D, E, 928 B
John XI, Pope, 931 A, 932 E, 936 A
John XII, Pope, 955 D, 962 A; deposed, 963 D, 964 B
John XIII, Pope, 965 D, 967 D, 968 H, 972 C
John XIV, Pope, 983 C, 984 B, C
John XV, Pope, 985 C, E, 993 H, 995 H, 996 B
John XVI (John Philagathus), anti-pope, 997 B, 998 A
John XVII, Pope, 1003 B, D
John XVIII, Pope, 1004 B, 1009 C
John XIX (Romanus, Senator of Rome), 1024 B, D, 1027 A, 1032 D
John XXI (Peter Juliani), Pope, 1276 C, E, 1277 B; as Petrus Hispanus, Port. physician, 1277 G
John XXII (Jacques Duèse), Pope (1316–34), 1316 C, 1317 A, 1318 H, 1319 C, 1327 H, 1330 B, 1332 C, 1334 D
contributes to canon law, 1317 H, 1331 H
prosecutes Spiritual Franciscans, 1318 H, 1323 H
reorganises missions, 1318 H, 1324 H
dispute with Lewis IV, 1323 D, 1324 A, B, 1326 E, 1328 A, B
John XXIII (Baldassare Cossa), Pope (1410–15), 1410 B, 1412 B, 1413 B, D, H, 1414 D, 1415 A, B, 1419 L, 1427 J
John I Tzimisces, Greek Emperor (969–76), 925 L, 969 D, 970 B, C, 972 B, 976 A; campaigns against Arabs, 958 E, 972 D, (973 C), 974 E, 975 B
John II Comnenus, Greek Emperor (1118–43), 1118 C, 1123 E, 1124 E; campaigns in Anatolia and Syria, 1137 E, 1138 B, 1142 C, 1143 B; chronicle of, 1183 K
John III Ducas Vatatzes, Greek Emperor, 1222 E, 1225 E, 1235 E, 1246 D, 1254 D
John IV Lascaris, Greek Emperor (b. 1250), 1258 C, D, 1261 C
John V Palaeologus, Greek Emperor (b. 1332; 1341–1391), 1341 B, 1369 D, 1376 E, 1391 A; civil war, 1341 D, 1343 E, 1347 A, 1352 A, 1354 D; war with Turks, 1366 C, 1367 E, 1371 C
John VI Cantacuzenus, Greek Emperor, 1341 D, 1343 E, 1347 A, 1352 A; deposed, 1354 D; as historian, 1383 K, L
John VII Palaeologus, Greek Emperor (b. 1390), 1425 C, 1437 D, 1438 A, 1439 C, 1448 D
John of Brienne, King of Jerusalem (b. 1148; 1210–25), 1210 D, 1225 D; Emperor of Constantinople, 1228 E; papal general, 1229 B; dies, 1237 A
John I, King of Aragon (b. 1350), 1387 A, 1395 B
John II, King of Navarre (b. 1397), 1425 C; King of Aragon and Sicily (1458–79), 1458 B, 1463 A, 1469 D, 1471 A, 1479 A; revolts against, 1461 C, 1462 B, 1472 D
John of Luxemburg, King of Bohemia (1310–46), 1310 C, 1315 E, 1320 E, 1322 C, 1329 E, 1335 B, D, 1336 E, 1346 C; fights in Italy, 1329 D, 1332 C, D, 1333 A, B, D
John I, King of Castile and Leon (b. 1358; 1379–90), 1379 B, 1380 B, 1381 B, 1387 B, 1390 D; war with Portugal, 1382 C, 1383 D, 1384 A, C, 1385 C
John II, King of Castile and Leon (b. 1405), 1406 D, 1412 B, 1415 D, 1431 E, 1452 C, 1454 C
John I, King of Denmark and Norway (1481–1513), 1481 B, 1483 A; and Sweden, 1483 C
John, King of England (1199–1216), 1167 L, 1199 B, 1201 G, 1212 F, 1213 F, 1216 D
Lord of Ireland, 1177 B, 1185 B, 1210 B
Count of Mortain, 1191 C, 1192 E, 1194 A
war with France, 1200 B, C, 1202 B, C, 1203 B, 1204 B, 1205 A, B, D, 1212 D, 1213 B, D, 1214 A, C
dispute with Pope, 1205 D, 1208 A, 1209 D, 1213 B, 1365 B
invades Scotland, 1209 C, 1216 A
war with Welsh, 1209 C, 1211 B, 1212 C, 1213 B
revolt against, 1215 B–D, 1216 B
John I, King of France, 1316 D
John II, King of France (1350–64), 1319 L, 1350 C, 1352 A, 1354 B, 1361 D, 1363 B, C; revolts against, 1350 D, 1354 A, 1356 B; captured, 1356 C, 1359 A, B, 1360 D, 1364 A
John I, King of Jerusalem and Cyprus, 1284 A, 1285 B
John III d'Albret, King of Navarre (d. 1516), 1483 A
John I the Great, King of Portugal (b. 1357; 1385–1433), 1384 A, 1385 B, C, 1386 B, 1415 C, 1433 C
John II the Perfect, King of Portugal (b. 1455; 1481–1495), 1481 C, 1483 B, 1484 C, 1488 G
John Balliol, King of Scotland (1292–6), 1292 D, 1294 B, 1296 C, 1313 L; son, 1332 C
John I, King of Sweden, 1220 E, 1223 E
John, Duke of Bedford (b. 1389), 1424 C, 1435 C
John, Duke of Berri, F. patron, 1340 L, 1392 C, 1410 J, 1411 J, 1413 J, 1416 L
John II, Duke of Brabant, 1312 F
John I, Margrave of Brandenburg, 1250 E, 1266 B
John III, Duke of Brittany, 1341 B
John de Montfort, claimant to Brittany, 1341 B, D, 1342 B, 1345 B, C
John IV de Montfort, Duke of Brittany (d. 1399), 1345 C, 1364 C, 1365 A, 1373 B, 1379 C, 1381 A, 1392 B, C, 1397 B
John V, Duke of Brittany (d. 1442), 1437 B, 1440 A
John sans Peur, Duke of Burgundy (1404–19), 1371 L, 1404 B, 1405 C, D, 1408 C; murders Orleans, 1407 D, 1408 A; war with Armagnacs, 1410 D, 1411 D, 1412 B, C, 1414 C, 1415 A, 1418 B; ally of Henry V, 1414 B, 1416 D; murdered, 1419 C
John of Luxemburg, Duke of Görlitz (d. 1395), 1378 D
John I, Count of Holland (b. 1281), 1299 D
John II of Avesnes, Count of Hainault (d. 1304), claimant to Flanders, 1280 A; Count of Holland and Zeeland, 1299 D, 1300 C
John of Gaunt, Duke of Lancaster, 1340 L, 1369 C, 1372 A, 1377 A, 1386 C, 1387 B, 1399 A
John of Anjou, claimant to Naples, 1460 C, 1462 C
'John of Burgundy', travel-author, 1372 G
John of Cologne, G. mason, 1442 J
John of Faenza, It. canonist, 1170 H
John of Garland, E. grammarian, 1220 G, K
John of Hexham, E. chronicler, 1154 K
John of Milan, It. botanist and physician, 1328 G
John of Monte Corvino, It. friar and envoy, 1289 G, 1294 H, 1304 H; Archbishop of Peking, 1307 H, 1328 L

John of Paris, F. polemicist (*c.* 1269–1306), 1302 F
John de Plano Carpini, It. friar and envoy, 1245 H, 1246 C
John of Salisbury, Bishop of Chartres, E. philosopher and historian (*c.* 1120–80), 1152 K, 1159 F, 1180 L
John of Ypres, Flemish travel-writer, 1383 G
John Alexander, Tsar of Bulgaria, 1331 B, 1361 E
John Asen. *See* Asen II
John Castriota I, King of Albania, 1432 E
John Castriota II, King of Albania, 1468 A, (1478 E)
John Crescentius, Patrician of Rome, 1003 B, 1012 A
John Henry of Bohemia, 1335 B, 1342 A
See also Giovanni; Jean; Johannes
Joinville, Jean, Sieur de, F. chronicler (*c.* 1224–1319), 1309 K, 1319 L
Jonas, St., Metropolitan of Russia (1448–61), 1461 H
Jordan, Bishop of Poznań (d. 984?), 968 H
Jordanus, friar and travel-author, 1330 G
Jordanus Nemorarius, G. mathematician, 1237 G
Jordi. *See* Sant Jordi
Josce of London, educational founder, 1180 H
Joscelin II, Count of Edessa (d. 1159), 1147 D, 1150 B
Joseph d'Arimathie (Robert de Borron), 1214 K
Josephus, Jewish historian (A.D. 38–*c.* 100), 1470 J
Jošt, Margrave of Moravia and Brandenburg, 1386 B; King of the Romans, 1410 D, 1411 A
Jottings of a Fool (Jien), 1220 K
Journal d'un Bourgeois de Paris (anon.), 1449 K
Jubayr, Abū-al-Husayn ibn-, Sp. M. traveller (1145–1217), 1185 G
Jubilee years, 1300 H, 1450 H
Judah ben Samuel ha-Levi, Sp. J. poet and philosopher, 1140 K
Judari w-al-Hasbah, Kitāb al- (al-Rāzī), 925 G
Judicio solis, De (Simon of Couvin), 1350 K
Judith (Botticelli), 1470 J
Jugement du roi de Navarre, Le (Guillaume de Machaut), 1377 K
Jules César, Li Hystore de (Jehan de Tuim), 1240 K
Juliana of Norwich, E. mystic, 1413 H
Jumièges, France, abbey, 1037 J
Junna, Emperor of Japan, 833 E
Jürched (*or* Ju-chen), tribe of Manchuria. *See* China
Juri II, King of Galicia (1325–1339), 1339 E
Juri I, Great Prince of Russia, 1155 E, 1157 E
Juri II, Great Prince of Vladimir, 1212 E, 1238 A
Juri III, Prince of Moscow, 1304 A; Grand Duke of Vladimir, 1319 E; deposed, 1322 E, 1324 E, 1325 E
Juri, Prince of Galich (b. 1374; d. 1434), claimant to Moscow, 1425 E, 1433 B, 1434 B, 1446 A
Jurists:
English. *See* Bracton, Henry; Fortescue, John; Glanville, Ranulph; Littleton, Thomas
French. *See* Ableiges, Jacques d'; Beaumanoir, Philippe de; Boutillier, Jean; Durandus, Guilelmus; Fontaines, Pierre de
German. *See* Freising, Ruprecht von
Greek. *See* Blastares, Matthew; Harmenopulos; Xiphilin, John; Zonaras, Joannes
Indian. *See* Candeśvara
Italian, of Bologna, 1100 F. *And see* Accursius; Azzo; Bartolus of Sassoferrato; Bulgarus; Cino da Pistoia; Gozzo of Orvieto; Hugolinus; Legnano, Giovanni da; Odofredus; Ubaldi, Baldus degli; Vacarius
Jurjan, Persia, 985 J; Ziyarid dynasty, 928 E, 1042 E
Jurjānī, Ismā'īl ibn-Husain al-, Per. physician, 1135 G
Jury system, 1166 F
Justice of the Emperor Otho (Dieric Bouts), 1470 J
Justices of the Peace, 1361 F, 1388 G
Justinian, Greek Emperor (527–65), code of, 886 F
Juwainī, 'Ala al-Dīn al-, Per. historian (*c.* 1233–83), 1260 K

K

Kabul, Afghanistan, 988 E
Kadensho (Zeami), 1443 K
Kadlubek, Vincent, Bishop of Cracow, Polish chronicler, 1161 L, 1223 K
Kaesŏng, Korea, 935 A
Kaffa, in Crimea, Russia, 1266 E, 1297 E, 1475 E
Kafiya, al- (ibn-al- Hajib), 1248 K
Kaifeng, China, 1126 E, G, 1215 E, 1234 E
Kaiqubād, Sultan of Delhi, 1287 E, 1290 B
Kairāwan, Tunisia, mosque, 830 J
Aghlabid dynasty, 800 E, 909 D; conquer Malta, 869 E; and Sicily, *q.v.*; *and see* Ibrāhīm I, Ziyādat-Allah I; Ibrāhīm II
Fātimid dynasty, 909 D; *and see* 'Ubaydullāh, Qā'im, Mansūr, Mu'izz (*continued under* Egypt)
Kākatīya, India, Hindu kingdom, 1262 E
Kakuyū ('Toba Sōjō'), Ja. painter (1053–1140), 1140 J
Kakuyid dynasty. *See* Isfahan
Kalbite dynasty. *See* Sicily
Kalhana, Indian poet and historian, 1148 K
Kālinga Vijaya-Bāhu, King of Ceylon, 1213 E
Kālinjar, India, 1202 E
Kalisz, Poland, Treaty of, 1343 C
Kalka, river, Russia, battles on, 1222 B, 1381 E
Kallundborg, Norway, Treaty of, 1376 D
Kalojan, Tsar of Bulgaria, 1197 E, 1204 D, 1205 A, B, 1206 C, 1207 C, D
Kamakura, Japan, 1185 B, 1333 E
Kamban, Indian poet, 1200 K
Kāmbojas, Indian tribe, 980 E
Kāmil I, Nāsir-ad-Dīn, Sultan of Egypt, 1218 C, 1219 H, 1220 C, 1227 D, 1229 A, E, 1238 A
Kāmil al-Sinā 'ah al-Tibbiyah (ibn-al-'Abbās), 994 G
Kāmil al-Sinā 'atayn (al-Baytar), 1340 G
Kāmil fi-al-Ta'rikh, Kitāb al- (ibn-al-Athīr), 1233 K
Kammu, Emperor of Japan (781–806), 806 E
Kamo Chōmei, Ja. hermit and writer (*c.* 1154–*c.* 1225), 1212 K
Kamp, W. Germany, abbey, 1123 H
Kampana, Indian prince, 1371 K
Kan'ami, Ja. actor (1333–84), 1384 K
Kanauj, India, Hindu Empire, 890 E, 916 E; capital of Pañchala, 1018 D, 1194 E
Kanawaza, Japan, school and library, 1270 H
Kao Ming, C. poet, 1356 J
Kao Tsung, Emperor of south China (1127–62), 1127 E
Karak, Jordan, 1239 D
Karakhanids, Turkish tribe, 960 E
Kara-Khitai (Western Liao), empire in east Turkestan, 1130 E, 1141 C, 1211 E
Karakorum, Outer Mongolia, capital of Great Khan, 1227 C, 1242 B, 1245 H, 1246 C, 1253 G; battle, 1277 E
Karaman Turks. *See* Rūm
Karelia, Finland, 1293 E
Kars, Turkey, 1064 E, 1209 E
Kāshānī, Abu'l-Qāsim al-, Per. writer on pottery, 1301 J
Kashmīr, Pakistan and India, Hindu kingdom, 883 G; history of, 1148 K; Muslim kingdom, 1346 E, 1416 H, 1470 J
Kasimov, Russia, Khanate of, 1452 E
Katīb al-Isfahānī, Muhammad 'Imād al-Dīn, Per. historian (1125–1201), 1201 K

Kauthal, India, battle, 1367 G
Kauza, Turkey, 1161 G
Kawākib al-Thābitah, Kitāb al- (al-Sūfī), 986 G
Kaykavus I, Sultan of Rūm (1210–19), 1217 J
Kaykhusraw I, Sultan of Rūm, 1204 E, 1210 B
Kaykhusraw II, Sultan of Rūm (1237–45), 1237 E, 1241 E, 1242 B
Kayqubād I, Sultan of Rūm (1219–37), 1230 C, 1231 C, 1237 E
Kayseri, Turkey, 1205 E; college, 1205 J; mosques and mausoleums, 1135 J, 1237 J, 1247 J, 1276 J
Kazakhstan, Russia, 1061 E, 1227 C
Kazan, Russia, Khanate of, 1487 C
Kells, Ireland, 804 J, 1152 H
Kemmu Code (Japanese), 1338 F
Kemp, John, Cardinal, Archbishop of Canterbury and Chancellor, 1454 A
Kemp, Margery, E. mystic, 1438 K
Kempis, Thomas à, Flemish mystic, 1379 L, 1425 H, 1471 H, L
Kenilworth, England, 1266 B, D
Kennedy, James, Bishop of St. Andrews (d. 1464/5), 1450 H
Kenneth MacAlpin, King of the Picts and Scots (843–58), 843 E, 858 E, 862 E, (877 E)
Kenneth II, King of Scotland (971–95), 971 E, 995 E, 1005 E
Kenneth III, King of Scotland, 997 E, 1000 E, 1005 E
Kent, England, 825 E; Earls of, *see* Odo, Edmund, Holand
Kerbōghā, atabeg of Mosul (d. 1102), 1098 B
Kēsh, Transoxiana, Russia, 1360 E
Khaidu, Mongol general, 1241 B
Khaidu, Mongol prince, 1268 E, 1277 E, 1301 E
Khail, Kitāb al- (al-Asma'ī), 827 G
Khajurāho, India, 999 J
Khaldūn, 'Abd-ar-Rahmān ibn-, Sp. M. historian and philosopher, 1332 L, 1406 K
Khallikān, Ahmad ibn-Muhammad ibn-, Syrian biographer (1211–82), 1282 K
Kharāj, Kitāb al- (Qudāma), 948 F
Kharaqī, Muhammad ibn-Ahmad al-, Per. astronomer, 1138 G
Khatīb, Lisān-ad-Dīn ibn-al-, Sp. M. physician and historian, 1313 L, 1374 G, K
Khayyām, 'Umar al-, Per. astronomer, mathematician and poet, 1044 L, 1074 G, 1079 G, 1123 G, K
Khazarī, Kitāb al- (Judah ha-Levi), 1140 K
Khazars, tribe of Russia, 850 E, 865 H, 965 E
Khāzini, Abū-l-Fath al-, Gk. (slave in Persia) physicist, 1121 G
Khidyr, Khan of the Golden Horde, 1361 E
Khirgiz, central Asian tribe, 840 E
Khizr Khan, Mongol conqueror of Delhi, 1405 D, 1414 B, 1421 B
Khitan (*or* Kitai), Mongol tribes. *See* China
Khmers. *See* Cambodia
Khorezm, Russia, 1387 E
Khujandī, Abū Mahmūd Hamīd al-, Arab astronomer (d. *c.* 1000), 994 G
Khunani, Russia, battle, 1221 A
Khurāsān, Persia:
  Tāhirid dynasty, 820 E, 872 E
  conquered by Saffārids, 872 E; Samanids, 900 E; Ghaznavids, 994 E
  under Seljuqs, 1037 E, 1050 E, 1104 A
  under Tīmūrids, 1382 E, 1447 E, 1459 E, 1469 E, 1470 C
Khurdādhbih, ibn-, Per. geographer (d. 848), 846 G
Khūrshāh, Rukn-ad-Dīn, Grand Master of Assassins, 1256 D
Khusraw Khan, usurper of Delhi, 1320 B, C
Khusraw, Muhammad Hasan, Indian M. poet, 1325 K
Khusraw, Nāsir-i, Per. poet and traveller (1003–88), 1088 G
Khwājū Kirmānī (Persian ms.), 1396 J
Khwārizm-Shāhs. *See* Persia
Khwārizm, Treasure of the King of (al-Jurjānī), 1135 G
Khwārizmī, Abū 'Abdallāh Muhammad, Per. scientific encyclopedeist (*fl. c.* 976), 976 G
Khwārizmī, Muhammad ben Mūsā al-, Per. mathematician and astronomer (d. 850), 850 G, 1126 G, 1145 G, 1187 G, 1307 G
Ki no Tomonori, Ja. poet (d. 906), 905 K
Ki no Tsurayuki, Ja. poet and traveller (833–946), 905 K, 935 K
Kiejstut of Kovno, Grand Prince of Lithuania (1381–2), 1348 E, 1381 E, 1382 E, 1401 A
Kiel, W. Germany, 1036 B
Kiev, Russia:
  taken by Vikings, 850 E, 878 E
  Princes of (Varangian Empire). *See*
    Oleg (878–913)
    Igor (913–45)
    Olga (regent, 945–62)
    Svjatoslav (945–72)
    Jaropolk I (972–7)
    Vladimir I (977–1015)
    Sviatopolk I (1015–19)
    Jaroslav (1019–55)
    Mstislav (1024–35)
    Isiaslav I (1055–78)
    Vsévolod I (1078–93)
    Sviatopolk II (1093–1113)
    Vladimir II (1113–25)
    Mstislav I (1125–32)
    Jaropolk II (1132–9)
    Vsévolod II (1139–46)
    Isiaslav II (1146–55)
    Juri I (1155–7)
    Andrew I (1157–9)
    Rostislav I (1159–67)
  attack Constantinople, 860 B, 865 E, 907 E, 911 E
  attacked by Pechenegs, 969 E
  'Golden Age' of, ends, 1055 A
  taken by Boleslav of Poland, 1069 A
  sacked; end of primacy in Russia, 1169 A
  taken by Mongols, 1240 E, 1247 E
  abandoned by Metropolitan, 1300 H
  defeated by Lithuania, 1320 E
  in Lithuania, sacked, 1482 C
  Cathedral, 1037 J; church, 991 J
  chronicles of, 1118 K, 1199 K
  laws, 1036 F
Kilia, Moldavia, Russia, 1484 E
Kilij Arslan I, Sultan of Rūm (1086–1107), 1086 E, 1092 E, 1096 D, 1097 B, C, 1107 C, 1117 E
Kilij Arslan II, Sultan of Rūm (d. 1192), 1156 E, 1161 G, 1169 E, 1174 E, 1176 C, 1188 E, J
Kilkenny, Ireland, 1366 A
Kim Pu-sik, Korean historian, 1145 K
Kindī, Abu-Yūsuf Ya'qub ibn-Ishāq al-, Arab philosopher, alchemist, astrologer, optician and musical theorist, 873 K
Kindī, al-, Eg. historian, 961 K
Kindi, The Apology of al-, 1141 K
King Alisaunder (anon.), 1300 K
King Horn, 1250 K
King's Mirror, 1247 F
King's Quair, The (James I), 1423 K
Kingdom of Lovers (Jan Ruysbroeck), 1381 H

Kingdoms, Christian, created:
Bavaria, 814 C
France, 843 C
Germany, 843 C
Lorraine, 843 C, 855 C
Scotland, 843 E
Brittany, 846 E
Provence, 855 C
Navarre, 857 E
Armenia, 885 E
Burgundy, 888 A
England, 954 E
Hungary, 1000 C
Poland, 1000 A, 1076 D, 1295 B; permanently, 1320 A
Sweden, 1000 E
Castile, 1033 E
Aragon, 1035 E
Zeta, 1040 E
Croatia, 1076 E
Serbia, 1084 E, 1217 E
Bohemia, 1085 B, 1158 A; permanently, 1198 E
Jerusalem, 1099 C
Sicily, 1130 C
Portugal, 1139 C, 1143 E
Cyprus, 1197 E
Armenia, Lesser, 1198 A
Bulgaria, 1204 D
Lithuania, 1251 E
Halich, 1254 E
Majorca, 1262 E
Trinacria, 1302 C
Albania, 1368 E
Kingston on Thames, England, Treaty of, 1217 C
Kinsale, Ireland, 1380 B
Kirkwall, Orkney Is., Scotland, Cathedral, 1137 J
Kirşehir, Turkey, 1250 J, 1268 J
Kisā'i, Per. grammarian, 805 K
Kissa-yōjō-ki (Eisai), 1191 G
Kitabatake Chikafusa, Ja. historian (1293–1354) 1354 K
Kitai. *See* Khitan; *also* Kara-Khitai
Kleidion, Bulgaria, battle, 1014 C
Klokotinitza, Greece, battle, 1230 B
Knolles, Robert, E. soldier, 1370 C, D
K'o Chiu-ssu, C. painter, 1312 L, 1365 J
Ko yō shō (Henchün Seiken), 1156 G
Kōbō Daishi. *See* Kūkai
Kogo-shūi, 808 K
Kokinshū (Ja. anthology), 905 K
Koloman, Tsar of Bulgaria, 1241 B, 1246 D
Kondurcha, river, Russia, battle on, 1391 B
Konjaku Monigatari, 1050 K
König Rother (anon.), 1150 K
Königsberg (*now* Kaliningrad), Poland, 1254 E, 1457 B, 1466 D
Konrad, Pfaffe, G. poet, 1150 K
Konungahella, Norway, 1101 E
Konungs skuggsjá, 1247 F
Konya (Iconium), Turkey, capital of Rūm, 1097 C, 1190 B, 1328 E; colleges, 1242 J, 1258 J; mausoleum, 1188 J; mosques, 1162 J, 1219 J
Koran, Latin translation of, 1143 H
Korea, 935 E
Silla dynasty (A.D. 668–935), 935 E
Koryŏ dynasty, 935 E, 1392 E
subject to Chin Empire, 1126 E
civil war, 1170 E
Ch'oe dictatorship, 1196 E, 1258 E
Mongol conquest, 1231 E, 1258 E
tributary to Ming Empire, 1369 E
Yi dynasty (1392–1910), 1392 E
capital at Kaesong, 935 A; at Seoul, 1394 E
civil service, examinations for, 958 F, 1393 F
description of (Hsü Ching), 1125 G
histories of, 1145 K, 1451 K
phonetic writing, 1446 K
printing, 1392 G
religions: Buddhism, 958 F, 1393 F; Confucianism, 1393 F
trade, 879 G
Koronowo, Poland, battle, 1410 D
Korybut, King of Bohemia, 1422 B, 1427 B
Koryŏ dynasty. *See* Korea
Koryŏ sa (Korean history), 1451 K
Köse Dagh, Turkey, battle, 1243 B
Košice, Czechoslovakia, Treaty of, 1491 A
Kossovopolje, Yugoslavia, battles, 1389 B, 1448 D
Koundoura, Greece, battle, 1204 E
Krak des Chevaliers, Syria, castle, 1271 B
Krishna III, King of Rāshtrakūta (936–66), 949 E
Kroissenbrunn, Austria, battle, 1260 C
Krum, Khan of the Bulgars, 809 E, 814 B
Krzyszkowo, Poland, 1157 E
Kuan Han-ch'ing, C. dramatist, 1300 K
Kuan-wu (Shao Yung), 1077 K
Kublai Khan, Great Khan of the Mongols (1260–94) and Emperor of China (1271–94), 1215 L, 1253 E, 1260 A, 1269 K, 1275 G, H, 1277 E, 1287 G, 1294 E; conquers China, 1258 E, 1260 H, 1261 E, 1271 E, 1273 E, 1276 E, 1279 E; attacks Japan, 1274 E, 1281 C, 1286 E; Dai Viet, 1286 E, 1287 E; and Java, 1292 E, 1293 E
Kudara-no-Kawanari, Ja. painter (782–853), 853 J
Kuei hai yü hêng chih (Fan Ch'êng-ta), 1193 G
Kūkai (Kōbō Daishi), Ja. Buddhist reformer (774–835), 806 H, 816 H
Kulbarga, India, 1345 E, 1367 J, 1422 J; Bāhmanī (Muslim) kingdom (of the Deccan), 1347 C, 1367 F, G, 1432 E, *and see* Fīrūz, Ahmad I; disintegrates, 1490 E; history of, 1359 K
Kulikovo, Russia, battle, 1380 C
Kulliyāt fī-al-Tibb, Kitāb al- (ibn-Rushd), 1160 G, 1255 G
Kulottunga III, Chola Emperor (d. 1218?), 1216 E
Kulm, Czechoslovakia, battle, 1126 A
Kulpa, Khan of the Golden Horde, 1359 E, 1360 E
Kumāra Kampana, Indian prince, 1370 E, K
Kumārapālacarita (Hemacandra), 1170 K
Kunovica, Mount, Yugoslavia, battle, 1444 A
Kuo Chung-shu, C. painter (*c.* 920–*c.* 977), 977 J
Kuo Hsi, C. painter (*c.* 1020–90), 1090 J
Kuo Shou-ching, C. astronomer (1231–1316), 1280 G
Kurya, Pecheneg leader, 972 B
Kutná Hora, Czechoslovakia, battles, 1304 E, 1422 A; mines, 1294 G; Treaty of, 1485 H
Kuyavia, Poland, 1335 D
Kyakunin isshu (Fuyiwara Teika), 1205 K
Kyeser, Konrad, G. writer on warfare (1366–1405), 1405 G
Kyōto (Heian), Japan, capital of, 806 E, 1183 E, 1333 E, 1336 E, 1338 F, 1392 E; monasteries, 1341 G; pavilions, 1397 J, 1483 J
Kyrenia, Cyprus, 1233 B

L

La Khai, King of Champa (1390–1400), 1390 A
Labour: riots, 1255 G, 1280 G; strikes, 1245 G, 1368 G; walk-out, 1274 G; *and see* Wages
Lacy, Henry, Earl of Lincoln and Salisbury (1251–1311), 1311 B

Ladislas (László) I, St., King of Hungary, 1077 B, 1091 E, 1095 C
Ladislas II, King of Hungary, 1161 C, 1162 A
Ladislas III, King of Hungary (b. 1199, d. 1205), 1204 E, 1205 E
Ladislas IV the Cuman, King of Hungary, 1272 C, 1278 C, 1290 C
Ladislas V, King of Hungary. *See* Vladislav III
Ladislas VI Postumus, King of Hungary and Bohemia, 1440 A, 1451 D, 1452 E, 1453 D, 1457 D
Ladislas VII, King of Hungary. *See* Vladislav II of Bohemia
Ladislas, King of Naples (b. 1376; 1386–1414), 1386 A, 1387 E, 1394 A, 1399 E, 1411 B, 1414 C; claims Hungary, 1395 B, 1403 C; wars against Popes, 1406 D, 1408 B, 1409 D, 1412 B, 1413 B
Lady with an Ermine (Leonardo), 1483 J
Laetus (*or* Laebo), Julius Pomponius, It. humanist (1425–98), 1425 L
Lahore, Pakistan, 1186 E, 1241 D; battle, 1287 E
Lai le Freine (Marie of France), 1185 K
Lais (Marie de France), 1165 K
Laiazzo, Turkey, naval battle off, 1294 E
Lal Ded, Indian poetess and mystic (b. 1347), 1380 K
Lalain, Jacques de, 'le bon chevalier', Belgian soldier, 1453 L; *Histoire* of, 1474 K
Lallā-vakyāni (Lal Ded), 1380 K
Lama'āt ('Irāqī), 1288 K
Lambert, Emperor and King of Italy, 894 D, 896 A, 898 D
Lambert, first Count of Maine, 846 E
Lambert of Hersfeld, G. chronicler, 1077 K
Lambert of St. Omer, F. geographer (d. 1125?), 1120 G
Lamentations Bourrien, Les (Henri Baude), 1486 K
Lan Na, Siam, Thai kingdom, 1296 E, 1311 E, 1325 E
Lancaster, England, Earls of, *see* Thomas, Henry of Grosmont; Dukes of, *see idem*, John of Gaunt
Landino, Francesco, It. musician (b. 1325), 1397 J
Landnámabók (Icelandic chronicle), 1148 K
Lando, Pope, 913 B, 914 A
Lando, Michele di, Florentine popular leader, 1378 C
Landolf IV, Prince of Capua-Benevento, 981 A
Lanfranc, Archbishop of Canterbury, It. theologian, 1070 C, 1089 L
Lanfranchi of Milan, It. surgeon, 1296 G
Langdarma, King of Tibet, 842 E
Langeais, France, castle, 994 E
Langenstein, Henry of, G. theologian (d. 1397), 1379 H, 1381 H
Langland, William, E. poet (*c.* 1332–*c.* 1400), 1377 K
Langtoft, Peter, E. poet-chronicler, (*fl. c.* 1307), 1307 K, 1338 K
Langton, Stephen, Cardinal, Archbishop of Canterbury, 1206 D, 1208 A, 1213 B, 1215 C, 1228 L
Lanval (Marie de France), 1185 K
Laon, France, 945 E, 950 E, 988 C; Bishop of, 991 A; Cathedral, 1160 J, 1190 J, 1205 J
Laos, kingdom of, 1353 E, 1479 E
Lapidario (of Alfonso X), 1279 G
Lapidum, Liber (Marbode), 1123 G
Largs, Scotland, battle, 1263 D
Larissa, Greece, 1215 E; battle, 1083 E
Last Judgement (Fra Angelico), 1447 J; (Roger van der Weyden), 1446 J
Last Supper (Castagno), 1445 J
Lateran Councils. *See* Councils, General
Latimer, Hugh, E. religious reformer (*c.* 1490–1555), 1490 L
Latini, Brunetto, It. poet, grammarian, moralist and encyclopedeist (*c.* 1220–*c.* 1295), 1267 K, 1295 K
Lattakieh, Syria, 1287 B
Latvia (Livonia), Russia, 1086 C, 1260 C; conversion of Livs of, 1184 H, 1201 E, 1204 E; history of, 1227 K
Lauda Sion (St. Thomas Aquinas), 1261 J
Laudi Spirituali (Bianco da Siena), 1367 K; (Jacopone da Todi), 1306 K
Laudibus Legum Angliae, De (John Fortescue), 1468 F
Laupen, Switzerland, battle, 1339 B
Laura, seen by Petrarch, 1327 K
Lausanne, Switzerland, 1448 C, 1449 B; Cathedral, 1219 J
Lausitz (Lusatia), Germany, 993 E, 1002 E, 1007 E, 1031 E, 1036 E, 1056 E, 1348 B; Sorbs, 806 E; *cf.* Görlitz
Law:
  capitularies. *See* Empire, Carolingian
  Church. *See* Canon Law; Canonists
  Codes and compilations:
    Arab, 1277 F
    Bohemian, 1294 F, G, 1350 F
    Burmese, 1210 F, 1306 F
    Chinese, 1397 F; Liao, 1036 F
    Danish, 1240 F
    English, 1118 F, 1180 F, 1268 F
    French, 1200 F, 1250 F, 1260 F, 1270 F, 1280 F, 1390 F; of towns, 1047 G, 1070 G
    German, 803 F, 1225 F, 1275 F, 1328 F
    Greek, 886 F, 1073 F, 1335 F
    Indian (Hindu), 1270 F
    Italian: Papal states, 1357 F; Sicily, 1231 F
    Japanese, 811 F, 833 F, 927 F, 1232 F, 1338 F
    Mongolian, 1206 F
    Norwegian, 1276 F
    Polish, 1347 F
    'Romania', of, 1322 F
    Russian, 1036 F
    Serbian, 1349 F
    Siamese, 1350 F
    Spanish, 1020 F, 1064 F, 1245 F, 1252 F, 1254 F, 1256 F
    Swedish, 1347 F
    Swiss, 1370 F
    Vietnamese, 1483 F
    Welsh, 949 F
  commercial, 1283 F, 1400 F
  courts. *See* Bohemia, Burgundy, England, Flanders, France, Germany
  forensic medicine, Chinese, 1248 G
  international, 1360 F, 1367 F
  Roman:
    revised, 879 F, 886 F
    vernacular summary, 1149 F
    banned at Paris University, 1219 H
    standard gloss (Accursius), 1260 F
  schools, Muslim, 820 F; *and see* Bologna, Constantinople, Montpellier, Orleans, Pavia
  writers on. *See* Jurists
  See also Charters of Liberties; Peace
Laxdaela, The (saga), 1200 K
Lay of Havelok the Dane, 1250 K
Layamon, E. chronicler, 1200 K
Laylā and Majnūn (Nizāmī), 1188 K
Lazar, Prince of Serbia, 1386 E, 1389 B
Lazarus, Gk. monastic founder, 1054 H
Le Dai Hanh, Emperor of Dai-co-viet (980–1005), 980 E, 981 E, 982 E
Le Loi, Emperor of Dai Viet (*as* Le Thai-to; 1428–33), 1418 E, 1428 E
Le Quy Ly, Emperor of Dai Viet (*as* Ho Quy), 1400 E

Le Thanh-tong, Emperor of Dai Viet (1460–97), 1471 E, 1479 E
Lea, river, England, 895 E
Leake, England, Treaty of, 1318 C
Leal Souvenir (Jan van Eyck), 1432 J
Lear, mythical British king, 1137 K, 1200 K
Learned Entertainments (Thomas of Štítný), 1401 H
Leaves of Jade (Fujiwara Kanezune), 1200 K
Lebena, Spain, 924 J
Lechfeld, river, W. Germany, battle, 955 C
Lectura in codicem (Cino da Pistoia), 1336 F
Łęczyca, Poland, Congress of, 1180 E
Leech Book (?Bald), 930 G
Leeds (Kent), England, castle, 1321 D
Legenda Aurea (Jacobus de Voragine), 1265 F
Leges Henrici Primi, 1118 F
Leges Walliae (Hywel Dda), 949 F
Leghorn, Italy, 1408 B, 1421 B
Legibus et Consuetudinibus Angliae, De (?Glanville), 1180 F; (Bracton), 1268 F
Legnano, Italy, battle, 1176 B
Legnano, Giovanni da, It. jurist (d. 1383), 1360 F, 1388 K
Leicester, England, 877 E; Earl of, *see* Montfort, Simon de
Leinster, Ireland, Kings of, 1169 B, 1171 B
Leipzig, E. Germany, University, 1409 H
Leitha, river, Austria, battle, 1242 E
Lemoine, John, Cardinal, F. educational founder, 1302 H
Lena, Spain, 905 J
Lenzen, E. Germany, battle, 929 C
Leo III, Pope (795–816), 800 D, 809 H, 816 B
Leo IV, Pope, 847 B, 855 C
Leo V, Pope, 903 C
Leo VI, Pope, 928 B, D
Leo VII, Pope, 936 A, 939 C
Leo VIII, Pope, 963 D, 964 B, 965 A
Leo IX (Bruno of Toul), Pope (b. 1002), 1048 D, 1049 H, 1051 E, 1053 B, E, 1054 B, H
Leo X (Giovanni de' Medici), Pope (1513–21), 1475 L
Leo V the Armenian, Greek Emperor, 813 B, 814 B, 815 H, 820 D
Leo VI the Philosopher, Greek Emperor (b. 866), 886 C, F, 887 E, 895 E, 896 E, 912 B; as author, 912 G
Leo II, Prince of Armenia (1186–1219), 1193 D; King, 1198 C, 1216 E, 1219 B
Leo VI, last King of Armenia, 1375 B, 1393 D
Leo the Deacon, Gk. chronicler, 992 K
Leo the Mathematician, Greek, 863 H
Leo of Ostia, It. chronicler (*c.* 1046–1115), 1094 K, 1139 K
Leo of Tripoli, Arab pirate, 904 C
Leoben, Austria, 1175 G
Leofgar, Bishop of Hereford, 1056 B
Leofric, Earl of Mercia, 1056 B
Leon, Spain, 988 E, 996 E; Cathedral, 1255 J
  Kingdom (of Oviedo *or* the Asturias). *See*
    Alfonso II (791–833)
    Ramiro I (833–50)
    Ordoño I (850–66)
    Alfonso III (866–910)
    Garcia I (910–14)
  Kings of Leon. *See*
    Ordoño II (914–23)
    Froila II (923–4)
    Alfonso IV (924–7)
    Ramiro II (927–52)
    Ordoño III (952–7)
    Sancho I (957–67)
    Ordoño IV (957–60)
    Ramiro III (967–82)
    Bermudo II (982–99)
    Alfonso V (999–1027)
    Bermudo III (1027–37)
    Ferdinand I of Castile (1037–65)
    Alfonso VI (1065–1109)
    Urracca (Queen, 1109–26)
    Alfonso VII of Castile (1126–57)
    Ferdinand II (1157–88)
    Alfonso IX (1188–1230)
  civil wars, 923 C, 952 E, 957 E, 960 E, 982 D, 1110 E, 1111 D
  subject to Caliph of Spain, 981 E, 988 E
  devastated by Moors, 1003 E
  Cortes of, 1188 F
  under interdict, 1202 E
  emancipation of serfs, 1215 F
  finally united to Castile, 1230 C
  laws, 1020 F
Leon the Iastrophist, Archbishop of Salonika, Gk. physician and inventor, 865 G
Leonardo da Vinci, It. painter (1452–1519), 1452 L, 1474 J, 1475 J, 1481 J, 1483 J; as inventor, 1480 G
Leonor, Queen and Regent of Portugal, 1440 E
Leopold IV the Liberal, Count of Austria, Duke of Bavaria, 1139 D, 1140 D, 1142 B
Leopold V, Duke of Austria (d. 1194), 1192 D, 1193 A
Leprosy, 1202 K, 1300 G
Lérida, Spain, Cathedral, 1203 J; University, 1300 H
Lesnovo, Yugoslavia, frescoes at, 1349 J
Leszek I, Duke of Poland, 892 E, 913 E
Leszek II the White, Prince of Cracow, 1202 E, 1205 E, 1227 D
Leszek III the Black, Grand Prince of Poland, 1279 E, 1282 E, 1288 E
Letters:
  Gilbert Foliot, 1187 K
  Guittone d'Arezzo, 1294 K
  John Hus, 1415 H
  Paston family, 1418 K
  Peter Abelard, 1142 K
Leventina, Switzerland, 1440 E, 1479 C
Levi ben Gerson (Gersonides), F. J. philosopher, theologian, astronomer and mathematician, 1288 L, 1321 G, 1323 K, 1329 G, K, 1342 G, 1343 G, 1344 L
Levy Hradec, Czechoslovakia, 875 J
Lewes, England, battle, 1264 B; *Song of*, 1264 K
Lewis IV the Bavarian, King of the Romans (1314–47), 1314 D, 1315 A, 1347 D
  war with Habsburgs, 1313 D, 1314 D, 1322 C, 1325 A
  Italian expeditions, 1323 C, 1327 B, 1328 A, C, 1329 D
  dispute with Pope, 1323 D, 1324 A, B, 1328 A, B, K, 1349 K
  dynastic schemes, 1324 B, 1330 C, 1335 B, 1342 A, 1345 C
  crowned as Emperor, 1328 A
  alliance with England, 1337 C, 1338 C, 1341 A
  revolt against, 1346 B, C
Lewis I the Great, King of Hungary (b. 1326; 1342–81), 1342 E, 1344 E, 1351 F, 1364 C, 1367 H, 1381 C
  war in Naples, 1345 D, 1348 A, B, 1350 E, 1352 A
  conquests in Balkans, 1345 E, 1358 A, 1362 E
  wars with Venice, 1356 E, 1357 C, 1358 A, 1369 E
  relations with Popes, 1360 C, 1379 B
  King of Poland (1370–81), 1339 E, 1370 D, 1374 F
Lexicons. *See* Dictionaries
Leyden, Nicholas of, Dutch sculptor, 1470 G
Leyre, France, abbey, 1085 J
Li Ch'eng, C. painter (*c.* 940–67), 967 J

Li Chi-fu, C. cartographer (758–814), 814 G
Li Chih-ch'ang, C. travel-writer, 1221 G
Li Ch'ing-chao, C. poetess (1084–1151 ?), 1151 K
Li Fang, C. encyclopedeist (924–95), 977 K
Li Ho, C. poet (791–817), 817 K
Li Hüang-hao, Emperor of Hsi Hsia, 1038 E
Li K'an, C. botanist, 1299 G
Li K'o-yung, leader of Sha-t'o, 884 E; Emperor (923–36), 923 E
Li Lung-mien, C. painter (*c.* 1070–1106), 1106 J
Li Shih (Hung Kua), 1184 K
Li Tse, Vietnamese historian and autobiographer, 1307 K
Li Yeh, C. mathematician, 1248 G
Liao dynasty. *See* China
Libel of English Policy, 1437 G
Liber Continens (Rhazes), 1279 G, 1486 G
Liber floridus (Lambert of St. Omer), 1120 G
Liber Regius (Haly Abbas), 994 G, 1127 G
Liber Solidus (ibn-Haiyān), 1076 K
Libraries. *See* Baghdād; Cairo, Herat; Kanawaza; Milan; Rome
Libre del feyts (James I of Aragon), 1276 K
Libre del orde de cavayleria (Raymond Lull), 1275 K
Libro du buen amor, El (Juan Ruiz), 1343 K
Libro de la prima navigatione, El (Alvise de Cá da mosto), 1464 G
Libro de las avas de caça (Lopez de Ayala), 1386 K
Libro de los engaños et los assayamientos de las mugeres, 1253 K
Libro de los Gatos (Climente Sánchez de Vercial), 1400 K
Libro d'Oltramare (Niccolò da Poggibonsi), 1349 K
Lichfield, England, Archbishopric, 803 H; Cathedral, 1250 J
Lieder (Heinrich von Veldeke), 1189 K
Liège, Belgium, 881 E, 1131 A, 1200 H; Cathedral school, 1000 H; iron industry, 1190 G, 1340 G; Bishops of, 1192 C; government of, 1316 F, 1373 F; revolts against, 1408 C, 1467 D, 1468 D; histories of, 1007 K, 1348 K, 1400 K
Liegnitz (*now* Legnica), Poland, battle, 1241 B
Lilium medicinae (Bernard of Gordon), 1303 G
Lille, France, 1312 E
'*Lille' Book of Stories, The*, 1225 K
Limburg, Holland, Duchy of, 1288 C, 1430 C
Limburg brothers, Flemish illuminators, 1410 J
Limburg an der Haardt, W. Germany, abbey, 1025 J
Limerick, Ireland, 967 E
Limoges, France, 1370 C, 1381 G; abbey, 1095 J; Cathedral, 1273 J
Lincoln, England, 877 E, 1301 A; battles, 1141 A, 1217 B; Bishops of, 1139 B, 1200 L, 1253 G, K, L; Cathedral, 1072 J, 1208 J, 1239 J, 1256 J
Lindholm, Denmark, Treaty of, 1395 B
Linières, Jean, F. astronomer (*fl.* 1320–55), 1350 G
Lipa, Henry of, Bohemian noble, 1320 E
Lipany, Czechoslovakia, battle, 1434 B
Lippi, Filippino, It. painter, (1457–1504), 1457 L, 1480 J, 1483 J, 1484 J, 1485 J, 1486 J, 1488 J
Lippi, Fra Filippo, It. painter (*c.* 1406–69), 1432 J, 1437 J, 1441 J, 1443 J, 1452 J, 1465 J, 1466 J, 1469 L
Lisān al-'Arab (ibn-Manzūr), 1311 K
Lisbon, Portugal, 844 C, 1093 E, 1147 D; besieged, 1179 E, 1372 A, 1382 C, 1384 C; Cathedral, 1150 J; University, 1290 H, 1308 H
Lisieux, France, 933 E; Bishops of, 852 K, 1382 G, K, L; Cathedral, 1180 J
Li-tai Ming-hua chin (C. paintings), 845 J
Litani, river, Lebanon, battle, 1179 B
Lithuania, Russia:
  becomes kingdom, 'converted', 1251 E, *and see* Mindovg
  raided by Mongols, 1259 E
  war with Teutonic Knights, 1260 C, 1285 E
  Grand Princes. *See*
    Gedymin (1315–41)
    Olgierd (1341–77)
    Jagiello (1377–81, 1382–)
    Kiejstut (1381–2)
  union to Poland, and conversion, 1383 E, 1387 J
  Grand Dukes. *See*
    Vitold (1401–30)
    Svidrigello (1430–2)
    Sigismund (1432–40)
    Casimir IV of Poland (1440–92)
  autonomy confirmed, 1413 D
  charter of liberties, 1447 B
  conspiracy, 1481 C
  Kiev in, 1482 C
  capital of. *See* Vilna
Little Flowers of St. Francis, The, 1330 K
Littleton, Thomas, E. jurist, 1481 F, L
Liu Hsü, C. historian (897–946), 946 K
Liu Tsung-yuan, C. poet (773–819), 819 K
Liubech, Russia, 1097 E
Liudolf, Duke of Swabia, 949 D, 953 E, 954 B, D
Liutpold, Bavarian margrave, 908 E
Liutprand of Cremona, It. diplomat and chronicler (*c.* 922–72), 958 K, 968 E, K
Living One, The (ibn-Tufayl), 1185 K
Livonia. *See* Latvia
Livre de la Prison, Le (Charles of Orleans), 1465 K
Livre des Fortunes et Adversitez (Jean Régnier), 1468 K
Livre du Chevalier de la Tour-Landry, 1371 K
Livre du Ciel et du Monde (Nicholas Oresme), 1382 G
Livre du voir-dit, Le (Guillaume de Machaut), 1377 K
Livre de Jostice et de Plet (anon.), 1260 F
Livre de Paix, Le (Christine de Pisan), 1412 K
Livre des Quatres Dames (Alain Chartier), 1416 K
Livre des trois vertus, Le (Christine de Pisan), 1415 K
Livre des faicts . . . du sage roi Charles, Le (Christine de Pisan), 1404 K
Livre des Mancières, Le (Étienne de Fougères), 1170 K
Livre des tournois (Réné of Anjou), 1460 K
Livs. *See* Latvia
Llewelyn ap Jorwerth, the Great, King of Gwynned (b. 1173; 1194–1240), 1200 E, 1208 E, 1240 B; wars with England, 1211 B, 1212 C, 1213 B, 1218 A, 1228 C, 1231 D, 1233 C
Llewelyn ap Gruffyd, King of Gwynned (1246–82), 1246 A, 1254 E; Prince of Wales, 1258 A, 1282 D; relations with England, 1259 C, 1262 E, 1267 C, 1277 B, D; brother, 1282 A
Lo Codi (Provençal), 1149 F
Lo Kuan-chung, C. fiction writer, 1400 K
Lochmaben, Scotland, castle, 1384 A
Lodi, Italy, peace of, 1454 B
Lohengrin (anon.), 1290 K; theme, 1212 K, 1287 K
Loiera, La, Sardinia, Italy, naval battle, 1353 C
Loire, river, France, 979 E
Lojsta, Sweden, palace, 1000 J
Lollards, E. heretics, 1401 H; rebel, 1414 A, 1431 B; tracts against, 1415 H, 1456 H; Scottish, 1408 H
Lombard League:
  oppose Frederick I, 1159 C, 1167 B, E, 1175 B, 1176 B, 1177 C, 1183 B
  ally with Henry VI, 1193 A
  oppose Frederick II, 1226 A, 1237 D
  others, 1252 A, 1265 A

Lombards:
Kings of, *see* Charlemagne; Conrad; Conrad III; Frederick I; Henry VII; Lewis IV. *Cf.* Italy
Italian principalities of. *See* Benevento; Capua; Salerno
history of (Paul the Deacon), 800 K
expelled from France, 1311 G
Lombardy, Italy, 1022 C, 1037 F, 1217 H; revolts against Germans, 997 E, 1002 A, 1014 B
London, England:
sacked by Vikings, 836 E, 842 E
taken by Danes, 871 E, 886 E, 895 E
annexed to Wessex, 911 E
attacked by Danes, 994 E, 1009 C, 1016 B
taken by barons, 1215 B, 1263 C, 1267 B, 1297 D
riots in, 1326 D, 1377 A
Peasants' Revolt, 1381 B
Treaties of, 1359 A, B, 1373 B
Lollard rising, 1414 A
riot, 1425 D
Cade's rebellion, 1450 C
astronomical tables for, 1149 G
Bishops of, 1179 F, 1187 K
chronicle of (Arnold), 1274 K
coal in, 1273 G
German merchants, 1157 F
places in:
Blackfriars, 1382 H
Cathedral, 1087 J
Charing Cross, 1291 J
College of Arms, 1484 F
Inns of Court, 1292 F
Guildhall, 1411 J
St. Bartholomew's priory and hospital, 1123 J; Fair, 1133 J
St. Thomas' hospital, 1215 G
Tower, 1088 J, 1466 C, 1483 B
See also Westminster
Longbow, 1298 G
Longchamp, William, Bishop of Ely (d. 1197), Justiciar of England, 1190 D, 1191 C, D
'Loosecoat Field', Empingham, England, 1470 A
Lopez, Fernão, Port. historian (d. 1459?), 1434 K
López de Ayala, Pedro, Sp. poet and historian (1332–1407), 1386 K, 1407 K
López de Mendoza Santillana, Sp. poet, 1398 L, 1458 K
Lorenzetti, Ambrogio, It. painter, 1319 J, 1337 J, 1342 J, 1348 L
Lorenzetti, Pietro, It. painter, 1320 J, 1329 J, 1330 J, 1340 J, 1341 J, 1342 J, 1348 L
Loria, Roger, Genoese admiral (d. 1305), 1284 B, 1287 B, 1300 B
Lorraine (Lotharingia), kingdom of, 855 C, 870 C, 875 D, 884 C, 888 D, 891 B; *and see* Lothar II, Charles the Bald, Charles the Simple, Otto II
Lorraine, France:
tribal duke of, 908 E
made German duchy, 925 E; *and see* Gilbert, Bruno, Charles, Godfrey
French invasions, 938 E, 978 D, 979 C, 980 C, 984 A
raided by Magyars, 954 E
German control reasserted, 1018 A, 1025 D
conquered by Charles of Burgundy, 1473 D, 1474 D, 1475 B
Lorris, France, Treaty of, 1243 A
Lorris, Guillaume de, F. poet (*fl.* 1237), 1237 K, 1305 K
Lorsch, W. Germany, 800 J
Lothair, King of France (b. 941; 954–86), 954 C, 960 E, 965 A, 977 E, 979 E, 985 A, 986 A, 988 C, 989 A; invades Lorraine, 978 A, 980 C, 984 A
Lothar I, Emperor (840–55), 840 B, 908 E
King of Bavaria, 814 C
joint-emperor, 817 C, 831 A
King of Italy, 823 E, 824 F
revolts against father, 829 E, 833 B, 834 A, 839 B
relations with brothers, 841 B, 842 A, B, 844 D, 847 E
partition of lands, 843 C, 855 C
Lothar II, Holy Roman Emperor (1133–7), 1075 L, 1133 B, 1137 D
Duke of Saxony, 1106 E, 1115 A, 1124 E
King of the Germans, 1125 C, 1126 A, 1131 A, 1134 E, 1135 C, 1136 C
revolts against, 1127 D, 1135 A
Italian expeditions, 1132 C, 1133 B, C, 1136 C, E
Lothar II, King of Italy, 948 B, 950 D
Lothar II, King of 'Lotharingia' (855–69), 855 C, 863 A, 865 A, 869 C; divorce of, 860 F, 861 E, 865 B
Louis I the Pious, Emperor (b. 778; 814–40), 814 A, 840 B
King of France, 806 A, 811 E, 813 C
concedes lands, 814 C, 817 C, 829 E, 839 B
blinds Bernard of Italy, 818 B, 822 E
attempts subdue Bretons, 818 C, 826 E
revolts against, 830 B, 831 B, 832 E, 833 B, D, 834 B
government of, 816 F, 833 F, 835 B
Church reform, 817 H, 818 H, 822 H
History of the Sons of (Nithard), 843 K
Louis II, Emperor and King of Italy (850–75), 847 E, 850 B, 852 B, 855 C, 863 A, 866 D, 871 A, 875 C
Louis III the Blind, King of Provence (887–927), 887 A, 888 A, 890 E, 927 E; King of Italy, 900 D; Emperor, 901 A; expelled, 902 E; blinded, 905 C
Louis, King of Aquitaine (781–806/13), 806 A
Louis the German, King of Bavaria (817–76), 817 C, 828 E, 845 A, 876 C
revolts against father, 830 B, 831 B, 832 E, 833 B, 834 A, 839 B, 840 B
wars against Lothar, 841 B, 842 A, B
treaties with brothers, 843 C, 844 D, 847 E
war against Moravia, 846 E, 874 E
invades France, 853 E, 858 C, 859 E
treaties with Charles the Bald, 860 B, 865 A, 869 C, 870 C
invades Lorraine, 875 D
Louis the Younger, King of Bavaria (880–2), 876 C, D, 879 B, 880 E, 882 A; poem about, 881 K
Louis the Child, King of the Germans (b. 893), 899 D, 910 E, 911 A
Louis I, King of France. *See* Louis I, Emperor
Louis II the Stammerer, King of France (b. 846), 877 D, 878 C, 879 B; King of Aquitaine, 866 C
Louis III, joint King of France (b. *c.* 863; 879–82), 879 B, D, 880 A, 881 C, 882 C, 893 A
Louis IV d'Outremer, King of France (b. 921), 936 B, 938 E, 939 C, 940 F, 943 E, 944 E, 945 E, 946 E, 950 E, 954 C
Louis V le Fainéant, King of France (b. *c.* 967), 986 A, 987 B; King of Aquitaine, 979 E
Louis VI the Fat, King of France (b. *c.* 1077; 1108–1137), 1108 C, 1124 C, 1127 A, E, 1128 C, 1131 D, 1136 B, 1137 C; wars with Henry I, 1109 A, 1113 A, 1117 E, 1119 C, D
Louis VII, King of France (b. *c.* 1120; 1137–80), 1131 D, 1137 C, 1142 E, 1152 A, 1162 C, 1179 D, 1180 C; on Crusade, 1147 B, D, 1148 A–C, 1149 C; relations with Henry II, 1151 C, 1159 C, 1169 A, 1173 A, 1174 C
Louis VIII, King of France (1223–6), 1187 L, 1223 C, 1224 B, 1226 B, D; invades England, 1216 B, 1217 B, C; annexes Toulouse, 1224 A, 1226 A, D

Louis IX, St., King of France (1226–70), 1234 B, 1241 G, 1243 J, 1246 A, 1249 C
minority, 1226 D, 1227 A, 1229 B
wars with Henry III, 1231 C, 1242 B, C, 1243 A, B
on Crusade, 1248 C, 1249 B, 1250 A, B, 1254 B, C
mission to Mongol court, 1253 E, G
mediation by, 1256 C, 1264 A
treaties with Aragon, 1258 B; and England, 1258 B, 1259 D
crusade to Tunis, 1270 C, G
government of, 1239 F, 1247 F, 1254 F, 1258 F, 1259 F, 1262 F, 1266 G
Établissements, 1270 F
canonised, 1297 C
Life of (Geoffrey de Beaulieu), 1274 K; (Joinville), 1309 K
Louis X Hutin, King of France (1314–16), 1289 L, 1314 D, 1315 B, C, 1316 B, D; King of Navarre, 1305 B
Louis XI, King of France (1461–83), 1423 L, 1461 C, 1463 D, 1464 G, 1467 G, 1469 C, 1471 G, 1475 J, 1483 C
as Dauphin, 1440 A, 1456 C
relations with Papacy, 1461 D, 1478 C
annexes Roussillon etc., 1462 B, 1463 A, 1473 A, 1475 A
revolts against, 1465 C, D, 1468 C, D, 1473 A
holds Estates-General, 1468 B
reconciles Margaret and Warwick, 1470 C
war with Burgundy, 1471 A, 1472 B, D, 1475 C
gains by reversion, 1472 B, 1480 C, 1481 G
mediates between Habsburgs and Swiss, 1474 A
war with England, 1474 C, 1475 C, 1480 E
plots against, 1475 C, D, 1477 C
annexes Burgundy, Artois, etc., 1477 A, C
war with Maximilian, 1479 C, 1482 D
account of (Commynes), 1489 K
Louis XII, King of France (b. 1462; 1498–1515), as Duke of Orleans, 1485 A, C, 1486 D, 1488 C
Louis of Taranto, King of Naples (b. 1320), 1346 C, 1350 E, 1362 B
Louis I, Duke of Anjou (b. 1339), 1380 B; King of Naples, 1382 B, 1384 C
Louis II, Duke of Anjou (b. 1377), 1384 C, 1385 B; King of Naples, 1387 E, 1390 C; expelled, 1399 E, 1409 D, 1411 B, 1417 B
Louis III, Duke of Anjou (b. 1403), 1417 B; heir to Naples, 1420 C, 1423 B, 1434 D
Louis, King of Sicily (b. 1338), 1342 C, 1355 D
Louis I of Nevers, Count of Flanders, 1322 C, 1323 B, 1328 C, 1337 D, 1346 C
Louis II de Maële, Count of Flanders (b. 1330), 1346 C, 1349 A, 1369 B, 1379 E, 1382 B, D, 1384 A
Louis, Duke of Orleans (and Touraine; b. 1372), 1387 B, 1405 C, D, 1406 D; murdered, 1407 D, 1408 A, 1410 D
Louis of Anjou, St., Bishop of Toulouse (b. 1275), 1298 L; painting, *St. Louis of Toulouse* (Martini), 1317 J
Louis of Évreux, claimant to Durazzo, 1376 E, 1379 E
Louvain, Belgium, battle, 891 C; University, 1311 H, 1425 H
Louviers, France, Treaties of, 856 A, 1196 A
Love of God (Bernard of Clairvaux), 1126 H
Lovel, Francis, Viscount, E. conspirator (d. 1487?), 1486 A
Loves of the Divine Hymns (St. Simeon), 1022 K
Loyala, Ignatius de, founder of the Jesuits (1491–1556), 1491 L
Lu Fa-yen, C. philologist (*fl. c.* 600), 1011 K
Lu T'ai, Siamese Buddhist cosmologist (d. *c.* 1370), 1345 K; as Dharmaja II, King of Sukhodaya (1347–61), 1349 E
Lu Yü, C. author (b. 750?), 804 G
Lu Yu, C. writer, 1329 G
Luang Prabang, Laos, 1353 E, 1479 E
Lubart, King of Halich (1339–49), 1339 E
Lübeck, W. Germany, 1143 G, 1147 B, 1181 E, 1191 E, 1226 G, 1227 C; and Hanse, 1241 G, 1252 G, 1259 G, 1282 G, 1283 G, 1418 G; canal, 1405 G; Cathedral, 1173 J; Treaty of, 1457 G
Lubusz, E. Germany, 1250 E
Lucca, Italy, 1264 E, 1279 E, 1306 B, 1314 B, 1317 E, 1320 E, 1328 C, 1337 E, 1342 C, 1400 A, 1408 A; tomb in Cathedral, 1406 J
Lucena, Spain, battle, 1483 B
Lucera, Italy, 1246 E, 1254 D
Lucerne, Switzerland, 1332 D
Lucidario (Sancho IV), 1295 K
Lucidator astronomiae (Pietro d'Abano), 1303 G
Lucius II, Pope, 1144 A, D, 1145 A
Lucius III (Ubald of Ostia), 1181 C, 1184 D, H, 1185 A, D
Lucka, E. Germany, battle, 1307 B
Ludford, England, battle, 1459 D
Ludmilla, St., widow of Bořivoj of Bohemia, 921 E
Ludwigslied (anon.), 881 K
Lughat-i-Furs (Asadī), 1060 K
Lulach, King of Scotland, 1057 C, 1058 A
Lull, Raymond, Catalan theologian and missionary (b. *c.* 1232), 1272 H, 1275 K, 1276 H, 1283 K, 1311 H, 1315 L
Lumphanan, Scotland, battle, 1057 C
Luna, Alvaro de, constable of Castile, 1452 C
Lunar Tables (Walcher of Malvern), 1108 G
Lund, Sweden, Archbishopric, 1104 H, 1258 E; Cathedral, 1146 J; church, 1000 J
Lüneburg Heath, W. Germany, battle, 880 A
Lupus, Servatus, Abbot of Ferrières, F. philologist, 862 K
Lusatia. *See* Lausitz
Lusatians, Slav tribe, 993 E
Lusignan, family of Poitou, 1242 B, C
Lusignan, Hugh de, 1200 C, 1202 C
Lusignan, L'histoire de (Jean d'Arras), 1387 K
Lute, Story of a (Kao Ming?), 1356 J
Luther, Martin, G. religious reformer (1483–1546), 1483 L
Luxemburg, Counts of, 1017 D, 1042 E, *and see* Henry VII; Duchy of, 1437 E, 1443 D
Ly dynasty. *See* Dai-co-viet
Ly Nhan-tong, Emperor of Dai Viet (b. 1065, d. 1128), 1076 E
Ly Thai-to, Emperor of Dai-co-viet (1010–29), 1010 E
Ly Thai-tong, Emperor of Dai-co-viet (1029–54), 1044 E
Ly Thanh-tong, Emperor of Dai-co-viet (1054–72), 1068 E
Lydgate, John, E. poet (*c.* 1370–*c.* 1451), 1412 K, 1420 K
Lyndwood, William, E. canonist (d. 1446), 1430 H
Lyons, France, 1244 D, 1305 D, 1310 E, 1467 G; Archbishops of, 841 H, 875 L, 1272 D; Cathedral, 1392 J; General Councils, 1245 C, H, 1274 C, H; Waldenses of, 1170 H, 1184 H
Lyra, Nicholas de, F. theologian (1279–1340), 1332 H, 1340 L
Lyutitzi, Slav tribe, 1036 E, 1056 E; *and see* Lausitz

M

Ma Kuan, C. travel-writer, 1451 G
Ma'ārif, Kitāb al- (ibn-Qutaybah), 889 K
Ma'arrī, Abū'l-'Alā' al-, Syrian poet (973–1058), 1058 K
Mabinogion, The, 1375 K
Mabuse, Jean (Jan Gossaert), Flemish artist (1470–1532), 1470 L
Macao, China, naval battle, 1279 E
Macbeth, King of Scotland, 1040 C, 1054 C, 1057 C
Macduff, Scottish noble, 1057 C
Macedonia, Yugoslavia, 1330 B
Machaut, Guillaume de, F. court poet and musician (*c.* 1300–77), 1364 J, 1377 K
Machiavelli, Niccolò, It. historian and writer on politics (1469–1527), 1469 L
Maclodio, Italy, battle, 1427 D
Mâcon, France, 1375 G
Madanī, Kashmīr, mosque, 1470 J
Madeira, island, 1418 G
Mādhava, Indian philosopher, 1386 H
Madhurā Vijayam (Gangā Devi), 1371 K
Madonna (sculpture; Giovanni Pisano), 1305 J
Madonna or *The Virgin*, paintings:
  Daddi, 1346 J
  Lorenzetti, Ambrogio, 1319 J
  and Child:
    Bellini, 1450 J
    Christus, 1417 J
    Crivelli, 1491 J
    Eyck, Jan van, 1434 J
    Lippi, Filippo, 1452 J
    Signorelli, 1490 J
  and Child and Angels (Mantegna), 1485 J
  and Child and two angels (Filippo Lippi), 1465 J
  and Child with St. Anthony (Filippino Lippi), 1480 J
  and Saints (Mantegna), 1457 J
  Coronation of:
    Bellini, 1473 J
    Filippo Lippi, 1441 J
  Death of (Hugo van der Goes), 1480 J
  degli Otto (Filippino Lippi), 1485 J
  della Misericordia (Uccello), 1445 J
  Enthroned:
    Cimabue, 1280 J
    Lorenzetti, Pietro, 1340 J
    Memling, 1480 J
  of Canon van der Paele (Jan van Eyck), 1436 J
  of the Chancellor Rolin (*idem*), 1435 J
  of the Fountain (*idem*), 1439 J
  of the Rocks (Leonardo), 1483 J
  with Four Saints (Roger van der Weyden), 1450 J
  with the Duke of Urbino (Piero della Francesca), 1472 J
Madrid, Spain, 932 E
Madura, India, Hindu kingdom, 1310 E; Muslim kingdom, 1335 E, 1370 E, 1371 K
Maerlant, Jacob van, Flemish poet-chronicler (1235?–1295?), 1283 K
Maes Moydog, Wales, battle, 1295 A
Maestà (Duccio), 1308 J; (Martini), 1315 J
Magdalen (Ghiberti), 1455 J
Magdeburg, E. Germany, 805 G, 1007 E; Archbishopric, 968 H, 1133 B; *and see* Adalbert, Norbert; Cathedral, 1207 J; monastery, 955 H
Magellan, Ferdinand, Port. navigator (1480–1521), 1480 L
Maghāzī, Kitāb al- (al-Wāqidi), 823 K
Magic, treatise against, 841 H; *and see* Witchcraft
Magisterium divinale (William of Auvergne), 1249 H
Magna Carta, 1215 B, C, F; reissues, 1216 D, 1217 D, 1225 A, F; confirmed, 1237 A, 1297 D, 1298 B, 1300 A, 1301 A, 1305 D
Magnet, floating (Chinese), 1020 G; (European), 1190 G
Magnetic needle, 1086 G, 1093 G; *cf.* Compass
Magnete, Epistola de (Peter Peregrinus), 1269 G
Magnus I the Good, King of Norway, 1035 D; and Denmark, 1042 B, 1047 D
Magnus II, King of Norway, 1066 C, 1068 B
Magnus III Bareleg, King of Norway, 1093 C, 1098 E, 1101 E, 1103 C
Magnus IV the Blind, King of Norway (d. 1139), 1130 A, 1135 A
[Magnus V, King of Norway, d. 1143]
Magnus VI, King of Norway (b. 1157), 1162 E, 1177 E, 1184 B
Magnus VII the Law-mender, King of Norway (b. 1238), 1263 D, 1266 C, 1276 F, 1280 B
Magnus VIII, King of Norway (b. 1316; d. 1374), 1319 B, 1343 E; King of Sweden (as Magnus II), 1319 C, 1347 F, 1360 C, E, 1362 C; deposed, 1363 D
Magnus I Barn-lock, King of Sweden (b. 1240), 1275 E, 1285 D, 1290 D
Magyars. *See* Hungary
Mahānādi, river, India, battle, 1244 B
Mahāvīri of Mysore, Indian mathematician, 830 G
Mahbaroth, The (Emanuel ben Solomon), 1331 K
Mahdī, The. *See* Muhammad ibn-Tūmart; Mu'awiya; Muntazar; 'Ubaydullāh
Mahdīyah, Tunisia, 1087 E, 1160 A
Mahīpāla, King of Kanauj, 916 E
Mahīpāla I, King of Bengal, 980 E
Mahmūd I, Nāsir-ad-Dīn, Sultan of Delhi, 1246 B, 1266 A
Mahmūd II, Shah of Delhi, 1393 A, 1413 A
Mahmūd, Emir of Ghaznī (998–1030), 971 L, 998 E, 1030 A, J; conquests, 1016 E; in India, 1001 D, 1009 E, 1018 D, 1025 A, 1026 E
Mahmūd I, Seljuq Sultan, 1092 D, 1094 E
Mahmudek, Khan of the Golden Horde (1445–65), 1445 C
Mahon, King of Munster, 967 E
Maiano, Benedetto da, It. architect (d. 1490), 1489 J
Maiestas Carolina, 1350 F
Mailberg, Austria, battle, 1082 E
Maimonides. *See* Moses ben Maimon
Maine, France, county, 846 E, 1048 E, 1062 E, 1083 E, 1087 C, 1099 E, 1113 A, 1151 C, 1480 C
Mainz, W. Germany, 1049 H, 1194 A, 1198 E; Archbishops of, 891 B, 973 E, 1115 D, 1226 B, 1241 C, 1344 H, 1405 C, *and see* Adolf of Nassau; Maurus; Cathedral, 978 J, 1009 J, 1060 J, 1181 J, 1250 J; mastersingers of, 1311 J; printing at, 1440 G, 1462 G; University, 1477 H
Maio of Bari, Emir of Naples, 1160 D
Maistre Pierre Pathelin (Guillaume Alexis?), 1464 K
Mājapāhit, Java, empire, 1377 E
Majorca, is., Spain, 1115 E; kingdom, 1262 E, 1344 A, *and see* James I, James II
Majrīti, Abū-l-Qāsim Maslamah al-, Sp. M. astronomer and mathematician, 1007 G
Makhluqāt wa-ghara' (al- Qazwini), 1283 G
Makura no Sōshi (Sei Shōnagon), 1000 K
Makuta, King of Thaton, 1057 E
Malacca, Malaya, kingdom, 1405 E, 1477 E
Malachy II, King of Tara, 980 E; High King of Ireland, 999 E
Malachy, St., Archbishop of Armagh, 1148 L
Malaga, Spain, 1489 C
Malatesta, lord of Rimini, 1312 E

Malatesta, Galeotto, lord of Rimini, 1355 B
Malatesta, Roberto, lord of Rimini, condottiere, 1469 C, 1482 C
Malatesta, Sigismondo (Piero della Francesca), 1451 J
Malatiya (Melitene) Turkey, 934 E, 1057 E; battle, 1067 E
Malaya, 1295 E, 1477 E; Empire, 1025 E
Malcolm I, King of Scotland (943–54), 943 E, 945 E, 954 E, 962 E
Malcolm II, King of Scotland, 1005 E, 1016 E, 1027 E, 1034 D
Malcolm III Canmore, King of Scotland (1058–93), 1054 C, 1057 C, 1058 A, 1094 E, 1097 D; invades England, 1061 E, 1070 E, 1079 E, 1091 E, 1093 D; does homage, 1072 B, 1091 E
Malcolm IV the Maiden, King of Scotland (b. 1131), 1153 B, 1157 E, 1160 E, 1164 E, 1165 D
Maldon, England, battle, 991 C; poem, 993 K
Maleficiorum, Libellus de improbacione (Arnold of Villanova), 1311 G; *cf. Malleus*
Malermi, Niccolò di, It. translator of Bible, 1471 H
Malestroit, France, Treaty of, 1343 A
Mali, Negro Empire, 1240 E, 1337 E, 1348 G
Mālik, ibn-, Per. poet, 1274 K
Malik Gazi, Seljuq noble, 1250 J
Malik Sarvar, Sultan of Jaunpur (1394–9), 1394 B
Malik Shah, Sultan of Persia (b. 1055), 1072 D, 1074 E, G, 1079 E, 1091 E, 1092 D, E
Malik Shah, Sultan of Rūm, 1107 C, 1117 E
Malik al Saleh, Sultan of Samudra, 1297 E
Malines, Belgium, Parlement of, 1473 F
Malipiero, Orio, Doge of Venice, 1179 B, 1192 B
Malipiero, Pasquale, Doge of Venice, 1457 D, 1462 B
Malleus Maleficiarum, 1487 H
Mallū Khan, ruler of Delhi, 1405 D
Malmesbury, England, monks of. *See* Oliver; Saewulf; William
Malory, Thomas, E. romance writer (d. 1471?), 1470 K, 1485 K
Malta (G.C.), 869 E, 1090 E
Mālwā, India, Hindu kingdom, 1060 E; Muslim kingdom, 1406 E
Mamay, Khan of the Golden Horde, 1381 E
Mamlūks. *See* Egypt
Ma'mūn, al-, Caliph (b. 786), 809 A, 813 C, G, 817 C, 818 E, 819 E, 820 E, 825 E, 830 K, 833 C, G
Ma'mūn, Abū-l-'Alā' al-, Almohad ruler in Spain and Morocco, 1227 C, 1229 C, E, 1232 D
Man, Isle of, England, 1000 E, 1098 E, 1266 C, 1313 E, 1333 B
Man in a Red Turban (Jan van Eyck), 1433 J
Man in the Panther's Skin, The (Shota Rustaveli), 1200 K
Manākh, Kitāb al- (ibn-al-Bannā), 1321 G
Manāzir, Kitāb al- (al-Hasan), 1039 G
Manchuria, China, tribes of. *See* Jürched (*under* China); Uighurs
'Mandeville, John de', travel-author, 1372 K
Mandeville, William de, Earl of Essex, 1189 D
Manekine, La (Philippe de Beaumanoir), 1276 K
Manetti, Giannozzo, It. humanist, 1396 L, 1459 L
Manfred, King of Sicily (1258–66), 1254 D, 1255 C, 1257 B, 1258 C, 1259 B, 1260 C, 1262 A, B, 1264 E, 1265 B, 1266 A
Manfredi, Giovanni de', lord of Faenza, 1350 A
Mangrai, King of Lan Na, 1296 E, 1311 E
Mangu-Temir, Khan of the Golden Horde, 1266 E, H, 1269 E, 1280 E
Maniaces, George, Gk. general, 1032 E, 1039 E, 1043 A
Manichaeism, heretical Christian doctrine, in China, 842 H; in Armenia, 867 H
Manny, Walter de, E. soldier (d. 1372), 1342 B
Mannyng, Robert, E. religious writer, poet and translator, 1303 K, 1338 K
Manrique, Jorge, Sp. poet (1440?–1479), 1479 K
Mans, Le, France, 1062 E, 1073 E, 1425 C, 1448 A; Cathedral, 1150 J, 1217 J, 1254 J
Mansa Musa, Emperor of Mali (1307–37), 1337 E
Mansūr, al-, Caliph of Kairāwan, 946 E, 948 E, 952 E *See also* Almanzor
Mansur Shah of Malacca, 1477 E
Mansūrah, Egypt, battle, 1250 A, B
Mantegna, Andrea, It. painter (1431–1506), 1431 L, 1448 J, 1457 J, 1458 J, 1460 J, 1485 J
Mantes, France, Cathedral, 1170 J; Treaty of, 1193 C
Mantua, Italy, 1090 B, 1091 B, 1226 A, 1397 A, 1398 B; castle, frescoes in, 1460 J; churches, 1460 J, 1470 J; Congress of, 1459 B; rules of, *see* Gonzaga
Manuale Sacerdotis (John Mirk), 1400 H
Manu-Dhammasattham (Wagaru), 1306 F
Manuel I Comnenus, Greek Emperor (1143–80), 1143 B, 1180 C, F; wars with Sicily, 1147 E, 1148 C, E, 1149 C, 1154 A, 1155 D, 1156 B, 1158 E; with Hungary, 1151 E, 1156 C; with Armenia and Antioch, 1158 B, 1159 B; with Venice, 1171 A, 1172 E; with Rūm, 1176 C; chronicle of, 1183 K
Manuel II Palaeologus, Greek Emperor (b. 1348), 1391 A, 1399 E, 1423 E, 1425 C
Manuel, Juan, Sp. writer of romances (1282–1349), 1349 K
Manuscripts, decorated:
  Arab, 1005 J
  Berri Books of Hours, 1410 J, 1411 J, 1413 J
  English, 1259 K, 1396 J
  French, 1296 J; *and see* Fouquet, Jean; Francis, Master; Pucelle, Jean
  Japanese, 1293 J
  Persian, 1314 K, 1335 J, 1396 J, 1488 J
  scriptoria, 800 H, 804 J, 821 H
  Utrecht Psalter, 832 J
Manuzio. *See* Aldus Manutius
Manzikert, Turkey, 1054 E; battle, 1071 C
Manzūr, Jamāl-ad-Dīn ibn-, Eg. philologist (1232–1311), 1311 K
Map, Walter, Welsh poet (*c.* 1140?–1209?), 1200 K
Mappa Mundi, Hereford, 1314 G
Mappae Clavicula, 1110 G
Mappemonde (Pierre de Beauvais), 1225 K
Maps, made by:
  Arabs, 950 G, 975 G, 985 G
  Chinese, 801 G, 814 G, 1137 G, 1331 F; celestial, 1092 G
  English, 1314 G, 1340 G
  French, 1120 G
  German, 1110 G
  Italians, 1119 G, 1321 G, 1352 G, 1436 G; portolans, 1311 G, 1367 G
  Persian, 851 G
  Spanish Jew, 1375 G
  Spanish Muslim, 1154 G
  earliest portolan, 1270 G
Maqāmāt (al-Hamadhānī), 1007 K; (al-Harīrī), 1122 K
Maqāsid al-Alhān (al-Qādir), 1418 J
Maqdisī, al-, Arab geographer and cartographer, 985 G
Maqrīzī, Taqi-ad-Dīn al-, Eg. historian, archaeologist and geographer (1364–1442), 1442 K
Mar, Donald, Earl of, Regent of Scotland, 1332 C
Marāghah, Persia, observatory, 1259 G
Māravarman Kulaśekhara, Pāndya Emperor (1269–1308/9), 1269 E, 1279 E
Māravarman Sundara, Pāndya Emperor, 1216 E

Marbach, W. Germany, alliance of, 1405 C
Marbode, Bishop of Rennes, F. medical author and poet (1035–1123), 1123 G
Marburg, W. Germany, church, 1235 J
'Marc the Greek', chemist, 1300 G
Marcel, Étienne, Parisian leader, 1355 D, 1356 D, 1358 A, C
Marcello, Niccolò, Doge of Venice, 1473 C, 1474 D
March, Earl of. *See* Mortimer, Roger
March, Auziàs, Catalan poet (1397–1459), 1459 K
Marco Polo. *See* Polo
Mareschalchiae, Liber (Giordano Ruffo), 1252 G
Margaret, Regent of Denmark (b. 1354; 1376–1412), 1362 C, 1376 B; and Norway, 1387 C; and Sweden, 1389 A, 1395 B, 1397 B, 1404 D, 1412 D
Margaret of Anjou, wife of Henry VI, 1429 L, 1444 B, 1445 B, 1447 H, 1482 L; Lancastrian leader, 1461 A, 1470 C, 1471 B
Margaret of Provence, wife of Louis IX, 1234 B
Margaret, St., Queen of Scotland, 1046 L, 1093 L; son, 1097 D
Margaret, 'the Maid of Norway', Queen of Scotland, 1286 A, 1289 D, 1290 C
Margaret 'Maultasch' of Carinthia, 1335 B, 1336 E, 1342 A, 1362 E
Margaret II, Countess of Flanders, 1280 A
Margaret, Countess of Hainault and Holland (d. 1356), 1345 C
Margut, France, 980 C
Maria, Queen of Jerusalem, 1205 B, 1210 D
Maria, Queen of Sicily, 1377 C, 1391 E, 1402 B
Maria Laach, Austria, Abbey, 1156 J
Marianus Scotus, Irish historian, 1028 L, 1083 K
Marie, wife of Philip III (d. 1321), 1296 G
Marie de France, F. poet, 1165 K, 1185 K
Marienburg (*now* Malborg), Poland, 1309 E, 1457 B
Marignolli, John of, It. friar, envoy and chronicler, 1340 H, 1359 K
Marigny, Enguerrand de, F. finance minister, 1315 B
Marīnids. *See* Morocco
Marino, Italy, battle, 1379 B
Marinus I (*alias* Martin II), Pope, 882 D, 884 B
Marinus II (*alias* Martin III), Pope, 942 D, 946 B
Marj as-Saffar, Syria, battle, 1303 E
Marlborough, England, Statute of, 1267 F
'Marmousets', F. councillors, 1388 D, 1392 C
Marozia, mistress and mother of Popes, 932 E
Marrakesh, Morocco, 1068 E, 1121 E, 1147 B, 1208 E, 1229 E, 1269 E
Marriage of clergy. *See* Clergy
Marseilles, France, 838 E, 1383 G, 1481 G
Marsh, Adam, E. friar and teacher at Oxford, 1257 H
Marshal, Richard, Earl of Pembroke, 1233 C, D, 1234 B
Marshal, William, Earl of Pembroke (b. 1146?), 1216 D, 1217 B, 1219 B; *Histoire* of, 1220 K
Marsigli, Luigi, It. humanist, 1394 K
Marsilio of Padua, It. political theorist, 1324 F, 1327 H, 1328 L
Martin IV (Simon de Brie), Pope, 1281 A–C, 1282 D, 1284 A, 1285 A
Martin V (Odo Colunna), Pope, 1417 D, H, 1420 A, C, 1423 B, C, 1428 A, 1428 H, 1431 A
Martin I, King of Aragon, 1395 B; and Sicily, 1409 C, 1410 B
Martin of Aragon, King of Sicily, 1391 E, 1402 B, 1409 C
Martin, F. mason, 1227 J
Martin Gallus, F. chronicler of Poland (?), 1112 K
Martin, Raymond, Sp. theologian (*c.* 1215–*c.* 1290), 1277 H
Martin of Troppau, Bohemian chronicler, 1278 K
Martini, Simone, It. painter, 1315 J, 1317 J, 1320 J, 1328 J, 1330 J, 1333 J, 1342 J, 1344 L
Martinus of Bologna, It. jurist, 1100 F
Martorell, Joanot, Catalan novelist (d. 1488?), 1490 K
Martyr Anglerius, Peter, It. historian (1459–1526), 1459 L
Martyrdom, forbidden, 852 H
Martyrologies (Eulogius), 859 H
Ma'rūf al-Karkhi of Baghdād, Sūfī saint, 815 H
Mary of Antioch, Greek Empress and Regent, 1180 C, 1182 C
Mary, Queen of Hungary (b. 1370), 1382 C, 1386 B, 1395 B
Mary of Burgundy, Countess of Flanders (b. 1457), 1477 A, C, 1478 A, 1482 A
Masaccio (Tomasso di Ser Giovanni di Mone), It. painter, 1401 L, 1425 J, 1426 J, 1428 L
Masālik al-absār (al-'Umari), 1348 G
Masālik w-al-Mamālik (ibn-Khurdādhbih), 846 G; (al-Istakhri), 950 G; (al-Bakri), 1094 G
Masar, Saracen leader, 852 B
Masarra, Muhammad ibn-'Abdallah ibn-, Sp. M. theologian, 931 H
Māsawayh, Yuhannā ibn-, Arab anatomist and ophthamologist (777–857), 857 G
Māsawayh al-Mārdini, Arab pharmacologist (925–1015), 1015 G
Māshā'allāh, Arab astronomer and meteorologist, 815 G
Masnavī (al-Rūmī), 1273 K
Masons. *See* Architects
Masovia, Poland, 1047 E, 1226 E, 1355 E
Masse'oth Rabbi Binjamin (Benjamin ben Jonah), 1173 G
Master of Game (Edward, Duke of York), 1410 K
Mastersingers, 1311 J
Masuccio, It. writer, 1476 K
Masuccio, Stefano, It. architect, 1291 L, 1388 L
Ma'sūd, 'Alā-ad-Dīn, Shah of Delhi, 1242 B, 1246 B
Ma'sūd I, Emir of Ghaznī, 1030 A, 1040 A
Ma'sūd III, Emir of Ghaznī (1089–1114), 1114 J
Ma'sūd I, Sultan of Rūm, 1117 E, 1156 E
Ma'sūdi, Abu-al-Hasan 'Ali al-, Arab historian and geographer, 956 G
Mateo, It. mason, 1168 J
Matfré de Bezier, F. poet, 1288 K
Mathematicians:
  Arab. *See* Aflah; Nasawi; Thābit; Wafā
  Belgian. *See* Franco of Liège
  Chinese. *See* Ch'in Chiu-shao; Chu Shih-chieh; Li Yeh; Shên Kua
  Egyptian. *See* Hasan; Mūsa ibn-Shakīr
  English. *See* Bradwardine, Thomas; Maudwith, John; Wallingford, Richard
  Greek. *See* Euclid; Leo the Mathematician
  French. *See* Abbo of Fleury; Alexander of Villedieu; Meurs, Jean de; Oresme, Nicholas
  French Jew. *See* Levi ben Gerson
  German. *See* Adelbold; Helperic; Hermann Contractus; Jordanus Nemorarius; Puerbach, Georg; Regiomontanus
  Indian. *See* Bhāskara; Mahāvīri; Śrīdhara
  Italian. *See* Borgo, Pietro; Campano, Giovanni; Fibonacci, Leonardo; Jacob of Florence
  Moroccan. *See* Bannā
  Persian. *See* Bīrūnī; Khayyām; Khwarizmī; Tūsī
  Spanish Muslim. *See* Majrīti
Matilda, Empress, 1167 L, 1114 A; marries Geoffrey Plantagenet, 1128 B; heir of Henry I, 1128 B, 1131 C; claims English crown, 1139 C, 1141 A, 1147 D, 1148 A

Matilda, wife of William the Conqueror, 1059 J
Matilda, Duchess of Saxony (1156–89), 1168 E
Matilda, Countess of Tuscany (b. 1046), 1089 E, 1091 B, 1095 E, 1102 E, 1115 C
Matīn, Kitāb al- (ibn-Haiyān), 1076 K
Matthew of Urfah, Armenian chronicler, 1144 K
Matthias of Arras, F. mason (d. 1352), 1344 J
Matthias of Cracow, Polish church critic, 1390 H
Matthias of Janov, Bohemian preacher, 1394 H
Matthias Corvinus (Hunyadi), King of Hungary (1458–90), 1443 L, 1458 A, 1463 E, 1465 F; fights Turks, 1463 D, 1475 E; conquests, 1467 E, 1469 B, 1478 D, E, 1485 B, 1490 B
Maturīdī, Abū'l-Mansūr al-, Per. philosopher, 944 K
Maudwith, John, E. mathematician and astronomer, 1310 G
Maulbronn, W. Germany, Abbey, 1146 J
Mauron, France, battle, 1352 C
Maurus of Salerno, It. surgeon, 1214 G
Maurus, Rabanus, Archbishop of Mainz (776–856), 856 H, L
Mauzé, France, battle, 1039 A
Māwardi, Abū'l-Hasan Habīb al-, Arab political theorist (972–1058). 1058 F
Mawsili, Ibrāhīm al-, Arab musician (742–804), 804 J
Mawsili, Muhammad ibn-Dāniyāl al-, Eg. writer on drama, 1310 K
Maximilian I Habsburg, Holy Roman Emperor (b. 1459; 1496–1519), Count of Flanders, 1477 C, 1478 A, 1479 C, 1482 D, 1488 A; King of the Romans, 1486 A, 1487 C, 1490 A, 1491 D; and Breton war, 1486 A, 1489 A, 1490 D
Maya, Mexico, Old Empire, 889 E; New Empire, 987 E, 1441 E
Mayapán, Mexico, 987 E, 999 E, 1441 E
Mayeul, St., Abbot of Cluny (from 963), 972 C, 994 L
Māzinī, Abū-Hāmid Muhammad al-, Sp. M. traveller and geographer (1080–1169), 1136 G, 1162 G
Meadows of Gold (al-Mas'ūdi), 956 G
Measles. *See* Small-pox
Meaux, France, 996 A, 1421 D, 1422 B, 1439 C; Cathedral, 1194 J
Mecca, Saudi Arabia, Black Stone of, 930 E, 951 E
Mechanics, treatises on, 860 G, 1121 G, 1206 G, 1382 G
Mechthild of Magdeburg, G. mystic-poetess, 1280 H
Mecklenburg, W. Germany, 955 D, 1229 E; Duke Albert of (d. 1379), 1363 D, 1367 D, 1369 D; *and see* Albert II
Medical Art, The Whole (ibn-al-'Abbās), 994 G
Medici, Cosimo de', ruler of Florence (b. 1389), 1434 D, 1439 K, 1464 C
Medici, Giovanni de', of Florence, 1429 L
Medici, Giuliano de', ruler of Florence, 1469 D, 1478 B
Medici, Lorenzo de', ruler of Florence (d. 1492), 1449 L, 1469 D, 1471 C, 1478 B, 1480 A; as poet and dramatist, 1489 K
Medici, Piero de', ruler of Florence, 1414 L, 1464 C, 1469 D
Medicine:
  alcohol for, 1100 G
  autopsy, first in China, 1145 G
  forensic, Chinese, 1248 G
  public health service, Chinese, 1102 G; first European commission, 1343 G
  quarantine, 1377 G, 1383 G
  schools of, Arab, 931 G, 978 G; European, *see* Bologna, Montpellier, Salerno; examinations in, 931 G, 1231 G
  translation of Greek into Arabic, 800 G, 873 G; of Arabic into Latin, first, 1087 G
  treatises on. *See* Physicians
  See also Diseases; Diet; Encyclopedias; Hospitals; Hygiene; Ophthalmologists; Pharmacologists; Surgeons; Surgery
Medicine, Canon of (Avicenna), 1037 G, 1187 G, 1288 G
Medina, Saudi Arabia, law-school, 820 F
Medina del Campo, Spain, Treaty of, 1489 A
Meditations (Ailred of Rievaulx), 1166 H
Meerssen, Holland, 847 E, F, 870 C
Megenburg, Conrad of, G. naturalist, 1351 G, 1374 L
Meissen, E. Germany, Cathedral, 1250 J; Margraves of, 1002 B, 1307 B
Mekhitur of Her, Armenian physician, 1184 G
Mekong Valley, Cambodia, 1295 E
Melfi, Italy, 1040 E, 1089 C; Treaty of, 1059 C
Melisande, Queen of Jerusalem, 1129 B, 1143 D
Melitene. *See* Malatiya
Melium (Richard Rolle), 1349 K
Melk, Austria, monastery, 1418 H
Mellifont, Ireland, abbey, 1142 J
Mellrichstadt, W. Germany, battle, 1078 C
Melno, Poland, Treaty of, 1422 C
Meloria, is., Italy, naval battle, 1284 C
Melque, Spain, church, 950 J
Melton, William, Archbishop of York (d. 1340), 1319 C
Melun, France, 866 E, 924 E, 996 A; Treaty of, 1226 B
Melun Diptych (Jean Fouquet), 1451 J
Mélusine fairy-wife theme, 1387 K
Memel, Lithuania, Russia, 1252 E
Memling, Hans, G. painter (d. 1494), 1475 J, 1478 J, 1480 J, 1485 J, 1489 J, 1491 J
Memmi, Lippo, It. painter (d. 1357), 1333 J
Memmo, Tribuno, Doge of Venice, 979 E, 991 E
Mémoires (Philippe de Commynes), 1489 K
Mena, Juan de la, Sp. poet, 1412 L, 1440 K, 1456 L
Ménagier de Paris, Le, 1394 K
Menam Valley, Cambodia and Siam, 1295 E, 1347 E
Mende, France, Bishop of. *See* Durandus
Mendicant Orders, four recognised, 1274 H; treatise against, 1360 F. *And see* Augustinian Friars; Carmelite Friars; Friars Minor; Friars Preachers; Minims; Poor Clares; Trinitarian Friars
Mendoza, Pedro Gonzalez de, Sp. explorer (1428–95), 1428 L
Mendoza Santillana. *See* López de Mendoza
Mêng-ch'i (Shên Kua), 1093 G
Mensura orbis terrae, De (Dicuil), 825 G
Méraugis de Portlesguez (Raoul de Houdenc), 1235 K
Mercia, England, kingdom of, 821 E, 825 E, 828 E, *and see* Coenwulf, Burgred; Danes in, 877 E, 910 E; Earldorman of, 911 E; Lady of, *see* Ethelfleda; annexed by Wessex, 918 B; Earls of, *see* Leofric, Edwin
Meridian. *See* Degree of meridian
Merlee, William, E. meteorologist (d. 1347), 1337 G, 1340 G
Merseburg, E. Germany, 1013 B, 1033 E, 1152 B; Bishop of, *see* Thietmar
Merswin, Rulman, G. mystic, 1370 H
Merton, England, Statute of, 1236 F
Merton, Walter de, Bishop of Rochester (d. 1277), 1264 H
Meshed, Persia, 1418 J
Mersivan, Turkey, battle, 1101 C
Mesembria, Bulgaria, 1307 E

Messina, Sicily, Italy, 843 E, 1061 C, 1190 D; naval battle, 965 E; Treaty of, 1191 A
Mesta, of Castile, 1273 G
Metal-work, Persian, 1163 J; at Mosul, 1232 J
Metallurgy, 1136 G, 1175 G; accounts of, 950 G (of twelfth century), 1100 G (earliest European), 1480 G; *and see* Iron manufacture
Meteorologists:
  Arab. *See* Māshā'allāh
  English. *See* Merlee, William
  German. *See* Dietrich of Freiburg
  Persian. *See* Fārisī
Methodius, St., apostle of Moravia, 862 H, 869 H, 870 H, 874 E, 875 E, 885 H, L
Methodus medendi (Joannes Actuarios), 1342 G
Methven, Scotland, battle, 1306 B
Metz, France, 1297 E, 1324 G, 1356 F; Treaty of, 1214 B
Meun, Jean de, F. poet, 1305 K
Meurs, Jean de, F. mathematician, astrologer and musical theorist (*fl.* 1313–50), 1343 G
Mexico:
  Toltec Empire, 999 E, 1168 E
  Aztecs in, 1168 E, 1300 E, 1325 E; Kings of, 1352 E, 1440 E, 1469 E
Mexico City (Tenochtitlán), 1325 E
Mézières, Philippe de, F. poet (1327–1405), 1376 F, 1389 K
Mezzarota, Cardinal Ludovico (Mantegna), 1458 J
Mi Fei, C. painter and calligrapher (1051–1107), 1107 J
Mibu no Tadamine, J. poet (*c.* 867–*c.* 965), 905 K
Michael I Rangabe, Greek Emperor, 811 C, 812 B, 813 B
Michael II the Amorian, Greek Emperor, 820 D, 822 E, 825 E, 829 E
Michael III, Greek Emperor, 842 A, 855 D, 856 E, 862 H, 863 C, 864 E, 866 B, C, 867 C
Michael IV the Paphlagonian, Greek Emperor, 1034 B, 1041 D, E
Michael V, Greek Emperor, 1041 D, 1042 B
Michael VI the Aged, Greek Emperor, 1056 C, 1057 C
Michael VII, Greek Emperor, 1071 D, 1075 E, 1078 A
Michael VIII Palaeologus, Greek Emperor (b. 1234), 1258 D, 1261 A, C, 1263 E, 1268 B, 1273 E, 1274 C, 1279 E, 1281 C, E, 1282 D
Michael, King of Serbia (1050–84), 1084 E
Michael I, Grand Prince of Vladimir, 1174 E, 1177 E
Michael II of Tver, Grand Duke of Vladimir, 1305 E, 1319 E
Michael of Antioch, Jacobite Patriarch, Syrian chronicler (1126–99), 1199 K
Michael Asen, Tsar of Bulgaria (1246–58), 1246 D
Michael Šišman, Tsar of Bulgaria, 1323 E, 1330 B
Michelangelo Buonarroti, It. sculptor and painter (1475–1564), 1475 L
Micheli, Domenico, Doge of Venice, 1117 E, 1130 E
Micheli, Vitale I, Doge of Venice, 1096 E, 1102 E
Micheli, Vitale II, Doge of Venice, 1156 E, 1173 B
Michelozzo Michelozzi, It. sculptor (1396–1472), 1452 J
Mico of St. Riquier, F. musical theorist, 825 K
Micrologus (Richard of Wendover), 1252 G
Micrologus de Disciplina Artis Musicae (Guido d'Arezzo), 1050 J
Middelburg, Holland, 1435 G
'Middle Ages', the term, 1464 K
Miecislas, Polish prince, 1146 E
Miedryrzecze, Poland, monastery, 996 H
Mieszko I, Duke of Poland, 963 E, 996 E, 967 E, 972 E, 973 E, 979 E, 985 E, 992 E
Mieszko II, King of Poland (1025–34), 1025 E, 1031 E, 1032 E, 1033 E, 1034 A, 1039 A
Mieszko III the Old, Grand Prince of Poland, 1173 D, 1177 E, 1201 E, 1202 E
Mignano, Italy, Treaty of, 1139 C
Milagros de Nuestra Señora, Los (Gonzalo de Berceo), 1235 K
Milal w-al-Nihal, Kitāb al- (al-Shahrastānī), 1128 H
Milan, Italy, 894 E, 1037 A, 1042 E, 1327 A
  Patarene movement, 1056 E, 1059 E, 1066 B, 1075 A, E
  wars with Frederick I, 1158 C, 1159 C, 1161 C, 1162 A, 1167 B, 1185 A
  under a rector, 1186 F
  wars with Frederick II, 1226 A, 1239 D
  under Torriani, 1257 E, 1259 C, 1263 D, 1265 C, 1278 A
  under Visconti, 1278 A, 1295 C, 1300 E
  Torriani restored, 1300 E, 1307 E, 1311 E
  ruled by Visconti (*q.v.*), *viz.*:
    Matteo I (1295–1300, 1311–22)
    Galeazzo I (1322–8)
    Azzo (1328–39)
    Luchino (1339–49)
    Giovanni (1349–54)
    Bernabo (1354–85)
    Galeazzo II (1354–78)
    Matteo II (1354–5)
    Gian Galeazzo (1378–1402; Duke from 1395)
    Giovanni Maria (Duke; 1402–12)
    Filippo Maria (Duke; 1412–47)
  Ambrosian Republic and war of succession, 1447 C, 1448 D, 1450 A
  Sforza (*q.v.*) Dukes. *See*
    Francesco (1450–66)
    Galeazzo Maria (1466–76)
    Gian Galeazzo (1476–94)
  canals, 1439 G
  Cathedral, 1386 J
  churches:
    Sant' Ambrogio, 840 G, 940 J, 1080 J, 1140 J
    S. Mariapresso, 1482 J
    S. Satiro, 876 J, 1482 J
    S. Vincenzo (basilica), 833 J
  library in, 1360 K
Mileševo, Yugoslavia, frescoes at, 1236 J
Milhamot Adonai (Levi ben Gerson), 1329 G, K
Milič, John, Bohemian church reformer, 1368 H, 1374 L
Military orders. *See* Alcántara; Avis; Christ; Hospitallers; Montesa; Santiago; Sword Brothers; Templars; Teutonic Knights
Mills:
  tidal, 1066 G, 1125 G
  water, for:
    irrigation, in Japan, 800 G; France, 1095 G
    hemp, in France, 1040 G
    fulling, in France, 1050 G
    corn, in England, 1087 G
    iron, in Europe, 1087 G, 1175 G, 1323 G; China, 1310 G
    saws, in Europe, 1271 G
    silk, in Italy, 1272 G; China, 1310 G
  wind, in Persia, 956 G; France, 1180 G
    tower-, in Europe, 1390 G
    for drainage, in Holland, 1404 G
Milsko, Poland, 1002 C
Minamoto no Shitagau, Ja. philologist (911–83), 983 K
Minamoto Sanetomo, Shogun of Japan, 1219 E
Minamoto Yoritomo, Shogun of Japan (b. 1147; 1185–99), 1180 E, F, 1184 E, 1185 B, 1189 E, 1199 E

Minamoto Yoshinaka, Ja. noble (1154–84), 1183 E, 1184 E
Minamoto Yoshitsune, Ja. noble (1159–89), 1184 E
Minchō, Ja. painter (1352–1431), 1431 J
Minden, W. Germany, Cathedral, 1064 J, 1270 J
Mindovg, ruler of Lithuania (b. 1219; 1246–63), 1251 E, 1252 E, 1260 C, 1263 E
Mineralogy. *See* Geology
Mines, metal, German, 964 G, 1136 G; Bohemian, 1294 G; French, 1471 G
Ming dynasty. *See* China
Ming-t'ien-li (Chou Ts'ung), 1065 G
Minhāj-ud-Dīn, Indian Muslim historian, 1260 K
Minims, Order of, 1436 H
Minnesingers, 1230 K; *and see* Hartmann von Aue; Hausen, Friedrich von; Wolfram von Eschenbach
Minorca, is., Spain, 1232 E
Minstrels, corporations of, French, 1321 J; English, 1469 J
Minūchirī, Per. poet, 1041 K
Mīr 'Ali of Tabriz, Per. illuminator, 1396 J
Mirabeau, France, battle, 1202 C
Miracle Plays, Mysteries and Moralities:
  Dunstable, 1100 K
  Le Jeu d'Adam, 1150 K
  Le Jeu de St. Nicholas, 1160 K
  El Misterio de los Reyes Magos, 1190 K
  The Harrowing of Hell, 1295 K
  The Chester Cycle, 1327 K
  Miracles de Notre-Dame, 1390 K
  Mystère du Concile de Bâle, 1432 K
  Mystère de la Passion, 1454 K
  Mystère du Vieil Testament, 1458 K
  Barlaam e Josafat, 1488 K
Mi'raj al-'ashiqin (Banda Nawāz), 1422 H
Miramar, Majorca, Spain, college, 1276 H
Mir'āt al-Zamān (ibn-al-Jawzi), 1257 K
Mirdāsid dynasty. *See* Aleppo
Mirfield, John, E. surgeon and physician, 1407 G
Mirk, John, Prior of Lilleshall, E. religious author and poet, 1400 H
Miroir de Phoebus (Gaston Phoebus de Foix), 1391 K, 1410 K
Mirror of Simple Souls (Jan Ruysbroeck), 1381 H
Mirror of the Eastland (Ja. chronicle), 1266 K
Mirror of the World (William Caxton), 1481 K
  Cf. Myreur
Mīrzā Swātī, Shah of Kashmīr (1346–9), 1346 E
Miscellanea (Politian), 1489 K
Miskawayh, Abū 'Alī Ahmad ibn-, Per. philosopher and historian, 1030 K
Missi of Carolingian Empire, 802 F, 835 B
Missions, Christian, in Asia, 1318 H, 1367 H; *and see* China (religions)
  See also Conversion
Missionary Society, 1253 H, 1324 H
Misterio de los Reyes Magos, El, 1190 K
Mistra, Greece, frescoes at, 1320 J
Mittelalterliche Hausbuch, 1480 G
Mizu-kagami (Nakayama), 1195 K
Mo fi chi yao (Shên Chi-sun), 1398 G
Mo shih (Lu Yo), 1329 G
Mocenigo, Giovanni, Doge of Venice, 1478 B, 1485 D
Mocenigo, Pietro, Doge of Venice, 1474 C, D, 1476 A
Mocenigo, Tomaso, Doge of Venice, 1414 A, 1423 B
Model City, The (al-Fārābī), 950 F
Modena, Italy, 1288 D, 1293 A, 1306 A, 1326 B; Cathedral, 1099 J; Duchy of, 1452 B
Modus tenendi parliamentum, 1320 F
Moerbeke, William of, Archbishop of Corinth, Flemish translator, 1261 K, 1286 K
Mohi, Hungary, battle, 1241 B
Mojmír, ruler of Moravia, 846 E
Mojmír (II), Prince of Moravia, 894 E
Molay, Jacques de, Grand Master of Templars, 1314 A
Moldavia, Roumania, 1387 E, 1467 E, 1484 E, 1485 C
Molesme, France, (monastic) Order of, 1075 H
Moissac, France, priory, 1115 J
Mon people. *See* Burma
Monachos, George, Gk. chronicler (*fl. c.* 842), 842 K, 948 K
Monarchia, De (Dante), 1312 F
Monasteries:
  Austria. *See* Melk
  China, 842 H, 845 H, J
  Czechoslovakia. *See* Břevnov; Prague
  England. *See* Bury St. Edmunds; Canterbury; Eynsham; Fountains; Glastonbury; Gloucester; London; Malmesbury; Peterborough; Ramsey; Rievaulx; St. Albans; Syon; Tewkesbury; Tintern; Waverley; Westminster
  France. *See* Bec; Caen; Centula; (La) Chaise-Dieu; Charlieu; (La) Charité-sur-Loire; Clairvaux; Cluny; Conques; Corbie; Déas; Dijon; (La) Ferté; Fleury; Fontenay; Fontevrault; Jumièges; Leyre; Limoges; Moissac; Mont-St.-Michel; Morimond; Murbach; Nevers; Paris; Pontigny; Reims; St. Martin du Canigou; Toulouse; Tournus; Tours; Vézelay
  Germany. *See* Bursfeld; Brauweiler; Corvey; Gernrode; Hersfeld; Hirsau; Kamp; Limburg an der Haardt; Magdeburg; Maria Laach; Maulbronn; Paderborn; Petersberg; Reichenau; Schaffhausen
  Greek Empire, 964 H. *And see* Constantinople; Mount Athos; Mount Galisius
  Holland. *See* Windesheim
  Ireland. *See* Mellifont
  Italy. *See* Assisi; Florence; Fossanova; Montecassino; Padua; Pavia; San Galgano
  Japan, 1341 G. *And see* Mount Hiei; Mount Koya
  Poland. *See* Miedryrzecze
  Portugal. *See* Alcobaça
  Russia. *See* Troitsa
  Scotland. *See* Iona
  Spain. *See* Cuxa; Ripoll; Roda; S. Juan de la Peña; S. Miguel de la Escalada
  Switzerland. *See* Einsiedeln; Hirsau; St. Gallen
  order of Louis the Pious for, 817 H
  plan for a, 820 J
  reformers. *See* Benedict XII; Benedict of Aniane; Bruno; Dunstan; Ethelwold; Gualberti; Innocent VIII; Mayeul; Nilus; Odo; Robert of Molesme; Stephen of Muret; William of Dijon
  See also Religious Orders
Mondino de'Luzzi, It. surgeon (*c.* 1275–1326), 1316 G
Mondeville, Henry de, F. surgeon, 1320 G
Moneta, De (Nicholas Oresme), 1382 G
Money:
  debasement of currency, 1295 G
  paper, 811 G, 1024 G, 1450 G
  See also Coins
Mongol Scroll (Ja. painting), 1293 J
Mongolia, 1227 C; Chinese campaigns in, 1410 E, 1414 E, 1422 E
Mongols (*or* Tartars):
  Great Khans. *See*
    Ghengiz (1206–27)
    Ogodai (1227–41)
    Guyuk (1246–8)
    Mongka (1251–9)
    Ariqboga (1260–1)

Kublai (1260–94)
envoys from Europe to, 1245 B, H, 1246 C, 1248 A, 1253 E, 1289 G
empire founded, 1206 B; divided, 1227 C; travel in, 1240 G; under Timur, 1367 E, H
conquests. *See* Champa; China; Dai Viet; Georgia; Hungary; India; Korea; Persia; Poland; Russia; Syria; *also esp.* Ghengiz; Timur
alphabet for, 1269 K
army, size of, 1227 F
capital. *See* Karakorum
converted to Islam, 1367 H
history of (al-Juwainī), 1260 K
language, studied in Europe, 1311 H
laws, 1206 F
Mongka, Great Khan of the Mongols (1251–9), 1251 C, 1254 C, 1258 E, 1259 C, 1260 A
Monks. *See* Religious Orders
Monmouth, Wales, battle, 1233 D
Monogatari. *See* Japan, literature
Monomach, Vladimir, Russian autobiographer, 1125 K
Monreale, Sicily, Italy, Cathedral, 1174 J; mosaics in, 1182 J
Mons-en-Pévèle, France, battle, 1304 C
Monstrelet, Enguerrand de, F. chronicler (*c.* 1390–1453), 1444 K
Montague, John, Earl of Salisbury, 1400 A
Montalvo, Garcia de, Sp. romance writer, 1475 K
Montaperto, Italy, battle, 1260 C
Montargis, France, battle, 1427 C
Monte, Pietro da, It. canonist, 1457 H, L
Montebello, Italy, Treaty of, 1175 B
Montecassino, Italy, abbey, 1071 J; chronicle of, 1094 K, 1139 K
Montecatini, Italy, battle, 1315 C
Montecatini, Ugolini da, It. balneologist (*c.* 1345–1425), 1425 G
Montefiascono, Italy, Treaty of, 1354 B
Monte Maggiore, Italy, battle, 1041 B
Montereau, France, 1419 C
Montesa, Spain, Order of, 1316 E
Montezuma I, Aztec king, 1440 E, 1469 E
Montfaucon, France, battle, 888 B
Montferrand, Syria, castle, 1137 C
Montferrat, William V, marquess of, 1290 C, 1292 A
Montfort, Amauri de, leader of Albigensian Crusade, 1219 B, 1224 A
Montfort, Guy son of Simon de, 1271 A
Montfort, John, Duke of Brittany. *See* John
Montfort, Simon de, leader of Albigenian Crusade, 1209 C, 1213 C, 1215 A, 1218 B
Montfort, Simon de, Earl of Leicester, 1238 A, 1250 E, 1251 B, 1252 B, 1263 B, C, 1264 B, K, 1265 C, F
Montgisard, Israel, battle, 1177 D
Montgomery, Wales, 1228 C; Treaty of, 1267 C
Montierender, France, church, 960 J
Montlhéry, France, battle, 1465 C
Montlouis, France, Treaty of, 1174 C
Montmirail, France, 1169 A
Montorio, Italy, battle, 1486 B
Montpellier, France, 1162 B, 1215 A, 1349 B; University, law schools, 1160 F, 1230 F; medical school, 1220 G
Montreuil-sur-mer, France, 948 E
Montserrat, Spain, church, 957 J
Mont-St.-Michel, France, abbey, 1024 J
Montulmo, Antonio de, It. astrologer, 1394 G
Monza, Italy, 1323 A, 1324 D
Moon, eclipse of, 1091 G
Morat, France, battle, 1476 B
Morava, river, Yugoslavia, battle, 1190 E
Moravia, Czechoslovakia:
conquered by Germans, 846 E, 870 E, 871 E
converted, 869 H, 885 H, 1063 H
independent. *See* Svátopluk I
civil war, 894 E
conquered by Magyars, 906 E
under Poland, 992 E
contested by Hungary and Bohemia, 1028 E, 1031 E
margravate founded, 1182 E
conquered by Bohemia, 1197 E
Mongol invasion, 1241 B
annexed to Bohemia, 1310 C, 1348 B; *and see* Jošt
ruled by lords, 1396 B
communion of Brethren, 1450 H
And see Bohemia
Moray, Scotland, Earl of. *See* Randolph, John
Morcar, Earl of Northumbria, 1065 E, 1068 E
More, Thomas, E. statesman and humanist (1478–1535), 1478 L
Morea, Greece, Latin principality, 1396 E; ruled by Greeks, 1432 E, 1448 D; conquered by Turks, 1423 E, 1448 D, 1460 E
Morgante Maggiore (Luigi Pulci), 1482 K
Morgarten, Switzerland, battle, 1315 D
Moribus, De Ingenuis (Pier Paulo Vergerio), 1398 H
Morimond, France, abbey, 1115 H
Morlaix, France, battle, 1342 C
Moro, Cristofero, Doge of Venice, 1462 B, 1471 D
Morocco:
ruled by Fātimids, 969 C
Almoravid (Murābit, Berber) dynasty. *See*
Yūsuf (1068–1106)
'Alī (1106–43)
Almohad dynasty. *See*
Muhammad (1121–9)
'Abd-al-Mu'min (1129–63)
Yūsuf I (1163–84)
Ya'qūb I (1184–99)
Nasir (1199–1214)
Yūsuf II (1214–24)
Ma'mūn (1229–32)
fall of, 1224 E, 1232 D, 1257 E, 1269 E
Marīnid dynasty, 1269 E, 1465 E; *and see* Ya'qūb III
Wattāsid dynasty, 1465 E
Berbers of, destroy Ghana, 1077 E
history of (ibn-Khaldūn), 1406 K
Morosini, Domenico, Doge of Venice, 1148 E, 1156 E
Morosini, Marino, Doge of Venice, 1249 C, 1252 E
Morosini, Michele, Doge of Venice, 1382 B, D
Morte d'Arthur (Thomas Malory), 1470 K, 1485 K
Mortemer, France, battle, 1054 A
Mortifiement de vaine plaisance (Réné of Anjou), 1480 K
Mortimer, Edmund, E. noble, 1402 B
Mortimer, Roger, Earl of March, 1325 A, 1326 C, 1330 A, D
Mortimer's Cross, England, battle, 1461 A
Morvan, Breton leader, 818 C
Morville-sur-Seille, France, 967 G
Mosaics. *See* Cefalù; Chios; Constantinople (Chora); Kiev; Monreale; Palermo; Salonika; Rome; Venice
Moscow, Russia, 1160 G
Princes of, *also* Grand Dukes of Vladimir. *See*
Juri III (1304–24)
Ivan I (*c.* 1330–41)
Simeon (1341–53)
Ivan II (1353–9)

Moscow, Russia—*contd.*
Princes of—*contd.*
Dmitri III (1359–89)
Vasili I (1389–1425)
Vasili II (1425–62)
Ivan III (1462–1505)
sacked by Mongols, 1238 A, 1382 C
becomes capital of Russia, 1332 E
attacked by Mongols, 1395 C, 1408 D
revolt in, 1446 A, 1447 A
independent of Mongols, 1462 A, 1476 E, 1481 E
Kremlin, 1367 J, 1485 K; cathedral in, 1475 J
Metropolitan at, 1326 H, 1332 E, 1461 H
Moses ben Ezra, Sp. J. poet and critic (1060–1139), 1139 K
Moses ben Joshua, F. J. physician and astrologer (*c.* 1290–*c.* 1362), 1350 G
Moses de Leon, Sp. J. cabalistic author, 1305 K
Moses ben Maimon (Maimonides), Sp. J. physician and philosopher (1135–1204), 1204 G, K, 1232 K
Moses Sephardi. *See* Pedro Alfonso
Mosinopolis, Greece, battle, 1185 C
Mosques. *See* Ajmer; ʿAmr; Ankara; Badaun; Bīdar; Cairo; Constantinople; Cordova; Delhi; Divrigi; Erzurum; Ispahan; Kairāwan; Kayseri; Konya; Kulbarga; Nigde; Mosul; Rabat; Sāmarra; Seville
Mosul, Iraq, 972 D
Atabegs. *See* Kerbōghā; Bursuqi
Zangid dynasty. *See*
Zangi (1127–46)
Sayf-ad-Dīn I (1146–9)
Qutb-ad-Dīn (1149–70)
Sayf-ad-Dīn II (1170–80)
ʿIzz-ad-Dīn (1180–93)
battle near, 1107 C
taken by Nūr-ad-Dīn, 1171 E
metal-work, 1232 J
mosque, 1145 J
Motu cordis, De (Alfred of Shareshel), 1210 G
Mount Athos, Greece, monasteries, 961 H
Mount Galisius, Turkey, monastery, 1054 H
Mount Hiei, Japan, monastery, 805 H; monk of, *see* Genshin
Mount Koya, Japan, monastery, 816 H
Mount Levunium, Bulgaria, battle, 1091 B
Mousqués, Philippe, F. poet, 1268 K
Mowbray, Robert, Earl of Northumberland, 1095 E
Mowbray, Thomas, Earl and Duke of Norfolk, 1388 A, 1398 C
Moycoba, Ireland, battle, 1103 C
Mozarabic architecture. *See* Architecture
Mstislav of Tmutarakan', joint ruler of Russia, 1024 E, 1035 E
Mstislav I, Prince of Kiev, 1125 E, 1132 E
Mszczvj, Prince of East Pomerania, 1294 E
Muʿāwiya, Ahmād ibn-, al-Mahdi, 893 E
Mu'ayyad Alhilli, Arab jurist, 1277 F
Muʿazzam, al-, ruler of Damascus, 1218 C, 1227 D
Mubārak I, Sultan of Delhi, 1316 B, 1317 E, 1320 B
Mubārak II, Shah of Delhi, 1421 B, 1435 A
Mubārak, Shah of East Bengal (1336–49), 1336 E
Mufarrij-ibn-Sālim, ruler of Bari, 853 E
Muhādarah, Kitāb al- (Moses ben Ezra), 1139 K
Muhammad, the Prophet (d. 632), 945 H; biographies of, 823 K, 1334 K
Muhammad ibn-Ghāzī, Danishmend ruler (1134–41), 1141 D
Muhammad ibn-Tūmart, al-Mahdi, Almohad ruler of Morocco, 1121 D, 1129 D
Muhammad Khan, of Delhi, 1285 A
Muhammad II (Tughluq), Ghiyāth-ad-Dīn, Shah of Delhi (1325–51), 1325 A, F, 1329 G, 1337 E, 1340 G, 1351 A; revolts against, 1327 E, 1329 E, 1335 E, 1336 B, E, 1339 E, 1345 E, 1346 E, 1347 C
Muhammad III, Shah of Delhi, 1390 D, 1393 A
Muhammad IV, Shah of Delhi, 1434 A, 1446 E
Muhammad, Ghiyāth-ad-Dīn, Sultan of Ghūr (1163–1203), 1203 E; Indian conquests, 1175 E, 1186 E, 1192 E, 1193 A, 1194 E, 1196 E, 1197 E, 1202 E
Muhammad bin Sām, Sultan of Ghūr, 1203 E, 1206 B
Muhammad ibn-Hūd, King of Granada, 1229 C, 1236 A
Muhammad I al-Ghālib, King of Granada, 1230 E, 1232 D, 1246 E, 1257 E, 1273 A, J
Muhammad II al-Faqīh, King of Granada, 1273 A, 1302 B
Muhammad III al-Maklūʿ, King of Granada, 1302 B, 1309 A
Muhammad IV, King of Granada, 1325 C, 1333 C
Muhammad V al-Ghānī, King of Granada, 1355 D, 1359 C, 1362 B, 1392 E
Muhammad VI, King of Granada, 1360 C, 1362 B
Muhammad VII al-Mustaʿīn, King of Granada, 1396 E, 1408 B
Muhammad VIII, King of Granada, 1417 E, 1427 E, 1429 E, 1431 E, 1432 B, 1445 E
Muhammad IX, King of Granada, 1427 E, 1429 E
Muhammad X, King of Granada, 1445 E, 1446 E, 1454 E
Muhammad XI abu-ʿAbdullah (Boabdil), King of Granada (d. 1533/4), 1482 E, 1483 B, 1485 E, 1489 D, 1491 D
Muhammad XII (al-Zaghall), King of Granada, 1485 E, 1489 D
Muhammad I, Ottoman Sultan, 1403 A, 1413 C, 1415 E, 1421 B
Muhammad II, Ottoman Sultan (b. 1430; 1451–81), 1451 A, 1463 J, 1481 E
liquidates Greek Empires, 1453 B, 1461 C
conquers Greece, 1455 E, 1456 E, 1460 E, 1470 C
war with Hungary, 1456 C, 1463 D, 1475 E
conquers Balkans, 1459 E, 1467 E, 1478 E
threatens Germany, 1471 B
war with Venice, 1474 C, 1479 C
takes Kaffa, 1475 E
attacks Rhodes, 1480 B, C
invades Italy, 1480 C, 1481 C
panegyric on, 1470 K
Muhammad I, Seljuq Sultan (1105–18), 1104 A
Muhammad I, Emir of Spain, 852 C, 886 E
Muhammad II, Caliph of Spain, 1009 E, 1010 E
Muhammad III, Caliph of Spain, 1023 E, 1025 E
Muhammad ibn-Kaulan, Syrian architect, 1219 J
Muhit, Kitāb al- (ibn-ʿAbbād), 995 K
Mühldorf, W. Germany, battle, 1322 C
Muhtadī, al-, Caliph of Baghdād, 869 B, 870 B
Mu'izz, al-, Caliph of Kairāwan, 952 E, 969 C, 971 E, 975 D
Mujāhid of Denia, Sp. M. leader, 1016 B
Mukhtasar Ta'rīkh al-Bashar (Abū-l-Fidā'), 1331 K
Muller, Johannes. *See* Regiomontanus
Mūltan, Pakistan, 1245 E, 1398 B; tombs, 1270 J, 1300 J, 1320 J
Munājāt (Ansārī), 1088 K
München-Gladbach, W. Germany, Cathedral, 1275 J
Mundhir, al-, Emir of Spain, 886 E, 888 E
Munich, W. Germany, 1157 G
Munqidh, Abū-l-Muzaffar Usāmah ibn-, Arab soldier, poet and autobiographer (d. 1188), 1182 K

Munster, Ireland, King of, 967 E
Muntāhā al-Idrāk (al-Kharaqī), 1138 G
Muntaner, Ramón, Catalan soldier, poet and chronicler (1265–1336), 1330 K, 1336 K
Muntassir, al-, Caliph of Baghdād, 861 D, 862 B
Muntazar, Muhammad al-, al-Mahdi, 878 H
Muqaddamah (ibn-Khaldūn), 1406 K
Muqni' fi al-Hisāb al-Hindi (al-Nasawi), 1041 G
Murābit dynasty. *See* Morocco
Murād I, Ottoman Sultan, 1359 E, 1361 E, 1366 E, 1371 C, 1375 B, 1385 E, 1386 E, 1389 B
Murād II, Ottoman Sultan (b. 1402; 1421–51), 1421 B, 1422 B, C, 1423 E, 1451 A; conquests, 1424 E, 1428 E, 1430 A, 1432 E, 1443 E, 1448 D; crusade against, 1440 E, 1441 E, 1442 E, 1443 E, 1444 A–D
Murasaki Shikibu (Lady Murasaki), Ja. novelist and court lady (978–*c.* 1031), 1010 K
Murbach, France, abbey, 1122 J
Murcia, Spain, Muslim kingdom, 1236 A, 1237 E, 1241 E, 1261 E, 1266 E
Muret, France, battle, 1213 C
Murimuth, Adam of, E. chronicler, 1347 K
Murūj al-Dhahab (al-Mas'ūdi), 956 G
Murs, Jean de, F. astronomer, 1318 G
Mūsa, Ottoman prince, 1411 A, 1413 C
Mūsa ibn-Shakir, sons of, Eg. mathematicians, 860 G
Musabbihi, al-, Eg. historian (976–1029), 1029 K
Mushrooms, treatise on (Ch'ên Jên-yü), 1245 G
Music:
- counterpoint, 1361 J
- degree in (Cambridge), 1463 J
- innovations, 912 K, 1050 J
- instruments: water-organ, 826 J; clavier, 1397 J
- minstrels incorporated, 1321 J, 1469 J
- 'new style', 1361 J
- opera (Chinese), 1356 J
- polyphony, 1364 J
- St. Bartholomew's Fair, 1133 J

Music, The Grand Book on (al-Fārābī), 950 J
Musica (Wilhelm of Hirsau), 1091 G
Musicians, composers:
- Arab. *See* Wāthiq
- English. *See* Dunstable, John
- Flemish. *See* Dufay, Guillaume
- French. *See* Basselin, Olivier; Machaut, Guillaume de
- German. *See* Notker Balbulus
- Italian. *See* Landino, Francesco
- Persian. *See* Mawsili

Musical theorists:
- Arab. *See* Kindi; Safī
- Chinese. *See* Shên Kua
- English. *See* Gregory of Bridlington; Odington, Walter; Tunsted, Simon
- French. *See* Meurs, Jean de; Mico of St. Riquier; Vitry, Philippe de
- German. *See* Frutolf of Bamberg; Hermann Contractus; Regino of Prüm; Wilhelm of Hirsau
- Italian. *See* Arezzo, Guido d'
- Persian. *See* Qādir
- Spanish Muslim. *See* Firnās; Sab'in
- Turkish. *See* Fārābī

Musicologists:
- Persian. *See* Isfahānī
- Spanish Muslim. *See* Rabbih

Musnad (Hanbal), 855 H
Musō Kokushi, Ja. monk and landscape gardener (1275–1351), 1341 G, 1351 J
Mussato, Albertino, It. poet, historian and humanist, 1261 L, 1329 K
Mustada, al-, Caliph of Baghdād, 908 D
Mustafā, Ottoman prince, 1422 C
Musta'īn, al-, Caliph of Baghdād, 862 B, 866 A
Mustansir, al-, Caliph of Baghdād (1226–42), 1234 H
Mustansir, al-, Caliph of Egypt (b. 1024), 1035 C, 1094 D
Musta'sim, al-, last Caliph of Baghdād (1242–58), 1258 A
Mustawfī, Hamdāllah, Per. poet, annalist and cosmologist (*c.* 1281–1350), 1330 K, 1333 K, 1340 G
Mu'tadid, al-, Caliph of Baghdād, 892 D, 902 A
Mu'tamid, al-, Caliph of Baghdād, 869 B, 885 E, 892 D
Mu'tamid, al-, King of Seville (1069–95), 1069 E, 1086 D
Mutannabī, Ahmad ibn-Husain al-, Syrian poet (915–65), 965 K
Mu'tasim, al-, Caliph of Baghdād, 833 C, 834 E, 836 E, 838 B, 842 A
Mutawakkil, al-, Caliph of Baghdād, 847 C, 855 E, 856 K, 861 D
Mu'tazz, al-, Caliph of Baghdād, 866 A, 869 B
Mu'tazz, ibn-al-, Arab poet, 908 K
Muwaffaq, Abu Mansūr, Per. physician and pharmacologist, 975 G
Muzaffar, 'Abd-al-Malik al-, Regent of Cordova, 1002 C, 1008 E
Muzaffar I, Sultan of Gujarāt (1407–11), 1407 E
Myreur des histors (Jean d'Outremeuse), 1400 K
Myriocephalum, Turkey, battle, 1176 C
Myriobiblon (Photius), 891 K
Mystère de la Passion (Arnoul Gréban), 1454 K
Mystère du Concile de Bâle, 1432 K
Mystère de Vieil Testament, 1458 K
Mystical Marriage of St. Catherine (Hans Memling), 1475 J
Mystics:
- Christian:
  - Belgian. *See* Denis the Carthusian; Harphius, Hendrik; Kempis, Thomas à; Petersen, Gerlac; Ruysbroeck, Jan
  - Dutch. *See* Devotio Moderna; Groot, Gerhard
  - English, 1380 H. *And see* Hilton, Walter; Juliana of Norwich; Kemp, Margery; Rolle, Richard
  - French. *See* Amaurists; Colette of Corbie; Porrette, Marguerite
  - German. *See* Brethren of the Free Spirit; Eckehart; Friends of God; Gertrude the Great; Hildegarde of Bingen; Mechthild; Merswin, Rulman; Suso, Heinrich
  - Greek. *See* Palamas, Gregory; Simeon
  - Italian. *See* Bernardino of Siena; Catherine of Bologna; Catherine of Siena; Joachim of Flora
- Muslim. *See* Abū-Sa'īd; Banda Nawāz; Fārid; *and under* Sūfīs

Myton, England, battle, 1319 C
Mzab, Algeria, Emir of, 800 E

N

Nabataean Agriculture (ibn-Wahshiyya), 800 G
Nadīm, ibn-al-, Arab bibliographer, 988 G
Näfels, Switzerland, battle, 1388 B
Nafīs, 'Alā' ad-Dīn ibn-al-, Eg. physician ,1288 G
Nagoričino, Yugoslavia, frescoes at, 1317
Nájera, Spain, battle, 1367 B

Nakayama Tadachika, Ja. historian and diarist (1131–95), 1195 K
Namur, Belgium, 1340 G, 1421 B
Nānak, Gurū, founder of the Sikhs (1469–1533), 1469 H
Nanchao, China, Thai kingdom, 829 E, 832 E, 863 E, 866 E, 1253 E
Nancy, France, battle, 1477 A; Treaty of, 1473 D
Nanking, China, 1356 E, 1367 E, 1420 E
Nanni di Banco, It. sculptor (*c.* 1384–1421), 1408 J, 1421 J
Nantes, France, 921 E; battle, 992 B; Cathedral, 1434 J; University, 1460 H
Naples, Italy:
ruled by Dukes, 837 E, 1028 E, 1030 E
besieged by Henry VI, 1191 C, 1194 C
taken by Conrad, 1253 D
naval battle, 1284 B
Black Death in, 1347 G
University, 1224 F
Naples, kingdom of*. *See*
Charles II (1285–1309)
Robert (1309–43)
Joanna I (1343–81)
Charles III (1381–6)
Ladislas (1386–1414)
Louis I (of Anjou; 1382–4)
Louis II (of Anjou; 1387–99)
Joanna II (1414–35)
Alfonso (V of Aragon; 1443–58)
Ferrante (1458–94)
Hungarian invasions, 1348 A, B, 1350 E
Angevin invasions, 1382 B, 1384 C, 1387 E, 1390 C, 1391 A, 1399 E, 1409 D, 1411 B
war of succession, 1420 C, 1423 B, 1435 A, 1442 B, 1443 A
Narahari of Kashmīr, Indian physician, 1242 G
Naranco, Spain, churches, 848 J
Narbonne, France, 1021 E, 1355 D; Capitulations of, 1415 D; Cathedral, 1272 J; Duchy, 1229 B
Nas, ibn-Sayyid al-, Eg. biographer, 1334 K
Nasawi, Ahmad al-, Arab mathematician, 1040 G
Nāsir, Muhammad al-, Almohad emperor, 1199 E, 1208 E, 1212 C, 1213 D, E
Nāsir II, al-Malik an-, ruler of Aleppo (d. 1260), 1250 C, 1251 A, 1253 B
Nāsir, Muhammad an-, Sultan of Egypt (b. 1285), 1293 E, 1303 E, 1340 E
Nāsir, an-, ruler of Karak, 1239 D
Nāsir al-Dīn Mahmūd, Indian M. prince, 1231 J
Nasr, King of Granada, 1309 A, 1314 A
Nasr ibn-Ahmad, ruler of Transoxiana (d. 892), 874 E
Nasrid dynasty. *See* Granada
Nathan ben Jeliel, It. J. Talmudic scholar (*c.* 1035–1106), 1101 H
Nativity (Dieric Bouts), 1445 J; (Roger van der Weyden), 1452 J; (Piero della Francesca), 1472 J
Natura Legis Naturae, De (John Fortescue), 1463 K
Natura rerum, De (Thomas de Chantimpré), 1246 G
Naturalists:
Chinese. *See* Ch'ên Jên-yü; Chia Ssŭ-tao
English. *See* Gervase of Tilbury
German. *See* Hildegarde of Bingen; Megenburg, Conrad of
See also Botanists
Naturis inferiorum et superiorum, Liber de (Daniel de Merlac), 1190 G
Naturis rerum, De (Alexander Neckham), 1217 G
Naumburg, E. Germany, Cathedral, 1250 J; 'Master of', 1250 J
Navarre, Spain, kingdom of, 857 E; *and see*
Garcia Ximenez (857–80)
Fortunus (880–905)
Sancho Garcia I (905–26)
Garcia I (926–70)
Sancho II (970–94)
Garcia II (994–1000)
Sancho III (1000–35)
Garcia III (1035–54)
Sancho IV (1054–76)
Sancho V of Aragon (1076–94)
Pedro I of Aragon (1094–1104)
Alfonso I of Aragon (1104–34)
Garcia IV (1134–50)
Sancho VI (1150–94)
Sancho VII (1194–1234)
Theobald I (1234–53)
Theobald II (1253–70)
Henry I (1270–4)
Joanna I (1274–1305)
Louis X of France (1305–16)
Philip V of France (1316–22)
Charles IV of France (1322–8)
Joanna II (1329–49)
Charles II (1349–87)
Charles III (1387–1425)
Blanche (1425–41)
John II (1425–79)
Carlos (1461)
Eleanor (1479)
Francis Phoebus (1479–83)
Catherine (1483–1512)
John III (1484–1512)
Navarrese Company, conquests in Greece, 1376 E, 1379 E, 1396 E
Navas de Tolosa, Las, Spain, battle, 1212 C
Navigatio sancti Brandani (Benedeiz), 1125 K
Navigation, school for, 1419 G; *and see* Compass, Maps
Navigators. *See* Bristol; Columbus, Christopher; Portugal
Naviglio Grande, Italy, 1179 G
Naxos, is., Greece, 1207 E
Neath, Wales, abbey, 1326 D
Neckham, Alexander, E. scientific encyclopedeist, 1157 L, 1217 G
Negro Empires. *See* Gao: Ghana; Mali
Negro slaves, in Iraq, 869 C, 883 E
Negropont, is., Greece, 1470 B
Německý Brod, Czechoslovakia, battle, 1422 A
Nemours, France, Duke of, 1477 C
Nennius, Welsh chronicler, 810 K
Neo-Platonism, 873 K, 1058 K
Nepal, kingdom of, 879 E
Nerez, Yugoslavia, frescoes at, 1165 J
Nesjar, Norway, naval battle, 1016 E
Nestor of Kiev, Russian chronicler, 1110 K
Nestorian Christians, 1275 H, 1287 G
Netter, Thomas, E. theologian, 1415 H, 1430 L
Neuss, W. Germany, 1201 B
Neustria, France, 880 A, 987 C; Marquesses of, *see* Robert the Strong, Odo, Robert, Hugh the Great, Hugh Capet
Neva, river, Russia, battle, 1240 C
Nevers, France, Cathedral, 1211 J, 1309 J; priory, 1097 J

* *Rectius* the kingdom of Sicily, but so styled here to distinguish from the separate kingdom in Sicily (*q.v.*).

Neville, Richard, Earl of Salisbury (1400–60), 1454 D, 1455 B, 1458 A, 1459 C, D, 1460 C
Neville, Richard, 'the Kingmaker', Earl of Warwick (1428–71), 1428 L, 1455 B, 1458 A, B; revolt against Henry VI, 1459 D, 1460 C, 1461 A; revolt against Edward IV, 1469 B, C, 1470 A, C, D, 1471 B
Neville's Cross, England, battle, 1346 D
Nevruz, Khan of the Golden Horde, 1360 E, 1361 E
New T'ang History, 805 K
Newark, England, 1216 D
Newcastle-upon-Tyne, England, castle, 1080 B; Coal trade, 1216 G, 1273 G; Treaty of, 1334 B
Newfoundland, Canada, 1491 G
Neyshabur, Persia, University, 1065 H; observatory, 1074 G
Ngo Quyen, King of Dai-co-Viet (939–44), 939 E
Ni Tsan, C. painter (1301–74), 1374 J
Niall Black-Knee, High King of Ireland, 919 C
Niani, Mali, 1337 E
Nibelungenlied, Das, 1200 K
Niccoli, Niccolò, It. humanist (1364–1437), 1437 L
Nicaea, Turkey, 1077 E, 1092 E, 1097 B, 1147 D; capital of Greek Empire, 1208 B, 1261 C; taken by Ottomans, 1300 E, 1304 E, 1331 A
Nice, France, 1419 D
Nicephorus I, Greek Emperor, 802 E, 805 E, 806 E, 807 E, 809 E, 811 C
Nicephorus II Phocas, Greek Emperor (963–9), 963 C, 964 H, 967 E, 968 E, 969 D; campaigns against Arabs, 957 B, 961 A, 962 D, 965 C, 966 E, 969 D
Nicephorus III Botaneiates, Greek Emperor, 1078 A, 1081 A
Nicephorus, St., Patriarch of Constantinople, Gk. historian, 815 H, 829 K
Nicheren, Ja. Buddhist (1212–82), 1282 H
Nicholas I, Pope, 858 B, H, 863 H, 865 A, B, 866 C, 867 D, H
Nicholas II (Gerard, Bishop of Florence), Pope, 1058 D, 1059 A–C, 1061 C
Nicholas III (John Gaetan), Pope, 1277 D, 1278 B, 1279 A, H, 1280 C
Nicholas IV (Jerome of Ascoli), Pope, 1288 B, 1289 B, E, G, H, 1290 C, 1291 H, 1292 B
Nicholas V (Peter of Corvara), anti-pope, 1328 B, C, 1330 C
Nicholas V (Tommaso Parentucelli), Pope, (b. 1398), 1447 A, 1448 A, 1452 A, 1453 A, 1454 C, 1455 B; humanist, 1450 J
Nicholas Canabus, Greek Emperor, 1204 A
Nicholas of Ely, E. mason, 1220 J
Nicholas de Guildford, E. poet, 1200 K
Nicobar Is., India, 1035 E
Nicomedia (*now* Izmit), Turkey, 1085 E, 1337 E
Nicopolis, Bulgaria, battle, 1396 C
Niederwildungen, W. Germany, 1404 J
Niels (Nicholas), King of Denmark, 1105 E, 1109 K, 1131 E, 1134 B, 1135 B
Niem, Dietrich of. *See* Dietrich
Nieszawa, Poland, 1454 F
Nigde, Turkey, mausoleum, 1312 J; mosque, 1223 J
Nihāyat al-Arab (al-Nuwayrī), 1322 F
Nihāyat al-idrak (al-Shīrāzi), 1311 G
Nijmegen, Holland, 1018 A, 1300 C
Nikitin, Athanasius, Russian merchant, 1470 G
Nilus, St., It. monastic reformer, 1005 L
Niš, Yugoslavia, 1386 E; battle, 1443 D
Nisibis, Syria, 972 D, 974 E, 1171 E, 1182 D
Nithard, Abbot of St. Riquier, Frankish chronicler (d. 844), 843 K
Nitiratnākara (Candeśvara), 1314 F
Nizām al-Mulk, Per. statesman (1018–92), 1065 H, 1087 F, 1092 E, F
Nizāmī, Ilyās ibn-Yūsuf, Per. poet (*c.* 1140–1209), 1188 K
Nizhni-Novgorod, Russia, 1391 E
Njal Saga, The, 1200 K
Nō plays (Zeami Motokiyo), 1443 K
Noah's Ark (Hugh of St. Victor), 1141 H
Nobla Leyczon, La, 1200 K
Nogaret, Guillaume, F. councillor (d. 1314), 1303 C
Nogay, ruler of Golden Horde, 1273 E, 1280 E, 1283 E, 1286 E, 1291 E, 1293 E, 1298 E, 1299 E
Noie, Le (Antonio Pucci), 1388 K
Noirmoutier, France, 843 E
Nola, Spain, battle, 1460 C
Nomenoë, Breton leader, 826 E, 845 D, 846 E, 851 A
Norbert, St., of Xanten, Archbishop of Magdeburg, monastic reformer, 1120 H, 1133 B, 1134 L
Nordalbingia (north of R. Elbe), W. Germany, 804 E
Norfolk, England, Duke of. *See* Mowbray, Thomas
Norham, England, 1291 B
Norman Conquest of England, 1066 D, 1080 J
Normandy, France, Duchy of, 911 E; *and see*
  Rollo (911–31)
  William Longsword (931–42)
  Richard I (942–96)
  Richard II (996–1026)
  Richard III (1026–7)
  Robert I (1027–35)
  William I of England (1035–87)
  Robert II (1087–1106)
  Henry I of England (1106–35)
  Stephen of England (1136–44)
  Geoffrey IV of Anjou (1148–50)
  Henry II of England (1150–89)
  Richard I of England (1189–99)
  John of England (1199–1204)
  Anjou independent of, 925 E
  under Hugh the Great, 956 B
  Ethelred in, 1013 E
  Truce of God in, 1042 F
  revolts in, 1047 E, 1053 E, 1074 E, 1077 E, 1112 E, 1117 E, 1123 E
  acquired by William II, 1096 E
  lost by Stephen, 1137 E, 1144 B
  inquest by Henry II, 1172 F
  conquered by Philip II, 1204 A, B
  renounced by Henry III, 1259 D
  anti-French revolts, 1346 C, 1356 B
  conquered by Henry V, 1417 C, 1418 C, 1419 A, 1420 B
  peasant revolts, 1434 E, 1435 D
  French conquest, 1449 D, 1450 B, C
  chronicles of, 1015 K, 1027 K, 1186 K
  legal customs, 1200 F, 1250 F
Normannicum tributum, 877 B
Norse Sagas. *See* Sagas
Northampton, England, 1164 D, 1264 B; assize of, 1176 F; battle, 1460 C; Parliament, 1426 A; Treaty of, 1328 B
Northumberland, England, claimed by Scotland, 1061 E, 1070 E, 1079 E, 1091 E, 1093 D, 1138 C, 1157 E, 1174 C; Earls of, *see* Mowbray (Thomas), Percy (Henry)
Northumbria, England, King of, 867 A; *and see* York; Earls of, *see* Siward, Tostig, Morcar, Comines, Waltheof, Walcher
Norton, Thomas, E. alchemist, 1477 G
Norway, Kings of, 810 E, 853 E; *and see*
  Harold I (900–33)
  Eric I (933–8)
  Haakon I (938–63)

O

Olbracht, claimant to Hungary, 1491 A
'Old Man of the Mountain'. *See* Sinān
Old Sarum, England, Cathedral, 1076 J
Oldcastle, John, E. knight and Lollard, 1414 A, 1417 D
Oldřich, Duke of Bohemia, 1012 E, 1028 E, 1031 E, 1034 E
Oleg, Regent of Novgorod and Kiev, 873 E, 878 E, 907 E, 913 E
Oléron, France, Treaty of, 1287 C
Olga, Regent of Kiev (d. 969), 945 E, 955 E, 959 E
Olgierd, Prince of Lithuania, 1341 E, 1348 E, 1363 E, 1370 A, 1377 E
Oliver, monk of Malmesbury, E. astrologer, 1070 G
Olmedo, Spain, battle, 1467 C
Olomuc (Olmütz), Czechoslovakia, 1107 E; bishopric of, 975 H, 1063 H; Treaty of, 1478 D
Omar Khayyam. *See* Khāyyām
Omni re scribili, De (Pico della Mirandola), 1486 K
Omnūm (Korean writing), 1446 K
Omortag, Khan of the Bulgars, 814 B, 831 E
Opera, Chinese, 1356 J
Ophthamologists:
  Arab. *See* Hunayn; Māsawayh
  Italian. *See* Beneventus Grassus
Optics, Correction of the (al-Fārisī), 1320 G; *also* al-Kindī, 873 K; al-Hasan, 1039 G; Witelo, 1274 G
Opus Maius (Roger Bacon), 1266 K
Opus Ruralium (Pietro dei Crescenzi), 1307 G
Opus Terrae Sanctae (Sanuto), 1321 G
Orah hayyim (Moses ben Joshua), 1350 G
Oranges, treatise on (Han Ch'an-chih), 1178 G
Oratio de hominis dignitate (Pico della Mirandola), 1486 K
Orbedo, river, Spain, battle, 874 E
Orcagna, Andrea, It. painter and sculptor, 1354 J, 1359 J
Ordelaffi, Francesco, lord of Cesena and Forli, 1356 A, 1357 B
Orderic Vitalis, Anglo-Norman chronicler, 1075 L, 1141 K
Orders. *See* Chivalry; Mendicant Orders; Military Orders; Religious Orders
Ordinall of Alchimy (Thomas Norton), 1477 G
Ordine docendi et studendi, De (Battista da Verona), 1458 H
Ordo Judiciarius (Tancred), 1215 H
Ordoño I, King of Oviedo, 850 E, 862 E, 866 B
Ordoño II, King of Leon, 914 E, 920 E, 923 C
Ordoño III, King of Leon, 952 E, 957 E
Ordoño IV the Bad, King of Leon, 957 C, 960 E
Oresme, Nicholas, Bishop of Lisieux, F. mathematician, astronomer and translator, 1382 G, K, L
Organ, water-, at Aachen, 826 J
Organon (Aristotle), 1128 G
Oriental studies, at Toledo, 1250 H
Origine urbis Venetiarum, De (Bernardo Giustinani), 1489 K
Orissa, India, pagodas, 1198 J, 1241 J
Orkhān, Ghāzi, Ottoman ruler, 1326 B, 1329 E, 1331 A, 1337 E, 1359 E
Orkney Is., Scotland, 1028 E, 1098 E, 1263 D, 1468 A
Orlando, Cape, Italy, naval battle, 1299 C
Orlando Innamorato (Boiardo), 1482 K
Orléannais, France, customal of, 1270 F
Orleans, France, 854 E, 1022 H, 1428 D, 1429 A, B, 1478 C; Bishop of, *see* Theodulf; cathedral school, 1000 H; Dukes of, *see* Louis, Charles, Louis XII; legal customs of, 1260 F; University, 1306 H; law school of, 1235 F
Ormulum, The, 1200 K
Ornithology, treatise on (Chinese), 1279 G
Orosius, Sp. historian and geographer (*c.* 390–*c.* 420), 892 K
Orseolo, Domenico, Doge of Venice, 1032 E
Orseolo, Ottone, Doge of Venice, 1009 A, 1026 E
Orseolo, Pietro, Doge of Venice, 976 C, 978 A
Orseolo, Pietro II, Doge of Venice, 991 E, 1009 A
Orsini, Napoleon, Cardinal, rector of Bologna, 1306 B
Orthodox Church. *See* Greek Church; Russia
Orvieto, Italy, 1271 A, 1354 B; Cathedral, 1282 J, 1347 J, 1447 J; Treaty of, 1281 C
Oscar, Danish king, 851 E
Ōshikōchi no Mitsune, Ja. poet (*c.* 859–*c.* 921), 905 K
Osilians, Balt tribe, converted, 1227 E
'Osmān I, Ghāzī, Ottoman ruler (from 1281?), 1259 L, 1301 C, 1304 E, 1326 B
Osmund, St., Bishop of Salisbury, 1099 L
Osnabrück, W. Germany, church, 1256 J
Ostrovo, Yugoslavia, battle, 1043 A
Oswald, St., Archbishop of York, 992 L
Otfrid of Weissenburg, G. theologian and poet, 868 K
Othée, Belgium, battle, 1408 C
Otia Imperialia (Gervase of Tilbury), 1212 G
Otranto, Italy, 1480 C, 1481 C
Otterburn, England, battle, 1388 C
Otto I the Great, Holy Roman Emperor (962–73), 912 L, 929 E, 959 E, 962 A, 973 B, 1006 C
  King of the Germans, 936 C, 947 E, 966 E
  occupies Burgundy, 938 E, 942 E
  defeats Magyars, 938 E, 955 C
  revolts against, 939 B, C, 953 E, 954 B, D
  relations with France, 940 E, 942 D, 946 E, 950 E
  and Italy, 941 E; King, 951 C, 952 C, 961 C, 963 D, 967 A
  founds bishoprics, 948 H, 955 H, 968 H, 973 E, 1007 D
  subjects Bohemia, 950 E, 973 E
  converts and conquers Wends, 948 H, 955 D, 956 E, 967 B
  controls Papacy, 963 D, 964 B
  subjects Poland, 963 E
  relations with Greeks, 968 E, 972 B
  life of (Liutprand), 958 K
Otto II, Holy Roman Emperor (967–83), 955 L, 967 D, 972 B, 974 E, 978 A, 979 E, 983 D
  King of Lorraine, 961 A, 977 E
  King of Italy, 961 C, 980 D, 982 C
  revolts against, 976 C, 978 A
  relations with France, 978 D, 980 C
Otto III, Holy Roman Emperor (996–1002), 980 L, 996 B, 998 A, F, 1000 A, 1002 A
  King of the Germans, 983 D, 984 A, B, 985 B, E, 993 E
  and Italy, 992 E, 997 E, 1000 E, 1001 A
Otto IV, Holy Roman Emperor (1209–?14), 1209 D, 1218 B
  King of the Romans, 1198 C, 1201 B, C, 1203 E, 1206 C, 1208 D
  Italian campaign, 1210 D
  German revolt, 1210 D, 1211 A, D
  allied with John, 1212 D, 1214 C
Otto of Nordheim, Duke of Bohemia, 1061 E; deprived, 1070 C, 1071 E, 1073 C, 1083 A
Otto III, Margrave of Brandenburg (d. 1267), 1250 E
Otto IV, Margrave of Brandenburg (d. 1309), 1296 A
Otto, Duke of Burgundy, 960 E, 965 E
Otto IV, Count of Burgundy, 1295 E, 1315 E
Otto, Duke of Swabia (d. 1047), 1045 B
Otto, Bishop of Bamberg, 1124 H
Otto, Bishop of Freising, G. chronicler, 1146 K, 1158 K, L
Otto of Kolmutz, claimant to Bohemia, 1126 A
Otto-William, Count of Burgundy, 1015 E, 1016 B

Ottokar I, Přemysl, Duke of Bohemia, 1197 E; King, 1198 E, 1203 E, 1207 E, 1212 C, 1216 E, 1222 F, 1224 E, 1230 E
Ottokar II, King of Bohemia (1253–78), Duke of Austria, 1246 E, 1248 E; King, 1253 E, 1254 E, 1273 D, 1278 C; conquests, 1251 E, 1259 E, 1260 C, 1262 C, 1269 E, 1274 E, 1277 D
Ottoman Turks. *See* Turkey
Ourique, Portugal, battle, 1139 C
Outremer. *See* Jerusalem, kingdom of
Outremeuse (*alias* Desprez), Jean d', Belgian poet (1338–1400), 1400 K
Ou-yang Hsiu, C. statesman, historian, archaeologist and botanist, 1007 L, 1072 F, G, K
Oviedo, Spain, 802 H, 914 E, 960 E; Cathedral, 802 J; churches, 830 J, 848 J; kingdom of, *see* Leon
Owain the Great, King of Gwynned, 1137 E, 1158 E, 1170 D
Owain ap Thomas, 'Prince of Wales' (d. 1378), 1372 B
Owl and the Nightingale, The, 1200 K
Oxford, England, 1213 F
  Earl of. *See* Vere, Robert de
  Provisions of, 1258 B
  University, 1110 H, 1133 H, 1149 H, 1214 H, 1253 K, 1257 H, 1324 H
    Colleges:
      All Souls, 1438 H
      Balliol, 1268 H
      Canterbury Hall, 1361 H
      Exeter, 1314 H
      Gloucester Hall, 1289 H
      Lincoln, 1429 H
      Magdalen, 1448 H
      Merton, 1264 H
      New College, 1379 H
      Oriel, 1324 H
      Queen's, 1341 H
      University, 1249 H
    Divinity school, 1480 J
    migrations from, 1209 H, 1238 H, 1334 H
    St. Scholastica's riot, 1355 H

P

Pactum Hlodovicianum, 817 H
Paderborn, W. Germany, 1017 J; Cathedral, 1009 J; priory, 1036 J
Padua, Italy, 1226 A, 1237 A, 1256 B, 1318 A; under Carrara lords, 1318 C, 1319 D, 1320 D, 1388 D, 1390 B, 1392 B; taken by Venice, 1405 D; monastery, 1421 H; University, 1222 H, 1392 K, 1397 K; works of art, 1305 J, 1306 J, 1376 J, 1448 J
Pagan, Burma, 849 E, 1287 E; King, *see* Aniruddha; temples, 1060 J, 1110 J
Painters:
  Chinese. *See* Chao Mêng-fu; Ch'ien Hsuan; Ching Hao; Fan K'uan; Huang Ch'üan; Huang Kung-weng; Hui Tsung; K'o Chiu-ssu; Kuo Chung-shu; Kuo Hsi; Li Ch'eng; Li Lung-mien; Mi Fei; Ni Tsan; T'ung Hou; Wang Meng; Wen T'ung; Wu Chen
  Dutch. *See* Bosch, Hieronymus; Bouts, Dieric
  Flemish. *See* Eyck, Hubert van; Eyck, Jan van; Goes, Hugo van der; Weyden, Roger van der
  French. *See* Fouquet, Jean
  German. *See* Christus, Petrus; Conrad of Soest; Memling, Hans; Wilhelm, Master
  Italian. *See* Angelico, Fra; Bellini, Giovanni; Botticelli, Sandro; Castagno, Andrea del; Cimabue; Crivelli, Carlo; Daddi, Bernardo; Domenico Veneziano; Duccio; Faenza, Francesco da; Francesca, Piero della; Gaddi, Taddeo; Gentile da Fabriano; Ghirlandaio, Domenico; Giotto; Leonardo da Vinci; Lippi, Filippino; Lippi, Fra Filippo; Lorenzetti, Ambrogio; Lorenzetto, Pietro; Mantegna, Andrea; Martini, Simone; Memmi, Lippo; Masaccio; Orcagna, Andrea; Paolo d'Avanzi; Perugino; Pisanello; Roberti, Ercole; Signorelli, Luca; Uccello, Paolo
  Japanese, 1293 J. *And see* Kakuyū; Kudara-no-Kawanari; Minchō; Takanobū
  Swiss. *See* Witz, Konrad
Paintings:
  catalogues of (Chinese), 845 J, 1135 J
  preserved (Chinese, etc.), 1035 H
  treatises on: Ching Hao, 960 J; Alberti, 1435 J
Paints and arts of the Romans (Heraclius), 950 G
Pāk Pattan, Pakistan, battle, 1405 D
Palaeologus, John, Greek noble, 1259 E
Palaeoogus, Thomas, Despot of the Morea, 1432 E
  See also Greek Empire
Palamas, St. Gregory, Gk. mystic, Archbishop of Salonika (b. 1295), 1341 H, 1351 H, 1359 H
Palatinate of the Rhine, Germany, 966 E, 1214 E; Electors of, *see* Rupert I, Rupert III
Paldolf, Prince of Salerno, 981 A
Paldolf I Ironhead, Prince of Capua-Benevento, 967 A, 980 A
Paldolf IV, Prince of Capua-Benevento, 1026 E, 1028 E, 1030 E, 1038 E
Palencia, Spain, 1114 D; University, 1212 H
Palermo, Sicily, Italy, 831 C, 1072 A, 1147 G, 1194 D; 'Sicilian Vespers', in, 1282 A; Cathedral, 1172 J; Martorana, mosaics in, 1151 J; Palatine chapel, 1132 J, 1143 J
Palestine, Israel and Jordan, conquests of, 937 E, 975 E, 983 E, 1187 C, D, 1253 B; *and see* Jerusalem, kingdom of
Pallava, India, Hindu kingdom (A.D. 325–897), 880 E, 897 E
Palma, Majorca, Spain, 1229 D; Cathedral, 1306 J; University, 1483 H
Palmiere, Matteo, It. writer (1406–75), 1475 K
Pamiers, France, Bishop of, 1301 D
Pampeluna, Spain, 806 E, 924 E
Pancalia, Turkey, battles, 978 B, 979 A
Pañchala, India, Hindu kingdom, 1018 D, 1194 E
Pandulf, Cardinal, legate in England (d. 1226), 1218 D, 1221 C
Pāndya, India, Hindu kingdom (A.D. 590–*c.* 915), 846 E, 880 E, 915 E; second empire, 1216 E, 1269 E, 1279 E
Pangal, India, battle, 1419 E
Pange lingua (St. Thomas Aquinas), 1263 J
Pannartz, G. printer, 1465 G
Pannonia. *See* Hungary
Panormia (Ivo of Chartres), 1115 H
Panormita. *See* Beccadelli, Antonio
Pantheism, Christian, 865 K; Muslim, 1191 K, 1240 K
Paolo d'Avanzi, Jacopo di, It. painter, 1376 J
Papacy, the:
  Popes. *See*
    Leo III (795–816)
    Stephen IV (816–17)
    Paschal I (817–24)
    Eugenius II (824–7)
    Valentine (827)
    Gregory IV (827–44)
    John (844)

Sergius II (844–7)
Leo IV (847–55)
Benedict III (855–8)
*Anastasius (855)
Nicholas I (858–67)
Adrian II (867–72)
John VIII (872–82)
Marinus I (882–4)
Adrian III (884–5)
Stephen V (885–91)
Formosus (891–6)
Boniface VI (896)
Stephen VI (896–7)
Romanus (897)
Theodore II (897)
John IX (898–900)
Benedict IV (900–3)
Leo V (903)
Christopher (903–4)
Sergius III (904–11)
Anastasius III (911–13)
Lando (913–14)
John X (914–28)
Leo VI (928)
Stephen VII (929–31)
John XI (931–5/6)
Leo VII (936–9)
Stephen VIII (939–42)
Marinus II (942–6)
Agapitus II (946–55)
John XII (955–63)
Leo VIII (963–5)
*Benedict V (964)
John XIII (965–72)
Benedict VI (973–4)
*Boniface VII (974–85)
Benedict VII (974–83)
John XIV (983–4)
John XV (985–96)
Gregory V (996–9)
*John XVI (997–8)
Silvester II (999–1003)
John XVII (1003)
John XVIII (1004–9)
Sergius IV (1009–12)
*Gregory (1012)
Benedict VIII (1012–24)
John XIX (1024–32)
Benedict IX (1032–45)
Silvester III (1045)
Gregory VI (1045–6)
Clement II (1046–7)
Damasus II (1047–8)
Leo IX (1048–54)
Victor II (1054–7)
Benedict X (1058–9)
Nicholas II (1059–61)
Alexander II (1061–73)
*Honorius II (1061–2)
Gregory VII (1073–85)
*Clement III (1080–1100)
Victor III (1086–7)
Urban II (1088–99)
Paschal II (1099–1118)
*Theoderic (1100)
*Albert (1102)
*Silvester IV (1105–11)
Gelasius II (1118–19)
*Gregory VIII (1118–21)
Calixtus II (1119–24)
Honorius II (1124–30)
Innocent II (1130–43)
*Anacletus II (1130–8)
*Victor IV (1138)
Celestine II (1143–4)
Lucius II (1144–5)
Eugenius III (1145–53)
Anastasius IV (1153–4)
Adrian IV (1154–9)
Alexander III (1159–81)
*Victor IV (1159–64)
*Paschal III (1164–8)
*Calixtus III (1168–78)
*Innocent III (1179–80)
Lucius III (1181–5)
Urban III (1185–7)
Gregory VIII (1188)
Clement III (1188–91)
Celestine III (1191–8)
Innocent III (1198–1216)
Honorius III (1216–27)
Gregory IX (1227–41)
Celestine IV (1241)
Vacancy
Innocent IV (1243–54)
Alexander IV (1254–61)
Urban IV (1261–4)
Clement IV (1265–8)
Vacancy
Gregory X (1271–6)
Innocent V (1276)
Adrian V (1276)
John XXI (1276–7)
Nicholas III (1277–80)
Martin IV (1280–5)
Honorius IV (1285–7)
Nicholas IV (1288–92)
Vacancy
Celestine V (1294)
Boniface VIII (1294–1303)
Benedict XI (1303–4)
Clement V (1305–14)
Vacancy
John XXII (1316–34)
*Nicholas V (1328–30)
Benedict XII (1334–42)
Clement VI (1342–52)
Innocent VI (1352–62)
Urban V (1362–70)
Gregory XI (1370–8)
Urban VI (Rome; 1378–89)
Clement VII (Avignon; 1378–94)
Boniface IX (Rome; 1389–1404)
Benedict XIII (Avignon; 1394–1417)
Innocent VII (Rome; 1404–6)
Gregory XII (Rome; 1406–15)
Alexander V (1409–10)
John XXIII (1410–15)
Vacancy
Martin V (1417–31)
*Clement VIII (1423–8)
*Benedict XIV (1423)
Eugenius IV (1431–47)
*Felix V (1439–49)
Nicholas V (1447–55)
Calixtus III (1455–8)
Pius II (1458–64)
Paul II (1464–71)
Sixtus IV (1471–84)
Innocent VIII (1484–92)
relations with Greek Church, *q.v.*

---

* Anti-popes.

Papacy, the—*contd.*
deposes archbishops, 863 H, 995 H
orders restoration of bishop, 865 A
'Pornocracy', 904 A
legate to settle dispute, 948 B
canonisation by, 993 H
creates kingdoms, 1000 C, 1076 D, E, 1084 E, 1204 D, 1217 E, 1251 E, 1254 E, 1295 B
sale of papacy, 1045 B
regulation of elections, 1059 B
creates vassal duchy, 1059 C
powers outlined, 1075 H
kings become vassals, 1089 E, 1090 E, 1143 E, 1179 E, 1204 D, 1213 D
registers begin, 1198 H
clergy first taxed, 1199 H, 1215 H, 1291 H; criticised, 1307 A
receives Comtât Venaissin, 1271 C
revenues divided with cardinals, 1289 H
at Avignon, 1309 H, 1348 A, 1376 H
courts reorganised, 1331 H, 1338 H
English legislation against, 1351 H, 1353 H, 1390 H, 1428 H
proposal to limit powers, 1352 D
Great Schism, 1378 H, 1417 H
plans to end, 1395 A, 1398 A, 1407 D, 1408 A, B
history of, 1410 H
Conciliar Movement, treatises of, 1379 H, 1380 H, 1381 H, 1433 H
Councils. *See* Pisa: Constance; Basel
treatises attacking, 1302 F, 1349 K, 1376 F, 1390 H, 1412 H
treatises defending, 1328 H, 1331 H, 1433 H
histories of: Abbo, 1004 K; Platina, 1479 K
Papal States, Italy, 817 H, 824 F
'Patrimony of St. Peter', 1102 E, 1115 C
imperial rights ceded to Pope, 1201 B, 1213 C, 1278 B, 1279 A, 1317 A, 1346 B
'parliament' in, 1207 F
'Donation of Constantine', 1236 C, 1440 H
collapse of authority, 1350 A
Egidian Constitution, 1357 F
legates in. *See* Albornoz; Poujet, Bertrand du
Paper, oldest Arabic, 866 G; made in Italy, 1272 G, 1340 G; in Germany, 1389 G
Papias the Lombard, It. philologist, 1063 K
Parachute, Leonardo's design for, 1480 G
Paradise of Wisdom (al-Tabarī), 850 G
Paramaraja I, King of Ayudhya (d. 1388), 1376 E
Paramaraja II, King of Ayudhya (1424–48), 1431 E
Paramesvara, first King of Malacca, 1405 E
Paramientos de la Caza, Los (Sancho VI), 1180 G
Parāntaka I, King of Cholas, 915 E, 949 E
Paravicius, It. translator, 1280 G
Parikramanabūlāvabodha (Gujarātī-Jaina), 1355 K
Paris, France, 1290 G, 1378 A, 1393 D, 1416 A
sacked by Vikings, 845 E, 856 D, 861 B
besieged, 885 D, 1360 B
riots in, 1358 A, C, 1382 A, 1383 A, 1413 B, C
and Burgundy-Armagnac feud, 1405 C, 1408 A, 1418 B
occupied by English, 1420 D, 1431 D, 1436 B
Treaties of, 1151 C, 1229 B, 1259 D, 1303 B, 1320 B, 1327 A
Bishops of, 886 L; *and see* Peter the Lombard
Bourgeois of, Journal of, 1449 K
Buildings:
Bastille, 1369 B, 1413 B
Nôtre Dame, 1163 J, 1200 J, 1220 J, 1250 J
Palais Royal, clock, 1370 G
St. Denis, abbey, 1137 J, 1140 J, 1231 J; abbot of, *see* Suger
St. Germain des Prés, 1005 J, 1163 J
Sainte-Chapelle, 1243 J
walls, 1209 E
Confrérie de la passion, 1398 H
friars, 1217 H, 1265 H
Parlement of, 1239 F, 1294 A, 1324 C, 1341 B; records of, 1254 F; regulations, 1278 F, 1454 F; Confraternity of lawyers, 1342 F
surgeons' guild, 1271 G
University:
cathedral school, 1000 H, 1121 H
school of William of Champeaux, 1108 H
school of Peter Abelard, 1113 H
royal charter, 1200 H
papal regulations, 1210 H, 1219 H, 1231 H, 1263 H
colleges:
Burgundy, 1332 H
Cardinal Lemoine, 1302 H
Dix-huit, 1180 H
Montaigu, 1314 H
Navarre, 1314 H
Sorbonne, 1257 H
oriental languages at, 1311 H
Paris, Matthew, E. chronicler and poet, 1259 K
Parlements. *See* Malines; Paris; Toulouse
Parler, Heinrich, G. mason, 1320 J
Parler, Heinrich (2), G. mason, 1377 J
Parler, Johannes, G. mason, 1354 J, 1357 J
Parler, Michael, G. mason, 1377 J
Parler, Peter, G. mason (1330–99), 1352 J, 1399 L
Parliament of Fowles, The (Geoffrey Chaucer), 1381 K
Parliaments, Cortes, Estates and other elected assemblies:
Bohemia, 1350 F
Brabant, 1312 F, 1356 F
Burgundy, 1463 E
Castile, 1250 F
Catalonia, 1218 F
England, 1213 F, 1254 F, 1265 F, 1275 F, 1295 F; *and see* England
Esthonia, 1315 F
France, 1302 B, 1314 F; *and see* France
Germany, 1255 F
Hungary, 1324 E
Iceland, 930 F
Ireland, 1297 F, 1366 A
Leon, 1188 F
Liège, 1316 F, 1373 F
Papal States, 1207 F
Poland, 1454 F
Portugal, 1254 F
Scotland, 1326 F, 1424 F, 1428 F
Sicily, 1232 F
Sweden, 1435 E
Valencia, 1283 F
Wales, 1404 B
Parma, Italy, 1037 D, 1247 B, 1248 A, 1316 E, 1326 C; Cathedral, 1106 J, 1117 J
Parr, Thomas, E. centenarian (1483?–1635), 1483 L
Particiaco, Angelo, Doge of Venice, 811 E, 827 E
Particiaco, Giovanni I, Doge of Venice, 829 E, 837 B
Particiaco, Giovanni II, Doge of Venice, 881 E, 887 B, C, 888 B
Particiaco, Giustiniani, Doge of Venice, 827 E, 829 E
Particiaco, Orso I, Doge of Venice, 864 A, 881 E
Particiaco, Orso II, Doge of Venice, 912 E, 932 E
Parzival (Wolfram von Eschenbach), 1212 K, 1336 K
Paschal I, Pope, 817 A, 823 E, 824 A
Paschal II (Rainer), Pope, 1099 C, 1103 H, 1104 E, 1111 A, 1112 B, 1117 A, 1118 A

Paschal III (Guido of Crema), anti-pope, 1164 B, 1167 C, 1168 C
Passau, W. Germany, bishop of, 942 H
Passion, Altarpiece of the (Hans Memling), 1491 J
Passionarius (Gariopontus), 1050 G
Paston family *Letters*, 1418 K
Patarines. *See* Milan
Patay, France, battle, 1429 B
Patras, Greece, 805 E
Patronio, Libro de (Juan Manuel), 1349 K
Paucapalea, It. canonist, 1150 H
Paul II (Marco Barbo), Pope, 1464 C, 1465 D, 1466 D, 1469 B, C, 1471 B, C
Paul the Deacon, It. chronicler, 800 K
Paulicians, Armenian heretics, 867 H, 872 E, 1114 H
Pauperie Salvatoris, De (Richard FitzRalph), 1360 F
Pavia, Italy, 894 E, 902 E, 924 E, 1004 B, 1315 D, 1332 D; coronations in, 876 A, 889 A, 900 D, 951 C, 961 C, 1155 B; synods, etc., 1018 H, 1022 C, 1037 A, 1046 D, 1160 A; General Council, 1423 B, C; Charterhouse, 1396 H; church, 1100 J; law school, 1000 F; University, 1361 H, 1398 H, 1412 H
Pazzi Conspiracy, 1478 B
Peace:
  constitution for empire, 1158 D
  'Day of Indulgence', 1043 D
  public, in Germany, 1269 B, 1371 F, 1383 F, 1389 B, 1441 F, 1467 F
  of God, in France, 989 F, 1010 F, 1040 F, 1042 F; Flanders, 1092 D; Empire, 1085 F
Pearl, The, 1375 K
Pecham, John, Archbishop of Canterbury, E. theologian, 1279 H, 1292 H, L
Pechenegs, Turkish tribe, in Russia, 895 E, 969 E, 972 B; raids by, 1033 E, 1036 E, 1048 E, 1064 E, 1071 E, 1087 E; settling, 1090 B; exterminated, 1122 E
Pecock, Reginald, Bishop of Chichester, E. theologian (d. 1460/1), 1455 H, 1456 H, 1457 H
Pecorone, Il (Giovanni de Firenze), 1378 K
Pécs, Hungary, Cathedral, 1150 J; University, 1367 H
Pedro I, King of Aragon and Navarre, 1095 B, 1096 E, 1104 C
Pedro II, King of Aragon, 1196 B, 1204 D, 1213 C
Pedro III the Great, King of Aragon (1276–85), 1276 C, 1280 E, 1281 E, 1283 F; and Sicily, 1262 B, 1282 A, B, D, 1284 A, 1285 D
Pedro IV the Ceremonious, King of Aragon, 1336 A, 1344 A, 1348 C, 1375 G, 1377 C, 1386 E, 1387 A
Pedro I the Cruel, King of Castile (b. 1336; 1349–69), 1349 A, 1362 B, 1365 C, 1367 B, 1369 A, 1372 A
Pedro I, King of Portugal (b. 1320; 1357–67), 1357 B, 1367 A, 1385 B
Pedro Alfonso (*born* Moses Sephardi), Sp. J. physician and fabulist (1062–1110), 1110 K
Pegolotti, Francesco Balducci, It. writer on commerce, 1340 G
Pegu (Hamsavati), Burma, capital of Mon kingdom, 825 E, 1035 E
Pei-shan Chiu-ching (Chui-chung), 1120 G
Peipus, Lake, Russia, battle, 1242 B
Peking, China:
  capital of Khitan, 936 E
  taken by Jürched, 1125 E, 1153 E
  taken by Mongols, 1215 E, 1261 E, 1367 E
  Ming capital, 1420 E, F, 1449 E
  Archbishoprics of, 1275 H, 1307 H
  canal to, 1289 G
  Christian mission in, 1294 H
  monk of, 1287 G
Pelacini, Biagio. *See* Blasius
Pelagius, It. cardinal and legate, 1218 D, 1220 C
Pelagonia, Greece, battle, 1259 E
Pelavicini, Oberto, Marquess of Cremona, 1252 A
Pelayo, Alvaro, Sp. theologian (*c.* 1280–1352), 1331 H
Pelekanon, Turkey, battle, 1329 E
Pèlerinage de Charlemagne, Le, 1150 K
Pembroke, Wales, Earls of. *See* FitzGilbert; Marshal; Valence, Aymer de; Hastings, John; Herbert, William
Penrith, England, 927 C
Peony, Chinese treatises on, 1070 G, 1072 G
Pepin I, King of Aquitaine (814–38), 814 C, 817 C, 838 E, 839 B; revolts, 830 B, 831 B, 832 E, 833 B, 834 A
Pepin II, King of Aquitaine (d. *c.* 864), 839 B, 841 B, 844 E, 845 B; deprived, 848 B, 852 C; resumed, 854 E
Pepin, King of Italy, 806 A, 810 C
Percevale le Gallois (Chrétien de Troyes), 1173 K
Percy, Henry, Earl of Northumberland, 1341 L, 1402 C, 1408 A
Percy, Henry, Earl of Northumberland (d. 1455), 1454 D
Percy, Henry, Earl of Northumberland, 1489 B
Percy, Henry 'Hotspur', E. noble, 1388 C, 1402 C, 1403 C
Pereyslavl, Russia, battle, 1068 E
Perfumery, Japanese treatise on, 1156 G
Pergamun, Turkey, 1211 D
Perigrinantes propter Christum (society), 1253 H, 1324 H
Perigueux, France, Cathedral, 1120 J
Pernau, Esthonia, Russia, 1315 F
Pero Niño, Count of Buelna, life of, 1450 K
Péronne, France, 1192 A, 1256 C, 1468 D
Perotti, Niccolò, It. grammarian (1430–80), 1473 K
Perpignan, France, 1409 D, 1463 A, 1473 A, 1475 A; Cathedral, 1433 J; University, 1351 H
Persia:
  disintegration of 'Abbasid Empire in. *See* Jurjan, Khurāsān, Sijistān, Transoxiana
  Buwayhids of Shīrāz, 946 A, 1055 D
  conquered by Seljuqs, 1037 E, 1040 A
  Seljuq Sultans. *See*
    Tughril Bey (1050–63)
    Alp Arslan (1063–72)
    Malik Shah (1072–92)
    Mahmūd I (1092–4)
    Barkiyāruq (1094–1105)
    Muhammad I (1105–18)
    Sanjar (1118–57)
    feudalism in, 1087 F
    disintegration, 1087 F, 1092 D, 1100 E, 1104 A, 1157 E
  conquered by Khwārizm-Shahs. *See*
    Tekish (1172–1200)
    'Alā'-ad-Dīn (1200–20)
    Jalāl-ad-Dīn (1220–31)
    in exile, 1244 C
  conquered by Mongols, 1219 B, 1220 D, J, 1221 D, 1222 B, 1225 E, 1231 C
  Ilkhans. *See*
    Hūlāgū (1256–65)
    Abāqa (1265–82)
    Tekuder (1282–4)
    Arghūn (1284–91)
    Ghazan (1295–1304)
    Uljāytū (1304–16)
    Abū Sa'īd (1316–35)
    European envoy to, 1289 G
    decline of, 1335 E, 1356 E
  conquered by Timur, 1382 E, 1386 E, 1393 E

Persia—*contd.*
decline of his empire, 1405 A; *and see* Khurāsān, Transoxiana
under White Sheep Turkomans, 1447 E, 1487 G
soi-disant Sultan of, 1470 C
calendar, 1074 G, 1079 G
ceramic industry, 1220 J, 1301 J
cultural revival, 874 E
history. *See* Historians
language, treatise on, 1344 K
lexicon, 1060 K
literature:
Isfahānī, 967 K
Hamadhānī, 1007 K
Firdausi, 1020 K
Tha'alibi, 1038 K
'Umar al-Khayyām, 1123 K
Nizāmī, 1181 K
Sa'dī, 1258 K
Rūmī, 1273 K
Cf. Arab literature; Poets
medical schools, 931 G
metal-work, 1163 J
trade with China, 879 G
Perspectiva Communis (John Pecham), 1292 G
Perth, Scotland, 1313 A, 1333 C; Treaty of, 1266 C
Peru, Incas of, 1200 E, 1471 E
Perugia, Italy, 1354 A, 1400 A; fountain, 1278 J; University, 1308 H
Perugino, It. painter (*c.* 1447–1523), 1478 J, 1481 J
Peruzzi, bankers of Florence, 1345 E
Peruzzi, Baldassare, It. architect and painter (1481–1536), 1481 L
Peshawar, Pakistan, battle, 1001 D
Peter de Courtenay, Emperor of Constantinople, 1216 B, 1217 E, 1221 A
Peter, Khan of the Bulgars, 927 B
Peter, Tsar of Bulgaria (1187–97); *as* Theodore, 1185 E, 1186 D; Tsar, 1187 E, 1190 E, 1196 E, 1197 E
Peter I, King of Cyprus, 1364 C, 1365 D
Peter the German, King of Hungary, 1038 C, 1042 B, 1044 C, 1046 C
Peter I, King of Sicily. *See* Pedro III of Aragon
Peter II, King of Sicily (b. 1305), 1337 A, 1342 C
Peter, Regent of Portugal, 1440 E, 1449 B
Peter, St., Metropolitan of Russia, 1326 H
Peter the Deacon, It. chronicler, 1139 K
Peter the Hermit, leader of crusade, 1096 C, 1115 L
Peter of Duisburg, G. chronicler, 1326 K
Peter the Lombard, Bishop of Paris, It. theologian (*c.* 1100–64), 1150 H, 1308 K
Peter of Piacenza, It. jurist, 1160 F
Peter of Toledo, Sp. translator, 1141 K
Peter the Venerable, Abbot of Cluny (b. 1094), 1122 H, 1156 L
Peter Deljan, Slav leader, 1040 E
See also Pedro, Petrus, Pierre
Peterborough, England, abbey (*now* Cathedral), 1118 J
Petersberg, E. Germany, monastery, 1120 J
Petersen, Gerlac, Flemish mystic, 1378 L, 1411 H
Petit Testament, Le (François Villon), 1456 K
Petrarch, Francesco, It. poet and humanist (1304–74), 1304 L, 1327 K, 1339 K, 1341 K, 1342 K, 1351 K, 1352 K, 1357 K, 1366 K, 1374 L
Petrocellus of Salerno, It. physician, 1035 G
Petronilla, Queen of Aragon, 1137 E, 1164 E
Petrus Comestor, F. theologian, 1198 K
Petrus Hispanus. *See* John XXI
Petrus Peregrinus, F. writer on lodestone, 1269 G
Petrus Petri, Sp. (?) mason (d. 1291), 1227 J
Pevensey, England, 1066 C
Pfaffe Amis, Der (Der Stricker), 1240 K
Pfaffenbrief (Swiss code), 1370 F
Phagspa, Mongol scholar, 1269 K
Pharmacologists:
Arab. *See* Māsawayh
Italian. *See* Platearius
Persian. *See* Muwaffaq; Sābūr
Spanish Muslim. *See* Baytār
Philadelphia (*now* Alashehir), Turkey, 1304 E
Philermo, Rhodes, Greece, 1306 D
Philip I, King of France (b. 1052; 1060–1108), 1059 B, 1060 C, 1071 A, 1101 E, 1108 C; and feudatories, 1068 E, 1079 A, 1080 E, 1094 E; abducts Countess of Anjou, 1092 E, 1095 D, 1104 E
Philip II Augustus, King of France (1180–23), 1165 L, 1179 D, 1180 B, C, 1185 E, 1200 H, 1207 D, 1209 E, 1212 D, 1223 C
gains Artois, etc., 1185 C, 1192 A, 1213 B
war with Henry II, 1187 E, 1188 A, D, 1189 C
on Crusade, 1190 C, 1191 B, C
war with Richard I, 1191 A, 1193 C, 1194 A, C, 1198 C, 1199 A
marriage to Ingeborg, 1193 C, 1195 B, 1196 B, 1200 C
war with John, 1200 B, 1202 B, 1203 B, 1204 A, B, 1205 A, 1206 B, D
invades England, 1213 B, 1216 B, 1217 C
victory at Bouvines, 1214 C, 1224 K
Philip III the Bold, King of France (1270–85), 1245 L, 1270 C, 1271 C, 1272 D, 1278 E, 1279 B, 1280 A; campaigns in Spain, 1276 E, 1279 D, 1284 A, 1285 C, D
Philip IV the Fair, King of France (1285–1314), 1268 L, 1284 C, 1285 D, 1301 H, 1310 E, 1314 D
fiscal measures, 1286 G, 1295 G, 1306 G, 1309 F, 1311 G, 1314 F, 1315 B
peace with Aragon, 1291 A, 1295 B
war with England, 1294 A, C, E, 1297 A, C, D, 1298 A, 1303 B
alliances, 1295 C, 1299 C, 1308 A
disputes with Pope, 1297 C, 1301 D, 1302 B
wars with Flanders, 1294 E, 1297 C, 1300 B, 1302 B, C, 1303 C, 1304 C, 1305 A, B, 1312 E, 1314 C
unrest against, 1303 A, 1314 D
attacks Templars 1307 D, 1308 B, C
Philip V the Long, King of France (b. *c.* 1294; 1317–22), 1316 B, 1317 A, 1318 A, 1320 B, F, 1322 A; wife, 1315 E, 1330 E
Philip VI of Valois, King of France (1328–50), 1293 L, 1328 A–C, 1329 B, 1340 G, 1341 A, 1346 C, 1349 C, 1350 C
banishes Robert of Artois, 1332 B, 1336 E
takes cross, 1332 C, 1336 E
shelters David, 1334 B, 1336 C
war with England, 1336 E, 1337 B, 1338 B, 1339 D, 1340 A, B, 1343 A, 1344 E, 1347 C
Philip II, Duke of Swabia, King of the Romans, 1198 A, C, E, 1205 A, 1206 C, 1207 A, 1208 B
Philip de Rouvres, Duke of Burgundy, 1361 D
Philip the Bold, Duke of Burgundy (1363–1404), 1342 L, 1363 C, 1392 C, 1404 B; Count of Flanders, 1369 B, 1384 A, 1385 D, 1386 F
Philip the Good, Duke of Burgundy (1419–67), 1396 L, 1419 C, 1425 J, 1429 A, 1453 C, 1456 C, 1457 G, 1463 E, 1467 B
ally of England, 1419 D, 1423 C, 1430 B
gains lands, 1421 B, 1424 D, 1425 B, 1428 C, 1430 C, 1437 E, 1443 D
war against England, 1435 C, 1436 C, 1439 C
Philip, Count of Flanders (1168–91), 1180 B, 1185 C
Philip of Thaon, F. poet, 1125 K
Philippa of Hainault, wife of Edward III, 1328 A

Philippe de Remy. *See* Beaumanoir
Philippis (William the Breton), 1224 K
Philippopolis (*now* Plovdiv), Bulgaria, 1114 H
Philobiblon (Richard de Bury), 1345 K
Philologists:
  Chinese. *See* Ch'en P'êng-nien; Lu Fa-yen; Sung Ch'i; Ting Tu
  Egyptian. *See* Abū-l-Barakāt; Manzūr
  French. *See* Lupus, Servatus
  Indian. *See* Hemacandra
  Italian. *See* Albertano of Brescio
  Japanese. *See* Minamoto no Shitagau
  Persian. *See* 'Abbād; Asadī; Duraid; Fāris; Fīrūzābādī; Qutaybah
  Spanish Muslim. *See* Abū Haiyān
  Turkish. *See* Jawhāri
Philosophers:
  Arab. *See* Ash'arī; Kindī; Tufayl
  Chinese. *See* Chou Tun-i; Chu Hsi; Han Yu; Shao Yung
  Dutch. *See* Agricola, Rudolphus
  English. *See* Bacon, Roger; Baconthorpe, John; Burley, Walter; Grosseteste, Robert; Ockham, William of
  French. *See* Abelard; Buridan, Jean; Gilbert de la Porrée; Roscelin; William of Champeaux; William of Conches
  French Jew. *See* Levi ben Gerson
  German. *See* Albert of Saxony; Albertus Magnus
  Greek. *See* Aristotle; Plato
  Indian. *See* Gujarātī-Jaina; Mādhava; Rāmānuja; Sankara
  Irish. *See* Erigena
  Italian. *See* Abano, Pietro d'; Aquinas; Boethius; Pico della Mirandola
  Persian. *See* Hamadhānī; Maturīdī; Miskawayh; Suhrawardi
  Scottish. *See* Duns Scotus
  Spanish Jews. *See* Judah ben Samuel; Moses ben Maimon; Solomon ben Gabīrōl
  Spanish Muslim. *See* 'Arabī; Bājjah; Khaldūn; Sab'in
  Turkish. *See* Fārābī
Philosophers, History of (al-Qiftī), 1248 G
Philosophia Mundi, De (William of Conches), 1154 K
Phnom Penh, Cambodia, 1434 E
Phocas, Nicephorus. *See* Nicephorus II
Phonetic dictionaries, Chinese, 1011 K, 1039 K, 1375 K; writing, Korean, 1446 K
Photius, Patriarch of Constantinople (*c.* 820–*c.* 891), 858 H, 863 H, 867 D, H, 877 H, 887 E, 891 K
Physica (Hildegarde of Bingen), 1179 G
Physicians:
  Arab. *See* Abbās; Joannes Afflacius
  Armenian. *See* Mekhitur
  Catalan. *See* Joannes Jacobi; Villanova, Arnold de
  Chinese. *See* Chia Ming; Ch'en Tzŭ-ming; Sung Tz'ŭ; Wên-jên Kuei
  Egyptian. *See* Nafīs
  Egyptian Jew. *See* Isrā'īli
  English. *See* Alfred of Shareshel; Arderne, John; Bald; Gaddesden, John of; Mirfield, John; Richard of Wendover
  French. *See* Ganivet, Jean; Giles of Corbeil; Gordon, Bernard de; Marbode
  French Jew. *See* Moses ben Joshua
  Greek. *See* Actuarios, Joannes; Galen; Hippocrates; Leon the Iastrosphist; Seth, Symeon
  Indian. *See* Narahari; Sureśvara
  Italian. *See* Abano, Pietro d'; Alderotti, Taddeo; Aldobrandon of Siena; Falcucci, Niccolò; Ferrari, Giovanni; Foligno, Gentile; Forlo, Jacopo da; Gariopontus; John of Milan; Petrocellus; Platearius; Simon of Genoa; Tossignano, Pietro de
  Japanese. *See* Yasuyori Tamba
  Persian. *See* Bīrunī; Jurjānī; Muwaffaq; Rashīd; Rāzī; Sīna; Tabarī
  Portuguese. *See* John XXI
  Spanish Jews. *See* Moses ben Maimon; Pedro Alfonso
  Spanish Muslim. *See* Baytār; Ghāfiqi; Khatīb; Rushd; Zahrāwi; Zuhr
  biographies of Greek and Arab, 1248 G, 1270 G
Physiologus, 1250 K
Pi Shêng, C. printer, 1045 G
Piacenza, Italy, 1095 A, 1159 C, 1236 C, 1337 E; Cathedral, 1122 J; University, 1248 H, 1398 H
Piast, Duke of Poland, 842 E, 861 E
Piast dynasty. *See* Poland
Picardy, France, 1471 A, 1482 D
Piccinino, Niccolò, It. condottiere (b. 1375), 1430 D, 1431 B, 1434 C, 1438 B, 1439 D, 1440 B, 1443 B, 1444 D
Piccolomini, Aeneas Silvius. *See* Pius II
Pico della Mirandola, Count Giovanni, It. philosopher (1463–94), 1463 L, 1486 K
Picquigny, France, Treaty of, 1475 C
Picts. *See* Scotland
Piedmont, Italy, 1275 D, 1359 E, 1418 D
Pierre de Beauvais, F. poet, 1225 K
Pierre de Montereau, F. mason, 1231 J
Piers Plowman (William Langland), 1377 K
Pietà (Giovanni Bellini), 1470 J
Pig, dissection of, 1110 G
Pigeons, carrier, 837 G
Pilgrim, Bishop of Passau, 942 H
Pilgrimages:
  to Santiago de Compostela, 813 H
  writers on:
    English. *See* Saewulf
    German. *See* Burchard of Mount Sion
    Icelandic. *See* Saemundarson, Nikulas
    Italian. *See* Fabri, Felix; Poggibonsi, Niccolò da
    Russian. *See* Daniel of Kiev
Pilleth, Wales, battle, 1402 B
Pillow Book, The (Sei Shōnagon), 1000 K
Pinya, Burma, Shan Kingdom, 1312 E
Piotrków, Poland, Statutes of, 1347 J
Pīr Muhammad, Mongol prince, 1398 B
Pisa, Italy:
  sacked by Vikings, 861 E; by Saracens, 1004 E, 1011 E
  conquests, 1006 E, 1016 B, 1034 E, 1087 E, 1133 E, 1323 E
  ally of Emperors, 1162 A, 1191 A
  defeated, 1270 E, 1284 C
  under Ugolino, 1289 E
  under Ugoccione, *q.v.*
  war with Florence, 1342 C
  under despots, 1370 D, 1392 D, 1398 C, 1399 A
  annexed by Florence, 1406 D
  General Council at, 1408 B, 1409 A, B
  Cathedral, 1063 J, 1299 J, 1302 J; Baptistery of, 1153 J, 1260 J; mosaic (Cimabue), 1302 J
  University, 1343 H, 1472 H
Pisa, Della Guerra di (Antonio Pucci), 1388 K
Pisan, Christine de, F. poetess and didactic prose writer (*c.* 1363–1431), 1399 K, 1402 K, 1404 K, 1412 K, 1415 K, 1431 L
Pisanello, Antonio, It. sculptor (1397–1455/6), 1397 L, 1415 J, 1423 J, 1431 J, 1437 J, 1448 J
Pisano, Andrea, It. sculptor, 1330 J, 1337 J, 1347 J, 1348 L

Pisano, Giovanni, It. sculptor and architect (d. *c.* 1320), 1278 J, 1297 J, 1299 J, 1302 J, 1305 J
Pisano, Niccolò, It. sculptor, 1260 J, 1265 J, 1278 J, L
Pistill of Suete Susan, The, 1370 K
Pistoia, Italy, 1306 B; works of art, 1297 J, 1353 J
Pitres, France, 856 C
Pittura, Della (Alberti), 1435 J
Pius II (Aeneas Silvius Piccolomini), Pope (b. 1405; 1458–64), 1405 L, 1458 C, 1460 H, 1462 G, 1464 L; crusade of, 1459 B, 1463 D, 1464 C; as humanist, historian and poet, 1440 K, 1444 K
Pizarro, Francisco, Sp. conqueror of Peru (*c.* 1471–1541), 1471 L
Pizigano, Francesco, It. cartographer, 1367 G
Plague, On (ibn-al-Khaṭīb), 1374 G
  See also Black Death
Planctu ecclesiae, De (Alvaro Pelayo), 1331 H
Planetarium, 888 G
Planetarium (Giovanni Dondi), 1364 G
Planisphere, 1154 G
Plantagenet, Geoffrey. *See* Geoffrey
Platearius, Matthaeus, It. physician and pharmacologist, 1161 G
Platina, Bartolomeo, It. historian, 1421 L, 1479 K, 1481 L
Plato, Gk. philosopher (d. 347 B.C.), translated, 1162 K
Plays. *See* Drama
Pleichfeld, W. Germany, battle, 1086 C
Plethon, Georgios Gemistos, Gk. scholar and diplomat (1356–1450), 1439 K
Pliska, Bulgaria, 809 E, 811 C
Plowce, Poland, battle, 1331 C
Po, river, Italy, battle on, 1431 B
Po-Chü-i, C. poet (772–846), 846 K
Podolia, Russia, 1377 E
Poema de Alfonso Onceno, 1350 K
Poema del Cid Campeador, 1140 K
Poeta Saxo (the Saxon poet), 890 K
Poetic Edda, The (the 'Elder Edda'), 1220 K
Poetry, Criticism of (Qudāma), 948 K
Poets:
  anon. (*Carmina Burana*), 1200 K
  Anglo-Norman. *See* Bernard de Morlaix; Langtoft, Peter; Paris, Matthew; Richard I; Thomas of Brittany; Wace
  Arab. *See* ʿAtāhiyah; ʿAttābī; Munqidh; Muʿtazz; Tammām
  Belgian. *See* Couvin, Simon; Maerlant, Jacob; Outremeuse, Jean d'
  Bohemian. *See* Dalimil; Tepl, Johann von
  Chinese. *See* Han Yü; Li Ch'ing-chao; Li Ho; Po Chü-i; Shao Yung; Su Tung-p'o; Yüan Chen
  Dutch. *See* Stoke, Melis
  Egyptian. *See* Būṣīrī; Fārid; Wafa
  English, anon., 800 K, 970 K, 975 K, 993 K, 1250 K, 1264 K, 1295 K, 1300 K, 1320 K, 1330 K, 1375 K. *And see* Chaucer, Geoffrey; Cynewulf; Ely, monk of; Hoccleve, Thomas; Langland, William; Mannyng, Robert; Map, Walter; Mirk, John; Nicholas de Guildford; Rolle, Richard; Thomas the Rhymer
  French, anon., 1170 K, 1180 K, 1200 K, 1260 K. *And see* Adam de la Halle; Adanet le Roi; Alan of Lille; Alexis, Guillaume; Angilbert; Baude, Henri; Baudry de Bourgueil; Beaumanoir, Philippe; Benoît de Sainte Maure; Bernard of Clairvaux; Béroul; Bertrand de Bar-sur-Aube; Bodel, Jean; Bonet, Honoré; Boucicaut; Bretel, Jacques; Butors, Bauduins; Charles, Duke of Orleans; Chartier, Alain; Chrétien de Troyes; Deschamps, Eustace; Évreux, Ambroise d'; Fontaine, Jehan de la; Fougères, Étienne de; Garnier de Point-Sainte-Maxence; Gautier de Metz; Gerbert de Montreuil; Giraud d'Amiens; Graindor de Douay; Guiot of Provins; Lorris, Guillaume de; Machaut, Guillaume; Marbode; Matfré de Bezier; Meun, Jean de; Mézières, Philippe de; Mousqués, Philippe; Odo of Meung; Philip of Thaon; Pierre de Beauvais; Pisan, Christine de; Rauol de Houdenc; Régnier, Jean; Renaud de Beaujeu; Robert de Borron; Rudel de Blaya; Saquet, Jakemon; Theobald I; Villon, François; William the Breton. *See also* Troubadours
  French Jew. *See* Bedersi
  Georgian. *See* Rustaveli, Shota
  German, anon., 820 K, 1150 K, 1200 K, 1240 K, 1290 K. *And see* Albert von Stade; Aue, Hartmann von; Ava; Beheim, Michael; Conrad von Würzburg; Eilhart von Oberg; Ekkehard; Ezzo of Bamberg; Gottfried von Strassburg; Hrotswith; Konrad, Pfaffe; Mechthild; Notker Balbulus; Notker Labeo; Otfrid of Weissenburg; Stricker, Der; Ulrich of Lichtenstein; Veldeke, Heinrich von; Walafrid Strabo. *See also* Mastersingers; Minnesingers
  Greek. *See* Prodromus, Theodore
  Icelandic, anon., 1200 K. *And see* Snorri Sturlason
  Indian. *See* Shand Bardāī; Gangā Devi; Hemacandra; Kalhana; Kamban; Lal Ded; Somadeva
  Indian Muslim. *See* Dihlavī; Khusraw; Isāmy
  Irish, 1391 K. *And see* Sedulius Scottus
  Italian. *See* Angiolieri, Cecco; Aquinas; Bianco da Siena; Boccaccio; Boiardo, Matteo; Cavalcanti, Guido; Cino da Pistoia; Compagni, Dino; Dante; Ferreto de' Ferreti; Francis, St.; Frezzi, Frederigo; Guinicelli, Guideo; Guittone d'Arezzo; Jacopo da Lentini; Jacopone da Todi; Latini, Brunetto; Medici, Lorenzo de'; Mussato, Albertino; Petrarch; Politian; Pucci, Antonio; Pulci, Bernardo; Pulci, Luigi; Rustico di Filippo; Sacchetti, Franco; Sannazaro, Jacopo; Sordel di Goito; Stabili, Francesco degli; Thomas of Celano; Uberti, Fazio degli; Vegio, Maffeo
  Italian Jew. *See* Emanuel ben Solomon
  Japanese, anon., 1205 K. *And see* Fujiwara Teika; Ise; Ki no Tomonori; Ki no Tsurayuki; Mibu no Tadamine; Ōshikōchi no Mitsune; Saigyō; Sugawara Michizane
  Persian. *See* Ansārī; 'Attār; Farrukhī; Firdausi; Hāfiz; Hanzala; 'Irāqī; Isfahānī; Khayyām; Khusraw; Mālik; Minūchihrī; Mustawfi; Nizāmī; Rūdakī; Rūmī; Sa'dī; Zākānī
  Polish, anon., 1408 K
  Portuguese, anon., 1350 K. *And see* Dinis
  Russian, anon., 1185 K, 1380 K
  Scottish, anon., 1370 K. *And see* Barbour, John; Henryson, Robert; James I
  Spanish, anon., 1225 K, 1340 K, 1350 K. *And see* Alfonso X; Gonzalo de Berceo; López de Ayala; López de Mendoza; Manrique, Jorge; Mena, Juan de la; Ruiz, Juan
  Spanish (Catalan). *See* Lull, Raymond; March, Auziàs; Muntaner, Ramón; Sant Jordi, Jordi da
  Spanish Jews. *See* Moses ben Ezra; Solomon ben Gabīrōl
  Spanish Muslim. *See* Hazm
  Swiss, anon., 1465 K
  Syrian. *See* Maʿarri; Mutannabī
  Turkish. *See* Ahmedī
  Welsh, anon., 1150 K. *And see* David ap Gwilym

Pogezanians, Prussian tribe, 1277 E
Poggibonsi, Niccolò da, It. friar and pilgrim-author, 1349 K
Poggibonzi, Italy, battle, 1479 C
Poggio, Gian Francesco (Bracciolini), It. humanist and historian (1381–1459), 1416 K, 1452 K, 1469 K, L
Poimanenon, Turkey, battles, 1204 D, 1225 E
Poiters, France, 1346 D, 1372 C; battle, 1356 C; Bishop of, *see* Gilbert de la Porrée; Cathedral, 1162 J; Church, 1025 J; County of, 845 B, 1039 A; University, 1432 H
Poitou, France, 1202 B, C, 1206 B, 1224 B, 1271 C, 1360 D, 1372 C, D, 1427 E
Poland:
  Dukes of Piast dynasty:
    legendary. *See* Piast; Ziemovit; Leszek I; Ziemomyslas
    historical. *See* Miesko I; Boleslav I
    kingdom created, 1000 A; abolished, 1033 E; *and see* Boleslav I, Mieszko II
  Dukes. *See* Casimir I; Boleslav II
  kingdom restored, 1076 D; ends, 1081 A; *and see* Boleslav II
  Dukes. *See* Vladislav I; Zbigiev; Boleslav III
  Grand Princes. *See*
    Vladislav II (1138–46)
    Boleslav IV (1146–73)
    Mieszko III (1173–7, 1201–2)
    Casimir II (1177–94)
  Princes at Cracow. *See*
    Leszek II (1202–27)
    Boleslav V (1227–79)
  Grand Princes. *See*
    Vladislav III (d. 1231)
    Henry I (1234–8)
    Henry II (1238–41)
    Boleslav V (1243–79)
    Leszek III (1279–88)
  kingdom restored, 1295 B; ends, 1296 A; *and see* Przemyslav II
  Grand Prince. *See* Vladislav I
  Kings. *See*
    Wenceslas II of Bohemia (*as* Václav, 1300–4)
    Vladislav I (1320–33)
    Casimir I (1333–70)
    Lewis I (of Hungary, 1370–82)
    Jadwiga (Queen, 1382–99)
    Jagiello (*as* Vladislav II, 1386–1434)
    Vladislav III (1434–44)
    Casimir IV (1447–92)
  conversion of, 966 E
  possesses Red Russia, 981 E, 1031 E, 1069 E
  fights Bohemia for Silesia, *q.v.*
  German claims to supremacy, 1018 K, 1028 E, 1157 E
  disintegration, 1031 E, 1033 E, 1034 A
  Bohemian invasion, 1038 E
  reconversion, 1044 H, 1058 D, 1076 D
  anarchy, 1081 E
  reform of church, 1103 H, 1123 H, 1215 H; under Magdeburg, 1133 B
  partition of Duchy, 1138 E
  civil war, 1194 B
  Mongol invasion, 1241 B, G
  German settlements, 1241 G, 1250 E, 1264 G
  Mongol raids, 1259 E, 1282 E, 1286 E, 1288 E
  defeat Jadzwings, 1264 E
  disintegration, 1279 D
  succession dispute, 1288 E
  cedes Little Poland, 1290 E
  Bohemian conquest, 1300 E, 1304 E
  end of Piast dynasty, 1370 D
  union to Lithuania, 1383 E
  capitals. *See* Gniezno; Cracow
  charters of liberties, 1374 F, 1454 F
  chronicles, 1112 K, 1223 K, 1480 K
  first poem, 1408 K
  law code, 1347 F
  Order of the White Eagle, 1325 E
  religious houses, 996 H, 1140 H
Polano, Pietro, Doge of Venice, 1130 E, 1148 E
Pole, William de la, Duke of Suffolk, 1450 A, B
Polei, Spain, battle, 891 B
Policraticus (John of Salisbury), 1159 K
Politics, writing on. *See* Government
Politian (Angelo Poliziano-Ambrogini), It. scholar, poet and dramatist (1454–94), 1454 L, 1479 K, 1480 K, 1489 K
Polo, Maffeo, It. merchant, 1260 G
Polo, Marco, It. traveller (1254–1324), 1254 L, 1271 G, 1275 G, 1292 G, 1295 G, 1298 G, 1324 L, 1375 G
Polychronicon (Ranulf Higden), 1352 K, 1387 K, 1482 K
Pomerania, E. Germany and Poland, 992 E, 1000 A, 1047 E
  Eastern:
    conquered by Denmark, 1210 E, 1229 E
    independent. *See* Swietopelk
    Polish, 1294 E
    won by Teutonic Knights, 1309 E, 1335 D, 1343 C
    under Poland, 1466 D
  Western:
    recovered by Poles, 1102 C, 1121 E, 1138 E
    conversion of, 1123 H, 1124 H
    becomes German, 1133 B, 1181 E, 1250 E, 1472 E, 1478 E
Pomezanians, Prussian tribe, 1236 E
Pomponazzi, Pietro, It. philosopher (1462–1525), 1462 L
Pomuk, John of, Bohemian ecclesiastic, 1393 A
Ponema juris (Michael Attaleiata), 1073 F
Ponthieu, France, 1279 B, 1360 B, 1369 B
Pontificale (Durandus), 1292 H
Pontigny, France, abbey, 1114 H, 1140 J, 1150 J, 1185 J
Pontius, Abbot of Cluny, 1122 H
Pontlevoi, France, battle, 1016 C
Pontoise, France, 1437 A, 1441 C
Pontvallain, France, battle of, 1370 D
Ponza, is., Italy, 845 E; battle of, 1435 C
Poor Clares, Order of, 1216 H
Popes. *See* Papacy
Porcaro, Stefano, Roman conspirator, 1453 A
Porcelain, Chinese, 1188 G
Porrette, Marguerite, F. mystic, 1310 H
Portinari Altarpiece (Hugo van der Goes), 1475 J
Portinari, Maria (Hans Memling), 1480 J
Portolans. *See* Maps
Portofino, Italy, battle, 1431 C
Porto Venere, Italy, 1408 A
Portrait of a Young Man (Dieric Bouts), 1462 J
Portsmouth, England, 1338 B
Portugal, 844 C, 1093 E
  created a county, 1095 E; *and see* Henry of Burgundy; Afonso I
  kings. *See*
    Afonso I (1139–85)
    Sancho I (1185–1211)
    Afonso II (1211–23)
    Sancho II (1223–48)
    Afonso III (1248–79)
    Dinis (1279–1325)
    Afonso IV (1325–57)
    Pedro I (1357–67)

Portugal—*contd.*
kings—*contd.*
Ferdinand I (1367–83)
John I (1385–1433)
Edward (1433–8)
Afonso V (1438–81)
John II (1481–95)
Moroccan invasion, 1184 B, C
papal fief, 1179 E, 1245 E
under interdicts, 1220 E, 1257 E
frontier defined, 1267 E
concordat with Church, 1289 E
alliance with England, 1373 B, 1386 B
claimed by Castile, 1383 D, 1384 A, C
conquers Canaries, 1425 E, 1480 A
conquers Tangier, 1437 E, 1471 C, 1480 A
capitals. *See* Braga; Lisbon
Cortes, 1254 F
Privilege of Union, 1287 F
discoveries by navigators of:
Madeira, 1418 G
Azores, 1431 G
Cape Verde, etc., 1446 G
Gambia, etc., 1455 G
Equator crossed, 1469 G
Fernando Po, 1471 G
Congo, 1482 G
Cape of Good Hope, 1488 G
first historian, 1434 K
Knights of Avis, 1179 E; of Christ, 1319 E
literature, 1325 K, 1350 K
wages and prices regulated, 1252 G
Po-shih Ch'ang-ch'ing chi (Po-Chü-i), 846 K
Postal services, Islamic, 809 G, 837 G, 846 G, 948 F; French, 1464 G
Postilla super Biblia (Nicholas de Lyra), 1332 H
Potestate Papae, De (John Wycliffe), 1379 H
Potestate regia et papali, De (John of Paris), 1302 F
Poujet, Bertrand de, F. cardinal and legate (1280–1352), 1319 C; campaigns in Italy, 1323 A–C, 1324 D, 1326 B, C, 1327 A, 1332 C, 1333 A, B, 1334 C
Poverty, apostolic, 1323 H
Povest' Vremennykh Let, 1118 K
Powys, Wales, 1208 E, 1258 A; Kings of, *see* Rhodri, Hywel, Gruffyd
Poznań, Poland, 1005 A; Bishopric, 968 H
Prachatitz, Peter von, G. mason, 1405 J
Practica (Petrocellus), 1035 G
Practica chirurgiae (Roger of Salerno), 1170 G
Practica de fistula (John Arderne), 1376 G
Practica geometriae (Fibonacci), 1220 G
Practica della mercatura (Francesco Pegolotti), 1340 G
Practica oculorum (Beneventus Grassus), 1130 G
Practica officii inquisitionis (Bernard Gui), 1323 H
Practica pars prima et secunda (Giovanni Matteo Ferrari), 1471 G
Praedestinacione Dei, De (Hincmar), 849 H
Praemunire, Statutes of, 1353 H, 1390 H, 1393 H
Prague, Czechoslovakia, 1393 A, 1401 B, 1408 H, 1410 H, 1419 C, 1420 C, 1448 C
Bishopric of, 973 E, 975 H, 1224 E, *and see* Adalbert; made archbishopric, 1344 H; Hussite Archbishop, 1471 L
Compacts of, 1433 D, 1436 C, 1485 H
Bethlehem Chapel, 1391 H, 1402 H
Cathedral, 1344 J, 1352 J, 1355 J
New Town, 1348 G
Old Town, 1235 G
Palace, 1333 J
religious houses, 967 H, 1347 H
University, 1348 H, 1385 H, 1403 H, 1409 H
Praguerie (French revolt), 1440 A
Prākrit, Indian vernacular, 1170 K
Pratāparudradeva II, King of Warangal, 1308 E
Prato, Italy, frescoes at, 1452 J
Praudharāya, King of Vijayanagar, 1486 E
Pravda Russkaia (Jaroslav), 1036 F
Precious Mirror of the Four Elements (Chu Shih-chieh), 1303 G
Predestination, 849 H, 851 H
Premonstratensian Order (of canons), 1120 H, 1140 H
Přemyslid dynasty. *See* Bohemia
Přemysl Ottokar. *See* Ottokar I
Prenzlau, E. Germany, Treaty of, 1472 E
Prés, Josquin des, Belgian musical composer (1445–1521), 1445 L
Presentation (Ambrogio Lorenzetti), 1342 J
Pressburg. *See* Bratislava
'Prester John', 1146 K
Pretiosa margarita novella (Pietro Buono), 1330 G
Prices, Arab treatise on, 815 G; regulated in Portugal, 1252 G
Prick of Conscience, The (Richard Rolle), 1349 K
Priests, Instructions for (John Mirk), 1400 H
Primavera (Botticelli), 1477 J
Printing:
China, 835 G, 868 G, 932 G, 1030 G, 1045 G, 1093 G, 1314 G
England, first illustrated book, 1481 G; *and see* Caxton, William
Flanders, of maps, 1478 G
France, 1375 G, 1381 G, 1392 G
Germany, 1440 G, 1462 G; woodcuts, 1147 G
Hungary, 1473 G
Italy, 1289 G, 1465 G; copperplate engravings, 1477 G; *and see* Aldus
Korea, 1392 G
Priories. *See* Monasteries
Prise d'Alexandrie, La (Guillaume de Machaut), 1377 K
Prithvī Rāj, last Hindu ruler of Delhi, 1192 E, K
Privileges. *See* Charters of Liberties
Procession of the Holy Ghost, 867 H, 1098 H
Prodromus, Theodorus, Gk. poet, 1160 K
Prokop, Andrew, the Great, Bohemian Hussite leader, 1426 B, 1434 B
Pronoia, 1118 F, 1180 F
Prophet's Mantle, The (al-Būsīri), 1296 K
Properietatibus Rerum, De (Bartholomew the Englishman), 1240 G, 1398 G
Prose Edda, The (the 'Younger Edda'), 1222 K
Prosody, treatise on (Micro), 825 K
Protat, Jules, F. printer, 1375 G
Provence, France, 860 E, 1217 H
kingdom of, 855 C, 861 E, 863 A, 933 E, 948 B; *and see* Boso, Louis the Blind
marquess of, 924 E
county of, 1112 E, 1167 E, 1246 A, 1480 C
Roman law in, 1149 F
troubadours of. *See* Troubadours
Proverbios (López de Mendoza), 1458 K
Provinciale (William Lyndwood), 1430 H
Provins, France, 996 A
Prüm, W. Germany, 881 E
Prussia, colonised, 1377 G; history of, 1326 K; annexed to Poland, 1454 A; (modern) kingdom of, 1473 F
Prussians, kill missionary, 997 H; defeat Poles, 1166 E; conquered and converted, 1226 E, *and see* Teutonic Knights
Przemyśl, Poland, 1018 C
Przemyslav, Prince of Greater Poland, 1290 E, 1294 E; King, 1295 B, 1296 A

Psellus, Michael, Gk. historian (1018–96), 1078 K
Psychology, in Ja. novel, 1010 K; treatise, 1277 G
Ptolemy, Gk. astronomer (*fl. c.* 150), translated, 827 G, 1160 G, 1175 G, 1478 G
Pucci, Antonio, It. poet, 1388 K
Pucelle, Jean, F. illuminator, 1327 J
Püchel von mein Geslechet (Ulman Stromer), 1407 K
Puerbach, Georg, G. mathematician (1423–61), 1461 L
Pugio fidei (Raymond Martin), 1277 H
Puiset, Hugh, Lord of Le, F. baron, 1080 E
Puiset, Hugh du, Bishop of Durham (d. 1195), 1189 D
Pulci, Bernardo, It. poet and dramatist, 1438 L, 1488 K
Pulci, Luigi, It. poet (1432–84), 1482 K
Pullus, Robert, It. canonist, 1133 G
Pulsibus, De (Giles of Corbeil), 1222 G
Punjab, India and Pakistan, Hindu kingdom, conquered by Ghaznavids, 986 E, 988 E, 1011 D; by Ghūrids, 1186 E; Mongol invasions, 1257 D, 1279 E, 1285 A, 1286 E, 1292 E, 1398 B, C; conquest, 1405 D; under Afghans, 1451 B
Pupilla Oculi (John de Burgh), 1385 H
Purbeck marble, 1179 J
Purport of Melodies (al-Qādir), 1418 J
Puy, Le, France, Bishop of, 1098 C
Pyinbya, King of Nanchao, 863 E
Pyu, Burmese kingdom, 832 E

Q

Qādir al-Jīlāni, 'Abd-al-, Per. religious reformer (1077–1166), 1166 H
Qādir ibn-Ghailī, 'Abd-al-, Per. musical theorist (d. 1435), 1405 J, 1418 J
Qādirite fraternity of Islam, 1166 H
Qā'im, Abu-al-Qāsim Muhammad al-, Caliph of Kairāwan, 934 E, 946 E
Qaisar ibn-Abī-al-Qasīm, Eg. astronomer (1178?–1251), 1225 G
Qā'it-bay, Sultan of Egypt (1468–95), 1468 E
Qalāwūn, Sayf-ad-Dīn, Sultan of Egypt, 1279 C, 1281 D, 1284 G, 1287 B, 1288 B, 1290 D
Qalqashandi, Ahmad al-, Eg. encyclopedeist, 1418 F
Qāmūs, al-(al-Firūzābādi), 1414 K
Qānūn fi al-Tibb, al- (ibn-Sīna), 1037 G, 1187 G, 1288 G
Qarmat, Hamdān, founder of Qarmatians, 890 E
Qarmatians, sect of Ismā'ites, 890 E, 899 E, 930 E, 951 E
Qatwān (Katvan) Steppe, Russia, battle, 1141 C
Qayrawān. *See* Kairāwan
Qazwini, Zakarīyya al-, Per. geographer (1203–83), 1283 G
Qiftī, Abū-al-Hasan ibn-al-, Eg. biographer (1172–1248), 1248 G
Qimhī, David, J. grammarian, 1235 K
Quadratorum, Liber (Fibonacci), 1225 G
Quadiregio (Frederigo Frezzi), 1403 K
Quadrilogue invectif (Alain Chartier), 1422 K
Quadripartitum de sinibus (Richard Wallingford), 1335 G
Quadripartitum numerorum (Jean de Meurs), 1343 G
Quaestiones (Duns Scotus), 1308 K
Quaestiones Naturales (Adelard), 1130 G
Quaestiones Octavi Libri Physicorum (Jean Buridan), 1359 G
Quarantine, 1377 G, 1383 G
Quaratesi Altarpiece (Gentile), 1425 J
Quattuor principalibus musices, De (Simon Tunsted), 1369 J
Qudāma ibn-Ja'far, Abū-l-Faraj, Arab literary critic, 948 F, K
Quedlinburg, E. Germany, 1054 E; church, 930 J
Quentovic, France, 842 E
Quercia, Jacopo della, It. sculptor, 1406 J, 1414 J, 1425 J, 1438 L
Querini, Mario, Venetian conspirator, 1310 B
Quetzacóatl, founder of Toltec Empire, 999 E
Quierz, France, 877 F
Quinque Compilationes Antiquae, 1226 H
Quintilian, *Institutio Oratorio*, 1416 K
Qutaybah, Muhammad ibn-Muslim ibn-, al-Dīnawari, Per. historian and philologist (828–89), 889 K
Qutb-ad-Dīn, atabeg of Mosul, 1170 E
Qūtīyah, ibn-al-, Sp. M. historian, 977 K
Qutuz, Sayf-ad-Dīn, Sultan of Egypt, 1259 D, 1260 D

R

Raab, river, Hungary, battle, 1044 C
Ra'bān, Syria, battle, 958 E
Rabat, Morocco, mosque, 1188 J
Rabban Sauma, monk of Peking and envoy (d. 1293), 1287 G
Rabbih, ibn-'Abd, Sp. M. musicologist, 940 J
Rabelais, François, F. satirist (1490?–1553), 1490 L
Radbertus, Paschasius, Abbot of Corbie, F. theologian, 831 H, 865 L
Radcot Bridge, England, battle, 1387 D
Radelchis, Prince of Benevento, 842 E
Radiyya, Queen of Delhi, 1236 B, 1240 B, D
Radoslav, joint king of Serbia, 1228 E
Radnald, Viking King of York (d. 921), 919 E
Ragusa. *See* Dubrovnik
Rahlat al-Kināni (ibn-Jubayr), 1185 G
Raimundus Lambardus, It. mason, 1175 J
Rainbows, treatises on, 1307 G, 1320 G
Rainulf I, Count of Poitiers, Duke of Aquitaine, 845 B
Rainulf of Alife, Duke of Apulia, 1136 E, 1138 B
Rainulf, Norman adventurer in Italy, 1030 E
Rais, Gilles de, F. noble, 1440 D
Rajāditya, Chola (Indian) prince, 949 E
Rājanighantu (Narahari), 1242 G
Rājarāja the Great, King of the Cholas (985–1016), 1016 E
Rajasanagara, King of Java, 1389 E
Rājatarangini (Kalhana), 1148 K
Rājendra III, last Chola king (1246–79), 1279 E
Rājendra-Choladeva I, King of the Cholas (1018–35), 1025 E, 1035 E
Ralf de Gael, Earl of East Anglia (d. *c.* 1100), 1075 E
Ralph de Diceto, E. chronicler (d. 1202?), 1199 K
Rama Khamheng, King of Sukhodaya (d. 1318?), 1295 E
Rāmachandra, King of Deogīr, 1307 E
Ramadhipati I, first King of Ayudhya (d. 1369), 1347 E, 1349 E, 1350 E, F
Rāmānuja, Indian philosopher, 1095 K
Rāmāyanam (or *Rāmāvatāram*; Kamban), 1200 K
Rambaldi, Benvenuto, de', It. writer on Dante (d. 1390), 1379 K
Ramiro I, King of Aragon, 1035 E, 1065 B
Ramiro II the Monk, King of Aragon, 1134 C, 1137 E
Ramiro I, King of Oviedo, 833 E, 850 E

Ramiro II, King of Leon, 927 E, 932 E, 937 E, 939 C, 952 E
Ramiro III, King of Leon (b. 962), 967 E, 982 D
Ramleh, Israel, battles, 1101 C, 1102 B, 1105 C
Ramsey, England, monk of, 1010 G
Randolph, John, Earl of Moray (d. 1346), 1332 D
Raoul, Duke of Burgundy, 921 E; King of France, 923 C, 924 E, 925 E, 931 E, 933 E, 935 E, 936 A
Raoul de Houdenc, F. poet, 1235 K
Raphael Sanzio, It. painter (1483–1520), 1483 L
Raqqah, al-, Syria, 877 G
Rasārnavasudhākara (Simhabhūpāla), 1350 K
Rascia, Serbia, 1100 E, 1169 E, 1196 E, 1217 E
Rashi. *See* Solomon ben Isaac
Rashīd-ad-Dīn, Per. physician and historian (*c.* 1247–1318), 1314 K, 1318 G, L
Rāshtrakūta, India, Hindu kingdom, 916 E, 949 E, 1156 E, 1167 E
Rationale divinorum officiorum (Durandus), 1286 H
Rationarium vite (Giovanni da Ravenna), 1408 K
Ratisbon. *See* Regensburg
Ravenna, Italy, 1014 A, 1231 D, 1240 C, 1289 G, 1441 A; Archbishops of, 863 H; *Lives of* (Agnellus), 840 K
Ravenna, Giovanni da, It. humanist-educationalist and autobiographer, 1408 K
Ravenspur, England, 1399 C
Ray (*now* Shahr Rey), Persia, ceramics industry, 1220 J; observatory, 994 G, 1074 G
Raymond of Poitiers, Prince of Antioch, 1137 E, 1142 C, 1148 D, 1149 B
Raymond IV, Count of Toulouse, crusader, 1095 D, 1101 B, C, 1105 A
Raymond VI, Count of Toulouse, 1209 B, 1213 C, 1218 C, 1219 B, 1222 C
Raymond VII, Count of Toulouse, 1219 B, 1222 C, 1225 A, 1226 A, D, 1229 B, 1242 B, C, 1243 A, 1249 C
Raymond, Archbishop of Toledo (d. 1149), 1125 K
Raymond of Marseilles, F. astronomer, 1140 G
Raymond-Berengar I, Count of Barcelona, 1064 F
Raymond-Berengar II, Count of Barcelona, 1090 E, 1091 E
Raymond-Berengar III, Count of Barcelona and Provence, 1112 E, 1113 E, 1115 E
Raymond-Berengar IV, Count of Barcelona, 1137 E, 1148 E, 1162 C
Raymond-Berengar II, Count of Provence, 1167 E
Raymond-Berengar IV, Count of Provence (1198–1245), 1246 A
Raymond-Roupen, King of Armenia, 1220 E
Rāzī (Rhazes), Abu-Bakr Muhammad ibn-Zakariyā' al-, Per. physician and alchemist (*c.* 865-925), 925 G, 1187 G, 1279 G, 1486 G
Razón feita de amor, La, 1225 K
Reading, England, 871 A, 1191 D
Reali di Francia, I (Andrea da Barberino), 1430 K
Realist philosophy, 1121 H
Receptae super nonum Almansoris (Pietro de Tossignano), 1398 G
Rechtsbuch (Ruprecht von Freising), 1328 F
Rectoribus Christianis, De (Sedulius Scottus), 848 K
Recuperatione terrae sanctae, De (Pierre Dubois), 1306 F
Recuyell of the Histories of Troye (William Caxton), 1474 K
'Redesdale, Robin of', E. rebel, 1469 B
Regensburg, Germany, 1156 C, 1158 A, 1189 B, 1274 E; Bishopric, 895 H, 973 E; Cathedral, 1272 J; church, 1020 J
Reggio, Italy, 1289 E, 1306 A
Reggio di Calabria, Italy, naval battle, 1006 E
Règime du corps, Le (Aldobrandon of Siena), 1257 G
Règime of a Solitary (ibn-Bājjah), 1138 K
Regimine principum, De (Giles of Rome), 1285 F; (Thomas Hoccleve), 1411 K; (Aquinas), 1274 F
Reginald, Prior of Canterbury, 1205 C
Reginar, Duke of Lorraine, 908 E
Regino of Prüm, G. canonist, chronicler and musical theorist, 906 F, 915 J, K
Regiomontaus (Johannes Muller), Bishop of Regensburg, G. mathematician and astronomer, 1436 L, 1474 G, 1475 G, L
Régnier, Jean, F. poet, 1468 K
Regularis concordia (St. Ethelwold), 970 H, 972 H
Regulis juris, De (Bulgarus), 1166 F
Regulis veteris et novi testamenti, De (Matthias of Janov), 1394 H
Reichenau, is., W. Germany, Minister, 819 J; abbot of, *see* Walafrid Strabo; monk of, *see* Hermann Contractus
Reims, France, 882 D, 937 E, 1049 H, 1119 E, 1148 H, 1359 D, 1360 A, 1429 C; Archbishops of, 940 F, *and see* Hincmar, Fulk, Hervé, Seulf, Hugh of Vermandois, Artaud, Adalbero, Arnulf, Silvester II; disputed election of, 948 B; Cathedral, 862 J, 1210 J, 1241 J; St. Remi's abbey, 1005 J, 1049 J, 1170 J; *History of the Church of Reims* (Flodoard), 966 K; *Recits d'un Menestrel de Reims*, 1260 K
Relatio de Standardo (Ailred), 1166 K
Relatio de legatione Constantinopolitana (Liutprand), 968 K
Relaxation of the Carmelite Rule (Filippo Lippi), 1432 J
Religion, comparative, 1064 H
Religion, The Revivification of the Sciences of (al-Ghazzāli), 1111 H
Religions and Sects, Book of (al-Shahrastānī), 1128 H
Religious movements, Christian. *See* Beghards; Béguins; Bohemia (Brethren); Capuciati; Flagellants; Milan (Patarines); Mystics; penitentiary, 1233 H; Waldenses. *See also* Buddhism; Islam
Religious Orders. *See* Augustinian; Benedictine; Brigittine; Camaldoli; Carthusian; Cistercian; Cluny; Fontevrault; Grandmont; Molesme; Premonstratensian; Reformed Communities, *viz.* Bursfeld, Melk, Padua; Savigny; Sempringham; Thiron; Vallombrosa
See also Monasteries
Remedia contra maleficia (Arnold of Villanova), 1311 G
Remi, St., Archbishop of Lyons, 875 L
Renaud de Beaujeu, F. poet, 1220 K
Réné II the Good, Duke of Anjou, etc., titular King of Jerusalem, Sicily, etc. (1409–1480), 1409 L, 1434 D, 1437 B, 1442 B, 1444 B, 1480 C; as author, 1460 K, 1480 K, L
Réné II, Duke of Upper Lorraine (b. 1451; d. 1508), 1473 D, 1476 B, 1486 B
Renfrew, Scotland, battle, 1164 E
Rennes, France, Bishop of, 1123 G
Rense, W. Germany, Declaration of, 1338 C
Repertorium aureum juris (Durandus), 1296 H
Repertorium utriuque juris (Pietro da Monte), 1457 H
Repkowe, Eike von, G. jurist (d. *c.* 1230), 1225 F
Repressor of Over Much Blaming of the Clergy (Reginald Pecock), 1455 H
Resby, John, Scottish Wycliffite, 1408 H
Resurrection (Piero della Francesca), 1470 J
Retra, Poland, 1124 E
Rettorica in volgar Fiorentino (Brunetto Latini), 1295 K
Reuchlin, Johann, G. Hebrew scholar and humanist (1455–1522) 1455 L
Reutlingen, W. Germany, battle, 1377 B

Revel, Esthonia, Russia, 1218 E
Revelations of Divine Love (Juliana of Norwich), 1413 H
Reynald of Châtillon, Prince of Antioch, 1156 B, 1158 D, 1159 B, 1160 D, 1182 E, 1187 C
Reynard the Fox, 1110 K
Reynard the Fox (Caxton), 1481 K
Rhazes. *See* Rāzī
Rhé, is., France, 821 E
Rhein, Poland, 1377 G
Rhine, Palatinate of, *see* Palatinate; towns of, Leagues of, 1226 D, 1254 C, D, 1257 E, 1381 C, 1384 C, 1385 A, 1388 D, 1389 B
Rhodes, is., Greece, 1204 D, 1248 E; under Hospitallers, 1306 D, 1308 C, 1480 B, C
Rhodri the Great, King of Gwynned, Powys and Seisyllwg, 878 E
Rhuddlan, Wales, Statute of, 1284 F
Rhyndacus, river, Turkey, battle, 1211 D
Rhys ap Tewdwr, King of Deheubarth, 1093 B
'Riade', E. Germany, battle, 933 A
Riazan, Russia, 1237 D
Ribe, Denmark, Bishopric, 948 H
Ribemont, France, Treaty of, 880 A
Rice, 1012 G, 1108 G
Rich, St. Edmund, Archbishop of Canterbury, 1240 L
Richard I Coeur de Lion, King of England (1189–1199), 1157 L, 1189 C, 1194 B, 1196 K, 1199 B
  Duke of Aquitaine, 1175 E, 1181 E, 1188 D, 1189 C
  on Crusade, 1189 D, 1190 C, D, 1191 A–C, 1192 A–C
  captured, 1192 D, 1193 A, B, 1194 A
  government in absence, 1189 D, 1190 D, 1191 D, 1194 F
  war against France, 1193 C, 1194 C, 1196 A, C, E, 1197 J, 1198 C, 1199 A
  as poet, 1199 K
  chronicle of, 1192 K
Richard II, King of England (b. 1367; 1377–99), 1377 B, 1380 A, 1390 F, 1397 J, 1400 A
  relations with France, 1378 B, C, 1391 A, 1396 A, D, 1397 B
  recognises Urban VI, 1378 D, 1381 C, 1383 B
  Peasants' Revolt, 1381 B
  marries Anne of Bohemia, 1382 A, 1394 B
  relations with Portugal, 1382 C, 1385 C, 1386 B
  war with Scotland, 1384 A, B, 1385 C
  disputes with magnates, 1386 D, 1387 C, D, 1388 A, 1389 B, 1397 D, 1398 A, C, 1399 A
  Irish expeditions, 1394 D, 1395 B, 1399 B
  deposed, 1399 C
Richard III, King of England (b. 1452; 1483–5), 1483 B, D, 1484 C, F, 1485 C; as Duke of Gloucester, 1482 C
Richard, King of the Romans (1257–72), 1209 L, 1257 A, 1259 A, 1262 C, 1269 B, 1272 B; as Earl of Cornwall, 1225 A, 1271 A
Richard the Justiciar, Count of Autun, 882 C; Duke of Burgundy, 877 F, 898 E, 915 E, 921 E
Richard I the Fearless, Duke of Normandy, 942 D, 996 E
Richard II the Good, Duke of Normandy, 996 E, 1026 E
Richard III, Duke of Normandy, 1026 E, 1027 E
Richard, Duke of York (b. 1411), 1437 A, 1450 C, 1452 A, 1454 A, D; captures Henry VI, 1455 B, D, 1456 A; reconciled with enemies, 1458 A; in revolt, 1459 D, 1460 D
Richard, Duke of York (b. 1473), 1483 B
Richard of Devizes, E. Chronicler, 1192 K
Richard fitz Nigel, Bishop of London and writer on Exchequer, 1179 F
Richard of St. Vannes, F. church reformer, 1046 H
Richard of Wendover, E. physician, 1252 G
Richemont, France, Arthur, Count of, 1427 E
Richer, monk of Reims, F. chronicler, 997 K
Richeut, 1170 K
Richsa, Queen and Regent of Poland, 1040 C
Rida, 'Ali al-, Per. leader of Shias, 817 C, 818 E
Ridwān, Seljuq ruler of Aleppo (d. 1113), 1095 E
Rienzo, Cola di, Tribune and Senator of Rome, 1313 L, 1347 B, D, 1354 C, D
Rievaulx, England, abbot of. *See* Ailred
Riga, Latvia, Russia, 1201 E, 1282 G, 1330 E; Bishop of, *see* Albert
Rijmkroniek (Melis Stoke), 1305 K
Rikkokushi (Ja. histories), 887 K
Rime, Le (Petrarch), 1341 K
Rime in vita e morte di Madonna Laura (Petrarch), 1366 K
Rimini, Italy, church, 1450 J; lords of, *see* Malatesta
Rinio, Benedetto, It. botanist, 1410 G
Riom, France, castle, 1385 J
Ripoll, Spain, abbey, 977 J, 1032 J
Ripon, England, 1318 B
Risalah (*The Apology of al-Kindi*), 1141 K
Risālat al-Ghufrān (al-Ma'arri), 1058 K
Risālat al-Sharafīya (Safī), 1294 B
Ristoro d'Arezzo, It. geologist, 1282 G
Riurik of Jutland, first Prince of Novgorod (d. 873 ?), 862 E
Riva, Italy, battle, 1439 D
Rivalto, Giordano de, It. prose writer, 1311 K
Rivaux, Peter des, E. civil servant, 1232 C, 1234 B
Road of Life (Moses ben Joshua), 1350 G
Robbia, Andrea della, It. sculptor (1435–1525), 1435 L, 1463 J
Robbia, Luca della, It. sculptor, 1400 L, 1431 J, 1464 J, 1482 L
Robert de Courtenay, Emperor of Constantinople, 1221 A, 1228 E
Robert (I), Marquess of Neustria, 921 E; King of France, 922 B, C, 923 B
Robert (II) the Pious, King of France (996–1031), 987 D, 996 D, 1006 C, 1010 F, 1015 E, 1022 C, 1031 C
Robert I Bruce, King of Scotland (1306–29), 1274 L, 1306 A–C, 1317 A, 1320 B, 1326 F, 1329 B; expels English, 1307 B, D, 1308 E, 1314 B, 1318 A; raids England, 1318 A, 1322 C, D, 1323 A, E, 1328 A, B; life (Barbour), 1373 K
Robert II Stewart, King of Scotland (b. 1316), 1371 A, 1390 B
Robert III, King of Scotland (b. *c.* 1337), 1390 B, E, 1406 B
Robert the Wise, King of Sicily (*i.e.* Naples; 1309–43), 1309 B, 1315 E, 1317 J, 1343 A
  operations in Tuscany, 1311 E, 1315 C, 1317 E, 1322 E, 1325 C, D
  opposes Henry VII, 1312 B, 1313 B, C
  vicar of Ferrara, 1310 B, 1317 C
  relieves Genoa, 1318 C
  lord of Brescia, 1319 A
Robert (Capet), Duke of Burgundy, 1032 E
Robert I the Frisian, Count of Flanders (1071–93), 1085 C, 1090 E, 1093 D
Robert III of Béthune, Count of Flanders, 1305 A, B, 1312 E, 1320 B, 1322 C
Robert IV of Cassel, Count of Flanders, 1323 B, 1328 C
Robert, Earl of Gloucester (b. *c.* 1090), 1138 B, 1141, A, D, 1147 D
Robert the Strong, Marquess of Neustria, 866 E; son, 885 D

Robert I the Devil, Duke of Normandy, 1027 E, 1035 C
Robert II Curthose, Duke of Normandy (b. *c.* 1052; 1087–1106), 1077 E, 1079 A, 1087 C, 1088 B, 1091 E, 1096 E, 1101 C, 1106 C, 1117 E, 1134 L
Robert of Bellême, Earl of Shrewsbury (d. 1113), 1102 E, 1112 E
Robert of Artois, F. noble, 1332 B, 1336 E, 1342 L
Robert de Borron, F. poet, 1214 K
Robert de Bougre, F. inquisitor, 1235 H
Robert of Chester, E. translator and astronomer, 1143 H, 1144 G, 1145 G, 1149 G
Robert the Englishman, astronomer, 1271 G
Robert of Geneva. *See* Clement VII
Robert de Luzarches, F. mason (d. *c.* 1236), 1220 J
Robert, St., Abbot of Molesme, founder of Cîteaux (1028–1111), 1075 H, 1098 H
Robert of Torigny, Anglo-Norman chronicler, 1186 K
Roberti, Ercole d'Antonio de', It. painter (*c.* 1452–96), 1480 J
Roccasecca, Italy, battle, 1411 B
Roccavione, Italy, battle, 1275 D
Roche, Adroin de la, Abbot of Cluny and legate, 1357 B
Roche, Otto de la, lord of Athens, 1204 D
Rochelle, La, France, naval battle, 1372 B
Rochester, England, castle, 1215 D; Cathedral, 1077 J
Rockingham, England, 1095 A
Roda, Spain, abbey, 958 J
Roderigo Jiménez de Rada, Archbishop of Toledo, Sp. historian (*c.* 1175–1248), 1248 K
Rodolph I of Auxerre, King of Burgundy, 888 A, D, 895 E, 911 D
Rodolph II, King of Burgundy, 911 D, 919 E, 924 E, 933 E, 937 C; King of Italy, 922 A, 923 C, 926 B
Rodolph III, King of Burgundy, 993 E, 1016 B, 1032 C
Rodriguez de la Cámara, Sp. novelist (1405?–1445?), 1430 K
Roeskild, Denmark, Treaty of, 1157 B
Roger I Guiscard, Great Count of Sicily (1085–1101), 1031 L, 1061 C, 1085 C, 1090 E, 1091 E, 1101 B
Roger II, King of Sicily (1130–54), 1097 L, 1130 C, D, 1147 G, 1154 A
  Count of Sicily, 1103 E, 1118 E
  Duke of Apulia, 1127 C, 1128 C
  revolt against, 1132 C, 1133 E
  attacked by Emperor, 1136 E
  war with Pope, 1138 A, 1139 B, C, 1144 D
  African conquests, 1146 E, 1153 E
  invades Greek Empire, 1147 E, 1148 C, E, 1149 C
  plots in Germany, 1150 A
  Book of (al-Edrisi), 1154 G
Roger Borsa, Duke of Apulia, 1085 C, 1111 A
Roger of Caen, Bishop of Salisbury (d. 1139), 1139 B
Roger FitzOsbern, Earl of Hereford, 1075 E
Roger of Hereford, E. astronomer, 1178 G
Roger of Hoveden, E. chronicler, 1201 K
Roger of Salerno, It. surgeon, 1170 G
Roger of Wendover, E. chronicler, 1237 K, L
Rokycana, John of, Hussite Archbishop of Prague, 1471 L
Roland, The Song of, 1095 K, 1150 K
Rolle, Richard, E. mystic poet, 1349 K, L
Rollo, Duke of Normandy, 911 E, 924 E, 931 E
Roma instaurata and *Roma triumphans* (Flavio Biondi), 1463 K
Romagna, Italy, 1278 B
Roman, Prince of Halich, 1205 E
Roman des fils du roi Constant (Bauduin Butors), 1294 K
Roman de Godefroi Bouillon, 1225 K
Roman de Troie (Benoît de Sainte-Maure), 1160 K
Roman de la Rose (Guillaume de Lorris), 1237 K; (Jean de Meun), 1305 K
Roman de la Violette (Gerbert de Violette), 1228 K
Roman History (Nicephorus Gregoras), 1359 K
Romanesque. *See* Architecture
Romania. *See* Greece
Romans de gestes. *See* Chansons de gestes
Romans, King of the. *See* Germany
Romanus, Pope, 897 C, D
Romanus I Lecapenus, Greek Emperor (d. 948), 920 D, 927 B, 944 D
Romanus II, Greek Emperor (959–63), 939 L, 959 D, 963A, 976 A
Romanus III, Greek Emperor, 1028 E, 1034 B
Romanus IV Diogenes, Greek Emperor, 1068 A, 1071 C, D
Rome, Italy:
  Charlemagne in, 800 D
  Saracen attacks, 846 C, 849 E
  fortified, 847 B
  revolts against Pope, 896 A, 897 C
  ruled by Duke Alberie, 932 E, 954 C, 955 D
  ruled by Crescenzi, 974 B, 996 C, 998 B, 1003 B, 1012 A
  Otto III in, 1000 E, 1001 A
  anti-German riot, 1014 A
  revolts against Pope, 1044 E, 1058 A
  attacked by Henry IV, 1081 B, 1083 B, 1084 A
  sacked by Normans, 1084 B
  recovered by Urban II, 1094 E
  anti-popes elected by, 1100 C, 1102 A
  Henry V in, 1117 A, 1118 A
  republic established, 1143 C, 1155 A
  anti-German riot, 1155 B
  Pope restored, 1165 D
  Frederick I in, 1167 B, C
  Tusculum razed by, 1191 B
  Pope expelled, 1234 E
  attacked by Frederick II, 1240 A
  general council called to, 1241 B
  republic established, 1252 E, 1253 D, 1255 D, 1257 B, 1259 E
  new anti-papal rising, 1267 B
  Charles of Anjou Senator of, 1268 B, 1278 B, 1281 A; expelled, 1284 A
  Henry VII in, 1312 B
  republic, and Lewis IV, 1328 A
  coronation of Petrarch as laureate, 1341 K
  under Cola di Rienzo, 1347 B, D, 1354 C, D
  under Giovanni di Vico, 1354 B
  Charles IV in, 1355 A, 1368 D
  Papacy restored to, 1367 D, 1370 C, 1377 A
  taken by Naples, 1408 B, 1413 B, 1417 C
  General Council in, 1413 H
  Papacy restored, 1420 C
  expelled by revolt, 1434 B, 1443 C
  republican conspiracy, 1453 A
  chief scholar, 897 K
  churches:
    Sta. Anastasia (basilica), 800 J
    Sta. Cecilia (basilica), mosaics, 817 J
    S. Clemente (basilica), 1100 J
    S. Giovanni in Lateran (basilica), 904 J; frescoes, 1431 J; councils in, 1059 B; General Councils, 1123 H, 1139 H, 1179 A, H, 1215 H
    S. Marco (basilica), mosaics, 827 J
    Sta. Maria in Domnica (basilica), mosaics, 817 J
    Sta. Maria in Trastavere (basilica), mosaics, 1145 J

Sta. Maria Sopra Minerva, 1280 J; frescoes, 1488 J
Sta. Prassede (basilica), mosaics, 817 J
S. Stefano degli Abessini (basilica), 815 J
University, 1303 H
Vatican, frescoes in chapel, 1446 J; Library, 1450 J; St. Peter's, 1450 J; Sistine Chapel, 1473 J, 1481 J
Romuald, St., It. monastic reformer, 1012 H, 1027 L
Romuald of Salerno, It. chronicler, 1181 K
Roncaglia, Italy, 1158 D
Roosebeke, Belgium, battle, 1382 D
Rōs, the, 850 E
Rosa anglica or *Medicinae* (John of Gaddesden), 1315 G
Roscelin, F. heretical theologian and philosopher (d. *c.* 1125), 1092 H
Rose-Garden, The (Sādi), 1258 K
'Roses, Wars of the'. *See* England (1450–87)
Rosillo, Italy, battle, 1361 B
Rostislav, Prince of Moravia, 846 E, 862 H, 870 E
Rostislav I, Prince of Kiev, 1159 E, 1167 E
Rostock, E. Germany, 1259 G; University, 1419 H
Roswitha. *See* Hrotswith
Rota, papal court, 1331 H
Rothad, Bishop of Soissons, 865 A
Rotrouenge (Richard I), 1199 K
Rouen, France, 840 E, 885 C, 911 E, 924 E, 944 E, 1144 B, 1204 B, 1382 A; held by English, 1418 C, 1419 A, 1431 B, 1449 D; Archbishop of, 1191 D; Cathedral, 1037 J, 1200 J, 1281 J, 1400 J; churches, 1318 J, 1434 J
Roulandesliet (Pfaffe Konrad), 1150 K
Round Table, The. *See* Arthurian Legends
Roupen I, first ruler of Lesser Armenia, 1080 E
Roupen II, Prince of Armenia (d. 1186), 1168 E
Rous, John, E. antiquary, 1491 K
Roussillon, France, County, 1217 E, 1462 B, 1463 A, 1473 A, 1475 A
Rouvray, France, battle, 1429 A
Rovine, Yugoslavia, battle, 1395 B
Roxburgh, Scotland, 1335 B, 1342 A, 1436 C, 1460 C
Rubaiyat (al-Khayyām), 1123 K
Rucellai Madonna (Duccio?), 1285 J
Rūdakī, Per. poet, 954 K
Rudau, Lithuania, Russia, battle, 1370 A
Rudel de Blaya, Jaufre, Provençal poet, 1150 K
Rudimenta grammatices (Niccolò Perotti), 1473 K
Rudolf I, Count of Habsburg, King of the Romans (b. 1218; 1273–91), 1268 B, 1273 D, 1274 C, 1278 B, 1279 A, 1285 C, 1291 C; war with Bohemia, 1276 D, 1278 C; promotes sons, 1282 D, 1290 C
Rudolf of Habsburg, King of Bohemia, 1305 D, 1307 C
Rudolf, Duke of Swabia (d. 1080), 1077 A, 1078 C, 1079 E, 1080 A, D, 1081 C
Rudolf of Ems, G. Chronicler, 1254 K
Rudolf of Strasbourg, G. mason, 1275 J
Rudrāmbā, Queen of Kākatīya (d. 1295), 1262 E
Rudravarman III, King of Champa (d. 1074), 1068 E
Rufinus, It. canonist, 1165 H
Ruiz, Juan, archpriest of Hita, Sp. poet (1283?–1350?), 1343 K
Rūjarī, al-Kitāb al- (*al-Edrisi*), 1154 G
Rūkh, Shāh, ruler of Transoxiana, 1405 A, 1414 B, 1443 K, 1447 E
Rule of a Recluse (Ailred of Rievaulx), 1166 H
Rūm, Turkey, Seljuq Sultanate. *See*
Sulaymān (1077–86)
Kilij Arslan I (1086–1107)
Malik Shāh (1107–17)
Ma'sūd I (1117–56)
Kilij Arslan II (1156–88)
Kaykhusraw I (1204–10)
Kaykavus I (1210–19)
Kayqubād I (1219–37)
Kaykhusraw II (1237–46)
partitioned, 1188 E
declines, 1237 E
under Mongols, 1277 B, 1299 B, 1307 E
conquered by Karaman Turks, 1328 E
conquered by Ottomans, 1394 E
Timur in, 1395 E
capitals. *See* Nicaea; Konya
Rūmī, Jalāl-ad-Dīn Muhammed al-, Per. Sūfī poet (1207–73), 1273 H, K
Rupert I, Elector Palatine (d. 1390), 1388 D
Rupert III, Elector Palatine, King of the Romans (b. 1352), 1400 C, 1401 D, 1405 C, 1410 B
Rupescissa, John of, Catalan alchemist, 1360 G
Ruralia Commoda (Pietro dei Crescenzi), 1307 G
Rusadan, Queen of Georgia (1223–47), 1223 E, 1231 C, 1243 B
Rushd (Averroes), Abū'l-Walīd ibn-, Sp. M. philosopher and physician (1126–98), 1126 L, 1160 G, 1198 K, L, 1220 K, 1255 G, 1256 K, 1272 K, 1277 H, 1323 K, 1346 H, 1482 G
Russia (European):
origin of name, 850 E
Viking empire. *See* Kiev
conversion of, 874 H, 955 E, 959 E, 961 H, 990 H
Bulgars in, 921 G
Red Russia won from Poland, 981 E, 1031 E, 1069 E
assist Polish dukes, 1047 E, 1076 D
Cumans in, 1061 E, 1068 E, 1097 E, 1111 E, 1185 K
presented to Pope, 1077 E
princes regulate inheritance, 1097 E
Polish invasions, 1138 E, 1169 E
federation disintegrates, 1139 E
primacy of Kiev ends, 1169 A. *And see* Vladimir
Mongol conquest, 1222 B*
Golden Horde, organised (the 'Tartar Yoke'), 1242 B. *And see*
Batu (1227–55)
Sartak (1255–6)
Ulagchi (1256–8)
Berke (1258–66)
Mangu-Temir (1266–80)
Tuda-Mangu (1280–7)
Tele-Buga (1287–91)
Tokhta (1291–1312)
Uzbeg (1312–41)
Tinibeg (1341–2)
Janibeg (1342–57)
Berdibeg (1357–9)
Kulpa (1359–60)
Nevruz (1360–1)
Tokhtamysh (1381–97)
Timur-Kutlugh (1397–1400)
Shadibeg (1400–7)
Bulat-Saltan (1407–10)
Timur-Khan (1410–11)
Jalāl-ad-Dīn (1412)
Ulug Mahmed (1419–45)
Mahmudek (1445–65)
Ahmad (1465–81)
tribute paid to, 1239 E, 1266 H
appoints Russian princes, 1247 E, 1252 E, *and see* Vladimir

* Entries for Christian Russia continue after Golden Horde.

Russia (European)—*contd.*
Golden Horde—*contd.*
ravages Poland, 1259 E
separate horde of Nogay (1273–99), *q.v.*
converted to Islam, 1312 E
defeated in Poland, 1344 E
Black Death in, 1346 G
disintegrates, 1361 E
defeated by Lithuania, 1363 E, 1377 E
and by Russians, 1378 E, 1380 C
reunited, 1381 E
recovers control of Russia, 1382 C, 1408 D
ravaged by Timur, 1395 C
ruled by Egidey, *q.v.*
disintegrates, invaded by Lithuania, 1397 E, 1399 C, 1406 E, 1408 C, 1411 E, 1412 E
satellite Khanate of Kasimov, 1452 E
loses control of Russia, 1462 A, 1476 E, 1481 E
defeated by Poles and Lithuanians, 1491 A
(Christian Russia *contd.*)
Moscow becomes capital, 1332 E, *and see* Moscow
Black Death in, 1352 G
Church, Orthodox, of, 990 H, 1266 H, 1326 H, 1461 H
German trade in, 1199 G, 1229 G, *and see* Novgorod
histories, 1110 K, 1118 K, 1199 K, 1448 K
literature:
Daniel of Kiev, 1107 G
Vladimir Monomach, 1125 K
The Campaign of Igor, 1185 K
Petition of Daniil Zatochnik, 1225 K
Zadonschchina, 1380 K
travellers in, 921 G, 1136 G
Rustah, ibn-, Per. geographer, 903 G
Rustaveli, Shota, Georgian poet, 1200 K
Rustico di Filippo, It. poet, 1280 K
Ruthenia, Russia, 1324 E
Ruybroek, William of, Flemish friar and missionary, 1253 E, G
Ruysbroeck, Jan, Flemish mystic, 1293 L, 1381 H
Ryo no gige, 833 F

S

Saadi ben Joseph. *See* Fayyūmi
Saaz, Czechoslovakia, battle, 1421 D
Sabbato, river, Italy, battle, 1133 E
Sabdapradīpa (Sureśvara), 1075 G
Sab'in, ibn-, Sp. M. philosopher and musical theorist, 1269 J
Sablé, France, Treaty of, 1488 C
Sabuktagīn, Sultan of Ghaznī (976–97), 986 E, 988 E, 994 E, 998 E
Sābūr ben Sahl, Per. pharmacologist, 869 G
Sacchetti, Franco, It. poet and short story writer (*c.* 1330–*c.* 1400), 1395 K
Sachsenhausen, W. Germany, Appeal of, 1324 B
Sachsenspiegel (Eike von Repkowe), 1225 F
Sächsische Weltchronik, 1237 K
Sacramentis Christiane Fidei, De (Hugh of St. Victor), 1141 H
Sacramento corporis et sanguinis domini nostri, De (Radbertus), 831 H
Sadaie. *See* Fujiwara Teika
Sa'd al-Musta'īn, King of Granada, 1445 E, 1446 E, 1454 E, 1462 E
Sa'dī, Muslih-ad-Dīn, Per. poet (1194–1291), 1258 K
Saemundarson, Nikulas, Icelandic pilgrim-author, 1158 G
Saewulf, monk of Malmesbury, E. pilgrim-author, 1104 G
Safadi, Khalīl ibn-Aibak al-, Arab biographer (*c.* 1297–1363), 1363 K
Safar-nāma (Khusraw), 1088 G
Safawi dynasty of Persia, 1405 A
Safed, Israel, castle, 1266 C
Sãffar, Ya'qūb ibn-al-Layth al-, Governor of Sijistān, 867 E, 872 E
Saffãrid dynasty. *See* Sijistān
Safī-ad-Dīn, Arab musical theorist, 1294 J
Sagas, Norse and Icelandic, 1120 K, 1148 K, 1200 K, 1220 K, 1222 K, 1225 K, 1284 K; German, 1450 K
Sāghānī, Abū Hāmid al-, Arab astronomer and instrument maker, 990 G
Sagrez, Portugal, 1419 G
Sague, Abyssinian Jewess, 925 E
Sahīh, al- (al-Bukhārī). 870 H; (ibn-al-Hajjāj), 874 H
Saichō, Ja. Buddhist reformer (767–822), 805 H
Sa'īd ibn-Husayn. *See* 'Ubaydullāh
Saigyō, Ja. poet (1118–90), 1190 K
St. Albans, England, abbey, 1077 J; chronicles of, 1422 K; clock in, 1326 F; *Registrum* of, 1465 K; battles at, 1455 B, 1458 A, 1461 A
St. Andrews, Scotland, 1304 A; University, 1413 H; college, 1450 H
Saint Aubin du Cormier, France, battle, 1488 C
St. Barbara (Jan van Eyck), 1437 J
St. Benoît sur Loire, France, Treaty of, 845 B; *and see* Fleury
St. Bertin, France, 1095 G
St. Brieuc, France, battle, 937 E
St. Christopher Triptych (Hans Memling), 1485 J
St. Clair-sur-Epte, France, 911 E
St. Cloud, France, battle, 1411 D
St. Denis. *See* Paris
St. Erasmus (Dieric Bouts), 1458 J
St. Gallen, Switzerland, abbey, 820 J, 830 J, 937 J, 1416 K; chronicle of, 1036 K; monks of, *see* Ekkehard, Notker
St. George (Donatello), 1416 J
St. George and the Princess (Pisanello), 1437 J
St. Gothard Pass, Switzerland, 1140 G, 1231 B
St. Jakob on the Birs, Switzerland, battle, 1444 C
St. Jerome (Piero della Francesca), 1450 J; (Ghirlandaio), 1480 J
St. Job (Giovanni Bellini), 1488 J
St. John (Cimabue), 1302 J
St. John the Baptist (Ghiberti), 1414 J
St. John the Evangelist (Donatello), 1413 J
St. John of Jerusalem, Knights of. *See* Hospitallers
S. Juan de la Peña, Spain, abbey, 1094 J
St. Lucy Altarpiece (Domenico Veneziano), 1445 J
Sainte-Mahé, France, naval battle, 1293 B
St. Malo, France, 1378 C
St. Mamede, Portugal, battle, 1128 E
St. Mark (Donatello), 1411 J
St. Martin-du-Canigou, France, abbey, 1001 J
St. Matthew (Ghiberti), 1419 J
S. Miguel de la Escalada, Spain, abbey, 912 J
St. Michael, (French) Order of, 1469 C
St. Omer, France, 1048 G, 1127 G; Treaty of, 1469 B
Saint-Pol, France, Count of, 1475 D
St. Quentin, France, 1047 G, 1213 B
St. Remi. *See* Reims
St. Riquier. *See* Centula
Saint-Sardos, France, 'war of', 1324 C, 1327 A
St. Sauvère de Vicomte, France, 1180 G
St. Sebastian (Mantegna), 1460 J
St. Stephen (Ghiberti), 1428 J
St. Ursula (Giovanni Bellini), 1450 J; *Shrine of* (Hans Memling), 1489 J

Saint-Vaast de la Hougue, France, 1346 C
Saintes, France, battle, 1242 C
Saints:
Ælfric, *Lives*, 995 K
St. Alban, 1259 K
Legenda Aurea, 1265 K, 1483 K
La Vie de Saint Louis, 1309 K
St. Francis, 1225 K, 1330 K
Filippo della Gazzaio, *Assempri*, 1422 K
See also Vida; *Vie*; *Vita*
Saiset, Bernard, Bishop of Pamiers, 1301 D
Salade, La (Antoine de la Salle), 1462 K
Saladin (Salāh-ad-Dīn), Sultan of Egypt and Syria (1175–93), 1138 L, 1167 C, 1173 E, 1175 B, 1176 J, 1188 G, 1193 A, 1196 E
vizir of Egypt, 1169 A, 1171 C, 1174 B
conquers Syria, 1174 D, 1176 B, 1182 D, 1183 B, C
war against Jerusalem, 1177 D, 1179 B, 1182 C, 1187 C, D, 1188 C
Crusade against, 1188 A, 1189 D, 1191 C, 1192 C
Salado, river, Spain, battle, 1340 D
Salamanca, Spain, 862 E; Cathedral, 1152 J; University, 1220 H, 1311 H
Salamia, Syria, battle, 1299 D
Salāmish, Badr-ad-Dīn, Sultan of Egypt (b. 1270), 1279 C
Salatgi, India, college, 945 H
Saleph (*now* Göksu), river, Turkey, 1190 B
Salerno, Italy, 871 A, 1085 B, 1191 C, 1192 E, 1194 C; Cathedral, 1084 J; Lombard princes of, 839 E, 842 E, 981 A, 1038 E, 1077 E; University, medical school, 1035 G, 1050 G, 1100 G, 1103 G, 1110 G, 1161 G, 1170 G, 1214 G, 1231 G
Salian dynasty. *See* Germany
Saliceto, William of, It. surgeon (*c.* 1210–*c.* 1280), 1275 G
Salimbene of Parma, It. chronicler (*c.* 1221–*c.* 1288), 1287 K
Salisbury, England, 1086 C, 1297 A; Bishops of, *see* Osmund, Roger of Caen; Cathedral, 1220 J, 1258 J, 1330 J; Earls of, *see* Montague (John), Neville (Richard); Treaty of, 1289 D; University, 1238 H
Salle, Antoine de la, F. writer (*c.* 1398–1470), 1462 K
Salnitsa, river, Russia, battle, 1111 E
Salome (Donatello), 1427 J
Salonika, Greece, 904 C, 1185 C, 1246 D, 1394 B, 1423 E, 1430 A; churches (with mosaics), 886 J, 1028 J, 1312 J; Latin kingdom of Thessalonica, 1207 C, 1224 E
Salt, *gabelle* (tax) on, 1286 G, 1341 F
Salutati, Coluccio, It. humanist (1331–1406), 1375 K, 1400 F, 1406 L
Sāluva Narasimha, King of Vijayanagar (d. 1491), 1486 E
Saluzzo, Italy, 1363 E; Thomas, marquess of, 1275 D
Salvio, Domenico, Doge of Venice, 1071 E, 1084 E
Salza, Hermann de, Grand Master of Teutonic Knights, 1210 E, 1230 E, 1239 A
Salzburg, Austria, *scriptorium* at, 821 J
Sāmānid dynasty. *See* Transoxiana
Samarqand, Russia, capital of Transoxiana, 809 A, 1016 E, 1369 E, 1437 G, 1469 E; battle, 1141 C; Rigistān, 1405 J
Sāmarra, Iraq, 836 E; mosque, 847 J
Sambians, Prussian tribe, 1263 E
Samguk sagi (Kim Pu-sik), 1145 K
Samogitia, Lithuania, Russia, 1411 A, 1435 E
Samudra, Sumatra, Indonesia, 1297 E
Samuel, Tsar of Bulgaria, 976 A, 987 E, 997 E, 998 E, 1003 B, 1014 D
Samuel ben Tibbon, Provençal J. translator, 1232 K
San Felice, Italy, battle, 1332 D
San Giovanni e San Paolo (Lorenzo de'Medici), 1489 K
San Kuo (Lo Kuan-Chung), 1400 K
San Galgano, Italy, abbey, 1218 J
San Germano, Italy, Treaty of, 1230 C
Sánchez de Vercial, Climente, Sp. anthologist and writer, 1400 K
Sancho I the Fat, King of Leon, 957 C, 960 E, 967 E
Sancho II, King of Castile, 1065 D, 1070 C, 1072 D
Sancho III, King of Castile, 1157 C, 1158 C
Sancho IV, King of Castile and Leon, 1284 B, 1295 E; as writer, 1295 K
Sancho Garcia I, King of Navarre, 905 E, 920 E, 926 E
Sancho II, King of Navarre, 970 E, 994 E
Sancho III the Great, King of Navarre, 1000 E, 1002 C, 1028 E, 1033 E; King of Spain, 1035 E
Sancho IV, King of Navarre, 1054 C, 1076 B
Sancho V Ramirez, King of Aragon, 1065 B; and Navarre, 1076 B, 1089 E, 1094 B
Sancho VI the Wise, King of Navarre, 1150 D, 1177 E, 1180 G, 1194 B
Sancho VII the Strong, King of Navarre, 1194 B, 1212 C, 1231 A, 1234 B
Sancho I, King of Portugal (b. *c.* 1155), 1185 D, 1189 C, 1191 E, 1211 A
Sancho II, King of Portugal (b. 1208), 1223 A, 1245 E, 1248 E
Sandwich, England, 1009 E, 1457 E; naval battle, 1217 C
Sanjar, Seljuq Sultan of Persia (1118–57), 1104 A, 1118 E, 1141 C, 1157 E
Sankara, Indian philosopher (*c.* 788–820?), 820 K
Sannazaro, Jacopo, It. poet (1458–1530), 1458 L, 1486 K
Sanok, Gregory of, Archbishop of Lwów, Polish humanist, 1477 L
Sant Jordi, Jordi de, Catalan poet (*c.* 1395–*c.* 1440), 1440 K
Santarem, Spain, 1093 E
Santiago de Compostela, Spain, 997 E; Cathedral, 879 J, 1075 J, 1168 J, 1188 J; Knights of, 1171 E; tomb of St. James, 813 H, 893 H, 997 J
Santiago de Peñalba, Spain, church, 919 J
Sanudo, Marco, Venetian Duke of the Archipelago, 1207 E
Sanuto, Marino, It. writer, 1321 G
Santillana. *See* López de Mendoza
Sapientia (Hrotswith), 962 K
Sapientza, is., Greece, naval battle, 1354 D
Saquet, Jakemon, F. poet, 1280 K
Saracenorum, Tractatus de Statu (William of Tripoli), 1273 K
Saracens (Muslim raiders in Mediterranean), sack Marseilles, 838 E; raid Switzerland, 940 E; conquer Sardinia, 1015 E, 1016 B; *and see* France, Garde-Freinet, Italy
Saragossa, Spain, 937 E, 1118 D, 1134 C
Sardinia, is., Italy, 934 E, 1015 E, 1016 B, 1323 E, 1336 K; King of, *see* Enzio
Sartak, Khan of the Golden Horde, 1255 E, 1256 E
Sarto, Andrea del, It. painter (1487–1531), 1487 L
Sarvadarśanasamgraha (Mādhava), 1386 H
Sarventikar, Turkey, battle, 1266 C
Sarzana, Italy, Treaty of, 1353 A
Sauchieburn, Scotland, battle, 1488 B
Saucourt, France, battle, 881 C
Savacz, Yugoslavia, 1475 E
Savigny, France, monastic order of, 1112 H, 1147 H
Savona, Italy, 1407 D

Savonarola, Girolamo, It. religious reformer (1452–98), 1452 L
Savoy, France, County, 1111 E, 1355 E, *and see* Amadeus VI; Duchy, 1416 A, *and see* Amadeus VIII
Sawtry, John, E. Lollard, 1401 H
Saxo Grammaticus, Danish chronicler (1140?–1216), 1208 K
Saxon dynasty. *See* Germany
Saxon poet, the, 890 K
Saxony, W. and E. Germany:
  conquered and converted, 804 E
  raided by Vikings, 829 E, 908 E
  ruled by Louis the Younger, 876 C, 882 C
  first Duke, 880 A
  raided by Magyars, 906 E, 924 E, 938 E
  Dukes (915–1002). *See* Germany, kings of
  revolt against Otto I, 939 B
  attack Poland, 963 E, 967 E
  revolts against Henry IV, 1071 E, 1073 C, 1074 A, 1075 B, D, 1076 E, 1080 A, 1088 E; and Henry V, 1113 E, 1115 A
  Dukes, 1011 E, *and see*
    Lothar II (1106–36)
    Henry the Proud (1136–8)
    Albert the Bear (1138/9–42)
    Henry the Lion (1142–80)
  revolt against Conrad, 1140 B
  Crusade against Wends, 1147 B, C
  Duchy divided, 1180 B
  recovered by Henry the Lion, 1189 D, 1190 B, 1191 E, 1194 A
  history of (Widukind), 973 K
  laws of, 803 F, 1225 F
  literature, 820 K, 890 K, 1237 K
Sāyana, Indian theologian, 1387 H
Sayf-ad-Dawla, Emir of Aleppo, 944 D, 953 E, 958 E 967 B
Sayf-ad-Dīn I, atabeg of Mosul (1146–9), 1146 C
Sayf-ad-Dīn II, atabeg of Mosul (1170–80), 1176 B, 1180 B
Scala, Antonio della, lord of Verona, 1387 D
Scala, Can Grande della, lord of Verona, 1311 E, 1318 A, 1319 D, 1320 D, 1329 C
Scala, Mastino della, lord of Verona, 1329 C, D, 1337 E, 1341 E
Scala Magna (Abū-l-Barakāt), 1316 K
Scalacronica (Thomas Grey), 1369 K
Scale of perfection (Walter Hilton), 1396 H
Scaliger, Julius Caesar, It. humanist (1484–1558), 1484 L
Scania, Sweden, 1360 E, 1369 D; Sound of, 1427 C
Schaffhausen, W. Germany, abbey, 1050 J
Schism, the Great. *See* Papacy
Schlestadt, W. Germany, 1474 B
Schleswig, W. Germany, 934 E, 1036 B, 1432 E, 1460 A; Bishopric, 948 H
Schools:
  in Carolingian Empire, 805 H, 818 H, 822 H
  cathedral, 826 H, 1000 H, 1078 H; *and see* Chartres
  humanist, 1398 H, 1458 H
  in England. *See* Eton; Winchester
  Japanese. *See* Kanazawa
  Muslim. *See* Cairo; Cordova
Shwabenspiegel, 1275 F
Schwäbisch Gmund, W. Germany, church, 1320 J
Schwanenritter, Der (Conrad von Würzburg), 1287 K
Schwänke:
  Der Stricker, *Der Pfaffe Amis*, 1240 K
Schwarz, Berthold, G. inventor of gunpowder, 1313 G
Schwerin, W. Germany, Count of, 1227 C, 1229 E
Schwyz. *See* Switzerland
Sciences, Index of (ibn-al-Nadīm), 988 G; (al-Warrāq), 995 G
Sciences, The Keys of the (al-Khwārizmī), 976 G
Scismate, De (Dietrich of Neim), 1410 H
Scone, Scotland, 'Stone of Destiny', 1296 C
Scot, Michael, Scottish translator and astronomer, 1217 G, 1220 K, 1235 K
Scotichronicon (John Fordun), 1383 K, 1449 K
Scotland:
  Scots and Picts united, 843 E
  Kings. *See*
    Kenneth MacAlpin (843–58)
    Donald I (858–62)
    Constantine I (862–77)
    Aed (877–8)
    Eochaiad (878–89)
    Donald II (889–900)
    Constantine II (900–43)
    Malcolm I (943–54)
    Indulf (954–62)
    Dub (962–6)
    Culen (966–71)
    Kenneth II (971–95)
    Constantine III (995–7)
    Kenneth III (997–1005)
    Malcolm II (1005–34)
    Duncan I (1034–40)
    Macbeth (1040–57)
    Lulach (1057–8)
    Malcolm III (1058–93)
    Donald III (1093–7)
    Duncan II (1094)
    Edgar (1097–1107)
    Alexander I (1107–24)
    David I (1124–53)
    Malcolm IV (1153–65)
    William I (1165–1214)
    Alexander II (1214–49)
    Alexander III (1249–86)
    Margaret (1286–90)
    John (Balliol; 1292–6)
    Robert I (1306–29)
    David II (1329–71)
    Stewarts
    Robert II (1371–90)
    Robert III (1390–1406)
    James I (1406–37)
    James II (1437–60)
    James III (1460–88)
    James IV (1488–1513)
  English invasion, 934 E
  Lothian annexed, 1016 E
  English campaigns in, 1072 B, 1080 B
  loses Cumberland and Westmorland, 1092 E
  feudalism in, 1153 B
  English invasions, 1209 C, 1216 A
  Border defined, 1237 A
  ruled by guardians, 1289 D, 1290 C
  'Great Cause' (of succession), 1291 B, 1292 D
  opposes Edward I, 1294 B
  'Auld Alliance', made, 1295 C
  Edward's campaigns, 1296 A–C, 1297 B, 1298 C, 1299 B, D, 1300 C, 1301 C, 1303 B, 1304 A, 1305 C
  War of Independence. *See* Robert I
  Declaration of Arbroath, 1320 B
  independence recognised, 1328 A, B
  claimed by Edward Balliol, 1332 C, D, 1333 B, C, 1334 B, C, 1356 A
  English invasions, 1335 A, C, 1336 C, D, 1341 B, 1342 A, B, 1355 D, 1356 A
  Black Death in, 1350 G

wars with England, 1384 A, B, 1385 C, 1400 C, 1402 C
ruled by regents. *See* Stewart, Robert; Stewart, Murdoch
wars with England, 1436 C, 1448 B, 1460 C, 1461 B, 1480 E, 1482 B, 1484 C
histories of, 1383 K, 1449 K
parliament, 1326 F, 1424 F, 1428 F
poetry:
The Pistill of Suete Susan, 1370 K
John Barbour, *The Brus*, 1373 K
James I, *The King's Quair*, 1423 K
Robert Henryson, *The Testament of Cresseid*, 1490 K
Screwjack, 1271 G
Scriptoria: Tours, 800 H, 804 J; Salzburg, 821 J
Scrope, Henry, Lord le, E. traitor, 1415 C
Scrope, Richard, Archbishop of York, 1405 B
Scrutinium Scripturae (Paul of Burgos), 1435 H, 1470 H
Sculptors:
Dutch. *See* Leyden, Nicholas of
Flemish. *See* Sluter, Claus
French. *See* Gislebert of Autun
German. *See* Naumburg, 'Master' of
Italian. *See* Arnolfo di Cambio; Donatello; Ghiberti, Lorenzo; Michelozzo; Nanni; Orcagna, Andrea; Pisano, Andrea; Pisano, Giovanni; Pisano, Niccolò; Quercia, Jacopo della; Robbia, Andrea della; Robbia, Luca della; Verrocchio, Andrea del
Sculpture, European revival, 1115 J; St. Denis, 1140 J; Chartres, 1219 J
Scutage, 1159 F
Scutari, Turkey, 1474 C
Scylitzes, Gk. chronicler, 1079 K
Sea of Jade (Wang Ying-lin), 1296 K
Seals, Chinese, 1307 K
Sebastea, Turkey, 1059 E; battle, 1067 E
Sebastiano del Piombo, It. painter (1485–1547), 1485 L
Sebastopol (Cherson), Russia, 989 E
Secretarium practicae medicinae (Joannes Jacobi), 1378 G
Secrets, The Book of (al-Rāzī), 925 G
Secretum (Petrarch), 1342 K
Secretum secretorum (attrib. to Aristotle), 1165 G
Sedacer, Guillem, Catalan alchemist (d. 1383), 1378 G
Sedacina totius alchimiae, 1378 G
Sedulius Scottus, Irish poet and grammarian, 848 K
Séez, France, Cathedral, 1220 J, 1270 J
Sefer ma'aseh hosheb (Levi ben Gerson), 1321 G
Sefer tekunah (Levi ben Gerson), 1329 G
Segarelli of Parma, It. heretical leader, 1300 H
Segeberg, W. Germany, battle, 1190 B
Segovia, Spain, archdeacon of, 1100 K
Sei Shōnagon, Ja. court lady and diarist (*c.* 965–1025), 1000 K
Seisyllwg, Wales, Kings of, 878 E, 949 E, F
Self-portrait (Albrecht Dürer), 1484 J
Seligenstadt, W. Germany, church, 821 J
Seljuq Turks, 956 E
conquer Persia, 1037 E, 1040 A; *and see* Persia
raid Armenia, 1045 E
attack Greek Empire, 1047 E, 1048 E, 1057 E, 1059 E
conquer Syria, *q.v.*
conquer Armenia and Anatolia, 1064 E, 1067 E, 1071 C, 1085 E; *and see* Rūm
expelled from Palestine, 1089 E
Sempach, Switzerland, battle, 1386 C; Covenant of, 1393 C
Sempringham, England, monastic order of, 1131 H
Sen Phu, King of Lan Na (d. 1334), 1325 E
Senegal, river, Senegal, 1446 G, 1455 G
Senlis, France, Treaty of, 1475 C
Sens, France, 1140 H; Cathedral, 822 H, 1140 J
Sentenario (Ferdinand III), 1252 F
Sententiarum libri IV (Peter the Lombard), 1150 H
Seo de Urgel, Spain, Cathedral, 1131 J, 1175 J
Seoul, Korea, 1394 E
Septem diebus et sex operum distinctionibus, De (Thierry of Chartres), 1155 L
Septennario (Alfonso the Wise), 1284 K
Sequences, The (Notker Balbulus), 912 K
Serbia, Yugoslavia:
subject to Bulgars and Greeks, 927 B
kingdom, 1084 E
in kingdom of Zeta, 1100 E
defeated by Greeks, 1123 E
independent state of Rascia in, 1180 C, 1196 E
becomes kingdom of Serbia, 1217 E; *and see*
Stephen (1217–28)
Radoslav (1228)
Vladislav (1228–43)
Stephen Uroš I (1243–76)
Stephen Dragutin (1276–82)
Stephen Uroš II (1282–1321)
Stephen Uroš III (1321–36)
Stephen Uroš IV (1336–55)
subjected to Mongols, 1293 E
collapse of empire, 1355 E, 1389 B
conquered by Turks, 1371 E, 1386 E, 1389 B, 1444 B, 1459 E
laws of, 1349 F
Sercambi, Giovanni, It. writer (1347–1424), 1424 K
Serchio, river, Italy, battle, 1430 D
Sergius II, Pope, 844 A, 847 A
Sergius III, Pope, 904 A, 911 B; son of, 931 A
Sergius IV, Pope, 1009 C, 1012 B
Sergius IV, Duke of Naples, 1028 E, 1030 E
Sergius, St., of Rádonezh, Russian monastic founder, 1335 H
Sermó de passatge de Sardenya (Ramón Muntaner), 1336 K
Sermo Lupi ad Anglos (Wulfstan), 1014 K
Sermones medicales septem (Niccolò Falcucci), 1411 G
Sermons (Giordano de Rivalto), 1311 K
Serres, Greece, 1345 C, 1361 E
Servatius (Heinrich von Veldeke), 1170 K
Servi Dei, Liber (Henry Bate), 1281 G
Seth, Symeon, Gk. physician, botanist and translator, 1080 G
Settepozzi, Greece, naval battle, 1263 E
Seulf, Archbishop of Reims, 922 C, 925 E
Seven Sacraments (Roger van der Weyden), 1453 J
Seville, Spain, 844 C, 891 B, 913 D, 1247 C, 1248 D; Muslim kingdom, 1042 E, 1069 E; Alcazar palace, 1360 J; Bishop of, *see* Isidore; Cathedral, 1402 J; mosque, 1172 J
Sex principiis, Liber de (Gilbert de la Porrée), 1154 K
Sext (canons), 1298 H
Sforza Attendolo, Giacomuzzo, It. condottiere (b. 1369), 1417 C, 1424 A
Sforza, Francesco, Duke of Milan (b. 1401; 1450–1466), as condottiere, 1424 A, 1431 B, 1439 D; wins Milan, 1441 D, 1447 C, 1448 C, D, 1450 A; as Duke, 1452 B, 1454 B, C, 1463 D, 1466 A
Sforza, Galeazzo Maria, Duke of Milan (b. 1444), 1466 A, 1476 D
Sforza, Gian Galeazzo, Duke of Milan (b. 1460; 1476–94), 1476 D, 1478 B, 1479 C, 1480 A, 1482 B

Sforza, Ludovico, il Moro (Duke of Milan, 1494–1505), 1451 L, 1479 C
Shādhili, 'Ali al-, founder of Muslim sect, 1258 H
Shādhilite fraternity, 1258 H
Shadibeg, Khan of the Golden Horde, 1400 E, 1407 E
Shāf'i, Muhammad ibn Idris al-, Arab religious reformer (767–820), 820 F, H
Shāfi'ite rite of Islam, 820 H
Shāhanshāh, title of, 983 E
Shāh-Nāma (Firdausī), 1020 K, 1335 J, 1359 K
Shahrastānī, Abū-l-Fath Muhammad al-, Per. historian and theologian (1076/7–1153), 1128 H
Shahrazād, 942 K
Shaizar, Syria, 1138 B
Shajar-ad-Durr, Sultanah of Egypt, 1250 B, 1257 B
Shakespeare, William, origins of sources of, 1110 K, 1137 K, 1160 K, 1208 K, 1378 K; *and see* Macbeth
Shami, Nizam-ad-Dīn al-, Per. biographer, 1403 K
Shang-tu ('Xanadu'), Mongolia, 1261 E
Shāns. *See* Assam; Burma
Shan-yüan, China, Treaty of, 1004 E
Shao-Yung, C. philosopher and poet (1101–77), 1077 K
Sharāi al-Islam (Mu'ayyad Alhilli), 1277 F
Sharp, Jack, E. Lollard, 1431 B
Sha-t'o, Turkish confederation, 878 E, 884 E
Sheep: Mesta of Castile, 1273 G
Sheherezade, 942 K
Shên Chi-sun, C. writer, 1398 G
Shên Kua, C. essayist (1030–93), 1093 G
Sherbourne, England, missal, 1396 J
Sherburn-in-Elmet, England, 1321 B
Shetland Is., Scotland, 1028 E, 1098 E, 1263 D, 1468 A
Shias, Muslim sect, leader of, 817 C; jurisprudence, 1277 F
Shih lei fu (Wu Shu), 1002 G
Shī'ite sect of Islam, 946 A, 969 C; college of theology, 1005 H; *and see* Ismā'ites
Shin Kokinshū, 1205 K
Shingon sect of Buddhism, 806 H, 816 H
Shinran, Ja. Buddhist founder (1173–1262), 1262 H
Shinsen Shōjiroku, 815 K
Ships, development of, 1180 G, 1279 G, 1466 G; dockyard, 1228 G
Shīrāz, Persia, Buwayhid dynasty of, 946 A, 1055 D
Shīrāzi, Qutb-ad-Dīn al-, Per. astronomer (1236–1311), 1311 G
Shīrkūh, Vizir of Egypt, 1169 A
Shogunate. *See* Japan
Shouh-shih li (Kuo Shou-ching), 1280 G
Shrewsbury, England, 1398 A; battle, 1403 C; Earls of, *see* Robert of Bellême; Talbot, John
Shu-shu Chiu-chang (Ch'in Chiu-Shao), 1247 G
Shuja ibn-Hanfar, Arab metalworker, 1232 J
Siam, Thais enter, 1253 E; their kingdoms, *see* Ayudhya, Lan Na, Sukhodaya; government, 1488 F; laws, 1350 F; literature: Lu T'ai, 1345 K
Sibylla, Queen of Jerusalem, 1186 C
Sic et non (Abelard), 1122 H
Sicily, is., Italy:
- conquered by Arabs, 827 B, 843 E, 859 E, 878 B, 902 C, 917 E
- Kalbite dynasty, 948 E
- Greek expedition to, 965 E
- civil war in, 1039 E, 1060 C
- first Normans in, 1016 E, 1030 E, 1034 E, 1039 E, 1040 E, 1041 B, 1046 B, 1051 E
- Norman conquest, 1053 B, 1061 C, 1072 A, 1091 E
- Counts of. *See* Guiscard, Robert; Roger I; Simon; Roger II
- Kingdom (with Naples, etc.), 1130 C, D; *and see*
  - Roger II (1130–54)
  - William I (1154–65)
  - William II (1165–89)
  - Tancred (1189–94)
  - William III (1194)
  - Henry VI (1194–7)
  - Frederick II (1198–1250)
  - Conrad IV (1250–4)
  - Conrad II (1254–8)
  - Manfred (1258–66)
  - Charles I (1266–85)
- history of (Falcandus), 1189 K
- revolts in, 1132 C, 1133 E, 1154 A, 1160 D, 1161 B
- conquered by Henry VI, 1191 B, C, 1194 C, D
- *Lex Augustalis*, 1231 F
- representative assembly, 1232 F
- Muslims deported from island, 1246 E
- offered to Edmund of England, 1254 A, 1255 B, 1258 D
- Angevin conquest, 1261 C, 1265 B, 1266 A
- revolt against, 1267 C, 1270 C
- 'Sicilian Vespers', 1282 A; war of, 1282 B, 1284 B, 1287 B, 1297 E, 1299 C, 1300 B, D
- Kingdom of Sicily (*only*, named Trinacria), 1302 C; *and see*
  - Pedro III of Aragon (1282–5)
  - James (1285–95)
  - Frederick II (1295–1337)
  - Peter II (1337–42)
  - Louis (1342–55)
  - Frederick III (1355–77)
  - Maria (1377–1402)
  - Martin (1391–1409)
  - annexed by Aragon, 1409 C

Siddhāntaśiromani (Bhāskara), 1150 G
'Sidrach', F. writer, 1243 G
Sidroe, Viking leader, 856 C
Siege of Thebes, The (John Lydgate), 1420 K
Siegfried, Archbishop of Mainz, 1241 C
Siena, Italy, 1259 B, 1270 E, 1279 E, 1354 A, 1385 A, 1399 C
- General council at, 1423 C, 1424 A
- Cathedral, 1230 J, 1265 J, 1284 J, 1308 J, 1339 J; Baptistery, 1427 J
- Fonte Gaia, 1414 J
- Palazzo Communale, 1288 J; frescoes, 1315 J, 1328 J, 1337 J
- University, 1203 H

Siervo libre de amor, El (Rodriguez de la Cámara), 1430 K
Siete Partidas (Alfonso X), 1256 F
Sifrewas, John, E. illuminator, 1396 J
Sigebert of Gembloux, Belgian historian (d. 1112), 1112 K, 1186 K
Sigefrid, Viking king, 885 D
Siger of Brabant, Belgian philosopher (*c.* 1230–90), 1277 A
Sigismund, Holy Roman Emperor (1433–7), 1368 L, 1433 B, 1437 D
- Margrave of Brandenburg, 1378 D, 1402 E, 1411 A
- King of Hungary, 1382 C, 1386 B, 1395 B, 1401 C
- influence in Bohemia, 1396 B, 1402 B
- wars with Turks, 1396 C, 1428 E
- wars with Venice, 1409 C, 1412 E, 1418 E
- King of the Romans, 1410 C, 1411 C
- grants titles, 1415 B, 1416 A, 1433 C
- promotes General Council, 1413 D, 1415 D
- ally of Henry V, 1416 A, C
- King of Bohemia, 1419 C; expelled, 1420 C, D, 1421 B, 1422 A; accepted, 1436 C

Sigismund, Grand Duke of Lithuania, 1432 C, 1435 C, 1440 E
Signorelli, Luca, It. painter (*c.* 1445–1523), 1490 J

Sigoli, Simone, It. travel-writer, 1390 G
Sigurd I, King of Norway, 1103 C, 1130 A
Sigurd II, King of Norway, 1135 D
Sigurd, brother of Harold of Norway, 1135 D
Sigurdsson, Amund, Norwegian leader, 1436 E
Sijistān, Persia and Afghanistan, 956 G; Saffārid dynasty of, 867 E, 872 E, 900 E, 908 E
Sikandar I, Shah of Delhi, 1393 A
Sikandar II Lodi, Shah of Delhi (1489–1517), 1489 C
Sikandar Butshikan, King of Kashmīr, 1416 H
Sikard, Duke of Benevento, 837 E, 839 E
Sikhs, founder of, 1469 H
Sikonolf, Prince of Salerno, 842 E
Sila fi Akhbar a'immat al-Andalūs, Kitab al- (ibn-Bashkuwāl), 1139 K
Silesia, Poland, 894 E
  contested by Bohemia and Poland, 999 E, 1000 A, 1038 E, 1041 B, 1050 E
  awarded to Poland, 1054 E, 1138 E
  German intervention, 1159 C
  divided by Poles, 1177 E
  Mongol invasion, 1241 B, G
  under Bohemia, 1335 D, 1348 B, 1458 A, 1491 A
Silistra (Dorystolum), Bulgaria, battle, 971 B
Silk manufacture:
  China, 1090 G, 1310 G
  France, 1467 G
  Greece, Sicily, 1147 G
  Italy, 1272 G, 1328 G
Silla dynasty. *See* Korea
Silsilat al-Tawārikh (anon.), 851 G
Silver mines, 1137 G, 1294 G
Silvester II (Gerbert of Aurillac), Pope (999–1003), Archbishop of Reims, 991 B, 995 H, 998 A; Pope, 999 B, 1000 C, 1003 B; as mathematician, 1003 G
Silvester III (Crescentius), Pope, 1045 A
Silvester IV, anti-pope, 1105 D, 1111 B
Simancas, Spain, battle, 939 C
Simeon, Prince of Moscow and Grand Duke of Vladimir, 1341 E, 1353 E
Simeon, St., Gk. mystic, 1022 K
Simeon, monk of Durham, E. chronicler, 1096 K, 1129 K
  See also Symeon
Simhabhūpala, Indian dramatist, 1350 K
Simnel, Lambert, E. pretender, 1487 B
Simon, Duke of Calabria and Count of Sicily, 1101 B, 1103 E
Simon of Genoa, It. physician, 1293 G
Simony, 1046 B, 1047 H, 1049 H, 1123 H; treatise against (Humbert), 1061 H
Simplici medicina, De (Platearius), 1161 G
Simplicibus, Liber de (Benedetto Rinio), 1410 G
Sīna (Avicenna), Abū 'Alī al-Husayn ibn-'Abd Allāh ibn-, Per. physician (980–1037), 980 L, 1037 G, 1187 G, 1288 G, 1472 G
Sinai, Journey to (Felix Fabri), 1348 G; (Simone Sigoli), 1390 G
Sinān, Rāshid-ad-Dīn, Assassin leader ('The Old Man of the Mountain'), 1192 B, 1193 E
Sind, India and Pakistan, 836 E, 1363 E
Sirmium, Yugoslavia, 1181 E
Sindbād the sailor, 851 G
Sindibad, The Book of, 1253 K
Siphra (Isaac al-Fez), 1103 H
Sinibus, chordis et arcubus, De (Levi ben Gerson), 1342 G
Sir Tristrem (Thomas the Rhymer), 1294 K
Sis, Turkey, 1375 B
Sita, river, Russia, battle, 1238 A
Sivas, Turkey:
  Danishmend emir of. *See* Ghāzī (1084–1134)
  collapse of their empire, 1141 D
  conquered by Rūm, 1169 E, 1174 E
  taken by Timur, 1395 E
  buildings: hospital, 1217 J; colleges, 1271 J
Siward, Earl of Northumbria, 1041 E, 1054 C, 1055 E
Sixtus IV (Francesco della Rovere), Pope (1471–84), 1414 L, 1471 C, 1472 E, 1475 H, 1478 C, 1484 C; war against Florence, 1478 B, 1480 A; war against Ferrara, 1482 B–D, 1483 A, C
Siyāsat-nāmah (Nizām-al-Mulk), 1092 F
Skanderbeg (George Castriota), ruler of Albania, 1443 E, 1444 B, 1462 C, 1466 E, 1468 A
Skellig, Michael, is., Eire, 823 J, 860 J
Skelton, John, E. poet (1460?–1529), 1460 L
Skoplje, Yugoslavia, 1282 E, 1346 B; battle, 1003 B
Skurdo, Prussian leader, 1283 E
Slave Kings. *See* Delhi
Slavonic script, 862 H; liturgy in, 880 H, 885 H
Slavs, in Balkans, 805 E, 887 C; *and see* Lusatians, Sorbs, Wends, Wiltzi; chronicles of missions to, 1171 K, 1212 K
Slovakia, Czechoslovakia, conversion of, 862 H
Slovo o Polku Igorevé, 1185 K
Sluter, Claus, Flemish sculptor, 1389 J, 1406 L
Sluys, Belgium, 1436 G; naval battle, 1340 B
Small-pox, treatise on (Wên-jên Kuei), 1323 G; and measles (al-Rāzī), 925 G
Smbat I, King of Armenia, 890 E, 914 E
Smbat II the Conqueror, King of Armenia, 977 E, 989 E
Smolensk, Russia, 1159 E, 1229 G, 1395 E, 1404 B
Smyrna, Turkey, 1092 E, 1300 E, 1344 D, 1402 D, 1424 E, 1472 E
Snorri Sturlason, Icelandic poet, 1178 L, 1222 K, 1225 K, 1241 L
Soběslav, Duke of Bohemia, 1111 E, 1125 E, 1126 A, 1140 E
Södermanland, Sweden, Duke Eric of, 1317 D, 1319 B, C
Sofia, Bulgaria, 809 E, 1127 E, 1385 E, 1443 D
Soissons, France, battle, 923 B; Bishop of, 865 A; Cathedral, 1200 J; church councils, 1092 H, 1121 H
Soliloquies (St. Augustine), 892 K
Solomon, King of Hungary (b. 1051), 1063 E, 1071 E; expelled, 1074 E, 1087 E
Solomon ben Gabīrōl (Avicebron), Sp. J. poet and philosopher (*c.* 1021–*c.* 1058), 1058 K, 1150 K
Solomon ben Isaac (Rashi), F. J. Talmudic and Biblical exegete, 1040 L, 1105 H
Solomonid dynasty. *See* Abyssinia
Solothurn, Switzerland, 1481 D
Somadeva, Indian poet and folk story collector, 1085 K
Somerled of the Isles, Scottish chieftain, 1164 E
Somerset, England, Dukes of. *See* Beaufort
Somme Rurale (Jean Boutillier), 1390 F
Somnāth (*now* Dwārka), India, 1025 A
Somnium Viridarii (Philippe de Mézières), 1376 F
Somosata, Syria, 958 E
Soncino, Italy, battle, 1431 B
Song of Canute, The (Monk of Ely), 1166 K
Song of Everlasting Remorse, The (Po-Chü-i), 846 K
Song of Lewes (anon.), 1264 K
Songe du Vergier, Le (Philippe de Mézières), 1376 F
Songe du vieil pelerin, Le (Philippe de Mézières), 1389 K
Sopočani, Yugoslavia, frescoes at, 1250 J
Soranzo, Giovanni, Doge of Venice, 1312 B, 1327 D

Sorbon, Robert de, F. founder of college, 1258 H
Sorbs, Slav tribe (of Lausitz, *q.v.*), 806 E
Sordello di Goito, It. poet, 1270 K
Sorel, Agnes, mistress of Charles VII (b. 1409), 1450 F
Sorø, Denmark, 1197 G
Souleuvres, France, Treaty of, 1475 C
Southwell, England, Minster, 1120 J
Spain:
  first general history of, 1248 K
  Black Death in, 1348 G
  Muslim. *See* Andalusia; Granada
  Christian:
    King of, 1035 E
    Emperors of, 1109 B, 1135 B
    See also Aragon; Castile; Leon; Navarre
    Spanish March. *See* Catalonia
    Inquisition in, 1477 H, 1483 H, 1488 H
    Jews massacred in, 1391 H; *and see* Jews
    literature:
      Cantore di mio Cid, 1140 K
      earliest religious drama, 1190 K
      first Castilian poets, 1225 K, 1235 K
      Libro de los engaños, 1253 K
      Alfonso the Wise, 1284 K
      El Caballero Cifar, 1340 K
      Juan Ruiz, 1343 K
      Juan Manuel, 1349 K
      Cancioneiros, 1350 K
      Poema de Alfonso Onceno, 1350 K
      López de Ayala, 1386 K, 1407 K
      Libro de los Gatos, 1400 K
      Pedro del Corral, 1403 K
      Rodriguez de la Cámara, 1430 K
      Cancionero General, 1440 K
      Cancionero de Baena, 1445 K
      López de Mendoza, 1458 K
      Garcia de Montalvo, 1475 K
      Jorge Manrique, 1477 K
      See also Catalonia
Spas: Turkish, 1161 G; Italian, 1425 G
Speaker of the Commons, 1376 F
Specchio della Croce (Domenico Cavalca), 1342 K
Spectacles, 1284 G, 1312 G, 1352 G
Speculum aureum (Hendrik Harphius), 1474 H
Speculum aureum de titulis beneficiorum (Matthias of Cracow), 1390 H
Speculum conversionis peccatorum (Denis the Carthusian), 1471 H
Speculum divinorum (Henry Bate), 1310 H
Speculum judiciale (Durandus), 1271 F
Speculum maius (Vincent of Beauvais), 1264 K, 1481 K
Speyer, W. Germany, 1178 D, 1280 G; Cathedral, 1030 J
Spieghel Historiael (Jacob van Maerlant), 1283 K
Spina, Alessandro della, It. inventor of spectacles, 1312 G
Spinning-wheel, 1280 G
Spinola, Francesco, Genoese leader, 1435 D
'Spiritual Society'. *See* Amaurists
Spoleto, Italy, 1400 A; Cathedral, frescoes in, 1465 J; Dukes of, *see* Guy, Lambert; March of, 967 A, 1152 E, 1174 D, 1198 D
Sport and games. *See* Chase; Chess; Falconry; Football; Hawking; Horses; Tennis
Spytihněv I, Prince of Bohemia, 895 E, H
Spytihněv II, Duke of Bohemia, 1055 E, 1061 E
Squaloribus curiae Romanae, De (Matthias of Cracow), 1390 H
Sri Parambiyan, India, battle, 880 E
Śrīdhara the Learned, Indian mathematician, 1020 G
Śrīvijaya, Sumatra, Indonesia, 1377 E
Ssŭ-ma Kuang, C. historian (1018/19–86), 1086 K, 1205 K
Ssu-yüan yü-chien (Chu Shih-chieh), 1303 G
Stabat Mater (Jacopone da Todi), 1306 K
Stabili, Francesco degli (Cecco d'Ascoli), It. poet and astrologer (1269–1327), 1327 H, K
Stade, Albert von. *See* Albert
Stained glass, 1140 J
Stafford, Henry, Duke of Buckingham, 1483 D
Staines, Scotland, battle, 1307 D
Stamford, England, 877 E, 1309 C; University, 1334 H
Stamford Bridge, England, battles, 1066 C, 1454 D
Standard, Battle of the, England, 1138 C, 1166 K
Stanislaus, St., Bishop of Cracow, 1079 B
Stanze per la Giostra, Le (Angelo Poliziano), 1479 K
Stapeldon, Walter, Bishop of Exeter, treasurer and founder (1261–1326), 1314 H, 1323 F, 1326 D
Star (French) Order of the, 1352 A
'Star Chamber Act', 1487 F
Star Raft, Description of the (Fei Hsin), 1436 G
Staraya Ladoga, Russia, frescoes at, 1180 J
Stars, Fixed (al-Sūfī), 986 G
Statesman's Book (John of Salisbury), 1159 F
Stavanger, Norway, Cathedral, 1150 J
Stavelot, Belgium, 881 E
Steinbach, W. Germany, church, 821 J
Stella alchimie (John Dombleday), 1384 G
Sten Sture, Regent of Sweden (d. 1503), 1471 D
Stenkil, King of Sweden, 1056 E
Steno, Michele, Doge of Venice, 1400 D, 1413 D
Stephen IV, Pope, 816 B, 817 A
Stephen V, Pope, 885 C, H, 890 E, 891 A, C
Stephen VI, Pope, 896 B, 897 C
Stephen VII, Pope, 929 A, 931 A
Stephen VIII, Pope, 939 C, 942 D
Stephen IX (Frederick of Lorraine), Pope, 1057 C, 1058 B
Stephen of Blois, King of England (1135–54), 1135 D, 1136 A, F, 1139 B; Duke of Normandy, 1136 B, 1137 E; war with Matilda, 1138 B, 1139 C, 1141 A, D; recognises Henry as heir, 1153 D, 1154 D
Stephen I (Géza), St., Duke of Hungary, 997 E; King, 1000 C, 1004 E, 1030 E, 1031 E, 1038 C
Stephen II Thunderbolt, King of Hungary (b. 1101), 1114 E, 1127 E, 1131 E
Stephen III, King of Hungary, 1161 B, 1163 B, 1173 A
Stephen IV, King of Hungary, 1162 A, 1163 B
Stephen V, King of Hungary, 1270 E, 1271 E, 1272 C
Stephen, Grand Župan of Rascia, 1196 E; King of Serbia, 1217 E, 1228 E
Stephen, Count of Champagne, 1037 D, 1038 E
Stephen, St., of Muret, F. monastic reformer, 1046 L, 1074 H, 1124 L
Stephen of Pisa, It. translator, 1227 G
Stephen Dragutin, King of Serbia (d. 1316), 1276 E, 1282 E
Stephen Držislav, King of Croatia, 997 E
Stephen Nemanja, Grand Župan of Rascia, 1169 E, 1172 E, 1180 C, 1189 E, 1190 E, 1196 E; son, 1243 E
Stephen Uroš I, King of Serbia, 1243 E, 1276 E
Stephen Uroš II Militin, King of Serbia, 1282 E, 1293 E, 1321 E
Stephen Uroš III Dečanski, King of Serbia, 1321 E, 1330 B, 1336 E
Stephen Uroš IV Dušan, King of Serbia, 1336 E, 1345 C, 1346 B, 1349 F, 1355 E
Stephen Vojuslav, King of Zeta, 1040 E
Steppes, Belgium, battle, 1213 D
Stettin (*now* Szczecin), Poland, 1121 E, 1181 E
Stewart dynasty. *See* Scotland

Stewart, Alexander, Duke of Albany (*c.* 1454–85?), 1479 C, 1482 B
Stewart, John, Earl of Mar, 1479 E
Stewart, Murdoch, Duke of Albany and Regent of Scotland, 1420 C, 1425 B
Stewart, Robert, Duke of Albany and Regent of Scotland, 1406 B, 1420 C
Stigand, Archbishop of Canterbury, 1070 C
Stiklestad, Norway, battle, 1030 C
Stirling, Scotland, battle, 1297 C; castle, 1299 D, 1314 B
Stirrup, first picture of, 840 G
Štítný, Thomas of, Czech preacher, 1401 H
Stock, Simon, first prior of Carmelites, 1265 H
Stockholm, Sweden, 1395 B
Stoke, East, England, battle, 1487 B
Stoke, Melis, Dutch poet and chronicler, 1305 K
Stralsund, E. Germany, Treaty of, 1369 D
Strangford Lough, Ireland, battle, 877 E
Strasbourg, France, 1474 B; Cathedral, 1015 J, 1275 J, 1277 J, 1439 J; Oaths of, 842 A, K; Peace of, 1189 B; Treaty of, 1299 C
Strascimir, Prince of Bulgaria, 1362 E
Strassburg, Lithuania, Russia, 1285 E
Strassburg, Gottfried von. *See* Gottfried
Stratford, John, Archbishop of Canterbury and Chancellor (d. 1348), 1340 D, 1341 B
Strathclyde, Scotland and England, Kingdom of, 927 C, 937 E, 945 E
Strawa, river, Lithuania, Russia, 1348 E
Stream of Kings (Kalhana), 1148 K
Stříbo, Czechoslovakia, battle, 1427 C
Stricker, Der, Rhenish poet, 1240 K
Strikes at Douai, 1245 G
Stromer, Nicholas, G. paper-maker, 1389 G
Stromer, Ulman, G. family chronicler (1329–1407), 1407 K
'Strongbow'. *See* FitzGilbert
Strozzi, Palla, Florentine noble and patron of humanists (1372–1462), 1434 D, 1462 L
Studenitza, Yugoslavia, frescoes at, 1314 J
Sturla Thordsson, Icelandic chronicler and saga writer (*c.* 1214–*c.* 1284), 1284 K
Sturlason. *See* Snorri
Sturlunga Saga, 1284 K
Styria, Austria, Duchy of, 1180 C, 1251 E, 1259 E, 1260 C, 1262 C, 1274 E; won by Habsburgs, 1276 D, 1282 D; *and see* Frederick III
Su Sung, C. astronomer, 1092 G
Su Tung-p'o, C. poet and essayist, 1036 L, 1101 K
Subh al-A'sha (al-Qalqashandi), 1418 F
Subiaco, Italy, 1465 G
Suda (Greek dictionary), 976 K
Sudan, 1173 E, 1314 E
Sudauen, Poland, 1435 E
Sudbury, Simon, Archbishop of Canterbury and Chancellor, 1381 B
Sudoměř, Czechslovakia, battle, 1420 A
Suez, Egypt, proposed canal, 809 G
Suffolk, England, Duke of. *See* Pole, William de la
Sūfī sect of Islam:
  first saint, 815 H; *and see* Dārāni, Hallāj, Hamadhāni
  literature, 1131 K, 1273 K
  mystics. *See* 'Arabī; Rūmī
  pantheist. *See* Suhrawardi
  theosophist. *See* Dhu-al-Nūn
Sūfī (Alsoufi), Abu'l-Husain al-, Per. astronomer and geographer (903–86), 903 L, 986 G, L, 1005 J
Sugawara Michizane, Ja. poet, 902 K
Suger, Abbot of St. Denis (1081–1151), 1140 J, 1145 K, 1151 L, 1231 J
Suhrawardi, Abū'l-Futūh al-, Per. Sūfī philosopher, 1191 K
Sukhodaya, Siam, Thai kingdom, 1230 E, 1295 E, 1349 E, 1376 E; *and see* Lu T'ai
Sülamish, governor of Rūm, 1299 B
Sulaymān, Caliph of Cordova, 1009 E, 1010 E, 1013 B, 1016 E
Sulaymān I, joint Ottoman Sultan, 1403 A, 1411 A
Sulaymān ibn-Qutlumish, first Sultan of Rūm, 1073 E, 1077 E, 1081 B, 1086 E
Sulaymān the Merchant, Arab traveller, 851 G
Sultan Han, Turkey, 1229 J
Sultānīyah, Persia, Archbishop of, 1318 H
Sultānpur. *See* Warangal
Sumangura, Negro ruler, 1377 E
Sumatra, Indonesia, 1025 E, 1292 G, 1297 E, 1377 E
Sumava, Czechoslovakia, battle, 1040 C
Sumer is icumen in, 1310 J
Summa (canon law):
  Bernard of Pavia, 1195 H
  Étienne of Tournai, 1168 H
  Hugoccio, 1180 H
  John of Faenza, 1170 H
  Paucapalea, 1150 H
  Rufinus, 1165 H
  Tedeschi, 1466 H
Summa Aurea (Hostiensis), 1271 H
Summa codicis et institutionum (Azzo), 1230 F
Summa de ecclesia (Juan de Torquemada), 1433 H
Summa de haeresibis (Guiu Terrena), 1340 H
Summa de potestate ecclesiastica (Agostino Trionfo), 1328 H
Summa digestorum (Hugolinus), 1233 F
Summa Theologiae:
  Alexander of Hales, 1245 H
  Henri de Gand, 1293 H
  St. Thomas Aquinas, 1274 H
Summa Theologica (Albertus Magnus), 1280 H
Summula respiciens facta mercatorum (Baldus), 1400 F
Sunām, India, battle, 1292 E
Sunderold, Archbishop of Mainz, 891 B
Sundiata, first Emperor of Mali, 1377 E
Sung dynasty. *See* China
Sung Ch'i, C. philologist and historian (998–1061), 1039 K, 1060 K
Sung Tz'ŭ, C. physician, 1248 G
Sunni Ali, Emperor of Gao, 1468 E
Super libros tegni Galeni (Jacopo da Forli), 1414 G
Sūrat al-Ard (al-Khwārizmī), 851 G
Sureśvara, Indian physician, 1075 G
Surgeons:
  French, guild of, 1271 G. *And see* Chauliac, Guy; Mondeville, Henry
  Italian. *See* Bartolomeo de Varignana; Bruno da Longoburgo; Lanfranchi; Maurus; Mondino de' Luzzi; Roger of Salerno; Saliceto, William of; Vigevano, Guido da
  Spanish Muslim. *See* Zahrāwi
Surgery. *See* Dissection
Surveying, treatise on (Hero), 938 G
Suryavarman II, King of Cambodia (1113–50), 1131 E, 1145 E, 1149 E, 1150 J
Suso, Heinrich, G. mystic (*c.* 1295–1366?), 1328 H
Sussex, England, 825 E
Sutri, Italy, 1046 D
Suzdal, Russia, princes of. *See* Juri; Andrew
Svátopluk I, Prince of Moravia, 870 E, 871 E, 874 E, 885 H, 892 E, 894 E
Svátopluk II, Prince of Moravia, 894 E
Svátopluk of Olomuc, Duke of Bohemia, 1107 E, 1109 E

Svein I Forkbeard, King of Denmark, 983 E, 994 E; and Sweden, 995 E; and Norway, 1000 E, 1003 E, 1009 C; and England, 1013 E, 1014 A
Svein II Estrithson, King of Denmark, 1047 D, 1069 C, 1074 B
Svein III, King of Denmark, 1147 E, 1152 B, 1154 E, 1156 E, 1157 B, D
Sverker I, King of Sweden (1129–50), 1129 E, 1150 E, 1163 E
Sverker II, King of Sweden (1192–1210), 1192 E, 1210 C, 1220 E
Sverre, King of Norway, 1177 E, 1184 B, 1202 A
Sviatopolk I, Prince of Kiev, 1015 E, 1018 C, 1019 E
Sviatopolk II, Prince of Kiev, 1093 E, 1113 B
Svidrigello, Grand Duke of Lithuania (1430–2), 1430 D, 1432 C, 1435 C
Svjatoslav, Grand Prince of Kiev, 945 E, 962 E, 965 E, 967 E, 969 E, 970 E, 971 B, C, 972 B
'Svold', Denmark, naval battle, 1000 E
Swabia, W. Germany:
  as Alemannia, *q.v.*
  Dukes of, 908 E, 1252 C; *and see* Burchard, Hermann, Liudolf, Ernest, Henry, Otto, Rudolf; Hohenstaufen, 1079 E, 1198 A, 1252 C
  Leagues of towns, 1376 B, 1377 B, 1381 C, 1384 C, 1385 A, 1388 C, 1389 B, 1487 C
  legal compilation, 1275 F
Sweden, Kings of, 810 E; *and see*
    Svein I of Denmark, 995 E
    Olaf the Tax-king, 1000 E
    Anund Jacob, 1026 E
    Edmund Slenme and Stenkil, 1056 E
    Halstan (1066–90)
    Inge I (1090–1112)
    Inge II (1118–29)
    Sverker I (1129–50)
    Eric, St. (1150–60)
    Charles VII (1162–8)
    Cnut Ericson (1168–92)
    Sverker II (1192–1210)
    Eric X (1210–20)
    John I (1220–3)
    Eric XI (1223–50)
    Waldemar (1250–75)
    Magnus I (1275–90)
    Birger II (1290–1319)
    Magnus VIII of Norway (1311–63)
    Albert II (1363–89)
    Eric VII of Denmark (1389–1439)
    Christopher III of Denmark (1441–8)
    Charles VIII (1448–70)
    Christian I of Denmark (1457–64)
    John I of Denmark (1481–1513)
  conversion of, 865 H, 1000 E
  'Wars of the Pretenders', 1155 E
  defeated in Russia, 1240 C
  feudalism in, 1290 D
  codification of laws, 1347 F
  united to Denmark and Norway, 1389 A
  revolt and regency of Charles Knutson, 1435 E, 1436 E, 1438 E, 1441 C
  interregnum and regency of Sten Sture, 1470 C, 1471 D, 1483 C
  first historian, 1486 K
'Sweet Dew-incident', 833 E
Sweynheym, G. printer, 1465 G
Swietopelk, ruler of Pomerania (1220–66), 1227 D, 1242 E, 1253 E, 1266 E
Swithin, St., Bishop of Winchester, 862 L
Switzerland, 940 E
  Uri freed from Habsburgs, 1231 B
  Schwyz, Uri and Unterwalden: Confederation of, recognised by emperors, 1240 D, 1309 B, 1315 A
  wars with Habsburgs, 1291 C, D, 1292 E, 1307 D, 1315 D, 1318 C, 1368 A, 1386 C, 1388 B, 1389 B
  accessions to, 1332 D, 1351 B, 1352 E, 1403 B, 1450 C
  defeats Frebourg, 1339 B
  Pfaffenbrief, 1370 F
  league with German towns, 1385 A
  Covenant of Sempach, 1393 C
  takes Aargau, 1415 E
  wars with Milan, 1422 B, 1440 E, 1479 C
  civil war, 1440 D, 1442 B
  war with Frederick III, 1442 B, 1444 C, 1446 B
  treaty with France, 1444 C
  war with Burgundy, 1469 B, 1474 A, B, 1476 A, B, 1477 A, 1478 A
  threat of disruption, 1481 D
  chronicle, 1348 K
  law, 1370 F
  literature:
    Ulrich Boner, 1349 K
    Ballad of William Tell, 1465 K
Sword Brothers of Latvia, 1204 E, 1237 E
Sy, Jean de, F. translator, 1355 H
Symeon, Khan of the Bulgars (893–927), 893 E, 895 E, 926 E, 927 B; attacks and claims Greek Empire, 896 E, 913 B, 917 C, 923 E, 924 E
Symeon the Logothete, Gk. chronicler, 948 K
Syncellos, Georgios, Gk. chronicler (d. 810), 810 K, 817 K
Synonyma medicinae (Simon of Genoa), 1293 G
Syon, England, nunnery, 1415 H
Syracuse, Sicily, Italy, 878 B, 965 E
Syria:
  conquered by Egypt, 877 E
  recovered by Caliph, 905 E
  conquered by Egypt, 937 E
  Hamdānids in, 940 D; *and see* Aleppo
  Greek campaigns in, 958 E, 962 D, 969 D, 972 D, 973 C, 974 E, 975 B
  Egyptians recover south, 983 E; defeat Greeks, 994 C
  Greek campaigns, 995 B, 999 D, 1032 E
  conquered by Seljuqs, 1065 E, 1067 E, 1071 C, 1074 E, 1104 A
  Crusading states. *See* Antioch; Edessa
  Greek campaigns, 1137 E, 1138 B, 1142 C, 1143 B
  conquered by Ayyūbids. *See* Damascus
  conquered by Mongols, 1259 C, 1260 A
  conquered by Egypt, 1260 C
  Mongol attacks, 1280 D, 1281 D, 1299 D, 1300 A, 1303 E, 1308 E
  conquered by Timur, 1400 E, 1401 A
  recovered by Egypt, 1405 A
  chronicle, 1199 K
  glassware, 1401 J
  poetry: al-Ma'arrī, 1058 K
Syriac Grammar (Bar Hebraeus), 1286 K
Syrian Lightning (al-Katīb), 1201 K
Szechuan, China, 829 E
Szeged, Hungary, Treaty of, 1444 B

T

Tabaqāt al-Kabir, Kitāb al- (al-Wāqidi), 823 K
Tabaqāt al-Uman (al-Andalusi), 1070 G
Tabarī, 'Ali ibn-Sahl Rabban al-, Per. physician and theologian, 850 G, 854 H
Tabarī, Abu-Ja'far Muhammad ibn-Jarīr al-, Per. historian (d. 923), 923 K, 1233 K

Taborites. *See* Bohemia
Tabriz, Persia, 1282 B, 1335 J, 1386 E, 1447 E
Tabrizī, 'Alā'-ad-Dīn al-, *alias* 'Alī al-Shatranji, Per. courtier and writer, 1405 K
Tabulae Alfonsinae, 1262 G
Tacticon (Leo VI), 912 G
Tadbir al-Mutawahhid (ibn-Bājjah), 1138 K
Taftazānī, al-, Per. theologian, 1389 H
Taghlib, Abū, Emir of Mosul, 972 D, 973 C
Taghri-Birdi, Abu-l-Mahāsin ibn-, Eg. historian (1411–69), 1469 K
Tagliacozzo, Italy, battle, 1268 C
Tāhir, governor of Khurāsān, 820 E
Tāhirid dynasty. *See* Khurāsān
Tahrir al-ahkām (ibn-Jamā'a), 1333 F
T'ai-ping yü-lan (Li Fang), 977 K
T'ai-Tsu. *See* Chao K'uang-yin
T'ai Tsung, Emperor of China, 976 E, 997 E
Taiheiki, 1374 K
Taillebourg, France, battle, 1242 C
Taillevent. *See* Tirel, Guillaume
Taira family, rules Japan, 1160 E, 1180 E, 1183 E, 1185 B
Takanobu, Ja. painter (1142–1205), 1205 J
Taketori Monogatari, 890 K
Takkōlam, India, battle, 949 E
Talbot, John, Lord, 1405 A; Earl of Shrewsbury, 1453 C
Tale of Genji, The (Lady Murasaki), 1010 K
Talenti, Francesco, It. architect, 1355 J
Tāliqān, Afghanistan, battle, 1040 A
Talkhis fi a'māl al-hisāb (ibn-al-Bannā), 1321 G
Talmudic scholars. *See* Isaac (Alphesi); Nathan ben Jeliel; Solomon ben Israel
Tamaron, Spain, battle, 1037 E
'Tamburlaine'. *See* Timur
Tamil literature, 1200 K
Ta-ming lü, 1397 F
Tammām, Abū, Arab poet (805–45), 845 K
Tancred, Count of Lecce, usurping King of Sicily, 1189 D, 1192 B, 1194 A
Tancred, Prince of Galilee and Regent of Antioch, 1101 A, 1111 A
Tancred, It. canonist, 1215 H
T'ang dynasty. *See* China
T'ang hui yao, 961 F
Tangier, Morocco, 1437 E, 1471 C, 1480 A
Tanguts. *See* Hsi Hsia
Tanjore, India, 846 E, 949 E; temple, 1009 J
Tannenburg. *See* Grunwald
Tao, Georgia, Russia, 1000 A; Prince of, *see* David
Tao-i-chi-lio (Wang Ta-yüan), 1349 G
Taoism, in China, 1260 H
Taormina, Sicily, Italy, 902 C
Tanqih al-Manāzur (al-Fārisī), 1320 G
Taqwim al-Buldān (Abū-l-Fidā'), 1321 G
Tara, Ireland, King of. *See* Malachy II
Tara Hill, Ireland, battle, 980 E
Taranto, Italy, 840 E, 880 E
Tarāori, India, battle, 1192 E
Tarascon, France, Treaty of, 1291 A
Ta'rikh al-Hind (al-Bīrunī), 1048 G
Ta'rikh al-Rusul w-al-Mulūk (al-Tabarī), 923 K
Ta'rikh-i-Firūz Shāhī (Baranī), 1352 K
Ta'rikh-i-guzida (Mustawfī), 1330 K
Ta'rikh-i-jahān gushā (al-Juwainī), 1260 K
Ta'rikh Iftitāh al-Andalus (ibn-al-Qūtīyah), 977 K
Tarquinia Madonna (Filippo Lippi), 1437 J
Tarragona, Spain, 1091 E; Cathedral, 1171 J, 1204 J
Tarshish (Moses ben Ezra), 1139 K
Tarsus, Turkey, 965 C
'Tartar Yoke'. *See* Russia
Tartars. *See* Mongols
Tasrif li-Man 'Azaz 'an al-Ta'alif (al-Zahrāwi), 1013 G
Tatars, Mongolian tribe, 1410 E, 1422 E
Tauler, John, G. mystic, 1361 H
Taunton, England, 1451 C
Tawq al-Hamāmah (ibn-Hazm), 1064 K
Taxatio (Nicholas IV), 1291 H
Taxation:
  'Abbāsid, 948 F
  Germany, 1471 B
  Hungary, 1465 F
  India, 1301 F
  See also Clergy; England; France
Tayf al-Khayāl (al-Mawsili), 1310 K
Taysir fi-al-Mudāwāh w-al-Tadbir (ibn-Zuhr), 1162 G, 1280 G
Tea, in Japan, 804 G, 1191 G; Ceremony, 1443 K; treatises on, 804 G, 1191 G
Technology:
  Artesian well, 1126 G
  bell-founding, 1100 G
  carpenter's brace, 1220 G, 1424 G; plane, 1220 G
  chemist's instruments, 1477 G
  crank and rod, 1423 G
  dredger, 1435 G
  needles, 1370 G
  parachute, 1480 G
  screw-jack, 1271 G
  spinning-wheel, 1280 G, 1298 G
  wheel-barrow, 1250 G
  See also Alcohol; Canals; Cannon; Ceramics; Clocks; Coal; Compass; Encyclopedias; Flight; Glass; Gunpowder; Horses; Ink; Iron manufacture; Magnet; Mechanics; Metallurgy; Mills (*inc.* water-power); Mines; Paper; Printing; Ships; Silk manufacture; Spectacles; Telegraph; War (manuals on)
Tedaldo, Italy, battle, 1309 C
Tedeschi, Niccolò de', It. cardinal and canonist (b. 1389), 1466 H
Tekish, Khwārizm Shah (1172–1200), 1194 E
Tekuder (Ahmad), Ilkhan of Persia, 1282 B, 1284 C
Tele-Buga, Khan of the Golden Horde, 1287 E, 1291 E
Telegraph, optical, 865 G
Telesio, Antonio, It. poet (1482–1534), 1482 L
Telingāna, India, Hindu kingdom, 1308 E, 1323 E
Tell, William, Swiss hero, 1307 D; *Ballad* of, 1465 K
Templars, Order of Knights, 1119 H, 1266 C; prosecuted, 1307 D, 1308 B, C, 1314 A; suppressed, 1312 B
Temples:
  Burmese. *See* Pagan
  Cambodian. *See* Angkor
  Indian. *See* Khajurāho; Orissa; Tanjore
Temujin. *See* Ghengiz Khan
Temür, Emperor of China and Great Khan, 1294 E, 1300 E, 1307 E
Tendai sect of Buddhism, 805 H
Tenedos, is., Greece, 1376 E, 1378 D
Tennis, 956 G
Tenochtitlán (Mexico City), 1325 E
Tenures (Thomas Littleton), 1481 F
Tephrice. *See* Divrigi
Tepl, Johann von, Bohemian writer (d. 1415?), 1405 K
Terek, river, Russia, battle, 1395 B
Terence, Roman dramatist (d. 159/8 B.C.), 962 K
Teresa, Queen and Regent of Portugal, 1128 E
Terrena, Guiu, Catalan theologian and historian (d. 1342), 1340 H

Tesaurus regis Francie (Guido da Vigevano), 1335 G
Tesoretto (Brunetto Latini), 1295 K
Testament maistre Jehan de Meung, Le, 1305 K
Testament of Cresseid, The (Robert Henryson), 1490 K
Tettenhall, England, battle, 910 C
Tetuan, Morocco, 1400 E
Teutonic Knights:
  founded as Order of the Cross, 1190 E, 1210 E
  conquer Prussia, 1226 E, 1230 E, 1236 E
  united with Sword Brothers, 1237 E
  defeated by Mongols, 1241 B
  defeated by Alexander Nevski, 1242 B
  revolts against, 1242 E, 1263 E, 1273 E, 1277 E, 1283 E
  foundations by, 1252 E, 1254 E, 1377 G
  war with Pomerania, 1253 E
  wars with Lithuanians, 1260 C, 1263 E, 1285 E, 1348 E, 1370 A
  headquarters of, 1291 E, 1309 E, 1457 B
  take Gdansk and East Pomerania, 1308 E, 1309 E
  occupy Esthonia, 1330 E, 1346 E
  war with Poland, 1331 C, 1335 D, 1339 C, 1343 C
  war with Denmark, 1360 C, 1398 B, 1404 D
  union of Poland and Lithuania against, 1383 E, 1410 C, D, 1411 A, 1414 E, 1422 C
  buy Neumark of Brandenburg, 1402 E; sell it, 1454 E
  conspire in Lithuania, 1432 C, 1435 C, D
  subjected to Poland, 1454 A, C, 1457 B, 1466 D
  war with Brandenburg, 1478 E
  history of, 1326 K
Tewkesbury, England, abbey, 1087 J; battle, 1471 B
Textiles. *See* Silk; Wool
Tha'ālibi, al-, Per. anthologist (961–1038), 1038 K
Thābit ibn-Qurra of Harrān, Arab astronomer, mathematician, physician and translator (825–901), 901 G
Thadominbya, Thai prince of Burma, 1364 E
Thais. *See* Burma; Cambodia; Nanchao; Siam
Thamar the Great, Queen of Georgia, 1184 E, 1209 E, 1212 E
Thanet, is., England, 851 E
Thang-long. *See* Hanoi
Thaton, Burma, Mon kingdom, 1057 E
Thebes, Greece, 1379 E
Theisir (Avenzoar), 1280 G
Thematibus, De (Constantine VII), 959 F
Theobald I, (IV as) Count of Champagne, King of Navarre (b. 1201), 1234 B, 1239 C, 1240 C, 1253 C; F. poet, 1253 K
Theobald II, King of Navarre, 1253 C, 1270 D
Theobald III Count of Blois, 1037 D, 1038 E, 1044 C
Theobald of Étampes, teacher at Oxford, 1110 H
Theoctistus, St., the Logothete, 855 D
Theoderic, anti-pope, 1100 C
Theodora, Greek Empress and Regent, 842 A, 855 D
Theodora, Greek Empress, 1042 B, 1055 A, 1056 C
Theodore II, Pope, 897 D
Theodore I Lascaris, Greek Emperor (1204–22), 1204 D, 1208 B, 1210 B, 1211 D, 1214 D, 1222 E; sons, 1225 E
Theodore II Lascaris, Greek Emperor (b. 1222), 1254 D, 1258 C
Theodore II, King of Lesser Armenia, 1143 B
Theodore of Gaza, Gk. grammarian, 1400 L, 1478 K
Theodore the Studite, Gk. theologian (759–826), 826 L
Theodore Svetoslav, Tsar of Bulgaria, 1307 E
Theodulf, Bishop of Orleans, 806 J, 818 H
Theologians:
  Belgian. *See* Bate, Henry; Gand, Henri de
  Egyptian (Coptic). *See* Abū-l-Barakāt
  English. *See* Alexander of Hales; Baconthorpe, John; Burgh, John de; FitzRalph, Richard; Mannyng, Robert; Netter, Thomas; Pecham, John; Pecock, Reginald; Wycliffe, John
  French. *See* Abelard; Agobard; Ailly, Pierre d'; Alignan, Benedict d'; Anselm of Laon; Berengar of Tours; Clamanges, Nicholas of; Gerson, Jean; Gui, Bernard; Hincmar; Hugh of St. Victor; Lyra, Nicholas de; Petrus Comestor; Roscelin; Thierry of Chartres; William of Auvergne; William of Champeaux
  French Jew. *See* Levi ben Gerson
  German. *See* Albertus Magnus; Cusa, Nicholas of; Gelnhausen, Conrad of; Gottschalk; Langenstein, Henry of; Maurus, Rabanus; Otfrid of Weissenburg; Walafrid Strabo
  Greek. *See* Barlaam; Theodore
  Irish. *See* Erigena
  Italian. *See* Anselm; Aquinas; Damian, Peter; Peter the Lombard; Trionfo, Agostino
  Scottish. *See* Duns Scotus
  Spanish. *See* Burgos, Paul of; Gundissalinus; Lull, Raymond; Martin, Raymond; Pelayo, Alvaro; Terrena, Guiu
  Spanish Jew. *See* Abraham ben Ezra
  See also Islam
Theophanes Confessor, Gk. historian (d. 817), 817 K, 1079 K
Theophano, German Empress and Regent, 972 B, 983 D, 984 B, 991 B
Theophilus, Greek Emperor, 829 E, 838 B, 842 A
'Theophilus', (G.?) writer on arts, 1100 G
Thesaurarum (Joannes Jacobi), 1378 G
Thesaurus pauperum (Petrus Hispanus), 1277 G
Thessalonica. *See* Salonika
Theutberga, wife of Lothar II, 860 E, 865 B
Thierry of Alsace, Count of Flanders (d. 1168), 1128 C
Thierry of Chartres, F. theologian, 1155 H
Thietmar, Bishop of Merseburg, G. chronicler, 1018 K
Thihathura, King of Pinya, 1312 E
Thinhkaba, Burmese king, 1358 E
Thiron, France, Congregation of, 1114 H
'Thirty', 'Battle of the', 1351 A
Thomas the Slav, pretender as 'Constantine VI', 825 E
Thomas, Duke of Clarence (b. 1388), 1421 A
Thomas of Woodstock, Earl of Buckingham (1355–1397), 1355 L, 1380 C, 1381 A; Duke of Gloucester, 1387 D, 1388 A, 1397 C
Thomas, Earl of Lancaster, 1311 A, 1312 B, 1316 A, 1318 C, 1320 B, 1322 A
Thomas of Brittany, Anglo-Norman poet, 1170 K
Thomas of Celano, It. friar, poet and biographer, 1255 K
Thomas de Chantimpré, Belgian scientist (*c.* 1200–*c.* 1275), 1244 G
Thomas de Cormont, F. mason, 1220 J
Thomas the Rhymer, E. poet, 1294 K
Thorn. *See* Toruń
Thoros, Prince of Armenia, 1156 B, 1158 D, 1168 E
Thouars, France, 1206 D
Thousand and one nights (al-Jahshiyari), 942 K
Thrace, Greece, 1343 E, 1359 E
Thuringia (E. and W. Germany), 908 E, 939 B; laws of, 803 F
Tiberias, Israel, 1187 C
Tibet, 821 E, 879 E, 1205 E, 1337 E; Buddhism in, 842 E, 1038 H, 1260 H; Lamas, 1260 H, 1392 H, 1473 H; paintings and mss., 1035 H; tribes, 1041 F, *and see* Hsi Hsia

Tidal-mills, 1066 G, 1125 G
Tides, treatise on, 886 G
Tiepolo, Bajamonte, Venetian conspirator, 1310 B
Tiepolo, Jacopo, Doge of Venice, 1229 E, 1249 C
Tiepolo, Lorenzo, Doge of Venice, 1268 C, 1275 C
Tīfāshī, Shihāb-ad-Dīn, Eg. mineralogist, 1154 G
Tiflis, Georgia, Russia, 1122 E, 1225 E, 1231 C, 1386 E
Timbuktu, Mali, 1337 E, 1468 E
Timur the Lame ('Tamburlaine'), Mongol Conqueror, 1335 L, 1367 E, H, 1405 A, J, K
wins Transoxiana, 1360 E, 1369 E
war with Golden Horde, 1381 E, 1385 E, 1386 E, 1387 E, 1389 E, 1391 B, 1395 B, C
wins Persia, 1382 E, 1386 E, 1387 D, 1393 E
and Iraq, 1392 E, 1393 E, 1401 C
and Asia Minor, 1395 E, 1402 C, D, 1404 E
invades India, 1398 B–D, 1399 A
wins Syria, 1400 E, 1401 A, J
biographies, 1403 K, 1435 K, 1454 K
Tīmūrids. *See* Khurāsān; Transoxiana
Timur-Khan, Khan of the Golden Horde, 1410 E, 1411 E
Timur-Kutlugh, Khan of the Golden Hoard, 1397 E, 1400 E
Tinchebrai, France, battle, 1106 C
Ting Tu, C. philologist (990–1053), 1039 K
Tinibeg, Khan of the Golden Horde, 1341 E, 1342 E
Tintern, Wales, abbey, 1131 J
Tipperary, Ireland, battle, 967 E
Tirant lo blanc (Joanot Martorell), 1490 K
Tirel, Guillaume (Taillevent), F. chef (*c.* 1315–*c.* 1395), 1377 K
Titurel (Wolfram), 1212 K
Tivoli, Italy, Treaty of, 1378 C
Toggenburg, Switzerland, 1440 D
Toghan Temur, Emperor of China (1333–67), 1367 E
Tokhta, Khan of the Golden Horde, 1291 E, 1293 E, 1298 E, 1299 E, 1312 E
Tokhtamysh, Khan of the Golden Horde (1381–97; d. 1405?), 1381 E, 1382 C, 1397 E, 1411 E; war with Timur, 1386 E, 1387 E, 1389 E, 1391 B, 1395 B, C
Toledan Tables (al-Zarqāli), 1087 G
Toledo, Spain, 806 E, 833 E, 874 E, 932 E, 1085 A
Archbishops of. *See* Eulogius; Raymond; Roderigo
Cathedral, 1227 J
school of oriental studies, 1250 H
synagogue, 1357 J
Treaties of, 1254 B, 1480 A
Tolentino, Nicholas of (Piero della Francesca), 1454 J; (Castagno), 1456 J
Tolfa, Italy, 1462 G
Tollán, Mexico, 999 E
Toltec Empire. *See* Mexico
Tomara, Indian tribe, 993 E
Tomislav, King of Croatia, 926 E
Tonarius (Frutolf), 1103 K
Tongres, Belgium, 881 E
Tönsberg, Norway, Treaty of, 1294 E
Topia, Charles, King of Albania, 1368 E
Torkil Knutson, Swedish noble, 1293 E
Tornabuoni, Lorenzo (Botticelli), 1486 J
Toro, Spain, battle, 1475 A
Toron, Lebanon, 1198 A
Torquemada, Juan de, Sp. cardinal and canonist (1388–1468), 1433 H, 1468 L
Torquemada, Tommaso de, Sp. inquisitor-general (*c.* 1420–98), 1483 H, 1488 H
Torre, Filippo della, despot of Milan, 1263 D, 1265 A
Torre, Guido della, captain of Milan, 1307 E
Torre, Martino della, despot of Milan, 1257 E, 1263 D
Torre, Napoleone della, despot of Milan, 1265 C, 1278 A
Torriani, restored in Milan, 1300 E
Tortona, Italy, 1155 A, 1323 A
Tortosa, Spain, 811 E, 1148 E
Toruń (Thorn), Poland, Treaties of, 1411 A, 1466 D
Tosa nikki (Ki no Tsurayuki), 935 K
Toscanelli, Paolo del Pozzo, It. astronomer, 1397 L, 1482 L
Tossignano, Pietro de, It. physician (d. *c.* 1407), 1398 G
Tostig, Earl of Northumbria, 1055 E, 1065 E, 1066 C
Toul, France, 1297 E; Cathedral, 1221 J, 1460 J; Treaty of, 1212 D
Toulouse, France, 1159 C, 1218 B, 1240 D; abbey, 1080 J; Cathedral, 1211 J, 1272 J; inquisition in, 1229 H; Parlement of, 1443 F; troubadors' academy, 1323 J; University, 1230 H
Counts of, 1173 A, 1271 E; *and see* Raymond IV; Raymond VI; Raymond VII; Alphonse
County, Albigenses of, 1167 H, 1205 H; Crusades against, 1179 A, 1207 D, 1209 B, C, 1213 C, 1215 A, D, 1218 B, E, 1219 B, 1224 A, 1226 A, D, 1229 B
Touraine, France, customal of, 1270 F; Duke of, *see* Louis, Duke of Orleans
Tour-Landry, le Chevalier de la, F. didactic writer (*fl.* 1346–89), 1371 K
Tournai, Belgium, Cathedral, 1110 J, 1160 J, 1240 J; Peace of, 1385 D; Treaty of, 1298 A
Tournaments, 1179 A; treatise on, 1460 K
Tournoi de Chauvency, Le (Jacques Bretel), 1285 K
Tournus, France, abbey, 960 J
Tours, France, 853 E, 903 E, 1038 E, 1044 C, 1189 C, 1468 B, 1484 A; abbey, 800 H, 804 J, 903 J, 997 J; Cathedral, 1000 H, 1240 J; Treaty of, 1444 B
Town-halls, etc. *See* Bruges; Brunswick; Brussels; Florence; London; Siena; Venice; Ypres
Towns. *See* Boroughs
Towton, England, battle, 1461 A
Tractatus de Bello (Giovanni da Legnano), 1360 F, 1388 K
Tractatus de jure regni et imperii (Lupold of Bebenburg), 1340 F
Tractatus de ponderibus (Blasius of Parma), 1416 G
Tractatus Fidei (Benedict d'Alignan), 1268 H
Tractus de vita curiali (Alain Chartier), 1440 K
Trade:
Arab, 851 G, 879 G; *and see* Caravanserais
Carolingian Empire, 805 F
Chinese, 851 G, 879 G, 1374 G
English, 1157 G, 1303 G; *Libel* on, 1437 G; shipowning, 1474 G
European:
St. Gothard opened, 1140 G
international mart, 1180 G; *and see* Champagne
commercial court, 1283 F
See also Hanse
handbook on, 1340 G
Japanese, 1341 G
Tradonico, Pietro, Doge of Venice, 837 B, 864 A
Traibhumikatha (Lu T'ai), 1345 K
'Trajan's Gate', Bulgaria, battle, 986 C
Tran Anh-tong, Emperor of Dai Viet (1293–1314), 1313 E
Tran Due-tong, Emperor of Dai Viet (1372–7), 1377 E
Tran Minh-tong, Emperor of Dai Viet (1314–29), 1318 E
Tran Thai-tong, Emperor of Dai Veit (b. 1208; 1225–58; d. 1277), 1216 D, 1225 E, 1257 E
Trani, Italy, battle, 1046 B; Cathedral, 1098 J
Translations:
Arabic, from Greek, 800 G, 827 G, 873 G, 901 G 997 G; from Hebrew, 942 H

Translations—*contd.*
English, from Flemish, 1481 K; from French, 1338 K, 1402 K, 1410 K, 1474 K, 1481 K; from Latin, 892 K, 1380 H, 1382 K, 1387 K, 1398 G, 1477 K, 1483 K
French, from Latin, 1240 K, 1355 H, 1382 K
German, from Latin, 1022 K
Greek, from Arabic, 1080 G
Hebrew, from Arabic, 1167 G, 1232 K, 1256 K
Italian, from Latin, 1471 H, 1477 H
Latin, from Arabic, 1087 G, 1100 G, K, 1103 G, 1125 K, 1126 G, 1127 G, 1128 G, 1141 K, 1143 G, H, 1144 G, 1145 G, 1165 G, 1175 G, 1187 G, 1217 G, 1220 K, 1235 K, 1255 G, 1272 K, 1279 G, 1280 G, 1313 G
from English, 998 K
from Greek, 897 K, 1160 G, 1162 K, 1193 G, 1252 K, 1253 G, 1261 K, 1286 K, 1435 K, 1439 K
from Hebrew, 1235 K
Spanish, from Arabic, 1284 G; from Latin and Hebrew, 1430 H
Transoxiana, Russia:
Sāmānid dynasty, 874 E, 900 E, 908 E, 994 E, 997 E; capital of, *see* Bukhāra
conquered by Īlek Khāns, 992 E, 997 E
by Seljuqs, 956 E, 1065 E, 1072 D
by Khwārizm-Shahs, 1214 E
by Mongols, 1219 E, 1220 A
by Timur, 1360 E, 1369 E, 1387 E
Tīmūrid dynasty, 1405 A, 1414 B, 1437 G, 1443 K, 1447 E, 1459 E, 1469 E
Transubstantiation, 831 H, 1381 H
Transylvania, Rumania, 1004 E, 1224 G, 1344 E, 1442 E
Trapani, Sicily, Italy, 1270 D; naval battle, 1264 E
Travel-writers:
Arab. *See* Fadlān; Sulaymān
Chinese. *See* Cheng Ho; Chiu Ch'ang-ch'un; Chou Ta-Kuan; Fei Hsin; Ma Huan; Rabban Sauma; Wang Ta-yüan
Flemish. *See* John of Ypres
French. *See* Baudry
Italian. *See* Contarini, Ambrogio; Conti, Niccolò de; Frescobaldi, Leonardo; John of Monte Corvino; Jordanus; Odoric of Pordenone; Polo, Marco; Sigoli, Simone
Japanese. *See* Ki no Tsurayuki
Moroccan. *See* Battūtah
Persian. *See* Khusraw
Portuguese. *See* Cá da Mosto, Alvise de
Russian. *See* Nikitin, Athanasius
Spanish Jews. *See* Benjamin ben Jonah; Ibrāhīm ibn Ia'qūb
Spanish Muslim. *See* Jubayr; Māzinī
fictitious, *viz.*, 'John de Mandeville', 1389 K
See also Pilgrimages
Travels to Tartary (Marco Polo), 1298 G
Traversari, Ambrogio, It. translator (b. 1386), 1439 K
Treasons, Statute of, 1352 F
Treatyse perteynynge to *Hawkynge, Huntynge* (Dame Juliana Berners), 1400 K
Trebbia, river, Italy battle, 889 A
Trebizond, Turkey, Greek Empire of, 1204 B, 1461 C
Trecento Novelle (Franco Sacchetti), 1395 K
Tree-Garden, The (Sādi), 1258 K
Tree of Battles (Honoré Bonet), 1388 K
Trémoille, Georges de la, F. Courtier, 1427 E, 1433 C
Trencavel, Raymond, of Toulouse, rebel, 1240 D
Très Ancien Coutumier de Normandie, 1200 F
Tresor, Li livres dou (Brunetto Latini), 1267 K
Trevisa, John of, E. translator (1326–1402), 1387 K, 1398 G, 1482 K
Treviso, Italy, 1237 A, 1339 E; fresco at, 1352 G
Trialogus (John Wycliffe), 1383 H
Triangulis planis et sphaericis, De (Regiomontanus), 1475 G
Tribhuvanadityavarman, Cambodian usurper, 1177 E
Tribuno, Pietro, Doge of Venice, 888 A, 912 E
Tribur, W. Germany, 887 D, 1076 D
Tricontai, Italy, battle, 1091 B
Trier, W. Germany, 881 E, 1473 C; Archbishops, 863 H, 1186 B; Cathedral, 1019 J; Church, 1235 J
Trigonometry, treatises on:
Abū'l-Wafa, 997 G
Jābir ibn-Aflah, 1145 G
John Maudwith, 1310 G
Richard of Wallingford, 1335 G
Levi ben Gerson, 1342 G
Trinacria. *See* Sicily
Trinitarian Friars, 1200 H
Trinitate et Fide Catholica, De Summa (John Pecham), 1292 H
Trinity (Masaccio), 1425 J
Trinity Altarpiece (Hugo van der Goes), 1478 J
Triomphe de l'amour, Le (Gaucelm Faidit), 1220 K
Trionfi, I (Petrarch), 1357 K
Trionfo, Agostino (Augustinus Triumphus), It. theologian (1243–1328), 1328 H
Tripartite Collection (Ivo of Chartres), 1115 H
Tripoli, Libya, 1146 E, 1161 E
Tripoli, Lebanon, 995 B, 1105 A, 1109 C, 1288 B
Trissino, Giangiorgio, It. tragic poet (1478–1550), 1478 L
Tristam, Nuño, Port. explorer, 1446 G
Tristan (Béroul), 1200 K; (Eilhart von Oberg), 1180 K
Tristan Theme:
Thomas, 1170 K
Marie de France, 1165 K
Thomas the Rhymer, 1294 K
Tristan und Isolde (Gottfried von Strassburg), 1210 K
Triumph of Caesar (Mantegna), 1485 J
Triumphs, The (Petrarch), 1357 K
Trivet, Nicholas, E. chronicler (b. *c.* 1263), 1328 K
Troan Chronicle, The, 1468 K
Troia, Italy, 1022 A, B; battle, 1462 C; Cathedral, 1093 J
Troilus (Albert von Stade), 1261 K
Troilus and Cressida Theme:
Benoît de Sainte-Maure, 1160 K
Boccaccio, 1350 K
Chaucer, 1384 K
Henryson, 1490 K
Troitsa monastery, Russia, 1335 H
Trojanische Krieg, Der (Conrad von Würzburg), 1287 K
Troncoso, Spain, Treaty of, 1387 B
Trono, Niccolò, Doge of Venice, 1471 D
Troubadours (Songs and Lyrics):
Rudel de Blaya, 1150 K
André le Chapelain, 1180 K
Girart de Roussillon, 1190 K
Bernart de Ventadour, 1195 K
Richard I, 1199 K
La Nobla Leyczon, 1200 K
Gaucelm Faidit, 1220 K
Trouville, Franco, 1417 C
Troy Book, The (John Lydgate), 1412 K
Troy Theme, The:
Benoît de Sainte-Maure, 1160 K
Albert von Stade, 1261 K

Guido de Columnis, 1287 K
Conrad von Würzburg, 1287 K
Boccaccio, 1350 K
Chaucer, 1384 K
Lydgate, 1412 K
Caxton's *Recuyell*, 1474 K
in national mythology, 1010 K, 1465 K; *and see* Brutus
Troyes, France, 878 C, 996 A; Cathedral, 1228 J, 1262 J; fair, 1114 G; Treaty of, 1420 B
Troylus and Cryseyde (Chaucer), 1384 K
Truce of God. *See* Peace
True Cross (Piero della Francesca), 1452 J
Trujillo, Spain, Treaty of, 1479 C
T'sê-fu yüan-kuei (Wang Ch'in-jo), 1005 F
Ts'e-yüan hai-ching (Li Yeh), 1248 G
Tsong Kapa, Tibetan Lama (1357–1419), 1392 H
Ts'u chih ching (Chia Ssŭ-tao), 1230 G
Tsurezure-gusa (Yoshida Kenkō), 1350 K
Tsutsumi Chúnagon, Ja. anthologist, 1200 K
Tu Yu, C. encyclopedeist, 812 F
Tuam, Ireland, Archbishopic of, 1152 H
Tübingen, W. Germany, University, 1477 H
Tuda-Mangu, Khan of the Golden Horde, 1280 E, 1287 E
Tudela, Spain, Treaty of, 1231 A
Tufayl, Abu-Bakr Muhammad ibn-, Arab novelist, 1185 K
Tughril Bey, first Seljuq Sultan (1055–63), 1040 A, 1050 E, 1054 E, 1055 D, 1063 C
Tughril III, last Seljuq Sultan of Iraq, 1194 E
Tuhfat al- Albāb (al-Māzinī), 1136 G, 1162 G
Tuhfat al- Nuzzār (ibn-Battūtah), 1354 G
Tuim, Jehan, F. translator, 1240 G
Tūlūn, Ahmad ibn-, Governor of Egypt (d. 884), 868 E, 872 G, 876 J, 877 E
Tulunid dynasty. *See* Egypt
Tuluy, ruler of Mongolia, 1227 C
Tungabhara, river, India, battle, 1422 E
Tun-huang, China, 1035 H
T'ung-chien chi-shih pen-mo (Yüan Shu), 1205 K
T'ung chih (Chêng Ch'iao), 1161 K
T'ung Hou, C. painter and art historian, 1329 J
T'ung Shu (*Chou Tun-i*), 1073 H
T'ung tien, 801 K; (Tu Yu), 812 F
Tunis, Tunisia, 909 D, 969 C, 1118 E, 1153 E, 1158 E, 1270 C, D, 1280 E
Tunsted, Simon, E. musical theorist, 1369 J
Tuqhluq I, Ghiyāth-ad-Dīn, Shah of Delhi, 1320 C, 1323 E, 1325 A
Tuqhluq II, Shah of Delhi, 1388 C, 1389 A
Tūrān Shāh, al- Mu'azzam, Sultan of Egypt, 1249 D, 1250 B
Tūrān-Shāh, brother of Saladin, 1173 E, 1174 E, 1176 E
Turfan, China, 840 E
Turgeis, Viking leader, 845 E
Turifa, Spain, battle, 1229 C
Turin, Italy, 1226 A, 1270 E; Treaty of, 1381 C
Turin, Très Belles Heures de, 1411 J
Turkestan, Russia, 956 E, 992 E; *and see* Chaghadai
Turkey, Ottoman Turks in, 1300 E; *and see*
'Osmān (*c.* 1288–1326)
Orkhān (1326–59)
Murād I (1359–89)
Bāyezīd I (1389–1403)
Sulaymān I (1403–11)
Muhammad I (1403–21)
Murād II (1421–51)
Muhammad II (1451–81)
Bāyezīd II (1481–1512)
Turkomans. *See* Azerbaijan; Persia
Turks, tribes or groups of, controlling Caliphate of Baghdād (*q.v.*); Delhi, 1246 B; *and see* Cumans, Ghaznī (for Ghaznavids), Karakhanids, Pechenegs, Persia (Khwārizm-Shāhs, Seljuqs), Rūm (Karamans, Seljuqs), Seljuq Turks, Sha-t'o, Sivas (Danishmends), Turkey (Ottomans), Uighur
grammar, 1313 K
poetry: al-Ahmedī, 1390 K
Tuscany, Italy, 1174 D, 1264 E, 1267 B, 1268 B, 1278 B, 1279 E, 1289 B, 1300 A, 1317 E; Countess of, *see* Matilda; Marquess of, *see* Welf VI
Tusculum, Italy, 1191 B; Counts of, 1012 B
Tūsī, Nasīr-ad-Dīn al-, Per. astronomer and mathematician (b. 1201), 1259 G, 1274 G
Tutush, Seljuq prince, 1079 E, 1086 E, 1094 E, 1095 E
Tuy, Spain, Treaty of, 1137 C
Tver, Russia, 1484 E; prince of, 1375 E
Twinger, Jakob, G. chronicler (*fl. c.* 1415), 1362 K
Tyler, Wat, E. rebel leader, 1381 B
Tyre, Lebanon, 1089 E, 1124 C, 1187 D
Tyrol, Austria, 1335 B, 1336 E, 1342 A, 1350 A; under Habsburgs, 1362 E, 1364 E, 1490 A; Count of, *see* Habsburg, Sigismund
Tyrranno, De (Salutati), 1400 F
Tzimisces, John. *See* John I, Greek Emperor
Tzŭ chieh t'ung chien (Ssŭ-ma Kuang), 1086 K

U

U Thong, Siam, 1347 E
Ubaldi, Baldo degli, It. jurist (b. 1327), 1400 F
Uberti, Fazio degli, It. poet, 1368 K
Uccello, Paolo, It. painter, 1397 L, 1425 J, 1436 J, 1443 J, 1445 J, 1454 J, 1465 J, 1475 L
Udaba', Mu'jam al- (Yāqūt), 1229 G
'Ubaydullāh al-Mahdī (Sa'īd ibn- Husayn), founder of Fātimids, 882 L, 909 D, 914 E, 917 E, 934 E
Uclés, Spain, battle, 1108 B
Ugolino, tyrant of Pisa, 1289 E
Ugra, river, Russia, 1408 C
Uguccione della Faggiuola, tyrant of Pisa, 1314 B, 1315 C, 1317 E, 1319 D
Uhtred, Earl of Northumbria, 1016 E
Uighur (Turkish) confederation in Manchuria (from 744), 832 E, 840 E, 842 H; books and mss. in Uighur, 1035 H
Ukraine, Russia, 1377 E, 1397 E; Cossacks of, 1412 E
Ulagchi, Khan of the Golden Horde, 1256 E, 1258 E
Ulf, Regent of Denmark 1026 E
Uljāytū, Muhammad, Sultan (Ilkhan) of Persia, 1307 E, 1308 E, 1316 E
Ulm, W. Germany, 1377 B; minster, 1377 J
Ulric, St., Bishop of Augsburg (d. 973), 993 H
Ulrich von Lichtenstein, G. poet and autobiographer (d. *c.* 1275), 1255 K
Ulug-Mahmed, Khan of the Golden Horde (1419–45), 1445 C
Ulūgh Beg, ruler of Transoxiana (b. 1394; 1447–9), *Tables* of, 1437 G
'Umar al-Mutawakkil, King of Badajoz (1068–94), 1094 A
'Umar, Shihāb-ad-Dīn, Sultan of Delhi (b. *c.* 1310) 1316 A
'Umari, ibn-Fadlallāh al-, Syrian geographer and historian (1301–49), 1348 G
Umayyad dynasty. *See* Andalusia
Unam Sanctam (Boniface VIII), 1302 D
Unique Necklace, The (Rabbih), 940 J

Unitate Intellectus, De (Albertus Magnus), 1256 K
Universal Mirror to help Government (Ssŭ-ma Kuang), 1086 K, 1205 K
Universities:
European, origin of, 1000 H; clerks at, 1298 H; *and see* Angers, Basel, Bologna, Bordeaux, Budapest, Caen, Cambridge, Coimbra, Cologne, Constantinople, Copenhagen, Cracow, Erfurt, Ferrara, Florence, Freiburg, Glasgow, Grenoble, Heidelberg, Leipzig, Lérida, Lisbon, Louvain, Mainz, Montpellier, Nantes, Naples, Northampton, Orleans, Oxford, Padua, Palencia, Palma, Paris, Pavia, Pécs, Perpignan, Perugia, Piacenza, Pisa, Poitiers, Prague, Rome, Rostock, St. Andrews, Salamanca, Salisbury, Siena, Stamford, Toulouse, Tübingen, Upsala, Valence, Valladolid, Vienna
in Dai Viet, 1076 H
Muslim, 1065 H; *and see* Baghdād, Cairo, Cordova
See also Colleges
Unterwalden. *See* Switzerland
Upsala, Sweden, Archbishop of, 1210 C; Cathedral, 1134 J; University, 1476 H
Urban II (Otto of Chatillon), Pope (1088–99), 1088 A, 1089 E, 1094 E, 1099 C; and First Crusade, 1089 C, 1095 A, D
Urban III (Humbert Crivelli), Pope, 1185 D, 1186 B–1186 D, 1187 D
Urban IV (James Pantaléon), Pope, 1261 C, 1262 A, 1263 D, H, 1264 D
Urban V (Guillaume de Grimoard), Pope (1362–70), 1362 C, 1363 B, D, 1365 B, 1370 D; war with Milan, 1363 A, 1364 A; attempts return to Rome, 1367 D, 1370 C
Urban VI (Bartolomeo Prignano), Pope (in Rome; 1378–89), 1378 B, C, 1381 B, 1389 D; and Great Schism, 1378 C, D, 1379 B, 1381 C, 1383 C
Urbino, Italy, Count of, 1430 D; painting at, 1465 J; paintings of Duke and Duchess (Piero della Francesca), 1470 J, 1472 J
Uri. *See* Switzerland
Urine, treatise on (al-Isrā'īli), 932 G; (Giles of Corbeil), 1222 G
Urracca, Queen of Castile and Leon (1109–26), 1109 E, 1112 E, 1126 A; breach with husband, Alfonso of Aragon, 1110 E, 1111 D, 1114 D
Usatges of Catalonia, 1064 F
Usaybi'ah, Ahmad ibn-abi, Syrian biographer (1203–70), 1270 G
Usk, river, Wales, battle, 1405 B
Usk, Adam of, Welsh chronicler, 1430 K
Usodimare, Antoniotto, Port. navigator, 1455 G
Ústi, Czechoslovakia, battle, 1426 B
Utrecht, Holland, 954 E; Cathedral, 1000 H, 1254 J; *Psalter*, 832 J; Treaty of, 1474 G
Utsubo Monogatari, 1000 K
Uzbeg, Khan of the Golden Horde, 1312 E, 1319 E, 1322 E, 1325 E, 1328 E, 1339 E, 1341 E
Uzun Hasan, ruler of the White Sheep Turkomans (1453–78), 1487 G

V

Vacarius, It. jurist, 1149 H
Václav, King of Poland. *See* Wenceslas II
Val de Dios, Spain, church, 893 J
Val de Junqueras, Spain, battle, 920 E
Val d'Ossola, Italy, 1422 B
Val-ès-Dunes, France, battle, 1047 E
Valais, Switzerland, 1403 B
Valence, France, University, 1452 H
Valence, Aymer de, Earl of Pembroke (*c.* 1270–1324), 1318 C
Valencia, Spain, 1085 B, 1094 E, 1099 E, 1238 C, 1309 E, 1316 E; Cathedral, 1262 J; commercial court, 1283 F; Cortes, 1283 F; 'Union' of, 1348 C
Valenciennes, France, 1006 C, 1007 E, 1009 E; Treaty of, 1337 C
Valenciennes, Henri de, F. crusader-chronicler (d. 1213?), 1216 K
Valentine, Pope, 827 C
Valla, Lorenzo, It. humanist and scholar (1405–57), 1405 L, 1432 K, 1435 K, 1440 H, 1457 K, L, 1471 K
Valladolid, Spain, University, 1346 H
Valle, Giovanni, It. mendicant reformer, 1334 H
Vallombrosa, Italy, monastic order of, 1038 H
Valois, France, 1213 B; Counts of, *see* Charles, Philip VI
Valpellage, Spain, battle, 1070 C
Vanagan, John, Armenian chronicler, 1251 K
Varangian Empire. *See* Kiev
Varangian guard, 988 C
Varangunavarman II, King of Pandya (862–80), 880 E
Varaville, France, battle, 1058 C
Vardan the Great, Armenian chronicler, 1271 K
Varna, Bulgaria, 1366 C; battle, 1444 D, 1447 B
Vasili, Grand Duke of Vladimir, 1272 E, 1276 E
Vasili I of Moscow, Grand Duke of Vladimir, 1389 B, 1391 E, 1398 E, 1406 E, 1408 C, D, 1425 E
Vasili II, Grand Duke of Moscow (b. 1410; 1425–62), 1425 E, 1433 B, 1434 B, 1445 C; blinded, 1446 A, 1447 A; extends power, 1452 E, 1453 E, 1462 A
Vasili Kosoy, claimant to Moscow, 1434 B
Vaudeville. *See Vaux-de-vire*
Vaudois. *See* Waldenses
Vaux-de-vire (Olivier Basselin), 1430 K
Vegio, Maffeo, It. poet, 1406 L, 1458 L
Velbužd, Bulgaria, battle, 1330 B
Veldeke, Heinrich von, G. poet (*fl.* 1170–90), 1170 K, 1189 K
Velluti, Donato, It. chronicler (1313–70), 1370 K
Velocitatum, De proportionibus (Thomas Bradwardine), 1349 G
Venaissin, France, Comtât, 1271 C
Vendôme, France, Treaty of, 1227 B
Vendramino, Andrea, Doge of Venice (b. 1400), 1476 A, 1478 B
Venetia, Italy, under Charlemagne, 805 E; under Greeks, 807 E, 810 C, 812 B; Saracen raid, 840 E
Veneto, Marine de, It. translator of Bible, 1477 H
Veneziano. *See* Domenico Veneziano
Venice, Italy:
Maurice dynasty of Doges (765–802), 802 E
defeat Pepin; city on Rialto, 810 C
popular election of Doges, 887 B, 888 B, 1032 E
battle with Slavs, 887 C
independence recognised, 992 E
trade in Greek Empire, 992 E, 1082 E
protectorate of Dalmatia, 998 E, 1115 E
defeat Muslim fleets, 1002 E, 1123 B
Consilium Sapientium founded, 1143 F
allies of Greek Empire, 1148 E
breach with Greeks, 1171 A
peace with Italian enemies, 1177 C
and Fourth Crusade, 1201 B
conquests from Greeks, 1202 B, 1204 D, 1207 E, 1212 E
trade in Latin Empire, 1261 A
war with Genoa, 1261 A, 1263 E, 1264 E
peace with Greeks, 1268 B
treaty with Sicily, 1281 C

war with Genoa, 1287 B, 1294 E, 1297 E, 1298 C, 1299 B
Teutonic Knights at, 1291 E
'closes' Great Council, 1298 C
War of Ferrarese Succession, 1308 A, C, 1310 B
Council of Ten, 1310 B, 1355 B, 1457 D
annexes Treviso, 1339 E
war with Genoa, 1352 A, 1353 C, 1354 D, 1355 B
war with Milan, 1354 A
conspiracy of Doge Falieri, 1355 B
wars with Hungary, 1356 E, 1357 C, 1358 A, 1369 E
War of Chioggia with Genoa, 1376 E, 1378 D, 1379 C, 1380 B, 1381 C
peace with Milan, 1400 A
rules Athens, 1403 A
takes Verona and Vicenza, 1404 E; and Padua, 1405 D
war with Hungary regains Dalmatia, 1409 C, 1412 E
defeats Turks, 1416 E
takes Friuli, 1418 E
holds Salonika, 1423 E, 1430 A
wars with Milan, 1425 D, 1426 A, 1427 D, 1428 B, 1431 B, C, 1432 B, 1433 B, 1434 C, 1438 B, 1439 D, 1441 D
annexes Ravenna, 1441 A
War of Milanese Succession, 1447 C, 1448 C, D, 1452 B, 1454 B, C
Doge Foscari deposed, 1457 D
war with Turks, 1470 C, 1474 C, 1479 A
war with Pope and Naples, 1478 B, 1480 A
War of Ferrara, 1482 B, C, 1483 A, 1484 C
buys Cyprus, 1489 A
Bank of, 1157 F
buildings, etc.:
Doge's Palace, 1310 J; frescoes, 1415 J
S. Marco, 1154 J; mosaics, 1063 J, 1425 J
S. Zaccaria, frescoes, 1442 J
statue, 1481 J
commission of Public Health, 1343 K
Doges. *See*:
Obelerius (802–11)
Particiaco, Angelo (811–27)
Particiaco, Giustiniani (827–9)
Particiaco, Giovanni I (829–37)
Tradonico, Pietro (837–64)
Particiaco, Orso (864–81)
Particiaco, Giovanni II (881–8)
Candiano, Pietro (887)
Tribuno, Pietro (888–912)
Particiaco, Orso II (912–32)
Candiano, Pietro II (932–9)
Badoero, Pietro (939–42)
Candiano, Pietro III (942–59)
Candiano, Pietro IV (959–76)
Orseolo, Pietro (976–8)
Candiano, Vitale (978–9)
Memmo, Tribuno (979–91)
Orseolo, Pietro II (991–1009)
Orseolo, Ottone (1009–26)
Barbolano, Pietro (1026–32)
Orseolo, Domenico (1032)
Orseolo, Flabanico (1032–43)
Contarino, Domenico I (1043–71)
Orseolo, Salvio (1071–84)
Falieri, Vitale (1084–96)
Micheli, Vitale I (1096–1102)
Falieri, Ordelafo (1102–17)
Micheli, Domenico (1117–30)
Polano, Pietro (1130–48)
Morosini, Domenico (1148–56)
Micheli, Vitale II (1156–73)
Ziano, Sebastiano (1173–7)
Malipiero, Orio (1177–92)
Dandolo, Enrico (1192–1205)
Ziano, Pietro (1205–29)
Tiepolo, Jacopo (1229–49)
Morosini, Giacomo (1249–52)
Zeno, Raniero (1252–68)
Tiepolo, Lorenzo (1268–75)
Contarino, Jacopo (1275–9)
Dandolo, Giovanni (1279–89)
Gradenigo, Pietro (1289–1311)
Giorgio, Marino (1311–12)
Soranzo, Giovanni (1312–27)
Dandolo, Francesco (1328–39)
Gradenigo, Bartolomeo (1339–42)
Dandolo, Andrea (1343–54)
Falieri, Marino (1354–5)
Gradenigo, Giovanni (1355–6)
Delfino, Giovanni (1356–61)
Celso, Lorenzo (1361–5)
Cornaro, Marco (1365–7)
Contarini, Andrea (1367–82)
Morosini, Michele (1382)
Vernieri, Antonio (1382–1400)
Steno, Michele (1400–13)
Mocenigo, Tomaso (1414–23)
Foscari, Francesco (1423–57)
Malipiero, Pasquale (1457–62)
Moro, Cristofero (1462–71)
Trono, Niccolò (1471–3)
Marcello, Niccolò (1473–4)
Mocenigo, Pietro (1474–6)
Vendramino, Andrea (1476–8)
Mocenigo, Giovanni (1478–85)
Barbarigo, Marco (1485–6)
Bargarigo, Agostino (1486–1501)
history (Bernado Giustiniani), 1489 K
industries, 1291 G, 1328 G
merchants. *See* Polo
Venosa, Italy, Cathedral, 1135 J
Vercelli, Italy, 1050 H, 1321 B; Bishop of, 997 E; Treaty of, 1193 A
Verde. *See* Cape Verde
Verdun, France, 984 A; Bishop and Count of, 1046 B; Cathedral, 1135 J; Treaty of, 843 C
Vere, Robert de, Earl of Oxford (1362–92), 1387 D
Verga, Judah, Port. J. astronomer (d. *c.* 1490), 1457 G
Vergerio, Pier Paolo, It. humanist-educationalist, 1398 H, 1428 L
Vermandois, France, 1213 B; Count of, *see* Herbert; customs of, 1260 F
Verneuil, France, battle, 1424 C
Vernieri, Antonio, Doge of Venice, 1382 D, 1400 D
Verona, Italy, 905 C, 1184 D, H, 1226 E, 1269 E, 1387 D, 1404 E; lords of, 1311 E, *and see* Scala; church, 990 J
Verona, Battista da, It. writer on education, 1458 H
Verona, Guarino da, It. humanist schoolmaster, 1370 L, 1458 H, 1460 L
Verrocchio, Andrea del, It. sculptor (*c.* 1435–88), 1481 J
Versinicia, Turkey, battle, 813 B
Vesconte, Pietro, It. cartographer, 1311 G
Vespasiano da Bisticci, It. bibliographer (1421–98), 1421 L
Vespucci, Amerigo, It. navigator (1451–1512), 1451 L
Veterinary surgeons:
Egyptian. *See* Baytar; Dimyāti
Italian. *See* Giordano Ruffo

Vexin, France, the Norman, 1151 C, 1160 D, 1193 C, 1196 E, 1198 C, 1200 B
Vézelay, France, 1146 B, 1190 C; abbey, 1096 J, 1120 J, 1185 J
Viaggio al Monte Sinai (Simone Sigoli), 1390 G
Viandier, Le (Taillevent), 1377 K
Viborg, Denmark, battle, 1157 D
Vicenza, Italy, 1226 A, 1236 D, 1341 E, 1387 D, 1404 E
Vick, Henri de, Belgian clockmaker, 1370 G
Vico, Giovanni di, Prefect of Rome, 1354 B, 1363 C
Victor II (Gebhard of Eichstadt), Pope, 1054 D, 1057 C
Victor III (Desiderius), Pope, 1086 B, 1087 C
Victor IV, anti-pope, 1138 A, B
Victor IV (Octavian), anti-pope, 1159 C, 1160 A, 1164 B
Victring, John of, Austrian chronicler, 1345 K
Vida de Sancto Domingo de Silos (Gonzalo de Berceo), 1235 K
Vida de Santa Oria (Gonzalo), 1235 K
Vie de Saint Alexis, La, 1040 K
Vie de Seint Auban, La (Matthew Paris), 1259 K
Vie de Sainte Eulalie, La, 885 K
Vie de Saint Louis, La (Jean de Joinville), 1309 K
Vienna, Austria, 1030 E, 1031 E, 1192 D
  Free City, 1237 A
  Habsburg capital, 1276 D, 1461 D
  Concordat of, 1448 A
  taken by Hungary, 1485 B, (1490 B)
  Cathedral, 1258 J, 1304 J, 1405 J, 1446 J
  St. Stephen's, 1470 J
  University, 1365 H
Vienna Diptych (Hugo van der Goes), 1470 J
Vienne, France, 1112 C; General Council, 1311 H, 1312 H; King of, 1365 B
  See also Dauphiné of Vienne
Vietnam, North. *See* Dai-co-viet; Dai Viet
Vietnam, South. *See* Champa
Vigevano, Guido da, It. surgeon and physician (*c.* 1280–*c.* 1345), 1335 G, 1345 G
Vijaya, S. Vietnam, 1000 E, 1044 E, 1149 E
Vijayabāhu I, King of Ceylon (1056–1101), 1070 E
Vijayālaya, founder of Chola Empire (d. *c.* 871), 846 E
Vijayanagar, India, Hindu Empire, 1336 B, 1367 F, G, 1370 E, 1404 E, 1419 E, 1422 E, 1486 E
Vikings and Danes, Norse raiders:
  sack Iona, 802 E
  invade Saxony, 829 E, 880 A
  attack Frisia, 834 E
  sack Quentovic, 842 E
  attack France and Spain, 844 C
  colonise Iceland, 847 G
  in Russia. *See* Kiev
  camp in France and Low Countries, 850 E
  raid Mediterranean, 859 E, 860 E, 861 E
  harry Rhineland and France, 881 E, 882 D
  move on to England and Lorraine, 884 C
  besiege Paris, raid Burgundy, 885 C, D
  in Lorraine and Belgium, 891 D
  colonise Greenland, 982 G
  reach North America, 1003 G, 1076 K
  See also England, France, Ireland
Vikramabāhu I, King of Ceylon (1029–41), 1029 E
Vikrāmanka, King of Rāshtrakūta, 1156 E
Villani, Giovanni, It. chronicler, 1348 K, L
Villanova, Arnold of, Catalan physician and alchemist, 1311 G
Villehardouin, Geoffrey of, Prince of Achaea, 1209 E
Villehardouin, Geoffroi de, F. chronicler (*c.* 1165–*c.* 1213), 1213 K, 1216 K
Villehardouin, William de, Prince of Achaea, 1278 B
Villon, François, F. poet (1431?–1466?), 1431 L, 1456 K, 1461 K, 1466 L
Vilna, Lithuania, Russia, 1341 E, 1447 B; Cathedral, 1387 J
Vincennes, France, Treaties of, 1341 A, 1381 A
Vincent of Beauvais, F. encyclopedeist (*c.* 1190–*c.* 1264), 1264 K, 1481 K
Vineland (Nova Scotia), 1003 G, 1076 K
Virgin, paintings of. *See Madonna*
Viribus herbarum, De (Odo of Meung), 1100 G
Viru, Esthonia, Russia, 1346 E
Visby, Gothland, Sweden, 1282 G, 1360 C, 1398 B; Cathedral, 1225 J
Visconti, Azzo, ruler of Milan (b. 1302), 1328 C, 1332 D, 1337 E, 1339 C
Visconti, Bernabò, ruler of Milan (1354–85), 1354 D, 1356 D; wars with Papacy, 1360 C, 1361 B, 1363 A, 1364 A, 1373 B, 1374 B; deposed, 1385 B, D
Visconti, Bianca, wife of Francesco Sforza, 1441 D
Visconti, Filippo Maria, Duke of Milan (b. 1391; 1412–47), 1412 B, 1447 C; annexes Genoa, 1421 D, 1435 D; wars with Swiss, 1422 B, 1440 E; with Italian powers, 1423 E, 1425 D, 1426 A, E, 1427 D, 1428 B, 1430 D, 1431 B, C, 1433 B, 1434 B, C, 1435 D, 1438 B, 1439 D, 1440 B, 1441 D; occupies Bologna, 1438 B, 1443 B; life of, 1477 K
Visconti, Galeazzo I, ruler of Milan (b. 1277), 1322 B, 1323 B, C, 1324 D, 1326 B, 1328 C
Visconti, Galeazzo II, joint ruler of Milan, 1354 D, 1360 H, 1378 C
Visconti, Gian Galeazzo, ruler and Duke of Milan (1378–1402), 1351 L, 1378 C, 1385 B, 1387 B, 1402 C
  gains in north Italy, 1379 A, 1386 E, 1387 D, 1388 D, 1390 B
  wars with Florence, etc., 1390 B, 1391 C, 1392 A, B, 1396 C, 1397 A, C, 1398 B, 1401 D, 1402 B
  created Duke, 1395 B
  gains in Tuscany, 1398 C, 1399 A, C, 1400 A
  as founder, 1386 J, 1396 H, 1398 H
Visconti, Giovanni, Archbishop of Milan (1343–54) and its ruler, 1349 A, 1350 D, 1351 D, 1352 B, 1353 A, C, 1354 A, D
Visconti, Giovanni Maria, Duke of Milan (b. 1388), 1402 C, 1412 B
Visconti, Luchino, ruler of Milan, 1339 C, 1349 A
Visconti, Matteo I, ruler of Milan (b. 1250), 1295 C, 1299 B; expelled, 1300 E; restored, 1311 E, 1315 D, 1321 B, 1322 A, B
Visconti, Matteo II, joint ruler of Milan (d. 1355), 1354 D
Visconti, Otto, Archbishop of Milan (b. 1208), 1263 D; secular ruler, 1278 A, 1295 C
Visconti, Tedald. *See* Gregory X
Visconti, Valentina, wife of Louis of Orleans, 1387 B
Visé, France, 942 D
Viseu, Portugal, 1027 B; Duke of, 1484 C
Vishnu-Vardhana, King of Halebīd, 1141 E
Vision of Piers Plowman, The (William Langland), 1377 K
Vistula, river, Poland, battle, 1344 E
Vita Caroli (Beneš of Weitmil), 1375 K
Vita civile, Della (Matteo Palmieri), 1475 K
Vita et moribus philosophorum (Walter Burley), 1345 K
Vita Karoli Magni (Einhard), 830 K
Vita Ludovici IX (Geoffroi de Beaulieu), 1274 K
Vita Nuova (Dante), 1300 K
Vita Philippi Mariae (Pier Candido Decembrio), 1477 K
Vita Sancti Anselmi (Eadmer), 1130 K
Vitalian Brethren, pirates, 1380 E

Vitas summorum Pontificum (Platina), 1479 K
Vitelleschi, Giovanni, Cardinal and legate, 1441 B
Viterbo, Italy, 1354 B
Vitkow, Czechoslovakia, battle, 1420 C
Vitold, Grand Duke of Lithuania (b. *c.* 1350, 1401–30), 1401 A, 1413 D, 1430 D, 1432 C
 wars with Russian princes, 1395 E, 1404 B, 1406 E, 1408 C
 conquers Ukraine, 1397 E, 1399 C, 1411 E, 1412 E
 wars with Teutonic Knights, 1410 C, 1411 A, 1414 E, 1422 C
Vitorial, El (Gutierre Diaz de Gamez), 1450 K
Vitry, Jacques de, F. cardinal and chronicler (1180–1240), 1240 K
Vitry, Philippe de, Bishop of Meaux, F. musician, 1291 L, 1343 G, 1361 J
Viyayarāya, Emperor of Vijayanagar (1422–6?), 1422 E
Vladimir, Russia, capital of Grand Princes of Russia, 1169 A
 Princes. *See*
  Andrew I (1169–74)
  Michael I (1174–7)
  Vsévolod III (1177–1212)
  Juri II (1212–38)
  Jaroslav II (1238–46)
 Grand Dukes appointed by Golden Horde. *See*
  Andrew II (1247–52)
  Alexander I Nevski (1252–63)
  Jaroslav III (1263–72)
  Vasili (1272–6)
  Dmitri I (1276–93)
  Andrew III (1280–1305)
  Michael II (1305–19)
  Juri III (1319–22)
  Dinitri II (1322–5)
  Alexander II (1325–8)
  Alexander III (1328–32)
  continued under Moscow
 sacked by Mongols, 1238 A, 1280 E, 1293 E
 Metropolitan see at, 1300 H
 Cathedral, 1158 J
 churches, 1190 J; frescoes, 1198 J
Vladimir, Khan of the Bulgars (889–93), 893 E
Vladimir, St., the Great, Prince of Kiev, 977 E, 981 E, 988 A, C, 989 E, 1015 E
Vladimir II Monomach, Prince of Kiev, 1113 B, 1125 E
Vladislav I, Duke of Bohemia (1111–25), 1111 E, 1114 E, 1125 E, 1040 E
Vladislav II (I as King), Duke of Bohemia, 1140 E, 1143 E; King, 1158 A, 1173 E
Vladislav II, King of Bohemia (b. *c.* 1456; 1471–1516), 1469 B, 1471 A, 1478 D, 1485 H; King of Hungary (as Ladislas VII), 1490 C, 1491 A, D
Vladislav I Hermann, Duke of Poland (b. 1043), 1081 A, 1102 C
Vladislav II, Grand Prince of Poland (b. 1104), 1138 E; expelled, 1146 E, 1158 C
Vladislav III, Grand Prince of Poland (b. 1168), 1231 E
Vladislav I Lokietek, King of Poland (b. 1260; 1320–33); as Vladislav IV, Grand Prince, 1296 A, 1300 E, 1304 E, 1308 D; King, 1320 A, 1325 E, 1326 E, 1331 C, 1333 A
Vladislav II, King of Poland. *See* Jagiello
Vladislav III, King of Poland (b. 1424; 1434–44), 1434 B, 1435 D; King of Hungary (as Ladislas V), 1439 D, 1440 E; Crusader, 1441 E, 1444 C, D, 1447 B
Vladislav, joint King of Serbia (1228–43), 1228 E
Vladislav Henry, Duke of Bohemia, 1197 E
Vladivoj, Duke of Bohemia, 1002 E, 1003 E
Vocabularium (Papias), 1063 K
Voiage and Travaile ('John de Mandeville'), 1372 G
Volhynia, Russia, 1339 E, 1366 E
Volkovysk, Russia, Treaty of, 1383 E
Volksbücher, 1450 K
Voluptate, De (Lorenzo Valla), 1432 K
Voragine, Jacobus de (Giacomo da Varaggio), Bishop of Genoa, It. hagiographer and chronicler (1230–98), 1265 K, 1298 K, 1483 K
Vordingborg, Denmark, Treaty of, 1435 C
Vorskla, river, Russia, battle, 1399 C
Vox Clamantis (John Gower), 1383 K
Voyage of Charlemagne, The, 1150 K
Voyages of the Eyes (al-'Umari), 1348 G
Vozha, river, Russia, battle, 1378 E
Vratislav I, Prince of Bohemia (d. *c.* 920), 921 E
Vratislav II, Duke of Bohemia, 1061 E, 1082 E; King, 1085 B, 1092 E
Vsévolod I, Prince of Kiev, 1078 E, 1093 E
Vsévolod II, Prince of Kiev, 1139 E, 1146 E
Vsévolod III, Grand Prince of Vladimir, 1177 E, 1212 E
Vukašin, King of Serbia, 1371 C
Vulgari Eloquentia, De (Dante), 1321 K
Vyborg, Russia, 1293 E
Vyšehrad, Czechoslovakia, battle, 1420 D
Vyšehrad, Hungary, Treaties of, 1335 D, 1339 E
Vyve-Saint-Bavon, Belgium, Treaty of, 1297 D

W

Wace (of Jersey), Norman poet and chronicler (*c.* 1100–*c.* 1175) 1155 K
Wafā al-Būzjānī, Abu'l-, Arab astronomer, mathematician and translator (*c.* 945–*c.* 997), 997 G
Wafa, ibn-, Eg. poet, 1357 K
Wāfī bi-l-wafayāt, Kitab al- (al-Safadi), 1363 K
Wagaru, ruler of Lower Burma (*c.* 1287–1306), 1306 F
Wages, regulated in England, 1351 G, 1388 G; in Portugal, 1252 G
Wahshiyya, ibn-, Arab writer on agriculture, 800 G
Wakefield, England, battle, 1460 D
Walafrid Strabo, Abbot of Reichenau, G. theologian, poet and herbalist (808/9–849), 849 H, K
Walcher, Bishop of Durham and Earl of Northumbria, 1080 B
Walcher of Malvern, E. astronomer (d. 1135), 1091 G, 1108 G
Waldemar I the Great, King of Denmark (b. 1131), 1157 B, D, 1181 E, 1182 B
Waldemar II the Victorious, King of Denmark (b. 1170), 1202 D, 1210 E, 1214 B, 1218 E, 1227 C, 1240 F, 1241 A
Waldemar IV Atterdag, King of Denmark (1340–75), 1340 E, 1346 E, 1362 C, 1364 C, 1375 A; war with Hanse, 1360 C, E, 1362 C, 1365 D, 1367 D, 1369 D
Waldemar, King of Sweden, 1250 A, 1275 E
Waldenses (Vaudois), F. heretics, 1170 H, 1184 H, 1217 H, 1488 H; of Lombardy, 1217 H
Waldhauser, Conrad, Austrian preacher (d. 1369), 1363 H
Waldo, Peter, merchant of Lyons and founder of Waldenses, 1170 H
Wales:
 native kings. *See* Gwynned; Powys
 English invasions, 1011 E, 1063 B, C
 Norman marcher lords, 1081 E, 1094 E, 1096 E
 South, last native King in, 1093 B

Wales—*contd.*
campaign of William II, 1097 E
rising, 1136 A
campaigns of Henry II, 1158 E, 1165 E
John's campaigns, 1209 D, 1211 B, 1212 C, 1213 B
campaigns of Henry III, 1218 A, 1228 C, 1231 D, 1241 E, 1259 C, 1262 E, 1267 C
Princes. *See*
Llewelyn ap Gruffyd (1258–82)
David ap Gruffyd (1282–3)
conquered by Edward I, 1277 B, D, 1282 A, C, 1283 B, D, 1284 F
revolts against, 1294 C, 1295 A, 1301 A
English Princes. *See* Edward II; Edward (the Black Prince); Henry V; Edward (1454–71); Edward V; Arthur
native 'princes'. *See* Owain ap Thomas; Glyn Dwr, Owain
revolt of Owain Glyn Dwr, 1400 C, D, 1401 D, 1402 C, 1403 C, D, 1404 B, C, 1405 A–C, 1409 A
parliament, 1404 B
Council for the Marches, 1473 F
Description (Gerald), 1188 K
Laws of Hywel Dda, 949 F
literature:
Nennius, 810 K
Black Book of Carmarthen, 1150 K
Eisteddfod, 1176 K
Mabinogion, 1375 K
Wallace, William, Scottish leader, 1297 B, C, 1305 C
Wallachia, Rumania, 1389 E, 1395 B, 1467 E
Wallingford, England, Treaty of, 1153 D
Wallingford, Richard, Abbot of St. Albans, E. astronomer and mathematician, 1291 L, 1326 G, 1335 G, L
Walsingham, Thomas, E. chronicler, 1422 K
Walter and Hildegund (Ekkehard), 937 K
Walter von der Vogelwiede, minnesinger, 1230 K
Walter, Hubert, Archbishop of Canterbury, justiciar and chancellor, 1180 F, 1194 F, 1205 C
Waltharii Poesis (Ekkehard), 937 L
Waltheof, Earl of Northumbria, 1075 E, 1076 B
Wamyōshō (Minamoto no Shitagau), 983 K
Wang An-shih, C. statesman (1021–86), 1076 F
Wang Chên, C. writer on agriculture, 1314 G
Wang Chien, Emperor of China, 935 E
Wang Ch'in-jo, C. encyclopedeist (d. 1024), 1005 F
Wang Hsien-Chih, C. peasant leader, 874 E, 878 E
Wang Kon, King of Korea, 935 A
Wang Kuan, C. botanist, 1070 G
Wang Meng, C. painter, 1385 J
Wang Ta-yüan, C. travel-writer, 1349 G
Wang Ying-lin, C. encyclopedist (1223–96), 1296 K
Wāqidi, Abū Muhammad ibn-'Umar al-, Arab historian (747–823), 823 K
War:
laws of (Legnano), 1360 F; (Bonet), 1388 K; (Indian), 1367 F
manuals on:
Leo VI, 912 G
Guido da Vigevano, 1335 G
Konrad Kyeser, 1405 G
Giovanni de' Fontana, 1415 G
Feuerwerkbuch, 1420 G
private, 989 F, 1040 F, 1258 F
War and Peace Theme:
Christine de Pisan, 1412 K
Alain Chartier, 1416 K
War, Great Northern, 1410 C, 1411 A
'War of the Eight Saints', 1376 B, 1378 C
'War of the Three Henries', 978 A
Warangal, India, 1308 E; renamed Sultānpur, 1323 E, 1345 E
Warbeck, Perkin, Flemish pretender to English throne (d. 1499), 1491 E
Wardlaw, Henry, Bishop of St. Andrews and founder (d. 1440), 1413 H
Warmstadt, E. Germany, battle, 1113 E
Warrāq, Muhammad ibn-Ishāq al-, Arab bibliographer, 995 G
'Wars of Pretenders', 1155 E
Wars of the Lord (Levi ben Gerson), 1329 K
'Wars of the Roses'. *See* England
Warsaw, Poland, process of, 1339 C
Warwick, England, Earls of. *See* Beauchamp; Neville, Richard
Warwick Rolls (John Rous), 1491 K
Wassenburg, W. Germany, battle, 1206 C
Waterford, Ireland, 1170 C, 1399 B
Water-Mirror (Nakayama), 1195 K
Water-power. *See* Mills
Wāthiq, al-, Caliph of Bagdād, 842 A, 847 C; as musician, 847 J
Wattāsids. *See* Morocco
Waverley, England, abbey, 1128 H
Waynflete, Willam, Bishop of Winchester and founder, 1448 H, 1486 L
Weather-forecasts, 1340 G
Wedding Feast (Botticelli), 1483 J
Wedmore, England, battle, 878 B
'Weibling' (Ghibelline), origin of, 1140 D
Weinsberg, W. Germany, battle, 1140 D
'Welf' (Guelf), origin of, 1140 D
Welf IV of Swabia, Duke of Bavaria (d. 1101), 1070 C, 1086 C
Welf V, Duke of Bavaria (d. 1120), 1089 E, 1095 E
Welf VI of Swabia (d. 1191), 1140 D, 1150 A; Marquess of Tuscany and Duke of Spoleto, 1152 E, 1174 D
Welfesholz, E. Germany, battle, 1115 A
Wells, England, Cathedral, 1188 J, 1220 J, 1319 J
Welshpool, Wales, battle, 1400 C
Wen T'ung, C. painter, 1079 J
Wencelas, St., Duke of Bohemia, 921 E, 928 E, 929 C
Wenceslas I, King of Bohemia, 1216 E, 1230 E, 1235 G, 1239 A, 1248 E, 1253 E
Wenceslas II, King of Bohemia (b. 1271; 1278–1305), 1278 C, 1294 F, 1300 G, 1301 A, 1305 B, 1310 C; Polish conquests, 1290 E, 1291 E; King of Poland (as Václav), 1300 E, 1304 E
Wenceslas III, King of Bohemia (b. 1288), 1305 B, C; King of Hungary, 1301 A, 1304 E
Wenceslas IV, King of the Romans (1376–1400), 1376 B, 1383 F, 1384 C, 1389 B, 1395 B, 1400 C; King of Bohemia (1378–1419), 1378 D, 1379 B, 1382 A, 1393 A, 1409 H, 1419 C; restricted by lords, 1394 B, 1396 B, 1401 B, 1402 B, 1403 D
Wenceslas, Duke of Brabant, 1356 F
Wends, Slav tribe (in N. Germany):
wars with Saxons, 880 A, 928 E
conquered, 929 C, 934 E, 955 D, 956 E, 983 E, 1005 A, 1147 B, C, 1160 C, 1162 C
converted, 929 C, 934 E, 948 H, 968 H, 1007 D, 1127 H
pagan temple of, 1124 E
See also Lyutitzi; Obotrites; Pomerania
Wên-jên Kuei, C. physician, 1323 G
Wen-tsung, Emperor of China (827–40), 833 E
Werner II, Count of Habsburg, 1096 E
Wessex, England, Earls of, *see* Godwin, Harold; Kings of, *see* England
Westminster, England:
Abbey, 1050 J, 1065 J, 1220 J, 1245 J, 1269 J, 1362 J
Common Pleas at, 1215 F

Hall, 1097 J, 1394 J
Provisions of, 1259 D, 1263 A, 1267 F
St. Stephen's, 1292 J
Statutes of, 1275 F, 1285 F, 1290 F, 1361 F
Westmorland, England, 945 E, 1092 E, 1157 E
Westphalia, W. Germany, 1180 B, 1371 F
Weyden, Roger van der, Flemish painter, 1435 J, 1446 J, 1450 J, 1452 J, 1453 J, 1464 L
Whethamstede, John Bostock of, Abbot of St. Albans, E. chronicler, 1465 K
Whittington, Richard, Mayor of London, 1423 L
Wichman, Count of Saxony, 963 E, 967 E
Widsith, 800 K
Widsith spoke, 975 K
Widukind, monk of Corvey, G. chronicler, 973 K
Wight, Isle of, England, 1377 C
Wilhelm, Master, of Cologne, G. painter, 1378 J
Wilhelm, Abbot of Hirsau, G. astronomer and musical theorist, 1091 G, J
Wilkomierz, Lithuania, Russia, battle, 1435 C
William I the Conqueror, King of England (1066–87), 1027 L, 1052 A, 1064 E, 1066 D, 1085 D, 1086 C, 1087 C
Duke of Normandy, 1035 C, 1054 A, 1058 C
conquers Maine, 1048 E, 1062 E, 1073 E, 1083 E, 1087 C
Norman revolts, 1047 E, 1053 E, 1074 E, 1077 E, 1079 A
conquers England, 1066 C, D, 1068 E, 1069 A, C, 1071 E
ecclesiastical policy, 1070 C, 1080 E
campaigns in Scotland, 1072 B, 1080 B
revolts in England, 1075 E, 1076 B, 1080 B, 1086 E
Welsh campaign, 1081 E
William II Rufus, King of England (b. *c.* 1058; 1087–1100), 1087 C, 1095 A, 1097 E, 1099 E, 1100 C
revolts in England, 1088 B, 1095 E
relations with Scotland, 1091 E, 1092 E
gains Normandy, 1091 E, 1094 E, 1096 E
William, Count of Holland, King of the Romans (b. *c.* 1227), 1247 D, 1252 A, C, 1255 F, 1256 A
William I the Lion, King of Scotland (b. 1142?), 1165 B, 1174 C, D, 1209 C, 1214 D
William I the Bad, King of Sicily (1154–65), 1154 A, 1156 B, 1159 C, 1160 A, 1165 B; revolts against, 1154 A, 1155 D, 1160 D, 1161 A, B; war with Greeks, 1156 B, 1157 E, 1158 E
William II, King of Sicily (b. 1154), 1165 B, 1185 B, C, 1189 D
William III, King of Sicily, 1194 A
William of Montferrat, King of Thessalonica, 1224 E
William I, Duke of Apulia, 1111 A, 1127 C
William V, Duke of Aquitaine (990–1029), 1025 E
William VIII, Duke of Aquitaine (1058–86), 1061 A; as Guy-Geoffrey, 1039 E
William Clito, claimant to Normandy, 1117 E, 1123 E; Count of Flanders, 1127 A, 1128 C
William III, Count of Holland and Hainault, 1328 A
William IV, Count of Holland and Hainault, 1345 C
William Longsword, Duke of Normandy, 931 E, 933 E, 942 D
William, son of Henry I (b. 1103), 1120 D
William of Auvergne, Bishop of Paris, F. theologian and scientist, 1249 H
William the Breton, F. poet, 1224 K
William of Champeaux, F. philosopher, 1121 H
William of Conches, F. philosopher, 1154 K
William of Dijon, F. monastic reformer (962–1031), 1031 L
William the Englishman, mason, 1179 J
William of Jumièges, F. chronicler, 1027 K
William, monk of Malmesbury, E. chronicler, 1142 K
William of Newburgh, E. chronicler (*c.* 1136–*c.* 1201), 1198 K
William, St., of Norwich, 1144 H
William of St. Cloud, F. astronomer, 1285 G, 1290 G, 1296 G
William of Sens, F. mason (d. 1179), 1174 J
William of Tripoli, crusader-state writer on Islam, 1273 K
William, Archbishop of Tyre, chronicler of crusades (1130–*c.* 1186), 1184 K
Wilton Diptych, 1397 J
Wiltzi, Slav tribe, 812 E
Winchelsea, England, naval battle, 1350 C
Winchelsey, Robert, Archbishop of Canterbury (d. 1313), 1306 A
Winchester, England, 1072 H, 1141 A; Bishops of, *see* Beaufort (Henry), Ethelwold, Swithin, Waynflete, Wykeham; Cathedral, 980 J, 1079 J, 1107 J, 1394 J; College, 1378 H
Windesheim, Holland, 1374 H; abbey, 1386 H
Windmills. *See* Mills
Windsor, England, Treaty of, 1386 B
Wine:
brandy, 1360 G
liqueurs, 1332 G
prohibited, 1301 F
treatise (Arnold de Villanova), 1311 G
vineyards in Bohemia, 1358 G
Winterthür, Switzerland, battle, 919 E
Winterthur, John of, Swiss chronicler, 1348 K
Wisdom of Illumination (al-Suhrawardi), 1191 K
Wiślica, Poland, statutes of, 1347 F
Wismar, E. Germany, 1259 G
Witchcraft:
alleged cases, 1310 H, 1440 D, 1441 D, 1452 C, 1460 H
laws against, 906 F, 1323 H, 1484 H
treatises:
Agobard, 841 H
Arnold of Villanova, 1311 G
Eustace Deschamps, 1406 G
Malleus Maleficarum, 1487 H
Witelo, Polish writer on optics (b. *c.* 1230), 1274 G
Wittlesbachs of Bavaria, 1214 E, 1487 C
Wittlesbach, Lewis I, Duke of Bavaria (1183–1231), 1231 C
Wittlesbach, Lewis of. *See* Lewis IV
Wittlesbach, Lewis I, Margrave of Brandenburg, 1324 B, 1326 E, 1342 A, 1350 A, 1351 D
Wittlesbach, Lewis II, Margrave of Brandenburg, 1351 D
Wittlesbach, Otto of, Duke of Bavaria (1180–3), 1180 C
Wittlesbach, Otto, Count Palatine of Bavaria (d. 1209), 1208 B
Wittlesbach, Otto V, Margrave of Brandenburg, 1351 D, 1373 D
Witz, Konrad, Swiss painter (*c.* 1405–*c.* 1445), 1435 J, 1444 J
Wolfram von Eschenbach, minnesinger (1170?–1220?), 1212 K, 1230 K, 1336 K
Wolsey, Thomas, E. cardinal and chancellor (*c.* 1475–1530), 1475 L
Woodcuts, 1147 G
Woodville, Anthony, Earl Rivers, E. translator (d. 1483), 1477 K
Woodville, Elizabeth, wife of Edward IV (d. 1492), 1464 B
Worcester, England, Cathedral, 1084 J
Worcestre, William, E. antiquary (b. 1415), 1478 K
World Conqueror, History of the (al-Juwainī), 1260 K

World Chronicle (Monachos), 842 K
World histories. *See* Historians (asterisked)
Worms, W. Germany, 1074 F, 1254 D; battle, 1388 D; Bishop, 1012 H; Cathedral, 1171 J; diets at, 1076 A, 1235 C, 1255 F, 1269 B; Treaties of, 839 B, 1122 C, 1193 B
Worringen, W. Germany, battle, 1288 C
Wroclaw (Breslau), Poland, 1235 H, 1241 G; battle, 1109 E; Princes of, *see* Henry I, Henry II
Wu Chen, C. painter (1280–1354), 1354 J
Wu Ching Tsung Yao, 1044 G
Wu Shu, C. encyclopedeist (947–1002), 1002 G
Wu-ch'iu Yen, C. archaeologist, 1307 K
Wulfric, St., E. hermit, 1154 H
Wulfstan, Archbishop of York, E. pastoral writer, 1014 K, 1023 K
Wulsi, St., E. hermit, 1097 H
Württemberg, W. Germany, Count of, 1388 C
Würzburg, W. Germany, diets at, 1121 C, 1165 B, 1180 A, 1196 B
Wycliffe, John, E. theologian (*c.* 1320–83/4), 1376 F, 1379 H, 1381 H, 1383 H, L; translates Bible, 1380 H; works condemned, 1377 A, H, 1382 H, 1403 H, 1410 H, 1413 H
Wycliffites. *See* Lollards
Wykeham, William of, Bishop of Winchester, chancellor and founder, 1323 L, 1371 A, 1378 H, 1379 H, 1404 L
Wynford, William, E. mason, 1394 J

X

'Xanadu'. *See* Shang-tu
XII Béguines (Jan Ruysbroeck), 1381 H
Ximines de Cisnéros, Francisco, Sp. cardinal and statesman (1436–1517), 1436 L
Xiphilin, John, Patriarch of Constantinople (1064–1075), Gk. jurist, 1045 H

Y

Yādava, India, Hindu Kingdom, 1270 F
Yādigār Muhammad, ruler of Khurāsān, 1469 E, 1470 C
Yanbū' al-Hayah (Solomon ben Gabirol), 1058 K
Yang Po Ku Vijaya, King of Champa, 1000 E
Yang-chou shao-yo-p'u (Wang Kuan), 1070 G
Ya'qub I al-Mansūr, Abū-Yūsuf, Emperor of Morocco, 1184 C, 1191 E, 1196 C, 1199 E
Ya'qūb III, Abū-Yūsuf, Emperor of Morocco (d. 1286), 1269 E, 1275 C
Ya'qūbi, ibn-Wādih al-, Arab geographer and historian, 891 G, K
Yāqūt ibn-'Abdullah al-Hamawi, Arab biographer and geographer (1179–1229), 1229 G, K
Yasa, Great, 1206 F
Yashuyori Tamba, Ja. physician, 982 G
Yasovarman I, King of Cambodia, 889 J
Yazdī, Sharaf-ad-Dīn 'Ali, Per. biographer, 1454 K
Yedo, Tokyo, Japan, castle, 1456 F
Yeh-lü A-pao-chi, ruler of the Khitan (872–926), 907 E
Yeh-lü Ta-shih, founder of Kara-Khitai, 1130 E
Yekuno Amlak, King of Abyssinia, 1270 E
Yellow River, China, 1289 G, 1333 G, 1351 E
Yemen, 1174 E, 1377 G
Yevele, Henry, E. mason, 1378 J, 1394 J, 1400 L
Yi Sŏng-gye, founder of Yi dynasty of Korea, 1392 E, 1393 F, 1394 E
Ying-yai-sheng-lan (Ma Huan), 1451 G
Ying-shih-hsii-chih (Chia Ming), 1368 G
Ymagines Historiarum (Ralph de Diceto), 1199 K
Yo Fei, Jürched general, 1141 E
Yolande, Empress and Regent of Constantinople, 1217 E
Yolande, Queen of Jerusalem and wife of Frederick II, 1225 D
York, England, 866 D
Danish kingdom, 875 E, 877 E, 910 C, 919 E, 939 E, 940 E, 944 E; second, 948 E, 952 E, 954 E
taken by Svein of Denmark, 1069 C
massacre of Jews, 1190 A
Treaty of, 1237 C
Statute of, 1322 B
Archbishop of, 1072 H; *and see* Oswald, Wulfstan, Melton, Scrope
Cathedral, 1080 J, 1291 J
Dukes of. *See* Edward; Richard
Yorkshire, 1068 E, 1069 A, C
Yorō Code, 833 F
Yoshida Kenkō, Ja. essayist (1283–1350), 1350 K
Yoshino, Japan, 1336 E
Yü hai (Wang Ying-lin), 1296 K
Yüan dynasty. *See* China
Yüan Chen, C. poet (779–831), 831 K
Yüan Shu, C. historian, 1205 K
Yucatán, Mexico, 889 E; Cocom dynasty (987–1441), 987 E
Yung-lo (Ch'eng-tsu), Emperor of China (b. 1360; 1403–24), 1403 E, 1405 E, 1417 F, 1420 E, 1424 E; conquests, 1407 E, 1409 E, 1418 E; wars with Mongols, 1410 E, 1414 E, 1422 E
Yung-lo Ta-tien, 1403 K
Yūnus, 'Ali ibn-, Eg. astronomer (979–1009), 1007 G
Yuriev, Esthonia, Russia, 1224 E
Yuriev-Polskij, Russia, cathedral, 1230 J
Yūsuf ibn-Tāshfīn, Emperor of Morocco (1061–1106), 1068 E, 1077 E, 1106 C; Spanish conquests, 1086 D, 1090 D, 1091 E, 1094 A
Yūsuf I, Abū-Ya'qūb, Emperor of Morocco, 1163 B, 1164 E, 1171 E, 1179 E, 1184 B, C
Yūsuf II, Abū-Ya'qūb, Emperor of Morocco, 1214 D, 1224 E
Yūsuf, emir of Azerbaijan, 914 E
Yūsuf I, King of Granada, 1333 C, E, 1354 D
Yūsuf II, King of Granada, 1392 E, 1396 E
Yūsuf III, King of Granada, 1408 B, 1417 E
Yūsuf IV, King of Granada, 1431 E, 1432 B
Yütz, France, Treaty of, 844 D
Ypres, Belgium, church, 1221 J; Cloth-hall, 1304 J

Z

Zabarella, Francesco, It. cardinal and canonist, 1339 L, 1417 H, L
Zadonschchina, 1380 K
Zafar-nāma (Mustawfī), 1333 K; (al-Shamī), 1403 K; (Yazdī), 1454 K
Zague, Abyssinian Jewess, 925 E
Zahara, Spain, 1481 E
Zāhir, al-, Caliph of Egypt (b. 1005), 1021 A, 1035 C
Zahrāwi (Abulcasis), Abū-l-Qāsim Khalaf al-, Sp. M. physician and surgeon, 1013 G
Zähringen, Germany, Dukes of, 1152 E, 1218 A
Zaid, Abū, al-Hasan al-Sīrafī, Arab geographer (d. 934), 920 G

Zain al-ʿAbidīn, Sultan of Kashmīr (1420–70), 1470 J
Zākānī, Per. poet, 1370 K
Zakonnik (Stephen Dušan), 1349 F
Zalaca, Spain, battle, 1086 D
Zamora, Spain, 893 E; battle, 981 E
Zangī, ʿImād-ad-Dīn, atabeg of Mosul, 1127 E, 1137 C, 1138 B, 1144 D, 1146 C
Zangid dynasty. *See* Aleppo; Mosul
Zapolino, Italy, battle, 1325 D
Zara (*now* Zadar), Yugoslavia, 1202 D, 1357 C; church, 812 J
Zara Yakub, Negus of Abyssinia (1434–68), 1445 D, 1468 H
Zarqāli (Arzachel), Abū-Ishaq Ibrahīm al-, Sp. M. astonomer and geographer (*c.* 1029–1087), 1087 G
Zaslaw, Russia, battle, 1491 A
Zawichost, Poland, battles, 1205 E, 1264 E
Zbigniev, joint Duke of Poland, 1102 C, 1107 E, 1109 E
Zeami Motokiyo, Ja. *Nō* dramatist (1363–1443), 1443 K
Zen Buddhism. *See* Japan
Zeno Ranieri, Doge of Venice, 1252 E, 1268 B
Zeta, Yugoslavia, Kingdom of, 1040 E, 1100 E
Ziano, Pietro, Doge of Venice, 1205 B, 1229 E
Ziano, Sebastiano, Doge of Venice, 1173 B, 1179 B
Ziemomyslas, Duke of Poland, 913 E
Ziemovit, Duke of Poland, 861 E, 892 E
Ziemowit II, Prince of Masovia, 1355 E
Zij (al-Battānī), 900 G
Zij al-Īl-Khāni (al-Tūsī), 1274 G
Zīrid dynasty, 972 E
Žiška, John, Bohemian Hussite leader, 1420 A, C, 1422 A, 1423 B, 1424 D
Ziyādat-Allah I, Caliph of Kairāwan (817–38), 827 B, 831 C
Ziyarid dynasty. *See* Jurjan
Zlatica, Bulgaria, battle, 1443 D
Zoe, Greek Empress, 1034 B, 1042 B
Zofingen, Switzerland, Treaty of, 1444 C
Zohar (Moses of Leon), 1305 K
Zonaras, Joannes, Gk. chronicler and jurist, 1145 K
Zoologists:
  Chinese. *See* Fu Kung
  Egyptian. *See* Damīrī
Zoynich, Voivode of Wallachia and Moldavia, 1467 E
Zug, Switzerland, 1352 E, 1368 A
Zuhr (Avenzoar), Abū-Marwān ibn-, Sp. M. physician (*c.* 1092–1162), 1162 G, 1280 G
Zuider Zee, Holland, 1287 G
Zurich, Switzerland, 1291 D, 1292 E, 1351 B; breach with Confederation, 1440 D, 1442 B, 1450 C; Treaties of, 1389 B, 1478 A
Zutphen, Holland, 1473 E
Zvonimir, King of Croatia, 1076 E
Zwentibold, King of Burgundy, 895 E
Zwettl, Austria, battle, 1427 A
Zwingli, Ulrich, Swiss reformer (1484–1531), 1484 L

X